CW00780297

Collins

Collins
Italian
Dictionary

HarperCollins Publishers
Westerhill Road
Bishopbriggs
Glasgow
G64 2QT
Great Britain

First Edition 2005

Previously published as Collins Pocket
Italian Dictionary

Latest Reprint 2006

© William Collins Sons & Co. Ltd. 1990
© HarperCollins Publishers 1996, 1999,
2002

ISBN-13   978-0-00-722394-7
ISBN-10   0-00-722394-3

Collins® and Bank of English® are
registered trademarks of HarperCollins
Publishers Limited

www.collins.co.uk

A catalogue record for this book is
available from the British Library

HarperCollins Publishers,
10 East 53rd Street, New York, NY 10022

HARPERCOLLINS POCKET ITALIAN
DICTIONARY.
Second US Edition 2002

ISBN-13   978-0-06-008452-3
ISBN-10   0-06-008452-9

Library of Congress Cataloging-in-
Publication Data has been applied for

www.harpercollins.com

First HarperCollins edition published
2000

HarperCollins books may be purchased
for educational, business, or sales
promotional use. For information,
please write to: Special Markets
Department, HarperCollins Publishers,
10 East 53rd Street, New York,
NY 10022

Typeset by Morton Word Processing
Ltd, Scarborough

Printed in Italy by Rotolito Lombarda
SpA

Acknowledgements
We would like to thank those authors
and publishers who kindly gave
permission for copyright material to be
used in the Collins Word Web. We
would also like to thank Times
Newspapers Ltd for providing valuable
data.

general editors/a cura di
Catherine E. Love • Michela Clari

with/hanno collaborato
Gabriella Bacchelli • Loredana Riu
Bob Grossmith

editorial staff/segreteria di redazione
Joyce Littlejohn • Isobel Gordon

series editor/collana a cura di
Lorna Sinclair Knight

INDICE/CONTENTS

I marchi registrati

I termini che a nostro parere
costituiscono un marchio
registrato sono stati designati
come tali. In ogni caso, né la
presenza né l'assenza di tale
designazione implicano alcuna
valutazione del loro reale stato
giuridico.

Note on trademarks

Words which we have reason to
believe constitute trademarks have
been designated as such. However,
neither the presence nor the
absence of such designation should
be regarded as affecting the legal
status of any trademark.

INTRODUZIONE

Questo dizionario è stato concepito e scritto per chi vuole imparare l'inglese per motivi di studio, lavoro o turismo.

La modernità e la ricchezza del lemmario e della fraseologia, l'elegante presentazione delle voci, l'uso del colore e il pratico formato fanno di questo dizionario un'opera unica nel suo genere.

Grazie ai giochi e agli esercizi che troverete nell'originale supplemento vi riuscirà facile e divertente imparare ad usare il dizionario così da trarne il massimo vantaggio.

I dizionari Collins sono sinonimo di qualità e modernità: vi ringraziamo di aver scelto il dizionario inglese Tascabile che siamo certi si rivelerà uno strumento di lavoro utile e piacevole da usarsi in ogni occasione.

COME USARE IL DIZIONARIO

Per imparare ad usare in modo efficace il dizionario è importante comprendere la funzione delle differenziazioni tipografiche, dei simboli e delle abbreviazioni usati nel testo. Vi forniamo pertanto qui di seguito alcuni chiarimenti in merito a tali convenzioni.

I lemmi

Sono le parole a colori elencate in ordine alfabetico. Il primo e l'ultimo lemma di ciascuna pagina appaiono al margine superiore.

Dove opportuno, informazioni sull'ambito d'uso o sul livello di formalità di certe parole vengono fornite tra parentesi in corsivo e spesso in forma abbreviata dopo la trascrizione fonetica (es. (COMM), (inf)).

In certi casi più parole con radice comune sono raggruppate sotto lo stesso lemma. Tali parole appaiono a colori ma in un carattere leggermente ridotto (es. **dolce, dolcezza**; **accept, acceptance**).

Esempi d'uso del lemma sono a loro volta in neretto ma in un carattere diverso dal lemma (es. **to be cold**).

La trascrizione fonetica
La trascrizione fonetica che illustra la corretta pronuncia del lemma è in parentesi quadra e segue immediatamente il lemma (es. **mezzo** ['mɛddzo]; **knead** [niːd]). L'elenco dei simboli fonetici è alle pagine xiv-xv.

Le traduzioni
Le traduzioni sono in carattere tondo e se si riferiscono a diversi significati del lemma sono separate da un punto e virgola. Spesso diverse traduzioni di un lemma sono introdotte da una o più parole in corsivo in parentesi tonda: la loro funzione è di chiarire a quale significato del lemma si riferisce la traduzione. Possono essere sinonimi, indicazioni di ambito d'uso o di registro del lemma (es. **party** (*POL*) (*team*) o (*celebration*), **laid back** (*inf*) etc.).

Le "parole chiave"
Un trattamento particolare è stato riservato a quelle parole che, per frequenza d'uso o complessità, necessitano una strutturazione più chiara ed esauriente (es. **da, di, avere** in italiano, **at, to, be, this** in inglese). Il simbolo ♦ e i numeri sono usati per guidarvi attraverso le varie distinzioni grammaticali e di significato. Dove necessario, ulteriori informazioni sono fornite in corsivo tra parentesi.

Informazioni grammaticali
Le parti del discorso (noun, adjective ecc.) sono espresse da abbreviazioni convenzionali in corsivo (*n, adj* ecc) e seguono la trascrizione fonetica del lemma.

Eventuali ulteriori informazioni grammaticali, come ad esempio le forme di un verbo irregolare o il plurale irregolare di un sostantivo, precedono tra parentesi la parte del discorso (es. **fall** (*pt* **fell**, *pp* **fallen**) *n*; **man** (*pl* **men**) *n*).

INTRODUCTION

We are delighted that you have decided to buy the Collins Italian Dictionary, and hope you will enjoy and benefit from using it at home, at school, on holiday or at work.

The innovative use of colour guides you quickly and efficiently to the word you want, and the comprehensive wordlist provides a wealth of modern and idiomatic phrases not normally found in a dictionary this size.

In addition, the supplement provides you with guidance on using the dictionary, along with entertaining ways of improving your dictionary skills.

We hope that you will enjoy using it and that it will significantly enhance your language studies.

USING YOUR COLLINS ITALIAN DICTIONARY

A wealth of information is presented in the dictionary, using various typefaces, sizes of type, symbols, abbreviations and brackets. The conventions and symbols used are explained in the following sections.

Headwords
The words you look up in a dictionary — "headwords" — are listed alphabetically. They are printed in **colour** for rapid identification. The two headwords appearing at the top of each page indicate the first and last word dealt with on the page in question.

Information about the usage or form of certain headwords is given in brackets after the phonetic spelling. This usually appears in abbreviated form and in italics (e.g. *(fam)*, *(comm)*).

Where appropriate, words related to headwords are grouped in the same entry (**illustrare, illustrazione; accept, acceptance**) in a slightly smaller type than the headword.

Common expressions in which the headword appears are shown in a different bold roman type (e.g. **aver freddo**).

Phonetic spellings
Where the phonetic spelling of headwords (indicating their pronunciation) is given, it will appear in square brackets immediately after the headword (e.g. **calza** ['kaltsa]; **knead** [niːd]). A list of these symbols is given on pages xiv-xv.

Translations
Headword translations are given in ordinary type and, where more than one meaning or usage exists, these are separated by a semi-colon. You will often find other words in italics in brackets before the translations. These offer suggested contexts in which the headword might appear (e.g. **duro** (*pietra*) or (*lavoro*)) or provide synonyms (e.g. **duro** (*ostinato*)).

"Key" words
Special status is given to certain Italian and English words which are considered as "key" words in each language. They may, for example, occur very frequently or have several types of usage (e.g. **da, di, avere; at, to, be, this**). A combination of lozenges and numbers helps you to distinguish different parts of speech and different meanings. Further helpful information is provided in brackets and in italics.

Grammatical information
Parts of speech are given in abbreviated form in italics after the phonetic spellings of headwords (e.g. *vt, av, cong*).

Genders of Italian nouns are indicated as follows: *sm* for a masculine and *sf* for a feminine noun. Feminine and irregular plural forms of nouns are also shown (**dottore, essa; droga, ghe**).

Feminine adjective endings are given as are plural forms (**opaco, a, chi, che**).

ABBREVIAZIONI

ABBREVIATIONS

abbreviazione	abbr	abbreviation
aggettivo	adj	adjective
amministrazione	ADMIN	administration
avverbio	adv	adverb
aeronautica, viaggi aerei	AER	flying, air travel
aggettivo	ag	adjective
agricoltura	AGR	agriculture
amministrazione	AMM	administration
anatomia	ANAT	anatomy
architettura	ARCHIT	architecture
articolo indeterminativo	art indet	indefinite article
attributivo	attrib	attributive
ausiliare	aus, aux	auxiliary
l'automobile	AUT	the motor car and motoring
avverbio	av	adverb
aeronautica, viaggi aerei	AVIAT	flying, air travel
biologia	BIOL	biology
botanica	BOT	botany
inglese della Gran Bretagna	BRIT	British English
consonante	C	consonant
chimica	CHIM, CHEM	chemistry
commercio, finanza, banca	COMM	commerce, finance, banking
comparativo	compar	comparative
informatica	COMPUT	computers
congiunzione	cong, conj	conjunction
edilizia	CONSTR	building
sostantivo usato come aggettivo, non può essere usato né come attributo, né dopo il sostantivo qualificato	cpd	compound element: noun used as adjective and which cannot follow the noun it qualifies
cucina	CUC, CULIN	cookery
davanti a	dav	before
articolo determinativo	def art	definite article
determinativo: articolo, aggettivo dimostrativo o indefinito etc	det	determiner: article, demonstrative etc
diminutivo	dimin	diminutive
diritto	DIR	law
economia	ECON	economics
edilizia	EDIL	building
elettricità, elettronica	ELETTR, ELEC	electricity, electronics
esclamazione	escl, excl	exclamation
femminile	f	feminine
familiare (! da evitare)	fam(!)	informal usage (! particularly offensive)
ferrovia	FERR	railways
figurato	fig	figurative use

fisiologia	FISIOL	physiology
fotografia	FOT	photography
(verbo inglese) la cui particella è inseparabile dal verbo	fus	(phrasal verb) where the particle cannot be separated from main verb
nella maggior parte dei sensi; generalmente	gen	in most or all senses; generally
geografia, geologia	GEO	geography, geology
geometria	GEOM	geometry
impersonale	impers	impersonal
articolo indeterminativo	indef art	indefinite article
familiare (! da evitare)	inf(!)	informal usage (! particularly offensive)
infinito	infin	infinitive
informatica	INFORM	computers
insegnamento, sistema scolastico e universitario	INS	schooling, schools and universities
invariabile	inv	invariable
irregolare	irreg	irregular
grammatica, linguistica	LING	grammar, linguistics
maschile	m	masculine
matematica	MAT(H)	mathematics
termine medico, medicina	MED	medical term, medicine
il tempo, meteorologia	METEOR	the weather, meteorology
maschile o femminile, secondo il sesso	m/f	either masculine or feminine depending on sex
esercito, linguaggio militare	MIL	military matters
musica	MUS	music
sostantivo	n	noun
nautica	NAUT	sailing, navigation
numerale (aggettivo, sostantivo)	num	numeral adjective or noun
	o.s.	oneself
peggiorativo	peg, pej	derogatory, pejorative
fotografia	PHOT	photography
fisiologia	PHYSIOL	physiology
plurale	pl	plural
politica	POL	politics
participio passato	pp	past participle
preposizione	prep	preposition
pronome	pron	pronoun
psicologia, psichiatria	PSIC, PSYCH	psychology, psychiatry
tempo passato	pt	past tense
qualcosa	qc	
qualcuno	qn	
religione, liturgia	REL	religions, church service
sostantivo	s	noun
	sb	somebody

ABBREVIAZIONI

ABBREVIATIONS

insegnamento, sistema scolastico e universitario	SCOL	schooling, schools and universities
singolare	sg	singular
soggetto (grammaticale)	sog	(grammatical) subject
	sth	something
congiuntivo	sub	subjunctive
soggetto (grammaticale)	subj	(grammatical) subject
superlativo	superl	superlative
termine tecnico, tecnologia	TECN, TECH	technical term, technology
telecomunicazioni	TEL	telecommunications
tipografia	TIP	typography, printing
televisione	TV	television
tipografia	TYP	typography, printing
inglese degli Stati Uniti	US	American English
vocale	V	vowel
verbo	vb	verb
verbo o gruppo verbale con funzione intransitiva	vi	verb or phrasal verb used intransitively
verbo riflessivo	vr	reflexive verb
verbo o gruppo verbale con funzione transitiva	vt	verb or phrasal verb used transitively
zoologia	ZOOL	zoology
marchio registrato	®	registered trademark
introduce un'equivalenza culturale	≈	introduces a cultural equivalent

TRASCRIZIONE FONETICA

PHONETIC TRANSCRIPTION

Consonants   Consonanti

NB p, b, t, d, k, g are not aspirated in Italian/sono seguite da un'aspirazione in inglese.

*pu*ppy	p	*p*adre
*b*aby	b	*b*ambino
*t*en*t*	t	*t*u*tt*o
*d*addy	d	*d*a*d*o
*c*ork *k*iss	k	*c*ane *ch*e
*ch*ord		
*g*ag *gu*ess	g	*g*ola *gh*iro
*s*o ri*c*e ki*ss*	s	*s*ano
cou*s*in bu*zz*	z	s*v*ago e*s*ame
*sh*eep *s*ugar	ʃ	*s*cena
plea*s*ure bei*g*e	ʒ	*g*arage
*ch*urch	tʃ	pe*c*e lan*ci*are
*j*udge *g*eneral	dʒ	*g*iro *gi*oco
*f*arm ra*ff*le	f	a*f*a *f*aro
*v*ery re*v*	v	*v*ero bra*v*o
*th*in ma*th*s	θ	
*th*at o*th*er	ð	
*l*ittle ba*ll*	l	*l*etto a*l*a
	ʎ	g*li*
*r*at b*r*at	r	*r*ete a*r*co
*m*ummy com*b*	m	*r*amo *m*adre
*n*o ra*n*	n	*n*o fuma*n*te
	ɲ	*gn*omo
si*ng*ing ba*n*k	ŋ	
*h*at re*h*eat	h	
*y*et	j	bu*i*o p*i*acere
*w*all be*w*ail	w	*u*omo g*u*aio
lo*ch*	x	

Vowels   Vocali

NB The pairing of some vowel sounds only indicates approximate equivalence./La messa in equivalenza di certi suoni indica solo una rassomiglianza approssimativa.

h*ee*l b*ea*d	iː i	v*i*no *i*dea
h*i*t p*i*ty	ɪ	
	e	st*e*lla *e*dera
s*e*t t*e*nt	ɛ	*e*poca ecc*e*tto
*a*pple b*a*t	æ a	m*a*mma
		*a*more
*a*fter c*a*r c*a*lm	ɑː	
f*u*n c*ou*sin	ʌ	
*o*ver ab*o*ve	ə	
*u*rn f*e*rn w*o*rk	əː	
w*a*sh p*o*t	ɔ	r*o*sa *o*cchio
b*o*rn c*o*rk	ɔː	
	o	p*o*nte *o*gnuno
	ø	f*ö*hn
f*u*ll s*oo*t	u	*u*tile z*u*cca
b*oo*n l*ew*d	uː	

Diphthongs   Dittonghi

ɪə	b*ee*r t*ie*r
ɛə	t*ea*r f*ai*r th*e*re
eɪ	d*a*te pl*ai*ce d*ay*
aɪ	l*i*fe b*uy* cr*y*
au	*ow*l f*ou*l n*ow*
əu	l*ow* n*o*
ɔɪ	b*oi*l b*oy* o*i*ly
uə	p*oo*r t*ou*r

Miscellaneous   Varie

* per l'inglese: la "r" finale viene pronunciata se seguita da una vocale.

ˈ precedes the stressed syllable/precede la sillaba accentata.

ITALIAN PRONUNCIATION

Vowels

Where the vowel e or the vowel o appears in a stressed syllable it can be either open [ɛ], [ɔ] or closed [e], [o]. As the open or closed pronunciation of these vowels is subject to regional variation, the distinction is of little importance to the user of this dictionary. Phonetic transcription for headwords containing these vowels will therefore only appear where other pronunciation difficulties are present.

Consonants

c before "e" or "i" is pronounced *tch*.

ch is pronounced like the "k" in "kit".

g before "e" or "i" is pronounced like the "j" in "jet".

gh is pronounced like the "g" in "get".

gl before "e" or "i" is normally pronounced like the "lli" in "million", and in a few cases only like the "gl" in "glove".

gn is pronounced like the "ny" in "canyon".

sc before "e" or "i" is pronounced *sh*.

z is pronounced like the "ts" in "stetson", or like the "d's" in "bird's-eye".

Headwords containing the above consonants and consonantal groups have been given full phonetic transcription in this dictionary.

NB All double written consonants in Italian are fully sounded: e.g. the "tt" in "tutto" is pronounced as in "ha*t t*rick".

ITALIANO – INGLESE
ITALIAN – ENGLISH

A, a

A *abbr* (= *autostrada*) ≈ M (= *motorway*)

PAROLA CHIAVE
---

a (*a+il* = **al**, *a+lo* = **allo**, *a+l'* = **all'**, *a+la* = **alla**, *a+i* = **ai**, *a+gli* = **agli**, *a+le* = **alle**) *prep* **1** (*stato in luogo*) at; (: *in*) in; **essere alla stazione** to be at the station; **essere ~ casa/~ scuola/~ Roma** to be at home/at school/in Rome; **è ~ 10 km da qui** it's 10 km from here, it's 10 km away
2 (*moto a luogo*) to; **andare ~ casa/~ scuola** to go home/to school
3 (*tempo*) at; (*epoca, stagione*) in; **alle cinque** at five (o'clock); **~ mezzanotte/Natale** at midnight/Christmas; **al mattino** in the morning; **~ maggio/primavera** in May/spring; **~ cinquant'anni** at fifty (years of age); **~ domani!** see you tomorrow!
4 (*complemento di termine*) to; **dare qc ~ qn** to give sth to sb
5 (*mezzo, modo*) with, by; **~ piedi/cavallo** on foot/horseback; **fatto ~ mano** made by hand, handmade; **una barca ~ motore** a motorboat; **~ uno ~ uno** one by one; **all'italiana** the Italian way, in the Italian fashion
6 (*rapporto*) a, per; (: *con prezzi*) at; **prendo 500.000 lire al mese** I get 500,000 lire a o per month; **pagato ~ ore** paid by the hour; **vendere qc ~ 2500 lire il chilo** to sell sth at 2,500 lire a o per kilo

abbacchi'ato, a [abbak'kjato] *ag* downhearted, in low spirits
abbagli'ante [abbaʎ'ʎante] *ag* dazzling; **~i** *smpl* (*AUT*): **accendere gli ~i** to put one's headlights on full (*BRIT*) o high (*US*) beam
abbagli'are [abbaʎ'ʎare] *vt* to dazzle; (*illudere*) to delude; **ab'baglio** *sm* blunder; **prendere un abbaglio** to

blunder, make a blunder
abbai'are *vi* to bark
abba'ino *sm* dormer window; (*soffitta*) attic room
abbando'nare *vt* to leave, abandon, desert; (*trascurare*) to neglect; (*rinunciare a*) to abandon, give up; **~rsi** *vr* to let o.s. go; **~rsi a** (*ricordi, vizio*) to give o.s. up to; **abban'dono** *sm* abandonment; neglect; (*SPORT*) withdrawal; (*fig*) abandon; **in abbandono** (*edificio, giardino*) neglected
abbas'sare *vt* to lower; (*radio*) to turn down; **~rsi** *vr* (*chinarsi*) to stoop; (*livello, sole*) to go down; (*fig: umiliarsi*) to demean o.s.; **~ i fari** (*AUT*) to dip o dim (*US*) one's lights
ab'basso *escl*: **~ il re!** down with the king!
abbas'tanza [abbas'tantsa] *av* (*a sufficienza*) enough; (*alquanto*) quite, rather, fairly; **non è ~ furbo** he's not shrewd enough; **un vino ~ dolce** quite a sweet wine; **averne ~ di qn/qc** to have had enough of sb/sth
ab'battere *vt* (*muro, casa*) to pull down; (*ostacolo*) to knock down; (*albero*) to fell; (: *sog: vento*) to bring down; (*bestie da macello*) to slaughter; (*cane, cavallo*) to destroy, put down; (*selvaggina, aereo*) to shoot down; (*fig: sog: malattia, disgrazia*) to lay low; **~rsi** *vr* (*avvilirsi*) to lose heart; **abbat'tuto, a** *ag* (*fig*) depressed
abba'zia [abbat'tsia] *sf* abbey
abbece'dario [abbetʃe'darjo] *sm* primer
abbel'lire *vt* (*ornare*) to embellish
abbeve'rare *vt* to water; **~rsi** *vr* to drink
'abbia *etc vb vedi* **avere**
abbicci [abbit'tʃi] *sm inv* alphabet; (*sillabario*) primer; (*fig*) rudiments *pl*
abbi'enti *smpl*: **gli ~** the well-to-do
abbiglia'mento [abbiʎʎa'mento] *sm* dress

no pl; (*indumenti*) clothes pl; (*industria*) clothing industry

abbigli'are [abbiʎˈʎare] *vt* to dress up

abbi'nare *vt*: ~ **(a)** to combine (with)

abbindo'lare *vt* (*fig*) to cheat, trick

abbocca'mento *sm* talks pl, meeting

abboc'care *vi* (*pesce*) to bite; (*tubi*) to join; ~ **(all'amo)** (*fig*) to swallow the bait

abboc'cato, a *ag* (*vino*) sweetish

abbona'mento *sm* subscription; (*alle ferrovie etc*) season ticket; **fare l'~** to take out a subscription (*o* season ticket)

abbo'narsi *vr*: ~ **a un giornale** to take out a subscription to a newspaper; ~ **al teatro/alle ferrovie** to take out a season ticket for the theatre/the train; **abbo'nato, a** *sm/f* subscriber; season-ticket holder

abbon'dante *ag* abundant, plentiful; (*giacca*) roomy

abbon'danza [abbonˈdantsa] *sf* abundance, plenty

abbon'dare *vi* to abound, be plentiful; ~ **in** *o* **di** to be full of, abound in

abbor'dabile (*persona*) approachable; (*prezzo*) reasonable

abbor'dare *vt* (*nave*) to board; (*persona*) to approach; (*argomento*) to tackle

abbotto'nare *vt* to button up, do up

abboz'zare [abbotˈtsare] *vt* to sketch, outline; (*SCULTURA*) to rough-hew; ~ **un sorriso** to give a hint of a smile;

ab'bozzo *sm* sketch, outline; (*DIR*) draft

abbracci'are [abbratˈtʃare] *vt* to embrace; (*persona*) to hug, embrace; (*professione*) to take up; (*contenere*) to include; **~rsi** *vr* to hug *o* embrace (one another); **ab'braccio** *sm* hug, embrace

abbrevi'are *vt* to shorten; (*parola*) to abbreviate

abbreviazi'one [abbrevjatˈtsjone] *sf* abbreviation

abbron'zante [abbronˈdzante] *ag* tanning, sun *cpd*

abbron'zare [abbronˈdzare] *vt* (*pelle*) to tan; (*metalli*) to bronze; **~rsi** *vr* to tan, get a tan; **abbronza'tura** *sf* tan, suntan

abbrusto'lire *vt* (*pane*) to toast; (*caffè*) to roast

abbru'tire *vt* to exhaust; to degrade

abbu'ono *sm* (*COMM*) allowance, discount; (*SPORT*) handicap

abdi'care *vi* to abdicate; ~ **a** to give up, renounce

aberrazi'one [aberratˈtsjone] *sf* aberration

a'bete *sm* fir (tree); ~ **rosso** spruce

abi'etto, a *ag* despicable, abject

'abile *ag* (*idoneo*): ~ **(a qc/a fare qc)** fit (for sth/to do sth); (*capace*) able; (*astuto*) clever; (*accorto*) skilful; ~ **al servizio militare** fit for military service; **abilità** *sf inv* ability; cleverness; skill

abili'tato, a *ag* qualified; (*TEL*) which has an outside line; **abilitazi'one** *sf* qualification

a'bisso *sm* abyss, gulf

abi'tacolo *sm* (*AER*) cockpit; (*AUT*) inside; (: *di camion*) cab

abi'tante *sm/f* inhabitant

abi'tare *vt* to live in, dwell in ♦ *vi*: ~ **in campagna/a Roma** to live in the country/in Rome; **abi'tato, a** *ag* inhabited; lived in ♦ *sm* (*anche*: **centro abitato**) built-up area; **abitazi'one** *sf* residence; house

'abito *sm* dress no pl; (*da uomo*) suit; (*da donna*) dress; (*abitudine, disposizione, REL*) habit; **~i** *smpl* (*vestiti*) clothes; **in ~ da sera** in evening dress

abitu'ale *ag* usual, habitual; (*cliente*) regular

abitu'are *vt*: ~ **qn a** to get sb used *o* accustomed to; **~rsi a** to get used to, accustom o.s. to

abitudi'nario, a *ag* of fixed habits ♦ *sm/f* regular customer

abi'tudine *sf* habit; **aver l'~ di fare qc** to be in the habit of doing sth; **d'~** usually; **per ~** from *o* out of habit

abo'lire *vt* to abolish; (*DIR*) to repeal

abomi'nevole *ag* abominable

abo'rigeno [aboriˈdʒeno] *sm* aborigine

abor'rire *vt* to abhor, detest

abor'tire *vi* (*MED*) to miscarry, have a

miscarriage; (: *deliberatamente*) to have an abortion; (*fig*) to miscarry, fail; **a'borto** *sm* miscarriage; abortion

abrasi'one *sf* abrasion; **abra'sivo, a** *ag*, *sm* abrasive

abro'gare *vt* to repeal, abrogate

A'bruzzo *sm*: **l'~, gli ~i** the Abruzzi

ABS [abɪese] *sigla m* (= *Anti-Blockier System*) ABS

'abside *sf* apse

a'bulico, a, ci, che *ag* lacking in will power

abu'sare *vi*: **~ di** to abuse, misuse; (*alcool*) to take to excess; (*approfittare, violare*) to take advantage of; **a'buso** *sm* abuse, misuse; excessive use

a.C. *av abbr* (= *avanti Cristo*) B.C.

a'cacia, cie [a'katʃa] *sf* (*BOT*) acacia

'acca *sf* letter H; **non capire un'~** not to understand a thing

acca'demia *sf* (*società*) learned society; (*scuola: d'arte, militare*) academy; **acca'demico, a, ci, che** *ag* academic ♦ *sm* academician

acca'dere *vb impers* to happen, occur; **acca'duto** *sm*: **raccontare l'accaduto** to describe what has happened

accalappi'are *vt* to catch

accal'carsi *vr*: **~ (in)** to crowd (into)

accal'darsi *vr* to grow hot

accalo'rarsi *vr* (*fig*) to get excited

accampa'mento *sm* camp

accam'pare *vt* to encamp; (*fig*) to put forward, advance; **~rsi** *vr* to camp

accani'mento *sm* fury; (*tenacia*) tenacity, perseverance

acca'nirsi *vr* (*infierire*) to rage; (*ostinarsi*) to persist; **acca'nito, a** *ag* (*odio, gelosia*) fierce, bitter; (*lavoratore*) assiduous, dogged; (*fumatore*) inveterate

ac'canto *av* near, nearby; **~ a** *prep* near, beside, close to

accanto'nare *vt* (*problema*) to shelve; (*somma*) to set aside

accapar'rare *vt* (*COMM*) to corner, buy up; **~rsi qc** (*fig: simpatia, voti*) to secure sth (for o.s.)

accapigli'arsi [akkapiʎ'ʎarsi] *vr* to come to

blows; (*fig*) to quarrel

accappa'toio *sm* bathrobe

accappo'nare *vi*: **far ~ la pelle a qn** to bring sb out in goose pimples

accarez'zare [akkaret'tsare] *vt* to caress, stroke, fondle; (*fig*) to toy with

acca'sarsi *vr* to set up house; to get married

accasci'arsi [akkaʃ'ʃarsi] *vr* to collapse; (*fig*) to lose heart

accat'tone, a *sm/f* beggar

accaval'lare *vt* (*gambe*) to cross; **~rsi** *vr* (*sovrapporsi*) to overlap; (*addensarsi*) to gather

acce'care [attʃe'kare] *vt* to blind ♦ *vi* to go blind

ac'cedere [at'tʃedere] *vi*: **~ a** to enter; (*richiesta*) to grant, accede to

accele'rare [attʃele'rare] *vt* to speed up ♦ *vi* (*AUT*) to accelerate; **~ il passo** to quicken one's pace; **accele'rato** *sm* (*FERR*) slow train; **accelera'tore** *sm* (*AUT*) accelerator; **accelerazi'one** *sf* acceleration

ac'cendere [at'tʃendere] *vt* (*fuoco, sigaretta*) to light; (*luce, televisione*) to put on, switch on, turn on; (*AUT: motore*) to switch on; (*COMM: conto*) to open; (*fig: suscitare*) to inflame, stir up; **~rsi** *vr* (*luce*) to come o go on; (*legna*) to catch fire, ignite; **accen'dino** *sm*, **accendi'sigaro** *sm* (cigarette) lighter

accen'nare [attʃen'nare] *vt* (*MUS*) to pick out the notes of; to hum ♦ *vi*: **~ a** (*fig: alludere a*) to hint at; (: *far atto di*) to make as if; **~ un saluto** (*con la mano*) to make as if to wave; (*col capo*) to half nod; **accenna a piovere** it looks as if it's going to rain

ac'cenno [at'tʃenno] *sm* (*cenno*) sign; nod; (*allusione*) hint

accensi'one [attʃen'sjone] *sf* (*vedi verbo*) lighting; switching on; opening; (*AUT*) ignition

accen'tare [attʃen'tare] *vt* (*parlando*) to stress; (*scrivendo*) to accent

ac'cento [at'tʃento] *sm* accent; (*FONETICA, fig*) stress; (*inflessione*) tone (of voice)

accen'trare [attʃen'trare] *vt* to centralize

accentu'are [attʃentu'are] *vt* to stress, emphasize; **~rsi** *vr* to become more noticeable

accerchi'are [attʃer'kjare] *vt* to surround, encircle

accerta'mento [attʃerta'mento] *sm* check; assessment

accer'tare [attʃer'tare] *vt* to ascertain; (*verificare*) to check; (*reddito*) to assess; **~rsi** *vr*: **~rsi (di)** to make sure (of)

ac'ceso, a [at'tʃeso] *pp di* **accendere ♦** *ag* lit; on; open; (*colore*) bright

acces'sibile [attʃes'sibile] *ag* (*luogo*) accessible; (*persona*) approachable; (*prezzo*) reasonable

ac'cesso [at'tʃesso] *sm* (*anche INFORM*) access; (*MED*) attack, fit; (*impulso violento*) fit, outburst

acces'sorio, a [attʃes'sɔrjo] *ag* secondary, of secondary importance; **~i** *smpl* accessories

ac'cetta [at'tʃetta] *sf* hatchet

accet'tabile [attʃet'tabile] *ag* acceptable

accet'tare [attʃet'tare] *vt* to accept; **~ di fare qc** to agree to do sth; **accettazi'one** *sf* acceptance; (*locale di servizio pubblico*) reception; **accettazione bagagli** (*AER*) check-in (desk)

ac'cetto, a [at'tʃetto] *ag*: **(ben) ~** welcome; (*persona*) well-liked

accezi'one [attʃet'tsjone] *sf* meaning

acchiap'pare [akkjap'pare] *vt* to catch

acci'acco, chi [at'tʃakko] *sm* ailment

acciaie'ria [attʃaje'ria] *sf* steelworks *sg*

acci'aio [at'tʃajo] *sm* steel

acci'dentale [attʃiden'tale] *ag* accidental

acciden'tato, a [attʃiden'tato] *ag* (*terreno etc*) uneven

acci'dente [attʃi'dɛnte] *sm* (*caso imprevisto*) accident; (*disgrazia*) mishap; **non si capisce un ~** it's as clear as mud; **~i!** (*fam: per rabbia*) damn (it)!; (*: per meraviglia*) good heavens!

accigli'ato, a [attʃiʎ'ʎato] *ag* frowning

ac'cingersi [at'tʃindʒersi] *vr*: **~ a fare qc** to be about to do sth

acciuf'fare [attʃuf'fare] *vt* to seize, catch

acci'uga, ghe [at'tʃuga] *sf* anchovy

accla'mare *vt* (*applaudire*) to applaud; (*eleggere*) to acclaim; **acclamazi'one** *sf* applause; acclamation

acclima'tare *vt* to acclimatize; **~rsi** *vr* to become acclimatized

ac'cludere *vt* to enclose; **ac'cluso, a** *pp di* **accludere ♦** *ag* enclosed

accocco'larsi *vr* to crouch

accogli'ente [akkoʎ'ʎɛnte] *ag* welcoming, friendly; **accogli'enza** *sf* reception; welcome

ac'cogliere [ak'kɔʎʎere] *vt* (*ricevere*) to receive; (*dare il benvenuto*) to welcome; (*approvare*) to agree to, accept; (*contenere*) to hold, accommodate

accol'lato, a *ag* (*vestito*) high-necked

accoltel'lare *vt* to knife, stab

ac'colto, a *pp di* **accogliere**

accoman'dita *sf* (*DIR*) limited partnership

accomia'tare *vt* to dismiss; **~rsi** *vr*: **~rsi (da)** to take one's leave (of)

accomoda'mento *sm* agreement, settlement

accomo'dante *ag* accommodating

accomo'dare *vt* (*aggiustare*) to repair, mend; (*riordinare*) to tidy; (*conciliare*) to settle; **~rsi** *vr* (*sedersi*) to sit down; **s'accomodi!** (*venga avanti*) come in!; (*si sieda*) take a seat!

accompagna'mento [akkompaɲɲa'mento] *sm* (*MUS*) accompaniment

accompa'gnare [akkompaɲ'ɲare] *vt* to accompany, come *o* go with; (*MUS*) to accompany; (*unire*) to couple; **~ la porta** to close the door gently

accompagna'tore, trice *sm/f* companion; **~ turistico** courier

accomu'nare *vt* to pool, share; (*avvicinare*) to unite

acconcia'tura [akkontʃa'tura] *sf* hairstyle

accondi'scendere [akkondiʃ'ʃɛndere] *vi*: **~ a** to agree *o* consent to; **accondi'sceso, a** *pp di* **accondiscendere**

acconsen'tire *vi*: **~ (a)** to agree *o* consent (to)

acconten'tare *vt* to satisfy; **~rsi di** to be satisfied with, content o.s. with

ac'conto *sm* part payment; **pagare una somma in ~** to pay a sum of money as a deposit

accoppi'are *vt* to couple, pair off; (BIOL) to mate; **~rsi** *vr* to pair off; to mate

acco'rato, a *ag* heartfelt

accorci'are [akkor'tʃare] *vt* to shorten; **~rsi** *vr* to become shorter

accor'dare *vt* to reconcile; (*colori*) to match; (MUS) to tune; (LING): **~ qc con qc** to make sth agree with sth; (DIR) to grant; **~rsi** *vr* to agree, come to an agreement; (*colori*) to match

ac'cordo *sm* agreement; (*armonia*) harmony; (MUS) chord; **essere d'~** to agree; **andare d'~** to get on well together; **d'~!** all right!, agreed!

ac'corgersi [ak'kordʒersi] *vr*: **~ di** to notice; (*fig*) to realize; **accorgi'mento** *sm* shrewdness *no pl*; (*espediente*) trick, device

ac'correre *vi* to run up

ac'corso, a *pp di* **accorrere**

ac'corto, a *pp di* **accorgersi** ♦ *ag* shrewd; **stare ~** to be on one's guard

accos'tare *vt* (*avvicinare*): **~ qc a** to bring sth near to, put sth near to; (*avvicinarsi a*) to approach; (*socchiudere: imposte*) to half-close; (: *porta*) to leave ajar ♦ *vi* (NAUT) to come alongside; **~rsi a** to draw near, approach; (*fig*) to support

accovacci'arsi [akkovat'tʃarsi] *vr* to crouch

accoz'zaglia [akkot'tsaʎʎa] (*peg*) *sf* (*di idee, oggetti*) jumble, hotchpotch

accredi'tare *vt* (*notizia*) to confirm the truth of; (COMM) to credit; (*diplomatico*) to accredit; **~rsi** *vr* (*fig*) to gain credit

ac'crescere [ak'kreʃʃere] *vt* to increase; **~rsi** *vr* to increase, grow; **accresci'tivo, a** *ag, sm* (LING) augmentative; **accresci'uto, a** *pp di* **accrescere**

accucci'arsi [akkut'tʃarsi] *vr* (*cane*) to lie down

accu'dire *vt* (*anche: vi*): **~ a** to attend to

accumu'lare *vt* to accumulate

accumula'tore *sm* (ELETTR) accumulator

accura'tezza [akkura'tettsa] *sf* care; accuracy

accu'rato, a *ag* (*diligente*) careful; (*preciso*) accurate

ac'cusa *sf* accusation; (DIR) charge; **la pubblica ~** the prosecution

accu'sare *vt*: **~ qn di qc** to accuse sb of sth; (DIR) to charge sb with sth; **~ ricevuta di** (COMM) to acknowledge receipt of

accu'sato, a *sm/f* accused; defendant

accusa'tore, 'trice *sm/f* accuser ♦ *sm* (DIR) prosecutor

a'cerbo, a [a'tʃerbo] *ag* bitter; (*frutta*) sour, unripe; (*persona*) immature

'acero ['atʃero] *sm* maple

a'cerrimo, a [a'tʃerrimo] *ag* very fierce

a'ceto [a'tʃeto] *sm* vinegar

ace'tone [atʃe'tone] *sm* nail varnish remover

A.C.I. ['atʃi] *sigla m = Automobile Club d'Italia*

'acido, a ['atʃido] *ag* (*sapore*) acid, sour; (CHIM) acid ♦ *sm* (CHIM) acid

'acino ['atʃino] *sm* berry; **~ d'uva** grape

'acne *sf* acne

'acqua *sf* water; (*pioggia*) rain; **~e** *sfpl* (*di mare, fiume etc*) waters; **fare ~** (NAUT) to leak, take in water; **~ in bocca!** mum's the word!; **~ corrente** running water; **~ dolce** fresh water; **~ minerale** mineral water; **~ potabile** drinking water; **~ salata** salt water; **~ tonica** tonic water

acqua'forte (*pl* **acque'forti**) *sf* etching

a'cquaio *sm* sink

acqua'ragia [akkwa'radʒa] *sf* turpentine

a'cquario *sm* aquarium; (*dello zodiaco*): **A~** Aquarius

acqua'santa *sf* holy water

ac'quatico, a, ci, che *ag* aquatic; (SPORT, SCIENZA) water *cpd*

acqua'vite *sf* brandy

acquaz'zone [akkwat'tsone] *sm* cloudburst, heavy shower

acque'dotto *sm* aqueduct; waterworks *pl*, water system

'acqueo, a *ag*: **vapore ~** water vapour

acque'rello *sm* watercolour

acqui'rente *sm/f* purchaser, buyer

acqui'sire *vt* to acquire

acquis'tare *vt* to purchase, buy; *(fig)* to gain; **a'cquisto** *sm* purchase; **fare acquisti** to go shopping

acqui'trino *sm* bog, marsh

acquo'lina *sf*: **far venire l'~ in bocca a qn** to make sb's mouth water

a'cquoso, a *ag* watery

'acre *ag* acrid, pungent; *(fig)* harsh, biting

a'crobata, i, e *sm/f* acrobat

acu'ire *vt* to sharpen

a'culeo *sm (ZOOL)* sting; *(BOT)* prickle

a'cume *sm* acumen, perspicacity

a'custica *sf (scienza)* acoustics *sg*; *(di una sala)* acoustics *pl*

a'cuto, a *ag (appuntito)* sharp, pointed; *(suono, voce)* shrill, piercing; *(MAT, LING, MED)* acute; *(MUS)* high-pitched; *(fig: dolore, desiderio)* intense; *(: perspicace)* acute, keen

ad *(before V) prep* = **a**

adagi'are [ada'dʒare] *vt* to lay *o* set down carefully; **~rsi** *vr* to lie down, stretch out

a'dagio [a'dadʒo] *av* slowly ♦ *sm (MUS)* adagio; *(proverbio)* adage, saying

adatta'mento *sm* adaptation

adat'tare *vt* to adapt; *(sistemare)* to fit; **~rsi (a)** *(ambiente, tempi)* to adapt (to); *(essere adatto)* to be suitable (for)

a'datto, a *ag*: **~ (a)** suitable (for), right (for)

addebi'tare *vt*: **~ qc a qn** to debit sb with sth

ad'debito *sm (COMM)* debit

adden'sare *vt* to thicken; **~rsi** *vr* to thicken; *(nuvole)* to gather

adden'tare *vt* to bite into

adden'trarsi *vr*: **~ in** to penetrate, go into

ad'dentro *av*: **essere molto ~ in qc** to be well-versed in sth

addestra'mento *sm* training

addes'trare *vt* to train; **~rsi** *vr* to train; **~rsi in qc** to practise *(BRIT) o* practice *(US)* sth

ad'detto, a *ag*: **~ a** *(persona)* assigned to; *(oggetto)* intended for ♦ *sm* employee; *(funzionario)* attaché; **~ commerciale/ stampa** commercial/press attaché; **gli ~i ai lavori** authorized personnel; *(fig)* those in the know

addì *av (AMM)*: **~ 3 luglio 1999** on the 3rd of July 1999 *(BRIT)*, on July 3rd 1999 *(US)*

addi'accio [ad'djattʃo] *sm (MIL)* bivouac; **dormire all'~** to sleep in the open

addi'etro *av (indietro)* behind; *(nel passato, prima)* before, ago

ad'dio *sm, escl* goodbye, farewell

addirit'tura *av (veramente)* really, absolutely; *(perfino)* even; *(direttamente)* directly, right away

ad'dirsi *vr*: **~ a** to suit, be suitable for

addi'tare *vt* to point out; *(fig)* to expose

addi'tivo *sm* additive

addizio'nare [addittsjo'nare] *vt (MAT)* to add (up); **addizi'one** *sf* addition

addob'bare *vt* to decorate; **ad'dobbo** *sm* decoration

addol'cire [addol'tʃire] *vt (caffè etc)* to sweeten; *(acqua, fig: carattere)* to soften; **~rsi** *vr (fig)* to mellow, soften

addolo'rare *vt* to pain, grieve; **~rsi (per)** to be distressed (by)

ad'dome *sm* abdomen

addomesti'care *vt* to tame

addormen'tare *vt* to put to sleep; **~rsi** *vr* to fall asleep, go to sleep

addos'sare *vt (appoggiare)*: **~ qc a qc** to lean sth against sth; *(fig)*: **~ la colpa a qn** to lay the blame on sb; **~rsi qc** *(responsabilità etc)* to shoulder sth

ad'dosso *av* on; **mettersi ~ il cappotto** to put one's coat on; **~ a** *(sopra)* on; *(molto vicino)* right next to; **stare ~ a qn** *(fig)* to breathe down sb's neck; **dare ~ a qn** *(fig)* to attack sb

ad'dotto, a *pp di* **addurre**

ad'durre *vt (DIR)* to produce; *(citare)* to cite

adegu'are *vt*: **~ qc a** to adjust *o* relate sth to; **~rsi** *vr* to adapt; **adegu'ato, a** *ag* adequate; *(conveniente)* suitable; *(equo)* fair

a'dempiere *vt* to fulfil, carry out

adem'pire *vt* = **adempiere**

ade'rente *ag* adhesive; *(vestito)* close-fitting ♦ *sm/f* follower; **ade'renza** *sf* adhesion; **aderenze** *sfpl* connections, contacts

ade'rire *vi* (*stare attaccato*) to adhere, stick; ~ **a** to adhere to, stick to; (*fig: società, partito*) to join; (: *opinione*) to support; (*richiesta*) to agree to

ades'care *vt* to lure, entice

adesi'one *sf* adhesion; (*fig*) agreement, acceptance; ade'sivo, a *ag, sm* adhesive

a'desso *av* (*ora*) now; (*or ora, poco fa*) just now; (*tra poco*) any moment now

adia'cente [adja'tʃɛnte] *ag* adjacent

adi'bire *vt* (*usare*): ~ **qc a** to turn sth into

adi'rarsi *vr*: ~ (**con** *o* **contro qn per qc**) to get angry (with sb over sth)

a'dire *vt* (*DIR*): ~ **le vie legali** to take legal proceedings

'adito *sm*: **dare** ~ **a** to give rise to

adocchi'are [adok'kjare] *vt* (*scorgere*) to catch sight of; (*occhieggiare*) to eye

adole'scente [adoleʃ'ʃɛnte] *ag, sm/f* adolescent; adole'scenza *sf* adolescence

adope'rare *vt* to use; ~**rsi** *vr* to strive; ~**rsi per qn/qc** to do one's best for sb/sth

ado'rare *vt* to adore; (*REL*) to adore, worship

adot'tare *vt* to adopt; (*decisione, ·provvedimenti*) to pass; adot'tivo, a *ag* (*genitori*) adoptive; (*figlio, patria*) adopted; adozi'one *sf* adoption

adri'atico, a, ci, che *ag* Adriatic ♦ *sm*: **l'A~, il mare A~** the Adriatic, the Adriatic Sea

adu'lare *vt* to adulate, flatter

adulte'rare *vt* to adulterate

adul'terio *sm* adultery

a'dulto, a *ag* adult; (*fig*) mature ♦ *sm* adult, grown-up

adu'nanza [adu'nantsa] *sf* assembly, meeting

adu'nare *vt* to assemble, gather; ~**rsi** *vr* to assemble, gather; adu'nata *sf* (*MIL*) parade, muster

a'dunco, a, chi, che *ag* hooked

a'ereo, a *ag* air *cpd*; (*radice*) aerial ♦ *sm* aerial; (*aeroplano*) plane; ~ **a reazione** jet (plane); ~ **da caccia** fighter (plane); ~ **di**

'linea airliner; ae'robica *sf* aerobics *sg*;
aerodi'namica *sf* aerodynamics *sg*;
aerodi'namico, a, ci, che *ag* aerodynamic; (*affusolato*) streamlined;
aero'nautica *sf* (*scienza*) aeronautics *sg*;
aeronautica militare air force;
aero'plano *sm* (aero)plane (*BRIT*), (air)plane (*US*)

aero'porto *sm* airport

aero'sol *sm inv* aerosol

'afa *sf* sultriness

af'fabile *ag* affable

affaccen'dato, a [affattʃen'dato] *ag* (*persona*) busy

affacci'arsi [affat'tʃarsi] *vr*: ~ (**a**) to appear (at)

affa'mato, a *ag* starving; (*fig*): ~ (**di**) eager (for)

affan'nare *vt* to leave breathless; (*fig*) to worry; ~**rsi** *vr*: ~**rsi per qn/qc** to worry about sb/sth; af'fanno *sm* breathlessness; (*fig*) anxiety, worry; affan'noso, a *ag* (*respiro*) difficult; (*fig*) troubled, anxious

af'fare *sm* (*faccenda*) matter, affair; (*COMM*) piece of business, (business) deal; (*occasione*) bargain; (*DIR*) case; (*fam: cosa*) thing; ~**i** *smpl* (*COMM*) business *sg*;
Ministro degli A~i esteri Foreign Secretary (*BRIT*), Secretary of State (*US*); affa'rista, i *sm* profiteer, unscrupulous businessman

affasci'nante [affaʃʃi'nante] *ag* fascinating

affasci'nare [affaʃʃi'nare] *vt* to bewitch; (*fig*) to charm, fascinate

affati'care *vt* to tire; ~**rsi** *vr* (*durar fatica*) to tire o.s. out

af'fatto *av* completely; **non ...** ~ not ... at all; **niente** ~ not at all

affer'mare *vt* (*dichiarare*) to maintain, affirm; ~**rsi** *vr* to assert o.s., make one's name known; affermazi'one *sf* affirmation, assertion; (*successo*) achievement

affer'rare *vt* to seize, grasp; (*fig: idea*) to grasp; ~**rsi** *vr*: ~**rsi a** to cling to

affet'tare *vt* (*tagliare a fette*) to slice; (*ostentare*) to affect; affet'tato, a *ag* sliced; affected ♦ *sm* sliced cold meat

affet'tivo, a *ag* emotional, affective

af'fetto *sm* affection; **affettu'oso, a** *ag* affectionate

affezio'narsi [affettsjo'narsi] *vr*: **~ a** to grow fond of

affian'care *vt* to place side by side; (*MIL*) to flank; (*fig*) to support; **~ qc a qc** to place sth next to *o* beside sth; **~rsi a qn** to stand beside sb

affia'tato, a *ag*: **essere molto ~i** to get on very well

affibbi'are *vt* (*fig: dare*) to give

affi'dabile *ag* reliable

affida'mento *sm* (*DIR: di bambino*) custody; (*fiducia*): **fare ~ su qn** to rely on sb; **non dà nessun ~** he's not to be trusted

affi'dare *vt*: **~ qc** *o* **qn a qn** to entrust sth *o* sb to sb; **~rsi** *vr*: **~rsi a** to place one's trust in

affievo'lirsi *vr* to grow weak

af'figgere [af'fiddʒere] *vt* to stick up, post up

affi'lare *vt* to sharpen

affili'arsi *vr*: **~ a** to become affiliated to

affi'nare *vt* to sharpen

affinché [affin'ke] *cong* in order that, so that

af'fine *ag* similar; **affinità** *sf inv* affinity

affio'rare *vi* to emerge

affissi'one *sf* billposting

af'fisso, a *pp di* **affiggere** ♦ *sm* bill, poster; (*LING*) affix

affit'tare *vt* (*dare in affitto*) to let, rent (out); (*prendere in affitto*) to rent; **af'fitto** *sm* rent; (*contratto*) lease

af'fliggere [af'fliddʒere] *vt* to torment; **~rsi** *vr* to grieve; **af'flitto, a** *pp di* **affliggere**; **afflizi'one** *sf* distress, torment

afflosci'arsi [afloʃ'farsi] *vr* to go limp

afflu'ente *sm* tributary; **afflu'enza** *sf* flow; (*di persone*) crowd

afflu'ire *vi* to flow; (*fig: merci, persone*) to pour in; **af'flusso** *sm* influx

affo'gare *vt, vi* to drown; **~rsi** *vr* to drown; (*deliberatamente*) to drown o.s.

affol'lare *vt* to crowd; **~rsi** *vr* to crowd;

affol'lato, a *ag* crowded

affon'dare *vt* to sink

affran'care *vt* to free, liberate; (*AMM*) to redeem; (*lettera*) to stamp; (*: meccanicamente*) to frank (*BRIT*), meter (*US*); **~rsi** *vr* to free o.s.; **affranca'tura** *sf* (*di francobollo*) stamping; franking (*BRIT*), metering (*US*); (*tassa di spedizione*) postage

af'franto, a *ag* (*esausto*) worn out; (*abbattuto*) overcome

af'fresco, schi *sm* fresco

affret'tare *vt* to quicken, speed up; **~rsi** *vr* to hurry; **~rsi a fare qc** to hurry *o* hasten to do sth

affron'tare *vt* (*pericolo etc*) to face; (*nemico*) to confront; **~rsi** *vr* (*reciproco*) to come to blows

af'fronto *sm* affront, insult

affumi'care *vt* to fill with smoke; to blacken with smoke; (*alimenti*) to smoke

affuso'lato, a *ag* tapering

a'foso, a *ag* sultry, close

'Africa *sf*: **l'~** Africa; **afri'cano, a** *ag, sm/f* African

afrodi'siaco, a, ci, che *ag, sm* aphrodisiac

a'genda [a'dʒenda] *sf* diary

a'gente [a'dʒente] *sm* agent; **~ di cambio** stockbroker; **~ di polizia** police officer; **agen'zia** *sf* agency; (*succursale*) branch; **agenzia di collocamento** employment agency; **agenzia immobiliare** estate agent's (office) (*BRIT*), real estate office (*US*); **agenzia pubblicitaria/viaggi** advertising/travel agency

agevo'lare [adʒevo'lare] *vt* to facilitate, make easy

a'gevole [a'dʒevole] *ag* easy; (*strada*) smooth

agganci'are [aggan'tʃare] *vt* to hook up; (*FERR*) to couple

ag'geggio [ad'dʒeddʒo] *sm* gadget, contraption

agget'tivo [addʒet'tivo] *sm* adjective

agghiacci'ante [aggjat'tʃante] *ag* chilling

agghin'darsi [aggin'darsi] *vr* to deck o.s. out

aggior'nare [addʒor'nare] *vt (opera, manuale)* to bring up-to-date; *(seduta etc)* to postpone; **~rsi** *vr* to bring (*o* keep) o.s. up-to-date; **aggior'nato, a** *ag* up-to-date

aggi'rare [addʒi'rare] *vt* to go round; *(fig: ingannare)* to trick; **~rsi** *vr* to wander about; **il prezzo s'aggira sul milione** the price is around the million mark

aggiudi'care [addʒudi'kare] *vt* to award; *(all'asta)* to knock down; **~rsi qc** to win sth

aggi'ungere [ad'dʒundʒere] *vt* to add; **aggi'unta** *sf* addition; **aggi'unto, a** *pp di* **aggiungere ♦** *ag* assistant *cpd* ♦ *sm* assistant

aggius'tare [addʒus'tare] *vt (accomodare)* to mend, repair; *(riassettare)* to adjust; *(fig: lite)* to settle; **~rsi** *vr (arrangiarsi)* to make do; *(con senso reciproco)* to come to an agreement

agglome'rato *sm (di rocce)* conglomerate; *(di legno)* chipboard; **~ urbano** built-up area

aggrap'parsi *vr*: **~ a** to cling to

aggra'vare *vt (aumentare)* to increase; *(appesantire: anche fig)* to weigh down, make heavy; *(pena)* to make worse; **~rsi** *vr* to worsen, become worse

aggrazi'ato, a [aggrat'tsjato] *ag* graceful

aggre'dire *vt* to attack, assault

aggre'gare *vt*: **~ qn a qc** to admit sb to sth; **~rsi** *vr* to join; **~rsi a** to join, become a member of

aggressi'one *sf* aggression; *(atto)* attack, assault

aggres'sivo, a *ag* aggressive

aggrot'tare *vt*: **~ le sopracciglia** to frown

aggrovigli'are [aggroviʎ'ʎare] *vt* to tangle; **~rsi** *vr (fig)* to become complicated

agguan'tare *vt* to catch, seize

aggu'ato *sm* trap; *(imboscata)* ambush; **tendere un ~ a qn** to set a trap for sb

agguer'rito, a *ag* fierce

agi'ato, a [a'dʒato] *ag (vita)* easy; *(persona)* well-off, well-to-do

'agile ['adʒile] *ag* agile, nimble; **agilità** *sf* agility, nimbleness

'agio ['adʒo] *sm* ease, comfort; **mettersi a proprio ~** to make o.s. at home *o* comfortable

a'gire [a'dʒire] *vi* to act; *(esercitare un'azione)* to take effect; *(TECN)* to work, function; **~ contro qn** *(DIR)* to take action against sb

agi'tare [adʒi'tare] *vt (bottiglia)* to shake; *(mano, fazzoletto)* to wave; *(fig: turbare)* to disturb; *(: incitare)* to stir (up); *(: dibattere)* to discuss; **~rsi** *vr (mare)* to be rough; *(malato, dormitore)* to toss and turn; *(bambino)* to fidget; *(emozionarsi)* to get upset; *(POL)* to agitate; **agi'tato, a** *ag* rough; restless; fidgety; upset, perturbed; **agitazi'one** *sf* agitation; *(POL)* unrest, agitation; **mettere in agitazione qn** to upset *o* distress sb

'agli ['aʎʎi] *prep + det vedi* **a**

'aglio ['aʎʎo] *sm* garlic

a'gnello [aɲ'ɲello] *sm* lamb

'ago *(pl* **'aghi**) *sm* needle

ago'nia *sf* agony

ago'nistico, a, ci, che *ag* athletic; *(fig)* competitive

agoniz'zare [agonid'dzare] *vi* to be dying

agopun'tura *sf* acupuncture

a'gosto *sm* August

a'graria *sf* agriculture

a'grario, a *ag* agrarian, agricultural; *(riforma)* land *cpd*

a'gricolo, a *ag* agricultural, farm *cpd*; **agricol'tore** *sm* farmer; **agricol'tura** *sf* agriculture, farming

agri'foglio [agri'fɔʎʎo] *sm* holly

agrimen'sore *sm* land surveyor

agritu'rismo *sm* farm holidays *pl*

'agro, a *ag* sour, sharp; **~dolce** *ag* bittersweet; *(salsa)* sweet and sour

a'grume *sm (spesso al pl: pianta)* citrus; *(: frutto)* citrus fruit

aguz'zare [agut'tsare] *vt* to sharpen; **~ gli orecchi** to prick up one's ears

a'guzzo, a [a'guttso] *ag* sharp

'ai *prep + det vedi* **a**

'Aia *sf*: **l'~** the Hague

'aia *sf* threshing floor

AIDS *sigla f o m* AIDS

ai'rone *sm* heron

aiu'ola *sf* flower bed

aiu'tante *sm/f* assistant ♦ *sm* (MIL)
adjutant; (NAUT) master-at-arms; **~ di
campo** aide-de-camp

aiu'tare *vt* to help; **~ qn (a fare)** to help sb
(to do)

ai'uto *sm* help, assistance, aid; (*aiutante*)
assistant; **venire in ~ di qn** to come to sb's
aid; **~ chirurgo** assistant surgeon

aiz'zare [ait'tsare] *vt* to incite; **~ i cani
contro qn** to set the dogs on sb

al *prep + det vedi* **a**

'ala (*pl* **'ali**) *sf* wing; **fare ~** to fall back,
make way; **~ destra / sinistra** (SPORT)
right/left wing

'alacre *ag* quick, brisk

a'lano *sm* Great Dane

a'lare *ag* wing *cpd*

'alba *sf* dawn

Alba'nia *sf*: **l'~** Albania

'albatro *sm* albatross

albeggi'are [albed'dʒare] *vi*, *vb impers* to
dawn

alberghi'ero, a [alber'gjero] *ag* hotel *cpd*

al'bergo, ghi *sm* hotel; **~ della gioventù**
youth hostel

'albero *sm* tree; (NAUT) mast; (TECN) shaft;
~ genealogico family tree; **~ a gomiti**
crankshaft; **~ di Natale** Christmas tree; **~
maestro** mainmast; **~ di trasmissione**
transmission shaft

albi'cocca, che *sf* apricot; **albi'cocco,
chi** *sm* apricot tree

'albo *sm* (*registro*) register, roll; (AMM)
notice board

'album *sm* album; **~ da disegno** sketch
book

al'bume *sm* albumen

'alce ['altʃe] *sm* elk

al'colico, a, ci, che *ag* alcoholic ♦ *sm*
alcoholic drink

alcoliz'zato, a [alkolid'dzato] *sm/f*
alcoholic

'alcool *sm* alcohol; **alco'olico** *etc*
= **alcolico** *etc*

al'cuno, a (*det*: *dav sm*: **alcun** +C, V,

alcuno +*s impura, gn, pn, ps, x, z; dav sf*:
alcuna +C, **alcun'** +V) *det* (*nessuno*): **non
... ~** no, not any; **~i, e** *det pl* some, a few;
non c'è ~a fretta there's no hurry, there
isn't any hurry; **senza alcun riguardo**
without any consideration ♦ *pron pl*: **~i, e**
some, a few

aldilà *sm*: **l'~** the after-life

alfa'beto *sm* alphabet

alfi'ere *sm* standard-bearer; (MIL) ensign;
(SCACCHI) bishop

'alga, ghe *sf* seaweed *no pl*, alga

'algebra *sf* algebra

Alge'ria [aldʒe'ria] *sf*: **l'~** Algeria

ali'ante *sm* (AER) glider

'alibi *sm inv* alibi

a'lice [a'litʃe] *sf* anchovy

alie'nare *vt* (DIR) to alienate, transfer;
(*rendere ostile*) to alienate; **~rsi qn** to
alienate sb; **alie'nato, a** *ag* alienated;
transferred; (*fuor di senno*) insane ♦ *sm*
lunatic, insane person; **alienazi'one** *sf*
alienation; transfer; insanity

ali'eno, a *ag* (*avverso*): **~ (da)** opposed
(to), averse (to) ♦ *sm/f* alien

alimen'tare *vt* to feed; (TECN) to feed; to
supply; (*fig*) to sustain ♦ *ag* food *cpd*; **~i**
smpl foodstuffs; (*anche*: **negozio di ~i**)
grocer's shop; **alimentazi'one** *sf* feeding;
supplying; sustaining; (*gli alimenti*) diet

ali'mento *sm* food; **~i** *smpl* (*cibo*) food *sg*;
(DIR) alimony

a'liquota *sf* share; (*d'imposta*) rate

alis'cafo *sm* hydrofoil

'alito *sm* breath

all. *abbr* (= *allegato*) encl.

'alla *prep + det vedi* **a**

allacci'are [allat'tʃare] *vt* (*scarpe*) to tie,
lace (up); (*cintura*) to do up, fasten; (*luce,
gas*) to connect; (*amicizia*) to form

alla'gare *vt* to flood; **~rsi** *vr* to flood

allar'gare *vt* to widen; (*vestito*) to let out;
(*aprire*) to open; (*fig: dilatare*) to extend

allar'mare *vt* to alarm

al'larme *sm* alarm; **~ aereo** air-raid
warning

allar'mismo *sm* scaremongering

allat'tare *vt* to feed

'alle *prep + det vedi* **a**

alle'anza [alle'antsa] *sf* alliance

alle'arsi *vr* to form an alliance; alle'ato, a *ag* allied ♦ *sm/f* ally

alle'gare *vt* (*accludere*) to enclose; (*DIR: citare*) to cite, adduce; (*denti*) to set on edge; alle'gato, a *ag* enclosed ♦ *sm* enclosure; (*di email*) attachment; **in allegato** enclosed

allegge'rire [alleddʒe'rire] *vt* to lighten, make lighter; (*fig: lavoro, tasse*) to reduce

alle'gria *sf* gaiety, cheerfulness

al'legro, a *ag* cheerful, merry; (*un po' brillo*) merry, tipsy; (*vivace: colore*) bright ♦ *sm* (*MUS*) allegro

allena'mento *sm* training

alle'nare *vt* to train; **~rsi** *vr* to train; allena'tore *sm* (*SPORT*) trainer, coach

allen'tare *vt* to slacken; (*disciplina*) to relax; **~rsi** *vr* to become slack; (*ingranaggio*) to work loose

aller'gia, 'gie [aller'dʒia] *sf* allergy; al'lergico, a, ci, che *ag* allergic

alles'tire *vt* (*cena*) to prepare; (*esercito, nave*) to equip, fit out; (*spettacolo*) to stage

allet'tare *vt* to lure, entice

alleva'mento *sm* breeding, rearing; (*luogo*) stock farm

alle'vare *vt* (*animale*) to breed, rear; (*bambino*) to bring up

allevi'are *vt* to alleviate

alli'bito, a *ag* astounded

allibra'tore *sm* bookmaker

allie'tare *vt* to cheer up, gladden

alli'evo *sm* pupil; (*apprendista*) apprentice; (*MIL*) cadet

alliga'tore *sm* alligator

alline'are *vt* (*persone, cose*) to line up; (*TIP*) to align; (*fig: economia, salari*) to adjust, align; **~rsi** *vr* to line up; (*fig: a idee*): **~rsi a** to come into line with

'allo *prep + det vedi* **a**

al'locco, a, chi, che *sm* tawny owl ♦ *sm/f* oaf

allocuzi'one [allokut'tsjone] *sf* address

al'lodola *sf* (sky)lark

alloggi'are [allod'dʒare] *vt* to accommodate ♦ *vi* to live; al'loggio *sm* lodging, accommodation (*BRIT*), accommodations (*US*)

allontana'mento *sm* removal; dismissal

allonta'nare *vt* to send away, send off; (*impiegato*) to dismiss; (*pericolo*) to avert, remove; (*estraniare*) to alienate; **~rsi** *vr*: **~rsi (da)** to go away (from); (*estraniarsi*) to become estranged (from)

al'lora *av* (*in quel momento*) then ♦ *cong* (*in questo caso*) well then; (*dunque*) well then, so; **la gente d'~** people then *o* in those days; **da ~ in poi** from then on

allor'ché [allor'ke] *cong* (*formale*) when, as soon as

al'loro *sm* laurel

'alluce ['allutʃe] *sm* big toe

alluci'nante [allutʃi'nante] *ag* awful; (*fam*) amazing

allucinazi'one [allutʃinat'tsjone] *sf* hallucination

al'ludere *vi*: **~ a** to allude to, hint at

al'luminio *sm* aluminium (*BRIT*), aluminum (*US*)

allun'gare *vt* to lengthen; (*distendere*) to prolong, extend; (*diluire*) to water down; **~rsi** *vr* to lengthen; (*ragazzo*) to stretch, grow taller; (*sdraiarsi*) to lie down, stretch out

allusi'one *sf* hint, allusion

al'luso, a *pp di* **alludere**

alluvi'one *sf* flood

al'meno *av* at least ♦ *cong*: **(se) ~** if only; **(se) ~ piovesse!** if only it would rain!

a'logeno, a [a'lɔdʒeno] *ag*: **lampada ~a** halogen lamp

a'lone *sm* halo

'Alpi *sfpl*: **le ~** the Alps

alpi'nismo *sm* mountaineering, climbing; alpi'nista, i, e *sm/f* mountaineer, climber

al'pino, a *ag* Alpine; mountain *cpd*

al'quanto *av* rather, a little; **~, a** *det* a certain amount of, some ♦ *pron* a certain amount; some; **~i, e** *det pl, pron pl* several, quite a few

alt *escl* halt!, stop!

alta'lena *sf* (*a funi*) swing; (*in bilico, anche fig*) seesaw

al'tare *sm* altar

alte'rare *vt* to alter, change; (*cibo*) to adulterate; (*registro*) to falsify; (*persona*) to irritate; **~rsi** *vr* to alter; (*cibo*) to go bad; (*persona*) to lose one's temper

al'terco, chi *sm* altercation, wrangle

alter'nare *vt* to alternate; **~rsi** *vr* to alternate; **alterna'tiva** *sf* alternative; **alterna'tivo, a** *ag* alternative; **alter'nato, a** *ag* alternate; (ELETTR) alternating; **alterna'tore** *sm* alternator

al'terno, a *ag* alternate; **a giorni ~i** on alternate days, every other day

al'tezza [al'tettsa] *sf* height; width, breadth; depth; pitch; (GEO) latitude; (*titolo*) highness; (*fig: nobiltà*) greatness; **essere all'~ di** to be on a level with; (*fig*) to be up to *o* equal to; **altez'zoso, a** *ag* haughty

al'ticcio, a, ci, ce [al'tittʃo] *ag* tipsy

altipi'ano *sm* = **altopiano**

alti'tudine *sf* altitude

'alto, a *ag* high; (*persona*) tall; (*tessuto*) wide, broad; (*sonno, acque*) deep; (*suono*) high(-pitched); (GEO) upper; (*: setten-trionale*) northern ♦ *sm* top (part) ♦ *av* high; (*parlare*) aloud, loudly; **il palazzo è ~ 20 metri** the building is 20 metres high; **ad ~a voce** aloud; **a notte ~a** in the dead of night; **in ~** up, upwards; at the top; **dall'~ in** *o* **al basso** up and down; **degli ~i e bassi** (*fig*) ups and downs; **~a fedeltà** high fidelity, hi-fi; **~a finanza** high finance; **~a moda** haute couture; **~a società** high society

alto'forno *sm* blast furnace

altolo'cato, a *ag* of high rank

altopar'lante *sm* loudspeaker

altopi'ano (*pl* **altipi'ani**) *sm* plateau, upland plain

altret'tanto, a *ag, pron* as much; (*pl*) as many ♦ *av* equally; **tanti auguri! — grazie, ~** all the best! — thank you, the same to you

'altri *pron inv* (*qualcuno*) somebody; (*: in espressioni negative*) anybody; (*un'altra persona*) another (person)

altri'menti *av* otherwise

'altro, a *det* 1 (*diverso*) other, different; **questa è un'~a cosa** that's another *o* a different thing

2 (*supplementare*) other; **prendi un ~ cioccolatino** have another chocolate; **hai avuto ~e notizie?** have you had any more *o* any other news?

3 (*nel tempo*): **l'~ giorno** the other day; **l'altr'anno** last year; **l'~ ieri** the day before yesterday; **domani l'~** the day after tomorrow; **quest'~ mese** next month

4: **d'~a parte** on the other hand

♦ *pron* 1 (*persona, cosa diversa o supplementare*): **un ~, un'~a** another (one); **lo farà un ~** someone else will do it; **~i, e others**; **gli ~i** (*la gente*) others, other people; **l'uno e l'~** both (of them); **aiutarsi l'un l'~** to help one another; **da un giorno all'~** from day to day; (*nel giro di 24 ore*) from one day to the next; (*da un momento all'altro*) any day now

2 (*sostantivato: solo maschile*) something else; (*: in espressioni interrogative*) anything else; **non ho ~ da dire** I have nothing else *o* I don't have anything else to say; **più che ~** above all; **se non ~** at least; **tra l'~** among other things; **ci mancherebbe ~!** that's all we need!; **non faccio ~ che lavorare** I do nothing but work; **contento? — ~ che!** are you pleased? — and how!; *vedi* **senza; noialtri; voialtri; tutto**

al'tronde *av*: **d'~** on the other hand

al'trove *av* elsewhere, somewhere else

al'trui *ag inv* other people's ♦ *sm*: **l'~** other people's belongings *pl*

altru'ista, i, e *ag* altruistic

al'tura *sf* (*rialto*) height, high ground; (*alto mare*) open sea; **pesca d'~** deep-sea fishing

a'lunno, a *sm/f* pupil

alve'are *sm* hive

'alveo *sm* riverbed

al'zare [al'tsare] *vt* to raise, lift; (*issare*) to hoist; (*costruire*) to build, erect; **~rsi** *vr* to rise; (*dal letto*) to get up; (*crescere*) to grow tall (*o* taller); **~ le spalle** to shrug one's shoulders; **~rsi in piedi** to stand up, get to one's feet; **al'zata** *sf* lifting, raising; **un'alzata di spalle** a shrug

a'mabile *ag* lovable; (*vino*) sweet

a'maca, che *sf* hammock

amalga'mare *vt* to amalgamate

a'mante *ag:* **~ di** (*musica etc*) fond of ♦ *sm/f* lover/mistress

a'mare *vt* to love; (*amico, musica, sport*) to like

amareggi'ato, a [amared'dʒato] *ag* upset, saddened

ama'rena *sf* sour black cherry

ama'rezza [ama'rettsa] *sf* bitterness

a'maro, a *ag* bitter ♦ *sm* bitterness; (*liquore*) bitters *pl*

ambasci'ata [ambaʃ'ʃata] *sf* embassy; (*messaggio*) message; **ambascia'tore, 'trice** *sm/f* ambassador/ambassadress

ambe'due *ag inv:* **~ i ragazzi** both boys ♦ *pron inv* both

ambien'tare *vt* to acclimatize; (*romanzo, film*) to set; **~rsi** *vr* to get used to one's surroundings

ambi'ente *sm* environment; (*fig: insieme di persone*) milieu; (*stanza*) room

am'biguo, a *ag* ambiguous

am'bire *vt* (*anche: vi:* **~ a**) to aspire to

'ambito *sm* sphere, field

ambizi'one [ambit'tsjone] *sf* ambition; **ambizi'oso, a** *ag* ambitious

'ambo *ag inv* both ♦ (*al gioco*) double

'ambra *sf* amber; **~ grigia** ambergris

ambu'lante *ag* itinerant ♦ *sm* peddler

ambu'lanza [ambu'lantsa] *sf* ambulance

ambula'torio *sm* (*studio medico*) surgery

a'meno, a *ag* pleasant; (*strano*) funny

A'merica *sf:* **l'~** America; **l'~ latina** Latin America; **ameri'cano, a** *ag, sm/f* American

ami'anto *sm* asbestos

a'mica *sf vedi* **amico**

ami'chevole [ami'kevole] *ag* friendly

ami'cizia [ami'tʃittsja] *sf* friendship; **~e** *sfpl* (*amici*) friends

a'mico, a, ci, che *sm/f* friend; (*fidanzato*) boyfriend/girlfriend; **~ del cuore** *o* **intimo** bosom friend

'amido *sm* starch

ammac'care *vt* (*pentola*) to dent; (*persona*) to bruise; **~rsi** *vr* to bruise

ammaes'trare *vt* (*animale*) to train

ammai'nare *vt* to lower, haul down

amma'larsi *vr* to fall ill; **amma'lato, a** *ag* ill, sick ♦ *sm/f* sick person; (*paziente*) patient

ammali'are *vt* (*fig*) to enchant, charm

am'manco, chi *sm* deficit

ammanet'tare *vt* to handcuff

ammas'sare *vt* (*ammucchiare*) to amass; (*raccogliere*) to gather together; **~rsi** *vr* to pile up; to gather; **am'masso** *sm* mass; (*mucchio*) pile, heap; (*ECON*) stockpile

ammat'tire *vi* to go mad

ammaz'zare [ammat'tsare] *vt* to kill; **~rsi** *vr* (*uccidersi*) to kill o.s.; (*rimanere ucciso*) to be killed; **~rsi di lavoro** to work o.s. to death

am'menda *sf* amends *pl*; (*DIR, SPORT*) fine

am'messo, a *pp di* **ammettere** ♦ *cong:* **~ che** supposing that

am'mettere *vt* to admit; (*riconoscere: fatto*) to acknowledge, admit; (*permettere*) to allow, accept; (*supporre*) to suppose

ammez'zato [ammed'dzato] *sm* (*anche:* **piano ~**) mezzanine, entresol

ammic'care *vi:* **~ (a)** to wink (at)

amminis'trare *vt* to run, manage; (*REL, DIR*) to administer; **amministra'tivo, a** *ag* administrative; **amministra'tore** *sm* administrator; (*di condominio*) flats manager; **amministratore delegato** managing director; **amministrazi'one** *sf* management; administration

ammiragli'ato [ammiraʎ'ʎato] *sm* admiralty

ammi'raglio [ammi'raʎʎo] *sm* admiral

ammi'rare *vt* to admire; **ammira'tore, 'trice** *sm/f* admirer; **ammirazi'one** *sf* admiration

ammissi'one *sf* admission

ammobili'ato, a *ag* furnished

am'modo *av* properly ♦ *ag inv* respectable, nice

am'mollo *sm*: **lasciare in ~** to leave to soak

ammo'niaca *sf* ammonia

ammoni'mento *sm* warning; admonishment

ammo'nire *vt* (*avvertire*) to warn; (*rimproverare*) to admonish; (*DIR*) to caution

ammon'tare *vi*: ~ **a** to amount to ♦ *sm* (total) amount

ammorbi'dente *sm* fabric conditioner

ammorbi'dire *vt* to soften

ammortiz'zare [ammortid'dzare] *vt* (*ECON*) to pay off, amortize; (: *spese d'impianto*) to write off; (*AUT*, *TECN*) to absorb, deaden; **ammortizza'tore** *sm* (*AUT*, *TECN*) shock-absorber

ammucchi'are [ammuk'kjare] *vt* to pile up, accumulate

ammuf'fire *vi* to go mouldy (*BRIT*) o moldy (*US*)

ammutina'mento *sm* mutiny

ammuto'lire *vi* to be struck dumb

amnis'tia *sf* amnesty

'amo *sm* (*PESCA*) hook; (*fig*) bait

a'modo *av* = **ammodo**

a'more *sm* love; **~i** *smpl* love affairs; **il tuo bambino è un ~** your baby's a darling; **fare l'~** o **all'~** to make love; **per ~** o **per forza** by hook or by crook; **amor proprio** self-esteem, pride; **amo'revole** *ag* loving, affectionate

a'morfo, a *ag* amorphous; (*fig: persona*) lifeless

amo'roso, a *ag* (*affettuoso*) loving, affectionate; (*d'amore: sguardo*) amorous; (: *poesia, relazione*) love *cpd*

ampi'ezza [am'pjettsa] *sf* width, breadth; spaciousness; (*fig: importanza*) scale, size

'ampio, a *ag* wide, broad; (*spazioso*) spacious; (*abbondante: vestito*) loose; (: *gonna*) full; (: *spiegazione*) ample, full

am'plesso *sm* intercourse

ampli'are *vt* (*ingrandire*) to enlarge; (*allargare*) to widen

amplifi'care *vt* to amplify; **amplifica'tore** *sm* (*TECN*, *MUS*) amplifier

am'polla *sf* (*vasetto*) cruet

ampu'tare *vt* (*MED*) to amputate

amu'leto *sm* lucky charm

anabbagli'ante [anabbaʎ'ʎante] *ag* (*AUT*) dipped (*BRIT*), dimmed (*US*); **~i** *smpl* dipped (*BRIT*) o dimmed (*US*) headlights

a'nagrafe *sf* (*registro*) register of births, marriages and deaths; (*ufficio*) registry office (*BRIT*), office of vital statistics (*US*)

anal'colico, a, ci, che *ag* non-alcoholic ♦ *sm* soft drink

analfa'beta, i, e *ag*, *sm/f* illiterate

anal'gesico, a, ci, che [anal'dʒɛziko] *ag*, *sm* analgesic

a'nalisi *sf inv* analysis; (*MED: esame*) test; ~ **grammaticale** parsing; **ana'lista, i, e** *sm/f* analyst; (*PSIC*) (psycho)analyst

analiz'zare [analid'dzare] *vt* to analyse; (*MED*) to test

analo'gia, 'gie [analo'dʒia] *sf* analogy

a'nalogo, a, ghi, ghe *ag* analogous

'ananas *sm inv* pineapple

anar'chia [anar'kia] *sf* anarchy; **a'narchico, a, ci, che** *ag* anarchic(al) ♦ *sm/f* anarchist

'ANAS *sigla f* (= *Azienda Nazionale Autonoma delle Strade*) national roads department

anato'mia *sf* anatomy; **ana'tomico, a, ci, che** *ag* anatomical; (*sedile*) contoured

'anatra *sf* duck

'anca, che *sf* (*ANAT*) hip

'anche ['anke] *cong* (*inoltre, pure*) also, too; (*perfino*) even; **vengo anch'io** I'm coming too; **~ se** even if

an'cora¹ *av* still; (*di nuovo*) again; (*di più*) some more; (*persino*): ~ **più forte** even stronger; **non ~** not yet; ~ **una volta** once more, once again; ~ **un po'** a little more; (*di tempo*) a little longer

'ancora² *sf* anchor; **gettare/levare l'~** to cast/weigh anchor; **anco'raggio** *sm* anchorage; **anco'rare** *vt* to anchor;

ancorarsi *vr* to anchor

anda'mento *sm* progress, movement; course; state

an'dante *ag* (*corrente*) current; (*di poco pregio*) cheap, second-rate ♦ *sm* (*MUS*) andante

an'dare *sm*: **a lungo ~** in the long run ♦ *vi* to go; (*essere adatto*): **~ a** to suit; (*piacere*): **il suo comportamento non mi va** I don't like the way he behaves; **ti va di andare al cinema?** do you feel like going to the cinema?; **andarsene** to go away; **questa camicia va lavata** this shirt needs a wash *o* should be washed; **~ a cavallo** to ride; **~ in macchina/aereo** to go by car/plane; **~ a fare qc** to go and do sth; **~ a pescare/ sciare** to go fishing/skiing; **~ a male** to go bad; **come va?** (*lavoro, progetto*) how are things?; **come va? — bene, grazie!** how are you? — fine, thanks!; **va fatto entro oggi** it's got to be done today; **ne va della nostra vita** our lives are at stake; **an'data** *sf* going; (*viaggio*) outward journey; **biglietto di sola andata** (*BRIT*) *o* one-way ticket; **biglietto di andata e ritorno** return (*BRIT*) *o* round-trip (*US*) ticket; **anda'tura** *sf* (*modo di andare*) walk, gait; (*SPORT*) pace; (*NAUT*) tack

an'dazzo [an'dattso] (*peg*) *sm*: **prendere un brutto ~** to take a turn for the worse

andirivi'eni *sm inv* coming and going

'andito *sm* corridor, passage

an'drone *sm* entrance hall

a'neddoto *sm* anecdote

ane'lare *vi*: **~ a** to long for, yearn for

a'nelito *sm* (*fig*): **~ di** longing *o* yearning for

a'nello *sm* ring; (*di catena*) link

a'nemico, a, ci, che *ag* anaemic

a'nemone *sm* anemone

aneste'sia *sf* anaesthesia; **anes'tetico, a, ci, che** *ag, sm* anaesthetic

anfite'atro *sm* amphitheatre

an'fratto *sm* ravine

an'gelico, a, ci, che [an'dʒeliko] *ag* angelic(al)

'angelo ['andʒelo] *sm* angel; **~ custode** guardian angel

anghe'ria [ange'ria] *sf* vexation

an'gina [an'dʒina] *sf* tonsillitis; **~ pectoris** angina

angli'cano, a *ag* Anglican

angli'cismo [angli'tʃizmo] *sm* anglicism

anglo'sassone *ag* Anglo-Saxon

ango'lare *ag* angular

angolazi'one [angolat'tsjone] *sf* (*FOT etc, fig*) angle

'angolo *sm* corner; (*MAT*) angle

an'goscia, sce [an'gɔʃʃa] *sf* deep anxiety, anguish *no pl*; **angosci'oso, a** *ag* (*d'angoscia*) anguished; (*che dà angoscia*) distressing, painful

angu'illa *sf* eel

an'guria *sf* watermelon

an'gustia *sf* (*ansia*) anguish, distress; (*povertà*) poverty, want

angusti'are *vt* to distress; **~rsi** *vr*: **~rsi (per)** to worry (about)

an'gusto, a *ag* (*stretto*) narrow

'anice ['anitʃe] *sm* (*CUC*) aniseed; (*BOT*) anise

a'nidride *sf* (*CHIM*): **~ carbonica/solforosa** carbon/sulphur dioxide

'anima *sf* soul; (*abitante*) inhabitant; **non c'era ~ viva** there wasn't a living soul

ani'male *sm, ag* animal; **~ domestico** pet

ani'mare *vt* to give life to, liven up; (*incoraggiare*) to encourage; **~rsi** *vr* to become animated, come to life; **ani'mato, a** *ag* animate; (*vivace*) lively, animated; (: *strada*) busy; **anima'tore, 'trice** *sm/f* guiding spirit; (*CINEMA*) animator; (*di festa*) life and soul; **animazi'one** *sf* liveliness; (*di strada*) bustle; (*CINEMA*) animation; **animazione teatrale** amateur dramatics

'animo *sm* (*mente*) mind; (*cuore*) heart; (*coraggio*) courage; (*disposizione*) character, disposition; **avere in ~ di fare qc** to intend *o* have a mind to do sth; **perdersi d'~** to lose heart

'anitra *sf* = **anatra**

anna'cquare *vt* to water down, dilute

annaffi'are *vt* to water; **annaffia'toio** *sm* watering can

an'nali *smpl* annals

annas'pare *vi* to flounder

an'nata *sf* year; (*importo annuo*) annual amount; **vino d'~** vintage wine

annebbi'are *vt* (*fig*) to cloud; **~rsi** *vr* to become foggy; (*vista*) to become dim

annega'mento *sm* drowning

anne'gare *vt, vi* to drown; **~rsi** *vr* (*accidentalmente*) to drown; (*deliberatamente*) to drown o.s.

anne'rire *vt* to blacken ♦ *vi* to become black

an'nesso, a *pp di* **annettere** ♦ *ag* attached; (*POL*) annexed; **... e tutti gli ~i e connessi** and so on and so forth

an'nettere *vt* (*POL*) to annex; (*accludere*) to attach

annichi'lire [anniki'lire] *vt* = **annichilare**

anni'darsi *vr* to nest

annien'tare *vt* to annihilate, destroy

anniver'sario *sm* anniversary

'anno *sm* year; **ha 8 ~i** he's 8 (years old)

anno'dare *vt* to knot, tie; (*fig: rapporto*) to form

annoi'are *vt* to bore; (*seccare*) to annoy; **~rsi** *vr* to be bored; to be annoyed

an'noso, a *ag* (*problema etc*) age-old

anno'tare *vt* (*registrare*) to note, note down; (*commentare*) to annotate; **annotazi'one** *sf* note; annotation

annove'rare *vt* to number

annu'ale *ag* annual

annu'ario *sm* yearbook

annu'ire *vi* to nod; (*acconsentire*) to agree

annul'lare *vt* to annihilate, destroy; (*contratto, francobollo*) to cancel; (*matrimonio*) to annul; (*sentenza*) to quash; (*risultati*) to declare void

annunci'are [annun'tʃare] *vt* to announce; (*dar segni rivelatori*) to herald; **annuncia'tore, 'trice** *sm/f* (*RADIO, TV*) announcer; **l'Annunciazi'one** *sf* the Annunciation

an'nuncio [an'nuntʃo] *sm* announcement; (*fig*) sign; **~ pubblicitario** advertisement; **~i economici** classified advertisements, small ads

'annuo, a *ag* annual, yearly

annu'sare *vt* to sniff, smell; **~ tabacco** to take snuff

'ano *sm* anus

anoma'lia *sf* anomaly

a'nomalo, a *ag* anomalous

a'nonimo, a *ag* anonymous ♦ *sm* (*autore*) anonymous writer (*o* painter *etc*); **società ~a** (*COMM*) joint stock company

anores'sia *sf* anorexia

anor'male *ag* abnormal ♦ *sm/f* subnormal person

ANSA *sigla f* (= *Agenzia Nazionale Stampa Associata*) press agency

'ansa *sf* (*manico*) handle; (*di fiume*) bend, loop

'ansia *sf* anxiety

ansi'età *sf* = **ansia**

ansi'mare *vi* to pant

ansi'oso, a *ag* anxious

'anta *sf* (*di finestra*) shutter; (*di armadio*) door

antago'nismo *sm* antagonism

an'tartico, a, ci, che *ag* Antarctic ♦ *sm*: **l'A~** the Antarctic

An'tartide *sf*: **l'~** Antarctica

antece'dente [antetʃe'dente] *ag* preceding, previous

ante'fatto *sm* previous events *pl*; previous history

antegu'erra *sm* pre-war period

ante'nato *sm* ancestor, forefather

an'tenna *sf* (*RADIO, TV*) aerial; (*ZOOL*) antenna, feeler; (*NAUT*) yard; **~ parabolica** satellite dish

ante'prima *sf* preview

anteri'ore *ag* (*ruota, zampa*) front; (*fatti*) previous, preceding

antia'ereo, a *ag* anti-aircraft

antia'tomico, a, ci, che *ag* anti-nuclear; **rifugio ~** fallout shelter

antibi'otico, a, ci, che *ag, sm* antibiotic

anti'camera *sf* anteroom; **fare ~** to wait (for an audience)

antichità [antiki'ta] *sf inv* antiquity; (*oggetto*) antique

antici'pare [antitʃi'pare] *vt* (*consegna,*

visita) to bring forward, anticipate; (*somma di denaro*) to pay in advance; (*notizia*) to disclose ♦ *vi* to be ahead of time; **anticipazi'one** *sf* anticipation; (*di notizia*) advance information; (*di somma di denaro*) advance; **an'ticipo** *sm* anticipation; (*di denaro*) advance; **in anticipo** early, in advance

an'tico, a, chi, che *ag* (*quadro, mobili*) antique; (*dell'antichità*) ancient; **all'~a** old-fashioned

anticoncezio'nale [antikontʃettsjo'nale] *sm* contraceptive

anticonfor'mista, i, e *ag, sm/f* nonconformist

anti'corpo *sm* antibody

antidepres'sivo *sm* antidepressant

an'tidoto *sm* antidote

anti'furto *sm* anti-theft device

anti'gelo [anti'dʒelo] *ag inv:* **(liquido)** ~ (*per motore*) antifreeze; (*per cristalli*) de-icer

An'tille *sfpl:* **le** ~ the West Indies

antin'cendio [antin'tʃendjo] *ag inv* fire *cpd*

antio'rario [antio'rarjo] *ag:* **in senso** ~ anticlockwise

anti'pasto *sm* hors d'œuvre

antipa'tia *sf* antipathy, dislike; **anti'patico, a, ci, che** *ag* unpleasant

antiquari'ato *sm* antique trade; **un oggetto d'~** an antique

anti'quario *sm* antique dealer

anti'quato, a *ag* antiquated, old-fashioned

antise'mita, i, e *ag* anti-Semitic

anti'settico, a, ci, che *ag, sm* antiseptic

antista'minico, a, ci, che *ag, sm* antihistamine

antolo'gia, 'gie [antolo'dʒia] *sf* anthology

antra'ce *sm* anthrax

anu'lare *ag* ring *cpd* ♦ *sm* third finger

'anzi ['antsi] *av* (*invece*) on the contrary; (*o meglio*) or rather, or better still

anzianità [antsjani'ta] *sf* old age; (*AMM*) seniority

anzi'ano, a [an'tsjano] *ag* old; (*AMM*) senior ♦ *sm/f* old person; senior member

anziché [antsi'ke] *cong* rather than

anzi'tutto [antsi'tutto] *av* first of all

apa'tia *sf* apathy, indifference

a'patico, a, ci, che *ag* apathetic

'ape *sf* bee

aperi'tivo *sm* apéritif

a'perto, a *pp di* **aprire** ♦ *ag* open; **all'~** in the open (air)

aper'tura *sf* opening; (*ampiezza*) width; (*FOT*) aperture; ~ **alare** wing span

'apice ['apitʃe] *sm* apex; (*fig*) height

ap'nea *sf:* **immergersi in** ~ to dive without breathing apparatus

a'postolo *sm* apostle

a'postrofo *sm* apostrophe

appa'gare *vt* to satisfy

ap'palto *sm* (*COMM*) contract; **dare/ prendere in** ~ **un lavoro** to let out/ undertake a job on contract

appan'nare *vt* (*vetro*) to mist; (*vista*) to dim; **~rsi** *vr* to mist over; to grow dim

appa'rato *sm* equipment, machinery; (*ANAT*) apparatus; ~ **scenico** (*TEATRO*) props *pl*

apparecchi'are [apparek'kjare] *vt* to prepare; (*tavola*) to set ♦ *vi* to set the table; **apparecchia'tura** *sf* equipment; (*macchina*) machine, device

appa'recchio [appa'rekkjo] *sm* device; (*aeroplano*) aircraft *inv*; ~ **televisivo/ telefonico** television set/telephone

appa'rente *ag* apparent; **appa'renza** *sf* appearance; **in** *o* **all'apparenza** apparently

appa'rire *vi* to appear; (*sembrare*) to seem, appear; **appari'scente** *ag* (*colore*) garish, gaudy; (*bellezza*) striking

ap'parso, a *pp di* **apparire**

apparta'mento *sm* flat (*BRIT*), apartment (*US*)

appar'tarsi *vr* to withdraw; **appar'tato, a** *ag* (*luogo*) secluded

apparte'nere *vi:* ~ **a** to belong to

appassio'nare *vt* to thrill; (*commuovere*) to move; **~rsi a qc** to take a great interest in sth; **appassio'nato, a** *ag* passionate; (*entusiasta*): **appassionato (di)** keen (on)

appas'sire *vi* to wither

appel'larsi *vr* (*ricorrere*): ~ **a** to appeal to; (*DIR*): ~ **contro** to appeal against; **ap'pello** *sm* roll-call; (*implorazione, DIR*) appeal; **fare**

appello a to appeal to

ap'pena *av* (*a stento*) hardly, scarcely; (*solamente, da poco*) just ♦ *cong* as soon as; **(non) ~ furono arrivati ...** as soon as they had arrived ...; **~ ... che** *o* **quando** no sooner ... than

ap'pendere *vt* to hang (up)

appen'dice [appen'ditʃe] *sf* appendix; **romanzo d'~** popular serial

appendi'cite [appendi'tʃite] *sf* appendicitis

Appen'nini *smpl*: **gli ~** the Apennines

appesan'tire *vt* to make heavy; **~rsi** *vr* to grow stout

ap'peso, a *pp di* **appendere**

appe'tito *sm* appetite; **appeti'toso, a** *ag* appetising; (*fig*) attractive, desirable

appia'nare *vt* to level; (*fig*) to smooth away, iron out

appiat'tire *vt* to flatten; **~rsi** *vr* to become flatter; (*farsi piatto*) to flatten o.s.; **~rsi al suolo** to lie flat on the ground

appic'care *vt*: **~ il fuoco a** to set fire to, set on fire

appicci'care [appittʃi'kare] *vt* to stick; **~rsi** *vr* to stick; (*fig: persona*) to cling

appi'eno *av* fully

appigli'arsi [appiʎ'ʎarsi] *vr*: **~ a** (*afferrarsi*) to take hold of; (*fig*) to cling to; **ap'piglio** *sm* hold; (*fig*) pretext

appiso'larsi *vr* to doze off

applau'dire *vt, vi* to applaud; **ap'plauso** *sm* applause

appli'care *vt* to apply; (*regolamento*) to enforce; **~rsi** *vr* to apply o.s.; **applicazi'one** *sf* application; enforcement

appoggi'are [appod'dʒare] *vt* (*mettere contro*): **~ qc a qc** to lean *o* rest sth against sth; (*fig: sostenere*) to support; **~rsi** *vr*: **~rsi a** to lean against; (*fig*) to rely upon; **ap'poggio** *sm* support

appollai'arsi *vr* (*anche fig*) to perch

ap'porre *vt* to affix

appor'tare *vt* to bring

apposita'mente *av* specially; (*apposta*) on purpose

ap'posito, a *ag* appropriate

ap'posta *av* on purpose, deliberately

appos'tarsi *vr* to lie in wait

ap'prendere *vt* (*imparare*) to learn

appren'dista, i, e *sm/f* apprentice

apprensi'one *sf* apprehension; **appren'sivo, a** *ag* apprehensive

ap'presso *av* (*accanto, vicino*) close by, near; (*dietro*) behind; (*dopo, più tardi*) after, later ♦ *ag inv* (*dopo*): **il giorno ~** the next day; **~ a** (*vicino a*) near, close to

appres'tare *vt* to prepare, get ready; **~rsi** *vr*: **~rsi a fare qc** to prepare *o* get ready to do sth

ap'pretto *sm* starch

apprezza'mento [apprettsa'mento] *sm* appreciation; (*giudizio*) opinion

apprez'zare [appret'tsare] *vt* to appreciate

ap'proccio [ap'prɔttʃo] *sm* approach

appro'dare *vi* (*NAUT*) to land; (*fig*): **non ~ a nulla** to come to nothing; **ap'prodo** *sm* landing; (*luogo*) landing-place

approfit'tare *vi*: **~ di** to make the most of; (*peg*) to take advantage of

approfon'dire *vt* to deepen; (*fig*) to study in depth

appropri'ato, a *ag* appropriate

approssi'marsi *vr*: **~ a** to approach

approssima'tivo, a *ag* approximate, rough; (*impreciso*) inexact, imprecise

appro'vare *vt* (*condotta, azione*) to approve of; (*candidato*) to pass; (*progetto di legge*) to approve; **approvazi'one** *sf* approval

approvvigio'nare [approvvidʒo'nare] *vt* to supply

appunta'mento *sm* appointment; (*amoroso*) date; **darsi ~** to arrange to meet (one another)

appun'tato *sm* (*CARABINIERI*) corporal

ap'punto *sm* note; (*rimprovero*) reproach ♦ *av* (*proprio*) exactly, just; **per l'~!, ~!** exactly!

appu'rare *vt* to check, verify

apribot'tiglie [apribot'tiʎʎe] *sm inv* bottle opener

a'prile *sm* April

a'prire *vt* to open; (*via, cadavere*) to open

up; (*gas, luce, acqua*) to turn on ♦ *vi* to open; **~rsi** *vr* to open; **~rsi a qn** to confide in sb, open one's heart to sb

apris'catole *sm inv* tin (*BRIT*) *o* can opener

a'**quario** *sm* = **acquario**

'**aquila** *sf* (*ZOOL*) eagle; (*fig*) genius

aqui'lone *sm* (*giocattolo*) kite; (*vento*) North wind

A'rabia Sau'dita *sf*: **l'~** Saudi Arabia

'**arabo, a** *ag*, *sm/f* Arab ♦ *sm* (*LING*) Arabic

a'**rachide** [a'rakide] *sf* peanut

ara'gosta *sf* crayfish; lobster

a'**rancia, ce** [a'rantʃa] *sf* orange; **aranci'ata** *sf* orangeade; **a'rancio** *sm* (*BOT*) orange tree; (*colore*) orange ♦ *ag inv* (*colore*) orange; **aranci'one** *ag inv*: **(color) arancione** bright orange

a'**rare** *vt* to plough (*BRIT*), plow (*US*)

a'**ratro** *sm* plough (*BRIT*), plow (*US*)

a'**razzo** [a'rattso] *sm* tapestry

arbi'trare *vt* (*SPORT*) to referee; to umpire; (*DIR*) to arbitrate

arbi'trario, a *ag* arbitrary

ar'**bitrio** *sm* will; (*abuso, sopruso*) arbitrary act

'**arbitro** *sm* arbiter, judge; (*DIR*) arbitrator; (*SPORT*) referee; (: *TENNIS, CRICKET*) umpire

ar'**busto** *sm* shrub

'**arca, che** *sf* (*sarcofago*) sarcophagus; **l'~ di Noè** Noah's ark

ar'**cangelo** [ar'kandʒelo] *sm* archangel

ar'**cata** *sf* (*ARCHIT, ANAT*) arch; (*ordine di archi*) arcade

archeolo'gia [arkeolo'dʒia] *sf* arch(a)eology; **arche'ologo, a, gi, ghe** *sm/f* arch(a)eologist

ar'**chetto** [ar'ketto] *sm* (*MUS*) bow

archi'tettare [arkitet'tare] *vt* (*fig: ideare*) to devise; (: *macchinare*) to plan, concoct

archi'tetto [arki'tetto] *sm* architect; **architet'tura** *sf* architecture

ar'**chivio** [ar'kivjo] *sm* archives *pl*; (*INFORM*) file

arci'**ere** [ar'tʃere] *sm* archer

ar'**cigno, a** [ar'tʃiɲɲo] *ag* grim, severe

arci'**vescovo** [artʃi'veskovo] *sm* archbishop

'**arco** *sm* (*arma, MUS*) bow; (*ARCHIT*) arch;

(*MAT*) arc

arcoba'leno *sm* rainbow

arcu'ato, a *ag* curved, bent

ar'**dente** *ag* burning; (*fig*) burning, ardent

ar'**dere** *vt*, *vi* to burn

ar'**desia** *sf* slate

ar'**dire** *vi* to dare ♦ *sm* daring; **ar'dito, a** *ag* brave, daring, bold; (*sfacciato*) bold

ar'**dore** *sm* blazing heat; (*fig*) ardour, fervour

'**arduo, a** *ag* arduous, difficult

'**area** *sf* area; (*EDIL*) land, ground

a'**rena** *sf* arena; (*per corride*) bullring; (*sabbia*) sand

are'narsi *vr* to run aground

areo'plano *sm* = **aeroplano**

'**argano** *sm* winch

argente'ria [ardʒente'ria] *sf* silverware, silver

Argen'tina [ardʒen'tina] *sf*: **l'~** Argentina; **argen'tino, a** *ag*, *sm/f* Argentinian

ar'**gento** [ar'dʒento] *sm* silver; **~ vivo** quicksilver

ar'**gilla** [ar'dʒilla] *sf* clay

'**argine** ['ardʒine] *sm* embankment, bank; (*diga*) dyke, dike

argo'mento *sm* argument; (*motivo*) motive; (*materia, tema*) subject

argu'ire *vt* to deduce

ar'**guto, a** *ag* sharp, quick-witted; **ar'guzia** *sf* wit; (*battuta*) witty remark

'**aria** *sf* air; (*espressione, aspetto*) air, look; (*MUS: melodia*) tune; (: *di opera*) aria; **mandare all'~ qc** to ruin *o* upset sth; **all'~ aperta** in the open (air)

'**arido, a** *ag* arid

arieggi'are [arjed'dʒare] *vt* (*cambiare aria*) to air; (*imitare*) to imitate

ari'**ete** *sm* ram; (*MIL*) battering ram; (*dello zodiaco*): **A~** Aries

a'**ringa, ghe** *sf* herring *inv*

'**arista** *sf* (*CUC*) chine of pork

aristo'cratico, a, ci, che *ag* aristocratic

arit'metica *sf* arithmetic

arlec'chino [arlek'kino] *sm* harlequin

'**arma, i** *sf* weapon, arm; (*parte dell'esercito*) arm; **chiamare alle ~i** to call up (BRIT), draft (US); **sotto le ~i** in the army (o forces); **alle ~i!** to arms!; **~ da fuoco** firearm

ar'**madio** sm cupboard; (per abiti) wardrobe; **~ a muro** built-in cupboard

armamen'**tario** sm equipment

arma'**mento** sm (MIL) armament; (: materiale) arms pl, weapons pl; (NAUT) fitting; manning

ar'**mare** vt to arm; (arma da fuoco) to cock; (NAUT: nave) to rig, fit out; to man; (EDIL: volta, galleria) to prop up, shore up; **~rsi** vr to arm o.s.; (MIL) to take up arms; ar'**mata** sf (MIL) army; (NAUT) fleet; arma'**tore** sm shipowner; arma'**tura** sf (struttura di sostegno) framework; (impalcatura) scaffolding; (STORIA) armour no pl, suit of armour

armeggi'**are** [armed'dʒare] vi: **~ (intorno a qc)** to mess about (with sth)

armis'**tizio** [armis'tittsjo] sm armistice

armo'**nia** sf harmony; ar'**monica, che** sf (MUS) harmonica; **~ a bocca** mouth organ; ar'**monico, a, ci, che** ag harmonic; (fig) harmonious; armoni'**oso** a ag harmonious

armoniz'**zare** [armonid'dzare] vt to harmonize; (colori, abiti) to match ♦ vi to be in harmony; to match

ar'**nese** sm tool, implement; (oggetto indeterminato) thing, contraption; **male in ~** (malvestito) badly dressed; (di salute malferma) in poor health; (di condizioni economiche) down-at-heel

'**arnia** sf hive

a'**roma, i** sm aroma; fragrance; **~i** smpl (CUC) herbs and spices; aromatera'**pia** sf aromatherapy; aro'**matico, a, ci, che** ag aromatic; (cibo) spicy

'**arpa** sf (MUS) harp

ar'**peggio** [ar'peddʒo] sm (MUS) arpeggio

ar'**pia** sf (anche fig) harpy

arpi'**one** sm (gancio) hook; (cardine) hinge; (PESCA) harpoon

arrabat'**tarsi** vr to do all one can, strive

arrabbi'**are** vi (cane) to be affected with rabies; **~rsi** vr (essere preso dall'ira) to get

angry, fly into a rage; arrabbi'**ato, a** ag rabid, with rabies; furious, angry

arraf'**fare** vt to snatch, seize; (sottrarre) to pinch

arrampi'**carsi** vr to climb (up)

arran'**care** vi to limp, hobble

arran'**giare** [arran'dʒare] vt to arrange; **~rsi** vr to manage, do the best one can

arre'**care** vt to bring; (causare) to cause

arreda'**mento** sm (studio) interior design; (mobili etc) furnishings pl

arre'**dare** vt to furnish; arreda'**tore, 'trice** sm/f interior designer; ar'**redo** sm fittings pl, furnishings pl

ar'**rendersi** vr to surrender

arres'**tare** vt (fermare) to stop, halt; (catturare) to arrest; **~rsi** vr (fermarsi) to stop; ar'**resto** sm (cessazione) stopping; (fermata) stop; (cattura, MED) arrest; **subire un arresto** to come to a stop o standstill; **mettere agli arresti** to place under arrest; **arresti domiciliari** house arrest sg

arre'**trare** vt, vi to withdraw; arre'**trato, a** ag (lavoro) behind schedule; (paese, bambino) backward; (numero di giornale) back cpd; arretrati smpl arrears

arric'**chire** [arrik'kire] vt to enrich; **~rsi** vr to become rich

arricci'**are** [arrit'tʃare] vt to curl

ar'**ringa, ghe** sf harangue; (DIR) address by counsel

arrischi'**are** [arris'kjare] vt to risk; **~rsi** vr to venture, dare; arrischi'**ato, a** ag risky; (temerario) reckless, rash

arri'**vare** vi to arrive; (accadere) to happen, occur; **~ a** (livello, grado etc) to reach; **lui arriva a Roma alle 7** he gets to o arrives at Rome at 7; **non ci arrivo** I can't reach it; (fig: non capisco) I can't understand it

arrive'**derci** [arrive'dertʃi] escl goodbye!

arrive'**derla** escl (forma di cortesia) goodbye!

arri'**vista, i, e** sm/f go-getter

ar'**rivo** sm arrival; (SPORT) finish, finishing line

arro'**gante** ag arrogant

arro'**lare** vb = **arruolare**

arros'sire *vi* (*per vergogna, timidezza*) to blush, flush; (*per gioia, rabbia*) to flush

arros'tire *vt* to roast; (*pane*) to toast; (*ai ferri*) to grill

ar'rosto *sm, ag inv* roast

arro'tare *vt* to sharpen; (*investire con un veicolo*) to run over

arroto'lare *vt* to roll up

arroton'dare *vt* (*forma, oggetto*) to round; (*stipendio*) to add to; (*somma*) to round off

arrovel'larsi *vr* to rack one's brains

arruf'fare *vt* to ruffle; (*fili*) to tangle; (*fig: questione*) to confuse

arruggi'nire [arruddʒi'nire] *vt* to rust; **~rsi** *vr* to rust; (*fig*) to become rusty

arruo'lare *vt* (*MIL*) to enlist; **~rsi** *vr* to enlist, join up

arse'nale *sm* (*MIL*) arsenal; (*cantiere navale*) dockyard

'arso, a *pp di* **ardere ♦** *ag* (*bruciato*) burnt; (*arido*) dry; **ar'sura** *sf* (*calore opprimente*) burning heat; (*siccità*) drought

'arte *sf* art; (*abilità*) skill

arte'fatto, a *ag* (*cibo*) adulterated; (*fig: modi*) artificial

ar'tefice [ar'tefitʃe] *sm/f* craftsman/woman; (*autore*) author

ar'teria *sf* artery

'artico, a, ci, che *ag* Arctic

artico'lare *ag* (*ANAT*) of the joints, articular ♦ *vt* to articulate; (*suddividere*) to divide, split up; **articolazi'one** *sf* articulation; (*ANAT, TECN*) joint

ar'ticolo *sm* article; **~ di fondo** (*STAMPA*) leader, leading article

'Artide *sm*: **l'~** the Arctic

artifici'ale [artifi'tʃale] *ag* artificial

arti'ficio [arti'fitʃo] *sm* (*espediente*) trick, artifice; (*ricerca di effetto*) artificiality

artigia'nato [artidʒa'nato] *sm* craftsmanship; craftsmen *pl*

artigi'ano, a [arti'dʒano] *sm/f* craftsman/woman

artiglie'ria [artiʎʎe'ria] *sf* artillery

ar'tiglio [ar'tiʎʎo] *sm* claw; (*di rapaci*) talon

ar'tista, i, e *sm/f* artist; **ar'tistico, a, ci, che** *ag* artistic

'arto *sm* (*ANAT*) limb

ar'trite *sf* (*MED*) arthritis

ar'trosi *sf* osteoarthritis

ar'zillo, a [ar'dzillo] *ag* lively, sprightly

a'scella [aʃʃella] *sf* (*ANAT*) armpit

ascen'dente [aʃʃen'dɛnte] *sm* ancestor; (*fig*) ascendancy; (*ASTR*) ascendant

ascensi'one [aʃʃen'sjone] *sf* (*ALPINISMO*) ascent; (*REL*): **l'A~** the Ascension

ascen'sore [aʃʃen'sore] *sm* lift

a'scesa [aʃ'ʃesa] *sf* ascent; (*al trono*) accession

a'scesso [aʃ'ʃesso] *sm* (*MED*) abscess

'ascia ['aʃʃa] (*pl* **asce**) *sf* axe

asciugaca'pelli [aʃʃugaka'pelli] *sm* hair-dryer

asciuga'mano [aʃʃuga'mano] *sm* towel

asciu'gare [aʃʃu'gare] *vt* to dry; **~rsi** *vr* to dry o.s.; (*diventare asciutto*) to dry

asci'utto, a [aʃ'ʃutto] *ag* dry; (*fig: magro*) lean; (: *burbero*) curt; **restare a bocca ~a** (*fig*) to be disappointed

ascol'tare *vt* to listen to; **ascolta'tore, 'trice** *sm/f* listener; **as'colto** *sm*: **essere** *o* **stare in ascolto** to be listening; **dare** *o* **prestare ascolto (a)** to pay attention (to)

as'falto *sm* asphalt

asfissi'are *vt* to suffocate

'Asia *sf*: **l'~** Asia; **asi'atico, a, ci, che** *ag, sm/f* Asiatic, Asian

a'silo *sm* refuge, sanctuary; **~ (d'infanzia)** nursery(-school); **~ nido** crèche; **~ politico** political asylum

'asino *sm* donkey, ass

A. S. L. *sigla f* (= *Azienda Sanitaria Locale*) local health centre

'asma *sf* asthma

'asola *sf* buttonhole

as'parago, gi *sm* asparagus *no pl*

aspet'tare *vt* to wait for; (*anche COMM*) to await; (*aspettarsi*) to expect ♦ *vi* to wait; **~rsi** *vr* to expect; **~ un bambino** to be expecting (a baby); **questo non me l'aspettavo** I wasn't expecting this; **aspetta'tiva** *sf* wait; expectation; **inferiore all'aspettativa** worse than expected; **essere in aspettativa** (*AMM*) to be on leave of absence

as'petto *sm* (*apparenza*) aspect, appearance, look; (*punto di vista*) point of view; di bell'~ good-looking

aspi'rante *ag* (*attore etc*) aspiring ♦ *sm/f* candidate, applicant

aspira'polvere *sm inv* vacuum cleaner

aspi'rare *vt* (*respirare*) to breathe in, inhale; (*sog: apparecchi*) to suck (up) ♦ *vi*: ~ a to aspire to; aspira'tore *sm* extractor fan

aspi'rina *sf* aspirin

aspor'tare *vt* (*anche MED*) to remove, take away

'aspro, a *ag* (*sapore*) sour, tart; (*odore*) acrid, pungent; (*voce, clima, fig*) harsh; (*superficie*) rough; (*paesaggio*) rugged

assaggi'are [assad'dʒare] *vt* to taste

assag'gini [assad'dʒini] *smpl* (*CUC*) *selection of first courses*

as'sai *av* (*molto*) a lot, much; (: *con ag*) very; (*a sufficienza*) enough ♦ *ag inv* (*quantità*) a lot of, much; (*numero*) a lot of, many; ~ contento very pleased

assa'lire *vt* to attack, assail

as'salto *sm* attack, assault

assapo'rare *vt* to savour

assassi'nare *vt* to murder; to assassinate; (*fig*) to ruin; assas'sinio *sm* murder; assassination; assas'sino, a *ag* murderous ♦ *sm/f* murderer; assassin

'asse *sm* (*TECN*) axle; (*MAT*) axis ♦ *sf* board; ~ da stiro ironing board

assedi'are *vt* to besiege; as'sedio *sm* siege

asse'gnare [assen'ɲare] *vt* to assign, allot; (*premio*) to award

as'segno [as'seɲɲo] *sm* allowance; (*anche*: ~ bancario) cheque (*BRIT*), check (*US*); contro ~ cash on delivery; ~ circolare bank draft; ~ sbarrato crossed cheque; ~ di viaggio traveller's cheque; ~ a vuoto dud cheque; ~i familiari ≈ child benefit *no pl*

assem'blea *sf* assembly

assen'nato, a *ag* sensible

as'senso *sm* assent, consent

as'sente *ag* absent; (*fig*) faraway, vacant;

as'senza *sf* absence

asses'sore *sm* (*POL*) councillor

asses'tare *vt* (*mettere in ordine*) to put in order, arrange; ~rsi *vr* to settle in; ~ un colpo a qn to deal sb a blow

asse'tato, a *ag* thirsty, parched

as'setto *sm* order, arrangement; (*NAUT, AER*) trim; in ~ di guerra on a war footing

assicu'rare *vt* (*accertare*) to ensure; (*infondere certezza*) to assure; (*fermare, legare*) to make fast, secure; (*fare un contratto di assicurazione*) to insure; ~rsi *vr* (*accertarsi*): ~rsi (di) to make sure (of); (*contro il furto etc*): ~rsi (contro) to insure o.s. (against); assicu'rata *sf* (*anche*: lettera assicurata) registered letter; assicu'rato, a *ag* insured; assicurazi'one *sf* assurance; insurance

assidera'mento *sm* exposure

as'siduo, a *ag* (*costante*) assiduous; (*frequentatore etc*) regular

assi'eme *av* (*insieme*) together; ~ a (together) with

assil'lare *vt* to pester, torment

as'sillo *sm* (*fig*) worrying thought

as'sise *sfpl* (*DIR*) assizes; Corte d'A~ Court of Assizes, ≈ Crown Court (*BRIT*)

assis'tente *sm/f* assistant; ~ sociale social worker; ~ di volo (*AER*) steward/stewardess

assis'tenza [assis'tɛntsa] *sf* assistance; ~ ospedaliera free hospital treatment; ~ sanitaria health service; ~ sociale welfare services *pl*

as'sistere *vt* (*aiutare*) to assist, help; (*curare*) to treat ♦ *vi*: ~ (a qc) (*essere presente*) to be present (at sth), to attend (sth)

'asso *sm* ace; piantare qn in ~ to leave sb in the lurch

associ'are [asso'tʃare] *vt* to associate; ~rsi *vr* to enter into partnership; ~rsi a to become a member of, join; (*dolori, gioie*) to share in; ~ qn alle carceri to take sb to prison

associazi'one [assotʃat'tsjone] *sf* association; (*COMM*) association, society; ~ a delinquere (*DIR*) criminal association

asso'dato, a *ag* well-founded

assogget'tare [assoddʒet'tare] *vt* to subject, subjugate

asso'lato, a *ag* sunny

assol'dare *vt* to recruit

as'solto, a *pp di* **assolvere**

assoluta'mente *av* absolutely

asso'luto, a *ag* absolute

assoluzi'one [assolut'tsjone] *sf* (*DIR*) acquittal; (*REL*) absolution

as'solvere *vt* (*DIR*) to acquit; (*REL*) to absolve; (*adempiere*) to carry out, perform

assomigli'are [assomiʎ'ʎare] *vi*: ~ **a** to resemble, look like

asson'nato, a *ag* sleepy

asso'pirsi *vr* to doze off

assor'bente *ag* absorbent ♦ *sm*: ~ **igienico** sanitary towel; ~ **interno** tampon

assor'bire *vt* to absorb

assor'dare *vt* to deafen

assorti'mento *sm* assortment

assor'tito, a *ag* assorted; matched; matching

as'sorto, a *ag* absorbed, engrossed

assottigli'are [assottiʎ'ʎare] *vt* to make thin, to thin; (*aguzzare*) to sharpen; (*ridurre*) to reduce; **~rsi** *vr* to grow thin; (*fig: ridursi*) to be reduced

assue'fare *vt* to accustom; **~rsi a** to get used to, accustom o.s. to

as'sumere *vt* (*impiegato*) to take on, engage; (*responsabilità*) to assume, take upon o.s.; (*contegno, espressione*) to assume, put on; (*droga*) to consume; **as'sunto, a** *pp di* **assumere** ♦ *sm* (*tesi*) proposition

assurdità *sf inv* absurdity; **dire delle ~** to talk nonsense

as'surdo, a *ag* absurd

'asta *sf* pole; (*vendita*) auction

astan'te'ria *sf* casualty department

as'temio, a *ag* teetotal ♦ *sm/f* teetotaller

aste'nersi *vr*: ~ **(da)** to abstain (from), refrain (from); (*POL*) to abstain (from)

aste'risco, schi *sm* asterisk

'astice ['astitʃe] *sm* lobster

asti'nenza [asti'nentsa] *sf* abstinence;

essere in crisi di ~ to suffer from withdrawal symptoms

'astio *sm* rancour, resentment

as'tratto, a *ag* abstract

'astro *sm* star

'astro... *prefisso*: **astrolo'gia** [astrolo'dʒia] *sf* astrology; **as'trologo, a, ghi, ghe** *sm/f* astrologer; **astro'nauta, i, e** *sm/f* astronaut; **astro'nave** *sf* space ship; **astrono'mia** *sf* astronomy; **astro'nomico, a, ci, che** *ag* astronomic(al)

as'tuccio [as'tuttʃo] *sm* case, box, holder

as'tuto, a *ag* astute, cunning, shrewd; **as'tuzia** *sf* astuteness, shrewdness; (*azione*) trick

A'tene *sf* Athens

ate'neo *sm* university

'ateo, a *ag, sm/f* atheist

at'lante *sm* atlas

at'lantico, a, ci, che *ag* Atlantic ♦ *sm*: **l'A~, l'Oceano A~** the Atlantic, the Atlantic Ocean

at'leta, i, e *sm/f* athlete; **at'letica** *sf* athletics *sg*; **atletica leggera** track and field events *pl*; **atletica pesante** weightlifting and wrestling

atmos'fera *sf* atmosphere

a'tomico, a, ci, che *ag* atomic; (*nucleare*) atomic, atom *cpd*, nuclear

'atomo *sm* atom

'atrio *sm* entrance hall, lobby

a'troce [a'trotʃe] *ag* (*che provoca orrore*) dreadful; (*terribile*) atrocious

attacca'mento *sm* (*fig*) attachment, affection

attacca'panni *sm* hook, peg; (*mobile*) hall stand

attac'care *vt* (*unire*) to attach; (*cucendo*) to sew on; (*far aderire*) to stick (on); (*appendere*) to hang (up); (*assalire: anche fig*) to attack; (*iniziare*) to begin, start; (*fig: contagiare*) to pass on ♦ *vi* to stick, adhere; **~rsi** *vr* to stick, adhere; (*trasmettersi per contagio*) to be contagious; (*afferrarsi*): **~rsi (a)** to cling (to); (*fig: affezionarsi*): **~rsi (a)** to become attached (to); ~ **discorso** to start a conversation; **at'tacco, chi** *sm* (*azione offensiva: anche fig*) attack; (*MED*) attack, fit; (*SCI*) binding; (*ELETTR*) socket

atteggia'mento [atteddʒa'mento] *sm* attitude

atteggi'arsi [atted'dʒarsi] *vr*: **~ a** to pose as

attem'pato, a *ag* elderly

at'tendere *vt* to wait for, await ♦ *vi*: **~ a** to attend to

atten'dibile *ag* (*storia*) credible; (*testimone*) reliable

atte'nersi *vr*: **~ a** to keep *o* stick to

atten'tare *vi*: **~ a** to make an attempt on; **atten'tato** attack; **attentato alla vita di qn** attempt on sb's life

at'tento, a *ag* attentive; (*accurato*) careful, thorough; **stare ~ a qc** to pay attention to sth; **~!** be careful!

attenu'ante *sf* (*DIR*) extenuating circumstance

attenu'are *vt* to attenuate; (*dolore, rumore*) to lessen, deaden; (*pena, tasse*) to alleviate; **~rsi** *vr* to ease, abate

attenzi'one [atten'tsjone] *sf* attention; **~!** watch out!, be careful!

atter'raggio [atter'raddʒo] *sm* landing

atter'rare *vt* to bring down ♦ *vi* to land

atter'rire *vt* to terrify

at'tesa *sf* waiting; (*tempo trascorso aspettando*) wait; **essere in attesa di qc** to be waiting for sth

at'teso, a *pp di* **attendere**

attes'tato *sm* certificate

'attico, ci *sm* attic

at'tiguo, a *ag* adjacent, adjoining

attil'lato, a *ag* (*vestito*) close-fitting

'attimo *sm* moment; **in un ~** in a moment

atti'nente *ag*: **~ a** relating to, concerning

atti'rare *vt* to attract

atti'tudine *sf* (*disposizione*) aptitude; (*atteggiamento*) attitude

atti'vare *vt* to activate; (*far funzionare*) to set going, start

attività *sf inv* activity; (*COMM*) assets *pl*

at'tivo, a *ag* active; (*COMM*) profit-making, credit *cpd* ♦ *sm* (*COMM*) assets *pl*; **in ~** in credit

attiz'zare [attit'tsare] *vt* (*fuoco*) to poke

'atto *sm* act; (*azione, gesto*) action, act, deed; (*DIR: documento*) deed, document; **~i** *smpl* (*di congressi etc*) proceedings; **mettere in ~** to put into action; **fare ~ di fare qc** to make as if to do sth

at'tonito, a *ag* dumbfounded, astonished

attorcigli'are [attortʃiʎ'ʎare] *vt* to twist; **~rsi** *vr* to twist

at'tore, 'trice *sm/f* actor/actress

at'torno *av* round, around, about; **~ a** round, around, about

at'tracco, chi *sm* (*NAUT*) docking *no pl*; berth

attra'ente *ag* attractive

at'trarre *vt* to attract; **attrat'tiva** *sf* (*fig: fascino*) attraction, charm; **at'tratto, a** *pp di* **attrarre**

attraversa'mento *sm*: **~ pedonale** pedestrian crossing

attraver'sare *vt* to cross; (*città, bosco, fig: periodo*) to go through; (*sog: fiume*) to run through

attra'verso *prep* through; (*da una parte all'altra*) across

attrazi'one [attrat'tsjone] *sf* attraction

attrez'zare [attret'tsare] *vt* to equip; (*NAUT*) to rig; **attrezza'tura** *sf* equipment *no pl*; rigging; **at'trezzo** *sm* tool, instrument; (*SPORT*) piece of equipment

attribu'ire *vt*: **~ qc a qn** (*assegnare*) to give *o* award sth to sb; (*quadro etc*) to attribute sth to sb; **attri'buto** *sm* attribute

at'trice [at'tritʃe] *sf vedi* **attore**

at'trito *sm* (*anche fig*) friction

attu'ale *ag* (*presente*) present; (*di attualità*) topical; (*che è in atto*) actual; **attualità** *sf inv* topicality; (*avvenimento*) current event; **attual'mente** *av* at the moment, at present

attu'are *vt* to carry out; **~rsi** *vr* to be realized

attu'tire *vt* to deaden, reduce

au'dace [au'datʃe] *ag* audacious, daring, bold; (*provocante*) provocative; (*sfacciato*) impudent, bold; **au'dacia** *sf* audacity, daring; boldness; provocativeness;

impudence

audiovi'sivo, a *ag* audiovisual

audizi'one [audit'tsjone] *sf* hearing; (*MUS*) audition

'auge ['audʒe] *sf*: **in ~** popular

augu'rare *vt* to wish; **~rsi qc** to hope for sth

au'gurio *sm* (*presagio*) omen; (*voto di benessere etc*) (good) wish; **essere di buon/cattivo ~** to be of good omen/be ominous; **fare gli ~i a qn** to give sb one's best wishes; **tanti ~i!** all the best!

'aula *sf* (*scolastica*) classroom; (*universitaria*) lecture theatre; (*di edificio pubblico*) hall

aumen'tare *vt, vi* to increase; **au'mento** *sm* increase

au'reola *sf* halo

au'rora *sf* dawn

ausili'are *ag, sm, sm/f* auxiliary

aus'picio [aus'pitʃo] *sm* omen; (*protezione*) patronage; **sotto gli ~i di** under the auspices of

aus'tero, a *ag* austere

Aus'tralia *sf*: **l'~** Australia; **australi'ano, a** *ag, sm/f* Australian

'Austria *sf*: **l'~** Austria; **aus'triaco, a, ci, che** *ag, sm/f* Austrian

au'tentico, a, ci, che *ag* authentic, genuine

au'tista, i *sm* driver

'auto *sf inv* car

autoabbronzante *sm, ag* self-tan

autoade'sivo, a *ag* self-adhesive ♦ *sm* sticker

autobiogra'fia *sf* autobiography

auto'botte *sf* tanker

'autobus *sm inv* bus

auto'carro *sm* lorry (*BRIT*), truck

autocorri'era *sf* coach, bus

au'tografo, a *ag, sm* autograph

auto'grill ® *sm inv* motorway restaurant

autogrù *sf inv* breakdown van

auto'linea *sf* bus company

au'toma, i *sm* automaton

auto'matico, a, ci, che *ag* automatic ♦ *sm* (*bottone*) snap fastener; (*fucile*) automatic

automazi'one [automat'tsjone] *sf* automation

auto'mezzo [auto'mɛddzo] *sm* motor vehicle

auto'mobile *sf* (motor) car

automobi'lista, i, e *sm/f* motorist

autono'leggio *sm* car hire

autono'mia *sf* autonomy; (*di volo*) range

au'tonomo, a *ag* autonomous, independent

autop'sia *sf* post-mortem, autopsy

auto'radio *sf inv* (*apparecchio*) car radio; (*autoveicolo*) radio car

au'tore, 'trice *sm/f* author

auto'revole *ag* authoritative; (*persona*) influential

autori'messa *sf* garage

autorità *sf inv* authority

autoriz'zare [autorid'dzare] *vt* (*permettere*) to authorize; (*giustificare*) to allow, sanction; **autorizzazi'one** *sf* authorization

autoscu'ola *sf* driving school

autos'top *sm* hitchhiking; **autostop'pista, i, e** *sm/f* hitchhiker

autos'trada *sf* motorway (*BRIT*), highway (*US*)

auto'treno *sm* articulated lorry (*BRIT*), semi (trailer) (*US*)

autove'icolo *sm* motor vehicle

auto'velox ® *sm inv* (police) speed camera

autovet'tura *sf* (motor) car

au'tunno *sm* autumn

avam'braccio [avam'brattʃo] (*pl* (*f*) **-cia**) *sm* forearm

avangu'ardia *sf* vanguard

a'vanti *av* (*stato in luogo*) in front; (*moto: andare, venire*) forward; (*tempo: prima*) before ♦ *prep* (*luogo*): **~ a** before, in front of; (*tempo*): **~ Cristo** before Christ ♦ *escl* (*entrate*) come (*o* go) in!; (*MIL*) forward!; (*coraggio*) come on! ♦ *sm inv* (*SPORT*) forward; **~ e indietro** backwards and forwards; **andare ~** to go forward; (*continuare*) to go on; (*precedere*) to go (on) ahead; (*orologio*) to be fast; **essere ~ negli studi** to be well advanced with one's studies avanza'mento [avantsa'mento] *sm* progress; promotion

avan'zare [avan'tsare] *vt* (*spostare in avanti*) to move forward, advance; (*domanda*) to put forward; (*promuovere*) to promote; (*essere creditore*): ~ **qc da qn** to be owed sth by sb ♦ *vi* (*andare avanti*) to move forward, advance; (*progredire*) to make progress; (*essere d'avanzo*) to be left, remain; **avan'zata** *sf* (MIL) advance; a'vanzo *sm* (*residuo*) remains *pl*, left-overs *pl*; (MAT) remainder; (COMM) surplus; **averne d'avanzo di qc** to have more than enough of sth; **avanzo di galera** jailbird

ava'ria *sf* (*guasto*) damage; (: *meccanico*) breakdown

a'varo, a *ag* avaricious, miserly ♦ *sm* miser

a'vena *sf* oats *pl*

PAROLA CHIAVE

a'vere *sm* (COMM) credit; **gli ~i** (*ricchezze*) wealth *sg*

♦ *vt* 1 (*possedere*) to have; **ha due bambini/una bella casa** she has (got) two children/a lovely house; **ha i capelli lunghi** he has (got) long hair; **non ho da mangiare/bere** I've (got) nothing to eat/ drink, I don't have anything to eat/drink

2 (*indossare*) to wear, have on; **aveva una maglietta rossa** he was wearing *o* he had on a red tee-shirt; **ha gli occhiali** he wears *o* has glasses

3 (*ricevere*) to get; **hai avuto l'assegno?** did you get *o* have you had the cheque?

4 (*età, dimensione*) to be; **ha 9 anni** he is 9 (years old); **la stanza ha 3 metri di lunghezza** the room is 3 metres in length; *vedi* **fame**; **paura** *etc*

5 (*tempo*): **quanti ne abbiamo oggi?** what's the date today?; **ne hai per molto?** will you be long?

6 (*fraseologia*): **avercela con qn** to be angry with sb; **cos'hai?** what's wrong *o* what's the matter (with you)?; **non ha niente a che vedere** *o* **fare con me** it's got nothing to do with me

♦ *vb aus* 1 to have; **aver bevuto/**

mangiato to have drunk/eaten

2 (+*da* +*infinito*): ~ **da fare qc** to have to do sth; **non hai che da chiederlo** you only have to ask him

---

'avi *smpl* ancestors, forefathers

aviazi'one [avjat'tsjone] *sf* aviation; (MIL) air force

avidità *sf* eagerness; greed

'avido, a *ag* eager; (*peg*) greedy

avo'cado *sm* avocado

a'vorio *sm* ivory

Avv. *abbr* = **avvocato**

avvalla'mento *sm* sinking *no pl*; (*effetto*) depression

avvalo'rare *vt* to confirm

avvam'pare *vi* (*incendio*) to flare up

avvantaggi'are [avvantad'dʒare] *vt* to favour; ~**rsi** *vr*: ~**rsi negli affari/sui concorrenti** to get ahead in business/of one's competitors

avvele'nare *vt* to poison

avve'nente *ag* attractive, charming

avveni'mento *sm* event

avve'nire *vi*, *vb impers* to happen, occur ♦ *sm* future

avven'tarsi *vr*: ~ **su** *o* **contro qn/qc** to hurl o.s. *o* rush at sb/sth

avven'tato, a *ag* rash, reckless

avven'tizio, a [avven'tittsjo] *ag* (*impiegato*) temporary; (*guadagno*) casual

av'vento *sm* advent, coming; (REL): **l'A~** Advent

avven'tore *sm* (regular) customer

avven'tura *sf* adventure; (*amorosa*) affair

avventu'rarsi *vr* to venture

avventu'roso, a *ag* adventurous

avve'rarsi *vr* to come true

av'verbio *sm* adverb

avver'sario, a *ag* opposing ♦ *sm* opponent, adversary

av'verso, a *ag* (*contrario*) contrary; (*sfavorevole*) unfavourable

avver'tenza [avver'tentsa] *sf* (*ammonimento*) warning; (*cautela*) care; (*premessa*) foreword; ~**e** *sfpl* (*istruzioni per l'uso*) instructions

avverti'mento *sm* warning

avver'tire *vt* (*avvisare*) to warn; (*rendere consapevole*) to inform, notify; (*percepire*) to feel

av'vezzo, a [av'vettso] *ag*: **~ a** used to

avvia'mento *sm* (*atto*) starting; (*effetto*) start; (*AUT*) starting; (*: dispositivo*) starter; (*COMM*) goodwill

avvi'are *vt* (*mettere sul cammino*) to direct; (*impresa, trattative*) to begin, start; (*motore*) to start; **~rsi** *vr* to set off, set out

avvicen'darsi [avvitʃen'darsi] *vr* to alternate

avvici'nare [avvitʃi'nare] *vt* to bring near; (*trattare con: persona*) to approach; **~rsi** *vr*: **~rsi (a qn/qc)** to approach (sb/sth), draw near (to sb/sth)

avvi'lire *vt* (*umiliare*) to humiliate; (*degradare*) to disgrace; (*scoraggiare*) to dishearten, discourage; **~rsi** *vr* (*abbattersi*) to lose heart

avvilup'pare *vt* (*avvolgere*) to wrap up

avvinaz'zato, a [avvinat'tsato] *ag* drunk

avvin'cente *ag* captivating

av'vincere [av'vintʃere] *vt* to charm, enthral

avvinghi'are [avvin'gjare] *vt* to clasp; **~rsi** *vr*: **~rsi a** to cling to

avvi'sare *vt* (*far sapere*) to inform; (*mettere in guardia*) to warn; **av'viso** *sm* warning; (*annuncio*) announcement; (*: affisso*) notice; (*inserzione pubblicitaria*) advertisement; **a mio avviso** in my opinion; **avviso di chiamata** (*TEL*) call waiting service

avvis'tare *vt* to sight

avvi'tare *vt* to screw down (*o* in)

avviz'zire [avvit'tsire] *vi* to wither

avvo'cato, 'essa *sm/f* (*DIR*) barrister (*BRIT*), lawyer; (*fig*) defender, advocate

av'volgere [av'voldʒere] *vt* to roll up; (*avviluppare*) to wrap up; **~rsi** *vr* (*avvilupparsi*) to wrap o.s. up

avvol'gibile *sm* roller blind (*BRIT*), blind

avvol'toio *sm* vulture

azi'enda [ad'dzjɛnda] *sf* business, firm, concern; **~ agricola** farm

azio'nare [attsjo'nare] *vt* to activate

azi'one [at'tsjone] *sf* action; (*COMM*) share; **azio'nista, i, e** *sm/f* (*COMM*) shareholder

a'zoto [ad'dzɔto] *sm* nitrogen

azzan'nare [attsan'nare] *vt* to sink one's teeth into

azzar'darsi [addzar'darsi] *vr*: **~ a fare** to dare (to) do; **azzar'dato, a** *ag* (*impresa*) risky; (*risposta*) rash

az'zardo [ad'dzardo] *sm* risk

azzec'care [attsek'kare] *vt* (*risposta etc*) to get right

azzuf'farsi [attsuf'farsi] *vr* to come to blows

az'zurro, a [ad'dzurro] *ag* blue ♦ *sm* (*colore*) blue; **gli ~i** (*SPORT*) the Italian national team

B, b

bab'beo *sm* simpleton

'babbo *sm* (*fam*) dad, daddy; **B~ Natale** Father Christmas

bab'buccia, ce [bab'buttʃa] *sf* slipper; (*per neonati*) bootee

ba'bordo *sm* (*NAUT*) port side

ba'cato, a *ag* worm-eaten, rotten

'bacca, che *sf* berry

baccalà *sm* dried salted cod; (*fig: peg*) dummy

bac'cano *sm* din, clamour

bac'cello [bat'tʃɛllo] *sm* pod

bac'chetta [bak'ketta] *sf* (*verga*) stick, rod; (*di direttore d'orchestra*) baton; (*di tamburo*) drumstick; **~ magica** magic wand

baci'are [ba'tʃare] *vt* to kiss; **~rsi** *vr* to kiss (one another)

baci'nella [batʃi'nɛlla] *sf* basin

ba'cino [ba'tʃino] *sm* basin; (*MINERALOGIA*) field, bed; (*ANAT*) pelvis; (*NAUT*) dock

'bacio ['batʃo] *sm* kiss

'baco, chi *sm* worm; **~ da seta** silkworm

ba'dare *vi* (*fare attenzione*) to take care, be careful; (*occuparsi di*): **~ a** to look after, take care of; (*dar ascolto*): **~ a** to pay attention to; **bada ai fatti tuoi!** mind your

own business!
ba'dia *sf* abbey
ba'dile *sm* shovel
'baffi *smpl* moustache *sg*; (*di animale*) whiskers; **ridere sotto i ~** to laugh up one's sleeve; **leccarsi i ~** to lick one's lips
ba'gagli [ba'gaʎʎi] *smpl* luggage *sg*; **fare i ~** to pack
bagagli'aio [bagaʎ'ʎajo] *sm* luggage van (*BRIT*) o car (*US*); (*AUT*) boot (*BRIT*), trunk (*US*)
bagli'ore [baʎ'ʎore] *sm* flash, dazzling light; **un ~ di speranza** a ray of hope
ba'gnante [baɲ'ɲante] *sm/f* bather
ba'gnare [baɲ'ɲare] *vt* to wet; (*inzuppare*) to soak; (*innaffiare*) to water; (*sog: fiume*) to flow through; (*: mare*) to wash, bathe; **~rsi** *vr* to get wet; (*al mare*) to go swimming o bathing; (*in vasca*) to have a bath
ba'gnato, a [baɲ'ɲato] *ag* wet
ba'gnino [baɲ'ɲino] *sm* lifeguard
'bagno ['baɲɲo] *sm* bath; (*locale*) bathroom; **~i** *smpl* (*stabilimento*) baths; **fare il ~** to have a bath; (*nel mare*) to go swimming o bathing; **fare il ~ a qn** to give sb a bath; **mettere a ~** to soak; **~ schiuma** bubble bath
bagnoma'ria [baɲɲoma'ria] *sm*: **cuocere a ~** to cook in a double saucepan
'baia *sf* bay
baio'netta *sf* bayonet
balbet'tare *vi* to stutter, stammer; (*bimbo*) to babble ♦ *vt* to stammer out
balbuzi'ente [balbut'tsjɛnte] *ag* stuttering, stammering
bal'cone *sm* balcony
baldac'chino [baldak'kino] *sm* canopy
bal'danza [bal'dantsa] *sf* self-confidence
'baldo, a *ag* bold, daring
bal'doria *sf*: **fare ~** to have a riotous time
ba'lena *sf* whale
bale'nare *vb impers*: **balena** there's lightning ♦ *vi* to flash; **mi balenò un'idea** an idea flashed through my mind; **ba'leno** *sm* flash of lightning; **in un baleno** in a flash

ba'lestra *sf* crossbow
ba'lia *sf*: **in ~ di** at the mercy of
'balla *sf* (*di merci*) bale; (*fandonia*) (tall) story
bal'lare *vt, vi* to dance; **bal'lata** *sf* ballad
balle'rina *sf* dancer; ballet dancer; (*scarpa*) ballet shoe
balle'rino *sm* dancer; ballet dancer
bal'letto *sm* ballet
'ballo *sm* dance; (*azione*) dancing *no pl*; **essere in ~** (*fig: persona*) to be involved; (*: cosa*) to be at stake
ballot'taggio [ballot'taddʒo] *sm* (*POL*) second ballot
balne'are *ag* seaside *cpd*; (*stagione*) bathing
balneazi'one *sf* bathing; **è vietata la ~** bathing strictly prohibited
ba'locco, chi *sm* toy
ba'lordo, a *ag* stupid, senseless
'balsamo *sm* (*aroma*) balsam; (*lenimento, fig*) balm
balu'ardo *sm* bulwark
'balza ['baltsa] *sf* (*dirupo*) crag; (*di stoffa*) frill
bal'zare [bal'tsare] *vi* to bounce; (*lanciarsi*) to jump, leap; **'balzo** *sm* bounce; jump, leap; (*del terreno*) crag
bam'bagia [bam'baddʒa] *sf* (*ovatta*) cotton wool (*BRIT*), absorbent cotton (*US*); (*cascame*) cotton waste
bam'bina *ag, sf vedi* **bambino**
bambi'naia *sf* nanny, nurse(maid)
bam'bino, a *sm/f* child
bam'boccio [bam'bɔttʃo] *sm* plump child; (*pupazzo*) rag doll
'bambola *sf* doll
bambù *sm* bamboo
ba'nale *ag* banal, commonplace
ba'nana *sf* banana; **ba'nano** *sm* banana tree
'banca, che *sf* bank; **~ dei dati** data bank
banca'rella *sf* stall
ban'cario, a *ag* banking, bank *cpd* ♦ *sm* bank clerk
banca'rotta *sf* bankruptcy; **fare ~** to go bankrupt

ban'chetto [ban'ketto] *sm* banquet

banchi'ere [ban'kjere] *sm* banker

ban'china [ban'kina] *sf* (*di porto*) quay; (*per pedoni, ciclisti*) path; (*di stazione*) platform; ~ **cedevole** (*AUT*) soft verge (*BRIT*) *o* shoulder (*US*)

'banco, chi *sm* bench; (*di negozio*) counter; (*di mercato*) stall; (*di officina*) (work-)bench; (*GEO, banca*) bank; ~ **di corallo** coral reef; ~ **degli imputati** dock; ~ **dei pegni** pawnshop; ~ **di prova** (*fig*) testing ground; ~ **dei testimoni** witness box

'Bancomat ® *sm inv* automated banking; (*tessera*) cash card

banco'nota *sf* banknote

'banda *sf* band; (*di stoffa*) band, stripe; (*lato, parte*) side; ~ **perforata** punch tape

banderu'ola *sf* (*METEOR*) weathercock

bandi'era *sf* flag, banner

ban'dire *vt* to proclaim; (*esiliare*) to exile; (*fig*) to dispense with

ban'dito *sm* outlaw, bandit

bandi'tore *sm* (*di aste*) auctioneer

'bando *sm* proclamation; (*esilio*) exile, banishment; ~ **alle chiacchiere!** that's enough talk!

'bandolo *sm*: **il ~ della matassa** (*fig*) the key to the problem

bar *sm inv* bar

'bara *sf* coffin

ba'racca, che *sf* shed, hut; (*peg*) hovel; **mandare avanti la ~** to keep things going

bara'onda *sf* hubbub, bustle

ba'rare *vi* to cheat

ba'ratro *sm* abyss

barat'tare *vt*: ~ **qc con** to barter sth for, swap sth for; ba'ratto *sm* barter

ba'rattolo *sm* (*di latta*) tin; (*di vetro*) jar; (*di coccio*) pot

'barba *sf* beard; **farsi la ~** to shave; **farla in ~ a qn** (*fig*) to do sth to sb's face; **che ~!** what a bore!

barbabi'etola *sf* beetroot (*BRIT*), beet (*US*); ~ **da zucchero** sugar beet

bar'barico, a, ci, che *ag* barbarian; barbaric

'barbaro, a *ag* barbarous; ~**i** *smpl*

barbarians

barbi'ere *sm* barber

bar'bone *sm* (*cane*) poodle; (*vagabondo*) tramp

bar'buto, a *ag* bearded

'barca, che *sf* boat; ~ **a remi** rowing boat; ~ **a vela** sail(ing) boat; barcai'olo *sm* boatman

barcol'lare *vi* to stagger

bar'cone *sm* (*per ponti di barche*) pontoon

ba'rella *sf* (*lettiga*) stretcher

ba'rile *sm* barrel, cask

ba'rista, i, e *sm/f* barman/maid; (*proprietario*) bar owner

ba'ritono *sm* baritone

bar'lume *sm* glimmer, gleam

ba'rocco, a, chi, che *ag, sm* baroque

ba'rometro *sm* barometer

ba'rone *sm* baron; baro'nessa *sf* baroness

'barra *sf* bar; (*NAUT*) helm; (*linea grafica*) line, stroke; (*obliqua*) slash

barri'care *vt* to barricade; barri'cata *sf* barricade

barri'era *sf* barrier; (*GEO*) reef

ba'ruffa *sf* scuffle

barzel'letta [bardzel'letta] *sf* joke, funny story

ba'sare *vt* to base, found; ~**rsi** *vr*: ~**rsi su** (*sog: fatti, prove*) to be based *o* founded on; (*: persona*) to base one's arguments on

'basco, a, schi, sche *ag* Basque ♦ *sm* (*copricapo*) beret

'base *sf* base; (*fig: fondamento*) basis; (*POL*) rank and file; **di ~** basic; **in ~ a** on the basis of, according to; **a ~ di caffè** coffee-based

ba'setta *sf* sideburn

ba'silica, che *sf* basilica

ba'silico *sm* basil

bassi'fondi *smpl*: **i ~** the slums

bas'sista *sm/f* bass player

'basso, a *ag* low; (*di statura*) short; (*meridionale*) southern ♦ *sm* bottom, lower part; (*MUS*) bass; **la ~a Italia** southern Italy

bassorili'evo *sm* bas-relief

'basta *escl* (that's) enough!, that will do!

bas'tardo, a *ag* (*animale, pianta*) hybrid,

crossbreed; (*persona*) illegitimate, bastard (*peg*) ♦ *sm/f* illegitimate child, bastard (*peg*)

bas'tare *vi*, *vb impers* to be enough, be sufficient; **~ a qn** to be enough for sb; **basta chiedere** *o* **che chieda a un vigile** you have only to *o* need only ask a policeman

basti'mento *sm* ship, vessel

basto'nare *vt* to beat, thrash

baston'cino [baston'tʃino] *sm* (*SCI*) ski pole; **~ di pesce** fish fingers

bas'tone *sm* stick; **~ da passeggio** walking stick

bat'taglia [bat'taʎʎa] *sf* battle; fight

bat'taglio [bat'taʎʎo] *sm* (*di campana*) clapper; (*di porta*) knocker

battagli'one [battaʎ'ʎone] *sm* battalion

bat'tello *sm* boat

bat'tente *sm* (*imposta: di porta*) wing, flap; (*: di finestra*) shutter; (*batacchio: di porta*) knocker; (*: di orologio*) hammer; **chiudere i ~i** (*fig*) to shut up shop

'battere *vt* to beat; (*grano*) to thresh; (*percorrere*) to scour ♦ *vi* (*bussare*) to knock; (*urtare*): **~ contro** to hit *o* strike against; (*pioggia, sole*) to beat down; (*cuore*) to beat; (*TENNIS*) to serve; **~rsi** *vr* to fight; **~ le mani** to clap; **~ i piedi** to stamp one's feet; **~ a macchina** to type; **~ bandiera italiana** to fly the Italian flag; **~ in testa** (*AUT*) to knock; **in un batter d'occhio** in the twinkling of an eye

bat'teri *smpl* bacteria

batte'ria *sf* battery; (*MUS*) drums *pl*

batte'rista *sm/f* drummer

bat'tesimo *sm* (*rito*) baptism; christening

battez'zare [batted'dzare] *vt* to baptize; to christen

batticu'ore *sm* palpitations *pl*

batti'mano *sm* applause

batti'panni *sm inv* carpet-beater

battis'tero *sm* baptistry

battis'trada *sm inv* (*di pneumatico*) tread; (*di gara*) pacemaker

battitap'peto *sm* vacuum cleaner

'battito *sm* beat, throb; **~ cardiaco** heartbeat

bat'tuta *sf* blow; (*di macchina da scrivere*) stroke; (*MUS*) bar; beat; (*TEATRO*) cue; (*frase spiritosa*) witty remark; (*di caccia*) beating; (*POLIZIA*) combing, scouring; (*TENNIS*) service

ba'ule *sm* trunk; (*AUT*) boot (*BRIT*), trunk (*US*)

'bava *sf* (*di animale*) slaver, slobber; (*di lumaca*) slime; (*di vento*) breath

bava'glino [bavaʎ'ʎino] *sm* bib

ba'vaglio [ba'vaʎʎo] *sm* gag

'bavero *sm* collar

Bavi'era *sf* Bavaria

ba'zar [bad'dzar] *sm inv* bazaar

baz'zecola [bad'dzekola] *sf* trifle

bazzi'care [battsi'kare] *vt* to frequent ♦ *vi*: **~ in/con** to frequent

BCE *sigla f* (= *Banca Centrale Europa*) ECB

be'ato, a *ag* blessed; (*fig*) happy; **~ te!** lucky you!

bebè *sm inv* baby

bec'caccia, ce [bek'kattʃa] *sf* woodcock

bec'care *vt* to peck; (*fig: raffreddore*) to catch; **~rsi qc** to catch sth

bec'cata *sf* peck

beccheggi'are [bekked'dʒare] *vi* to pitch

bec'chino [bek'kino] *sm* gravedigger

'becco, chi *sm* beak, bill; (*di caffettiera etc*) spout; lip

Be'fana *sf see box*; (*Epifania*) Epiphany; (*donna brutta*): **b~** hag, witch

---

Befana

---

i The **Befana** is a national holiday on the feast of the Epiphany. It takes its name from a legendary old woman, **la Befana**, who comes down the chimney during the night leaving gifts for children who have been good, and coal for those who have not.

'beffa *sf* practical joke; **farsi ~ di qn** to make a fool of sb; bef'fardo, a *ag* scornful, mocking; bef'fare *vt* (*anche*: **beffarsi di**) to make a fool of, mock

'bega, ghe *sf* quarrel

'begli ['beʎʎi] *ag vedi* **bello**
'bei *ag vedi* **bello**
bel *ag vedi* **bello**
be'lare *vi* to bleat
'belga, gi, ghe *ag, sm/f* Belgian
'Belgio ['beldʒo] *sm:* il ~ Belgium
bel'lezza [bel'lettsa] *sf* beauty
'bella *sf* (SPORT) decider; *vedi anche* **bello**

PAROLA CHIAVE

'bello, a (*ag: dav sm* bel +C, bell' +V,
bello +s impura, gn, pn, ps, x, z, pl bei +C,
begli +s impura etc o V) 1 (*oggetto,
donna, paesaggio*) beautiful, lovely; (*uomo*)
handsome; (*tempo*) beautiful, fine, lovely;
le belle arti fine arts
2 (*quantità*): una ~a cifra a considerable
sum of money; un bel niente absolutely
nothing
3 (*rafforzativo*): è una truffa ~a e buona!
it's a real fraud!; è bell'e finito it's already
finished
♦ *sm* 1 (*bellezza*) beauty; (*tempo*) fine
weather
2: adesso viene il ~ now comes the best
bit; sul più ~ at the crucial point; cosa fai
di ~? are you doing anything interesting?
♦ *av:* fa ~ the weather is fine, it's fine

'belva *sf* wild animal
belve'dere *sm inv* panoramic viewpoint
benché [ben'ke] *cong* although
'benda *sf* bandage; (*per gli occhi*) blindfold;
ben'dare *vt* to bandage; to blindfold
'bene *av* well; (*completamente, affatto*): è
ben difficile it's very difficult ♦ *ag inv:*
gente ~ well-to-do people ♦ *sm* good; ~i
smpl (*averi*) property *sg*, estate *sg*; io sto
~/poco ~ I'm well/not very well; va ~ all
right; volere un ~ dell'anima a qn to love
sb very much; un uomo per ~ a
respectable man; fare ~ to do the right
thing; fare ~ a (*salute*) to be good for; fare
del ~ a qn to do sb a good turn; ~i di
consumo consumer goods
bene'detto, a *pp di* **benedire** ♦ *ag*
blessed, holy

bene'dire *vt* to bless; to consecrate;
benedizi'one *sf* blessing
benedu'cato, a *ag* well-mannered
benefi'cenza [benefi'tʃɛntsa] *sf* charity
bene'ficio [bene'fitʃo] *sm* benefit; con ~
d'inventario (*fig*) with reservations
be'nefico, a, ci, che *ag* beneficial;
charitable
beneme'renza [beneme'rɛntsa] *sf* merit
bene'merito, a *ag* meritorious
be'nessere *sm* well-being
benes'tante *ag* well-to-do
benes'tare *sm* consent, approval
be'nevolo, a *ag* benevolent
be'nigno, a [be'niɲɲo] *ag* kind, kindly;
(*critica etc*) favourable; (*MED*) benign
benin'teso *av* of course
bensi *cong* but (rather)
benve'nuto, a *ag, sm* welcome; dare il ~
a qn to welcome sb
ben'zina [ben'dzina] *sf* petrol (BRIT), gas
(US); fare ~ to get petrol (BRIT) o gas (US); ~
verde unleaded (petrol); benzi'naio *sm*
petrol (BRIT) o gas (US) pump attendant
'bere *vt* to drink; darla a ~ a qn (*fig*) to
fool sb
ber'lina *sf* (AUT) saloon (car) (BRIT), sedan
(US)
Ber'lino *sf* Berlin
ber'noccolo *sm* bump; (*inclinazione*) flair
ber'retto *sm* cap
bersagli'are [bersaʎ'ʎare] *vt* to shoot at;
(*colpire ripetutamente, fig*) to bombard
ber'saglio [ber'saʎʎo] *sm* target
bes'temmia *sf* curse; (REL) blasphemy
bestemmi'are *vi* to curse, swear; to
blaspheme ♦ *vt* to curse, swear at; to
blaspheme
'bestia *sf* animal; andare in ~ (*fig*) to fly
into a rage; besti'ale *ag* beastly; animal
cpd; (*fam*): fa un freddo bestiale it's
bitterly cold; besti'ame *sm* livestock;
(*bovino*) cattle *pl*
'bettola (*peg*) *sf* dive
be'tulla *sf* birch
be'vanda *sf* drink, beverage
bevi'tore, 'trice *sm/f* drinker

be'vuta *sf* drink

be'vuto, a *pp di* **bere**

bi'ada *sf* fodder

bianche'ria [bjanke'ria] *sf* linen; ~ **intima** underwear; ~ **da donna** ladies' underwear, lingerie

bi'anco, a, chi, che *ag* white; (*non scritto*) blank ♦ *sm* white; (*intonaco*) whitewash ♦ *sm/f* white, white man/ woman; **in** ~ (*foglio, assegno*) blank; (*notte*) sleepless; **in** ~ **e nero** (*TV, FOT*) black and white; **mangiare in** ~ to follow a bland diet; **pesce in** ~ boiled fish; **andare in** ~ (*non riuscire*) to fail; ~ **dell'uovo** egg-white

biasi'mare *vt* to disapprove of, censure; bi'asimo *sm* disapproval, censure

'bibbia *sf* (*anche fig*) bible

bibe'ron *sm inv* feeding bottle

'bibita *sf* (soft) drink

biblio'teca, che *sf* library; (*mobile*) bookcase; bibliote'cario, a *sm/f* librarian

bicarbo'nato *sm*: ~ **(di sodio)** bicarbonate (of soda)

bicchi'ere [bik'kjɛre] *sm* glass

bici'cletta [bitʃi'kletta] *sf* bicycle; **andare in** ~ to cycle

bidé *sm inv* bidet

bi'dello, a *sm/f* (*INS*) janitor

bi'done *sm* drum, can; (*anche*: ~ **dell'immondizia**) (dust)bin; (*fam: truffa*) swindle; **fare un** ~ **a qn** (*fam*) to let sb down; to cheat sb

bien'nale *ag* biennial

Biennale di Venezia

ⓘ The **Biennale di Venezia** is an international contemporary art festival, which takes place every two years at Giardini. In its current form, it includes exhibits from the countries taking part, a thematic exhibition and a section for young artists.

---

bi'ennio *sm* period of two years

bi'etola *sf* beet

bifor'carsi *vr* to fork; biforcazi'one *sf* fork

bighello'nare [bigello'nare] *vi* to loaf (about)

bigiotte'ria [bidʒotte'ria] *sf* costume jewellery; (*negozio*) jeweller's (*selling only costume jewellery*)

bigli'ardo [biʎ'ʎardo] *sm* = **biliardo**

bigliet'taio, a *sm/f* (*in treno*) ticket inspector; (*in autobus*) conductor

bigliette'ria [biʎʎette'ria] *sf* (*di stazione*) ticket office; booking office; (*di teatro*) box office

bigli'etto [biʎ'ʎetto] *sm* (*per viaggi, spettacoli etc*) ticket; (*cartoncino*) card; (*anche*: ~ **di banca**) (bank)note; ~ **d'auguri/da visita** greetings/visiting card; ~ **d'andata e ritorno** return (ticket), round-trip ticket (*US*)

bignè [biɲ'ɲe] *sm inv* cream puff

bigo'dino *sm* roller, curler

bi'gotto, a *ag* over-pious ♦ *sm/f* church fiend

bi'lancia, ce [bi'lantʃa] *sf* (*pesa*) scales *pl*; (: *di precisione*) balance; (*dello zodiaco*): **B~** Libra; ~ **commerciale/dei pagamenti** balance of trade/payments; **bilanci'are** *vt* (*pesare*) to weigh; (: *fig*) to weigh up; (*pareggiare*) to balance

bi'lancio [bi'lantʃo] *sm* (*COMM*) balance (-sheet); (*statale*) budget; **fare il** ~ **di** (*fig*) to assess; ~ **consuntivo** (final) balance; ~ **preventivo** budget

'bile *sf* bile; (*fig*) rage, anger

bili'ardo *sm* billiards *sg*; billiard table

'bilico, chi *sm*: **essere in** ~ to be balanced; **tenere qn in** ~ (*fig*) to keep sb in suspense

bi'lingue *ag* bilingual

bili'one *sm* (*mille milioni*) thousand million; (*milione di milioni*) billion (*BRIT*), trillion (*US*)

'bimbo, a *sm/f* little boy/girl

bimen'sile *ag* fortnightly

bimes'trale *ag* two-monthly, bimonthly

bi'nario, a *ag* (*sistema*) binary ♦ *sm* (railway) track *o* line; (*piattaforma*) platform; ~ **morto** dead-end track

bi'nocolo *sm* binoculars *pl*

bio... *prefisso*: bio'chimica [bio'kimika] *sf*

biochemistry; **biodegra'dabile** *ag*
biodegradable; **biogra'fia** *sf* biography;
biolo'gia *sf* biology; **bio'logico, a, ci,
che** *ag* biological

bi'ondo, a *ag* blond, fair

bir'bante *sm* rogue, rascal

biri'chino, a [biri'kino] *ag* mischievous
♦ *sm/f* scamp, little rascal

bi'rillo *sm* skittle (*BRIT*), pin (*US*); **~i** *smpl*
(*gioco*) skittles *sg* (*BRIT*), bowling (*US*)

'biro ® *sf inv* biro ®

'birra *sf* beer; **a tutta ~** (*fig*) at top speed;
birra chiara ≈ lager; **birra scura** ≈ stout;
birre'ria *sf* ≈ bierkeller

bis *escl, sm inv* encore

bis'betico, a, ci, che *ag* ill-tempered,
crabby

bisbigli'are [bisbi'ʎʎare] *vt, vi* to whisper

'bisca, sche *sf* gambling-house

'biscia, sce ['biʃʃa] *sf* snake; **~ d'acqua**
grass snake

bis'cotto *sm* biscuit

bises'tile *ag*: **anno ~** leap year

bis'lungo, a, ghi, ghe *ag* oblong

bis'nonno, a *sm/f* great grandfather/
grandmother

biso'gnare [bizoɲ'ɲare] *vb impers*: **bisogna
che tu parta/lo faccia** you'll have to go/
do it; **bisogna parlargli** we'll (*o* I'll) have
to talk to him

bi'sogno [bi'zoɲɲo] *sm* need; **~i** *smpl*: **fare
i propri ~i** to relieve o.s.; **avere ~ di qc/di
fare qc** to need sth/to do sth; **al ~, in
caso di ~** if need be; **biso'gnoso, a** *ag*
needy, poor; **bisognoso di** in need of,
needing

bis'tecca, che *sf* steak, beefsteak

bisticci'are [bistit'tʃare] *vi* to quarrel,
bicker; **~rsi** *vr* to quarrel, bicker;
bis'ticcio *sm* quarrel, squabble; (*gioco di
parole*) pun

'bisturi *sm* scalpel

bi'sunto, a *ag* very greasy

'bitter *sm inv* bitters *pl*

bi'vacco, chi *sm* bivouac

'bivio *sm* fork; (*fig*) dilemma

'bizza ['biddza] *sf* tantrum; **fare le ~e**

(*bambino*) to be naughty

biz'zarro, a [bid'dzarro] *ag* bizarre, strange

biz'zeffe [bid'dzɛffe]: **a ~** *av* in plenty,
galore

blan'dire *vt* to soothe; to flatter

'blando, a *ag* mild, gentle

bla'sone *sm* coat of arms

blate'rare *vi* to chatter

blin'dato, a *ag* armoured

bloc'care *vt* to block; (*isolare*) to isolate,
cut off; (*porto*) to blockade; (*prezzi, beni*) to
freeze; (*meccanismo*) to jam; **~rsi** *vr*
(*motore*) to stall; (*freni, porta*) to jam, stick;
(*ascensore*) to stop, get stuck

bloc'chetto [blok'ketto] *sm* notebook; (*di
biglietti*) book

'blocco, chi *sm* block; (*MIL*) blockade; (*dei
fitti*) restriction; (*quadernetto*) pad; (*fig:
unione*) coalition; (*il bloccare*) blocking;
isolating, cutting-off; blockading; freezing;
jamming; **in ~** (*nell'insieme*) as a whole;
(*COMM*) in bulk; **~ cardiaco** cardiac arrest

blu *ag inv, sm* dark blue

'blusa *sf* (*camiciotto*) smock; (*camicetta*)
blouse

'boa *sm inv* (*ZOOL*) boa constrictor; (*sciarpa*)
feather boa ♦ *sf* buoy

bo'ato *sm* rumble, roar

bo'bina *sf* reel, spool; (*di pellicola*) spool;
(*di film*) reel; (*ELETTR*) coil

'bocca, che *sf* mouth; **in ~ al lupo!** good
luck!

boc'caccia, ce [bok'kattʃa] *sf* (*malalingua*)
gossip; **fare le ~ce** to pull faces

boc'cale *sm* jug; **~ da birra** tankard

boc'cetta [bot'tʃetta] *sf* small bottle

boccheggi'are [bokked'dʒare] *vi* to gasp

boc'chino [bok'kino] *sm* (*di sigaretta,
sigaro: cannella*) cigarette-holder; cigar-
holder; (*di pipa, strumenti musicali*)
mouthpiece

'boccia, ce ['bottʃa] *sf* bottle; (*da vino*)
decanter, carafe; (*palla*) bowl; **gioco delle
~ce** bowls *sg*

bocci'are [bot'tʃare] *vt* (*proposta, progetto*)
to reject; (*INS*) to fail; (*BOCCE*) to hit;
boccia'tura *sf* failure

bocci'olo [bot'tʃɔlo] *sm* bud
boc'cone *sm* mouthful, morsel
boc'coni *av* face downwards
'boia *sm inv* executioner; hangman
boi'ata *sf* botch
boicot'tare *vt* to boycott
'bolide *sm* meteor; **come un ~** like a flash, at top speed
'bolla *sf* bubble; (*MED*) blister; **~ papale** papal bull; **~ di consegna** (*COMM*) delivery note
bol'lare *vt* to stamp; (*fig*) to brand
bol'lente *ag* boiling; boiling hot
bol'letta *sf* bill; (*ricevuta*) receipt; **essere in ~** to be hard up
bollet'tino *sm* bulletin; (*COMM*) note; **~ meteorologico** weather report; **~ di spedizione** consignment note
bol'lire *vt, vi* to boil; **bol'lito** *sm* (*CUC*) boiled meat
bolli'tore *sm* (*CUC*) kettle; (*per riscaldamento*) boiler
'bollo *sm* stamp; **~ per patente** *driving licence tax*
'bomba *sf* bomb; **~ atomica** atom bomb
bombarda'mento *sm* bombardment; bombing
bombar'dare *vt* to bombard; (*da aereo*) to bomb
bombardi'ere *sm* bomber
bom'betta *sf* bowler (hat)
'bombola *sf* cylinder
bo'naccia, ce [bo'nattʃa] *sf* dead calm
bo'nario, a *ag* good-natured, kind
bo'nifica, che *sf* reclamation; reclaimed land
bo'nifico, ci *sm* (*riduzione, abbuono*) discount; (*versamento a terzi*) credit transfer
bontà *sf* goodness; (*cortesia*) kindness; **aver la ~ di fare qc** to be good *o* kind enough to do sth
borbot'tare *vi* to mumble
'borchia ['borkja] *sf* stud
borda'tura *sf* (*SARTORIA*) border, trim
bor'deaux [bor'dɔ] *ag inv, sm inv* maroon
'bordo *sm* (*NAUT*) ship's side; (*orlo*) edge; (*striscia di guarnizione*) border, trim; **a ~ di**

(*nave, aereo*) aboard, on board; (*macchina*) in
bor'gata *sf* (*in campagna*) hamlet
bor'ghese [bor'geze] *ag* (*spesso peg*) middle-class; bourgeois; **abito ~** civilian dress; **borghe'sia** *sf* middle classes *pl*; bourgeoisie
'borgo, ghi *sm* (*paesino*) village; (*quartiere*) district; (*sobborgo*) suburb
'boria *sf* self-conceit, arrogance
boro'talco *sm* talcum powder
bor'raccia, ce [bor'rattʃa] *sf* canteen, water-bottle
'borsa *sf* bag; (*anche:* **~ da signora**) handbag; (*ECON*): **la B~ (valori)** the Stock Exchange; **~ nera** black market; **~ della spesa** shopping bag; **~ di studio** grant; **borsai'olo** *sm* pickpocket; **borsel'lino** *sm* purse; **bor'setta** *sf* handbag; **bor'sista, i, e** *sm/f* (*ECON*) speculator; (*INS*) grant-holder
bos'caglia [bos'kaʎʎa] *sf* woodlands *pl*
boscai'olo *sm* woodcutter; forester
'bosco, schi *sm* wood; **bos'coso, a** *ag* wooded
'bossolo *sm* cartridge-case
bo'tanica *sf* botany
bo'tanico, a, ci, che *ag* botanical ♦ *sm* botanist
'botola *sf* trap door
'botta *sf* blow; (*rumore*) bang
'botte *sf* barrel, cask
bot'tega, ghe *sf* shop; (*officina*) workshop; **botte'gaio, a** *sm/f* shopkeeper; **botte'ghino** *sm* ticket office; (*del lotto*) public lottery office
bot'tiglia [bot'tiʎʎa] *sf* bottle; **bottiglie'ria** *sf* wine shop
bot'tino *sm* (*di guerra*) booty; (*di rapina, furto*) loot
'botto *sm* bang; crash; **di ~** suddenly
bot'tone *sm* button; **attaccare ~ a qn** (*fig*) to buttonhole sb
bo'vino, a *ag* bovine; **~i** *smpl* cattle
boxe [bɔks] *sf* boxing
'bozza ['bɔttsa] *sf* draft; sketch; (*TIP*) proof; **boz'zetto** *sm* sketch**

'**bozzolo** [ˈbɔttsolo] *sm* cocoon

BR *sigla fpl* = **Brigate Rosse**

brac'care *vt* to hunt

brac'cetto [bratˈtʃetto] *sm*: **a ~** arm in arm

bracci'ale [bratˈtʃale] *sm* bracelet; (*distintivo*) armband; **braccia'letto** *sm* bracelet, bangle

bracci'ante [bratˈtʃante] *sm* (*AGR*) day labourer

bracci'ata [bratˈtʃata] *sf* (*nel nuoto*) stroke

'**braccio** [ˈbrattʃo] (*pl(f)* **braccia**) *sm* (*ANAT*) arm; (*pl(m)* **bracci**: *di gru, fiume*) arm; (: *di edificio*) wing; **~ di mare** sound; **bracci'olo** *sm* (*appoggio*) arm

'**bracco, chi** *sm* hound

bracconi'ere *sm* poacher

'**brace** [ˈbratʃe] *sf* embers *pl*; **braci'ere** *sm* brazier

braci'ola [braˈtʃɔla] *sf* (*CUC*) chop

bra'mare *vt*: **~ qc/di fare** to long for sth/ to do

'**branca, che** *sf* branch

'**branchia** [ˈbrankja] *sf* (*ZOOL*) gill

'**branco, chi** *sm* (*di cani, lupi*) pack; (*di pecore*) flock; (*peg: di persone*) gang, pack

branco'lare *vi* to grope, feel one's way

'**branda** *sf* camp bed

bran'dello *sm* scrap, shred; **a ~i** in tatters, in rags

bran'dire *vt* to brandish

'**brano** *sm* piece; (*di libro*) passage

bra'sato *sm* braised beef

Bra'sile *sm*: **il ~** Brazil; **brasili'ano, a** *ag*, *sm/f* Brazilian

'**bravo, a** *ag* (*abile*) clever, capable, skilful; (*buono*) good, honest; (: *bambino*) good; (*coraggioso*) brave; **~!** well done!; (*a teatro*) bravo!

bra'vura *sf* cleverness, skill

'**breccia, ce** [ˈbrettʃa] *sf* breach

bre'tella *sf* (*AUT*) link; **~e** *sfpl* (*di calzoni*) braces

'**breve** *ag* brief, short; **in ~** in short

brevet'tare *vt* to patent

bre'vetto *sm* patent; **~ di pilotaggio** pilot's licence (*BRIT*) *o* license (*US*)

'**brezza** [ˈbreddza] *sf* breeze

'**bricco, chi** *sm* jug; **~ del caffè** coffeepot

bric'cone, a *sm/f* rogue, rascal

briciola [ˈbritʃola] *sf* crumb

briciolo [ˈbritʃolo] *sm* (*specie fig*) bit

'**briga, ghe** *sf* (*fastidio*) trouble, bother; **pigliarsi la ~ di fare qc** to take the trouble to do sth

brigadi'ere *sm* (*dei carabinieri etc*) ≈ sergeant

bri'gante *sm* bandit

bri'gata *sf* (*MIL*) brigade; (*gruppo*) group, party; **B~e Rosse** (*POL*) Red Brigades

'**briglia** [ˈbriʎʎa] *sf* rein; **a ~ sciolta** at full gallop; (*fig*) at full speed

bril'lante *ag* bright; (*anche fig*) brilliant; (*che luccica*) shining ♦ *sm* diamond

bril'lare *vi* to shine; (*mina*) to blow up ♦ *vt* (*mina*) to set off

'**brillo, a** *ag* merry, tipsy

'**brina** *sf* hoarfrost

brin'dare *vi*: **~ a qn/qc** to drink to *o* toast sb/sth

'**brindisi** *sm inv* toast

'**brio** *sm* liveliness, go

bri'oche [briˈɔʃ] *sf inv* brioche

bri'oso, a *ag* lively

bri'tannico, a, ci, che *ag* British

'**brivido** *sm* shiver; (*di ribrezzo*) shudder; (*fig*) thrill

brizzo'lato, a [brittsoˈlato] *ag* (*persona*) going grey; (*barba, capelli*) greying

'**brocca, che** *sf* jug

broc'cato *sm* brocade

'**broccolo** *sm* broccoli *sg*

'**brodo** *sm* broth; (*per cucinare*) stock; **~ ristretto** consommé

brogli'accio [broʎˈʎattʃo] *sm* scribbling pad

'**broglio** [ˈbrɔʎʎo] *sm*: **~ elettorale** gerrymandering

bron'chite [bronˈkite] *sf* (*MED*) bronchitis

'**broncio** [ˈbrontʃo] *sm* sulky expression; **tenere il ~** to sulk

'**bronco, chi** *sm* bronchial tube

bronto'lare *vi* to grumble; (*tuono, stomaco*) to rumble

'**bronzo** [ˈbrondzo] *sm* bronze

'browser ['brauzer] *sm inv* (INFORM)
browser
bru'care *vt* to browse on, nibble at
brucia'pelo [brutʃa'pelo]: **a ~** *av* point-
blank
bruci'are [bru'tʃare] *vt* to burn; (*scottare*) to
scald ♦ *vi* to burn; brucia'tore *sm*
burner; brucia'tura *sf* (*atto*) burning *no*
pl; (*segno*) burn; (*scottatura*) scald;
bruci'ore *sm* burning *o* smarting
sensation; **bruciore di stomaco** heartburn
'bruco, chi *sm* caterpillar; grub
brughi'era [bru'gjera] *sf* heath, moor
bruli'care *vi* to swarm
'brullo, a *ag* bare, bleak
'bruma *sf* mist
'bruno, a *ag* brown, dark; (*persona*)
dark(-haired)
'brusco, a, schi, sche *ag* (*sapore*)
sharp; (*modi, persona*) brusque, abrupt;
(*movimento*) abrupt, sudden
bru'sio *sm* buzz, buzzing
bru'tale *ag* brutal
'bruto, a *ag* (*forza*) brute *cpd* ♦ *sm* brute
brut'tezza [brut'tettsa] *sf* ugliness
'brutto, a *ag* ugly; (*cattivo*) bad; (*malattia,
strada, affare*) nasty, bad; **~ tempo** bad
weather; brut'tura *sf* (*cosa brutta*) ugly
thing; (*sudiciume*) filth; (*azione meschina*)
mean action
Bru'xelles [bry'sɛl] *sf* Brussels
BSE [biesse'e] *sigla f* (= *encefalopatia
spongiforme bovina*) BSE
bub'bone *sm* swelling
'buca, che *sf* hole; (*avvallamento*) hollow;
~ delle lettere letterbox
buca'neve *sm inv* snowdrop
bu'care *vt* (*forare*) to make a hole (*o* holes)
in; (*pungere*) to pierce; (*biglietto*) to punch;
~rsi *vr* (*di eroina*) to mainline; **~ una
gomma** to have a puncture
bu'cato *sm* (*operazione*) washing; (*panni*)
wash, washing
'buccia, ce ['buttʃa] *sf* skin, peel
bucherel'lare [bukerel'lare] *vt* to riddle
with holes
'buco, chi *sm* hole

bu'dello *sm* (ANAT: *pl(f)* ~a) bowel, gut;
(*fig: tubo*) tube; (*vicolo*) alley
bu'dino *sm* pudding
'bue *sm* ox; **carne di ~** beef
'bufalo *sm* buffalo
bu'fera *sf* storm
'buffo, a *ag* funny; (TEATRO) comic
buf'fone *sm* buffoon; (*peg*) clown
bu'gia, 'gie [bu'dʒia] *sf* lie; **dire una ~** to
tell a lie; bugi'ardo, a *ag* lying, deceitful
♦ *sm/f* liar
bugi'gattolo [budʒi'gattolo] *sm* poky little
room
'buio, a *ag* dark ♦ *sm* dark, darkness
'bulbo *sm* (BOT) bulb; **~ oculare** eyeball
Bulga'ria *sf*: **la ~** Bulgaria
bul'lone *sm* bolt
buona'notte *escl* good night! ♦ *sf*: **dare
la ~ a** to say good night to
buona'sera *escl* good evening!
buongi'orno [bwon'dʒorno] *escl* good
morning (*o* afternoon)!
buongus'taio, a *sm/f* gourmet
buon'gusto *sm* good taste

bu'ono, a (*ag: dav sm* buon +C *o* V,
buono +*s impura, gn, pn, ps, x, z; dav sf*
buon' +*V*) *ag* 1 (*gen*) good; **un buon
pranzo** a good lunch; **(stai) ~!** behave!
2 (*benevolo*): **~ (con)** good (to), kind (to)
3 (*giusto, valido*) right; **al momento ~** at
the right moment
4 (*adatto*): **~ a/da** fit for/to; **essere ~ a
nulla** to be no good *o* use at anything
5 (*auguri*): **buon anno!** happy New Year!;
buon appetito! enjoy your meal!; **buon
compleanno!** happy birthday!; **buon
divertimento!** have a nice time!; **~a
fortuna!** good luck!; **buon riposo!** sleep
well!; **buon viaggio!** bon voyage!, have a
good trip!
6: **a buon mercato** cheap; **di buon'ora**
early; **buon senso** common sense; **alla ~a**
ag simple ♦ *av* without any fuss
♦ *sm* 1 (*bontà*) goodness, good
2 (COMM) voucher, coupon; **~ di cassa**

cash voucher; **~ di consegna** delivery note; **~ del Tesoro** Treasury bill

---

buontem'pone, a *sm/f* jovial person

burat'tino *sm* puppet

'burbero, a *ag* surly, gruff

'burla *sf* prank, trick; **bur'lare** *vt*: **burlare qc/qn, burlarsi di qc/qn** to make fun of sth/sb

burocra'zia [burokrat'tsia] *sf* bureaucracy

bur'rasca, sche *sf* storm

'burro *sm* butter

bur'rone *sm* ravine

bus'care *vt* (*anche*: **~rsi**: *raffreddore*) to get, catch; **buscarle** (*fam*) to get a hiding

bus'sare *vi* to knock

'bussola *sf* compass

'busta *sf* (*da lettera*) envelope; (*astuccio*) case; **in ~ aperta/chiusa** in an unsealed/sealed envelope; **~ paga** pay packet

busta'rella *sf* bribe, backhander

'busto *sm* bust; (*indumento*) corset, girdle; **a mezzo ~** (*foto*) half-length

buttafu'ori *sm inv* bouncer

but'tare *vt* to throw; (*anche*: **~ via**) to throw away; **~ giù** (*scritto*) to scribble down; (*cibo*) to gulp down; (*edificio*) to pull down, demolish; (*pasta, verdura*) to put into boiling water

C, c

ca'bina *sf* (*di nave*) cabin; (*da spiaggia*) beach hut; (*di autocarro, treno*) cab; (*di aereo*) cockpit; (*di ascensore*) cage; **~ telefonica** call *o* (tele)phone box; **cabi'nato** *sm* cabin cruiser

ca'cao *sm* cocoa

'caccia ['kattʃa] *sf* hunting; (*con fucile*) shooting; (*inseguimento*) chase; (*cacciagione*) game ♦ *sm inv* (*aereo*) fighter; (*nave*) destroyer; **~ grossa** big-game hunting; **~ all'uomo** manhunt

cacciabombardi'ere [kattʃabombar'djere] *sm* fighter-bomber

cacciagi'one [kattʃa'dʒone] *sf* game

cacci'are [kat'tʃare] *vt* to hunt; (*mandar via*) to chase away; (*ficcare*) to shove, stick ♦ *vi* to hunt; **~rsi** *vr*: **dove s'è cacciata la mia borsa?** where has my bag got to?; **~rsi nei guai** to get into trouble; **~ fuori qc** to whip *o* pull sth out; **~ un urlo** to let out a yell; **cacci'atore** *sm* hunter; **cacciatore di frodo** poacher

caccia'vite [kattʃa'vite] *sm inv* screwdriver

'cactus *sm inv* cactus

ca'davere *sm* (dead) body, corpse

ca'dente *ag* falling; (*casa*) tumbledown

ca'denza [ka'dɛntsa] *sf* cadence; (*ritmo*) rhythm; (*MUS*) cadenza

ca'dere *vi* to fall; (*denti, capelli*) to fall out; (*tetto*) to fall in; **questa gonna cade bene** this skirt hangs well; **lasciar ~** (*anche fig*) to drop; **~ dal sonno** to be falling asleep on one's feet; **~ dalle nuvole** (*fig*) to be taken aback

ca'detto, a *ag* younger; (*squadra*) junior *cpd* ♦ *sm* cadet

ca'duta *sf* fall; **la ~ dei capelli** hair loss

caffè *sm inv* coffee; (*locale*) café; **~ macchiato** coffee with a dash of milk; **~ macinato** ground coffee

caffel'latte *sm inv* white coffee

caffetti'era *sf* coffeepot

cagio'nare [kadʒo'nare] *vt* to cause

cagio'nevole [kadʒo'nevole] *ag* delicate, weak

cagli'are [kaʎ'ʎare] *vi* to curdle

'cagna ['kaɲɲa] *sf* (*ZOOL, peg*) bitch

ca'gnesco, a, schi, sche [kaɲ'ɲesko] *ag* (*fig*): **guardare qn in ~** to scowl at sb

cala'brone *sm* hornet

cala'maio *sm* inkpot; inkwell

cala'maro *sm* squid

cala'mita *sf* magnet

calamità *sf inv* calamity, disaster

ca'lare *vt* (*far discendere*) to lower; (*MAGLIA*) to decrease ♦ *vi* (*discendere*) to go (*o* come) down; (*tramontare*) to set, go down; **~ di peso** to lose weight

'calca *sf* throng, press

cal'cagno [kal'kaɲɲo] *sm* heel

cal'care *sm* limestone ♦ *vt* (*premere coi*

piedi) to tread, press down; (*premere con forza*) to press down; (*mettere in rilievo*) to stress; ~ **la mano** to overdo it, exaggerate

'calce ['kaltʃe] *sm*: **in ~** at the foot of the page ♦ *sf* lime; ~ **viva** quicklime

calces'truzzo [kaltʃes'truttso] *sm* concrete

calci'are [kal'tʃare] *vt, vi* to kick; calcia'tore *sm* footballer

'calcio ['kaltʃo] *sm* (*pedata*) kick; (*sport*) football, soccer; (*di pistola, fucile*) butt; (*CHIM*) calcium; ~ **d'angolo** (*SPORT*) corner (kick); ~ **di punizione** (*SPORT*) free kick

'calco, chi *sm* (*ARTE*) casting, moulding; cast, mould

calco'lare *vt* to calculate, work out, reckon; (*ponderare*) to weigh (up); calcola'tore, 'trice *ag* calculating ♦ *sm* calculator; (*fig*) calculating person; **calcolatore elettronico** computer; calcola'trice *sf* calculator

'calcolo *sm* (*anche MAT*) calculation; (*infinitesimale etc*) calculus; (*MED*) stone; **fare i propri ~i** (*fig*) to weigh the pros and cons; **per ~** out of self-interest

cal'daia *sf* boiler

caldeggi'are [kalded'dʒare] *vt* to support

'caldo, a *ag* warm; (*molto ~*) hot; (*fig: appassionato*) keen; hearty ♦ *sm* heat; **ho ~** I'm warm; I'm hot; **fa ~** it's warm; it's hot

calen'dario *sm* calendar

'calibro *sm* (*di arma*) calibre, bore; (*TECN*) callipers *pl*; (*fig*) calibre; **di grosso ~** (*fig*) prominent

'calice ['kalitʃe] *sm* goblet; (*REL*) chalice

ca'ligine [ka'lidʒine] *sf* fog; (*mista con fumo*) smog

'callo *sm* callus; (*ai piedi*) corn

'calma *sf* calm

cal'mante *sm* tranquillizer

cal'mare *vt* to calm; (*lenire*) to soothe; ~rsi *vr* to grow calm, calm down; (*vento*) to abate; (*dolori*) to ease

calmi'ere *sm* controlled price

'calmo, a *ag* calm, quiet

'calo *sm* (*COMM: di prezzi*) fall; (: *di volume*) shrinkage; (: *di peso*) loss

ca'lore *sm* warmth; heat; **in ~** (*ZOOL*) on heat

calo'ria *sf* calorie

calo'roso, a *ag* warm

calpes'tare *vt* to tread on, trample on; "**è vietato ~ l'erba**" "keep off the grass"

ca'lunnia *sf* slander; (*scritta*) libel

cal'vario *sm* (*fig*) affliction, cross

cal'vizie [kal'vittsje] *sf* baldness

'calvo, a *ag* bald

'calza ['kaltsa] *sf* (*da donna*) stocking; (*da uomo*) sock; **fare la ~** to knit; ~**e di nailon** nylons, (nylon) stockings

cal'zare [kal'tsare] *vt* (*scarpe, guanti: mettersi*) to put on; (: *portare*) to wear ♦ *vi* to fit; calza'tura *sf* footwear

calzet'tone [kaltset'tone] *sm* heavy knee-length sock

cal'zino [kal'tsino] *sm* sock

calzo'laio [kaltso'lajo] *sm* shoemaker; (*che ripara scarpe*) cobbler; calzole'ria *sf* (*negozio*) shoe shop

calzon'cini [kaltson'tʃini] *smpl* shorts

cal'zone [kal'tsone] *sm* trouser leg; (*CUC*) *savoury turnover made with pizza dough*; ~**i** *smpl* (*pantaloni*) trousers (*BRIT*), pants (*US*)

cambi'ale *sf* bill (of exchange); (*pagherò cambiario*) promissory note

cambia'mento *sm* change

cambi'are *vt* to change; (*modificare*) to alter, change; (*barattare*): ~ **(qc con qn/ qc)** to exchange (sth with sb/for sth) ♦ *vi* to change, alter; ~**rsi** *vr* (*d'abito*) to change; ~ **casa** to move (house); ~ **idea** to change one's mind; ~ **treno** to change trains

'cambio *sm* change; (*modifica*) alteration, change; (*scambio, COMM*) exchange; (*corso dei cambi*) rate (of exchange); (*TECN, AUT*) gears *pl*; **in ~ di** in exchange for; **dare il ~ a qn** to take over from sb

'camera *sf* room; (*anche*: ~ **da letto**) bedroom; (*POL*) chamber, house; ~ **ardente** mortuary chapel; ~ **d'aria** inner tube; (*di pallone*) bladder; **C~ di Commercio** Chamber of Commerce; **C~ dei Deputati** Chamber of Deputies, ≈ House of

Commons (*BRIT*), ≈ House of Representatives (*US*); **~ a gas** gas chamber; **~ a un letto / a due letti / matrimoniale** single/twin-bedded/double room; **~ oscura** (*FOT*) dark room

came'rata, i, e *sm/f* companion, mate ♦ *sf* dormitory

cameri'era *sf* (*domestica*) maid; (*che serve a tavola*) waitress; (*che fa le camere*) chambermaid

cameri'ere *sm* (man)servant; (*di ristorante*) waiter

came'rino *sm* (*TEATRO*) dressing room

'camice ['kamitʃe] *sm* (*REL*) alb; (*per medici etc*) white coat

cami'cetta [kami'tʃetta] *sf* blouse

ca'micia, cie [ka'mitʃa] *sf* (*da uomo*) shirt; (*da donna*) blouse; **~ di forza** straitjacket

cami'netto *sm* hearth, fireplace

ca'mino *sm* chimney; (*focolare*) fireplace, hearth

'camion *sm inv* lorry (*BRIT*), truck (*US*); camion'cino *sm* van

cam'mello *sm* (*ZOOL*) camel; (*tessuto*) camel hair

cammi'nare *vi* to walk; (*funzionare*) to work, go; cammi'nata *sf* walk

cam'mino *sm* walk; (*sentiero*) path; (*itinerario, direzione, tragitto*) way; **mettersi in ~** to set *o* start off

camo'milla *sf* camomile; (*infuso*) camomile tea

ca'morra *sf* camorra; racket

ca'moscio [ka'mɔʃʃo] *sm* chamois; **di ~** (*scarpe, borsa*) suede *cpd*

cam'pagna [kam'paɲɲa] *sf* country, countryside; (*POL, COMM, MIL*) campaign; **in ~** in the country; **andare in ~** to go to the country; **fare una ~** to campaign; campa'gnola *sf* (*AUT*) cross-country vehicle; campa'gnolo, a *ag* country *cpd*

cam'pale *ag* field *cpd*; (*fig*): **una giornata ~** a hard day

cam'pana *sf* bell; (*anche*: **~ di vetro**) bell jar; campa'nella *sf* small bell; (*di tenda*) curtain ring; campa'nello *sm* (*all'uscio, da tavola*) bell

campa'nile *sm* bell tower, belfry; campani'lismo *sm* parochialism

cam'pare *vi* to live; (*tirare avanti*) to get by, manage

cam'pato, a *ag*: **~ in aria** unfounded

campeggi'are [kamped'dʒare] *vi* to camp; (*risaltare*) to stand out; campeggia'tore, 'trice *sm/f* camper; cam'peggio *sm* camping; (*terreno*) camp site; **fare (del) campeggio** to go camping

cam'pestre *ag* country *cpd*, rural

Campidoglio

ⓘ The **Campidoglio**, one of the Seven Hills of Rome, is the site of the *Comune di Roma.*

---

campio'nario, a *ag*: **fiera ~a** a trade fair ♦ *sm* collection of samples

campio'nato *sm* championship

campi'one, 'essa *sm/f* (*SPORT*) champion ♦ *sm* (*COMM*) sample

'campo *sm* field; (*MIL*) field; (*: accampamento*) camp; (*spazio delimitato: sportivo etc*) ground; (*di quadro*) background; **i ~i** (*campagna*) the countryside; **~ da aviazione** airfield; **~ di battaglia** (*MIL, fig*) battlefield; **~ di golf** golf course; **~ da tennis** tennis court; **~ visivo** field of vision

campo'santo (*pl* **campisanti**) *sm* cemetery

camuf'fare *vt* to disguise

'Canada *sm*: **il ~** Canada; cana'dese *ag*, *sm/f* Canadian ♦ *sf* (*anche*: **tenda canadese**) ridge tent

ca'naglia [ka'naʎʎa] *sf* rabble, mob; (*persona*) scoundrel, rogue

ca'nale *sm* (*anche fig*) channel; (*artificiale*) canal

'canapa *sf* hemp; **~ indiana** (*droga*) cannabis

cana'rino *sm* canary

cancel'lare [kantʃel'lare] *vt* (*con la gomma*) to rub out, erase; (*con la penna*) to strike out; (*annullare*) to annul, cancel; (*disdire*) to cancel

cancelle'ria [kantʃelle'ria] *sf* chancery; (*materiale per scrivere*) stationery

cancelli'ere [kantʃel'ljere] *sm* chancellor; (*di tribunale*) clerk of the court

can'cello [kan'tʃello] *sm* gate

can'crena *sf* gangrene

'cancro *sm* (*MED*) cancer; (*dello zodiaco*): **C~** Cancer

candeg'gina [kanded'dʒina] *sf* bleach

can'dela *sf* candle; **~ (di accensione)** (*AUT*) spark(ing) plug

cande'labro *sm* candelabra

candeli'ere *sm* candlestick

candi'dato, a *sm/f* candidate; (*aspirante a una carica*) applicant

'candido, a *ag* white as snow; (*puro*) pure; (*sincero*) sincere, candid

can'dito, a *ag* candied

can'dore *sm* brilliant white; purity; sincerity, candour

'cane *sm* dog; (*di pistola, fucile*) cock; **fa un freddo ~** it's bitterly cold; **non c'era un ~** there wasn't a soul; **~ da caccia/uardia** hunting/guard dog; **~ lupo** alsatian

ca'nestro *sm* basket

'canfora *sf* camphor

cangi'ante [kan'dʒante] *ag* iridescent

can'guro *sm* kangaroo

ca'nile *sm* kennel; (*di allevamento*) kennels *pl*; **~ municipale** dog pound

ca'nino, a *ag, sm* canine

'canna *sf* (*pianta*) reed; (*: indica, da zucchero*) cane; (*bastone*) stick, cane; (*di fucile*) barrel; (*di organo*) pipe; (*fam: droga*) joint; **~ da pesca** (fishing) rod; **~ da zucchero** sugar cane

can'nella *sf* (*CUC*) cinnamon

cannel'loni *smpl* pasta tubes stuffed with sauce and baked

cannocchi'ale [kannok'kjale] *sm* telescope

can'none *sm* (*MIL*) gun; (*: STORIA*) cannon; (*tubo*) pipe, tube; (*piega*) box pleat; (*fig*) ace

can'nuccia, ce [kan'nuttʃa] *sf* (drinking) straw

ca'noa *sf* canoe

'canone *sm* canon, criterion; (*mensile, annuo*) rent; fee

ca'nonico, ci *sm* (*REL*) canon

ca'noro, a *ag* (*uccello*) singing, song *cpd*

canot'taggio [kanot'taddʒo] *sm* rowing

canotti'era *sf* vest

ca'notto *sm* small boat, dinghy; canoe

cano'vaccio [kano'vattʃo] *sm* (*tela*) canvas; (*strofinaccio*) duster; (*trama*) plot

can'tante *sm/f* singer

can'tare *vt, vi* to sing; **cantau'tore, 'trice** *sm/f* singer-composer

canti'ere *sm* (*EDIL*) (building) site; (*anche:* **~ navale**) shipyard

canti'lena *sf* (*filastrocca*) lullaby; (*fig*) sing-song voice

can'tina *sf* cellar; (*bottega*) wine shop

'canto *sm* song; (*arte*) singing; (*REL*) chant; chanting; (*poesia*) poem, lyric; (*parte di una poesia*) canto; (*parte, lato*): **da un ~** on the one hand; **d'altro ~** on the other hand

canto'nata *sf* corner; **prendere una ~** (*fig*) to blunder

can'tone *sm* (*in Svizzera*) canton

can'tuccio [kan'tuttʃo] *sm* corner, nook

canzo'nare [kantso'nare] *vt* to tease

can'zone [kan'tsone] *sf* song; (*POESIA*) canzone; **canzoni'ere** *sm* (*MUS*) songbook; (*LETTERATURA*) collection of poems

'caos *sm inv* chaos; **ca'otico, a, ci, che** *ag* chaotic

C.A.P. *sigla m* = **codice di avviamento postale**

ca'pace [ka'patʃe] *ag* able, capable; (*ampio, vasto*) large, capacious; **sei ~ di farlo?** can you *o* are you able to do it?; **capacità** *sf inv* ability; (*DIR, di recipiente*) capacity; **capaci'tarsi** *vr* to understand

ca'panna *sf* hut

capan'none *sm* (*AGR*) barn; (*fabbricato industriale*) (factory) shed

ca'parbio, a *ag* stubborn

ca'parra *sf* deposit, down payment

ca'pello *sm* hair; **~i** *smpl* (*capigliatura*) hair *sg*

capez'zale [kapet'tsale] *sm* bolster; (*fig*)

bedside

ca'**pezzolo** [ka'pettsolo] *sm* nipple

capi'**enza** [ka'pjentsa] *sf* capacity

capiglia'**tura** [kapiʎʎa'tura] *sf* hair

ca'**pire** *vt* to understand

capi'**tale** *ag* (*mortale*) capital; (*fondamentale*) main, chief ♦ *sf* (*città*) capital ♦ *sm* (ECON) capital; **capita'lismo** *sm* capitalism; **capita'lista, i, e** *ag, sm/f* capitalist

capitane'**ria** *sf*: ~ **di porto** port authorities *pl*

capi'**tano** *sm* captain

capi'**tare** *vi* (*giungere casualmente*) to happen to go, find o.s.; (*accadere*) to happen; (*presentarsi: cosa*) to turn up, present itself ♦ *vb impers* to happen; **mi è capitato un guaio** I've had a spot of trouble

capi'**tello** *sm* (ARCHIT) capital

ca'**pitolo** *sm* chapter

capi'**tombolo** *sm* headlong fall, tumble

'**capo** *sm* head; (*persona*) head, leader; (: *in ufficio*) head, boss; (: *in tribù*) chief; (*di oggetti*) head; top; end; (GEO) cape; **andare a** ~ to start a new paragraph; **da** ~ over again; ~ **di bestiame** head *inv* of cattle; ~ **di vestiario** item of clothing

'**capo...** *prefisso*: **capocu'oco, chi** *sm* head cook; **Capo'danno** *sm* New Year; **capo'fitto: a capofitto** *av* headfirst, headlong; **capo'giro** *sm* dizziness *no pl*; **capola'voro, i** *sm* masterpiece; **capo'linea** (*pl* **capi'linea**) *sm* terminus; **capo'lino** *sm*: **fare capolino** to peep out (*o in etc*); **capolu'ogo** (*pl* **-ghi** *o* **capilu'oghi**) *sm* chief town, administrative centre

capo'**rale** *sm* (MIL) lance corporal (BRIT), private first class (US)

'**capo...** *prefisso*: **capostazi'one** (*pl* **capistazi'one**) *sm* station master; **capo'treno** (*pl* **capi'treno** *o* **capo'treni**) *sm* guard

capo'**volgere** [kapo'vɔldʒere] *vt* to overturn; (*fig*) to reverse; **~rsi** *vr* to overturn; (*barca*) to capsize; (*fig*) to be

reversed; **capo'volto, a** *pp di* **capovolgere**

'**cappa** *sf* (*mantello*) cape, cloak; (*del camino*) hood

cap'**pella** *sf* (REL) chapel; **cappel'lano** *sm* chaplain

cap'**pello** *sm* hat

'**cappero** *sm* caper

cap'**pone** *sm* capon

cap'**potto** *sm* (over)coat

cappuc'**cino** [kapput'tʃino] *sm* (*frate*) Capuchin monk; (*bevanda*) cappuccino, *frothy white coffee*

cap'**puccio** [kap'puttʃo] *sm* (*copricapo*) hood; (*della biro*) cap

'**capra** *sf* (she-)goat; **ca'pretto** *sm* kid

ca'**priccio** [ka'prittʃo] *sm* caprice, whim; (*bizza*) tantrum; **fare i ~i** to be very naughty; **capricci'oso, a** *ag* capricious, whimsical; naughty

Capri'**corno** *sm* Capricorn

capri'**ola** *sf* somersault

capri'**olo** *sm* roe deer

'**capro** *sm*: ~ **espiatorio** scapegoat

'**capsula** *sf* capsule; (*di arma, per bottiglie*) cap

cap'**tare** *vt* (RADIO, TV) to pick up; (*cattivarsi*) to gain, win

cara'**bina** *sf* rifle

carabini'**ere** *sm member of Italian military police force*

---

carabinieri

Originally part of the armed forces, the **carabinieri** *are police who now perform both military and civil duties and include paratroop units and mounted divisions.*

---

ca'**raffa** *sf* carafe

cara'**mella** *sf* sweet

ca'**rattere** *sm* character; (*caratteristica*) characteristic, trait; **avere un buon** ~ to be good-natured; **caratte'ristica, che** *sf* characteristic, trait, peculiarity; **caratte'ristico, a, ci, che** *ag* characteristic; **caratteriz'zare** *vt* to characterize

car'bone *sm* coal
carbu'rante *sm* (motor) fuel
carbura'tore *sm* carburettor
car'cassa *sf* carcass; (*fig: peg: macchina etc*) (old) wreck
carce'rato, a [kartʃe'rato] *sm/f* prisoner
'carcere ['kartʃere] *sm* prison; (*pena*) imprisonment
carci'ofo [kar'tʃɔfo] *sm* artichoke
car'diaco, a, ci, che *ag* cardiac, heart *cpd*
cardi'nale *ag, sm* cardinal
'cardine *sm* hinge
'cardo *sm* thistle
ca'renza [ka'rɛntsa] *sf* lack, scarcity; (*vitaminica*) deficiency
cares'tia *sf* famine; (*penuria*) scarcity, dearth
ca'rezza [ka'rettsa] *sf* caress; **carez'zare** *vt* to caress, stroke
'carica, che *sf* (*mansione ufficiale*) office, position; (*MIL, TECN, ELETTR*) charge; **ha una forte ~ di simpatia** he's very likeable; *vedi anche* **carico**
caricabatte'ria *sm inv* battery charger
cari'care *vt* (*merce, INFORM*) to load; (*orologio*) to wind up; (*batteria, MIL*) to charge
'carico, a, chi, che *ag* (*che porta un peso*): **~ di** loaded *o* laden with; (*fucile*) loaded; (*orologio*) wound up; (*batteria*) charged; (*colore*) deep; (*caffè, tè*) strong ♦ *sm* (*il caricare*) loading; (*ciò che si carica*) load; (*fig: peso*) burden, weight; **persona a ~ dependent**; **essere a ~ di qn** (*spese etc*) to be charged to sb
'carie *sf* (*dentaria*) decay
ca'rino, a *ag* (*grazioso*) lovely, pretty, nice; (*riferito a uomo, anche simpatico*) nice
carità *sf* charity; **per ~!** (*escl di rifiuto*) good heavens, no!
carnagi'one [karna'dʒone] *sf* complexion
car'nale *ag* (*amore*) carnal
'carne *sf* flesh; (*bovina, ovina etc*) meat; **~ di manzo/maiale/pecora** beef/pork/mutton; **~ tritata** mince (*BRIT*), hamburger meat (*US*), minced (*BRIT*) *o* ground (*US*) meat
car'nefice [kar'nefitʃe] *sm* executioner; (*alla forca*) hangman
carne'vale *sm* carnival

---

carnevale

ℹ️ **Carnevale** *is the period between Epiphany and the start of Lent. People wear fancy dress, and there are parties, processions of floats and bonfires. It culminates immediately before Lent in the festivities of* **martedì grasso** *(Shrove Tuesday).*

---

car'noso, a *ag* fleshy
'caro, a *ag* (*amato*) dear; (*costoso*) dear, expensive
ca'rogna [ka'roɲɲa] *sf* carrion; (*fig: fam*) swine
ca'rota *sf* carrot
caro'vana *sf* caravan
caro'vita *sm* high cost of living
carpenti'ere *sm* carpenter
car'pire *vt*: **~ qc a qn** (*segreto etc*) to get sth out of sb
car'poni *av* on all fours
car'rabile *ag* suitable for vehicles; **"passo ~"** "keep clear"
car'raio, a *ag*: **passo ~** driveway
carreggi'ata [karred'dʒata] *sf* carriageway (*BRIT*), (road)way
car'rello *sm* trolley; (*AER*) undercarriage; (*CINEMA*) dolly; (*di macchina da scrivere*) carriage
carri'era *sf* career; **fare ~** to get on; **a gran ~** at full speed
carri'ola *sf* wheelbarrow
'carro *sm* cart, wagon; **~ armato** tank; **~ attrezzi** breakdown van
car'rozza [kar'rɔttsa] *sf* carriage, coach
carrozze'ria [karrottse'ria] *sf* body, coachwork (*BRIT*); (*officina*) coachbuilder's workshop (*BRIT*), body shop
carroz'zina [karrot'tsina] *sf* pram (*BRIT*), baby carriage (*US*)
'carta *sf* paper; (*al ristorante*) menu; (*GEO*) map; plan; (*documento, da gioco*) card; (*costituzione*) charter; **~e** *sfpl* (*documenti*) papers, documents; **alla ~** (*al ristorante*) à

la carte; **~ assegni** bank card; **~
assorbente** blotting paper; **~ bollata** *o* **da
bollo** official stamped paper; **~ di credito**
credit card; **~ (geografica)** map; **~
d'identità** identity card; **~ igienica** toilet
paper; **~ d'imbarco** (*AER, NAUT*) boarding
card; **~ da lettere** writing paper; **~ libera**
(*AMM*) unstamped paper; **~ da parati**
wallpaper; **~ stradale** road map; **~ verde**
(*AUT*) green card; **~ vetrata** sandpaper; **~
da visita** visiting card

carta**car'bone** (*pl* cartecar'bone) *sf*
carbon paper

car**'taccia, ce** [kar'tattʃa] *sf* waste paper

carta**'pecora** *sf* parchment

carta**'pesta** *sf* papier-mâché

car**'teggio** [kar'teddʒo] *sm* correspondence

car**'tella** *sf* (*scheda*) card; (*INFORM; custodia:
di cartone*) folder; (*: di uomo d'affari etc*)
briefcase; (*: di scolaro*) schoolbag, satchel;
~ clinica (*MED*) case sheet

car**'tello** *sm* sign; (*pubblicitario*) poster;
(*stradale*) sign, signpost; (*ECON*) cartel; (*in
dimostrazioni*) placard; cartel**'lone** *sm*
(*pubblicitario*) advertising poster; (*della
tombola*) scoring frame; (*TEATRO*) playbill;
tenere il cartellone (*spettacolo*) to have a
long run

carti**'era** *sf* paper mill

car**'tina** *sf* (*AUT, GEO*) map

car**'toccio** [kar'tɔttʃo] *sm* paper bag

carto**le'ria** *sf* stationer's (shop)

carto**'lina** *sf* postcard; **~ postale** ready-
stamped postcard

car**'tone** *sm* cardboard; (*ARTE*) cartoon; **~i
animati** *smpl* (*CINEMA*) cartoons

car**'tuccia, ce** [kar'tuttʃa] *sf* cartridge

'casa *sf* house; (*in senso astratto*) home;
(*COMM*) firm, house; **essere a ~** to be at
home; **vado a ~ mia/tua** I'm going
home/to your house; **~ di cura** nursing
home; **~ dello studente** student hostel; **~e
popolari** ≈ council houses (*o* flats) (*BRIT*),
≈ public housing units (*US*); **vino della ~**
house wine

ca**'sacca, che** *sf* military coat; (*di fantino*)
blouse

casa**'linga, ghe** *sf* housewife

casa**'lingo, a, ghi, ghe** *ag* household,
domestic; (*fatto a casa*) home-made;
(*semplice*) homely; (*amante della casa*)
home-loving; **~ghi** *smpl* household articles;
cucina ~a plain home cooking

cas**'care** *vi* to fall; cas**'cata** *sf* fall;
(*d'acqua*) cascade, waterfall

ca**'scina** [kaʃʃina] *sf* farmstead

'casco, schi *sm* helmet; (*del parrucchiere*)
hair-dryer; (*di banane*) bunch

casei**'ficio** [kazei'fitʃo] *sm* creamery

ca**'sella** *sf* pigeon-hole; **~ postale** post
office box

casel**'lario** *sm* filing cabinet; **~ giudiziale**
court records *pl*

ca**'sello** *sm* (*di autostrada*) toll-house

ca**'serma** *sf* barracks *pl*

ca**'sino** (*fam*) *sm* brothel; (*confusione*) row,
racket

casi**nò** *sm inv* casino

'caso *sm* chance; (*fatto, vicenda*) event,
incident; (*possibilità*) possibility; (*MED, LING*)
case; **a ~** at random; **per ~** by chance, by
accident; **in ogni ~, in tutti i ~i** in any case,
at any rate; **al ~** should the opportunity
arise; **nel ~ che** in case; **~ mai** if by
chance; **~ limite** borderline case

caso**'lare** *sm* cottage

'cassa *sf* case, crate, box; (*bara*) coffin;
(*mobile*) chest; (*involucro: di orologio etc*)
case; (*macchina*) cash register, till; (*luogo di
pagamento*) checkout (counter); (*fondo*)
fund; (*istituto bancario*) bank; **~
automatica prelievi** cash dispenser; **~
continua** night safe; **~ integrazione:
mettere in ~ integrazione** ≈ to lay off; **~
mutua** *o* **malattia** health insurance
scheme; **~ di risparmio** savings bank; **~
toracica** (*ANAT*) chest

cassa**'forte** (*pl* casse**'forti**) *sf* safe

cassa**'panca** (*pl* cassa**'panche** *o*
casse**'panche**) *sf* settle

casse**'rola** *sf* = **casseruola**

casseru**'ola** *sf* saucepan

cas**'setta** *sf* box; (*per registratore*) cassette;
(*CINEMA, TEATRO*) box-office takings *pl*; **film**

di ~ box-office draw; **~ di sicurezza** strongbox; **~ delle lettere** letterbox
cas'setto *sm* drawer; **casset'tone** *sm* chest of drawers
cassi'ere, a *sm/f* cashier; (*di banca*) teller
casso'netto *sm* wheelie-bin
'casta *sf* caste
cas'tagna [kas'taɲɲa] *sf* chestnut
cas'tagno [kas'taɲɲo] *sm* chestnut (tree)
cas'tano, a *ag* chestnut (brown)
cas'tello *sm* castle; (*TECN*) scaffolding
casti'gare *vt* to punish; **cas'tigo, ghi** *sm* punishment
castità *sf* chastity
cas'toro *sm* beaver
cas'trare *vt* to castrate; to geld; to doctor (*BRIT*), fix (*US*)
casu'ale *ag* chance *cpd*; (*INFORM*) random *cpd*
cata'comba *sf* catacomb
ca'talogo, ghi *sm* catalogue
catarifran'gente [katarifran'dʒɛnte] *sm* (*AUT*) reflector
ca'tarro *sm* catarrh
ca'tasta *sf* stack, pile
ca'tasto *sm* land register; land registry office
ca'tastrofe *sf* catastrophe, disaster
catego'ria *sf* category
ca'tena *sf* chain; **~ di montaggio** assembly line; **~e da neve** (*AUT*) snow chains; **cate'naccio** *sm* bolt
cate'ratta *sf* cataract; (*chiusa*) sluice-gate
cati'nella *sf*: **piovere a ~e** to pour
ca'tino *sm* basin
ca'trame *sm* tar
'cattedra *sf* teacher's desk; (*di docente*) chair
catte'drale *sf* cathedral
catti'veria *sf* malice, spite; naughtiness; (*atto*) spiteful act; (*parole*) malicious *o* spiteful remark
cattività *sf* captivity
cat'tivo, a *ag* bad; (*malvagio*) bad, wicked; (*turbolento: bambino*) bad, naughty; (*: mare*) rough; (*odore, sapore*) nasty, bad
cat'tolico, a, ci, che *ag, sm/f* (Roman)
Catholic
cat'tura *sf* capture
cattu'rare *vt* to capture
caucciù [kaut'tʃu] *sm* rubber
'causa *sf* cause; (*DIR*) lawsuit, case, action; **a ~ di, per ~ di** because of; **fare** *o* **muovere ~ a qn** to take legal action against sb
cau'sare *vt* to cause
cau'tela *sf* caution, prudence
caute'lare *vt* to protect; **~rsi** *vr*: **~rsi (da)** to take precautions (against)
'cauto, a *ag* cautious, prudent
cauzi'one [kaut'tsjone] *sf* security; (*DIR*) bail
cav. *abbr* = **cavaliere**
'cava *sf* quarry
caval'care *vt* (*cavallo*) to ride; (*muro*) to sit astride; (*sog: ponte*) to span; **caval'cata** *sf* ride; (*gruppo di persone*) riding party
cavalca'via *sm inv* flyover
cavalci'oni [kaval'tʃoni]: **a ~ di** *prep* astride
cavali'ere *sm* rider; (*feudale, titolo*) knight; (*soldato*) cavalryman; (*al ballo*) partner; **cavalle'resco, a, schi, sche** *ag* chivalrous; **cavalle'ria** *sf* (*di persona*) chivalry; (*milizia a cavallo*) cavalry
cavalle'rizzo, a [kavalle'rittso] *sm/f* riding instructor; circus rider
caval'letta *sf* grasshopper
caval'letto *sm* (*FOT*) tripod; (*da pittore*) easel
ca'vallo *sm* horse; (*SCACCHI*) knight; (*AUT: anche: ~ vapore*) horsepower; (*dei pantaloni*) crotch; **a ~** on horseback; **a ~ di** astride, straddling; **~ di battaglia** (*fig*) hobby-horse; **~ da corsa** racehorse
ca'vare *vt* (*togliere*) to draw out, extract, take out; (*: giacca, scarpe*) to take off; (*: fame, sete, voglia*) to satisfy; **cavarsela** to manage, get on all right; (*scamparla*) to get away with it
cava'tappi *sm inv* corkscrew
ca'verna *sf* cave
'cavia *sf* guinea pig
cavi'ale *sm* caviar
ca'viglia [ka'viʎʎa] *sf* ankle
ca'villo *sm* quibble

'cavo, a *ag* hollow ♦ *sm* (ANAT) cavity; (*corda*, ELETTR, TEL) cable

cavolfi'ore *sm* cauliflower

'cavolo *sm* cabbage; (*fam*): **non m'importa un ~** I don't give a damn; **~ di Bruxelles** Brussels sprout

cazzuo'la [kat'tswɔla] *sf* trowel

c / c *abbr* = **conto corrente**

CCD *sigla m* = **Centro Cristiano Democratico**

CD *sm inv* CD

CD-ROM [tʃidi'rɔm] *sm inv* CD-ROM

C. d. u. *sigla m* = **Cristiano Democratici Uniti**

C.E. [tʃe] *sigla f* (= *Comunità Europea*) EC

ce [tʃe] *pron*, *av vedi* **ci**

'cece ['tʃetʃe] *sm* chickpea

cecità [tʃetʃi'ta] *sf* blindness

'ceco, a ['tʃɛko] *ag*, *sm/f* Czech; **la Repubblica ~a** the Czech Republic

Cecoslo'vacchia [tʃekoslo'vakkja] *sf*: **la ~** Czechoslovakia

'cedere ['tʃedere] *vt* (*concedere: posto*) to give up; (DIR) to transfer, make over ♦ *vi* (*cadere*) to give way, subside; **~ (a)** to surrender (to), yield (to), give in (to); ce'devole *ag* (*terreno*) soft; (*fig*) yielding

'cedola ['tʃedola] *sf* coupon; voucher

'cedro ['tʃedro] *sm* cedar; (*albero da frutto*, *frutto*) citron

'ceffo ['tʃeffo] (*peg*) *sm* ugly mug

cef'fone [tʃef'fone] *sm* slap, smack

ce'lare [tʃe'lare] *vt* to conceal; **~rsi** to hide

cele'brare [tʃele'brare] *vt* to celebrate; celebrazi'one *sf* celebration

'celebre ['tʃelebre] *ag* famous, celebrated; celebrità *sf inv* fame; (*persona*) celebrity

'celere ['tʃelere] *ag* fast, swift; (*corso*) crash *cpd*

ce'leste [tʃe'leste] *ag* celestial; heavenly; (*colore*) sky-blue

'celibe ['tʃelibe] *ag* single, unmarried

'cella ['tʃella] *sf* cell

'cellula ['tʃellula] *sf* (BIOL, ELETTR, POL) cell; cellu'lare *sm* cellphone

cellu'lite [tʃellu'lite] *sf* cellulite

cemen'tare [tʃemen'tare] *vt* (*anche fig*) to cement

ce'mento [tʃe'mento] *sm* cement

'cena ['tʃena] *sf* dinner; (*leggera*) supper

ce'nare [tʃe'nare] *vi* to dine, have dinner

'cencio ['tʃentʃo] *sm* piece of cloth, rag; (*per spolverare*) duster

'cenere ['tʃenere] *sf* ash

'cenno ['tʃenno] *sm* (*segno*) sign, signal; (*gesto*) gesture; (*col capo*) nod; (*con la mano*) wave; (*allusione*) hint, mention; (*breve esposizione*) short account; **far ~ di sì/no** to nod (one's head)/shake one's head

censi'mento [tʃensi'mento] *sm* census

cen'sura [tʃen'sura] *sf* censorship; censor's office; (*fig*) censure

cente'nario, a [tʃente'narjo] *ag* (*che ha cento anni*) hundred-year-old; (*che ricorre ogni cento anni*) centennial, centenary *cpd* ♦ *sm/f* centenarian ♦ *sm* centenary

cen'tesimo, a [tʃen'tezimo] *ag*, *sm* hundredth

cen'tigrado, a [tʃen'tigrado] *ag* centigrade; **20 gradi ~i** 20 degrees centigrade

cen'timetro [tʃen'timetro] *sm* centimetre

centi'naio [tʃenti'najo] (*pl(f)* **-aia**) *sm*: **un ~ (di)** a hundred; about a hundred

'cento ['tʃento] *num* a hundred, one hundred

cen'trale [tʃen'trale] *ag* central ♦ *sf*: **~ telefonica** (telephone) exchange; **~ elettrica** electric power station; centrali'nista *sm/f* operator; centra'lino *sm* (telephone) exchange; (*di albergo etc*) switchboard

cen'trare [tʃen'trare] *vt* to hit the centre of; (TECN) to centre

cen'trifuga [tʃen'trifuga] *sf* spin-dryer

'centro ['tʃentro] *sm* centre; **~ civico** civic centre; **~ commerciale** shopping centre; (*città*) commercial centre

'ceppo ['tʃeppo] *sm* (*di albero*) stump; (*pezzo di legno*) log

'cera ['tʃera] *sf* wax; (*aspetto*) appearance

ce'ramica, che [tʃe'ramika] *sf* ceramic; (ARTE) ceramics *sg*

cerbi'atto [tʃer'bjatto] *sm* (ZOOL) fawn

'cerca ['tʃerka] *sf*: **in** *o* **alla ~ di** in search of

cer'care [tʃer'kare] *vt* to look for, search for

♦ vi: ~ **di fare qc** to try to do sth
'**cerchia** ['tʃerkja] sf circle
'**cerchio** ['tʃerkjo] sm circle; (giocattolo, di botte) hoop
cere'**ale** [tʃere'ale] sm cereal
ceri'**monia** [tʃeri'mɔnja] sf ceremony
ce'**rino** [tʃe'rino] sm wax match
'**cernia** ['tʃernja] sf (ZOOL) stone bass
cerni'**era** [tʃer'njera] sf hinge; ~ **lampo** zip (fastener) (BRIT), zipper (US)
'**cernita** ['tʃernita] sf selection
'**cero** ['tʃero] sm (church) candle
ce'**rotto** [tʃe'rɔtto] sm sticking plaster
certa'**mente** [tʃerta'mente] av certainly
cer'**tezza** [tʃer'tettsa] sf certainty
certifi'**cato** [tʃertifi'kato] sm certificate; ~ **medico/di nascita** medical/birth certificate

PAROLA CHIAVE

'**certo, a** ['tʃerto] ag (sicuro): ~ **(di/che)** certain o sure (of/that)
♦ det 1 (tale) certain; **un ~ signor Smith** a (certain) Mr Smith
2 (qualche; con valore intensivo) some; **dopo un ~ tempo** after some time; **un fatto di una ~a importanza** a matter of some importance; **di una ~a età** past one's prime, not so young
♦ pron: ~**i, e** pl some
♦ av (certamente) certainly; (senz'altro) of course; **di ~** certainly; **no (di) ~!, ~ che no!** certainly not!; **sì** ~ yes indeed, certainly

cer'**vello, i** [tʃer'vello] (ANAT: pl(f) -a) sm brain
'**cervo, a** ['tʃervo] sm/f stag/doe ♦ sm deer
ce'**sello** [tʃe'zello] sm chisel
ce'**soie** [tʃe'zoje] sfpl shears
ces'**puglio** [tʃes'puʎʎo] sm bush
ces'**sare** [tʃes'sare] vi, vt to stop, cease; ~ **di fare qc** to stop doing sth
'**cesso** ['tʃesso] (fam) sm (gabinetto) bog
'**cesta** ['tʃesta] sf (large) basket
ces'**tino** [tʃes'tino] sm basket; (per la carta straccia) wastepaper basket; ~ **da viaggio** (FERR) packed lunch (o dinner)
'**cesto** ['tʃesto] sm basket

'**ceto** ['tʃeto] sm (social) class
cetrio'**lino** [tʃetrio'lino] sm gherkin
cetri'**olo** [tʃetri'ɔlo] sm cucumber
CFC sm inv (= clorofluorocarburo) CFC
cfr. abbr (= confronta) cf
CGIL sigla f (= Confederazione Generale Italiana del Lavoro) trades union organization
chat line sf inv chatline
chattare vi (INFORM) to chat

PAROLA CHIAVE

che [ke] pron 1 (relativo: persona: soggetto) who; (: oggetto) whom, that; (: cosa, animale) which, that; **il ragazzo ~ è venuto** the boy who came; **l'uomo ~ io vedo** the man (whom) I see; **il libro ~ è sul tavolo** the book which o that is on the table; **il libro ~ vedi** the book (which o that) you see; **la sera ~ ti ho visto** the evening I saw you
2 (interrogativo, esclamativo) what; ~ **(cosa) fai?** what are you doing?; **a ~ (cosa) pensi?** what are you thinking about?; **non sa ~ (cosa) fare** he doesn't know what to do
3 (indefinito): **quell'uomo ha un ~ di losco** there's something suspicious about that man; **un certo non so ~** an indefinable something
♦ det 1 (interrogativo: tra tanti) what; (: tra pochi) which; ~ **tipo di film preferisci?** what sort of film do you prefer?; ~ **vestito ti vuoi mettere?** what (o which) dress do you want to put on?
2 (esclamativo: seguito da aggettivo) how; (: seguito da sostantivo) what; ~ **buono!** how delicious!; ~ **bel vestito!** what a lovely dress!
♦ cong 1 (con proposizioni subordinate) that; **credo ~ verrà** I think he'll come; **voglio ~ tu studi** I want you to study; **so ~ tu c'eri** I know (that) you were there; **non ~: non ~ sia sbagliato, ma ...** not that it's wrong, but ...
2 (finale) so that; **vieni qua, ~ ti veda** come here, so (that) I can see you

3 (*temporale*): **arriva** ~ **eri già partito** you had already left when I arrived; **sono anni** ~ **non lo vedo** I haven't seen him for years

4 (*in frasi imperative, concessive*): ~ **venga pure!** let him come by all means!; ~ **tu sia benedetto!** may God bless you!

5 (*comparativo: con più, meno*) than; *vedi anche* **più; meno; così** *etc*

cheti'chella [keti'kɛlla]: **alla** ~ *av* stealthily, unobtrusively

---

PAROLA CHIAVE

chi [ki] *pron* 1 (*interrogativo: soggetto*) who; (: *oggetto*) who, whom; ~ **è?** who is it?; **di** ~ **è questo libro?** whose book is this?, whose is this book?; **con** ~ **parli?** who are you talking to?; **a** ~ **pensi?** who are you thinking about?; ~ **di voi?** which of you?; **non so a** ~ **rivolgermi** I don't know who to ask

2 (*relativo*) whoever, anyone who; **dillo a** ~ **vuoi** tell whoever you like

3 (*indefinito*): ~ ... ~ ... some ... others ...; ~ **dice una cosa,** ~ **dice un'altra** some say one thing, others say another

---

chiacchie'rare [kjakkje'rare] *vi* to chat; (*discorrere futilmente*) to chatter; (*far pettegolezzi*) to gossip; **chiacchie'rata** *sf* chat; (*far due* o **quattro chiacchiere** to have a chat; **chiacchie'rone, a** *ag* talkative, chatty; gossipy ♦ *sm/f* chatterbox; gossip

chia'mare [kja'mare] *vt* to call; (*rivolgersi a qn*) to call (in), send for; ~**rsi** *vr* (*aver nome*) to be called; **mi chiamo Paolo** my name is Paolo, I'm called Paolo; ~ **alle armi** to call up; ~ **in giudizio** to summon; **chia'mata** *sf* (*TEL*) call; (*MIL*) call-up

chia'rezza [kja'rettsa] *sf* clearness; clarity

chia'rire [kja'rire] *vt* to make clear; (*fig: spiegare*) to clear up, explain; ~**rsi** *vr* to become clear

chi'aro, a [kjaro] *ag* clear; (*luminoso*) clear, bright; (*colore*) pale, light

chiaroveg'gente [kjaroved'dʒɛnte] *sm/f* clairvoyant

chi'asso [kjasso] *sm* uproar, row; **chias'soso, a** *ag* noisy, rowdy; (*vistoso*) showy, gaudy

chi'ave [kjave] *sf* key ♦ *ag inv* key *cpd*; ~ **d'accensione** (*AUT*) ignition key; ~ **inglese** monkey wrench; ~ **di volta** keystone; **chiavis'tello** *sm* bolt

chi'azza [kjattsa] *sf* stain; splash

'chicco, chi [kikko] *sm* grain; (*di caffè*) bean; ~ **d'uva** grape

chi'edere [kjedere] *vt* (*per sapere*) to ask; (*per avere*) to ask for ♦ *vi*: ~ **di qn** to ask after sb; (*al telefono*) to ask o want sb; ~ **qc a qn** to ask sb sth; to ask sb for sth

chi'erico, ci [kjeriko] *sm* cleric; altar boy

chi'esa [kjeza] *sf* church

chi'esto, a *pp di* **chiedere**

'chiglia [kiʎʎa] *sf* keel

'chilo [kilo] *sm* kilo; **chilo'grammo** *sm* kilogram(me); **chilome'traggio** *sm* ≈ mileage; ~**metraggio illimitato** unlimited mileage; **chi'lometro** *sm* kilometre

'chimica [kimika] *sf* chemistry

'chimico, a, ci, che [kimiko] *ag* chemical ♦ *sm/f* chemist

'china [kina] *sf* (*pendio*) slope, descent; (*inchiostro*) Indian ink

chi'nare [ki'nare] *vt* to lower, bend; ~**rsi** *vr* to stoop, bend

chi'nino [ki'nino] *sm* quinine

chi'occiola [kjɔttʃola] *sf* snail; **scala a** ~ spiral staircase

chi'odo [kjɔdo] *sm* nail; (*fig*) obsession

chi'oma [kjɔma] *sf* (*capelli*) head of hair

chi'osco, schi [kjɔsko] *sm* kiosk, stall

chi'ostro [kjɔstro] *sm* cloister

chiro'mante [kiro'mante] *sm/f* palmist

chirur'gia [kirur'dʒia] *sf* surgery; ~ **estetica** cosmetic surgery; **chi'rurgo, ghi** o **gi** *sm* surgeon

chissà [kis'sa] *av* who knows, I wonder

chi'tarra [ki'tarra] *sf* guitar

chi'udere [kjudere] *vt* to close, shut; (*luce, acqua*) to put off, turn off; (*definitivamente: fabbrica*) to close down, shut down;

(strada) to close; (recingere) to enclose; (porre termine a) to end ♦ vi to close, shut; to close down, shut down; to end; **~rsi** vr to shut, close; (ritirarsi: anche fig) to shut o.s. away; (ferita) to close up

chi'unque [ki'unkwe] pron (relativo) whoever; (indefinito) anyone, anybody; **~ sia** whoever it is

chi'uso, a ['kjuso] pp di **chiudere** ♦ sf (di corso d'acqua) sluice, lock; (recinto) enclosure; (di discorso etc) conclusion, ending; chiu'sura sf (vedi **chiudere**) closing; shutting; closing o shutting down; enclosing; putting o turning off; ending; (dispositivo) catch; fastening; fastener

---

PAROLA CHIAVE

ci [tʃi] (dav lo, la, li, le, ne diventa **ce**) pron **1** (personale: complemento oggetto) us; (: a noi: complemento di termine) (to) us; (: riflessivo) ourselves; (: reciproco) each other, one another; (impersonale): **~ si veste** we get dressed; **~ ha visti** he's seen us; **non ~ ha dato niente** he gave us nothing; **~ vestiamo** we get dressed; **~ amiamo** we love one another o each other
2 (dimostrativo: di ciò, su ciò, in ciò etc) about (o on o of) it; **non so cosa far~** I don't know what to do about it; **che c'entro io?** what have I got to do with it? ♦ av (qui) here; (lì) there; (moto attraverso luogo): **~ passa sopra un ponte** a bridge passes over it; **non ~ passa più nessuno** nobody comes this way any more; **esser~** vedi **essere**

---

cia'batta [tʃa'batta] sf slipper; (pane) ciabatta
ci'alda ['tʃalda] sf (CUC) wafer
ciam'bella [tʃam'bɛlla] sf (CUC) ring-shaped cake; (salvagente) rubber ring
ci'ao ['tʃao] escl (all'arrivo) hello!; (alla partenza) cheerio! (BRIT), bye!
cias'cuno, a [tʃas'kuno] (det: dav sm: **ciascun** +C, V, **ciascuno** +s impura, gn, pn, ps, x, z; dav sf: **ciascuna** +C, **ciascun'** +V) det every, each; (ogni) every ♦ pron each

(one); (tutti) everyone, everybody
ci'barie [tʃi'barje] sfpl foodstuffs
'cibo ['tʃibo] sm food
ci'cala [tʃi'kala] sf cicada
cica'trice [tʃika'tritʃe] sf scar
'cicca ['tʃikka] sf cigarette end
'ciccia ['tʃittʃa] (fam) sf fat
cice'rone [tʃitʃe'rone] sm guide
ci'clismo [tʃi'klizmo] sm cycling; ci'clista, i, e sm/f cyclist
'ciclo ['tʃiklo] sm cycle; (di malattia) course
ciclomo'tore [tʃiklomo'tore] sm moped
ci'clone [tʃi'klone] sm cyclone
ci'cogna [tʃi'koɲɲa] sf stork
ci'coria [tʃi'kɔria] sf chicory
ci'eco, a, chi, che ['tʃɛko] ag blind ♦ sm/f blind man/woman
ci'elo ['tʃɛlo] sm sky; (REL) heaven
'cifra ['tʃifra] sf (numero) figure; numeral; (somma di denaro) sum, figure; (monogramma) monogram, initials pl; (codice) code, cipher
'ciglio, i ['tʃiʎʎo] (delle palpebre: pl(f) ciglia) sm (margine) edge, verge; (eye)lash; (eye)lid; (sopracciglio) eyebrow
'cigno ['tʃiɲɲo] sm swan
cigo'lare [tʃigo'lare] vi to squeak, creak
'Cile ['tʃile] sm: **il ~** Chile
ci'lecca [tʃi'lekka] sf: **far ~** to fail
cili'egia, gie o ge [tʃi'ljedʒa] sf cherry; cili'egio sm cherry tree
cilin'drata [tʃilin'drata] sf (AUT) (cubic) capacity; **una macchina di grossa ~** a big-engined car
ci'lindro [tʃi'lindro] sm cylinder; (cappello) top hat
'cima ['tʃima] sf (sommità) top; (di monte) top, summit; (estremità) end; **in ~ a** at the top of; **da ~ a fondo** from top to bottom; (fig) from beginning to end
'cimice ['tʃimitʃe] sf (ZOOL) bug; (puntina) drawing pin (BRIT), thumbtack (US)
cimini'era [tʃimi'njera] sf chimney; (di nave) funnel
cimi'tero [tʃimi'tero] sm cemetery
'Cina ['tʃina] sf: **la ~** China
cin'cin [tʃin'tʃin] escl cheers!

cin cin [tʃin'tʃin] *escl* = **cincin**

cinema ['tʃinema] *sm inv* cinema; **cine'presa** *sf* cine-camera

ci'nese [tʃi'nese] *ag, sm/f, sm* Chinese *inv*

cingere ['tʃindʒere] *vt* (*attorniare*) to surround, encircle

cinghia ['tʃingja] *sf* strap; (*cintura, TECN*) belt

cinghi'ale [tʃin'gjale] *sm* wild boar

cinguet'tare [tʃingwet'tare] *vi* to twitter

cinico, a, ci, che ['tʃiniko] *ag* cynical ♦ *sm/f* cynic; **ci'nismo** *sm* cynicism

cin'quanta [tʃin'kwanta] *num* fifty; **cinquan'tesimo, a** *num* fiftieth

cinquan'tina [tʃinkwan'tina] *sf* (*serie*): **una ~ (di)** about fifty; (*età*): **essere sulla ~** to be about fifty

cinque ['tʃinkwe] *num* five; **avere ~ anni** to be five (years old); **il ~ dicembre 1999** the fifth of December 1999; **alle ~ (*ora*)** at five (o'clock)

cinque'cento [tʃinkwe'tʃento] *num* five hundred ♦ *sm*: **il C~** the sixteenth century

cinto, a ['tʃinto] *pp di* **cingere**

cin'tura [tʃin'tura] *sf* belt; **~ di salvataggio** lifebelt (*BRIT*), life preserver (*US*); **~ di sicurezza** (*AUT, AER*) safety *o* seat belt

ciò [tʃɔ] *pron* this; that; **~ che** what; **~ nonostante** *o* **nondimeno** nevertheless, in spite of that

ci'occa, che ['tʃɔkka] *sf* (*di capelli*) lock

ciocco'lata [tʃokko'lata] *sf* chocolate; (*bevanda*) (hot) chocolate; **cioccola'tino** *sm* chocolate; **ciocco'lato** *sm* chocolate

cioè [tʃo'ɛ] *av* that is (to say)

ciondo'lare [tʃondo'lare] *vi* to dangle; (*fig*) to loaf (about); **ci'ondolo** *sm* pendant

ci'otola ['tʃotola] *sf* bowl

ci'ottolo [tʃ'ottolo] *sm* pebble; (*di strada*) cobble(stone)

ci'polla [tʃi'polla] *sf* onion; (*di tulipano etc*) bulb

ci'presso [tʃi'presso] *sm* cypress (tree)

cipria ['tʃiprja] *sf* (face) powder

Cipro ['tʃipro] *sm* Cyprus

circa ['tʃirka] *av* about, roughly ♦ *prep* about, concerning; **a mezzogiorno ~** about midday

circo, chi ['tʃirko] *sm* circus

circo'lare [tʃirko'lare] *vi* to circulate; (*AUT*) to drive (along), move (along) ♦ *ag* circular ♦ *sf* (*AMM*) circular; (*di autobus*) circle (line); **circolazi'one** *sf* circulation; (*AUT*): **la circolazione** (the) traffic

circolo ['tʃirkolo] *sm* circle

circon'dare [tʃirkon'dare] *vt* to surround

circonfe'renza [tʃirkonfe'rentsa] *sf* circumference

circonvallazi'one [tʃirkonvallat'tsjone] *sf* ring road (*BRIT*), beltway (*US*); (*per evitare una città*) by-pass

circos'critto, a [tʃirkos'kritto] *pp di* **circoscrivere**

circos'crivere [tʃirkos'krivere] *vt* to circumscribe; (*fig*) to limit, restrict; **circoscrizi'one** *sf* (*AMM*) district, area; **circoscrizione elettorale** constituency

circos'petto, a [tʃirkos'petto] *ag* circumspect, cautious

circos'tante [tʃirkos'tante] *ag* surrounding, neighbouring

circos'tanza [tʃirkos'tantsa] *sf* circumstance; (*occasione*) occasion

cir'cuito [tʃir'kuito] *sm* circuit

CISL *sigla f* (= *Confederazione Italiana Sindacati Lavoratori*) *trades union organization*

ciste ['tʃiste] *sf* = **cisti**

cis'terna [tʃis'terna] *sf* tank, cistern

cisti ['tʃisti] *sf* cyst

C.I.T. [tʃit] *sigla f* = **Compagnia Italiana Turismo**

ci'tare [tʃi'tare] *vt* (*DIR*) to summon; (*autore*) to quote; (*a esempio, modello*) to cite; **citazi'one** *sf* summons *sg*; quotation; (*di persona*) mention

ci'tofono [tʃi'tɔfono] *sm* entry phone; (*in uffici*) intercom

città [tʃit'ta] *sf inv* town; (*importante*) city; **~ universitaria** university campus

cittadi'nanza [tʃittadi'nantsa] *sf* citizens *pl*; (*DIR*) citizenship

citta'dino, a [tʃitta'dino] *ag* town *cpd*; city *cpd* ♦ *sm/f* (*di uno Stato*) citizen; (*abitante* *di città*) townsman, city dweller

ci'uco, a, chi, che ['tʃuko] *sm/f* ass

ci'uffo ['tʃuffo] *sm* tuft

ci'vetta [tʃi'vetta] *sf* (*ZOOL*) owl; (*fig: donna*) flirt ♦ *ag inv*: **auto/nave ~** decoy car/ship

'civico, a, ci, che ['tʃiviko] *ag* civic; (*museo*) municipal, town *cpd*; city *cpd*

ci'vile [tʃi'vile] *ag* civil; (*non militare*) civilian; (*nazione*) civilized ♦ *sm* civilian

civilizzazi'one [tʃiviliddzat'tsjone] *sf* civilization

civiltà [tʃivil'ta] *sf* civilization; (*cortesia*) civility

'clacson *sm inv* (*AUT*) horn

cla'more *sm* (*frastuono*) din, uproar, clamour; (*fig*) outcry; **clamo'roso, a** *ag* noisy; (*fig*) sensational

clandes'tino, a *ag* clandestine; (*POL*) underground, clandestine; (*immigrato*) illegal ♦ *sm/f* stowaway

clari'netto *sm* clarinet

'classe *sf* class; **di ~** (*fig*) with class; of excellent quality

'classico, a, ci, che *ag* classical; (*tradizionale: moda*) classic(al) ♦ *sm* classic; classical author

clas'sifica *sf* classification; (*SPORT*) placings *pl*

classifi'care *vt* to classify; (*candidato, compito*) to grade; **~rsi** *vr* to be placed

'clausola *sf* (*DIR*) clause

'clava *sf* club

clavi'cembalo [klavi'tʃembalo] *sm* harpsichord

cla'vicola *sf* (*ANAT*) collar bone

cle'mente *ag* merciful; (*clima*) mild; **cle'menza** *sf* mercy, clemency; mildness

'clero *sm* clergy

clic'care *vi* (*INFORM*): **~ su** to click on

cli'ente *sm/f* customer, client; **clien'tela** *sf* customers *pl*, clientèle

'clima, i *sm* climate; **cli'matico, a, ci, che** *ag* climatic; **stazione climatica** health resort; **climatizzatore** *sm* air conditioning system; **climatizzazi'one** *sf* (*TECN*) air conditioning

'clinica, che *sf* (*scienza*) clinical medicine;

(*casa di cura*) clinic, nursing home; (*settore d'ospedale*) clinic

'clinico, a, ci, che *ag* clinical ♦ *sm* (*medico*) clinician

clo'aca, che *sf* sewer

'cloro *sm* chlorine

cloro'formio *sm* chloroform

club *sm inv* club

c.m. *abbr* = **corrente mese**

coabi'tare *vi* to live together

coagu'lare *vt* to coagulate ♦ *vi* to coagulate; (*latte*) to curdle; **~rsi** *vr* to coagulate; to curdle

coalizi'one [koalit'tsjone] *sf* coalition

co'atto, a *ag* (*DIR*) compulsory, forced

'COBAS *sigla mpl* (= *Comitati di base*) *independent trades unions*

Coca'Cola ® *sf* Coca-Cola ®

coca'ina *sf* cocaine

cocci'nella [kottʃi'nella] *sf* ladybird (*BRIT*), ladybug (*US*)

'coccio ['kɔttʃo] *sm* earthenware; (*vaso*) earthenware pot; **~i** *smpl* (*frammenti*) fragments (of pottery)

cocci'uto, a [kot'tʃuto] *ag* stubborn, pigheaded

'cocco, chi *sm* (*pianta*) coconut palm; (*frutto*): **noce di ~** coconut ♦ *sm/f* (*fam*) darling

cocco'drillo *sm* crocodile

cocco'lare *vt* to cuddle, fondle

co'cente [ko'tʃente] *ag* (*anche fig*) burning

co'comero *sm* watermelon

co'cuzzolo [ko'kuttsolo] *sm* top; (*di capo, cappello*) crown

'coda *sf* tail; (*fila di persone, auto*) queue (*BRIT*), line (*US*); (*di abiti*) train; **con la ~ dell'occhio** out of the corner of one's eye; **mettersi in ~** to queue (up) (*BRIT*), line up (*US*); to join the queue (*BRIT*) o line (*US*); **~ di cavallo** (*acconciatura*) ponytail

co'dardo, a *ag* cowardly ♦ *sm/f* coward

'codice ['koditʃe] *sm* code; **~ di avviamento postale** postcode (*BRIT*), zip code (*US*); **~ fiscale** tax code; **~ della strada** highway code

coe'rente *ag* coherent; **coe'renza** *sf*

coherence

coe'taneo, a *ag, sm/f* contemporary

'**cofano** *sm* (*AUT*) bonnet (*BRIT*), hood (*US*); (*forziere*) chest

'**cogli** [ˈkoʎʎi] *prep + det =* **con + gli**; *vedi* **con**

'**cogliere** [ˈkɔʎʎere] *vt* (*fiore, frutto*) to pick, gather; (*sorprendere*) to catch, surprise; (*bersaglio*) to hit; (*fig: momento opportuno etc*) to grasp, seize, take; (: *capire*) to grasp; **~ qn in flagrante** *o* **in fallo** to catch sb red-handed

co'gnato, a [koɲˈɲato] *sm/f* brother-/sister-in-law

co'gnome [koɲˈɲome] *sm* surname

'**coi** *prep + det =* **con + i**; *vedi* **con**

coinci'denza [kointʃiˈdentsa] *sf* coincidence; (*FERR, AER, di autobus*) connection

coin'cidere [koinˈtʃidere] *vi* to coincide; **coin'ciso, a** *pp di* **coincidere**

coin'volgere [koinˈvɔldʒere] *vt*: **~ in** to involve in; **coin'volto, a** *pp di* **coinvolgere**

col *prep + det =* **con + il**; *vedi* **con**

cola'brodo *sm inv* strainer

cola'pasta *sm inv* colander

co'lare *vt* (*liquido*) to strain; (*pasta*) to drain; (*oro fuso*) to pour ♦ *vi* (*sudore*) to drip; (*botte*) to leak; (*cera*) to melt; **~ a picco** *vt, vi* (*nave*) to sink

co'lata *sf* (*di lava*) flow; (*FONDERIA*) casting

colazi'one [kolatˈtsjone] *sf* (*anche:* **prima ~**) breakfast; (*anche:* **seconda ~**) lunch; **fare ~** to have breakfast (*o* lunch)

co'lei *pron vedi* **colui**

co'lera *sm* (*MED*) cholera

'**colica** *sf* (*MED*) colic

'**colla** *sf* glue; (*di farina*) paste

collabo'rare *vi* to collaborate; **~ a** to collaborate on; (*giornale*) to contribute to; **collabora'tore, 'trice** *sm/f* collaborator; contributor

col'lana *sf* necklace; (*collezione*) collection, series

col'lant [kɔˈlɑ̃] *sm inv* tights *pl*

col'lare *sm* collar

col'lasso *sm* (*MED*) collapse

collau'dare *vt* to test, try out; **col'laudo** *sm* testing *no pl*; test

'**colle** *sm* hill

col'lega, ghi, ghe *sm/f* colleague

collega'mento *sm* connection; (*MIL*) liaison

colle'gare *vt* to connect, join, link; **~rsi** *vr* (*RADIO, TV*) to link up; **~rsi con** (*TEL*) to get through to

col'legio [kolˈlɛdʒo] *sm* college; (*convitto*) boarding school; **~ elettorale** (*POL*) constituency

'**collera** *sf* anger

col'lerico, a, ci, che *ag* quick-tempered, irascible

col'letta *sf* collection

collettività *sf* community

collet'tivo, a *ag* collective; (*interesse*) general, everybody's; (*biglietto, visita etc*) group *cpd* ♦ *sm* (*POL*) (political) group

col'letto *sm* collar

collezio'nare [kollettsjoˈnare] *vt* to collect

collezi'one [kolletˈtsjone] *sf* collection

colli'mare *vi* to correspond, coincide

col'lina *sf* hill

col'lirio *sm* eyewash

collisi'one *sf* collision

'**collo** *sm* neck; (*di abito*) neck, collar; (*pacco*) parcel; **~ del piede** instep

colloca'mento *sm* (*impiego*) employment; (*disposizione*) placing, arrangement

collo'care *vt* (*libri, mobili*) to place; (*COMM: merce*) to find a market for

col'loquio *sm* conversation, talk; (*ufficiale, per un lavoro*) interview; (*INS*) preliminary oral exam

col'mare *vt*: **~ di** (*anche fig*) to fill with; (*dare in abbondanza*) to load *o* overwhelm with; '**colmo, a** *ag*: **colmo (di)** full (of) ♦ *sm* summit, top; (*fig*) height; **al colmo della disperazione** in the depths of despair; **è il colmo!** it's the last straw!

co'lombo, a *sm/f* dove; pigeon

co'lonia *sf* colony; (*per bambini*) holiday camp; (**acqua di**) **~** (eau de) cologne; **coloni'ale** *ag* colonial ♦ *sm/f* colonist, settler

co'**lonna** *sf* column; **~ vertebrale** spine, spinal column

colon'**nello** *sm* colonel

co'**lono** *sm* (*coltivatore*) tenant farmer

colo'**rante** *sm* colouring

colo'**rare** *vt* to colour; (*disegno*) to colour in

co'**lore** *sm* colour; **a ~i** in colour, colour *cpd*; **farne di tutti i ~i** to get up to all sorts of mischief

colo'**rito, a** *ag* coloured; (*viso*) rosy, pink; (*linguaggio*) colourful ♦ *sm* (*tinta*) colour; (*carnagione*) complexion

co'**loro** *pron pl vedi* **colui**

co'**losso** *sm* colossus

'**colpa** *sf* fault; (*biasimo*) blame; (*colpevolezza*) guilt; (*azione colpevole*) offence; (*peccato*) sin; **di chi è la ~?** whose fault is it?; **è ~ sua** it's his fault; **per ~ di** through, owing to; **col'pevole** *ag* guilty

col'**pire** *vt* to hit, strike; (*fig*) to strike; **rimanere colpito da qc** to be amazed *o* struck by sth

'**colpo** *sm* (*urto*) knock; (: *affettivo*) blow, shock; (: *aggressivo*) blow; (*di pistola*) shot; (*MED*) stroke; (*rapina*) raid; **di ~** suddenly; **fare ~** to make a strong impression; **~ di grazia** coup de grâce; **~ di scena** (*TEATRO*) coup de théâtre; (*fig*) dramatic turn of events; **~ di sole** sunstroke; **~ di Stato** coup d'état; **~ di telefono** phone call; **~ di testa** (sudden) impulse *o* whim; **~ di vento** gust (of wind)

coltel'**lata** *sf* stab

col'**tello** *sm* knife; **~ a serramanico** clasp knife

colti'**vare** *vt* to cultivate; (*verdura*) to grow, cultivate; **coltiva'tore** *sm* farmer; **coltivazi'one** *sf* cultivation; growing

'**colto, a** *pp di* **cogliere** ♦ *ag* (*istruito*) cultured, educated

'**coltre** *sf* blanket

col'**tura** *sf* cultivation

co'**lui** (*f* co'**lei**, *pl* co'**loro**) *pron* the one; **~ che parla** the one *o* the man *o* the person who is speaking; **colei che amo** the one *o*

the woman *o* the person (whom) I love

'**coma** *sm inv* coma

comanda'**mento** *sm* (*REL*) commandment

coman'**dante** *sm* (*MIL*) commander, commandant; (*di reggimento*) commanding officer; (*NAUT, AER*) captain

coman'**dare** *vi* to be in command ♦ *vt* to command; (*imporre*) to order, command; **~ a qn di fare** to order sb to do; **co'mando** *sm* (*ingiunzione*) order, command; (*autorità*) command; (*TECN*) control

co'**mare** *sf* (*madrina*) godmother

combaci'**are** [kombaˈtʃare] *vi* to meet; (*fig: coincidere*) to coincide

com'**battere** *vt, vi* to fight; **combatti'mento** *sm* fight; fighting *no pl*; (*di pugilato*) match

combi'**nare** *vt* to combine; (*organizzare*) to arrange; (*fam: fare*) to make, cause; **combinazi'one** *sf* combination; (*caso fortuito*) coincidence; **per combinazione** by chance

combus'**tibile** *ag* combustible ♦ *sm* fuel

com'**butta** (*peg*) *sf*: **in ~** in league

PAROLA CHIAVE

'**come** *av* **1** (*alla maniera di*) like; **ti comporti ~ lui** you behave like him *o* like he does; **bianco ~ la neve** (as) white as snow; **~ se** as if, as though

2 (*in qualità di*) as a; **lavora ~ autista** he works as a driver

3 (*interrogativo*) how; **~ ti chiami?** what's your name?; **~ sta?** how are you?; **com'è il tuo amico?** what is your friend like?; **~?** (*prego?*) pardon?, sorry?; **~ mai?** how come?; **~ mai non ci hai avvertiti?** why on earth didn't you warn us?

4 (*esclamativo*): **~ sei bravo!** how clever you are!; **~ mi dispiace!** I'm terribly sorry! ♦ *cong* **1** (*in che modo*) how; **mi ha spiegato ~ l'ha conosciuto** he told me how he met him

2 (*correlativo*) as; (*con comparativi di maggioranza*) than; **non è bravo ~ pensavo** he isn't as clever as I thought; **è meglio di ~ pensassi** it's better than I thought

3 (*appena che, quando*) as soon as; **~ arrivò, iniziò a lavorare** as soon as he arrived, he set to work; *vedi* **così**; **tanto**

'**comico, a, ci, che** *ag* (*TEATRO*) comic; (*buffo*) comical ♦ *sm* (*attore*) comedian, comic actor

co'**mignolo** [ko'miɲɲolo] *sm* chimney top

cominci'**are** [komin'tʃare] *vt, vi* to begin, start; **~ a fare/col fare** to begin to do/by doing

comi'**tato** *sm* committee

comi'**tiva** *sf* party, group

co'**mizio** [ko'mittsjo] *sm* (*POL*) meeting, assembly

com'**mando** *sm inv* commando (squad)

com'**media** *sf* comedy; (*opera teatrale*) play; (: *che fa ridere*) comedy; (*fig*) playacting *no pl*; **commedi'ante** (*peg*) *sm/f* third-rate actor/actress; (*fig*) sham

commemo'**rare** *vt* to commemorate

commenda'**tore** *sm* official title *awarded for services to one's country*

commen'**tare** *vt* to comment on; (*testo*) to annotate; (*RADIO, TV*) to give a commentary on; **commenta'tore, 'trice** *sm/f* commentator; com'**mento** *sm* comment; (*a un testo, RADIO, TV*) commentary

commerci'**ale** [kommer'tʃale] *ag* commercial, trading; (*peg*) commercial

commerci'**ante** [kommer'tʃante] *sm/f* trader, dealer; (*negoziante*) shopkeeper

commerci'**are** [kommer'tʃare] *vt, vi*: **~ in** to deal *o* trade in

com'**mercio** [kom'mertʃo] *sm* trade, commerce; **essere in ~** (*prodotto*) to be on the market *o* on sale; **essere nel ~** (*persona*) to be in business

com'**messa** *sf* (*COMM*) order

com'**messo, a** *pp di* **commettere** ♦ *sm/f* shop assistant (*BRIT*), sales clerk (*US*) ♦ *sm* (*impiegato*) clerk; **~ viaggiatore** commercial traveller

commes'**tibile** *ag* edible; **~i** *smpl* foodstuffs

com'**mettere** *vt* to commit

com'**miato** *sm* leave-taking

commi'**nare** *vt* (*DIR*) to threaten; to inflict

commissari'**ato** *sm* (*AMM*) commissionership; (: *sede*) commissioner's office; (: *di polizia*) police station

commis'**sario** *sm* commissioner; (*di pubblica sicurezza*) ≈ (police) superintendent (*BRIT*), (police) captain (*US*); (*SPORT*) steward; (*membro di commissione*) member of a committee *o* board

commissio'**nario** *sm* (*COMM*) agent, broker

commissi'**one** *sf* (*incarico*) errand; (*comitato, percentuale*) commission; (*COMM: ordinazione*) order

commit'**tente** *sm/f* (*COMM*) purchaser, customer

com'**mosso, a** *pp di* **commuovere**

commo'**vente** *ag* moving

commozi'**one** [kommot'tsjone] *sf* emotion, deep feeling; **~ cerebrale** (*MED*) concussion

commu'**overe** *vt* to move, affect; **~rsi** *vr* to be moved

commu'**tare** *vt* (*pena*) to commute; (*ELETTR*) to change *o* switch over

co'**mò** *sm inv* chest of drawers

como'**dino** *sm* bedside table

comodi'**tà** *sf inv* comfort; convenience

'**comodo, a** *ag* comfortable; (*facile*) easy; (*conveniente*) convenient; (*utile*) useful, handy ♦ *sm* comfort; convenience; **con ~** at one's convenience *o* leisure; **fare il proprio ~** to do as one pleases; **far ~** to be useful *o* handy

compae'**sano, a** *sm/f* fellow countryman; person from the same town

com'**pagine** [kom'padʒine] *sf* (*squadra*) team

compa'**gnia** [kompaɲ'ɲia] *sf* company; (*gruppo*) gathering

com'**pagno, a** [kom'paɲɲo] *sm/f* (*di classe, gioco*) companion; (*POL*) comrade

compa'**rare** *vt* to compare

compara'**tivo, a** *ag, sm* comparative

compa'**rire** *vi* to appear; com'**parsa** *sf* appearance; (*TEATRO*) walk-on; (*CINEMA*)

extra; **comparso, a** *pp di* **comparire**
compartecipazi'one [kompar-
tetʃipat'tsjone] *sf* sharing; *(quota)* share; ~
agli utili profit-sharing
comparti'mento *sm* compartment;
(AMM) district
compas'sato, a *ag (persona)* composed
compassi'one *sf* compassion, pity; **avere**
~ **di qn** to feel sorry for sb, to pity sb
com'passo *sm* (pair of) compasses *pl*;
callipers *pl*
compa'tibile *ag (scusabile)* excusable;
(conciliabile, INFORM) compatible
compa'tire *vt (aver compassione di)* to
sympathize with, feel sorry for; *(scusare)* to
make allowances for
com'patto, a *ag* compact; *(roccia)* solid;
(folla) dense; *(fig: gruppo, partito)* united
com'pendio *sm* summary; *(libro)*
compendium
compen'sare *vt (equilibrare)* to
compensate for, make up for; ~ **qn di**
(rimunerare) to pay *o* remunerate sb for;
(risarcire) to pay compensation to sb for;
(fig: fatiche, dolori) to reward sb for;
com'penso *sm* compensation; payment,
remuneration; reward; **in compenso**
(d'altra parte) on the other hand
'compera *sf (acquisto)* purchase; **fare le**
~**e** to do the shopping
compe'rare *vt* = **comprare**
compe'tente *ag* competent; *(mancia)* apt,
suitable; **compe'tenza** *sf* competence;
competenze *sfpl (onorari)* fees
com'petere *vi* to compete, vie; *(DIR:*
spettare): ~ **a** to lie within the competence
of; **competizi'one** *sf* competition
compia'cente [kompja'tʃɛnte] *ag*
courteous, obliging; **compia'cenza** *sf*
courtesy
compia'cere [kompja'tʃere] *vi*: ~ **a** to
gratify, please ♦ *vt* to please; ~**rsi** *vr*
(provare soddisfazione): ~**rsi di** *o* **per qc** to
be delighted at sth; *(rallegrarsi)*: ~**rsi con**
qn to congratulate sb; *(degnarsi)*: ~**rsi di**
fare to be so good as to do;
compiaci'uto, a *pp di* **compiacere**

compi'angere [kom'pjandʒere] *vt* to
sympathize with, feel sorry for;
compi'anto, a *pp di* **compiangere**
'compiere *vt (concludere)* to finish,
complete; *(adempiere)* to carry out, fulfil;
~**rsi** *vr (avverarsi)* to be fulfilled, come true;
~ **gli anni** to have one's birthday
compi'lare *vt (modulo)* to fill in;
(dizionario, elenco) to compile
com'pire *vt* = **compiere**
compi'tare *vt* to spell out
'compito *sm (incarico)* task, duty; *(dovere)*
duty; *(INS)* exercise; *(: a casa)* piece of
homework; **fare i ~i** to do one's homework
com'pito, a *ag* well-mannered, polite
comple'anno *sm* birthday
complemen'tare *ag* complementary;
(INS: materia) subsidiary
comple'mento *sm* complement; *(MIL)*
reserve (troops); ~ **oggetto** *(LING)* direct
object
complessità *sf* complexity
comples'sivo, a *ag (globale)*
comprehensive, overall; *(totale: cifra)* total
com'plesso, a *ag* complex ♦ *sm (PSIC,*
EDIL) complex; *(MUS: corale)* ensemble;
(: orchestrina) band; *(: di musica pop)*
group; **in** *o* **nel** ~ on the whole
comple'tare *vt* to complete
com'pleto, a *ag* complete; *(teatro,*
autobus) full ♦ *sm* suit; **al** ~ full; *(tutti*
presenti) all present
compli'care *vt* to complicate; ~**rsi** *vr* to
become complicated; **complicazi'one** *sf*
complication
'complice ['komplitʃe] *sm/f* accomplice
complimen'tarsi *vr*: ~ **con** to
congratulate
compli'mento *sm* compliment; ~**i** *smpl*
(cortesia eccessiva) ceremony *sg*; *(ossequi)*
regards, compliments; ~**i!** congratulations!;
senza ~**i!** don't stand on ceremony!; make
yourself at home!; help yourself!
complot'tare *vt* to plot, conspire
com'plotto *sm* plot, conspiracy
compo'nente *sm/f* member ♦ *sm*
component

componi'mento *sm* (*DIR*) settlement; (*INS*) composition; (*poetico, teatrale*) work

com'porre *vt* (*musica, testo*) to compose; (*mettere in ordine*) to arrange; (*DIR: lite*) to settle; (*TIP*) to set; (*TEL*) to dial

comporta'mento *sm* behaviour

compor'tare *vt* (*implicare*) to involve; **~rsi** *vr* to behave

composi'tore, 'trice *sm/f* composer; (*TIP*) compositor, typesetter

composizi'one [kompozit'tsjone] *sf* composition; (*DIR*) settlement

com'posta *sf* (*CUC*) stewed fruit *no pl*; (*AGR*) compost; *vedi anche* **composto**

compos'tezza [kompos'tettsa] *sf* composure; decorum

com'posto, a *pp di* **comporre ♦** *ag* (*persona*) composed, self-possessed; (*: decoroso*) dignified; (*formato da più elementi*) compound *cpd* ♦ *sm* compound

com'prare *vt* to buy; **compra'tore, 'trice** *sm/f* buyer, purchaser

com'prendere *vt* (*contenere*) to comprise, consist of; (*capire*) to understand

comprensi'one *sf* understanding

compren'sivo, a *ag* (*prezzo*): **~ di** inclusive of; (*indulgente*) understanding

com'preso, a *pp di* **comprendere ♦** *ag* (*incluso*) included

com'pressa *sf* (*MED: garza*) compress; (*: pastiglia*) tablet; *vedi anche* **compresso**

compressi'one *sf* compression

com'presso, a *pp di* **comprimere ♦** *ag* (*vedi comprimere*) pressed; compressed; repressed

com'primere *vt* (*premere*) to press; (*FISICA*) to compress; (*fig*) to repress

compro'messo, a *pp di* **compromettere ♦** *sm* compromise

compro'mettere *vt* to compromise

compro'vare *vt* to confirm

com'punto, a *ag* contrite

compu'tare *vt* to calculate

com'puter *sm inv* computer

computiste'ria *sf* accounting, bookkeeping

'computo *sm* calculation

comu'nale *ag* municipal, town *cpd*, ≈ borough *cpd*

co'mune *ag* common; (*consueto*) common, everyday; (*di livello medio*) average; (*ordinario*) ordinary ♦ *sm* (*AMM*) town council; (*: sede*) town hall ♦ *sf* (*di persone*) commune; **fuori del ~** out of the ordinary; **avere in ~** to have in common, share; **mettere in ~** to share

comuni'care *vt* (*notizia*) to pass on, convey; (*malattia*) to pass on; (*ansia etc*) to communicate; (*trasmettere: calore etc*) to transmit, communicate; (*REL*) to administer communion to ♦ *vi* to communicate; **~rsi** *vr* (*propagarsi*): **~rsi a** to spread to; (*REL*) to receive communion

comuni'cato *sm* communiqué; **~ stampa** press release

comunicazi'one [komunikat'tsjone] *sf* communication; (*annuncio*) announcement; (*TEL*): **~ (telefonica)** (telephone) call; **dare la ~ a qn** to put sb through; **ottenere la ~** to get through

comuni'one *sf* communion; **~ di beni** (*DIR*) joint ownership of property

comu'nismo *sm* communism; **comu'nista, i, e** *ag, sm/f* communist

comunità *sf inv* community; **C~ Europea** European Community

co'munque *cong* however, no matter how ♦ *av* (*in ogni modo*) in any case; (*tuttavia*) however, nevertheless

con *prep* with; **partire col treno** to leave by train; **~ mio grande stupore** to my great astonishment; **~ tutto ciò** for all that

co'nato *sm*: **~ di vomito** retching

'conca, che *sf* (*GEO*) valley

con'cedere [kon'tʃedere] *vt* (*accordare*) to grant; (*ammettere*) to admit, concede; **~rsi qc** to treat o.s. to sth, to allow o.s. sth

concentra'mento [kontʃentra'mento] *sm* concentration

concen'trare [kontʃen'trare] *vt* to concentrate; **~rsi** *vr* to concentrate; **concentrazi'one** *sf* concentration

conce'pire [kontʃe'pire] *vt* (*bambino*) to conceive; (*progetto, idea*) to conceive (of);

(*metodo, piano*) to devise

con'cernere [kon'tʃɛrnere] *vt* to concern

concer'tare [kontʃer'tare] *vt* (*MUS*) to harmonize; (*ordine*) to devise, plan; ~rsi *vr* to agree

con'certo [kon'tʃɛrto] *sm* (*MUS*) concert; (: *componimento*) concerto

concessio'nario [kontʃessjo'narjo] *sm* (*COMM*) agent, dealer

con'cesso, a [kon'tʃɛsso] *pp di* concedere

con'cetto [kon'tʃetto] *sm* (*pensiero, idea*) concept; (*opinione*) opinion

concezi'one [kontʃet'tsjone] *sf* conception

con'chiglia [kon'kiʎʎa] *sf* shell

'concia ['kontʃa] *sf* (*di pelle*) tanning; (*di tabacco*) curing; (*sostanza*) tannin

conci'are [kon'tʃare] *vt* (*pelli*) to tan; (*tabacco*) to cure; (*fig: ridurre in cattivo stato*) to beat up; ~rsi *vr* (*sporcarsi*) to get in a mess; (*vestirsi male*) to dress badly

concili'are [kontʃi'ljare] *vt* to reconcile; (*contravvenzione*) to pay on the spot; (*sonno*) to be conducive to, induce; ~rsi qc to gain *o* win sth (for o.s.); ~rsi qn to win sb over; ~rsi con to be reconciled with; conciliazi'one *sf* reconciliation; (*DIR*) settlement

con'cilio [kon'tʃiljo] *sm* (*REL*) council

con'cime [kon'tʃime] *sm* manure; (*chimico*) fertilizer

con'ciso, a [kon'tʃizo] *ag* concise, succinct

conci'tato, a [kontʃi'tato] *ag* excited, emotional

concitta'dino, a [kontʃitta'dino] *sm/f* fellow citizen

con'cludere *vt* to conclude; (*portare a compimento*) to conclude, finish, bring to an end; (*operare positivamente*) to achieve ♦ *vi* (*essere convincente*) to be conclusive; ~rsi *vr* to come to an end, close; conclusi'one *sf* conclusion; (*risultato*) result; conclu'sivo, a *ag* conclusive; (*finale*) final; con'cluso, a *pp di* concludere

concor'danza [konkor'dantsa] *sf* (*anche LING*) agreement

concor'dare *vt* (*tregua, prezzo*) to agree

on; (*LING*) to make agree ♦ *vi* to agree; concor'dato *sm* agreement; (*REL*) concordat

con'corde *ag* (*d'accordo*) in agreement; (*simultaneo*) simultaneous

concor'rente *sm/f* competitor; (*INS*) candidate; concor'renza *sf* competition

con'correre *vi*: ~ (in) (*MAT*) to converge *o* meet (in); ~ (a) (*competere*) to compete (for); (: *INS: a una cattedra*) to apply (for); (*partecipare: a un'impresa*) to take part (in), contribute (to); con'corso, a *pp di* concorrere ♦ *sm* competition; (*INS*) competitive examination; concorso di colpa (*DIR*) contributory negligence

con'creto, a *ag* concrete

concussi'one *sf* (*DIR*) extortion

condan'nare *vt* (*DIR*): ~ a to sentence to; ~ per to convict of; (*disapprovare*) to condemn; condan'nato, a *sm/f* convict

conden'sare *vt* to condense; ~rsi *vr* to condense; condensazi'one *sf* condensation

condi'mento *sm* seasoning; dressing

con'dire *vt* to season; (*insalata*) to dress

condi'videre *vt* to share; condi'viso, a *pp di* condividere

condizio'nale [kondittsjo'nale] *ag* conditional ♦ *sm* (*LING*) conditional ♦ *sf* (*DIR*) suspended sentence

condizio'nare [kondittsjo'nare] *vt* to condition; ad aria condizionata air-conditioned; condiziona'tore *sm* air conditioner

condizi'one [kondit'tsjone] *sf* condition; ~i *sfpl* (*di pagamento etc*) terms, conditions; a ~ che on condition that, provided that

condogli'anze [kondoʎ'ʎantse] *sfpl* condolences

condo'minio *sm* joint ownership; (*edificio*) jointly-owned building

condo'nare *vt* (*DIR*) to remit; con'dono *sm* remission; condono fiscale *conditional amnesty for people evading tax*

con'dotta *sf* (*modo di comportarsi*)

conduct, behaviour; (*di un affare etc*) handling; (*di acqua*) piping; (*incarico sanitario*) country medical practice *controlled by a local authority*

con'dotto, a *pp di* condurre ♦ *ag*: **medico ~** local authority doctor (*in country district*) ♦ *sm* (*canale, tubo*) pipe, conduit; (*ANAT*) duct

condu'cente [kondu'tʃɛnte] *sm* driver

con'durre *vt* to conduct; (*azienda*) to manage; (*accompagnare: bambino*) to take; (*automobile*) to drive; (*trasportare: acqua, gas*) to convey, conduct; (*fig*) to lead ♦ *vi* to lead; **condursi** *vr* to behave, conduct o.s.

condut'tore *ag*: **filo ~** (*fig*) thread ♦ *sm* (*di mezzi pubblici*) driver; (*FISICA*) conductor

con'farsi *vr*: **~ a** to suit, agree with

confederazi'one [konfederat'tsjone] *sf* confederation

confe'renza [konfe'rɛntsa] *sf* (*discorso*) lecture; (*riunione*) conference; **~ stampa** press conference; **conferenzi'ere, a** *sm/f* lecturer

confe'rire *vt*: **~ qc a qn** to give sth to sb, bestow sth on sb ♦ *vi* to confer

con'ferma *sf* confirmation

confer'mare *vt* to confirm

confes'sare *vt* to confess; **~rsi** *vr* to confess; **andare a ~rsi** (*REL*) to go to confession; **confessio'nale** *ag, sm* confessional; **confessi'one** *sf* confession; (*setta religiosa*) denomination; **confes'sore** *sm* confessor

con'fetto *sm* sugared almond; (*MED*) pill

confezio'nare [konfettsjo'nare] *vt* (*vestito*) to make (up); (*merci, pacchi*) to package

confezi'one [konfet'tsjone] *sf* (*di abiti: da uomo*) tailoring; (*: da donna*) dressmaking; (*imballaggio*) packaging; **~ regalo** gift pack; **~i per signora** ladies' wear; **~i da uomo** menswear

confic'care *vt*: **~ qc in** to hammer *o* drive sth into; **~rsi** *vr* to stick

confi'dare *vi*: **~ in** to confide in, rely on ♦ *vt* to confide; **~rsi con qn** to confide in sb; **confi'dente** *sm/f* (*persona amica*)

confidant/confidante; (*informatore*) informer; **confi'denza** *sf* (*familiarità*) intimacy, familiarity; (*fiducia*) trust, confidence; (*rivelazione*) confidence; **confidenzi'ale** *ag* familiar, friendly; (*segreto*) confidential

configu'rarsi *vr*: **~ a** to assume the shape *o* form of

confi'nare *vi*: **~ con** to border on ♦ *vt* (*POL*) to intern; (*fig*) to confine; **~rsi** *vr* (*isolarsi*): **~rsi in** to shut o.s. up in

Confin'dustria *sigla f* (= *Confederazione Generale dell'Industria Italiana*) *employers' association;* ≈ CBI (*BRIT*)

con'fine *sm* boundary; (*di paese*) border, frontier

con'fino *sm* internment

confis'care *vt* to confiscate

con'flitto *sm* conflict

conflu'enza [konflu'ɛntsa] *sf* (*di fiumi*) confluence; (*di strade*) junction

conflu'ire *vi* (*fiumi*) to flow into each other, meet; (*strade*) to meet

con'fondere *vt* to mix up, confuse; (*imbarazzare*) to embarrass; **~rsi** *vr* (*mescolarsi*) to mingle; (*turbarsi*) to be confused; (*sbagliare*) to get mixed up

confor'mare *vt* (*adeguare*): **~ a** to adapt *o* conform to; **~rsi** *vr*: **~rsi (a)** to conform (to)

confor'tare *vt* to comfort, console; **confor'tevole** *ag* (*consolante*) comforting; (*comodo*) comfortable; **con'forto** *sm* comfort, consolation

confron'tare *vt* to compare

con'fronto *sm* comparison; **in** *o* **a ~ di** in comparison with, compared to; **nei miei** (*o* **tuoi** *etc*) **~i** towards me (*o* you *etc*)

confusi'one *sf* confusion; (*chiasso*) racket, noise; (*imbarazzo*) embarrassment

con'fuso, a *pp di* confondere ♦ *ag* (*vedi confondere*) confused; embarrassed

confu'tare *vt* to refute

conge'dare [kondʒe'dare] *vt* to dismiss; (*MIL*) to demobilize; **~rsi** *vr* to take one's leave; **con'gedo** *sm* (*anche MIL*) leave; **prendere congedo da qn** to take one's leave of sb; **congedo assoluto** (MIL) discharge

conge'gnare [kondʒeɲ'ɲare] vt to construct, put together; **con'gegno** sm device, mechanism

conge'lare [kondʒe'lare] vt to freeze; **~rsi** vr to freeze; **congela'tore** sm freezer

congestio'nare [kondʒestjo'nare] vt to congest

congesti'one [kondʒes'tjone] sf congestion

conget'tura [kondʒet'tura] sf conjecture

con'giungere [kon'dʒundʒere] vt to join (together); **~rsi** vr to join (together)

congiunti'vite [kondʒunti'vite] sf conjunctivitis

congiun'tivo [kondʒun'tivo] sm (LING) subjunctive

congi'unto, a [kon'dʒunto] pp di **congiungere** ♦ ag (unito) joined ♦ sm/f relative

congiun'tura [kondʒun'tura] sf (giuntura) junction, join; (ANAT) joint; (circostanza) juncture; (ECON) economic situation

congiunzi'one [kondʒun'tsjone] sf (LING) conjunction

congi'ura [kon'dʒura] sf conspiracy; **congiu'rare** vi to conspire

conglome'rato sm (GEO) conglomerate; (fig) conglomeration; (EDIL) concrete

congratu'larsi vr: **~ con qn per qc** to congratulate sb on sth

congratulazi'oni [kongratulat'tsjoni] sfpl congratulations

con'grega, ghe sf band, bunch

con'gresso sm congress

congu'aglio [kon'gwaʎʎo] sm balancing, adjusting; (somma di denaro) balance

coni'are vt to mint, coin; (fig) to coin

co'niglio [ko'niʎʎo] sm rabbit

coniu'gare [konju'gare] vt (LING) to conjugate; **~rsi** vr to get married; **coniu'gato, a** ag (sposato) married; **coniugazi'one** sf (LING) conjugation

'coniuge ['kɔnjudʒe] sm/f spouse

connazio'nale [konnattsjo'nale] sm/f fellow-countryman/woman

connessi'one sf connection

con'nesso, a pp di **connettere**

con'nettere vt to connect, join ♦ vi (fig) to think straight

conni'vente ag conniving

conno'tati smpl distinguishing marks

'cono sm cone; **~ gelato** ice-cream cone

cono'scente [konoʃʃente] sm/f acquaintance

cono'scenza [konoʃʃentsa] sf (il sapere) knowledge no pl; (persona) acquaintance; (facoltà sensoriale) consciousness no pl; **perdere ~** to lose consciousness

co'noscere [ko'noʃʃere] vt to know; **ci siamo conosciuti a Firenze** we (first) met in Florence; **conosci'tore, 'trice** sm/f connoisseur; **conosci'uto, a** pp di **conoscere** ♦ ag well-known

con'quista sf conquest

conquis'tare vt to conquer; (fig) to gain, win

consa'crare vt (REL) to consecrate; (: sacerdote) to ordain; (dedicare) to dedicate; (fig: uso etc) to sanction; **~rsi a** to dedicate o.s. to

consangu'ineo, a sm/f blood relation

consa'pevole ag: **~ di** aware o conscious of; **consapevo'lezza** sf awareness, consciousness

'conscio, a, sci, sce ['kɔnʃo] ag: **~ di** aware o conscious of

consecu'tivo, a ag consecutive; (successivo: giorno) following, next

con'segna [kon'seɲɲa] sf delivery; (merce consegnata) consignment; (custodia) care, custody; (MIL: ordine) orders pl; (: punizione) confinement to barracks; **pagamento alla ~** cash on delivery; **dare qc in ~ a qn** to entrust sth to sb

conse'gnare [konseɲ'ɲare] vt to deliver; (affidare) to entrust, hand over; (MIL) to confine to barracks

consegu'enza [konse'gwentsa] sf consequence; **per o di ~** consequently

consegu'ire vt to achieve ♦ vi to follow

con'senso sm approval, consent

consen'tire vi: **~ a** to consent o agree to ♦ vt to allow, permit

con'serva sf (CUC) preserve; ~ di frutta jam; ~ di pomodoro tomato purée
conser'vare vt (CUC) to preserve; (custodire) to keep; (: dalla distruzione etc) to preserve, conserve; ~rsi vr to keep
conserva'tore, 'trice sm/f (POL) conservative
conservazi'one [konservat'tsjone] sf preservation; conservation
conside'rare vt to consider; (reputare) to consider, regard; considerazi'one sf consideration; (stima) regard, esteem; prendere in considerazione to take into consideration; conside'revole ag considerable
consigli'are [konsiʎ'ʎare] vt (persona) to advise; (metodo, azione) to recommend, advise, suggest; ~rsi vr: ~rsi con qn to ask sb for advice; consigli'ere, a sm/f adviser ♦ sm: consigliere d'amministrazione board member; consigliere comunale town councillor; con'siglio sm (suggerimento) advice no pl, piece of advice; (assemblea) council; consiglio d'amministrazione board; il Consiglio dei Ministri (POL) ≈ the Cabinet; Consiglio d'Europa Council of Europe
consis'tente ag thick; solid; (fig) sound, valid; consis'tenza sf consistency, thickness; solidity; validity
con'sistere vi: ~ in to consist of; consis'tito, a pp di consistere
conso'lare ag consular ♦ vt (confortare) to console, comfort; (rallegrare) to cheer up; ~rsi vr to be comforted; to cheer up
conso'lato sm consulate
consolazi'one [konsolat'tsjone] sf consolation, comfort
'console¹ sm consul
con'sole² [kon'sɔl] sf (quadro di comando) console
conso'nante sf consonant
'consono, a ag: ~ a consistent with, consonant with
con'sorte sm/f consort
con'sorzio [kon'sɔrtsjo] sm consortium

con'stare vi: ~ di to consist of ♦ vb impers: mi consta che it has come to my knowledge that, it appears that
consta'tare vt to establish, verify; constatazi'one sf observation; constatazione amichevole jointly-agreed statement for insurance purposes
consu'eto, a ag habitual, usual; consue'tudine sf habit, custom; (usanza) custom
consu'lente sm/f consultant; consu'lenza sf consultancy
consul'tare vt to consult; ~rsi vr: ~rsi con qn to seek the advice of sb; consultazi'one sf consultation; consultazioni sfpl (POL) talks, consultations
consul'torio sm: ~ familiare family planning clinic
consu'mare vt (logorare: abiti, scarpe) to wear out; (usare) to consume, use up; (mangiare, bere) to consume; (DIR) to consummate; ~rsi vr to wear out; to be used up; (anche fig) to be consumed; (combustibile) to burn out; consuma'tore sm consumer; consumazi'one sf (bibita) drink; (spuntino) snack; (DIR) consummation; consu'mismo sm consumerism; con'sumo sm consumption; wear; use
consun'tivo sm (ECON) final balance
con'tabile ag accounts cpd, accounting ♦ sm/f accountant; contabili'tà sf (attività, tecnica) accounting, accountancy; (insieme dei libri etc) books pl, accounts pl; (ufficio) accounts department
contachi'lometri [kontaki'lɔmetri] sm inv ≈ mileometer
conta'dino, a sm/f countryman/woman; farm worker; (peg) peasant
contagi'are [konta'dʒare] vt to infect
con'tagio [kon'tadʒo] sm infection; (per contatto diretto) contagion; (epidemia) epidemic; contagi'oso, a ag infectious; contagious
conta'gocce [konta'gottʃe] sm inv (MED) dropper
contami'nare vt to contaminate

con'tante sm cash; **pagare in ~i** to pay cash

con'tare vt to count; (considerare) to consider ♦ vi to count, be of importance; **~ su qn** to count o rely on sb; **~ di fare qc** to intend to do sth; **conta'tore** sm meter

contat'tare vt to contact

con'tatto sm contact

'conte sm count

conteggi'are [konted'dʒare] vt to charge, put on the bill; **con'teggio** sm calculation

con'tegno [kon'teɲɲo] sm (comportamento) behaviour; (atteggiamento) attitude; **darsi un ~** to act nonchalant; to pull o.s. together

contem'plare vt to contemplate, gaze at; (DIR) to make provision for

contemporanea'mente av simultaneously; at the same time

contempo'raneo, a ag, sm/f contemporary

conten'dente sm/f opponent, adversary

con'tendere vi (competere) to compete; (litigare) to quarrel ♦ vt: **~ qc a qn** to contend with o be in competition with sb for sth

conte'nere vt to contain; **conteni'tore** sm container

conten'tare vt to please, satisfy; **~rsi di** to be satisfied with, content o.s. with

conten'tezza [konten'tettsa] sf contentment

con'tento, a ag pleased, glad; **~ di** pleased with

conte'nuto sm contents pl; (argomento) content

con'tesa sf dispute, argument

con'teso, a pp di **contendere**

con'tessa sf countess

contes'tare vt (DIR) to notify; (fig) to dispute; **contestazi'one** sf (DIR) notification; dispute; (protesta) protest

con'testo sm context

con'tiguo, a ag: **~ (a)** adjacent (to)

continen'tale ag, sm/f continental

conti'nente ag continent ♦ sm (GEO) continent; (: terra ferma) mainland

contin'gente [kontin'dʒɛnte] ag contingent ♦ sm (COMM) quota; (MIL) contingent; contin'genza [kon'tingentsa] sf circumstance; (ECON): **(indennità di) contingenza** cost-of-living allowance

continu'are vt to continue (with), go on with ♦ vi to continue, go on; **~ a fare qc** to go on o continue doing sth; **continuazi'one** sf continuation

continu'ità sf continuity

con'tinuo, a ag (numerazione) continuous; (pioggia) continual, constant; (ELETTR): **corrente ~a** direct current; **di ~** continually

'conto sm (calcolo) calculation; (COMM, ECON) account; (di ristorante, albergo) bill; (fig: stima) consideration, esteem; **fare i ~i con qn** to settle one's account with sb; **fare ~ su qn/qc** to count o rely on sb; **rendere ~ a qn di qc** to be accountable to sb for sth; **tener ~ di qn/qc** to take sb/sth into account; **per ~ di** on behalf of; **per ~ mio** as far as I'm concerned; **a ~i fatti, in fin dei ~i** all things considered; **~ corrente** current account; **~ alla rovescia** countdown

con'torcere [kon'tortʃere] vt to twist; **~rsi** vr to twist, writhe

contor'nare vt to surround

con'torno sm (linea) outline, contour; (ornamento) border; (CUC) vegetables pl

con'torto, a pp di **contorcere**

contrabbandi'ere, a sm/f smuggler

contrab'bando sm smuggling, contraband; **merce di ~** contraband, smuggled goods pl

contrab'basso sm (MUS) (double) bass

contraccambi'are vt (favore etc) to return

contraccet'tivo, a [kontrattʃet'tivo] ag, sm contraceptive

contrac'colpo sm rebound; (di arma da fuoco) recoil; (fig) repercussion

con'trada sf street; district

contrad'detto, a pp di **contraddire**

contrad'dire vt to contradict; **contraddit'torio, a** ag contradictory; (sentimenti) conflicting ♦ sm (DIR) cross-examination; **contraddizi'one** *sf* contradiction

contraf'fare *vt* (*persona*) to mimic; (*alterare: voce*) to disguise; (*firma*) to forge, counterfeit; **contraf'fatto, a** *pp di* **contraffare** ♦ *ag* counterfeit; **contraffazi'one** *sf* mimicking *no pl*; disguising *no pl*; forging *no pl*; (*cosa contraffatta*) forgery

contrap'peso *sm* counterbalance, counterweight

contrap'porre *vt*: ~ **qc a qc** to counter sth with sth; (*paragonare*) to compare sth with sth; **contrap'posto, a** *pp di* **contrapporre**

contraria'mente *av*: ~ **a** contrary to

contrari'are *vt* (*contrastare*) to thwart, oppose; (*irritare*) to annoy, bother; **~rsi** *vr* to get annoyed

contrarietà *sf* adversity; (*fig*) aversion

con'trario, a *ag* opposite; (*sfavorevole*) unfavourable ♦ *sm* opposite; **essere ~ a qc** (*persona*) to be against sth; **in caso ~** otherwise; **avere qc in ~** to have some objection; **al ~** on the contrary

con'trarre *vt* to contract; **contrarsi** *vr* to contract

contrasse'gnare [kontrassen'nare] *vt* to mark; **contras'segno** *sm* (*distintivo*) distinguishing mark; **spedire in contrassegno** to send C.O.D.

contras'tare *vt* (*avversare*) to oppose; (*impedire*) to bar; (*negare: diritto*) to contest, dispute ♦ *vi*: ~ **(con)** (*essere in disaccordo*) to contrast (with); (*lottare*) to struggle (with); **con'trasto** *sm* contrast; (*litigio*) dispute

contrat'tacco *sm* counterattack

contrat'tare *vt*, *vi* to negotiate

contrat'tempo *sm* hitch

con'tratto, a *pp di* **contrarre** ♦ *sm* contract; **contrattu'ale** *ag* contractual

contravvenzi'one [contravven'tsjone] *sf* contravention; (*ammenda*) fine

contrazi'one [kontrat'tsjone] *sf* contraction; (*di prezzi etc*) reduction

contribu'ente *sm/f* taxpayer; ratepayer

(*BRIT*), property tax payer (*US*)

contribu'ire *vi* to contribute; **contri'buto** *sm* contribution; (*tassa*) tax

'contro *prep* against; **~ di me/lui** against me/him; **pastiglie ~ la tosse** throat lozenges; **~ pagamento** (*COMM*) on payment ♦ *prefisso*: **contro'battere** *vt* (*fig: a parole*) to answer back; (: *confutare*) to refute; **controfi'gura** *sf* (*CINEMA*) double; **controfir'mare** *vt* to countersign

control'lare *vt* (*accertare*) to check; (*sorvegliare*) to watch, control; (*tenere nel proprio potere, fig: dominare*) to control; **con'trollo** *sm* check; watch; control; **controllo delle nascite** birth control; **control'lore** *sm* (*FERR, AUTOBUS*) (ticket) inspector

controprodu'cente [kontroprodu'tʃɛnte] *ag* counterproductive

contro'senso *sm* (*contraddizione*) contradiction in terms; (*assurdità*) nonsense

controspio'naggio [kontrospio'naddʒo] *sm* counterespionage

contro'versia *sf* controversy; (*DIR*) dispute

contro'verso, a *ag* controversial

contro'voglia [kontro'vɔʎʎa] *av* unwillingly

contu'macia [kontu'matʃa] *sf* (*DIR*) default

contusi'one *sf* (*MED*) bruise

convale'scente [konvaleʃ'ʃɛnte] *ag, sm/f* convalescent; **convale'scenza** *sf* convalescence

convali'dare *vt* (*AMM*) to validate; (*fig: sospetto, dubbio*) to confirm

con'vegno [kon'venno] *sm* (*incontro*) meeting; (*congresso*) convention, congress; (*luogo*) meeting place

conve'nevoli *smpl* civilities

conveni'ente *ag* suitable; (*vantaggioso*) profitable; (: *prezzo*) cheap; **conveni'enza** *sf* suitability; advantage; cheapness; **le convenienze** *sfpl* social conventions

conve'nire *vi* (*riunirsi*) to gather, assemble; (*concordare*) to agree; (*tornare utile*) to be worthwhile ♦ *vb impers*: **conviene fare questo** it is advisable to do this; **conviene andarsene** we should go; **ne convengo** I agree

con'vento *sm* (*di frati*) monastery; (*di suore*) convent

convenzio'nale [konventsjo'nale] *ag* conventional

convenzi'one [konven'tsjone] *sf* (*DIR*) agreement; (*nella società*) convention; **le ~i** *sfpl* social conventions

conver'sare *vi* to have a conversation, converse

conversazi'one [konversat'tsjone] *sf* conversation; **fare ~** to chat, have a chat

conversi'one *sf* conversion; **~ ad U** (*AUT*) U-turn

conver'tire *vt* (*trasformare*) to change; (*POL, REL*) to convert; **~rsi** *vr*: **~rsi (a)** to be converted (to)

con'vesso, a *ag* convex

con'vincere [kon'vintʃere] *vt* to convince; **~ qn di qc** to convince sb of sth; **~ qn a fare qc** to persuade sb to do sth; con'vinto, a *pp di* **convincere**; convinzi'one *sf* conviction, firm belief

convis'suto, a *pp di* **convivere**

con'vivere *vi* to live together

convo'care *vt* to call, convene; (*DIR*) to summon; convocazi'one *sf* meeting; summons *sg*

convogli'are [konvoʎ'ʎare] *vt* to convey; (*dirigere*) to direct, send; con'voglio *sm* (*di veicoli*) convoy; (*FERR*) train

convulsi'one *sf* convulsion

con'vulso, a *ag* (*pianto*) violent, convulsive; (*attività*) feverish

coope'rare *vi*: **~ (a)** to cooperate (in); coopera'tiva *sf* cooperative; cooperazi'one *sf* cooperation

coordi'nare *vt* to coordinate; coordi'nate *sfpl* (*MAT, GEO*) coordinates; coordi'nati *smpl* (*MODA*) coordinates

co'perchio [ko'perkjo] *sm* cover; (*di pentola*) lid

co'perta *sf* cover; (*di lana*) blanket; (*da viaggio*) rug; (*NAUT*) deck

coper'tina *sf* (*STAMPA*) cover, jacket

co'perto, a *pp di* **coprire** ♦ *ag* covered; (*cielo*) overcast ♦ *sm* place setting; (*posto a*

tavola) place; (*al ristorante*) cover charge; **~ di** covered in *o* with

coper'tone *sm* (*AUT*) rubber tyre

coper'tura *sf* (*anche ECON, MIL*) cover; (*di edificio*) roofing

'copia *sf* copy; **brutta / bella ~** rough/final copy

copi'are *vt* to copy; copia'trice *sf* copier, copying machine

copi'one *sm* (*CINEMA, TEATRO*) script

'coppa *sf* (*bicchiere*) goblet; (*per frutta, gelato*) dish; (*trofeo*) cup, trophy; **~ dell'olio** oil sump (*BRIT*) *o* pan (*US*)

'coppia *sf* (*di persone*) couple; (*di animali, SPORT*) pair

coprifu'oco, chi *sm* curfew

copri'letto *sm* bedspread

co'prire *vt* to cover; (*occupare: carica, posto*) to hold; **~rsi** *vr* (*cielo*) to cloud over; (*vestirsi*) to wrap up, cover up; (*ECON*) to cover o.s.; **~rsi di** (*macchie, muffa*) to become covered in

co'raggio [ko'raddʒo] *sm* courage, bravery; **~!** (*forza!*) come on!; (*animo!*) cheer up!; coraggi'oso, a *ag* courageous, brave

co'rallo *sm* coral

co'rano *sm* (*REL*) Koran

co'razza [ko'rattsa] *sf* armour; (*di animali*) carapace, shell; (*MIL*) armour(-plating); coraz'zata *sf* battleship

corbelle'ria *sf* stupid remark; **~e** *sfpl* nonsense *no pl*

'corda *sf* cord; (*fune*) rope; (*spago, MUS*) string; **dare ~ a qn** to let sb have his (*o* her) way; **tenere sulla ~ qn** to keep sb on tenterhooks; **tagliare la ~** to slip away, sneak off; **~e vocali** vocal cords

cordi'ale *ag* cordial, warm ♦ *sm* (*bevanda*) cordial

cor'doglio [kor'dɔʎʎo] *sm* grief; (*lutto*) mourning

cor'done *sm* cord, string; (*linea: di polizia*) cordon; **~ ombelicale** umbilical cord

Co'rea *sf*: **la ~** Korea

coreogra'fia *sf* choreography

cori'andolo *sm* (*BOT*) coriander; **~i** *smpl* confetti *sg* cori'carsi *vr* to go to bed

'corna *sfpl vedi* corno

cor'nacchia [kor'nakkja] *sf* crow

corna'musa *sf* bagpipes *pl*

cor'netta *sf* (*MUS*) cornet; (*TEL*) receiver

cor'netto *sm* (*CUC*) croissant; (*gelato*) cone

cor'nice [kor'nitʃe] *sf* frame; (*fig*) setting, background

cornici'one [korni'tʃone] *sm* (*di edificio*) ledge; (*ARCHIT*) cornice

'corno (*pl(f)* **-a**) *sm* (*ZOOL*) horn; (*pl(m)* **-i**: *MUS*) horn; **fare le ~a a qn** to be unfaithful to sb

Corno'vaglia [korno'vaʎʎa] *sf*: **la ~** Cornwall

cor'nuto, a *ag* (*con corna*) horned; (*fam!*: *marito*) cuckolded ♦ *sm* (*fam!*) cuckold; (: *insulto*) bastard (*!*)

'coro *sm* chorus; (*REL*) choir

co'rona *sf* crown; (*di fiori*) wreath; coro'nare *vt* to crown

'corpo *sm* body; (*militare, diplomatico*) corps *inv*; **prendere ~** to take shape; **a ~ a ~** hand-to-hand; (*fig*) **di ballo** corps de ballet; **~ insegnante** teaching staff

corpo'rale *ag* bodily; (*punizione*) corporal

corpora'tura *sf* build, physique

corporazi'one [korporat'tsjone] *sf* corporation

corpu'lento, a *ag* stout

corre'dare *vt*: **~ di** to provide *o* furnish with; cor'redo *sm* equipment; (*di sposa*) trousseau

cor'reggere [kor'rɛddʒere] *vt* to correct; (*compiti*) to correct, mark

cor'rente *ag* (*acqua: di fiume*) flowing; (: *di rubinetto*) running; (*moneta, prezzo*) current; (*comune*) everyday ♦ *sm*: **essere al ~ (di)** to be well-informed (about); **mettere al ~ (di)** to inform (of) ♦ *sf* (*d'acqua*) current, stream; (*spiffero*) draught; (*ELETTR, METEOR*) current; (*fig*) trend, tendency; **la vostra lettera del 5 ~ mese** (*COMM*) your letter of the 5th of this month; **corrente'mente** *av* commonly; **parlare una lingua correntemente** to speak a language fluently

'correre *vi* to run; (*precipitarsi*) to rush; (*partecipare a una gara*) to race, run; (*fig*: *diffondersi*) to go round ♦ *vt* (*SPORT: gara*) to compete in; (*rischio*) to run; (*pericolo*) to face; **~ dietro a qn** to run after sb; **corre voce che ...** it is rumoured that ...

cor'retto, a *pp di* correggere ♦ *ag* (*comportamento*) correct, proper; **caffè ~ al cognac** coffee laced with brandy

correzi'one [korret'tsjone] *sf* correction; marking; **~ di bozze** proofreading

corri'doio *sm* corridor

corri'dore *sm* (*SPORT*) runner; (: *su veicolo*) racer

corri'era *sf* coach (*BRIT*), bus

corri'ere *sm* (*diplomatico, di guerra, postale*) courier; (*COMM*) carrier

corrispet'tivo *sm* (*somma*) amount due

corrispon'dente *ag* corresponding ♦ *sm/f* correspondent

corrispon'denza [korrispon'dentsa] *sf* correspondence

corris'pondere *vi* (*equivalere*): **~ (a)** to correspond (to) ♦ *vt* (*stipendio*) to pay; (*fig*: *amore*) to return; **corris'posto, a** *pp di* corrispondere

corrobo'rare *vt* to strengthen, fortify; (*fig*) to corroborate, bear out

cor'rodere *vt* to corrode; **~rsi** *vr* to corrode

cor'rompere *vt* to corrupt; (*comprare*) to bribe

corrosi'one *sf* corrosion

cor'roso, a *pp di* corrodere

cor'rotto, a *pp di* corrompere ♦ *ag* corrupt

corrucci'arsi [korrut'tʃarsi] *vr* to grow angry *o* vexed

corru'gare *vt* to wrinkle; **~ la fronte** to knit one's brows

corruzi'one [korrut'tsjone] *sf* corruption; bribery

'corsa *sf* running *no pl*; (*gara*) race; (*di autobus, taxi*) journey, trip; **fare una ~** to run, dash; (*SPORT*) to run a race

cor'sia *sf* (*AUT, SPORT*) lane; (*di ospedale*) ward

cor'sivo *sm* cursive (writing); (*TIP*) italics *pl*

'corso, a *pp di* correre ♦ *sm* course; (*strada cittadina*) main street; (*di unità monetaria*) circulation; (*di titoli, valori*) rate, price; in ~ in progress, under way; (*annata*) current; ~ d'acqua river, stream; (*artificiale*) waterway; ~ d'aggiornamento refresher course; ~ serale evening class

'corte *sf* (court)yard; (*DIR, regale*) court; fare la ~ a qn to court sb; ~ marziale court-martial

cor'teccia, ce [kor'tettʃa] *sf* bark

corteggi'are [korted'dʒare] *vt* to court

cor'teo *sm* procession

cor'tese *ag* courteous; corte'sia *sf* courtesy; per cortesia ... excuse me, please ...

cortigi'ana [korti'dʒana] *sf* courtesan

cortigi'ano, a [korti'dʒano] *sm/f* courtier

cor'tile *sm* (court)yard

cor'tina *sf* curtain; (*anche fig*) screen

'corto, a *ag* short; essere a ~ di qc to be short of sth; ~ circuito short-circuit

'corvo *sm* raven

'cosa *sf* thing; (*faccenda*) affair, matter, business *no pl*; (che) ~? what?; (che) cos'è? what is it?; a ~ pensi? what are you thinking about?

'coscia, sce ['kɔʃʃa] *sf* thigh; ~ di pollo (*CUC*) chicken leg

cosci'ente [koʃ'ʃɛnte] *ag* conscious; ~ di conscious *o* aware of; cosci'enza *sf* conscience; (*consapevolezza*) consciousness; coscienzi'oso, a *ag* conscientious

cosci'otto [koʃ'ʃɔtto] *sm* (*CUC*) leg

cos'critto *sm* (*MIL*) conscript

PAROLA CHIAVE

così *av* 1 (*in questo modo*) like this, (in) this way; (*in tal modo*) so; le cose stanno ~ this is the way things stand; non ho detto ~! I didn't say that!; come stai? – (e) ~ how are you? — so-so; e ~ via and so on; per ~ dire so to speak

2 (*tanto*) so; ~ lontano so far away; un ragazzo ~ intelligente such an intelligent boy

♦ *ag inv* (*tale*): non ho mai visto un film ~ I've never seen such a film

♦ *cong* 1 (*perciò*) so, therefore

2: ~ ... come as ... as; non è ~ bravo come te he's not as good as you; ~ ... che so ... that

---

cosid'detto, a *ag* so-called

cos'metico, a, ci, che *ag, sm* cosmetic

cos'pargere [kos'pardʒere] *vt*: ~ di to sprinkle with; cos'parso, a *pp di* cospargere

cos'petto *sm*: al ~ di in front of; in the presence of

cos'picuo, a *ag* considerable, large

cospi'rare *vi* to conspire; cospirazi'one *sf* conspiracy

'costa *sf* (*tra terra e mare*) coast(line); (*litorale*) shore; (*ANAT*) rib; la C~ Azzurra the French Riviera

cos'tante *ag* constant; (*persona*) steadfast ♦ *sf* constant

cos'tare *vi, vt* to cost; ~ caro to be expensive, cost a lot

cos'tata *sf* (*CUC*) large chop

cos'tato *sm* (*ANAT*) ribs *pl*

costeggi'are [kosted'dʒare] *vt* to be close to; to run alongside

cos'tei *pron vedi* costui

costi'era *sf* stretch of coast

costi'ero, a *ag* coastal, coast *cpd*

costitu'ire *vt* (*comitato, gruppo*) to set up, form; (*sog: elementi, parti: comporre*) to make up, constitute; (*rappresentare*) to constitute; (*DIR*) to appoint; ~rsi alla polizia to give o.s. up to the police

costituzio'nale [kostituttsjo'nale] *ag* constitutional

costituzi'one [kostitut'tsjone] *sf* setting up; building up; constitution

'costo *sm* cost; a ogni *o* qualunque ~, a tutti i ~i at all costs

'costola *sf* (*ANAT*) rib

cos'toro *pron pl vedi* costui

cos'toso, a *ag* expensive, costly

cos'tretto, a *pp di* costringere

cos'tringere [kos'trindʒere] *vt*: ~ qn a fare

qc to force sb to do sth; **costrizi'one** *sf* coercion

costru'ire *vt* to construct, build; **costruzi'one** *sf* construction, building

cos'tui (*f* **cos'tei**, *pl* **cos'toro**) *pron* (*soggetto*) he/she; *pl* they; (*complemento*) him/her; *pl* them; **si può sapere chi è ~?** (*peg*) just who is that fellow?

cos'tume *sm* (*uso*) custom; (*foggia di vestire, indumento*) costume; **~i** *smpl* (*condotta morale*) morals, morality *sg*; **~ da bagno** bathing *o* swimming costume (*BRIT*), swimsuit; (*da uomo*) bathing *o* swimming trunks *pl*

co'tenna *sf* bacon rind

co'togna [ko'toɲɲa] *sf* quince

coto'letta *sf* (*di maiale, montone*) chop; (*di vitello, agnello*) cutlet

co'tone *sm* cotton; **~ idrofilo** cotton wool (*BRIT*), absorbent cotton (*US*)

'cotta *sf* (*fam: innamoramento*) crush

'cottimo *sm*: **lavorare a ~** to do piecework

'cotto, a *pp di* **cuocere** ♦ *ag* cooked; (*fam: innamorato*) head-over-heels in love; **ben ~** (*carne*) well done

cot'tura *sf* cooking; (*in forno*) baking; (*in umido*) stewing

co'vare *vt* to hatch; (*fig: malattia*) to be sickening for; (: *odio, rancore*) to nurse ♦ *vi* (*fuoco, fig*) to smoulder

'covo *sm* den

co'vone *sm* sheaf

'cozza ['kɔttsa] *sf* mussel

coz'zare [kot'tsare] *vi*: **~ contro** to bang into, collide with

C.P. *abbr* (= *casella postale*) P.O. Box

crack [kræk] *sm inv* (*droga*) crack

'crampo *sm* cramp

'cranio *sm* skull

cra'tere *sm* crater

cra'vatta *sf* tie

cre'anza [kre'antsa] *sf* manners *pl*

cre'are *vt* to create; **cre'ato** *sm* creation; **crea'tore, 'trice** *ag* creative ♦ *sm* creator; **crea'tura** *sf* creature; (*bimbo*) baby, infant; **creazi'one** *sf* creation; (*fondazione*) foundation, establishment

cre'dente *sm/f* (*REL*) believer

cre'denza [kre'dɛntsa] *sf* belief; (*armadio*) sideboard

credenzi'ali [kreden'tsjali] *sfpl* credentials

'credere *vt* to believe ♦ *vi*: **~ in, ~ a** to believe in; **~ qn onesto** to believe sb (to be) honest; **~ che** to believe *o* think that; **~rsi furbo** to think one is clever

'credito *sm* (*anche COMM*) credit; (*reputazione*) esteem, repute; **comprare a ~** to buy on credit

'credo *sm inv* creed

'crema *sf* cream; (*con uova, zucchero etc*) custard; **~ solare** sun cream

cre'mare *vt* to cremate

Crem'lino *sm*: **il ~** the Kremlin

'crepa *sf* crack

cre'paccio [kre'pattʃo] *sm* large crack, fissure; (*di ghiacciaio*) crevasse

crepacu'ore *sm* broken heart

cre'pare *vi* (*fam: morire*) to snuff it, kick the bucket; **~ dalle risa** to split one's sides laughing

crepi'tare *vi* (*fuoco*) to crackle; (*pioggia*) to patter

cre'puscolo *sm* twilight, dusk

'crescere ['kreʃʃere] *vi* to grow ♦ *vt* (*figli*) to raise; **'crescita** *sf* growth; **cresci'uto, a** *pp di* **crescere**

'cresima *sf* (*REL*) confirmation

'crespo, a *ag* (*capelli*) frizzy; (*tessuto*) puckered ♦ *sm* crêpe

'cresta *sf* crest; (*di polli, uccelli*) crest, comb

'creta *sf* chalk; clay

cre'tino, a *ag* stupid ♦ *sm/f* idiot, fool

cric *sm inv* (*TECN*) jack

'cricca, che *sf* clique

cri'ceto [kri'tʃeto] *sm* hamster

crimi'nale *ag, sm/f* criminal

'crimine *sm* (*DIR*) crime

'crine *sm* horsehair; **crini'era** *sf* mane

crisan'temo *sm* chrysanthemum

'crisi *sf inv* crisis; (*MED*) attack, fit; **~ di nervi** attack *o* fit of nerves

cristalliz'zare [kristalid'dzare] *vi* to crystallize; (*fig*) to become fossilized; **~rsi**

vr to crystallize; to become fossilized
cris'tallo *sm* crystal
cristia'nesimo *sm* Christianity
cristi'ano, a *ag, sm/f* Christian
'Cristo *sm* Christ
cri'terio *sm* criterion; (*buon senso*) (common) sense
'critica, che *sf* criticism; la ~ (*attività*) criticism; (*persone*) the critics *pl*; *vedi anche* **critico**
criti'care *vt* to criticize
'critico, a, ci, che *ag* critical ♦ *sm* critic
Croa'zia [kroa'ttsja] *sf* Croatia
croc'cante *ag* crisp, crunchy
'croce ['krotʃe] *sf* cross; in ~ (*di traverso*) crosswise; (*fig*) on tenterhooks; la C~ **Rossa** the Red Cross
croce'figgere *etc* [krotʃe'fiddʒere] = **crocifiggere** *etc*
croce'via *sm inv* crossroads *sg*
croci'ata [kro'tʃata] *sf* crusade
cro'cicchio [kro'tʃikkjo] *sm* crossroads *sg*
croci'era [kro'tʃera] *sf* (*viaggio*) cruise; (*ARCHIT*) transept
croci'figgere [krotʃi'fiddʒere] *vt* to crucify; crocifissi'one *sf* crucifixion; croci'fisso, a *pp di* **crocifiggere**
crogi'olo [kro'dʒɔlo] *sm* (*fig*) melting pot
crol'lare *vi* to collapse; 'crollo *sm* collapse; (*di prezzi*) slump, sudden fall
cro'mato, a *ag* chromium-plated
'cromo *sm* chrome, chromium
'cronaca, che *sf* (*STAMPA*) news *sg*; (: *rubrica*) column; (*TV, RADIO*) commentary; **fatto** *o* **episodio di** ~ news item; ~ **nera** crime news *sg*; crime column
'cronico, a, ci, che *ag* chronic
cro'nista, i *sm* (*STAMPA*) reporter
cronolo'gia [kronolo'dʒia] *sf* chronology
cro'nometro *sm* chronometer; (*a scatto*) stopwatch
'crosta *sf* crust
cros'tacei [kros'tatʃei] *smpl* shellfish
cros'tata *sf* (*CUC*) tart
cros'tino *sm* (*CUC*) croûton; (: *da antipasto*) canapé
'cruccio ['kruttʃo] *sm* worry, torment

cruci'verba *sm inv* crossword (puzzle)
cru'dele *ag* cruel; crudel'tà *sf* cruelty
'crudo, a *ag* (*non cotto*) raw; (*aspro*) harsh, severe
cru'miro (*peg*) *sm* blackleg (*BRIT*), scab
'crusca *sf* bran
crus'cotto *sm* (*AUT*) dashboard
CSI *sigla f inv* (= Comunità Stati Indipendenti) CIS
'Cuba *sf* Cuba
cu'betto *sm*: ~ **di ghiaccio** ice cube
'cubico, a, ci, che *ag* cubic
'cubo, a *ag* cubic ♦ *sm* cube; **elevare al** ~ (*MAT*) to cube
cuc'cagna [kuk'kaɲɲa] *sf*: **paese della** ~ land of plenty; **albero della** ~ greasy pole (*fig*)
cuc'cetta [kut'tʃetta] *sf* (*FERR*) couchette; (*NAUT*) berth
cucchiai'ata [kukkja'jata] *sf* spoonful
cucchia'ino [kukkja'ino] *sm* teaspoon; coffee spoon
cucchi'aio [kuk'kjajo] *sm* spoon
'cuccia, ce ['kuttʃa] *sf* dog's bed; **a ~!** down!
'cucciolo ['kuttʃolo] *sm* cub; (*di cane*) puppy
cu'cina [ku'tʃina] *sf* (*locale*) kitchen; (*arte culinaria*) cooking, cookery; (*le vivande*) food, cooking; (*apparecchio*) cooker; ~ **componibile** fitted kitchen; cuci'nare *vt* to cook
cu'cire [ku'tʃire] *vt* to sew, stitch; cuci'trice *sf* stapler; cuci'tura *sf* sewing, stitching; (*costura*) seam
cucù *sm inv* = **cuculo**
cu'culo *sm* cuckoo
'cuffia *sf* bonnet, cap; (*da infermiera*) cap; (*da bagno*) (bathing) cap; (*per ascoltare*) headphones *pl*, headset
cu'gino, a [ku'dʒino] *sm/f* cousin

─────────────────
| PAROLA CHIAVE |
─────────────────

'cui *pron* 1 (*nei complementi indiretti: persona*) whom; (: *oggetto, animale*) which; **la persona/le persone a ~ accennavi** the person/people you were referring to *o* to

whom you were referring; **i libri di ~
parlavo** the books I was talking about *o*
about which I was talking; **il quartiere in ~
abito** the district where I live; **la ragione
per ~** the reason why
2 (*inserito tra articolo e sostantivo*) whose;
la donna i ~ figli sono scomparsi the
woman whose children have disappeared;
il signore, dal ~ figlio ho avuto il libro
the man from whose son I got the book

---

culi'naria *sf* cookery
'culla *sf* cradle
cul'lare *vt* to rock
culmi'nare *vi*: **~ con** to culminate in
'culmine *sm* top, summit
'culo (*fam!*) *sm* arse (*Brit!*), ass (*US!*); (*fig:
fortuna*): **aver ~** to have the luck of the
devil
'culto *sm* (*religione*) religion; (*adorazione*)
worship; (*venerazione: anche fig*) cult
cul'tura *sf* culture; education, learning;
cultu'rale *ag* cultural
cumula'tivo, a *ag* cumulative; (*prezzo*)
inclusive; (*biglietto*) group *cpd*
'cumulo *sm* (*mucchio*) pile, heap; (*METEOR*)
cumulus
'cuneo *sm* wedge
cu'netta *sf* (*avvallamento*) dip; (*di scolo*)
gutter
cu'oca *sf vedi* cuoco
cu'ocere ['kwɔtʃere] *vt* (*alimenti*) to cook;
(*mattoni etc*) to fire ♦ *vi* to cook; **~ al forno**
(*pane*) to bake; (*arrosto*) to roast; cu'oco,
a, chi, che *sm/f* cook; (*di ristorante*) chef
cu'oio *sm* leather; **~ capelluto** scalp
cu'ore *sm* heart; **~i** *smpl* (*CARTE*) hearts;
avere buon ~ to be kind-hearted; **stare a
~ a qn** to be important to sb
cupi'digia [kupi'didʒa] *sf* greed,
covetousness
'cupo, a *ag* dark; (*suono*) dull; (*fig*)
gloomy, dismal
'cupola *sf* dome; cupola
'cura *sf* care; (*MED: trattamento*) (course of)
treatment; **aver ~ di** (*occuparsi di*) to look
after; **a ~ di** (*libro*) edited by; **~**

dimagrante diet
cu'rare *vt* (*malato, malattia*) to treat;
(*: guarire*) to cure; (*aver cura di*) to take
care of; (*testo*) to edit; **~rsi** *vr* to take care
of o.s.; (*MED*) to follow a course of
treatment; **~rsi di** to pay attention to
cu'rato *sm* parish priest; (*protestante*) vicar,
minister
cura'tore, 'trice *sm/f* (*DIR*) trustee; (*di
antologia etc*) editor
curio'sare *vi* to look round, wander
round; (*tra libri*) to browse; **~ nei negozi** to
look *o* wander round the shops
curiosità *sf inv* curiosity; (*cosa rara*) curio,
curiosity
curi'oso, a *ag* curious; **essere ~ di** to be
curious about
cur'sore *sm* (*INFORM*) cursor
'curva *sf* curve; (*stradale*) bend, curve
cur'vare *vt* to bend ♦ *vi* (*veicolo*) to take a
bend; (*strada*) to bend, curve; **~rsi** *vr* to
bend; (*legno*) to warp
'curvo, a *ag* curved; (*piegato*) bent
cusci'netto [kuʃʃi'netto] *sm* pad; (*TECN*)
bearing ♦ *ag inv*: **stato ~** buffer state; **~ a
sfere** ball bearing
cu'scino [kuʃ'ʃino] *sm* cushion; (*guanciale*)
pillow
'cuspide *sf* (*ARCHIT*) spire
cus'tode *sm/f* keeper, custodian
cus'todia *sf* care; (*DIR*) custody; (*astuccio*)
case, holder
custo'dire *vt* (*conservare*) to keep;
(*assistere*) to look after, take care of; (*fare la
guardia*) to guard
'cute *sf* (*ANAT*) skin
C.V. *abbr* (= *cavallo vapore*) h.p.
cybercaffè [tʃiberka'fe] *sm inv* cybercafé

D, d

da (*da+il* = **dal**, *da+lo* = **dallo**, *da+l'*
= **dall'**, *da+la* = **dalla**, *da+i* = **dai**, *da+gli*
= **dagli**, *da+le* = **dalle**) *prep* 1 (*agente*) by;

dipinto ~ un grande artista painted by a great artist
2 (*causa*) with; **tremare dalla paura** to tremble with fear
3 (*stato in luogo*) at; **abito ~ lui** I'm living at his house *o* with him; **sono dal giornalaio/~ Francesco** I'm at the newsagent's/Francesco's (house)
4 (*moto a luogo*) to; (*moto per luogo*) through; **vado ~ Pietro/dal giornalaio** I'm going to Pietro's (house)/to the newsagent's; **sono passati dalla finestra** they came in through the window
5 (*provenienza, allontanamento*) from; **arrivare/partire ~ Milano** to arrive/depart from Milan; **scendere dal treno/dalla macchina** to get off the train/out of the car; **si trova a 5 km ~ qui** it's 5 km from here
6 (*tempo: durata*) for; (: *a partire da: nel passato*) since; (: *nel futuro*) from; **vivo qui ~ un anno** I've been living here for a year; **è dalle 3 che ti aspetto** I've been waiting for you since 3 (o'clock); **~ oggi in poi** from today onwards; **~ bambino** as a child, when I (*o* he *etc*) was a child
7 (*modo, maniera*) like; **comportarsi ~ uomo** to behave like a man; **l'ho fatto ~ me** I did it (by) myself
8 (*descrittivo*): **una macchina ~ corsa** a racing car; **una ragazza dai capelli biondi** a girl with blonde hair; **un vestito ~ 100.000 lire** a 100,000 lire dress

da 'capo *av* = **daccapo**
dac'capo *av* (*di nuovo*) (once) again; (*dal principio*) all over again, from the beginning
'dado *sm* (*da gioco*) dice *o* die; (*CUC*) stock (*BRIT*) *o* bouillon (*US*) cube; (*TECN*) (screw)nut; **giocare a ~i** to play dice
daf'fare *sm* work, toil
'dagli ['daʎʎi] *prep + det vedi* **da**
'dai *prep + det vedi* **da**
'daino *sm* (*fallow*) deer *inv*; (*pelle*) buckskin
dal *prep + det vedi* **da**
dall' *prep + det vedi* **da**
'dalla *prep + det vedi* **da**
'dalle *prep + det vedi* **da**
'dallo *prep + det vedi* **da**
dal'tonico, a, ci, che *ag* colour-blind
'dama *sf* lady; (*nei balli*) partner; (*gioco*) draughts *sg* (*BRIT*), checkers *sg* (*US*)
damigi'ana [dami'dʒana] *sf* demijohn
da'naro *sm* = **denaro**
da'nese *ag* Danish ♦ *sm/f* Dane ♦ *sm* (*LING*) Danish
Dani'marca *sf*: **la ~** Denmark
dan'nare *vt* (*REL*) to damn; **~rsi** *vr* (*fig: tormentarsi*) to be worried to death; **far ~ qn** to drive sb mad; **dannazi'one** *sf* damnation
danneggi'are [danned'dʒare] *vt* to damage; (*rovinare*) to spoil; (*nuocere*) to harm
'danno *sm* damage; (*a persona*) harm, injury; **~i** *smpl* (*DIR*) damages; **dan'noso, a** *ag*: **dannoso (a, per)** harmful (to), bad (for)
Da'nubio *sm*: **il ~** the Danube
'danza ['dantsa] *sf*: **la ~** dancing; **una ~** a dance
dan'zare [dan'tsare] *vt, vi* to dance
dapper'tutto *av* everywhere
dap'poco *ag inv* inept, worthless
dap'prima *av* at first
'dare *sm* (*COMM*) debit ♦ *vt* to give; (*produrre: frutti, suono*) to produce ♦ *vi* (*guardare*): **~ su** to look (out); **~rsi** *vr*: **~rsi a** to dedicate o.s. to; **~rsi al commercio** to go into business; **~rsi al bere** to take to drink; **~ da mangiare a qn** to give sb sth to eat; **~ per certo qc** to consider sth certain; **~ per morto qn** to give sb up for dead; **~rsi per vinto** to give in
'darsena *sf* dock; dockyard
'data *sf* date; **~ di nascita** date of birth
da'tare *vt* to date ♦ *vi*: **~ da** to date from
'dato, a *ag* (*stabilito*) given ♦ *sm* datum; **~i** *smpl* data *pl*; **~ che** given that; **un ~ di fatto** a fact; **~ sensibili** personal information
da'tore, trice *sm/f*: **~ di lavoro** employer
'dattero *sm* date

dattilogra'fare *vt* to type; **dattilogra'fia** *sf* typing; **datti'lografo, a** *sm/f* typist

da'vanti *av* in front; (*dirimpetto*) opposite ♦ *ag inv* front ♦ *sm* front; **~ a** in front of; facing, opposite; (*in presenza di*) before, in front of

davan'zale [davan'tsale] *sm* windowsill

d'a'vanzo [da'vantso] *av* more than enough

dav'vero *av* really, indeed

'dazio ['dattsjo] *sm* (*somma*) duty; (*luogo*) customs *pl*

DC *sigla f* = **Democrazia Cristiana**

d. C. *ad abbr* (= *dopo Cristo*) A.D.

'dea *sf* goddess

'debito, a *ag* due, proper ♦ *sm* debt; (*COMM: dare*) debit; **a tempo ~** at the right time; **debi'tore, 'trice** *sm/f* debtor

'debole *ag* weak, feeble; (*suono*) faint; (*luce*) dim ♦ *sm* weakness; **debo'lezza** *sf* weakness

debut'tare *vi* to make one's début; **de'butto** *sm* début

deca'denza [deka'dɛntsa] *sf* decline; (*DIR*) loss, forfeiture

decaffei'nato, a *ag* decaffeinated

decan'tare *vt* to praise, sing the praises of

decapi'tare *vt* to decapitate

decappot'tabile *ag, sf* convertible

dece'duto, a [detʃe'duto] *ag* deceased

de'cennio [de'tʃɛnnjo] *sm* decade

de'cente [de'tʃɛnte] *ag* decent, respectable, proper; (*accettabile*) satisfactory, decent

de'cesso [de'tʃɛsso] *sm* death

de'cidere [de'tʃidere] *vt*: **~ qc** to decide on sth; (*questione, lite*) to settle sth; **~ di fare/che** to decide to do/that; **~ di qc** (*sog: cosa*) to determine sth; **~rsi (a fare)** to decide (to do), make up one's mind (to do)

deci'frare [detʃi'frare] *vt* to decode; (*fig*) to decipher, make out

deci'male [detʃi'male] *ag* decimal

'decimo, a ['detʃimo] *num* tenth

de'cina [de'tʃina] *sf* ten; (*circa dieci*): **una ~ (di)** about ten

decisi'one [detʃi'zjone] *sf* decision;

prendere una ~ to make a decision

de'ciso, a [de'tʃizo] *pp di* **decidere**

declas'sare *vt* to downgrade; to lower in status

decli'nare *vi* (*pendio*) to slope down; (*fig: diminuire*) to decline ♦ *vt* to decline

declinazi'one *sf* (*LING*) declension

de'clino *sm* decline

decodifica'tore *sm* (*TEL*) decoder

decol'lare *vi* (*AER*) to take off; **de'collo** *sm* take-off

decolo'rare *vt* to bleach

decom'porre *vt* to decompose; **decomporsi** *vr* (*vi*) to decompose; **decom'posto, a** *pp di* **decomporre**

deconge'lare [dekondʒe'lare] *vt* to defrost

deco'rare *vt* to decorate; **decora'tore, 'trice** *sm/f* (*interior*) decorator; **decorazi'one** *sf* decoration

de'coro *sm* decorum; **deco'roso, a** *ag* decorous, dignified

de'correre *vi* to pass, elapse; (*avere effetto*) to run, have effect; **de'corso, a** *pp di* **decorrere** ♦ *sm* (*evoluzione: anche MED*) course

de'crepito, a *ag* decrepit

de'crescere [de'kreʃʃere] *vi* (*diminuire*) to decrease, diminish; (*acque*) to subside, go down; (*prezzi*) to go down; **decresci'uto, a** *pp di* **decrescere**

de'creto *sm* decree; **~ legge** *decree with the force of law*

'dedalo *sm* maze, labyrinth

'dedica, che *sf* dedication

dedi'care *vt* to dedicate

'dedito, a *ag*: **~ a** (*studio etc*) dedicated *o* devoted to; (*vizio*) addicted to

de'dotto, a *pp di* **dedurre**

de'durre *vt* (*concludere*) to deduce; (*defalcare*) to deduct; **deduzi'one** *sf* deduction

defal'care *vt* to deduct

defe'rente *ag* respectful, deferential

defe'rire *vt*: **~ a** (*DIR*) to refer to

defezi'one [defet'tsjone] *sf* defection, desertion

defici'ente [defi'tʃɛnte] *ag* (*mancante*): **~ di**

deficient in; (*insufficiente*) insufficient
♦ *sm/f* mental defective; (*peg: cretino*) idiot

'**deficit** ['defifit] *sm inv* (ECON) deficit

defi'**nire** *vt* to define; (*risolvere*) to settle;
defini'**tivo, a** *ag* definitive, final;
definizi'**one** *sf* definition; settlement

deflet'**tore** *sm* (AUT) quarter-light

de'**flusso** *sm* (*della marea*) ebb

defor'**mare** *vt* (*alterare*) to put out of
shape; (*corpo*) to deform; (*pensiero, fatto*)
to distort; ~**rsi** *vr* to lose its shape

de'**forme** *ag* deformed; disfigured;
deformità *sf inv* deformity

defrau'**dare** *vt*: ~ **qn di qc** to defraud sb
of sth, cheat sb out of sth

de'**funto, a** *ag* late *cpd* ♦ *sm/f* deceased

degene'**rare** [dedʒene'rare] *vi* to
degenerate; de'**genere** *ag* degenerate

de'**gente** [de'dʒɛnte] *sm/f* (*in ospedale*) in-
patient

'**degli** ['deʎʎi] *prep + det vedi* **di**

de'**gnarsi** [deɲ'narsi] *vr*: ~ **di fare** to deign
o condescend to do

'**degno, a** *ag* dignified; ~ **di** worthy of; ~
di lode praiseworthy

degra'**dare** *vt* (MIL) to demote; (*privare
della dignità*) to degrade; ~**rsi** *vr* to
demean o.s.

degustazi'**one** [degustat'tsjone] *sf*
sampling, tasting

'**dei** *prep + det vedi* **di**

del *prep + det vedi* **di**

dela'**tore**, '**trice** *sm/f* police informer

'**delega, ghe** *sf* (*procura*) proxy

dele'**gare** *vt* to delegate; dele'**gato** *sm*
delegate

dele'**terio, a** *ag* damaging; (*per salute etc*)
harmful

del'**fino** *sm* (ZOOL) dolphin; (STORIA)
dauphin; (*fig*) probable successor

delibe'**rare** *vt* to come to a decision on
♦ *vi* (DIR): ~ (**su qc**) to rule (on sth)

delica'**tezza** [delika'tettsa] *sf* delicacy;
frailty; thoughtfulness; tactfulness

deli'**cato, a** *ag* delicate; (*salute*) delicate,
frail; (*fig: gentile*) thoughtful, considerate;
(*: che dimostra tatto*) tactful

deline'**are** *vt* to outline; ~**rsi** *vr* to be
outlined; (*fig*) to emerge

delin'**quente** *sm/f* criminal, delinquent; ~
abituale regular offender, habitual
offender; delin'**quenza** *sf* criminality,
delinquency; **delinquenza minorile**
juvenile delinquency

deli'**rare** *vi* to be delirious, rave; (*fig*) to
rave

de'**lirio** *sm* delirium; (*ragionamento
insensato*) raving; (*fig*): **andare / mandare
in** ~ to go/send into a frenzy

de'**litto** *sm* crime

de'**lizia** [de'littsja] *sf* delight; delizi'**oso, a**
ag delightful; (*cibi*) delicious

dell' *prep + det vedi* **di**

'**della** *prep + det vedi* **di**

'**delle** *prep + det vedi* **di**

'**dello** *prep + det vedi* **di**

delta'**plano** *sm* hang-glider; **volo col** ~
hang-gliding

de'**ludere** *vt* to disappoint; delusi'**one** *sf*
disappointment; de'**luso, a** *pp di*
deludere

de'**manio** *sm* state property

de'**menza** [de'mɛntsa] *sf* dementia;
(*stupidità*) foolishness

demo'**cratico, a, ci, che** *ag* democratic

demo'**crazia** [demokrat'tsia] *sf* democracy

democristi'**ano, a** *ag, sm/f* Christian
Democrat

demo'**lire** *vt* to demolish

'**demone** *sm* demon

de'**monio** *sm* demon, devil; **il D**~ the Devil

de'**naro** *sm* money

denomi'**nare** *vt* to name;
denominazi'**one** *sf* name;
denomination; **denominazione d'origine
controllata** *label guaranteeing the quality
and origin of a wine*

densità *sf inv* density

'**denso, a** *ag* thick, dense

den'**tale** *ag* dental

'**dente** *sm* tooth; (*di forchetta*) prong; **al** ~
(CUC: *pasta*) al dente; ~**i del giudizio**
wisdom teeth; denti'**era** *sf* (set of) false
teeth *pl*

denti'fricio [denti'fritʃo] *sm* toothpaste
den'tista, i, e *sm/f* dentist
'dentro *av* inside; (*in casa*) indoors; (*fig: nell'intimo*) inwardly ♦ *prep*: ~ **(a)** in; **piegato in** ~ folded over; **qui/là** ~ in here/there; ~ **di sé** (*pensare, brontolare*) to oneself
de'nuncia, ce *o* cie [de'nuntʃa] *sf* denunciation; declaration; ~ **dei redditi** (income) tax return
denunci'are [denun'tʃare] *vt* to denounce; (*dichiarare*) to declare
de'nunzia *etc* [de'nuntsja] = **denuncia** *etc*
denutrizi'one [denutrit'tsjone] *sf* malnutrition
deodo'rante *sm* deodorant
depe'rire *vi* to waste away
depila'torio, a *ag* hair-removing *cpd*, depilatory
dépli'ant [depli'ã] *sm inv* leaflet; (*opuscolo*) brochure
deplo'revole *ag* deplorable
de'porre *vt* (*depositare*) to put down; (*rimuovere: da una carica*) to remove; (*: re*) to depose; (*DIR*) to testify
depor'tare *vt* to deport
deposi'tare *vt* (*gen, GEO, ECON*) to deposit; (*lasciare*) to leave; (*merci*) to store
de'posito *sm* deposit; (*luogo*) warehouse; depot; (*: MIL*) depot; ~ **bagagli** left-luggage office
deposizi'one [depozit'tsjone] *sf* deposition; (*da una carica*) removal
de'posto, a *pp di* **deporre**
depra'vato, a *ag* depraved ♦ *sm/f* degenerate
depre'dare *vt* to rob, plunder
depressi'one *sf* depression
de'presso, a *pp di* **deprimere** ♦ *ag* depressed
deprez'zare [depret'tsare] *vt* (*ECON*) to depreciate
de'primere *vt* to depress
depu'rare *vt* to purify
depu'tato *sm* (*POL*) deputy, ≈ Member of Parliament (*BRIT*), ≈ Member of Congress (*US*)

deragli'are [deraʎ'ʎare] *vi* to be derailed; **far** ~ to derail
dere'litto, a *ag* derelict
dere'tano (*fam*) *sm* bottom, buttocks *pl*
de'ridere *vt* to mock, deride; de'riso, a *pp di* **deridere**
de'riva *sf* (*NAUT, AER*) drift; **andare alla** ~ (*anche fig*) to drift
deri'vare *vi*: ~ **da** to derive from ♦ *vt* to derive; (*corso d'acqua*) to divert; derivazi'one *sf* derivation; diversion
derma'tologo, a, gi, ghe *sm/f* dermatologist
der'rate *sfpl*: ~ **alimentari** foodstuffs
deru'bare *vt* to rob
des'critto, a *pp di* **descrivere**
des'crivere *vt* to describe; descrizi'one *sf* description
de'serto, a *ag* deserted ♦ *sm* (*GEO*) desert; **isola ~a** desert island
deside'rare *vt* to want, wish for; (*sessualmente*) to desire; ~ **fare/che qn faccia** to want *o* wish to do/sb to do; **desidera fare una passeggiata?** would you like to go for a walk?
desi'derio *sm* wish; (*più intenso, carnale*) desire
deside'roso, a *ag*: ~ **di** longing *o* eager for
desi'nenza [dezi'nɛntsa] *sf* (*LING*) ending, inflexion
de'sistere *vi*: ~ **da** to give up, desist from; desis'tito, a *pp di* **desistere**
deso'lato, a *ag* (*paesaggio*) desolate; (*persona: spiacente*) sorry
des'tare *vt* to wake (up); (*fig*) to awaken, arouse; ~**rsi** *vr* to wake (up)
desti'nare *vt* to destine; (*assegnare*) to appoint, assign; (*indirizzare*) to address; ~ **qc a qn** to intend to give sth to sb, intend sb to have sth; destina'tario, a *sm/f* (*di lettera*) addressee
destinazi'one [destinat'tsjone] *sf* destination; (*uso*) purpose
des'tino *sm* destiny, fate
destitu'ire *vt* to dismiss, remove
'desto, a *ag* (wide) awake

'**destra** *sf* (*mano*) right hand; (*parte*) right (side); (*POL*): **la ~** the Right; **a ~** (*essere*) on the right; (*andare*) to the right

destreggi'arsi [destred'dʒarsi] *vr* to manoeuvre (*BRIT*), maneuver (*US*)

des'trezza [des'trettsa] *sf* skill, dexterity

'**destro, a** *ag* right, right-hand

dete'nere *vt* (*incarico, primato*) to hold; (*proprietà*) to have, possess; (*in prigione*) to detain, hold; **dete'nuto, a** *sm/f* prisoner; **detenzi'one** *sf* holding; possession; detention

deter'gente [deter'dʒɛnte] *ag* detergent; (*crema, latte*) cleansing ♦ *sm* detergent

deterio'rare *vt* to damage; **~rsi** *vr* to deteriorate

determi'nare *vt* to determine; **determinazi'one** *sf* determination; (*decisione*) decision

deter'sivo *sm* detergent

detes'tare *vt* to detest, hate

de'trarre *vt*: **~ (da)** to deduct (from), take away (from); **de'tratto, a** *pp di* **detrarre**; **detrazi'one** *sf* deduction; **detrazione d'imposta** tax allowance

de'trito *sm* (*GEO*) detritus

'**detta** *sf*: **a ~ di** according to

dettagli'are [dettaʎ'ʎare] *vt* to detail, give full details of

det'taglio [det'taʎʎo] *sm* detail; (*COMM*): **il ~** retail; **al ~** (*COMM*) retail; separately

det'tare *vt* to dictate; **~ legge** (*fig*) to lay down the law; **det'tato** *sm* dictation; **detta'tura** *sf* dictation

'**detto, a** *pp di* **dire** ♦ *ag* (*soprannominato*) called, known as; (*già nominato*) above-mentioned ♦ *sm* saying; **~ fatto** no sooner said than done

detur'pare *vt* to disfigure; (*moralmente*) to sully

devas'tare *vt* to devastate; (*fig*) to ravage

devi'are *vi*: **~ (da)** to turn off (from) ♦ *vt* to divert; **deviazi'one** *sf* (*anche AUT*) diversion

devo'luto, a *pp di* **devolvere**

devoluzi'one [devolut'tsjone] *sf* (*DIR*) devolution, transfer

de'volvere *vt* (*DIR*) to transfer, devolve

de'voto, a *ag* (*REL*) devout, pious; (*affezionato*) devoted

devozi'one [devot'tsjone] *sf* devoutness; (*anche REL*) devotion

---

PAROLA CHIAVE

---

di (*di+il* = **del**, *di+lo* = **dello**, *di+l'* = **dell'**, *di+la* = **della**, *di+i* = **dei**, *di+gli* = **degli**, *di+le* = **delle**) *prep* 1 (*possesso, specificazione*) of; (*composto da, scritto da*) by; **la macchina ~ Paolo/mio fratello** Paolo's/my brother's car; **un amico ~ mio fratello** a friend of my brother's, one of my brother's friends; **un quadro ~ Botticelli** a painting by Botticelli

2 (*caratterizzazione, misura*) of; **una casa ~ mattoni** a brick house, a house made of bricks; **un orologio d'oro** a gold watch; **un bimbo ~ 3 anni** a child of 3, a 3-year-old child

3 (*causa, mezzo, modo*) with; **tremare ~ paura** to tremble with fear; **morire ~ cancro** to die of cancer; **spalmare ~ burro** to spread with butter

4 (*argomento*) about, of; **discutere ~ sport** to talk about sport

5 (*luogo: provenienza*) from; out of; **essere ~ Roma** to be from Rome; **uscire ~ casa** to come out of *o* leave the house

6 (*tempo*) in; **d'estate/d'inverno** in (the) summer/winter; **~ notte** by night, at night; **~ mattina/sera** in the morning/evening; **~ lunedì** on Mondays

♦ *det* (*una certa quantità di*) some; (*: negativo*) any; (*: interrogativo*) any, some; **del pane** (some) bread; **delle caramelle** (some) sweets; **degli amici miei** some friends of mine; **vuoi del vino?** do you want some *o* any wine?

---

dia'bete *sm* diabetes *sg*

di'acono *sm* (*REL*) deacon

dia'dema, i *sm* diadem; (*di donna*) tiara

dia'framma, i *sm* (*divisione*) screen; (*ANAT, FOT, contraccettivo*) diaphragm

di'agnosi [di'aɲɲozi] *sf* diagnosis *sg*

diago'nale *ag, sf* diagonal
dia'gramma, i *sm* diagram
dia'letto *sm* dialect
di'alisi *sf* dialysis *sg*
di'alogo, ghi *sm* dialogue
dia'mante *sm* diamond
di'ametro *sm* diameter
di'amine *escl:* **che ~ ...?** what on earth ...?
diaposi'tiva *sf* transparency, slide
di'ario *sm* diary
diar'rea *sf* diarrhoea
di'avolo *sm* devil
di'battere *vt* to debate, discuss; **~rsi** *vr* to struggle; **di'battito** *sm* debate, discussion
dicas'tero *sm* ministry
di'cembre [di'tʃembre] *sm* December
dice'ria [ditʃe'ria] *sf* rumour, piece of gossip
dichia'rare [dikja'rare] *vt* to declare; **dichiarazi'one** *sf* declaration
dician'nove [ditʃan'nɔve] *num* nineteen
dicias'sette [ditʃas'sette] *num* seventeen
dici'otto [di'tʃɔtto] *num* eighteen
dici'tura [ditʃi'tura] *sf* words *pl*, wording
di'eci ['djetʃi] *num* ten; **die'cina** *sf* = **decina**
'diesel ['dizəl] *sm inv* diesel engine
di'eta *sf* diet; **essere a ~** to be on a diet
di'etro *av* behind; (*in fondo*) at the back ♦ *prep* behind; (*tempo: dopo*) after ♦ *sm* back, rear ♦ *ag inv* back *cpd*; **le zampe di ~** the hind legs; **~ richiesta** on demand; (*scritta*) on application
di'fatti *cong* in fact, as a matter of fact
di'fendere *vt* to defend; **difen'sivo, a** *ag* defensive ♦ *sf:* **stare sulla difensiva** (*anche fig*) to be on the defensive; **difen'sore, a** *sm/f* defender; **avvocato difensore** counsel for the defence; **di'fesa** *sf* defence; **di'feso, a** *pp di* **difendere**
difet'tare *vi* to be defective; **~ di** to be lacking in, lack; **difet'tivo, a** *ag* defective
di'fetto *sm* (*mancanza*): **~ di** lack of; shortage of; (*di fabbricazione*) fault, flaw, defect; (*morale*) fault, failing, defect; (*fisico*) defect; **far ~** to be lacking; **in ~** at fault; in the wrong; **difet'toso, a** *ag* defective, faulty

diffa'mare *vt* to slander; to libel
diffe'rente *ag* different
diffe'renza [diffe'rentsa] *sf* difference; **a ~ di** unlike
differenzi'are [differen'tsjare] *vt* to differentiate; **~rsi da** to differentiate o.s. from; to differ from
diffe'rire *vt* to postpone, defer ♦ *vi* to be different
dif'ficile [dif'fitʃile] *ag* difficult; (*persona*) hard to please, difficult (to please); (*poco probabile*): **è ~ che sia libero** it is unlikely that he'll be free ♦ *sm* difficult part; difficulty; **difficoltà** *sf inv* difficulty
dif'fida *sf* (*DIR*) warning, notice
diffi'dare *vi:* **~ di** to be suspicious *o* distrustful of ♦ *vt* (*DIR*) to warn; **~ qn dal fare qc** to warn sb not to do sth, caution sb against doing sth; **diffi'dente** *ag* suspicious, distrustful; **diffi'denza** *sf* suspicion, distrust
dif'fondere *vt* (*luce, calore*) to diffuse; (*notizie*) to spread, circulate; **~rsi** *vr* to spread; **diffusi'one** *sf* diffusion; spread; (*anche di giornale*) circulation; (*FISICA*) scattering; **dif'fuso, a** *pp di* **diffondere** ♦ *ag* (*malattia, fenomeno*) widespread
difi'lato *av* (*direttamente*) straight, directly; (*subito*) straight away
difte'rite *sf* (*MED*) diphtheria
'diga, ghe *sf* dam; (*portuale*) breakwater
dige'rente [didʒe'rente] *ag* (*apparato*) digestive
dige'rire [didʒe'rire] *vt* to digest; **digesti'one** *sf* digestion; **diges'tivo, a** *ag* digestive ♦ *sm* (*after-dinner*) liqueur
digi'tale [didʒi'tale] *ag* digital; (*delle dita*) finger *cpd*, digital ♦ *sf* (*BOT*) foxglove
digi'tare [didʒi'tare] *vt, vi* (*INFORM*) to key (in)
digiu'nare [didʒu'nare] *vi* to starve o.s.; (*REL*) to fast; **digi'uno, a** *ag:* **essere digiuno** not to have eaten ♦ *sm* fast; **a digiuno** on an empty stomach
dignità [diɲɲi'ta] *sf inv* dignity; **digni'toso, a** *ag* dignified
'DIGOS ['digɔs] *sigla f* (= *Divisione*

Investigazioni Generali e Operazioni Speciali) police department dealing with political security

digri'gnare [digriɲˈɲare] *vt*: ~ **i denti** to grind one's teeth

dila'gare *vi* to flood; *(fig)* to spread

dilani'are *vt (preda)* to tear to pieces

dilapi'dare *vt* to squander, waste

dila'tare *vt* to dilate; *(gas)* to cause to expand; *(passaggio, cavità)* to open (up); **~rsi** *vr* to dilate; *(FISICA)* to expand

dilazio'nare [dilattsjoˈnare] *vt* to delay, defer; **dilazi'one** *sf* delay; *(COMM: di pagamento etc)* extension; *(rinvio)* postponement

dilegu'are *vi* to vanish, disappear; **~rsi** *vr* to vanish, disappear

di'lemma, i *sm* dilemma

dilet'tante *sm/f* dilettante; *(anche SPORT)* amateur

dilet'tare *vt* to give pleasure to, delight; **~rsi** *vr*: **~rsi di** to take pleasure in, enjoy

di'letto, a *ag* dear, beloved ♦ *sm* pleasure, delight

dili'gente [diliˈdʒente] *ag (scrupoloso)* diligent; *(accurato)* careful, accurate; **dili'genza** *sf* diligence; care; *(carrozza)* stagecoach

dilu'ire *vt* to dilute

dilun'garsi *vr (fig)*: ~ **su** to talk at length on *o* about

diluvi'are *vb impers* to pour (down)

di'luvio *sm* downpour; *(inondazione, fig)* flood

dima'grire *vi* to get thinner, lose weight

dime'nare *vt* to wave, shake; **~rsi** *vr* to toss and turn; *(fig)* to struggle; ~ **la coda** *(sog: cane)* to wag its tail

dimensi'one *sf* dimension; *(grandezza)* size

dimenti'canza [dimentiˈkantsa] *sf* forgetfulness; *(errore)* oversight, slip; **per ~** inadvertently

dimenti'care *vt* to forget; **~rsi di qc** to forget sth

di'messo, a *pp di* **dimettere** ♦ *ag (voce)* subdued; *(uomo, abito)* modest, humble

dimesti'chezza [dimestiˈkettsa] *sf* familiarity

di'mettere *vt*: ~ **qn da** to dismiss sb from; *(dall'ospedale)* to discharge sb from; **~rsi (da)** to resign (from)

dimez'zare [dimedˈdzare] *vt* to halve

diminu'ire *vt* to reduce, diminish; *(prezzi)* to bring down, reduce ♦ *vi* to decrease, diminish; *(rumore)* to die down, die away; *(prezzi)* to fall, go down; **diminuzi'one** *sf* decreasing, diminishing

dimissi'oni *sfpl* resignation *sg*; **dare** *o* **presentare le ~** to resign, hand in one's resignation

di'mora *sf* residence

dimo'rare *vi* to reside

dimos'trare *vt* to demonstrate, show; *(provare)* to prove, demonstrate; **~rsi** *vr*: **~rsi molto abile** to show o.s. *o* prove to be very clever; **dimostra 30 anni** he looks about 30 (years old); **dimostrazi'one** *sf* demonstration; proof

di'namica *sf* dynamics *sg*

di'namico, a, ci, che *ag* dynamic

dina'mite *sf* dynamite

'dinamo *sf inv* dynamo

di'nanzi [diˈnantsi]: ~ **a** *prep* in front of

dini'ego, ghi *sm* refusal; denial

dinocco'lato, a *ag* lanky

din'torno *av* round, (round) about; **~i** *smpl* outskirts; **nei ~i di** in the vicinity *o* neighbourhood of

'dio *(pl* **'dei)** *sm* god; **D~** God; **gli dei** the gods; **D~ mio!** my goodness!, my God!

di'ocesi [diˈɔtʃezi] *sf inv* diocese

dipa'nare *vt (lana)* to wind into a ball; *(fig)* to disentangle, sort out

diparti'mento *sm* department

dipen'dente *ag* dependent ♦ *sm/f* employee; **dipen'denza** *sf* dependence; **essere alle dipendenze di qn** to be employed by sb *o* in sb's employ

di'pendere *vi*: ~ **da** to depend on; *(finanziariamente)* to be dependent on; *(derivare)* to come from, be due to; **di'peso, a** *pp di* **dipendere**

di'pingere [diˈpindʒere] *vt* to paint;

di'pinto, a *pp di* **dipingere** ♦ *sm* painting
di'ploma, i *sm* diploma
diplo'mare *vt* to award a diploma to,
graduate (*US*); **~rsi** *vr* to obtain a diploma,
graduate (*US*)
diplo'matico, a, ci, che *ag* diplomatic
♦ *sm* diplomat
diploma'zia [diplomat'tsia] *sf* diplomacy
di'porto : imbarcazione da ~ *sf* pleasure
craft
dira'dare *vt* to thin (out); (*visite*) to
reduce, make less frequent; **~rsi** *vr* to
disperse; (*nebbia*) to clear (up)
dira'mare *vt* to issue ♦ *vi* (*strade*) to
branch; **~rsi** *vr* to branch
'dire *vt* to say; (*segreto, fatto*) to tell; **~ qc a
qn** to tell sb sth; **~ a qn di fare qc** to tell
sb to do sth; **~ di sì/no** to say yes/no; **si
dice che ...** they say that ...; **si direbbe
che ...** it looks (*o* sounds) as though ...;
dica, signora? (*in un negozio*) yes,
Madam, can I help you?
di'retto, a *pp di* **dirigere** ♦ *ag* direct ♦ *sm*
(*FERR*) through train
diret'tore, 'trice *sm/f* (*di azienda*)
director; manager/ess; (*di scuola
elementare*) head (teacher) (*BRIT*), principal
(*US*); **~ d'orchestra** conductor; **~ vendite**
sales director *o* manager
direzi'one [diret'tsjone] *sf* board of
directors; management; (*senso di
movimento*) direction; **in ~ di** in the
direction of, towards
diri'gente [diri'dʒɛnte] *sm/f* executive; (*POL*)
leader ♦ *ag*: **classe ~** ruling class
di'rigere [di'ridʒere] *vt* to direct; (*impresa*)
to run, manage; (*MUS*) to conduct; **~rsi** *vr*:
~rsi verso *o* **a** to make *o* head for
dirim'petto *av* opposite; **~ a** opposite,
facing
di'ritto, a *ag* straight; (*onesto*) straight,
upright ♦ *av* straight, directly; **andare ~** to
go straight on ♦ *sm* right side; (*TENNIS*)
forehand; (*MAGLIA*) plain stitch; (*prerogativa*)
right; (*leggi, scienza*): **il ~** law; **~i** *smpl*
(*tasse*) duty *sg*; **stare ~** to stand up
straight; **aver ~ a qc** to be entitled to sth;

~i d'autore royalties
dirit'tura *sf* (*SPORT*) straight; (*fig*) rectitude
diroc'cato, a *ag* tumbledown, in ruins
dirot'tare *vt* (*nave, aereo*) to change the
course of; (*aereo: sotto minaccia*) to hijack;
(*traffico*) to divert ♦ *vi* (*nave, aereo*) to
change course; **dirotta'tore, 'trice** *sm/f*
hijacker
di'rotto, a *ag* (*pioggia*) torrential; (*pianto*)
unrestrained; **piovere a ~** to pour;
piangere a ~ to cry one's heart out
di'rupo *sm* crag, precipice
disabi'tato, a *ag* uninhabited
disabitu'arsi *vr*: **~ a** to get out of the
habit of
disac'cordo *sm* disagreement
disadat'tato, a *ag* (*PSIC*) maladjusted
disa'dorno, a *ag* plain, unadorned
disagi'ato, a [diza'dʒato] *ag* poor, needy;
(*vita*) hard
di'sagio [di'zadʒo] *sm* discomfort; (*disturbo*)
inconvenience; (*fig: imbarazzo*)
embarrassment; **essere a ~** to be ill at ease
disappro'vare *vt* to disapprove of;
disapprovazi'one *sf* disapproval
disap'punto *sm* disappointment
disar'mare *vt, vi* to disarm; **di'sarmo** *sm*
(*MIL*) disarmament
di'sastro *sm* disaster
disat'tento, a *ag* inattentive;
disattenzi'one *sf* carelessness, lack of
attention
disa'vanzo [diza'vantso] *sm* (*ECON*) deficit
disavven'tura *sf* misadventure, mishap
dis'brigo, ghi *sm* (*prompt*) clearing up *o*
settlement
dis'capito *sm*: **a ~ di** to the detriment of
dis'carica, che *sf* (*di rifiuti*) rubbish tip *o*
dump
discen'dente [diʃʃen'dɛnte] *ag* descending
♦ *sm/f* descendant
di'scendere [diʃ'ʃɛndere] *vt* to go (*o come*)
down ♦ *vi* to go (*o come*) down; (*strada*)
to go down; (*smontare*) to get off; **~ da**
(*famiglia*) to be descended from; **~ dalla
macchina/dal treno** to get out of the
car/out of *o* off the train; **~ da cavallo** to

dismount, get off one's horse

di'scepolo, a [diʃʃepolo] *sm/f* disciple

di'scernere [diʃʃɛrnere] *vt* to discern

di'scesa [diʃʃesa] *sf* descent; (*pendio*) slope; **in ~** (*strada*) downhill *cpd*, sloping; ~ **libera** (*SCI*) downhill (race)

di'sceso, a [diʃʃeso] *pp di* **discendere**

disci'ogliere [diʃʃɔʎʎere] *vt* to dissolve; (*fondere*) to melt; ~**rsi** *vr* to dissolve; to melt; **disci'olto, a** *pp di* **disciogliere**

disci'plina [diʃʃiplina] *sf* discipline; **discipli'nare** *ag* disciplinary ♦ *vt* to discipline

'disco, schi *sm* disc; (*SPORT*) discus; (*fonografico*) record; (*INFORM*) disk; ~ **orario** (*AUT*) parking disc; ~ **rigido** (*INFORM*) hard disk; ~ **volante** flying saucer

discol'pare *vt* to clear of blame

disco'noscere [diskonoʃʃere] *vt* (*figlio*) to disown; (*meriti*) to ignore, disregard; **disconosci'uto, a** *pp di* **disconoscere**

dis'corde *ag* conflicting, clashing; **dis'cordia** *sf* discord; (*dissidio*) disagreement, clash

dis'correre *vi*: ~ **(di)** to talk (about)

dis'corso, a *pp di* **discorrere** ♦ *sm* speech; (*conversazione*) conversation, talk

dis'costo, a *ag* faraway, distant ♦ *av* far away; ~ **da** far from

disco'teca, che *sf* (*raccolta*) record library; (*locale*) disco

discre'panza [diskre'pantsa] *sf* disagreement

dis'creto, a *ag* discreet; (*abbastanza buono*) reasonable, fair; **discrezi'one** *sf* discretion; (*giudizio*) judgment, discernment; **a discrezione di** at the discretion of

discriminazi'one [diskriminat'tsjone] *sf* discrimination

discussi'one *sf* discussion; (*litigio*) argument; **fuori ~** out of the question

dis'cusso, a *pp di* **discutere**

dis'cutere *vt* to discuss, debate; (*contestare*) to question ♦ *vi* (*conversare*): ~ **(di)** to discuss; (*litigare*) to argue

disde'gnare [disde'ɲɲare] *vt* to scorn

dis'detta *sf* (*di prenotazione etc*) cancellation; (*sfortuna*) bad luck

dis'detto, a *pp di* **disdire**

dis'dire *vt* (*prenotazione*) to cancel; (*DIR*): ~ **un contratto d'affitto** to give notice (to quit)

dise'gnare [disen'ɲare] *vt* to draw; (*progettare*) to design; (*fig*) to outline

disegna'tore, 'trice *sm/f* designer

di'segno [di'seɲɲo] *sm* drawing; design; outline; ~ **di legge** (*DIR*) bill

diser'bante *sm* weed-killer

diser'tare *vt, vi* to desert; **diser'tore** *sm* (*MIL*) deserter

dis'fare *vt* to undo; (*valigie*) to unpack; (*meccanismo*) to take to pieces; (*neve*) to melt; ~**rsi** *vr* to come undone; (*neve*) to melt; ~ **il letto** to strip the bed; ~**rsi di qn** (*liberarsi*) to get rid of sb; **dis'fatta** *sf* (*sconfitta*) rout; **dis'fatto, a** *pp di* **disfare**

dis'gelo [diz'dʒelo] *sm* thaw

dis'grazia [diz'grattsja] *sf* (*sventura*) misfortune; (*incidente*) accident, mishap; **disgrazi'ato, a** *ag* unfortunate ♦ *sm/f* wretch

disgre'gare *vt* to break up; ~**rsi** *vr* to break up

disgu'ido *sm* hitch; ~ **postale** error in postal delivery

disgus'tare *vt* to disgust; ~**rsi** *vr*: ~**rsi di** to be disgusted by

dis'gusto *sm* disgust; **disgus'toso, a** *ag* disgusting

disidra'tare *vt* to dehydrate

disil'ludere *vt* to disillusion, disenchant

disimpa'rare *vt* to forget

disinfet'tante *ag, sm* disinfectant

disinfet'tare *vt* to disinfect

disini'bito, a *ag* uninhibited

disinte'grare *vt, vi* to disintegrate

disinteres'sarsi *vr*: ~ **di** to take no interest in

disinte'resse *sm* indifference; (*generosità*) unselfishness

disintossi'care *vt* (*alcolizzato, drogato*) to treat for alcoholism (*o* drug addiction); ~ **l'organismo** to clear out one's system

disin'volto, a *ag* casual, free and easy; **disinvol'tura** *sf* casualness, ease

disles'sia *sf* dyslexia

dislo'care *vt* to station, position

dismi'sura *sf* excess; **a ~** to excess, excessively

disobbe'dire *etc* = **disubbidire** *etc*

disoccu'pato, a *ag* unemployed ♦ *sm/f* unemployed person; **disoccupazi'one** *sf* unemployment

diso'nesto, a *ag* dishonest

diso'nore *sm* dishonour, disgrace

di'sopra *av* (*con contatto*) on top; (*senza contatto*) above; (*al piano superiore*) upstairs ♦ *ag inv* (*superiore*) upper ♦ *sm inv* top, upper part

disordi'nato, a *ag* untidy; (*privo di misura*) irregular, wild

di'sordine *sm* (*confusione*) disorder, confusion; (*sregolatezza*) debauchery

disorien'tare *vt* to disorientate; **~rsi** *vr* (*fig*) to get confused, lose one's bearings

di'sotto *av* below, underneath; (*in fondo*) at the bottom; (*al piano inferiore*) downstairs ♦ *ag inv* (*inferiore*) lower; bottom *cpd* ♦ *sm inv* (*parte inferiore*) lower part; bottom

dis'paccio [dis'pattʃo] *sm* dispatch

'dispari *ag inv* odd, uneven

dis'parte: in ~ *av* (*da lato*) aside, apart; **tenersi** *o* **starsene in ~** to keep to o.s., hold o.s. aloof

dispendi'oso, a *ag* expensive

dis'pensa *sf* pantry, larder; (*mobile*) sideboard; (*DIR*) exemption; (*REL*) dispensation; (*fascicolo*) number, issue

dispen'sare *vt* (*elemosine, favori*) to distribute; (*esonerare*) to exempt

dispe'rare *vi*: ~ (**di**) to despair (of); **~rsi** *vr* to despair; **dispe'rato, a** *ag* (*persona*) in despair; (*caso, tentativo*) desperate; **disperazi'one** *sf* despair

dis'perdere *vt* (*disseminare*) to disperse; (*MIL*) to scatter, rout; (*fig: consumare*) to waste, squander; **~rsi** *vr* to disperse; to scatter; **dis'perso, a** *pp di* **disperdere** ♦ *sm/f* missing person

dis'petto *sm* spite *no pl*, spitefulness *no pl*; **fare un ~ a qn** to play a (nasty) trick on sb; **a ~ di** in spite of; **dispet'toso, a** *ag* spiteful

dispia'cere [dispja'tʃere] *sm* (*rammarico*) regret, sorrow; (*dolore*) grief; **~i** *smpl* (*preoccupazioni*) troubles, worries ♦ *vi*: ~ **a** to displease ♦ *vb impers*: **mi dispiace (che)** I am sorry (that); **se non le dispiace, me ne vado adesso** if you don't mind, I'll go now; **dispiaci'uto, a** *pp di* **dispiacere** ♦ *ag* sorry

dispo'nibile *ag* available; **disponibilità** *sf inv* (*di biglietti, camere*) availability; (*gentilezza*) helpfulness; (*spec pl: FIN*) liquid assets *pl*

dis'porre *vt* (*sistemare*) to arrange; (*preparare*) to prepare; (*DIR*) to order; (*persuadere*): ~ **qn a** to incline *o* dispose sb towards ♦ *vi* (*decidere*) to decide; (*usufruire*): ~ **di** to use, have at one's disposal; (*essere dotato*): ~ **di** to have; **disporsi** *vr* (*ordinarsi*) to place o.s., arrange o.s.

disposi'tivo *sm* (*meccanismo*) device

disposizi'one [dispozit'tsjone] *sf* arrangement, layout; (*stato d'animo*) mood; (*tendenza*) bent, inclination; (*comando*) order; (*DIR*) provision, regulation; **a ~ di qn** at sb's disposal

dis'posto, a *pp di* **disporre**

disprez'zare [dispret'tsare] *vt* to despise

dis'prezzo [dis'prettso] *sm* contempt

'disputa *sf* dispute, quarrel

dispu'tare *vt* (*contendere*) to dispute, contest; (*gara*) to take part in ♦ *vi* to quarrel; ~ **di** to discuss; **~rsi qc** to fight for sth

dissan'guare *vt* (*fig: persona*) to bleed white; (: *patrimonio*) to suck dry; **~rsi** *vr* (*MED*) to lose blood; (*fig: rovinarsi*) to ruin o.s.

dissec'care *vt* to dry up; **~rsi** *vr* to dry up

dissemi'nare *vt* to scatter; (*fig: notizie*) to spread

dis'senso *sm* dissent; (*disapprovazione*) disapproval

dissente'ria _sf_ dysentery
dissen'tire _vi_: ~ **(da)** to disagree (with)
dissertazi'one [dissertat'tsjone] _sf_
dissertation
disser'vizio [disser'vittsjo] _sm_ inefficiency
disses'tare _vt_ (_ECON_) to ruin; **dis'sesto**
_sm_ (financial) ruin
disse'tante _ag_ refreshing
dis'sidio _sm_ disagreement
dis'simile _ag_ different, dissimilar
dissimu'lare _vt_ (_fingere_) to dissemble;
(_nascondere_) to conceal
dissi'pare _vt_ to dissipate; (_scialacquare_) to
squander, waste
dis'solto, a _pp di_ **dissolvere**
disso'luto, a _pp di_ **dissolvere** ♦ _ag_
dissolute, licentious
dis'solvere _vt_ to dissolve; (_neve_) to melt;
(_fumo_) to disperse; **~rsi** _vr_ to dissolve; to
melt; to disperse
dissu'adere _vt_: ~ **qn da** to dissuade sb
from; **dissu'aso, a** _pp di_ **dissuadere**
distac'care _vt_ to detach, separate; (_SPORT_)
to leave behind; **~rsi** _vr_ to be detached;
(_fig_) to stand out; **~rsi da** (_fig: allontanarsi_)
to grow away from
dis'tacco, chi _sm_ (_separazione_)
separation; (_fig: indifferenza_) detachment;
(_SPORT_): **vincere con un ~ di ...** to win by
a distance of ...
dis'tante _av_ far away ♦ _ag_: ~ **(da)** distant
(from), far away (from)
dis'tanza [dis'tantsa] _sf_ distance
distanzi'are [distan'tsjare] _vt_ to space out,
place at intervals; (_SPORT_) to outdistance;
(_fig: superare_) to outstrip, surpass
dis'tare _vi_: **distiamo pochi chilometri da
Roma** we are only a few kilometres (away)
from Rome
dis'tendere _vt_ (_coperta_) to spread out;
(_gambe_) to stretch (out); (_mettere a giacere_)
to lay; (_rilassare: muscoli, nervi_) to relax;
~rsi _vr_ (_rilassarsi_) to relax; (_sdraiarsi_) to lie
down; **disten'sione** _sf_ stretching;
relaxation; (_POL_) détente
dis'tesa _sf_ expanse, stretch
dis'teso, a _pp di_ **distendere**

distil'lare _vt_ to distil
distille'ria _sf_ distillery
dis'tinguere _vt_ to distinguish
dis'tinta _sf_ (_nota_) note; (_elenco_) list
distin'tivo, a _ag_ distinctive; distinguishing
♦ _sm_ badge
dis'tinto, a _pp di_ **distinguere** ♦ _ag_
(_dignitoso ed elegante_) distinguished; **~i
saluti** (_in lettera_) yours faithfully
distinzi'one [distin'tsjone] _sf_ distinction
dis'togliere [dis'tɔʎʎere] _vt_: ~ **da** to take
away from; (_fig_) to dissuade from;
dis'tolto, a _pp di_ **distogliere**
distorsi'one _sf_ (_MED_) sprain; (_FISICA,
OTTICA_) distortion
dis'trarre _vt_ to distract; (_divertire_) to
entertain, amuse; **distrarsi** _vr_ (_non fare
attenzione_) to be distracted, let one's mind
wander; (_svagarsi_) to amuse _o_ enjoy o.s.;
dis'tratto, a _pp di_ **distrarre** ♦ _ag_ absent-
minded; (_disattento_) inattentive;
distrazi'one _sf_ absent-mindedness;
inattention; (_svago_) distraction,
entertainment
dis'tretto _sm_ district
distribu'ire _vt_ to distribute; (_CARTE_) to
deal (out); (_posta_) to deliver; (_lavoro_) to
allocate, assign; (_ripartire_) to share out;
distribu'tore _sm_ (_di benzina_) petrol (_BRIT_)
_o_ gas (_US_) pump; (_AUT, ELETTR_) distributor;
(_automatico_) vending machine;
distribuzi'one _sf_ distribution; delivery
distri'care _vt_ to disentangle, unravel
dis'truggere [dis'truddʒere] _vt_ to destroy;
dis'trutto, a _pp di_ **distruggere**;
distruzi'one _sf_ destruction
distur'bare _vt_ to disturb, trouble; (_sonno,
lezioni_) to disturb, interrupt; **~rsi** _vr_ to put
o.s. out
dis'turbo _sm_ trouble, bother,
inconvenience; (_indisposizione_) (slight)
disorder, ailment; **~i** _smpl_ (_RADIO, TV_) static
_sg_
disubbidi'ente _ag_ disobedient;
disubbidi'enza _sf_ disobedience
disubbi'dire _vi_: ~ **(a qn)** to disobey (sb)
disugu'ale _ag_ unequal; (_diverso_) different;

(*irregolare*) uneven

disu'mano, a *ag* inhuman

di'suso *sm*: andare *o* cadere in ~ to fall into disuse

'dita *fpl di* dito

di'tale *sm* thimble

'dito (*pl(f)* 'dita) *sm* finger; (*misura*) finger, finger's breadth; ~ (del piede) toe

'ditta *sf* firm, business

ditta'tore *sm* dictator

ditta'tura *sf* dictatorship

dit'tongo, ghi *sm* diphthong

di'urno, a *ag* day *cpd*, daytime *cpd*

'diva *sf vedi* divo

diva'gare *vi* to digress

divam'pare *vi* to flare up, blaze up

di'vano *sm* sofa; divan

divari'care *vt* to open wide

di'vario *sm* difference

dive'nire *vi* = diventare

diven'tare *vi* to become; ~ famoso/professore to become famous/a teacher

dive'nuto, a *pp di* divenire

di'verbio *sm* altercation

di'vergere [di'vɛrdʒere] *vi* to diverge

diversifi'care *vt* to diversify, vary; to differentiate

diversi'one *sf* diversion

diversità *sf inv* difference, diversity; (*varietà*) variety

diver'sivo *sm* diversion, distraction

di'verso, a *ag* (*differente*): ~ (da) different (from); ~i, e *det pl* several, various; (*COMM*) sundry ♦ *pron pl* several (people), many (people)

diver'tente *ag* amusing

diverti'mento *sm* amusement, pleasure; (*passatempo*) pastime, recreation

diver'tire *vt* to amuse, entertain; ~rsi *vr* to amuse *o* enjoy o.s.

divi'dendo *sm* dividend

di'videre *vt* (*anche MAT*) to divide; (*distribuire, ripartire*) to divide (up), split (up); ~rsi *vr* (*separarsi*) to separate; (*strade*) to fork

divi'eto *sm* prohibition; "~ di sosta" (*AUT*) "no parking"

divinco'larsi *vr* to wriggle, writhe

divinità *sf inv* divinity

di'vino, a *ag* divine

di'visa *sf* (*MIL etc*) uniform; (*COMM*) foreign currency

divisi'one *sf* division

di'viso, a *pp di* dividere

'divo, a *sm/f* star

divo'rare *vt* to devour

divorzi'are [divor'tsjare] *vi*: ~ (da qn) to divorce (sb); divorzi'ato, a *sm/f* divorcee

di'vorzio [di'vortsjo] *sm* divorce

divul'gare *vt* to divulge, disclose; (*rendere comprensibile*) to popularize; ~rsi *vr* to spread

dizio'nario [ditsjo'narjo] *sm* dictionary

dizi'one [dit'tsjone] *sf* diction; pronunciation

do *sm* (*MUS*) C; (: *solfeggiando*) do(h)

DOC [dɔk] *abbr* (= *denominazione di origine controllata*) label guaranteeing the quality of wine

'doccia, ce ['dottʃa] *sf* (*bagno*) shower; fare la ~ to have a shower

do'cente [do'tʃɛnte] *ag* teaching ♦ *sm/f* teacher; (*di università*) lecturer

'docile ['dɔtʃile] *ag* docile

documen'tare *vt* to document; ~rsi *vr*: ~rsi (su) to gather information *o* material (about)

documen'tario *sm* documentary

docu'mento *sm* document; ~i *smpl* (*d'identità etc*) papers

'dodici ['doditʃi] *num* twelve

do'gana *sf* (*ufficio*) customs *pl*; (*tassa*) (customs) duty; passare la ~ to go through customs; doga'nale *ag* customs *cpd*; dogani'ere *sm* customs officer

'doglie ['dɔʎʎe] *sfpl* (*MED*) labour *sg*, labour pains

'dolce ['doltʃe] *ag* sweet; (*carattere, persona*) gentle, mild; (*fig: mite: clima*) mild; (*non ripido: pendio*) gentle ♦ *sm* (*sapore dolce*) sweetness, sweet taste; (*CUC: portata*) sweet, dessert; (: *torta*) cake; dol'cezza *sf* sweetness; softness; mildness; gentleness; dolcifi'cante *sm* sweetener; dolci'umi *smpl* sweets

do'lente *ag* sorrowful, sad

do'lere *vi* to be sore, hurt, ache; ~rsi *vr* to complain; (*essere spiacente*): ~rsi di to be sorry for; mi duole la testa my head aches, I've got a headache

'dollaro *sm* dollar

'dolo *sm* (*DIR*) malice

Dolo'miti *sfpl*: le ~ the Dolomites

do'lore *sm* (*fisico*) pain; (*morale*) sorrow, grief; dolo'roso, a *ag* painful; sorrowful, sad

do'loso, a *ag* (*DIR*) malicious

do'manda *sf* question; (*richiesta*) demand; (*: cortese*) request; (*DIR: richiesta scritta*) application; (*ECON*): la ~ demand; fare una ~ a qn to ask sb a question; fare ~ (per un lavoro) to apply (for a job)

doman'dare *vt* (*per avere*) to ask for; (*per sapere*) to ask; (*esigere*) to demand; ~rsi *vr* to wonder; ~ qc a qn to ask sb for sth; to ask sb sth

do'mani *av* tomorrow ♦ *sm*: il ~ (*il futuro*) the future; (*il giorno successivo*) the next day; ~ l'altro the day after tomorrow

do'mare *vt* to tame

domat'tina *av* tomorrow morning

do'menica, che *sf* Sunday; di *o* la ~ on Sundays; domeni'cale *ag* Sunday *cpd*

do'mestica, che *sf vedi* domestico

do'mestico, a, ci, che *ag* domestic ♦ *sm/f* servant, domestic

domi'cilio [domi'tʃiljo] *sm* (*DIR*) domicile, place of residence

domi'nare *vt* to dominate; (*fig: sentimenti*) to control, master ♦ *vi* to be in the dominant position; ~rsi *vr* (*controllarsi*) to control o.s.; ~ su (*fig*) to surpass, outclass; dominazi'one *sf* domination

do'minio *sm* dominion; (*fig: campo*) field, domain

do'nare *vt* to give, present; (*per beneficenza etc*) to donate ♦ *vi* (*fig*): ~ a to suit, become; ~ sangue to give blood; dona'tore, 'trice *sm/f* donor; donatore di sangue/di organi blood/organ donor

dondo'lare *vt* (*cullare*) to rock; ~rsi *vr* to

swing, sway; 'dondolo *sm*: sedia / cavallo a dondolo rocking chair/horse

'donna *sf* woman; ~ di casa housewife; home-loving woman; ~ di servizio maid

donnai'olo *sm* ladykiller

'donnola *sf* weasel

'dono *sm* gift

'doping *sm inv* drug abuse

'dopo *av* (*tempo*) afterwards; (*: più tardi*) later; (*luogo*) after, next ♦ *prep* after ♦ *cong* (*temporale*): ~ mangiato va a dormire after having eaten *o* after a meal he goes for a sleep ♦ *ag inv*: il giorno ~ the following day; un anno ~ a year later; ~ di me / lui after me/him

dopo'barba *sm inv* after-shave

dopodo'mani *av* the day after tomorrow

dopogu'erra *sm* postwar years *pl*

dopo'pranzo [dopo'prandzo] *av* after lunch (*o* dinner)

doposcì [dopoʃˈʃi] *sm inv* après-ski outfit

doposcu'ola *sm inv* school club offering extra tuition and recreational facilities

dopo'sole *sm inv* aftersun (lotion) ♦ *ag inv* aftersun

dopo'tutto *av* (*tutto considerato*) after all

doppi'aggio [dop'pjaddʒo] *sm* (*CINEMA*) dubbing

doppi'are *vt* (*NAUT*) to round; (*SPORT*) to lap; (*CINEMA*) to dub

'doppio, a *ag* double; (*fig: falso*) double-dealing, deceitful ♦ *sm* (*quantità*): il ~ (di) twice as much (*o* many), double the amount (*o* number) of; (*SPORT*) doubles *pl* ♦ *av* double

doppi'one *sm* duplicate (copy)

doppio'petto *sm* double-breasted jacket

do'rare *vt* to gild; (*CUC*) to brown; do'rato, a *ag* golden; (*ricoperto d'oro*) gilt, gilded; dora'tura *sf* gilding

dormicchi'are [dormik'kjare] *vi* to doze

dormigli'one, a [dormiʎˈʎone] *sm/f* sleepyhead

dor'mire *vt, vi* to sleep; andare a ~ to go to bed; dor'mita *sf*: farsi una dormita to have a good sleep

dormi'torio *sm* dormitory

dormi'veglia [dormi'veʎʎa] *sm* drowsiness

'**dorso** *sm* back; (*di montagna*) ridge, crest; (*di libro*) spine; **a ~ di cavallo** on horseback

do'sare *vt* to measure out; (*MED*) to dose

'**dose** *sf* quantity, amount; (*MED*) dose

'**dosso** *sm* (*rilievo*) rise; (*di strada*) bump; (*dorso*): **levarsi di ~ i vestiti** to take one's clothes off

do'tare *vt*: **~ di** to provide *o* supply with; **dotazi'one** *sf* (*insieme di beni*) endowment; (*di macchine etc*) equipment

'**dote** *sf* (*di sposa*) dowry; (*assegnata a un ente*) endowment; (*fig*) gift, talent

Dott. *abbr* (= *dottore*) Dr.

'**dotto, a** *ag* (*colto*) learned ♦ *sm* (*sapiente*) scholar; (*ANAT*) duct

dotto'rato *sm* degree; **~ di ricerca** doctorate, doctor's degree

dot'tore, essa *sm/f* doctor

dot'trina *sf* doctrine

Dott.ssa *abbr* (= *dottoressa*) Dr.

'**dove** *av* (*gen*) where; (*in cui*) where, in which; (*dovunque*) wherever ♦ *cong* (*mentre, laddove*) whereas; **~ sei?/vai?** where are you?/are you going?; **dimmi dov'è** tell me where it is; **di ~ sei?** where are you from?; **per ~ si passa?** which way should we go?; **la città ~ abito** the town where *o* in which I live; **siediti ~ vuoi** sit wherever you like

do'vere *sm* (*obbligo*) duty ♦ *vt* (*essere debitore*): **~ qc (a qn)** to owe (sb) sth ♦ *vi* (*seguito dall'infinito: obbligo*) to have to; **rivolgersi a chi di ~** to apply to the appropriate authority *o* person; **lui deve farlo** he has to do it, he must do it; **è dovuto partire** he had to leave; **ha dovuto pagare** he had to pay; (: *intenzione*): **devo partire domani** I'm (due) to leave tomorrow; (: *probabilità*): **dev'essere tardi** it must be late; **come si deve** (*lavorare, comportarsi*) properly; **una persona come si deve** a respectable person

dove'roso, a *ag* (right and) proper

do'vunque *av* (*in qualunque luogo*) wherever; (*dappertutto*) everywhere; **~ io**

vada wherever I go

do'vuto, a *ag* (*causato*): **~ a** due to

doz'zina [dod'dzina] *sf* dozen; **una ~ di uova** a dozen eggs

dozzi'nale [doddzi'nale] *ag* cheap, second-rate

dra'gare *vt* to dredge

'**drago, ghi** *sm* dragon

'**dramma, i** [dre'dramma] *sm* drama; **dram'matico, a, ci, che** *ag* dramatic; **drammatiz'zare** *vt* to dramatize; **dramma'turgo, ghi** *sm* playwright, dramatist

drappeggi'are [draped'dʒare] *vt* to drape

drap'pello *sm* (*MIL*) squad; (*gruppo*) band, group

'**drastico, a, ci, che** *ag* drastic

dre'naggio [dre'naddʒo] *sm* drainage

dre'nare *vt* to drain

'**dritto, a** *ag, av* = **diritto**

driz'zare [drit'tsare] *vt* (*far tornare dritto*) to straighten; (*innalzare: antenna, muro*) to erect; **~rsi** *vr*: **~rsi (in piedi)** to stand up; **~ le orecchie** to prick up one's ears

'**droga, ghe** *sf* (*sostanza aromatica*) spice; (*stupefacente*) drug; **dro'gare** *vt* to season, spice; to drug, dope; **drogarsi** *vr* to take drugs; **dro'gato, a** *sm/f* drug addict

droghe'ria [droge'ria] *sf* grocer's shop (*BRIT*), grocery (store) (*US*)

DS *sigla mpl* = **Democratici di Sinistra**

'**dubbio, a** *ag* (*incerto*) doubtful, dubious; (*ambiguo*) dubious ♦ *sm* (*incertezza*) doubt; **avere il ~ che** to be afraid that, suspect that; **mettere in ~ qc** to question sth; **dubbi'oso, a** *ag* doubtful, dubious

dubi'tare *vi*: **~ di** to doubt; (*risultato*) to be doubtful of

Dub'lino *sf* Dublin

'**duca, chi** *sm* duke

du'chessa [du'kessa] *sf* duchess

'**due** *num* two

due'cento [due'tʃento] *num* two hundred

due'pezzi [due'pettsi] *sm* (*costume da bagno*) two-piece swimsuit; (*abito femminile*) two-piece suit

du'etto *sm* duet

'dunque *cong* (*perciò*) so, therefore; (*riprendendo il discorso*) well (then) ♦ *sm inv*: **venire al ~** to come to the point

du'omo *sm* cathedral

'duplex *sm inv* (*TEL*) party line

dupli'cato *sm* duplicate

'duplice ['duplitʃe] *ag* double, twofold; **in ~ copia** in duplicate

du'rante *prep* during

du'rare *vi* to last; **~ fatica a** to have difficulty in; du'rata *sf* length (of time); duration; dura'turo, a *ag* lasting

du'rezza [du'rettsa] *sf* hardness; stubbornness; harshness; toughness

'duro, a *ag* (*pietra, lavoro, materasso, problema*) hard; (*persona: ostinato*) stubborn, obstinate; (*: severo*) harsh, hard; (*voce*) harsh; (*carne*) tough ♦ *sm* hardness; (*difficoltà*) hard part; (*persona*) tough guy; **tener ~** to stand firm, hold out; **~ d'orecchi** hard of hearing

du'rone *sm* hard skin

DVD *sigla m* (= *digital versatile* (*or*) *video disc*) DVD

E, e

e (*dav V spesso* ed) *cong* and; **~ lui?** what about him?; **~ compralo!** well buy it then!

E. *abbr* (= *est*) E

è *vb vedi* essere

'ebano *sm* ebony

eb'bene *cong* well (then)

eb'brezza [eb'brettsa] *sf* intoxication

'ebbro, a *ag* drunk; **~ di** (*gioia etc*) beside o.s. *o* wild with

'ebete *ag* stupid, idiotic

ebollizi'one [ebolliţ'tsjone] *sf* boiling; **punto di ~** boiling point

e'braico, a, ci, che *ag* Hebrew, Hebraic ♦ *sm* (*LING*) Hebrew

e'breo, a *ag* Jewish ♦ *sm/f* Jew/Jewess

'Ebridi *sfpl*: **le (isole) ~** the Hebrides

ecc *av abbr* (= *eccetera*) etc

ecce'denza [ettʃe'dɛntsa] *sf* excess, surplus

ec'cedere [et'tʃedere] *vt* to exceed ♦ *vi* to go too far; **~ nel bere/mangiare** to indulge in drink/food to excess

eccel'lente [ettʃel'lɛnte] *ag* excellent; eccel'lenza *sf* excellence; (*titolo*) Excellency

ec'cellere [et'tʃellere] *vi*: **~ (in)** to excel (at); ec'celso, a *pp di* eccellere

ec'centrico, a, ci, che [et'tʃɛntriko] *ag* eccentric

ecces'sivo, a [ettʃes'sivo] *ag* excessive

ec'cesso [et'tʃɛsso] *sm* excess; **all'~** (*gentile, generoso*) to excess, excessively; **~ di velocità** (*AUT*) speeding

ec'cetera [et'tʃetera] *av* et cetera, and so on

ec'cetto [et'tʃetto] *prep* except, with the exception of; **~ che** except, other than; **~ che (non)** unless

eccettu'are [ettʃettu'are] *vt* to except

eccezio'nale [ettʃetsjo'nale] *ag* exceptional

eccezi'one [ettʃet'tsjone] *sf* exception; (*DIR*) objection; **a ~ di** with the exception of, except for; **d'~** exceptional

ec'cidio [et'tʃidio] *sm* massacre

ecci'tare [ettʃi'tare] *vt* (*curiosità, interesse*) to excite, arouse; (*folla*) to incite; **~rsi** *vr* to get excited; (*sessualmente*) to become aroused; eccitazi'one *sf* excitement

'ecco *av* (*per dimostrare*): **~ il treno!** here's *o* here comes the train!; (*dav pron*): **~mi!** here I am!; **~ne uno!** here's one (of them)!; (*dav pp*): **~ fatto!** there, that's it done!

echeggi'are [eked'dʒare] *vi* to echo

e'clissi *sf* eclipse

'eco (*pl*(*m*) 'echi) *sm o f* echo

ecogra'fia *sf* (*MED*) scan

ecolo'gia [ekolo'dʒia] *sf* ecology

econo'mia *sf* economy; (*scienza*) economics *sg*; (*risparmio: azione*) saving; **fare ~** to economize, make economies; eco'nomico, a, ci, che *ag* economic; (*poco costoso*) economical; econo'mista, i *sm* economist; economiz'zare *vt, vi* to save; e'conomo, a *ag* thrifty ♦ *sm/f* (*INS*) bursar

E'CU ['eku] *sm inv* (= *Unità monetaria europea*) ECU *n*

ed *cong vedi* e

'edera *sf* ivy

e'dicola *sf* newspaper kiosk *o* stand (*US*)

edifi'care *vt* to build; (*fig: teoria, azienda*) to establish; (*indurre al bene*) to edify

edi'ficio [edi'fitʃo] *sm* building

e'dile *ag* building *cpd*; edi'lizia *sf* building, building trade; edi'lizio, a *ag* building *cpd*

Edim'burgo *sf* Edinburgh

edi'tore, 'trice *ag* publishing *cpd* ♦ *sm/f* publisher; (*curatore*) editor; edito'ria *sf* publishing; editori'ale *ag* publishing *cpd* ♦ *sm* editorial, leader

edizi'one [edit'tsjone] *sf* edition; (*tiratura*) printing

edu'care *vt* to educate; (*gusto, mente*) to train; ~ **qn a fare** to train sb to do; edu'cato, a *ag* polite, well-mannered; educazi'one *sf* education; (*familiare*) upbringing; (*comportamento*) (good) manners *pl*; **educazione fisica** (*INS*) physical training *o* education

effemi'nato, a *ag* effeminate

effet'tivo, a *ag* (*reale*) real, actual; (*impiegato, professore*) permanent; (*MIL*) regular ♦ *sm* (*MIL*) strength; (*di patrimonio etc*) sum total

ef'fetto *sm* effect; (*COMM: cambiale*) bill; (*fig: impressione*) impression; **in ~i** in fact, actually; ~ **serra** greenhouse effect; effettu'are *vt* to effect, carry out

effi'cace [effi'katʃe] *ag* effective

effici'ente [effi'tʃente] *ag* efficient; effici'enza *sf* efficiency

ef'fimero, a *ag* ephemeral

E'geo [e'dʒɛo] *sm*: **l'~, il mare** ~ the Aegean (Sea)

E'gitto [e'dʒitto] *sm*: **l'~** Egypt

egizi'ano, a [edʒit'tsjano] *ag, sm/f* Egyptian

'egli ['eʎʎi] *pron* he; ~ **stesso** he himself

ego'ismo *sm* selfishness, egoism; ego'ista, i, e *ag* selfish, egoistic ♦ *sm/f* egoist

egr. *abbr* = **egregio**

e'gregio, a, gi, gie [e'grɛdʒo] *ag* (*nelle lettere*): **E~ Signore** Dear Sir

eguagli'anza *etc* [egwaʎ'ʎantsa]

= **uguaglianza** *etc*

E.I. *abbr* = **Esercito Italiano**

elabo'rare *vt* (*progetto*) to work out, elaborate; (*dati*) to process; elabora'tore *sm* (*INFORM*): **elaboratore elettronico** computer; elaborazi'one *sf* elaboration; **elaborazione dei dati** data processing

elasticiz'zato, a [elastitʃid'dzato] *ag* stretch *cpd*

e'lastico, a, ci, che *ag* elastic; (*fig: andatura*) springy; (*: decisione, vedute*) flexible ♦ *sm* (*di gomma*) rubber band; (*per il cucito*) elastic *no pl*

ele'fante *sm* elephant

ele'gante *ag* elegant

e'leggere [e'ledere] *vt* to elect

elemen'tare *ag* elementary; **le (scuole) ~i** *sfpl* primary (*BRIT*) *o* grade (*US*) school

ele'mento *sm* element; (*parte componente*) element, component, part; **~i** *smpl* (*della scienza etc*) elements, rudiments

ele'mosina *sf* charity, alms *pl*; **chiedere l'~** to beg

elen'care *vt* to list

e'lenco, chi *sm* list; ~ **telefonico** telephone directory

e'letto, a *pp di* **eleggere** ♦ *sm/f* (*nominato*) elected member; eletto'rale *ag* electoral, election *cpd*; eletto'rato *sm* electorate; elet'tore, 'trice *sm/f* voter, elector

elet'trauto *sm inv* workshop for car electrical repairs; (*tecnico*) car electrician

elettri'cista, i [elettri'tʃista] *sm* electrician

elettricità [elettritʃi'ta] *sf* electricity

e'lettrico, a, ci, che *ag* electric(al)

elettriz'zare [elettrid'dzare] *vt* to electrify

e'lettro... *prefisso*: elettrocar'dio'gramma, i *sm* electrocardiogram; elettrodo'mestico, a, ci, che *ag*: **apparecchi elettrodomestici** domestic (electrical) appliances; elet'trone *sm* electron; elet'tronica *sf* electronics *sg*; elet'tronico, a, ci, che *ag* electronic

ele'vare *vt* to raise; (*edificio*) to erect; (*multa*) to impose

elezi'one [elet'tsjone] *sf* election; **~i** *sfpl* (*POL*) election(s)

'elica, che *sf* propeller

eli'cottero *sm* helicopter

elimi'nare *vt* to eliminate; **elimina'toria** *sf* eliminating round

'elio *sm* helium

elisoc'corso *sm* helicopter ambulance

'ella *pron* she; (*forma di cortesia*) you; **~ stessa** she herself; you yourself

el'metto *sm* helmet

e'logio [e'lɔdʒo] *sm* (*discorso, scritto*) eulogy; (*lode*) praise (*di solito no pl*)

elo'quente *ag* eloquent

e'ludere *vt* to evade; **elu'sivo, a** *ag* evasive

e-mail *sf inv* e-mail

ema'nare *vt* to send out, give off; (*fig: leggi, decreti*) to issue ♦ *vi:* **~ da** to come from

emanci'pare [emantʃi'pare] *vt* to emancipate; **~rsi** *vr* (*fig*) to become liberated *o* emancipated

embri'one *sm* embryo

emenda'mento *sm* amendment

emen'dare *vt* to amend

emer'genza [emer'dʒentsa] *sf* emergency; **in caso di ~** in an emergency

e'mergere [e'mɛrdʒere] *vi* to emerge; (*sommergibile*) to surface; (*fig: distinguersi*) to stand out; **e'merso, a** *pp di* **emergere**

e'messo, a *pp di* **emettere**

e'mettere *vt* (*suono, luce*) to give out, emit; (*onde radio*) to send out; (*assegno, francobollo, ordine*) to issue

emi'crania *sf* migraine

emi'grare *vi* to emigrate; **emigrazi'one** *sf* emigration

emi'nente *ag* eminent, distinguished

emis'fero *sm* hemisphere; **~ boreale/ australe** northern/southern hemisphere

emissi'one *sf* (*vedi* emettere) emission; sending out; issue; (*RADIO*) broadcast

emit'tente *ag* (*banca*) issuing; (*RADIO*) broadcasting, transmitting ♦ *sf* (*RADIO*) transmitter

emorra'gia, 'gie [emorra'dʒia] *sf* haemorrhage

emor'roidi *sfpl* haemorrhoids *pl* (*BRIT*), hemorrhoids *pl* (*US*)

emo'tivo, a *ag* emotional

emozio'nante [emottsjo'nante] *ag* exciting, thrilling

emozio'nare [emottsjo'nare] *vt* (*appassionare*) to thrill, excite; (*commuovere*) to move; (*innervosire*) to upset; **~rsi** *vr* to be excited; to be moved; to be upset

emozi'one [emot'tsjone] *sf* emotion; (*agitazione*) excitement

'empio, a *ag* (*sacrilego*) impious; (*spietato*) cruel, pitiless; (*malvagio*) wicked, evil

emulsi'one *sf* emulsion

enciclope'dia [entʃiklope'dia] *sf* encyclopaedia

endove'noso, a *ag* (*MED*) intravenous

'ENEL ['enel] *sigla m* (= *Ente Nazionale per l'Energia Elettrica*) *national electricity company*

ener'gia, 'gie [ener'dʒia] *sf* (*FISICA*) energy; (*fig*) energy, strength, vigour; **~ eolica** wind power; **~ solare** solar energy, solar power; **e'nergico, a, ci, che** *ag* energetic, vigorous

'enfasi *sf* emphasis; (*peg*) bombast, pomposity; **en'fatico, a, ci, che** *ag* emphatic; pompous

en'nesimo, a *ag* (*MAT, fig*) nth; **per l'~a volta** for the umpteenth time

e'norme *ag* enormous, huge; **enormità** *sf inv* enormity, huge size; (*assurdità*) absurdity; **non dire enormità!** don't talk nonsense!

'ente *sm* (*istituzione*) body, board, corporation; (*FILOSOFIA*) being

en'trambi, e *pron pl* both (of them) ♦ *ag pl:* **~ i ragazzi** both boys, both of the boys

en'trare *vi* to go (*o* come) in; **~ in** (*luogo*) to enter, go (*o* come) into; (*trovar posto, poter stare*) to fit into; (*essere ammesso a: club etc*) to join, become a member of; **~ in automobile** to get into the car; **far ~ qn** (*visitatore etc*) to show sb in; **questo non c'entra** (*fig*) that's got nothing to do with it; **en'trata** *sf* entrance, entry; **entrate** *sfpl* (*COMM*) receipts, takings; (*ECON*) income *sg*

'**entro** *prep* (*temporale*) within

entusias'mare *vt* to excite, fill with enthusiasm; **~rsi (per qc/qn)** to become enthusiastic (about sth/sb); **entusi'asmo** *sm* enthusiasm; **entusi'asta, i, e** *ag* enthusiastic ♦ *sm/f* enthusiast; **entusi'astico, a, ci, che** *ag* enthusiastic

enunci'are [enun'tʃare] *vt* (*teoria*) to set out

epa'tite *sf* hepatitis

'**epico, a, ci, che** *ag* epic

epide'mia *sf* epidemic

epi'dermide *sf* skin, epidermis

Epifa'nia *sf* Epiphany

epiles'sia *sf* epilepsy

e'pilogo, ghi *sm* conclusion

epi'sodio *sm* episode

e'piteto *sm* epithet

'**epoca, che** *sf* (*periodo storico*) age, era; (*tempo*) time; (*GEO*) age

ep'pure *cong* and yet, nevertheless

equa'tore *sm* equator

equazi'one [ekwat'tsjone] *sf* (*MAT*) equation

e'questre *ag* equestrian

equi'latero, a *ag* equilateral

equili'brare *vt* to balance; **equi'librio** *sm* balance, equilibrium; **perdere l'~** to lose one's balance

e'quino, a *ag* horse *cpd*, equine

equipaggi'are [ekwipad'dʒare] *vt* (*di persone*) to man; (*di mezzi*) to equip; **equi'paggio** *sm* crew

equipa'rare *vt* to make equal

equità *sf* equity, fairness

equitazi'one [ekwitat'tsjone] *sf* (horse-)riding

equiva'lente *ag, sm* equivalent; **equiva'lenza** *sf* equivalence

equivo'care *vi* to misunderstand; **e'quivoco, a, ci, che** *ag* equivocal, ambiguous; (*sospetto*) dubious ♦ *sm* misunderstanding; **a scanso di equivoci** to avoid any misunderstanding; **giocare sull'equivoco** to equivocate

'**equo, a** *ag* fair, just

'**era** *sf* era

'**erba** *sf* grass; (*aromatica, medicinale*) herb;

in ~ (*fig*) budding; **er'baccia, ce** *sf* weed

e'rede *sm/f* heir; **eredità** *sf* (*DIR*) inheritance; (*BIOL*) heredity; **lasciare qc in eredità a qn** to leave *o* bequeath sth to sb; **eredi'tare** *vt* to inherit; **eredi'tario, a** *ag* hereditary

ere'mita, i *sm* hermit

ere'sia *sf* heresy; **e'retico, a, ci, che** *ag* heretical ♦ *sm/f* heretic

e'retto, a *pp di* **erigere** ♦ *ag* erect, upright; **erezi'one** *sf* (*FISIOL*) erection

er'gastolo *sm* (*DIR: pena*) life imprisonment

'**erica** *sf* heather

e'rigere [e'ridʒere] *vt* to erect, raise; (*fig: fondare*) to found

ERM *sigla* (= *Meccanismo dei tassi di cambio*) ERM *n*

ermel'lino *sm* ermine

er'metico, a, ci, che *ag* hermetic

'**ernia** *sf* (*MED*) hernia

e'roe *sm* hero

ero'gare *vt* (*somme*) to distribute; (*gas, servizi*) to supply

e'roico, a, ci, che *ag* heroic

ero'ina *sf* heroine; (*droga*) heroin

ero'ismo *sm* heroism

erosi'one *sf* erosion

e'rotico, a, ci, che *ag* erotic

er'rare *vi* (*vagare*) to wander, roam; (*sbagliare*) to be mistaken

er'rore *sm* error, mistake; (*morale*) error; **per ~** by mistake

'**erta** *sf* steep slope; **stare all'~** to be on the alert

erut'tare *vt* (*sog: vulcano*) to throw out, belch

eruzi'one [erut'tsjone] *sf* eruption

esacer'bare [ezatʃer'bare] *vt* to exacerbate

esage'rare [ezadʒe'rare] *vt* to exaggerate ♦ *vi* to exaggerate; (*eccedere*) to go too far; **esagerazi'one** *sf* exaggeration

e'sagono *sm* hexagon

esal'tare *vt* to exalt; (*entusiasmare*) to excite, stir; **esal'tato, a** *sm/f* fanatic

e'same *sm* examination; (*INS*) exam, examination; **fare *o* dare un ~** to sit *o* take an exam; **~ del sangue** blood test

esami'nare *vt* to examine

e'sanime *ag* lifeless

esaspe'rare *vt* to exasperate; to exacerbate; **~rsi** *vr* to become annoyed *o* exasperated; **esasperazi'one** *sf* exasperation

esatta'mente *av* exactly; accurately, precisely

esat'tezza [ezat'tettsa] *sf* exactitude, accuracy, precision

e'satto, a *pp di* **esigere** ♦ *ag* (*calcolo, ora*) correct, right, exact; (*preciso*) accurate, precise; (*puntuale*) punctual

esat'tore *sm* (*di imposte etc*) collector

esau'dire *vt* to grant, fulfil

esauri'ente *ag* exhaustive

esauri'mento *sm* exhaustion; **~ nervoso** nervous breakdown

esau'rire *vt* (*stancare*) to exhaust, wear out; (*provviste, miniera*) to exhaust; **~rsi** *vr* to exhaust o.s., wear o.s. out; (*provviste*) to run out; **esau'rito, a** *ag* exhausted; (*merci*) sold out; **registrare il tutto esaurito** (*TEATRO*) to have a full house; **e'sausto, a** *ag* exhausted

'esca (*pl* **'esche**) *sf* bait

escande'scenza [eskandeʃ'ʃentsa] *sf*: **dare in ~e** to lose one's temper, fly into a rage

'esce *etc* ['eʃe] *vb vedi* **uscire**

eschi'mese [eski'mese] *ag, sm/f* Eskimo

escla'mare *vi* to exclaim, cry out; **esclamazi'one** *sf* exclamation

es'cludere *vt* to exclude

esclu'siva *sf* (*DIR, COMM*) exclusive *o* sole rights *pl*

esclu'sivo, a *ag* exclusive

es'cluso, a *pp di* **escludere**

'esco *etc vb vedi* **uscire**

escogi'tare [eskodʒi'tare] *vt* to devise, think up

escursi'one *sf* (*gita*) excursion, trip; (: *a piedi*) hike, walk; (*METEOR*) range

ese'crare *vt* to loathe, abhor

esecu'tivo, a *ag, sm* executive

esecu'tore, 'trice *sm/f* (*MUS*) performer; (*DIR*) executor

esecuzi'one [ezekut'tsjone] *sf* execution, carrying out; (*MUS*) performance; **~ capitale** execution

esegu'ire *vt* to carry out, execute; (*MUS*) to perform, execute

e'sempio *sm* example; **per ~** for example, for instance; **fare un ~** to give an example; **esem'plare** *ag* exemplary ♦ *sm* example; (*copia*) copy; **esemplifi'care** *vt* to exemplify

esen'tare *vt*: **~ qn/qc da** to exempt sb/ sth from

e'sente *ag*: **~ da** (*dispensato da*) exempt from; (*privo di*) free from; **esenzi'one** *sf* exemption

e'sequie *sfpl* funeral rites; funeral service *sg*

eser'cente [ezer'tʃɛnte] *sm/f* trader, dealer; shopkeeper

eserci'tare [ezertʃi'tare] *vt* (*professione*) to practise (*BRIT*), practice (*US*); (*allenare: corpo, mente*) to exercise, train; (*diritto*) to exercise; (*influenza, pressione*) to exert; **~rsi** *vr* to practise; **~rsi alla lotta** to practise fighting; **esercitazi'one** *sf* (*scolastica, militare*) exercise

e'sercito [e'zertʃito] *sm* army

eser'cizio [ezer'tʃittsjo] *sm* practice; exercising; (*fisico, di matematica*) exercise; (*ECON*) financial year; (*azienda*) business, concern; **in ~** (*medico etc*) practising

esi'bire *vt* to exhibit, display; (*documenti*) to produce, present; **~rsi** *vr* (*attore*) to perform; (*fig*) to show off; **esibizi'one** *sf* exhibition; (*di documento*) presentation; (*spettacolo*) show, performance

esi'gente [ezi'dʒɛnte] *ag* demanding; **esi'genza** *sf* demand, requirement

e'sigere [e'zidʒere] *vt* (*pretendere*) to demand; (*richiedere*) to demand, require; (*imposte*) to collect

e'siguo, a *ag* small, slight

'esile *ag* (*persona*) slender, slim; (*stelo*) thin; (*voce*) faint

esili'are *vt* to exile; **e'silio** *sm* exile

e'simere *vt*: **~ qn/qc da** to exempt sb/sth from; **~rsi** *vr*: **~rsi da** to get out of

esis'tenza [ezis'tɛntsa] *sf* existence

e'sistere *vi* to exist

esis'tito, a *pp di* **esistere**

esi'tare *vi* to hesitate; esitazi'one *sf* hesitation

'esito *sm* result, outcome

'esodo *sm* exodus

esone'rare *vt* to exempt

e'sordio *sm* début

esor'tare *vt*: ~ **qn a fare** to urge sb to do

e'sotico, a, ci, che *ag* exotic

es'pandere *vt* to expand; (*confini*) to extend; (*influenza*) to extend, spread; **~rsi** *vr* to expand; **espansi'one** *sf* expansion; **espan'sivo, a** *ag* expansive, communicative

espatri'are *vi* to leave one's country

espedi'ente *sm* expedient

es'pellere *vt* to expel

esperi'enza [espe'rjɛntsa] *sf* experience

esperi'mento *sm* experiment

es'perto, a *ag, sm* expert

espi'are *vt* to atone for

espi'rare *vt, vi* to breathe out

espli'care *vt* (*attività*) to carry out, perform

es'plicito, a [es'plitʃito] *ag* explicit

es'plodere *vi* (*anche fig*) to explode ♦ *vt* to fire

esplo'rare *vt* to explore; **esplora'tore** *sm* explorer; **giovane esploratore** (boy) scout

esplosi'one *sf* explosion; **esplo'sivo, a** *ag, sm* explosive; **es'ploso, a** *pp di* **esplodere**

espo'nente *sm/f* (*rappresentante*) representative

es'porre *vt* (*merci*) to display; (*quadro*) to exhibit, show; (*fatti, idee*) to explain, set out; (*porre in pericolo, FOT*) to expose

espor'tare *vt* to export; **esportazi'one** *sf* exportation; export

esposizi'one [espozit'tsjone] *sf* displaying; exhibiting; setting out; (*anche FOT*) exposure; (*mostra*) exhibition; (*narrazione*) explanation, exposition

es'posto, a *pp di* **esporre** ♦ *ag*: ~ **a nord**

facing north ♦ *sm* (*AMM*) statement, account; (: *petizione*) petition

espressi'one *sf* expression

espres'sivo, a *ag* expressive

es'presso, a *pp di* **esprimere** ♦ *ag* express ♦ *sm* (*lettera*) express letter; (*anche*: **treno ~**) express train; (*anche*: **caffè ~**) espresso

es'primere *vt* to express

espulsi'one *sf* expulsion; **es'pulso, a** *pp di* **espellere**

'essa (*pl* **'esse**) *pron f vedi* **esso**

es'senza [es'sɛntsa] *sf* essence; **essenzi'ale** *ag* essential; **l'essenziale** the main *o* most important thing

---

PAROLA CHIAVE

'essere *sm* being; ~ **umano** human being ♦ *vb copulativo* **1** (*con attributo, sostantivo*) to be; **sei giovane/simpatico** you are *o* you're young/nice; **è medico** he is *o* he's a doctor

2 (*+di: appartenere*) to be; **di chi è la penna?** whose pen is it?; **è di Carla** it is *o* it's Carla's, it belongs to Carla

3 (*+di: provenire*) to be; **è di Venezia** he is *o* he's from Venice

4 (*data, ora*): **è il 15 agosto/lunedì** it is *o* it's the 15th of August/Monday; **che ora è?, che ore sono?** what time is it?; **è l'una** it is *o* it's one o'clock; **sono le due** it is *o* it's two o'clock

5 (*costare*): **quant'è?** how much is it?; **sono 20.000 lire** it's 20,000 lire

♦ *vb aus* **1** (*attivo*): ~ **arrivato/venuto** to have arrived/come; **è già partita** she has already left

2 (*passivo*) to be; ~ **fatto da** to be made by; **è stata uccisa** she has been killed

3 (*riflessivo*): **si sono lavati** they washed, they got washed

4 (*+da +infinito*): **è da farsi subito** it must be *o* it is to be done immediately

♦ *vi* **1** (*esistere, trovarsi*) to be; **sono a casa** I'm at home; ~ **in piedi/seduto** to be standing/sitting

2: **esserci: c'è** there is; **ci sono** there are;

che c'è? what's the matter?, what is it?; **ci sono!** (*fig: ho capito*) I get it!; *vedi anche* **ci** ♦ *vb impers*: **è tardi/Pasqua** it's late/Easter; **è possibile che venga** he may come; **è così** that's the way it is

'**esso, a** *pron* it; (*riferito a persona: soggetto*) he/she; (: *complemento*) him/her; **~i, e** *pron pl* they; (*complemento*) them

est *sm* east

'**estasi** *sf* ecstasy

es'tate *sf* summer

es'tendere *vt* to extend; **~rsi** *vr* (*diffondersi*) to spread; (*territorio, confini*) to extend; **estensi'one** *sf* extension; (*di superficie*) expanse; (*di voce*) range

esteri'ore *ag* outward, external

ester'nare *vt* to express

es'terno, a *ag* (*porta, muro*) outer, outside; (*scala*) outside; (*alunno, impressione*) external ♦ *sm* outside, exterior ♦ *sm/f* (*allievo*) day pupil; **per uso ~** for external use only

'**estero, a** *ag* foreign ♦ *sm*: **all'~** abroad

es'teso, a *pp di* **estendere** ♦ *ag* extensive, large; **scrivere per ~** to write in full

es'tetico, a, ci, che *ag* aesthetic ♦ *sf* (*disciplina*) aesthetics *sg*; (*bellezza*) attractiveness; **este'tista, i, e** *sm/f* beautician

'**estimo** *sm* valuation; (*disciplina*) surveying

es'tinguere *vt* to extinguish, put out; (*debito*) to pay off; **~rsi** *vr* to go out; (*specie*) to become extinct; **es'tinto, a** *pp di* **estinguere**; **estin'tore** *sm* (fire) extinguisher; **estinzi'one** *sf* putting out; (*di specie*) extinction

estir'pare *vt* (*pianta*) to uproot, pull up; (*fig: vizio*) to eradicate

es'tivo, a *ag* summer *cpd*

es'torcere [es'tɔrtʃere] *vt*: **~ qc (a qn)** to extort sth (from sb); **es'torto, a** *pp di* **estorcere**

estradizi'one [estradit'tsjone] *sf* extradition

es'traneo, a *ag* foreign ♦ *sm/f* stranger; **rimanere ~ a qc** to take no part in sth

es'trarre *vt* to extract; (*minerali*) to mine; (*sorteggiare*) to draw; **es'tratto, a** *pp di* **estrarre** ♦ *sm* extract; (*di documento*)

abstract; **estratto conto** statement of account; **estratto di carne** (CUC) meat extract; **estratto di nascita** birth certificate; **estrazi'one** *sf* extraction; mining; drawing *no pl*; draw

estremità *sf inv* extremity, end ♦ *sfpl* (ANAT) extremities

es'tremo, a *ag* extreme; (*ultimo: ora, tentativo*) final, last ♦ *sm* extreme; (*di pazienza, forze*) limit, end; **~i** *smpl* (AMM: *dati essenziali*) details, particulars; **l'~ Oriente** the Far East

'**estro** *sm* (*capriccio*) whim, fancy; (*ispirazione creativa*) inspiration; **es'troso, a** *ag* whimsical, capricious; inspired

estro'verso, a *ag, sm* extrovert

'**esule** *sm/f* exile

età *sf inv* age; **all'~ di 8 anni** at the age of 8, at 8 years of age; **ha la mia ~** he (*o* she) is the same age as me *o* as I am; **raggiungere la maggiore ~** to come of age; **essere in ~ minore** to be under age

'**etere** *sm* ether; **e'tereo, a** *ag* ethereal

eternità *sf* eternity

e'terno, a *ag* eternal

etero'geneo, a [etero'dʒɛneo] *ag* heterogeneous

'**etica** *sf* ethics *sg*; *vedi anche* **etico**

eti'chetta [eti'ketta] *sf* label; (*cerimoniale*): **l'~** etiquette

'**etico, a, ci, che** *ag* ethical

etimolo'gia, 'gie [etimolo'dʒia] *sf* etymology

Eti'opia *sf*: **l'~** Ethiopia

'**Etna** *sm*: **l'~** Etna

'**etnico, a, ci, che** *ag* ethnic

e'trusco, a, schi, sche *ag, sm/f* Etruscan

'**ettaro** *sm* hectare (= *10,000 m²*)

'**etto** *sm abbr* = **ettogrammo**

etto'grammo *sm* hectogram(me) (= *100 grams*)

Eucaris'tia *sf*: **l'~** the Eucharist

'**euro** *sm inv* (*divisa*) euro

eurocity [euro'siti] *sm* international express train

Euro'landia *sf* Euroland

train

Eu'ropa *sf*: **l'~** Europe; **euro'peo, a** *ag, sm/f* European

evacu'are *vt* to evacuate

e'vadere *vi* (*fuggire*): **~ da** to escape from ♦ *vt* (*sbrigare*) to deal with, dispatch; (*tasse*) to evade

evan'gelico, a, ci, che [evan'dʒɛliko] *ag* evangelical

evapo'rare *vi* to evaporate; **evaporazi'one** *sf* evaporation

evasi'one *sf* (*vedi evadere*) escape; dispatch; **~ fiscale** tax evasion

eva'sivo, a *ag* evasive

e'vaso, a *pp di* **evadere** ♦ *sm* escapee

eveni'enza [eve'njɛntsa] *sf*: **pronto(a) per ogni ~** ready for any eventuality

e'vento *sm* event

eventu'ale *ag* possible

eventual'mente *av* if necessary

evi'dente *ag* evident, obvious; **evi'denza** *sf* obviousness; **mettere in evidenza** to point out, highlight; **evidenzi'are** *vt* to emphasize; (*con evidenziatore*) to highlight; **evidenzia'tore** *sm* highlighter

evi'tare *vt* to avoid; **~ di fare** to avoid doing; **~ qc a qn** to spare sb sth

'evo *sm* age, epoch

evo'care *vt* to evoke

evo'luto, a *pp di* **evolvere** ♦ *ag* (*civiltà*) (highly) developed, advanced; (*persona*) independent

evoluzi'one [evolut'tsjone] *sf* evolution

e'volversi *vr* to evolve

ev'viva *escl* hurrah!; **~ il re!** long live the king!, hurrah for the king!

ex *prefisso* ex, former

'extra *ag inv* first-rate; top-quality ♦ *sm inv* extra; **extracomuni'tario, a** *ag* from outside the EC ♦ *sm/f* non-EC citizen; **extraconiu'gale** *ag* extramarital

F, f

fa *vb vedi* **fare** ♦ *sm inv* (MUS) F; (: *solfeggiando la scala*) fa ♦ *av*: **10 anni ~** 10 years ago

fabbi'sogno [fabbi'zoɲɲo] *sm* needs *pl*, requirements *pl*

'fabbrica *sf* factory; **fabbri'cante** *sm* manufacturer, maker; **fabbri'care** *vt* to build; (*produrre*) to manufacture, make; (*fig*) to fabricate, invent

'fabbro *sm* (black)smith

fac'cenda [fat'tʃɛnda] *sf* matter, affair; (*cosa da fare*) task, chore

fac'chino [fak'kino] *sm* porter

'faccia, ce ['fattʃa] *sf* face; (*di moneta, medaglia*) side; **~ a ~** face to face

facci'ata [fat'tʃata] *sf* façade; (*di pagina*) side

'faccio ['fattʃo] *vb vedi* **fare**

'facile ['fatʃile] *ag* easy; (*disposto*): **~ a** inclined to, prone to; (*probabile*): **è ~ che piova** it's likely to rain; **facilità** *sf* easiness; (*disposizione, dono*) aptitude; **facili'tare** *vt* to make easier

facino'roso, a [fatʃino'roso] *ag* violent

facoltà *sf inv* faculty; (*autorità*) power

facolta'tivo, a *ag* optional; (*fermata d'autobus*) request *cpd*

fac'simile *sm* facsimile

'faggio ['faddʒo] *sm* beech

fagi'ano [fa'dʒano] *sm* pheasant

fagio'lino [fadʒo'lino] *sm* French (BRIT) o string bean

fagi'olo [fa'dʒɔlo] *sm* bean

fa'gotto *sm* bundle; (MUS) bassoon; **far ~** (*fig*) to pack up and go

'fai *vb vedi* **fare**

'falce ['faltʃe] *sf* scythe; **falci'are** *vt* to cut; (*fig*) to mow down

'falco, chi *sm* hawk

fal'cone *sm* falcon

'falda *sf* layer, stratum; (*di cappello*) brim; (*di cappotto*) tails *pl*; (*di monte*) lower slope; (*di tetto*) pitch

fale'gname [faleɲˈɲame] *sm* joiner
fal'lace [falˈlatʃe] *ag* misleading
falli'mento *sm* failure; bankruptcy
fal'lire *vi* (*non riuscire*): **~ (in)** to fail (in); (*DIR*) to go bankrupt ♦ *vt* (*colpo, bersaglio*) to miss; **fal'lito, a** *ag* unsuccessful; bankrupt ♦ *sm/f* bankrupt
'fallo *sm* error, mistake; (*imperfezione*) defect, flaw; (*SPORT*) foul; fault; **senza ~** without fail
falò *sm inv* bonfire
fal'sare *vt* to distort, misrepresent; **fal'sario** *sm* forger; counterfeiter; **falsifi'care** *vt* to forge; (*monete*) to forge, counterfeit
'falso, a *ag* false; (*errato*) wrong; (*falsificato*) forged; fake; (: *oro, gioielli*) imitation *cpd* ♦ *sm* forgery; **giurare il ~** to commit perjury
'fama *sf* fame; (*reputazione*) reputation, name
'fame *sf* hunger; **aver ~** to be hungry; **fa'melico, a, ci, che** *ag* ravenous
fa'miglia [faˈmiʎʎa] *sf* family
famili'are *ag* (*della famiglia*) family *cpd*; (*ben noto*) familiar; (*rapporti, atmosfera*) friendly; (*LING*) informal, colloquial ♦ *sm/f* relative, relation; **familiarità** *sf* familiarity; friendliness; informality
fa'moso, a *ag* famous, well-known
fa'nale *sm* (*AUT*) light, lamp (*BRIT*); (*luce stradale, NAUT*) light; (*di faro*) beacon
fa'natico, a, ci, che *ag* fanatical; (*del teatro, calcio etc*): **~ di** *o* **per** mad *o* crazy about ♦ *sm/f* fanatic; (*tifoso*) fan
fanci'ullo, a [fanˈtʃullo] *sm/f* child
fan'donia *sf* tall story; **~e** *sfpl* (*assurdità*) nonsense *sg*
fan'fara *sf* (*musica*) fanfare
'fango, ghi *sm* mud; **fan'goso, a** *ag* muddy
'fanno *vb vedi* **fare**
fannul'lone *a sm/f* idler, loafer
fantasci'enza [fantaʃˈʃentsa] *sf* science fiction
fanta'sia *sf* fantasy, imagination; (*capriccio*) whim, caprice ♦ *ag inv*: **vestito ~**

patterned dress
fan'tasma, i *sm* ghost, phantom
fan'tastico, a, ci, che *ag* fantastic; (*potenza, ingegno*) imaginative
'fante *sm* infantryman; (*CARTE*) jack, knave (*BRIT*); **fante'ria** *sf* infantry
fan'toccio [fanˈtɔttʃo] *sm* puppet
fara'butto *sm* crook
fard *sm inv* blusher
far'dello *sm* bundle; (*fig*) burden

PAROLA CHIAVE

'fare *sm* **1** (*modo di fare*): **con ~ distratto** absent-mindedly; **ha un ~ simpatico** he has a pleasant manner
2: **sul far del giorno/della notte** at daybreak/nightfall
♦ *vt* **1** (*fabbricare, creare*) to make; (: *casa*) to build; (: *assegno*) to make out; **~ un pasto/una promessa/un film** to make a meal/a promise/a film; **~ rumore** to make a noise
2 (*effettuare: lavoro, attività, studi*) to do; (: *sport*) to play; **cosa fa?** (*adesso*) what are you doing?; **cosa fa?** (*di professione*) what do you do?; **~ psicologia/italiano** (*INS*) to do psychology/Italian; **~ un viaggio** to go on a trip *o* journey; **~ una passeggiata** to go for a walk; **~ la spesa** to do the shopping
3 (*funzione*) to be; (*TEATRO*) to play, be; **~ il medico** to be a doctor; **~ il malato** (*fingere*) to act the invalid
4 (*suscitare: sentimenti*): **~ paura a qn** to frighten sb; **(non) fa niente** (*non importa*) it doesn't matter
5 (*ammontare*): **3 più 3 fa 6** 3 and 3 are *o* make 6; **fanno 6.000 lire** that's 6,000 lire; **Roma fa 2.000.000 di abitanti** Rome has 2,000,000 inhabitants; **che ora fai?** what time do you make it?
6 (*+infinito*): **far ~ qc a qn** (*obbligare*) to make sb do sth; (*permettere*) to let sb do sth; **fammi vedere** let me see; **far partire il motore** to start (up) the engine; **far riparare la macchina/costruire una casa** to get *o* have the car repaired/a house built
7: **~rsi**: **~rsi una gonna** to make o.s. a

skirt; **~rsi un nome** to make a name for o.s.; **~rsi la permanente** to get a perm; **~rsi tagliare i capelli** to get one's hair cut; **~rsi operare** to have an operation
8 (*fraseologia*): **farcela** to succeed, manage; **non ce la faccio più** I can't go on; **ce la faremo** we'll make it; **me l'hanno fatta!** (*imbrogliare*) I've been done!; **lo facevo più giovane** I thought he was younger; **fare sì/no con la testa** to nod/shake one's head
♦ *vi* 1 (*agire*) to act, do; **fate come volete** do as you like; **~ presto** to be quick; **~ da** to act as; **non c'è niente da ~** it's no use; **saperci ~ con qn/qc** to know how to deal with sb/sth; **faccia pure!** go ahead!
2 (*dire*) to say; **"davvero?" fece** "really?" he said
3: **~ per** (*essere adatto*) to be suitable for; **~ per ~ qc** to be about to do sth; **fece per andarsene** he made as if to leave
4: **~rsi: si fa così** you do it like this, this is the way it's done; **non si fa così!** (*rimprovero*) that's no way to behave!; **la festa non si fa** the party is off
5: **~ a gara con qn** to compete *o* vie with sb; **~ a pugni** to come to blows; **~ in tempo a ~** to be in time to do
♦ *vb impers*: **fa bel tempo** the weather is fine; **fa caldo/freddo** it's hot/cold; **fa notte** it's getting dark
♦ *vr*: **~rsi** 1 (*diventare*) to become; **~rsi prete** to become a priest; **~rsi grande/vecchio** to grow tall/old
2 (*spostarsi*): **~rsi avanti/indietro** to move forward/back
3 (*fam: drogarsi*) to be a junkie

far'falla *sf* butterfly
fa'rina *sf* flour
farma'cia, 'cie [farma'tʃia] *sf* pharmacy; (*negozio*) chemist's (shop) (*BRIT*), pharmacy; **farma'cista, i, e** *sm/f* chemist (*BRIT*), pharmacist
'farmaco, ci *o* **chi** *sm* drug, medicine
'faro *sm* (*NAUT*) lighthouse; (*AER*) beacon; (*AUT*) headlight

'farsa *sf* farce
'fascia, sce ['faʃʃa] *sf* band, strip; (*MED*) bandage; (*di sindaco, ufficiale*) sash; (*parte di territorio*) strip, belt; (*di contribuenti etc*) group, band; **essere in ~sce** (*anche fig*) to be in one's infancy; **~ oraria** time band
fasci'are [faʃʃare] *vt* to bind; (*MED*) to bandage
fa'scicolo [faʃʃikolo] *sm* (*di documenti*) file, dossier; (*di rivista*) issue, number; (*opuscolo*) booklet, pamphlet
'fascino ['faʃʃino] *sm* charm, fascination
'fascio ['faʃʃo] *sm* bundle, sheaf; (*di fiori*) bunch; (*di luce*) beam; (*POL*): **il F~** the Fascist Party
fa'scismo [faʃʃizmo] *sm* fascism
'fase *sf* phase; (*TECN*) stroke; **fuori ~** (*motore*) rough
fas'tidio *sm* bother, trouble; **dare ~ a qn** to bother *o* annoy sb; **sento ~ allo stomaco** my stomach's upset; **avere ~i con la polizia** to have trouble *o* bother with the police; **fastidi'oso, a** *ag* annoying, tiresome
'fasto *sm* pomp, splendour
'fata *sf* fairy
fa'tale *ag* fatal; (*inevitabile*) inevitable; (*fig*) irresistible; **fatalità** *sf inv* inevitability; (*avversità*) misfortune; (*fato*) fate, destiny
fa'tica, che *sf* hard work; (*sforzo*) effort; (*di metalli*) fatigue; **a ~** with difficulty; **fare ~ a fare qc** to have a job doing sth; **fati'care** *vi* to toil; **faticare a fare qc** to have difficulty doing sth; **fati'coso, a** *ag* tiring, exhausting; (*lavoro*) laborious
'fato *sm* fate, destiny
'fatto, a *pp di* **fare** ♦ *ag*: **un uomo ~** a grown man; **~ a mano/in casa** hand-/home-made ♦ *sm* (*fatto*) fact; (*azione*) deed; (*avvenimento*) event, occurrence; (*di romanzo, film*) action, story; **cogliere qn sul ~** to catch sb red-handed; **il ~ sta** *o* **è che** the fact remains is that; **in ~ di** as for, as far as ... is concerned
fat'tore *sm* (*AGR*) farm manager; (*MAT, elemento costitutivo*) factor; **~ di protezione** (*di lozione solare*) factor

fatto'ria *sf* farm; farmhouse

fatto'rino *sm* errand-boy; *(di ufficio)* office-boy; *(d'albergo)* porter

fat'tura *sf* (COMM) invoice; *(di abito)* tailoring; *(malia)* spell

fattu'rare *vt* (COMM) to invoice

fattu'rato *sm* (COMM) turnover

'fatuo, a *ag* vain, fatuous

'fauna *sf* fauna

fau'tore, trice *sm/f* advocate, supporter

fa'villa *sf* spark

'favola *sf* (fiaba) fairy tale; *(d'intento morale)* fable; *(fandonia)* yarn; **favo'loso, a** *ag* fabulous; *(incredibile)* incredible

fa'vore *sm* favour; **per ~** please; **fare un ~ a qn** to do sb a favour; **favo'revole** *ag* favourable

favo'rire *vt* to favour; *(il commercio, l'industria, le arti)* to promote, encourage; **vuole ~?** won't you help yourself?; **favorisca in salotto** please come into the sitting room; **favo'rito, a** *ag, sm/f* favourite

fazzo'letto [fattso'letto] *sm* handkerchief; *(per la testa)* (head)scarf; **~ di carta** tissue

feb'braio *sm* February

'febbre *sf* fever; **aver la ~** to have a high temperature; **~ da fieno** hay fever; **feb'brile** *ag* (anche fig) feverish

'feccia, ce ['fettʃa] *sf* dregs *pl*

'fecola *sf* potato flour

fecondazi'one [fekondat'tsjone] *sf* fertilization; **~ artificiale** artificial insemination

fe'condo, a *ag* fertile

'fede *sf* (credenza) belief, faith; (REL) faith; *(fiducia)* faith, trust; *(fedeltà)* loyalty; *(anello)* wedding ring; *(attestato)* certificate; **aver ~ in qn** to have faith in sb; **in buona/cattiva ~** in good/bad faith; **"in ~"** (DIR) "in witness whereof"; **fe'dele** *ag:* **fedele (a)** faithful (to) ♦ *sm/f* follower; **i fedeli** (REL) the faithful; **fedeltà** *sf* faithfulness; *(coniugale)* fidelity; **alta fedeltà** (RADIO) high fidelity

'federa *sf* pillowslip, pillowcase

fede'rale *ag* federal

'fegato *sm* liver; (fig) guts *pl*, nerve

'felce ['feltʃe] *sf* fern

fe'lice [fe'litʃe] *ag* happy; *(fortunato)* lucky; **felicità** *sf* happiness

felici'tarsi [felitʃi'tarsi] *vr* (congratularsi): **~ con qn per qc** to congratulate sb on sth

fe'lino, a *ag, sm* feline

'felpa *sf* sweatshirt

'feltro *sm* felt

'femmina *sf* (ZOOL, TECN) female; *(figlia)* girl, daughter; *(spesso peg)* woman; **femmi'nile** *ag* feminine; *(sesso)* female; *(lavoro, giornale, moda)* woman's ♦ *sm* (LING) feminine; **femmi'nismo** *sm* feminism

'fendere *vt* to cut through; **fendi'nebbia** *sm inv* (AUT) fog lamp

fe'nomeno *sm* phenomenon

'feretro *sm* coffin

feri'ale *ag:* **giorno ~** weekday

'ferie *sfpl* holidays (BRIT), vacation *sg* (US); **andare in ~** to go on holiday *o* vacation

fe'rire *vt* to injure; *(deliberatamente: MIL etc)* to wound; *(colpire)* to hurt; **fe'rita** *sf* injury, wound; **fe'rito, a** *sm/f* wounded *o* injured man/woman

'ferma *sf* (MIL) (period of) service; (CACCIA): **cane da ~** pointer

fer'maglio [fer'maʎʎo] *sm* clasp; *(per documenti)* clip

fer'mare *vt* to stop, halt; (POLIZIA) to detain, hold ♦ *vi* to stop; **~rsi** *vr* to stop, halt; **~rsi a fare qc** to stop to do sth

fer'mata *sf* stop; **~ dell'autobus** bus stop

fer'mento *sm* (anche fig) ferment; *(lievito)* yeast

fer'mezza [fer'mettsa] *sf* (fig) firmness, steadfastness

'fermo, a *ag* still, motionless; *(veicolo)* stationary; *(orologio)* not working; *(saldo: anche fig)* firm; *(voce, mano)* steady ♦ *escl* stop!; keep still! ♦ *sm* (chiusura) catch, lock; (DIR): **~ di polizia** police detention

'fermo 'posta *av, sm inv* poste restante (BRIT), general delivery (US)

fe'roce [fe'rɔtʃe] *ag* (animale) fierce, ferocious; *(persona)* cruel, fierce; *(fame,*

dolore) raging; **le bestie ~i** wild animals
ferra'gosto *sm* (*festa*) feast of the
Assumption; (*periodo*) August holidays *pl*

---
ferragosto

i **Ferragosto** *is a national holiday which
falls on 15 August and is the most
important holiday of the summer season.
Most people extend it by taking the days
around the 15th off too. Consequently
during this period, most of industry and
commerce is at a standstill.*

---

ferra'menta *sfpl*: **negozio di ~**
ironmonger's (*BRIT*), hardware shop *o* store
(*US*)
fer'rato, a *ag* (*FERR*): **strada ~a** railway
(*BRIT*) *o* railroad (*US*) line; (*fig*): **essere ~ in**
to be well up in
'ferro *sm* iron; **una bistecca ai ~i** a grilled
steak; **~ battuto** wrought iron; **~ da calza**
knitting needle; **~ di cavallo** horseshoe; **~
da stiro** iron
ferro'via *sf* railway (*BRIT*), railroad (*US*);
ferrovi'ario, a *ag* railway *cpd* (*BRIT*),
railroad *cpd* (*US*); **ferrovi'ere** *sm*
railwayman (*BRIT*), railroad man (*US*)
'fertile *ag* fertile; **fertiliz'zante** *sm*
fertilizer
'fervido, a *ag* fervent
fer'vore *sm* fervour, ardour
'fesso, a *pp di* **fendere** ♦ *ag* (*fam: sciocco*)
crazy, cracked
fes'sura *sf* crack, split; (*per gettone,
moneta*) slot
'festa *sf* (*religiosa*) feast; (*pubblica*) holiday;
(*compleanno*) birthday; (*onomastico*) name
day; (*ricevimento*) celebration, party; **far ~**
to have a holiday; to live it up; **far ~ a qn**
to give sb a warm welcome

---
festa della Repubblica

i *The* **festa della Repubblica**, *which
takes place on 2 June, celebrates the
founding of the Italian Republic after the
fall of the monarchy and the subsequent
referendum in 1946. It is marked by*

---

military parades and political speeches.

---

festeggi'are [fested'dʒare] *vt* to celebrate;
(*persona*) to have a celebration for
fes'tino *sm* party; (*con balli*) ball
fes'tivo, a *ag* (*atmosfera*) festive; **giorno ~**
holiday
fes'toso, a *ag* merry, joyful
fe'ticcio [fe'tittʃo] *sm* fetish
'feto *sm* foetus (*BRIT*), fetus (*US*)
'fetta *sf* slice
fettuc'cine [fettut'tʃine] *sfpl* (*CUC*) ribbon-
shaped pasta
FF.SS. *abbr* = **Ferrovie dello Stato**
fi'aba *sf* fairy tale
fi'acca *sf* weariness; (*svogliatezza*)
listlessness
fiac'care *vt* to weaken
fi'acco, a, chi, che *ag* (*stanco*) tired,
weary; (*svogliato*) listless; (*debole*) weak;
(*mercato*) slack
fi'accola *sf* torch
fi'ala *sf* phial
fi'amma *sf* flame
fiam'mante *ag* (*colore*) flaming; **nuovo ~**
brand new
fiam'mifero *sm* match
fiam'mingo, a, ghi, ghe *ag* Flemish
♦ *sm/f* Fleming ♦ *sm* (*LING*) Flemish; **i
F~ghi** the Flemish
fiancheggi'are [fjanked'dʒare] *vt* to
border; (*fig*) to support, back (up); (*MIL*) to
flank
fi'anco, chi *sm* side; (*MIL*) flank; **di ~**
sideways, from the side; **a ~ a ~** side by
side
fi'asco, schi *sm* flask; (*fig*) fiasco; **fare ~**
to fail
fi'ato *sm* breath; (*resistenza*) stamina; **avere
il ~ grosso** to be out of breath; **prendere
~** to catch one's breath; **~i** *smpl* (*MUS*)
wind instruments; **strumento a ~** wind
instrument
'fibbia *sf* buckle
'fibra *sf* fibre; (*fig*) constitution
fic'care *vt* to push, thrust, drive; **~rsi** *vr*
(*andare a finire*) to get to

'**fico, chi** *sm* (*pianta*) fig tree; (*frutto*) fig; ~ **d'India** prickly pear; ~ **secco** dried fig

fidanza'mento [fidantsaˈmento] *sm* engagement

fidan'zarsi [fidanˈtsarsi] *vr* to get engaged; **fidan'zato, a** *sm/f* fiancé/fiancée

fi'darsi *vr*: ~ **di** to trust; **fi'dato, a** *ag* reliable, trustworthy

'**fido, a** *ag* faithful, loyal ♦ *sm* (COMM) credit

fi'ducia [fiˈdutʃa] *sf* confidence, trust; **incarico di** ~ position of trust, responsible position; **persona di** ~ reliable person

fi'ele *sm* (*fig*) bitterness

fie'nile *sm* barn; hayloft

fi'eno *sm* hay

fi'era *sf* fair

fie'rezza [fjeˈrettsa] *sf* pride

fi'ero, a *ag* proud; (*audace*) bold

'**fifa** (*fam*) *sf*: **aver** ~ to have the jitters

'**figlia** [ˈfiʎʎa] *sf* daughter

figli'astro, a [fiʎˈʎastro] *sm/f* stepson/daughter

'**figlio** [ˈfiʎʎo] *sm* son; (*senza distinzione di sesso*) child; ~ **di papà** spoilt, wealthy young man; ~ **unico** only child; **figli'occio, a, ci, ce** *sm/f* godchild, godson/daughter

fi'gura *sf* figure; (*forma, aspetto esterno*) form, shape; (*illustrazione*) picture, illustration; **far** ~ to look smart; **fare una brutta** ~ to make a bad impression

figu'rare *vi* to appear ♦ *vt*: **~rsi qc** to imagine sth; **~rsi** *vr*: **figurati!** imagine that!; **ti do noia? — ma figurati!** am I disturbing you? — not at all!

figura'tivo, a *ag* figurative

figu'rina *sf* figurine; (*cartoncino*) picture card

'**fila** *sf* row, line; (*coda*) queue; (*serie*) series, string; **di** ~ in succession; **fare la** ~ to queue; **in** ~ **indiana** in single file

filantro'pia *sf* philanthropy

fi'lare *vt* to spin ♦ *vi* (*baco, ragno*) to spin; (*formaggio fuso*) to go stringy; (*discorso*) to hang together; (*fam: amoreggiare*) to go steady; (*muoversi a forte velocità*) to go at full speed; ~ **diritto** (*fig*) to toe the line; ~ **via** to dash off

filas'trocca, che *sf* nursery rhyme

filate'lia *sf* philately, stamp collecting

fi'lato, a *ag* spun ♦ *sm* yarn; **3 giorni ~i** 3 days running *o* on end

fi'letto *sm* (*di vite*) thread; (*di carne*) fillet

fili'ale *ag* filial ♦ *sf* (*di impresa*) branch

fili'grana *sf* (*in oreficeria*) filigree; (*su carta*) watermark

film *sm inv* film; **fil'mare** *vt* to film

'**filo** *sm* (*anche fig*) thread; (*filato*) yarn; (*metallico*) wire; (*di lama, rasoio*) edge; **per ~ e per segno** in detail; ~ **d'erba** blade of grass; ~ **interdentale** dental floss; ~ **di perle** string of pearls; ~ **spinato** barbed wire; **con un** ~ **di voce** in a whisper

'**filobus** *sm inv* trolley bus

filon'cino [filonˈtʃino] *sm* ≈ French stick

fi'lone *sm* (*di minerali*) seam, vein; (*pane*) ≈ Vienna loaf; (*fig*) trend

filoso'fia *sf* philosophy; **fi'losofo, a** *sm/f* philosopher

fil'trare *vt, vi* to filter

'**filtro** *sm* filter; ~ **dell'olio** (AUT) oil filter

fin *av, prep* = **fino**

fi'nale *ag* final ♦ *sm* (*di opera*) end, ending; (: *MUS*) finale ♦ *sf* (SPORT) final; **finalità** *sf* (*scopo*) aim, purpose; **final'mente** *av* finally, at last

fi'nanza [fiˈnantsa] *sf* finance; ~**e** *sfpl* (*di individuo, Stato*) finances; **finanzi'ario, a** *ag* financial; **finanzi'ere** *sm* financier; (*doganale*) customs officer; (*della tributaria*) inland revenue official

finché [finˈke] *cong* (*per tutto il tempo che*) as long as; (*fino al momento in cui*) until; **aspetta ~ io (non) sia ritornato** wait until I get back

'**fine** *ag* (*lamina, carta*) thin; (*capelli, polvere*) fine; (*vista, udito*) keen, sharp; (*persona: raffinata*) refined, distinguished; (*osservazione*) subtle ♦ *sf* end ♦ *sm* aim, purpose; (*esito*) result, outcome; **secondo ~** ulterior motive; **in** *o* **alla** ~ in the end, finally; ~ **settimana** *sm o f inv* weekend

fi'nestra *sf* window; **fines'trino** *sm* (*di*

treno, auto) window

'fingere ['findʒere] *vt* to feign; (*supporre*) to imagine, suppose; **~rsi** *vr*: **~rsi ubriaco/pazzo** to pretend to be drunk/mad; **~ di fare** to pretend to do

fini'mondo *sm* pandemonium

fi'nire *vt* to finish ♦ *vi* to finish, end; **~ di fare** (*compiere*) to finish doing; (*smettere*) to stop doing; **~ in galera** to end up *o* finish up in prison; **fini'tura** *sf* finish

finlan'dese *ag, sm* (*LING*) Finnish ♦ *sm/f* Finn

Fin'landia *sf*: **la ~** Finland

'fino, a *ag* (*capelli, seta*) fine; (*oro*) pure; (*fig: acuto*) shrewd ♦ *av* (*spesso troncato in* **fin**: *pure, anche*) even ♦ *prep* (*spesso troncato in* **fin**: *tempo*): **fin quando?** till when?; (: *luogo*): **fin qui** as far as here; **~ a** (*tempo*) until, till; (*luogo*) as far as, (up) to; **fin da domani** from tomorrow onwards; **fin da ieri** since yesterday; **fin dalla nascita** from *o* since birth

fi'nocchio [fi'nɔkkjo] *sm* fennel; (*fam: peg: omosessuale*) queer

fi'nora *av* up till now

'finta *sf* pretence, sham; (*SPORT*) feint; **far ~a (di fare)** to pretend (to do)

'finto, a *pp di* **fingere** ♦ *ag* false; artificial

finzi'one [fin'tsjone] *sf* pretence, sham

fi'occo, chi *sm* (*di nastro*) bow; (*di stoffa, lana*) flock; (*di neve*) flake; (*NAUT*) jib; **coi ~chi** (*fig*) first-rate; **~chi di granoturco** cornflakes

fi'ocina ['fjɔtʃina] *sf* harpoon

fi'oco, a, chi, che *ag* faint, dim

fi'onda *sf* catapult

fio'raio, a *sm/f* florist

fi'ore *sm* flower; **~i** *smpl* (*CARTE*) clubs; **a fior d'acqua** on the surface of the water; **avere i nervi a fior di pelle** to be on edge

fioren'tino, a *ag* Florentine

fio'retto *sm* (*SCHERMA*) foil

fio'rire *vi* (*rosa*) to flower; (*albero*) to blossom; (*fig*) to flourish

Fi'renze [fi'rentse] *sf* Florence

'firma *sf* signature

fir'mare *vt* to sign; **un abito firmato** a designer suit

fisar'monica, che *sf* accordion

fis'cale *ag* fiscal, tax *cpd*; **medico ~** doctor employed by Social Security to verify cases of sick leave

fischi'are [fis'kjare] *vi* to whistle ♦ *vt* to whistle; (*attore*) to boo, hiss

'fischio ['fiskjo] *sm* whistle

'fisco *sm* tax authorities *pl*, ≈ Inland Revenue (*BRIT*), ≈ Internal Revenue Service (*US*)

'fisica *sf* physics *sg*

'fisico, a, ci, che *ag* physical ♦ *sm/f* physicist ♦ *sm* physique

fisiolo'gia [fizjolo'dʒia] *sf* physiology

fisiono'mia *sf* face, physiognomy

fisiotera'pia *sf* physiotherapy

fis'sare *vt* to fix, fasten; (*guardare intensamente*) to stare at; (*data, condizioni*) to fix, establish, set; (*prenotare*) to book; **~rsi su** (*sog: sguardo, attenzione*) to focus on; (*fig: idea*) to become obsessed with; **fissazi'one** *sf* (*PSIC*) fixation

'fisso, a *ag* fixed; (*stipendio, impiego*) regular ♦ *av*: **guardare ~ qc/qn** to stare at sth/sb

'fitta *sf* sharp pain; *vedi anche* **fitto**

fit'tizio, a *ag* fictitious, imaginary

'fitto, a *ag* thick, dense; (*pioggia*) heavy ♦ *sm* depths *pl*, middle; (*affitto, pigione*) rent

fi'ume *sm* river

fiu'tare *vt* to smell, sniff; (*sog: animale*) to scent; (*fig: inganno*) to get wind of, smell; **~ tabacco/cocaina** to take snuff/cocaine; **fi'uto** *sm* (*sense of*) smell; (*fig*) nose

fla'gello [fla'dʒello] *sm* scourge

fla'grante *ag*: **cogliere qn in ~** to catch sb red-handed

fla'nella *sf* flannel

flash [flaʃ] *sm inv* (*FOT*) flash; (*giornalistico*) newsflash

'flauto *sm* flute

'flebile *ag* faint, feeble

'flemma *sf* (*calma*) coolness, phlegm

fles'sibile *ag* pliable; (*fig: che si adatta*) flexible 'flesso, a *pp di* flettere

flessu'oso, a *ag* supple, lithe

'flettere *vt* to bend

'flipper *sm inv* pinball machine

F.lli *abbr* (= *fratelli*) Bros.

'flora *sf* flora

'florido, a *ag* flourishing; (*fig*) glowing with health

'floscio, a, sci, sce ['flɔʃʃo] *ag* (*cappello*) floppy, soft; (*muscoli*) flabby

'flotta *sf* fleet

'fluido, a *ag*, *sm* fluid

flu'ire *vi* to flow

flu'oro *sm* fluorine

fluo'ruro *sm* fluoride

'flusso *sm* flow; (*FISICA, MED*) flux; ~ e riflusso ebb and flow

fluttu'are *vi* (*mare*) to rise and fall; (*ECON*) to fluctuate

fluvi'ale *ag* river *cpd*, fluvial

'foca, che *sf* (*ZOOL*) seal

fo'caccia, ce [fo'kattʃa] *sf* kind of pizza; (*dolce*) bun

'foce ['fotʃe] *sf* (*GEO*) mouth

foco'laio *sm* (*MED*) centre of infection; (*fig*) hotbed

foco'lare *sm* hearth, fireside; (*TECN*) furnace

'fodera *sf* (*di vestito*) lining; (*di libro, poltrona*) cover; fode'rare *vt* to line; to cover

'fodero *sm* (*di spada*) scabbard; (*di pugnale*) sheath; (*di pistola*) holster

'foga *sf* enthusiasm, ardour

'foggia, ge ['fɔddʒa] *sf* (*maniera*) style; (*aspetto*) form, shape

'foglia ['fɔʎʎa] *sf* leaf; ~ d'argento/d'oro silver/gold leaf; fogli'ame *sm* foliage, leaves *pl*

'foglio ['fɔʎʎo] *sm* (*di carta*) sheet (of paper); (*di metallo*) sheet; ~ rosa (*AUT*) provisional licence; ~ di via (*DIR*) expulsion order; ~ volante pamphlet

'fogna ['foɲɲa] *sf* drain, sewer; fogna'tura *sf* drainage, sewerage

föhn [føːn] *sm inv* hair dryer

folgo'rare *vt* (*sog: fulmine*) to strike down; (*: alta tensione*) to electrocute

'folla *sf* crowd, throng

'folle *ag* mad, insane; (*TECN*) idle; in ~ (*AUT*) in neutral

fol'lia *sf* folly, foolishness; foolish act; (*pazzia*) madness, lunacy

'folto, a *ag* thick

fomen'tare *vt* to stir up, foment

fon *sm inv* hair dryer

fondamen'tale *ag* fundamental, basic

fonda'mento *sm* foundation; ~a *sfpl* (*EDIL*) foundations

fon'dare *vt* to found; (*fig: dar base*): ~ qc su to base sth on; fondazi'one *sf* foundation

'fondere *vt* (*neve*) to melt; (*metallo*) to fuse, melt; (*fig: colori*) to merge, blend; (*: imprese, gruppi*) to merge ♦ *vi* to melt; ~rsi *vr* to melt; (*fig: partiti, correnti*) to unite, merge; fonde'ria *sf* foundry

'fondo, a *ag* deep ♦ *sm* (*di recipiente, pozzo*) bottom; (*di stanza*) back; (*quantità di liquido che resta, deposito*) dregs *pl*; (*sfondo*) background; (*unità immobiliare*) property, estate; (*somma di denaro*) fund; (*SPORT*) long-distance race; ~i *smpl* (*denaro*) funds; a notte ~a at dead of night; in ~ a at the bottom of; at the back of; (*strada*) at the end of; andare a ~ (*nave*) to sink; conoscere a ~ to know inside out; dar ~ a (*fig: provviste, soldi*) to use up; in ~ (*fig*) after all, all things considered; andare fino in ~ a (*fig*) to examine thoroughly; a ~ perduto (*COMM*) without security; ~i di caffè coffee grounds; ~i di magazzino old *o* unsold stock *sg*

fo'netica *sf* phonetics *sg*

fon'tana *sf* fountain

'fonte *sf* spring, source; (*fig*) source ♦ *sm*: ~ battesimale (*REL*) font

fon'tina *sm* sweet full-fat hard cheese from Val d'Aosta

fo'raggio [fo'raddʒo] *sm* fodder, forage

fo'rare *vt* to pierce, make a hole in; (*pallone*) to burst; (*biglietto*) to punch; ~ una gomma to burst a tyre (*BRIT*) *o* tire (*US*)

'**forbici** ['fɔrbitʃi] *sfpl* scissors

'**forca, che** *sf* (AGR) fork, pitchfork; (*patibolo*) gallows *sg*

for'**cella** [for'tʃella] *sf* (TECN) fork; (*di monte*) pass

for'**chetta** [for'ketta] *sf* fork

for'**cina** [for'tʃina] *sf* hairpin

'**forcipe** ['fɔrtʃipe] *sm* forceps *pl*

fo'**resta** *sf* forest

foresti'**ero, a** *ag* foreign ♦ *sm/f* foreigner

'**forfora** *sf* dandruff

forgi'**are** *vt* to forge

'**forma** *sf* form; (*aspetto esteriore*) form, shape; (DIR: *procedura*) procedure; (*per calzature*) last; (*stampo da cucina*) mould; ~**e** *sfpl* (*del corpo*) figure, shape; **le ~e** (*convenzioni*) appearances; **essere in ~** to be in good shape

formag'**gino** [formad'dʒino] *sm* processed cheese

for'**maggio** [for'maddʒo] *sm* cheese

for'**male** *ag* formal; **formalità** *sf inv* formality

for'**mare** *vt* to form, shape, make; (*numero di telefono*) to dial; (*fig: carattere*) to form, mould; ~**rsi** *vr* to form, take shape; for'**mato** *sm* format, size; **formazi'one** *sf* formation; (*fig: educazione*) training

for'**mica, che** *sf* ant; **formi'caio** *sm* anthill

formico'**lare** *vi* (*anche fig*): ~ **di** to be swarming with; **mi formicola la gamba** I've got pins and needles in my leg; **formico'lio** *sm* pins and needles *pl*; swarming

formi'**dabile** *ag* powerful, formidable; (*straordinario*) remarkable

'**formula** *sf* formula; ~ **di cortesia** courtesy form

formu'**lare** *vt* to formulate; to express

for'**nace** [for'natʃe] *sf* (*per laterizi etc*) kiln; (*per metalli*) furnace; ~ **a microonde** microwave oven

for'**naio** *sm* baker

for'**nello** *sm* (*elettrico, a gas*) ring; (*di pipa*) bowl

for'**nire** *vt*: ~ **qn di qc**, ~ **qc a qn** to provide *o* supply sb with sth, to supply sth to sb

'**forno** *sm* (*di cucina*) oven; (*panetteria*) bakery; (TECN: *per calce etc*) kiln; (: *per metalli*) furnace; ~ **a microonde** microwave oven

'**foro** *sm* (*buco*) hole; (STORIA) forum; (*tribunale*) (law) court

'**forse** *av* perhaps, maybe; (*circa*) about; **essere in ~** to be in doubt

forsen'**nato, a** *ag* mad, insane

'**forte** *ag* strong; (*suono*) loud; (*spesa*) considerable, great; (*passione, dolore*) great, deep ♦ *av* strongly; (*velocemente*) fast; (*a voce alta*) loud(ly); (*violentemente*) hard ♦ *sm* (*edificio*) fort; (*specialità*) forte, strong point; **essere ~ in qc** to be good at sth

for'**tezza** [for'tettsa] *sf* (*morale*) strength; (*luogo fortificato*) fortress

for'**tuito, a** *ag* fortuitous, chance

for'**tuna** *sf* (*destino*) fortune, luck; (*buona sorte*) success, fortune; (*eredità, averi*) fortune; **per ~** luckily, fortunately; **di ~** makeshift, improvised; **atterraggio di ~** emergency landing; **fortu'nato, a** *ag* lucky, fortunate; (*coronato da successo*) successful

'**forza** ['fɔrtsa] *sf* strength; (*potere*) power; (FISICA) force; ~**e** *sfpl* (*fisiche*) strength *sg*; (MIL) forces ♦ *escl* come on!; **per ~** against one's will; (*naturalmente*) of course; **a viva ~** by force; **a ~ di** by dint of; ~ **maggiore** circumstances beyond one's control; **la ~ pubblica** the police *pl*; **le ~e armate** the armed forces; ~**e dell'ordine** the forces of law and order

for'**zare** [for'tsare] *vt* to force; ~ **qn a fare** to force sb to do; for'**zato, a** *ag* forced ♦ *sm* (DIR) prisoner sentenced to hard labour

fos'**chia** [fos'kia] *sf* mist, haze

'**fosco, a, schi, sche** *ag* dark, gloomy

'**fosforo** *sm* phosphorous

'**fossa** *sf* pit; (*di cimitero*) grave; ~ **biologica** septic tank

fos'**sato** *sm* ditch; (*di fortezza*) moat

fos'**setta** *sf* dimple

'fossile *ag, sm* fossil

'fosso *sm* ditch; (*MIL*) trench

'foto *sf* photo ♦ *prefisso*: foto'copia *sf* photocopy; fotocopi'are *vt* to photocopy; fotogra'fare *vt* to photograph; fotogra'fia *sf* (*procedimento*) photography; (*immagine*) photograph; **fare una fotografia** to take a photograph; **una fotografia a colori/in bianco e nero** a colour/black and white photograph; fo'tografo, a *sm/f* photographer; fotoro'manzo *sm* romantic picture story; foto'tessera *sf* passport-size photo

fra *prep* = **tra**

fracas'sare *vt* to shatter, smash; **~rsi** *vr* to shatter, smash; (*veicolo*) to crash; fra'casso *sm* smash; crash; (*baccano*) din, racket

'fradicio, a, ci, ce ['fradit∫o] *ag* (*molto bagnato*) soaking (wet); **ubriaco ~** blind drunk

'fragile ['fradʒile] *ag* fragile; (*fig: salute*) delicate

'fragola *sf* strawberry

fra'gore *sm* roar; (*di tuono*) rumble

frago'roso, a *ag* deafening

fra'grante *ag* fragrant

frain'tendere *vt* to misunderstand; frain'teso, a *pp di* **fraintendere**

fram'mento *sm* fragment

'frana *sf* landslide; (*fig: persona*): **essere una ~** to be useless; fra'nare *vi* to slip, slide down

fran'cese [fran't∫eze] *ag* French ♦ *sm/f* Frenchman/woman ♦ *sm* (*LING*) French; **i F~i** the French

fran'chezza [fran'kettsa] *sf* frankness, openness

'Francia ['frant∫a] *sf*: **la ~** France

'franco, a, chi, che *ag* (*COMM*) free; (*sincero*) frank, open, sincere ♦ *sm* (*moneta*) franc; **farla ~a** (*fig*) to get off scot-free; **~ di dogana** duty-free; **prezzo ~ fabbrica** ex-works price; **~ tiratore** *sm* sniper

franco'bollo *sm* (postage) stamp

fran'gente [fran'dʒɛnte] *sm* (*onda*) breaker; (*scoglio emergente*) reef; (*circostanza*) situation, circumstance

'frangia, ge ['frandʒa] *sf* fringe

frantu'mare *vt* to break into pieces, shatter; **~rsi** *vr* to break into pieces, shatter

frap'pé *sm* milk shake

'frasca, sche *sf* (leafy) branch

'frase *sf* (*LING*) sentence; (*locuzione, espressione, MUS*) phrase; **~ fatta** set phrase

'frassino *sm* ash (tree)

frastagli'ato, a [frasta∫.'∫ato] *ag* (*costa*) indented, jagged

frastor'nare *vt* to daze; to befuddle

frastu'ono *sm* hubbub, din

'frate *sm* friar, monk

fratel'lanza [fratel'lantsa] *sf* brotherhood; (*associazione*) fraternity

fratel'lastro *sm* stepbrother

fra'tello *sm* brother; **~i** *smpl* brothers; (*nel senso di fratelli e sorelle*) brothers and sisters

fra'terno, a *ag* fraternal, brotherly

frat'tanto *av* in the meantime, meanwhile

frat'tempo *sm*: **nel ~** in the meantime, meanwhile

frat'tura *sf* fracture; (*fig*) split, break

frazi'one [frat'tsjone] *sf* fraction; (*di comune*) small town

'freccia, ce ['frett∫a] *sf* arrow; **~ di direzione** (*AUT*) indicator

fred'dare *vt* to shoot dead

fred'dezza [fred'dettsa] *sf* coldness

'freddo, a *ag, sm* cold; **fa ~** it's cold; **aver ~** to be cold; **a ~** (*fig*) deliberately; freddo'loso, a *ag* sensitive to the cold

fred'dura *sf* pun

fre'gare *vt* to rub; (*fam: truffare*) to take in, cheat; (: *rubare*) to swipe, pinch; **fregarsene** (*fam!*): **chi se ne frega?** who gives a damn (about it)?

fre'gata *sf* rub; (*fam*) swindle; (*NAUT*) frigate

'fregio ['fredʒo] *sm* (*ARCHIT*) frieze; (*ornamento*) decoration

'fremere *vi*: **~ di** to tremble *o* quiver with; 'fremito *sm* tremor, quiver

fre'nare *vt* (*veicolo*) to slow down; (*cavallo*) to rein in; (*lacrime*) to restrain, hold back

♦ *vi* to brake; **~rsi** *vr* (*fig*) to restrain o.s., control o.s.; **fre'nata** *sf*: **fare una frenata** to brake

frene'sia *sf* frenzy

'**freno** *sm* brake; (*morso*) bit; **~ a disco** disc brake; **~ a mano** handbrake; **tenere a ~** to restrain

frequen'tare *vt* (*scuola, corso*) to attend; (*locale, bar*) to go to, frequent; (*persone*) to see (often)

fre'quente *ag* frequent; **di ~** frequently; **fre'quenza** *sf* frequency; (*INS*) attendance

fres'chezza [fres'kettsa] *sf* freshness

'**fresco, a, schi, sche** *ag* fresh; (*temperatura*) cool; (*notizia*) recent, fresh ♦ *sm*: **godere il ~** to enjoy the cool air; **stare ~** (*fig*) to be in for it; **mettere al ~** to put in a cool place

'**fretta** *sf* hurry, haste; **in ~** in a hurry; **in ~ e furia** in a mad rush; **aver ~** to be in a hurry; **fretto'loso, a** *ag* (*persona*) in a hurry; (*lavoro etc*) hurried, rushed

fri'abile *ag* (*terreno*) friable; (*pasta*) crumbly

'**friggere** ['friddʒere] *vt* to fry ♦ *vi* (*olio etc*) to sizzle

'**frigido, a** ['friʒido] *ag* (*MED*) frigid

'**frigo** *sm* fridge

frigo'rifero, a *ag* refrigerating ♦ *sm* refrigerator

fringu'ello *sm* chaffinch

frit'tata *sf* omelette; **fare una ~** (*fig*) to make a mess of things

frit'tella *sf* (*CUC*) fritter

'**fritto, a** *pp di* **friggere** ♦ *ag* fried ♦ *sm* fried food; **~ misto** mixed fry

frit'tura *sf* (*CUC*): **~ di pesce** mixed fried fish

'**frivolo, a** *ag* frivolous

frizi'one [frit'tsjone] *sf* friction; (*di pelle*) rub, rub-down; (*AUT*) clutch

friz'zante [frid'dzante] *ag* (*anche fig*) sparkling

fro'dare *vt* to defraud, cheat

'**frode** *sf* fraud; **~ fiscale** tax evasion

'**frollo, a** *ag* (*carne*) tender; (: *di selvaggina*) high; **pasta ~a** short(crust) pastry

'**fronda** *sf* (leafy) branch; (*di partito politico*) internal opposition

fron'tale *ag* frontal; (*scontro*) head-on

'**fronte** *sf* (*ANAT*) forehead; (*di edificio*) front, façade ♦ *sm* (*MIL, POL, METEOR*) front; **a ~**, **di ~** facing, opposite; **di ~ a** (*posizione*) opposite, facing, in front of; (*a paragone di*) compared with

fronteggi'are [fronted'dʒare] *vt* (*avversari, difficoltà*) to face, stand up to; (*spese*) to cope with

fronti'era *sf* border, frontier

'**fronzolo** ['frondzolo] *sm* frill

frot'tola *sf* fib; **~e** *sfpl* (*assurdità*) nonsense *sg*

fru'gare *vi* to rummage ♦ *vt* to search

frul'lare *vt* (*CUC*) to whisk ♦ *vi* (*uccelli*) to flutter; **frul'lato** *sm* milk shake; fruit drink; **frulla'tore** *sm* electric mixer; **frul'lino** *sm* whisk

fru'mento *sm* wheat

fru'scio [fruʃ'ʃio] *sm* rustle; rustling; (*di acque*) murmur

'**frusta** *sf* whip; (*CUC*) whisk

frus'tare *vt* to whip

frus'tino *sm* riding crop

frus'trare *vt* to frustrate

'**frutta** *sf* fruit; (*portata*) dessert; **~ candita/secca** candied/dried fruit

frut'tare *vi* to bear dividends, give a return

frut'teto *sm* orchard

frutti'vendolo, a *sm/f* greengrocer (*BRIT*), produce dealer (*US*)

'**frutto** *sm* fruit; (*fig: risultato*) result(s); (*ECON: interesse*) interest; (: *reddito*) income; **~i di mare** seafood *sg*

FS *abbr* = **Ferrovie dello Stato**

fu *vb vedi* **essere** ♦ *ag inv*: **il ~ Paolo Bianchi** the late Paolo Bianchi

fuci'lare [futʃi'lare] *vt* to shoot; **fuci'lata** *sf* rifle shot

fu'cile [fu'tʃile] *sm* rifle, gun; (*da caccia*) shotgun, gun

fu'cina [fu'tʃina] *sf* forge

'**fuga** *sf* escape, flight; (*di gas, liquidi*) leak; (*MUS*) fugue; **~ di cervelli** brain drain

fu'gace [fu'gatʃe] *ag* fleeting, transient

fug'gevole [fud'dʒevole] _ag_ fleeting

fuggi'asco, a, schi, sche [fud'dʒasko] _ag, sm/f_ fugitive

fuggi'fuggi [fuddʒi'fuddʒi] _sm_ scramble, stampede

fug'gire [fud'dʒire] _vi_ to flee, run away; (_fig: passar veloce_) to fly ♦ _vt_ to avoid; **fuggi'tivo, a** _sm/f_ fugitive, runaway

ful'gore _sm_ brilliance, splendour

fu'liggine [fu'liddʒine] _sf_ soot

fulmi'nare _vt_ (_sog: fulmine_) to strike; (_: elettricità_) to electrocute; (_con arma da fuoco_) to shoot dead; (_fig: con lo sguardo_) to look daggers at

'fulmine _sm_ thunderbolt; lightning _no pl_

fu'mare _vi_ to smoke; (_emettere vapore_) to steam ♦ _vt_ to smoke; **fu'mata** _sf_ (_segnale_) smoke signal; **farsi una fumata** to have a smoke; **fuma'tore, 'trice** _sm/f_ smoker

fu'metto _sm_ comic strip; **giornale** _sm_ **a ~i** comic

'fumo _sm_ smoke; (_vapore_) steam; (_il fumare tabacco_) smoking; **~i** _smpl_ (_industriali etc_) fumes; **i ~i dell'alcool** the after-effects of drink; **vendere ~** to deceive, cheat; **~ passivo** passive smoking; **fu'moso, a** _ag_ smoky; (_fig_) muddled

fu'nambolo, a _sm/f_ tightrope walker

'fune _sf_ rope, cord; (_più grossa_) cable

'funebre _ag_ (_rito_) funeral; (_aspetto_) gloomy, funereal

fune'rale _sm_ funeral

'fungere ['fundʒere] _vi_: **~ da** to act as

'fungo, ghi _sm_ fungus; (_commestibile_) mushroom; **~ velenoso** toadstool

funico'lare _sf_ funicular railway

funi'via _sf_ cable railway

funzio'nare [funtsjo'nare] _vi_ to work, function; (_fungere_): **~ da** to act as

funzio'nario [funtsjo'narjo] _sm_ official

funzi'one [fun'tsjone] _sf_ function; (_carica_) post, position; (_REL_) service; **in ~** (_meccanismo_) in operation; **in ~ di** (_come_) as; **fare la ~ di qn** (_farne le veci_) to take sb's place

fu'oco, chi _sm_ fire; (_fornello_) ring; (_FOT, FISICA_) focus; **dare ~ a qc** to set fire to sth;

far ~ (_sparare_) to fire; **~ d'artificio** firework

fuorché [fwor'ke] _cong, prep_ except

fu'ori _av_ outside; (_all'aperto_) outdoors, outside; (_fuori di casa, SPORT_) out; (_esclamativo_) get out! ♦ _prep_: **~ (di)** out of, outside ♦ _sm_ outside; **lasciar ~ qc/qn** to leave sth/sb out; **far ~ qn** (_fam_) to kill sb, do sb in; **essere ~ di sé** to be beside o.s.; **~ luogo** (_inopportuno_) out of place, uncalled for; **~ mano** out of the way, remote; **~ pericolo** out of danger; **~ uso** old-fashioned; obsolete

fu'ori... _prefisso_: **fuori'bordo** _sm inv_ speedboat (with outboard motor); outboard motor; **fuori'classe** _sm/f inv_ (undisputed) champion; **fuorigi'oco** _sm_ offside; **fuori'legge** _sm/f inv_ outlaw; **fuori'serie** _ag inv_ (_auto etc_) custom-built ♦ _sf_ custom-built car; **fuori'strada** _sm_ (_AUT_) cross-country vehicle; **fuor(i)u'scito, a** _sm/f_ exile; **fuorvi'are** _vt_ to mislead; (_fig_) to lead astray ♦ _vi_ to go astray

'furbo, a _ag_ clever, smart; (_peg_) cunning

fu'rente _ag_: **~ (contro)** furious (with)

fur'fante _sm_ rascal, scoundrel

fur'gone _sm_ van

'furia _sf_ (_ira_) fury, rage; (_fig: impeto_) fury, violence; (_fretta_) rush; **a ~ di** by dint of; **andare su tutte le ~e** to get into a towering rage; **furi'bondo, a** _ag_ furious

furi'oso, a _ag_ furious

fu'rore _sm_ fury; (_esaltazione_) frenzy; **far ~** to be all the rage

fur'tivo, a _ag_ furtive

'furto _sm_ theft; **~ con scasso** burglary

'fusa _sfpl_: **fare le ~** to purr

fu'sibile _sm_ (_ELETTR_) fuse

fusi'one _sf_ (_di metalli_) fusion, melting; (_colata_) casting; (_COMM_) merger; (_fig_) merging

'fuso, a _pp di_ **fondere** ♦ _sm_ (_FILATURA_) spindle; **~ orario** time zone

fus'tagno [fus'taɲɲo] _sm_ corduroy

fus'tino _sm_ (_di detersivo_) tub

'fusto _sm_ stem; (_ANAT, di albero_) trunk; (_recipiente_) drum, can

fu'turo, a *ag, sm* future

G, g

gab'bare *vt* to take in, dupe; **~rsi** *vr*: **~rsi di qn** to make fun of sb

'gabbia *sf* cage; (*da imballaggio*) crate; **~ dell'ascensore** lift (*BRIT*) *o* elevator (*US*) shaft; **~ toracica** (*ANAT*) rib cage

gabbi'ano *sm* (sea)gull

gabi'netto *sm* (*MED etc*) consulting room; (*POL*) ministry; (*WC*) toilet, lavatory; (*INS: di fisica etc*) laboratory

'gaffe [gaf] *sf inv* blunder

gagli'ardo, a [gaʎ'ʎardo] *ag* strong, vigorous

'gaio, a *ag* cheerful, gay

'gala *sf* (*sfarzo*) pomp; (*festa*) gala

ga'lante *ag* gallant, courteous; (*avventura*) amorous; galante'ria *sf* gallantry

galantu'omo (*pl* galantu'omini) *sm* gentleman

ga'lassia *sf* galaxy

gala'teo *sm* (good) manners *pl*

gale'otto *sm* (*rematore*) galley slave; (*carcerato*) convict

ga'lera *sf* (*NAUT*) galley; (*prigione*) prison

'galla *sf*: a **~** afloat; **venire a ~** to surface, come to the surface; (*fig: verità*) to come out

galleggi'ante [galled'dʒante] *ag* floating ♦ *sm* (*di pescatore, lenza, TECN*) float

galleggi'are [galled'dʒare] *vi* to float

galle'ria *sf* (*traforo*) tunnel; (*ARCHIT, d'arte*) gallery; (*TEATRO*) circle; (*strada coperta con negozi*) arcade

'Galles *sm*: **il ~** Wales; **gal'lese** *ag, sm* (*LING*) Welsh ♦ *sm/f* Welshman/woman

gal'letta *sf* cracker

gal'lina *sf* hen

'gallo *sm* cock

gal'lone *sm* piece of braid; (*MIL*) stripe; (*unità di misura*) gallon

galop'pare *vi* to gallop

ga'loppo *sm* gallop; **al** *o* **di ~** at a gallop

'gamba *sf* leg; (*asta: di lettera*) stem; **in ~** (*in buona salute*) well; (*bravo, sveglio*) bright, smart; **prendere qc sotto ~** (*fig*) to treat sth too lightly

gambe'retto *sm* shrimp

'gambero *sm* (*di acqua dolce*) crayfish; (*di mare*) prawn

'gambo *sm* stem; (*di frutta*) stalk

'gamma *sf* (*MUS*) scale; (*di colori, fig*) range

ga'nascia, sce [ga'naʃʃa] *sf* jaw; **~sce del freno** (*AUT*) brake shoes

'gancio ['gantʃo] *sm* hook

'gangheri ['gangeri] *smpl*: **uscire dai ~** (*fig*) to fly into a temper

'gara *sf* competition; (*SPORT*) competition; contest; match; (: *corsa*) race; **fare a ~** to compete, vie

ga'rage [ga'raʒ] *sm inv* garage

garan'tire *vt* to guarantee; (*debito*) to stand surety for; (*dare per certo*) to assure

garan'zia [garan'tsia] *sf* guarantee; (*pegno*) security

gar'bato, a *ag* courteous, polite

'garbo *sm* (*buone maniere*) politeness, courtesy; (*di vestito etc*) grace, style

gareggi'are [gared'dʒare] *vi* to compete

garga'rismo *sm* gargle; **fare i ~i** to gargle

ga'rofano *sm* carnation; **chiodo di ~** clove

'garza ['gardza] *sf* (*per bende*) gauze

gar'zone [gar'dzone] *sm* (*di negozio*) boy

gas *sm inv* gas; **a tutto ~** at full speed; **dare ~** (*AUT*) to accelerate

ga'solio *sm* diesel (oil)

ga's(s)ato, a *ag* (*bibita*) aerated, fizzy

gas'sosa *sf* fizzy drink

gas'soso, a *ag* gaseous; gassy

gastrono'mia *sf* gastronomy

gat'tino *sm* kitten

'gatto, a *sm/f* cat, tomcat/she-cat; **~ selvatico** wildcat; **~ delle nevi** (*AUT, SCI*) snowcat

gatto'pardo *sm*: **~ africano** serval; **~ americano** ocelot

'gaudio *sm* joy, happiness

ga'vetta *sf* (*MIL*) mess tin; **venire dalla ~** (*MIL, fig*) to rise from the ranks

'gazza ['gaddza] *sf* magpie

gaz'zella [gad'dzɛlla] *sf* gazelle

gaz'zetta [gad'dzetta] *sf* news sheet; **G~ Ufficiale** official publication containing details of new laws

gel [dʒɛl] *sm inv* gel

ge'lare [dʒe'lare] *vt, vi, vb impers* to freeze; ge'lata *sf* frost

gelate'ria [dʒelate'ria] *sf* ice-cream shop

gela'tina [dʒela'tina] *sf* gelatine; **~ esplosiva** dynamite; **~ di frutta** fruit jelly

ge'lato, a [dʒe'lato] *ag* frozen ♦ *sm* ice cream

'gelido, a ['dʒɛlido] *ag* icy, ice-cold

'gelo ['dʒɛlo] *sm* (*temperatura*) intense cold; (*brina*) frost; (*fig*) chill; ge'lone *sm* chilblain

gelo'sia [dʒelo'sia] *sf* jealousy

ge'loso, a [dʒe'loso] *ag* jealous

'gelso ['dʒɛlso] *sm* mulberry (tree)

gelso'mino [dʒelso'mino] *sm* jasmine

ge'mello, a [dʒe'mɛllo] *ag, sm/f* twin; **~i** *smpl* (*di camicia*) cufflinks; (*dello zodiaco*): **G~i** Gemini *sg*

'gemere ['dʒɛmere] *vi* to moan, groan; (*cigolare*) to creak; 'gemito *sm* moan, groan

'gemma ['dʒɛmma] *sf* (*BOT*) bud; (*pietra preziosa*) gem

gene'rale [dʒene'rale] *ag, sm* general; **in ~** (*per sommi capi*) in general terms; (*di solito*) usually, in general; generalità *sfpl* (*dati d'identità*) particulars; generaliz'zare *vt, vi* to generalize; general'mente *av* generally

gene'rare [dʒene'rare] *vt* (*dar vita*) to give birth to; (*produrre*) to produce; (*causare*) to arouse; (*TECN*) to produce, generate; genera'tore *sm* (*TECN*) generator; generazi'one *sf* generation

'genere ['dʒɛnere] *sm* kind, type, sort; (*BIOL*) genus; (*merce*) article, product; (*LING*) gender; (*ARTE, LETTERATURA*) genre; **in ~** generally, as a rule; **il ~ umano** mankind; **~i alimentari** foodstuffs

ge'nerico, a, ci, che [dʒe'nɛriko] *ag* generic; (*vago*) vague, imprecise

'genero ['dʒɛnero] *sm* son-in-law

generosità [dʒenerosi'ta] *sf* generosity

gene'roso, a [dʒene'roso] *ag* generous

ge'netica [dʒe'nɛtika] *sf* genetics *sg*

ge'netico, a, ci, che [dʒe'nɛtiko] *ag* genetic

gen'giva [dʒen'dʒiva] *sf* (*ANAT*) gum

geni'ale [dʒen'jale] *ag* (*persona*) of genius; (*idea*) ingenious, brilliant

'genio ['dʒɛnjo] *sm* genius; **andare a ~ a qn** to be to sb's liking, appeal to sb

geni'tale [dʒeni'tale] *ag* genital; **~i** *smpl* genitals

geni'tore [dʒeni'tore] *sm* parent, father o mother; **i miei ~i** my parents, my father and mother

gen'naio [dʒen'najo] *sm* January

'Genova ['dʒɛnova] *sf* Genoa

gen'taglia [dʒen'taʎʎa] (*peg*) *sf* rabble

'gente ['dʒɛnte] *sf* people *pl*

gen'tile [dʒen'tile] *ag* (*persona, atto*) kind; (: *garbato*) courteous, polite; (*nelle lettere*): **G~ Signore** Dear Sir; (: *sulla busta*): **G~ Signor Fernando Villa** Mr Fernando Villa; genti'lezza *sf* kindness; courtesy, politeness; **per gentilezza** (*per favore*) please

gentilu'omo [dʒenti'lwɔmo] (*pl* gentilu'omini) *sm* gentleman

genu'ino, a [dʒenu'ino] *ag* (*prodotto*) natural; (*persona, sentimento*) genuine, sincere

geogra'fia [dʒeogra'fia] *sf* geography

geolo'gia [dʒeolo'dʒia] *sf* geology

ge'ometra, i, e [dʒe'ɔmetra] *sm/f* (*professionista*) surveyor

geome'tria [dʒeome'tria] *sf* geometry; geo'metrico, a, ci, che *ag* geometric(al)

gerar'chia [dʒerar'kia] *sf* hierarchy

ge'rente [dʒe'rɛnte] *sm/f* manager/ manageress

'gergo, ghi ['dʒɛrgo] *sm* jargon; slang

geria'tria [dʒerja'tria] *sf* geriatrics *sg*

Ger'mania [dʒer'manja] *sf*: **la ~** Germany; **la ~ occidentale/orientale** West/East Germany

'germe ['dʒɛrme] *sm* germ; (*fig*) seed

germogli'are [dʒermoʎ'ʎare] *vi* to sprout; to germinate; **ger'moglio** *sm* shoot; bud
gero'glifico, ci [dʒero'glifiko] *sm* hieroglyphic
'gesso ['dʒɛsso] *sm* chalk; (*SCULTURA, MED, EDIL*) plaster; (*statua*) plaster figure; (*minerale*) gypsum
gesti'one [dʒes'tjone] *sf* management
ges'tire [dʒes'tire] *vt* to run, manage
'gesto ['dʒɛsto] *sm* gesture
ges'tore [dʒes'tore] *sm* manager
Gesù [dʒe'zu] *sm* Jesus
gesu'ita, i [dʒezu'ita] *sm* Jesuit
get'tare [dʒet'tare] *vt* to throw; (*anche:* ~ **via**) to throw away *o* out; (*SCULTURA*) to cast; (*EDIL*) to lay; (*acqua*) to spout; (*grido*) to utter; **~rsi** *vr:* **~rsi in** (*sog: fiume*) to flow into; ~ **uno sguardo su** to take a quick look at; **get'tata** *sf* (*di cemento, gesso, metalli*) cast; (*diga*) jetty
'getto ['dʒɛtto] *sm* (*di gas, liquido, AER*) jet; **a** ~ **continuo** uninterruptedly; **di** ~ (*fig*) straight off, in one go
get'tone [dʒet'tone] *sm* token; (*per giochi*) counter; (*: roulette etc*) chip; ~ **telefonico** telephone token
ghiacci'aio [gjat'tʃajo] *sm* glacier
ghiacci'are [gjat'tʃare] *vt* to freeze; (*fig*): ~ **qn** to make sb's blood run cold ♦ *vi* to freeze, ice over; **ghiacci'ato, a** *ag* frozen; (*bevanda*) ice-cold
ghi'accio [gj'attʃo] *sm* ice
ghiacci'olo [gjat'tʃɔlo] *sm* icicle; (*tipo di gelato*) ice lolly (*BRIT*), popsicle (*US*)
ghi'aia ['gjaja] *sf* gravel
ghi'anda ['gjanda] *sf* (*BOT*) acorn
ghi'andola ['gjandola] *sf* gland
ghigliot'tina [giʎʎot'tina] *sf* guillotine
ghi'gnare [gin'nare] *vi* to sneer
ghi'otto, a [gj'otto] *ag* greedy; (*cibo*) delicious, appetizing; **ghiot'tone, a** *sm/f* glutton
ghiri'goro [giri'gɔro] *sm* scribble, squiggle
ghir'landa [gir'landa] *sf* garland, wreath
'ghiro ['giro] *sm* dormouse
'ghisa ['giza] *sf* cast iron
già [dʒa] *av* already; (*ex, in precedenza*)

formerly ♦ *escl* of course!, yes indeed!
gi'acca, che ['dʒakka] *sf* jacket; ~ **a vento** windcheater (*BRIT*), windbreaker (*US*)
giacché [dʒak'ke] *cong* since, as
giac'chetta [dʒak'ketta] *sf* (light) jacket
gia'cenza [dʒa'tʃɛntsa] *sf:* **merce in** ~ goods in stock; **~e di magazzino** unsold stock
gia'cere [dʒa'tʃere] *vi* to lie; **giaci'mento** *sm* deposit
gia'cinto [dʒa'tʃinto] *sm* hyacinth
gi'ada ['dʒada] *sf* jade
giaggi'olo [dʒad'dʒɔlo] *sm* iris
giagu'aro [dʒa'gwaro] *sm* jaguar
gi'allo ['dʒallo] *ag* yellow; (*carnagione*) sallow ♦ *sm* yellow; (*anche: romanzo* ~) detective novel; (*anche:* **film** ~) detective film; ~ **dell'uovo** yolk
giam'mai [dʒam'mai] *av* never
Giap'pone [dʒap'pone] *sm* Japan; **giappo'nese** *ag, sm/f, sm* Japanese *inv*
gi'ara ['dʒara] *sf* jar
giardi'naggio [dʒardi'nadd3o] *sm* gardening
giardini'era [dʒardi'njera] *sf* (*misto di sottaceti*) mixed pickles *pl*
giardini'ere, a [dʒardi'njere] *sm/f* gardener
giar'dino [dʒar'dino] *sm* garden; ~ **d'infanzia** nursery school; ~ **pubblico** public gardens *pl*, (public) park; ~ **zoologico** zoo
giarretti'era [dʒarret'tjera] *sf* garter
giavel'lotto [dʒavel'lɔtto] *sm* javelin
gi'gante, 'essa [dʒi'gante] *sm/f* giant ♦ *ag* giant, gigantic; (*COMM*) giant-size; **gigan'tesco, a, schi, sche** *ag* gigantic
'giglio ['dʒiʎʎo] *sm* lily
gilè [dʒi'le] *sm inv* waistcoat
gin [dʒin] *sm inv* gin
gine'cologo, a, gi, ghe [dʒine'kɔlogo] *sm/f* gynaecologist
gi'nepro [dʒi'nepro] *sm* juniper
gi'nestra [dʒi'nestra] *sf* (*BOT*) broom
Gi'nevra [dʒi'nevra] *sf* Geneva
gingil'larsi [dʒindʒil'larsi] *vr* to fritter away one's time; (*giocare*): **~ con** to fiddle with

gin'gillo [dʒin'dʒillo] *sm* plaything

gin'nasio [dʒin'nazjo] *sm* the 4th and 5th *year of secondary school in Italy*

gin'nasta, i, e [dʒin'nasta] *sm/f* gymnast; gin'nastica *sf* gymnastics *sg*; (*esercizio fisico*) keep-fit exercises; (*INS*) physical education

gi'nocchio [dʒi'nɔkkjo] (*pl(m)* gi'nocchi *o pl(f)* gi'nocchia) *sm* knee; stare in ~ to kneel, be on one's knees; mettersi in ~ to kneel, go down on one's knees; ginocchi'oni *av* on one's knees

gio'care [dʒo'kare] *vt* to play; (*scommettere*) to stake, wager, bet; (*ingannare*) to take in ♦ *vi* to play; (*a roulette etc*) to gamble; (*fig*) to play a part, be important; ~ a (*gioco, sport*) to play; (*cavalli*) to bet on; ~rsi la carriera to put one's career at risk; gioca'tore, 'trice *sm/f* player; gambler

gio'cattolo [dʒo'kattolo] *sm* toy

gio'chetto [dʒo'ketto] *sm* (*tranello*) trick; (*fig*): è un ~ it's child's play

gi'oco, chi ['dʒɔko] *sm* game; (*divertimento, TECN*) play; (*al casinò*) gambling; (*CARTE*) hand; (*insieme di pezzi etc necessari per un gioco*) set; per ~ for fun; fare il doppio ~ con qn to double-cross sb; ~ d'azzardo game of chance; ~ degli scacchi chess set; i Giochi Olimpici the Olympic Games

giocoli'ere [dʒoko'ljere] *sm* juggler

gio'coso, a [dʒo'koso] *ag* playful, jesting

gi'ogo, ghi ['dʒogo] *sm* yoke

gi'oia ['dʒɔja] *sf* joy, delight; (*pietra preziosa*) jewel, precious stone

gioielle'ria [dʒojelle'ria] *sf* jeweller's craft; jeweller's (shop)

gioielli'ere, a [dʒojel'ljere] *sm/f* jeweller

gioi'ello [dʒo'jello] *sm* jewel, piece of jewellery; i miei ~i my jewels *o* jewellery

gioi'oso, a [dʒo'joso] *ag* joyful

Gior'dania [dʒor'danja] *sf*: la ~ Jordan

giorna'laio, a [dʒorna'lajo] *sm/f* newsagent (*BRIT*), newsdealer (*US*)

gior'nale [dʒor'nale] *sm* newspaper; (*diario*) journal, diary; (*COMM*) journal; ~ di bordo log; ~ radio news *sg*

giornali'ero, a [dʒorna'ljero] *ag* daily; (*che varia: umore*) changeable ♦ *sm* day labourer

giorna'lismo [dʒorna'lizmo] *sm* journalism

giorna'lista, i, e [dʒorna'lista] *sm/f* journalist

gior'nata [dʒor'nata] *sf* day; ~ lavorativa working day

gi'orno ['dʒorno] *sm* day; (*opposto alla notte*) day, daytime; (*luce del* ~) daylight; al ~ per day; di ~ by day; al ~ d'oggi nowadays

giorno dei morti

🛈 **Il giorno dei Morti**, All Souls' Day, falls on 2 November. On that day, relatives make a special visit to the graves of loved ones, to lay flowers.

gi'ostra ['dʒɔstra] *sf* (*per bimbi*) merry-go-round; (*torneo storico*) joust

gi'ovane ['dʒovane] *ag* young; (*aspetto*) youthful ♦ *sm/f* youth/girl, young man/woman; i ~i young people; giova'nile *ag* youthful; (*scritti*) early; (*errore*) of youth; giova'notto *sm* young man

gio'vare [dʒo'vare] *vi*: ~ a (*essere utile*) to be useful to; (*far bene*) to be good for ♦ *vb impers* (*essere bene, utile*) to be useful; ~rsi di qc to make use of sth

giovedì [dʒove'di] *sm inv* Thursday; di *o* il ~ on Thursdays

gioventù [dʒoven'tu] *sf* (*periodo*) youth; (*i giovani*) young people *pl*, youth

giovi'ale [dʒo'vjale] *ag* jovial, jolly

giovi'nezza [dʒovi'nettsa] *sf* youth

gira'dischi [dʒira'diski] *sm inv* record player

gi'raffa [dʒi'raffa] *sf* giraffe

gi'randola [dʒi'randola] *sf* (*fuoco d'artificio*) Catherine wheel; (*giocattolo*) toy windmill; (*banderuola*) weather vane, weathercock

gi'rare [dʒi'rare] *vt* (*far ruotare*) to turn; (*percorrere, visitare*) to go round; (*CINEMA*) to shoot; to make; (*COMM*) to endorse ♦ *vi* to turn; (*più veloce*) to spin; (*andare in giro*) to wander, go around; ~rsi *vr* to turn; ~

attorno to go round; to revolve round; **far ~ la testa a qn** to make sb dizzy; (*fig*) to turn sb's head

girar'rosto [dʒirar'rɔsto] *sm* (*CUC*) spit

gira'sole [dʒira'sole] *sm* sunflower

gi'rata [dʒi'rata] *sf* (*passeggiata*) stroll; (*con veicolo*) drive; (*COMM*) endorsement

gira'volta [dʒira'vɔlta] *sf* twirl, turn; (*curva*) sharp bend; (*fig*) about-turn

gi'revole [dʒi'revole] *ag* revolving, turning

gi'rino [dʒi'rino] *sm* tadpole

'giro [dʒiro] *sm* (*circuito, cerchio*) circle; (*di chiave, manovella*) turn; (*viaggio*) tour, excursion; (*passeggiata*) stroll, walk; (*in macchina*) drive; (*in bicicletta*) ride; (*SPORT: della pista*) lap; (*di denaro*) circulation; (*CARTE*) hand; (*TECN*) revolution; **prendere in ~ qn** (*fig*) to pull sb's leg; **fare un ~** to go for a walk (*o* a drive *o* a ride); **andare in ~** to go about, walk around; **a stretto ~ di posta** by return of post; **nel ~ di un mese** in a month's time; **essere nel ~** (*fig*) to belong to a circle (of friends); **~ d'affari** (*COMM*) turnover; **~ di parole** circumlocution; **~ di prova** (*AUT*) test drive; **~ turistico** sightseeing tour; **giro'collo** *sm*: **a girocollo** crew-neck *cpd*

gironzo'lare [dʒirondzo'lare] *vi* to stroll about

'gita ['dʒita] *sf* excursion, trip; **fare una ~** to go for a trip, go on an outing

gi'tano, a [dʒi'tano] *sm/f* gipsy

giù [dʒu] *av* down; (*dabbasso*) downstairs; **in ~** downwards, down; **~ di lì** (*pressappoco*) thereabouts; **bambini dai 6 anni in ~** children aged 6 and under; **~ per: cadere ~ per le scale** to fall down the stairs; **essere ~** (*fig: di salute*) to be run down; (*: di spirito*) to be depressed

giub'botto [dʒub'bɔtto] *sm* jerkin; **~ antiproiettile** bulletproof vest

gi'ubilo ['dʒubilo] *sm* rejoicing

giudi'care [dʒudi'kare] *vt* to judge; (*accusato*) to try; (*lite*) to arbitrate in; **~ qn/qc bello** to consider sb/sth (to be) beautiful

gi'udice ['dʒuditʃe] *sm* judge; **~ conciliatore** justice of the peace; **~ istruttore** examining (*BRIT*) *o* committing (*US*) magistrate; **~ popolare** member of a jury

giu'dizio [dʒu'dittsjo] *sm* judgment; (*opinione*) opinion; (*DIR*) judgment, sentence; (*: processo*) trial; (*: verdetto*) verdict; **aver ~** to be wise *o* prudent; **citare in ~** to summons; **giudizi'oso, a** *ag* prudent, judicious

gi'ugno ['dʒuɲɲo] *sm* June

glul'lare [dʒul'lare] *sm* jester

giu'menta [dʒu'menta] *sf* mare

gi'unco, chi ['dʒunko] *sm* rush

gi'ungere ['dʒundʒere] *vi* to arrive ♦ *vt* (*mani etc*) to join; **~ a** to arrive at, reach

gi'ungla ['dʒungla] *sf* jungle

gi'unta ['dʒunta] *sf* addition; (*organo esecutivo, amministrativo*) council, board; **per ~a** into the bargain, in addition; **~a militare** military junta

gi'unto, a ['dʒunto] *pp di* **giungere** ♦ *sm* (*TECN*) coupling, joint; **giun'tura** *sf* joint

giuo'care [dʒwo'kare] *etc* = **giocare** *etc*

giura'mento [dʒura'mento] *sm* oath; **~ falso** perjury

giu'rare [dʒu'rare] *vt* to swear ♦ *vi* to swear, take an oath; **giu'rato, a** *ag*: **nemico giurato** sworn enemy ♦ *sm/f* juror, juryman/woman

giu'ria [dʒu'ria] *sf* jury

giu'ridico, a, ci, che [dʒu'ridiko] *ag* legal

giustifi'care [dʒustifi'kare] *vt* to justify; **giustificazi'one** *sf* justification; (*INS*) (note of) excuse

gius'tizia [dʒus'tittsja] *sf* justice; **giustizi'are** *vt* to execute, put to death; **giustizi'ere** *sm* executioner

gi'usto, a ['dʒusto] *ag* (*equo*) fair, just; (*vero*) true, correct; (*adatto*) right, suitable; (*preciso*) exact, correct ♦ *av* (*esattamente*) exactly, precisely; (*per l'appunto, appena*) just; **arrivare ~** to arrive just in time; **ho ~ bisogno di te** you're just the person I need

glaci'ale [gla'tʃale] *ag* glacial

gli [ʎi] (*dav V, s impura, gn, pn, ps, x, z*) *det mpl* the ♦ *pron* (*a lui*) to him; (*a esso*) to it; (*in coppia con lo, la, li, le, ne: a lui, a lei, a loro etc*): **gliele do** I'm giving them to him (*o* her *o* them); *vedi anche* **il**

gli'ela ['ʎela] *etc vedi* **gli**

glo'bale *ag* overall

'globo *sm* globe

'globulo *sm* (ANAT): ~ **rosso/bianco** red/white corpuscle

'gloria *sf* glory; **glori'oso, a** *ag* glorious

glos'sario *sm* glossary

'gnocchi ['ɲɔkki] *smpl* (CUC) small dumplings made of semolina pasta or potato

'gobba *sf* (ANAT) hump; (*protuberanza*) bump

'gobbo, a *ag* hunchbacked; (*ricurvo*) round-shouldered ♦ *sm/f* hunchback

'goccia, ce ['gottʃa] *sf* drop; **goccio'lare** *vi, vt* to drip

go'dere *vi* (*compiacersi*): ~ **(di)** to be delighted (at), rejoice (at); (*trarre vantaggio*): ~ **di** to benefit from ♦ *vt* to enjoy; **~rsi la vita** to enjoy life; **~sela** to have a good time, enjoy o.s.; **godi'mento** *sm* enjoyment

'goffo, a *ag* clumsy, awkward

'gola *sf* (ANAT) throat; (*golosità*) gluttony, greed; (*di camino*) flue; (*di monte*) gorge; **fare** ~ (*anche fig*) to tempt

golf *sm inv* (SPORT) golf; (*maglia*) cardigan

'golfo *sm* gulf

go'loso, a *ag* greedy

'gomito *sm* elbow; (*di strada etc*) sharp bend

go'mitolo *sm* ball

'gomma *sf* rubber; (*per cancellare*) rubber, eraser; (*di veicolo*) tyre (BRIT), tire (US); ~ **americana** *o* **da masticare** chewing gum; ~ **a terra** flat tyre (BRIT) *o* tire (US); **gommapi'uma** ® *sf* foam rubber; **gom'mone** *sm* rubber dinghy

'gondola *sf* gondola; **gondoli'ere** *sm* gondolier

gonfa'lone *sm* banner

gonfi'are *vt* (*pallone*) to blow up, inflate; (*dilatare, ingrossare*) to swell; (*fig: notizia*) to exaggerate; **~rsi** *vr* to swell; (*fiume*) to rise; **'gonfio, a** *ag* swollen; (*stomaco*) bloated; (*vela*) full; **gonfi'ore** *sm* swelling

gongo'lare *vi* to look pleased with o.s.; ~ **di gioia** to be overjoyed

'gonna *sf* skirt; ~ **pantalone** culottes *pl*

'gonzo ['gondzo] *sm* simpleton, fool

gorgheggi'are [gorged'dʒare] *vi* to warble; to trill

'gorgo, ghi *sm* whirlpool

gorgogli'are [gorgoʎ'ʎare] *vi* to gurgle

go'rilla *sm inv* gorilla; (*guardia del corpo*) bodyguard

'gotta *sf* gout

gover'nante *sm/f* ruler ♦ *sf* (*di bambini*) governess; (*donna di servizio*) housekeeper

gover'nare *vt* (*stato*) to govern, rule; (*pilotare, guidare*) to steer; (*bestiame*) to tend, look after; **governa'tivo, a** *ag* government *cpd*; **governa'tore** *sm* governor

go'verno *sm* government

gozzovigli'are [gottsoviʎ'ʎare] *vi* to make merry, carouse

gpl *sigla m* (= *gas di petrolio liquefatto*) lpg

gracchi'are [grak'kjare] *vi* to caw

graci'dare [gratʃi'dare] *vi* to croak

'gracile ['gratʃile] *ag* frail, delicate

gra'dasso *sm* boaster

gradazi'one [gradat'tsjone] *sf* (*sfumatura*) gradation; ~ **alcolica** alcoholic content, strength

gra'devole *ag* pleasant, agreeable

gradi'mento *sm* pleasure, satisfaction; **è di suo ~?** is it to your liking?

gradi'nata *sf* flight of steps; (*in teatro, stadio*) tiers *pl*

gra'dino *sm* step; (ALPINISMO) foothold

gra'dire *vt* (*accettare con piacere*) to accept; (*desiderare*) to wish, like; **gradisce una tazza di tè?** would you like a cup of tea?; **gra'dito, a** *ag* pleasing; welcome

'grado *sm* (MAT, FISICA *etc*) degree; (*stadio*) degree, level; (MIL, *sociale*) rank; **essere in ~ di fare** to be in a position to do

gradu'ale *ag* gradual

gradu'are *vt* to grade; **gradu'ato, a** *ag* (*esercizi*) graded; (*scala, termometro*) graduated ♦ *sm* (MIL) non-commissioned officer

'graffa *sf* (*gancio*) clip; (*segno grafico*) brace

graffi'are *vt* to scratch

'graffio *sm* scratch

gra'fia *sf* spelling; (*scrittura*) handwriting

'grafica *sf* graphic arts *pl*

'grafico, a, ci, che *ag* graphic ♦ *sm* graph; (*persona*) graphic designer

gra'migna [gra'miɲɲa] *sf* weed; couch grass

gram'matica, che *sf* grammar; grammati'cale *ag* grammatical

'grammo *sm* gram(me)

gran *ag vedi* **grande**

'grana *sf* (*granello, di minerali, corpi spezzati*) grain; (*fam: seccatura*) trouble; (: *soldi*) cash ♦ *sm inv* Parmesan (cheese)

gra'naio *sm* granary, barn

gra'nata *sf* (*proiettile*) grenade

Gran Bre'tagna [-bre'taɲɲa] *sf*: **la ~** Great Britain

'granchio ['grankjo] *sm* crab; (*fig*) blunder; **prendere un ~** (*fig*) to blunder

grandango'lare *sm* wide-angle lens *sg*

'grande (*qualche volta* gran +*C*, grand' +*V*) *ag* (*grosso, largo, vasto*) big, large; (*alto*) tall; (*lungo*) long; (*in sensi astratti*) great ♦ *sm/f* (*persona adulta*) adult, grown-up; (*chi ha ingegno e potenza*) great man/ woman; **fare le cose in ~** to do things in style; **una gran bella donna** a very beautiful woman; **non è una gran cosa** *o* **un gran che** it's nothing special; **non ne so gran che** I don't know very much about it

grandeggi'are [granded'dʒare] *vi* (*emergere per grandezza*): **~ su** to tower over; (*darsi arie*) to put on airs

gran'dezza [gran'dettsa] *sf* (*dimensione*) size; magnitude; (*fig*) greatness; **in ~ naturale** lifesize

grandi'nare *vb impers* to hail

'grandine *sf* hail

gran'duca, chi *sm* grand duke

gra'nello *sm* (*di cereali, uva*) seed; (*di frutta*) pip; (*di sabbia, sale etc*) grain

gra'nita *sf* kind of water ice

gra'nito *sm* granite

'grano *sm* (*in quasi tutti i sensi*) grain; (*frumento*) wheat; (*di rosario, collana*) bead; **~ di pepe** peppercorn

gran'turco *sm* maize

'grappa *sf* rough, strong brandy

'grappolo *sm* bunch, cluster

gras'setto *sm* (*TIP*) bold (type)

'grasso, a *ag* fat; (*cibo*) fatty; (*pelle*) greasy; (*terreno*) rich; (*fig: guadagno, annata*) plentiful ♦ *sm* (*di persona, animale*) fat; (*sostanza che unge*) grease; gras'soccio, a, ci, ce *ag* plump

'grata *sf* grating

gra'ticola *sf* grill

gra'tifica, che *sf* bonus

'gratis *av* free, for nothing

grati'tudine *sf* gratitude

'grato, a *ag* grateful; (*gradito*) pleasant, agreeable

gratta'capo *sm* worry, headache

grattaci'elo [gratta'tʃɛlo] *sm* skyscraper

grat'tare *vt* (*pelle*) to scratch; (*raschiare*) to scrape; (*pane, formaggio, carote*) to grate; (*fam: rubare*) to pinch ♦ *vi* (*stridere*) to grate; (*AUT*) to grind; **~rsi** *vr* to scratch o.s.; **gratta e vinci** ≈ scratch card

grat'tugia, gie [grat'tudʒa] *sf* grater; grattugi'are [grattu'dʒare] *vt* to grate; **pane grattugiato** breadcrumbs *pl*

gra'tuito, a *ag* free; (*fig*) gratuitous

gra'vare *vt* to burden ♦ *vi*: **~ su** to weigh on

'grave *ag* (*danno, pericolo, peccato etc*) grave, serious; (*responsabilità*) heavy, grave; (*contegno*) grave, solemn; (*voce, suono*) deep, low-pitched; (*LING*): **accento ~** grave accent; **un malato ~** a person who is seriously ill

gravi'danza [gravi'dantsa] *sf* pregnancy

'gravido, a *ag* pregnant

gravità *sf* seriousness; (*anche FISICA*) gravity

gra'voso, a *ag* heavy, onerous

'grazia ['grattsja] *sf* grace; (*favore*) favour; (*DIR*) pardon; grazi'are *vt* (*DIR*) to pardon

'grazie ['grattsje] *escl* thank you!; **~ mille!** *o* **tante!** *o* **infinite!** thank you very much!; **~**

a thanks to

grazi'oso, a [grat'tsjoso] *ag* charming, delightful; (*gentile*) gracious

'Grecia ['grɛtʃa] *sf*: **la ~** Greece; **'greco, a, ci, che** *ag, sm/f*, sm Greek

'gregge ['greddʒe] (*pl(f)* **-i**) *sm* flock

'greggio, gi ['greddʒo] *sm* (*anche*: **petrolio ~**) crude (oil)

grembi'ule *sm* apron; (*sopravveste*) overall

'grembo *sm* lap; (*ventre della madre*) womb

gre'mito, a *ag*: **~ (di)** packed o crowded (with)

'gretto, a *ag* mean, stingy; (*fig*) narrow-minded

'greve *ag* heavy

'grezzo, a ['greddzo] *ag* raw, unrefined; (*diamante*) rough, uncut; (*tessuto*) unbleached

gri'dare *vi* (*per chiamare*) to shout, cry (out); (*strillare*) to scream, yell ♦ *vt* to shout (out), yell (out); **~ aiuto** to cry o shout for help

'grido (*pl(m)* **-i** *o pl(f)* **-a**) *sm* shout, cry; scream, yell; (*di animale*) cry; **di ~** famous

'grigio, a, gi, gie ['gridʒo] *ag, sm* grey

'griglia ['griʎʎa] *sf* (*per arrostire*) grill; (*ELETTR*) grid; (*inferriata*) grating; **alla ~** (*CUC*) grilled; **grigli'ata** (*CUC*) grill

gril'letto *sm* trigger

'grillo *sm* (*ZOOL*) cricket; (*fig*) whim

grimal'dello *sm* picklock

'grinta *sf* grim expression; (*SPORT*) fighting spirit

'grinza ['grintsa] *sf* crease, wrinkle; (*ruga*) wrinkle; **non fare una ~** (*fig: ragionamento*) to be faultless; **grin'zoso, a** *ag* creased; wrinkled

gris'sino *sm* bread-stick

'gronda *sf* eaves *pl*

gron'daia *sf* gutter

gron'dare *vi* to pour; (*essere bagnato*): **~ di** to be dripping with ♦ *vt* to drip with

'groppa *sf* (*di animale*) back, rump; (*fam: dell'uomo*) back, shoulders *pl*

'groppo *sm* tangle; **avere un ~ alla gola** (*fig*) to have a lump in one's throat

gros'sezza [gros'settsa] *sf* size; thickness

gros'sista, i, e (*COMM*) wholesaler

'grosso, a *ag* big, large; (*di spessore*) thick; (*grossolano: anche fig*) coarse; (*grave, insopportabile*) serious, great; (*tempo, mare*) rough ♦ *sm*: **il ~ di** the bulk of; **un pezzo ~** (*fig*) a VIP, a bigwig; **farla ~a** to do something very stupid; **dirle ~e** to tell tall stories; **sbagliarsi di ~** to be completely wrong

grosso'lano, a *ag* rough, coarse; (*fig*) coarse, crude; (: *errore*) stupid

grosso'modo *av* roughly

'grotta *sf* cave; grotto

grot'tesco, a, schi, sche *ag* grotesque

grovi'era *sm o f* gruyère (cheese)

gro'viglio [gro'viʎʎo] *sm* tangle; (*fig*) muddle

gru *sf inv* crane

'gruccia, ce ['gruttʃa] *sf* (*per camminare*) crutch; (*per abiti*) coat-hanger

gru'gnire [gruɲ'ɲire] *vi* to grunt; **gru'gnito** *sm* grunt

'grugno ['gruɲɲo] *sm* snout; (*fam: faccia*) mug

'grullo, a *ag* silly, stupid

'grumo *sm* (*di sangue*) clot; (*di farina etc*) lump

'gruppo *sm* group; **~ sanguigno** blood group

gruvi'era *sm o f* = **groviera**

guada'gnare [gwadaɲ'ɲare] *vt* (*ottenere*) to gain; (*soldi, stipendio*) to earn; (*vincere*) to win; (*raggiungere*) to reach

gua'dagno [gwa'daɲɲo] *sm* earnings *pl*; (*COMM*) profit; (*vantaggio, utile*) advantage, gain; **~ lordo/netto** gross/net earnings *pl*

gu'ado *sm* ford; **passare a ~** to ford

gu'ai *escl*: **~ a te** (*o* **lui** *etc*)! woe betide you (*o* him *etc*)!

gua'ina *sf* (*fodero*) sheath; (*indumento per donna*) girdle

gu'aio *sm* trouble, mishap; (*inconveniente*) trouble, snag

gua'ire *vi* to whine, yelp

gu'ancia, ce ['gwantʃa] *sf* cheek

guanci'ale [gwan'tʃale] *sm* pillow

gu'anto sm glove

gu'arda... prefisso: ~'boschi sm inv forester; ~'caccia sm inv gamekeeper; ~'coste sm inv coastguard; (nave) coastguard patrol vessel; ~'linee sm inv (SPORT) linesman

guar'dare vt (con lo sguardo: osservare) to look at; (film, televisione) to watch; (custodire) to look after, take care of ♦ vi to look; (badare): ~ a to pay attention to; (luoghi: esser orientato): ~ a to face; ~rsi vr to look at o.s.; ~rsi da (astenersi) to refrain from; (stare in guardia) to beware of; ~rsi dal fare to take care not to do; guarda di non sbagliare try not to make a mistake; ~ a vista qn to keep a close watch on sb

guarda'roba sm inv wardrobe; (locale) cloakroom; guardarobi'ere, a sm/f cloakroom attendant

gu'ardia sf (individuo, corpo) guard; (sorveglianza) watch; fare la ~ a qc/qn to guard sth/sb; stare in ~ (fig) to be on one's guard; di ~ (medico) on call; ~ carceraria (prison) warder; ~ del corpo bodyguard; ~ di finanza (corpo) customs pl; (persona) customs officer; ~ medica emergency doctor service

Guardia di finanza

ⓘ The Guardia di finanza is a military body which deals with infringements of the laws relating to income tax and monopolies. It reports to the Ministers of Finance, Justice or Agriculture.

guardi'ano, a sm/f (di carcere) warder; (di villa etc) caretaker; (di museo) custodian; (di zoo) keeper; ~ notturno night watchman

guar'dingo, a, ghi, ghe ag wary, cautious

guardi'ola sf porter's lodge; (MIL) look-out tower

guard'rail [ga:dreil] sm inv crash barrier

guarigi'one [gwari'dʒone] sf recovery

gua'rire vt (persona, malattia) to cure; (ferita) to heal ♦ vi to recover, be cured; to

heal (up)

guarnigi'one [gwarni'dʒone] sf garrison

guar'nire vt (ornare: abiti) to trim; (CUC) to garnish; guarnizi'one sf trimming; garnish; (TECN) gasket

guasta'feste sm/f inv spoilsport

guas'tare vt to spoil, ruin; (meccanismo) to break; ~rsi vr (cibo) to go bad; (meccanismo) to break down; (tempo) to change for the worse

gu'asto, a ag (non funzionante) broken; (: telefono etc) out of order; (andato a male) bad, rotten; (: dente) decayed, bad; (fig: corrotto) depraved ♦ sm breakdown; (avaria) failure; ~ al motore engine failure

gu'ercio, a, ci, ce ['gwertʃo] ag cross-eyed

gu'erra sf war; (tecnica: atomica, chimica etc) warfare; fare la ~ (a) to wage war (against); ~ mondiale world war; guerri'ero, a ag warlike ♦ sm warrior; guer'riglia sf guerrilla warfare; guerrigli'ero sm guerrilla

'gufo sm owl

gu'ida sf guidebook; (comando, direzione) guidance, direction; (AUT) driving; (tappeto, di tenda, cassetto) runner; ~ a destra/ sinistra (AUT) right-/left-hand drive; ~ telefonica telephone directory; ~ turistica tourist guide

gui'dare vt to guide; (squadra, rivolta) to lead; (auto) to drive; (aereo, nave) to pilot; sai ~? can you drive?; guida'tore, trice sm/f (conducente) driver

guin'zaglio [gwin'tsaʎʎo] sm leash, lead

gu'isa sf: a ~ di like, in the manner of

guiz'zare [gwit'tsare] vi to dart; to flicker; to leap

'guscio ['guʃʃo] sm shell

gus'tare vt (cibi) to taste; (: assaporare con piacere) to enjoy, savour; (fig) to enjoy, appreciate ♦ vi: ~ a to please; non mi gusta affatto I don't like it at all

'gusto sm taste; (sapore) flavour; (godimento) enjoyment; al ~ di fragola strawberry-flavoured; mangiare di ~ to eat heartily; prenderci ~: ci ha preso ~ he's

acquired a taste for it, he's got to like it;
gus'toso, a *ag* tasty; (*fig*) agreeable

H, h

h *abbr* = **ora**; **altezza**
ha *etc* [a] *vb vedi* **avere**
ha'cker [hæˈkəˈ] *sm inv* hacker
hall [hɔl] *sf inv* hall, foyer
'handicap [ˈhandikap] *sm inv* handicap;
   handicap'pato, a *ag* handicapped
   ♦ *sm/f* handicapped person, disabled
   person
'hanno [ˈanno] *vb vedi* **avere**
'hascisc [ˈhaʃiʃ] *sm* hashish
'herpes [ˈɛrpes] *sm* (*MED*) herpes *sg*; ~
   zoster shingles *sg*
ho [ɔ] *vb vedi* **avere**
'hobby [ˈhɔbi] *sm inv* hobby
'hockey [ˈhɔki] *sm* hockey; ~ **su ghiaccio**
   ice hockey
'hostess [ˈhoustis] *sf inv* air hostess (*BRIT*) o
   stewardess
ho'tel *sm inv* hotel

I, i

i *det mpl* the
i'ato *sm* hiatus
ibernazi'one [ibernatˈtsjone] *sf* hibernation
'ibrido, a *ag*, *sm* hybrid
i'cona *sf* (*REL, INFORM, fig*) icon
Id'dio *sm* God
i'dea *sf* idea; (*opinione*) opinion, view;
   (*ideale*) ideal; **dare l'~ di** to seem, look like;
   ~ **fissa** obsession; **neanche** o **neppure per**
   ~**!** certainly not!
ide'ale *ag*, *sm* ideal
ide'are *vt* (*immaginare*) to think up,
   conceive; (*progettare*) to plan
i'dentico, a, ci, che *ag* identical
identifi'care *vt* to identify;
   identificazi'one *sf* identification
identità *sf inv* identity
ideolo'gia, 'gie [ideoloˈdʒia] *sf* ideology

idi'oma, i *sm* idiom, language;
   idio'matico, a, ci, che *ag* idiomatic;
   frase idiomatica idiom
idi'ota, i, e *ag* idiotic ♦ *sm/f* idiot
idola'trare *vt* to worship; (*fig*) to idolize
'idolo *sm* idol
idoneità *sf* suitability
i'doneo, a *ag*: ~ **a** suitable for, fit for; (*MIL*)
   fit for; (*qualificato*) qualified for
i'drante *sm* hydrant
idra'tante *ag* moisturizing ♦ *sm*
   moisturizer
i'draulica *sf* hydraulics *sg*
i'draulico, a, ci, che *ag* hydraulic ♦ *sm*
   plumber
idroe'lettrico, a, ci, che *ag*
   hydroelectric
i'drofilo, a *ag vedi* **cotone**
i'drogeno [iˈdrɔdʒeno] *sm* hydrogen
idros'calo *sm* seaplane base
idrovo'lante *sm* seaplane
i'ena *sf* hyena
i'eri *av*, *sm* yesterday; **il giornale di** ~
   yesterday's paper; ~ **l'altro** the day before
   yesterday; ~ **sera** yesterday evening
igi'ene [iˈdʒɛne] *sf* hygiene; ~ **pubblica**
   public health; **igi'enico, a, ci, che** *ag*
   hygienic; (*salubre*) healthy
i'gnaro, a [iɲˈɲaro] *ag*: ~ **di** unaware of,
   ignorant of
i'gnobile [iɲˈɲɔbile] *ag* despicable, vile
igno'rante [iɲɲoˈrante] *ag* ignorant
igno'rare [iɲɲoˈrare] *vt* (*non sapere, conoscere*)
   to be ignorant o unaware of, not to know;
   (*fingere di non vedere, sentire*) to ignore
i'gnoto, a [iɲˈɲɔto] *ag* unknown

─── PAROLA CHIAVE ───

il (*pl* (*m*) **i**; *diventa* **lo** (*pl* **gli**) *davanti a s
   impura, gn, pn, ps, x, z; f* **la** (*pl* **le**)) *det m*
   1 the; ~ **libro/lo studente/l'acqua** the
   book/the student/the water; **gli scolari** the
   pupils
   2 (*astrazione*): ~ **coraggio/l'amore/la
   giovinezza** courage/love/youth
   3 (*tempo*): ~ **mattino/la sera** in the
   morning/evening; ~ **venerdì** *etc*

(*abitualmente*) on Fridays *etc*; (*quel giorno*) on (the) Friday *etc*; **la settimana prossima** next week

4 (*distributivo*) a, an; **2.500 lire ~ chilo/paio** 2,500 lire a *o* per kilo/pair

5 (*partitivo*) some, any; **hai messo lo zucchero?** have you added sugar?; **hai comprato ~ latte?** did you buy (some *o* any) milk?

6 (*possesso*): **aprire gli occhi** to open one's eyes; **rompersi la gamba** to break one's leg; **avere i capelli neri/~ naso rosso** to have dark hair/a red nose

7 (*con nomi propri*): **~ Petrarca** Petrarch; **~ Presidente Clinton** President Clinton; **dov'è la Francesca?** where's Francesca?

8 (*con nomi geografici*): **~ Tevere** the Tiber; **l'Italia** Italy; **~ Regno Unito** the United Kingdom; **l'Everest** Everest

'**ilare** *ag* cheerful; **ilarità** *sf* hilarity, mirth

illazi'one [illat'tsjone] *sf* inference, deduction

ille'gale *ag* illegal

illeg'gibile [illed'dʒibile] *ag* illegible

ille'gittimo, a [ille'dʒittimo] *ag* illegitimate

il'leso, a *ag* unhurt, unharmed

illi'bato, a *ag*: **donna ~a** virgin

illimi'tato, a *ag* boundless; unlimited

ill.mo *abbr* = **illustrissimo**

il'ludere *vt* to deceive, delude; **~rsi** *vr* to deceive o.s., delude o.s.

illumi'nare *vt* to light up, illuminate; (*fig*) to enlighten; **~rsi** *vr* to light up; **~ a giorno** to floodlight; **illuminazi'one** *sf* lighting; illumination; floodlighting; (*fig*) flash of inspiration

illusi'one *sf* illusion; **farsi delle ~i** to delude o.s.

illusio'nismo *sm* conjuring

il'luso, a *pp di* **illudere**

illus'trare *vt* to illustrate; **illustra'tivo, a** *ag* illustrative; **illustrazi'one** *sf* illustration

il'lustre *ag* eminent, renowned; **illus'trissimo, a** *ag* (*negli indirizzi*) very revered

imbacuc'care *vt* to wrap up; **~rsi** *vr* to wrap up

imbal'laggio [imbal'laddʒo] *sm* packing *no pl*

imbal'lare *vt* to pack; (*AUT*) to race; **~rsi** *vr* (*AUT*) to race

imbalsa'mare *vt* to embalm

imbambo'lato, a *ag* (*sguardo*) vacant, blank

imban'dire *vt*: **~ un pranzo** to prepare a lavish meal

imbaraz'zare [imbarat'tsare] *vt* (*mettere a disagio*) to embarrass; (*ostacolare: movimenti*) to hamper

imba'razzo [imba'rattso] *sm* (*disagio*) embarrassment; (*perplessità*) puzzlement, bewilderment; **~ di stomaco** indigestion

imbarca'dero *sm* landing stage

imbar'care *vt* (*passeggeri*) to embark; (*merci*) to load; **~rsi** *vr*: **~rsi su** to board; **~rsi per l'America** to sail for America; **~rsi in** (*fig: affare etc*) to embark on

imbarcazi'one [imbarkat'tsjone] *sf* (small) boat, (small) craft *inv*; **~ di salvataggio** lifeboat

im'barco, chi *sm* embarkation; loading; boarding; (*banchina*) landing stage

imbas'tire *vt* (*cucire*) to tack; (*fig: abbozzare*) to sketch, outline

im'battersi *vr*: **~ in** (*incontrare*) to bump *o* run into

imbat'tibile *ag* unbeatable, invincible

imbavagli'are [imbavaʎ'ʎare] *vt* to gag

imbec'cata *sf* (*TEATRO*) prompt

imbe'cille [imbe'tʃille] *ag* idiotic ♦ *sm/f* idiot; (*MED*) imbecile

imbel'lire *vt* to adorn, embellish ♦ *vi* to grow more beautiful

im'berbe *ag* beardless

im'bevere *vt* to soak; **~rsi** *vr*: **~rsi di** to soak up, absorb

imbian'care *vt* to whiten; (*muro*) to whitewash ♦ *vi* to become *o* turn white

imbian'chino [imbjan'kino] *sm* (house) painter, painter and decorator

imboc'care *vt* (*bambino*) to feed; (*entrare: strada*) to enter, turn into

imbocca'tura *sf* mouth; (*di strada, porto*)

entrance; (MUS, del morso) mouthpiece
im'bocco, chi sm entrance
imbos'care vt to hide; ~rsi vr (MIL) to evade military service
imbos'cata sf ambush
imbottigli'are [imbottiʎˈʎare] vt to bottle; (NAUT) to blockade; (MIL) to hem in; ~rsi vr to be stuck in a traffic jam
imbot'tire vt to stuff; (giacca) to pad; imbot'tita sf quilt; imbot'tito, a ag stuffed; (giacca) padded; **panino imbottito** filled roll; imbotti'tura sf stuffing; padding
imbrat'tare vt to dirty, smear, daub
imbrigli'are [imbriʎˈʎare] vt to bridle
imbroc'care vt (fig) to guess correctly
imbrogli'are [imbroʎˈʎare] vt to mix up; (fig: raggirare) to deceive, cheat; (: confondere) to confuse, mix up; ~rsi vr to get tangled; (fig) to become confused; im'broglio sm (groviglio) tangle; (situazione confusa) mess; (truffa) swindle, trick; imbrogli'one, a sm/f cheat, swindler
imbronci'ato, a ag sulky
imbru'nire vi, vb impers to grow dark; **all'~** at dusk
imbrut'tire vt to make ugly ♦ vi to become ugly
imbu'care vt to post
imbur'rare vt to butter
im'buto sm funnel
imi'tare vt to imitate; (riprodurre) to copy; (assomigliare) to look like; imitazi'one sf imitation
immaco'lato, a ag spotless; immaculate
immagazzi'nare [immagaddziˈnare] vt to store
immagi'nare [immadʒiˈnare] vt to imagine; (supporre) to suppose; (inventare) to invent; **s'immagini!** don't mention it!, not at all!; immagi'nario, a ag imaginary; immaginazi'one sf imagination; (cosa immaginata) fancy
im'magine [imˈmadʒine] sf image; (rappresentazione grafica, mentale) picture
imman'cabile ag certain; unfailing

im'mane ag (smisurato) enormous; (spaventoso) terrible
immangi'abile [immanˈdʒabile] ag inedible
immatrico'lare vt to register; ~rsi vr (INS) to matriculate, enrol; immatricolazi'one sf registration; matriculation, enrolment
imma'turo, a ag (frutto) unripe; (persona) immature; (prematuro) premature
immedesi'marsi vr: ~ **in** to identify with
immediata'mente av immediately, at once
immedi'ato, a ag immediate
im'memore ag: ~ **di** forgetful of
im'menso, a ag immense
im'mergere [imˈmerdʒere] vt to immerse, plunge; ~rsi vr to plunge; (sommergibile) to dive, submerge; (dedicarsi a): ~rsi **in** to immerse o.s. in
immeri'tato, a ag undeserved
immeri'tevole ag undeserving, unworthy
immersi'one sf immersion; (di sommergibile) submersion, dive; (di palombaro) dive
im'merso, a pp di **immergere**
im'mettere vt: ~ **(in)** to introduce (into); ~ **dati in un computer** to enter data on a computer
immi'grato, a sm/f immigrant; immigrazi'one sf immigration
immi'nente ag imminent
immischi'are [immisˈkjare] vt: ~ **qn in** to involve sb in; ~rsi **in** to interfere o meddle in
immissi'one sf (di aria, gas) intake; ~ **di dati** (INFORM) data entry
im'mobile ag motionless, still; ~i smpl (anche: **beni ~i**) real estate sg; immobili'are ag (DIR) property cpd; immobilità sf stillness; immobility
immo'desto, a ag immodest
immo'lare vt to sacrifice, immolate
immon'dizia [immonˈdittsja] sf dirt, filth; (spesso al pl: spazzatura, rifiuti) rubbish no pl, refuse no pl
im'mondo, a ag filthy, foul
immo'rale ag immoral
immor'tale ag immortal

im'mune *ag* (*esente*) exempt; (MED, DIR) immune; **immunità** *sf* immunity; **immunità parlamentare** parliamentary privilege

immu'tabile *ag* immutable; unchanging

impacchet'tare [impakket'tare] *vt* to pack up

impacci'are [impat'tʃare] *vt* to hinder, hamper; **impacci'ato, a** *ag* awkward, clumsy; (*imbarazzato*) embarrassed; **im'paccio** *sm* obstacle; (*imbarazzo*) embarrassment; (*situazione imbarazzante*) awkward situation

im'pacco, chi *sm* (MED) compress

impadro'nirsi *vr*: **~ di** to seize, take possession of; (*fig: apprendere a fondo*) to master

impa'gabile *ag* priceless

impagi'nare [impadʒi'nare] *vt* (TIP) to paginate, page (up)

impagli'are [impaʎ'ʎare] *vt* to stuff (with straw)

impa'lato, a *ag* (*fig*) stiff as a board

impalca'tura *sf* scaffolding

impalli'dire *vi* to turn pale; (*fig*) to fade

impa'nare *vt* (CUC) to dip in breadcrumbs

impanta'narsi *vr* to sink (in the mud); (*fig*) to get bogged down

impappi'narsi *vr* to stammer, falter

impa'rare *vt* to learn

imparen'tarsi *vr*: **~ con** to marry into

'impari *ag inv* (*disuguale*) unequal; (*dispari*) odd

impar'tire *vt* to bestow, give

imparzi'ale [impar'tsjale] *ag* impartial, unbiased

impas'sibile *ag* impassive

impas'tare *vt* (*pasta*) to knead

im'pasto *sm* (*l'impastare: di pane*) kneading; (*di cemento*) mixing; (*pasta*) dough; (*anche fig*) mixture

im'patto *sm* impact

impau'rire *vt* to scare, frighten ♦ *vi* (*anche: ~rsi*) to become scared *o* frightened

im'pavido, a *ag* intrepid, fearless

impazi'ente [impat'tsjɛnte] *ag* impatient; **impazi'enza** *sf* impatience

impaz'zata [impat'tsata] *sf*: **all'~** (*precipitosamente*) at breakneck speed

impaz'zire [impat'tsire] *vi* to go mad; **~ per qn/qc** to be crazy about sb/sth

impec'cabile *ag* impeccable

impedi'mento *sm* obstacle, hindrance

impe'dire *vt* (*vietare*): **~ a qn di fare** to prevent sb from doing; (*ostruire*) to obstruct; (*impacciare*) to hamper, hinder

impe'gnare [impeɲ'ɲare] *vt* (*dare in pegno*) to pawn; (*onore etc*) to pledge; (*prenotare*) to book, reserve; (*obbligare*) to oblige; (*occupare*) to keep busy; (MIL: *nemico*) to engage; **~rsi** *vr* (*vincolarsi*): **~rsi a fare** to undertake to do; (*mettersi risolutamente*): **~rsi in qc** to devote o.s. to sth; **~rsi con qn** (*accordarsi*) to come to an agreement with sb; **impegna'tivo, a** *ag* binding; (*lavoro*) demanding, exacting; **impe'gnato, a** *ag* (*occupato*) busy; (*fig: romanzo, autore*) committed, engagé

im'pegno [im'peɲɲo] *sm* (*obbligo*) obligation; (*promessa*) promise, pledge; (*zelo*) diligence, zeal; (*compito, d'autore*) commitment

impel'lente *ag* pressing, urgent

impene'trabile *ag* impenetrable

impen'narsi *vr* (*cavallo*) to rear up; (AER) to nose up; (*fig*) to bridle

impen'sato, a *ag* unforeseen, unexpected

impensie'rire *vt* to worry; **~rsi** *vr* to worry

impe'rare *vi* (*anche fig*) to reign, rule

impera'tivo, a *ag, sm* imperative

impera'tore, 'trice *sm/f* emperor/empress

imperdo'nabile *ag* unforgivable, unpardonable

imper'fetto, a *ag* imperfect ♦ *sm* (LING) imperfect (tense); **imperfezi'one** *sf* imperfection

imperi'ale *ag* imperial

imperi'oso, a *ag* (*persona*) imperious; (*motivo, esigenza*) urgent, pressing

impe'rizia [impe'rittsja] *sf* lack of experience

imperma'lirsi *vr* to take offence

imperme'abile *ag* waterproof ♦ *sm* raincoat

imperni'are *vt*: ~ **qc su** to hinge sth on; *(fig)* to base sth on; ~**rsi** *vr (fig)*: ~**rsi su** to be based on

im'pero *sm* empire; *(forza, autorità)* rule, control

imperscru'tabile *ag* inscrutable

imperso'nale *ag* impersonal

imperso'nare *vt* to personify; *(TEATRO)* to play, act (the part of)

imperter'rito, a *ag* fearless, undaunted; impassive

imperti'nente *ag* impertinent

imperver'sare *vi* to rage

'impeto *sm (moto, forza)* force, impetus; *(assalto)* onslaught; *(fig: impulso)* impulse; *(: slancio)* transport; **con ~** energetically, vehemently

impet'tito, a *ag* stiff, erect

impetu'oso, a *ag (vento)* strong, raging; *(persona)* impetuous

impian'tare *vt (motore)* to install; *(azienda, discussione)* to establish, start

impi'anto *sm (installazione)* installation; *(apparecchiature)* plant; *(sistema)* system; ~ **elettrico** wiring; ~ **sportivo** sports complex; ~**i di risalita** *(SCI)* ski lifts

impiastricci'are [impjastrit'tʃare] *vt* = **impiastrare**

impi'astro *sm* poultice

impic'care *vt* to hang; ~**rsi** *vr* to hang o.s.

impicci'are [impit'tʃare] *vt* to hinder, hamper; ~**rsi** *vr* to meddle, interfere; **im'piccio** *sm (ostacolo)* hindrance; *(seccatura)* trouble, bother; *(affare imbrogliato)* mess; **essere d'impiccio** to be in the way

impie'gare *vt (usare)* to use, employ; *(spendere: denaro, tempo)* to spend; *(investire)* to invest; **impie'gato, a** *sm/f* employee

impi'ego, ghi *sm (uso)* use; *(occupazione)* employment; *(posto di lavoro)* (regular) job, post; *(ECON)* investment

impieto'sire *vt* to move to pity; ~**rsi** *vr* to be moved to pity

impie'trire *vt (fig)* to petrify

impigli'are [impiʎ'ʎare] *vt* to catch, entangle; ~**rsi** *vr* to get caught up *o* entangled

impi'grire *vt* to make lazy ♦ *vi (anche:* ~**rsi)** to grow lazy

impli'care *vt* to imply; *(coinvolgere)* to involve; **implicazi'one** *sf* implication

im'plicito, a [im'plitʃito] *ag* implicit

implo'rare *vt* to implore; *(pietà etc)* to beg for

impolve'rare *vt* to cover with dust; ~**rsi** *vr* to get dusty

impo'nente *ag* imposing, impressive

impo'nibile *ag* taxable ♦ *sm* taxable income

impopo'lare *ag* unpopular

im'porre *vt* to impose; *(costringere)* to force, make; *(far valere)* to impose, enforce; **imporsi** *vr (persona)* to assert o.s.; *(cosa: rendersi necessario)* to become necessary; *(aver successo: moda, attore)* to become popular; ~ **a qn di fare** to force sb to do, make sb do

impor'tante *ag* important; **impor'tanza** *sf* importance; **dare importanza a qc** to attach importance to sth; **darsi importanza** to give o.s. airs

impor'tare *vt (introdurre dall'estero)* to import ♦ *vi* to matter, be important ♦ *vb impers (essere necessario)* to be necessary; *(interessare)* to matter; **non importa!** it doesn't matter!; **non me ne importa!** I don't care!; **importazi'one** *sf* importation; *(merci importate)* imports *pl*

im'porto *sm* (total) amount

importu'nare *vt* to bother

impor'tuno, a *ag* irksome, annoying

imposizi'one [impozit'tsjone] *sf* imposition; order, command; *(onere, imposta)* tax

imposses'sarsi *vr*: ~ **di** to seize, take possession of

impos'sibile *ag* impossible; **fare l'~** to do one's utmost, do all one can; **impossibilità** *sf* impossibility; **essere nell'impossibilità di fare qc** to be unable to do sth

im'posta *sf (di finestra)* shutter; *(tassa)* tax; **~ sul reddito** income tax; **~ sul valore aggiunto** value added tax *(BRIT)*, sales tax *(US)*

impos'tare *vt (imbucare)* to post; *(preparare)* to plan, set out; *(avviare)* to begin, start off; *(voce)* to pitch

im'posto, a *pp di* **imporre**

impo'tente *ag* weak, powerless; *(anche MED)* impotent

impove'rire *vt* to impoverish ♦ *vi (anche:* **~rsi)** to become poor

imprati'cabile *ag (strada)* impassable; *(campo da gioco)* unplayable

imprati'chirsi [imprati'kirsi] *vr:* **~rsi in qc** to practise *(BRIT)* o practice *(US)* sth

impre'gnare [impreɲ'ɲare] *vt:* **~ (di)** *(imbevere)* to soak o impregnate (with); *(riempire: anche fig)* to fill (with)

imprendi'tore *sm (industriale)* entrepreneur; *(appaltatore)* contractor; **piccolo ~** small businessman

im'presa *sf (iniziativa)* enterprise; *(azione)* exploit; *(azienda)* firm, concern

impre'sario *sm (TEATRO)* manager, impresario; **~ di pompe funebri** funeral director

imprescin'dibile [impreʃʃin'dibile] *ag* not to be ignored

impressio'nante *ag* impressive; upsetting

impressio'nare *vt* to impress; *(turbare)* to upset; *(FOT)* to expose; **~rsi** *vr* to be easily upset

impressi'one *sf* impression; *(fig: sensazione)* sensation, feeling; *(stampa)* printing; **fare ~** *(colpire)* to impress; *(turbare)* to frighten, upset; **fare buona/cattiva ~ a** to make a good/bad impression on

im'presso, a *pp di* **imprimere**

impres'tare *vt:* **~ qc a qn** to lend sth to sb

impreve'dibile *ag* unforeseeable; *(persona)* unpredictable

imprevi'dente *ag* lacking in foresight

impre'visto, a *ag* unexpected, unforeseen

♦ *sm* unforeseen event; **salvo ~i** unless anything unexpected happens

imprigio'nare [impridʒo'nare] *vt* to imprison

im'primere *vt (anche fig)* to impress, stamp; *(comunicare: movimento)* to transmit, give

impro'babile *ag* improbable, unlikely

im'pronta *sf* imprint, impression, sign; *(di piede, mano)* print; *(fig)* mark, stamp; **~ digitale** fingerprint

impro'perio *sm* insult

im'proprio, a *ag* improper; **arma ~a** offensive weapon

improvvisa'mente *av* suddenly; unexpectedly

improvvi'sare *vt* to improvise; **~rsi** *vr:* **~rsi cuoco** to (decide to) act as cook; **improvvi'sata** *sf* (pleasant) surprise

improv'viso, a *ag (imprevisto)* unexpected; *(subitaneo)* sudden; **all'~** unexpectedly; suddenly

impru'dente *ag* unwise, rash

impu'dente *ag* impudent

impu'dico, a, chi, che *ag* immodest

impu'gnare [impuɲ'ɲare] *vt* to grasp, grip; *(DIR)* to contest

impul'sivo, a *ag* impulsive

im'pulso *sm* impulse

impun'tarsi *vr* to stop dead, refuse to budge; *(fig)* to be obstinate

impu'tare *vt (ascrivere):* **~ qc a** to attribute sth to; *(DIR: accusare):* **~ qn di** to charge sb with, accuse sb of; **impu'tato, a** *sm/f (DIR)* accused, defendant; **imputazi'one** *sf (DIR)* charge

imputri'dire *vi* to rot

PAROLA CHIAVE

---

in *(in+il = nel, in+lo = nello, in+l' = nell', in+la = nella, in+i = nei, in+gli = negli, in+le = nelle) prep* **1** *(stato in luogo)* in; **vivere ~ Italia/città** to live in Italy/town; **essere ~ casa/ufficio** to be at home/the office; **se fossi ~ te** if I were you

2 *(moto a luogo)* to; *(: dentro)* into; **andare ~ Germania/città** to go to Germany/

town; **andare ~ ufficio** to go to the office;
entrare ~ macchina/casa to get into the
car/go into the house
3 (*tempo*) in; **nel 1999** in 1999; **~
giugno/estate** in June/summer
4 (*modo, maniera*) in; **~ silenzio** in silence;
~ abito da sera in evening dress; **~
guerra** at war; **~ vacanza** on holiday;
Maria Bianchi ~ Rossi Maria Rossi née
Bianchi
5 (*mezzo*) by; **viaggiare ~ autobus/treno**
to travel by bus/train
6 (*materia*) made of; **~ marmo** made of
marble, marble *cpd*; **una collana ~ oro** a
gold necklace
7 (*misura*) in; **siamo ~ quattro** there are
four of us; **~ tutto** in all
8 (*fine*): **dare ~ dono** to give as a gift;
spende tutto ~ alcool he spends all his
money on drink; **~ onore di** in honour of

inabi'tabile *ag* uninhabitable
inacces'sibile [inattʃes'sibile] *ag* (*luogo*)
inaccessible; (*persona*) unapproachable
inaccet'tabile [inattʃet'tabile] *ag*
unacceptable
ina'datto, a *ag*: **~ (a)** unsuitable *o* unfit
(for)
inadegu'ato, a *ag* inadequate
inadempi'enza [inadem'pjentsa] *sf*: **~ (a)**
non-fulfilment (of)
inaffer'rabile *ag* elusive; (*concetto, senso*)
difficult to grasp
inalbe'rarsi *vr* (*fig*) to flare up, fly off the
handle
inalte'rabile *ag* unchangeable; (*colore*)
fast, permanent; (*affetto*) constant
inalte'rato, a *ag* unchanged
inami'dato, a *ag* starched
inani'mato, a *ag* inanimate; (*senza vita:
corpo*) lifeless
inappa'gabile *ag* insatiable
inappel'labile *ag* (*decisione*) final,
irrevocable; (*DIR*) final, not open to appeal
inappe'tenza [inappe'tentsa] *sf* (*MED*) lack
of appetite
inappun'tabile *ag* irreproachable

inar'care *vt* (*schiena*) to arch; (*sopracciglia*)
to raise; **~rsi** *vr* to arch
inari'dire *vt* to make arid, dry up ♦ *vi*
(*anche: ~rsi*) to dry up, become arid
inaspet'tato, a *ag* unexpected
inas'prire *vt* (*disciplina*) to tighten up,
make harsher; (*carattere*) to embitter; **~rsi**
vr to become harsher; to become bitter; to
become worse
inattac'cabile *ag* (*anche fig*) unassailable;
(*alibi*) cast-iron
inatten'dibile *ag* unreliable
inat'teso, a *ag* unexpected
inattu'abile *ag* impracticable
inau'dito, a *ag* unheard of
inaugu'rare *vt* to inaugurate, open;
(*monumento*) to unveil
inavver'tenza [inavver'tentsa] *sf*
carelessness, inadvertence
incagli'are [inkaʎ'ʎare] *vi* (*NAUT: anche:
~rsi*) to run aground
incal'lito, a *ag* calloused; (*fig*) hardened,
inveterate; (: *insensibile*) hard
incal'zare [inkal'tsare] *vt* to follow *o* pursue
closely; (*fig*) to press ♦ *vi* (*urgere*) to be
pressing; (*essere imminente*) to be
imminent
incammi'nare *vt* (*fig: avviare*) to start up;
~rsi *vr* to set off
incande'scente [inkandeʃ'ʃɛnte] *ag*
incandescent, white-hot
incan'tare *vt* to enchant, bewitch; **~rsi** *vr*
(*rimanere intontito*) to be spellbound; to be
in a daze; (*meccanismo: bloccarsi*) to jam;
incanta'tore, 'trice *ag* enchanting,
bewitching ♦ *sm/f* enchanter/enchantress;
incan'tesimo *sm* spell, charm;
incan'tevole *ag* charming, enchanting
in'canto *sm* spell, charm, enchantment;
(*asta*) auction; **come per ~** as if by magic;
mettere all'~ to put up for auction
inca'pace [inka'patʃe] *ag* incapable;
incapacità *sf* inability; (*DIR*) incapacity
incapo'nirsi *vr* to be stubborn, be
determined
incap'pare *vi*: **~ in qc/qn** (*anche fig*) to
run into sth/sb

incapricci'arsi [inkaprit'tʃarsi] *vr*: **~ di** to take a fancy to *o* for

incapsu'lare *vt* (*dente*) to crown

incarce'rare [inkartʃe'rare] *vt* to imprison

incari'care *vt*: **~ qn di fare** to give sb the responsibility of doing; **~rsi di** to take care *o* charge of; **incari'cato, a** *ag*: **incaricato (di)** in charge (of), responsible (for) ♦ *sm/f* delegate, representative; **professore incaricato** *teacher with a temporary appointment*

in'carico, chi *sm* task, job

incar'nare *vt* to embody; **~rsi** *vr* to be embodied; (*REL*) to become incarnate

incarta'mento *sm* dossier, file

incar'tare *vt* to wrap (in paper)

incas'sare *vt* (*merce*) to pack (in cases); (*gemma: incastonare*) to set; (*ECON: riscuotere*) to collect; (*PUGILATO: colpi*) to take, stand up to; **in'casso** *sm* cashing, encashment; (*introito*) takings *pl*

incasto'nare *vt* to set; **incastona'tura** *sf* setting

incas'trare *vt* to fit in, insert; (*fig: intrappolare*) to catch; **~rsi** *vr* (*combaciare*) to fit together; (*restare bloccato*) to become stuck; **in'castro** *sm* slot, groove; (*punto di unione*) joint

incate'nare *vt* to chain up

incatra'mare *vt* to tar

incatti'vire *vt* to make wicked; **~rsi** *vr* to turn nasty

in'cauto, a *ag* imprudent, rash

inca'vare *vt* to hollow out; **in'cavo** *sm* hollow; (*solco*) groove

incendi'are [intʃen'djare] *vt* to set fire to; **~rsi** *vr* to catch fire, burst into flames

incendi'ario, a [intʃen'djarjo] *ag* incendiary ♦ *sm/f* arsonist

in'cendio [in'tʃendjo] *sm* fire

incene'rire [intʃene'rire] *vt* to burn to ashes, incinerate; (*cadavere*) to cremate; **~rsi** *vr* to be burnt to ashes

in'censo [in'tʃenso] *sm* incense

incensu'rato, a [intʃensu'rato] *ag* (*DIR*): **essere ~** to have a clean record

incen'tivo [intʃen'tivo] *sm* incentive

incep'pare [intʃep'pare] *vt* to obstruct, hamper; **~rsi** *vr* to jam

ince'rata [intʃe'rata] *sf* (*tela*) tarpaulin; (*impermeabile*) oilskins *pl*

incer'tezza [intʃer'tettsa] *sf* uncertainty

in'certo, a [in'tʃerto] *ag* uncertain; (*irresoluto*) undecided, hesitating ♦ *sm* uncertainty

in'cetta [in'tʃetta] *sf* buying up; **fare ~ di qc** to buy up sth

inchi'esta [in'kjesta] *sf* investigation, inquiry

inchi'nare [inki'nare] *vt* to bow; **~rsi** *vr* to bend down; (*per riverenza*) to bow; (: *donna*) to curtsy; **in'chino** *sm* bow; curtsy

inchio'dare [inkjo'dare] *vt* to nail (down); **~ la macchina** (*AUT*) to jam on the brakes

inchi'ostro [in'kjɔstro] *sm* ink; **~ simpatico** invisible ink

inciam'pare [intʃam'pare] *vi* to trip, stumble

inci'ampo [in'tʃampo] *sm* obstacle; **essere d'~ a qn** (*fig*) to be in sb's way

inci'dente [intʃi'dente] *sm* accident; **~ d'auto** car accident

inci'denza [intʃi'dentsa] *sf* incidence; **avere una forte ~ su qc** to affect sth greatly

in'cidere [in'tʃidere] *vi*: **~ su** to bear upon, affect ♦ *vt* (*tagliare incavando*) to cut into; (*ARTE*) to engrave; to etch; (*canzone*) to record

in'cinta [in'tʃinta] *ag f* pregnant

incipri'are [intʃi'prjare] *vt* to powder

in'circa [in'tʃirka] *av*: **all'~** more or less, very nearly

incisi'one [intʃi'zjone] *sf* cut; (*disegno*) engraving; etching; (*registrazione*) recording; (*MED*) incision

in'ciso, a [in'tʃizo] *pp di* **incidere** ♦ *sm*: **per ~** incidentally, by the way

inci'tare [intʃi'tare] *vt* to incite

inci'vile [intʃi'vile] *ag* uncivilized; (*villano*) impolite

incl. *abbr* (= *incluso*) encl.

incli'nare *vt* to tilt; **~rsi** *vr* (*barca*) to list; (*aereo*) to bank; **incli'nato, a** *ag* sloping; **inclinazi'one** *sf* slope; (*fig*) inclination, tendency; in'cline *ag*: **incline a** inclined to

in'cludere *vt* to include; (*accludere*) to enclose; in'cluso, a *pp di* includere ♦ *ag* included; enclosed

incoe'rente *ag* incoherent; (*contraddittorio*) inconsistent

in'cognita [in'koɲɲita] *sf* (MAT, *fig*) unknown quantity

in'cognito, a [in'koɲɲito] *ag* unknown ♦ *sm*: in ~ incognito

incol'lare *vt* to glue, gum; (*unire con colla*) to stick together

incolon'nare *vt* to draw up in columns

inco'lore *ag* colourless

incol'pare *vt*: ~ qn di to charge sb with

in'colto, a *ag* (*terreno*) uncultivated; (*trascurato: capelli*) neglected; (*persona*) uneducated

in'colume *ag* safe and sound, unhurt

incom'benza [inkom'bɛntsa] *sf* duty, task

in'combere *vi* (*sovrastare minacciando*): ~ su to threaten, hang over

incominci'are [inkomin'tʃare] *vi, vt* to begin, start

in'comodo *sm* inconvenience

incompe'tente *ag* incompetent

incompi'uto, a *ag* unfinished, incomplete

incom'pleto, a *ag* incomplete

incompren'sibile *ag* incomprehensible

incom'preso, a *ag* not understood; misunderstood

inconce'pibile [inkontʃe'pibile] *ag* inconceivable

inconcili'abile [inkontʃi'ljabile] *ag* irreconcilable

inconclu'dente *ag* inconclusive; (*persona*) ineffectual

incondizio'nato, a [inkondittsjo'nato] *ag* unconditional

inconfu'tabile *ag* irrefutable

incongru'ente *ag* inconsistent

inconsa'pevole *ag*: ~ di unaware of, ignorant of

in'conscio, a, sci, sce [in'kɔnʃo] *ag* unconscious ♦ *sm* (PSIC): l'~ the unconscious

inconsis'tente *ag* insubstantial; unfounded

inconsu'eto, a *ag* unusual

incon'sulto, a *ag* rash

incon'trare *vt* to meet; (*difficoltà*) to meet with; ~rsi *vr* to meet

incontras'tabile *ag* incontrovertible, indisputable

in'contro *av*: ~ a (*verso*) towards ♦ *sm* meeting; (SPORT) match; meeting; ~ di calcio football match

inconveni'ente *sm* drawback, snag

incoraggia'mento [inkoraddʒa'mento] *sm* encouragement

incoraggi'are [inkorad'dʒare] *vt* to encourage

incornici'are [inkorni'tʃare] *vt* to frame

incoro'nare *vt* to crown; incoronazi'one *sf* coronation

incorpo'rare *vt* to incorporate; (*fig: annettere*) to annex

in'correre *vi*: ~ in to meet with, run into

incosci'ente [inkoʃ'ʃente] *ag* (*inconscio*) unconscious; (*irresponsabile*) reckless, thoughtless; incosci'enza *sf* unconsciousness; recklessness, thoughtlessness

incre'dibile *ag* incredible, unbelievable

in'credulo, a *ag* incredulous, disbelieving

incremen'tare *vt* to increase; (*dar sviluppo a*) to promote

incre'mento *sm* (*sviluppo*) development; (*aumento numerico*) increase, growth

incresci'oso, a [inkreʃ'ʃoso] *ag* (*incidente etc*) regrettable

incres'parsi *vr* (*acqua*) to ripple; (*capelli*) to go frizzy; (*pelle, tessuto*) to wrinkle

incrimi'nare *vt* (DIR) to charge

incri'nare *vt* to crack; (*fig: rapporti, amicizia*) to cause to deteriorate; ~rsi *vr* to crack; to deteriorate; incri'natura *sf* crack; (*fig*) rift

incroci'are [inkro'tʃare] *vt* to cross; (*incontrare*) to meet ♦ *vi* (NAUT, AER) to cruise; ~rsi *vr* (*strade*) to cross, intersect; (*persone, veicoli*) to pass each other; ~ le braccia/le gambe to fold one's arms/cross one's legs; **incrocia'tore** *sm* cruiser

in'crocio [in'krotʃo] *sm* (*anche FERR*) crossing; (*di strade*) crossroads

incros'tare *vt* to encrust

incuba'trice [inkuba'tritʃe] *sf* incubator

'incubo *sm* nightmare

in'cudine *sf* anvil

incu'rante *ag*: ~ **(di)** heedless (of), careless (of)

incurio'sire *vt* to make curious; **~rsi** *vr* to become curious

incursi'one *sf* raid

incur'vare *vt* to bend, curve; **~rsi** *vr* to bend, curve

in'cusso, a *pp di* **incutere**

incusto'dito, a *ag* unguarded, unattended

in'cutere *vt*: ~ **timore/rispetto a qn** to strike fear into sb/command sb's respect

'indaco *sm* indigo

indaffa'rato, a *ag* busy

inda'gare *vt* to investigate

in'dagine [in'dadʒine] *sf* investigation, inquiry; (*ricerca*) research, study

indebi'tarsi *vr* to run *o* get into debt

in'debito, a *ag* undue; undeserved

indebo'lire *vt, vi* (*anche*: **~rsi**) to weaken

inde'cente [inde'tʃente] *ag* indecent; **inde'cenza** *sf* indecency

inde'ciso, a [inde'tʃizo] *ag* indecisive; (*irresoluto*) undecided

inde'fesso, a *ag* untiring, indefatigable

indefi'nito, a *ag* (*anche LING*) indefinite; (*impreciso, non determinato*) undefined

in'degno, a [in'deɲno] *ag* (*atto*) shameful; (*persona*) unworthy

indelica'tezza [indelika'tettsa] *sf* tactlessness

indemoni'ato, a *ag* possessed (by the devil)

in'denne *ag* unhurt, uninjured; **indennità** *sf inv* (*rimborso: di spese*) allowance; (: *di perdita*) compensation, indemnity; **indennità di contingenza** cost-of-living allowance; **indennità di trasferta** travel expenses *pl*

indenniz'zare [indennid'dzare] *vt* to compensate; **inden'nizzo** *sm* (*somma*) compensation, indemnity

indero'gabile *ag* binding

'India *sf*: **l'~** India; **indi'ano, a** *ag* Indian ♦ *sm/f* (*d'India*) Indian; (*d'America*) Native American, (American) Indian

indiavo'lato, a *ag* possessed (by the devil); (*vivace, violento*) wild

indi'care *vt* (*mostrare*) to show, indicate; (: *col dito*) to point to, point out; (*consigliare*) to suggest, recommend; **indica'tivo, a** *ag* indicative ♦ *sm* (*LING*) indicative (mood); **indica'tore** *sm* (*elenco*) guide; directory; (*TECN*) gauge; indicator; **indicatore di velocità** (*AUT*) speedometer; **indicatore della benzina** fuel gauge; **indicazi'one** *sf* indication; (*informazione*) piece of information

'indice ['inditʃe] *sm* index; (*fig*) sign; (*dito*) index finger, forefinger; ~ **di gradimento** (*RADIO, TV*) popularity rating

indi'cibile [indi'tʃibile] *ag* inexpressible

indietreggi'are [indietred'dʒare] *vi* to draw back, retreat

indi'etro *av* back; (*guardare*) behind, back; (*andare, cadere*: *anche*: **all'~**) backwards; **rimanere** ~ to be left behind; **essere** ~ (*col lavoro*) to be behind; (*orologio*) to be slow; **rimandare qc** ~ to send sth back

indi'feso, a *ag* (*città etc*) undefended; (*persona*) defenceless

indiffe'rente *ag* indifferent; **indiffe'renza** *sf* indifference

in'digeno, a [in'didʒeno] *ag* indigenous, native ♦ *sm/f* native

indi'gente [indi'dʒɛnte] *ag* poverty-stricken, destitute; **indi'genza** *sf* extreme poverty

indigesti'one [indidʒes'tjone] *sf* indigestion

indi'gesto, a [indi'dʒɛsto] *ag* indigestible

indi'gnare [indiɲ'ɲare] *vt* to fill with indignation; **~rsi** *vr* to get indignant

indimenti'cabile *ag* unforgettable

indipen'dente *ag* independent; **indipen'denza** *sf* independence

in'dire *vt* (*concorso*) to announce; (*elezioni*) to call

indi'retto, a *ag* indirect

indiriz'zare [indirit'tsare] *vt* (*dirigere*) to direct; (*mandare*) to send; (*lettera*) to address

indi'rizzo [indi'rittso] *sm* address; (*direzione*) direction; (*avvio*) trend, course

indis'creto, a *ag* indiscreet

indis'cusso, a *ag* unquestioned

indispen'sabile *ag* indispensable, essential

indispet'tire *vt* to irritate, annoy ♦ *vi* (*anche*: **~rsi**) to get irritated *o* annoyed

in'divia *sf* endive

individu'ale *ag* individual; **individualità** *sf* individuality

individu'are *vt* (*dar forma distinta a*) to characterize; (*determinare*) to locate; (*riconoscere*) to single out

indi'viduo *sm* individual

indizi'ato, a *ag* suspected ♦ *sm/f* suspect

in'dizio [in'dittsjo] *sm* (*segno*) sign, indication; (*POLIZIA*) clue; (*DIR*) piece of evidence

'indole *sf* nature, character

indolen'zito, a [indolen'tsito] *ag* stiff, aching; (*intorpidito*) numb

indo'lore *ag* painless

indo'mani *sm*: **l'~** the next day, the following day

Indo'nesia *sf*: **l'~** Indonesia

indos'sare *vt* (*mettere indosso*) to put on; (*avere indosso*) to have on; **indossa'tore, 'trice** *sm/f* model

in'dotto, a *pp di* **indurre**

indottri'nare *vt* to indoctrinate

indovi'nare *vt* (*scoprire*) to guess; (*immaginare*) to imagine, guess; (*il futuro*) to foretell; **indovi'nato, a** *ag* successful; (*scelta*) inspired; **indovi'nello** *sm* riddle; **indovi'no, a** *sm/f* fortuneteller

indubbia'mente *av* undoubtedly

in'dubbio, a *ag* certain, undoubted

indugi'are [indu'dʒare] *vi* to take one's time, delay

in'dugio [in'dudʒo] *sm* (*ritardo*) delay; **senza ~** without delay

indul'gente [indul'dʒɛnte] *ag* indulgent;

(*giudice*) lenient; **indul'genza** *sf* indulgence; leniency

in'dulgere [in'duldʒere] *vi*: **~ a** (*accondiscendere*) to comply with; (*abbandonarsi*) to indulge in; **in'dulto, a** *pp di* **indulgere** ♦ *sm* (*DIR*) pardon

indu'mento *sm* article of clothing, garment; **~i** *smpl* (*vestiti*) clothes

indu'rire *vt* to harden ♦ *vi* (*anche*: **~rsi**) to harden, become hard

in'durre *vt*: **~ qn a fare qc** to induce *o* persuade sb to do sth; **~ qn in errore** to mislead sb

in'dustria *sf* industry; **industri'ale** *ag* industrial ♦ *sm* industrialist

industri'arsi *vr* to do one's best, try hard

industri'oso, a *ag* industrious, hardworking

induzi'one [indut'tsjone] *sf* induction

inebe'tito, a *ag* dazed, stunned

inebri'are *vt* (*anche fig*) to intoxicate; **~rsi** *vr* to become intoxicated

inecce'pibile [inettʃe'pibile] *ag* unexceptionable

i'nedia *sf* starvation

i'nedito, a *ag* unpublished

ineffi'cace [ineffi'katʃe] *ag* ineffective

ineffici'ente [ineffi'tʃɛnte] *ag* inefficient

inegu'ale *ag* unequal; (*irregolare*) uneven

ine'rente *ag*: **~ a** concerning, regarding

i'nerme *ag* unarmed; defenceless

inerpi'carsi *vr*: **~ (su)** to clamber (up)

i'nerte *ag* inert; (*inattivo*) indolent, sluggish

i'nerzia *sf* inertia; indolence, sluggishness

ine'satto, a *ag* (*impreciso*) inexact; (*erroneo*) incorrect; (*AMM: non riscosso*) uncollected

inesis'tente *ag* non-existent

inesperi'enza [inespe'rjɛntsa] *sf* inexperience

ines'perto, a *ag* inexperienced

i'netto, a *ag* (*incapace*) inept; (*che non ha attitudine*): **~ (a)** unsuited (to)

ine'vaso, a *ag* (*ordine, corrispondenza*) outstanding

inevi'tabile *ag* inevitable

i'nezia [i'nettsja] *sf* trifle, thing of no

importance

infagot'tare *vt* to bundle up, wrap up; **~rsi** *vr* to wrap up

infal'libile *ag* infallible

infa'mante *ag* defamatory

in'fame *ag* infamous; (*fig: cosa, compito*) awful, dreadful

infan'gare *vt* to cover with mud; (*fig: reputazione*) to sully

infan'tile *ag* child *cpd*; childlike; (*adulto, azione*) childish; **letteratura ~** children's books *pl*

in'fanzia [in'fantsja] *sf* childhood; (*bambini*) children *pl*; **prima ~** babyhood, infancy

infari'nare *vt* to cover with (*o* sprinkle with *o* dip in) flour; **infarina'tura** *sf* (*fig*) smattering

in'farto *sm* (MED) heart attack

infasti'dire *vt* to annoy, irritate; **~rsi** *vr* to get annoyed *o* irritated

infati'cabile *ag* tireless, untiring

in'fatti *cong* as a matter of fact, in fact, actually

infatu'arsi *vr*: **~ di** to become infatuated with, fall for; **infatuazi'one** *sf* infatuation

in'fausto, a *ag* unpropitious, unfavourable

infe'condo, a *ag* infertile

infe'dele *ag* unfaithful; **infedeltà** *sf* infidelity

infe'lice [infe'litʃe] *ag* unhappy; (*sfortunato*) unlucky, unfortunate; (*inopportuno*) inopportune, ill-timed; (*mal riuscito: lavoro*) bad, poor; **infelicità** *sf* unhappiness

inferi'ore *ag* lower; (*per intelligenza, qualità*) inferior ♦ *sm/f* inferior; **~ a** (*numero, quantità*) less *o* smaller than; (*meno buono*) inferior to; **~ alla media** below average; **inferiorità** *sf* inferiority

inferme'ria *sf* infirmary; (*di scuola, nave*) sick bay

infermi'ere, a *sm/f* nurse

infermità *sf inv* illness; infirmity

in'fermo, a *ag* (*ammalato*) ill; (*debole*) infirm

infer'nale *ag* infernal; (*proposito, complotto*) diabolical

in'ferno *sm* hell

inferri'ata *sf* grating

infervo'rarsi *vr* to get excited, get carried away

infes'tare *vt* to infest

infet'tare *vt* to infect; **~rsi** *vr* to become infected; **infet'tivo, a** *ag* infectious; **in'fetto, a** *ag* infected; (*acque*) polluted, contaminated; **infezi'one** *sf* infection

infiac'chire [infjak'kire] *vt* to weaken ♦ *vi* (*anche*: **~rsi**) to grow weak

infiam'mabile *ag* inflammable

infiam'mare *vt* to set alight; (*fig*, MED) to inflame; **~rsi** *vr* to catch fire; (MED) to become inflamed; **infiammazi'one** *sf* (MED) inflammation

in'fido, a *ag* unreliable, treacherous

infie'rire *vi*: **~ su** (*fisicamente*) to attack furiously; (*verbalmente*) to rage at

in'figgere [in'fiddʒere] *vt*: **~ qc in** to thrust *o* drive sth into

infi'lare *vt* (*ago*) to thread; (*mettere: chiave*) to insert; (: *anello, vestito*) to slip *o* put on; (*strada*) to turn into, take; **~rsi** *vr*: **~rsi in** to slip into; (*indossare*) to slip on; **~ l'uscio** to slip in; to slip out

infil'trarsi *vr* to penetrate, seep through; (MIL) to infiltrate; **infiltrazi'one** *sf* infiltration

infil'zare [infil'tsare] *vt* (*infilare*) to string together; (*trafiggere*) to pierce

'infimo, a *ag* lowest

in'fine *av* finally; (*insomma*) in short

infinità *sf* infinity; (*in quantità*): **un'~ di** an infinite number of

infi'nito, a *ag* infinite; (LING) infinitive ♦ *sm* infinity; (LING) infinitive; **all'~** (*senza fine*) endlessly

infinocchi'are [infinok'kjare] (*fam*) *vt* to hoodwink

infischi'arsi [infis'kjarsi] *vr*: **~ di** not to care about

in'fisso, a *pp di* **infiggere** ♦ *sm* fixture; (*di porta, finestra*) frame

infit'tire *vt, vi* (*anche*: **~rsi**) to thicken

inflazi'one [inflat'tsjone] *sf* inflation

in'fliggere [in'fliddʒere] *vt* to inflict; **in'flitto, a** *pp di* **infliggere**

influ'ente *ag* influential; influ'enza *sf* influence; (*MED*) influenza, flu

influ'ire *vi*: ~ su to influence

in'flusso *sm* influence

infol'tire *vt*, *vi* to thicken

infon'dato, a *ag* unfounded, groundless

in'fondere *vt*: ~ qc in qn to instill sth in sb

infor'care *vt* to fork (up); (*bicicletta, cavallo*) to get on; (*occhiali*) to put on

infor'mare *vt* to inform, tell; ~rsi *vr*: ~rsi (di *o* su) to inquire (about)

infor'matica *sf* computer science

informa'tivo, a *ag* informative

informa'tore *sm* informer

informazi'one [informat'tsjone] *sf* piece of information; prendere ~i sul conto di qn to get information about sb; chiedere un'~ to ask for (some) information

in'forme *ag* shapeless

informico'larsi *vr* = informicolirsi

informico'lirsi *vr* to have pins and needles

infor'tunio *sm* accident; ~ sul lavoro industrial accident, accident at work

infos'sarsi *vr* (*terreno*) to sink; (*guance*) to become hollow; infos'sato, a *ag* hollow; (*occhi*) deep-set; (: *per malattia*) sunken

in'frangere [in'frandʒere] *vt* to smash; (*fig: legge, patti*) to break; ~rsi *vr* to smash, break; infran'gibile *ag* unbreakable; in'franto, a *pp di* infrangere ♦ *ag* broken

infrazi'one [infrat'tsjone] *sf*: ~ a breaking of, violation of

infredda'tura *sf* slight cold

infreddo'lito, a *ag* cold, chilled

infruttu'oso, a *ag* fruitless

infu'ori *av* out; all'~ outwards; all'~ di (*eccetto*) except, with the exception of

infuri'are *vi* to rage; ~rsi *vr* to fly into a rage

infusi'one *sf* infusion

in'fuso, a *pp di* infondere ♦ *sm* infusion

Ing. *abbr* = ingegnere

ingabbi'are *vt* to cage

ingaggi'are [ingad'dʒare] *vt* (*assumere con compenso*) to take on, hire; (*SPORT*) to sign on; (*MIL*) to engage; in'gaggio *sm* hiring;

signing on

ingan'nare *vt* to deceive; (*fisco*) to cheat; (*eludere*) to dodge, elude; (*fig: tempo*) to while away ♦ *vi* (*apparenza*) to be deceptive; ~rsi *vr* to be mistaken, be wrong; ingan'nevole *ag* deceptive

in'ganno *sm* deceit, deception; (*azione*) trick; (*menzogna, frode*) cheat, swindle; (*illusione*) illusion

ingarbugli'are [ingarbuʎ'ʎare] *vt* to tangle; (*fig*) to confuse, muddle; ~rsi *vr* to become confused *o* muddled

inge'gnarsi [indʒen'narsi] *vr* to do one's best, try hard; ~ per vivere to live by one's wits

inge'gnere [indʒen'nere] *sm* engineer; ~ civile/navale civil/naval engineer; ingegne'ria *sf* engineering; ~ genetica genetic engineering

in'gegno [in'dʒenɲo] *sm* (*intelligenza*) intelligence, brains *pl*; (*capacità creativa*) ingenuity; (*disposizione*) talent; inge'gnoso, a *ag* ingenious, clever

ingelo'sire [indʒelo'zire] *vt* to make jealous ♦ *vi* (*anche*: ~rsi) to become jealous

in'gente [in'dʒente] *ag* huge, enormous

ingenuità [indʒenui'ta] *sf* ingenuousness

in'genuo, a [in'dʒenuo] *ag* ingenuous, naïve

inge'rire [indʒe'rire] *vt* to ingest

inges'sare [indʒes'sare] *vt* (*MED*) to put in plaster; ingessa'tura *sf* plaster

Inghil'terra [ingil'terra] *sf*: l'~ England

inghiot'tire [ingjot'tire] *vt* to swallow

ingial'lire [indʒal'lire] *vi* to go yellow

ingigan'tire [indʒigan'tire] *vt* to enlarge, magnify ♦ *vi* to become gigantic *o* enormous

inginocchi'arsi [indʒinok'kjarsi] *vr* to kneel (down)

ingiù [in'dʒu] *av* down, downwards

ingiunzi'one [indʒun'tsjone] *sf* injunction

ingi'uria [in'dʒurja] *sf* insult; (*fig: danno*) damage; ingiuri'are *vt* to insult, abuse; ingiuri'oso, a *ag* insulting, abusive

ingius'tizia [indʒus'tittsja] *sf* injustice

ingi'usto, a [in'dʒusto] *ag* unjust, unfair

in'glese *ag* English ♦ *sm/f* Englishman/ woman *sm* (*LING*) English; **gli I~i** the English; **andarsene** *o* **filare all'~** to take French leave

ingoi'are *vt* to gulp (down); (*fig*) to swallow (up)

ingol'fare *vt* (*motore*) to flood; **~rsi** *vr* to flood

ingom'brante *ag* cumbersome

ingom'brare *vt* (*strada*) to block; (*stanza*) to clutter up; **in'gombro, a** *ag* (*strada, passaggio*) blocked ♦ *sm* obstacle; **essere d'ingombro** to be in the way

in'gordo, a *ag*: ~ **di** greedy for

in'gorgo, ghi *sm* blockage, obstruction; (*anche*: ~ **stradale**) traffic jam

ingoz'zare [ingot'tsare] *vt* (*animali*) to fatten; (*fig: persona*) to stuff; **~rsi** *vr*: **~rsi (di)** to stuff o.s. (with)

ingra'naggio [ingra'naddʒo] *sm* (*TECN*) gear; (*di orologio*) mechanism; **gli ~i della burocrazia** the bureaucratic machinery

ingra'nare *vi* to mesh, engage ♦ *vt* to engage; **~ la marcia** to get into gear

ingrandi'mento *sm* enlargement; extension

ingran'dire *vt* (*anche FOT*) to enlarge; (*estendere*) to extend; (*OTTICA, fig*) to magnify ♦ *vi* (*anche*: **~rsi**) to become larger *o* bigger; (*aumentare*) to grow, increase; (*espandersi*) to expand

ingras'sare *vt* to make fat; (*animali*) to fatten; (*lubrificare*) to oil, lubricate ♦ *vi* (*anche*: **~rsi**) to get fat, put on weight

in'grato, a *ag* ungrateful; (*lavoro*) thankless, unrewarding

ingredi'ente *sm* ingredient

in'gresso *sm* (*porta*) entrance; (*atrio*) hall; (*l'entrare*) entrance, entry; (*facoltà di entrare*) admission; **"~ libero"** "admission free"

ingros'sare *vt* to increase; (*folla, livello*) to swell ♦ *vi* (*anche*: **~rsi**) to increase; to swell

in'grosso *av*: **all'~** (*COMM*) wholesale; (*all'incirca*) roughly, about

ingua'ribile *ag* incurable

'inguine *sm* (*ANAT*) groin

ini'bire *vt* to forbid, prohibit; (*PSIC*) to inhibit; **inibizi'one** *sf* prohibition; inhibition

iniet'tare *vt* to inject; **~rsi** *vr*: **~rsi di sangue** (*occhi*) to become bloodshot; **iniezi'one** *sf* injection

inimi'carsi *vr*: ~ **con qn** to fall out with sb

ininter'rotto, a *ag* unbroken; uninterrupted

iniquità *sf inv* iniquity; (*atto*) wicked action

inizi'ale [init'tsjale] *ag, sf* initial

inizi'are [init'tsjare] *vi, vt* to begin, start; ~ **qn a** to initiate sb into; (*pittura etc*) to introduce sb to; ~ **a fare qc** to start doing sth

inizia'tiva [inittsja'tiva] *sf* initiative; ~ **privata** private enterprise

i'nizio [i'nittsjo] *sm* beginning; **all'~** at the beginning, at the start; **dare ~ a qc** to start sth, get sth going

innaffi'are *etc* = **annaffiare** etc

innal'zare [innal'tsare] *vt* (*sollevare, alzare*) to raise; (*rizzare*) to erect; **~rsi** *vr* to rise

innamo'rarsi *vr*: ~ (**di qn**) to fall in love (with sb); **innamo'rato, a** *ag* (*che nutre amore*): **innamorato (di)** in love (with); (*appassionato*): **innamorato di** very fond of ♦ *sm/f* lover; sweetheart

in'nanzi [in'nantsi] *av* (*stato in luogo*) in front, ahead; (*moto a luogo*) forward, on; (*tempo: prima*) before ♦ *prep* (*prima*) before; ~ **a** in front of; **innanzi'tutto** *av* first of all

in'nato, a *ag* innate

innatu'rale *ag* unnatural

inne'gabile *ag* undeniable

innervo'sire *vt*: ~ **qn** to get on sb's nerves; **~rsi** *vr* to get irritated *o* upset

innes'care *vt* to prime

innes'tare *vt* (*BOT, MED*) to graft; (*TECN*) to engage; (*inserire: presa*) to insert; **in'nesto** *sm* graft; grafting *no pl*; (*TECN*) clutch; (*ELETTR*) connection

'inno *sm* hymn; ~ **nazionale** national anthem

inno'cente [inno'tʃɛnte] *ag* innocent;

inno'cenza *sf* innocence

in'nocuo, a *ag* innocuous, harmless

innova'tivo, a *ag* innovative

innume'revole *ag* innumerable

ino'doro, a *ag* odourless

inol'trare *vt* (AMM) to pass on, forward; **~rsi** *vr* (*addentrarsi*) to advance, go forward

i'noltre *av* besides, moreover

inon'dare *vt* to flood; **inondazi'one** *sf* flooding *no pl*; flood

inope'roso, a *ag* inactive, idle

inoppor'tuno, a *ag* untimely, ill-timed; inappropriate; (*momento*) inopportune

inorgo'glire [inorgoʎ'ʎire] *vt* to make proud ♦ *vi* (*anche:* **~rsi**) to become proud; **~rsi di qc** to pride o.s. on sth

inor'dire *vt* to horrify ♦ *vi* to be horrified

inospi'tale *ag* inhospitable

inosser'vato, a *ag* (*non notato*) unobserved; (*non rispettato*) not observed, not kept

inossi'dabile *ag* stainless

inqua'drare *vt* (*foto, immagine*) to frame; (*fig*) to situate, set

inquie'tare *vt* (*turbare*) to disturb, worry; **~rsi** *vr* to worry, become anxious; (*impazientirsi*) to get upset

inqui'eto, a *ag* restless; (*preoccupato*) worried, anxious; **inquie'tudine** *sf* anxiety, worry

inqui'lino, a *sm/f* tenant

inquina'mento *sm* pollution

inqui'nare *vt* to pollute

inqui'sire *vt, vi* to investigate; **inquisi'tore, 'trice** *ag* (*sguardo*) inquiring; **inquisizi'one** *sf* (STORIA) inquisition

insabbi'are *vt* (*fig: pratica*) to shelve; **~rsi** *vr* (*arenarsi: barca*) to run aground; (*fig: pratica*) to be shelved

insac'cati *smpl* (CUC) sausages

insa'lata *sf* salad; **~ mista** mixed salad; **insalati'era** *sf* salad bowl

insa'lubre *ag* unhealthy

insa'nabile *ag* (*piaga*) which cannot be healed; (*situazione*) irremediable; (*odio*) implacable

insangui'nare *vt* to stain with blood

insa'puta *sf*: **all'~ di qn** without sb knowing

insce'nare [inʃe'nare] *vt* (TEATRO) to stage, put on; (*fig*) to stage

insedi'are *vt* to install; **~rsi** *vr* to take up office; (*popolo, colonia*) to settle

in'segna [in'seɲɲa] *sf* sign; (*emblema*) sign, emblem; (*bandiera*) flag, banner; **~e** *sfpl* (*decorazioni*) insignia *pl*

insegna'mento [inseɲɲa'mento] *sm* teaching

inse'gnante [insen'ɲante] *ag* teaching ♦ *sm/f* teacher

inse'gnare [insen'ɲare] *vt, vi* to teach; **~ a qn qc** to teach sb sth; **~ a qn a fare qc** to teach sb (how) to do sth

insegui'mento *sm* pursuit, chase

insegu'ire *vt* to pursue, chase

inselvati'chire [inselvati'kire] *vi* (*anche:* **~rsi**) to grow wild

insena'tura *sf* inlet, creek

insen'sato, a *ag* senseless, stupid

insen'sibile *ag* (*nervo*) insensible; (*persona*) indifferent

inse'rire *vt* to insert; (ELETTR) to connect; (*allegare*) to enclose; (*annuncio*) to put in, place; **~rsi** *vr* (*fig*): **~rsi in** to become part of; **in'serto** *sm* (*pubblicazione*) insert

inservi'ente *sm/f* attendant

inserzi'one [inser'tsjone] *sf* insertion; (*avviso*) advertisement; **fare un'~ sul giornale** to put an advertisement in the paper

insetti'cida, i [insetti'tʃida] *sm* insecticide

in'setto *sm* insect

insi'curo, a *ag* insecure

in'sidia *sf* snare, trap; (*pericolo*) hidden danger; **insidi'are** *vt*: **~ la vita di qn** to make an attempt on sb's life

insi'eme *av* together ♦ *prep*: **~ a** *o* **con** together with ♦ *sm* whole; (MAT, *servizio, assortimento*) set; (MODA) ensemble, outfit; **tutti ~** all together; **tutto ~** all together; (*in una volta*) at one go; **nell'~** on the whole; **d'~** (*veduta etc*) overall

in'signe [in'sinɲe] *ag (persona)* famous, distinguished; *(città, monumento)* notable

insignifi'cante [insinɲifi'kante] *ag* insignificant

insi'gnire [insiɲ'ɲire] *vt*: ~ **qn di** to honour *o* decorate sb with

insin'cero, a [insin'tʃero] *ag* insincere

insinda'cabile *ag* unquestionable

insinu'are *vt (introdurre)*: ~ **qc in** to slip *o* slide sth into; *(fig)* to insinuate, imply; ~**rsi** *vr*: ~**rsi in** to seep into; *(fig)* to creep into; to worm one's way into

in'sipido, a *ag* insipid

insis'tente *ag* insistent; persistent

in'sistere *vi*: ~ **su qc** to insist on sth; ~ **in qc/a fare** *(perseverare)* to persist in sth/in doing; **insis'tito, a** *pp di* **insistere**

insoddis'fatto, a *ag* dissatisfied

insoffe'rente *ag* intolerant

insolazi'one [insolat'tsjone] *sf (MED)* sunstroke

inso'lente *ag* insolent; **insolen'tire** *vi* to grow insolent ♦ *vt* to insult, be rude to

in'solito, a *ag* unusual, out of the ordinary

inso'luto, a *ag (non risolto)* unsolved

in'somma *av (in conclusione)* in short; *(dunque)* well ♦ *escl* for heaven's sake!

in'sonne *ag* sleepless; **in'sonnia** *sf* insomnia, sleeplessness

insonno'lito, a *ag* sleepy, drowsy

insoppor'tabile *ag* unbearable

in'sorgere [in'sordʒere] *vi (ribellarsi)* to rise up, rebel; *(apparire)* to come up, arise

in'sorto, a *pp di* **insorgere** ♦ *sm/f* rebel, insurgent

insospet'tire *vt* to make suspicious ♦ *vi (anche:* ~**rsi***)* to become suspicious

inspi'rare *vt* to breathe in, inhale

in'stabile *ag (carico, indole)* unstable; *(tempo)* unsettled; *(equilibrio)* unsteady

instal'lare *vt* to install; ~**rsi** *vr (sistemarsi)*: ~**rsi in** to settle in; **installazi'one** *sf* installation

instan'cabile *ag* untiring, indefatigable

instau'rare *vt* to introduce, institute

instra'dare *vt*: ~ **(verso)** to direct (towards)

insuc'cesso [insut'tʃɛsso] *sm* failure, flop

insudici'are [insudi'tʃare] *vt* to dirty; ~**rsi** *vr* to get dirty

insuffici'ente [insuffi'tʃɛnte] *ag* insufficient; *(compito, allievo)* inadequate; **insuffici'enza** *sf* insufficiency; inadequacy; *(INS)* fail

insu'lare *ag* insular

insu'lina *sf* insulin

in'sulso, a *ag (sciocco)* inane, silly; *(persona)* dull, insipid

insul'tare *vt* to insult, affront

in'sulto *sm* insult, affront

insussis'tente *ag* non-existent

intac'care *vt (fare tacche)* to cut into; *(corrodere)* to corrode; *(fig: cominciare ad usare: risparmi)* to break into; *(: ledere)* to damage

intagli'are [intaʎ'ʎare] *vt* to carve; **in'taglio** *sm* carving

intan'gibile [intan'dʒibile] *ag* untouchable; inviolable

in'tanto *av (nel frattempo)* meanwhile, in the meantime; *(per cominciare)* just to begin with; ~ **che** while

in'tarsio *sm* inlaying *no pl*, marquetry *no pl*; inlay

inta'sare *vt* to choke (up), block (up); *(AUT)* to obstruct, block; ~**rsi** *vr* to become choked *o* blocked

intas'care *vt* to pocket

in'tatto, a *ag* intact; *(puro)* unsullied

intavo'lare *vt* to start, enter into

inte'grale *ag* complete; *(pane, farina)* wholemeal *(BRIT)*, whole-wheat *(US)*; *(MAT)*: **calcolo** ~ integral calculus

inte'grante *ag*: **parte** ~ integral part

inte'grare *vt* to complete; *(MAT)* to integrate; ~**rsi** *vr (persona)* to become integrated

integrità *sf* integrity

'integro, a *ag (intatto, intero)* complete, whole; *(retto)* upright

intelaia'tura *sf* frame; *(fig)* structure, framework

intel'letto *sm* intellect; **intellettu'ale** *ag, sm/f* intellectual

intelli'gente [intelli'dʒente] *ag* intelligent; **intelli'genza** *sf* intelligence

intem'perie *sfpl* bad weather *sg*

intempes'tivo, a *ag* untimely

inten'dente *sm*: **~ di Finanza** inland (*BRIT*) *o* internal (*US*) revenue officer; **inten'denza** *sf*: **intendenza di Finanza** inland (*BRIT*) *o* internal (*US*) revenue office

in'tendere *vt* (*avere intenzione*): **~ fare qc** to intend *o* mean to do sth; (*comprendere*) to understand; (*udire*) to hear; (*significare*) to mean; **~rsi** *vr* (*conoscere*): **~rsi di** to know a lot about, be a connoisseur of; (*accordarsi*) to get on (well); **intendersela con qn** (*avere una relazione amorosa*) to have an affair with sb; **intendi'mento** *sm* (*intelligenza*) understanding; (*proposito*) intention; **intendi'tore, 'trice** *sm/f* connoisseur, expert

intene'rire *vt* (*fig*) to move (to pity); **~rsi** *vr* (*fig*) to be moved

inten'sivo, a *ag* intensive

in'tenso, a *ag* intense

in'tento, a *ag* (*teso, assorto*): **~ (a)** intent (on), absorbed (in) ♦ *sm* aim, purpose

intenzio'nale [intentsjo'nale] *ag* intentional

intenzi'one [inten'tsjone] *sf* intention; (*DIR*) intent; **avere ~ di fare qc** to intend *o* to do sth, have the intention of doing sth

interat'tivo, a *ag* interactive

interca'lare *sm* pet phrase, stock phrase ♦ *vt* to insert

interca'pedine *sf* gap, cavity

intercet'tare [intertʃet'tare] *vt* to intercept

intercity [intəsi'ti] *sm inv* (*FERR*) ≈ intercity (train)

inter'detto, a *pp di* **interdire** ♦ *ag* forbidden, prohibited; (*sconcertato*) dumbfounded ♦ *sm* (*REL*) interdict

inter'dire *vt* to forbid, prohibit, ban; (*REL*) to interdict; (*DIR*) to deprive of civil rights; **interdizi'one** *sf* prohibition, ban

interessa'mento *sm* interest

interes'sante *ag* interesting; **essere in stato ~** to be expecting (a baby)

interes'sare *vt* to interest; (*concernere*) to concern, be of interest to; (*far intervenire*): **~ qn a** to draw sb's attention to ♦ *vi*: **~ a** to interest, matter to; **~rsi** *vr* (*mostrare interesse*): **~rsi a** to take an interest in, be interested in; (*occuparsi*): **~rsi di** to take care of

inte'resse *sm* (*anche COMM*) interest

inter'faccia, ce [inter'fattʃa] *sf* (*INFORM*) interface

interfe'renza [interfe'rentsa] *sf* interference

interfe'rire *vi* to interfere

interiezi'one [interjet'tsjone] *sf* exclamation, interjection

interi'ora *sfpl* entrails

interi'ore *ag* interior, inner, inside, internal; (*fig*) inner

inter'ludio *sm* (*MUS*) interlude

inter'medio, a *ag* intermediate

inter'mezzo [inter'meddzo] *sm* (*intervallo*) interval; (*breve spettacolo*) intermezzo

inter'nare *vt* (*arrestare*) to intern; (*MED*) to commit (to a mental institution)

inter'nauta *sm/f* (Inter)net surfer

internazio'nale [internattsjo'nale] *ag* international

'Internet ['internet] *sf* Internet; **in ~** on the Internet

in'terno, a *ag* (*di dentro*) internal, interior, inner; (*: mare*) inland; (*nazionale*) domestic; (*allievo*) boarding ♦ *sm* inside, interior; (*di paese*) interior; (*fodera*) lining; (*di appartamento*) flat (number); (*TEL*) extension ♦ *sm/f* (*INS*) boarder; **~i** *smpl* (*CINEMA*) interior shots; **all'~** inside; **Ministero degli I~i** Ministry of the Interior, ≈ Home Office (*BRIT*), Department of the Interior (*US*)

in'tero, a *ag* (*integro, intatto*) whole, entire; (*completo, totale*) complete; (*numero*) whole; (*non ridotto: biglietto*) full; (*latte*) full-cream

interpel'lare *vt* to consult

inter'porre *vt* (*ostacolo*): **~ qc a qc** to put sth in the way of sth; (*influenza*) to use; **interporsi** *vr* to intervene; **interporsi fra** (*mettersi in mezzo*) to come between; **inter'posto, a** *pp di* **interporre**

interpre'tare *vt* to interpret; **in'terprete** *sm/f* interpreter; (*TEATRO*) actor/actress, performer; (*MUS*) performer

interregio'nale [interredʒo'nale] *sm* long

distance train (*stopping frequently*)
interro'gare *vt* to question; (*INS*) to test;
interroga'tivo, a *ag* (*occhi, sguardo*)
questioning, inquiring; (*LING*) interrogative
♦ *sm* question; (*fig*) mystery;
interroga'torio, a *ag* interrogatory,
questioning ♦ *sm* (*DIR*) questioning *no pl*;
interrogazi'one *sf* questioning *no pl*;
(*INS*) oral test
inter'rompere *vt* to interrupt; (*studi,
trattative*) to break off, interrupt; ~**rsi** *vr* to
break off, stop; **inter'rotto, a** *pp di*
interrompere
interrut'tore *sm* switch
interruzi'one [interrut'tsjone] *sf*
interruption; break
interse'care *vt* to intersect; ~**rsi** *vr* to
intersect
inter'stizio [inter'stittsjo] *sm* interstice,
crack
interur'bana *sf* trunk *o* long-distance call
interur'bano, a *ag* inter-city; (*TEL:
chiamata*) trunk *cpd*, long-distance;
(*: telefono*) long-distance
inter'vallo *sm* interval; (*spazio*) space, gap
interve'nire *vi* (*partecipare*): ~ **a** to take
part in; (*intromettersi: anche POL*) to
intervene; (*MED: operare*) to operate;
inter'vento *sm* participation;
(*intromissione*) intervention; (*MED*)
operation; **fare un intervento nel corso di**
(*dibattito, programma*) to take part in
inter'vista *sf* interview; **intervis'tare** *vt*
to interview
in'tesa *sf* understanding; (*accordo*)
agreement, understanding
in'teso, a *pp di* **intendere** ♦ *ag* agreed;
siamo ~i? OK?
intes'tare *vt* (*lettera*) to address;
(*proprietà*): ~ **a** to register in the name of;
~ **un assegno a qn** to make out a cheque
to sb; **intestazi'one** *sf* heading; (*su carta
da lettere*) letterhead
intes'tino, a *ag* (*lotte*) internal, civil ♦ *sm*
(*ANAT*) intestine
inti'mare *vt* to order, command;
intimazi'one *sf* order, command

intimidazi'one [intimidat'tsjone] *sf*
intimidation
intimi'dire *vt* to intimidate ♦ *vi* (*anche:
~**rsi**) to grow shy
intimità *sf* intimacy; privacy; (*familiarità*)
familiarity
'intimo, a *ag* intimate; (*affetti, vita*) private;
(*fig: profondo*) inmost ♦ *sm* (*persona*)
intimate *o* close friend; (*dell'animo*)
bottom, depths *pl*; **parti ~e** (*ANAT*) private
parts
intimo'rire *vt* to frighten; ~**rsi** *vr* to
become frightened
in'tingolo *sm* sauce; (*pietanza*) stew
intiriz'zire [intirid'dzire] *vt* to numb ♦ *vi*
(*anche*: ~**rsi**) to go numb
intito'lare *vt* to give a title to; (*dedicare*) to
dedicate
intolle'rabile *ag* intolerable
intolle'rante *ag* intolerant
in'tonaco, ci *o* **chi** *sm* plaster
into'nare *vt* (*canto*) to start to sing;
(*armonizzare*) to match; ~**rsi** *vr* (*colori*) to
go together; ~**rsi a** (*carnagione*) to suit;
(*abito*) to go with, match
inton'tire *vt* to stun, daze ♦ *vi* (*anche*:
~**rsi**) to be stunned *o* dazed
in'toppo *sm* stumbling block, obstacle
in'torno *av* around; ~ **a** (*attorno a*) around;
(*riguardo, circa*) about
intorpi'dire *vt* to numb; (*fig*) to make
sluggish ♦ *vi* (*anche*: ~**rsi**) to grow numb;
(*fig*) to become sluggish
intossi'care *vt* to poison;
intossicazi'one *sf* poisoning
intralci'are [intral'tʃare] *vt* to hamper, hold
up
intransi'tivo, a *ag, sm* intransitive
intrapren'dente *ag* enterprising, go-
ahead
intra'prendere *vt* to undertake
intrat'tabile *ag* intractable
intratte'nere *vt* to entertain; to engage in
conversation; ~**rsi** *vr* to linger; ~**rsi su qc**
to dwell on sth
intrave'dere *vt* to catch a glimpse of; (*fig*)
to foresee

intrecci'are [intret'tʃare] vt (capelli) to plait, braid; (intessere: anche fig) to weave, interweave, intertwine; **~rsi** vr to intertwine, become interwoven; **~ le mani** to clasp one's hands; **in'treccio** sm (fig: trama) plot, story

intri'gare vi to manoeuvre (BRIT), maneuver (US); scheme; **in'trigo, ghi** sm plot, intrigue

in'trinseco, a, ci, che ag intrinsic

in'triso, a ag: **~ (di)** soaked (in)

intro'durre vt to introduce; (chiave etc): **~ qc in** to insert sth into; (persone: far entrare) to show in; **introdursi** vr (moda, tecniche) to be introduced; **introdursi in** (persona: penetrare) to enter; (: entrare furtivamente) to steal o slip into; **introduzi'one** sf introduction

in'troito sm income, revenue

intro'mettersi vr to interfere, meddle; (interporsi) to intervene

in'truglio [in'truʎʎo] sm concoction

intrusi'one sf intrusion; interference

in'truso, a sm/f intruder

intu'ire vt to perceive by intuition; (rendersi conto) to realize; **in'tuito** sm intuition; (perspicacia) perspicacity; **intuizi'one** sf intuition

inu'mano, a ag inhuman

inumi'dire vt to dampen, moisten; **~rsi** vr to become damp o wet

i'nutile ag useless; (superfluo) pointless, unnecessary; **inutilità** sf uselessness; pointlessness

inutil'mente av unnecessarily; (senza risultato) in vain

inva'dente ag (fig) interfering, nosey

in'vadere vt to invade; (affollare) to swarm into, overrun; (sog: acque) to flood

inva'ghirsi [inva'girsi] vr: **~ di** to take a fancy to

invalidità sf infirmity; disability; (DIR) invalidity

in'valido, a ag (infermo) infirm, invalid; (al lavoro) disabled; (DIR: nullo) invalid ♦ sm/f invalid; disabled person

in'vano av in vain

invasi'one sf invasion

in'vaso, a pp di **invadere**

inva'sore, invadi'trice [invadi'tritʃe] ag invading ♦ sm invader

invecchi'are [invek'kjare] vi (persona) to grow old; (vino, popolazione) to age; (moda) to become dated ♦ vt to age; (far apparire più vecchio) to make look older

in'vece [in'vetʃe] av instead; (al contrario) on the contrary; **~ di** instead of

inve'ire vi: **~ contro** to rail against

inven'tare vt to invent; (pericoli, pettegolezzi) to make up, invent

inven'tario sm inventory; (COMM) stocktaking no pl

inven'tivo, a ag inventive ♦ sf inventiveness

inven'tore sm inventor

invenzi'one [inven'tsjone] sf invention; (bugia) lie, story

inver'nale ag winter cpd; (simile all'inverno) wintry

in'verno sm winter

invero'simile ag unlikely

inversi'one sf inversion; reversal; **"divieto d'~"** (AUT) "no U-turns"

in'verso, a ag opposite; (MAT) inverse ♦ sm contrary, opposite; **in senso ~** in the opposite direction; **in ordine ~** in reverse order

inver'tire vt to invert, reverse; **~ la marcia** (AUT) to do a U-turn; **inver'tito, a** sm/f homosexual

investi'gare vt, vi to investigate; **investiga'tore, trice** sm/f investigator, detective; **investigazi'one** sf investigation, inquiry

investi'mento sm (ECON) investment

inves'tire vt (denaro) to invest; (sog: veicolo: pedone) to knock down; (: altro veicolo) to crash into; (apostrofare) to assail; (incaricare): **~ qn di** to invest sb with

invi'are vt to send; **invi'ato, a** sm/f envoy; (STAMPA) correspondent

in'vidia sf envy; **invidi'are** vt: **invidiare qn (per qc)** to envy sb for sth; **invidiare qc a qn** to envy sb sth; **invidi'oso, a** ag envious

in'vio, 'vii *sm* sending; *(insieme di merci)* consignment; *(tasto)* return

invipe'rito, a *ag* furious

invischi'are [invis'kjare] *vt (fig):* **~ qn in** to involve sb in; **~rsi** *vr:* **~rsi (con qn/in qc)** to get mixed up *o* involved (with sb/in sth)

invi'sibile *ag* invisible

invi'tare *vt* to invite; **~ qn a fare** to invite sb to do; **invi'tato, a** *sm/f* guest; **in'vito** *sm* invitation

invo'care *vt (chiedere: aiuto, pace)* to cry out for; *(appellarsi: la legge, Dio)* to appeal to, invoke

invogli'are [invoʎ'ʎare] *vt:* **~ qn a fare** to tempt sb to do, induce sb to do

involon'tario, a *ag (errore)* unintentional; *(gesto)* involuntary

invol'tino *sm (CUC)* roulade

in'volto *sm (pacco)* parcel; *(fagotto)* bundle

in'volucro *sm* cover, wrapping

involuzi'one [involut'tsjone] *sf (di stile)* convolutedness; *(regresso):* **subire un'~** to regress

inzacche'rare [intsakke'rare] *vt* to spatter with mud

inzup'pare [intsup'pare] *vt* to soak; **~rsi** *vr* to get soaked

'io *pron* I ♦ *sm inv:* **l'~** the ego, the self; **~ stesso(a)** I myself

i'odio *sm* iodine

l'onio *sm:* **lo ~, il mar ~** the Ionian (Sea)

iperrmer'cato *sm* hypermarket

ipertensi'one *sf* high blood pressure

iper'testo *sm* hypertext; **ipertestuale** *ag* hypertext(ual)

ip'nosi *sf* hypnosis; **ipno'tismo** *sm* hypnotism; **ipnotiz'zare** *vt* to hypnotize

ipocri'sia *sf* hypocrisy

i'pocrita, i, e *ag* hypocritical ♦ *sm/f* hypocrite

ipo'teca, che *sf* mortgage; **ipote'care** *vt* to mortgage

i'potesi *sf inv* hypothesis; **ipo'tetico, a, ci, che** *ag* hypothetical

'ippica *sf* horseracing

'ippico, a, ci, che *ag* horse *cpd*

ippocas'tano *sm* horse chestnut

ip'podromo *sm* racecourse

ippo'potamo *sm* hippopotamus

'ira *sf* anger, wrath

l'ran *sm:* **l'~** Iran

l'raq *sm:* **l'~** Iraq

'iride *sf (arcobaleno)* rainbow; *(ANAT, BOT)* iris

Ir'landa *sf:* **l'~** Ireland; **l'~ del Nord** Northern Ireland, Ulster; **la Repubblica d'~** Eire, the Republic of Ireland; **irlan'dese** *ag* Irish ♦ *sm/f* Irishman/woman; **gli Irlandesi** the Irish

iro'nia *sf* irony; **i'ronico, a, ci, che** *ag* ironic(al)

irradi'are *vt* to radiate; *(sog: raggi di luce: illuminare)* to shine on ♦ *vi (diffondersi: anche:* **~rsi)** to radiate

irragio'nevole [irradʒo'nevole] *ag* irrational; unreasonable

irrazio'nale [irrattsjo'nale] *ag* irrational

irre'ale *ag* unreal

irrecupe'rabile *ag* irretrievable; *(fig: persona)* irredeemable

irrecu'sabile *ag (offerta)* not to be refused; *(prova)* irrefutable

irrego'lare *ag* irregular; *(terreno)* uneven

irremo'vibile *ag (fig)* unyielding

irrepa'rabile *ag* irreparable; *(fig)* inevitable

irrepe'ribile *ag* nowhere to be found

irrequi'eto, a *ag* restless

irresis'tibile *ag* irresistible

irrespon'sabile *ag* irresponsible

irridu'cibile [irridu'tʃibile] *ag* irreducible; *(fig)* indomitable

irri'gare *vt (annaffiare)* to irrigate; *(sog: fiume etc)* to flow through; **irrigazi'one** *sf* irrigation

irrigi'dire [irridʒi'dire] *vt* to stiffen; **~rsi** *vr* to stiffen

irri'sorio, a *ag* derisory

irri'tare *vt (mettere di malumore)* to irritate, annoy; *(MED)* to irritate; **~rsi** *vr (stizzirsi)* to become irritated *o* annoyed; *(MED)* to become irritated; **irritazi'one** *sf* irritation; annoyance

ir'rompere *vi:* **~ in** to burst into

irro'rare vt to sprinkle; (AGR) to spray

irru'ente ag (fig) impetuous, violent

irruzi'one sf: **fare ~ in** to burst into; (sog: polizia) to raid

'irto, a ag bristly; **~ di** bristling with

is'critto, a pp di **iscrivere ♦** sm/f member; **per** o **in ~** in writing

is'crivere vt to register, enter; (persona): **~ (a)** to register (in), enrol (in); **~rsi** vr: **~rsi (a)** (università) to register o enrol (at); (esame, concorso) to register o enter (for); **iscrizi'one** sf (epigrafe etc) inscription; (a scuola, società) enrolment, registration; (registrazione) registration

Is'lam sm: **l'~** Islam

Is'landa sf: **l'~** Iceland

'isola sf island; **~ pedonale** (AUT) pedestrian precinct

isola'mento sm isolation; (TECN) insulation

iso'lante ag insulating **♦** sm insulator

iso'lare vt to isolate; (TECN) to insulate; (: acusticamente) to soundproof; **iso'lato, a** ag isolated; insulated **♦** sm (gruppo di edifici) block

ispetto'rato sm inspectorate

ispet'tore sm inspector

ispezio'nare [ispettsjo'nare] vt to inspect; **ispezi'one** sf inspection

'ispido, a ag bristly, shaggy

ispi'rare vt to inspire; **~rsi** vr: **~rsi a** to draw one's inspiration from

Isra'ele sm: **l'~** Israel; **israeli'ano, a** ag, sm/f Israeli

is'sare vt to hoist

istan'taneo, a ag instantaneous **♦** sf (FOT) snapshot

is'tante sm instant, moment; **all'~, sull'~** instantly, immediately

is'tanza [is'tantsa] sf petition, request

is'terico, a, ci, che ag hysterical

iste'rismo sm hysteria

isti'gare vt to incite; **istigazi'one** sf incitement; **istigazione a delinquere** (DIR) incitement to crime

is'tinto sm instinct

istitu'ire vt (fondare) to institute, found; (porre: confronto) to establish; (intraprendere: inchiesta) to set up

isti'tuto sm institute; (di università) department; (ente, DIR) institution; **~ di bellezza** beauty salon

istituzi'one [istitut'tsjone] sf institution

'istmo sm (GEO) isthmus

'istrice ['istritʃe] sm porcupine

istri'one (peg) sm ham actor

istru'ire vt (insegnare) to teach; (ammaestrare) to train; (informare) to instruct, inform; (DIR) to prepare; **istrut'tore, 'trice** sm/f instructor **♦** ag: **giudice istruttore** vedi **giudice**; **istrut'toria** sf (DIR) (preliminary) investigation and hearing; **istruzi'one** sf education; training; (direttiva) instruction

I'talia sf: **l'~** Italy

itali'ano, a ag Italian **♦** sm/f Italian **♦** sm (LING) Italian; **gli I~i** the Italians

itine'rario sm itinerary

itte'rizia [itte'rittsja] sf (MED) jaundice

'ittico, a, ci, che ag fish cpd; fishing cpd

lugos'lavia etc = **Jugoslavia** etc

i'uta sf jute

I.V.A. ['iva] sigla f (= imposta sul valore aggiunto) VAT

J, j

jazz [dʒaz] sm jazz

jeans [dʒinz] smpl jeans

Jugos'lavia [jugoz'lavja] sf: **la ~** Yugoslavia; **la ex-~** former Yugoslavia; **jugos'lavo, a** ag, sm/f Yugoslav(ian)

'juta ['juta] sf = **iuta**

K, k

K abbr (INFORM) K

k abbr (= kilo) k

karatè sm karate

Kg abbr (= chilogrammo) kg

'killer sm inv gunman, hired gun

'kiwi ['kiwi] sm inv kiwi fruit

km *abbr* (= *chilometro*) km
koso'varo, a *sm/f, ag* Kosovar
'krapfen *sm inv* (*CUC*) doughnut

L, l

l' *det vedi* **la; lo; il**
la¹ (*dav V* **l'**) *det f* the ♦ *pron* (*oggetto: persona*) her; (: *cosa*) it; (: *forma di cortesia*) you; *vedi anche* **il**
la² *sm inv* (*MUS*) A; (: *solfeggiando*) la
là *av* there; **di ~** (*da quel luogo*) from there; (*in quel luogo*) in there; (*dall'altra parte*) over there; **di ~ di** beyond; **per di ~** that way; **più in ~** further on; (*tempo*) later on; **fatti in ~** move up; **~ dentro/sopra/sotto** in/up (*o* on)/under there; *vedi anche* **quello**
'labbro (*pl(f)*: **labbra**: *solo nel senso ANAT*) *sm* lip
labi'rinto *sm* labyrinth, maze
labora'torio *sm* (*di ricerca*) laboratory; (*di arti, mestieri*) workshop
labori'oso, a *ag* (*faticoso*) laborious; (*attivo*) hard-working
labu'rista, i, e *ag* Labour (*BRIT*) *cpd* ♦ *sm/f* Labour Party member (*BRIT*)
'lacca, che *sf* lacquer
'laccio ['lattʃo] *sm* noose; (*legaccio, tirante*) lasso; (*di scarpa*) lace; **~ emostatico** tourniquet
lace'rare [latʃe'rare] *vt* to tear to shreds, lacerate; **~rsi** *vr* to tear; **'lacero, a** *ag* (*logoro*) torn, tattered; (*MED*) lacerated
'lacrima *sf* tear; **in ~e** in tears; **lacri'mare** *vi* to water; **lacri'mogeno, a** *ag*: **gas lacrimogeno** tear gas
la'cuna *sf* (*fig*) gap
'ladro *sm* thief; **ladro'cinio** *sm* theft, larceny
laggiù [lad'dʒu] *av* down there; (*di là*) over there
la'gnarsi [laɲ'ɲarsi] *vr*: **~ (di)** to complain (about)
'lago, ghi *sm* lake
la'guna *sf* lagoon

'laico, a, ci, che *ag* (*apostolato*) lay; (*vita*) secular; (*scuola*) non-denominational ♦ *sm/f* layman/woman
'lama *sm inv* (*ZOOL*) llama; (*REL*) lama ♦ *sf* blade
lam'bire *vt* to lick; to lap
lamen'tare *vt* to lament; **~rsi** *vr* (*emettere lamenti*) to moan, groan; (*rammaricarsi*): **~rsi (di)** to complain (about); **lamen'tela** *sf* complaining *no pl*; **lamen'tevole** *ag* (*voce*) complaining, plaintive; (*destino*) pitiful; **la'mento** *sm* moan, groan; wail; **lamen'toso, a** *ag* plaintive
la'metta *sf* razor blade
lami'era *sf* sheet metal
'lamina *sf* (*lastra sottile*) thin sheet (*o* layer *o* plate); **~ d'oro** gold leaf; gold foil; **lami'nare** *vt* to laminate; **lami'nato, a** *ag* laminated; (*tessuto*) lamé ♦ *sm* laminate
'lampada *sf* lamp; **~ a gas** gas lamp; **~ da tavolo** table lamp
lampa'dario *sm* chandelier
lampa'dina *sf* light bulb; **~ tascabile** pocket torch (*BRIT*) *o* flashlight (*US*)
lam'pante *ag* (*fig: evidente*) crystal clear, evident
lampeggi'are [lamped'dʒare] *vi* (*luce, fari*) to flash ♦ *vb impers*: **lampeggia** there's lightning; **lampeggia'tore** *sm* (*AUT*) indicator
lampi'one *sm* street light *o* lamp (*BRIT*)
'lampo *sm* (*METEOR*) flash of lightning; (*di luce, fig*) flash; **~i** *smpl* lightning *no pl* ♦ *ag inv*: **cerniera ~** zip (fastener) (*BRIT*), zipper (*US*); **guerra ~** blitzkrieg
lam'pone *sm* raspberry
'lana *sf* wool; **~ d'acciaio** steel wool; **pura ~ vergine** pure new wool; **~ di vetro** glass wool
lan'cetta [lan'tʃetta] *sf* (*indice*) pointer, needle; (*di orologio*) hand
'lancia ['lantʃa] *sf* (*arma*) lance; (: *picca*) spear; (*di pompa antincendio*) nozzle; (*imbarcazione*) launch
lanciafi'amme [lantʃa'fjamme] *sm inv* flamethrower
lanci'are [lan'tʃare] *vt* to throw, hurl, fling;

(*SPORT*) to throw; (*far partire: automobile*) to get up to full speed; (*bombe*) to drop; (*razzo, prodotto, moda*) to launch; **~rsi** *vr*: **~rsi contro/su** to throw *o* hurl *o* fling o.s. against/on; **~rsi in** (*fig*) to embark on

lanci'nante [lantʃi'nante] *ag* (*dolore*) shooting, throbbing; (*grido*) piercing

'lancio ['lantʃo] *sm* throwing *no pl*; throw; dropping *no pl*; drop; launching *no pl*; launch; **~ del peso** putting the shot

'landa *sf* (*GEO*) moor

'languido, a *ag* (*fiacco*) languid, weak; (*tenero, malinconico*) languishing

langu'ore *sm* weakness, languor

lani'ficio [lani'fitʃo] *sm* woollen mill

la'noso, a *ag* woolly

lan'terna *sf* lantern; (*faro*) lighthouse

la'nugine [la'nudʒine] *sf* down

lapi'dario, a *ag* (*fig*) terse

'lapide *sf* (*di sepolcro*) tombstone; (*commemorativa*) plaque

'lapis *sm inv* pencil

Lap'ponia *sf* Lapland

'lapsus *sm inv* slip

'laptop ['læptɔp] *sm inv* laptop (computer)

'lardo *sm* bacon fat, lard

lar'ghezza [lar'gettsa] *sf* width; breadth; looseness; generosity; **~ di vedute** broad-mindedness

'largo, a, ghi, ghe *ag* wide; broad; (*maniche*) wide; (*abito: troppo ampio*) loose; (*fig*) generous ♦ *sm* width; breadth; (*mare aperto*): **il ~** the open sea ♦ *sf*: **stare** *o* **tenersi alla ~a (da qn/qc)** to keep one's distance (from sb/sth), keep away (from sb/sth); **~ due metri** two metres wide; **~ di spalle** broad-shouldered; **di ~ghe vedute** broad-minded; **su ~a scala** on a large scale; **di manica ~a** generous, open-handed; **al ~ di Genova** off the coast of) Genoa; **farsi ~ tra la folla** to push one's way through the crowd

'larice ['laritʃe] *sm* (*BOT*) larch

larin'gite [larin'dʒite] *sf* laryngitis

'larva *sf* larva; (*fig*) shadow

la'sagne [la'zaɲɲe] *sfpl* lasagna *sg*

lasci'are [laʃ'ʃare] *vt* to leave;

(*abbandonare*) to leave, abandon, give up; (*cessare di tenere*) to let go of ♦ *vb aus*: **~ fare qn** to let sb do; **~ andare** *o* **perdere** to let things go their own way; **~ stare qc/qn** to leave sth/sb alone; **~rsi** *vr* (*persone*) to part; (*coppia*) to split up; **~rsi andare** to let o.s. go

'lascito ['laʃʃito] *sm* (*DIR*) legacy

'laser ['lazer] *ag, sm inv*: **(raggio) ~** laser (beam)

lassa'tivo, a *ag, sm* laxative

'lasso *sm*: **~ di tempo** interval, lapse of time

lassù *av* up there

'lastra *sf* (*di pietra*) slab; (*di metallo, FOT*) plate; (*di ghiaccio, vetro*) sheet; (*radiografica*) X-ray (plate)

lastri'cato *sm* paving

late'rale *ag* lateral, side *cpd*; (*uscita, ingresso etc*) side *cpd* ♦ *sm* (*CALCIO*) half-back

late'rizio [late'rittsjo] *sm* (perforated) brick

lati'fondo *sm* large estate

la'tino, a *ag, sm* Latin; **~-ameri'cano, a** *ag* Latin-American

lati'tante *sm/f* fugitive (from justice)

lati'tudine *sf* latitude

'lato, a *ag* (*fig*) wide, broad ♦ *sm* side; (*fig*) aspect, point of view; **in senso ~** broadly speaking

la'trare *vi* to bark

la'trina *sf* public lavatory

'latta *sf* tin (plate); (*recipiente*) tin, can

lat'taio, a *sm/f* milkman/woman; dairyman/woman

lat'tante *ag* unweaned

'latte *sm* milk; **~ detergente** cleansing milk *o* lotion; **~ in polvere** dried *o* powdered milk; **~ scremato** skimmed milk; **latte'ria** *sf* dairy; **latti'cini** *smpl* dairy products

lat'tina *sf* (*di birra etc*) can

lat'tuga, ghe *sf* lettuce

'laurea *sf* degree; **laurearsi** *vr* to graduate; **laure'ato, a** *ag, sm/f* graduate

'lauro *sm* laurel

'lauto, a *ag* (*pranzo, mancia*) lavish

'lava *sf* lava

la'vabo *sm* washbasin

la'vaggio [la'vaddʒo] *sm* washing *no pl*; ~ **del cervello** brainwashing *no pl*

la'vagna [la'vaɲɲa] *sf* (GEO) slate; (*di scuola*) blackboard

la'vanda *sf* (*anche* MED) wash; (BOT) lavender; lavan'daia *sf* washerwoman; lavande'ria *sf* laundry; **lavanderia automatica** launderette; **lavanderia a secco** dry-cleaner's; lavan'dino *sm* sink

lavapi'atti *sm/f* dishwasher

la'vare *vt* to wash; ~rsi *vr* to wash, have a wash; ~ **a secco** to dry-clean; ~rsi le mani/i denti to wash one's hands/clean one's teeth

lava'secco *sm o f inv* drycleaner's

lavasto'viglie [lavasto'viʎʎe] *sm o f inv* (*macchina*) dishwasher

lava'trice [lava'tritʃe] *sf* washing machine

lava'tura *sf* washing *no pl*; ~ **di piatti** dishwater

lavo'rante *sm/f* worker

lavo'rare *vi* to work; (*fig: bar, studio etc*) to do good business ♦ *vt* to work; ~rsi qn (*persuaderlo*) to work on sb; ~ **a** to work on; ~ **a maglia** to knit; lavora'tivo, a *ag* working; lavora'tore, 'trice *sm/f* worker ♦ *ag* working; lavorazi'one *sf* (*gen*) working; (*di legno, pietra*) carving; (*di film*) making; (*di prodotto*) manufacture; (*modo di esecuzione*) workmanship; lavo'rio *sm* intense activity

la'voro *sm* work; (*occupazione*) job, work *no pl*; (*opera*) piece of work, job; (ECON) labour; ~i forzati hard labour *sg*; ~i pubblici public works

le *det fpl* the ♦ *pron* (*oggetto*) them; (: a lei, a essa) (to) her; (: *forma di cortesia*) (to) you; *vedi anche* il

le'ale *ag* loyal; (*sincero*) sincere; (*onesto*) fair; lealtà *sf* loyalty; sincerity; fairness

'lebbra *sf* leprosy

'lecca 'lecca *sm inv* lollipop

leccapi'edi (*peg*) *sm/f inv* toady, bootlicker

lec'care *vt* to lick; (*sog: gatto: latte etc*) to lick *o* lap up; (*fig*) to flatter; ~rsi i baffi to lick one's lips

'leccio ['lettʃo] *sm* holm oak, ilex

leccor'nia *sf* titbit, delicacy

'lecito, a ['lɛtʃito] *ag* permitted, allowed

'ledere *vt* to damage, injure

'lega, ghe *sf* league; (*di metalli*) alloy

le'gaccio [le'gattʃo] *sm* string, lace

le'gale *ag* legal ♦ *sm* lawyer; legaliz'zare *vt* to authenticate; (*regolarizzare*) to legalize

le'game *sm* (*corda, fig: affettivo*) tie, bond; (*nesso logico*) link, connection

le'gare *vt* (*prigioniero, capelli, cane*) to tie (up); (*libro*) to bind; (CHIM) to alloy; (*fig: collegare*) to bind, join ♦ *vi* (*far lega*) to unite; (*fig*) to get on well

le'gato *sm* (REL) legate; (DIR) legacy, bequest

lega'tura *sf* (*di libro*) binding; (MUS) ligature

le'genda [le'dʒɛnda] *sf* (*di carta geografica etc*) = leggenda

'legge ['leddʒe] *sf* law

leg'genda [led'dʒɛnda] *sf* (*narrazione*) legend; (*di carta geografica etc*) key, legend

'leggere ['leddʒere] *vt, vi* to read

legge'rezza [leddʒe'rettsa] *sf* lightness; thoughtlessness; fickleness

leg'gero, a [led'dʒero] *ag* light; (*agile, snello*) nimble, agile, light; (*tè, caffè*) weak; (*fig: non grave, piccolo*) slight; (: *spensierato*) thoughtless; (: *incostante*) fickle; free and easy; **alla ~a** thoughtlessly

leggi'adro, a [led'dʒadro] *ag* pretty, lovely; (*movimenti*) graceful

leg'gio, 'gii [led'dʒio] *sm* lectern; (MUS) music stand

legisla'tura [ledʒizla'tura] *sf* legislature

legislazi'one [ledʒizlat'tsjone] *sf* legislation

le'gittimo, a [le'dʒittimo] *ag* legitimate; (*fig: giustificato, lecito*) justified, legitimate; **~a difesa** (DIR) self-defence

'legna ['leɲɲa] *sf* firewood; le'gname *sm* wood, timber

'legno ['leɲɲo] *sm* wood; (*pezzo di ~*) piece of wood; **di ~** wooden; ~ **compensato** plywood; **le'gnoso, a** *ag* wooden; woody; *(carne)* tough

le'gumi *smpl* (*BOT*) pulses

'lei *pron (soggetto)* she; *(oggetto: per dare rilievo, con preposizione)* her; *(forma di cortesia: anche: L~)* you ♦ *sm:* **dare del ~ a qn** to address sb as "lei"; **~ stessa** she herself; you yourself

'lembo *sm (di abito, strada)* edge; *(striscia sottile: di terra)* strip

'lemma, i *sm* headword

'lemme 'lemme *av* (very) very slowly

'lena *sf (fig)* energy, stamina

le'nire *vt* to soothe

lenta'mente *av* slowly

'lente *sf (OTTICA)* lens *sg;* **~ d'ingran-dimento** magnifying glass; **~i a contatto** *o* **corneali** contact lenses

len'tezza [len'tettsa] *sf* slowness

len'ticchia [len'tikkja] *sf (BOT)* lentil

len'tiggine [len'tiddʒine] *sf* freckle

'lento, a *ag* slow; *(molle: fune)* slack; *(non stretto: vite, abito)* loose ♦ *sm (ballo)* slow dance

'lenza ['lɛntsa] *sf* fishing-line

lenzu'olo [len'tswɔlo] *sm* sheet; **~a** *sfpl* pair of sheets

le'one *sm* lion; *(dello zodiaco):* **L~** Leo

lepo'rino, a *ag:* **labbro ~** harelip

'lepre *sf* hare

'lercio, a, ci, cie ['lertʃo] *ag* filthy

'lesbica, che *sf* lesbian

lesi'nare *vt* to be stingy with ♦ *vi:* **~ (su)** to skimp (on), be stingy (with)

lesi'one *sf (MED)* lesion; *(DIR)* injury, damage; *(EDIL)* crack

'leso, a *pp di* **ledere** ♦ *ag (offeso)* injured; **parte ~a** *(DIR)* injured party

les'sare *vt (CUC)* to boil

'lessico, ci *sm* vocabulary; lexicon

'lesso, a *ag* boiled ♦ *sm* boiled meat

'lesto, a *ag* quick; *(agile)* nimble; **~ di mano** *(per rubare)* light-fingered; *(per picchiare)* free with one's fists

le'tale *ag* lethal; fatal

leta'maio *sm* dunghill

le'tame *sm* manure, dung

le'targo, ghi *sm* lethargy; *(ZOOL)* hibernation

le'tizia [le'tittsja] *sf* joy, happiness

'lettera *sf* letter; **~e** *sfpl (letteratura)* literature *sg; (studi umanistici)* arts (subjects); **alla ~** literally; **in ~e** in words, in full; **lette'rale** *ag* literal

lette'rario, a *ag* literary

lette'rato, a *ag* well-read, scholarly

lettera'tura *sf* literature

let'tiga, ghe *sf (barella)* stretcher

let'tino *sm* cot *(BRIT)*, crib *(US)*

'letto *sm, pp di* **leggere** ♦ *sm* bed; **andare a ~** to go to bed; **~ a castello** bunk beds *pl;* **~ a una piazza/a due piazze** *o* **matrimoniale** single/double bed

let'tore, 'trice *sm/f* reader; *(INS)* (foreign language) assistant *(BRIT)*, (foreign) teaching assistant *(US)* ♦ *sm (TECN):* **~ ottico** optical character reader

let'tura *sf* reading

leuce'mia [leutʃe'mia] *sf* leukaemia

'leva *sf* lever; *(MIL)* conscription; **far ~ su qn** to work on sb; **~ del cambio** *(AUT)* gear lever

le'vante *sm* east; *(vento)* East wind; **il L~** the Levant

le'vare *vt (occhi, braccio)* to raise; *(sollevare, togliere: tassa, divieto)* to lift; *(indumenti)* to take off, remove; *(rimuovere)* to take away; (*: dal di sopra*) to take off; (*: dal di dentro*) to take out; **~rsi** *vr* to get up; *(sole)* to rise; **le'vata** *sf (di posta)* collection

leva'toio, a *ag:* **ponte ~** drawbridge

leva'tura *sf* intelligence, mental capacity

levi'gare *vt* to smooth; *(con carta vetrata)* to sand

levri'ere *sm* greyhound

lezi'one [let'tsjone] *sf* lesson; *(UNIV)* lecture; **fare ~** to teach; to lecture; **dare una ~ a qn** to teach sb a lesson

lezi'oso, a [let'tsjoso] *ag* affected; simpering

'lezzo ['leddzo] *sm* stench, stink

li *pron pl (oggetto)* them

lì *av* there; **di** *o* **da ~** from there; **per di ~** that way; **di ~ a pochi giorni** a few days

later; ~ **per** ~ there and then; at first;
essere ~ **(~) per fare** to be on the point
of doing, be about to do; ~ **dentro** in
there; ~ **sotto** under there; ~ **sopra** on
there; up there; *vedi anche* **quello**
liba'nese *ag, sm/f* Lebanese *inv*
Li'bano *sm*: **il** ~ the Lebanon
'libbra *sf (peso)* pound
li'beccio [li'bettʃo] *sm* south-west wind
li'bello *sm* libel
li'bellula *sf* dragonfly
libe'rale *ag, sm/f* liberal
liberaliz'zare [liberalid'dzare] *vt* to
liberalize
libe'rare *vt (rendere libero: prigioniero)* to
release; *(: popolo)* to free, liberate;
(sgombrare: passaggio) to clear; *(: stanza)*
to vacate; *(produrre: energia)* to release;
~rsi *vr*: **~rsi di qc/qn** to get rid of sth/sb;
libera'tore, 'trice *ag* liberating ♦ *sm/f*
liberator; liberazi'one *sf* liberation,
freeing; release; rescuing

Liberazione
---

i The **Liberazione** is a national holiday
which falls on 25 April. It
commemorates the liberation of Italy at the
end of the Second World War.

'libero, a *ag* free; *(strada)* clear; *(non
occupato: posto etc)* vacant; not taken;
empty; not engaged; ~ **di fare qc** free to
do sth; ~ **da** free from; ~ **arbitrio** free will;
~ **professionista** self-employed
professional person; ~ **scambio** free trade;
libertà *sf inv* freedom; *(tempo disponibile)*
free time ♦ *sfpl (licenza)* liberties; **in libertà
provvisoria/vigilata** released without
bail/on probation
'Libia *sf*: **la** ~ Libya; 'libico, a, ci, che *ag,
sm/f* Libyan
li'bidine *sf* lust
li'braio *sm* bookseller
li'brarsi *vr* to hover
libre'ria *sf (bottega)* bookshop; *(stanza)*
library; *(mobile)* bookcase
li'bretto *sm* booklet; *(taccuino)* notebook;

(MUS) libretto; ~ **degli assegni** cheque
book; ~ **di circolazione** *(AUT)* logbook; ~ **di
risparmio** *(savings)* bank-book, passbook;
~ **universitario** student's report book
'libro *sm* book; ~ **di cassa** cash book; ~
mastro ledger; ~ **paga** payroll; ~ **di testo**
textbook
li'cenza [li'tʃɛntsa] *sf (permesso)* permission,
leave; *(di pesca, caccia, circolazione)* permit,
licence; *(MIL)* leave; *(INS)* school leaving
certificate; *(libertà)* liberty; licence;
licentiousness; **andare in** ~ *(MIL)* to go on
leave
licenzia'mento [litʃentsja'mento] *sm*
dismissal
licenzi'are [litʃen'tsjare] *vt (impiegato)* to
dismiss; *(COMM: per eccesso di personale)* to
make redundant; *(INS)* to award a
certificate to; **~rsi** *vr (impiegato)* to resign,
hand in one's notice; *(INS)* to obtain one's
school-leaving certificate
li'ceo [li'tʃɛo] *sm (INS)* secondary *(BRIT)* o
high *(US)* school *(for 14- to 19-year-olds)*
'lido *sm* beach, shore
li'eto, a *ag* happy, glad; **"molto ~"** *(nelle
presentazioni)* "pleased to meet you"
li'eve *ag* light; *(di poco conto)* slight;
(sommesso: voce) faint, soft
lievi'tare *vi (anche fig)* to rise ♦ *vt* to
leaven
li'evito *sm* yeast; ~ **di birra** brewer's yeast
'ligio, a, gi, gie ['lidʒo] *ag* faithful, loyal
'lilla *sm inv* lilac
'lillà *sm inv* lilac
'lima *sf* file
limacci'oso, a [limat'tʃoso] *ag* slimy;
muddy
li'mare *vt* to file (down); *(fig)* to polish
'limbo *sm (REL)* limbo
li'metta *sf* nail file
limi'tare *vt* to limit, restrict; *(circoscrivere)*
to bound, surround; limita'tivo, a *ag*
limiting, restricting; limi'tato, a *ag*
limited, restricted
'limite *sm* limit; *(confine)* border, boundary;
~ **di velocità** speed limit
li'mitrofo, a *ag* neighbouring

limo'nata *sf* lemonade (*BRIT*), (lemon) soda (*US*); lemon squash (*BRIT*), lemonade (*US*)

li'mone *sm* (*pianta*) lemon tree; (*frutto*) lemon

'limpido, a *ag* clear; (*acqua*) limpid, clear

'lince ['lintʃe] *sf* lynx

linci'are *vt* to lynch

'lindo, a *ag* tidy, spick and span; (*biancheria*) clean

'linea *sf* line; (*di mezzi pubblici di trasporto: itinerario*) route; (: *servizio*) service; **a grandi ~e** in outline; **mantenere la ~** to look after one's figure; **aereo di ~** airliner; **nave di ~** liner; **volo di ~** scheduled flight; **~ aerea** airline; **~ cortesia ~ di partenza/ d'arrivo** (*SPORT*) starting/finishing line; **~ di tiro** line of fire

linea'menti *smpl* features; (*fig*) outlines

line'are *ag* linear; (*fig*) coherent, logical

line'etta *sf* (*trattino*) dash; (*d'unione*) hyphen

lin'gotto *sm* ingot, bar

'lingua *sf* (*ANAT, CUC*) tongue; (*idioma*) language; **mostrare la ~** to stick out one's tongue; **di ~ italiana** Italian-speaking; **~ madre** mother tongue; **una ~ di terra** a spit of land

lingu'aggio [lin'gwaddʒo] *sm* language

lingu'etta *sf* (*di strumento*) reed; (*di scarpa, TECN*) tongue; (*di busta*) flap

lingu'istica *sf* linguistics *sg*

'lino *sm* (*pianta*) flax; (*tessuto*) linen

li'noleum *sm inv* linoleum, lino

liposuzi'one [liposut'tsjone] *sf* liposuction

lique'fare *vt* (*render liquido*) to liquefy; (*fondere*) to melt; **~rsi** *vr* to liquefy; to melt

liqui'dare *vt* (*società, beni; persona: uccidere*) to liquidate; (*persona: sbarazzarsene*) to get rid of; (*conto, problema*) to settle; (*COMM: merce*) to sell off, clear; **liquidazi'one** *sf* liquidation; settlement; clearance sale

liquidità *sf* liquidity

'liquido, a *ag, sm* liquid; **~ per freni** brake fluid

liqui'rizia [likwi'rittsja] *sf* liquorice

li'quore *sm* liqueur

'lira *sf* (*unità monetaria*) lira; (*MUS*) lyre; **~ sterlina** pound sterling

'lirica, che *sf* (*poesia*) lyric poetry; (*componimento poetico*) lyric; (*MUS*) opera

'lirico, a, ci, che *ag* lyric(al); (*MUS*) lyric; **cantante/teatro ~** opera singer/house

'lisca, sche *sf* (*di pesce*) fishbone

lisci'are [liʃ'ʃare] *vt* to smooth; (*fig*) to flatter

'liscio, a, sci, sce ['liʃʃo] *ag* smooth; (*capelli*) straight; (*mobile*) plain; (*bevanda alcolica*) neat; (*fig*) straightforward, simple ♦ *av:* **andare ~** to go smoothly; **passarla ~a** to get away with it

'liso, a *ag* worn out, threadbare

'lista *sf* (*elenco*) list; **~ elettorale** electoral roll; **~ delle vivande** menu; **~ delle spese** shopping list

lis'tino *sm* list; **~ dei cambi** (*foreign*) exchange rate; **~ dei prezzi** price list

Lit. *abbr* = **lire italiane**

'lite *sf* quarrel, argument; (*DIR*) lawsuit

liti'gare *vi* to quarrel; (*DIR*) to litigate

li'tigio [li'tidʒo] *sm* quarrel; **litigi'oso, a** *ag* quarrelsome; (*DIR*) litigious

litogra'fia *sf* (*sistema*) lithography; (*stampa*) lithograph

lito'rale *ag* coastal, coast *cpd* ♦ *sm* coast

'litro *sm* litre

livel'lare *vt* to level, make level; **~rsi** *vr* to become level; (*fig*) to level out, balance out

li'vello *sm* level; (*fig*) level, standard; **ad alto ~** (*fig*) high-level; **~ del mare** sea level

'livido, a *ag* livid; (*per percosse*) bruised, black and blue; (*cielo*) leaden ♦ *sm* bruise

li'vore *sm* malice, spite

Li'vorno *sf* Livorno, Leghorn

li'vrea *sf* livery

'lizza ['littsa] *sf* lists *pl*; **scendere in ~** (*anche fig*) to enter the lists

lo (*dav s impura, gn, pn, ps, x, z; dav V* **l'**) *det m* the ♦ *pron* (*oggetto: persona*) him; (: *cosa*) it; **~ sapevo** I knew it; **~ so** I know; **sii buono, anche se lui non ~ è** be good, even if he isn't; *vedi anche* **il**

lo'cale *ag* local ♦ *sm* room; (*luogo pubblico*) premises *pl*; **~ notturno** nightclub;

località *sf inv* locality; **localiz'zare** *vt* (*circoscrivere*) to confine, localize; (*accertare*) to locate, place

lo'canda *sf* inn; **locandi'ere, a** *sm/f* innkeeper

loca'tario, a *sm/f* tenant

loca'tore, 'trice *sm/f* landlord/lady

locazi'one [lokat'tsjone] *sf* (*da parte del locatario*) renting *no pl*; (*da parte del locatore*) renting out *no pl*, letting *no pl*; **(contratto di)** ~ lease; **(canone di)** ~ rent; **dare in** ~ to rent out, let

locomo'tiva *sf* locomotive

locomo'tore *sm* electric locomotive

locomozi'one [lokomot'tsjone] *sf* locomotion; **mezzi di** ~ vehicles, means of transport

lo'custa *sf* locust

locuzi'one [lokut'tsjone] *sf* phrase, expression

lo'dare *vt* to praise

'lode *sf* praise; (*INS*): **laurearsi con 110 e** ~ ≈ to graduate with a first-class honours degree (*BRIT*), graduate summa cum laude (*US*)

'loden *sm inv* (*stoffa*) loden; (*cappotto*) loden overcoat

lo'devole *ag* praiseworthy

loga'ritmo *sm* logarithm

'loggia, ge ['lɔddʒa] *sf* (*ARCHIT*) loggia; (*circolo massonico*) lodge; **loggi'one** *sm* (*di teatro*): **il loggione** the Gods *sg*

'logica *sf* logic

'logico, a, ci, che ['lɔdʒiko] *ag* logical

logo'rare *vt* to wear out; (*sciupare*) to waste; **~rsi** *vr* to wear out; (*fig*) to wear o.s. out

logo'rio *sm* wear and tear; (*fig*) strain

'logoro, a *ag* (*stoffa*) worn out, threadbare; (*persona*) worn out

lom'baggine [lom'baddʒine] *sf* lumbago

Lombar'dia *sf*: **la** ~ Lombardy

lom'bata *sf* (*taglio di carne*) loin

'lombo *sm* (*ANAT*) loin

lom'brico, chi *sm* earthworm

londi'nese *ag* London *cpd* ♦ *sm/f* Londoner

'Londra *sf* London

lon'gevo, a [lon'dʒevo] *ag* long-lived

longi'tudine [londʒi'tudine] *sf* longitude

lonta'nanza [lonta'nantsa] *sf* distance; absence

lon'tano, a *ag* (*distante*) distant, faraway; (*assente*) absent; (*vago: sospetto*) slight, remote; (*tempo: remoto*) far-off, distant; (*parente*) distant, remote ♦ *av* far; **è ~a la casa?** is it far to the house?, is the house far from here?; **è ~ un chilometro** it's a kilometre away *o* a kilometre from here; **più** ~ farther; **da** *o* **di** ~ from a distance; ~ **da** a long way from; **alla ~a** slightly, vaguely

'lontra *sf* otter

lo'quace [lo'kwatʃe] *ag* talkative, loquacious; (*fig: gesto etc*) eloquent

'lordo, a *ag* dirty, filthy; (*peso, stipendio*) gross

'loro *pron pl* (*oggetto, con preposizione*) them; (*complemento di termine*) to them; (*soggetto*) they; (*forma di cortesia: anche:* **L~**) you; to you; **il(la)** ~, **i(le)** ~ *det* their; (*forma di cortesia: anche:* **L~**) your ♦ *pron* theirs; (*forma di cortesia: anche:* **L~**) yours; ~ **stessi(e)** they themselves; you yourselves

'losco, a, schi, sche *ag* (*fig*) shady, suspicious

'lotta *sf* struggle, fight; (*SPORT*) wrestling; ~ **libera** all-in wrestling; **lot'tare** *vi* to fight, struggle; to wrestle; **lotta'tore, trice** *sm/f* wrestler

lotte'ria *sf* lottery; (*di gara ippica*) sweepstake

'lotto *sm* (*gioco*) (state) lottery; (*parte*) lot; (*EDIL*) site

lozi'one [lot'tsjone] *sf* lotion

lubrifi'cante *sm* lubricant

lubrifi'care *vt* to lubricate

luc'chetto [luk'ketto] *sm* padlock

lucci'care [luttʃi'kare] *vi* to sparkle, glitter, twinkle

'luccio ['luttʃo] *sm* (*ZOOL*) pike

'lucciola ['luttʃola] *sf* (*ZOOL*) firefly; glowworm

'luce ['lutʃe] *sf* light; (*finestra*) window; **alla**

~ di by the light of; **fare ~ su qc** (*fig*) to shed *o* throw light on sth; **~ del sole/della luna** sun/moonlight; **lu'cente** *ag* shining

lucer'nario [lutʃer'narjo] *sm* skylight

lu'certola [lu'tʃertola] *sf* lizard

luci'dare [lutʃi'dare] *vt* to polish

lucida'trice [lutʃida'tritʃe] *sf* floor polisher

'lucido, a ['lutʃido] *ag* shining, bright; (*lucidato*) polished; (*fig*) lucid ♦ *sm* shine, lustre; (*per scarpe etc*) polish; (*disegno*) tracing

'lucro *sm* profit, gain; **lu'croso, a** *ag* lucrative, profitable

'luglio ['luʎʎo] *sm* July

'lugubre *ag* gloomy

'lui *pronome* (*soggetto*) he; (*oggetto: per dare rilievo, con preposizione*) him; **~ stesso** he himself

lu'maca, che *sf* slug; (*chiocciola*) snail

'lume *sm* light; (*lampada*) lamp; (*fig*): **chiedere ~i a qn** to ask sb for advice; **a ~ di naso** (*fig*) by rule of thumb

lumi'naria *sf* (*per feste*) illuminations *pl*

lumi'noso, a *ag* (*che emette luce*) luminous; (*cielo, colore, stanza*) bright; (*sorgente*) of light, light *cpd*; (*fig: sorriso*) bright, radiant

'luna *sf* moon; **~ nuova/piena** new/full moon; **~ di miele** honeymoon

'luna park *sm inv* amusement park, funfair

lu'nare *ag* lunar, moon *cpd*

lu'nario *sm* almanac; **sbarcare il ~** to make ends meet

lu'natico, a, ci, che *ag* whimsical, temperamental

lunedì *sm inv* Monday; **di** *o* **il ~** on Mondays

lun'gaggine [lun'gaddʒine] *sf* slowness; **~i della burocrazia** red tape

lun'ghezza [lun'gettsa] *sf* length; **~ d'onda** (*FISICA*) wavelength

'lungi ['lundʒi]: **~ da** *prep* far from

'lungo, a, ghi, ghe *ag* long; (*lento: persona*) slow; (*diluito: caffè, brodo*) weak, watery, thin ♦ *sm* length ♦ *prep* along; **~ 3 metri** 3 metres long; **a ~** for a long time; **a ~ andare** in the long run; **di gran ~a**

(*molto*) by far; **andare in ~** *o* **per le lunghe** to drag on; **saperla ~a** to know what's what; **in ~ e in largo** far and wide, all over; **~ il corso dei secoli** throughout the centuries

lungo'mare *sm* promenade

lu'notto *sm* (*AUT*) rear *o* back window; **~ termico** heated rear window

lu'ogo, ghi *sm* place; (*posto: di incidente etc*) scene, site; (*punto, passo di libro*) passage; **in ~ di** instead of; **in primo ~** in the first place; **aver ~** to take place; **dar ~ a** to give rise to; **~ comune** commonplace; **~ di nascita** birthplace; (*AMM*) place of birth; **~ di provenienza** place of origin

luogote'nente *sm* (*MIL*) lieutenant

lu'para *sf* sawn-off shotgun

'lupo, a *sm/f* wolf

'luppolo *sm* (*BOT*) hop

'lurido, a *ag* filthy

lu'singa, ghe *sf* (*spesso al pl*) flattery *no pl*

lusin'gare *vt* to flatter; **lusinghi'ero, a** *ag* flattering, gratifying

lus'sare *vt* (*MED*) to dislocate

Lussem'burgo *sm* (*stato*): **il ~** Luxembourg ♦ *sf* (*città*) Luxembourg

'lusso *sm* luxury; **di ~** luxury *cpd*; **lussu'oso, a** *ag* luxurious

lussureggi'ante [lussured'dʒante] *ag* luxuriant

lus'suria *sf* lust

lus'trare *vt* to polish, shine

lustras'carpe *sm/f inv* shoeshine

lus'trino *sm* sequin

'lustro, a *ag* shiny; (*pelo*) glossy ♦ *sm* shine, gloss; (*fig*) prestige, glory; (*quinquennio*) five-year period

'lutto *sm* mourning; **essere in/portare il ~** to be in/wear mourning; **luttu'oso, a** *ag* mournful, sad

M, m

ma *cong* but; **~ insomma!** for goodness sake!; **~ no!** of course not!

'**macabro, a** *ag* gruesome, macabre

macché [mak'ke] *escl* not at all!, certainly not!

macche'roni [makke'rɔni] *smpl* macaroni *sg*

'**macchia** ['makkja] *sf* stain, spot; (*chiazza di diverso colore*) spot; splash, patch; (*tipo di boscaglia*) scrub; **alla ~** (*fig*) in hiding; **macchi'are** *vt* (*sporcare*) to stain, mark; **macchiarsi** *vr* (*persona*) to get o.s. dirty; (*stoffa*) to stain; to get stained *o* marked

'**macchina** ['makkina] *sf* machine; (*motore, locomotiva*) engine; (*automobile*) car; (*fig: meccanismo*) machinery; **andare in ~** (*AUT*) to go by car; (*STAMPA*) to go to press; **~ da cucire** sewing machine; **~ fotografica** camera; **~ da presa** cine *o* movie camera; **~ da scrivere** typewriter; **~ a vapore** steam engine

macchi'nare [makki'nare] *vt* to plot

macchi'nario [makki'narjo] *sm* machinery

macchi'netta [makki'netta] (*fam*) *sf* (*caffettiera*) percolator; (*accendino*) lighter

macchi'nista, i [makki'nista] *sm* (*di treno*) engine-driver; (*di nave*) engineer

macchi'noso, a [makki'noso] *ag* complex, complicated

mace'donia [matʃe'dɔnja] *sf* fruit salad

macel'laio [matʃel'lajo] *sm* butcher

macel'lare [matʃel'lare] *vt* to slaughter, butcher; **macelle'ria** *sf* butcher's (shop); **ma'cello** *sm* (*mattatoio*) slaughterhouse, abattoir (*BRIT*); (*fig*) slaughter, massacre; (*: disastro*) shambles

mace'rare [matʃe'rare] *vt* to macerate; (*CUC*) to marinate; **~rsi** *vr* (*fig*): **~rsi in** to be consumed with

ma'cerie [ma'tʃɛrje] *sfpl* rubble *sg*, debris *sg*

ma'cigno [ma'tʃiɲɲo] *sm* (*masso*) rock, boulder

'**macina** ['matʃina] *sf* (*pietra*) millstone; (*macchina*) grinder; **macinacaffè** *sm inv* coffee grinder; **macina'pepe** *sm inv* peppermill

maci'nare [matʃi'nare] *vt* to grind; (*carne*) to mince (*BRIT*), grind (*US*); **maci'nato** *sm* meal, flour; (*carne*) minced (*BRIT*) *o* ground (*US*) meat

maci'nino [matʃi'nino] *sm* coffee grinder; peppermill

'**madido, a** *ag*: **~ (di)** wet *o* moist (with)

Ma'donna *sf* (*REL*) Our Lady

mador'nale *ag* enormous, huge

'**madre** *sf* mother; (*matrice di bolletta*) counterfoil ♦ *ag inv* mother *cpd*; **ragazza ~** unmarried mother; **scena ~** (*TEATRO*) principal scene; (*fig*) terrible scene

madre'lingua *sf* mother tongue, native language

madre'perla *sf* mother-of-pearl

ma'drina *sf* godmother

maestà *sf inv* majesty; **maes'toso, a** *ag* majestic

ma'estra *sf vedi* **maestro**

maes'trale *sm* north-west wind, mistral

maes'tranze [maes'trantse] *sfpl* workforce *sg*

maes'tria *sf* mastery, skill

ma'estro, a *sm/f* (*INS: anche*: **~ di scuola** *o* **elementare**) primary (*BRIT*) *o* grade school (*US*) teacher; (*esperto*) expert ♦ *sm* (*artigiano, fig: guida*) master; (*MUS*) maestro ♦ *ag* (*principale*) main; (*di grande abilità*) masterly, skilful; **~ d'asilo** nursery teacher; **~ di cerimonie** master of ceremonies

'**mafia** *sf* Mafia; **mafi'oso** *sm* member of the Mafia

'**maga** *sf* sorceress

ma'gagna [ma'gaɲɲa] *sf* defect, flaw, blemish; (*noia, guaio*) problem

ma'gari *escl* (*esprime desiderio*): **~ fosse vero!** if only it were true!; **ti piacerebbe andare in Scozia?** — **~!** would you like to go to Scotland? — and how! ♦ *av* (*anche*) even; (*forse*) perhaps

magaz'zino [magad'dzino] *sm* warehouse; **grande ~** department store

'**maggio** ['maddʒo] *sm* May

maggio'rana [maddʒo'rana] *sf* (BOT) (sweet) marjoram

maggio'ranza [maddʒo'rantsa] *sf* majority

maggio'rare [maddʒo'rare] *vt* to increase, raise

maggior'domo [maddʒor'dɔmo] *sm* butler

maggi'ore [mad'dʒore] *ag (comparativo: più grande)* bigger, larger; taller; greater; *(: più vecchio: sorella, fratello)* older, elder; *(: di grado superiore)* senior; *(: più importante, MIL, MUS)* major; *(superlativo)* biggest, largest; tallest; greatest; oldest, eldest ♦ *sm/f (di grado)* superior; *(di età)* elder; *(MIL)* major; *(: AER)* squadron leader; **la maggior parte** the majority; **andare per la ~** *(cantante etc)* to be very popular; **maggio'renne** *ag* of age ♦ *sm/f* person who has come of age; **maggior'mente** *av* much more; *(con senso superlativo)* most

ma'gia [ma'dʒia] *sf* magic; **'magico, a, ci, che** *ag* magic; *(fig)* fascinating, charming, magical

'magio ['madʒo] *sm* (REL): **i re Magi** the Magi, the Three Wise Men

magis'tero [madʒis'tero] *sm*: **facoltà di M~** ≈ teachers' training college; **magis'trale** *ag* primary (BRIT) *o* grade school (US) teachers', primary (BRIT) *o* grade school (US) teaching *cpd*; skilful

magis'trato [madʒis'trato] *sm* magistrate; **magistra'tura** *sf* magistrature; *(magistrati)*: **la magistratura** the Bench

'maglia ['maʎʎa] *sf* stitch; *(lavoro ai ferri)* knitting *no pl*; *(tessuto, SPORT)* jersey; *(maglione)* jersey, sweater; *(di catena)* link; *(di rete)* mesh; **~ diritta/rovescia** plain/ purl; **maglie'ria** *sf* knitwear; *(negozio)* knitwear shop; **magli'etta** *sf (canottiera)* vest; *(tipo camicia)* T-shirt; **magli'ficio** *sm* knitwear factory

'maglio ['maʎʎo] *sm* mallet; *(macchina)* power hammer

magli'one *sm* sweater, jumper

ma'gnanimo, a [maɲ'ɲanimo, a] *ag* magnanimous

ma'gnete [maɲ'ɲete] *sm* magnet; **ma'gnetico, a, ci, che** *ag* magnetic

magne'tofono [maɲɲe'tɔfono] *sm* tape recorder

ma'gnifico, a, ci, che [maɲ'ɲifiko] *ag* magnificent, splendid; *(ospite)* generous

'magno, a ['maɲɲo] *ag*: **aula ~a** main hall

ma'gnolia [maɲ'ɲɔlja] *sf* magnolia

'mago, ghi *sm (stregone)* magician, wizard; *(illusionista)* magician

ma'grezza [ma'grettsa] *sf* thinness

'magro, a *ag* (very) thin, skinny; *(carne)* lean; *(formaggio)* low-fat; *(fig: scarso, misero)* meagre, poor; *(: meschino: scusa)* poor, lame; **mangiare di ~** not to eat meat

'mai *av (nessuna volta)* never; *(talvolta)* ever; **non ... ~** never; **~ più** never again; **come ~?** why *(o how)* on earth?; **chi/dove/ quando ~?** whoever/wherever/whenever?

mai'ale *sm* (ZOOL) pig; *(carne)* pork

mail *sf inv* e-mail

maio'nese *sf* mayonnaise

'mais *sm inv* maize

mai'uscola *sf* capital letter

mai'uscolo, a *ag (lettera)* capital; *(fig)* enormous, huge

mal *av, sm vedi* **male**

malac'corto, a *ag* rash, careless

mala'fede *sf* bad faith

mala'lingua *(pl* **male'lingue)** *sf* gossip(monger)

mala'mente *av* badly; dangerously

malan'dato, a *ag (persona: di salute)* in poor health; *(: di condizioni finanziarie)* badly off; *(trascurato)* shabby

ma'lanno *sm (disgrazia)* misfortune; *(malattia)* ailment

mala'pena *sf*: **a ~** hardly, scarcely

mala'sorte *sf* bad luck

mala'ticcio, a [mala'tittʃo] *ag* sickly

ma'lato, a *ag* ill, sick; *(gamba)* bad; *(pianta)* diseased ♦ *sm/f* sick person; *(in ospedale)* patient; **malat'tia** *sf (infettiva etc)* illness, disease; *(cattiva salute)* illness, sickness; *(di pianta)* disease

malau'gurio *sm* bad *o* ill omen

mala'vita *sf* underworld

mala'voglia [mala'vɔʎʎa] *sf*: **di ~** unwillingly, reluctantly

mal'concio, a, ci, ce [mal'kontʃo] *ag* in a sorry state

malcon'tento *sm* discontent

malcos'tume *sm* immorality

mal'destro, a *ag* (*inabile*) inexpert, inexperienced; (*goffo*) awkward

maldi'cenza [maldi'tʃentsa] *sf* malicious gossip

maldis'posto, a *ag*: ~ **(verso)** ill-disposed (towards)

'male *av* badly ♦ *sm* (*ciò che è ingiusto, disonesto*) evil; (*danno, svantaggio*) harm; (*sventura*) misfortune; (*dolore fisico, morale*) pain, ache; **di ~ in peggio** from bad to worse; **sentirsi ~** to feel ill; **far ~** (*dolere*) to hurt; **far ~ alla salute** to be bad for one's health; **far del ~ a qn** to hurt *o* harm sb; **restare** *o* **rimanere ~** to be sorry; to be disappointed; to be hurt; **andare a ~** to go bad; **come va? — non c'è ~** how are you? — not bad; **mal di cuore** heart trouble; **~ di dente** toothache; **mal di mare** seasickness; **avere mal di gola/testa** to have a sore throat/a headache; **aver ~ ai piedi** to have sore feet

male'detto, a *pp di* **maledire** ♦ *ag* cursed, damned; (*fig: fam*) damned, blasted

male'dire *vt* to curse; **maledizi'one** *sf* curse; **maledizione!** damn it!

maledu'cato, a *ag* rude, ill-mannered

male'fatta *sf* misdeed

male'ficio [male'fitʃo] *sm* witchcraft

ma'lefico, a, ci, che *ag* (*influsso, azione*) evil

ma'lessere *sm* indisposition, slight illness; (*fig*) uneasiness

ma'levolo, a *ag* malevolent

malfa'mato, a *ag* notorious

mal'fatto, a *ag* (*persona*) deformed; (*oggetto*) badly made; (*lavoro*) badly done

malfat'tore, 'trice *sm/f* wrongdoer

mal'fermo, a *ag* unsteady, shaky; (*salute*) poor, delicate

malformazi'one [malformat'tsjone] *sf* malformation

malgo'verno *sm* maladministration

mal'grado *prep* in spite of, despite ♦ *cong* although; **mio** (*o* **tuo** *etc*) **~** against my (*o* your *etc*) will

mali'gnare [malin'ɲare] *vi*: ~ **su** to malign, speak ill of

ma'ligno, a [ma'liɲɲo] *ag* (*malvagio*) malicious, malignant; (*MED*) malignant

malinco'nia *sf* melancholy, gloom; **malin'conico, a, ci, che** *ag* melancholy

malincu'ore: a ~ *av* reluctantly, unwillingly

malintenzio'nato, a [malintentsjo'nato] *ag* ill-intentioned

malin'teso, a *ag* misunderstood; (*riguardo, senso del dovere*) mistaken, wrong ♦ *sm* misunderstanding

ma'lizia [ma'littsja] *sf* (*malignità*) malice; (*furbizia*) cunning; (*espediente*) trick; **malizi'oso, a** *ag* malicious; cunning; (*vivace, birichino*) mischievous

mal'loppo *sm* (*involto*) bundle; (*fam: refurtiva*) loot

malme'nare *vt* to beat up

mal'messo, a *ag* shabby

malnu'trito, a *ag* undernourished

ma'locchio [ma'lɔkkjo] *sm* evil eye

ma'lora *sf*: **andare in ~** to go to the dogs

ma'lore *sm* (sudden) illness

mal'sano, a *ag* unhealthy

malsi'curo, a *ag* unsafe

'Malta *sf* Malta

'malta *sf* (*EDIL*) mortar

mal'tempo *sm* bad weather

'malto *sm* malt

maltrat'tare *vt* to ill-treat

malu'more *sm* bad mood; (*irritabilità*) bad temper; (*discordia*) ill feeling; **di ~** in a bad mood

mal'vagio, a, gi, gie [mal'vadʒo] *ag* wicked, evil

malversazi'one [malversat'tsjone] *sf* (*DIR*) embezzlement

mal'visto, a *ag*: ~ **(da)** disliked (by), unpopular (with)

malvi'vente *sm* criminal

malvolenti'eri *av* unwillingly, reluctantly

'mamma *sf* mummy, mum; ~ **mia!** my

goodness!

mam'mella sf (ANAT) breast; (di vacca, capra etc) udder

mam'mifero sm mammal

'mammola sf (BOT) violet

ma'nata sf (colpo) slap; (quantità) handful

'manca sf left (hand); **a destra e a ~** left, right and centre, on all sides

man'canza [man'kantsa] sf lack; (carenza) shortage, scarcity; (fallo) fault; (imperfezione) failing, shortcoming; **per ~ di tempo** through lack of time; **in ~ di meglio** for lack of anything better

man'care vi (essere insufficiente) to be lacking; (venir meno) to fail; (sbagliare) to be wrong, make a mistake; (non esserci) to be missing, not to be there; (essere lontano): **~ (da)** to be away (from) ♦ vt to miss; **~ di** to lack; **~ a** (promessa) to fail to keep; **tu mi manchi** I miss you; **mancò poco che morisse** he very nearly died; **mancano ancora 10 sterline** we're still £10 short; **manca un quarto alle 6** it's a quarter to 6; **man'cato, a** ag (tentativo) unsuccessful; (artista) failed

'mancia, ce ['mantʃa] sf tip; **~ competente** reward

manci'ata [man'tʃata] sf handful

man'cino, a [man'tʃino] ag (braccio) left; (persona) left-handed; (fig) underhand

'manco av (nemmeno): **~ per sogno** o **per idea!** not on your life!

man'dante sm/f (di delitto) instigator

manda'rancio [manda'rantʃo] sm clementine

man'dare vt to send; (far funzionare: macchina) to drive; (emettere) to send out; (: grido) to give, utter, let out; **~ a chiamare qn** to send for sb; **~ avanti** (fig: famiglia) to provide for; (: fabbrica) to run, look after; **~ giù** to send down; (anche fig) to swallow; **~ via** to send away; (licenziare) to fire

manda'rino sm mandarin (orange); (cinese) mandarin

man'data sf (quantità) lot, batch; (di chiave) turn; **chiudere a doppia ~** to double-lock

man'dato sm (incarico) commission; (DIR: provvedimento) warrant; (di deputato etc) mandate; (ordine di pagamento) postal o money order; **~ d'arresto** warrant for arrest

man'dibola sf mandible, jaw

'mandorla sf almond; **'mandorlo** sm almond tree

'mandria sf herd

maneggi'are [maned'dʒare] vt (creta, cera) to mould, work, fashion; (arnesi, utensili) to handle; (: adoperare) to use; (fig: persone, denaro) to handle, deal with; **ma'neggio** sm moulding; handling; use; (intrigo) plot, scheme; (per cavalli) riding school

ma'nesco, a, schi, sche ag free with one's fists

ma'nette sfpl handcuffs

manga'nello sm club

manga'nese sm manganese

mange'reccio, a, ci, ce [mandʒe'rettʃo] ag edible

mangi'are [man'dʒare] vt to eat; (intaccare) to eat into o away; (CARTE, SCACCHI etc) to take ♦ vi to eat ♦ sm eating; (cibo) food; (cucina) cooking; **~rsi le parole** to mumble; **~rsi le unghie** to bite one's nails; **mangia'toia** sf feeding-trough

man'gime [man'dʒime] sm fodder

'mango, ghi sm mango

ma'nia sf (PSIC) mania; (fig) obsession, craze; **ma'niaco, a, ci, che** ag suffering from a mania; **maniaco (di)** obsessed (by), crazy (about)

'manica sf sleeve; (fig: gruppo) gang, bunch; (GEO): **la M~, il Canale della M~** the (English) Channel; **essere di ~ larga/ stretta** to be easy-going/strict; **~ a vento** (AER) wind sock

mani'chino [mani'kino] sm (di sarto, vetrina) dummy

'manico, ci sm handle; (MUS) neck

mani'comio sm mental hospital; (fig) madhouse

mani'cotto sm muff; (TECN) coupling; sleeve

mani'cure *sm o f inv* manicure ♦ *sf inv* manicurist

mani'era *sf* way, manner; (*stile*) style, manner; **~e** *sfpl* (*comportamento*) manners; **in ~ che** so that; **in ~ da** so as to; **in tutte le ~e** at all costs

manie'rato, a *ag* affected

manifat'tura *sf* (*lavorazione*) manufacture; (*stabilimento*) factory

manifes'tare *vt* to show, display; (*esprimere*) to express; (*rivelare*) to reveal, disclose ♦ *vi* to demonstrate; **~rsi** *vr* to show o.s.; **~rsi amico** to prove o.s. (to be) a friend; **manifestazi'one** *sf* show, display; expression; (*sintomo*) sign, symptom; (*dimostrazione pubblica*) demonstration; (*cerimonia*) event

mani'festo, a *ag* obvious, evident ♦ *sm* poster, bill; (*scritto ideologico*) manifesto

ma'niglia [ma'niʎʎa] *sf* handle; (*sostegno: negli autobus etc*) strap

manipo'lare *vt* to manipulate; (*alterare: vino*) to adulterate; **manipolazi'one** *sf* manipulation; adulteration

---

mani pulite

i **Mani pulite** is a term used to describe the judicial operation which identified, gathered evidence against, and brought to trial a number of politicians and industrialists implicated in bribery and corruption scandals. See also **Tangentopoli**.

'manna *sf* (*REL*) manna; (*fig*) godsend

man'naia *sf* (*del boia*) (executioner's) axe; (*per carni*) cleaver

man'naro: lupo ~ *sm* werewolf

'mano, i *sf* hand; (*strato: di vernice etc*) coat; **di prima ~** (*notizia*) first-hand; **di seconda ~** second-hand; **man ~** little by little, gradually; **man ~ che** as; **darsi** *o* **stringersi la ~** to shake hands; **mettere le ~i avanti** (*fig*) to safeguard o.s.; **restare a ~i vuote** to be left empty-handed; **venire alle ~i** to come to blows; **a ~** by hand; **~i in alto!** hands up!

mano'dopera *sf* labour

mano'messo, a *pp di* **manomettere**

ma'nometro *sm* gauge, manometer

mano'mettere *vt* (*alterare*) to tamper with; (*aprire indebitamente*) to break open illegally

ma'nopola *sf* (*dell'armatura*) gauntlet; (*guanto*) mitt; (*di impugnatura*) hand-grip; (*pomello*) knob

manos'critto, a *ag* handwritten ♦ *sm* manuscript

mano'vale *sm* labourer

mano'vella *sf* handle; (*TECN*) crank

ma'novra *sf* manoeuvre (*BRIT*), maneuver (*US*); (*FERR*) shunting; **mano'vrare** *vt* (*veicolo*) to manoeuvre (*BRIT*), maneuver (*US*); (*macchina, congegno*) to operate; (*fig: persona*) to manipulate ♦ *vi* to manoeuvre

manro'vescio [manro'veʃʃo] *sm* slap (*with back of hand*)

man'sarda *sf* attic

mansi'one *sf* task, duty, job

mansu'eto, a *ag* gentle, docile

man'tello *sm* cloak; (*fig: di neve etc*) blanket, mantle; (*ZOOL*) coat

mante'nere *vt* to maintain; (*adempiere: promesse*) to keep, abide by; (*provvedere a*) to support, maintain; **~rsi** *vr*: **~rsi calmo/giovane** to stay calm/young; **manteni'mento** *sm* maintenance

'mantice ['mantitʃe] *sm* bellows *pl*

'manto *sm* cloak; **~ stradale** road surface

manu'ale *ag* manual ♦ *sm* (*testo*) manual, handbook

ma'nubrio *sm* handle; (*di bicicletta etc*) handlebars *pl*; (*SPORT*) dumbbell

manu'fatto *sm* manufactured article

manutenzi'one [manuten'tsjone] *sf* maintenance, upkeep; (*d'impianti*) maintenance, servicing

'manzo ['mandzo] *sm* (*ZOOL*) steer; (*carne*) beef

'mappa *sf* (*GEO*) map; **mappa'mondo** *sm* map of the world; (*globo girevole*) globe

mara'tona *sf* marathon

'marca, che *sf* (*COMM: di prodotti*) brand; (*contrassegno, scontrino*) ticket, check;

prodotto di ~ (*di buona qualità*) high-class product; **~ da bollo** official stamp

mar'care *vt* (*munire di contrassegno*) to mark; (*a fuoco*) to brand; (*SPORT: gol*) to score; (: *avversario*) to mark; (*accentuare*) to stress; **~ visita** (*MIL*) to report sick

'Marche ['marke] *sfpl*: **le ~** the Marches (*region of central Italy*)

mar'chese, a [mar'keze] *sm/f* marquis *o* marquess/marchioness

marchi'are [mar'kjare] *vt* to brand; 'marchio *sm* (*di bestiame, COMM, fig*) brand; **marchio depositato** registered trademark; **marchio di fabbrica** trademark

'marcia, ce ['martʃa] *sf* (*anche MUS, MIL*) march; (*funzionamento*) running; (*il camminare*) walking; (*AUT*) gear; **mettere in ~** to start; **mettersi in ~** to get moving; **far ~ indietro** (*AUT*) to reverse; (*fig*) to back-pedal

marciapi'ede [martʃa'pjede] *sm* (*di strada*) pavement (*BRIT*), sidewalk (*US*); (*FERR*) platform

marci'are [mar'tʃare] *vi* to march; (*andare: treno, macchina*) to go; (*funzionare*) to run, work

'marcio, a, ci, ce ['martʃo] *ag* (*frutta, legno*) rotten, bad; (*MED*) festering; (*fig*) corrupt, rotten

mar'cire [mar'tʃire] *vi* (*andare a male*) to go bad, rot; (*suppurare*) to fester; (*fig*) to rot, waste away

'marco, chi *sm* (*unità monetaria*) mark

'mare *sm* sea; **in ~** at sea; **andare al ~** (*in vacanza etc*) to go to the seaside; **il M~ del Nord** the North Sea

ma'rea *sf* tide; **alta/bassa ~** high/low tide

mareggi'ata [mared'dʒata] *sf* heavy sea

mare'moto *sm* seaquake

maresci'allo [mareʃ'ʃallo] *sm* (*MIL*) marshal; (: *sottufficiale*) warrant officer

marga'rina *sf* margarine

marghe'rita [marge'rita] *sf* (*ox-eye*) daisy, marguerite; (*di stampante*) daisy wheel

'margine ['mardʒine] *sm* margin; (*di bosco, via*) edge, border

ma'rina *sf* navy; (*costa*) coast; (*quadro*)

seascape; **~ militare/mercantile** navy/merchant navy (*BRIT*) *o* marine (*US*)

mari'naio *sm* sailor

mari'nare *vt* (*CUC*) to marinate; **~ la scuola** to play truant; **mari'nata** *sf* marinade

ma'rino, a *ag* sea *cpd*, marine

mario'netta *sf* puppet

mari'tare *vt* to marry; **~rsi** *vr*: **~rsi a** *o* **con qn** to marry sb, get married to sb

ma'rito *sm* husband

ma'rittimo, a *ag* maritime, sea *cpd*

mar'maglia [mar'maʎʎa] *sf* mob, riff-raff

marmel'lata *sf* jam; (*di agrumi*) marmalade

mar'mitta *sf* (*recipiente*) pot; (*AUT*) silencer; **~ catalitica** catalytic converter

'marmo *sm* marble

mar'mocchio [mar'mɔkkjo] (*fam*) *sm* tot, kid

mar'motta *sf* (*ZOOL*) marmot

Ma'rocco *sm*: **il ~** Morocco

mar'rone *ag inv* brown ♦ *sm* (*BOT*) chestnut

mar'sala *sm inv* (*vino*) Marsala

mar'sina *sf* tails *pl*, tail coat

mar'supio *sm* pouch; (*per denaro*) bum bag; (*per neonato*) sling

marte'dì *sm inv* Tuesday; **di** *o* **il ~** on Tuesdays; **~ grasso** Shrove Tuesday

martel'lare *vt* to hammer ♦ *vi* (*pulsare*) to throb; (: *cuore*) to thump

mar'tello *sm* hammer; (*di uscio*) knocker

marti'netto *sm* (*TECN*) jack

'martire *sm/f* martyr; **mar'tirio** *sm* martyrdom; (*fig*) agony, torture

'martora *sf* marten

martori'are *vt* to torment, torture

mar'xista, i, e *ag, sm/f* Marxist

marza'pane [martsa'pane] *sm* marzipan

'marzo ['martso] *sm* March

mascal'zone [maskal'tsone] *sm* rascal, scoundrel

ma'scella [maʃ'ʃella] *sf* (*ANAT*) jaw

'maschera ['maskera] *sf* mask; (*travestimento*) disguise; (: *per un ballo etc*) fancy dress; (*TEATRO, CINEMA*) usher/

usherette; (*personaggio del teatro*) stock character; **masche'rare** *vt* to mask; (*travestire*) to disguise; to dress up; (*fig: celare*) to hide, conceal; (*MIL*) to camouflage; **~rsi da** (*travestirsi*) to disguise o.s. as; to dress up as; (*fig*) to masquerade as

mas'chile [mas'kile] *ag* masculine; (*sesso, popolazione*) male; (*abiti*) men's; (*per ragazzi: scuola*) boys'

'maschio, a ['maskjo] *ag* (*BIOL*) male; (*virile*) manly ♦ *sm* (*anche ZOOL, TECN*) male; (*uomo*) man; (*ragazzo*) boy; (*figlio*) son

masco'lino, a *ag* masculine

'massa *sf* mass; (*di errori etc*): **una ~ di** heaps of, masses of; (*di gente*) mass, multitude; (*ELETTR*) earth; **in ~** (*COMM*) in bulk; (*tutti insieme*) en masse; **adunata in ~** mass meeting; **di ~** (*cultura, manifestazione*) mass *cpd*

mas'sacro *sm* massacre, slaughter; (*fig*) mess, disaster

mas'saggio [mas'saddʒo] *sm* massage

mas'saia *sf* housewife

masse'rizie [masse'rittsje] *sfpl* (household) furnishings

mas'siccio, a, ci, ce [mas'sittʃo] *ag* (*oro, legno*) solid; (*palazzo*) massive; (*corporatura*) stout ♦ *sm* (*GEO*) massif

'massima *sf* (*sentenza, regola*) maxim; (*METEOR*) maximum temperature; **in linea di ~** generally speaking; *vedi anche* **massimo**

massi'male *sm* maximum

'massimo, a *ag, sm* maximum; **al ~** at (the) most

'masso *sm* rock, boulder

mas'sone *sm* freemason; **massone'ria** *sf* freemasonry

mas'tello *sm* tub

masti'care *vt* to chew

'mastice ['mastitʃe] *sm* mastic; (*per vetri*) putty

mas'tino *sm* mastiff

ma'tassa *sf* skein

mate'matica *sf* mathematics *sg*

mate'matico, a, ci, che *ag*

mathematical ♦ *sm/f* mathematician

materas'sino *sm* mat; (*gonfiabile*) air bed

mate'rasso *sm* mattress; **~ a molle** spring *o* interior-sprung mattress

ma'teria *sf* (*FISICA*) matter; (*TECN, COMM*) material, matter *no pl*; (*disciplina*) subject; (*argomento*) subject matter, material; **~e prime** raw materials; **in ~ di** (*per quanto concerne*) on the subject of

materi'ale *ag* material; (*fig: grossolano*) rough, rude ♦ *sm* material; (*insieme di strumenti etc*) equipment *no pl*, materials *pl*

maternità *sf* motherhood, maternity; (*reparto*) maternity ward

ma'terno, a *ag* (*amore, cura etc*) maternal, motherly; (*nonno*) maternal; (*lingua, terra*) mother *cpd*

ma'tita *sf* pencil

ma'trice [ma'tritʃe] *sf* matrix; (*COMM*) counterfoil; (*fig: origine*) background

ma'tricola *sf* (*registro*) register; (*numero*) registration number; (*nell'università*) freshman, fresher

ma'trigna [ma'triɲɲa] *sf* stepmother

matrimoni'ale *ag* matrimonial, marriage *cpd*

matri'monio *sm* marriage, matrimony; (*durata*) marriage, married life; (*cerimonia*) wedding

ma'trona *sf* (*fig*) matronly woman

mat'tina *sf* morning; **matti'nata** *sf* morning; (*spettacolo*) matinée, afternoon performance; **mattini'ero, a** *ag*: **essere mattiniero** to be an early riser

mat'tino *sm* morning

'matto, a *ag* mad, crazy; (*fig: falso*) false, imitation ♦ *sm/f* madman/woman; **avere una voglia ~a di qc** to be dying for sth

mat'tone *sm* brick; (*fig*): **questo libro/film è un ~** this book/film is heavy going

matto'nella *sf* tile

matu'rare *vi* (*anche: ~rsi*) (*frutta, grano*) to ripen; (*ascesso*) to come to a head; (*fig: persona, idea, ECON*) to mature ♦ *vt* to ripen; to (make) mature

maturità *sf* maturity; (*di frutta*) ripeness, maturity; (*INS*) school-leaving examination,

≈ GCE A-levels (*BRIT*)

ma'turo, a *ag* mature; (*frutto*) ripe, mature

maxiprocesso *n* criminal trial involving large numbers of co-accused

'mazza ['mattsa] *sf* (*bastone*) club; (*martello*) sledge-hammer; (*SPORT*: *da golf*) club; (: *da baseball, cricket*) bat

maz'zata [mat'tsata] *sf* (*anche fig*) heavy blow

'mazzo ['mattso] *sm* (*di fiori, chiavi etc*) bunch; (*di carte da gioco*) pack

me *pron* me; ~ **stesso(a)** myself; **sei bravo quanto** ~ you are as clever as I (am) *o* as me

me'andro *sm* meander

mec'canica, che *sf* mechanics *sg*; (*attività tecnologica*) mechanical engineering; (*meccanismo*) mechanism

mec'canico, a, ci, che *ag* mechanical ♦ *sm* mechanic

mecca'nismo *sm* mechanism

me'daglia [me'daʎʎa] *sf* medal; medagli'one *sm* (*ARCHIT*) medallion; (*gioiello*) locket

me'desimo, a *ag* same; (*in persona*): **io** ~ I myself

'media *sf* average; (*MAT*) mean; (*INS*: *voto*) end-of-term average; **in** ~ on average; *vedi anche* **medio**

medi'ano, a *ag* median; (*valore*) mean ♦ *sm* (*CALCIO*) half-back

medi'ante *prep* by means of

medi'are *vt* (*fare da mediatore*) to act as mediator in; (*MAT*) to average

media'tore, 'trice *sm/f* mediator; (*COMM*) middle man, agent

medica'mento *sm* medicine, drug

medi'care *vt* to treat; (*ferita*) to dress; medicazi'one *sf* treatment, medication; dressing

medi'cina [medi'tʃina] *sf* medicine; ~ **legale** forensic medicine; **medici'nale** *ag* medicinal ♦ *sm* drug, medicine

'medico, a, ci, che *ag* medical ♦ *sm* doctor; ~ **generico** general practitioner, GP

medie'vale *ag* medieval

'medio, a *ag* average; (*punto, ceto*) middle; (*altezza, statura*) medium ♦ *sm* (*dito*) middle finger; **licenza ~a** leaving certificate awarded at the end of 3 years of secondary education; **scuola ~a** first 3 years of secondary school

medi'ocre *ag* mediocre, poor

medioe'vale *ag* = **medievale**

medio'evo *sm* Middle Ages *pl*

medi'tare *vt* to ponder over, meditate on; (*progettare*) to plan, think out ♦ *vi* to meditate

mediter'raneo, a *ag* Mediterranean; **il (mare) M~** the Mediterranean (Sea)

me'dusa *sf* (*ZOOL*) jellyfish

me'gafono *sm* megaphone

'meglio ['meʎʎo] *av, ag inv* better; (*con senso superlativo*) best ♦ *sm* (*la cosa migliore*): **il** ~ the best (thing); **faresti** ~ **ad andartene** you had better leave; **alla** ~ as best one can; **andar di bene in** ~ to get better and better; **fare del proprio** ~ to do one's best; **per il** ~ for the best; **aver la** ~ **su qn** to get the better of sb

'mela *sf* apple; ~ **cotogna** quince

mela'grana *sf* pomegranate

melan'zana [melan'dzana] *sf* aubergine (*BRIT*), eggplant (*US*)

me'lenso, a *ag* dull, stupid

mel'lifluo, a (*peg*) *ag* sugary, honeyed

'melma *sf* mud, mire

'melo *sm* apple tree

melo'dia *sf* melody

me'lone *sm* (*musk*)melon

'membro *sm* member; (*pl(f)* ~**a**: *arto*) limb

memo'randum *sm inv* memorandum

me'moria *sf* memory; ~**e** *sfpl* (*opera autobiografica*) memoirs; **a** ~ (*imparare, sapere*) by heart; **a** ~ **d'uomo** within living memory; **memori'ale** *sm* (*raccolta di memorie*) memoirs *pl*; (*DIR*) memorial

mena'dito: **a** ~ *av* perfectly, thoroughly; **sapere qc a** ~ to have sth at one's fingertips

me'nare *vt* to lead; (*picchiare*) to hit, beat; (*dare: colpi*) to deal; ~ **la coda** (*cane*) to wag its tail

mendi'cante *sm/f* beggar

mendi'care *vt* to beg for ♦ *vi* to beg

PAROLA CHIAVE

'**meno** *av* 1 (*in minore misura*) less; **dovresti mangiare ~** you should eat less, you shouldn't eat so much
2 (*comparativo*): **~ ... di** not as ... as, less ... than; **sono ~ alto di te** I'm not as tall as you (are), I'm less tall than you (are); **~ ... che** not as ... as, less ... than; **~ che mai** less than ever; **è ~ intelligente che ricco** he's more rich than intelligent; **~ fumo più mangio** the less I smoke the more I eat
3 (*superlativo*) least; **il ~ dotato degli studenti** the least gifted of the students; **è quello che compro ~ spesso** it's the one I buy least often
4 (*MAT*) minus; **8 ~ 5** 8 minus 5, 8 take away 5; **sono le 8 ~ un quarto** it's a quarter to 8; **~ 5 gradi** 5 degrees below zero, minus 5 degrees; **mille lire in ~** a thousand lire less
5 (*fraseologia*): **quanto ~ poteva telefonare** he could at least have phoned; **non so se accettare o ~** I don't know whether to accept or not; **fare a ~ di qc/qn** to do without sth/sb; **non potevo fare a ~ di ridere** I couldn't help laughing; **~ male!** thank goodness!; **~ male che sei arrivato** it's a good job that you've come
♦ *ag inv* (*tempo, denaro*) less; (*errori, persone*) fewer; **ha fatto ~ errori di tutti** he made fewer mistakes than anyone, he made the fewest mistakes of all
♦ *sm inv* 1: **il ~** (*il minimo*) the least; **parlare del più e del ~** to talk about this and that
2 (*MAT*) minus
♦ *prep* (*eccetto*) except (for), apart from; **a ~ che, a ~ di** unless; **a ~ che non piova** unless it rains; **non posso, a ~ di prendere ferie** I can't, unless I take some leave

---

meno'mare *vt* (*danneggiare*) to maim, disable
meno'pausa *sf* menopause

'**mensa** *sf* (*locale*) canteen; (: *MIL*) mess; (: *nelle università*) refectory
men'sile *ag* monthly ♦ *sm* (*periodico*) monthly (magazine); (*stipendio*) monthly salary
'mensola *sf* bracket; (*ripiano*) shelf; (*ARCHIT*) corbel
'**menta** *sf* mint; (*anche*: **~ piperita**) peppermint; (*bibita*) peppermint cordial; (*caramella*) mint, peppermint
men'tale *ag* mental; **mentalità** *sf inv* mentality
'**mente** *sf* mind; **imparare/sapere qc a ~** to learn/know sth by heart; **avere in ~ qc** to have sth in mind; **passare di ~ a qn** to slip sb's mind
men'tire *vi* to lie
'**mento** *sm* chin
men'tolo *sm* menthol
'**mentre** *cong* (*temporale*) while; (*avversativo*) whereas
menù *sm inv* menu; **~ turistico** set menu
menzio'nare [mentsjo'nare] *vt* to mention
menzi'one [men'tsjone] *sf* mention; **fare ~ di** to mention
men'zogna [men'tsɲɲa] *sf* lie
mera'viglia [mera'viʎʎa] *sf* amazement, wonder; (*persona, cosa*) marvel, wonder; **a ~** perfectly, wonderfully; **meravigli'are** *vt* to amaze, astonish; **meravigliarsi (di)** to marvel (at); (*stupirsi*) to be amazed (at), be astonished (at); **meravigli'oso, a** *ag* wonderful, marvellous
mer'cante *sm* merchant; **~ d'arte** art dealer; **mercanteggi'are** *vt* (*onore, voto*) to sell ♦ *vi* to bargain, haggle; **mercan'tile** *ag* commercial, mercantile; (*nave, marina*) merchant *cpd* ♦ *sm* (*nave*) merchantman; **mercan'zia** *sf* merchandise, goods *pl*
mer'cato *sm* market; **~ dei cambi** exchange market; **~ nero** black market
'**merce** ['mertʃe] *sf* goods *pl*, merchandise; **~ deperibile** perishable goods *pl*
mercé [mer'tʃe] *sf* mercy
merce'nario, a [mertʃe'narjo] *ag, sm* mercenary

merce'ria [mertʃe'ria] *sf* (*articoli*) haberdashery (*BRIT*), notions *pl* (*US*); (*bottega*) haberdasher's shop (*BRIT*), notions store (*US*)

mercole'dì *sm inv* Wednesday; **di** *o* **il ~** on Wednesdays; **~ delle Ceneri** Ash Wednesday

---
mercoledì delle ceneri

ⓘ **Mercoledì delle ceneri**, *in the Catholic Church, marks the beginning of Lent. On that day, people go to church and are marked on the forehead with ash from the burning of the blessed olive branch. Ash Wednesday is a day of fasting, abstinence and penitence.*

mer'curio *sm* mercury

'merda (*fam!*) *sf* shit (!)

me'renda *sf* afternoon snack

meridi'ana *sf* (*orologio*) sundial

meridi'ano, a *ag* meridian; midday *cpd*, noonday ♦ *sm* meridian

meridio'nale *ag* southern ♦ *sm/f* southerner

meridi'one *sm* south

me'ringa, ghe *sf* (*CUC*) meringue

meri'tare *vt* to deserve, merit ♦ *vb impers*: **merita andare** it's worth going

meri'tevole *ag* worthy

'merito *sm* merit; (*valore*) worth; **in ~ a** as regards, with regard to; **dare ~ a qn di** to give sb credit for; **finire a pari ~** to finish joint first (*o* second *etc*); to tie; **meri'torio, a** *ag* praiseworthy

mer'letto *sm* lace

'merlo *sm* (*ZOOL*) blackbird; (*ARCHIT*) battlement

mer'luzzo [mer'luttso] *sm* (*ZOOL*) cod

mes'chino, a [mes'kino] *ag* wretched; (*scarso*) scanty, poor; (*persona: gretta*) mean; (*: limitata*) narrow-minded, petty

mesco'lanza [mesko'lantsa] *sf* mixture

mesco'lare *vt* to mix; (*vini, colori*) to blend; (*mettere in disordine*) to mix up, muddle up; (*carte*) to shuffle; **~rsi** *vr* to mix; to blend; to get mixed up; (*fig*): **~rsi**

in to get mixed up in, meddle in

'mese *sm* month

'messa *sf* (*REL*) mass; (*il mettere*): **~ in moto** starting; **~ in piega** set; **~ a punto** (*TECN*) adjustment; (*AUT*) tuning; (*fig*) clarification; **~ in scena = messinscena**

messag'gero [messad'dʒero] *sm* messenger

mes'saggio [mes'saddʒo] *sm* message

mes'sale *sm* (*REL*) missal

'messe *sf* harvest

Mes'sia *sm inv* (*REL*): **il ~** the Messiah

'Messico *sm*: **il ~** Mexico

messin'scena [messin'ʃena] *sf* (*TEATRO*) production

'messo, a *pp di* **mettere** ♦ *sm* messenger

mesti'ere *sm* (*professione*) job; (*: manuale*) trade; (*: artigianale*) craft; (*fig: abilità nel lavoro*) skill, technique; **essere del ~** to know the tricks of the trade

'mesto, a *ag* sad, melancholy

'mestolo *sm* (*CUC*) ladle

mestruazi'one [mestruat'tsjone] *sf* menstruation

'meta *sf* destination; (*fig*) aim, goal

metà *sf inv* half; (*punto di mezzo*) middle; **dividere qc a** *o* **per ~** to divide sth in half, halve sth; **fare a ~ (di qc con qn)** to go halves (with sb in sth); **a ~ prezzo** at half price; **a ~ strada** halfway

me'tafora *sf* metaphor

me'tallico, a, ci, che *ag* (*di metallo*) metal *cpd*; (*splendore, rumore etc*) metallic

me'tallo *sm* metal

metalmec'canico, a, ci, che *ag* engineering *cpd* ♦ *sm* engineering worker

me'tano *sm* methane

meteorolo'gia [meteorolo'dʒia] *sf* meteorology; **meteoro'logico, a, ci, che** *ag* meteorological, weather *cpd*

me'ticcio, a, ci, ce [me'tittʃo] *sm/f* half-caste, half-breed

me'todico, a, ci, che *ag* methodical

'metodo *sm* method

'metrica *sf* metrics *sg*; **'metrico, a, ci, che** *ag* metric; (*POESIA*) metrical

'metro *sm* metre; (*nastro*) tape measure;

(asta) (metre) rule

metropoli'tana *sf* underground, subway

metropoli'tano, a *ag* metropolitan

'mettere *vt* to put; *(abito)* to put on; (: *portare*) to wear; *(installare: telefono)* to put in; *(fig: provocare)*: **~ fame/allegria a qn** to make sb hungry/happy; *(supporre)*: **mettiamo che …** let's suppose *o* say that … ; **~rsi** *vr (persona)* to put o.s.; *(oggetto)* to go; *(disporsi: faccenda)* to turn out; **~rsi a sedere** to sit down; **~rsi a letto** to get into bed; *(per malattia)* to take to one's bed; **~rsi il cappello** to put on one's hat; **~rsi a** *(cominciare)* to begin to, start to; **~rsi al lavoro** to set to work; **~rsi con qn** *(in società)* to team up with sb; *(in coppia)* to start going out with sb; **~rci:** **~rci molta cura/molto tempo** to take a lot of care/a lot of time; **ci ho messo 3 ore per venire** it's taken me 3 hours to get here; **~rcela tutta** to do one's best; **~ a tacere qn/qc** to keep sb/sth quiet; **~ su casa** to set up house; **~ su un negozio** to start a shop; **~ via** to put away

'mezza ['mɛddza] *sf*: **la ~** half-past twelve *(in the afternoon)*; *vedi anche* **mezzo**

mez'zadro [med'dzadro] *sm (AGR)* sharecropper

mezza'luna [meddza'luna] *sf* half-moon; *(dell'islamismo)* crescent; *(coltello)* (semicircular) chopping knife

mezza'nino [meddza'nino] *sm* mezzanine (floor)

mez'zano, a [med'dzano] *ag (medio)* average, medium; *(figlio)* middle *cpd* ♦ *sm/f (ruffiano)* pimp

mezza'notte [meddza'nɔtte] *sf* midnight

'mezzo, a ['mɛddzo] *ag* half; **un ~ litro/panino** half a litre/roll ♦ *av* half-; **~ morto** half-dead ♦ *sm (metà)* half; *(parte centrale: di strada etc)* middle; *(per raggiungere un fine)* means *sg*; *(veicolo)* vehicle; *(nell'indicare l'ora)*: **le nove e ~** half past nine; **mezzogiorno e ~** half past twelve; **~i** *smpl (possibilità economiche)* means; **di ~a età** middle-aged; **un soprabito di ~a stagione** a spring *(o* autumn) coat; **di ~**

middle, in the middle; **andarci di ~** *(patir danno)* to suffer; **levarsi** *o* **togliersi di ~** to get out of the way; **in ~ a** in the middle of; **per** *o* **a ~ di** by means of; **~i di comunicazione di massa** mass media *pl;* **~i pubblici** public transport *sg;* **~i di trasporto** means of transport

mezzogi'orno [meddzo'dʒorno] *sm* midday, noon; **a ~** at 12 (o'clock) *o* midday *o* noon; **il ~ d'Italia** southern Italy

mez'z'ora [med'dzora] *sf* half-hour, half an hour

mi *(dav lo, la, li, le, ne diventa* **me)** *pron (oggetto)* me; *(complemento di termine)* to me; *(riflessivo)* myself ♦ *sm (MUS)* E; (: *solfeggiando la scala)* mi

'mia *vedi* **mio**

miago'lare *vi* to miaow, mew

'mica *av (fam)*: **non … ~** not … at all; **non sono ~ stanco** I'm not a bit tired; **non sarà ~ partito?** he wouldn't have left, would he?; **~ male** not bad

'miccia, ce ['mittʃa] *sf* fuse

micidi'ale [mitʃi'djale] *ag* fatal; *(dannosissimo)* deadly

mi'crofono *sm* microphone

micros'copio *sm* microscope

mi'dollo *(pl(f)* **~a)** *sm (ANAT)* marrow; **~ osseo** bone marrow

'mie *vedi* **mio**

mi'ei *vedi* **mio**

mi'ele *sm* honey

mi'etere *vt (AGR)* to reap, harvest; *(fig: vite)* to take, claim

'miglia ['miʎʎa] *sfpl di* **miglio**

migli'aio [miʎ'ʎajo] *(pl(f)* **~a)** *sm* thousand; **un ~ (di)** about a thousand; **a ~a** by the thousand, in thousands

'miglio ['miʎʎo] *sm (BOT)* millet; *(pl(f)* **~a:** *unità di misura)* mile; **~ marino** *o* **nautico** nautical mile

migliora'mento [miʎʎora'mento] *sm* improvement

miglio'rare [miʎʎo'rare] *vt, vi* to improve

migli'ore [miʎ'ʎore] *ag (comparativo)* better; *(superlativo)* best ♦ *sm:* **il ~** the best (thing) ♦ *sm/f:* **il(la) ~** the best (person); **il**

miglior vino di questa regione the best wine in this area

'mignolo ['miɲɲolo] *sm* (ANAT) little finger, pinkie; (: *dito del piede*) little toe

mi'grare *vi* to migrate

'mila *pl di* mille

Mi'lano *sf* Milan

miliar'dario, a *sm/f* millionaire

mili'ardo *sm* thousand million, billion (US)

mili'are *ag*: **pietra** ~ milestone

mili'one *sm* million; **due ~i di lire** two million lire

mili'tante *ag, sm/f* militant

mili'tare *vi* (MIL) to be a soldier, serve; (*fig: in un partito*) to be a militant ♦ *ag* military ♦ *sm* serviceman; **fare il** ~ to do one's military service

'milite *sm* soldier

millanta'tore, 'trice *sm/f* boaster

'mille (*pl* mila) *num* a *o* one thousand; **dieci mila** ten thousand

mille'foglie [mille'fɔʎʎe] *sm inv* (CUC) cream *o* vanilla slice

mil'lennio *sm* millennium

millepi'edi *sm inv* centipede

mil'lesimo, a *ag, sm* thousandth

milli'grammo *sm* milligram(me)

mil'limetro *sm* millimetre

'milza ['miltsa] *sf* (ANAT) spleen

mimetiz'zare [mimetid'dzare] *vt* to camouflage; **~rsi** *vr* to camouflage o.s.

'mimica *sf* (*arte*) mime

'mimo *sm* (*attore, componimento*) mime

mi'mosa *sf* mimosa

'mina *sf* (*esplosiva*) mine; (*di matita*) lead

mi'naccia, ce [mi'nattʃa] *sf* threat; **minacci'are** *vt* to threaten; **minacciare qn di morte** to threaten to kill sb; **minacciare di fare qc** to threaten to do sth; **minacci'oso, a** *ag* threatening

mi'nare *vt* (MIL) to mine; (*fig*) to undermine

mina'tore *sm* miner

mina'torio, a *ag* threatening

mine'rale *ag, sm* mineral

mine'rario, a *ag* (*delle miniere*) mining; (*dei minerali*) ore *cpd*

mi'nestra *sf* soup; ~ **in brodo/di verdure** noodle/vegetable soup; **mines'trone** *sm* thick vegetable and pasta soup

mingher'lino, a [minger'lino] *ag* thin, slender

'mini *ag inv* mini ♦ *sf inv* miniskirt

minia'tura *sf* miniature

mini'disc *sm inv* Minidisc ®

mini'era *sf* mine

mini'gonna *sf* miniskirt

'minimo, a *ag* minimum, least, slightest; (*piccolissimo*) very small, slight; (*il più basso*) lowest, minimum ♦ *sm* minimum; **al** ~ at least; **girare al** ~ (AUT) to idle

minis'tero *sm* (POL, REL) ministry; (*governo*) government; **M~ delle Finanze** Ministry of Finance, ≈ Treasury

mi'nistro *sm* (POL, REL) minister

mino'ranza [mino'rantsa] *sf* minority

mino'rato, a *ag* handicapped ♦ *sm/f* physically (*o* mentally) handicapped person

mi'nore *ag* (*comparativo*) less; (*più piccolo*) smaller; (*numero*) lower; (*inferiore*) lower, inferior; (*meno importante*) minor; (*più giovane*) younger; (*superlativo*) least; smallest; lowest; youngest ♦ *sm/f* = **minorenne**

mino'renne *ag* under age ♦ *sm/f* minor, person under age

mi'nuscolo, a *ag* (*scrittura, carattere*) small; (*piccolissimo*) tiny ♦ *sf* small letter

mi'nuta *sf* rough copy, draft

mi'nuto, a *ag* tiny, minute; (*pioggia*) fine; (*corporatura*) delicate, fine ♦ *sm* (*unità di misura*) minute; **al** ~ (COMM) retail

'mio (*f* 'mia, *pl* mi'ei, 'mie) *det*: **il** ~, **la mia** *etc* my ♦ *pron*: **il** ~, **la mia** *etc* mine; **i miei** my family; **un** ~ **amico** a friend of mine

'miope *ag* short-sighted

'mira *sf* (*anche fig*) aim; **prendere la** ~ to take aim; **prendere di** ~ **qn** (*fig*) to pick on sb

mi'rabile *ag* admirable, wonderful

mi'racolo *sm* miracle

mi'raggio [mi'raddʒo] *sm* mirage

mi'rare *vi*: ~ **a** to aim at

mi'rino *sm* (TECN) sight; (FOT) viewer, viewfinder

mir'tillo *sm* bilberry (*BRIT*), blueberry (*US*), whortleberry

mi'scela [miʃʃela] *sf* mixture; (*di caffè*) blend

miscel'lanea [miʃʃel'lanea] *sf* miscellany

'mischia ['miskja] *sf* scuffle; (*RUGBY*) scrum, scrummage

mischi'are [mis'kjare] *vt* to mix, blend; **~rsi** *vr* to mix, blend

mis'cuglio [mis'kuʎʎo] *sm* mixture, hotchpotch, jumble

mise'rabile *ag* (*infelice*) miserable, wretched; (*povero*) poverty-stricken; (*di scarso valore*) miserable

mi'seria *sf* extreme poverty; (*infelicità*) misery; **~e** *sfpl* (*del mondo etc*) misfortunes, troubles; **porca ~!** (*fam*) blast!, damn!

miseri'cordia *sf* mercy, pity

'misero, a *ag* miserable, wretched; (*povero*) poverty-stricken; (*insufficiente*) miserable

mis'fatto *sm* misdeed, crime

mi'sogino [mi'zɔdʒino] *sm* misogynist

'missile *sm* missile

missio'nario, a *ag, sm/f* missionary

missi'one *sf* mission

misteri'oso, a *ag* mysterious

mis'tero *sm* mystery

'misto, a *ag* mixed; (*scuola*) mixed, coeducational ♦ *sm* mixture

mis'tura *sf* mixture

mi'sura *sf* measure; (*misurazione, dimensione*) measurement; (*taglia*) size; (*provvedimento*) measure, step; (*moderazione*) moderation; (*MUS*) time; (: *divisione*) bar; (*fig: limite*) bounds *pl*, limit; **nella ~ in cui** inasmuch as, insofar as; **(fatto) su ~** made to measure

misu'rare *vt* (*ambiente, stoffa*) to measure; (*terreno*) to survey; (*abito*) to try on; (*pesare*) to weigh; (*fig: parole etc*) to weigh up; (: *spese, cibo*) to limit ♦ *vi* to measure; **~rsi** *vr*: **~rsi con qn** to have a confrontation with sb; to compete with sb; **misu'rato, a** *ag* (*ponderato*) measured; (*moderato*) moderate

'mite *ag* mild

miti'gare *vt* to mitigate, lessen; (*lenire*) to soothe, relieve; **~rsi** *vr* (*odio*) to subside; (*tempo*) to become milder

'mito *sm* myth; **mitolo'gia, 'gie** *sf* mythology

'mitra *sf* (*REL*) mitre ♦ *sm inv* (*arma*) sub-machine gun

mitraglia'trice [mitraʎʎa'tritʃe] *sf* machine gun

mit'tente *sm/f* sender

'mobile *ag* mobile; (*parte di macchina*) moving; (*DIR: bene*) movable, personal ♦ *sm* (*arredamento*) piece of furniture; **~i** *smpl* (*mobilia*) furniture *sg*

mo'bilia *sf* furniture

mobili'are *ag* (*DIR*) personal, movable

mo'bilio *sm* = **mobilia**

mobili'tare *vt* to mobilize

mocas'sino *sm* moccasin

mocci'oso, a [mot'tʃoso, a] *sm/f* (*peg*) snotty(-nosed) kid

'moccolo *sm* (*di candela*) candle-end; (*fam: bestemmia*) oath; (: *moccio*) snot; **reggere il ~** to play gooseberry (*BRIT*), act as chaperon

'moda *sf* fashion; **alla ~, di ~** fashionable, in fashion

modalità *sf inv* formality

mo'della *sf* model

model'lare *vt* (*creta*) to model, shape; **~rsi** *vr*: **~rsi su** to model o.s. on

mo'dello *sm* model; (*stampo*) mould ♦ *ag inv* model *cpd*

'modem *sm inv* modem

mode'rare *vt* to moderate; **~rsi** *vr* to restrain o.s.; **mode'rato, a** *ag* moderate

modera'tore, 'trice *sm/f* moderator

mo'derno, a *ag* modern

mo'destia *sf* modesty

mo'desto, a *ag* modest

'modico, a, ci, che *ag* reasonable, moderate

mo'difica, che *sf* modification

modifi'care *vt* to modify, alter; **~rsi** *vr* to alter, change

mo'dista *sf* milliner

'modo *sm* way, manner; (*mezzo*) means,

way; (*occasione*) opportunity; (*LING*) mood; (*MUS*) mode; **~i** *smpl* (*comportamento*) manners; **a suo ~**, **a ~ suo** in his own way; **ad** *o* **in ogni ~** anyway; **di** *o* **in ~ che** so that; **in ~ da** so as to; **in tutti i ~i** at all costs; (*comunque sia*) anyway; (*in ogni caso*) in any case; **in qualche ~** somehow or other; **~ di dire** turn of phrase; **per ~ di dire** so to speak

modu'lare *vt* to modulate; **modulazi'one** *sf* modulation; **modulazione di frequenza** frequency modulation

'modulo *sm* (*modello*) form; (*ARCHIT, lunare, di comando*) module

'mogano *sm* mahogany

'mogio, a, gi, gie ['mɔdʒo] *ag* down in the dumps, dejected

'moglie ['mɔʎʎe] *sf* wife

mo'ine *sfpl* cajolery *sg*; (*leziosità*) affectation *sg*

'mola *sf* millstone; (*utensile abrasivo*) grindstone

mo'lare *sm* (*dente*) molar

'mole *sf* mass; (*dimensioni*) size; (*edificio grandioso*) massive structure

moles'tare *vt* to bother, annoy; **mo'lestia** *sf* annoyance, bother; **recar molestia a qn** to bother sb; **mo'lesto, a** *ag* annoying

'molla *sf* spring; **~e** *sfpl* (*per camino*) tongs

mol'lare *vt* to release, let go; (*NAUT*) to ease; (*fig: ceffone*) to give ♦ *vi* (*cedere*) to give in

'molle *ag* soft; (*muscoli*) flabby

mol'letta *sf* (*per capelli*) hairgrip; (*per panni stesi*) clothes peg

mol'lica, che *sf* crumb, soft part

mol'lusco, schi *sm* mollusc

'molo *sm* mole, breakwater; jetty

mol'teplice [mol'teplitʃe] *ag* (*formato di più elementi*) complex; **~i** *pl* (*svariati: interessi, attività*) numerous, various

moltipli'care *vt* to multiply; **~rsi** *vr* to multiply; to increase in number; **moltiplicazi'one** *sf* multiplication

---

PAROLA CHIAVE

'molto, a *det* (*quantità*) a lot of, much; (*numero*) a lot of, many; **~ pane/carbone** a lot of bread/coal; **~a gente** a lot of people, many people; **~i libri** a lot of books, many books; **non ho ~ tempo** I haven't got much time; **per ~ (tempo)** for a long time

♦ *av* 1 a lot, (very) much; **viaggia ~** he travels a lot; **non viaggia ~** he doesn't travel much *o* a lot

2 (*intensivo: con aggettivi, avverbi*) very; (: *con participio passato*) (very) much; **~ buono** very good; **~ migliore**, **~ meglio** much *o* a lot better

♦ *pron* much, a lot; **~i, e** *pron pl* many, a lot; **~i pensano che ...** many (people) think ...

---

momen'taneo, a *ag* momentary, fleeting

mo'mento *sm* moment; **da un ~ all'altro** at any moment; (*all'improvviso*) suddenly; **al ~ di fare** just as I was (*o* you were *o* he was *etc*) doing; **per il ~** for the time being; **dal ~ che** ever since; (*dato che*) since; **a ~i** (*da un ~ all'altro*) any time *o* moment now; (*quasi*) nearly

'monaca, che *sf* nun

'Monaco *sf* Monaco; **~ (di Baviera)** Munich

'monaco, ci *sm* monk

mo'narca, chi *sm* monarch; **monar'chia** *sf* monarchy

monas'tero *sm* (*di monaci*) monastery; (*di monache*) convent; **mo'nastico, a, ci, che** *ag* monastic

'monco, a, chi, che *ag* maimed; (*fig*) incomplete

mon'dano, a *ag* (*anche fig*) worldly; (*dell'alta società*) society *cpd*; fashionable

mon'dare *vt* (*frutta, patate*) to peel; (*piselli*) to shell; (*pulire*) to clean

mondi'ale *ag* (*campionato, popolazione*) world *cpd*; (*influenza*) world-wide

'mondo *sm* world; (*grande quantità*): **un ~ di** lots of, a host of; **il bel ~** high society mo'nello, a *sm/f* street urchin; (*ragazzo vivace*) scamp, imp

mo'neta *sf* coin; (*ECON: valuta*) currency; (*denaro spicciolo*) (small) change; ~ **estera** foreign currency; ~ **legale** legal tender; **mone'tario, a** *ag* monetary

mongo'loide *ag*, *sm/f* (*MED*) mongol

'monito *sm* warning

'monitor *sm inv* (*TECN, TV*) monitor

monolo'cale *sm* studio flat

mono'polio *sm* monopoly

mo'notono, a *ag* monotonous

monsi'gnore [monsiɲˈɲore] *sm* (*REL: titolo*) Your (*o* His) Grace

mon'sone *sm* monsoon

monta'carichi [monta'kariki] *sm inv* hoist, goods lift

mon'taggio [mon'taddʒo] *sm* (*TECN*) assembly; (*CINEMA*) editing

mon'tagna [mon'taɲɲa] *sf* mountain; (*zona montuosa*): **la** ~ the mountains *pl*; **andare in** ~ to go to the mountains; ~**e russe** roller coaster *sg*, big dipper *sg* (*BRIT*); **monta'gnoso, a** *ag* mountainous

monta'naro, a *ag* mountain *cpd* ♦ *sm/f* mountain dweller

mon'tano, a *ag* mountain *cpd*; alpine

mon'tare *vt* to go (*o* come) up; (*cavallo*) to ride; (*apparecchiatura*) to set up, assemble; (*CUC*) to whip; (*ZOOL*) to cover; (*incastonare*) to mount, set; (*CINEMA*) to edit; (*FOT*) to mount ♦ *vi* to go (*o* come) up; (*a cavallo*): ~ **bene/male** to ride well/badly; (*aumentare di livello, volume*) to rise; ~**rsi** *vr* to become big-headed; ~ **qc** to exaggerate sth; ~ **qn** *o* **la testa a qn** to turn sb's head; ~ **in bicicletta/macchina/treno** to get on a bicycle/into a car/on a train; ~ **a cavallo** to get on *o* mount a horse

monta'tura *sf* assembling *no pl*; (*di occhiali*) frames *pl*; (*di gioiello*) mounting, setting; (*fig*): ~ **pubblicitaria** publicity stunt

'monte *sm* mountain; **a** ~ upstream; **mandare a** ~ **qc** to upset sth, cause sth to fail; **il M~ Bianco** Mont Blanc; ~ **di pietà** pawnshop

mon'tone *sm* (*ZOOL*) ram; **carne di** ~ mutton

montu'oso, a *ag* mountainous

monu'mento *sm* monument

mo'quette [mɔˈkɛt] *sf inv* fitted carpet

'mora *sf* (*del rovo*) blackberry; (*del gelso*) mulberry; (*DIR*) delay; (*: somma*) arrears *pl*

mo'rale *ag* moral ♦ *sf* (*scienza*) ethics *sg*, moral philosophy; (*complesso di norme*) moral standards *pl*, morality; (*condotta*) morals *pl*; (*insegnamento morale*) moral ♦ *sm* morale; **essere giù di** ~ to be feeling down; **moralità** *sf* morality; (*condotta*) morals *pl*

'morbido, a *ag* soft; (*pelle*) soft, smooth

mor'billo *sm* (*MED*) measles *sg*

'morbo *sm* disease

mor'boso, a *ag* (*fig*) morbid

mor'dace [mor'datʃe] *ag* biting, cutting

mor'dente *sm* (*fig: di satira, critica*) bite; (*: di persona*) drive

'mordere *vt* to bite; (*addentare*) to bite into

mori'bondo, a *ag* dying, moribund

morige'rato, a [moridʒeˈrato] *ag* of good morals

mo'rire *vi* to die; (*abitudine, civiltà*) to die out; ~ **di fame** to die of hunger; (*fig*) to be starving; ~ **di noia/paura** to be bored/scared to death; **fa un caldo da** ~ it's terribly hot

mormo'rare *vi* to murmur; (*brontolare*) to grumble

'moro, a *ag* dark(-haired); dark(-complexioned); **i M~i** *smpl* (*STORIA*) the Moors

mo'roso, a *ag* in arrears ♦ *sm/f* (*fam: innamorato*) sweetheart

'morsa *sf* (*TECN*) vice; (*fig: stretta*) grip

morsi'care *vt* to nibble (at), gnaw (at); (*sog: insetto*) to bite

'morso, a *pp di* **mordere** ♦ *sm* bite; (*di insetto*) sting; (*parte della briglia*) bit; ~**i della fame** pangs of hunger

mor'taio *sm* mortar

mor'tale *ag*, *sm* mortal; **mortalità** *sf* mortality, death rate 'morte *sf* death

mortifi'care *vt* to mortify

'morto, a *pp di* morire ♦ *ag* dead ♦ *sm/f* dead man/woman; i ~i the dead; fare il ~ (*nell'acqua*) to float on one's back; il Mar M~ the Dead Sea

mor'torio *sm* (*anche fig*) funeral

mo'saico, ci *sm* mosaic

'Mosca *sf* Moscow

'mosca, sche *sf* fly; ~ cieca blind-man's-buff

mos'cato *sm* muscatel (wine)

mosce'rino [moʃʃe'rino] *sm* midge, gnat

mos'chea [mos'kɛa] *sf* mosque

mos'chetto [mos'ketto] *sm* musket

'moscio, a, sci, sce ['mɔʃʃo] *ag* (*fig*) lifeless

mos'cone *sm* (*ZOOL*) bluebottle; (*barca*) pedalo; (: *a remi*) *kind of pedalo with oars*

'mossa *sf* movement; (*nel gioco*) move

'mosso, a *pp di* muovere ♦ *ag* (*mare*) rough; (*capelli*) wavy; (*FOT*) blurred

mos'tarda *sf* mustard

'mostra *sf* exhibition, show; (*ostentazione*) show; in ~ on show; far ~ di (*fingere*) to pretend; far ~ di sé to show off

mos'trare *vt* to show; ~rsi *vr* to appear

'mostro *sm* monster; mostru'oso, a *ag* monstrous

mo'tel *sm inv* motel

moti'vare *vt* (*causare*) to cause; (*giustificare*) to justify, account for; motivazi'one *sf* justification; motive; (*PSIC*) motivation

mo'tivo *sm* (*causa*) reason, cause; (*movente*) motive; (*letterario*) (central) theme; (*disegno*) motif, design, pattern; (*MUS*) motif; per quale ~? why?, for what reason?

'moto *sm* (*anche FISICA*) motion; (*movimento, gesto*) movement; (*esercizio fisico*) exercise; (*sommossa*) rising, revolt; (*commozione*) feeling, impulse ♦ *sf inv* (*motocicletta*) motorbike; mettere in ~ to set in motion; (*AUT*) to start up

motoci'cletta [mototʃi'kletta] *sf* motorcycle; motoci'clismo *sm* motorcycling, motorcycle racing;

motoci'clista, i, e *sm/f* motorcyclist

mo'tore, 'trice *ag* motor; (*TECN*) driving ♦ *sm* engine, motor; a ~ motor *cpd*, power-driven; ~ a combustione interna/a reazione internal combustion/jet engine; ~ di ricerca search engine; moto'rino *sm* moped; motorino di avviamento (*AUT*) starter; motoriz'zato, a *ag* (*truppe*) motorized; (*persona*) having a car *o* transport

motos'cafo *sm* motorboat

'motto *sm* (*battuta scherzosa*) witty remark; (*frase emblematica*) motto, maxim

'mouse ['maus] *sm inv* (*INFORM*) mouse

mo'vente *sm* motive

movimen'tare *vt* to liven up

movi'mento *sm* movement; (*fig*) activity, hustle and bustle; (*MUS*) tempo, movement

mozi'one [mot'tsjone] *sf* (*POL*) motion

moz'zare [mot'tsare] *vt* to cut off; (*coda*) to dock; ~ il fiato *o* il respiro a qn (*fig*) to take sb's breath away

mozza'rella [mottsa'rella] *sf* mozzarella

mozzi'cone [mottsi'kone] *sm* stub, butt, end; (*anche*: ~ di sigaretta) cigarette end

'mozzo ['mottso] *sm* (*NAUT*) ship's boy

'mucca, che *sf* cow

'mucchio ['mukkjo] *sm* pile, heap; (*fig*): un ~ di lots of, heaps of

'muco, chi *sm* mucus

'muffa *sf* mould, mildew

mug'gire [mud'dʒire] *vi* (*vacca*) to low, moo; (*toro*) to bellow; (*fig*) to roar; mug'gito *sm* low, moo; bellow; roar

mu'ghetto [mu'getto] *sm* lily of the valley

mu'gnaio, a [mun'ɲajo] *sm/f* miller

mugo'lare *vi* (*cane*) to whimper, whine; (*fig: persona*) to moan

muli'nare *vi* to whirl, spin (round and round)

muli'nello *sm* (*moto vorticoso*) eddy, whirl; (*di canna da pesca*) reel

mu'lino *sm* mill; ~ a vento windmill

'mulo *sm* mule

'multa *sf* fine; mul'tare *vt* to fine

'multiplo, a *ag, sm* multiple

multiproprietà *sf inv* time-share

'mummia *sf* mummy

'mungere ['mundʒere] *vt* (*anche fig*) to milk

munici'pale [munitʃi'pale] *ag* municipal; town *cpd*

muni'cipio [muni'tʃipjo] *sm* town council, corporation; (*edificio*) town hall

mu'nire *vt*: ~ qc/qn di to equip sth/sb with

munizi'oni [munit'tsjoni] *sfpl* (*MIL*) ammunition *sg*

'munto, a *pp di* mungere

mu'overe *vt* to move; (*ruota, macchina*) to drive; (*sollevare: questione, obiezione*) to raise, bring up; (: *accusa*) to make, bring forward; ~rsi *vr* to move; muoviti! hurry up!, get a move on!

'mura *sfpl vedi* muro

mu'raglia [mu'raʎʎa] *sf* (high) wall

mu'rale *ag* wall *cpd*; mural

mu'rare *vt* (*persona, porta*) to wall up

mura'tore *sm* mason; bricklayer

'muro *sm* wall; ~a *sfpl* (*cinta cittadina*) walls; a ~ wall *cpd*; (*armadio etc*) built-in; ~ del suono sound barrier; mettere al ~ (*fucilare*) to shoot *o* execute (by firing squad)

'muschio ['muskjo] *sm* (*ZOOL*) musk; (*BOT*) moss

musco'lare *ag* muscular, muscle *cpd*

'muscolo *sm* (*ANAT*) muscle

mu'seo *sm* museum

museru'ola *sf* muzzle

'musica *sf* music; ~ da ballo/camera dance/chamber music; musi'cale *ag* musical; musi'cista, i, e *sm/f* musician

'muso *sm* muzzle; (*di auto, aereo*) nose; tenere il ~ to sulk; mu'sone, a *sm/f* sulky person

'muta *sf* (*di animali*) moulting; (*di serpenti*) sloughing; (*per immersioni subacquee*) diving suit; (*gruppo di cani*) pack

muta'mento *sm* change

mu'tande *sfpl* (*da uomo*) (under) pants; mutan'dine *sfpl* (*da donna, bambino*) pants (*BRIT*), briefs

mu'tare *vt*, *vi* to change, alter; mutazi'one *sf* change, alteration; (*BIOL*) mutation; mu'tevole *ag* changeable

muti'lare *vt* to mutilate, maim; (*fig*) to mutilate, deface; muti'lato, a *sm/f* disabled person (*through loss of limbs*)

mu'tismo *sm* (*MED*) mutism; (*atteggiamento*) (stubborn) silence

'muto, a *ag* (*MED*) dumb; (*emozione, dolore, CINEMA*) silent; (*LING*) silent, mute; (*carta geografica*) blank; ~ per lo stupore *etc* speechless with amazement *etc*

'mutua *sf* (*anche: cassa ~*) health insurance scheme

mutu'are *vt* (*fig*) to borrow

mutu'ato, a *sm/f* member of a health insurance scheme

'mutuo, a *ag* (*reciproco*) mutual ♦ *sm* (*ECON*) (long-term) loan

N, n

N. *abbr* (= *nord*) N

'nacchere ['nakkere] *sfpl* castanets

'nafta *sf* naphtha; (*per motori diesel*) diesel oil

nafta'lina *sf* (*CHIM*) naphthalene; (*tarmicida*) mothballs *pl*

'naia *sf* (*MIL*) slang term for national service

'nailon *sm* nylon

'nanna *sf* (*linguaggio infantile*): andare a ~ to go to beddy-byes

'nano, a *ag*, *sm/f* dwarf

napole'tano, a *ag*, *sm/f* Neapolitan

'Napoli *sf* Naples

'nappa *sf* tassel

nar'ciso [nar'tʃizo] *sm* narcissus

nar'cosi *sf* narcosis

nar'cotico, ci *sm* narcotic

na'rice [na'ritʃe] *sf* nostril

nar'rare *vt* to tell the story of, recount; narra'tiva *sf* (*branca letteraria*) fiction; narra'tivo, a *ag* narrative; narra'tore, 'trice *sm/f* narrator; narrazi'one *sf* narration; (*racconto*) story, tale

na'sale *ag* nasal

'nascere ['naʃʃere] *vi* (*bambino*) to be born; (*pianta*) to come *o* spring up; (*fiume*) to rise, have its source; (*sole*) to rise; (*dente*) to come through; (*fig: derivare, conseguire*): ~ **da** to arise from, be born out of; **è nata nel 1952** she was born in 1952; '**nascita** *sf* birth

nas'condere *vt* to hide, conceal; **~rsi** *vr* to hide; nascon'diglio *sm* hiding place; nascon'dino *sm* (*gioco*) hide-and-seek; nas'costo, a *pp di* nascondere ♦ *ag* hidden; **di nascosto** secretly

na'sello *sm* (ZOOL) hake

'naso *sm* nose

'nastro *sm* ribbon; (*magnetico, isolante, SPORT*) tape; ~ **adesivo** adhesive tape; ~ **trasportatore** conveyor belt

nas'turzio [nas'turtsjo] *sm* nasturtium

na'tale *ag* of one's birth ♦ *sm* (REL): **N~** Christmas; (*giorno della nascita*) birthday; natalità *sf* birth rate; nata'lizio, a *ag* (*del Natale*) Christmas *cpd*

na'tante *sm* craft *inv*, boat

'natica, che *sf* (ANAT) buttock

na'tio, a, 'tii, 'tie *ag* native

Nativnever *sf* (REL) Nativity

na'tivo, a *ag*, *sm/f* native

'nato, a *pp di* nascere ♦ *ag*: **un attore ~** a born actor; **~a Pieri** née Pieri

na'tura *sf* nature; **pagare in ~** to pay in kind; **~ morta** still life

natu'rale *ag* natural; natura'lezza *sf* naturalness; natura'lista, i, e *sm/f* naturalist

naturaliz'zare [naturalid'dzare] *vt* to naturalize

natural'mente *av* naturally; (*certamente, sì*) of course

naufra'gare *vi* (*nave*) to be wrecked; (*persona*) to be shipwrecked; (*fig*) to fall through; nau'fragio *sm* shipwreck; (*fig*) ruin, failure; 'naufrago, ghi *sm* castaway, shipwreck victim

'nausea *sf* nausea; nausea'bondo, a *ag* nauseating, sickening; nause'are *vt* to nauseate, make (feel) sick

'nautica *sf* (art of) navigation

'nautico, a, ci, che *ag* nautical

na'vale *ag* naval

na'vata *sf* (*anche:* ~ **centrale**) nave; (*anche:* ~ **laterale**) aisle

'nave *sf* ship, vessel; ~ **cisterna** tanker; ~ **da guerra** warship; ~ **passeggeri** passenger ship

na'vetta *sf* shuttle; (*servizio di collegamento*) shuttle (service)

navi'cella [navi'tʃɛlla] *sf* (*di aerostato*) gondola; ~ **spaziale** spaceship

navi'gare *vi* to sail; ~ **in Internet** to surf the Net; navigazi'one *sf* navigation

na'viglio [na'viʎʎo] *sm* (*canale artificiale*) canal; ~ **da pesca** fishing fleet

nazio'nale [nattsjo'nale] *ag* national ♦ *sf* (SPORT) national team; naziona'lismo *sm* nationalism; nazionalità *sf inv* nationality

nazi'one [nat'tsjone] *sf* nation

PAROLA CHIAVE

---

ne *pron* **1** (*di lui, lei, loro*) of him/her/them; about him/her/them; ~ **riconosco la voce** I recognize his (*o* her) voice

2 (*di questa, quella cosa*) of it; about it; ~ **voglio ancora** I want some more (of it *o* them); **non parliamone più!** let's not talk about it any more!

3 (*con valore partitivo*): **hai dei libri? – sì,** ~ **ho** have you any books? — yes, I have (some); **hai del pane? – no, non** ~ **ho** have you any bread? — no, I haven't any; **quanti anni hai? –** ~ **ho 17** how old are you? — I'm 17

♦ *av* (*moto a luogo: da lì*) from there; ~ **vengo ora** I've just come from there

---

né *cong*: ~ ... ~ neither ... nor; ~ **l'uno** ~ **l'altro lo vuole** neither of them wants it; **non parla** ~ **l'italiano** ~ **il tedesco** he speaks neither Italian nor German, he doesn't speak either Italian or German; **non piove** ~ **nevica** it isn't raining or snowing

ne'anche [ne'anke] *av*, *cong* not even; **non** ... ~ not even; ~ **se volesse potrebbe venire** he couldn't come even if he wanted to; **non l'ho visto —** ~ **io** I didn't see him — neither did I *o* I didn't either; ~ **per idea** *o* **sogno!** not on your life!

'**nebbia** *sf* fog; *(foschia)* mist; **nebbi'oso, a** *ag* foggy; misty

nebu'loso, a *ag (atmosfera)* hazy; *(fig)* hazy, vague

necessaria'mente [netʃessarja'mente] *av* necessarily

neces'sario, a [netʃes'sarjo] *ag* necessary

necessità [netʃessi'ta] *sf inv* necessity; *(povertà)* need, poverty; **necessi'tare** *vt* to require ♦ *vi (aver bisogno):* **necessitare di** to need

necro'logio [nekro'lɔdʒo] *sm* obituary notice

ne'fando, a *ag* infamous, wicked

ne'fasto, a *ag* inauspicious, ill-omened

ne'gare *vt* to deny; *(rifiutare)* to deny, refuse; **~ di aver fatto/che** to deny having done/that; **nega'tivo, a** *ag, sf, sm* negative; **negazi'one** *sf* negation

ne'gletto, a *ag (trascurato)* neglected

'negli ['neʎʎi] *prep +det vedi* **in**

negli'gente [negli'dʒente] *ag* negligent, careless; **negli'genza** *sf* negligence, carelessness

negozi'ante [negot'tsjante] *sm/f* trader, dealer; *(bottegaio)* shopkeeper *(BRIT)*, storekeeper *(US)*

negozi'are [negot'tsjare] *vt* to negotiate ♦ *vi:* **~ in** to trade *o* deal in; **negozi'ato** *sm* negotiation

ne'gozio [ne'gɔttsjo] *sm (locale)* shop *(BRIT)*, store *(US)*

'negro, a *ag, sm/f* Negro

'nei *prep +det vedi* **in**

nel *prep +det vedi* **in**

nell' *prep +det vedi* **in**

'nella *prep +det vedi* **in**

'nelle *prep +det vedi* **in**

'nello *prep +det vedi* **in**

'nembo *sm (METEOR)* nimbus

ne'mico, a, ci, che *ag* hostile; *(MIL)* enemy *cpd* ♦ *sm/f* enemy; **essere ~ di** to be strongly averse *o* opposed to

nem'meno *av, cong* = **neanche**

'nenia *sf* dirge; *(motivo monotono)* monotonous tune

'neo *sm* mole; *(fig)* (slight) flaw

'**neo...** *prefisso* neo...

'**neon** *sm (CHIM)* neon

neo'nato, a *ag* newborn ♦ *sm/f* newborn baby

neozelan'dese [neoddzelan'dese] *ag* New Zealand *cpd* ♦ *sm/f* New Zealander

nep'pure *av, cong* = **neanche**

'**nerbo** *sm* lash; *(fig)* strength, backbone; **nerbo'ruto, a** *ag* muscular; robust

ne'retto *sm (TIP)* bold type

'**nero, a** *ag* black; *(scuro)* dark ♦ *sm* black; **il Mar N~** the Black Sea

nerva'tura *sf (ANAT)* nervous system; *(BOT)* veining; *(ARCHIT, TECN)* rib

'**nervo** *sm (ANAT)* nerve; *(BOT)* vein; **avere i ~i** to be on edge; **dare sui ~i a qn** to get on sb's nerves; **ner'voso, a** *ag* nervous; *(irritabile)* irritable ♦ *sm (fam):* **far venire il nervoso a qn** to get on sb's nerves

'**nespola** *sf (BOT)* medlar; *(fig)* blow, punch; '**nespolo** *sm* medlar tree

'**nesso** *sm* connection, link

PAROLA CHIAVE
---

nes'suno, a *(det: dav sm* **nessun** +C, V, **nessuno** +s impura, gn, pn, ps, x, z; *dav sf* **nessuna** +C, **nessun'** +V) *det* **1** *(non uno)* no, *espressione negativa* +any; **non c'è nessun libro** there isn't any book, there is no book; **nessun altro** no one else, nobody else; **nessun'altra cosa** nothing else; **in nessun luogo** nowhere

2 *(qualche)* any; **hai ~a obiezione?** do you have any objections?

♦ *pron* **1** *(non uno)* no one, nobody, *espressione negativa* +any(one); *(: cosa)* none, *espressione negativa* +any; **~ è venuto, non è venuto ~** nobody came

2 *(qualcuno)* anyone, anybody; **ha telefonato ~?** did anyone phone?

---

net'tare[1] *vt* to clean

'**nettare**[2] *sm* nectar

net'tezza [net'tettsa] *sf* cleanness, cleanliness; **~ urbana** cleansing department

'**netto, a** *ag (pulito)* clean; *(chiaro)* clear, clear-cut; *(deciso)* definite; *(ECON)* net nettur'bino *sm* dustman (*BRIT*), garbage collector (*US*)

neu'rosi *sf* = **nevrosi**

neu'trale *ag* neutral; **neutralità** *sf* neutrality; **neutraliz'zare** *vt* to neutralize

'neutro, a *ag* neutral; (*LING*) neuter ♦ *sm* (*LING*) neuter

'neve *sf* snow; **nevi'care** *vb impers* to snow; **nevi'cata** *sf* snowfall

ne'vischio [ne'viskjo] *sm* sleet

ne'voso, a *ag* snowy; snow-covered

nevral'gia [nevral'dʒia] *sf* neuralgia

nevras'tenico, a, ci, che *ag* (*MED*) neurasthenic; (*fig*) hot-tempered

ne'vrosi *sf* neurosis

'nibbio *sm* (*ZOOL*) kite

'nicchia ['nikkja] *sf* niche; (*naturale*) cavity, hollow

nicchi'are [nik'kjare] *vi* to shilly-shally, hesitate

'nichel ['nikel] *sm* nickel

nico'tina *sf* nicotine

'nido *sm* nest; **a ~ d'ape** (*tessuto etc*) honeycomb *cpd*

PAROLA CHIAVE

ni'ente *pron* 1 (*nessuna cosa*) nothing; ~ **può fermarlo** nothing can stop him; ~ **di ~** absolutely nothing; **nient'altro** nothing else; **nient'altro che** nothing but, just, only; ~ **affatto** not at all, in the least; **come se ~ fosse** as if nothing had happened; **cose da ~** trivial matters; **per ~** (*gratis, invano*) for nothing

2 (*qualcosa*): **hai bisogno di ~?** do you need anything?

3: **non ... ~** nothing, *espressione negativa* +anything; **non ho visto ~** I saw nothing, I didn't see anything; **non ho ~ da dire** I have nothing *o* haven't anything to say ♦ *sm* nothing; **un bel ~** absolutely nothing; **basta un ~ per farla piangere** the slightest thing is enough to make her cry ♦ *av* (*in nessuna misura*): **non ... ~** not ... at all; **non è (per) ~ buono** it isn't good at all

---

nientedi'meno *av* actually, even ♦ *escl* really!, I say!

niente'meno *av*, *escl* = **nientedimeno**

'Nilo *sm*: **il ~** the Nile

'ninfa *sf* nymph

nin'fea *sf* water lily

ninna-'nanna *sf* lullaby

'ninnolo *sm* (*gingillo*) knick-knack

ni'pote *sm/f* (*di zii*) nephew/niece; (*di nonni*) grandson/daughter, grand-child

'nitido, a *ag* clear; (*specchio*) bright

ni'trato *sm* nitrate

'nitrico, a, ci, che *ag* nitric

ni'trire *vi* to neigh

ni'trito *sm* (*di cavallo*) neighing *no pl*; neigh; (*CHIM*) nitrite

nitroglice'rina [nitroglitʃe'rina] *sf* nitroglycerine

no *av* (*risposta*) no; **vieni o ~?** are you coming or not?; **perché ~?** why not?; **lo conosciamo? – tu ~ ma io sì** do we know him? — you don't but I do; **verrai, ~?** you'll come, won't you?

'nobile *ag* noble ♦ *sm/f* noble, nobleman/ woman; **nobili'are** *ag* noble; **nobiltà** *sf* nobility; (*di azione*) nobleness

'nocca, che *sf* (*ANAT*) knuckle

noccio'ola [not'tʃɔla] *ag inv* (*colore*) hazel, light brown ♦ *sf* hazelnut

noccio'lina [nottʃo'lina] *sf*: ~ **americana** peanut

'nocciolo¹ ['nɔttʃolo] *sm* (*di frutto*) stone; (*fig*) heart, core

noc'ciolo² [not'tʃɔlo] *sm* (*albero*) hazel

'noce ['notʃe] *sm* (*albero*) walnut tree ♦ *sf* (*frutto*) walnut; ~ **moscata** nutmeg

no'civo, a [no'tʃivo] *ag* harmful, noxious

'nodo *sm* (*di cravatta, legname, NAUT*) knot; (*AUT, FERR*) junction; (*MED, ASTR, BOT*) node; (*fig: legame*) bond, tie; (: *punto centrale*) heart, crux; **avere un ~ alla gola** to have a lump in one's throat; **no'doso, a** *ag* (*tronco*) gnarled

'noi *pron* (*soggetto*) we; (*oggetto: per dare rilievo, con preposizione*) us; ~ **stessi(e)** we ourselves; (*oggetto*) ourselves

'noia sf boredom; (disturbo, impaccio) bother no pl, trouble no pl; avere qn/qc a ~ not to like sb/sth; mi è venuto a ~ I'm tired of it; dare ~ a to annoy; avere delle ~e con qn to have trouble with sb

noi'altri pron we

noi'oso, a ag boring; (fastidioso) annoying, troublesome

noleggi'are [noled'dʒare] vt (prendere a noleggio) to hire (BRIT), rent; (dare a noleggio) to hire out (BRIT), rent (out); (aereo, nave) to charter; no'leggio sm hire (BRIT), rental; charter

'nolo sm hire (BRIT), rental; charter; (per trasporto merci) freight; prendere/dare a ~ qc to hire/hire out sth

'nomade ag nomadic ♦ sm/f nomad

'nome sm name; (LING) noun; in/a ~ di in the name of; di o per ~ (chiamato) called, named; conoscere qn di ~ to know sb by name; ~ d'arte stage name; ~ di battesimo Christian name; ~ di famiglia surname

no'mea sf notoriety

no'mignolo [no'miɲɲolo] sm nickname

'nomina sf appointment

nomi'nale ag nominal; (LING) noun cpd

nomi'nare vt to name; (eleggere) to appoint; (citare) to mention

nomina'tivo, a ag (LING) nominative; (ECON) registered ♦ sm (LING: anche: caso ~) nominative (case); (AMM) name

non av not ♦ prefisso non-; vedi affatto; appena etc

nonché [non'ke] cong (tanto più, tanto meno) let alone; (e inoltre) as well as

noncu'rante ag: ~ (di) careless (of), indifferent (to); noncu'ranza sf carelessness, indifference

nondi'meno cong (tuttavia) however; (nonostante) nevertheless

'nonno, a sm/f grandfather/mother; (in senso più familiare) grandma/grandpa; ~i smpl grandparents

non'nulla sm inv: un ~ nothing, a trifle

'nono, a ag, sm ninth

nonos'tante prep in spite of,

notwithstanding ♦ cong although, even though

nontiscordardimé sm inv (BOT) forget-me-not

nord sm North ♦ ag inv north; northern; il Mare del N~ the North Sea; nor'dest sm north-east; 'nordico, a, ci, che ag nordic, northern European; nor'dovest sm north-west

'norma sf (principio) norm; (regola) regulation, rule; (consuetudine) custom, rule; a ~ di legge according to law, as laid down by law

nor'male ag normal; standard cpd; normalità sf normality; normaliz'zare vt to normalize, bring back to normal

normal'mente av normally

norve'gese [norve'dʒese] ag, sm/f, sm Norwegian

Nor'vegia [nor'vedʒa] sf: la ~ Norway

nostal'gia [nostal'dʒia] sf (di casa, paese) homesickness; (del passato) nostalgia; nos'talgico, a, ci, che ag homesick; nostalgic

nos'trano, a ag local; national; home-produced

'nostro, a det: il(la) ~(a) etc our ♦ pron: il(la) ~(a) etc ours ♦ sm: il ~ our money; our belongings; i ~i our family; our own people; è dei ~i he's one of us

'nota sf (segno) mark; (comunicazione scritta, MUS) note; (fattura) bill; (elenco) list; degno di ~ noteworthy, worthy of note

no'tabile ag notable ♦ sm prominent citizen

no'taio sm notary

no'tare vt (segnare: errori) to mark; (registrare) to note (down), write down; (rilevare, osservare) to note, notice; farsi ~ to get o.s. noticed

no'tevole ag (talento) notable, remarkable; (peso) considerable

no'tifica, che sf notification

notifi'care vt (DIR): ~ qc a qn to notify sb of sth, give sb notice of sth

no'tizia [no'tittsja] sf (piece of) news sg; (informazione) piece of information; ~e sfpl (*informazioni*) news *sg*; information *sg*; notizi'ario *sm* (RADIO, TV, STAMPA) news *sg*

'noto, a *ag* (well-)known

notorietà *sf* fame; notoriety

no'torio, a *ag* well-known; (*peg*) notorious

not'tambulo, a *sm/f* night-bird (*fig*)

not'tata *sf* night

'notte *sf* night; **di** ~ at night; (*durante la notte*) in the night, during the night; ~ **bianca** sleepless night; **notte'tempo** *av* at night; during the night

not'turno, a *ag* nocturnal; (*servizio, guardiano*) night *cpd*

no'vanta *num* ninety; **novan'tesimo, a** *num* ninetieth; **novan'tina** *sf*: **una novantina (di)** about ninety

'nove *num* nine

nove'cento [nove'tʃɛnto] *num* nine hundred ♦ *sm*: **il N~** the twentieth century

no'vella *sf* (LETTERATURA) short story

novel'lino, a *ag* (*pivello*) green, inexperienced

no'vello, a *ag* (*piante, patate*) new; (*insalata, verdura*) early; (*sposo*) newly-married

no'vembre *sm* November

novi'lunio *sm* (ASTR) new moon

novità *sf inv* novelty; (*innovazione*) innovation; (*cosa originale, insolita*) something new; (*notizia*) (piece of) news *sg*; **le ~ della moda** the latest fashions

no'vizio, a [no'vittsjo] *sm/f* (REL) novice; (*tirocinante*) beginner, apprentice

nozi'one [not'tsjone] *sf* notion, idea; **~i** *sfpl* (*rudimenti*) basic knowledge *sg*, rudiments

'nozze ['nɔttse] *sfpl* wedding *sg*, marriage *sg*; ~ **d'argento/d'oro** silver/golden wedding *sg*

ns. *abbr* (COMM) = **nostro**

'nube *sf* cloud; **nubi'fragio** *sm* cloudburst

'nubile *ag* (*donna*) unmarried, single

'nuca *sf* nape of the neck

nucle'are *ag* nuclear

'nucleo *sm* nucleus; (*gruppo*) team, unit, group; (MIL, POLIZIA) squad; **il ~ familiare** the family unit

nu'dista, i, e *sm/f* nudist

'nudo, a *ag* (*persona*) bare, naked, nude; (*membra*) bare, naked; (*montagna*) bare ♦ *sm* (ARTE) nude

'nugolo *sm*: **un ~ di** a whole host of

'nulla *pron, av* = **niente** ♦ *sm*: **il ~** nothing

nulla'osta *sm inv* authorization

nullità *sf inv* nullity; (*persona*) nonentity

'nullo, a *ag* useless, worthless; (DIR) null (and void); (SPORT): **incontro ~** draw

nume'rale *ag, sm* numeral

nume'rare *vt* to number; **numerazi'one** *sf* numbering; (*araba, decimale*) notation

nu'merico, a, ci, che *ag* numerical

'numero *sm* number; (*romano, arabo*) numeral; (*di spettacolo*) act, turn; ~ **civico** house number; ~ **di telefono** telephone number; **nume'roso, a** *ag* numerous, many; (*con sostantivo sg*) large

'nunzio ['nuntsjo] *sm* (REL) nuncio

nu'ocere ['nwɔtʃere] *vi*: ~ **a** to harm, damage; **nuoci'uto, a** *pp di* **nuocere**

nu'ora *sf* daughter-in-law

nuo'tare *vi* to swim; (*galleggiare: oggetti*) to float; **nuota'tore, 'trice** *sm/f* swimmer; **nu'oto** *sm* swimming

nu'ova *sf* (*notizia*) (piece of) news *sg*; *vedi anche* **nuovo**

nuova'mente *av* again

Nu'ova Ze'landa [-dze'landa] *sf*: **la ~** New Zealand

nu'ovo, a *ag* new; **di ~** again; ~ **fiammante** *o* **di zecca** brand-new

nutri'ente *ag* nutritious, nourishing

nutri'mento *sm* food, nourishment

nu'trire *vt* to feed; (*fig: sentimenti*) to harbour, nurse; **nutri'tivo, a** *ag* nutritional; (*alimento*) nutritious; **nutrizi'one** *sf* nutrition

'nuvola *sf* cloud; **nuvo'loso, a** *ag* cloudy

nuzi'ale [nut'tsjale] *ag* nuptial; wedding *cpd*

O, o

o (*dav V spesso* **od**) *cong* or; **~ ... ~** either ... or; **~ l'uno ~ l'altro** either (of them)

O. *abbr* (= *ovest*) W

'oasi *sf inv* oasis

obbedi'ente *etc* = **ubbidiente** *etc*

obbli'gare *vt* (*costringere*): **~ qn a fare** to force *o* oblige sb to do; (*DIR*) to bind; **~rsi** *vr*: **~rsi a fare** to undertake to do; **obbli'gato, a** *ag* (*costretto, grato*) obliged; (*percorso, tappa*) set, fixed; **obbliga'torio, a** *ag* compulsory, obligatory; **obbligazi'one** *sf* (*COMM*) bond, debenture; **'obbligo, ghi** *sm* obligation; (*dovere*) duty; **avere l'obbligo di fare** to be obliged to do; **essere d'obbligo** (*discorso, applauso*) to be called for

ob'brobrio *sm* disgrace; (*fig*) eyesore

o'beso, a *ag* obese

obiet'tare *vt*: **~ che** to object that; **~ su qc** to object to sth, raise objections concerning sth

obiet'tivo, a *ag* objective ♦ *sm* (*OTTICA, FOT*) lens *sg*, objective; (*MIL, fig*) objective

obiet'tore *sm* objector; **~ di coscienza** conscientious objector

obiezi'one [objet'tsjone] *sf* objection

obi'torio *sm* morgue, mortuary

o'bliquo, a *ag* oblique; (*inclinato*) slanting; (*fig*) devious, underhand

oblite'rare *vt* (*biglietto*) to stamp; (*francobollo*) to cancel

oblò *sm inv* porthole

o'blungo, a, ghi, ghe *ag* oblong

'oboe *sm* (*MUS*) oboe

'oca (*pl* **'oche**) *sf* goose

occasi'one *sf* (*caso favorevole*) opportunity; (*causa, motivo, circostanza*) occasion; (*COMM*) bargain; **d'~** (*a buon prezzo*) bargain *cpd*; (*usato*) secondhand

occhi'aia [ok'kjaja] *sf* eye socket; **avere le ~e** to have shadows under one's eyes

occhi'ali [ok'kjali] *smpl* glasses, spectacles; **~ da sole** sunglasses; **~ da vista** (prescription) glasses

occhi'ata [ok'kjata] *sf* look, glance; **dare un'~ a** to have a look at

occhi'ello [ok'kjɛllo] *sm* buttonhole; (*asola*) eyelet

'occhio ['ɔkkjo] *sm* eye; **~!** careful!, watch out!; **a ~ nudo** with the naked eye; **a quattr'~i** privately, tête-à-tête; **dare all'~** *o* **nell'~ a qn** to catch sb's eye; **fare l'~ a qc** to get used to sth; **tenere d'~ qn** to keep an eye on sb; **vedere di buon/mal ~ qc** to look favourably/unfavourably on sth

occhio'lino [okkjo'lino] *sm*: **fare l'~ a qn** to wink at sb

occiden'tale [ottʃiden'tale] *ag* western ♦ *sm/f* Westerner

occi'dente [ottʃi'dɛnte] *sm* west; (*POL*): **l'O~** the West; **a ~** in the west

oc'cipite [ot'tʃipite] *sm* back of the head, occiput

oc'cludere *vt* to block; **occlusi'one** *sf* blockage, obstruction; **oc'cluso, a** *pp di* **occludere**

occor'rente *ag* necessary ♦ *sm* all that is necessary

occor'renza [okkor'rɛntsa] *sf* necessity, need; **all'~** in case of need

oc'correre *vi* to be needed, be required ♦ *vb impers*: **occorre farlo** it must be done; **occorre che tu parta** you must leave, you'll have to leave; **mi occorrono i soldi** I need the money; **oc'corso, a** *pp di* **occorrere**

occul'tare *vt* to hide, conceal

oc'culto, a *ag* hidden, concealed; (*scienze, forze*) occult

occu'pare *vt* to occupy; (*manodopera*) to employ; (*ingombrare*) to occupy, take up; **~rsi** *vr* to occupy o.s., to keep busy; (*impiegarsi*) to get a job; **~rsi di** (*interessarsi*) to take an interest in; (*prendersi cura di*) to look after, take care of; **occu'pato, a** *ag* (*MIL, POL*) occupied; (*persona: affaccendato*) busy; (*posto, sedia*) taken; (*toilette, TEL*) engaged; **occupazi'one** *sf* occupation; (*impiego,* *lavoro*) job; (*ECON*) employment

o'ceano [o'tʃeano] *sm* ocean

'ocra *sf* ochre

ocu'lare *ag* ocular, eye *cpd*; **testimone ~** eye witness

ocu'lato, a *ag* (*attento*) cautious, prudent; (*accorto*) shrewd

ocu'lista, i, e *sm/f* eye specialist, oculist

'ode *sf* ode

odi'are *vt* to hate, detest

odi'erno, a *ag* today's, of today; (*attuale*) present

'odio *sm* hatred; **avere in ~ qc/qn** to hate *o* detest sth/sb; odi'oso, a *ag* hateful, odious

odo'rare *vt* (*annusare*) to smell; (*profumare*) to perfume, scent ♦ *vi*: **~ (di)** to smell (of); odo'rato *sm* sense of smell

o'dore *sm* smell; **gli ~i** *smpl* (*CUC*) (aromatic) herbs; odo'roso, a *ag* sweet-smelling

of'fendere *vt* to offend; (*violare*) to break, violate; (*insultare*) to insult; (*ferire*) to hurt; **~rsi** *vr* (*con senso reciproco*) to insult one another; (*risentirsi*): **~rsi (di)** to take offence (at), be offended (by); offen'sivo, a *ag*, *sf* offensive

offe'rente *sm* (*in aste*): **al maggior ~** to the highest bidder

of'ferta *sf* offer; (*donazione, anche REL*) offering; (*in gara d'appalto*) tender; (*in aste*) bid; (*ECON*) supply; **"~e d'impiego"** "situations vacant"; **fare un'~a** to make an offer; to tender; to bid

of'ferto, a *pp di* offrire

of'fesa *sf* insult, affront; (*MIL*) attack; (*DIR*) offence; *vedi anche* offeso

of'feso, a *pp di* offendere ♦ *ag* offended; (*fisicamente*) hurt, injured ♦ *sm/f* offended party; **essere ~ con qn** to be annoyed with sb; **parte ~a** (*DIR*) plaintiff

offi'cina [offi'tʃina] *sf* workshop

of'frire *vt* to offer; **~rsi** *vr* (*proporsi*) to offer (o.s.), volunteer; (*occasione*) to present itself; (*esporsi*): **~rsi a** to expose o.s. to; **ti offro da bere** I'll buy you a drink

offus'care *vt* to obscure, darken; (*fig:*

intelletto) to dim, cloud; (*: fama*) to obscure, overshadow; **~rsi** *vr* to grow dark; to cloud, grow dim; to be obscured

ogget'tivo, a [oddʒet'tivo] *ag* objective

og'getto [od'dʒetto] *sm* object; (*materia, argomento*) subject (matter); **~i smarriti** lost property *sg*

'oggi ['ɔddʒi] *av, sm* today; **~ a otto** a week today; **oggigi'orno** *av* nowadays

OGM *sigla m* (= *organismo geneticamente modificato*) GMO

'ogni ['oɲɲi] *det* every, each; (*tutti*) all; (*con valore distributivo*) every; **~ uomo è mortale** all men are mortal; **viene ~ due giorni** he comes every two days; **~ cosa** everything; **ad ~ costo** at all costs, at any price; **in ~ luogo** everywhere; **~ tanto** every so often; **~ volta che** every time that

Ognis'santi [oɲɲis'santi] *sm* All Saints' Day

o'gnuno [oɲ'ɲuno] *pron* everyone, everybody

'ohi *escl* oh!; (*esprimente dolore*) ow!

ohi'mè *escl* oh dear!

O'landa *sf*: **l'~** Holland; olan'dese *ag* Dutch ♦ *sm* (*LING*) Dutch ♦ *sm/f* Dutchman/woman; **gli Olandesi** the Dutch

oleo'dotto *sm* oil pipeline

ole'oso, a *ag* oily; (*che contiene olio*) oil-yielding

ol'fatto *sm* sense of smell

oli'are *vt* to oil

oli'era *sf* oil cruet

olim'piadi *sfpl* Olympic games; o'limpico, a, ci, che *ag* Olympic

'olio *sm* oil; **sott'~** (*CUC*) in oil; **~ di fegato di merluzzo** cod liver oil; **~ d'oliva** olive oil; **~ di semi** vegetable oil

o'liva *sf* olive; oli'vastro, a *ag* olive(-coloured); (*carnagione*) sallow; oli'veto *sm* olive grove; o'livo *sm* olive tree

'olmo *sm* elm

oltraggi'are [oltrad'dʒare] *vt* to outrage

ol'traggio [ol'traddʒo] *sm* outrage; offence, insult; **~ al pudore** (*DIR*) indecent behaviour; oltraggi'oso, a *ag* offensive

ol'tralpe *av* beyond the Alps

ol'tranza [ol'trantsa] *sf*: **a ~** to the last, to

the bitter end

'oltre *av* (*più in là*) further; (*di più: aspettare*) longer, more ♦ *prep* (*di là da*) beyond, over, on the other side of; (*più di*) more than, over; (*in aggiunta a*) besides; (*eccetto*): **~ a** except, apart from; **oltre'mare** *av* overseas; **oltre'modo** *av* extremely; **oltrepas'sare** *vt* to go beyond, exceed

o'maggio [o'maddʒo] *sm* (*dono*) gift; (*segno di rispetto*) homage, tribute; **~i** *smpl* (*complimenti*) respects; **rendere ~ a** to pay homage *o* tribute to; **in ~** (*copia, biglietto*) complimentary

ombe'lico, chi *sm* navel

'ombra *sf* (*zona non assolata, fantasma*) shade; (*sagoma scura*) shadow; **sedere all'~** to sit in the shade; **restare nell'~** (*fig*) to remain in obscurity

om'brello *sm* umbrella; **ombrel'lone** *sm* beach umbrella

om'bretto *sm* eyeshadow

om'broso, a *ag* shady, shaded; (*cavallo*) nervous, skittish; (*persona*) touchy, easily offended

ome'lia *sf* (*REL*) homily, sermon

omeopa'tia *sf* homoeopathy

omertà *sf* conspiracy of silence

o'messo, a *pp di* omettere

o'mettere *vt* to omit, leave out; **~ di fare** to omit *o* fail to do

omi'cida, i, e [omi'tʃida] *ag* homicidal, murderous ♦ *sm/f* murderer/eress

omi'cidio [omi'tʃidjo] *sm* murder; **~ colposo** culpable homicide

omissi'one *sf* omission; **~ di soccorso** (*DIR*) failure to stop and give assistance

omogeneiz'zato [omodʒeneid'dzato] *sm* baby food

omo'geneo, a [omo'dʒeneo] *ag* homogeneous

omolo'gare *vt* to approve, recognize; to ratify

o'monimo, a *sm/f* namesake ♦ *sm* (*LING*) homonym

omosessu'ale *ag, sm/f* homosexual

'oncia, ce ['ontʃa] *sf* ounce

'onda *sf* wave; **mettere** *o* **mandare in ~** (*RADIO, TV*) to broadcast; **andare in ~** (*RADIO, TV*) to go on the air; **~e corte/ medie/lunghe** short/medium/long wave; **on'data** *sf* wave, billow; (*fig*) wave, surge; **a ondate** in waves; **ondata di caldo** heatwave

ondeggi'are [onded'dʒare] *vi* (*acqua*) to ripple; (*muoversi sulle onde: barca*) to rock, roll; (*fig: muoversi come le onde, barcollare*) to sway; (: *essere incerto*) to waver

'onere *sm* burden; **~i fiscali** taxes; **one'roso, a** *ag* (*fig*) heavy, onerous

onestà *sf* honesty

o'nesto, a *ag* (*probo, retto*) honest; (*giusto*) fair; (*casto*) chaste, virtuous

'onice ['onitʃe] *sf* onyx

onnipo'tente *ag* omnipotent

ono'mastico, ci *sm* name-day

ono'ranze [ono'rantse] *sfpl* honours; **~ funebri** funeral (service)

ono'rare *vt* to honour; (*far onore a*) to do credit to; **~rsi** *vr*: **~rsi di** to feel honoured at, be proud of

ono'rario, a *ag* honorary ♦ *sm* fee

o'nore *sm* honour; **in ~ di** in honour of; **fare gli ~i di casa** to play host (*o* hostess); **fare ~ a** to honour; (*pranzo*) to do justice to; (*famiglia*) to be a credit to; **farsi ~** to distinguish o.s.; **ono'revole** *ag* honourable ♦ *sm/f* (*POL*) ≈ Member of Parliament (*BRIT*), ≈ Congressman/woman (*US*); **onorifi'cenza** *sf* honour; decoration; **ono'rifico, a, ci, che** *ag* honorary

'onta *sf* shame, disgrace

on'tano *sm* (*BOT*) alder

'O.N.U. ['ɔnu] *sigla f* (= *Organizzazione delle Nazioni Unite*) UN, UNO

o'paco, a, ci, che *ag* (*vetro*) opaque; (*metallo*) dull, matt

o'pale *sm o f* opal

'opera *sf* work; (*azione rilevante*) action, deed, work; (*MUS*) work; opus; (: *melodramma*) opera; (: *teatro*) opera house; (*ente*) institution, organization; **~ d'arte** work of art; **~ lirica** (grand) opera;

~e pubbliche public works

ope'raio, a *ag* working-class; workers'
♦ *sm/f* worker; **classe ~a** working class

ope'rare *vt* to carry out, make; (*MED*) to
operate on ♦ *vi* to operate, work; (*rimedio*)
to act, work; (*MED*) to operate; **~rsi** *vr*
(*MED*) to have an operation; **~rsi
d'appendicite** to have one's appendix out;
opera'tivo, a *ag* operative, operating;
opera'tore, 'trice *sm/f* operator; (*TV,
CINEMA*) cameraman; **operatore
economico** agent, broker; **operatore
turistico** tour operator; **opera'torio, a** *ag*
(*MED*) operating; **operazi'one** *sf*
operation

ope'retta *sf* (*MUS*) operetta, light opera

ope'roso, a *ag* busy, active, hard-working

opini'one *sf* opinion; **~ pubblica** public
opinion

'oppio *sm* opium

oppo'nente *ag* opposing ♦ *sm/f* opponent

op'porre *vt* to oppose; **opporsi** *vr*:
opporsi (a qc) to oppose (sth); to object
(to sth); **~ resistenza/un rifiuto** to offer
resistance/refuse

opportu'nista, i, e *sm/f* opportunist

opportunità *sf inv* opportunity;
(*convenienza*) opportuneness, timeliness

oppor'tuno, a *ag* timely, opportune

opposi'tore, 'trice *sm/f* opposer,
opponent

opposizi'one [oppozit'tsjone] *sf*
opposition; (*DIR*) objection

op'posto, a *pp di* **opporre** ♦ *ag* opposite;
(*opinioni*) conflicting ♦ *sm* opposite,
contrary; **all'~** on the contrary

oppressi'one *sf* oppression

oppres'sivo, a *ag* oppressive

op'presso, a *pp di* **opprimere**

oppres'sore *sm* oppressor

op'primere *vt* (*premere, gravare*) to weigh
down; (*estenuare: sog: caldo*) to suffocate,
oppress; (*tiranneggiare: popolo*) to oppress

op'pure *cong* or (else)

op'tare *vi*: **~ per** to opt for

o'puscolo *sm* booklet, pamphlet

opzi'one [op'tsjone] *sf* option

'ora¹ *sf* (*60 minuti*) hour; (*momento*) time;
che ~ è?, che ~e sono? what time is it?;
non veder l'~ di fare to long to do, look
forward to doing; **di buon'~** early; **alla
buon'~!** at last!; **~ di cena** dinner time; **~
legale** *o* **estiva** summer time (*BRIT*),
daylight saving time (*US*); **~ locale** local
time; **~ di pranzo** lunchtime; **~ di punta**
(*AUT*) rush hour

ora² *av* (*adesso*) now; (*poco fa*): **è uscito
proprio ~** he's just gone out; (*tra poco*)
presently, in a minute; (*correlativo*): **~ ... ~**
now ... now; **d'~ in avanti** *o* **poi** from now
on; **or ~** just now, a moment ago; **5 anni
or sono** 5 years ago; **~ come ~** right now,
at present

o'racolo *sm* oracle

'orafo *sm* goldsmith

o'rale *ag, sm* oral

ora'mai *av* = **ormai**

o'rario, a *ag* hourly; (*fuso, segnale*) time
cpd; (*velocità*) per hour ♦ *sm* timetable,
schedule; (*di ufficio, visite etc*) hours *pl*,
time(s *pl*); **in ~** on time

o'rata *sf* (*ZOOL*) sea bream

ora'tore, 'trice *sm/f* speaker; orator

ora'toria *sf* (*arte*) oratory

ora'torio, a *ag* oratorical ♦ *sm* (*REL*)
oratory; (*MUS*) oratorio

ora'zione [orat'tsjone] *sf* (*REL*) prayer;
(*discorso*) speech, oration

or'bene *cong* so, well (then)

'orbita *sf* (*ASTR, FISICA*) orbit; (*ANAT*)
(eye-)socket

or'chestra [or'kestra] *sf* orchestra;
orches'trare *vt* to orchestrate; (*fig*) to
mount, stage-manage

orchi'dea [orki'dɛa] *sf* orchid

'orco, chi *sm* ogre

'orda *sf* horde

or'digno [or'diɲɲo] *sm* (*esplosivo*) explosive
device

ordi'nale *ag, sm* ordinal

ordina'mento *sm* order, arrangement;
(*regolamento*) regulations *pl*, rules *pl*; **~
scolastico/giuridico** education/legal
system

ordi'nanza [ordi'nantsa] *sf* (*DIR, MIL*) order; (*persona: MIL*) orderly, batman; **d'~** (*MIL*) regulation *cpd*

ordi'nare *vt* (*mettere in ordine*) to arrange, organize; (*COMM*) to order; (*prescrivere: medicina*) to prescribe; (*comandare*): **~ a qn di fare qc** to order *o* command sb to do sth; (*REL*) to ordain

ordi'nario, a *ag* (*comune*) ordinary; everyday; standard; (*grossolano*) coarse, common ♦ *sm* ordinary; (*INS: di università*) full professor

ordi'nato, a *ag* tidy, orderly

ordinazi'one [ordinat'tsjone] *sf* (*COMM*) order; (*REL*) ordination; **eseguire qc su ~** to make sth to order

'ordine *sm* order; (*carattere*): **d'~ pratico** of a practical nature; **all'~** (*COMM: assegno*) to order; **di prim'~** first-class; **fino a nuovo ~** until further notice; **essere in ~** (*documenti*) to be in order; (*stanza, persona*) to be tidy; **mettere in ~** to put in order, tidy (up); **~ del giorno** (*di seduta*) agenda; (*MIL*) order of the day; **~ di pagamento** (*COMM*) order for payment; **l'~ pubblico** law and order; **~i (sacri)** (*REL*) holy orders

or'dire *vt* (*fig*) to plot, scheme; **or'dito** *sm* (*di tessuto*) warp

orec'chino [orek'kino] *sm* earring

o'recchio [o'rekkjo] (*pl(f*) **o'recchie**) *sm* (*ANAT*) ear

orecchi'oni [orek'kjoni] *smpl* (*MED*) mumps *sg*

o'refice [o'refitʃe] *sm* goldsmith; jeweller; **orefice'ria** *sf* (*arte*) goldsmith's art; (*negozio*) jeweller's (shop)

'orfano, a *ag* orphan(ed) ♦ *sm/f* orphan; **~ di padre/madre** fatherless/motherless; **orfano'trofio** *sm* orphanage

orga'netto *sm* barrel organ; (*fam: armonica a bocca*) mouth organ; (: *fisarmonica*) accordion

or'ganico, a, ci, che *ag* organic ♦ *sm* personnel, staff

organi'gramma, i *sm* organization chart

orga'nismo *sm* (*BIOL*) organism; (*corpo umano*) body; (*AMM*) body, organism

organiz'zare [organid'dzare] *vt* to organize; **~rsi** *vr* to get organized; **organizza'tore, 'trice** *ag* organizing ♦ *sm/f* organizer; **organizzazi'one** *sf* organization

'organo *sm* organ; (*di congegno*) part; (*portavoce*) spokesman, mouthpiece

or'gasmo *sm* (*FISIOL*) orgasm; (*fig*) agitation, anxiety

'orgia, ge ['ɔrdʒa] *sf* orgy

or'goglio [or'gɔʎʎo] *sm* pride; **orgogli'oso, a** *ag* proud

orien'tale *ag* oriental; eastern; east

orienta'mento *sm* positioning; orientation; direction; **senso di ~** sense of direction; **perdere l'~** to lose one's bearings; **~ professionale** careers guidance

orien'tare *vt* (*situare*) to position; (*fig*) to direct, orientate; **~rsi** *vr* to find one's bearings; (*fig: tendere*) to tend, lean; (: *indirizzarsi*): **~rsi verso** to take up, go in for

ori'ente *sm* east; **l'O~** the East, the Orient; **a ~** in the east

o'rigano *sm* oregano

origi'nale [oridʒi'nale] *ag* original; (*bizzarro*) eccentric ♦ *sm* original; **originalità** *sf* originality; eccentricity

origi'nare [oridʒi'nare] *vt* to bring about, produce ♦ *vi*: **~ da** to arise *o* spring from

origi'nario, a [oridʒi'narjo] *ag* original; **essere ~ di** to be a native of; (*provenire da*) to originate from; to be native to

o'rigine [o'ridʒine] *sf* origin; **all'~** originally; **d'~ inglese** of English origin; **dare ~ a** to give rise to

origli'are [oriʎ'ʎare] *vi*: **~ (a)** to eavesdrop (on)

o'rina *sf* urine

ori'nare *vi* to urinate ♦ *vt* to pass; **orina'toio** *sm* (*public*) urinal

ori'undo, a *ag*: **essere ~ di Milano** *etc* to be of Milanese *etc* extraction *o* origin ♦ *sm/f* person of foreign extraction *o* origin

orizzon'tale [oriddzon'tale] *ag* horizontal

oriz'zonte [orid'dzonte] *sm* horizon

or'lare *vt* to hem

'**orlo** *sm* edge, border; (*di recipiente*) rim, brim; (*di vestito etc*) hem

'**orma** *sf* (*di persona*) footprint; (*di animale*) track; (*impronta, traccia*) mark, trace

or'**mai** *av* by now, by this time; (*adesso*) now; (*quasi*) almost, nearly

ormeggi'**are** [ormed'dʒare] *vt* (*NAUT*) to moor; or'**meggio** *sm* (*atto*) mooring *no pl*; (*luogo*) moorings *pl*

or'**mone** *sm* hormone

ornamen'**tale** *ag* ornamental, decorative

orna'**mento** *sm* ornament, decoration

or'**nare** *vt* to adorn, decorate; **~rsi** *vr*: **~rsi (di)** to deck o.s. (out) (with); or'**nato, a** *ag* ornate

ornitolo'**gia** [ornitolo'dʒia] *sf* ornithology

'**oro** *sm* gold; **d'~, in ~** gold *cpd*; **d'~** (*colore, occasione*) golden; (*persona*) marvellous

orologe'**ria** [orolodʒe'ria] *sf* watchmaking *no pl*; watchmaker's (shop); clockmaker's (shop); **bomba a ~** time bomb

orologi'**aio** [orolo'dʒajo] *sm* watchmaker; clockmaker

oro'**logio** [oro'lɔdʒo] *sm* clock; (*da tasca, da polso*) watch; **~ da polso** wristwatch; **~ al quarzo** quartz watch

o'**roscopo** *sm* horoscope

or'**rendo, a** *ag* (*spaventoso*) horrible, awful; (*bruttissimo*) hideous

or'**ribile** *ag* horrible

'**orrido, a** *ag* fearful, horrid

orripi'**lante** *ag* hair-raising, horrifying

or'**rore** *sm* horror; **avere in ~ qn/qc** to loathe *o* detest sb/sth; **mi fanno ~** I loathe *o* detest them

orsacchi'**otto** [orsak'kjɔtto] *sm* teddy bear

'**orso** *sm* bear; **~ bruno/bianco** brown/polar bear

or'**taggio** [or'taddʒo] *sm* vegetable

or'**tensia** *sf* hydrangea

or'**tica, che** *sf* (stinging) nettle

orti'**caria** *sf* nettle rash

'**orto** *sm* vegetable garden, kitchen garden; (*AGR*) market garden (*BRIT*), truck farm (*US*)

orto'**dosso, a** *ag* orthodox

ortogra'**fia** *sf* spelling

orto'**lano, a** *sm/f* (*venditore*) greengrocer (*BRIT*), produce dealer (*US*)

ortope'**dia** *sf* orthopaedics *sg*; orto'**pedico, a, ci, che** *ag* orthopaedic ♦ *sm* orthopaedic specialist

orzai'**olo** [ordza'jɔlo] *sm* (*MED*) stye

or'**zata** [or'dzata] *sf* barley water

'**orzo** ['ordzo] *sm* barley

o'**sare** *vt, vi* to dare; **~ fare** to dare (to) do

oscenità [offeni'ta] *sf inv* obscenity

o'**sceno, a** [of'feno] *ag* obscene; (*ripugnante*) ghastly

oscil'**lare** [offil'lare] *vi* (*pendolo*) to swing; (*dondolare: al vento etc*) to rock; (*variare*) to fluctuate; (*TECN*) to oscillate; (*fig*): **~ fra** to waver *o* hesitate between; oscillazi'**one** *sf* oscillation; (*di prezzi, temperatura*) fluctuation

oscura'**mento** *sm* darkening; obscuring; (*in tempo di guerra*) blackout

oscu'**rare** *vt* to darken, obscure; (*fig*) to obscure; **~rsi** *vr* (*cielo*) to darken, cloud over; (*persona*): **si oscurò in volto** his face clouded over

os'**curo, a** *ag* dark; (*fig*) obscure; humble, lowly ♦ *sm*: **all'~** in the dark; **tenere qn all'~ di qc** to keep sb in the dark about sth

ospe'**dale** *sm* hospital; ospedali'**ero, a** *ag* hospital *cpd*

ospi'**tale** *ag* hospitable; ospitalità *sf* hospitality

ospi'**tare** *vt* to give hospitality to; (*sog: albergo*) to accommodate

'**ospite** *sm/f* (*persona che ospita*) host/hostess; (*persona ospitata*) guest

os'**pizio** [os'pittsjo] *sm* (*per vecchi etc*) home

'**ossa** *sfpl vedi* **osso**

ossa'**tura** *sf* (*ANAT*) skeletal structure, frame; (*TECN, fig*) framework

'**osseo, a** *ag* bony; (*tessuto etc*) bone *cpd*

os'**sequio** *sm* deference, respect; **~i** *smpl* (*saluto*) respects, regards; ossequi'**oso, a** *ag* obsequious

osser'**vanza** [osser'vantsa] *sf* observance

osser'**vare** *vt* to observe, watch; (*esaminare*) to examine; (*notare, rilevare*) to notice, observe; (DIR: la legge) to observe, respect; (mantenere: silenzio) to keep, observe; **far ~ qc a qn** to point sth out to sb; **osserva'tore, 'trice** ag observant, perceptive ♦ sm/f observer;

osserva'torio sm (ASTR) observatory; (MIL) observation post; **osservazi'one** sf observation; (di legge etc) observance; (considerazione critica) observation, remark; (rimprovero) reproof; **in osservazione** under observation

ossessio'nare vt to obsess, haunt; (tormentare) to torment, harass

ossessi'one sf obsession

os'sesso, a ag (spiritato) possessed

os'sia cong that is, to be precise

ossi'buchi [ossi'buki] smpl di **ossobuco**

ossi'dare vt to oxidize; **~rsi** vr to oxidize

'ossido sm oxide; **~ di carbonio** carbon monoxide

ossige'nare [ossidʒe'nare] vt to oxygenate; (decolorare) to bleach; **acqua ossigenata** hydrogen peroxide

os'sigeno sm oxygen

'osso (pl(f) **ossa** nel senso ANAT) sm bone; **d'~** (bottone etc) of bone, bone cpd

osso'buco (pl **ossi'buchi**) sm (CUC) marrowbone; (: piatto) stew made with knuckle of veal in tomato sauce

os'suto, a ag bony

ostaco'lare vt to block, obstruct

os'tacolo sm obstacle; (EQUITAZIONE) hurdle, jump

os'taggio [os'taddʒo] sm hostage

'oste, os'tessa sm/f innkeeper

osteggi'are [osted'dʒare] vt to oppose, be opposed to

os'tello sm: **~ della gioventù** youth hostel

osten'tare vt to make a show of, flaunt; **ostentazi'one** sf ostentation, show

oste'ria sf inn

os'tessa sf vedi **oste**

os'tetrica sf midwife; **os'tetrico, a, ci, che** ag obstetric ♦ sm obstetrician

'ostia sf (REL) host; (per medicinali) wafer

'ostico, a, ci, che ag (fig) harsh; hard, difficult; unpleasant

os'tile ag hostile; **ostilità** sf inv hostility ♦ sfpl (MIL) hostilities

osti'narsi vr to insist, dig one's heels in; **~ a fare** to persist (obstinately) in doing; **osti'nato, a** ag (caparbio) obstinate; (tenace) persistent, determined; **ostinazi'one** sf obstinacy; persistence

'ostrica, che sf oyster

ostru'ire vt to obstruct, block; **ostruzi'one** sf obstruction, blockage

'otre sm (recipiente) goatskin

ottago'nale ag octagonal

ot'tagono sm octagon

ot'tanta num eighty; **ottan'tesimo, a** num eightieth; **ottan'tina** sf: **una ottantina (di)** about eighty

ot'tava sf octave

ot'tavo, a num eighth

ottempe'rare vi: **~ a** to comply with, obey

otte'nere vt to obtain, get; (risultato) to achieve, obtain

'ottica sf (scienza) optics sg; (FOT: lenti, prismi etc) optics pl

'ottico, a, ci, che ag (della vista: nervo) optic; (dell'ottica) optical ♦ sm optician

ottima'mente av excellently, very well

otti'mismo sm optimism; **otti'mista, i, e** sm/f optimist

'ottimo, a ag excellent, very good

'otto num eight

ot'tobre sm October

otto'cento [otto'tʃɛnto] num eight hundred ♦ sm: **l'O~** the nineteenth century

ot'tone sm brass; **gli ~i** (MUS) the brass

ottu'rare vt to close (up); (dente) to fill; **ottura'tore** sm (FOT) shutter; (nelle armi) breechblock; **otturazi'one** sf closing (up); (dentaria) filling

ot'tuso, a ag (MAT, fig) obtuse; (suono) dull

o'vaia sf (ANAT) ovary

o'vale ag, sm oval

o'vatta sf cotton wool; (per imbottire) padding, wadding; **ovat'tare** vt (fig: smorzare) to muffle

ovazi'one [ovat'tsjone] sf ovation

over'dose ['ouvədəʊs] sf inv overdose

'ovest *sm* west

o'vile *sm* pen, enclosure

o'vino, a *ag* sheep *cpd*, ovine

ovulazi'one [ovulat'tsjone] *sf* ovulation

'ovulo *sm* (FISIOL) ovum

o'vunque *av* = **dovunque**

ov'vero *cong* (*ossia*) that is, to be precise; (*oppure*) or (else)

ovvi'are *vi*: ~ **a** to obviate

'ovvio, a *ag* obvious

ozi'are [ot'tsjare] *vi* to laze, idle

'ozio ['ɔttsjo] *sm* idleness; (*tempo libero*) leisure; **ore d'~** leisure time; **stare in ~** to be idle; **ozi'oso, a** *ag* idle

o'zono [o'dzɔno] *sm* ozone

P, p

P *abbr* (= *parcheggio*) P; (AUT: = *principiante*) L

pa'cato, a *ag* quiet, calm

'pacca *sf* pat

pac'chetto [pak'ketto] *sm* packet; ~ **azionario** (COMM) shareholding

pacchi'ano, a [pak'kjano] *ag* vulgar

'pacco, chi *sm* parcel; (*involto*) bundle

'pace ['patʃe] *sf* peace; **darsi ~** to resign o.s.; **fare la ~ con** to make it up with

pacifi'care [patʃifi'kare] *vt* (*riconciliare*) to reconcile, make peace between; (*mettere in pace*) to pacify

pa'cifico, a, ci, che [pa'tʃifiko] *ag* (*persona*) peaceable; (*vita*) peaceful; (*fig: indiscusso*) indisputable; (: *ovvio*) obvious, clear ♦ *sm*: **il P~, l'Oceano P~** the Pacific (Ocean)

paci'fista, i, e [patʃi'fista] *sm/f* pacifist

pa'della *sf* frying pan; (*per infermi*) bedpan

padigli'one [padiʎ'ʎone] *sm* pavilion

'Padova *sf* Padua

'padre *sm* father; ~**i** *smpl* (*antenati*) forefathers

pa'drino *sm* godfather

padro'nanza [padro'nantsa] *sf* command, mastery

pa'drone, a *sm/f* master/mistress;

(*proprietario*) owner; (*datore di lavoro*) employer; **essere ~ di sé** to be in control of o.s.; ~ **di casa** (*ospite*) host/hostess; (*per gli inquilini*) landlord/lady; **padroneggi'are** *vt* (*fig: sentimenti*) to master, control; (: *materia*) to master, know thoroughly; **padroneggiarsi** *vr* to control o.s.

pae'saggio [pae'zaddʒo] *sm* landscape

pae'sano, a *ag* country *cpd* ♦ *sm/f* villager; countryman/woman

pa'ese *sm* (*nazione*) country, nation; (*terra*) country, land; (*villaggio*) village; (*small*) town; ~ **di provenienza** country of origin; **i P~i Bassi** the Netherlands

paf'futo, a *ag* chubby, plump

'paga, ghe *sf* pay, wages *pl*

paga'mento *sm* payment

pa'gano, a *ag*, *sm/f* pagan

pa'gare *vt* to pay; (*acquisto, fig: colpa*) to pay for; (*contraccambiare*) to repay, pay back ♦ *vi* to pay; **quanto l'hai pagato?** how much did you pay for it?; ~ **con carta di credito** to pay by credit card; ~ **in contanti** to pay cash

pa'gella [pa'dʒɛlla] *sf* (INS) report card

'paggio ['paddʒo] *sm* page(boy)

pagherò [page'rɔ] *sm inv* acknowledgement of a debt, IOU

'pagina ['padʒina] *sf* page; ~**e gialle** Yellow Pages

'paglia ['paʎʎa] *sf* straw

pagliac'cetto [paʎʎat'tʃetto] *sm* (*per bambini*) rompers *pl*

pagli'accio [paʎ'ʎattʃo] *sm* clown

pagli'etta [paʎ'ʎetta] *sf* (*cappello per uomo*) (straw) boater; (*per tegami etc*) steel wool

pa'gnotta [pan'ɲɔtta] *sf* round loaf

'paio (*pl*(*f*) 'paia) *sm* pair; **un ~ di** (*alcuni*) a couple of

pai'olo *sm* (*copper*) pot

'pala *sf* shovel; (*di remo, ventilatore, elica*) blade; (*di ruota*) paddle

pa'lato *sm* palate

pa'lazzo [pa'lattso] *sm* (*reggia*) palace; (*edificio*) building; ~ **di giustizia** courthouse; ~ **dello sport** sports stadium

---

Rome has a number of palazzi, which are now associated with various government departments and political figures or groups. Palazzo Chigi, in Piazza Colonna, dates from the 16th century and has, since 1961, been the Prime Minister's office and the place where the cabinet meets. Palazzo Madama, also built in the 16th century, has been the seat of the Senate since 1871. Palazzo di Montecitorio, which was completed in 1694, has housed the Camera dei deputati since 1870. Palazzo Viminale, which takes its name from the hill in Rome on which it stands, is the home of the Ministry of the Interior.

'**palco, chi** *sm* (TEATRO) box; (*tavolato*) platform, stand; (*ripiano*) layer

palco'scenico, ci [palkoʃˈʃeniko] *sm* (TEATRO) stage

pale'sare *vt* to reveal, disclose; **~rsi** *vr* to reveal *o* show o.s.

pa'lese *ag* clear, evident

Pales'tina *sf*: **la ~** Palestine

pa'lestra *sf* gymnasium; (*esercizio atletico*) exercise; (*fig*) training ground, school

pa'letta *sf* spade; (*per il focolare*) shovel; (*del capostazione*) signalling disc

pa'letto *sm* stake, peg; (*spranga*) bolt

'**palio** *sm* (*gara*): **il P~** horse race run at Siena; **mettere qc in ~** to offer sth as a prize

---

The palio is a horse race which takes place in a number of Italian towns, the most famous being the one in Siena. This is usually held twice a year on 2 July and 16 August in the Piazza del Campo, Siena. 10 of the 17 contrade or districts take part, each represented by a horse and rider. The winner is the first horse to complete the course, whether it has a rider or not.

'**palla** *sf* ball; (*pallottola*) bullet; **~ canestro** *sm* basketball; **~ nuoto** *sm* water polo; **~ ovale** rugby ball; **~ volo** *sm* volleyball

palleggi'are [palledˈdʒare] *vi* (CALCIO) to practise with the ball; (TENNIS) to knock up

pallia'tivo *sm* palliative; (*fig*) stopgap measure

'**pallido, a** *ag* pale

pal'lina *sf* (*bilia*) marble

pallon'cino [pallonˈtʃino] *sm* balloon; (*lampioncino*) Chinese lantern

pal'lone *sm* (*palla*) ball; (CALCIO) football; (*aerostato*) balloon; **gioco del ~** football

pal'lore *sm* pallor, paleness

pal'lottola *sf* pellet; (*proiettile*) bullet

'**palma** *sf* (ANAT) = **palmo**; (BOT, *simbolo*) palm; **~ da datteri** date palm

'**palmo** *sm* (ANAT) palm; **restare con un ~ di naso** to be badly disappointed

'**palo** *sm* (*legno appuntito*) stake; (*sostegno*) pole; **fare da** *o* **il ~** (*fig*) to act as look-out

palom'baro *sm* diver

pa'lombo *sm* (*pesce*) dogfish

pal'pare *vt* to feel, finger

'**palpebra** *sf* eyelid

palpi'tare *vi* (*cuore, polso*) to beat; (: *più forte*) to pound, throb; (*fremere*) to quiver; '**palpito** *sm* (*del cuore*) beat; (*fig: d'amore etc*) throb

paltò *sm inv* overcoat

pa'lude *sf* marsh, swamp; **palu'doso, a** *ag* marshy, swampy

pa'lustre *ag* marsh *cpd*, swamp *cpd*

'**pampino** *sm* vine leaf

'**panca, che** *sf* bench

pancarrè *sm* sliced square bread

pan'cetta [panˈtʃetta] *sf* (CUC) bacon

pan'chetto [panˈketto] *sm* stool; footstool

pan'china [panˈkina] *sf* garden seat; (*di giardino pubblico*) (park) bench

'**pancia, ce** [ˈpantʃa] *sf* belly, stomach; **mettere** *o* **fare ~** to be getting a paunch; **avere mal di ~** to have stomachache *o* a sore stomach

panci'otto [panˈtʃɔtto] *sm* waistcoat

'pancreas *sm inv* pancreas
'panda *sm inv* panda
pande'monio *sm* pandemonium
'pane *sm* bread; (*pagnotta*) loaf (of bread); (*forma*): **un ~ di burro** a pat of butter; **guadagnarsi il ~** to earn one's living; **~ a cassetta** sliced bread; **~ di Spagna** sponge cake; **~ integrale** wholemeal bread; **~ tostato** toast
panette'ria *sf* (*forno*) bakery; (*negozio*) baker's (shop), bakery
panetti'ere, a *sm/f* baker
panet'tone *sm* a kind of spiced brioche with sultanas, eaten at Christmas
'panfilo *sm* yacht
pangrat'tato *sm* breadcrumbs *pl*
'panico, a, ci, che *ag, sm* panic
pani'ere *sm* basket
pani'ficio [pani'fitʃo] *sm* (*forno*) bakery; (*negozio*) baker's (shop), bakery
pa'nino *sm* roll; **~ caldo** toasted sandwich; **~ imbottito** filled roll; sandwich; **panino'teca** *sf* sandwich bar
'panna *sf* (*CUC*) cream; (*TECN*) = **panne**; **~ da cucina** cooking cream; **~ montata** whipped cream
'panne *sf inv*: **essere in ~** (*AUT*) to have broken down
pan'nello *sm* panel; **~ solare** solar panel
'panno *sm* cloth; **~i** *smpl* (*abiti*) clothes; **mettiti nei miei ~i** (*fig*) put yourself in my shoes
pan'nocchia [pan'nɔkkja] *sf* (*di mais etc*) ear
panno'lino *sm* (*per bambini*) nappy (*BRIT*), diaper (*US*)
pano'rama, i *sm* panorama; pano'ramico, a, ci, che *ag* panoramic; **strada panoramica** scenic route
panta'loni *smpl* trousers (*BRIT*), pants (*US*), pair *sg* of trousers *o* pants
pan'tano *sm* bog
pan'tera *sf* panther
pan'tofola *sf* slipper
panto'mima *sf* pantomime
pan'zana [pan'tsana] *sf* fib, tall story
pao'nazzo, a [pao'nattso] *ag* purple

'papa, i *sm* pope
papà *sm inv* dad(dy)
pa'pale *ag* papal
pa'pato *sm* papacy
pa'pavero *sm* poppy
'papera *sf* (*fig*) slip of the tongue, blunder; *vedi anche* **papero**
'papero, a *sm/f* (*ZOOL*) gosling
pa'piro *sm* papyrus
'pappa *sf* baby cereal
pappa'gallo *sm* parrot; (*fig: uomo*) Romeo, wolf
pappa'gorgia, ge [pappa'gordʒa] *sf* double chin
pap'pare *vt* (*fam: anche*: **~rsi**) to gobble up
'para *sf*: **suole di ~** crepe soles
pa'rabola *sf* (*MAT*) parabola; (*REL*) parable
para'brezza [para'breddza] *sm inv* (*AUT*) windscreen (*BRIT*), windshield (*US*)
paraca'dute *sm inv* parachute
para'carro *sm* kerbstone (*BRIT*), curbstone (*US*)
para'diso *sm* paradise
parados'sale *ag* paradoxical
para'dosso *sm* paradox
para'fango, ghi *sm* mudguard
paraf'fina *sf* paraffin, paraffin wax
para'fulmine *sm* lightning conductor
pa'raggi [pa'raddʒi] *smpl*: **nei ~** in the vicinity, in the neighbourhood
parago'nare *vt*: **~ con/a** to compare with/to
para'gone *sm* comparison; (*esempio analogo*) analogy, parallel; **reggere al ~** to stand comparison
pa'ragrafo *sm* paragraph
pa'ralisi *sf* paralysis; para'litico, a, ci, che *ag, sm/f* paralytic
paraliz'zare [paralid'dzare] *vt* to paralyze
paral'lela *sf* parallel (line); **~e** *sfpl* (*attrezzo ginnico*) parallel bars
paral'lelo, a *ag* parallel ♦ *sm* (*GEO*) parallel; (*comparazione*): **fare un ~ tra** to draw a parallel between
para'lume *sm* lampshade
pa'rametro *sm* parameter

para'noia *sf* paranoia; para'noico, a, ci, che *ag*, *sm/f* paranoid
para'occhi [para'ɔkki] *smpl* blinkers
para'petto *sm* balustrade
para'piglia [para'piʎʎa] *sm* commotion, uproar
pa'rare *vt* (*addobbare*) to adorn, deck; (*proteggere*) to shield, protect; (*scansare: colpo*) to parry; (*CALCIO*) to save ♦ *vi*: **dove vuole andare a ~?** what are you driving at?; **~rsi** *vr* (*presentarsi*) to appear, present o.s.
para'sole *sm inv* parasol, sunshade
paras'sita, i *sm* parasite
pa'rata *sf* (*SPORT*) save; (*MIL*) review, parade
para'tia *sf* (*di nave*) bulkhead
para'urti *sm inv* (*AUT*) bumper
para'vento *sm* folding screen; **fare da ~ a qn** (*fig*) to shield sb
par'cella [par'tʃella] *sf* account, fee (*of lawyer etc*)
parcheggi'are [parked'dʒare] *vt* to park; par'cheggio *sm* parking *no pl*; (*luogo*) car park; (*singolo posto*) parking space
par'chimetro [par'kimetro] *sm* parking meter
'parco[1], chi *sm* park; (*spazio per deposito*) depot; (*complesso di veicoli*) fleet
'parco[2], a, chi, che *ag*: ~ **(in)** (*sobrio*) moderate (in); (*avaro*) sparing (with)
pa'recchio, a [pa'rekkjo] *det* quite a lot of; (*tempo*) quite a lot of, a long; **~i, e** *det pl* quite a lot of, several ♦ *pron* quite a lot, quite a bit; (*tempo*) quite a while, a long time; **~i, e** *pron pl* quite a lot, several ♦ *av* (*con ag*) quite, rather; (*con vb*) quite a lot, quite a bit
pareggi'are [pared'dʒare] *vt* to make equal; (*terreno*) to level, make level; (*bilancio, conti*) to balance ♦ *vi* (*SPORT*) to draw; pa'reggio *sm* (*ECON*) balance; (*SPORT*) draw
pa'rente *sm/f* relative, relation
paren'tela *sf* (*vincolo di sangue, fig*) relationship
pa'rentesi *sf* (*segno grafico*) bracket, parenthesis; (*frase incisa*) parenthesis; (*digressione*) parenthesis, digression
pa'rere *sm* (*opinione*) opinion; (*consiglio*) advice, opinion; **a mio ~** in my opinion ♦ *vi* to seem, appear ♦ *vb impers*: **pare che** it seems *o* appears that, they say that; **mi pare che** it seems to me that; **mi pare di sì** I think so; **fai come ti pare** do as you like; **che ti pare del mio libro?** what do you think of my book?
pa'rete *sf* wall
'pari *ag inv* (*uguale*) equal, same; (*in giochi*) equal; drawn, tied; (*MAT*) even ♦ *sm inv* (*POL: di Gran Bretagna*) ≈ peer ♦ *sm/f inv* peer, equal; **copiato ~** copied word for word; **alla ~** on the same level; **ragazza alla ~** au pair girl; **mettersi alla ~ con** to place o.s. on the same level as; **mettersi in ~ con** to catch up with; **andare di ~ passo con qn** to keep pace with sb
Pa'rigi [pa'ridʒi] *sf* Paris
pa'riglia [pa'riʎʎa] *sf* pair; **rendere la ~** to give tit for tat
parità *sf* parity, equality; (*SPORT*) draw, tie
parlamen'tare *ag* parliamentary ♦ *sm/f* ≈ Member of Parliament (*BRIT*), ≈ Congressman/woman (*US*) ♦ *vi* to negotiate, parley
parla'mento *sm* parliament
parlan'tina (*fam*) *sf* talkativeness; **avere ~** to have the gift of the gab
par'lare *vi* to speak, talk; (*confidare cose segrete*) to talk ♦ *vt* to speak; **~ (a qn) di** to speak *o* talk (to sb) about; parla'torio *sm* (*di carcere etc*) visiting room; (*REL*) parlour
parmigi'ano [parmi'dʒano] *sm* (*grana*) Parmesan (cheese)
paro'dia *sf* parody
pa'rola *sf* word; (*facoltà*) speech; **~e** *sfpl* (*chiacchiere*) talk *sg*; **chiedere la ~** to ask permission to speak; **prendere la ~** to take the floor; **~ d'onore** word of honour; **~ d'ordine** (*MIL*) password; **~e incrociate** crossword (puzzle) *sg*; paro'laccia, ce *sf* bad word, swearword
par'rocchia [par'rɔkkja] *sf* parish; parish church
'parroco, ci *sm* parish priest

par'rucca, che *sf* wig
parrucchi'ere, a [parruk'kjɛre] *sm/f* hairdresser ♦ *sm* barber
parsi'monia *sf* frugality, thrift
'parso, a *pp di* **parere**
'parte *sf* part; (*lato*) side; (*quota spettante a ciascuno*) share; (*direzione*) direction; (*POL*) party; faction; (*DIR*) party; **a ~** *ag* separate ♦ *av* separately; **scherzi a ~** joking aside; **a ~ ciò** apart from that; **da ~** (*in disparte*) to one side, aside; **d'altra ~** on the other hand; **da ~ di** (*per conto di*) on behalf of; **da ~ mia** as far as I'm concerned, as for me; **da ~ a ~** right through; **da ogni ~** on all sides, everywhere; (*moto da luogo*) from all sides; **da nessuna ~** nowhere; **da questa ~** (*in questa direzione*) this way; **prendere ~ a qc** to take part in sth; **mettere da ~** to put aside; **mettere qn a ~ di** to inform sb of
parteci'pare [partetʃi'pare] *vi*: **~ a** to take part in, participate in; (*utili etc*) to share in; (*spese etc*) to contribute to; (*dolore, successo di qn*) to share (in); **partecipazi'one** *sf* participation; sharing; (*ECON*) interest; **partecipazione agli utili** profit-sharing; **partecipazioni di nozze** *wedding announcement card*; **par'tecipe** *ag* participating; **essere partecipe di** to take part in, participate in; to share (in); (*consapevole*) to be aware of
parteggi'are [parted'dʒare] *vi*: **~ per** to side with, be on the side of
par'tenza [par'tɛntsa] *sf* departure; (*SPORT*) start; **essere in ~** to be about to leave, be leaving
parti'cella [parti'tʃɛlla] *sf* particle
parti'cipio [parti'tʃipjo] *sm* participle
partico'lare *ag* (*specifico*) particular; (*proprio*) personal, private; (*speciale*) special, particular; (*caratteristico*) distinctive, characteristic; (*fuori dal comune*) peculiar ♦ *sm* detail, particular; **in ~** in particular, particularly; **particolarità** *sf inv* particularity; detail; characteristic, feature
partigi'ano, a [parti'dʒano] *ag* partisan ♦ *sm* (*MIL*) partisan

par'tire *vi* to go, leave; (*allontanarsi*) to go (*o drive etc*) away *o* off; (*petardo, colpo*) to go off; (*fig: avere inizio, SPORT*) to start; **sono partita da Roma alle 7** I left Rome at 7; **il volo parte da Ciampino** the flight leaves from Ciampino; **a ~ da** from
par'tita *sf* (*COMM*) lot, consignment; (*ECON: registrazione*) entry, item; (*CARTE, SPORT: gioco*) game; (*: competizione*) match, game; **~ di caccia** hunting party; **~ IVA** VAT registration number
par'tito *sm* (*POL*) party; (*decisione*) decision, resolution; (*persona da maritare*) match
parti'tura *sf* (*MUS*) score
'parto *sm* (*MED*) delivery, (child)birth; labour; **parto'rire** *vt* to give birth to; (*fig*) to produce
parzi'ale [par'tsjale] *ag* (*limitato*) partial; (*non obiettivo*) biased, partial
'pascere ['paʃʃere] *vt* (*brucare*) to graze on; (*far pascolare*) to graze, pasture; **pasci'uto, a** *pp di* **pascere**
pasco'lare *vt, vi* to graze
'pascolo *sm* pasture
'Pasqua *sf* Easter; **pas'quale** *ag* Easter *cpd*; **Pas'quetta** *sf* Easter Monday
pas'sabile *ag* fairly good, passable
pas'saggio [pas'saddʒo] *sm* passing *no pl*, passage; (*traversata*) crossing *no pl*, passage; (*luogo, prezzo della traversata, brano di libro etc*) passage; (*su veicolo altrui*) lift (*BRIT*), ride; (*SPORT*) pass; (*persona*) passing through; **~ pedonale/a livello** pedestrian/level (*BRIT*) *o* grade (*US*) crossing
passamon'tagna [passamon'taɲɲa] *sm inv* balaclava
pas'sante *sm/f* passer-by ♦ *sm* loop
passa'porto *sm* passport
pas'sare *vi* (*andare*) to go; (*veicolo, pedone*) to pass (by), go by; (*fare una breve sosta: postino etc*) to come, call; (*: amico: per fare una visita*) to call *o* drop in; (*sole, aria, luce*) to get through; (*trascorrere: giorni, tempo*) to pass, go by; (*fig: proposta di legge*) to be passed; (*: dolore*) to pass, go away; (*CARTE*) to pass ♦ *vt* (*attraversare*) to cross; (*trasmettere: messaggio*): **~ qc a qn**

to pass sth on to sb; (*dare*): **~ qc a qn** to pass sth to sb, give sb sth; (*trascorrere: tempo*) to spend; (*superare: esame*) to pass; (*triturare: verdura*) to strain; (*approvare*) to pass, approve; (*oltrepassare, sorpassare: anche fig*) to go beyond, pass; (*fig: subire*) to go through; **~ da ... a** to pass from ... to; **~ di padre in figlio** to be handed down *o* to pass from father to son; **~ per** (*anche fig*) to go through; **~ per stupido/un genio** to be taken for a fool/a genius; **~ sopra** (*anche fig*) to pass over; **~ attraverso** (*anche fig*) to go through; **~ alla storia** to pass into history; **~ a un esame** to go up (to the next class) after an exam; **~ inosservato** to go unnoticed; **~ di moda** to go out of fashion; **le passo il Signor X** (*al telefono*) here is Mr X; I'm putting you through to Mr X; **lasciar ~ qn/qc** to let sb/sth through; **come te la passi?** how are you getting on *o* along?

pas'sata *sf*: **dare una ~ di vernice a qc** to give sth a coat of paint; **dare una ~ al giornale** to have a look at the paper, skim through the paper

passa'tempo *sm* pastime, hobby

pas'sato, a *ag* past; (*sfiorito*) faded ♦ *sm* past; (*LING*) past (tense); **~ prossimo** (*LING*) present perfect; **~ remoto** (*LING*) past historic; **~ di verdura** (*CUC*) vegetable purée

passaver'dura *sm inv* vegetable mill

passeg'gero, a [passed'dʒero] *ag* passing ♦ *sm/f* passenger

passeggi'are [passed'dʒare] *vi* to go for a walk; (*in veicolo*) to go for a drive; **passeggi'ata** *sf* walk; drive; (*luogo*) promenade; **fare una passeggiata** to go for a walk (*o* drive); **passeg'gino** *sm* pushchair (*BRIT*), stroller (*US*); **pas'seggio** *sm* walk, stroll; (*luogo*) promenade

passe'rella *sf* footbridge; (*di nave, aereo*) gangway; (*pedana*) catwalk

'passero *sm* sparrow

pas'sibile *ag*: **~ di** liable to

passi'one *sf* passion

pas'sivo, a *ag* passive ♦ *sm* (*LING*) passive;

(*ECON*) debit; (: *complesso dei debiti*) liabilities *pl*

'passo *sm* step; (*andatura*) pace; (*rumore*) (foot)step; (*orma*) footprint; (*passaggio, fig: brano*) passage; (*valico*) pass; **a ~ d'uomo** at walking pace; **~ (a) ~** step by step; **fare due *o* quattro ~i** to go for a walk *o* a stroll; **di questo ~** at this rate; **"~ carraio"** "vehicle entrance — keep clear"

'pasta *sf* (*CUC*) dough; (: *impasto per dolce*) pastry; (: *anche*: **~ alimentare**) pasta; (*massa molle di materia*) paste; (*fig: indole*) nature; **~e** *sfpl* (*pasticcini*) pastries; **~ in brodo** noodle soup

pastasci'utta [pastaʃʃutta] *sf* pasta

pas'tella *sf* batter

pas'tello *sm* pastel

pas'ticca, che *sf* = pastiglia

pasticce'ria [pastittʃe'ria] *sf* (*pasticcini*) pastries *pl*, cakes *pl*; (*negozio*) cake shop; (*arte*) confectionery

pasticci'are [pastit'tʃare] *vt* to mess up, make a mess of ♦ *vi* to make a mess

pasticci'ere, a [pastit'tʃere] *sm/f* pastrycook; confectioner

pas'ticcio [pas'tittʃo] *sm* (*CUC*) pie; (*lavoro disordinato, imbroglio*) mess; **trovarsi nei ~i** to get into trouble

pasti'ficio [pasti'fitʃo] *sm* pasta factory

pas'tiglia [pas'tiʎʎa] *sf* pastille, lozenge

pas'tina *sf* small pasta shapes used in soup

'pasto *sm* meal

pas'tore *sm* shepherd; (*REL*) pastor, minister; (*anche*: **cane ~**) sheepdog; **~ tedesco** (*ZOOL*) Alsatian, German shepherd

pastoriz'zare [pastorid'dzare] *vt* to pasteurize

pas'toso, a *ag* doughy; pasty; (*fig: voce, colore*) mellow, soft

pas'trano *sm* greatcoat

pa'tata *sf* potato; **~e fritte** chips (*BRIT*), French fries; **pata'tine** *sfpl* (*potato*) crisps; **~ fritte** chips

pata'trac *sm* (*crollo: anche fig*) crash

paté *sm inv* pâté

pa'tella *sf* (*ZOOL*) limpet

pa'tema, i *sm* anxiety, worry
pa'tente *sf* licence; (*anche:* ~ **di guida**)
driving licence (*BRIT*), driver's license (*US*)
paternità *sf* paternity, fatherhood
pa'terno, a *ag* (*affetto, consigli*) fatherly;
(*casa, autorità*) paternal
pa'tetico, a, ci, che *ag* pathetic;
(*commovente*) moving, touching
pa'tibolo *sm* gallows *sg*, scaffold
'patina *sf* (*su rame etc*) patina; (*sulla lingua*)
fur, coating
pa'tire *vt, vi* to suffer
pa'tito, a *sm/f* enthusiast, fan, lover
patolo'gia [patolo'dʒia] *sf* pathology;
pato'logico, a, ci, che *ag* pathological
'patria *sf* homeland
patri'arca, chi *sm* patriarch
pa'trigno [pa'triɲɲo] *sm* stepfather
patri'monio *sm* estate, property; (*fig*)
heritage
patri'ota, i, e *sm/f* patriot; **patri'ottico,
a, ci, che** *ag* patriotic; **patriot'tismo** *sm*
patriotism
patroci'nare [patrotʃi'nare] *vt* (*DIR:
difendere*) to defend; (*sostenere*) to sponsor,
support; **patro'cinio** *sm* defence,
support, sponsorship
patro'nato *sm* patronage; (*istituzione
benefica*) charitable institution *o* society
pa'trono *sm* (*REL*) patron saint; (*socio di
patronato*) patron; (*DIR*) counsel
'patta *sf* flap; (*dei pantaloni*) fly
patteggia'mento [patteddʒa'mento] *sm*
(*DIR*) plea bargaining
patteggi'are [patted'dʒare] *vt, vi* to
negotiate; (*DIR*) to plea-bargain
patti'naggio [patti'naddʒo] *sm* skating
patti'nare *vi* to skate; ~ **sul ghiaccio** to
ice-skate; **pattina'tore, 'trice** *sm/f*
skater; **'pattino¹** *sm* skate; (*di slitta*)
runner; (*AER*) skid; (*TECN*) sliding block;
pattini (da ghiaccio) (ice) skates; **pattini a
rotelle** roller skates; **pat'tino²** *sm* (*barca*)
kind of pedalo with oars
'patto *sm* (*accordo*) pact, agreement;
(*condizione*) term, condition; **a ~ che** on
condition that

pat'tuglia [pat'tuʎʎa] *sf* (*MIL*) patrol
pattu'ire *vt* to reach an agreement on
pattumi'era *sf* (dust)bin (*BRIT*), ashcan (*US*)
pa'ura *sf* fear; **aver ~ di/di fare/che** to be
frightened *o* afraid of/of doing/that; **far ~ a**
to frighten; **per ~ di/che** for fear of/that;
pau'roso, a *ag* (*che fa paura*) frightening;
(*che ha paura*) fearful, timorous
'pausa *sf* (*sosta*) break; (*nel parlare, MUS*)
pause
pavi'mento *sm* floor
pa'vone *sm* peacock; **pavoneggi'arsi** *vr*
to strut about, show off
pazien'tare [pattsjen'tare] *vi* to be patient
pazi'ente [pat'tsjɛnte] *ag, sm/f* patient;
pazi'enza *sf* patience
paz'zesco, a, schi, sche [pat'tsesko] *ag*
mad, crazy
paz'zia [pat'tsia] *sf* (*MED*) madness, insanity;
(*azione*) folly; (*di azione, decisione*)
madness, folly
'pazzo, a ['pattso] *ag* (*MED*) mad, insane;
(*strano*) wild, mad ♦ *sm/f* madman/
woman; **~ di** (*gioia, amore etc*) crazy
with; **~ per qc/qn** mad *o* crazy about sth/
sb
PCI *sigla m* = **Partito Comunista Italiano**
'pecca, che *sf* defect, flaw, fault
peccami'noso, a *ag* sinful
pec'care *vi* to sin; (*fig*) to err
pec'cato *sm* sin; **è un ~ che** it's a pity
that; **che ~!** what a shame *o* pity!
pecca'tore, 'trice *sm/f* sinner
'pece ['petʃe] *sf* pitch
Pe'chino [pe'kino] *sf* Beijing
'pecora *sf* sheep; **peco'raio** *sm* shepherd;
peco'rino *sm* sheep's milk cheese
peculi'are *ag*: ~ **di** peculiar to
pe'daggio [pe'daddʒo] *sm* toll
pedago'gia [pedago'dʒia] *sf* pedagogy,
educational methods *pl*
peda'lare *vi* to pedal; (*andare in bicicletta*)
to cycle
pe'dale *sm* pedal
pe'dana *sf* footboard; (*SPORT: nel salto*)
springboard; (*: nella scherma*) piste
pe'dante *ag* pedantic ♦ *sm/f* pedant

pe'data sf (impronta) footprint; (colpo) kick;
prendere a ~e qn/qc to kick sb/sth
pede'rasta, i sm pederast; homosexual
pedi'atra, i, e sm/f paediatrician;
pedia'tria sf paediatrics sg
pedi'cure sm/f inv chiropodist
pe'dina sf (della dama) draughtsman (BRIT),
draftsman (US); (fig) pawn
pedi'nare vt to shadow, tail
pedo'nale ag pedestrian
pe'done, a sm/f pedestrian ♦ sm (SCACCHI)
pawn
'peggio ['pɛddʒo] av, ag inv worse
♦ sm o f: **il o la ~** the worst; **alla ~** at
worst, if the worst comes to the worst;
peggiora'mento sm worsening; peggio'rare vt to make worse, worsen ♦ vi
to grow worse, worsen; peggiora-
ra'tivo, a ag pejorative; peggi'ore ag
(comparativo) worse; (superlativo)
worst ♦ sm/f: **il(la) peggiore** the worst
(person)
'pegno ['pɛɲɲo] sm (DIR) security, pledge;
(nei giochi di società) forfeit; (fig) pledge,
token; **dare in ~ qc** to pawn sth
pe'lare vt (spennare) to pluck; (spellare) to
skin; (sbucciare) to peel; (fig) to make pay
through the nose; **~rsi** vr to go bald
pe'lato, a ag: **pomodori ~i** tinned
tomatoes
pel'lame sm skins pl, hides pl
'pelle sf skin; (di animale) skin, hide; (cuoio)
leather; **avere la ~ d'oca** to have goose
pimples o goose flesh
pellegri'naggio [pellegri'naddʒo] sm
pilgrimage
pelle'grino, a sm/f pilgrim
pelle'rossa (pl pelli'rosse) sm/f Red
Indian
pellette'ria sf leather goods pl; (negozio)
leather goods shop
pelli'cano sm pelican
pellicce'ria [pellittʃe'ria] sf (negozio)
furrier's (shop)
pel'liccia, ce [pel'littʃa] sf (mantello di
animale) coat, fur; (indumento) fur coat
pel'licola sf (membrana sottile) film, layer;
(FOT, CINEMA) film

'pelo sm hair; (pelame) coat, hair; (pelliccia)
fur; (di tappeto) pile; (di liquido) surface;
**per un ~: per un ~ non ho perduto il
treno** I very nearly missed the train; **c'è
mancato un ~ che affogasse** he escaped
drowning by the skin of his teeth;
pe'loso, a ag hairy
'peltro sm pewter
pe'luria sf down
'pena sf (DIR) sentence; (punizione)
punishment; (sofferenza) sadness no pl,
sorrow; (fatica) trouble no pl, effort;
(difficoltà) difficulty; **far ~** to be pitiful; **mi
fai ~** I feel sorry for you; **prendersi o darsi
la ~ di fare** to go to the trouble of doing;
~ di morte death sentence; **~ pecuniaria**
fine; pe'nale ag penal; penalità sf inv
penalty; penaliz'zare vt (SPORT) to
penalize
pe'nare vi (patire) to suffer; (faticare) to
struggle
pen'dente ag hanging; leaning ♦ sm
(ciondolo) pendant; (orecchino) drop
earring; pen'denza sf slope, slant; (grado
d'inclinazione) gradient; (ECON) outstanding
account
'pendere vi (essere appeso): **~ da** to hang
from; (essere inclinato) to lean; (fig:
incombere): **~ su** to hang over
pen'dice [pen'ditʃe] sf: **alle ~i del monte** at
the foot of the mountain
pen'dio, 'dii sm slope, slant; (luogo in
pendenza) slope
'pendola sf pendulum clock
pendo'lare sm/f commuter
pendo'lino sm high-speed train
'pendolo sm (peso) pendulum; (anche:
orologio a ~) pendulum clock
'pene sm penis
pene'trante ag piercing, penetrating
pene'trare vi to come o get in ♦ vt to
penetrate; **~ in** to enter; (sog: proiettile) to
penetrate; (: acqua, aria) to go o come into
penicil'lina [penitʃil'lina] sf penicillin
pe'nisola sf peninsula
peni'tenza [peni'tɛntsa] sf penitence;

(*punizione*) penance
penitenzi'ario [peniten'tsjarjo] *sm* prison
'**penna** *sf* (*di uccello*) feather; (*per scrivere*)
pen; **~e** *sfpl* (*CUC*) quills (*type of pasta*); **~
stilografica/a sfera** fountain/ballpoint pen
penna'rello *sm* felt(-tip) pen
pennel'lare *vi* to paint
pen'nello *sm* brush; (*per dipingere*)
(paint)brush; **a ~** (*perfettamente*) to
perfection, perfectly; **~ per la barba**
shaving brush
pen'nino *sm* nib
pen'none *sm* (*NAUT*) yard; (*stendardo*)
banner, standard
pe'nombra *sf* half-light, dim light
pe'noso, a *ag* painful, distressing;
(*faticoso*) tiring, laborious
pen'sare *vi* to think ♦ *vt* to think;
(*inventare, escogitare*) to think out; **~ a** to
think of; (*amico, vacanze*) to think of *o*
about; (*problema*) to think about; **~ di fare
qc** to think of doing sth; **ci penso io** I'll
see to *o* take care of it
pensi'ero *sm* thought; (*modo di pensare,
dottrina*) thinking *no pl*; (*preoccupazione*)
worry, care, trouble; **stare in ~ per qn** to
be worried about sb; **pensie'roso, a** *ag*
thoughtful
'**pensile** *ag* hanging
pensi'lina *sf* (*per autobus*) bus shelter
pensio'nante *sm/f* (*presso una famiglia*)
lodger; (*di albergo*) guest
pensio'nato, a *sm/f* pensioner
pensi'one *sf* (*al prestatore di lavoro*)
pension; (*vitto e alloggio*) board and
lodging; (*albergo*) boarding house; **andare
in ~** to retire; **mezza ~** half board; **~
completa** full board
pen'soso, a *ag* thoughtful, pensive, lost in
thought
pentapar'tito *sm* five-party government
Pente'coste *sf* Pentecost, Whit Sunday
(*BRIT*)
penti'mento *sm* repentance, contrition
pen'tirsi *vr*: **~ di** to repent of;
(*rammaricarsi*) to regret, be sorry for
'**pentola** *sf* pot; **~ a pressione** pressure

cooker
pe'nultimo, a *ag* last but one (*BRIT*), next
to last, penultimate
pe'nuria *sf* shortage
penzo'lare [pendzo'lare] *vi* to dangle, hang
loosely; **penzo'loni** *av* dangling, hanging
down; **stare penzoloni** to dangle, hang
down
'**pepe** *sm* pepper; **~ macinato/in grani**
ground/whole pepper
pepero'nata *sf* (*CUC*) stewed peppers,
tomatoes and onions
pepe'rone *sm* pepper, capsicum;
(*piccante*) chili
pe'pita *sf* nugget

PAROLA CHIAVE
---

per *prep* **1** (*moto attraverso luogo*) through; **i
ladri sono passati ~ la finestra** the
thieves got in (*o* out) through the window;
l'ho cercato ~ tutta la casa I've searched
the whole house *o* all over the house for it
2 (*moto a luogo*) for, to; **partire ~ la
Germania/il mare** to leave for Germany/
the sea; **il treno ~ Roma** the Rome train,
the train for *o* to Rome
3 (*stato in luogo*): **seduto/sdraiato ~ terra**
sitting/lying on the ground
4 (*tempo*) for; **~ anni/lungo tempo** for
years/a long time; **~ tutta l'estate**
throughout the summer, all summer long;
lo rividi ~ Natale I saw him again at
Christmas; **lo faccio ~ lunedì** I'll do it for
Monday
5 (*mezzo, maniera*) by; **~ lettera/via
aerea/ferrovia** by letter/airmail/rail;
prendere qn ~ un braccio to take sb by
the arm
6 (*causa, scopo*) for; **assente ~ malattia**
absent because of *o* through *o* owing to
illness; **ottimo ~ il mal di gola** excellent for
sore throats
7 (*limitazione*) for; **è troppo difficile ~ lui**
it's too difficult for him; **~ quel che mi
riguarda** as far as I'm concerned; **~ poco
che sia** however little it may be; **~ questa
volta ti perdono** I'll forgive you this time

8 (*prezzo, misura*) for; (*distributivo*) a, per; **venduto ~ 3 milioni** sold for 3 million; **1000 lire ~ persona** 1000 lire *o* per person; **uno ~ volta** one at a time; **uno ~ uno** one by one; **5 ~ cento** 5 per cent; **3 ~ 4 fa 12** 3 times 4 equals 12; **dividere/ moltiplicare 12 ~ 4** to divide/multiply 12 by 4

9 (*in qualità di*) as; (*al posto di*) for; **avere qn ~ professore** to have sb as a teacher; **ti ho preso ~ Mario** I mistook you for Mario, I thought you were Mario; **dare ~ morto qn** to give sb up for dead

10 (*seguito da vb: finale*): **~ fare qc** (so as) to do sth, in order to do sth; (: *causale*): **~ aver fatto qc** for having done sth; (: *consecutivo*): **è abbastanza grande ~ andarci da solo** he's big enough to go on his own

'**pera** *sf* pear
pe'**raltro** *av* moreover, what's more
per'**bene** *ag inv* respectable, decent ♦ *av* (*con cura*) properly, well
percentu'**ale** [pert∫entu'ale] *sf* percentage
perce'**pire** [pert∫e'pire] *vt* (*sentire*) to perceive; (*ricevere*) to receive; **percezi'one** *sf* perception

---

PAROLA CHIAVE

perché [per'ke] *av* why why; **~ no?** why not?; **~ non vuoi andarci?** why don't you want to go?; **spiegami ~ l'hai fatto** tell me why you did it

♦ *cong* 1 (*causale*) because; **non posso uscire ~ ho da fare** I can't go out because *o* as I've a lot to do

2 (*finale*) in order that, so that; **te lo do ~ tu lo legga** I'm giving it to you so (that) you can read it

3 (*consecutivo*): **è troppo forte ~ si possa batterlo** he's too strong to be beaten

♦ *sm inv* reason; **il ~ di** the reason for

---

perciò [per't∫ɔ] *cong* so, for this (*o* that) reason
per'**correre** *vt* (*luogo*) to go all over;

(: *paese*) to travel up and down, go all over; (*distanza*) to cover
per'**corso, a** *pp di* **percorrere** ♦ *sm* (*tragitto*) journey; (*tratto*) route
per'**cossa** *sf* blow
per'**cosso, a** *pp di* **percuotere**
percu'**otere** *vt* to hit, strike
percussi'**one** *sf* percussion; **strumenti a ~** (*MUS*) percussion instruments
'**perdere** *vt* to lose; (*lasciarsi sfuggire*) to miss; (*sprecare: tempo, denaro*) to waste ♦ *vi* to lose; (*serbatoio etc*) to leak; **~rsi** *vr* (*smarrirsi*) to get lost; (*svanire*) to disappear, vanish; **saper ~** to be a good loser; **lascia ~!** forget it!, never mind!
perdigi'**orno** [perdi'dʒorno] *sm/f inv* idler, waster
'**perdita** *sf* loss; (*spreco*) waste; (*fuoriuscita*) leak; **siamo in ~** (*COMM*) we are running at a loss; **a ~ d'occhio** as far as the eye can see
perdo'**nare** *vt* to pardon, forgive; (*scusare*) to excuse, pardon
per'**dono** *sm* forgiveness; (*DIR*) pardon
perdu'**rare** *vi* to go on, last
perduta'**mente** *av* desperately, passionately
per'**duto, a** *pp di* **perdere**
peregri'**nare** *vi* to wander, roam
pe'**renne** *ag* eternal, perpetual, perennial; (*BOT*) perennial
peren'**torio, a** *ag* peremptory; (*definitivo*) final
per'**fetto, a** *ag* perfect ♦ *sm* (*LING*) perfect (tense)
perfezio'**nare** [perfettsjo'nare] *vt* to improve, perfect; **~rsi** *vr* to improve
perfezi'**one** [perfet'tsjone] *sf* perfection
'**perfido, a** *ag* perfidious, treacherous
per'**fino** *av* even
perfo'**rare** *vt* to perforate; to punch a hole (*o* holes) in; (*banda, schede*) to punch; (*trivellare*) to drill; **perfora'trice** *sf* (*TECN*) boring *o* drilling machine; (*INFORM*) card punch; **perforazi'one** *sf* perforation; punching; drilling; (*INFORM*) punch; (*MED*) perforation

perga'mena *sf* parchment

'pergola *sf (per rampicanti)* pergola

perico'lante *ag* precarious

pe'ricolo *sm* danger; **mettere in** ~ to endanger, put in danger; **perico'loso, a** *ag* dangerous

perife'ria *sf (di città)* outskirts *pl*

pe'rifrasi *sf* circumlocution

pe'rimetro *sm* perimeter

peri'odico, a, ci, che *ag* periodic(al); *(MAT)* recurring ♦ *sm* periodical

pe'riodo *sm* period

peripe'zie [peripet'tsie] *sfpl* ups and downs, vicissitudes

pe'rire *vi* to perish, die

pe'rito, a *ag* expert, skilled ♦ *sm/f* expert; *(agronomo, navale)* surveyor; **un** ~ **chimico** a qualified chemist

pe'rizia [pe'rittsja] *sf (abilità)* ability; *(giudizio tecnico)* expert opinion; expert's report

'perla *sf* pearl; **per'lina** *sf* bead

perlus'trare *vt* to patrol

perma'loso, a *ag* touchy

perma'nente *ag* permanent ♦ *sf* permanent wave, perm; **perma'nenza** *sf* permanence; *(soggiorno)* stay

perma'nere *vi* to remain

perme'are *vt* to permeate

per'messo, a *pp di* **permettere** ♦ *sm (autorizzazione)* permission, leave; *(dato a militare, impiegato)* leave; *(licenza)* licence, permit; *(MIL: foglio)* pass; **~?, è ~?** *(posso entrare?)* may I come in?; *(posso passare?)* excuse me; ~ **di lavoro/pesca** work/ fishing permit; ~ **di soggiorno** residence permit

per'mettere *vt* to allow, permit; ~ **a qn qc/di fare** to allow sb sth/to do; **~rsi qc/ di fare** to allow o.s. sth/to do; *(avere la possibilità)* to afford sth/to do

per'nacchia [per'nakkja] *(fam) sf*: **fare una** ~ to blow a raspberry

per'nice [per'nitʃe] *sf* partridge

'perno *sm* pivot

pernot'tare *vi* to spend the night, stay overnight

'pero *sm* pear tree

però *cong (ma)* but; *(tuttavia)* however, nevertheless

pero'rare *vt (DIR, fig)*: ~ **la causa di qn** to plead sb's case

perpendico'lare *ag, sf* perpendicular

perpe'trare *vt* to perpetrate

perpetu'are *vt* to perpetuate

per'petuo, a *ag* perpetual

per'plesso, a *ag* perplexed; uncertain, undecided

perqui'sire *vt* to search; **perquisizi'one** *sf* (police) search

persecu'tore *sm* persecutor

persecuzi'one [persekut'tsjone] *sf* persecution

persegu'ire *vt* to pursue

persegui'tare *vt* to persecute

perseve'rante *ag* persevering

perseve'rare *vi* to persevere

'Persia *sf*: **la** ~ Persia

persi'ana *sf* shutter; ~ **avvolgibile** roller shutter

persi'ano, a *ag, sm/f* Persian

'persico, a, ci, che *ag*: **il golfo P~** the Persian Gulf

per'sino *av* = **perfino**

persis'tente *ag* persistent

per'sistere *vi* to persist; ~ **a fare** to persist in doing; **persis'tito, a** *pp di* **persistere**

'perso, a *pp di* **perdere**

per'sona *sf* person; *(qualcuno)*: **una** ~ someone, somebody, *espressione interrogativa* +anyone *o* anybody; **~e** *sfpl* people; **non c'è** ~ **che ...** there's nobody who ..., there isn't anybody who ...

perso'naggio [perso'naddʒo] *sm (persona ragguardevole)* personality, figure; *(tipo)* character, individual; *(LETTERATURA)* character

perso'nale *ag* personal ♦ *sm* staff; personnel; *(figura fisica)* build

personalità *sf inv* personality

personifi'care *vt* to personify; to embody

perspi'cace [perspi'katʃe] *ag* shrewd, discerning

persu'adere *vt*: ~ **qn (di qc/a fare)** to

persuade sb (of sth/to do); **persuasi'one** *sf* persuasion; **persua'sivo, a** *ag* persuasive; **persu'aso, a** *pp di* **persuadere**

per'tanto *cong* (*quindi*) so, therefore

'pertica, che *sf* pole

perti'nente *ag*: ~ **(a)** relevant (to), pertinent (to)

per'tosse *sf* whooping cough

per'tugio [per'tudʒo] *sm* hole, opening

perturbazi'one [perturbat'tsjone] *sf* disruption; perturbation; ~ **atmosferica** atmospheric disturbance

per'vadere *vt* to pervade; **per'vaso, a** *pp di* **pervadere**

perve'nire *vi*: ~ **a** to reach, arrive at, come to; (*venire in possesso*): **gli pervenne una fortuna** he inherited a fortune; **far ~ qc a** to have sth sent to; **perve'nuto, a** *pp di* **pervenire**

per'verso, a *ag* depraved; perverse

p. es. *abbr* (= *per esempio*) e.g.

'pesa *sf* weighing *no pl*; weighbridge

pe'sante *ag* heavy

pe'sare *vt* to weigh ♦ *vi* (*avere un peso*) to weigh; (*essere pesante*) to be heavy; (*fig*) to carry weight; ~ **su** (*fig*) to lie heavy on; to influence; to hang over

'pesca (*pl* **pesche**: *frutto*) *sf* peach; (*il pescare*) fishing; **andare a ~** to go fishing; ~ **di beneficenza** (*lotteria*) lucky dip; ~ **con la lenza** angling

pes'care *vt* (*pesce*) to fish for; to catch; (*qc nell'acqua*) to fish out; (*fig: trovare*) to get hold of, find; **andare a ~** to go fishing

pesca'tore *sm* fisherman; angler

'pesce ['peʃʃe] *sm* fish *gen inv*; **P~i** (*dello zodiaco*) Pisces; ~ **d'aprile!** April Fool!; ~ **spada** swordfish; **pesce'cane** *sm* shark

pesce d'aprile

i **Il pesce d'aprile** *is a practical joke played on 1 April. It takes its name from the traditional prank of surreptitiously sticking a paper fish on someone's back.*

pesche'reccio [peske'rettʃo] *sm* fishing

boat

pesche'ria [peske'ria] *sf* fishmonger's (shop) (*BRIT*), fish store (*US*)

pesci'vendolo, a [peʃʃi'vendolo] *sm/f* fishmonger (*BRIT*), fish merchant (*US*)

'pesco, schi *sm* peach tree

pes'coso, a *ag* abounding in fish

'peso *sm* weight; (*SPORT*) shot; **rubare sul** ~ to give short weight; **essere di ~ a qn** (*fig*) to be a burden to sb; ~ **lordo/netto** gross/net weight; ~ **piuma/mosca/gallo/ medio/massimo** (*PUGILATO*) feather/fly/ bantam/middle/heavyweight

pessi'mismo *sm* pessimism; **pessi'mista, i, e** *ag* pessimistic ♦ *sm/f* pessimist

'pessimo, a *ag* very bad, awful

pes'tare *vt* to tread on, trample on; (*sale, pepe*) to grind; (*uva, aglio*) to crush; (*fig: picchiare*): ~ **qn** to beat sb up

'peste *sf* plague; (*persona*) nuisance, pest

pes'tello *sm* pestle

pesti'lenza [pesti'lɛntsa] *sf* pestilence; (*fetore*) stench

'pesto, a *ag*: **c'è buio ~** it's pitch-dark; **occhio ~** black eye ♦ *sm* (*CUC*) sauce made with basil, garlic, cheese and oil

'petalo *sm* (*BOT*) petal

pe'tardo *sm* firecracker, banger (*BRIT*)

petizi'one [petit'tsjone] *sf* petition

'peto (*fam!*) *sm* fart (*!*)

petrol'chimica [petrol'kimika] *sf* petrochemical industry

petroli'era *sf* (*nave*) oil tanker

petro'lifero, a *ag* oil-bearing; oil *cpd*

pe'trolio *sm* oil, petroleum; (*per lampada, fornello*) paraffin

pettego'lare *vi* to gossip

pettego'lezzo [pettego'leddzo] *sm* gossip *no pl*; **fare ~i** to gossip

pet'tegolo, a *ag* gossipy ♦ *sm/f* gossip

petti'nare *vt* to comb (the hair of); **~rsi** *vr* to comb one's hair; **pettina'tura** *sf* (*acconciatura*) hairstyle

'pettine *sm* comb; (*ZOOL*) scallop

petti'rosso *sm* robin

'petto *sm* chest; (*seno*) breast, bust; (*CUC: di*

carne bovina) brisket; (: *di pollo etc*) breast; **a doppio ~** (*abito*) double-breasted; **petto'ruto, a** *ag* broad-chested; full-breasted

petu'lante *ag* insolent

pe'tunia *sf* (BOT) petunia

'pezza ['pɛttsa] *sf* piece of cloth; (*toppa*) patch; (*cencio*) rag, cloth

pez'zato, a [pet'tsato] *ag* piebald

pez'zente [pet'tsɛnte] *sm/f* beggar

'pezzo ['pɛttso] *sm* (*gen*) piece; (*brandello*, *frammento*) piece, bit; (*di macchina*, *arnese etc*) part; (STAMPA) article; (*di tempo*): **aspettare un ~** to wait quite a while *o* some time; **in** *o* **a ~i** in pieces; **andare in ~i** to break into pieces; **un bel ~ d'uomo** a fine figure of a man; **abito a due ~i** two-piece suit; **~ di cronaca** (STAMPA) report; **~ grosso** (*fig*) bigwig; **~ di ricambio** spare part

pia'cente [pja'tʃɛnte] *ag* attractive

pia'cere [pja'tʃere] *vi* to please; **una ragazza che piace** a likeable girl; an attractive girl; **~ a: mi piace** I like it; **quei ragazzi non mi piacciono** I don't like those boys; **gli piacerebbe andare al cinema** he would like to go to the cinema ♦ *sm* pleasure; (*favore*) favour; "**~!**" (*nelle presentazioni*) "pleased to meet you!"; **con ~** certainly, with pleasure; **per ~!** please; **fare un ~ a qn** to do sb a favour; **pia'cevole** *ag* pleasant, agreeable; **piaci'uto, a** *pp di* **piacere**

pi'aga, ghe *sf* (*lesione*) sore; (*ferita: anche fig*) wound; (*fig: flagello*) scourge, curse; (: *persona*) pest, nuisance

piagnis'teo [pjaɲɲis'tɛo] *sm* whining, whimpering

piagnuco'lare [pjaɲɲuko'lare] *vi* to whimper

pi'alla *sf* (*arnese*) plane; **pial'lare** *vt* to plane

pi'ana *sf* stretch of level ground; (*più estesa*) plain

pianeggi'ante [pjaned'dʒante] *ag* flat, level

piane'rottolo *sm* landing

pia'neta *sm* (ASTR) planet

pi'angere ['pjandʒere] *vi* to cry, weep; (*occhi*) to water ♦ *vt* to cry, weep; (*lamentare*) to bewail, lament; **~ la morte di qn** to mourn sb's death

pianifi'care *vt* to plan; **pianificazi'one** *sf* planning

pia'nista, i, e *sm/f* pianist

pi'ano, a *ag* (*piatto*) flat, level; (MAT) plane; (*chiaro*) clear, plain ♦ *av* (*adagio*) slowly; (*a bassa voce*) softly; (*con cautela*) slowly, carefully ♦ *sm* (MAT) plane; (GEO) plain; (*livello*) level, plane; (*di edificio*) floor; (*programma*) plan; (MUS) piano; **pian ~** very slowly; (*poco a poco*) little by little; **in primo/secondo ~** in the foreground/background; **di primo ~** (*fig*) prominent, high-ranking

piano'forte *sm* piano, pianoforte

pi'anta *sf* (BOT) plant; (ANAT: *anche*: **~ del piede**) sole (of the foot); (*grafico*) plan; (*topografica*) map; **in ~ stabile** on the permanent staff; **piantagi'one** *sf* plantation; **pian'tare** *vt* to plant; (*conficcare*) to drive *o* hammer in; (*tenda*) to put up, pitch; (*fig: lasciare*) to leave, desert; **~rsi** *vr*: **~rsi davanti a qn** to plant o.s. in front of sb; **piantala!** (*fam*) cut it out!

pianter'reno *sm* ground floor

pian'tina *sf* (*carta*) map

pi'anto, a *pp di* **piangere** ♦ *sm* tears *pl*, crying

pian'tone *sm* (*vigilante*) sentry, guard; (*soldato*) orderly; (AUT) steering column

pia'nura *sf* plain

pi'astra *sf* plate; (*di pietra*) slab; (*di fornello*) hotplate; **~ di registrazione** tape deck; **panino alla ~** ≈ toasted sandwich

pias'trella *sf* tile

pias'trina *sf* (MIL) identity disc

piatta'forma *sf* (*anche fig*) platform

piat'tino *sm* saucer

pi'atto, a *ag* flat; (*fig: scialbo*) dull ♦ *sm* (*recipiente, vivanda*) dish; (*portata*) course; (*parte piana*) flat (part); **~i** *smpl* (MUS) cymbals; **~ fondo** soup dish; **~ forte** main course; **~ del giorno** dish of the day, plat du jour; **~ del giradischi** turntable

pi'azza ['pjattsa] *sf* square; (COMM) market; **far ~ pulita** to make a clean sweep; **~ d'armi** (MIL) parade ground; **piaz'zale** *sm* (large) square

piaz'zare [pjat'tsare] *vt* to place; (COMM) to market, sell; **~rsi** *vr* (SPORT) to be placed

piaz'zista, i [pjat'tsista] *sm* (COMM) commercial traveller

piaz'zola [pjat'tsɔla] *sf* (AUT) lay-by

'picca, che *sf* pike; **~che** *sfpl* (CARTE) spades

pic'cante *ag* hot, pungent; (fig) racy; biting

pic'carsi *vr*: **~ di fare** to pride o.s. on one's ability to do; **~ per qc** to take offence at sth

pic'chetto [pik'ketto] *sm* (MIL, di scioperanti) picket; (di tenda) peg

picchi'are [pik'kjare] *vt* (persona: colpire) to hit, strike; (: prendere a botte) to beat (up); (battere) to beat; (sbattere) to bang ♦ *vi* (bussare) to knock; (: con forza) to bang; (colpire) to hit, strike; (sole) to beat down; **picchi'ata** *sf* (AER) dive

picchiet'tare [pikkjet'tare] *vt* (punteggiare) to spot, dot; (colpire) to tap

'picchio ['pikkjo] *sm* woodpecker

pic'cino, a [pit'tʃino] *ag* tiny, very small

piccio'naia [pittʃo'naja] *sf* pigeon-loft; (TEATRO): **la ~** the gods *sg*

picci'one [pit'tʃone] *sm* pigeon

'picco, chi *sm* peak; **a ~** vertically

'piccolo, a *ag* small; (oggetto, mano, di età: bambino) small, little (dav sostantivo); (di breve durata: viaggio) short; (fig) mean, petty ♦ *sm/f* child, little one; **~i** *smpl* (di animale) young *pl*; **in ~** in miniature

pic'cone *sm* pick(-axe)

pic'cozza [pik'kɔttsa] *sf* ice-axe

pic'nic *sm inv* picnic

pi'docchio [pi'dɔkkjo] *sm* louse

pi'ede *sm* foot; (di mobile) leg; **in ~i** standing; **a ~i** on foot; **a ~i nudi** barefoot; **su due ~i** (fig) at once; **prendere ~** (fig) to gain ground, catch on; **sul ~ di guerra** (MIL) ready for action; **~ di porco** crowbar

piedes'tallo *sm* pedestal

piedipi'atti *sm inv* (peg) cop

pi'ega, ghe *sf* (piegatura, GEO) fold; (di gonna) pleat; (di pantaloni) crease; (grinza) wrinkle, crease; **prendere una brutta ~** (fig) to take a turn for the worse

pie'gare *vt* to fold; (braccia, gambe, testa) to bend ♦ *vi* to bend; **~rsi** *vr* to bend; (fig): **~rsi (a)** to yield (to), submit (to); **pieghet'tare** *vt* to pleat; **pie'ghevole** *ag* pliable, flexible; (porta) folding

Pie'monte *sm*: **il ~** Piedmont

pi'ena *sf* (di fiume) flood, spate

pi'eno, a *ag* full; (muro, mattone) solid ♦ *sm* (colmo) height, peak; (carico) full load; **~ di** full of; **in ~ giorno** in broad daylight; **fare il ~ (di benzina)** to fill up (with petrol)

pietà *sf* pity; (REL) piety; **senza ~** pitiless, merciless; **avere ~ di** (compassione) to pity, feel sorry for; (misericordia) to have pity *o* mercy on

pie'tanza [pje'tantsa] *sf* dish, course

pie'toso, a *ag* (compassionevole) pitying, compassionate; (che desta pietà) pitiful

pi'etra *sf* stone; **~ preziosa** precious stone, gem; **pie'traia** *sf* (terreno) stony ground; **pietrifi'care** *vt* to petrify; (fig) to transfix, paralyze

'piffero *sm* (MUS) pipe

pigi'ama, i [pi'dʒama] *sm* pyjamas *pl*

'pigia 'pigia ['pidʒa'pidʒa] *sm* crowd, press

pigi'are [pi'dʒare] *vt* to press

pigi'one [pi'dʒone] *sf* rent

pigli'are [piʎ'ʎare] *vt* to take, grab; (afferrare) to catch

'piglio ['piʎʎo] *sm* look, expression

pig'meo, a *sm/f* pygmy

'pigna ['piɲɲa] *sf* pine cone

pi'gnolo, a [piɲ'ɲɔlo] *ag* pernickety

pigno'rare [piɲɲo'rare] *vt* to distrain

pigo'lare *vi* to cheep, chirp

pi'grizia [pi'grittsja] *sf* laziness

'pigro, a *ag* lazy

'pila *sf* (catasta, di ponte) pile; (ELETTR) battery; (torcia) torch (BRIT), flashlight

pi'lastro *sm* pillar

'pile ['pail] sm inv fleece

'pillola sf pill; **prendere la ~** to be on the pill

pi'lone sm (di ponte) pier; (di linea elettrica) pylon

pi'lota, i, e sm/f pilot; (AUT) driver ♦ ag inv pilot cpd; **~ automatico** automatic pilot; **pilo'tare** vt to pilot; to drive

pinaco'teca, che sf art gallery

pi'neta sf pinewood

ping-'pong [piŋ'pɔŋ] sm table tennis

'pingue ag fat, corpulent

pingu'ino sm (ZOOL) penguin

'pinna sf (di pesce) fin; (di cetaceo, per nuotare) flipper

'pino sm pine (tree); pi'nolo sm pine kernel

'pinza ['pintsa] sf pliers pl; (MED) forceps pl; (ZOOL) pincer

pinzette [pin'tsette] sfpl tweezers

'pio, a, 'pii, 'pie ag pious; (opere, istituzione) charitable, charity cpd

pi'oggia, ge ['pjɔddʒa] sf rain; **~ acida** acid rain

pi'olo sm peg; (di scala) rung

piom'bare vi to fall heavily; (gettarsi con impeto): **~ su** to fall upon, assail ♦ vt (dente) to fill; **piomba'tura** sf (di dente) filling

piom'bino sm (sigillo) (lead) seal; (del filo a piombo) plummet; (PESCA) sinker

pi'ombo sm (CHIM) lead; **a ~** (cadere) straight down; **senza ~** (benzina) unleaded

pioni'ere, a sm/f pioneer

pi'oppo sm poplar

pi'overe vb impers to rain ♦ vi (fig: scendere dall'alto) to rain down; (lettere, regali) to pour into; **pioviggi'nare** vb impers to drizzle; **pio'voso, a** ag rainy

pi'ovra sf octopus

'pipa sf pipe

pipì (fam) sf: **fare ~** to have a wee (wee)

pipis'trello sm (ZOOL) bat

pi'ramide sf pyramid

pi'rata, i sm pirate; **~ della strada** hit-and-run driver

Pire'nei smpl: **i ~** the Pyrenees

'pirico, a, ci, che ag: **polvere ~a** gunpowder

pi'rofilo, a ag heat-resistant; pi'rofila sf heat-resistant dish

pi'roga, ghe sf dug-out canoe

pi'romane sm/f pyromaniac; arsonist

pi'roscafo sm steamer, steamship

pisci'are [piʃʃare] (fam!) vi to piss (!), pee (!)

pi'scina [piʃʃina] sf (swimming) pool; (stabilimento) (swimming) baths pl

pi'sello sm pea

piso'lino sm nap

'pista sf (traccia) track, trail; (di stadio) track; (di pattinaggio) rink; (da sci) run; (AER) runway; (di circo) ring; **~ da ballo** dance floor

pis'tacchio [pis'takkjo] sm pistachio (tree); pistachio (nut)

pis'tola sf pistol, gun

pis'tone sm piston

pi'tone sm python

pit'tore, 'trice sm/f painter; pitto'resco, a, schi, sche ag picturesque

pit'tura sf painting; pittu'rare vt to paint

┌─── *PAROLA CHIAVE* ───────────┐

più av 1 (in maggiore quantità) more; **~ del solito** more than usual; **in ~, di ~** more; **ne voglio di ~** I want some more; **ci sono 3 persone in o di ~** there are 3 more o extra people; **~ o meno** more or less; **per di ~** (inoltre) what's more, moreover

2 (comparativo) more, aggettivo corto +...er; **~ ... di/che** more ... than; **lavoro ~ di te/Paola** I work harder than you/Paola; **è ~ intelligente che ricco** he's more intelligent than rich

3 (superlativo) most, aggettivo corto +...est; **il ~ grande/intelligente** the biggest/most intelligent; **è quello che compro ~ spesso** that's the one I buy most often; **al ~ presto** as soon as possible; **al ~ tardi** at the latest

4 (negazione): **non ... ~** no more, no longer; **non ho ~ soldi** I've got no more money, I don't have any more money; **non**

lavoro ~ I'm no longer working, I don't work any more; **a ~ non posso** (*gridare*) at the top of one's voice; (*correre*) as fast as one can

5 (*MAT*) plus; **4 ~ 5 fa 9** 4 plus 5 equals 9; **~ 5 gradi** 5 degrees above freezing, plus 5 ♦ *prep* plus

♦ *ag inv* 1 : **~ ... (di)** more ... (than); **~ denaro/tempo** more money/time; **~ persone di quante ci aspettassimo** more people than we expected

2 (*numerosi, diversi*) several; **l'aspettai per ~ giorni** I waited for it for several days

♦ *sm* 1 (*la maggior parte*): **il ~ è fatto** most of it is done

2 (*MAT*) plus (sign)

3 : **i ~** the majority

piucchepper'fetto [pjukkepper'fetto] *sm* (*LING*) pluperfect, past perfect

pi'uma *sf* feather; **piu'maggio** *sm* plumage, feathers *pl*; **piu'mino** *sm* (*eider*)down; (*per letto*) eiderdown; (: *tipo danese*) duvet, continental quilt; (*giacca*) quilted jacket (*with goose-feather padding*); (*per cipria*) powder puff; (*per spolverare*) feather duster

piut'tosto *av* rather; **~ che** (*anziché*) rather than

pi'vello, a *sm/f* greenhorn

'pizza ['pittsa] *sf* pizza; **pizze'ria** *sf* place *where pizzas are made, sold or eaten*

pizzi'cagnolo, a [pittsi'kaɲɲolo] *sm/f* specialist grocer

pizzi'care [pittsi'kare] *vt* (*stringere*) to nip, pinch; (*pungere*) to sting; to bite; (*MUS*) to pluck ♦ *vi* (*prudere*) to itch, be itchy; (*cibo*) to be hot *o* spicy

pizziche'ria [pittsike'ria] *sf* delicatessen (*shop*)

'pizzico, chi ['pittsiko] *sm* (*pizzicotto*) pinch, nip; (*piccola quantità*) pinch, dash; (*d'insetto*) sting; bite

pizzi'cotto [pittsi'kɔtto] *sm* pinch, nip

'pizzo ['pittso] *sm* (*merletto*) lace; (*barbetta*) goatee beard

pla'care *vt* to placate, soothe; **~rsi** *vr* to

calm down

'placca, che *sf* plate; (*con iscrizione*) plaque; (*anche:* **~ dentaria**) (dental) plaque; **plac'care** *vt* to plate; **placcato in oro/argento** gold-/silver-plated

'placido, a ['platʃido] *ag* placid, calm

plagi'are [pla'dʒare] *vt* (*copiare*) to plagiarize; **'plagio** *sm* plagiarism

pla'nare *vi* (*AER*) to glide

'plancia, ce ['plantʃa] *sf* (*NAUT*) bridge

plane'tario, a *ag* planetary ♦ *sm* (*locale*) planetarium

'plasma *sm* plasma

plas'mare *vt* to mould, shape

'plastica, che *sf* (*arte*) plastic arts *pl*; (*MED*) plastic surgery; (*sostanza*) plastic

'plastico, a, ci, che *ag* plastic ♦ *sm* (*rappresentazione*) relief model; (*esplosivo*): **bomba al ~** plastic bomb

plasti'lina ® *sf* plasticine ®

'platano *sm* plane tree

pla'tea *sf* (*TEATRO*) stalls *pl*

'platino *sm* platinum

pla'tonico, a, ci, che *ag* platonic

plau'sibile *ag* plausible

'plauso *sm* (*fig*) approval

ple'baglia [ple'baʎʎa] (*peg*) *sf* rabble, mob

'plebe *sf* common people; **ple'beo, a** *ag* plebeian; (*volgare*) coarse, common

ple'nario, a *ag* plenary

pleni'lunio *sm* full moon

'plettro *sm* plectrum

pleu'rite *sf* pleurisy

'plico, chi *sm* (*pacco*) parcel; **in ~ a parte** (*COMM*) under separate cover

plo'tone *sm* (*MIL*) platoon; **~ d'esecuzione** firing squad

'plumbeo, a *ag* leaden

plu'rale *ag, sm* plural; **pluralità** *sf* plurality; (*maggioranza*) majority

plusva'lore *sm* (*ECON*) surplus

pneu'matico, a, ci, che *ag* inflatable; pneumatic ♦ *sm* (*AUT*) tyre (*BRIT*), tire (*US*)

po' *av, sm vedi* **poco**

PAROLA CHIAVE

'poco, a, chi, che *ag* (*quantità*) little, not

much; (*numero*) few, not many; ~ **pane/denaro/spazio** little *o* not much bread/money/space; **~che persone/idee** few *o* not many people/ideas; **ci vediamo tra ~** (*sottinteso: tempo*) see you soon
♦ *av* 1 (*in piccola quantità*) little, not much; (*numero limitato*) few, not many; **guadagna ~** he doesn't earn much, he earns little
2 (*con ag, av*) (a) little, not very; **sta ~ bene** he isn't very well; **è ~ più vecchia di lui** she's a little *o* slightly older than him
3 (*tempo*): ~ **dopo/prima** shortly afterwards/before; **il film dura ~** the film doesn't last very long; **ci vediamo molto ~** we don't see each other very often, we hardly ever see each other
4: **un po'** a little, a bit; **è un po' corto** it's a little *o* bit short; **arriverà fra un po'** he'll arrive shortly *o* in a little while
5: **a dir ~** to say the least; **a ~ a ~** little by little; **per ~ non cadevo** I nearly fell; **è una cosa da ~** it's nothing, it's of no importance; **una persona da ~** a worthless person
♦ *pron* (a) little; **~chi, che** *pron pl* (*persone*) few (people); (*cose*) few
♦ *sm* 1 little; **vive del ~ che ha** he lives on the little he has
2: **un po'** a little; **un po' di zucchero** a little sugar; **un bel po' di denaro** quite a lot of money; **un po' per ciascuno** a bit each

po'**dere** *sm* (*AGR*) farm
po**de'roso, a** *ag* powerful
pode**stà** *sm inv* (*nel fascismo*) podesta, mayor
'**podio** *sm* dais, platform; (*MUS*) podium
po'**dismo** *sm* (*SPORT*) track events *pl*
po'**ema, i** *sm* poem
poe**sia** *sf* (*arte*) poetry; (*componimento*) poem
po'**eta, 'essa** *sm/f* poet/poetess; po**e'tico, a, ci, che** *ag* poetic(al)
poggi'**are** [pod'dʒare] *vt* to lean, rest; (*posare*) to lay, place; **poggia'testa** *sm*

inv (*AUT*) headrest
'**poggio** ['poddʒo] *sm* hillock, knoll
poggi'**olo** [pod'dʒɔlo] *sm* balcony
'**poi** *av* then; (*alla fine*) finally, at last; **e ~** (*inoltre*) and besides; **questa ~ (è bella)!** (*ironico*) that's a good one!
poi**ché** [poi'ke] *cong* since, as
'**poker** *sm* poker
po'**lacco, a, chi, che** *ag* Polish ♦ *sm/f* Pole
po'**lare** *ag* polar
po'**lemica, che** *sf* controversy
po'**lemico, a, ci, che** *ag* polemic(al), controversial
po'**lenta** *sf* (*CUC*) sort of thick porridge *made with maize flour*
poliambula'**torio** *sm* health centre
poli'**clinico, ci** *sm* general hospital, polyclinic
poli'**estere** *sm* polyester
'**polio(mie'lite)** *sf* polio(myelitis)
'**polipo** *sm* polyp
polisti'**rolo** *sm* polystyrene
poli'**tecnico, ci** *sm* postgraduate technical college
po'**litica, che** *sf* politics *sg*; (*linea di condotta*) policy; *vedi anche* **politico**
politiciz'**zare** [politit∫id'dzare] *vt* to politicize
po'**litico, a, ci, che** *ag* political ♦ *sm/f* politician
poli'**zia** [polit'tsia] *sf* police; ~ **giudiziaria** ≈ Criminal Investigation Department (*BRIT*), ≈ Federal Bureau of Investigation (*US*); ~ **stradale** traffic police; polizi'**esco, a, schi, sche** *ag* police *cpd*; (*film, romanzo*) detective *cpd*; polizi'**otto** *sm* policeman; **cane poliziotto** police dog; **donna poliziotto** policewoman

---

polizia di stato

ⓘ The function of the **polizia di stato** is to maintain public order, to uphold the law and prevent and investigate crime. They are a civil body, reporting to the Minister of the Interior.

'po'lizza [po'littsa] *sf* (*COMM*) bill; ~ **di assicurazione** insurance policy; ~ **di carico** bill of lading
pol'laio *sm* henhouse
pol'lame *sm* poultry
pol'lastro *sm* (*ZOOL*) cockerel
'pollice ['pollitʃe] *sm* thumb
'polline *sm* pollen
'pollo *sm* chicken
pol'mone *sm* lung; ~ **d'acciaio** (*MED*) iron lung; polmo'nite *sf* pneumonia
'polo *sm* (*GEO, FISICA*) pole; (*gioco*) polo; **il ~ sud/nord** the South/North Pole
Po'lonia *sf*: **la ~** Poland
'polpa *sf* flesh, pulp; (*carne*) lean meat
pol'paccio [pol'pattʃo] *sm* (*ANAT*) calf
polpas'trello *sm* fingertip
pol'petta *sf* (*CUC*) meatball; polpet'tone *sm* (*CUC*) meatloaf
'polpo *sm* octopus
pol'poso, a *ag* fleshy
pol'sino *sm* cuff
'polso *sm* (*ANAT*) wrist; (*pulsazione*) pulse; (*fig: forza*) drive, vigour
pol'tiglia [pol'tiʎʎa] *sf* (*composto*) mash, mush; (*di fango e neve*) slush
pol'trire *vi* to laze about
pol'trona *sf* armchair; (*TEATRO: posto*) seat in the front stalls (*BRIT*) o orchestra (*US*)
pol'trone *ag* lazy, slothful
'polvere *sf* dust; (*anche: ~ **da sparo***) (gun)powder; (*sostanza ridotta minutissima*) powder, dust; **latte in ~** dried o powdered milk; **caffè in ~** instant coffee; **sapone in ~** soap powder; polveri'era *sf* (*MIL*) (gun)powder magazine; polveriz'zare *vt* to pulverize; (*nebulizzare*) to atomize; (*fig*) to crush, pulverize; to smash; polve'rone *sm* thick cloud of dust; polve'roso, a *ag* dusty
po'mata *sf* ointment, cream
po'mello *sm* knob
pomeridi'ano, a *ag* afternoon *cpd*; **nelle ore ~e** in the afternoon
pome'riggio [pome'riddʒo] *sm* afternoon
'pomice ['pomitʃe] *sf* pumice
'pomo *sm* (*mela*) apple; (*ornamentale*) knob; (*di sella*) pommel; ~ **d'Adamo** (*ANAT*) Adam's apple
pomo'doro *sm* tomato
'pompa *sf* pump; (*sfarzo*) pomp (and ceremony); **~e funebri** funeral parlour *sg* (*BRIT*), undertaker's *sg*; pom'pare *vt* to pump; (*trarre*) to pump out; (*gonfiare d'aria*) to pump up
pom'pelmo *sm* grapefruit
pompi'ere *sm* fireman
pom'poso, a *ag* pompous
ponde'rare *vt* to ponder over, consider carefully
ponde'roso, a *ag* (*anche fig*) weighty
po'nente *sm* west
'ponte *sm* bridge; (*di nave*) deck; (*: anche: ~ **di comando***) bridge; (*impalcatura*) scaffold; **fare il ~** (*fig*) to take the extra day off (*between 2 public holidays*); **governo ~** interim government; ~ **aereo** airlift; ~ **sospeso** suspension bridge
pon'tefice [pon'tefitʃe] *sm* (*REL*) pontiff
pontifi'care *vi* (*anche fig*) to pontificate
ponti'ficio, a, ci, cie [ponti'fitʃo] *ag* papal
popo'lano, a *ag* popular, of the people
popo'lare *ag* popular; (*quartiere, clientela*) working-class ♦ *vt* (*rendere abitato*) to populate; **~rsi** *vr* to fill with people, get crowded; popolarità *sf* popularity; popolazi'one *sf* population
'popolo *sm* people; popo'loso, a *ag* densely populated
'poppa *sf* (*di nave*) stern; (*seno*) breast
pop'pare *vt* to suck
poppa'toio *sm* (*feeding*) bottle
porcel'lana [portʃel'lana] *sf* porcelain, china; piece of china
porcel'lino, a [portʃel'lino] *sm/f* piglet
porche'ria [porke'ria] *sf* filth, muck; (*fig: oscenità*) obscenity; (*: azione disonesta*) dirty trick; (*: cosa mal fatta*) rubbish
por'cile [por'tʃile] *sm* pigsty
por'cino, a [por'tʃino] *ag* of pigs, pork *cpd* ♦ *sm* (*fungo*) type of edible mushroom
'porco, ci *sm* pig; (*carne*) pork
porcos'pino *sm* porcupine

'porgere ['pɔrdʒere] *vt* to hand, give; (*tendere*) to hold out

pornogra'fia *sf* pornography; **porno'grafico, a, ci, che** *ag* pornographic

'poro *sm* pore; **po'roso, a** *ag* porous

'porpora *sf* purple

'porre *vt* (*mettere*) to put; (*collocare*) to place; (*posare*) to lay (down), put (down); (*fig: supporre*): **poniamo (il caso) che ...** let's suppose that ...; **porsi** *vr* (*mettersi*): **porsi a sedere/in cammino** to sit down/set off; **~ una domanda a qn** to ask sb a question, put a question to sb

'porro *sm* (*BOT*) leek; (*MED*) wart

'porta *sf* door; (*SPORT*) goal; **~e** *sfpl* (*di città*) gates; **a ~e chiuse** (*DIR*) in camera

'porta... *prefisso* **portaba'gagli** *sm inv* (*facchino*) porter; (*AUT, FERR*) luggage rack; **porta'cenere** *sm inv* ashtray; **portachi'avi** *sm inv* keyring; **porta'cipria** *sm inv* powder compact; **porta'erei** *sf inv* (*nave*) aircraft carrier; **portafi'nestra** (*pl* **portefi'nestre**) *sf* French window; **porta'foglio** *sm* wallet; (*POL, BORSA*) portfolio; **portafor'tuna** *sm inv* lucky charm; mascot; **portagi'oie** *sm inv* jewellery box

por'tale *sm* (*di chiesa*, *INFORM*) portal

porta'lettere *sm/f inv* postman/woman (*BRIT*), mailman/woman (*US*)

porta'mento *sm* carriage, bearing

portamo'nete *sm inv* purse

por'tante *ag* (*muro etc*) supporting, load-bearing

portan'tina *sf* sedan chair; (*per ammalati*) stretcher

por'tare *vt* (*sostenere, sorreggere: peso, bambino, pacco*) to carry; (*indossare: abito, occhiali*) to wear; (*: capelli lunghi*) to have; (*avere: nome, titolo*) to have, bear; (*recare*): **~ qc a qn** to take (*o* bring) sth to sb; (*fig: sentimenti*) to bear; **~rsi** *vr* (*recarsi*) to go; **~ avanti** (*discorso, idea*) to pursue; **~ via** to take away; (*rubare*) to take; **~ i bambini a spasso** to take the children for a walk; **~ fortuna** to bring good luck

portasiga'rette *sm inv* cigarette case

por'tata *sf* (*vivanda*) course; (*AUT*) carrying (*o* loading) capacity; (*di arma*) range; (*volume d'acqua*) (rate of) flow; (*fig: limite*) scope, capability; (*: importanza*) impact, import; **alla ~ di tutti** (*conoscenza*) within everybody's capabilities; (*prezzo*) within everybody's means; **a/fuori ~ (di)** within/out of reach (of); **a ~ di mano** within (arm's) reach

por'tatile *ag* portable

por'tato, a *ag*: **~ a** inclined *o* apt to

porta'tore, 'trice *sm/f* (*anche COMM*) bearer; (*MED*) carrier

portau'ovo *sm inv* eggcup

porta'voce [porta'votʃe] *sm/f inv* spokesman/woman

por'tento *sm* wonder, marvel

porticci'olo [portit'tʃolo] *sm* marina

'portico, ci *sm* portico

porti'era *sf* (*AUT*) door

porti'ere *sm* (*portinaio*) concierge, caretaker; (*di hotel*) porter; (*nel calcio*) goalkeeper

porti'naio, a *sm/f* concierge, caretaker

portine'ria *sf* caretaker's lodge

'porto, a *pp di* **porgere** ♦ *sm* (*NAUT*) harbour, port ♦ *sm inv* port (wine); **~ d'armi** (*documento*) gun licence

Porto'gallo *sm*: **il ~** Portugal; **porto'ghese** *ag, sm/f, sm* Portuguese *inv*

por'tone *sm* main entrance, main door

portu'ale *ag* harbour *cpd*, port *cpd* ♦ *sm* dock worker

porzi'one [por'tsjone] *sf* portion, share; (*di cibo*) portion, helping

'posa *sf* (*FOT*) exposure; (*atteggiamento, di modello*) pose

posa'cenere [posa'tʃenere] *sm inv* ashtray

po'sare *vt* to put (down), lay (down) ♦ *vi* (*ponte, edificio, teoria*): **~ su** to rest on; (*FOT, atteggiarsi*) to pose; **~rsi** *vr* (*aereo*) to land; (*uccello*) to alight; (*sguardo*) to settle

po'sata *sf* piece of cutlery; **~e** *sfpl* (*servizio*) cutlery *sg*

po'sato, a *ag* serious

pos'critto *sm* postscript

posi'tivo, a *ag* positive

posizi'one [pozit'tsjone] *sf* position; **prendere ~** (*fig*) to take a stand; **luci di ~** (*AUT*) sidelights

posolo'gia, 'gie [pozolo'dʒia] *sf* dosage, directions *pl* for use

pos'porre *vt* to place after; (*differire*) to postpone, defer; pos'posto, a *pp di* **posporre**

posse'dere *vt* to own, possess; (*qualità, virtù*) to have, possess; possedi'mento *sm* possession

posses'sivo, a *ag* possessive

pos'sesso *sm* ownership *no pl*; possession

posses'sore *sm* owner

pos'sibile *ag* possible ♦ *sm*: **fare tutto il ~** to do everything possible; **nei limiti del ~** as far as possible; **al più tardi ~** as late as possible; possibilità *sf inv* possibility ♦ *sfpl* (*mezzi*) means; **aver la possibilità di fare** to be in a position to do; to have the opportunity to do

possi'dente *sm/f* landowner

'posta *sf* (*servizio*) post, postal service; (*corrispondenza*) post, mail; (*ufficio postale*) post office; (*nei giochi d'azzardo*) stake; **~e** *sfpl* (*amministrazione*) post office; **~ aerea** airmail; **~ elettronica** E-mail, e-mail, electronic mail; **~ e Telecomunicazioni** Postmaster General; posta'giro *sm* post office cheque, postal giro (*BRIT*); pos'tale *ag* postal, post office *cpd*

post'bellico, a, ci, che *ag* postwar

posteggi'are [posted'dʒare] *vt, vi* to park; posteggia'tore, trice *sm/f* car park attendant; pos'teggio *sm* car park (*BRIT*), parking lot (*US*); (*di taxi*) rank (*BRIT*), stand (*US*)

postelegra'fonico, a, ci, che *ag* postal and telecommunications *cpd*

'poster *sm inv* poster

posteri'ore *ag* (*dietro*) back; (*dopo*) later ♦ *sm* (*fam: sedere*) behind

pos'ticcio, a, ci, ce [pos'tittʃo] *ag* false ♦ *sm* hairpiece

postici'pare [postitʃi'pare] *vt* to defer, postpone

pos'tilla *sf* marginal note

pos'tino *sm* postman (*BRIT*), mailman (*US*)

'posto, a *pp di* porre ♦ *sm* (*sito, posizione*) place; (*impiego*) job; (*spazio libero*) room, space; (*di parcheggio*) space; (*sedile: al teatro, in treno etc*) seat; (*MIL*) post; **a ~** (*in ordine*) in place, tidy; (*fig*) settled; (: *persona*) reliable; **al ~ di** in place of; **sul ~** on the spot; **mettere a ~** to tidy (up), put in order; (*faccende*) to straighten out; **~ di blocco** roadblock; **~ di polizia** police station

pos'tribolo *sm* brothel

'postumo, a *ag* posthumous; (*tardivo*) belated; **~i** *smpl* (*conseguenze*) after-effects, consequences

po'tabile *ag* drinkable; **acqua ~** drinking water

po'tare *vt* to prune

po'tassio *sm* potassium

po'tente *ag* (*nazione*) strong, powerful; (*veleno, farmaco*) potent, strong; po'tenza *sf* power; (*forza*) strength

potenzi'ale [poten'tsjale] *ag, sm* potential

PAROLA CHIAVE

po'tere *sm* power; **al ~** (*partito etc*) in power; **~ d'acquisto** purchasing power ♦ *vb aus* 1 (*essere in grado di*) can, be able to; **non ha potuto ripararlo** he couldn't *o* he wasn't able to repair it; **non è potuto venire** he couldn't *o* he wasn't able to come; **spiacente di non poter aiutare** sorry not to be able to help

2 (*avere il permesso*) can, may, be allowed to; **posso entrare?** can *o* may I come in?; **si può sapere dove sei stato?** where on earth have you been?

3 (*eventualità*) may, might, could; **potrebbe essere vero** it might *o* could be true; **può aver avuto un incidente** he may *o* might *o* could have had an accident; **può darsi** perhaps; **può darsi *o* essere che non venga** he may *o* might not come

4 (*augurio*): **potessi almeno parlargli!** if only I could speak to him!

5 (*suggerimento*): **potresti almeno scusarti!** you could at least apologize! ♦ *vt* can, be able to; **può molto per noi** he can do a lot for us; **non ne posso più** (*per stanchezza*) I'm exhausted; (*per rabbia*) I can't take any more

potestà *sf* (*potere*) power; (*DIR*) authority

'**povero, a** *ag* poor; (*disadorno*) plain, bare ♦ *sm/f* poor man/woman; **i ~i** the poor; **~ di** lacking in, having little; **povertà** *sf* poverty

'**pozza** ['pottsa] *sf* pool

poz'zanghera [pot'tsangera] *sf* puddle

'**pozzo** ['pottso] *sm* well; (*cava: di carbone*) pit; (*di miniera*) shaft; **~ petrolifero** oil well

pran'zare [pran'dzare] *vi* to dine, have dinner; to lunch, have lunch

'**pranzo** ['prandzo] *sm* dinner; (*a mezzogiorno*) lunch

'**prassi** *sf* usual procedure

'**pratica, che** *sf* practice; (*esperienza*) experience; (*conoscenza*) knowledge, familiarity; (*tirocinio*) training, practice; (*AMM: affare*) matter, case; (: *incartamento*) file, dossier; **in ~** (*praticamente*) in practice; **mettere in ~** to put into practice

prati'cabile *ag* (*progetto*) practicable, feasible; (*luogo*) passable, practicable

prati'cante *sm/f* apprentice, trainee; (*REL*) (regular) churchgoer

prati'care *vt* to practise; (*SPORT: tennis etc*) to play; (: *nuoto, scherma etc*) to go in for; (*eseguire: apertura, buco*) to make; **~ uno sconto** to give a discount

'**pratico, a, ci, che** *ag* practical; **~ di** (*esperto*) experienced o skilled in; (*familiare*) familiar with

'**prato** *sm* meadow; (*di giardino*) lawn

preav'viso *sm* notice; **telefonata con ~** personal o person to person call

pre'cario, a *ag* precarious; (*INS*) temporary

precauzi'one [prekaut'tsjone] *sf* caution, care; (*misura*) precaution

prece'dente [pretʃe'dɛnte] *ag* previous ♦ *sm* precedent; **il discorso/film ~** the previous o preceding speech/film; **senza ~i**

unprecedented; **~i penali** criminal record *sg*; **prece'denza** *sf* priority, precedence; (*AUT*) right of way

pre'cedere [pre'tʃedere] *vt* to precede, go (o come) before

pre'cetto [pre'tʃetto] *sm* precept; (*MIL*) call-up notice

precet'tore [pretʃet'tore] *sm* (private) tutor

precipi'tare [pretʃipi'tare] *vi* (*cadere*) to fall headlong; (*fig: situazione*) to get out of control ♦ *vt* (*gettare dall'alto in basso*) to hurl, fling; (*fig: affrettare*) to rush; **~rsi** *vr* (*gettarsi*) to hurl o fling o.s.; (*affrettarsi*) to rush; **precipitazi'one** *sf* (*METEOR*) precipitation; (*fig*) haste; **precipi'toso, a** *ag* (*caduta, fuga*) headlong; (*fig: avventato*) rash, reckless; (: *affrettato*) hasty, rushed

preci'pizio [pretʃi'pittsjo] *sm* precipice; **a ~** (*fig: correre*) headlong

preci'sare [pretʃi'zare] *vt* to state, specify; (*spiegare*) to explain (in detail)

precisi'one [pretʃi'zjone] *sf* precision; accuracy

pre'ciso, a [pre'tʃizo] *ag* (*esatto*) precise; (*accurato*) accurate, precise; (*deciso: idee*) precise, definite; (*uguale*): **2 vestiti ~i** 2 dresses exactly the same; **sono le 9 ~e** it's exactly 9 o'clock

pre'cludere *vt* to block, obstruct; **pre'cluso, a** *pp di* **precludere**

pre'coce [pre'kɔtʃe] *ag* early; (*bambino*) precocious; (*vecchiaia*) premature

precon'cetto [prekon'tʃetto] *sm* preconceived idea, prejudice

precur'sore *sm* forerunner, precursor

'**preda** *sf* (*bottino*) booty; (*animale, fig*) prey; **essere ~ di** to fall prey to; **essere in ~ a** to be prey to; **preda'tore** *sm* predator

predeces'sore, a [predetʃes'sore] *sm/f* predecessor

predesti'nare *vt* to predestine

pre'detto, a *pp di* **predire**

'**predica, che** *sf* sermon; (*fig*) lecture, talking-to

predi'care *vt, vi* to preach

predi'cato *sm* (*LING*) predicate

predi'letto, a *pp di* prediligere ♦ *ag, sm/f* favourite

predilezi'one [predilet'tsjone] *sf* fondness, partiality; avere una ~ per qc/qn to be partial to sth/fond of sb

predi'ligere [predi'lidʒere] *vt* to prefer, have a preference for

pre'dire *vt* to foretell, predict

predis'porre *vt* to get ready, prepare; ~ qn a qc to predispose sb to sth; predis'posto, a *pp di* predisporre

predizi'one [predit'tsjone] *sf* prediction

predomi'nare *vi* to predominate; predo'minio *sm* predominance; supremacy

prefabbri'cato, a *ag* (EDIL) prefabricated

prefazi'one [prefat'tsjone] *sf* preface, foreword

prefe'renza [prefe'rentsa] *sf* preference; preferenzi'ale *ag* preferential; corsia ~ bus and taxi lane

prefe'rire *vt* to prefer, like better; ~ il caffè al tè to prefer coffee to tea, like coffee better than tea; prefe'rito, a *ag* favourite

pre'fetto *sm* prefect; prefet'tura *sf* prefecture

pre'figgersi [pre'fiddʒersi] *vr*: ~ uno scopo to set o.s. a goal

pre'fisso, a *pp di* prefiggere ♦ *sm* (LING) prefix; (TEL) dialling (BRIT) *o* dial (US) code

pre'gare *vi* to pray ♦ *vt* (REL) to pray to; (implorare) to beg; (chiedere): ~ qn di fare to ask sb to do; farsi ~ to need coaxing *o* persuading

pre'gevole [pre'dʒevole] *ag* valuable

preghi'era [pre'gjera] *sf* (REL) prayer; (domanda) request

pregi'ato, a [pre'dʒato] *ag* (di valore) valuable; vino ~ vintage wine

'pregio ['predʒo] *sm* (stima) esteem, regard; (qualità) (good) quality, merit; (valore) value, worth

pregiudi'care [predʒudi'kare] *vt* to prejudice, harm, be detrimental to; pregiudi'cato, a *sm/f* (DIR) previous offender

preglu'dizlo [predʒu'dittsjo] *sm* (idea errata) prejudice; (danno) harm *no pl*

'pregno, a ['preɲɲo] *ag* (saturo): ~ di full of, saturated with

'prego *escl* (a chi ringrazia) don't mention it!; (invitando qn ad accomodarsi) please sit down!; (invitando qn ad andare prima) after you!

pregus'tare *vt* to look forward to

preis'torico, a, ci, che *ag* prehistoric

pre'lato *sm* prelate

prele'vare *vt* (denaro) to withdraw; (campione) to take; (sog: polizia) to take, capture

preli'evo *sm* (di denaro) withdrawal; (MED): fare un ~ (di) to take a sample (of)

prelimi'nare *ag* preliminary; ~i *smpl* preliminary talks; preliminaries

pre'ludio *sm* prelude

pré-ma'man [prema'mã] *sm inv* maternity dress

prema'turo, a *ag* premature

premeditazi'one [premeditat'tsjone] *sf* (DIR) premeditation; con ~ *ag* premeditated ♦ *av* with intent

'premere *vt* to press ♦ *vi*: ~ su to press down on; (fig) to put pressure on; ~ a (fig: importare) to matter to

pre'messa *sf* introductory statement, introduction

pre'messo, a *pp di* premettere

pre'mettere *vt* to put before; (dire prima) to start by saying, state first

premi'are *vt* to give a prize to; (fig: merito, onestà) to reward

'premio *sm* prize; (ricompensa) reward; (COMM) premium; (AMM: indennità) bonus

premu'nirsi *vr*: ~ di to provide o.s. with; ~ contro to protect o.s. from, guard o.s. against

pre'mura *sf* (fretta) haste, hurry; (riguardo) attention, care; premu'roso, a *ag* thoughtful, considerate

prena'tale *ag* antenatal

'prendere *vt* to take; (andare a prendere) to get, fetch; (ottenere) to get; (guadagnare) to get, earn; (catturare: ladro, *pesce*) to catch; (*collaboratore, dipendente*) to take on; (*passeggero*) to pick up; (*chiedere: somma, prezzo*) to charge, ask; (*trattare: persona*) to handle ♦ *vi* (*colla, cemento*) to set; (*pianta*) to take; (*fuoco: nel camino*) to catch; (*voltare*): **~ a destra** to turn (to the) right; **~rsi** *vr* (*azzuffarsi*): **~rsi a pugni** to come to blows; **prendi qualcosa?** (*da bere, da mangiare*) would you like something to eat (*o* drink)?; **prendo un caffè** I'll have a coffee; **~ qn/ qc per** (*scambiare*) to take sb/sth for; **~ fuoco** to catch fire; **~ parte a** to take part in; **~rsi cura di qn/ qc** to look after sb/sth; **prendersela** (*adirarsi*) to get annoyed; (*preoccuparsi*) to get upset, worry

prendi'sole *sm inv* sundress
preno'tare *vt* to book, reserve; **prenotazi'one** *sf* booking, reservation
preoccu'pare *vt* to worry; to preoccupy; **~rsi** *vr*: **~rsi di qn/qc** to worry about sb/ sth; **~rsi per qn** to be anxious for sb; **preoccupazi'one** *sf* worry, anxiety
prepa'rare *vt* to prepare; (*esame, concorso*) to prepare for; **~rsi** *vr* (*vestirsi*) to get ready; **~rsi a qc/a fare** to get ready *o* prepare (o.s.) for sth/to do; **~ da mangiare** to prepare a meal; **prepara'tivi** *smpl* preparations; **prepa'rato** *sm* (*prodotto*) preparation; **preparazi'one** *sf* preparation
preposizi'one [prepozit'tsjone] *sf* (*LING*) preposition
prepo'tente *ag* (*persona*) domineering, arrogant; (*bisogno, desiderio*) overwhelming, pressing ♦ *sm/f* bully; **prepo'tenza** *sf* arrogance; arrogant behaviour
'presa *sf* taking *no pl*; catching *no pl*; (*di città*) capture; (*indurimento: di cemento*) setting; (*appiglio, SPORT*) hold; (*di acqua, gas*) (supply) point; (*ELETTR*): **~ (di corrente)** socket; (: *al muro*) point; (*piccola quantità: di sale etc*) pinch; (*CARTE*) trick; **far ~** (*colla*) to set; **far ~ sul pubblico** to catch the public's imagination; **~ d'aria** air inlet; **essere alle ~e con** (*fig*) to be struggling

with
pre'sagio [pre'zadʒo] *sm* omen
presa'gire [preza'dʒire] *vt* to foresee
'presbite *ag* long-sighted
presbi'terio *sm* presbytery
pre'scindere [preʃ'ʃindere] *vi*: **~ da** to leave out of consideration; **a ~ da** apart from
pres'critto, a *pp di* **prescrivere**
pres'crivere *vt* to prescribe; **prescrizi'one** *sf* (*MED, DIR*) prescription; (*norma*) rule, regulation
presen'tare *vt* to present; (*far conoscere*): **~ qn (a)** to introduce sb (to); (*AMM: inoltrare*) to submit; **~rsi** *vr* (*recarsi, farsi vedere*) to present o.s., appear; (*farsi conoscere*) to introduce o.s.; (*occasione*) to arise; **~rsi come candidato** (*POL*) to stand as a candidate; **~rsi bene/male** to have a good/poor appearance; **presentazi'one** *sf* presentation; introduction
pre'sente *ag* present; (*questo*) this ♦ *sm* present; **i ~i** those present; **aver ~ qc/qn** to remember sth/sb
presenti'mento *sm* premonition
pre'senza [pre'zentsa] *sf* presence; (*aspetto esteriore*) appearance; **~ di spirito** presence of mind
pre'sepe, pre'sepio *sm* crib
preser'vare *vt* to protect; to save; **preserva'tivo** *sm* sheath, condom
'preside *sm/f* (*INS*) head (teacher) (*BRIT*), principal (*US*); (*di facoltà universitaria*) dean
presi'dente *sm* (*POL*) president; (*di assemblea, COMM*) chairman; **~ del consiglio** prime minister; **presiden'tessa** *sf* president; president's wife; chairwoman; **presi'denza** *sf* presidency; office of president; chairmanship
presidi'are *vt* to garrison; **pre'sidio** *sm* garrison
presi'edere *vt* to preside over ♦ *vi*: **~ a** to direct, be in charge of
'preso, a *pp di* **prendere**
'pressa *sf* (*TECN*) press

pressap'poco *av* about, roughly
pres'sare *vt* to press
pressi'one *sf* pressure; **far ~ su qn** to put pressure on sb; **~ sanguigna** blood pressure
'presso *av* (*vicino*) nearby, close at hand
♦ *prep* (*vicino a*) near; (*accanto a*) beside, next to; (*in casa di*): **~ qn** at sb's home; (*nelle lettere*) care of, c/o; (*alle dipendenze di*): **lavora ~ di noi** he works for *o* with us
♦ *smpl*: **nei ~i di** near, in the vicinity of
pressuriz'zare [pressurid'dzare] *vt* to pressurize
presta'nome (*peg*) *sm/f inv* figurehead
pres'tante *ag* good-looking
pres'tare *vt*: **~ (qc a qn)** to lend (sb sth *o* sth to sb); **~rsi** *vr* (*offrirsi*): **~rsi a fare** to offer to do; (*essere adatto*): **~rsi a** to lend itself to, be suitable for; **~ aiuto** to lend a hand; **~ attenzione** to pay attention; **~ fede a qc/qn** to give credence to sth/sb; **~ orecchio** to listen; **prestazi'one** *sf* (*TECN, SPORT*) performance; **prestazioni** *sfpl* (*di persona: servizi*) services
prestigia'tore, 'trice [prestidʒa'tore] *sm/f* conjurer
pres'tigio [pres'tidʒo] *sm* (*fama*) prestige; (*illusione*): **gioco di ~** conjuring trick
'prestito *sm* lending *no pl*; loan; **dar in ~** to lend; **prendere in ~** to borrow
'presto *av* (*tra poco*) soon; (*in fretta*) quickly; (*di buon'ora*) early; **a ~** see you soon; **fare ~ a fare qc** to hurry up and do sth; (*non costare fatica*) to have no trouble doing sth; **si fa ~ a criticare** it's easy to criticize
pre'sumere *vt* to presume, assume; **pre'sunto, a** *pp di* **presumere**
presuntu'oso, a *ag* presumptuous
presunzi'one [prezun'tsjone] *sf* presumption
presup'porre *vt* to suppose; to presuppose
'prete *sm* priest
preten'dente *sm/f* pretender ♦ *sm* (*corteggiatore*) suitor
pre'tendere *vt* (*esigere*) to demand,

require; (*sostenere*): **~ che** to claim that; **pretende di aver sempre ragione** he thinks he's always right
pretenzi'oso, a [preten'tsjoso] *ag* pretentious
pre'tesa *sf* (*esigenza*) claim, demand; (*presunzione, sfarzo*) pretentiousness; **senza ~e** unpretentious
pre'teso, a *pp di* **pretendere**
pre'testo *sm* pretext, excuse
pre'tore *sm* magistrate; **pre'tura** *sf* magistracy; (*sede*) magistrate's court
preva'lente *ag* prevailing; **preva'lenza** *sf* predominance
preva'lere *vi* to prevail; **pre'valso, a** *pp di* **prevalere**
preve'dere *vt* (*indovinare*) to foresee; (*presagire*) to foretell; (*considerare*) to make provision for
pre'vendita *sf* advance booking
preve'nire *vt* (*anticipare*) to forestall; to anticipate; (*evitare*) to avoid, prevent
preven'tivo, a *ag* preventive ♦ *sm* (*COMM*) estimate
prevenzi'one [preven'tsjone] *sf* prevention; (*preconcetto*) prejudice
previ'dente *ag* showing foresight; prudent; **previ'denza** *sf* foresight; **istituto di previdenza** provident institution; **previdenza sociale** social security (*BRIT*), welfare (*US*)
previsi'one *sf* forecast, prediction; **~i meteorologiche** *o* **del tempo** weather forecast *sg*
pre'visto, a *pp di* **prevedere** ♦ *sm*: **più/meno del ~** more/less than expected
prezi'oso, a [pret'tsjoso] *ag* precious; invaluable ♦ *sm* jewel; valuable
prez'zemolo [pret'tsemolo] *sm* parsley
'prezzo ['prettso] *sm* price; **~ d'acquisto/di vendita** buying/selling price
prigi'one [pri'dʒone] *sf* prison; **prigio'nia** *sf* imprisonment; **prigioni'ero, a** *ag* captive ♦ *sm/f* prisoner
'prima *sf* (*TEATRO*) first night; (*CINEMA*) première; (*AUT*) first gear; *vedi anche* **primo**
♦ *av* before; (*in anticipo*) in advance,

beforehand; (*per l'addietro*) at one time, formerly; (*più presto*) sooner, earlier; (*in primo luogo*) first ♦ *cong*: ~ **di fare/che parta** before doing/he leaves; ~ **di** before; ~ **o poi** sooner or later

pri'mario, a *ag* primary; (*principale*) chief, leading, primary ♦ *sm* (MED) chief physician

pri'mato *sm* supremacy; (SPORT) record

prima'vera *sf* spring; **primave'rile** *ag* spring *cpd*

primeggi'are [primed'dʒare] *vi* to excel, be one of the best

primi'tivo, a *ag* primitive; original

pri'mizie [pri'mittsje] *sfpl* early produce *sg*

'primo, a *ag* first; (*fig*) initial; basic; prime ♦ *sm/f* first (one) ♦ *sm* (CUC) first course; (*in date*): **il ~ luglio** the first of July; **le ~e ore del mattino** the early hours of the morning; **ai ~i di maggio** at the beginning of May; **viaggiare in ~a** to travel first-class; **in ~ luogo** first of all, in the first place; **di prim'ordine** *o* **~a qualità** first-class, first-rate; **in un ~ tempo** at first; **~a donna** leading lady; (*di opera lirica*) prima donna

primo'genito, a [primo'dʒenito] *ag, sm/f* firstborn

'primula *sf* primrose

princi'pale [printʃi'pale] *ag* main, principal ♦ *sm* manager, boss

princi'pato [printʃi'pato] *sm* principality

'principe ['printʃipe] *sm* prince; ~ **ereditario** crown prince; **princi'pessa** *sf* princess

principi'ante [printʃi'pjante] *sm/f* beginner

prin'cipio [prin'tʃipjo] *sm* (*inizio*) beginning, start; (*origine*) origin, cause; (*concetto, norma*) principle; **al** *o* **in ~** at first; **per ~** on principle

pri'ore *sm* (REL) prior

priorità *sf* priority

priori'tario, a *ag* priority; **posta prioritaria** first-class mail

'prisma, i *sm* prism

pri'vare *vt*: ~ **qn di** to deprive sb of; **~rsi di** to go *o* do without

pri'vato, a *ag* private ♦ *sm/f* private citizen; **in ~** in private

privazi'one [privat'tsjone] *sf* privation, hardship

privilegi'are [privile'dʒare] *vt* to grant a privilege to

privi'legio [privi'lɛdʒo] *sm* privilege

'privo, a *ag*: ~ **di** without, lacking

pro *prep* for, on behalf of ♦ *sm inv* (*utilità*) advantage, benefit; **a che ~?** what's the use?; **il ~ e il contro** the pros and cons

pro'babile *ag* probable, likely; **probabilità** *sf inv* probability

pro'blema, i *sm* problem

pro'boscide [pro'bɔʃʃide] *sf* (*di elefante*) trunk

procacci'are [prokat'tʃare] *vt* to get, obtain

pro'cedere [pro'tʃɛdere] *vi* to proceed; (*comportarsi*) to behave; (*iniziare*) to start; ~ **a** to start; ~ **contro** (DIR) to start legal proceedings against; **procedi'mento** *sm* procedure; (*di avvenimenti*) course; (TECN) process; **procedimento penale** (DIR) criminal proceedings; **proce'dura** *sf* (DIR) procedure

proces'sare [protʃes'sare] *vt* (DIR) to try

processi'one [protʃes'sjone] *sf* procession

pro'cesso [pro'tʃɛsso] *sm* (DIR) trial; proceedings *pl*; (*metodo*) process

pro'cinto [pro'tʃinto] *sm*: **in ~ di fare** about to do, on the point of doing

procla'mare *vt* to proclaim

procre'are *vt* to procreate

pro'cura *sf* (DIR) proxy; power of attorney; (*ufficio*) attorney's office

procu'rare *vt*: ~ **qc a qn** (*fornire*) to get *o* obtain sth for sb; (*causare: noie etc*) to bring *o* give sb sth

procura'tore, 'trice *sm/f* (DIR) ≈ solicitor; (: *chi ha la procura*) attorney; proxy; ~ **generale** (*in corte d'appello*) public prosecutor; (*in corte di cassazione*) Attorney General; ~ **della Repubblica** (*in corte d'assise, tribunale*) public prosecutor

prodi'gare *vt* to be lavish with; **~rsi per qn** to do all one can for sb

pro'digio [pro'didʒo] *sm* marvel, wonder; (*persona*) prodigy; **prodigi'oso, a** *ag* prodigious; phenomenal

'**prodigo, a, ghi, ghe** *ag* lavish, extravagant

pro'dotto, a *pp di* produrre ♦ *sm* product; **~i agricoli** farm produce *sg*

pro'durre *vt* to produce; produttività *sf* productivity; produt'tivo, a *ag* productive; produt'tore, 'trice *sm/f* producer; produzi'one *sf* production; (*rendimento*) output

pro'emio *sm* introduction, preface

Prof. *abbr* (= *professore*) Prof

profa'nare *vt* to desecrate

pro'fano, a *ag* (*mondano*) secular; profane; (*sacrilego*) profane

profe'rire *vt* to utter

profes'sare *vt* to profess; (*medicina etc*) to practise

professio'nale *ag* professional

professi'one *sf* profession; professio'nista, i, e *sm/f* professional

profes'sore, 'essa *sm/f* (*INS*) teacher; (*: di università*) lecturer; (*: titolare di cattedra*) professor

pro'feta, i *sm* prophet; profe'zia *sf* prophecy

pro'ficuo, a *ag* useful, profitable

profi'larsi *vr* to stand out, be silhouetted; to loom up

profi'lattico *sm* condom

pro'filo *sm* profile; (*breve descrizione*) sketch, outline; **di ~** in profile

pro'fitto *sm* advantage, profit, benefit; (*fig: progresso*) progress; (*COMM*) profit

profondità *sf inv* depth

pro'fondo, a *ag* deep; (*rancore, meditazione*) profound ♦ *sm* depth(s *pl*), bottom; **~ 8 metri** 8 metres deep

'profugo, a, ghi, ghe *sm/f* refugee

profu'mare *vt* to perfume ♦ *vi* to be fragrant; **~rsi** *vr* to put on perfume *o* scent

profume'ria *sf* perfumery; (*negozio*) perfume shop

pro'fumo *sm* (*prodotto*) perfume, scent; (*fragranza*) scent, fragrance

profusi'one *sf* profusion; **a ~** in plenty

proget'tare [prodʒet'tare] *vt* to plan;

(*edificio*) to plan, design; **pro'getto** *sm* plan; (*idea*) plan, project; **progetto di legge** bill

pro'gramma, i *sm* programme; (*TV, RADIO*) programmes *pl*; (*INS*) syllabus, curriculum; (*INFORM*) program; program'mare *vt* (*TV, RADIO*) to put on; (*INFORM*) to program; (*ECON*) to plan; programma'tore, 'trice *sm/f* (*INFORM*) computer programmer

progre'dire *vi* to progress, make progress

progres'sivo, a *ag* progressive

pro'gresso *sm* progress *no pl*; **fare ~i** to make progress

proi'bire *vt* to forbid, prohibit; proibi'tivo, a *ag* prohibitive; proibizi'one *sf* prohibition

proiet'tare *vt* (*gen, GEOM, CINEMA*) to project; (*: presentare*) to show, screen; (*luce, ombra*) to throw, cast, project; proi'ettile *sm* projectile, bullet (*o shell etc*); proiet'tore *sm* (*CINEMA*) projector; (*AUT*) headlamp; (*MIL*) searchlight; proiezi'one *sf* (*CINEMA*) projection; showing

'prole *sf* children *pl*, offspring

prole'tario, a *ag, sm* proletarian

prolife'rare *vi* (*fig*) to proliferate

pro'lisso, a *ag* verbose

'prologo, ghi *sm* prologue

pro'lunga, ghe *sf* (*di cavo etc*) extension

prolun'gare *vt* (*discorso, attesa*) to prolong; (*linea, termine*) to extend

prome'moria *sm inv* memorandum

pro'messa *sf* promise

pro'messo, a *pp di* promettere

pro'mettere *vt* to promise ♦ *vi* to be *o* look promising; **~ a qn di fare** to promise sb that one will do

promi'nente *ag* prominent

promiscuità *sf* promiscuousness

promon'torio *sm* promontory, headland

pro'mosso, a *pp di* promuovere

promo'tore, trice *sm/f* promoter, organizer

promozi'one [promot'tsjone] *sf* promotion

promul'gare *vt* to promulgate

promu'overe *vt* to promote

proni'pote *sm/f* (*di nonni*) great-grandchild, great-grandson/granddaughter; (*di zii*) great-nephew/niece; ~i *smpl* (*discendenti*) descendants

pro'nome *sm* (*LING*) pronoun

pro'nostico, ci *sm* forecast, prediction

pron'tezza [pron'tettsa] *sf* readiness; quickness, promptness

'pronto, a *ag* ready; (*rapido*) fast, quick, prompt; ~! (*TEL*) hello!; ~ all'ira quick-tempered; ~ soccorso first aid

prontu'ario *sm* manual, handbook

pro'nuncia [pro'nuntʃa] *sf* pronunciation

pronunci'are [pronun'tʃare] *vt* (*parola, sentenza*) to pronounce; (*dire*) to utter; (*discorso*) to deliver; ~rsi *vr* to declare one's opinion; pronunci'ato, a *ag* (*spiccato*) pronounced, marked; (*sporgente*) prominent

pro'nunzia *etc* [pro'nuntsja] = pronuncia *etc*

propa'ganda *sf* propaganda

propa'gare *vt* (*notizia, malattia*) to spread; (*REL, BIOL*) to propagate; ~rsi *vr* to spread; (*BIOL*) to propagate; (*FISICA*) to be propagated

pro'pendere *vi*: ~ per to favour, lean towards; propensi'one *sf* inclination, propensity; pro'penso, a *pp di* propendere

propi'nare *vt* to administer

pro'pizio, a [pro'pittsjo] *ag* favourable

pro'porre *vt* (*suggerire*): ~ qc (a qn) to suggest sth (to sb); (*candidato*) to put forward; (*legge, brindisi*) to propose; ~ di fare to suggest *o* propose doing; proporsi di fare to propose *o* intend to do; proporsi una meta to set o.s. a goal

proporzio'nale [proportsjo'nale] *ag* proportional

proporzio'nare [proportsjo'nare] *vt*: ~ qc a to proportion *o* adjust sth to

proporzi'one [propor'tsjone] *sf* proportion; in ~ a in proportion to

pro'posito *sm* (*intenzione*) intention, aim; (*argomento*) subject, matter; a ~ di regarding, with regard to; di ~ (*apposta*) deliberately, on purpose; a ~ by the way; capitare a ~ (*cosa, persona*) to turn up at the right time

proposizi'one [propozit'tsjone] *sf* (*LING*) clause; (: *periodo*) sentence

pro'posta *sf* proposal; (*suggerimento*) suggestion; ~a di legge bill

pro'posto, a *pp di* proporre

proprietà *sf inv* (*ciò che si possiede*) property *gen no pl*, estate; (*caratteristica*) property; (*correttezza*) correctness; proprie'tario, a *sm/f* owner; (*di albergo etc*) proprietor, owner; (*per l'inquilino*) landlord/lady

'proprio, a *ag* (*possessivo*) own; (: *impersonale*) one's; (*esatto*) exact, correct, proper; (*senso, significato*) literal; (*LING: nome*) proper; (*particolare*): ~ di characteristic of, peculiar to ♦ *av* (*precisamente*) just, exactly; (*davvero*) really; (*affatto*): non ... ~ not ... at all; l'ha visto con i (suoi) ~i occhi he saw it with his own eyes

'prora *sf* (*NAUT*) bow(s *pl*), prow

'proroga, ghe *sf* extension; postponement; proro'gare *vt* to extend; (*differire*) to postpone, defer

pro'rompere *vi* to burst out; pro'rotto, a *pp di* prorompere

'prosa *sf* prose; pro'saico, a, ci, che *ag* (*fig*) prosaic, mundane

pro'sciogliere [proʃ'ʃɔʎʎere] *vt* to release; (*DIR*) to acquit; prosci'olto, a *pp di* prosciogliere

prosciu'gare [proʃʃu'gare] *vt* (*terreni*) to drain, reclaim; ~rsi *vr* to dry up

prosci'utto [proʃ'ʃutto] *sm* ham; ~ cotto/crudo cooked/cured ham

prosegui'mento *sm* continuation; buon ~! all the best!; (*a chi viaggia*) enjoy the rest of your journey!

prosegu'ire *vt* to carry on with, continue ♦ *vi* to carry on, go on

prospe'rare *vi* to thrive; prosperità *sf* prosperity; 'prospero, a *ag* (*fiorente*) flourishing, thriving, prosperous;

prospe'roso, a *ag* (*robusto*) hale and hearty; (: *ragazza*) buxom

prospet'tare *vt* (*esporre*) to point out, show; ~rsi *vr* to look, appear

prospet'tiva *sf* (ARTE) perspective; (*veduta*) view; (*fig: previsione, possibilità*) prospect

pros'petto *sm* (DISEGNO) elevation; (*veduta*) view, prospect; (*facciata*) façade, front; (*tabella*) table; (*sommario*) summary

prospici'ente [prospi'tʃɛnte] *ag*: ~ qc facing *o* overlooking sth

prossimità *sf* nearness, proximity; **in ~ di** near (to), close to

'prossimo, a *ag* (*vicino*): ~ a near (to), close to; (*che viene subito dopo*) next; (*parente*) close ♦ *sm* neighbour, fellow man

prosti'tuta *sf* prostitute; prostituzi'one *sf* prostitution

pros'trare *vt* (*fig*) to exhaust, wear out; ~rsi *vr* (*fig*) to humble o.s.

protago'nista, i, e *sm/f* protagonist

pro'teggere [pro'tɛddʒere] *vt* to protect

proteggi'slip [protɛddʒi'zlip] *sm inv* panty liner

prote'ina *sf* protein

pro'tendere *vt* to stretch out; pro'teso, a *pp di* protendere

pro'testa *sf* protest

protes'tante *ag, sm/f* Protestant

protes'tare *vt, vi* to protest; ~rsi *vr*: ~rsi innocente *etc* to protest one's innocence *o* that one is innocent *etc*

protet'tivo, a *ag* protective

pro'tetto, a *pp di* proteggere

protet'tore, 'trice *sm/f* protector; (*sostenitore*) patron

protezi'one [protet'tsjone] *sf* protection; (*patrocinio*) patronage

protocol'lare *vt* to register ♦ *ag* formal; of protocol; proto'collo *sm* protocol; (*registro*) register of documents

pro'totipo *sm* prototype

pro'trarre *vt* (*prolungare*) to prolong; pro'tratto, a *pp di* protrarre

protube'ranza [protube'rantsa] *sf* protuberance, bulge

'prova *sf* (*esperimento, cimento*) test, trial; (*tentativo*) attempt, try; (MAT, *testimonianza, documento etc*) proof; (DIR) evidence *no pl*, proof; (INS) exam, test; (TEATRO) rehearsal; (*di abito*) fitting; **a ~ di** (*in testimonianza di*) as proof of; **a ~ di fuoco** fireproof; **fino a ~ contraria** until it is proved otherwise; **mettere alla ~** to put to the test; **giro di ~** test *o* trial run; **~ generale** (TEATRO) dress rehearsal

pro'vare *vt* (*sperimentare*) to test; (*tentare*) to try, attempt; (*assaggiare*) to try, taste; (*sperimentare in sé*) to experience; (*sentire*) to feel; (*cimentare*) to put to the test; (*dimostrare*) to prove; (*abito*) to try on; **~ a fare** to try *o* attempt to do

proveni'enza [prove'njentsa] *sf* origin, source

prove'nire *vi*: ~ da to come from

pro'venti *smpl* revenue *sg*

prove'nuto, a *pp di* provenire

pro'verbio *sm* proverb

pro'vetta *sf* test tube; **bambino in ~** test-tube baby

pro'vetto, a *ag* skilled, experienced

pro'vincia, ce *o* cie [pro'vintʃa] *sf* province; provinci'ale *ag* provincial; **(strada) provinciale** main road (BRIT), highway (US)

pro'vino *sm* (CINEMA) screen test; (*campione*) specimen

provo'cante *ag* (*attraente*) provocative

provo'care *vt* (*causare*) to cause, bring about; (*eccitare: riso, pietà*) to arouse; (*irritare, sfidare*) to provoke; provoca'torio, a *ag* provocative; provocazi'one *sf* provocation

provve'dere *vi* (*disporre*): ~ (a) to provide (for); (*prendere un provvedimento*) to take steps, act; provvedi'mento *sm* measure; (*di previdenza*) precaution

provvi'denza [provvi'dɛntsa] *sf*: la ~ providence; provvidenzi'ale *ag* providential

provvigi'one [provvi'dʒone] *sf* (COMM) commission

provvi'sorio, a *ag* temporary

prov'vista *sf* provision, supply

'prua *sf* (*NAUT*) = **prora**

pru'dente *ag* cautious, prudent; (*assennato*) sensible, wise; pru'denza *sf* prudence, caution; wisdom

'prudere *vi* to itch, be itchy

'prugna ['pruɲɲa] *sf* plum; ~ **secca** prune

prurigi'noso, a [pruridʒi'noso] *ag* itchy

pru'rito *sm* itchiness *no pl*; itch

P.S. *abbr* (= *postscriptum*) P.S.; (*POLIZIA*) = **Pubblica Sicurezza**

pseu'donimo *sm* pseudonym

PSI *sigla m* = **Partito Socialista Italiano**

psicana'lista, i, e *sm/f* psychoanalyst

'psiche ['psike] *sf* (*PSIC*) psyche

psichi'atra, i, e [psi'kjatra] *sm/f* psychiatrist; psichi'atrico, a, ci, che *ag* psychiatric

'psichico, a, ci, che ['psikiko] *ag* psychological

psicolo'gia [psikolo'dʒia] *sf* psychology; psico'logico, a, ci, che *ag* psychological; psi'cologo, a, gi, ghe *sm/f* psychologist

psico'patico, a, ci, che *ag* psychopathic ♦ *sm/f* psychopath

P.T. *abbr* = **Posta e Telegrafi**

pubbli'care *vt* to publish

pubblicazi'one [pubblikat'tsjone] *sf* publication; ~i (matrimoniali) *sfpl* (marriage) banns

pubbli'cista, i, e [pubbli'tʃista] *sm/f* (*STAMPA*) occasional çontributor

pubblicità [pubblitʃi'ta] *sf* (*diffusione*) publicity; (*attività*) advertising; (*annunci nei giornali*) advertisements *pl*; pubblici'tario, a *ag* advertising *cpd*; (*trovata, film*) publicity *cpd*

'pubblico, a, ci, che *ag* public; (*statale: scuola etc*) state *cpd* ♦ *sm* public; (*spettatori*) audience; in ~ in public; ~ funzionario civil servant; P~ Ministero Public Prosecutor's Office; la P~a Sicurezza the police

'pube *sm* (*ANAT*) pubis

pubertà *sf* puberty

'pudico, a, ci, che *ag* modest

pu'dore *sm* modesty

puericul'tura *sf* paediatric nursing; infant care

pue'rile *ag* childish

pugi'lato [pudʒi'lato] *sm* boxing

'pugile ['pudʒile] *sm* boxer

pugna'lare [puɲɲa'lare] *vt* to stab

pu'gnale [puɲ'ɲale] *sm* dagger

'pugno ['puɲɲo] *sm* fist; (*colpo*) punch; (*quantità*) fistful

'pulce ['pultʃe] *sf* flea

pul'cino [pul'tʃino] *sm* chick

pu'ledro, a *sm/f* colt/filly

pu'leggia, ge [pu'leddʒa] *sf* pulley

pu'lire *vt* to clean; (*lucidare*) to polish; pu'lita *sf* quick clean; pu'lito, a *ag* (*anche fig*) clean; (*ordinato*) neat, tidy; puli'tura *sf* cleaning; pulitura a secco dry cleaning; puli'zia *sf* cleaning; cleanness; fare le pulizie to do the cleaning *o* the housework

'pullman *sm inv* coach

pul'lover *sm inv* pullover, jumper

pullu'lare *vi* to swarm, teem

pul'mino *sm* minibus

'pulpito *sm* pulpit

pul'sante *sm* (push-)button

pul'sare *vi* to pulsate, beat; pulsazi'one *sf* beat

pul'viscolo *sm* fine dust

'puma *sm inv* puma

pun'gente [pun'dʒɛnte] *ag* prickly; stinging; (*anche fig*) biting

'pungere ['pundʒere] *vt* to prick; (*sog: insetto, ortica*) to sting; (: *freddo*) to bite

pungigli'one [pundʒiʎ'ʎone] *sm* sting

pu'nire *vt* to punish; punizi'one *sf* punishment; (*SPORT*) penalty

'punta *sf* point; (*parte terminale*) tip, end; (*di monte*) peak; (*di costa*) promontory; (*minima parte*) touch, trace; in ~ di piedi on tip-toe; ore di ~ peak hours; uomo di ~ front-rank *o* leading man

pun'tare *vt* (*piedi a terra, gomiti sul tavolo*) to plant; (*dirigere: pistola*) to point; (*scommettere*) to bet ♦ *vi* (*mirare*): ~ a to aim at; ~ su (*dirigersi*) to head *o* make for; (*fig: contare*) to count *o* rely on

pun'tata *sf (gita)* short trip; *(scommessa)* bet; *(parte di opera)* instalment; **romanzo a ~e** serial

punteggia'tura [puntedddʒa'tura] *sf (LING)* punctuation

pun'teggio [pun'teddʒo] *sm* score

puntel'lare *vt* to support

pun'tello *sm* prop, support

puntigli'oso, a [puntiʎ'ʎoso] *ag* punctilious

pun'tina *sf:* **~ da disegno** drawing pin

pun'tino *sm* dot; **fare qc a ~** to do sth properly

'punto, a *pp di* **pungere** ♦ *sm (segno, macchiolina)* dot; *(LING)* full stop; *(MAT, momento, di punteggio, fig: argomento)* point; *(posto)* spot; *(a scuola)* mark; *(nel cucire, nella maglia, MED)* stitch ♦ *av:* **non ... ~** not at all; **due ~i** *sm (LING)* colon; **sul ~ di fare** (just) about to do; **fare il ~** *(NAUT)* to take a bearing; *(fig):* **fare il ~ della situazione** to take stock of the situation; to sum up the situation; **alle 6 in ~** at 6 o'clock sharp *o* on the dot; **essere a buon ~** to have reached a satisfactory stage; **mettere a ~** to adjust; *(motore)* to tune; *(cannocchiale)* to focus; *(fig)* to settle; **di ~ in bianco** point-blank; **~ cardinale** point of the compass, cardinal point; **~ debole** weak point; **~ esclamativo/interrogativo** exclamation/question mark; **~ di riferimento** landmark; *(fig)* point of reference; **~ di vendita** retail outlet; **~ e virgola** semicolon; **~ di vista** *(fig)* point of view; **~i di sospensione** suspension points

puntu'ale *ag* punctual; **puntualità** *sf* punctuality

pun'tura *sf (di ago)* prick; *(di insetto)* sting, bite; *(MED)* puncture; *(: iniezione)* injection; *(dolore)* sharp pain

punzecchi'are [puntsek'kjare] *vt* to prick; *(fig)* to tease

'pupa *sf* doll

pu'pazzo [pu'pattso] *sm* puppet

pu'pilla *sf (ANAT)* pupil

pu'pillo, a *sm/f (DIR)* ward; *(prediletto)* favourite, pet

purché [pur'ke] *cong* provided that, on condition that

'pure *cong (tuttavia)* and yet, nevertheless; *(anche se)* even if ♦ *av (anche)* too, also; **pur di** *(al fine di)* just to; **faccia ~!** go ahead!, please do!

purè *sm (CUC)* purée; *(: di patate)* mashed potatoes

pu'rea *sf* = **purè**

pu'rezza [pu'rettsa] *sf* purity

'purga, ghe *sf (MED)* purging *no pl*; purge; *(POL)* purge

pur'gante *sm (MED)* purgative, purge

pur'gare *vt (MED, POL)* to purge; *(pulire)* to clean

purga'torio *sm* purgatory

purifi'care *vt* to purify; *(metallo)* to refine

puri'tano, a *ag, sm/f* puritan

'puro, a *ag* pure; *(acqua)* clear, limpid; *(vino)* undiluted; **puro'sangue** *sm/f inv* thoroughbred

pur'troppo *av* unfortunately

'pustola *sf* pimple

puti'ferio *sm* rumpus, row

putre'fare *vi* to putrefy, rot; **putre'fatto, a** *pp di* **putrefare**

'putrido, a *ag* putrid, rotten

put'tana *(fam!) sf* whore (!)

'puzza ['puttsa] *sf* = **puzzo**

puz'zare [put'tsare] *vi* to stink

'puzzo ['puttso] *sm* stink, foul smell

'puzzola ['puttsola] *sf* polecat

puzzo'lente [puttso'lɛnte] *ag* stinking

Q, q

qua *av* here; **in ~** *(verso questa parte)* this way; **da un anno in ~** for a year now; **da quando in ~?** since when?; **per di ~** *(passare)* this way; **al di ~ di** *(fiume, strada)* on this side of; **~ dentro/fuori** *etc* in/out here *etc*; *vedi anche* **questo**

qua'derno *sm* notebook; *(per scuola)* exercise book

qua'drante *sm* quadrant; *(di orologio)* face

qua'drare *vi (bilancio)* to balance, tally;

(descrizione) to correspond ♦ vt (MAT) to square; **non mi quadra** I don't like it;
qua'drato, a ag square; (fig: equilibrato) level-headed, sensible; (: peg) square ♦ sm (MAT) square; (PUGILATO) ring; **5 al quadrato** 5 squared
qua'dretto sm: **a ~i** (tessuto) checked; (foglio) squared
quadri'foglio [kwadri'fɔʎʎo] sm four-leaf clover
'quadro sm (pittura) painting, picture; (quadrato) square; (tabella) table, chart; (TECN) board, panel; (TEATRO) scene; (fig: scena, spettacolo) sight; (: descrizione) outline, description; **~i** smpl (POL) party organizers; (MIL) cadres; (COMM) managerial staff; (CARTE) diamonds
'quadruplo, a ag, sm quadruple
quaggiù [kwad'dʒu] av down here
'quaglia ['kwaʎʎa] sf quail

'qualche ['kwalke] det 1 some, a few; (in interrogative) any; **ho comprato ~ libro** I've bought some o a few books; **~ volta** sometimes; **hai ~ sigaretta?** have you any cigarettes?
2 (uno): **c'è ~ medico?** is there a doctor?; **in ~ modo** somehow
3 (un certo, parecchio) some; **un personaggio di ~ rilievo** a figure of some importance
4: **~ cosa = qualcosa**

qualche'duno [kwalke'duno] pron = qualcuno
qual'cosa pron something; (in espressioni interrogative) anything; **qualcos'altro** something new; anything else; **~ di nuovo** something new; anything new; **~ da mangiare** something to eat; anything to eat; **c'è ~ che non va?** is there something o anything wrong?
qual'cuno pron (persona) someone, somebody; (: in espressioni interrogative) anyone, anybody; (alcuni) some; **~ è favorevole a noi** some are on our side;

qualcun altro someone o somebody else; anyone o anybody else

'quale (spesso troncato in qual) det 1 (interrogativo) what; (: scegliendo tra due o più cose o persone) which; **~ uomo/denaro?** what man/money?; which man/money?; **~i sono i tuoi programmi?** what are your plans?; **~ stanza preferisci?** which room do you prefer?
2 (relativo: come): **il risultato fu ~ ci si aspettava** the result was as expected
3 (esclamativo) what; **~ disgrazia!** what bad luck!
♦ pron 1 (interrogativo) which; **~ dei due scegli?** which of the two do you want?
2 (relativo): **il(la) ~** (persona: soggetto) who; (: oggetto, con preposizione) whom; (cosa) which; (possessivo) whose; **suo padre, il ~ è avvocato, ...** his father, who is a lawyer, ...; **il signore con il ~ parlavo** the gentleman to whom I was speaking; **l'albergo al ~ ci siamo fermati** the hotel where we stayed o which we stayed at; **la signora della ~ ammiriamo la bellezza** the lady whose beauty we admire
3 (relativo: in elenchi) such as, like; **piante ~i l'edera** plants like o such as ivy; **~ sindaco di questa città** as mayor of this town

qua'lifica, che sf qualification; (titolo) title
qualifi'care vt to qualify; (definire): **~ qn/qc come** to describe sb/sth as; **~rsi** vr (anche SPORT) to qualify; qualifica'tivo, a ag qualifying; qualificazi'one sf: **gara di qualificazione** (SPORT) qualifying event
qualità sf inv quality; **in ~ di** in one's capacity as
qua'lora cong in case, if
qual'siasi det inv = qualunque
qua'lunque det inv any; (quale che sia) whatever; (discriminativo) whichever; (posposto: mediocre) poor, indifferent; ordinary; **mettiti un vestito ~** put on any old dress; **~ cosa** anything; **~ cosa**

accada whatever happens; **a ~ costo** at any cost, whatever the cost; **l'uomo ~** the man in the street; **~ persona** anyone, anybody

'**quando** *cong, av* when; **~ sarò ricco** when I'm rich; **da ~** (*dacché*) since; (*interrogativo*): **da ~ sei qui?** how long have you been here?; **quand'anche** even if

quantità *sf inv* quantity; (*gran numero*): **una ~ di** a great deal of, a lot of; **in grande ~** in large quantities; **quanti'tativo** *sm* (*COMM*) amount, quantity

┌─────────────────┐
│ *PAROLA CHIAVE* │
└─────────────────┘

'**quanto, a** *det* 1 (*interrogativo: quantità*) how much; (: *numero*) how many; **~ pane/denaro?** how much bread/money?; **~i libri/ragazzi?** how many books/boys?; **~ tempo?** how long?; **~i anni hai?** how old are you?

2 (*esclamativo*): **~e storie!** what a lot of nonsense!; **~ tempo sprecato!** what a waste of time!

3 (*relativo: quantità*) as much ... as; (: *numero*) as many ... as; **ho ~ denaro mi occorre** I have as much money as I need; **prendi ~i libri vuoi** take as many books as you like

♦ *pron* 1 (*interrogativo: quantità*) how much; (: *numero*) how many; (: *tempo*) how long; **~ mi dai?** how much will you give me?; **~i me ne hai portati?** how many did you bring me?; **da ~ sei qui?** how long have you been here?; **~i ne abbiamo oggi?** what's the date today?

2 (*relativo: quantità*) as much as; (: *numero*) as many as; **farò ~ posso** I'll do as much as I can; **possono venire ~i sono stati invitati** all those who have been invited can come

♦ *av* 1 (*interrogativo: con ag, av*) how; (: *con vb*) how much; **~ stanco ti sembrava?** how tired did he seem to you?; **~ corre la tua moto?** how fast can your motorbike go?; **~ costa?** how much

does it cost?; **quant'è?** how much is it?

2 (*esclamativo: con ag, av*) how; (: *con vb*) how much; **~ sono felice!** how happy I am!; **sapessi ~ abbiamo camminato!** if you knew how far we've walked!; **studierò ~ posso** I'll study as much as *o* all I can; **~ prima** as soon as possible

3: **in ~** (*in qualità di*) as; (*perché, per il fatto che*) as, since; **(in) ~ a** (*per ciò che riguarda*) as for, as regards

4: **per ~** (*nonostante, anche se*) however; **per ~ si sforzi, non ce la farà** try as he may, he won't manage it; **per ~ sia brava, fa degli errori** however good she may be, she makes mistakes; **per ~ io sappia** as far as I know

└─────────────────────────────────────┘

quan'tunque *cong* although, though

qua'ranta *num* forty

quaran'tena *sf* quarantine

quaran'tesimo, a *num* fortieth

quaran'tina *sf*: **una ~ (di)** about forty

qua'resima *sf*: **la ~** Lent

'**quarta** *sf* (*AUT*) fourth (gear); *vedi anche* **quarto**

quar'tetto *sm* quartet(te)

quarti'ere *sm* district, area; (*MIL*) quarters *pl*; **~ generale** headquarters *pl*

'**quarto, a** *ag* fourth ♦ *sm* fourth; (*quarta parte*) quarter; **le 6 e un ~** a quarter past six; **~ d'ora** quarter of an hour; **~i di finale** quarter final

'**quarzo** ['kwartso] *sm* quartz

'**quasi** *av* almost, nearly ♦ *cong* (*anche*: **~ che**) as if; **(non) ... ~ mai** hardly ever; **~ ~ me ne andrei** I've half a mind to leave

quassù *av* up here

'**quatto, a** *ag* crouched, squatting; (*silenzioso*) silent; **~ ~** very quietly; stealthily

quat'tordici [kwat'torditʃi] *num* fourteen

quat'trini *smpl* money *sg*, cash *sg*

'**quattro** *num* four; **in ~ e quattr'otto** in less than no time; **quattro'cento** *num* four hundred ♦ *sm*: **il Quattrocento** the fifteenth century; **quattro'mila** *num* four thousand

---

'**quello, a** (*dav sm* **quel** +*C*, **quell'** +*V*, **quello** +*s* impura, *gn, pn, ps, x, z; pl* **quei** +*C*, **quegli** +*V o s* impura, *gn, pn, ps, x, z; dav sf* **quella** +*C*, **quell'** +*V; pl* **quelle**) *det* that; those *pl*; **~a casa** that house; **quegli uomini** those men; **voglio ~a camicia (lì** *o* **là)** I want that shirt

♦ *pron* **1** (*dimostrativo*) that (one); those (ones) *pl*; (*ciò*) that; **conosci ~a?** do you know that woman?; **prendo ~ bianco** I'll take the white one; **chi è ~?** who's that?; **prendi ~!** take that one (there)
2 (*relativo*): **~(a) che** (*persona*) the one (who); (*cosa*) the one (which), the one (that); **~i(e) che** (*persone*) those who; (*cose*) those which; **è lui ~ che non voleva venire** he's the one who didn't want to come; **ho fatto ~ che potevo** I did what I could

'**quercia, ce** [ˈkwertʃa] *sf* oak (tree); (*legno*) oak

que'**rela** *sf* (*DIR*) (legal) action; **quere'lare** *vt* to bring an action against

que'**sito** *sm* question, query; problem

questio'**nario** *sm* questionnaire

questi'**one** *sf* problem, question; (*controversia*) issue; (*litigio*) quarrel; **in ~** in question; **è ~ di tempo** it's a matter *o* question of time

'**questo, a** *det* **1** (*dimostrativo*) this; these *pl*; **io prendo ~ libro (qui** *o* **qua)** this book; **io prendo ~ cappotto, tu quello** I'll take this coat, you take that one; **quest'oggi** today; **~a sera** this evening
2 (*enfatico*): **non fatemi più prendere di ~e paure** don't frighten me like that again

♦ *pron* (*dimostrativo*) this (one); these (ones) *pl*; (*ciò*) this; **prendo ~ (qui** *o* **qua)** I'll take this one; **preferisci ~ o quelli?** do you prefer these (ones) or those (ones)?; **~ intendevo io** this is what I meant; **vengono Paolo e Luca: ~ da Roma,**

quello da Palermo Paolo and Luca are coming: the former from Palermo, the latter from Rome

---

ques'**tore** *sm* ≈ chief constable (*BRIT*), ≈ police commissioner (*US*)

'**questua** *sf* collection of alms

ques'**tura** *sf* police headquarters *pl*

qui *av* here; **da** *o* **di ~** from here; **di ~ in avanti** from now on; **di ~ a poco/una settimana** in a little while/a week's time; **~ dentro/sopra/vicino** in/up/near here; *vedi anche* **questo**

quie'**tanza** [kwjeˈtantsa] *sf* receipt

quie'**tare** *vt* to calm, soothe

qui'**ete** *sf* quiet, quietness; calmness; stillness; peace

qui'**eto, a** *ag* quiet; (*notte*) calm, still; (*mare*) calm

'**quindi** *av* then ♦ *cong* therefore, so

'**quindici** [ˈkwinditʃi] *num* fifteen; **~ giorni** a fortnight (*BRIT*), two weeks

quindi'**cina** [kwindiˈtʃina] *sf* (*serie*): **una ~ (di)** about fifteen; **fra una ~ di giorni** in a fortnight

quin'**quennio** *sm* period of five years

quin'**tale** *sm* quintal (*100 kg*)

'**quinte** *sfpl* (*TEATRO*) wings

'**quinto, a** *num* fifth

i The **Quirinale**, which takes its name from the hill in Rome on which it stands, is the official residence of the Presidente della Repubblica.

'**quota** *sf* (*parte*) quota, share; (*AER*) height, altitude; (*IPPICA*) odds *pl*; **prendere/ perdere ~** (*AER*) to gain/lose height *o* altitude; **~ d'iscrizione** enrolment fee; (*a club*) membership fee

quo'**tare** *vt* (*BORSA*) to quote; **quotazi'one** *sf* quotation

quotidi'**ano, a** *ag* daily; (*banale*) everyday ♦ *sm* (*giornale*) daily (paper)

quozi'**ente** [kwotˈtsjente] *sm* (*MAT*) quotient; **~ d'intelligenza** intelligence quotient, IQ

R, r

ra'barbaro sm rhubarb

'rabbia sf (ira) anger, rage; (accanimento, furia) fury; (MED: idrofobia) rabies sg

rab'bino sm rabbi

rabbi'oso, a ag angry, furious; (facile all'ira) quick-tempered; (forze, acqua etc) furious, raging; (MED) rabid, mad

rabbo'nire vt to calm down; ~rsi vr to calm down

rabbrivi'dire vi to shudder, shiver

rabbui'arsi vr to grow dark

raccapez'zarsi [rakkapet'tsarsi] vr: non ~ to be at a loss

raccapricci'ante [rakkaprit'tʃante] ag horrifying

raccatta'palle sm inv (SPORT) ballboy

raccat'tare vt to pick up

rac'chetta [rak'ketta] sf (per tennis) racket; (per ping-pong) bat; ~ da neve snowshoe; ~ da sci ski stick

racchi'udere [rak'kjudere] vt to contain; racchi'uso, a pp di racchiudere

rac'cogliere [rak'kɔʎʎere] vt to collect; (raccattare) to pick up; (frutti, fiori) to pick, pluck; (AGR) to harvest; (approvazione, voti) to win; ~rsi vr to gather; (fig) to gather one's thoughts; to meditate; raccogli'mento sm meditation; raccogli'tore sm (cartella) folder, binder; raccoglitore ad anelli ring binder

rac'colta sf collecting no pl; collection; (AGR) harvesting no pl, gathering no pl; harvest, crop; (adunata) gathering

rac'colto, a pp di raccogliere ♦ ag (persona: pensoso) thoughtful; (luogo: appartato) secluded, quiet ♦ sm (AGR) crop, harvest

raccoman'dare vt to recommend; (affidare) to entrust; (esortare): ~ a qn di non fare to tell o warn sb not to do; ~rsi vr: ~rsi a qn to commend o.s. to sb; mi raccomando! don't forget!;

rabarbaro → radura

raccoman'data sf (anche: lettera raccomandata) recorded-delivery letter; raccomandazi'one sf recommendation

raccon'tare vt: ~ (a qn) (dire) to tell (sb); (narrare) to relate (to sb), tell (sb) about; rac'conto sm telling no pl, relating no pl; (fatto raccontato) story, tale

raccorci'are [rakkor'tʃare] vt to shorten

rac'cordo sm (TECN: giunto) connection, joint; (AUT: di autostrada) slip road (BRIT), entrance (o exit) ramp (US); ~ anulare (AUT) ring road (BRIT), beltway (US)

ra'chitico, a, ci, che [ra'kitiko] ag suffering from rickets; (fig) scraggy, scrawny

racimo'lare [ratʃimo'lare] vt (fig) to scrape together, glean

'rada sf (natural) harbour

'radar sm radar

raddol'cire [raddol'tʃire] vt (persona, carattere) to soften; (fig: tempo) to grow milder; (persona) to soften, mellow

raddoppi'are vt, vi to double

raddriz'zare [raddrit'tsare] vt to straighten; (fig: correggere) to put straight, correct

'radere vt (barba) to shave off; (mento) to shave; (fig: rasentare) to graze; to skim; ~rsi vr to shave (o.s.); ~ al suolo to raze to the ground

radi'are vt to strike off

radia'tore sm radiator

radiazi'one [radjat'tsjone] sf (FISICA) radiation; (cancellazione) striking off

radi'cale ag radical ♦ sm (LING) root

ra'dicchio [ra'dikkjo] sm chicory

ra'dice [ra'ditʃe] sf root

'radio sf inv radio ♦ sm (CHIM) radium; radioat'tivo, a ag radioactive; radiodiffusi'one sf (radio) broadcasting; radiogra'fare vt to X-ray; radiogra'fia sf radiography; (foto) X-ray photograph

radi'oso, a ag radiant

'rado, a ag (capelli) sparse, thin; (visite) infrequent; di ~ rarely

radu'nare vt, to gather, assemble; ~rsi vr to gather, assemble; ra'duno sm meeting

ra'dura sf clearing

raffazzo'nato [raffattso'nato] _ag_ patched up

raf'fermo, a _ag_ stale

'raffica, che _sf_ (METEOR) gust (of wind); (_di colpi: scarica_) burst of gunfire

raffigu'rare _vt_ to represent

raffi'nare _vt_ to refine; **raffina'tezza** _sf_ refinement; **raffi'nato, a** _ag_ refined; **raffine'ria** _sf_ refinery

raffor'zare [raffor'tsare] _vt_ to reinforce

raffredda'mento _sm_ cooling

raffred'dare _vt_ to cool; (_fig_) to dampen, have a cooling effect on; **~rsi** _vr_ to grow cool _o_ cold; (_prendere un raffreddore_) to catch a cold; (_fig_) to cool (off)

raffred'dato, a _ag_ (MED): **essere ~** to have a cold

raffred'dore _sm_ (MED) cold

raf'fronto _sm_ comparison

'rafia _sf_ (_fibra_) raffia

ra'gazzo, a [ra'gattso] _sm/f_ boy/girl; (_fam: fidanzato_) boyfriend/girlfriend

raggi'ante [rad'dʒante] _ag_ radiant, shining

'raggio ['raddʒo] _sm_ (_di sole etc_) ray; (MAT, _distanza_) radius; (_di ruota etc_) spoke; **~ d'azione** range; **~i X** X-rays

raggi'rare [raddʒi'rare] _vt_ to take in, trick; **rag'giro** _sm_ trick

raggi'ungere [rad'dʒundʒere] _vt_ to reach; (_persona: riprendere_) to catch up (with); (_bersaglio_) to hit; (_fig: meta_) to achieve; **raggi'unto, a** _pp di_ **raggiungere**

raggomito'larsi _vr_ to curl up

raggranel'lare _vt_ to scrape together

raggrup'pare _vt_ to group (together)

raggu'aglio [rag'gwaʎʎo] _sm_ (_informazione_) piece of information

raggua'rdevole _ag_ (_degno di riguardo_) distinguished, notable; (_notevole: somma_) considerable

ragiona'mento [radʒona'mento] _sm_ reasoning _no pl_; arguing _no pl_; argument

ragio'nare [radʒo'nare] _vi_ to reason; **~ di** (_discorrere_) to talk about

ragi'one [ra'dʒone] _sf_ reason; (_dimostrazione, prova_) argument, reason; (_diritto_) right; **aver ~** to be right; **aver ~ di**

qn to get the better of sb; **dare ~ a qn** to agree with sb; to prove sb right; **perdere la ~** to become insane; (_fig_) to take leave of one's senses; **in ~ di** at the rate of; to the amount of; according to; **a o con ~** rightly, justly; **~ sociale** (COMM) corporate name; **a ragion veduta** after due consideration

ragione'ria [radʒone'ria] _sf_ accountancy; accounts department

ragio'nevole [radʒo'nevole] _ag_ reasonable

ragioni'ere, a [radʒo'njere] _sm/f_ accountant

ragli'are [raʎ'ʎare] _vi_ to bray

ragna'tela [raɲɲa'tela] _sf_ cobweb, spider's web

'ragno ['raɲɲo] _sm_ spider

ragù _sm inv_ (CUC) meat sauce; stew

RAI-TV [raiti'vu] _sigla f_ = **Radio televisione italiana**

rallegra'menti _smpl_ congratulations

ralle'grare _vt_ to cheer up; **~rsi** _vr_ to cheer up; (_provare allegrezza_) to rejoice; **~rsi con qn** to congratulate sb

rallen'tare _vt_ to slow down; (_fig_) to lessen, slacken ♦ _vi_ to slow down

raman'zina [raman'dzina] _sf_ lecture, telling-off

'rame _sm_ (CHIM) copper

rammari'carsi _vr_: **~ (di)** (_rincrescersi_) to be sorry (about), regret; (_lamentarsi_) to complain (about); **ram'marico, chi** _sm_ regret

rammen'dare _vt_ to mend; (_calza_) to darn; **ram'mendo** _sm_ mending _no pl_; darning _no pl_; mend; darn

rammen'tare _vt_ to remember, recall; (_richiamare alla memoria_): **~ qc a qn** to remind sb of sth; **~rsi** _vr_: **~rsi (di qc)** to remember (sth)

rammol'lire _vt_ to soften ♦ _vi_ (_anche_: **~rsi**) to go soft

'ramo _sm_ branch

ramo'scello [ramoʃ'ʃello] _sm_ twig

'rampa _sf_ flight (of stairs); **~ di lancio** launching pad

rampi'cante _ag_ (BOT) climbing

ram'pone *sm* harpoon; (*ALPINISMO*) crampon

'rana *sf* frog

'rancido, a ['rantʃido] *ag* rancid

ran'core *sm* rancour, resentment

ran'dagio, a, gi, gie *o* ge [ran'dadʒo] *ag* (*gatto, cane*) stray

ran'dello *sm* club, cudgel

'rango, ghi *sm* (*condizione sociale, MIL: riga*) rank

rannicchi'arsi [rannik'kjarsi] *vr* to crouch, huddle

rannuvo'larsi *vr* to cloud over, become overcast

ra'nocchio [ra'nɔkkjo] *sm* (edible) frog

'rantolo *sm* wheeze; (*di agonizzanti*) death rattle

'rapa *sf* (*BOT*) turnip

ra'pace [ra'patʃe] *ag* (*animale*) predatory; (*fig*) rapacious, grasping ♦ *sm* bird of prey

ra'pare *vt* (*capelli*) to crop, cut very short

'rapida *sf* (*di fiume*) rapid; *vedi anche* rapido

rapida'mente *av* quickly, rapidly

rapidità *sf* speed

'rapido, a *ag* fast, quick, rapid ♦ *sm* (*FERR*) express (train)

rapi'mento *sm* kidnapping; (*fig*) rapture

ra'pina *sf* robbery; ~ a mano armata armed robbery; rapi'nare *vt* to rob; rapina'tore, 'trice *sm/f* robber

ra'pire *vt* (*cose*) to steal; (*persone*) to kidnap; (*fig*) to enrapture, delight; rapi'tore, 'trice *sm/f* kidnapper

rappor'tare *vt* (*confrontare*) to compare; (*riprodurre*) to reproduce

rap'porto *sm* (*resoconto*) report; (*legame*) relationship; (*MAT, TECN*) ratio; ~i *smpl* (*fra persone, paesi*) relations; ~i sessuali sexual intercourse *sg*

rap'prendersi *vr* to coagulate, clot; (*latte*) to curdle

rappre'saglia [rappre'saʎʎa] *sf* reprisal, retaliation

rappresen'tante *sm/f* representative; rappresen'tanza *sf* delegation, deputation; (*COMM: ufficio, sede*) agency

rappresen'tare *vt* to represent; (*TEATRO*) to perform; rappresentazi'one *sf* representation; performing *no pl*; (*spettacolo*) performance

rap'preso, a *pp di* rapprendere

rapso'dia *sf* rhapsody

rara'mente *av* seldom, rarely

rare'fatto, a *ag* rarefied

'raro, a *ag* rare

ra'sare *vt* (*barba etc*) to shave off; (*siepi, erba*) to trim, cut; ~rsi *vr* to shave (o.s.)

raschi'are [ras'kjare] *vt* to scrape; (*macchia, fango*) to scrape off ♦ *vi* to clear one's throat

rasen'tare *vt* (*andar rasente*) to keep close to; (*sfiorare*) to skim along (*o* over); (*fig*) to border on

ra'sente *prep*: ~ (a) close to, very near

'raso, a *pp di* radere ♦ *ag* (*barba*) shaved; (*capelli*) cropped; (*con misure di capacità*) level; (*pieno: bicchiere*) full to the brim ♦ *sm* (*tessuto*) satin; ~ terra close to the ground; un cucchiaio ~ a level spoonful

ra'soio *sm* razor; ~ elettrico electric shaver *o* razor

ras'segna [ras'seɲɲa] *sf* (*MIL*) inspection, review; (*esame*) inspection; (*resoconto*) review, survey; (*pubblicazione letteraria etc*) review; (*mostra*) exhibition, show; passare in ~ (*MIL, fig*) to review

rasse'gnare [rasseɲ'ɲare] *vt*: ~ le dimissioni to resign, hand in one's resignation; ~rsi *vr* (*accettare*): ~rsi (a qc/ a fare) to resign o.s. (to sth/to doing); rassegnazi'one *sf* resignation

rasse'renarsi *vr* (*tempo*) to clear up

rasset'tare *vt* to tidy, put in order; (*aggiustare*) to repair, mend

rassicu'rare *vt* to reassure

rasso'dare *vt* to harden, stiffen

rassomigli'anza [rassomiʎ'ʎantsa] *sf* resemblance

rassomigli'are [rassomiʎ'ʎare] *vi*: ~ a to resemble, look like

rastrel'lare *vt* to rake; (*fig: perlustrare*) to comb

rastrelli'era *sf* rack; (*per piatti*) dish rack

ras'trello *sm* rake

'rata *sf* (*quota*) instalment; **pagare a ~e** to pay by instalments *o* on hire purchase (*BRIT*)

ratifi'care *vt* (*DIR*) to ratify

'ratto *sm* (*DIR*) abduction; (*ZOOL*) rat

rattop'pare *vt* to patch; rat'toppo *sm* patching *no pl*; patch

rattrap'pirsi *vr* to get stiff

rattris'tare *vt* to sadden; ~**rsi** *vr* to become sad

'rauco, a, chi, che *ag* hoarse

rava'nello *sm* radish

ravi'oli *smpl* ravioli *sg*

ravve'dersi *vr* to mend one's ways

ravvici'nare [ravvitʃi'nare] *vt* (*avvicinare*): ~ **qc a** to bring sth nearer to; (: *due tubi*) to bring closer together; (*riconciliare*) to reconcile, bring together

ravvi'sare *vt* to recognize

ravvi'vare *vt* to revive; (*fig*) to brighten up, enliven; ~**rsi** *vr* to revive; to brighten up

razio'cinio [ratsjo'tʃinjo] *sm* reasoning *no pl*; reason; (*buon senso*) common sense

razio'nale [rattsjo'nale] *ag* rational

razio'nare [rattsjo'nare] *vt* to ration

razi'one [rat'tsjone] *sf* ration; (*porzione*) portion, share

'razza ['rattsa] *sf* race; (*ZOOL*) breed; (*discendenza, stirpe*) stock, race; (*sorta*) sort, kind

raz'zia [rat'tsia] *sf* raid, foray

razzi'ale [rat'tsjale] *ag* racial

raz'zismo [rat'tsizmo] *sm* racism, racialism

raz'zista, i, e [rat'tsista] *ag, sm/f* racist, racialist

'razzo ['raddzo] *sm* rocket

razzo'lare [rattso'lare] *vi* (*galline*) to scratch about

re *sm inv* king; (*MUS*) D; (: *solfeggiando*) re

rea'gire [rea'dʒire] *vi* to react

re'ale *ag* real; (*di, da re*) royal ♦ *sm*: **il ~** reality; (*di, da re*) royal ♦ *sm*: **il ~** reality; rea'lismo *sm* realism; rea'lista, i, e *sm/f* realist; (*POL*) royalist

realiz'zare [realid'dzare] *vt* (*progetto etc*) to realize, carry out; (*sogno, desiderio*) to realize, fulfil; (*scopo*) to achieve; (*COMM: titoli etc*) to realize; (*CALCIO etc*) to score; ~**rsi** *vr* to be realized; realizzazi'one *sf* realization; fulfilment; achievement

real'mente *av* really, actually

realtà *sf inv* reality

re'ato *sm* offence

reat'tore *sm* (*FISICA*) reactor; (*AER: aereo*) jet; (: *motore*) jet engine

reazio'nario, a [reattsjo'narjo] *ag* (*POL*) reactionary

reazi'one [reat'tsjone] *sf* reaction

recapi'tare *vt* to deliver

re'capito *sm* (*indirizzo*) address; (*consegna*) delivery

re'care *vt* (*portare*) to bring; (*avere su di sé*) to carry, bear; (*cagionare*) to cause, bring; ~**rsi** *vr* to go

re'cedere [re'tʃedere] *vi* to withdraw

recensi'one [retʃen'sjone] *sf* review; recen'sire *vt* to review

re'cente [re'tʃente] *ag* recent; **di ~** recently; recente'mente *av* recently

recessi'one [retʃes'sjone] *sf* (*ECON*) recession

re'cidere [re'tʃidere] *vt* to cut off, chop off

reci'divo, a [retʃi'divo] *sm/f* (*DIR*) second (*o* habitual) offender, recidivist

re'cinto [re'tʃinto] *sm* enclosure; (*ciò che recinge*) fence; surrounding wall

recipi'ente [retʃi'pjente] *sm* container

re'ciproco, a, ci, che [re'tʃiproko] *ag* reciprocal

re'ciso, a [re'tʃizo] *pp di* **recidere**

'recita ['rɛtʃita] *sf* performance

reci'tare [retʃi'tare] *vt* (*poesia, lezione*) to recite; (*dramma*) to perform; (*ruolo*) to play *o* act (the part of); recitazi'one *sf* recitation; (*di attore*) acting

recla'mare *vi* to complain ♦ *vt* (*richiedere*) to demand

ré'clame [re'klam] *sf inv* advertising *no pl*; advertisement, advert (*BRIT*), ad (*fam*)

re'clamo *sm* complaint

reclusi'one *sf* (*DIR*) imprisonment

're'cluta *sf* recruit; reclu'tare *vt* to recruit

re'condito, a *ag* secluded; (*fig*) secret,

hidden

recriminazi'one [rekriminat'tsjone] *sf* recrimination

recrude'scenza [rekrudeʃ'ʃentsa] *sf* fresh outbreak

recupe'rare *vt* = **ricuperare**

redargu'ire *vt* to rebuke

re'datto, a *pp di* **redigere**; **redat'tore, 'trice** *sm/f* (*STAMPA*) editor; (: *di articolo*) writer; (*di dizionario etc*) compiler; **redattore capo** chief editor; **redazi'one** *sf* editing; writing; (*sede*) editorial office(s); (*personale*) editorial staff; (*versione*) version

reddi'tizio, a [reddi'tittsjo] *ag* profitable

'reddito *sm* income; (*dello Stato*) revenue; (*di un capitale*) yield

re'dento, a *pp di* **redimere**

redenzi'one [reden'tsjone] *sf* redemption

re'digere [re'didʒere] *vt* to write; (*contratto*) to draw up

'redini *sfpl* reins

'reduce ['rɛdutʃe] *ag*: ~ **da** returning from, back from ♦ *sm/f* survivor

refe'rendum *sm inv* referendum

refe'renza [refe'rentsa] *sf* reference

re'ferto *sm* medical report

refet'torio *sm* refectory

refrat'tario, a *ag* refractory

refrige'rare [refridʒe'rare] *vt* to refrigerate; (*rinfrescare*) to cool, refresh

rega'lare *vt* to give (as a present), make a present of

re'gale *ag* regal

re'galo *sm* gift, present

re'gata *sf* regatta

reg'gente [red'dʒente] *sm/f* regent

'reggere ['rɛddʒere] *vt* (*tenere*) to hold; (*sostenere*) to support, bear, hold up; (*portare*) to carry, bear; (*resistere*) to withstand; (*dirigere: impresa*) to manage, run; (*governare*) to rule, govern; (*LING*) to take, be followed by ♦ *vi* (*resistere*): ~ **a** to stand up to, hold out against; (*sopportare*): ~ **a** to stand; (*durare*) to last; (*fig: teoria etc*) to hold water; ~**rsi** *vr* (*stare ritto*) to stand

'reggia, ge ['rɛddʒa] *sf* royal palace

reggi'calze [reddʒi'kaltse] *sm inv* suspender belt

reggi'mento [reddʒi'mento] *sm* (*MIL*) regiment

reggi'petto [reddʒi'pɛtto] *sm* bra

reggi'seno [reddʒi'sɛno] *sm* bra

re'gia, 'gie [re'dʒia] *sf* (*TV, CINEMA etc*) direction

re'gime [re'dʒime] *sm* (*POL*) regime; (*DIR: aureo, patrimoniale etc*) system; (*MED*) diet; (*TECN*) (engine) speed

re'gina [re'dʒina] *sf* queen

'regio, a, gi, gie ['rɛdʒo] *ag* royal

regio'nale [redʒo'nale] *ag* regional ♦ *sm* local train (*stopping frequently*)

regi'one [re'dʒone] *sf* region; (*territorio*) region, district, area

re'gista, i, e [re'dʒista] *sm/f* (*TV, CINEMA etc*) director

regis'trare [redʒis'trare] *vt* (*AMM*) to register; (*COMM*) to enter; (*notare*) to note, take note of; (*canzone, conversazione, sog: strumento di misura*) to record; (*mettere a punto*) to adjust, regulate; (*bagagli*) to check in; **registra'tore** *sm* (*strumento*) recorder, register; (*magnetofono*) tape recorder; **registratore di cassa** cash register; **registrazi'one** *sf* recording; (*AMM*) registration; (*COMM*) entry; (*di bagagli*) check-in

re'gistro [re'dʒistro] *sm* (*libro, MUS, TECH*) register; ledger; logbook; (*DIR*) registry

re'gnare [reɲ'ɲare] *vi* to reign, rule

'regno ['reɲɲo] *sm* kingdom; (*periodo*) reign; (*fig*) realm; **il ~ animale/vegetale** the animal/vegetable kingdom; **il R~ Unito** the United Kingdom

'regola *sf* rule; **a ~ d'arte** duly; perfectly; **in ~** in order

rego'labile *ag* adjustable

regola'mento *sm* (*complesso di norme*) regulations *pl*; (*di debito*) settlement; ~ **di conti** (*fig*) settling of scores

rego'lare *ag* regular; (*in regola: domanda*) in order, lawful ♦ *vt* to regulate, control; (*apparecchio*) to adjust, regulate; (*questione, conto, debito*) to settle; ~**rsi** *vr* (*moderarsi*): ~**rsi nel bere/nello spendere** to control one's drinking/spending; (*comportarsi*) to behave, act; **regolarità** *sf inv* regularity

'**regolo** *sm* ruler; **~ calcolatore** slide rule

reinte'grare *vt* (*energie*) to recover; (*in una carica*) to reinstate

rela'tivo, a *ag* relative

relazi'one [relat'tsjone] *sf* (*fra cose, persone*) relation(ship); (*resoconto*) report, account; **~i** *sfpl* (*conoscenze*) connections

rele'gare *vt* to banish; (*fig*) to relegate

religi'one [reli'dʒone] *sf* religion; **religi'oso, a** *ag* religious ♦ *sm/f* monk/nun

re'liquia *sf* relic

re'litto *sm* wreck; (*fig*) down-and-out

re'mare *vi* to row

remini'scenze [reminiʃʃɛntse] *sfpl* reminiscences

remissi'one *sf* remission

remis'sivo, a *ag* submissive, compliant

'**remo** *sm* oar

re'moto, a *ag* remote

'**rendere** *vt* (*ridare*) to return, give back; (: *saluto etc*) to return; (*produrre*) to yield, bring in; (*esprimere, tradurre*) to render; **qc possibile** to make sth possible; **~rsi utile** to make o.s. useful; **~rsi conto di qc** to realize sth

rendi'conto *sm* (*rapporto*) report, account; (*AMM, COMM*) statement of account

rendi'mento *sm* (*reddito*) yield; (*di manodopera, TECN*) efficiency; (*capacità di produrre*) output; (*di studenti*) performance

'**rendita** *sf* (*di individuo*) private *o* unearned income; (*COMM*) revenue; **~ annua** annuity

'**rene** *sm* kidney

'**reni** *sfpl* back *sg*

reni'tente *ag* reluctant, unwilling; **~ ai consigli di qn** unwilling to follow sb's advice; **essere ~ alla leva** (*MIL*) to fail to report for military service

'**renna** *sf* reindeer *inv*

'**Reno** *sm*: **il ~** the Rhine

'**reo, a** *sm/f* (*DIR*) offender

re'parto *sm* department, section; (*MIL*) detachment

repel'lente *ag* repulsive

repen'taglio [repen'taʎʎo] *sm*: **mettere a ~** to jeopardize, risk

repen'tino, a *ag* sudden, unexpected

repe'rire *vt* to find, trace

re'perto *sm* (*ARCHEOLOGIA*) find; (*MED*) report; (*DIR: anche*: **~ giudiziario**) exhibit

reper'torio *sm* (*TEATRO*) repertory; (*elenco*) index, (*alphabetical*) list

'**replica, che** *sf* repetition; reply, answer; (*obiezione*) objection; (*TEATRO, CINEMA*) repeat performance; (*copia*) replica

repli'care *vt* (*ripetere*) to repeat; (*rispondere*) to answer, reply

repressi'one *sf* repression

re'presso, a *pp di* **reprimere**

re'primere *vt* to suppress, repress

re'pubblica, che *sf* republic; **repubbli'cano, a** *ag, sm/f* republican

repu'tare *vt* to consider, judge

reputazi'one [reputat'tsjone] *sf* reputation

'**requie** *sf*: **senza ~** unceasingly

requi'sire *vt* to requisition

requi'sito *sm* requirement

'**resa** *sf* (*l'arrendersi*) surrender; (*restituzione, rendimento*) return; **~ dei conti** rendering of accounts; (*fig*) day of reckoning

resi'dente *ag* resident; **resi'denza** *sf* residence; **residenzi'ale** *ag* residential

re'siduo, a *ag* residual, remaining ♦ *sm* remainder; (*CHIM*) residue

'**resina** *sf* resin

resis'tente *ag* (*che resiste*): **~ a** resistant to; (*forte*) strong; (*duraturo*) long-lasting, durable; **~ al caldo** heat-resistant; **resis'tenza** *sf* resistance; (*di persona: fisica*) stamina, endurance; (: *mentale*) endurance, resistance

---

Resistenza

i *The* **Resistenza** *in Italy fought against the Nazis and the Fascists during the Second World War. Members of the Resistance spanned a wide political spectrum and played a vital role in the Liberation and in the formation of the new democratic government at the end* *of the war.*

re'sistere *vi* to resist; **~ a** (*assalto, tentazioni*) to resist; (*dolore, sog: pianta*) to withstand; (*non patir danno*) to be resistant to; **resis'tito, a** *pp di* **resistere**

'**reso, a** *pp di* **rendere**

reso'conto *sm* report, account

res'pingere [res'pindʒere] *vt* to drive back, repel; (*rifiutare*) to reject; (*INS: bocciare*) to fail; **res'pinto, a** *pp di* **respingere**

respi'rare *vi* to breathe; (*fig*) to get one's breath; to breathe again ♦ *vt* to breathe (in), inhale; **respira'tore** *sm* respirator; **respirazi'one** *sf* breathing; **respirazione artificiale** artificial respiration; **res'piro** *sm* breathing *no pl*; (*singolo atto*) breath; (*fig*) respite, rest; **mandare un respiro di sollievo** to give a sigh of relief

respon'sabile *ag* responsible ♦ *sm/f* person responsible; (*capo*) person in charge; **~ di** responsible for; (*DIR*) liable for; **responsabilità** *sf inv* responsibility; (*legale*) liability

res'ponso *sm* answer

'**ressa** *sf* crowd, throng

res'tare *vi* (*rimanere*) to remain, stay; (*avanzare*) to be left, remain; **~ orfano/ cieco** to become o be left an orphan/ become blind; **~ d'accordo** to agree; **non resta più niente** there's nothing left; **restano pochi giorni** there are only a few days left

restau'rare *vt* to restore; **restaurazi'one** *sf* (*POL*) restoration; **res'tauro** *sm* (*di edifici etc*) restoration

res'tio, a, 'tii, 'tie *ag*: **~ a** reluctant to

restitu'ire *vt* to return, give back; (*energie, forze*) to restore

'**resto** *sm* remainder, rest; (*denaro*) change; (*MAT*) remainder; **~i** *smpl* (*di cibo*) leftovers; (*di città*) remains; **del ~** moreover, besides; **~i mortali** (*mortal*) remains

res'tringere [res'trindʒere] *vt* to reduce; (*vestito*) to take in; (*stoffa*) to shrink; (*fig*) to restrict, limit; **~rsi** *vr* (*strada*) to narrow; (*stoffa*) to shrink; **restrizi'one** *sf*

restriction

'**rete** *sf* net; (*fig*) trap, snare; (*di recinzione*) wire netting; (*AUT, FERR, di spionaggio etc*) network; **segnare una ~** (*CALCIO*) to score a goal; **~ del letto** (*sprung*) bed base

reti'cente [reti'tʃɛnte] *ag* reticent

retico'lato *sm* grid; (*rete*) wire netting; (*di filo spinato*) barbed wire (fence)

'**retina** *sf* (*ANAT*) retina

re'torica *sf* rhetoric

re'torico, a, ci, che *ag* rhetorical

retribu'ire *vt* to pay; **retribuzi'one** *sf* payment

'**retro** *sm inv* back ♦ *av* (*dietro*): **vedi ~** see over(leaf)

retro'cedere [retro'tʃedere] *vi* to withdraw ♦ *vt* (*CALCIO*) to relegate; (*MIL*) to degrade

re'trogrado, a *ag* (*fig*) reactionary, backward-looking

retro'marcia [retro'martʃa] *sf* (*AUT*) reverse; (: *dispositivo*) reverse gear

retro'scena [retroʃ'ʃena] *sm inv* (*TEATRO*) backstage; **i ~** (*fig*) the behind-the-scenes activities

retrospet'tivo, a *ag* retrospective

retrovi'sore *sm* (*AUT*) (rear-view) mirror

'**retta** *sf* (*MAT*) straight line; (*di convitto*) charge for bed and board; (*fig: ascolto*): **dar ~ a** to listen to, pay attention to

rettango'lare *ag* rectangular

ret'tangolo, a *ag* right-angled ♦ *sm* rectangle

ret'tifica, che *sf* rectification, correction

rettifi'care *vt* (*curva*) to straighten; (*fig*) to rectify, correct

'**rettile** *sm* reptile

retti'lineo, a *ag* rectilinear

retti'tudine *sf* rectitude, uprightness

'**retto, a** *pp di* **reggere** ♦ *ag* straight; (*MAT*): **angolo ~** right angle; (*onesto*) honest, upright; (*giusto, esatto*) correct, proper, right

ret'tore *sm* (*REL*) rector; (*di università*) ≈ chancellor

reuma'tismo *sm* rheumatism

reve'rendo, a *ag*: **il ~ padre Belli** the Reverend Father Belli

rever'sibile *ag* reversible

revisio'nare *vt* (*conti*) to audit; (*TECN*) to overhaul, service; (*DIR: processo*) to review

revisi'one *sf* auditing *no pl*; audit; servicing *no pl*; overhaul; review; revision

revi'sore *sm*: ~ **di conti/bozze** auditor/proofreader

'revoca *sf* revocation

revo'care *vt* to revoke

re'volver *sm inv* revolver

riabili'tare *vt* to rehabilitate

riagganci'are [riaggan'tʃare] *vt* (*TEL*) to hang up

rial'zare [rial'tsare] *vt* to raise, lift; (*alzare di più*) to heighten, raise; (*aumentare: prezzi*) to increase, raise ♦ *vi* (*prezzi*) to rise, increase, raise; **ri'alzo** *sm* (*di prezzi*) increase, rise; (*sporgenza*) rise

rianimazi'one [rianimat'tsjone] *sf* (*MED*) resuscitation; **centro di** ~ intensive care unit

riap'pendere *vt* to rehang; (*TEL*) to hang up

ria'prire *vt* to reopen, open again; **~rsi** *vr* to reopen, open again

ri'armo *sm* (*MIL*) rearmament

rias'setto *sm* (*di stanza etc*) rearrangement; (*ordinamento*) reorganization

rias'sumere *vt* (*riprendere*) to resume; (*impiegare di nuovo*) to re-employ; (*sintetizzare*) to summarize; **rias'sunto, a** *pp di* **riassumere** ♦ *sm* summary

ria'vere *vt* to have again; (*avere indietro*) to get back; (*riacquistare*) to recover; **~rsi** *vr* to recover

riba'dire *vt* (*fig*) to confirm

ri'balta *sf* flap; (*TEATRO: proscenio*) front of the stage; (*fig*) limelight; **luci della** ~ footlights *pl*

ribal'tabile *ag* (*sedile*) tip-up

ribal'tare *vt, vi* (*anche:* **~rsi**) to turn over, tip over

ribas'sare *vt* to lower, bring down ♦ *vi* to come down, fall; **ri'basso** *sm* reduction, fall

ri'battere *vt* to return, hit back; (*confutare*)

to refute; ~ **che** to retort that

ribel'larsi *vr*: ~ **(a)** to rebel (against); **ri'belle** *ag* (*soldati*) rebel; (*ragazzo*) rebellious ♦ *sm/f* rebel; **ribelli'one** *sf* rebellion

'ribes *sm inv* currant; ~ **nero** blackcurrant; ~ **rosso** redcurrant

ribol'lire *vi* (*fermentare*) to ferment; (*fare bolle*) to bubble, boil; (*fig*) to seethe

ri'brezzo [ri'breddzo] *sm* disgust, loathing; **far** ~ **a** to disgust

ribut'tante *ag* disgusting, revolting

rica'dere *vi* to fall again; (*scendere a terra, fig: nel peccato etc*) to fall back; (*vestiti, capelli etc*) to hang (down); (*riversarsi: fatiche, colpe*): ~ **su** to fall on; **rica'duta** *sf* (*MED*) relapse

rical'care *vt* (*disegni*) to trace; (*fig*) to follow faithfully

rica'mare *vt* to embroider

ricambi'are *vt* to change again; (*contraccambiare*) to repay, return; **ri'cambio** *sm* exchange, return; (*FISIOL*) metabolism; **ricambi** *smpl* (*TECN*) spare parts

ri'camo *sm* embroidery

ricapito'lare *vt* to recapitulate, sum up

ricari'care *vt* (*arma, macchina fotografica*) to reload; (*pipa*) to refill; (*orologio*) to rewind; (*batteria*) to recharge

ricat'tare *vt* to blackmail; **ricatta'tore, 'trice** *sm/f* blackmailer; **ri'catto** *sm* blackmail

rica'vare *vt* (*estrarre*) to draw out, extract; (*ottenere*) to obtain, gain; **ri'cavo** *sm* proceeds *pl*

ric'chezza [rik'kettsa] *sf* wealth; (*fig*) richness; ~**e** *sfpl* (*beni*) wealth *sg*, riches

'riccio, a ['rittʃo] *ag* curly ♦ *sm* (*ZOOL*) hedgehog; (*: anche:* ~ **di mare**) sea urchin; **'ricciolo** *sm* curl; **ricci'uto, a** *ag* curly

'ricco, a, chi, che *ag* rich; (*persona, paese*) rich, wealthy ♦ *sm/f* rich man/woman; **i ~chi** the rich; ~ **di** full of; rich in

ri'cerca, che [ri'tʃerka] *sf* search; (*indagine*) investigation, inquiry; (*studio*): **la** ~ research; **una** ~ piece of research

ricer'care [ritʃer'kare] *vt (motivi, cause)* to look for, try to determine; *(successo, piacere)* to pursue; *(onore, gloria)* to seek; **ricer'cato, a** *ag (apprezzato)* much sought-after; *(affettato)* studied, affected ♦ *sm/f (POLIZIA)* wanted man/woman

ri'cetta [ri'tʃetta] *sf (MED)* prescription; *(CUC)* recipe

ricettazi'one [ritʃettat'tsjone] *sf (DIR)* receiving (stolen goods)

ri'cevere [ri'tʃevere] *vt* to receive; *(stipendio, lettera)* to get, receive; *(accogliere: ospite)* to welcome; *(vedere: cliente, rappresentante etc)* to see; **ricevi'mento** *sm* receiving *no pl; (festa)* reception; **ricevi'tore** *sm (TECN)* receiver; **ricevito'ria** *sf* lottery *o* pools office; **rice'vuta** *sf* receipt; **ricevuta fiscale** receipt for tax purposes; **ricezi'one** *sf (RADIO, TV)* reception

richia'mare [rikja'mare] *vt (chiamare indietro, ritelefonare)* to call back; *(ambasciatore, truppe)* to recall; *(rimproverare)* to reprimand; *(attirare)* to attract, draw; **~rsi a** *(riferirsi a)* to refer to; **richi'amo** *sm* call; recall; reprimand; attraction

richi'edere [ri'kjɛdere] *vt* to ask again for; *(chiedere indietro)*: **~ qc** to ask for sth back; *(chiedere: per sapere)* to ask; *(: per avere)* to ask for; *(AMM: documenti)* to apply for; *(esigere)* to need, require; **richi'esta** *sf (domanda)* question; *(AMM)* application, request; *(esigenza)* demand, request; **a richiesta** on request; **richi'esto, a** *pp di* **richiedere**

rici'clare [ritʃi'klare] *vt* to recycle

'ricino ['ritʃino] *sm*: **olio di ~** castor oil

ricognizi'one [rikoɲɲit'tsjone] *sf (MIL)* reconnaissance; *(DIR)* recognition, acknowledgement

ricominci'are [rikomin'tʃare] *vt, vi* to start again, begin again

ricom'pensa *sf* reward

ricompen'sare *vt* to reward

riconcili'are [rikontʃi'ljare] *vt* to reconcile; **~rsi** *vr* to be reconciled; **riconciliazi'one** *sf* reconciliation

ricono'scente [rikonoʃ'ʃɛnte] *ag* grateful; **ricono'scenza** *sf* gratitude

rico'noscere [riko'noʃʃere] *vt* to recognize; *(DIR: figlio, debito)* to acknowledge; *(ammettere: errore)* to admit, acknowledge; **riconosci'mento** *sm* recognition; acknowledgement; *(identificazione)* identification; **riconosci'uto, a** *pp di* **riconoscere**

ricopi'are *vt* to copy

rico'prire *vt (coprire)* to cover; *(occupare: carica)* to hold

ricor'dare *vt* to remember, recall; *(richiamare alla memoria)*: **~ qc a qn** to remind sb of sth; **~rsi** *vr*: **~rsi (di)** to remember; **~rsi di qc/di aver fatto** to remember sth/having done

ri'cordo *sm* memory; *(regalo)* keepsake, souvenir; *(di viaggio)* souvenir; **~i** *smpl (memorie)* memoirs

ricor'rente *ag* recurrent, recurring; **ricor'renza** *sf* recurrence; *(festività)* anniversary

ri'correre *vi (ripetersi)* to recur; **~ a** *(rivolgersi)* to turn to; *(: DIR)* to appeal to; *(servirsi di)* to have recourse to; **ri'corso, a** *pp di* **ricorrere** ♦ *sm* recurrence; *(DIR)* appeal; **far ricorso a = ricorrere a**

ricostitu'ente *ag (MED)*: **cura ~** tonic

ricostru'ire *vt (casa)* to rebuild; *(fatti)* to reconstruct; **ricostruzi'one** *sf* rebuilding *no pl*; reconstruction

ri'cotta *sf* soft white unsalted cheese made from sheep's milk

ricove'rare *vt* to give shelter to; **~ qn in ospedale** to admit sb to hospital

ri'covero *sm* shelter, refuge; *(MIL)* shelter; *(MED)* admission (to hospital)

ricre'are *vt* to recreate; *(fig: distrarre)* to amuse

ricreazi'one [rikreat'tsjone] *sf* recreation, entertainment; *(INS)* break

ri'credersi *vr* to change one's mind

ricupe'rare *vt (rientrare in possesso di)* to recover, get back; *(tempo perduto)* to make up for; *(NAUT)* to salvage; *(: naufraghi)* to rescue; *(delinquente)* to rehabilitate; **~ lo**

svantaggio (SPORT) to close the gap
ridacchi'are [ridak'kjare] vi to snigger
ri'dare vt to return, give back
'**ridere** vi to laugh; (deridere, beffare): ~ **di** to laugh at, make fun of
ri'detto, a pp di **ridire**
ri'dicolo, a ag ridiculous, absurd
ridimensio'nare vt to reorganize; (fig) to see in the right perspective
ri'dire vt to repeat; (criticare) to find fault with; to object to; **trova sempre qualcosa da ~** he always manages to find fault
ridon'dante ag redundant
ri'dotto, a pp di **ridurre** ♦ ag (biglietto) reduced; (formato) small
ri'durre vt (anche CHIM, MAT) to reduce; (prezzo, spese) to cut, reduce; (accorciare: opera letteraria) to abridge; (: RADIO, TV) to adapt; **ridursi** vr (diminuirsi) to be reduced, shrink; **ridursi a** to be reduced to; **ridursi pelle e ossa** to be reduced to skin and bone; **ridut'tore** sm (ELEC) adaptor; **riduzi'one** sf reduction; abridgement; adaptation
riem'pire vt to fill (up); (modulo) to fill in o out; **~rsi** vr to fill (up); **~ qc di** to fill sth (up) with
rien'tranza [rien'trantsa] sf recess; indentation
rien'trare vi (entrare di nuovo) to go (o come) back in; (tornare) to return; (fare una rientranza) to curve inwards; to be indented; (riguardare): **~ in** to be included among, form part of; **ri'entro** sm (ritorno) return; (di astronave) re-entry
riepilo'gare vt to summarize ♦ vi to recapitulate
ri'fare vt to do again; (ricostruire) to make again; (nodo) to tie again, do up again; (imitare) to imitate, copy; **~rsi** vr (risarcirsi): **~rsi di** to make up for; (vendicarsi): **~rsi di qc su qn** to get one's own back on sb for sth; (riferirsi): **~rsi a** to go back to; to follow; **~ il letto** to make the bed; **~rsi una vita** to make a new life for o.s.; **ri'fatto, a** pp di **rifare**
riferi'mento sm reference; **in** o **con ~ a**

with reference to
rife'rire vt (riportare) to report ♦ vi to do a report; **~rsi** vr: **~rsi a** to refer to
rifi'nire vt to finish off, put the finishing touches to; **rifini'tura** sf finishing touch; **rifiniture** sfpl (di mobile, auto) finish sg
rifiu'tare vt to refuse; **~ di fare** to refuse to do; **rifi'uto** sm refusal; **rifiuti** smpl (spazzatura) rubbish sg, refuse sg
riflessi'one sf (FISICA, meditazione) reflection; (il pensare) thought, reflection; (osservazione) remark
rifles'sivo, a ag (persona) thoughtful, reflective; (LING) reflexive
ri'flesso, a pp di **riflettere** ♦ sm (di luce, allo specchio) reflection; (FISIOL) reflex; **di** o **per ~** indirectly
ri'flettere vt to reflect ♦ vi to think; **~rsi** vr to be reflected; **~ su** to think over
riflet'tore sm reflector; (proiettore) floodlight; searchlight
ri'flusso sm flowing back; (della marea) ebb; **un'epoca di ~** an era of nostalgia
ri'fondere vt to refund, repay
ri'forma sf reform; **la R~** (REL) the Reformation
rifor'mare vt to re-form; (REL, POL) to reform; (MIL: recluta) to declare unfit for service; (: soldato) to invalid out, discharge; **riforma'torio** sm (DIR) community home (BRIT), reformatory (US)
riforni'mento sm supplying, providing; restocking; **~i** smpl (provviste) supplies, provisions
rifor'nire vt (provvedere): **~ di** to supply o provide with; (fornire di nuovo: casa etc) to restock
rifrazi'one [rifrat'tsjone] sf refraction
rifug'gire [rifud'dʒire] vi to escape again; (fig): **~ da** to shun
rifugi'arsi [rifu'dʒarsi] vr to take refuge; **rifugi'ato, a** sm/f refugee
ri'fugio [ri'fudʒo] sm refuge, shelter; (in montagna) shelter; **~ antiaereo** air-raid shelter
'**riga, ghe** sf line; (striscia) stripe; (di persone, cose) line, row; (regolo) ruler;

(*scriminatura*) parting; **mettersi in ~** to line up; **a ~ghe** (*foglio*) lined; (*vestito*) striped

ri'gagnolo [ri'gaɲɲolo] *sm* rivulet

ri'gare *vt* (*foglio*) to rule ♦ *vi*: **~ diritto** (*fig*) to toe the line

rigatti'ere *sm* junk dealer

riget'tare [ridʒet'tare] *vt* (*gettare indietro*) to throw back; (*fig: respingere*) to reject; (*vomitare*) to bring *o* throw up; ri'getto *sm* (*anche MED*) rejection

rigidità [ridʒidi'ta] *sf* rigidity; stiffness; severity, rigours *pl*; strictness

'rigido, a ['ridʒido] *ag* rigid, stiff; (*membra etc: indurite*) stiff; (*METEOR*) harsh, severe; (*fig*) strict

rigi'rare [ridʒi'rare] *vt* to turn; **~rsi** *vr* to turn round; (*nel letto*) to turn over; **~ qc tra le mani** to turn sth over in one's hands; **~ il discorso** to change the subject

'rigo, ghi *sm* line; (*MUS*) staff, stave

rigogli'oso, a [rigoʎ'ʎoso] *ag* (*pianta*) luxuriant; (*fig: commercio, sviluppo*) thriving

ri'gonfio, a *ag* swollen

ri'gore *sm* (*METEOR*) harshness, rigours *pl*; (*fig*) severity, strictness; (*anche: **calcio di ~***) penalty; **di ~** compulsory; **a rigor di termini** strictly speaking; **rigo'roso, a** *ag* (*severo: persona, ordine*) strict; (*preciso*) rigorous

rigover'nare *vt* to wash (up)

riguar'dare *vt* to look at again; (*considerare*) to regard, consider; (*concernere*) to regard, concern; **~rsi** *vr* (*aver cura di sé*) to look after o.s.

rigu'ardo *sm* (*attenzione*) care; (*considerazione*) regard, respect; **~ a** concerning, with regard to; **non aver ~i nell'agire/nel parlare** to act/speak freely

rilasci'are [rilaʃ'ʃare] *vt* (*rimettere in libertà*) to release; (*AMM: documenti*) to issue; ri'lascio *sm* release; issue

rilas'sare *vt* to relax; **~rsi** *vr* to relax; (*fig: disciplina*) to become slack

rile'gare *vt* (*libro*) to bind; **rilega'tura** *sf* binding

ri'leggere [ri'leddʒere] *vt* to reread, read again; (*rivedere*) to read over

ri'lento: **a ~** *av* slowly

rileva'mento *sm* (*topografico, statistico*) survey; (*NAUT*) bearing

rile'vante *ag* considerable; important

rile'vare *vt* (*ricavare*) to find; (*notare*) to notice; (*mettere in evidenza*) to point out; (*venire a conoscere: notizia*) to learn; (*raccogliere: dati*) to gather, collect; (*TOPOGRAFIA*) to survey; (*MIL*) to relieve; (*COMM*) to take over

rili'evo *sm* (*ARTE, GEO*) relief; (*fig: rilevanza*) importance; (*TOPOGRAFIA*) survey; **dar ~ a** *o* **mettere in ~ qc** (*fig*) to bring sth out, highlight sth

rilut'tante *ag* reluctant; **rilut'tanza** *sf* reluctance

'rima *sf* rhyme; (*verso*) verse

riman'dare *vt* to send again; (*restituire, rinviare*) to send back, return; (*differire*): **~ qc (a)** to postpone sth *o* put sth off (till); (*fare riferimento*): **~ qn a** to refer sb to; **essere rimandato** (*INS*) to have to repeat one's exams

ri'mando *sm* (*rinvio*) return; (*dilazione*) postponement; (*riferimento*) cross-reference

rima'nente *ag* remaining ♦ *sm* rest, remainder; **i ~i** (*persone*) the rest of them, the others; **rima'nenza** *sf* rest, remainder; **rimanenze** *sfpl* (*COMM*) unsold stock *sg*

rima'nere *vi* (*restare*) to remain, stay; (*avanzare*) to be left, remain; (*restare stupito*) to be amazed; (*restare, mancare*): **rimangono poche settimane a Pasqua** there are only a few weeks left till Easter; **rimane da vedere se** it remains to be seen whether; (*diventare*): **~ vedovo** to be left a widower; (*trovarsi*): **~ sorpreso** to be surprised

ri'mare *vt*, *vi* to rhyme

rimargi'nare [rimardʒi'nare] *vt*, *vi* (*anche*: **~rsi**) to heal

ri'masto, a *pp di* **rimanere**

rima'sugli [rima'suʎʎi] *smpl* leftovers

rimbal'zare [rimbal'tsare] *vi* to bounce back, rebound; (*proiettile*) to ricochet; **rim'balzo** *sm* rebound; ricochet

rimbam'bito, a *ag* senile, in one's dotage

rimboc'care *vt* (*coperta*) to tuck in; (*maniche, pantaloni*) to turn *o* roll up

rimbom'bare *vi* to resound

rimbor'sare *vt* to pay back, repay; **rim'borso** *sm* repayment

rimedi'are *vi:* ~ **a** to remedy ♦ *vt* (*fam: procurarsi*) to get *o* scrape together

ri'medio *sm* (*medicina*) medicine; (*cura, fig*) remedy, cure

rimesco'lare *vt* to mix well, stir well; (*carte*) to shuffle; **sentirsi ~ il sangue** (*per paura*) to feel one's blood run cold; (*per rabbia*) to feel one's blood boil

ri'messa *sf* (*locale: per veicoli*) garage; (: *per aerei*) hangar; (*COMM: di merce*) consignment; (: *di denaro*) remittance; (*TENNIS*) return; (*CALCIO: anche:* ~ **in gioco**) throw-in

ri'messo, a *pp di* **rimettere**

ri'mettere *vt* (*mettere di nuovo*) to put back; (*indossare di nuovo*): ~ **qc** to put sth back on, put sth on again; (*affidare*) to entrust; (: *decisione*) to refer; (*condonare*) to remit; (*COMM: merci*) to deliver; (: *denaro*) to remit; (*vomitare*) to bring up; (*perdere: anche:* **rimetterci**) to lose; **~rsi al bello** (*tempo*) to clear up; **~rsi in salute** to get better, recover one's health

'rimmel ® *sm inv* mascara

rimoder'nare *vt* to modernize

rimon'tare *vt* (*meccanismo*) to reassemble; (: *tenda*) to put up again ♦ *vi* (*salire di nuovo*): ~ **in** (*macchina, treno*) to get back into; (*SPORT*) to close the gap

rimorchi'are [rimor'kjare] *vt* to tow; (*fig: ragazza*) to pick up; **rimorchia'tore** *sm* (*NAUT*) tug(boat)

ri'morchio [ri'mɔrkjo] *sm* tow; (*veicolo*) trailer

ri'morso *sm* remorse

rimozi'one [rimot'tsjone] *sf* removal; (*da un impiego*) dismissal; (*PSIC*) repression

rim'pasto *sm* (*POL*) reshuffle

rimpatri'are *vi* to return home ♦ *vt* to repatriate; **rim'patrio** *sm* repatriation

rimpi'angere [rim'pjandʒere] *vt* to regret; (*persona*) to miss; **rimpi'anto, a** *pp di*

rimpiangere ♦ *sm* regret

rimpiat'tino *sm* hide-and-seek

rimpiaz'zare [rimpjat'tsare] *vt* to replace

rimpiccio'lire [rimpittʃo'lire] *vt* to make smaller ♦ *vi* (*anche:* **~rsi**) to become smaller

rimpin'zare [rimpin'tsare] *vt:* ~ **di** to cram *o* stuff with

rimprove'rare *vt* to rebuke, reprimand; **rim'provero** *sm* rebuke, reprimand

rimugi'nare [rimudʒi'nare] *vt* (*fig*) to turn over in one's mind

rimunerazi'one [rimunerat'tsjone] *sf* remuneration; (*premio*) reward

rimu'overe *vt* to remove; (*destituire*) to dismiss

Rinasci'mento [rinaʃʃi'mento] *sm:* **il ~** the Renaissance

ri'nascita [ri'naʃʃita] *sf* rebirth, revival

rinca'rare *vt* to increase the price of ♦ *vi* to go up, become more expensive

rinca'sare *vi* to go home

rinchi'udere [rin'kjudere] *vt* to shut (*o* lock) up; **~rsi** *vr:* **~rsi in** to shut o.s. up in; **~rsi in se stesso** to withdraw into o.s.; **rinchi'uso, a** *pp di* **rinchiudere**

rin'correre *vt* to chase, run after; **rin'corsa** *sf* short run; **rin'corso, a** *pp di* **rincorrere**

rin'crescere [rin'kreʃʃere] *vb impers:* **mi rincresce che/di non poter fare** I'm sorry that/I can't do, I regret that/being unable to do; **rincresci'mento** *sm* regret; **rincresci'uto, a** *pp di* **rincrescere**

rincu'lare *vi* (*arma*) to recoil

rinfacci'are [rinfat'tʃare] *vt* (*fig*): ~ **qc a qn** to throw sth in sb's face

rinfor'zare [rinfor'tsare] *vt* to reinforce, strengthen ♦ *vi* (*anche:* **~rsi**) to grow stronger; **rin'forzo** *sm:* **mettere un rinforzo a** to strengthen; **di rinforzo** (*asse, sbarra*) strengthening; (*esercito*) supporting; (*personale*) extra, additional; **rinforzi** *smpl* (*MIL*) reinforcements

rinfran'care *vt* to encourage, reassure

rinfres'care *vt* (*atmosfera, temperatura*) to cool (down); (*abito, pareti*) to freshen up

♦ vi (tempo) to grow cooler; **~rsi** vr (ristorarsi) to refresh o.s.; (lavarsi) to freshen up; **rin'fresco, schi** sm (festa) party; **rinfreschi** smpl refreshments

rin'fusa sf: **alla ~** in confusion, higgledy-piggledy

ringhi'are [rin'gjare] vi to growl, snarl

ringhi'era [rin'gjera] sf railing; (delle scale) banister(s pl)

ringiova'nire [rindʒova'nire] vt (sog: vestito, acconciatura etc): **~ qn** to make sb look younger; (: vacanze etc) to rejuvenate ♦ vi (anche: **~rsi**) to become (o look) younger

ringrazia'mento [ringrattsja'mento] sm thanks pl

ringrazi'are [ringrat'tsjare] vt to thank; **~ qn di qc** to thank sb for sth

rinne'gare vt (fede) to renounce; (figlio) to disown, repudiate; **rinne'gato, a** sm/f renegade

rinnova'mento sm renewal; (economico) revival

rinno'vare vt to renew; (ripetere) to repeat, renew; **rin'novo** sm (di contratto) renewal; **"chiuso per rinnovo dei locali"** "closed for alterations"

rinoce'ronte [rinotʃe'ronte] sm rhinoceros

rino'mato, a ag renowned, celebrated

rinsal'dare vt to strengthen

rintoc'care vi (campana) to toll; (orologio) to strike

rintracci'are [rintrat'tʃare] vt to track down

rintro'nare vi to boom, roar ♦ vt (assordare) to deafen; (stordire) to stun

ri'nuncia [ri'nuntʃa] etc = **rinunzia** etc

ri'nunzia [ri'nuntsja] sf renunciation

rinunzi'are [rinun'tsjare] vi: **~ a** to give up, renounce

rinve'nire vt to find, recover; (scoprire) to discover, find out ♦ vi (riprendere i sensi) to come round; (fiori) to revive

rinvi'are vt (rimandare indietro) to send back, return; (differire): **~ qc (a)** to postpone sth o put sth off (till); to adjourn sth (till); (fare un rimando): **~ qn a** to refer sb to

rinvigo'rire vt to strengthen

rin'vio, 'vii sm (rimando) return; (differimento) postponement; (: di seduta) adjournment; (in un testo) cross-reference

ri'one sm district, quarter

riordi'nare vt (rimettere in ordine) to tidy; (riorganizzare) to reorganize

riorganiz'zare [riorganid'dzare] vt to reorganize

ripa'gare vt to repay

ripa'rare vt (proteggere) to protect, defend; (correggere: male, torto) to make up for; (: errore) to put right; (aggiustare) to repair ♦ vi (mettere rimedio): **~ a** to make up for; **~rsi** vr (rifugiarsi) to take refuge o shelter; **riparazi'one** sf (di un torto) reparation; (di guasto, scarpe) repairing no pl; repair; (risarcimento) compensation

ri'paro sm (protezione) shelter, protection; (rimedio) remedy

ripar'tire vt (dividere) to divide up; (distribuire) to share out ♦ vi to set off again; to leave again

ripas'sare vi to come (o go) back ♦ vt (scritto, lezione) to go over (again); **ri'passo** sm revision (BRIT), review (US)

ripen'sare vi to think; (cambiare pensiero) to change one's mind; (tornare col pensiero): **~ a** to recall

ripercu'otersi vr: **~ su** (fig) to have repercussions on

ripercussi'one sf (fig): **avere una ~** o **delle ~i su** to have repercussions on

ripes'care vt (pesce) to catch again; (persona, cosa) to fish out; (fig: ritrovare) to dig out

ri'petere vt to repeat; (ripassare) to go over; **ripetizi'one** sf repetition; (di lezione) revision; **ripetizioni** sfpl (INS) private tutoring o coaching sg

ripi'ano sm (di mobile) shelf

ri'picca sf: **per ~** out of spite

'ripido, a ag steep

ripie'gare vt to refold; (piegare più volte) to fold (up) ♦ vi (MIL) to retreat, fall back; (fig: accontentarsi): **~ su** to make do with; **~rsi** vr to bend; **ripi'ego, ghi** sm expedient

ripi'eno, a *ag* full; (*CUC*) stuffed; (: *panino*) filled ♦ *sm* (*CUC*) stuffing

ri'porre *vt* (*porre al suo posto*) to put back, replace; (*mettere via*) to put away; (*fiducia, speranza*): **~ qc in qn** to place *o* put sth in sb

ripor'tare *vt* (*portare indietro*) to bring (*o* take) back; (*riferire*) to report; (*citare*) to quote; (*vittoria*) to gain; (*successo*) to have; (*MAT*) to carry; **~rsi a** (*anche fig*) to go back to; (*riferirsi a*) to refer to; **~ danni** to suffer damage

ripo'sare *vt, vi* to rest; **~rsi** *vr* to rest; **ri'poso** *sm* rest; (*MIL*): **riposo!** at ease!; **a riposo** (*in pensione*) retired; **giorno di riposo** day off

ripos'tiglio [ripos'tiʎʎo] *sm* lumber-room

ri'posto, a *pp di* **riporre**

ri'prendere *vt* (*prigioniero, fortezza*) to recapture; (*prendere indietro*) to take back; (*ricominciare: lavoro*) to resume; (*andare a prendere*) to fetch, come back for; (*riassumere: impiegati*) to take on again, re-employ; (*rimproverare*) to tell off; (*restringere: abito*) to take in; (*CINEMA*) to shoot; **~rsi** *vr* to recover; (*correggersi*) to correct o.s.; **ri'presa** *sf* recapture; resumption; (*economica, da malattia, emozione*) recovery; (*AUT*) acceleration *no pl*; (*TEATRO, CINEMA*) rerun; (*CINEMA: presa*) shooting *no pl*; shot; (*SPORT*) second half; (: *PUGILATO*) round; **a più riprese** on several occasions, several times; **ripreso, a** *pp di* **riprendere**

ripristi'nare *vt* to restore

ripro'durre *vt* to reproduce; **riprodursi** *vr* (*BIOL*) to reproduce; (*riformarsi*) to form again; **riproduzi'one** *sf* reproduction; **riproduzione vietata** all rights reserved

ripudi'are *vt* to repudiate, disown

ripu'gnante [ripuɲ'ɲante] *ag* disgusting, repulsive

ripu'gnare [ripuɲ'ɲare] *vi*: **~ a qn** to repel *o* disgust sb

ripu'lire *vt* to clean up; (*sog: ladri*) to clean out; (*perfezionare*) to polish, refine

ri'quadro *sm* square; (*ARCHIT*) panel

ri'saia *sf* paddy field

risa'lire *vi* (*ritornare in su*) to go back up; **~ a** (*ritornare con la mente*) to go back to; (*datare da*) to date back to, go back to

risal'tare *vi* (*fig: distinguersi*) to stand out; (*ARCHIT*) to project, jut out; **ri'salto** *sm* prominence; (*sporgenza*) projection; **mettere** *o* **porre in risalto qc** to make sth stand out

risa'nare *vt* (*guarire*) to heal, cure; (*palude*) to reclaim; (*economia*) to improve; (*bilancio*) to reorganize

risa'puto, a *ag*: **è ~ che ...** everyone knows that ..., it is common knowledge that ...

risarci'mento [risartʃi'mento] *sm*: **~ (di)** compensation (for)

risar'cire [risar'tʃire] *vt* (*cose*) to pay compensation for; (*persona*): **~ qn di qc** to compensate sb for sth

ri'sata *sf* laugh

riscalda'mento *sm* heating; **~ centrale** central heating

riscal'dare *vt* (*scaldare*) to heat; (: *mani, persona*) to warm; (*minestra*) to reheat; **~rsi** *vr* to warm up

riscat'tare *vt* (*prigioniero*) to ransom, pay a ransom for; (*DIR*) to redeem; **~rsi** *vr* (*da disonore*) to redeem o.s.; **ris'catto** *sm* ransom; redemption

rischia'rare [riskja'rare] *vt* (*illuminare*) to light up; (*colore*) to make lighter; **~rsi** *vr* (*tempo*) to clear up; (*cielo*) to clear; (*fig: volto*) to brighten up; **~rsi la voce** to clear one's throat

rischi'are [ris'kjare] *vt* to risk ♦ *vi*: **~ di fare qc** to risk *o* run the risk of doing sth

'rischio ['riskjo] *sm* risk; **rischi'oso, a** *ag* risky, dangerous

risciac'quare [riʃʃa'kware] *vt* to rinse

riscon'trare *vt* (*rilevare*) to find; **ris'contro** *sm* confirmation; (*lettera di risposta*) reply

ris'cossa *sf* (*riconquista*) recovery, reconquest; *vedi anche* **riscosso**

riscossi'one *sf* collection

ris'cosso, a *pp di* **riscuotere**

ris'cuotere vt (ritirare: somma) to collect; (: stipendio) to draw, collect; (assegno) to cash; (fig: successo etc) to win, earn; ~rsi vr: ~rsi (da) to shake o.s. (out of), rouse o.s. (from)

risenti'mento sm resentment

risen'tire vt to hear again; (provare) to feel ♦ vi: ~ di to feel (o show) the effects of; ~rsi vr: ~rsi di o per to take offence at, resent

risen'tito, a ag resentful

ri'serbo sm reserve

ri'serva sf reserve; (di caccia, pesca) preserve; (restrizione, di indigeni) reservation; di ~ (provviste etc) in reserve

riser'vare vt (tenere in serbo) to keep, put aside; (prenotare) to book, reserve; ~rsi vr: ~rsi di fare qc to intend to do sth

riserva'tezza sf reserve

riser'vato, a ag (prenotato, fig: persona) reserved; (confidenziale) confidential

risi'edere vi: ~ a o in to reside in

'risma sf (di carta) ream; (fig) kind, sort

'riso (pl(f) ~a: il ridere) sm: il ~ laughter; (pianta) rice ♦ pp di ridere

riso'lino sm snigger

ri'solto, a pp di risolvere

risolu'tezza [risolu'tettsa] sf determinatione

riso'luto, a ag determined, resolute

risoluzi'one [risolut'tsjone] sf solving no pl; (MAT) solution; (decisione, di immagine) resolution

ri'solvere vt (difficoltà, controversia) to resolve; (problema) to solve; (decidere): ~ di fare to resolve to do; ~rsi vr (decidersi): ~rsi a fare to make up one's mind to do; (andare a finire): ~rsi in to end up, turn out; ~rsi in nulla to come to nothing

riso'nanza [riso'nantsa] sf resonance; aver vasta ~ (fig: fatto etc) to be known far and wide

riso'nare vt, vi = risuonare

ri'sorgere [ri'sordʒere] vi to rise again; risorgi'mento sm revival; il Risorgimento (STORIA) the Risorgimento

---

> **Risorgimento**
>
> *i* The **Risorgimento** *was the political movement which led to the proclamation of the Kingdom of Italy in 1861, and eventually to unification (1871).*

ri'sorsa sf expedient, resort; ~e sfpl (naturali, finanziarie etc) resources; persona piena di ~e resourceful person

ri'sorto, a pp di risorgere

ri'sotto sm (CUC) risotto

risparmi'are vt to save; (non uccidere) to spare ♦ vi to save; ~ qc a qn to spare sb sth

ris'parmio sm saving no pl; (denaro) savings pl

rispec'chiare [rispek'kjare] vt to reflect

rispet'tabile ag respectable

rispet'tare vt to respect; farsi ~ to command respect

rispet'tivo, a ag respective

ris'petto sm respect; ~i smpl (saluti) respects, regards; ~ a (in paragone a) compared to; (in relazione a) as regards, as for; rispet'toso, a ag respectful

ris'plendere vi to shine

ris'pondere vi to answer, reply; (freni) to respond; ~ a (domanda) to answer, reply to; (persona) to answer; (invito) to reply to; (provocazione, sog: veicolo, apparecchio) to respond to; (corrispondere a) to correspond to; (: speranze, bisogno) to answer; ~ di to answer for; ris'posta sf answer, reply; in risposta a in reply to; risposto, a pp di rispondere

'rissa sf brawl

ristabi'lire vt to re-establish, restore; (persona: sog: riposo etc) to restore to health; ~rsi vr to recover

rista'gnare [ristaɲ'ɲare] vi (acqua) to become stagnant; (sangue) to cease flowing; (fig: industria) to stagnate; ris'tagno sm stagnation

ris'tampa sf reprinting no pl; reprint

risto'rante sm restaurant

risto'rarsi vr to have something to eat and

drink; (*riposarsi*) to rest, have a rest;
ris'toro *sm* (*bevanda, cibo*) refreshment;
servizio di ristoro (*FERR*) refreshments *pl*
ristret'tezza [ristret'tettsa] *sf* (*strettezza*)
narrowness; (*fig: scarsezza*) scarcity, lack;
(*: meschinità*) meanness; **~e** *sfpl* (*povertà*)
financial straits
ris'tretto, a *pp di* **restringere** ♦ *ag*
(*racchiuso*) enclosed, hemmed in; (*angusto*)
narrow; (*limitato*) **~ (a)** restricted *o* limited
(to); (*CUC: brodo*) thick; (*: caffè*) extra
strong
risucchi'are [risuk'kjare] *vt* to suck in
risul'tare *vi* (*dimostrarsi*) to prove (to be),
turn out (to be); (*riuscire*): **~ vincitore** to
emerge as the winner; **~ da** (*provenire*) to
result from, be the result of; **mi risulta che
...** I understand that ...; **non mi risulta** not
as far as I know; **risul'tato** *sm* result
risuo'nare *vi* (*rimbombare*) to resound
risurrezi'one [risurret'tsjone] *sf* (*REL*)
resurrection
risusci'tare [risuʃʃi'tare] *vt* to resuscitate,
restore to life; (*fig*) to revive, bring back
♦ *vi* to rise (from the dead)
ris'veglio [riz'veʎʎo] *sm* waking up; (*fig*)
revival
ris'volto *sm* (*di giacca*) lapel; (*di
pantaloni*) turn-up; (*di manica*) cuff; (*di
tasca*) flap; (*di libro*) inside flap; (*fig*)
implication
ritagli'are [rita'ʎʎare] *vt* (*tagliar via*) to cut
out; **ri'taglio** *sm* (*di giornale*) cutting,
clipping; (*di stoffa etc*) scrap; **nei ritagli di
tempo** in one's spare time
ritar'dare *vi* (*persona, treno*) to be late;
(*orologio*) to be slow ♦ *vt* (*rallentare*) to
slow down; (*impedire*) to delay, hold up;
(*differire*) to postpone, delay;
ritarda'tario, a *sm/f* latecomer
ri'tardo *sm* delay; (*di persona aspettata*)
lateness *no pl*; (*fig: mentale*) backwardness;
in ~ late
ri'tegno [ri'teɲɲo] *sm* restraint
rite'nere *vt* (*trattenere*) to hold back;
(*: somma*) to deduct; (*giudicare*) to
consider, believe; **rite'nuta** *sf* (*sul salario*)

deduction
riti'rare *vt* to withdraw; (*POL: richiamare*) to
recall; (*andare a prendere: pacco etc*) to
collect, pick up; **~rsi** *vr* to withdraw; (*da
un'attività*) to retire; (*stoffa*) to shrink;
(*marea*) to recede; **riti'rata** *sf* (*MIL*) retreat;
(*latrina*) lavatory; **ri'tiro** *sm* withdrawal;
recall; collection; (*luogo appartato*) retreat
'ritmo *sm* rhythm; (*fig*) rate; (*: della vita*)
pace, tempo
'rito *sm* rite; **di ~** usual, customary
ritoc'care *vt* (*disegno, fotografia*) to touch
up; (*testo*) to alter; **ri'tocco, chi** *sm*
touching up *no pl*; alteration
ritor'nare *vi* to return, go (*o* come) back;
(*ripresentarsi*) to recur; (*ridiventare*): **~ ricco**
to become rich again ♦ *vt* (*restituire*) to
return, give back
ritor'nello *sm* refrain
ri'torno *sm* return; **essere di ~** to be back;
avere un ~ di fiamma (*AUT*) to backfire;
(*fig: persona*) to be back in love again
ritorsi'one *sf* retaliation
ri'trarre *vt* (*trarre indietro, via*) to withdraw;
(*distogliere: sguardo*) to turn away;
(*rappresentare*) to portray, depict; (*ricavare*)
to get, obtain
ritrat'tare *vt* (*disdire*) to retract, take back;
(*trattare nuovamente*) to deal with again
ri'tratto, a *pp di* **ritrarre** ♦ *sm* portrait
ri'troso, a *ag* (*restio*): **~ (a)** reluctant (to);
(*schivo*) shy; **andare a ~** to go backwards
ritro'vare *vt* to find; (*salute*) to regain;
(*persona*) to find; to meet again; **~rsi** *vr*
(*essere, capitare*) to find o.s.; (*raccapezzarsi*)
to find one's way; (*con senso reciproco*) to
meet (again); **ri'trovo** *sm* meeting place;
ritrovo notturno night club
'ritto, a *ag* (*in piedi*) standing, on one's
feet; (*levato in alto*) erect, raised; (*: capelli*)
standing on end; (*posto verticalmente*)
upright
ritu'ale *ag, sm* ritual
riuni'one *sf* (*adunanza*) meeting;
(*riconciliazione*) reunion
riu'nire *vt* (*ricongiungere*) to join (together);
(*riconciliare*) to reunite, bring together

(again); **~rsi** *vr* (*adunarsi*) to meet; (*tornare insieme*) to be reunited

riu'scire [riuʃˈʃire] *vi* (*uscire di nuovo*) to go out again, go back out; (*aver esito: fatti, azioni*) to go, turn out; (*aver successo*) to succeed, be successful; (*essere, apparire*) to be, prove; (*raggiungere il fine*) to manage, succeed; **~ a fare qc** to manage to do *o* succeed in doing *o* be able to do sth; **riu'scita** *sf* (*esito*) result, outcome; (*buon esito*) success

'riva *sf* (*di fiume*) bank; (*di lago, mare*) shore

ri'vale *sm/f* rival; **rivalità** *sf* rivalry

ri'valsa *sf* (*rivincita*) revenge

rivalu'tare *vt* (ECON) to revalue

rivan'gare *vt* (*ricordi etc*) to dig up (again)

rive'dere *vt* to see again; (*ripassare*) to revise; (*verificare*) to check

rive'lare *vt* to reveal; (*divulgare*) to reveal, disclose; (*dare indizio*) to reveal, show; **~rsi** *vr* (*manifestarsi*) to be revealed; **~rsi onesto** *etc* to prove to be honest *etc*; **rivela'tore** *sm* (TECN) detector; (FOT) developer; **rivelazi'one** *sf* revelation

rivendi'care *vt* to claim, demand

ri'vendita *sf* (*bottega*) retailer's (shop)

rivendi'tore, 'trice *sm/f* retailer; **~ autorizzato** (COMM) authorized dealer

ri'verbero *sm* (*di luce, calore*) reflection; (*di suono*) reverberation

rive'renza [rive'rɛntsa] *sf* reverence; (*inchino*) bow; curtsey

rive'rire *vt* (*rispettare*) to revere; (*salutare*) to pay one's respects to

river'sare *vt* (*anche fig*) to pour; **~rsi** *vr* (*fig: persone*) to pour out

rivesti'mento *sm* covering; coating

rives'tire *vt* to dress again; (*ricoprire*) to cover; to coat; (*fig: carica*) to hold; **~rsi** *vr* to get dressed again; to change (one's clothes)

rivi'era *sf* coast; **la ~ ligure** the Italian Riviera

ri'vincita [ri'vintʃita] *sf* (SPORT) return match; (*fig*) revenge

rivis'suto, a *pp di* **rivivere**

ri'vista *sf* review; (*periodico*) magazine, review; (TEATRO) revue; variety show

ri'vivere *vi* (*riacquistare forza*) to come alive again; (*tornare in uso*) to be revived ♦ *vt* to relive

ri'volgere [ri'vɔldʒere] *vt* (*attenzione, sguardo*) to turn, direct; (*parole*) to address; **~rsi** *vr* to turn round; (*fig: dirigersi per informazioni*) to turn to; **~rsi a** to go and see, go and speak to; (: *ufficio*) to enquire at

ri'volta *sf* revolt, rebellion

rivol'tare *vt* to turn over; (*con l'interno all'esterno*) to turn inside out; (*disgustare: stomaco*) to upset, turn; **~rsi** *vr* (*ribellarsi*): **~rsi (a)** to rebel (against)

rivol'tella *sf* revolver

ri'volto, a *pp di* **rivolgere**

rivoluzio'nare [rivoluttsjo'nare] *vt* to revolutionize

rivoluzio'nario, a [rivoluttsjo'narjo] *ag, sm/f* revolutionary

rivoluzi'one [rivolut'tsjone] *sf* revolution

riz'zare [rit'tsare] *vt* to raise, erect; **~rsi** *vr* to stand up; (*capelli*) to stand on end

'roba *sf* stuff, things *pl*; (*possessi, beni*) belongings *pl*, things *pl*, possessions *pl*; **~ da mangiare** things *pl* to eat, food; **~ da matti** sheer madness *o* lunacy

'robot *sm inv* robot

ro'busto, a *ag* robust, sturdy; (*solido: catena*) strong

'rocca, che *sf* fortress

rocca'forte *sf* stronghold

roc'chetto [rok'ketto] *sm* reel, spool

'roccia, ce ['rɔttʃa] *sf* rock; **fare ~** (SPORT) to go rock climbing; **roc'cioso, a** *ag* rocky

ro'daggio [ro'daddʒo] *sm* running (BRIT) *o* breaking (US) in; **in ~** running (BRIT) *o* breaking (US) in

'Rodano *sm*: **il ~** the Rhone

'rodere *vt* to gnaw (at); (*distruggere poco a poco*) to eat into

rodi'tore *sm* (ZOOL) rodent

rodo'dendro *sm* rhododendron

'rogna ['rɔɲɲa] *sf* (MED) scabies *sg*; (*fig*) bother, nuisance

ro'gnone [ɾoɲˈɲone] *sm* (CUC) kidney

'rogo, ghi *sm* (*per cadaveri*) (funeral) pyre; (*supplizio*): **il ~** the stake

rol'lio *sm* roll(ing)

'Roma *sf* Rome

Roma'nia *sf*: **la ~** Romania

ro'manico, a, ci, che *ag* Romanesque

ro'mano, a *ag*, *sm/f* Roman

romanti'cismo [romantiˈtʃizmo] *sm* romanticism

ro'mantico, a, ci, che *ag* romantic

ro'manza [roˈmandza] *sf* (MUS, LETTERATURA) romance

roman'zesco, a, schi, sche [romanˈdzesko] *ag* (*stile, personaggi*) fictional; (*fig*) storybook *cpd*

romanzi'ere [romanˈdzjere] *sm* novelist

ro'manzo, a [roˈmandzo] *ag* (LING) romance *cpd* ♦ *sm* novel; **~ d'appendice** serial (story)

rom'bare *vi* to rumble, thunder, roar

'rombo *sm* rumble, thunder, roar; (MAT) rhombus; (ZOOL) turbot; brill

ro'meno, a *ag*, *sm/f*, *sm* = **rumeno, a**

'rompere *vt* to break; (*fidanzamento*) to break off ♦ *vi* to break; **~rsi** *vr* to break; **mi rompe le scatole** (*fam*) he (*o* she) is a pain in the neck; **~rsi un braccio** to break an arm; **rompi'capo** *sm* worry, headache; (*indovinello*) puzzle; (*in enigmistica*) brainteaser; **rompighi'accio** *sm* (NAUT) icebreaker; **rompis'catole** (*fam*) *sm/f inv* pest, pain in the neck

'ronda *sf* (MIL) rounds *pl*, patrol

ron'della *sf* (TECN) washer

'rondine *sf* (ZOOL) swallow

ron'done *sm* (ZOOL) swift

ron'zare [ronˈdzare] *vi* to buzz, hum

ron'zino [ronˈdzino] *sm* (*peg: cavallo*) nag

ron'zio [ronˈdzio] *sm* buzzing

'rosa *sf* rose ♦ *ag inv*, *sm* pink; ro'saio *sm* (*pianta*) rosebush, rose tree; (*giardino*) rose garden; ro'sario *sm* (REL) rosary; ro'sato, a *ag* pink, rosy ♦ *sm* (*vino*) rosé (wine); ro'seo, a *ag* (*anche fig*) rosy

rosicchi'are [rosikˈkjare] *vt* to gnaw (at); (*mangiucchiare*) to nibble (at)

rosma'rino *sm* rosemary

'roso, a *pp di* **rodere**

roso'lare *vt* (CUC) to brown

roso'lia *sf* (MED) German measles *sg*, rubella

ro'sone *sm* rosette; (*vetrata*) rose window

'rospo *sm* (ZOOL) toad

ros'setto *sm* (*per labbra*) lipstick

'rosso, a *ag*, *sm*, *sm/f* red; **il mar R~** the Red Sea; **~ d'uovo** egg yolk; ros'sore *sm* flush, blush

rosticce'ria [rostittʃeˈria] *sf* shop selling roast meat and other cooked food

ro'tabile *ag* (*percorribile*): **strada ~** roadway; (FERR): **materiale ~** rolling stock

ro'taia *sf* rut, track; (FERR) rail

ro'tare *vt*, *vi* to rotate; rotazi'one *sf* rotation

rote'are *vt*, *vi* to whirl; **~ gli occhi** to roll one's eyes

ro'tella *sf* small wheel; (*di mobile*) castor

roto'lare *vt*, *vi* to roll; **~rsi** *vr* to roll (about)

'rotolo *sm* roll; **andare a ~i** (*fig*) to go to rack and ruin

ro'tonda *sf* rotunda

ro'tondo, a *ag* round

'rotta *sf* (AER, NAUT) course, route; (MIL) rout; **a ~ di collo** at breakneck speed; **essere in ~ con qn** to be on bad terms with sb

rot'tame *sm* fragment, scrap, broken bit; **~i** *smpl* (*di nave, aereo etc*) wreckage *sg*

'rotto, a *pp di* **rompere** ♦ *ag* broken; (*calzoni*) torn, split; **per il ~ della cuffia** by the skin of one's teeth

rot'tura *sf* breaking *no pl*; break; breaking off; (MED) fracture, break

rou'lotte [ruˈlɔt] *sf* caravan

ro'vente *ag* red-hot

'rovere *sm* oak

rovesci'are [roveʃˈʃare] *vt* (*versare in giù*) to pour; (: *accidentalmente*) to spill; (*capovolgere*) to turn upside down; (*gettare a terra*) to knock down; (: *fig: governo*) to overthrow; (*piegare all'indietro: testa*) to throw back; **~rsi** *vr* (*sedia, macchina*) to overturn; (barca) to capsize; (liquido) to spill; (fig: situazione) to be reversed

ro'vescio, sci [ro'veʃʃo] sm other side, wrong side; (della mano) back; (di moneta) reverse; (pioggia) sudden downpour; (fig) setback; (MAGLIA: anche: punto ~) purl (stitch); (TENNIS) backhand (stroke); a ~ upside-down; inside-out; capire qc a ~ to misunderstand sth

ro'vina sf ruin; andare in ~ (andare a pezzi) to collapse; (fig) to go to rack and ruin

rovi'nare vi to collapse, fall down ♦ vt (danneggiare, fig) to ruin; rovi'noso, a ag disastrous; damaging; violent

rovis'tare vt (casa) to ransack; (tasche) to rummage in (o through)

'rovo sm (BOT) blackberry bush, bramble bush

'rozzo, a ['roddzo] ag rough, coarse

'ruba sf: andare a ~ to sell like hot cakes

ru'bare vt to steal; ~ qc a qn to steal sth from sb

rubi'netto sm tap, faucet (US)

ru'bino sm ruby

ru'brica, che sf (STAMPA) column; (quadernetto) index book; address book

'rude ag tough, rough

'rudere sm (rovina) ruins pl

rudimen'tale ag rudimentary, basic

rudi'menti smpl rudiments; basic principles; basic knowledge sg

ruffi'ano sm pimp

'ruga, ghe sf wrinkle

'ruggine ['ruddʒine] sf rust

rug'gire [rud'dʒire] vi to roar

rugi'ada [ru'dʒada] sf dew

ru'goso, a ag wrinkled

rul'lare vi (tamburo, nave) to roll; (aereo) to taxi

rul'lino sm (FOT) spool; (: pellicola) film

'rullo sm (di tamburi) roll; (arnese cilindrico, TIP) roller; ~ compressore steam roller; ~ di pellicola roll of film

rum sm rum

ru'meno, a ag, sm/f, sm Romanian

rumi'nare vt (ZOOL) to ruminate

ru'more sm: un ~ a noise, a sound; (fig) a rumour; il ~ noise; rumo'roso, a ag noisy

ru'olo sm (TEATRO, fig) role, part; (elenco) roll, register, list; di ~ permanent, on the permanent staff

ru'ota sf wheel; ~ anteriore/posteriore front/back wheel; ~ di scorta spare wheel

ruo'tare vt, vi = rotare

'rupe sf cliff

ru'rale ag rural, country cpd

ru'scello [ruʃ'ʃello] sm stream

'ruspa sf excavator

rus'sare vi to snore

'Russia sf: la ~ Russia; 'russo, a ag, sm/f, sm Russian

'rustico, a, ci, che ag rustic; (fig) rough, unrefined

rut'tare vi to belch; 'rutto sm belch

'ruvido, a ag rough, coarse

ruzzo'lare [ruttso'lare] vi to tumble down; ruzzo'loni av: cadere ruzzoloni to tumble down

S, s

S. abbr (= sud) S

sa vb vedi sapere

'sabato sm Saturday; di o il ~ on Saturdays

'sabbia sf sand; ~e mobili quicksand(s); sabbi'oso, a ag sandy

sabo'taggio [sabo'taddʒo] sm sabotage

sabo'tare vt to sabotage

'sacca, che sf bag; (bisaccia) haversack; ~ da viaggio travelling bag

sacca'rina sf saccharin(e)

sac'cente [sat'tʃente] sm/f know-all (BRIT), know-it-all (US)

saccheggi'are [sakked'dʒare] vt to sack, plunder; sac'cheggio sm sack(ing)

sac'chetto [sak'ketto] sm (small) bag; (small) sack

'sacco, chi sm bag; (per carbone etc) sack; (ANAT, BIOL) sac; (tela) sacking; (saccheggio) sack(ing); (fig: grande quantità): un ~ di lots of, heaps of; ~ a pelo sleeping bag; ~ per i rifiuti bin bag

sacer'dote [satʃer'dɔte] *sm* priest; **sacer'dozio** *sm* priesthood

sacra'mento *sm* sacrament

sacrifi'care *vt* to sacrifice; **~rsi** *vr* to sacrifice o.s.; (*privarsi di qc*) to make sacrifices

sacri'ficio [sakri'fitʃo] *sm* sacrifice

sacri'legio [sacri'lɛdʒo] *sm* sacrilege

'sacro, a *ag* sacred

'sadico, a, ci, che *ag* sadistic ♦ *sm/f* sadist

sa'etta *sf* arrow; (*fulmine: anche fig*) thunderbolt; flash of lightning

sa'fari *sm inv* safari

sa'gace [sa'gatʃe] *ag* shrewd, sagacious

sag'gezza [sad'dʒettsa] *sf* wisdom

saggi'are [sad'dʒare] *vt* (*metalli*) to assay; (*fig*) to test

'saggio, a, gi, ge ['saddʒo] *ag* wise ♦ *sm* (*persona*) sage; (*esperimento*) test; (*fig: prova*) proof; (*campione*) sample; (*scritto*) essay

Sagit'tario [sadʒit'tarjo] *sm* Sagittarius

'sagoma *sf* (*profilo*) outline, profile; (*forma*) form, shape; (*TECN*) template; (*bersaglio*) target; (*fig: persona*) character

'sagra *sf* festival

sagres'tano *sm* sacristan; sexton

sagres'tia *sf* sacristy

Sa'hara [sa'ara] *sm*: **il (deserto del) ~** the Sahara (Desert)

'sai *vb vedi* **sapere**

'sala *sf* hall; (*stanza*) room; **~ d'aspetto** waiting room; **~ da ballo** ballroom; **~ per concerti** concert hall; **~ da gioco** gaming room; **~ operatoria** operating theatre; **~ da pranzo** dining room

sa'lame *sm* salami *no pl*, salami sausage

sala'moia *sf* (*CUC*) brine

sa'lare *vt* to salt

sa'lario *sm* pay, wages *pl*

sa'lato, a *ag* (*sapore*) salty; (*CUC*) salted, salt *cpd*; (*fig: prezzo*) steep, stiff

sal'dare *vt* (*congiungere*) to join, bind; (*parti metalliche*) to solder; (*: con saldatura autogena*) to weld; (*conto*) to settle, pay; **salda'tura** *sf* soldering; welding; (*punto*

saldato) soldered joint; weld

sal'dezza [sal'dettsa] *sf* firmness; strength

'saldo, a *ag* (*resistente, forte*) strong, firm; (*fermo*) firm, steady, stable; (*fig*) firm, steadfast ♦ *sm* (*svendita*) sale; (*di conto*) settlement; (*ECON*) balance

'sale *sm* salt; (*fig*): **ha poco ~ in zucca** he doesn't have much sense; **~ fino/grosso** table/cooking salt

'salice ['salitʃe] *sm* willow; **~ piangente** weeping willow

sali'ente *ag* (*fig*) salient, main

sali'era *sf* salt cellar

sa'lina *sf* saltworks *sg*

sa'lino, a *ag* saline

sa'lire *vi* to go (*o* come) up; (*aereo etc*) to climb, go up; (*passeggero*) to get on; (*sentiero, prezzi, livello*) to go up, rise ♦ *vt* (*scale, gradini*) to go (*o* come) up; **~ su** to climb (up); **~ sul treno/sull'autobus** to board the train/the bus; **~ in macchina** to get into the car; **sa'lita** *sf* climb, ascent; (*erta*) hill, slope; **in salita** *ag, av* uphill

sa'liva *sf* saliva

'salma *sf* corpse

'salmo *sm* psalm

sal'mone *sm* salmon

sa'lone *sm* (*stanza*) sitting room, lounge; (*in albergo*) lounge; (*su nave*) lounge, saloon; (*mostra*) show, exhibition; **~ di bellezza** beauty salon

sa'lotto *sm* lounge, sitting room; (*mobilio*) lounge suite

sal'pare *vi* (*NAUT*) to set sail; (*anche*: **~ l'ancora**) to weigh anchor

'salsa *sf* (*CUC*) sauce; **~ di pomodoro** tomato sauce

sal'siccia, ce [sal'sittʃa] *sf* pork sausage

sal'tare *vi* to jump, leap; (*esplodere*) to blow up, explode; (*: valvola*) to blow out; (*venir via*) to pop off; (*non aver luogo: corso etc*) to be cancelled ♦ *vt* to jump (over), leap (over); (*fig: pranzo, capitolo*) to skip, miss (out); (*CUC*) to sauté; **far ~** to blow up; to burst open; **~ fuori** (*fig: apparire all'improvviso*) to turn up

saltel'lare *vi* to skip; to hop

saltim'banco *sm* acrobat

'salto *sm* jump; (*SPORT*) jumping; **fare un ~** to jump, leap; **fare un ~ da qn** to pop over to sb's (place); **~ in alto/lungo** high/long jump; **~ con l'asta** pole vaulting; **~ mortale** somersault

saltu'ario, a *ag* occasional, irregular

sa'lubre *ag* healthy, salubrious

salume'ria *sf* delicatessen

sa'lumi *smpl* salted pork meats

salu'tare *ag* healthy; (*fig*) salutary, beneficial ♦ *vt* (*incontrandosi*) to greet; (*congedandosi*) to say goodbye to; (*MIL*) to salute

sa'lute *sf* health; **~!** (*a chi starnutisce*) bless you!; (*nei brindisi*) cheers!; **bere alla ~ di qn** to drink (to) sb's health

sa'luto *sm* (*gesto*) wave; (*parola*) greeting; (*MIL*) salute; **~i** *smpl* (*formula di cortesia*) greetings; **cari ~i** best regards; **vogliate gradire i nostri più distinti ~i** Yours faithfully

salvacon'dotto *sm* (*MIL*) safe-conduct

salva'gente [salva'dʒɛnte] *sm* (*NAUT*) lifebuoy; (*ciambella*) life belt; (*giubbotto*) lifejacket; (*stradale*) traffic island

salvaguar'dare *vt* to safeguard

sal'vare *vt* to save; (*trarre da un pericolo*) to rescue; (*proteggere*) to protect; **~rsi** *vr* to save o.s.; (*per scampare*) to escape; **salva'taggio** *sm* rescue; **salva'tore, 'trice** *sm/f* saviour

'salve (*fam*) *escl* hi!

sal'vezza [sal'vettsa] *sf* salvation; (*sicurezza*) safety

'salvia *sf* (*BOT*) sage

salvi'etta *sf* napkin; **~ umidificata** baby wipe

'salvo, a *ag* safe, unhurt, unharmed; (*fuori pericolo*) safe, out of danger ♦ *sm*: **in ~** safe ♦ *prep* (*eccetto*) except; **mettere qc in ~** to put sth in a safe place; **~ che** (*a meno che*) unless; (*eccetto che*) except (that); **~ imprevisti** barring accidents

sam'buco *sm* elder (tree)

san *ag vedi* **santo**

sa'nare *vt* to heal, cure; (*economia*) to put right

san'cire [san'tʃire] *vt* to sanction

'sandalo *sm* (*BOT*) sandalwood; (*calzatura*) sandal

'sangue *sm* blood; **farsi cattivo ~** to fret, get in a state; **~ freddo** (*fig*) sang-froid, calm; **a ~ freddo** in cold blood; **sangu'igno, a** *ag* blood *cpd*; (*colore*) blood-red; **sangui'nare** *vi* to bleed; **sangui'noso, a** *ag* bloody; **sangui'suga** *sf* leech

sanità *sf* health; (*salubrità*) healthiness; **Ministero della S~** Department of Health; **~ mentale** sanity

sani'tario, a *ag* health *cpd*; (*condizioni*) sanitary ♦ *sm* (*AMM*) doctor; (*impianti*) **~i** *smpl* bathroom *o* sanitary fittings

'sanno *vb vedi* **sapere**

'sano, a *ag* healthy; (*denti, costituzione*) healthy, sound; (*integro*) whole, unbroken; (*fig: politica, consigli*) sound; **~ di mente** sane; **di ~a pianta** completely, entirely; **~ e salvo** safe and sound

sant' *ag vedi* **santo**

santifi'care *vt* to sanctify; (*feste*) to observe

santità *sf* sanctity; holiness; **Sua/Vostra ~** (*titolo di Papa*) His/Your Holiness

'santo, a *ag* holy; (*fig*) saintly; (*seguito da nome proprio*) saint ♦ *sm/f* saint; **la S~a Sede** the Holy See

santu'ario *sm* sanctuary

sanzio'nare [santsjo'nare] *vt* to sanction

sanzi'one [san'tsjone] *sf* sanction; (*penale, civile*) sanction, penalty

sa'pere *vt* to know; (*essere capace di*): **so nuotare** I know how to swim, I can swim ♦ *vi*: **~ di** (*aver sapore*) to taste of; (*aver odore*) to smell of ♦ *sm* knowledge; **far ~ qc a qn** to inform sb about sth, let sb know sth; **mi sa che non sia vero** I don't think that's true

sapi'enza [sa'pjentsa] *sf* wisdom

sa'pone *sm* soap; **~ da bucato** washing soap; **sapo'netta** *sf* cake *o* bar *o* tablet of soap

sa'pore *sm* taste, flavour; **sapo'rito, a** *ag* tasty

sappi'amo *vb vedi* **sapere**

saraci'nesca [saratʃi'neska] *sf* (*serranda*) rolling shutter

sar'casmo *sm* sarcasm *no pl*; sarcastic remark

Sar'degna [sar'deɲɲa] *sf*: **la ~** Sardinia

sar'dina *sf* sardine

'sardo, a *ag, sm/f* Sardinian

'sarto, a *sm/f* tailor/dressmaker; **sarto'ria** *sf* tailor's (shop); dressmaker's (shop); (*casa di moda*) fashion house; (*arte*) couture

'sasso *sm* stone; (*ciottolo*) pebble; (*masso*) rock

sas'sofono *sm* saxophone

sas'soso, a *ag* stony; pebbly

'Satana *sm* Satan; **sa'tanico, a, ci, che** *ag* satanic, fiendish

sa'tellite *sm, ag* satellite

'satira *sf* satire

'saturo, a *ag* saturated; (*fig*): **~ di** full of

'sauna *sf* sauna

Sa'voia *sf* Savoy

savoi'ardo, a *ag* of Savoy, Savoyard ♦ *sm* (*biscotto*) sponge finger

sazi'are [sat'tsjare] *vt* to satisfy, satiate; **~rsi** *vr*: **~rsi (di)** to eat one's fill (of); (*fig*): **~rsi di** to grow tired *o* weary of

'sazio, a ['sattsjo] *ag*: **~ (di)** sated (with), full (of); (*fig: stufo*) fed up (with), sick (of)

sba'dato, a *ag* careless, inattentive

sbadigli'are [zbadiʎ'ʎare] *vi* to yawn; **sba'diglio** *sm* yawn

sbagli'are [zbaʎ'ʎare] *vt* to make a mistake in, get wrong ♦ *vi* to make a mistake, be mistaken, be wrong; (*operare in modo non giusto*) to err; **~rsi** *vr* to make a mistake, be mistaken, be wrong; **~ la mira/strada** to miss one's aim/take the wrong road; **'sbaglio** *sm* mistake, error; (*morale*) error; **fare uno sbaglio** to make a mistake

sbal'lare *vt* (*merce*) to unpack ♦ *vi* (*nel fare un conto*) to overestimate; (*fam: gergo della droga*) to get high

sballot'tare *vt* to toss (about)

sbalor'dire *vt* to stun, amaze ♦ *vi* to be stunned, be amazed; **sbalordi'tivo, a** *ag* amazing; (*prezzo*) incredible, absurd

sbal'zare [zbal'tsare] *vt* to throw, hurl ♦ *vi* (*balzare*) to bounce; (*saltare*) to leap, bound; **'sbalzo** *sm* (*spostamento improvviso*) jolt, jerk; **a sbalzi** jerkily; (*fig*) in fits and starts; **uno sbalzo di temperatura** a sudden change in temperature

sban'dare *vi* (NAUT) to list; (AER) to bank; (AUT) to skid; **~rsi** *vr* (*folla*) to disperse

sbandie'rare *vt* (*bandiera*) to wave; (*fig*) to parade, show off

sbaragli'are [zbaraʎ'ʎare] *vt* (MIL) to rout; (*in gare sportive etc*) to beat, defeat

sba'raglio [zba'raʎʎo] *sm* rout; defeat; **gettarsi allo ~** to risk everything

sbaraz'zarsi [zbarat'tsarsi] *vr*: **~ di** to get rid of, rid o.s. of

sbar'care *vt* (*passeggeri*) to disembark; (*merci*) to unload ♦ *vi* to disembark; **'sbarco** *sm* disembarkation; unloading; (MIL) landing

'sbarra *sf* bar; (*di passaggio a livello*) barrier; (DIR): **presentarsi alla ~** to appear before the court

sbarra'mento *sm* (*stradale*) barrier; (*diga*) dam, barrage; (MIL) barrage

sbar'rare *vt* (*strada etc*) to block, bar; (*assegno*) to cross; **~ il passo** to bar the way; **~ gli occhi** to open one's eyes wide

'sbattere *vt* (*porta*) to slam, bang; (*tappeti, ali, CUC*) to beat; (*urtare*) to knock, hit ♦ *vi* (*porta, finestra*) to bang; (*agitarsi: ali, vele etc*) to flap; **me ne sbatto!** (*fam*) I don't give a damn!; **sbat'tuto, a** *ag* (*viso, aria*) dejected, worn out; (*uovo*) beaten

sba'vare *vi* to dribble; (*colore*) to smear, smudge

sbia'dire *vi, vt* to fade; **~rsi** *vr* to fade; **sbia'dito, a** *ag* faded; (*fig*) colourless, dull

sbian'care *vt* to whiten; (*tessuto*) to bleach ♦ *vi* (*impallidire*) to grow pale *o* white

sbi'eco, a, chi, che *ag* (*storto*) squint, askew; **di ~**: **guardare qn di ~** (*fig*) to look askance at sb; **tagliare una stoffa di ~** to cut a material on the bias

sbigot'tire *vt* to dismay, stun ♦ *vi* (*anche*: **~rsi**) to be dismayed

sbilanci'are [zbilan'tʃare] *vt* to throw off balance; **~rsi** *vr* (perdere l'equilibrio) to overbalance, lose one's balance; (*fig: compromettersi*) to compromise o.s.

sbirci'are [zbir'tʃare] *vt* to cast sidelong glances at, eye

'sbirro (*peg*) *sm* cop

sbizzar'rirsi [zbiddzar'rirsi] *vr* to indulge one's whims

sbloc'care *vt* to unblock, free; (*freno*) to release; (*prezzi, affitti*) to decontrol

sboc'care *vi*: **~ in** (*fiume*) to flow into; (*strada*) to lead into; (*persona*) to come (out) into; (*fig: concludersi*) to end (up) in

sboc'cato, a *ag* (*persona*) foul-mouthed; (*linguaggio*) foul

sbocci'are [zbot'tʃare] *vi* (*fiore*) to bloom, open (out)

'sbocco, chi *sm* (*di fiume*) mouth; (*di strada*) end; (*di tubazione, COMM*) outlet; (*uscita: anche fig*) way out; **siamo in una situazione senza ~chi** there's no way out of this for us

sbol'lire *vi* (*fig*) to cool down, calm down

'sbornia (*fam*) *sf*: **prendersi una ~** to get plastered

sbor'sare *vt* (*denaro*) to pay out

sbot'tare *vi*: **~ in una risata/per la collera** to burst out laughing/explode with anger

sbotto'nare *vt* to unbutton, undo

sbrai'tare *vi* to yell, bawl

sbra'nare *vt* to tear to pieces

sbricio'lare [zbritʃo'lare] *vt* to crumble; **~rsi** *vr* to crumble

sbri'gare *vt* to deal with; **~rsi** *vr* to hurry (up); **sbriga'tivo, a** *ag* (*persona, modo*) quick, expeditious; (*giudizio*) hasty

sbrindel'lato, a *ag* tattered, in tatters

sbrodo'lare *vt* to stain, dirty

'sbronza ['zbrontsa] (*fam*) *sf* (*ubriaco*): **prendersi una ~** to get plastered

'sbronzo, a [zbrontso] (*fam*) *ag* plastered

sbruf'fone, a *sm/f* boaster

sbu'care *vi* to come out, emerge; (*improvvisamente*) to pop out (o up)

sbucci'are [zbut'tʃare] *vt* (*arancia, patata*)

to peel; (*piselli*) to shell; **~rsi un ginocchio** to graze one's knee

sbudel'larsi *vr*: **~ dalle risa** to split one's sides laughing

sbuf'fare *vi* (*persona, cavallo*) to snort; (: *ansimare*) to puff, pant; (*treno*) to puff; **'sbuffo** *sm* (*di aria, fumo, vapore*) puff; **maniche a sbuffo** puff(ed) sleeves

'scabbia *sf* (*MED*) scabies *sg*

sca'broso, a *ag* (*fig: difficile*) difficult, thorny; (: *imbarazzante*) embarrassing; (: *sconcio*) indecent

scacchi'era [skak'kjera] *sf* chessboard

scacci'are [skat'tʃare] *vt* to chase away o out, drive away o out

'scacco, chi *sm* (*pezzo del gioco*) chessman; (*quadretto di scacchiera*) square; (*fig*) setback, reverse; **~chi** *smpl* (*gioco*) chess *sg*; **a ~chi** (*tessuto*) check(ed); **scacco'matto** *sm* checkmate

sca'dente *ag* shoddy, of poor quality

sca'denza [ska'dentsa] *sf* (*di cambiale, contratto*) maturity; (*di passaporto*) expiry date; **a breve/lunga ~** short-/long-term; **data di ~** expiry date

sca'dere *vi* (*contratto etc*) to expire; (*debito*) to fall due; (*valore, forze, peso*) to decline, go down

sca'fandro *sm* (*di palombaro*) diving suit; (*di astronauta*) space-suit

scaf'fale *sm* shelf; (*mobile*) set of shelves

'scafo *sm* (*NAUT, AER*) hull

scagio'nare [skadʒo'nare] *vt* to exonerate, free from blame

'scaglia ['skaʎʎa] *sf* (*ZOOL*) scale; (*scheggia*) chip, flake

scagli'are [skaʎ'ʎare] *vt* (*lanciare: anche fig*) to hurl, fling; **~rsi** *vr*: **~rsi su o contro** to hurl o fling o.s. at; (*fig*) to rail at

scaglio'nare [skaʎʎo'nare] *vt* (*pagamenti*) to space out, spread out; (*MIL*) to echelon; **scagli'one** *sm* echelon; (*GEO*) terrace; **a scaglioni** in groups

'scala *sf* (*a gradini etc*) staircase, stairs *pl*; (*a pioli, di corda*) ladder; (*MUS, GEO, di colori, valori, fig*) scale; **~e** *sfpl* (*scalinata*) stairs; **su vasta ~/~ ridotta** on a large/small scale; **~ a libretto** stepladder; **~ mobile** escalator; (*ECON*) sliding scale; **~ mobile (dei salari)** index-linked pay scale

---
Scala

ⓘ Milan's world-famous **la Scala** *theatre first opened its doors in 1778 with a performance of Salieri's opera, "L'Europa riconosciuta". It suffered serious damage in the bombing of Milan in 1943 and reopened in 1946 with a concert conducted by Toscanini. It also has a famous classical dance school.*

---

sca'lare *vt* (*ALPINISMO, muro*) to climb, scale; (*debito*) to scale down, reduce; sca'lata *sf* scaling *no pl*, climbing *no pl*; (*arrampicata, fig*) climb; scala'tore, 'trice *sm/f* climber

scalda'bagno [skalda'baɲɲo] *sm* waterheater

scal'dare *vt* to heat; **~rsi** *vr* to warm up, heat up; (*al fuoco, al sole*) to warm o.s.; (*fig*) to get excited

scal'fire *vt* to scratch

scali'nata *sf* staircase

sca'lino *sm* (*anche fig*) step; (*di scala a pioli*) rung

'scalo *sm* (*NAUT*) slipway; (*: porto d'approdo*) port of call; (*AER*) stopover; **fare ~ (a)** (*NAUT*) to call (at), put in (at); (*AER*) to land (at), make a stop (at); **~ merci** (*FERR*) goods (*BRIT*) *o* freight yard

scalop'pina *sf* (*CUC*) escalope

scal'pello *sm* chisel

scal'pore *sm* noise, row; **far ~** (*notizia*) to cause a sensation *o* a stir

'scaltro, a *ag* cunning, shrewd

'scalzo, a ['skaltso] *ag* barefoot

scambi'are *vt* to exchange; (*confondere*): **~ qn/qc per** to take *o* mistake sb/sth for; **mi hanno scambiato il cappello** they've given me the wrong hat

scambi'evole *ag* mutual, reciprocal

'scambio *sm* exchange; (*FERR*) points *pl*; **fare (uno) ~** to make a swap

scampa'gnata [skampaɲ'ɲata] *sf* trip to the country

scam'pare *vt* (*salvare*) to rescue, save; (*evitare: morte, prigione*) to escape ♦ *vi*: **~ (a qc)** to survive (sth), escape (sth); **scamparla bella** to have a narrow escape

'scampo *sm* (*salvezza*) escape; (*ZOOL*) prawn; **cercare ~ nella fuga** to seek safety in flight

'scampolo *sm* remnant

scana'latura *sf* (*incavo*) channel, groove

scandagli'are [skanda'ʎʎare] *vt* (*NAUT*) to sound; (*fig*) to sound out; to probe

scandaliz'zare [skandalid'dzare] *vt* to shock, scandalize; **~rsi** *vr* to be shocked

'scandalo *sm* scandal

Scandi'navia *sf*: **la ~** Scandinavia; scandi'navo, a *ag, sm/f* Scandinavian

scan'dire *vt* (*versi*) to scan; (*parole*) to articulate, pronounce distinctly; **~ il tempo** (*MUS*) to beat time

scan'nare *vt* (*animale*) to butcher, slaughter; (*persona*) to cut *o* slit the throat of

'scanno *sm* seat, bench

scansafa'tiche [skansafa'tike] *sm/f inv* idler, loafer

scan'sare *vt* (*rimuovere*) to move (aside), shift; (*schivare: schiaffo*) to dodge; (*sfuggire*) to avoid; **~rsi** *vr* to move aside

scan'sia *sf* shelves *pl*; (*per libri*) bookcase

'scanso *sm*: **a ~ di** in order to avoid, as a precaution against

scanti'nato *sm* basement

scanto'nare *vi* to turn the corner; (*svignarsela*) to sneak off

scapacci'one [skapat'tʃone] *sm* clout

scapes'trato, a *ag* dissolute

'scapito *sm*: **a ~ di** to the detriment of

'scapola *sf* shoulder blade

'scapolo *sm* bachelor

scappa'mento *sm* (*AUT*) exhaust

scap'pare *vi* (*fuggire*) to escape; (*andare via in fretta*) to rush off; **lasciarsi ~ un'occasione** to let an opportunity go by; **~ di prigione** to escape from prison; **~ di mano** (*oggetto*) to slip out of one's hands; **~ di mente a qn** to slip sb's mind; **mi**

scappò detto I let it slip; **scap'pata** sf quick visit o call; **scappa'tella** sf escapade; **scappa'toia** sf way out

scara'beo sm beetle

scarabocchi'are [skarabok'kjare] vt to scribble, scrawl; **scara'bocchio** sm scribble, scrawl

scara'faggio [skara'faddʒo] sm cockroach

scaraven'tare vt to fling, hurl

scarce'rare [skartʃe'rare] vt to release (from prison)

scardi'nare vt: ~ **una porta** to take a door off its hinges

'scarica, che sf (di più armi) volley of shots; (di sassi, pugni) hail, shower; (ELETTR) discharge; ~ **di mitra** burst of machine-gun fire

scari'care vt (merci, camion etc) to unload; (passeggeri) to set down, put off; (arma) to unload; (: sparare, ELETTR) to discharge; (sog: corso d'acqua) to empty, pour; (fig: liberare da un peso) to unburden, relieve; **~rsi** vr (orologio) to run o wind down; (batteria, accumulatore) to go flat o dead; (fig: rilassarsi) to unwind; (: sfogarsi) to let off steam; **scarica'tore** sm (di porto) docker

'scarico, a, chi, che ag unloaded; (orologio) run down; (accumulatore) dead, flat ♦ sm (di merci, materiali) unloading; (di immondizie) dumping, tipping (BRIT); (TECN: deflusso) draining; (: dispositivo) drain; (AUT) exhaust

scarlat'tina sf scarlet fever

scar'latto, a ag scarlet

'scarno, a ag thin, bony

'scarpa sf shoe; **~e da ginnastica/tennis** gym/tennis shoes

scar'pata sf escarpment

scar'pone sm boot; **~i da sci** ski-boots

scarseggi'are [skarsed'dʒare] vi to be scarce; ~ **di** to be short of, lack

scar'sezza [skar'settsa] sf scarcity, lack

'scarso, a ag (insufficiente) insufficient, meagre; (povero: annata) poor, lean; (INS: voto) poor; ~ **di** lacking in; **3 chili ~i** just under 3 kilos, barely 3 kilos

scarta'mento sm (FERR) gauge; ~ **normale/ridotto** standard/narrow gauge

scar'tare vt (pacco) to unwrap; (idea) to reject; (MIL) to declare unfit for military service; (carte da gioco) to discard; (CALCIO) to dodge (past) ♦ vi to swerve

'scarto sm (cosa scartata, anche COMM) reject; (di veicolo) swerve; (differenza) gap, difference

scassi'nare vt to break, force

'scasso sm vedi **furto**

scate'nare vt (fig) to incite, stir up; **~rsi** vr (temporale) to break; (rivolta) to break out; (persona: infuriarsi) to fly into a rage

'scatola sf box; (di latta) tin (BRIT), can; **cibi in ~** tinned (BRIT) o canned foods; ~ **cranica** cranium

scat'tare vt (fotografia) to take ♦ vi (congegno, molla etc) to be released; (balzare) to spring up; (SPORT) to put on a spurt; (fig: per l'ira) to fly into a rage; ~ **in piedi** to spring to one's feet

'scatto sm (dispositivo) release; (: di arma da fuoco) trigger mechanism; (rumore) click; (balzo) jump, start; (SPORT) spurt; (fig: di ira etc) fit; (: di stipendio) increment; **di ~** suddenly

scatu'rire vi to gush, spring

scaval'care vt (ostacolo) to pass (o climb) over; (fig) to get ahead of, overtake

sca'vare vt (terreno) to dig; (legno) to hollow out; (pozzo, galleria) to bore; (città sepolta etc) to excavate

'scavo sm excavating no pl; excavation

'scegliere ['ʃeʎʎere] vt to choose, select

sce'icco, chi [ʃe'ikko] sm sheik

scelle'rato, a [ʃelle'rato] ag wicked, evil

scel'lino [ʃel'lino] sm shilling

'scelta ['ʃelta] sf choice; selection; **di prima ~** top grade o quality; **frutta o formaggi a ~** choice of fruit or cheese

'scelto, a ['ʃelto] pp di **scegliere** ♦ ag (gruppo) carefully selected; (frutta, verdura) choice, top quality; (MIL: specializzato) crack cpd, highly skilled

sce'mare [ʃe'mare] vt, vi to diminish

'scemo, a ['ʃemo] ag stupid, silly

'scempio ['ʃempjo] *sm* slaughter, massacre; (*fig*) ruin; far ~ di (*fig*) to play havoc with, ruin

'scena ['ʃɛna] *sf* (*gen*) scene; (*palcoscenico*) stage; le ~e (*fig: teatro*) the stage; fare una ~ to make a scene; andare in ~ to be staged *o* put on *o* performed; mettere in ~ to stage

sce'nario [ʃe'narjo] *sm* scenery; (*di film*) scenario

sce'nata [ʃe'nata] *sf* row, scene

'scendere ['ʃendere] *vi* to go (*o* come) down; (*strada, sole*) to go down; (*notte*) to fall; (*passeggero: fermarsi*) to get out, alight; (*fig: temperatura, prezzi*) to go *o* come down, fall, drop ♦ *vt* (*scale, pendio*) to go (*o* come) down; ~ dalle scale to go (*o* come) down the stairs; ~ dal treno to get off *o* out of the train; ~ dalla macchina to get out of the car; ~ da cavallo to dismount, get off one's horse

'scenico, a, ci, che ['ʃɛniko] *ag* stage *cpd*, scenic

scervel'lato, a [ʃervel'lato] *ag* feather-brained, scatterbrained

'sceso, a ['ʃeso] *pp di* scendere

'scettico, a, ci, che ['ʃɛttiko] *ag* sceptical

'scettro ['ʃɛttro] *sm* sceptre

'scheda ['skɛda] *sf* (*index*) card; ~ elettorale ballot paper; ~ telefonica phone card; sche'dare *vt* (*dati*) to file; (*libri*) to catalogue; (*registrare: anche POLIZIA*) to put on one's files; sche'dario *sm* file; (*mobile*) filing cabinet

'scheggia, ge ['skɛddʒa] *sf* splinter, sliver

'scheletro ['skɛletro] *sm* skeleton

'schema, i ['skɛma] *sm* (*diagramma*) diagram, sketch; (*progetto, abbozzo*) outline, plan

'scherma ['skɛrma] *sf* fencing

scher'maglia [sker'maʎʎa] *sf* (*fig*) skirmish

'schermo ['skɛrmo] *sm* shield, screen; (*CINEMA, TV*) screen

scher'nire [sker'nire] *vt* to mock, sneer at; 'scherno *sm* mockery, derision

scher'zare [sker'tsare] *vi* to joke

'scherzo ['skɛrtso] *sm* joke; (*tiro*) trick;

(*MUS*) scherzo; è uno ~! (*una cosa facile*) it's child's play!, it's easy!; per ~ in jest; for a joke *o* a laugh; fare un brutto ~ a qn to play a nasty trick on sb; scher'zoso, a *ag* (*tono, gesto*) playful; (*osservazione*) facetious; è un tipo scherzoso he likes a joke

schiaccia'noci [skjattʃa'notʃi] *sm inv* nutcracker

schiacci'are [skjat'tʃare] *vt* (*dito*) to crush; (*noci*) to crack; ~ un pisolino to have a nap

schiaffeggi'are [skjaffed'dʒare] *vt* to slap

schi'affo [skjaffo] *sm* slap

schiamaz'zare [skjamat'tsare] *vi* to squawk, cackle

schian'tare [skjan'tare] *vt* to break, tear apart; ~rsi *vr* to break (up), shatter; schi'anto *sm* (*rumore*) crash; tearing sound; è uno schianto! (*fam*) it's (*o* he's *o* she's) terrific!; di schianto all of a sudden

schia'rire [skja'rire] *vt* to lighten, make lighter ♦ *vi* (*anche*: ~rsi) to grow lighter; (*tornar sereno*) to clear, brighten up; ~rsi la voce to clear one's throat

schiavitù [skjavi'tu] *sf* slavery

schi'avo, a ['skjavo] *sm/f* slave

schi'ena ['skjɛna] *sf* (*ANAT*) back; schie'nale *sm* (*di sedia*) back

schi'era ['skjɛra] *sf* (*MIL*) rank; (*gruppo*) group, band

schiera'mento [skjera'mento] *sm* (*MIL, SPORT*) formation; (*fig*) alliance

schie'rare [skje'rare] *vt* (*esercito*) to line up, draw up, marshal; ~rsi *vr* to line up; (*fig*): ~rsi con *o* dalla parte di/contro qn to side with/oppose sb

schi'etto, a ['skjɛtto] *ag* (*puro*) pure; (*fig*) frank, straightforward; sincere

'schifo ['skifo] *sm* disgust; fare ~ (*essere fatto male, dare pessimi risultati*) to be awful; mi fa ~ it makes me sick, it's disgusting; quel libro è uno ~ that book's rotten; schi'foso, a *ag* disgusting, revolting; (*molto scadente*) rotten, lousy

schioc'care [skjɔk'kare] *vt* (*frusta*) to crack; (*dita*) to snap; (*lingua*) to click; ~ le labbra to smack one's lips

schi'udere ['skjudere] *vt* to open; **~rsi** *vr* to open

schi'uma ['skjuma] *sf* foam; (*di sapone*) lather; (*di latte*) froth; (*fig: feccia*) scum; **schiu'mare** *vt* to skim ♦ *vi* to foam

schi'uso, a ['skjuso] *pp di* **schiudere**

schi'vare [ski'vare] *vt* to dodge, avoid

'schivo, a ['skivo] *ag* (*ritroso*) stand-offish, reserved; (*timido*) shy

schiz'zare [skit'tsare] *vt* (*spruzzare*) to spurt, squirt; (*sporcare*) to splash, spatter; (*fig: abbozzare*) to sketch ♦ *vi* to spurt, squirt; (*saltar fuori*) to dart up (*o* off *etc*)

schizzi'noso, a [skittsi'noso] *ag* fussy, finicky

'schizzo ['skittso] *sm* (*di liquido*) spurt, splash, spatter; (*abbozzo*) sketch

sci [ʃi] *sm* (*attrezzo*) ski; (*attività*) skiing; **~ nautico** water-skiing

'scia ['ʃia] (*pl* **'scie**) *sf* (*di imbarcazione*) wake; (*di profumo*) trail

scià [ʃa] *sm inv* shah

sci'abola ['ʃabola] *sf* sabre

scia'callo [ʃa'kallo] *sm* jackal

sciac'quare [ʃak'kware] *vt* to rinse

scia'gura [ʃa'gura] *sf* disaster, calamity; misfortune; **sciagu'rato, a** *ag* unfortunate; (*malvagio*) wicked

scialac'quare [ʃalak'kware] *vt* to squander

scia'lare [ʃa'lare] *vi* to lead a life of luxury

sci'albo, a [ʃ'albo] *ag* pale, dull; (*fig*) dull, colourless

sci'alle ['ʃalle] *sm* shawl

scia'luppa [ʃa'luppa] *sf* (*anche:* **~ di salvataggio**) lifeboat

sci'ame ['ʃame] *sm* swarm

scian'cato, a [ʃan'kato] *ag* lame

sci'are [ʃi'are] *vi* to ski

sci'arpa ['ʃarpa] *sf* scarf; (*fascia*) sash

scia'tore, 'trice [ʃia'tore] *sm/f* skier

sci'atto, a [ʃ'atto] *ag* (*persona*) slovenly, unkempt

scien'tifico, a, ci, che [ʃen'tifiko] *ag* scientific

sci'enza ['ʃɛntsa] *sf* science; (*sapere*) knowledge; **~e** *sfpl* (*INS*) science *sg*; **~e**

naturali natural sciences; **scienzi'ato, a** *sm/f* scientist

'scimmia ['ʃimmja] *sf* monkey; **scimmiot'tare** *vt* to ape, mimic

scimpanzé [ʃimpan'tse] *sm inv* chimpanzee

scimu'nito, a [ʃimu'nito] *ag* silly, idiotic

'scindere ['ʃindere] *vt* to split (up); **~rsi** *vr* to split (up)

scin'tilla [ʃin'tilla] *sf* spark; **scintil'lare** *vi* to spark; (*acqua, occhi*) to sparkle

scioc'chezza [ʃok'kettsa] *sf* stupidity *no pl*; stupid *o* foolish thing; **dire ~e** to talk nonsense

sci'occo, a, chi, che ['ʃɔkko] *ag* stupid, foolish

sci'ogliere ['ʃɔʎʎere] *vt* (*nodo*) to untie; (*capelli*) to loosen; (*persona, animale*) to untie, release; (*fig: persona*): **~ da** to release from; (*neve*) to melt; (*nell'acqua: zucchero etc*) to dissolve; (*fig: mistero*) to solve; (*porre fine a: contratto*) to cancel; (: *società, matrimonio*) to dissolve; (: *riunione*) to bring to an end; **~rsi** *vr* to loosen, come untied; to melt; to dissolve; (*assemblea etc*) to break up; **~ i muscoli** to limber up

sciol'tezza [ʃol'tettsa] *sf* agility; suppleness; ease

sci'olto, a ['ʃɔlto] *pp di* **sciogliere** ♦ *ag* loose; (*agile*) agile, nimble; supple; (*disinvolto*) free and easy; **versi ~i** (*POESIA*) blank verse

sciope'rante [ʃope'rante] *sm/f* striker

sciope'rare [ʃope'rare] *vi* to strike, go on strike

sci'opero ['ʃɔpero] *sm* strike; **fare ~** to strike; **~ bianco** work-to-rule (*BRIT*), slowdown (*US*); **~ selvaggio** wildcat strike; **~ a singhiozzo** on-off strike

scip'pare [ʃip'pare] *vt*: **~ qn** to snatch sb's bag; **mi hanno scippato** they snatched my bag

sci'rocco [ʃi'rɔkko] *sm* sirocco

sci'roppo [ʃi'rɔppo] *sm* syrup

'scisma, i ['ʃizma] *sm* (*REL*) schism

scissi'one [ʃis'sjone] *sf* (*anche fig*) split, division; (*FISICA*) fission

'scisso, a ['ʃisso] *pp di* **scindere**

sciu'pare [ʃu'pare] *vt* (*abito, libro, appetito*) to spoil, ruin; (*tempo, denaro*) to waste; **~rsi** *vr* to get spoilt *o* ruined; (*rovinarsi la salute*) to ruin one's health

scivo'lare [ʃivo'lare] *vi* to slide *o* glide along; (*involontariamente*) to slip, slide; **'scivolo** *sm* slide; (*TECN*) chute; **scivo'loso, a** *ag* slippery

scle'rosi *sf* sclerosis

scoc'care *vt* (*freccia*) to shoot ♦ *vi* (*guizzare*) to shoot up; (*battere: ora*) to strike

scocci'are [skot'tʃare] (*fam*) *vt* to bother, annoy; **~rsi** *vr* to be bothered *o* annoyed

sco'della *sf* bowl

scodinzo'lare [skodintso'lare] *vi* to wag its tail

scogli'era [skoʎ'ʎera] *sf* reef; cliff

'scoglio ['skɔʎʎo] *sm* (*al mare*) rock

scoi'attolo *sm* squirrel

scolapi'atti *sm inv* drainer (*for plates*)

sco'lare *ag*: **età ~** school age ♦ *vt* to drain ♦ *vi* to drip

scola'resca *sf* schoolchildren *pl*, pupils *pl*

sco'laro, a *sm/f* pupil, schoolboy/girl

sco'lastico, a, ci, che *ag* school *cpd*; scholastic

scol'lare *vt* (*staccare*) to unstick; **~rsi** *vr* to come unstick

scolla'tura *sf* neckline

'scolo *sm* drainage

scolo'rire *vt* to fade; to discolour ♦ *vi* (*anche*: **~rsi**) to fade; to become discoloured; (*impallidire*) to turn pale

scol'pire *vt* to carve, sculpt

scombi'nare *vt* to mess up, upset

scombusso'lare *vt* to upset

scom'messa *sf* bet, wager

scom'messo, a *pp di* **scommettere**

scom'mettere *vt, vi* to bet

scomo'dare *vt* to trouble, bother; to disturb; **~rsi** *vr* to put o.s. out; **~rsi a fare** to go to the bother *o* trouble of doing

'scomodo, a *ag* uncomfortable; (*sistemazione, posto*) awkward, inconvenient

scompa'rire *vi* (*sparire*) to disappear,

vanish; (*fig*) to be insignificant; **scom'parsa** *sf* disappearance; **scom'parso, a** *pp di* **scomparire**

scomparti'mento *sm* compartment

scom'parto *sm* compartment, division

scompigli'are [skompiʎ'ʎare] *vt* (*cassetto, capelli*) to mess up, disarrange; (*fig: piani*) to upset; **scom'piglio** *sm* mess, confusion

scom'porre *vt* (*parola, numero*) to break up; (*CHIM*) to decompose; **scomporsi** *vr* (*fig*) to get upset, lose one's composure; **scom'posto, a** *pp di* **scomporre** ♦ *ag* (*gesto*) unseemly; (*capelli*) ruffled, dishevelled

sco'munica *sf* excommunication

scomuni'care *vt* to excommunicate

sconcer'tare [skontʃer'tare] *vt* to disconcert, bewilder

'sconcio, a, ci, ce ['skontʃo] *ag* (*osceno*) indecent, obscene ♦ *sm* disgrace

sconfes'sare *vt* to renounce, disavow; to repudiate

scon'figgere [skon'fiddʒere] *vt* to defeat, overcome

sconfi'nare *vi* to cross the border; (*in proprietà privata*) to trespass; (*fig*): **~ da** to stray *o* digress from; **sconfi'nato, a** *ag* boundless, unlimited

scon'fitta *sf* defeat

scon'fitto, a *pp di* **sconfiggere**

scon'forto *sm* despondency

scongiu'rare [skondʒu'rare] *vt* (*implorare*) to entreat, beseech, implore; (*eludere: pericolo*) to ward off, avert; **scongi'uro** *sm* entreaty; (*esorcismo*) exorcism; **fare gli scongiuri** to touch wood (*BRIT*), knock on wood (*US*)

scon'nesso, a *ag* incoherent

sconosci'uto, a [skonoʃ'ʃuto] *ag* unknown; new, strange ♦ *sm/f* stranger; unknown person

sconquas'sare *vt* to shatter, smash

sconside'rato, a *ag* thoughtless, rash

sconsigli'are [skonsiʎ'ʎare] *vt*: **~ qc a qn** to advise sb against sth; **~ qn dal fare qc** to advise sb not to do *o* against doing sth

sconso'lato, a *ag* inconsolable; desolate

scon'tare *vt* (COMM: *detrarre*) to deduct; (: *debito*) to pay off; (: *cambiale*) to discount; (*pena*) to serve; (*colpa, errori*) to pay for, suffer for

scon'tato, a *ag* (*previsto*) foreseen, taken for granted; **dare per ~ che** to take it for granted that

scon'tento, a *ag*: ~ **(di)** dissatisfied (with) ♦ *sm* dissatisfaction

'sconto *sm* discount; **fare uno ~** to give a discount

scon'trarsi *vr* (*treni etc*) to crash, collide; (*venire ad uno scontro, fig*) to clash; ~ **con** to crash into, collide with

scon'trino *sm* ticket

'scontro *sm* clash, encounter; crash, collision

scon'troso, a *ag* sullen, surly; (*permaloso*) touchy

sconveni'ente *ag* unseemly, improper

scon'volgere [skon'vɔldʒere] *vt* to throw into confusion, upset; (*turbare*) to shake, disturb, upset; **scon'volto, a** *pp di* **sconvolgere**

'scopa *sf* broom; (CARTE) Italian card game; **sco'pare** *vt* to sweep

sco'perta *sf* discovery

sco'perto, a *pp di* **scoprire** ♦ *ag* uncovered; (*capo*) uncovered, bare; (*macchina*) open; (MIL) exposed, without cover; (*conto*) overdrawn

'scopo *sm* aim, purpose; **a che ~?** what for?

scoppi'are *vi* (*spaccarsi*) to burst; (*esplodere*) to explode; (*fig*) to break out; ~ **in pianto** *o* **a piangere** to burst out crying; ~ **dalle risa** *o* **dal ridere** to split one's sides laughing

scoppiet'tare *vi* to crackle

'scoppio *sm* explosion; (*di tuono, arma etc*) crash, bang; (*fig: di rabbia, ira*) fit, outburst; (: *di guerra*) outbreak; **a ~ ritardato** delayed-action

sco'prire *vt* to discover; (*liberare da ciò che copre*) to uncover; (: *monumento*) to unveil; ~**rsi** *vr* to put on lighter clothes; (*fig*) to give o.s. away

scoraggi'are [skorad'dʒare] *vt* to discourage; ~**rsi** *vr* to become discouraged, lose heart

scorcia'toia [skortʃa'toja] *sf* short cut

'scorcio ['skortʃo] *sm* (ARTE) foreshortening; (*di secolo, periodo*) end, close

scor'dare *vt* to forget; ~**rsi** *vr*: ~**rsi di qc/ di fare** to forget sth/to do

'scorgere ['skɔrdʒere] *vt* to make out, distinguish, see

sco'ria *sf* (*di metalli*) slag; (*vulcanica*) scoria; ~**e radioattive** (FISICA) radioactive waste *sg*

'scorno *sm* ignominy, disgrace

scorpacci'ata [skorpat'tʃata] *sf*: **fare una ~ (di)** to stuff o.s. (with), eat one's fill (of)

scorpi'one *sm* scorpion; (*dello zodiaco*): **S~** Scorpio

scorraz'zare [skorrat'tsare] *vi* to run about

'scorrere *vt* (*giornale, lettera*) to run *o* skim through ♦ *vi* (*liquido, fiume*) to run, flow; (*fune*) to run; (*cassetto, porta*) to slide easily; (*tempo*) to pass (by)

scor'retto, a *ag* incorrect; (*sgarbato*) impolite; (*sconveniente*) improper

scor'revole *ag* (*porta*) sliding; (*fig: stile*) fluent, flowing

scorri'banda *sf* (MIL) raid; (*escursione*) trip, excursion

'scorsa *sf* quick look, glance

'scorso, a *pp di* **scorrere** ♦ *ag* last

scor'soio, a *ag*: **nodo ~** noose

'scorta *sf* (*di personalità, convoglio*) escort; (*provvista*) supply, stock; **scor'tare** *vt* to escort

scor'tese *ag* discourteous, rude; **scorte'sia** *sf* discourtesy, rudeness; (*azione*) discourtesy

scorti'care *vt* to skin

'scorto, a *pp di* **scorgere**

'scorza ['skɔrdza] *sf* (*di albero*) bark; (*di agrumi*) peel, skin

sco'sceso, a [skoʃ'ʃeso] *ag* steep

'scossa *sf* jerk, jolt, shake; (ELETTR, *fig*) shock

'scosso, a *pp di* **scuotere** ♦ *ag* (*turbato*) shaken, upset scos'tante *ag* (*fig*) off-putting (*BRIT*), unpleasant

scos'tare *vt* to move (away), shift; **~rsi** *vr* to move away

scostu'mato, a *ag* immoral, dissolute

scot'tare *vt* (*ustionare*) to burn; (*: con liquido bollente*) to scald ♦ *vi* to burn; (*caffè*) to be too hot; **scotta'tura** *sf* burn; scald

'scotto, a *ag* overcooked ♦ *sm* (*fig*): **pagare lo ~ (di)** to pay the penalty (for)

sco'vare *vt* to drive out, flush out; (*fig*) to discover

'Scozia ['skɔttsia] *sf*: **la ~** Scotland; **scoz'zese** *ag* Scottish ♦ *sm/f* Scot

scredi'tare *vt* to discredit

screpo'lare *vt* to crack; **~rsi** *vr* to crack; **screpola'tura** *sf* cracking *no pl*; crack

screzi'ato, a [skret'tsjato] *ag* streaked

'screzio ['skrɛttsjo] *sm* disagreement

scricchio'lare [skrikkjo'lare] *vi* to creak, squeak

'scricciolo ['skrittʃolo] *sm* wren

'scrigno ['skriɲɲo] *sm* casket

scrimina'tura *sf* parting

'scritta *sf* inscription

'scritto, a *pp di* **scrivere** ♦ *ag* written ♦ *sm* writing; (*lettera*) letter, note; **~i** *smpl* (*letterari etc*) writing *sg*

scrit'toio *sm* writing desk

scrit'tore, 'trice *sm/f* writer

scrit'tura *sf* writing; (*COMM*) entry; (*contratto*) contract; (*REL*): **la Sacra S~** the Scriptures *pl*; **~e** *sfpl* (*COMM*) accounts, books

scrittu'rare *vt* (*TEATRO, CINEMA*) to sign up, engage; (*COMM*) to enter

scriva'nia *sf* desk

'scrivere *vt* to write; **come si scrive?** how is it spelt?, how do you write it?

scroc'cone *sm/f* scrounger

'scrofa *sf* (*ZOOL*) sow

scrol'lare *vt* to shake; **~rsi** *vr* (*anche fig*) to give o.s. a shake; **~ le spalle/il capo** to shrug one's shoulders/shake one's head

scrosci'are [skroʃ'ʃare] *vi* (*pioggia*) to pour down, pelt down; (*torrente, fig: applausi*) to thunder, roar; '**scroscio** *sm* pelting; thunder, roar; (*di applausi*) burst

scros'tare *vt* (*intonaco*) to scrape off, strip; **~rsi** *vr* to peel off, flake off

'scrupolo *sm* scruple; (*meticolosità*) care, conscientiousness

scru'tare *vt* to scrutinize; (*intenzioni, causa*) to examine, scrutinize

scruti'nare *vt* (*voti*) to count; **scru'tinio** *sm* (*votazione*) ballot; (*insieme delle operazioni*) poll; (*INS*) (*meeting for*) *assignment of marks at end of a term or year*

scu'cire [sku'tʃire] *vt* (*orlo etc*) to unpick, undo

scude'ria *sf* stable

scu'detto *sm* (*SPORT*) (championship) shield; (*distintivo*) badge

'scudo *sm* shield

scul'tore, 'trice *sm/f* sculptor

scul'tura *sf* sculpture

scu'ola *sf* school; **~ elementare/ materna/media** primary (*BRIT*) *o* grade (*US*)/nursery/secondary (*BRIT*) *o* high (*US*) school; **~ guida** driving school; **~ dell'obbligo** compulsory education; **~e serali** evening classes, night school *sg*; **~ tecnica** technical college

scu'otere *vt* to shake; **~rsi** *vr* to jump, be startled; (*fig: muoversi*) to rouse o.s., stir o.s.; (*: turbarsi*) to be shaken

'scure *sf* axe

'scuro, a *ag* dark; (*fig: espressione*) grim ♦ *sm* darkness; dark colour; (*imposta*) (window) shutter; **verde/rosso** *etc* **~** dark green/red *etc*

scur'rile *ag* scurrilous

'scusa *sf* apology; (*pretesto*) excuse; **chiedere ~ a qn (per)** to apologize to sb (for); **chiedo ~** I'm sorry; (*disturbando etc*) excuse me

scu'sare *vt* to excuse; **~rsi** *vr*: **~rsi (di)** to apologize (for); **(mi) scusi** I'm sorry; (*per richiamare l'attenzione*) excuse me

sde'gnato, a [zdeɲ'ɲato] *ag* indignant, angry

'sdegno ['zdeɲɲo] *sm* scorn, disdain;

sde'gnoso, a *ag* scornful, disdainful

sdoga'nare *vt (merci)* to clear through customs

sdolci'nato, a [zdoltʃi'nato] *ag* mawkish, oversentimental

sdrai'arsi *vr* to stretch out, lie down

'sdraio *sm*: sedia a ~ deck chair

sdruccio'levole [zdruttʃo'levole] *ag* slippery

PAROLA CHIAVE

se *pron vedi* si
 ♦ *cong* 1 *(condizionale, ipotetica)* if; ~ nevica non vengo I won't come if it snows; sarei rimasto ~ me l'avessero chiesto I would have stayed if they'd asked me; non puoi fare altro ~ non telefonare all you can do is phone; ~ mai if, if ever; siamo noi ~ mai che le siamo grati it is we who should be grateful to you; ~ no *(altrimenti)* or (else), otherwise
 2 *(in frasi dubitative, interrogative indirette)* if, whether; non so ~ scrivere o telefonare I don't know whether *o* if I should write or phone

---

sé *pron (gen)* oneself; *(esso, essa, lui, lei, loro)* itself; himself; herself; themselves; ~ stesso(a) *pron* oneself; itself; himself; herself; ~ stessi(e) *pron pl* themselves

seb'bene *cong* although, though

sec. *abbr (= secolo)* c

'secca *sf (del mare)* shallows *pl; vedi anche* secco

sec'care *vt* to dry; *(prosciugare)* to dry up; *(fig: importunare)* to annoy, bother ♦ *vi* to dry; to dry up; ~rsi *vr* to dry; to dry up; *(fig)* to grow annoyed; secca'tura *sf (fig)* bother *no pl*, trouble *no pl*

secchi'ello *sm* bucket; ~ del ghiaccio ice bucket

'secchio ['sekkjo] *sm* bucket, pail

'secco, a, chi, che *ag* dry; *(fichi, pesce)* dried; *(foglie, ramo)* withered; *(magro: persona)* thin, skinny; *(fig: risposta, modo di fare)* curt, abrupt; *(: colpo)* clean, sharp ♦ *sm (siccità)* drought; restarci ~ *(fig:*

morire sul colpo) to drop dead; mettere in ~ *(barca)* to beach; rimanere a ~ *(fig)* to be left in the lurch

seco'lare *ag* age-old, centuries-old; *(laico, mondano)* secular

'secolo *sm* century; *(epoca)* age

se'conda *sf (AUT)* second (gear); viaggiare in ~ to travel second-class; *vedi anche* secondo

secon'dario, a *ag* secondary

se'condo, a *ag* second ♦ *sm* second; *(di pranzo)* main course ♦ *prep* according to; *(nel modo prescritto)* in accordance with; ~ me in my opinion, to my mind; di ~a classe second-class; di ~a mano second-hand; a ~a di according to; in accordance with

'sedano *sm* celery

seda'tivo, a *ag, sm* sedative

'sede *sf* seat; *(di ditta)* head office; *(di organizzazione)* headquarters *pl*; ~ sociale registered office

seden'tario, a *ag* sedentary

se'dere *vi* to sit, be seated; ~rsi *vr* to sit down ♦ *sm (deretano)* behind, bottom

'sedia *sf* chair

sedi'cente [sedi'tʃɛnte] *ag* self-styled

'sedici ['seditʃi] *num* sixteen

se'dile *sm* seat; *(panchina)* bench

se'dotto, a *pp di* sedurre

sedu'cente [sedu'tʃɛnte] *ag* seductive; *(proposta)* very attractive

se'durre *vt* to seduce

se'duta *sf* session, sitting; *(riunione)* meeting; ~ spiritica séance; ~ stante *(fig)* immediately

seduzi'one [sedut'tsjone] *sf* seduction; *(fascino)* charm, appeal

'sega, ghe *sf* saw

se'gale *sf* rye

se'gare *vt* to saw; *(recidere)* to saw off; sega'tura *sf (residuo)* sawdust

'seggio ['sɛddʒo] *sm* seat; ~ elettorale polling station

'seggiola ['sɛddʒola] *sf* chair; seggio'lino *sm* seat; *(per bambini)* child's chair; seggio'lone *sm (per bambini)* highchair

seggio'via [seddʒo'via] _sf_ chairlift
seghe'ria [sege'ria] _sf_ sawmill
segna'lare [seɲɲa'lare] _vt_ (_manovra etc_) to signal; to indicate; (_annunciare_) to announce; to report; (_fig: far conoscere_) to point out; (: _persona_) to single out; **~rsi** _vr_ (_distinguersi_) to distinguish o.s.
se'gnale [seɲ'ɲale] _sm_ signal; (_cartello_): **~ stradale** road sign; **~ d'allarme** alarm; (_FERR_) communication cord; **~ orario** (_RADIO_) time signal; **segna'letica** _sf_ signalling, signposting; **segnaletica stradale** road signs _pl_
segna'libro [seɲɲa'libro] _sm_ bookmark
se'gnare [seɲ'ɲare] _vt_ to mark; (_prendere nota_) to note; (_indicare_) to indicate, mark; (_SPORT: goal_) to score; **fare ~ di sì/no** to nod (one's head)/shake one's head; **fare ~ a qn di fermarsi** to motion (to) sb to stop; **cogliere** _o_ **colpire nel ~** (_fig_) to hit the mark
segre'gare _vt_ to segregate, isolate; **segregazi'one** _sf_ segregation
segre'tario, a _sm/f_ secretary; **~ comunale** town clerk; **S~ di Stato** Secretary of State
segrete'ria _sf_ (_di ditta, scuola_) (secretary's) office; (_d'organizzazione internazionale_) secretariat; (_POL etc: carica_) office of Secretary; **~ telefonica** answering service
segre'tezza [segre'tettsa] _sf_ secrecy
se'greto, a _ag_ secret ♦ _sm_ secret; secrecy _no pl_; **in ~** in secret, secretly
segu'ace [se'gwatʃe] _sm/f_ follower, disciple
segu'ente _ag_ following, next
segu'ire _vt_ to follow; (_frequentare: corso_) to attend ♦ _vi_ to follow; (_continuare: testo_) to continue
segui'tare _vt_ to continue, carry on with ♦ _vi_ to continue, carry on
'seguito _sm_ (_scorta_) suite, retinue; (_discepoli_) followers _pl_; (_favore_) following;

(_continuazione_) continuation; (_conseguenza_) result; **di ~** at a stretch, on end; **in ~** later on; **in ~ a, a ~ di** following; (_a causa di_) as a result of, owing to
'sei _vb vedi_ **essere** ♦ _num_ six
sei'cento [sei'tʃɛnto] _num_ six hundred ♦ _sm_: **il S~** the seventeenth century
selci'ato [sel'tʃato] _sm_ cobbled surface
selezio'nare [selettsjo'nare] _vt_ to select
selezi'one [selet'tsjone] _sf_ selection
'sella _sf_ saddle; **sel'lare** _vt_ to saddle
selvag'gina [selvad'dʒina] _sf_ (_animali_) game
sel'vaggio, a, gi, ge [sel'vaddʒo] _ag_ wild; (_tribù_) savage, uncivilized; (_fig_) savage, brutal ♦ _sm/f_ savage
sel'vatico, a, ci, che _ag_ wild
se'maforo _sm_ (_AUT_) traffic lights _pl_
sem'brare _vi_ to seem ♦ _vb impers_: **sembra che** it seems that; **mi sembra che** it seems to me that; I think (that); **~ di essere** to seem to be
'seme _sm_ seed; (_sperma_) semen; (_CARTE_) suit
se'mestre _sm_ half-year, six-month period
'semi... _prefisso_ semi...; **semi'cerchio** _sm_ semicircle; **semifi'nale** _sf_ semifinal; **semi'freddo** _sm_ ice-cream cake
'semina _sf_ (_AGR_) sowing
semi'nare _vt_ to sow
semi'nario _sm_ seminar; (_REL_) seminary
seminter'rato _sm_ basement; (_appartamento_) basement flat
sem'mai = **se mai**; _vedi_ **se**
'semola _sf_: **~ di grano duro** durum wheat
semo'lino _sm_ semolina
'semplice ['semplitʃe] _ag_ simple; (_di un solo elemento_) single; **semplice'mente** _av_ simply; **semplicità** _sf_ simplicity
'sempre _av_ always; (_ancora_) still; **posso ~ tentare** I can always _o_ still try; **da ~** always; **per ~** forever; **una volta per ~** once and for all; **~ che** provided (that); **~ più** more and more; **~ meno** less and less
sempre'verde _ag, sm o f_ (_BOT_) evergreen
'senape _sf_ (_CUC_) mustard
se'nato _sm_ senate; **sena'tore, 'trice**

sm/f senator

'senno *sm* judgment, (common) sense; **col ~ di poi** with hindsight

sennò *av* = **se no**; *vedi* **se**

'seno *sm* (ANAT: *petto, mammella*) breast; (: *grembo, fig*) womb; (: *cavità*) sinus

sen'sato, a *ag* sensible

sensazio'nale [sensattsjo'nale] *ag* sensational

sensazi'one [sensat'tsjone] *sf* feeling, sensation; **avere la ~ che** to have a feeling that; **fare ~** to cause a sensation, create a stir

sen'sibile *ag* sensitive; (*ai sensi*) perceptible; (*rilevante, notevole*) appreciable, noticeable; **~ a** sensitive to; **sensibilità** *sf* sensitivity

'senso *sm* (FISIOL, *istinto*) sense; (*impressione, sensazione*) feeling, sensation; (*significato*) meaning, sense; (*direzione*) direction; **~i** *smpl* (*coscienza*) consciousness *sg*; (*sensualità*) senses; **ciò non ha ~** that doesn't make sense; **fare ~ a** (*ripugnare*) to disgust, repel; **~ comune** common sense; **in ~ orario/antiorario** clockwise/anticlockwise; **a ~ unico** (*strada*) one-way

sensu'ale *ag* sensual; sensuous; **sensualità** *sf* sensuality; sensuousness

sen'tenza [sen'tentsa] *sf* (DIR) sentence; (*massima*) maxim; **sentenzi'are** *vi* (DIR) to pass judgment

senti'ero *sm* path

sentimen'tale *ag* sentimental; (*vita, avventura*) love *cpd*

senti'mento *sm* feeling

senti'nella *sf* sentry

sen'tire *vt* (*percepire al tatto, fig*) to feel; (*udire*) to hear; (*ascoltare*) to listen to; (*odore*) to smell; (*avvertire con il gusto, assaggiare*) to taste ♦ *vi*: **~ di** (*avere sapore*) to taste of; (*avere odore*) to smell of; **~rsi** *vr* (*uso reciproco*) to be in touch; **~rsi bene/male** to feel well/unwell *o* ill; **~rsi di fare qc** (*essere disposto*) to feel like doing sth

sen'tito, a *ag* (*sincero*) sincere, warm; **per ~ dire** by hearsay

'senza ['sentsa] *prep, cong* without; **~ dir** nulla without saying a word; **fare ~ qc** to do without sth; **~ di me** without me; **~ che io lo sapessi** without me *o* my knowing; **senz'altro** of course, certainly; **~ dubbio** no doubt; **~ scrupoli** unscrupulous; **~ amici** friendless

sepa'rare *vt* to separate; (*dividere*) to divide; (*tenere distinto*) to distinguish; **~rsi** *vr* (*coniugi*) to separate, part; (*amici*) to part, leave each other; **~rsi da** (*coniuge*) to separate *o* part from; (*amico, socio*) to part company with; (*oggetto*) to part with; **sepa'rato, a** *ag* (*letti, conto etc*) separate; (*coniugi*) separated; **separazi'one** *sf* separation

se'polcro *sm* sepulchre

se'polto, a *pp di* **seppellire**

seppel'lire *vt* to bury

'seppia *sf* cuttlefish ♦ *ag inv* sepia

se'quenza [se'kwentsa] *sf* sequence

seques'trare *vt* (DIR) to impound; (*rapire*) to kidnap; **se'questro** *sm* (DIR) impoundment; **sequestro di persona** kidnapping

'sera *sf* evening; **di ~** in the evening; **domani ~** tomorrow evening, tomorrow night; **se'rale** *ag* evening *cpd*; **se'rata** *sf* evening; (*ricevimento*) party

ser'bare *vt* to keep; (*mettere da parte*) to put aside; **~ rancore/odio verso qn** to bear sb a grudge/hate sb

serba'toio *sm* tank; (*cisterna*) cistern

'serbo *sm*: **mettere/tenere** *o* **avere in ~ qc** to put/keep sth aside

se'reno, a *ag* (*tempo, cielo*) clear; (*fig*) serene, calm

ser'gente [ser'dʒɛnte] *sm* (MIL) sergeant

'serie *sf inv* (*successione*) series *inv*; (*gruppo, collezione*) set; (SPORT) division; league; (COMM): **modello di ~/fuori ~** standard/custom-built model; **in ~** in quick succession; (COMM) mass *cpd*

serietà *sf* seriousness; reliability

'serio, a *ag* serious; (*impiegato*) responsible, reliable; (*ditta, cliente*) reliable, dependable; **sul ~** (*davvero*) really, truly; (*seriamente*) seriously, in earnest

ser'mone *sm* sermon
serpeggi'are [serped'dʒare] *vi* to wind;
(*fig*) to spread
ser'pente *sm* snake; ~ **a sonagli**
rattlesnake
'serra *sf* greenhouse; hothouse
ser'randa *sf* roller shutter
ser'rare *vt* to close, shut; (*a chiave*) to
lock; (*stringere*) to tighten; ~ **i pugni/i**
denti to clench one's fists/teeth; ~ **le file**
to close ranks
serra'tura *sf* lock
'serva *sf vedi* servo
ser'vire *vt* to serve; (*clienti: al ristorante*) to
wait on; (: *al negozio*) to serve, attend to;
(*fig: giovare*) to aid, help; (*CARTE*) to deal
♦ *vi* (*TENNIS*) to serve; (*essere utile*): ~ **a qn**
to be of use to sb; ~ **a qc/a fare** (*utensile
etc*) to be used for sth/for doing; ~ (**a qn**)
da to serve as (for sb); ~**rsi** *vr* (*usare*): ~**rsi**
di to use; (*prendere: cibo*): ~**rsi (di)** to help
o.s. (to); (*essere cliente abituale*): ~**rsi da** to
be a regular customer at, go to
servitù *sf* servitude; slavery; (*personale di
servizio*) servants *pl*, domestic staff
servizi'evole [servit'tʃevole] *ag* obliging,
willing to help
ser'vizio [ser'vittsjo] *sm* service; (*al
ristorante: sul conto*) service (charge);
(*STAMPA, TV, RADIO*) report; (*da tè, caffè etc*)
set, service; (*di casa*) kitchen and
bathroom; (*ECON*) services; **essere di ~** to
be on duty; **fuori ~** (*telefono etc*) out of
order; ~ **compreso** service included; ~
militare military service; ~**i segreti** secret
service *sg*
'servo, a *sm/f* servant
ses'santa *num* sixty; sessan'tesimo, a
num sixtieth
sessan'tina *sf*: **una ~ (di)** about sixty

ⓘ **Sessantotto**, '68, *refers to 1968 when
the student protest movement intensified
and influenced other parts of society,
leading to major political and social change.
Left-wing groups flourished, schools and*

*universities became more democratic and
the referendum on divorce was held.*

sessi'one *sf* session
'sesso *sm* sex; sessu'ale *ag* sexual, sex
cpd
ses'tante *sm* sextant
'sesto, a *ag, sm* sixth
'seta *sf* silk
'sete *sf* thirst; **avere ~** to be thirsty
'setola *sf* bristle
'setta *sf* sect
set'tanta *num* seventy; settan'tesimo, a
num seventieth
settan'tina *sf*: **una ~ (di)** about seventy
'sette *num* seven
sette'cento [sette'tʃento] *num* seven
hundred ♦ *sm*: **il S~** the eighteenth
century
set'tembre *sm* September
settentrio'nale *ag* northern
settentri'one *sm* north
setti'mana *sf* week; settima'nale *ag, sm*
weekly

ⓘ *The* **settimana bianca** *is a winter-
sports holiday taken by many Italians.*

'settimo, a *ag, sm* seventh
set'tore *sm* sector
severità *sf* severity
se'vero, a *ag* severe
sevizi'are [sevit'tsjare] *vt* to torture
se'vizie [se'vittsje] *sfpl* torture *sg*
sezio'nare [settsjo'nare] *vt* to divide into
sections; (*MED*) to dissect
sezi'one [set'tsjone] *sf* section
sfaccen'dato, a [sfattʃen'dato] *ag* idle
sfacci'ato, a [sfat'tʃato] *ag* (*maleducato*)
cheeky, impudent; (*vistoso*) gaudy
sfa'celo [sfa'tʃɛlo] *sm* (*fig*) ruin, collapse
sfal'darsi *vr* to flake (off)
sfa'mare *vt* to feed; (*sog: cibo*) to fill
'sfarzo ['sfartso] *sm* pomp, splendour
sfasci'are [sfaʃ'ʃare] *vt* (*ferita*) to
unbandage; (*distruggere*) to smash, shatter;

~rsi *vr* (*rompersi*) to smash, shatter

sfa'tare *vt* (*leggenda*) to explode

sfavil'lare *vi* to spark, send out sparks; (*risplendere*) to sparkle

sfavo'revole *ag* unfavourable

'sfera *sf* sphere; **'sferico, a, ci, che** *ag* spherical

sfer'rare *vt* (*fig: colpo*) to land, deal; (: *attacco*) to launch

sfer'zare [sfer'tsare] *vt* to whip; (*fig*) to lash out at

sfi'brare *vt* (*indebolire*) to exhaust, enervate

'sfida *sf* challenge

sfi'dare *vt* to challenge; (*fig*) to defy, brave

sfi'ducia [sfi'dutʃa] *sf* distrust, mistrust

sfigu'rare *vt* (*persona*) to disfigure; (*quadro, statua*) to deface ♦ *vi* (*far cattiva figura*) to make a bad impression

sfi'lare *vt* (*ago*) to unthread; (*abito, scarpe*) to slip off ♦ *vi* (*truppe*) to march past; (*atleti*) to parade; **~rsi** *vr* (*perle etc*) to come unstrung; (*orlo, tessuto*) to fray; (*calza*) to run, ladder; **sfi'lata** *sf* march past; parade; **sfilata di moda** fashion show

'sfinge ['sfindʒe] *sf* sphinx

sfi'nito, a *ag* exhausted

sfio'rare *vt* to brush (against); (*argomento*) to touch upon

sfio'rire *vi* to wither, fade

sfo'cato, a *ag* (*FOT*) out of focus

sfoci'are [sfo'tʃare] *vi*: **~ in** to flow into; (*fig: malcontento*) to develop into

sfode'rato, a *ag* (*vestito*) unlined

sfo'gare *vt* to vent, pour out; **~rsi** *vr* (*sfogare la propria rabbia*) to give vent to one's anger; (*confidarsi*): **~rsi (con)** to pour out one's feelings (to); **non sfogarti su di me!** don't take your bad temper out on me!

sfoggi'are [sfod'dʒare] *vt, vi* to show off

'sfoglia ['sfoʎʎa] *sf* sheet of pasta dough; **pasta ~** (*CUC*) puff pastry

sfogli'are [sfoʎ'ʎare] *vt* (*libro*) to leaf through

'sfogo, ghi *sm* (*eruzione cutanea*) rash; (*fig*) outburst; **dare ~ a** (*fig*) to give vent to

sfolgo'rante *ag* (*luce*) blazing; (*fig: vittoria*) brilliant

sfol'lare *vt* to empty, clear ♦ *vi* to disperse; **~ da** (*città*) to evacuate

sfon'dare *vt* (*porta*) to break down; (*scarpe*) to wear a hole in; (*cesto, scatola*) to burst, knock the bottom out of; (*MIL*) to break through ♦ *vi* (*riuscire*) to make a name for o.s.

'sfondo *sm* background

sfor'mato *sm* (*CUC*) type of soufflé

sfor'nare *vt* (*pane etc*) to take out of the oven; (*fig*) to churn out

sfor'nito, a *ag*: **~ di** lacking in, without; (*negozio*) out of

sfor'tuna *sf* misfortune, ill luck *no pl*; **avere ~** to be unlucky; **sfortu'nato, a** *ag* unlucky; (*impresa, film*) unsuccessful

sfor'zare [sfor'tsare] *vt* to force; (*voce, occhi*) to strain; **~rsi** *vr*: **~rsi di** *o* **a** *o* **per fare** to try hard to do

'sforzo ['sfortso] *sm* effort; (*tensione eccessiva, TECN*) strain; **fare uno ~** to make an effort

sfrat'tare *vt* to evict; **'sfratto** *sm* eviction

sfrecci'are [sfret'tʃare] *vi* to shoot *o* flash past

sfregi'are [sfre'dʒare] *vt* to slash, gash; (*persona*) to disfigure; (*quadro*) to deface; **'sfregio** *sm* gash; scar; (*fig*) insult

sfre'nato, a *ag* (*fig*) unrestrained, unbridled

sfron'tato, a *ag* shameless

sfrutta'mento *sm* exploitation

sfrut'tare *vt* (*terreno*) to overwork, exhaust; (*miniera*) to exploit, work; (*fig: operai, occasione, potere*) to exploit

sfug'gire [sfud'dʒire] *vi* to escape; **~ a** (*custode*) to escape (from); (*morte*) to escape; **~ a qn** (*dettaglio, nome*) to escape sb; **~ di mano a qn** to slip out of sb's hand (*o* hands); **sfug'gita: di sfuggita** *ad* (*rapidamente, in fretta*) in passing

sfu'mare *vt* (*colori, contorni*) to soften, shade off ♦ *vi* to shade (off), fade; (*fig: svanire*) to vanish, disappear; (: *speranze*) to come to nothing

sfuma'tura *sf* shading off *no pl*; (*tonalità*) shade, tone; (*fig*) touch, hint

sfuri'ata *sf* (*scatto di collera*) fit of anger; (*rimprovero*) sharp rebuke

sga'bello *sm* stool

sgabuz'zino [zgabud'dzino] *sm* lumber room

sgambet'tare *vi* to kick one's legs about

sgam'betto *sm*: **far lo ~ a qn** to trip sb up; (*fig*) to oust sb

sganasci'arsi [zganaʃʃarsi] *vr*: **~ dalle risa** to roar with laughter

sganci'are [zgan'tʃare] *vt* to unhook; (*FERR*) to uncouple; (*bombe: da aereo*) to release, drop; (*fig: fam: soldi*) to fork out; **~rsi** *vr* (*fig*): **~rsi (da)** to get away (from)

sganghe'rato, a [zgange'rato] *ag* (*porta*) off its hinges; (*auto*) ramshackle; (*risata*) wild, boisterous

sgar'bato, a *ag* rude, impolite

'sgarbo *sm*: **fare uno ~ a qn** to be rude to sb

sgattaio'lare *vi* to sneak away *o* off

sge'lare [zdʒe'lare] *vi, vt* to thaw

'sghembo, a ['zgembo] *ag* (*obliquo*) slanting; (*storto*) crooked

sghignaz'zare [zgiɲɲat'tsare] *vi* to laugh scornfully

sgob'bare (*fam*) *vi* (*scolaro*) to swot; (*operaio*) to slog

sgoccio'lare [zgottʃo'lare] *vt* (*vuotare*) to drain (to the last drop) ♦ *vi* (*acqua*) to drip; (*recipiente*) to drain; **'sgoccioli** *smpl*: **essere agli ~** (*provviste*) to be nearly finished; (*periodo*) to be nearly over

sgo'larsi *vr* to talk (*o* shout *o* sing) o.s. hoarse

sgomb(e)'rare *vt* to clear; (*andarsene da: stanza*) to vacate; (*evacuare*) to evacuate

'sgombro, a *ag*: **~ (di)** clear (of), free (from) ♦ *sm* (*ZOOL*) mackerel; (*anche:* **sgombero**) clearing; vacating; evacuation; (*: trasloco*) removal

sgomen'tare *vt* to dismay; **sgo'mento, a** *ag* dismayed ♦ *sm* dismay, consternation

sgonfi'are *vt* to let down, deflate; **~rsi** *vr* to go down

'sgorbio *sm* blot; scribble

sgor'gare *vi* to gush (out)

sgoz'zare [zgot'tsare] *vt* to cut the throat of

sgra'devole *ag* unpleasant, disagreeable

sgra'dito, a *ag* unpleasant, unwelcome

sgra'nare *vt* (*piselli*) to shell; **~ gli occhi** to open one's eyes wide

sgran'chirsi [zgran'kirsi] *vr* to stretch; **~ le gambe** to stretch one's legs

sgranocchi'are [zgranok'kjare] *vt* to munch

'sgravio *sm*: **~ fiscale** tax relief

sgrazi'ato, a [zgrat'tsjato] *ag* clumsy, ungainly

sgreto'lare *vt* to cause to crumble; **~rsi** *vr* to crumble

sgri'dare *vt* to scold; **sgri'data** *sf* scolding

sguai'ato, a *ag* coarse, vulgar

sgual'cire [zgwal'tʃire] *vt* to crumple (up), crease

sgual'drina (*peg*) *sf* slut

sgu'ardo *sm* (*occhiata*) look, glance; (*espressione*) look (in one's eye)

'sguattero *sm/f* dishwasher (*person*)

sguaz'zare [zgwat'tsare] *vi* (*nell'acqua*) to splash about; (*nella melma*) to wallow; **~ nell'oro** to be rolling in money

sguinzagli'are [zgwintsaʎ'ʎare] *vt* to let off the leash; (*fig: persona*): **~ qn dietro a qn** to set sb on sb

sgusci'are [zguʃ'ʃare] *vt* to shell ♦ *vi* (*sfuggire di mano*) to slip; **~ via** to slip *o* slink away

'shampoo ['ʃampo] *sm inv* shampoo

shock [ʃɔk] *sm inv* shock

PAROLA CHIAVE

si[1] (*dav lo, la, li, le, ne diventa* **se**) *pron*

1 (*riflessivo: maschile*) himself; (*: femminile*) herself; (*: neutro*) itself; (*: impersonale*) oneself; (*: pl*) themselves; **lavarsi** to wash (oneself); **~ è tagliato** he has cut himself; **~ credono importanti** they think a lot of themselves

2 (*riflessivo: con complemento oggetto*): **lavarsi le mani** to wash one's hands; **~ sta**

lavando i capelli he (*o* she) is washing his (*o* her) hair

3 (*reciproco*) one another, each other; **si amano** they love one another *o* each other

4 (*passivo*): **~ ripara facilmente** it is easily repaired

5 (*impersonale*): **~ dice che ...** they *o* people say that ...; **~ vede che è vecchio** one *o* you can see that it's old

6 (*noi*) we; **tra poco ~ parte** we're leaving soon

si² *sm* (MUS) B; (*solfeggiando la scala*) ti

sì *av* yes; **un giorno ~ e uno no** every other day

'sia *cong*: **~ ... ~** (*o ... o*): **~ che lavori, ~ che non lavori** whether he works or not; (*tanto ... quanto*): **verranno ~ Luigi ~ suo fratello** both Luigi and his brother will be coming

si'amo *vb vedi* **essere**

sibi'lare *vi* to hiss; (*fischiare*) to whistle; **'sibilo** *sm* hiss; whistle

si'cario *sm* hired killer

sicché [sik'ke] *cong* (*perciò*) so (that), therefore; (*e quindi*) (and) so

siccità [sittʃi'ta] *sf* drought

sic'come *cong* since, as

Si'cilia [si'tʃilja] *sf*: **la ~** Sicily; **sicili'ano, a** *ag, sm/f* Sicilian

si'cura *sf* safety catch; (AUT) safety lock

sicu'rezza [siku'rettsa] *sf* safety; security; (*fiducia*) confidence; (*certezza*) certainty; **di ~ safety** *cpd*; **la ~ stradale** road safety

si'curo, a *ag* safe; (*ben difeso*) secure; (*fiducioso*) confident; (*certo*) sure, certain; (*notizia, amico*) reliable; (*esperto*) skilled ♦ *av* (*anche*: **di ~**) certainly; **essere/ mettere al ~** to be safe/put in a safe place; **~ di sé** self-confident, sure of o.s.; **sentirsi ~** to feel safe *o* secure

siderur'gia [siderur'dʒia] *sf* iron and steel industry

'sidro *sm* cider

si'epe *sf* hedge

si'ero *sm* (MED) serum; **sieronega'tivo, a** *ag* HIV-negative; **sieroposi'tivo, a** *ag* HIV-positive

si'esta *sf* siesta, (afternoon) nap

si'ete *vb vedi* **essere**

si'filide *sf* syphilis

si'fone *sm* siphon

Sig. *abbr* (= *signore*) Mr

siga'retta *sf* cigarette

'sigaro *sm* cigar

Sigg. *abbr* (= *signori*) Messrs

sigil'lare [sidʒil'lare] *vt* to seal

si'gillo [si'dʒillo] *sm* seal

'sigla *sf* initials *pl*; acronym, abbreviation; **~ automobilistica** *abbreviation of province on vehicle number plate*; **~ musicale** signature tune

si'glare *vt* to initial

Sig.na *abbr* (= *signorina*) Miss

signifi'care [siɲɲifi'kare] *vt* to mean; **significa'tivo, a** *ag* significant; **signifi'cato** *sm* meaning

si'gnora [siɲ'ɲora] *sf* lady; **la ~ X** Mrs X; **buon giorno S~/Signore/Signorina** good morning; (*deferente*) good morning Madam/Sir/Madam; (*quando si conosce il nome*) good morning Mrs/Mr/Miss X; **Gentile S~/Signore/Signorina** (*in una lettera*) Dear Madam/Sir/Madam; **il signor Rossi e ~** Mr Rossi and his wife; **~e e signori** ladies and gentlemen

si'gnore [siɲ'ɲore] *sm* gentleman; (*padrone*) lord, master; (REL): **il S~** the Lord; **il signor X** Mr X; **i ~i Bianchi** (*coniugi*) Mr and Mrs Bianchi; *vedi anche* **signora**

signo'rile [siɲɲo'rile] *ag* refined

signo'rina [siɲɲo'rina] *sf* young lady; **la ~ X** Miss X; *vedi anche* **signora**

Sig.ra *abbr* (= *signora*) Mrs

silenzia'tore [silentsja'tore] *sm* silencer

si'lenzio [si'lɛntsjo] *sm* silence; **fare ~** to be quiet, stop talking; **silenzi'oso, a** *ag* silent, quiet

si'licio [si'litʃo] *sm* silicon

'sillaba *sf* syllable

silu'rare *vt* to torpedo; (*fig: privare del comando*) to oust

si'luro *sm* torpedo

simboleggi'are [simboled'dʒare] *vt* to

symbolize

'**simbolo** sm symbol

'**simile** ag (analogo) similar; (di questo tipo):
un uomo ~ such a man, a man like this;
libri ~i such books; **~ a** similar to; **i suoi ~i**
one's fellow men; one's peers

simme'tria sf symmetry

simpa'tia sf (qualità) pleasantness;
(inclinazione) liking; **avere ~ per qn** to like
sb, have a liking for sb; **sim'patico, a,
ci, che** ag (persona) nice, pleasant,
likeable; (casa, albergo etc) nice, pleasant

simpatiz'zare [simpatid'dzare] vi: **~ con** to
take a liking to

sim'posio sm symposium

simu'lare vt to sham, simulate; (TECN) to
simulate; **simulazi'one** sf shamming;
simulation

simul'taneo, a ag simultaneous

sina'goga, ghe sf synagogue

since'rità [sintʃeri'ta] sf sincerity

sin'cero, a [sin'tʃero] ag sincere; genuine;
heartfelt

'**sincope** sf syncopation; (MED) blackout

sinda'cale ag (trade-)union cpd;
sindaca'lista, i, e sm/f trade unionist

sinda'cato sm (di lavoratori) (trade)
union; (AMM, ECON, DIR) syndicate, trust,
pool

'**sindaco, ci** sm mayor

sinfo'nia sf (MUS) symphony

singhioz'zare [singjot'tsare] vi to sob; to
hiccup

singhi'ozzo [sin'gjottso] sm sob; (MED)
hiccup; **avere il ~** to have the hiccups; **a ~**
(fig) by fits and starts

singo'lare ag (insolito) remarkable,
singular; (LING) singular ♦ sm (LING)
singular; (TENNIS): **~ maschile/femminile**
men's/women's singles

'**singolo, a** ag single, individual ♦ sm
(persona) individual; (TENNIS) = **singolare**

si'**nistra, ghe** sf (POL) left (wing); **a ~** on the left;
(direzione) to the left

si'**nistro, a** ag left, left-hand; (fig) sinister
♦ sm (incidente) accident

'**sino** prep = **fino**

si'**nonimo** sm synonym; **~ di** synonymous
with

sin'**tassi** sf syntax

'**sintesi** sf synthesis; (riassunto) summary,
résumé

sin'**tetico, a, ci, che** ag synthetic

sintetiz'**zare** [sintetid'dzare] vt to
synthesize; (riassumere) to summarize

sinto'**matico, a, ci, che** ag
symptomatic

'**sintomo** sm symptom

sinu'**oso, a** ag (strada) winding

si'**pario** sm (TEATRO) curtain

si'**rena** sf (apparecchio) siren; (nella
mitologia, fig) siren, mermaid

'**Siria** sf: **la ~** Syria

si'**ringa, ghe** sf syringe

'**sismico, a, ci, che** ag seismic

sis'**mografo** sm seismograph

sis'**tema, i** sm system; method, way

siste'**mare** vt (mettere a posto) to tidy, put
in order; (risolvere: questione) to sort out,
settle; (procurare un lavoro a) to find a job
for; (dare un alloggio a) to settle, find
accommodation for; **~rsi** vr (problema) to
be settled; (persona: trovare alloggio) to
find accommodation (BRIT) o accommodations (US); (: trovarsi un lavoro) to get
fixed up with a job; **ti sistemo io!** I'll soon
sort you out!

siste'**matico, a, ci, che** ag systematic

sistemazi'**one** [sistemat'tsjone] sf
arrangement; order; settlement;
employment; accommodation (BRIT),
accommodations (US)

'**sito** sm (Internet) Website

situ'**are** vt to site, situate; **situ'ato, a** ag:
situato a/su situated at/on

situazi'**one** [situat'tsjone] sf situation

ski-lift ['ski:lift] sm inv ski tow

slacci'**are** [zlat'tʃare] vt to undo, unfasten

slanci'**ato, a** [zlan'tʃato] ag slender

'**slancio** sm dash, leap; (fig) surge; **di ~**
impetuously

sla'**vato, a** ag faded, washed out; (fig:
viso, occhi) pale, colourless

'**slavo, a** ag Slav(onic), Slavic

sle'ale *ag* disloyal; (*concorrenza etc*) unfair

sle'gare *vt* to untie

slip [zlip] *sm inv* briefs *pl*

'slitta *sf* sledge; (*trainata*) sleigh

slit'tare *vi* to slip, slide; (*AUT*) to skid

slo'gare *vt* (*MED*) to dislocate

sloggi'are [zlod'dʒare] *vt* (*inquilino*) to turn out ♦ *vi* to move out

slo'vacco, a, chi, che *ag*, *sm/f* Slovak

Slovenia [zlo'venja] *sf* Slovenia

smacchi'are [zmak'kjare] *vt* to remove stains from; smacchia'tore *sm* stain remover

'smacco, chi *sm* humiliating defeat

smagli'ante [zmaʎ'ʎante] *ag* brilliant, dazzling

smaglia'tura [zmaʎʎa'tura] *sf* (*su maglia, calza*) ladder; (*della pelle*) stretch mark

smalizi'ato, a [smalit'tsjato] *ag* shrewd, cunning

smal'tare *vt* to enamel; (*ceramica*) to glaze; (*unghie*) to varnish

smal'tire *vt* (*merce*) to sell off; (*rifiuti*) to dispose of; (*cibo*) to digest; (*peso*) to lose; (*rabbia*) to get over; ~ la sbornia to sober up

'smalto *sm* (*anche: di denti*) enamel; (*per ceramica*) glaze; ~ per unghie nail varnish

'smania *sf* agitation, restlessness; (*fig*): ~ di thirst for, craving for; avere la ~ addosso to have the fidgets; avere la ~ di fare to be desperate to do

smantel'lare *vt* to dismantle

smarri'mento *sm* loss; (*fig*) bewilderment; dismay

smar'rire *vt* to lose; (*non riuscire a trovare*) to mislay; ~rsi *vr* (*perdersi*) to lose one's way, get lost; (*: oggetto*) to go astray; smar'rito, a *ag* (*sbigottito*) bewildered

smasche'rare [zmaske'rare] *vt* to unmask

smemo'rato, a *ag* forgetful

smen'tire *vt* (*negare*) to deny; (*testimonianza*) to refute; smen'tita *sf* denial; retraction

sme'raldo *sm* emerald

smerci'are [zmer'tʃare] *vt* (*COMM*) to sell; (*: svendere*) to sell off

'smesso, a *pp di* smettere

'smettere *vt* to stop; (*vestiti*) to stop wearing ♦ *vi* to stop, cease; ~ di fare to stop doing

'smilzo, a ['zmiltso] *ag* thin, lean

sminu'ire *vt* to diminish, lessen; (*fig*) to belittle

sminuz'zare [zminut'tsare] *vt* to break into small pieces; to crumble

smis'tare *vt* (*pacchi etc*) to sort; (*FERR*) to shunt

smisu'rato, a *ag* boundless, immeasurable; (*grandissimo*) immense, enormous

smobili'tare *vt* to demobilize

smo'dato, a *ag* immoderate

smoking ['sməukiŋ] *sm inv* dinner jacket

smon'tare *vt* (*mobile, macchina etc*) to take to pieces, dismantle; (*fig: scoraggiare*) to dishearten ♦ *vi* (*scendere: da cavallo*) to dismount; (*: da treno*) to get off; (*terminare il lavoro*) to stop (work); ~rsi *vr* to lose heart; to lose one's enthusiasm

'smorfia *sf* grimace; (*atteggiamento lezioso*) simpering; fare ~e to make faces; to simper; smorfi'oso, a *ag* simpering

'smorto, a *ag* (*viso*) pale, wan; (*colore*) dull

smor'zare [zmor'tsare] *vt* (*suoni*) to deaden; (*colori*) to tone down; (*luce*) to dim; (*sete*) to quench; (*entusiasmo*) to dampen; ~rsi *vr* (*suono, luce*) to fade; (*entusiasmo*) to dampen

'smosso, a *pp di* smuovere

smotta'mento *sm* landslide

SMS *sigla m* (= *short message system*) SMS

'smunto, a *ag* haggard, pinched

smu'overe *vt* to move, shift; (*fig: commuovere*) to move; (*: dall'inerzia*) to rouse, stir; ~rsi *vr* to move, shift

smus'sare *vt* (*angolo*) to round off, smooth; (*lama etc*) to blunt; ~rsi *vr* to become blunt

snatu'rato, a *ag* inhuman, heartless

'snello, a *ag* (*agile*) agile; (*svelto*) slender, slim

sner'vare *vt* to enervate, wear out

sni'dare *vt* to drive out, flush out

snob'bare *vt* to snub

sno'bismo *sm* snobbery

snoccio'lare [znottʃo'lare] *vt* (*frutta*) to stone; (*fig: orazioni*) to rattle off

sno'dare *vt* (*rendere agile, mobile*) to loosen; **~rsi** *vr* to come loose; (*articolarsi*) to bend; (*strada, fiume*) to wind

so *vb vedi* **sapere**

so'ave *ag* sweet, gentle, soft

sobbal'zare [sobbal'tsare] *vi* to jolt, jerk; (*trasalire*) to jump, start; **sob'balzo** *sm* jerk, jolt; jump, start

sobbar'carsi *vr*: **~ a** to take on, undertake

sob'borgo, ghi *sm* suburb

sobil'lare *vt* to stir up, incite

'sobrio, a *ag* sober

socchi'udere [sok'kjudere] *vt* (*porta*) to leave ajar; (*occhi*) to half-close; **socchi'uso, a** *pp di* **socchiudere**

soc'correre *vt* to help, assist; **soc'corso, a** *pp di* **soccorrere** ♦ *sm* help, aid, assistance; **soccorsi** *smpl* relief *sg*, aid *sg*; **soccorso stradale** breakdown service

soci'ale [so'tʃale] *ag* social; (*di associazione*) club *cpd*, association *cpd*

socia'lismo [sotʃa'lizmo] *sm* socialism; **socia'lista, i, e** *ag, sm/f* socialist

società [sotʃe'ta] *sf inv* society; (*sportiva*) club; (*COMM*) company; **~ per azioni** limited (*BRIT*) *o* incorporated (*US*) company; **~ a responsabilità limitata** *type of limited liability company*

soci'evole [so'tʃevole] *ag* sociable

'socio ['sɔtʃo] *sm* (*DIR, COMM*) partner; (*membro di associazione*) member

'soda *sf* (*CHIM*) soda; (*bibita*) soda (water)

soda'lizio [soda'littsjo] *sm* association, society

soddisfa'cente [soddisfa'tʃente] *ag* satisfactory

soddis'fare *vt, vi*: **~ a** to satisfy; (*impegno*) to fulfil; (*debito*) to pay off; (*richiesta*) to meet, comply with; **soddis'fatto, a** *pp di* **soddisfare** ♦ *ag* satisfied; **soddisfatto di** happy *o* satisfied with; pleased with; **soddisfazi'one** *sf* satisfaction

'sodo, a *ag* firm, hard; (*uovo*) hard-boiled ♦ *av* (*picchiare, lavorare*) hard; (*dormire*)

soundly

sofà *sm inv* sofa

soffe'renza [soffe'rentsa] *sf* suffering

sof'ferto, a *pp di* **soffrire**

soffi'are *vt* to blow; (*notizia, segreto*) to whisper ♦ *vi* to blow; (*sbuffare*) to puff (and blow); **~rsi il naso** to blow one's nose; **~ qc/qn a qn** (*fig*) to pinch *o* steal sth/sb from sb; **~ via qc** to blow sth away

'soffice ['sɔffitʃe] *ag* soft

'soffio *sm* (*di vento*) breath; **~ al cuore** heart murmur

sof'fitta *sf* attic

sof'fitto *sm* ceiling

soffo'care *vi* (*anche: ~rsi*) to suffocate, choke ♦ *vt* to suffocate, choke; (*fig*) to stifle, suppress

sof'friggere [sof'friddʒere] *vt* to fry lightly

sof'frire *vt* to suffer, endure; (*sopportare*) to bear, stand ♦ *vi* to suffer; to be in pain; **~ (di) qc** (*MED*) to suffer from sth

sof'fritto, a *pp di* **soffriggere** ♦ *sm* (*CUC*) *fried mixture of herbs, bacon and onions*

sofisti'cato, a *ag* sophisticated; (*vino*) adulterated

sogget'tivo, a [soddʒet'tivo] *ag* subjective

sog'getto, a [sod'dʒetto] *ag*: **~ a** (*sottomesso*) subject to; (*esposto: a variazioni, danni etc*) subject *o* liable to ♦ *sm* subject

soggezi'one [soddʒet'tsjone] *sf* subjection; (*timidezza*) awe; **avere ~ di qn** to stand in awe of sb; to be ill at ease in sb's presence

sogghi'gnare [soggiɲ'ɲare] *vi* to sneer

soggior'nare [soddʒor'nare] *vi* to stay; **soggi'orno** *sm* (*invernale, marino*) stay; (*stanza*) living room

sog'giungere [sod'dʒundʒere] *vt* to add

'soglia ['sɔʎʎa] *sf* doorstep; (*anche fig*) threshold

sogli'ola ['sɔʎʎola] *sf* (*ZOOL*) sole

so'gnare [soɲ'ɲare] *vt, vi* to dream; **~ a occhi aperti** to daydream; **sogna'tore, 'trice** *sm/f* dreamer

'sogno ['soɲɲo] *sm* dream

'soia *sf* (*BOT*) soya

sol *sm* (*MUS*) G; (*: solfeggiando*) so(h)

so'laio sm (soffitta) attic

sola'mente av only, just

so'lare ag solar, sun cpd

'solco, chi sm (scavo, fig: ruga) furrow; (incavo) rut, track; (di disco) groove

sol'dato sm soldier; ~ **semplice** private

'soldo sm (fig): **non avere un ~** to be penniless; **non vale un ~** it's not worth a penny; **~i** smpl (denaro) money sg

'sole sm sun; (luce) sun(light); (tempo assolato) sun(shine); **prendere il ~** to sunbathe

soleggi'ato, a [soled'dʒato] ag sunny

so'lenne ag solemn; solennità sf solemnity; (festività) holiday, feast day

sol'fato sm (CHIM) sulphate

soli'dale ag: **essere ~ (con)** to be in agreement (with)

solidarietà sf solidarity

'solido, a ag solid; (forte, robusto) sturdy, solid; (fig: ditta) sound, solid ♦ sm (MAT) solid

soli'loquio sm soliloquy

so'lista, i, e ag solo ♦ sm/f soloist

solita'mente av usually, as a rule

soli'tario, a ag (senza compagnia) solitary, lonely; (solo, isolato) solitary, lone; (deserto) lonely ♦ sm (gioiello, gioco) solitaire

'solito, a ag usual; **essere ~ fare** to be in the habit of doing; **di ~** usually; **più tardi del ~** later than usual; **come al ~** as usual

soli'tudine sf solitude

solleci'tare [solletʃi'tare] vt (lavoro) to speed up; (persona) to urge on; (chiedere con insistenza) to press for, request urgently; (stimolare): **~ qn a fare** to urge sb to do; sollecitazi'one sf entreaty, request; (fig) incentive; (TECN) stress

sol'lecito, a [sol'letʃito] ag prompt, quick ♦ sm (lettera) reminder; solleci'tudine sf promptness, speed

solleti'care vt to tickle

sol'letico sm tickling; **soffrire il ~** to be ticklish

solleva'mento sm raising; lifting; revolt; **~ pesi** (SPORT) weight-lifting

solle'vare vt to lift, raise; (fig: persona: alleggerire): ~ **(da)** to relieve (of); (: dar conforto) to comfort, relieve; (: questione) to raise; (: far insorgere) to stir (to revolt); ~rsi vr to rise; (fig: riprendersi) to recover; (: ribellarsi) to rise up

solli'evo sm relief; (conforto) comfort

'solo, a ag alone; (in senso spirituale: isolato) lonely; (unico): **un ~ libro** only one book, a single book; (con ag numerale): **veniamo noi tre ~i** just o only the three of us are coming ♦ av (soltanto) only, just; **non ~ ... ma anche** not only ... but also; **fare qc da ~** to do sth (all) by oneself

sol'tanto av only

so'lubile ag (sostanza) soluble

soluzi'one [solut'tsjone] sf solution

sol'vente ag, sm solvent

'soma sf: **bestia da ~** beast of burden

so'maro sm ass, donkey

somigli'anza [somiʎ'ʎantsa] sf resemblance

somigli'are [somiʎ'ʎare] vi: **~ a** to be like, resemble; (nell'aspetto fisico) to look like; ~rsi vr to be (o look) alike

'somma sf (MAT) sum; (di denaro) sum (of money)

som'mare vt to add up; (aggiungere) to add; **tutto sommato** all things considered

som'mario, a ag (racconto, indagine) brief; (giustizia) summary ♦ sm summary

som'mergere [som'mɛrdʒere] vt to submerge

sommer'gibile [sommer'dʒibile] sm submarine

som'merso, a pp di **sommergere**

som'messo, a ag (voce) soft, subdued

somminis'trare vt to give, administer

sommità sf inv summit, top; (fig) height

'sommo, a ag highest; (rispetto etc) highest, greatest; (poeta, artista) great, outstanding; **per ~i capi** briefly, covering the main points

som'mossa sf uprising

so'nare etc = **suonare** etc

son'daggio [son'daddʒo] sm sounding; probe; boring, drilling; (indagine) survey; **~ d'opinioni** opinion poll

son'dare vt (NAUT) to sound; (atmosfera,

piaga) to probe; (*MINERALOGIA*) to bore, drill; (*fig: opinione etc*) to survey, poll

so'netto *sm* sonnet

son'nambulo, a *sm/f* sleepwalker

sonnecchi'are [sonnek'kjare] *vi* to doze, nod

son'nifero *sm* sleeping drug (*o* pill)

'sonno *sm* sleep; **prendere ~** to fall asleep; **aver ~** to be sleepy

'sono *vb vedi* **essere**

so'noro, a *ag* (*ambiente*) resonant; (*voce*) sonorous, ringing; (*onde, film*) sound *cpd*

sontu'oso, a *ag* sumptuous; lavish

sopo'rifero, a *ag* soporific

soppe'sare *vt* to weigh in one's hand(s), feel the weight of; (*fig*) to weigh up

soppi'atto: **di ~** *av* secretly; furtively

soppor'tare *vt* (*reggere*) to support; (*subire: perdita, spese*) to bear, sustain; (*soffrire: dolore*) to bear, endure; (*sog: cosa: freddo*) to withstand; (*sog: persona: freddo, vino*) to take; (*tollerare*) to put up with, tolerate

sop'presso, a *pp di* **sopprimere**

sop'primere *vt* (*carica, privilegi, testimone*) to do away with; (*pubblicazione*) to suppress; (*parola, frase*) to delete

'sopra *prep* (*gen*) on; (*al di sopra di, più in alto di*) above; over; (*riguardo a*) on, about ♦ *av* on top; (*attaccato, scritto*) on it; (*al di sopra*) above; (*al piano superiore*) upstairs; **donne ~ i 30 anni** women over 30 (years of age); **abito di ~** I live upstairs; **dormirci ~** (*fig*) to sleep on it

so'prabito *sm* overcoat

soprac'ciglio [soprat'tʃiʎʎo] (*pl(f)* **soprac'ciglia**) *sm* eyebrow

sopracco'perta *sf* (*di letto*) bedspread; (*di libro*) jacket

sopraf'fare *vt* to overcome, overwhelm; sopraf'fatto, a *pp di* **sopraffare**

sopraf'fino, a *ag* (*pranzo, vino*) excellent

sopraggi'ungere [soprad'dʒundʒere] *vi* (*giungere all'improvviso*) to arrive (unexpectedly); (*accadere*) to occur (unexpectedly)

sopral'luogo, ghi *sm* (*di esperti*)

inspection; (*di polizia*) on-the-spot investigation

sopram'mobile *sm* ornament

soprannatu'rale *ag* supernatural

sopran'nome *sm* nickname

so'prano, a *sm/f* (*persona*) soprano ♦ *sm* (*voce*) soprano

soprappensi'ero *av* lost in thought

sopras'salto *sm*: **di ~** with a start; suddenly

soprasse'dere *vi*: **~ a** to delay, put off

soprat'tutto *av* (*anzitutto*) above all; (*specialmente*) especially

sopravvalu'tare *vt* to overestimate

soprav'vento *sm*: **avere/prendere il ~ su** to have/get the upper hand over

sopravvis'suto, a *pp di* **sopravvivere**

soprav'vivere *vi* to survive; (*continuare a vivere*): **~ (in)** to live on (in); **~ a** (*incidente etc*) to survive; (*persona*) to outlive

soprele'vata *sf* (*strada*) flyover; (*ferrovia*) elevated railway

soprinten'dente *sm/f* supervisor; (*statale: di belle arti etc*) keeper; soprinten'denza *sf* supervision; (*ente*): **soprintendenza alle Belle Arti** *government department responsible for monuments and artistic treasures*

so'pruso *sm* abuse of power; **subire un ~** to be abused

soq'quadro *sm*: **mettere a ~** to turn upside-down

sor'betto *sm* sorbet, water ice

sor'bire *vt* to sip; (*fig*) to put up with

'sorcio, ci ['sortʃo] *sm* mouse

'sordido, a *ag* sordid; (*fig: gretto*) stingy

sor'dina *sf*: **in ~** softly; (*fig*) on the sly

sordità *sf* deafness

'sordo, a *ag* deaf; (*rumore*) muffled; (*dolore*) dull; (*odio, rancore*) veiled ♦ *sm/f* deaf person; sordo'muto, a *ag* deaf-and-dumb ♦ *sm/f* deaf-mute

so'rella *sf* sister; sorel'lastra *sf* stepsister

sor'gente [sor'dʒente] *sf* (*d'acqua*) spring; (*di fiume, FISICA, fig*) source

'sorgere ['sordʒere] *vi* to rise; (*scaturire*) to spring, rise; (*fig: difficoltà*) to arise

sormon'tare *vt* (*fig*) to overcome, surmount

sorni'one, a *ag* sly

sorpas'sare *vt* (*AUT*) to overtake; (*fig*) to surpass; (: *eccedere*) to exceed, go beyond; **~ in altezza** to be higher than; (*persona*) to be taller than; **sor'passo** *sm* (*AUT*) overtaking

sorpren'dente *ag* surprising

sor'prendere *vt* (*cogliere: in flagrante etc*) to catch; (*stupire*) to surprise; **~rsi** *vr*: **~rsi (di)** to be surprised (at); **sor'presa** *sf* surprise; **fare una sorpresa a qn** to give sb a surprise; **sor'preso, a** *pp di* **sorprendere**

sor'reggere [sor'rɛddʒere] *vt* to support, hold up; (*fig*) to sustain; **sor'retto, a** *pp di* **sorreggere**

sor'ridere *vi* to smile; **sor'riso, a** *pp di* **sorridere** ♦ *sm* smile

'sorso *sm* sip

'sorta *sf* sort, kind; **di ~** whatever, of any kind, at all

'sorte *sf* (*fato*) fate, destiny; (*evento fortuito*) chance; **tirare a ~** to draw lots

sor'teggio [sor'tɛddʒo] *sm* draw

sorti'legio [sorti'lɛdʒo] *sm* witchcraft *no pl*; (*incantesimo*) spell; **fare un ~ a qn** to cast a spell on sb

sor'tita *sf* (*MIL*) sortie

'sorto, a *pp di* **sorgere**

sorvegli'anza [sorveʎ'ʎantsa] *sf* watch; supervision; (*POLIZIA, MIL*) surveillance

sorvegli'are [sorveʎ'ʎare] *vt* (*bambino, bagagli, prigioniero*) to watch, keep an eye on; (*malato*) to watch over; (*territorio, casa*) to watch *o* keep watch over; (*lavori*) to supervise

sorvo'lare *vt* (*territorio*) to fly over ♦ *vi*: **~ su** (*fig*) to skim over

'sosia *sm inv* double

sos'pendere *vt* (*appendere*) to hang (up); (*interrompere, privare di una carica*) to suspend; (*rimandare*) to defer; (*appendere*) to hang; **sospensi'one** *sf* (*anche CHIM, AUT*) suspension; deferment; **sos'peso, a** *pp di* **sospendere** ♦ *ag* (*appeso*): **sospeso**

a hanging on (*o* from); (*treno, autobus*) cancelled; **in sospeso** in abeyance; (*conto*) outstanding; **tenere in sospeso** (*fig*) to keep in suspense

sospet'tare *vt* to suspect ♦ *vi*: **~ di** to suspect; (*diffidare*) to be suspicious of

sos'petto, a *ag* suspicious ♦ *sm* suspicion; **sospet'toso, a** *ag* suspicious

sos'pingere [sos'pindʒere] *vt* to drive, push; **sos'pinto, a** *pp di* **sospingere**

sospi'rare *vi* to sigh ♦ *vt* to long for, yearn for; **sos'piro** *sm* sigh

'sosta *sf* (*fermata*) stop, halt; (*pausa*) pause, break; **senza ~** non-stop, without a break

sostan'tivo *sm* noun, substantive

sos'tanza [sos'tantsa] *vt* substance; **~e** *sfpl* (*ricchezze*) wealth *sg*, possessions; **in ~** in short, to sum up; **sostanzi'oso, a** *ag* (*cibo*) nourishing, substantial

sos'tare *vi* (*fermarsi*) to stop (for a while), stay; (*fare una pausa*) to take a break

sos'tegno [sos'tɛɲɲo] *sm* support

soste'nere *vt* to support; (*prendere su di sé*) to take on, bear; (*resistere*) to withstand, stand up to; (*affermare*): **~ che** to maintain that; **~rsi** *vr* to hold o.s. up, support o.s.; (*fig*) to keep up one's strength; **~ gli esami** to sit exams; **sosteni'tore, 'trice** *sm/f* supporter

sostenta'mento *sm* maintenance, support

soste'nuto, a *ag* (*stile*) elevated; (*velocità, ritmo*) sustained; (*prezzo*) high ♦ *sm/f*: **fare il(la) ~(a)** to be standoffish, keep one's distance

sostitu'ire *vt* (*mettere al posto di*): **~ qn/qc a** to substitute sb/sth for; (*prendere il posto di: persona*) to substitute for; (: *cosa*) to take the place of

sosti'tuto, a *sm/f* substitute

sostituzi'one [sostitut'tsjone] *sf* substitution; **in ~ di** as a substitute for, in place of

sotta'ceti [sotta'tʃeti] *smpl* pickles

sot'tana *sf* (*sottoveste*) underskirt; (*gonna*) skirt; (*REL*) soutane, cassock

sotter'fugio [sotter'fudʒo] *sm* subterfuge

sotter'raneo, a *ag* underground ♦ *sm* cellar

sotter'rare *vt* to bury

sottigli'ezza [sottiλ'λettsa] *sf* thinness; slimness; (*fig: acutezza*) subtlety; shrewdness; **~e** *sfpl* (*pedanteria*) quibbles

sot'tile *ag* thin; (*figura, caviglia*) thin, slim, slender; (*fine: polvere, capelli*) fine; (*fig: leggero*) light; (*: vista*) sharp, keen; (*: olfatto*) fine, discriminating; (*: mente*) subtle; shrewd ♦ *sm*: **non andare per il ~** not to mince matters

sottin'tendere *vt* (*intendere qc non espresso*) to understand; (*implicare*) to imply; **sottin'teso, a** *pp di* **sottintendere** ♦ *sm* allusion; **parlare senza sottintesi** to speak plainly

'sotto *prep* (*gen*) under; (*più in basso di*) below ♦ *av* underneath, beneath; below; **(al piano) di ~** downstairs; **~ forma di** in the form of; **~ il monte** at the foot of the mountain; **siamo ~ Natale** it's nearly Christmas; **~ la pioggia/il sole** in the rain/sun(shine); **~ terra** underground; **chiuso ~ vuoto** vacuum-packed

sottoline'are *vt* to underline; (*fig*) to emphasize, stress

sottoma'rino, a *ag* (*flora*) submarine; (*cavo, navigazione*) underwater ♦ *sm* (*NAUT*) submarine

sotto'messo, a *pp di* **sottomettere**

sotto'mettere *vt* to subdue, subjugate; **~rsi** *vr* to submit

sottopas'saggio [sottopas'saddʒo] *sm* (*AUT*) underpass; (*pedonale*) subway, underpass

sotto'porre *vt* (*costringere*) to subject; (*fig: presentare*) to submit; **sottoporsi** *vr* to submit; **sottoporsi a** (*subire*) to undergo; **sotto'posto, a** *pp di* **sottoporre**

sottos'critto, a *pp di* **sottoscrivere**

sottos'crivere *vt* to sign ♦ *vi*: **~ a** to subscribe to; **sottoscrizi'one** *sf* signing; subscription

sottosegre'tario *sm*: **~ di Stato** Under-Secretary of State (*BRIT*), Assistant Secretary

of State (*US*)

sotto'sopra *av* upside-down

sotto'terra *av* underground

sotto'titolo *sm* subtitle

sottovalu'tare *vt* to underestimate

sotto'veste *sf* underskirt

sotto'voce [sotto'votʃe] *av* in a low voice

sot'trarre *vt* (*MAT*) to subtract, take away; **~ qn/qc a** (*togliere*) to remove sb/sth from; (*salvare*) to save *o* rescue sb/sth from; **~ qc a qn** (*rubare*) to steal sth from sb; **sottrarsi** *vr*: **sottrarsi a** (*sfuggire*) to escape; (*evitare*) to avoid; **sot'tratto, a** *pp di* **sottrarre**; **sottrazi'one** *sf* subtraction; removal

sovi'etico, a, ci, che *ag* Soviet ♦ *sm/f* Soviet citizen

sovraccari'care *vt* to overload

sovrannatu'rale *ag* = **soprannaturale**

so'vrano, a *ag* sovereign; (*fig: sommo*) supreme ♦ *sm/f* sovereign, monarch

sovrap'porre *vt* to place on top of, put on top of

sovras'tare *vi*: **~ a** (*vallata, fiume*) to overhang; (*fig*) to hang over, threaten ♦ *vt* to overhang; to hang over, threaten

sovrinten'dente *etc* = **soprintendente** *etc*

sovru'mano, a *ag* superhuman

sovvenzi'one [sovven'tsjone] *sf* subsidy, grant

sovver'sivo, a *ag* subversive

'sozzo, a [ˈsottso] *ag* filthy, dirty

S.p.A. *abbr* = **società per azioni**

spac'care *vt* to split, break; (*legna*) to chop; **~rsi** *vr* to split, break; **spacca'tura** *sf* split

spacci'are [spat'tʃare] *vt* (*vendere*) to sell (off); (*mettere in circolazione*) to circulate; (*droga*) to peddle, push; **~rsi** *vr*: **~rsi per** (*farsi credere*) to pass o.s. off as, pretend to be; **spaccia'tore, 'trice** *sm/f* (*di droga*) pusher; (*di denaro falso*) dealer; **'spaccio** *sm* (*di merce rubata, droga*): **spaccio (di)** trafficking (in); (*in denaro falso*): **spaccio (di)** passing (of); (*vendita*) sale; (*bottega*) shop

'spacco, chi *sm* (*fenditura*) split, crack;

(*strappo*) tear; (*di gonna*) slit
spac'cone *sm/f* boaster, braggart
'**spada** *sf* sword
spae'sato, a *ag* disorientated, lost
spa'ghetti [spa'ɡetti] *smpl* (*CUC*) spaghetti *sg*
'**Spagna** ['spaɲɲa] *sf*: **la ~** Spain; **spa'gnolo, a** *ag* Spanish ♦ *sm/f* Spaniard ♦ *sm* (*LING*) Spanish; **gli Spagnoli** the Spanish
'**spago, ghi** *sm* string, twine
spai'ato, a *ag* (*calza, guanto*) odd
spalan'care *vt* to open wide; **~rsi** *vr* to open wide
spa'lare *vt* to shovel
'**spalla** *sf* shoulder; (*fig: TEATRO*) stooge; **~e** *sfpl* (*dorso*) back; **spalleggi'are** *vt* to back up, support
spalli'era *sf* (*di sedia etc*) back; (*di letto: da capo*) head(board); (: *da piedi*) foot(board); (*GINNASTICA*) wall bars *pl*
spal'lina *sf* (*bretella*) strap; (*imbottita*) shoulder pad
spal'mare *vt* to spread
'**spalti** *smpl* (*di stadio*) terracing
spandere ['spandere] *vt* to spread; (*versare*) to pour (out); **~rsi** *vr* to spread; '**spanto, a** *pp di* **spandere**
spa'rare *vt* to fire ♦ *vi* (*far fuoco*) to fire; (*tirare*) to shoot; **spara'toria** *sf* exchange of shots
sparecchi'are [sparek'kjare] *vt*: **~ (la tavola)** to clear the table
spa'reggio [spa'reddʒo] *sm* (*SPORT*) play-off
'**spargere** ['spardʒere] *vt* (*sparpagliare*) to scatter; (*versare: vino*) to spill; (: *lacrime, sangue*) to shed; (*diffondere*) to spread; (*emanare*) to give off (*o* out); **~rsi** *vr* to spread; **spargi'mento** *sm* scattering, strewing; spilling; shedding; **spargimento di sangue** bloodshed
spa'rire *vi* to disappear, vanish
spar'lare *vi*: **~ di** to run down, speak ill of
'**sparo** *sm* shot
sparpagli'are [sparpaʎ'ʎare] *vt* to scatter; **~rsi** *vr* to scatter
'**sparso, a** *pp di* **spargere** ♦ *ag* scattered;

(*sciolto*) loose
spar'tire *vt* (*eredità, bottino*) to share out; (*avversari*) to separate
spar'tito *sm* (*MUS*) score
sparti'traffico *sm inv* (*AUT*) central reservation (*BRIT*), median (strip) (*US*)
spa'ruto, a *ag* (*viso etc*) haggard
sparvi'ero *sm* (*ZOOL*) sparrowhawk
spasi'mante *sm* suitor
'**spasimo** *sm* pang; '**spasmo** *sm* (*MED*) spasm; **spas'modico, a, ci, che** *ag* (*angoscioso*) agonizing; (*MED*) spasmodic
spassio'nato, a *ag* dispassionate, impartial
'**spasso** *sm* (*divertimento*) amusement, enjoyment; **andare a ~** to go out for a walk; **essere a ~** (*fig*) to be out of work; **mandare qn a ~** (*fig*) to give sb the sack
'**spatola** *sf* spatula; (*di muratore*) trowel
spau'racchio [spau'rakkjo] *sm* scarecrow
spau'rire *vt* to frighten, terrify
spa'valdo, a *ag* arrogant, bold
spaventa'passeri *sm inv* scarecrow
spaven'tare *vt* to frighten, scare; **~rsi** *vr* to be frightened, be scared; to get a fright; **spa'vento** *sm* fear, fright; **far spavento a qn** to give sb a fright; **spaven'toso, a** *ag* frightening, terrible; (*fig: fam*) tremendous, fantastic
spazien'tire [spattsjen'tire] *vi* (*anche*: **~rsi**) to lose one's patience
'**spazio** ['spattsjo] *sm* space; **~ aereo** airspace; **spazi'oso, a** *ag* spacious
spazzaca'mino [spattsaka'mino] *sm* chimney sweep
spazza'neve [spattsa'neve] *sm inv* snowplough
spaz'zare [spat'tsare] *vt* to sweep; (*foglie etc*) to sweep up; (*cacciare*) to sweep away; **spazza'tura** *sf* sweepings *pl*; (*immondizia*) rubbish; **spaz'zino** *sm* street sweeper
'**spazzola** ['spattsola] *sf* brush; **~ per abiti** clothesbrush; **~ da capelli** hairbrush; **spazzo'lare** *vt* to brush; **spazzo'lino** *sm* (small) brush; **spazzolino da denti** toothbrush

specchi'arsi [spek'kjarsi] *vr* to look at o.s. in a mirror; (*riflettersi*) to be mirrored, be reflected

'**specchio** ['spɛkkjo] *sm* mirror

speci'ale [spe'tʃale] *ag* special; **specia'lista, i, e** *sm/f* specialist; **specialità** *sf inv* speciality; (*branca di studio*) special field, speciality; **specializ'zarsi** *vr*: **specializzarsi (in)** to specialize (in); **special'mente** *av* especially, particularly

'**specie** ['spɛtʃe] *sf inv* (BIOL, BOT, ZOOL) species *inv*; (*tipo*) kind, sort ♦ *av* especially, particularly; **una ~ di** a kind of; **fare ~ a qn** to surprise sb; **la ~ umana** mankind

specifi'care [spetʃifi'kare] *vt* to specify, state

spe'cifico, a, ci, che [spe'tʃifiko] *ag* specific

specu'lare *vi*: **~ su** (COMM) to speculate in; (*sfruttare*) to exploit; (*meditare*) to speculate on; **speculazi'one** *sf* speculation

spe'dire *vt* to send; **spedizi'one** *sf* sending; (*collo*) consignment; (*scientifica etc*) expedition

'**spegnere** ['spɛɲɲere] *vt* (*fuoco, sigaretta*) to put out, extinguish; (*apparecchio elettrico*) to turn o switch off; (*gas*) to turn off; (*fig: suoni, passioni*) to stifle; (*debito*) to extinguish; **~rsi** *vr* to go out; to go off; (*morire*) to pass away

spel'lare *vt* (*scuoiare*) to skin; (*scorticare*) to graze; **~rsi** *vr* to peel

'**spendere** *vt* to spend

spen'nare *vt* to pluck

spensie'rato, a *ag* carefree

'**spento, a** *pp di* **spegnere** ♦ *ag* (*suono*) muffled; (*colore*) dull; (*sigaretta*) out; (*civiltà, vulcano*) extinct

spe'ranza [spe'rantsa] *sf* hope

spe'rare *vt* to hope for ♦ *vi*: **~ in** to trust in; **~ che/di fare** to hope that/to do; **lo spero, spero di sì** I hope so

sper'duto, a *ag* (*isolato*) out-of-the-way; (*persona: smarrita, a disagio*) lost

spergi'uro, a [sper'dʒuro] *sm/f* perjurer

♦ *sm* perjury

sperimen'tale *ag* experimental

sperimen'tare *vt* to experiment with, test; (*fig*) to test, put to the test

'**sperma, i** *sm* sperm

spe'rone *sm* spur

sperpe'rare *vt* to squander

'**spesa** *sf* (*somma di denaro*) expense; (*costo*) cost; (*acquisto*) purchase; (*fam: acquisto del cibo quotidiano*) shopping; **~e** *sfpl* (*soldi spesi*) expenses; (COMM) costs; charges; **fare la ~** to do the shopping; **a ~e di** (*a carico di*) at the expense of; **~e generali** overheads; **~e postali** postage *sg*; **~e di viaggio** travelling expenses

'**speso, a** *pp di* **spendere**

'**spesso, a** *ag* (*fitto*) thick; (*frequente*) frequent ♦ *av* often; **~e volte** frequently, often

spes'sore *sm* thickness

spet'tabile (*abbr:* **Spett.**: *in lettere*) *ag*: **~ ditta X** Messrs X and Co.

spet'tacolo *sm* (*rappresentazione*) performance, show; (*vista, scena*) sight; **dare ~ di sé** to make an exhibition o a spectacle of o.s.; **spettaco'loso, a** *ag* spectacular

spet'tare *vi*: **~ a** (*decisione*) to be up to; (*stipendio*) to be due to; **spetta a te decidere** it's up to you to decide

spetta'tore, 'trice *sm/f* (CINEMA, TEATRO) member of the audience; (*di avvenimento*) onlooker, witness

spetti'nare *vt*: **~ qn** to ruffle sb's hair; **~rsi** *vr* to get one's hair in a mess

'**spettro** *sm* (*fantasma*) spectre; (FISICA) spectrum

'**spezie** ['spɛttsje] *sfpl* (CUC) spices

spez'zare [spet'tsare] *vt* (*rompere*) to break; (*fig: interrompere*) to break up; **~rsi** *vr* to break

spezza'tino [spettsa'tino] *sm* (CUC) stew

spezzet'tare [spettset'tare] *vt* to break up (o chop) into small pieces

'**spia** *sf* spy; (*confidente della polizia*) informer; (ELETTR) indicating light; warning light; (*fessura*) peep-hole; (*fig: sintomo*) sign, indication

spia'cente [spja'tʃɛnte] *ag* sorry; **essere ~ di qc/di fare qc** to be sorry about sth/for doing sth

spia'cevole [spja'tʃevole] *ag* unpleasant

spi'aggia, ge ['spjaddʒa] *sf* beach; **~ libera** public beach

spia'nare *vt* (*terreno*) to level, make level; (*edificio*) to raze to the ground; (*pasta*) to roll out; (*rendere liscio*) to smooth (out)

spi'ano *sm*: **a tutto ~** (*lavorare*) non-stop, without a break; (*spendere*) lavishly

spian'tato, a *ag* penniless, ruined

spi'are *vt* to spy on

spi'azzo ['spjattso] *sm* open space; (*radura*) clearing

spic'care *vt* (*assegno, mandato di cattura*) to issue ♦ *vi* (*risaltare*) to stand out; **~ il volo** to fly off; (*fig*) to spread one's wings; **~ un balzo** to leap; **spic'cato, a** *ag* (*marcato*) marked, strong; (*notevole*) remarkable

'spicchio ['spikkjo] *sm* (*di agrumi*) segment; (*di aglio*) clove; (*parte*) piece, slice

spicci'are [spit'tʃare] *vt* to finish off quickly; **~rsi** *vr* to hurry up

'spicciolo, a ['spittʃolo] *ag*: **moneta ~a, ~i** *smpl* (small) change

'spicco, chi *sm*: **di ~** outstanding; (*tema*) main, principal; **fare ~** to stand out

spie'dino *sm* (*utensile*) skewer; (*pietanza*) kebab

spi'edo *sm* (*CUC*) spit

spie'gare *vt* (*far capire*) to explain; (*tovaglia*) to unfold; (*vele*) to unfurl; **~rsi** *vr* to explain o.s., make o.s. clear; **~ qc a qn** to explain sth to sb; **spiegazi'one** *sf* explanation

spiegaz'zare [spjegat'tsare] *vt* to crease, crumple

spie'tato, a *ag* ruthless, pitiless

spiffe'rare (*fam*) *vt* to blurt out, blab

'spiga, ghe (*BOT*) ear

spigli'ato, a [spiʎ'ʎato] *ag* self-possessed, self-confident

'spigolo *sm* corner; (*MAT*) edge

'spilla *sf* brooch; (*da cravatta, cappello*) pin; **~ di sicurezza** *o* **da balia** safety pin

spil'lare *vt* (*vino, fig*) to tap; **~ denaro/ notizie a qn** to tap sb for money/ information

'spillo *sm* pin

spi'lorcio, a, ci, ce [spi'lortʃo] *ag* mean, stingy

'spina *sf* (*BOT*) thorn; (*ZOOL*) spine, prickle; (*di pesce*) bone; (*ELETTR*) plug; (*di botte*) bunghole; **birra alla ~** draught beer; **~ dorsale** (*ANAT*) backbone

spi'nacio [spi'natʃo] *sm* spinach; (*CUC*): **~i** spinach *sg*

'spingere ['spindʒere] *vt* to push; (*condurre: anche fig*) to drive; (*stimolare*): **~ qn a fare** to urge *o* press sb to do; **~rsi** *vr* (*inoltrarsi*) to push on, carry on; **~rsi troppo lontano** (*anche fig*) to go too far

spi'noso, a *ag* thorny, prickly

'spinta *sf* (*urto*) push; (*FISICA*) thrust; (*fig: stimolo*) incentive, spur; (*: appoggio*) string-pulling *no pl*; **dare una ~a a qn** (*fig*) to pull strings for sb

'spinto, a *pp di* **spingere**

spio'naggio [spio'naddʒo] *sm* espionage, spying

spi'overe *vi* to stop raining

'spira *sf* coil

spi'raglio [spi'raʎʎo] *sm* (*fessura*) chink, narrow opening; (*raggio di luce, fig*) glimmer, gleam

spi'rale *sf* spiral; (*contraccettivo*) coil; **a ~** spiral(-shaped)

spi'rare *vi* (*vento*) to blow; (*morire*) to expire, pass away

spiri'tato, a *ag* possessed; (*fig: persona, espressione*) wild

spiri'tismo *sm* spiritualism

'spirito *sm* (*REL, CHIM, disposizione d'animo, di legge etc, fantasma*) spirit; (*pensieri, intelletto*) mind; (*arguzia*) wit; (*umorismo*) humour, wit; **lo S~ Santo** the Holy Spirit *o* Ghost

spirito'saggine [spirito'saddʒine] *sf* witticism; (*peg*) wisecrack

spiri'toso, a *ag* witty

spiritu'ale *ag* spiritual

'**splendere** *vi* to shine

'**splendido, a** *ag* splendid; (*splendente*) shining; (*sfarzoso*) magnificent, splendid

splen'dore *sm* splendour; (*luce intensa*) brilliance, brightness

spodes'tare *vt* to deprive of power; (*sovrano*) to depose

spogli'are [spoʎˈʎare] *vt* (*svestire*) to undress; (*privare, fig: depredare*): ~ **qn di qc** to deprive sb of sth; (*togliere ornamenti: anche fig*): ~ **qn/qc di** to strip sb/sth of; ~**rsi** *vr* to undress, strip; ~**rsi di** (*ricchezze etc*) to deprive o.s. of, give up; (*pregiudizi*) to rid o.s. of; **spoglia'toio** *sm* dressing room; (*di scuola etc*) cloakroom; (*SPORT*) changing room; '**spoglie** [ˈspɔʎʎe] *sfpl* (*salma*) remains; (*preda*) spoils, booty *sg*; *vedi anche* **spoglio**; '**spoglio, a** *ag* (*pianta, terreno*) bare; (*privo*): **spoglio di** stripped of, lacking in, without ♦ *sm* (*di voti*) counting

'**spola** *sf* (*bobina di filo*) cop; **fare la ~ (fra)** to go to and fro *o* shuttle (between)

spol'pare *vt* to strip the flesh off

spolve'rare *vt* (*anche CUC*) to dust; (*con spazzola*) to brush; (*con battipanni*) to beat; (*fig*) to polish off ♦ *vi* to dust

'**sponda** *sf* (*di fiume*) bank; (*di mare, lago*) shore; (*bordo*) edge

spon'taneo, a *ag* spontaneous; (*persona*) unaffected, natural

spopo'lare *vt* to depopulate ♦ *vi* (*attirare folla*) to draw the crowds; ~**rsi** *vr* to become depopulated

spor'care *vt* to dirty, make dirty; (*fig*) to sully, soil; ~**rsi** *vr* to get dirty

spor'cizia [sporˈtʃittsja] *sf* (*stato*) dirtiness; (*sudiciume*) dirt, filth; (*cosa sporca*) dirt *no pl*, something dirty

'**sporco, a, chi, che** *ag* dirty, filthy

spor'genza [sporˈdʒɛntsa] *sf* projection

'**sporgere** [ˈspɔrdʒere] *vt* to put out, stretch out ♦ *vi* (*venire in fuori*) to stick out; ~**rsi** *vr* to lean out; ~ **querela contro qn** (*DIR*) to take legal action against sb

sport *sm inv* sport

'**sporta** *sf* shopping bag

spor'tello *sm* (*di treno, auto etc*) door; (*di banca, ufficio*) window, counter; ~ **automatico** (*BANCA*) cash dispenser, automated telling machine

spor'tivo, a *ag* (*gara, giornale, centro*) sports *cpd*; (*persona*) sporty; (*abito*) casual; (*spirito, atteggiamento*) sporting

'**sporto, a** *pp di* **sporgere**

'**sposa** *sf* bride; (*moglie*) wife

sposa'lizio [spozaˈlittsjo] *sm* wedding

spo'sare *vt* to marry; (*fig: idea, fede*) to espouse; ~**rsi** *vr* to get married, marry; ~**rsi con qn** to marry sb, get married to sb; **spo'sato, a** *ag* married

'**sposo** *sm* (bride)groom; (*marito*) husband; **gli ~i** *smpl* the newlyweds

spos'sato, a *ag* exhausted, weary

spos'tare *vt* to move, shift; (*cambiare: orario*) to change; ~**rsi** *vr* to move

'**spranga, ghe** *sf* (*sbarra*) bar

'**sprazzo** [ˈsprattso] *sm* (*di sole etc*) flash; (*fig: di gioia etc*) burst

spre'care *vt* to waste; ~**rsi** *vr* (*persona*) to waste one's energy; '**spreco** *sm* waste

spre'gevole [spreˈdʒevole] *ag* contemptible, despicable

spregiudi'cato, a [spredʒudiˈkato] *ag* unprejudiced, unbiased; (*peg*) unscrupulous

'**spremere** *vt* to squeeze

spre'muta *sf* fresh juice; ~ **d'arancia** fresh orange juice

sprez'zante [spretˈtsante] *ag* scornful, contemptuous

sprigio'nare [spridʒoˈnare] *vt* to give off, emit; ~**rsi** *vr* to emanate; (*uscire con impeto*) to burst out

spriz'zare [spritˈtsare] *vt, vi* to spurt; ~ **gioia/salute** to be bursting with joy/health

sprofon'dare *vi* to sink; (*casa*) to collapse; (*suolo*) to give way, subside; ~**rsi** *vr*: ~**rsi in** (*poltrona*) to sink into; (*fig*) to become immersed *o* absorbed in

spro'nare *vt* to spur (on)

'**sprone** *sm* (*sperone, fig*) spur

sproporzio'nato, a [sproportsjoˈnato] *ag* disproportionate, out of all proportion

sproporzi'one [spropor'tsjone] *sf* disproportion

sproposi'tato, a *ag* (*lettera, discorso*) full of mistakes; (*fig: costo*) excessive, enormous

spro'posito *sm* blunder; **a ~** at the wrong time; (*rispondere, parlare*) irrelevantly

sprovve'duto, a *ag* inexperienced, naïve

sprov'visto, a *ag* (*mancante*): **~ di** lacking in, without; **alla ~a** unawares

spruz'zare [sprut'tsare] *vt* (*a nebulizzazione*) to spray; (*aspergere*) to sprinkle; (*inzaccherare*) to splash; **'spruzzo** *sm* spray; splash

'spugna ['spuɲɲa] *sf* (ZOOL) sponge; (*tessuto*) towelling; **spu'gnoso, a** *ag* spongy

'spuma *sf* (*schiuma*) foam; (*bibita*) fizzy drink

spu'mante *sm* sparkling wine

spumeggi'ante [spumed'dʒante] *ag* (*birra*) foaming; (*vino, fig*) sparkling

spu'mone *sm* (CUC) mousse

spun'tare *vt* (*coltello*) to break the point of; (*capelli*) to trim ♦ *vi* (*uscire: germogli*) to sprout; (: *capelli*) to begin to grow; (: *denti*) to come through; (*apparire*) to appear (suddenly); **~rsi** *vr* to become blunt, lose its point; **spuntarla** (*fig*) to make it, win through

spun'tino *sm* snack

'spunto *sm* (TEATRO, MUS) cue; (*fig*) starting point; **dare lo ~ a** (*fig*) to give rise to

spur'gare *vt* (*fogna*) to clean, clear

spu'tare *vt* to spit out; (*fig*) to belch (out) ♦ *vi* to spit; **'sputo** *sm* spittle *no pl*, spit *no pl*

'squadra *sf* (*strumento*) (set) square; (*gruppo*) team, squad; (*di operai*) gang, squad; (MIL) squad; (: AER, NAUT) squadron; (SPORT) team; **lavoro a ~e** teamwork

squa'drare *vt* to square, make square; (*osservare*) to look at closely

squa'driglia [skwa'driʎʎa] *sf* (AER) flight; (NAUT) squadron

squa'drone *sm* squadron

squagli'arsi [skwaʎ'ʎarsi] *vr* to melt; (*fig*) to sneak off

squa'lifica *sf* disqualification

squalifi'care *vt* to disqualify

'squallido, a *ag* wretched, bleak

squal'lore *sm* wretchedness, bleakness

'squalo *sm* shark

'squama *sf* scale; **squa'mare** *vt* to scale; **squamarsi** *vr* to flake *o* peel (off)

squarcia'gola [skwartʃa'gola]: **a ~** *av* at the top of one's voice

squarci'are [skwar'tʃare] *vt* to rip (open); (*fig*) to pierce

squar'tare *vt* to quarter, cut up

squattri'nato, a *ag* penniless

squili'brato, a *ag* (PSIC) unbalanced; **squi'librio** *sm* (*differenza, sbilancio*) imbalance; (PSIC) unbalance

squil'lante *ag* shrill, sharp

squil'lare *vi* (*campanello, telefono*) to ring (out); (*tromba*) to blare; **'squillo** *sm* ring, ringing *no pl*; blare; **ragazza** *f* **squillo** *inv* call girl

squi'sito, a *ag* exquisite; (*cibo*) delicious; (*persona*) delightful

squit'tire *vi* (*uccello*) to squawk; (*topo*) to squeak

sradi'care *vt* to uproot; (*fig*) to eradicate

sragio'nare [zradʒo'nare] *vi* to talk nonsense, rave

srego'lato, a *ag* (*senza ordine: vita*) disorderly; (*smodato*) immoderate; (*dissoluto*) dissolute

S.r.l. *abbr* = **società a responsabilità limitata**

'stabile *ag* stable, steady; (*tempo: non variabile*) settled; (TEATRO: *compagnia*) resident ♦ *sm* (*edificio*) building

stabili'mento *sm* (*edificio*) establishment; (*fabbrica*) plant, factory

stabi'lire *vt* to establish; (*fissare: prezzi, data*) to fix; (*decidere*) to decide; **~rsi** *vr* (*prendere dimora*) to settle

stac'care *vt* (*levare*) to detach, remove; (*separare: anche fig*) to separate, divide; (*strappare*) to tear off (*o* out); (*scandire: parole*) to pronounce clearly; (SPORT) to leave behind; **~rsi** *vr* (*bottone etc*) to come off; (*scostarsi*): **~rsi (da)** to move away (from); (*fig: separarsi*): **~rsi da** to leave; **non ~ gli occhi da qn** not to take one's eyes off sb

'**stadio** *sm* (SPORT) stadium; (*periodo, fase*) phase, stage

'**staffa** *sf* (*di sella,* TECN) stirrup; **perdere le ~e** (*fig*) to fly off the handle

staf'**fetta** *sf* (*messo*) dispatch rider; (SPORT) relay race

stagio'**nale** [stadʒo'nale] *ag* seasonal

stagio'**nare** [stadʒo'nare] *vt* (*legno*) to season; (*formaggi, vino*) to mature

stagi'**one** [sta'dʒone] *sf* season; **alta/bassa ~** high/low season

stagli'**arsi** [staʎ'ʎarsi] *vr* to stand out, be silhouetted

'**stagno, a** ['stanno] *ag* watertight; (*a tenuta d'aria*) airtight ♦ *sm* (*acquitrino*) pond; (CHIM) tin

sta'**gnola** [stan'nɔla] *sf* tinfoil

'**stalla** *sf* (*per bovini*) cowshed; (*per cavalli*) stable

stal'**lone** *sm* stallion

sta'**mani** *av* = **stamattina**

stamat'**tina** *av* this morning

stam'**becco, chi** *sm* ibex

'**stampa** *sf* (TIP, FOT: *tecnica*) printing; (*impressione, copia fotografica*) print; (*insieme di quotidiani, giornalisti etc*) press; "**~e**" *sfpl* "printed matter"

stam'**pante** *sf* (INFORM) printer

stam'**pare** *vt* to print; (*pubblicare*) to publish; (*coniare*) to strike, coin; (*imprimere: anche fig*) to impress

stampa'**tello** *sm* block letters *pl*

stam'**pella** *sf* crutch

'**stampo** *sm* mould; (*fig: indole*) type, kind, sort

sta'**nare** *vt* to drive out

stan'**care** *vt* to tire, make tired; (*annoiare*) to bore; (*infastidire*) to annoy; **~rsi** *vr* to get tired, tire o.s. out; **~rsi (di)** to grow weary (of), grow tired (of)

stan'**chezza** [stan'kettsa] *sf* tiredness, fatigue

'**stanco, a, chi, che** *ag* tired; **~ di** tired of, fed up with

'**stanga, ghe** *sm* bar; (*di carro*) shaft

stan'**gata** *sf* (*colpo: anche fig*) blow; (*cattivo risultato*) poor result; (CALCIO) shot

sta'**notte** *av* tonight; (*notte passata*) last night

'**stante** *prep*: **a sé ~** (*appartamento, casa*) independent, separate

stan'**tio, a,** '**tii,** '**tie** *ag* stale; (*burro*) rancid; (*fig*) old

stan'**tuffo** *sm* piston

'**stanza** ['stantsa] *sf* room; (POESIA) stanza; **~ da letto** bedroom

stanzi'**are** [stan'tsjare] *vt* to allocate

stap'**pare** *vt* to uncork; to uncap

'**stare** *vi* (*restare in un luogo*) to stay, remain; (*abitare*) to stay, live; (*essere situato*) to be, be situated; (*anche*: **~ in piedi**) to be, stand; (*essere, trovarsi*) to be; (*dipendere*): **se stesse in me** if it were up to me, if it depended on me; (*seguito da gerundio*): **sta studiando** he's studying; **starci** (*esserci spazio*): **nel baule non ci sta più niente** there's no more room in the boot; (*accettare*) to accept; **ci stai?** is that okay with you?; **~ a** (*attenersi a*) to follow, stick to; (*seguito dall'infinito*): **stiamo a discutere** we're talking; (*toccare a*): **sta a te giocare** it's your turn to play; **~ per fare qc** to be about to do sth; **come sta?** how are you?; **io sto bene/male** I'm very well/not very well; **~ a qn** (*abiti etc*) to fit sb; **queste scarpe mi stanno strette** these shoes are tight for me; **il rosso ti sta bene** red suits you

starnu'**tire** *vi* to sneeze; star'**nuto** *sm* sneeze

sta'**sera** *av* this evening, tonight

sta'**tale** *ag* state *cpd*; government *cpd* ♦ *sm/f* state employee, local authority employee; (*nell'amministrazione*) ≈ civil servant

sta'**tista, i** *sm* statesman

sta'**tistica** *sf* statistics *sg*

'**stato, a** *pp di* **essere; stare** ♦ *sm* (*condizione*) state, condition; (POL) state; (DIR) status; **essere in ~ d'accusa** (DIR) to be committed for trial; **~ d'assedio/**

d'emergenza state of siege/emergency; **~ civile** (AMM) marital status; **~ maggiore** (MIL) staff; **gli S~i Uniti (d'America)** the United States (of America)

'**statua** sf statue

statuni'tense ag United States cpd, of the United States

sta'tura sf (ANAT) height, stature; (fig) stature

sta'tuto sm (DIR) statute; constitution

sta'volta av this time

stazio'nario, a [stattsjo'narjo] ag stationary; (fig) unchanged

stazi'one [stat'tsjone] sf station; (balneare, termale) resort; **~ degli autobus** bus station; **~ balneare** seaside resort; **~ ferroviaria** railway (BRIT) o railroad (US) station; **~ invernale** winter sports resort; **~ di polizia** police station (in small town); **~ di servizio** service o petrol (BRIT) o filling station

'stecca, che sf stick; (di ombrello) rib; (di sigarette) carton; (MED) splint; (stonatura): **fare una ~** to sing (o play) a wrong note

stec'cato sm fence

stec'chito, a [stek'kito] ag: **lasciar ~ qn** (fig) to leave sb flabbergasted; **morto ~** stone dead

'stella sf star; **~ alpina** (BOT) edelweiss; **~ di mare** (ZOOL) starfish

'stelo sm stem; (asta) rod; **lampada a ~** standard lamp

'stemma, i sm coat of arms

stempe'rare vt to dilute; to dissolve; (colori) to mix

sten'dardo sm standard

'stendere vt (braccia, gambe) to stretch (out); (tovaglia) to spread (out); (bucato) to hang out; (mettere a giacere) to lay (down); (spalmare: colore) to spread; (mettere per iscritto) to draw up; **~rsi** vr (coricarsi) to stretch out, lie down; (estendersi) to extend, stretch

stenodatti'lografo, a sm/f shorthand typist (BRIT), stenographer (US)

stenogra'fare vt to take down in shorthand; stenogra'fia sf shorthand

sten'tare vi: **~ a fare** to find it hard to do, have difficulty doing

'stento sm (fatica) difficulty; **~i** smpl (privazioni) hardship sg, privation sg; **a ~** with difficulty, barely

'sterco sm dung

stereo('fonico, a, ci, che) ag stereo(phonic)

'sterile ag sterile; (terra) barren; (fig) futile, fruitless; sterilità sf sterility

steriliz'zare [sterilid'dzare] vt to sterilize; sterilizzazi'one sf sterilization

ster'lina sf pound (sterling)

stermi'nare vt to exterminate, wipe out

stermi'nato, a ag immense; endless

ster'minio sm extermination, destruction

'sterno sm (ANAT) breastbone

'sterpo sm dry twig; **~i** smpl brushwood sg

ster'zare [ster'tsare] vt, vi (AUT) to steer; 'sterzo sm steering; (volante) steering wheel

'steso, a pp di **stendere**

'stesso, a ag same; (rafforzativo: in persona, proprio): **il re ~** the king himself o in person ♦ pron: **lo(la) ~(a)** the same (one); **i suoi ~i avversari lo ammirano** even his enemies admire him; **fa lo ~** it doesn't matter; **per me è lo ~** it's all the same to me, it doesn't matter to me; vedi **io; tu** etc

ste'sura sf drafting no pl, drawing up no pl; draft

'stigmate sfpl (REL) stigmata

sti'lare vt to draw up, draft

'stile sm style; sti'lista, i sm designer

stil'lare vi (trasudare) to ooze; (gocciolare) to drip; stilli'cidio sm (fig) continual pestering (o moaning etc)

stilo'grafica, che sf (anche: **penna ~**) fountain pen

'stima sf esteem; valuation; assessment; estimate

sti'mare vt (persona) to esteem, hold in high regard; (terreno, casa etc) to value; (stabilire in misura approssimativa) to estimate, assess; (ritenere): **~ che** to consider that; **~rsi fortunato** to consider o.s. (to be) lucky

stimo'lare vt to stimulate; (incitare): ~ qn (a fare) to spur sb on (to do)

'stimolo sm (anche fig) stimulus

'stinco, chi sm shin; shinbone

'stingere ['stindʒere] vt, vi (anche: ~rsi) to fade; 'stinto, a pp di stingere

sti'pare vt to cram, pack; ~rsi vr (accalcarsi) to crowd, throng

sti'pendio sm salary

'stipite sm (di porta, finestra) jamb

stipu'lare vt (redigere) to draw up

sti'rare vt (abito) to iron; (distendere) to stretch; (strappare: muscolo) to strain; ~rsi vr to stretch (o.s.); stira'tura sf ironing

'stirpe sf birth, stock; descendants pl

stiti'chezza [stiti'kettsa] sf constipation

'stitico, a, ci, che ag constipated

'stiva sf (di nave) hold

sti'vale sm boot

'stizza ['stittsa] sf anger, vexation; stiz'zirsi vr to lose one's temper; stiz'zoso, a ag (persona) quick-tempered, irascible; (risposta) angry

stocca'fisso sm stockfish, dried cod

stoc'cata sf (colpo) stab, thrust; (fig) gibe, cutting remark

'stoffa sf material, fabric; (fig): aver la ~ di to have the makings of

'stola sf stole

'stolto, a ag stupid, foolish

'stomaco, chi sm stomach; dare di ~ to vomit, be sick

sto'nare vt to sing (o play) out of tune ♦ vi to be out of tune, sing (o play) out of tune; (fig) to be out of place, jar; (: colori) to clash; stona'tura sf (suono) false note

stop sm inv (TEL) stop; (AUT: cartello) stop sign; (: fanalino d'arresto) brake-light

'stoppa sf tow

stop'pino sm wick; (miccia) fuse

'storcere ['stɔrtʃere] vt to twist; ~rsi vr to writhe, twist; ~ il naso (fig) to turn up one's nose; ~rsi la caviglia to twist one's ankle

stor'dire vt (intontire) to stun, daze; ~rsi vr: ~rsi col bere to dull one's senses with

drink; stor'dito, a ag stunned

'storia sf (scienza, avvenimenti) history; (racconto, bugia) story; (faccenda, questione) business no pl; (pretesto) excuse, pretext; ~e sfpl (smancerie) fuss sg; 'storico, a, ci, che ag historic(al) ♦ sm historian

stori'one sm (ZOOL) sturgeon

stor'mire vi to rustle

'stormo sm (di uccelli) flock

stor'nare vt (COMM) to transfer

'storno sm (ZOOL) starling

storpi'are vt to cripple, maim; (fig: parole) to mangle; (: significato) to twist

'storpio, a ag crippled, maimed

'storta sf (distorsione) sprain, twist

'storto, a pp di storcere ♦ ag (chiodo) twisted, bent; (gamba, quadro) crooked

sto'viglie [sto'viʎʎe] sfpl dishes pl, crockery

'strabico, a, ci, che ag squint-eyed; (occhi) squint

stra'bismo sm squinting

stra'carico, a, chi, che ag overloaded

strac'chino [strak'kino] sm type of soft cheese

stracci'are [strat'tʃare] vt to tear

'straccio, a, ci, ce ['strattʃo] ag: carta ~a waste paper ♦ sm rag; (per pulire) cloth, duster

stra'cotto, a ag overcooked ♦ sm (CUC) beef stew

'strada sf road; (di città) street; (cammino, via, fig) way; farsi ~ (fig) to do well for o.s.; essere fuori ~ (fig) to be on the wrong track; ~ facendo on the way; ~ senza uscita dead end; stra'dale ag road cpd

strafalci'one [strafal'tʃone] sm blunder, howler

stra'fare vi to overdo it; stra'fatto, a pp di strafare

strafot'tente ag: è ~ he doesn't give a damn, he couldn't care less

'strage ['stradʒe] sf massacre, slaughter

stralu'nato, a ag (occhi) rolling; (persona) beside o.s., very upset

stramaz'zare [stramat'tsare] vi to fall heavily

'strambo, a *ag* strange, queer

strampa'lato, a *ag* odd, eccentric

stra'nezza [stra'nettsa] *sf* strangeness

strango'lare *vt* to strangle; ~rsi *vr* to choke

strani'ero, a *ag* foreign ♦ *sm/f* foreigner

'strano, a *ag* strange, odd

straordi'nario, a *ag* extraordinary; (*treno etc*) special ♦ *sm* (*lavoro*) overtime

strapaz'zare [strapat'tsare] *vt* to ill-treat; ~rsi *vr* to tire o.s. out, overdo things; stra'pazzo *sm* strain, fatigue; da strapazzo (*fig*) third-rate

strapi'ombo *sm* overhanging rock; a ~ overhanging

strapo'tere *sm* excessive power

strap'pare *vt* (*gen*) to tear, rip; (*pagina etc*) to tear off, tear out; (*sradicare*) to pull up; (*togliere*): ~ qc a qn to snatch sth from sb; (*fig*) to wrest sth from sb; ~rsi *vr* (*lacerarsi*) to rip, tear; (*rompersi*) to break; ~rsi un muscolo to tear a muscle; 'strappo *sm* pull, tug; tear, rip; fare uno strappo alla regola to make an exception to the rule; strappo muscolare torn muscle

strari'pare *vi* to overflow

strasci'care [straʃʃi'kare] *vt* to trail; (*piedi*) to drag; ~ le parole to drawl

'strascico, chi ['straʃʃiko] *sm* (*di abito*) train; (*conseguenza*) after-effect

strata'gemma, i [strata'dʒɛmma] *sm* stratagem

strate'gia, 'gie [strate'dʒia] *sf* strategy; stra'tegico, a, ci, che *ag* strategic

'strato *sm* layer; (*rivestimento*) coat, coating; (*GEO, fig*) stratum; (*METEOR*) stratus; ~ di ozono ozone layer

strava'gante *ag* odd, eccentric; strava'ganza *sf* eccentricity

stra'vecchio, a [stra'vɛkkjo] *ag* very old

stra'vizio [stra'vittsjo] *sm* excess

stra'volgere [stra'vɔldʒere] *vt* (*volto*) to contort; (*fig: animo*) to trouble deeply; (: *verità*) to twist, distort; stra'volto, a *pp di* stravolgere

strazi'are [strat'tsjare] *vt* to torture, torment; 'strazio *sm* torture; (*fig: cosa fatta male*): essere uno ~ to be appalling

'strega, ghe *sf* witch

stre'gare *vt* to bewitch

stre'gone *sm* (*mago*) wizard; (*di tribù*) witch doctor

stre'gua *sf*: alla ~ di by the same standard as

stre'mare *vt* to exhaust

'stremo *sm* very end; essere allo ~ to be at the end of one's tether

'strenna *sf* Christmas present

strepi'toso, a *ag* clamorous, deafening; (*fig: successo*) resounding

stres'sante *ag* stressful

'stretta *sf* (*di mano*) grasp; (*finanziaria*) squeeze; (*fig: dolore, turbamento*) pang; una ~a di mano a handshake; essere alle ~e to have one's back to the wall; *vedi anche* stretto

stretta'mente *av* tightly; (*rigorosamente*) strictly

stret'tezza [stret'tettsa] *sf* narrowness

'stretto, a *pp di* stringere ♦ *ag* (*corridoio, limiti*) narrow; (*gonna, scarpe, nodo, curva*) tight; (*intimo: parente, amico*) close; (*rigoroso: osservanza*) strict; (*preciso: significato*) precise, exact ♦ *sm* (*braccio di mare*) strait; a denti ~i with clenched teeth; lo ~ necessario the bare minimum; stret'toia *sf* bottleneck; (*fig*) tricky situation

stri'ato, a *ag* streaked

'stridere *vi* (*porta*) to squeak; (*animale*) to screech, shriek; (*colori*) to clash; 'stridulo, a *ag* shrill

stril'lare *vt, vi* to scream, shriek; 'strillo *sm* scream, shriek

stril'lone *sm* newspaper seller

strimin'zito, a [strimin'tsito] *ag* (*misero*) shabby; (*molto magro*) skinny

strimpel'lare *vt* (*MUS*) to strum

'stringa, ghe *sf* lace

strin'gato, a *ag* (*fig*) concise

'stringere ['strindʒere] *vt* (*avvicinare due cose*) to press (together), squeeze (together); (*tenere stretto*) to hold tight, clasp, clutch; (*pugno, mascella, denti*) to clench; (*labbra*) to compress; (*avvitare*) to tighten; (*abito*) to take in; (*sog: scarpe*) to pinch, be tight for; (*fig: concludere: patto*) to make; (*: accelerare: passo, tempo*) to quicken ♦ *vi* (*essere stretto*) to be tight; (*tempo: incalzare*) to be pressing; **~rsi** *vr* (*accostarsi*): **~rsi a** to press o.s. up against; **~ la mano a qn** to shake sb's hand; **~ gli occhi** to screw up one's eyes

'**striscia, sce** ['striʃʃa] *sf* (*di carta, tessuto etc*) strip; (*riga*) stripe; **~sce (pedonali)** zebra crossing *sg*

strisci'are [striʃ'ʃare] *vt* (*piedi*) to drag; (*muro, macchina*) to graze ♦ *vi* to crawl, creep

'strisci o ['striʃʃo] *sm* graze; (*MED*) smear; **colpire di ~** to graze

strito'lare *vt* to grind

striz'zare [strit'tsare] *vt* (*panni*) to wring (out); **~ l'occhio** to wink

'strofa *sf* strophe

strofi'naccio [strofi'nattʃo] *sm* duster, cloth; (*per piatti*) dishcloth; (*per pavimenti*) floorcloth

strofi'nare *vt* to rub

stron'care *vt* to break off; (*fig: ribellione*) to suppress, put down; (*: film, libro*) to tear to pieces

stropicci'are [stropit'tʃare] *vt* to rub

stroz'zare [strot'tsare] *vt* (*soffocare*) to choke, strangle; **~rsi** *vr* to choke; strozza'tura *sf* (*restringimento*) narrowing; (*di strada etc*) bottleneck

'struggersi ['struddʒersi] *vr* (*fig*): **~ di** to be consumed with

strumen'tale *ag* (*MUS*) instrumental

strumentaliz'zare [strumentalid'dzare] *vt* to exploit, use to one's own ends

stru'mento *sm* (*arnese, fig*) instrument, tool; (*MUS*) instrument; **~ a corda o ad arco/a fiato** stringed/wind instrument

'strutto *sm* lard

strut'tura *sf* structure; struttu'rare *vt* to structure

'struzzo ['struttso] *sm* ostrich

stuc'care *vt* (*muro*) to plaster; (*vetro*) to

putty; (*decorare con stucchi*) to stucco

stuc'chevole [stuk'kevole] *ag* nauseating; (*fig*) tedious, boring

'stucco, chi *sm* plaster; (*da vetri*) putty; (*ornamentale*) stucco; **rimanere di ~** (*fig*) to be dumbfounded

stu'dente, 'essa *sm/f* student; (*scolaro*) pupil, schoolboy/girl; studen'tesco, a, schi, sche *ag* student *cpd*; school *cpd*

studi'are *vt* to study

'studio *sm* studying; (*ricerca, saggio, stanza*) study; (*di professionista*) office; (*di artista, CINEMA, TV, RADIO*) studio; **~i** *smpl* (*INS*) studies; **~ medico** doctor's surgery (*BRIT*) o office (*US*)

studi'oso, a *ag* studious, hard-working ♦ *sm/f* scholar

'stufa *sf* stove; **~ elettrica** electric fire o heater

stu'fare *vt* (*CUC*) to stew; (*fig: fam*) to bore; stu'fato *sm* (*CUC*) stew; 'stufo, a (*fam*) *ag*: **essere stufo di** to be fed up with, be sick and tired of

stu'oia *sf* mat

stupefa'cente [stupefa'tʃente] *ag* stunning, astounding ♦ *sm* drug, narcotic

stu'pendo, a *ag* marvellous, wonderful

stupi'daggine [stupi'daddʒine] *sf* stupid thing to do o say

stupidità *sf* stupidity

'stupido, a *ag* stupid

stu'pire *vt* to amaze, stun ♦ *vi* (*anche*: **~rsi**): **~ (di)** to be amazed (at), be stunned (by)

stu'pore *sm* amazement, astonishment

'stupro *sm* rape

stu'rare *vt* (*lavandino*) to clear

stuzzica'denti [stuttsika'denti] *sm* toothpick

stuzzi'care [stuttsi'kare] *vt* (*ferita etc*) to poke (at), prod (at); (*fig*) to tease; (*: appetito*) to whet; (*: curiosità*) to stimulate; **~ i denti** to pick one's teeth

---

PAROLA CHIAVE

su (*su +il* = **sul**, *su +lo* = **sullo**, *su +l'* = **sull'**, *su +la* = **sulla**, *su +i* = **sui**, *su +gli*

= **sugli, su** +**le** = **sulle**) *prep* 1 *(gen)* on; *(moto)* on(to); *(in cima a)* on (top of); **mettilo sul tavolo** put it on the table; **un paesino sul mare** a village by the sea 2 *(argomento)* about, on; **un libro ~ Cesare** a book on *o* about Caesar 3 *(circa)* about; **costerà sui 3 milioni** it will cost about 3 million; **una ragazza sui 17 anni** a girl of about 17 (years of age) 4: **~ misura** made to measure; **~ richiesta** on request; **3 casi ~ dieci** 3 cases out of 10

♦ *av* 1 *(in alto, verso l'alto)* up; **vieni ~** come on up; **guarda ~** look up; **~ le mani!** hands up!; **in ~** *(verso l'alto)* up(wards); *(in poi)* onwards; **dai 20 anni in ~** from the age of 20 onwards

2 *(addosso)* on; **cos'hai ~?** what have you got on?

♦ *escl* come on!; **~ coraggio!** come on, cheer up!

'sua *vedi* **suo**

su'bacqueo, a *ag* underwater ♦ *sm* skindiver

sub'buglio [sub'buʎʎo] *sm* confusion, turmoil

subcosci'ente [subkoʃ'ʃɛnte] *ag, sm* subconscious

'subdolo, a *ag* underhand, sneaky

suben'trare *vi*: **~ a qn in qc** to take over sth from sb

su'bire *vt* to suffer, endure

subis'sare *vt (fig)*: **~ di** to overwhelm with, load with

subi'taneo, a *ag* sudden

'subito *av* immediately, at once, straight away

subodo'rare *vt (insidia etc)* to smell, suspect

subordi'nato, a *ag* subordinate; *(dipendente)*: **~ a** dependent on, subject to

subur'bano, a *ag* suburban

suc'cedere [sut'tʃɛdere] *vi (prendere il posto di qn)*: **~ a** to succeed; *(venire dopo)*: **~ a** to follow; *(accadere)* to happen; **~rsi** *vr* to follow each other; **~ al trono** to succeed to

the throne; **successi'one** *sf* succession; **succes'sivo, a** *ag* successive; **suc'cesso, a** *pp di* **succedere** ♦ *sm* *(esito)* outcome; *(buona riuscita)* success; **di successo** *(libro, personaggio)* successful

succhi'are [suk'kjare] *vt* to suck (up); **succhi'otto** *sm (per bambino)* dummy

suc'cinto, a [sut'tʃinto] *ag (discorso)* succinct; *(abito)* brief

'succo, chi *sm* juice; *(fig)* essence, gist; **~ di frutta** fruit juice; **suc'coso, a** *ag* juicy; *(fig)* pithy

succur'sale *sf* branch (office)

sud *sm* south ♦ *ag inv* south; *(lato)* south, southern

Su'dafrica *sm*: **il ~** South Africa; **sudafri'cano, a** *ag, sm/f* South African

Suda'merica *sm*: **il ~** South America; **sudameri'cano, a** *ag, sm/f* South American

su'dare *vi* to perspire, sweat; **~ freddo** to come out in a cold sweat; **su'data** *sf* sweat; **ho fatto una bella sudata per finirlo in tempo** it was a real sweat to get it finished in time

sud'detto, a *ag* above-mentioned

sud'dito, a *sm/f* subject

suddi'videre *vt* to subdivide

su'dest *sm* south-east

'sudicio, a, ci, ce ['sudit ʃo] *ag* dirty, filthy; **sudici'ume** *sm* dirt, filth

su'dore *sm* perspiration, sweat

su'dovest *sm* south-west

'sue *vedi* **suo**

suffici'ente [suffi'tʃɛnte] *ag* enough, sufficient; *(borioso)* self-important; *(INS)* satisfactory; **suffici'enza** *sf* self-importance; pass mark; **a sufficienza** enough; **ne ho avuto a sufficienza!** I've had enough of this!

suf'fisso *sm (LING)* suffix

suf'fragio [suf'fradʒo] *sm (voto)* vote; **~ universale** universal suffrage

suggel'lare [suddʒel'lare] *vt (fig)* to seal

suggeri'mento [suddʒeri'mento] *sm* suggestion; *(consiglio)* piece of advice, advice *no pl*

sugge'rire [suddʒe'rire] *vt* (*risposta*) to tell; (*consigliare*) to advise; (*proporre*) to suggest; (TEATRO) to prompt;

suggeri'tore, 'trice *sm/f* (TEATRO) prompter

suggestio'nare [suddʒestjo'nare] *vt* to influence

suggesti'one [suddʒes'tjone] *sf* (PSIC) suggestion

sugges'tivo, a [suddʒes'tivo] *ag* (*paesaggio*) evocative; (*teoria*) interesting, attractive

'sughero ['sugero] *sm* cork

'sugli ['suʎʎi] *prep +det vedi* **su**

'sugo, ghi *sm* (*succo*) juice; (*di carne*) gravy; (*condimento*) sauce; (*fig*) gist, essence

'sui *prep +det vedi* **su**

sui'cida, i, e [sui'tʃida] *ag* suicidal ♦ *sm/f* suicide

suici'darsi [suitʃi'darsi] *vr* to commit suicide

sui'cidio [sui'tʃidjo] *sm* suicide

su'ino, a *ag*: **carne ~a** pork ♦ *sm* pig; **~i** *smpl* swine *pl*

sul *prep + det vedi* **su**

sull' *prep + det vedi* **su**

'sulla *prep + det vedi* **su**

'sulle *prep + det vedi* **su**

'sullo *prep + det vedi* **su**

sulta'nina *ag f*: (**uva**) **~** sultana

sul'tano *sm/f* sultan/sultana

'sunto *sm* summary

'suo (*f* **'sua**, *pl* **'sue, su'oi**) *det*: **il ~, la sua** *etc* (*di lui*) his; (*di lei*) her; (*di esso*) its; (*con valore indefinito*) one's, his/her; (*forma di cortesia: anche*: **S~**) your ♦ *pron*: **il ~, la sua** *etc* his; hers; yours; **i suoi** his (*o* her *o* one's *o* your) family

su'ocero, a ['swotʃero] *sm/f* father/mother-in-law; **i ~i** *smpl* father-and-mother-in-law

su'oi *vedi* **suo**

su'ola *sf* (*di scarpa*) sole

su'olo *sm* (*terreno*) ground; (*terra*) soil

suo'nare *vt* (MUS) to play; (*campana*) to ring; (*ore*) to strike; (*clacson, allarme*) to

sound ♦ *vi* to play; (*telefono, campana*) to ring; (*ore*) to strike; (*clacson, fig: parole*) to sound

suone'ria *sf* alarm

su'ono *sm* sound

su'ora *sf* (REL) sister

'super *sf* (*anche*: **benzina ~**) ≈ four-star (petrol) (BRIT), premium (US)

supe'rare *vt* (*oltrepassare: limite*) to exceed, surpass; (*percorrere*) to cover; (*attraversare: fiume*) to cross; (*sorpassare: veicolo*) to overtake; (*fig: essere più bravo di*) to surpass, outdo; (*: difficoltà*) to overcome; (*: esame*) to get through; **~ qn in altezza/peso** to be taller/heavier than sb; **ha superato la cinquantina** he's over fifty (years of age)

su'perbia *sf* pride; **su'perbo, a** *ag* proud; (*fig*) magnificent, superb

superfici'ale [superfi'tʃale] *ag* superficial

super'ficie, ci [super'fitʃe] *sf* surface

su'perfluo, a *ag* superfluous

superi'ore *ag* (*piano, arto, classi*) upper; (*più elevato: temperatura, livello*): **~ (a)** higher (than); (*migliore*): **~ (a)** superior (to); **~, a** *sm/f* (*anche* REL) superior; **superiorità** *sf* superiority

superla'tivo, a *ag, sm* superlative

supermer'cato *sm* supermarket

su'perstite *ag* surviving ♦ *sm/f* survivor

superstizi'one [superstit'tsjone] *sf* superstition; **superstizi'oso, a** *ag* superstitious

super'strada *sf* ≈ (toll-free) motorway

su'pino, a *ag* supine

suppel'lettile *sf* furnishings *pl*

supper'giù [supper'dʒu] *av* more or less, roughly

supplemen'tare *ag* extra; (*treno*) relief *cpd*; (*entrate*) additional

supple'mento *sm* supplement

sup'plente *sm/f* temporary member of staff; supply (*o* substitute) teacher

'supplica, che *sf* (*preghiera*) plea; (*domanda scritta*) petition, request

suppli'care *vt* to implore, beseech

sup'plire *vi*: **~ a** to make up for,

compensate for

sup'plizio [sup'plittsjo] sm torture

sup'porre vt to suppose

sup'porto sm (sostegno) support

sup'posta sf (MED) suppository

sup'posto, a pp di supporre

su'premo, a ag supreme

surge'lare [surdʒe'lare] vt to (deep-)freeze; surge'lati smpl frozen food sg

sur'plus sm inv (ECON) surplus

surriscal'dare vt to overheat

surro'gato sm substitute

suscet'tibile [suʃʃet'tibile] ag (sensibile) touchy, sensitive

susci'tare [suʃʃi'tare] vt to provoke, arouse

su'sina sf plum; su'sino sm plum (tree)

sussegu'ire vt to follow; ~rsi vr to follow one another

sus'sidio sm subsidy

sus'sistere vi to exist; (essere fondato) to be valid o sound

sussul'tare vi to shudder

sussur'rare vt, vi to whisper, murmur; sus'surro sm whisper, murmur

sutu'rare vt (MED) to stitch up, suture

sva'gare vt (distrarre) to distract; (divertire) to amuse; ~rsi vr to amuse o.s.; to enjoy o.s.

'svago, ghi sm (riposo) relaxation; (ricreazione) amusement; (passatempo) pastime

svaligi'are [zvali'dʒare] vt to rob, burgle (BRIT), burglarize (US)

svalu'tare vt (ECON) to devalue; (fig) to belittle; ~rsi vr (ECON) to be devalued; svalutazi'one sf devaluation

sva'nire vi to disappear, vanish

svan'taggio [zvan'taddʒo] sm disadvantage; (inconveniente) drawback, disadvantage

svapo'rare vi to evaporate

svari'ato, a ag varied; various

'svastica sf swastika

sve'dese ag Swedish ♦ sm/f Swede ♦ sm (LING) Swedish

'sveglia ['zveʎʎa] sf waking up; (orologio) alarm (clock); ~ telefonica alarm call

svegli'are [zveʎ'ʎare] vt to wake up; (fig) to awaken, arouse; ~rsi vr to wake up; (fig) to be revived, reawaken

'sveglio, a ['zveʎʎo] ag awake; (fig) quick-witted

sve'lare vt to reveal

'svelto, a ag (passo) quick; (mente) quick, alert; alla ~a quickly

'svendita sf (COMM) (clearance) sale

sveni'mento sm fainting fit, faint

sve'nire vi to faint

sven'tare vt to foil, thwart

sven'tato, a ag (distratto) scatterbrained; (imprudente) rash

svento'lare vt, vi to wave, flutter

sven'trare vt to disembowel

sven'tura sf misfortune; sventu'rato, a ag unlucky, unfortunate

sve'nuto, a pp di svenire

svergo'gnato, a [zvergoɲ'ɲato] ag shameless

sver'nare vi to spend the winter

sves'tire vt to undress; ~rsi vr to get undressed

'Svezia ['zvettsja] sf: la ~ Sweden

svez'zare [zvet'tsare] vt to wean

svi'are vt to divert; (fig) to lead astray; ~rsi vr to go astray

svi'gnarsela [zviɲ'ɲarsela] vr to slip away, sneak off

svilup'pare vt to develop; ~rsi vr to develop

svi'luppo sm development

'svincolo sm (stradale) motorway (BRIT) o expressway (US) intersection

svisce'rare [zviʃʃe'rare] vt (fig: argomento) to examine in depth; svisce'rato, a ag (amore) passionate; (lodi) obsequious

'svista sf oversight

svi'tare vt to unscrew

'Svizzera ['zvittsera] sf: la ~ Switzerland

'svizzero, a ['zvittsero] ag, sm/f Swiss

svogli'ato, a [zvoʎ'ʎato] ag listless; (pigro) lazy

svolaz'zare [zvolat'tsare] vi to flutter

'svolgere ['zvoldʒere] vt to unwind; (srotolare) to unroll; (fig: argomento) to

develop; (: *piano, programma*) to carry out;
~**rsi** *vr* to unwind; to unroll; (*fig: aver
luogo*) to take place; (: *procedere*) to go on;
svolgi'mento *sm* development; carrying
out; (*andamento*) course
'**svolta** *sf* (*atto*) turning *no pl*; (*curva*) turn,
bend; (*fig*) turning-point
svol'tare *vi* to turn
'**svolto, a** *pp di* **svolgere**
svuo'tare *vt* to empty (out)

T, t

tabac'caio, a *sm/f* tobacconist
tabacche'ria [tabakke'ria] *sf* tobacconist's
(shop)
ta'bacco, chi *sm* tobacco
ta'bella *sf* (*tavola*) table; (*elenco*) list
tabel'lone *sm* (*pubblicitario*) billboard; (*con
orario*) timetable board
taber'nacolo *sm* tabernacle
tabu'lato *sm* (INFORM) printout
'**tacca, che** *sf* notch, nick
tac'cagno, a [tak'kaɲɲo] *ag* mean, stingy
tac'chino [tak'kino] *sm* turkey
tacci'are [tat'tʃare] *vt*: ~ **qn di** to accuse sb
of
'**tacco, chi** *sm* heel; ~**chi a spillo** stiletto
heels
taccu'ino *sm* notebook
ta'cere [ta'tʃere] *vi* to be silent *o* quiet;
(*smettere di parlare*) to fall silent ♦ *vt* to
keep to oneself, say nothing about; **far ~
qn** to make sb be quiet; (*fig*) to silence sb
ta'chimetro [ta'kimetro] *sm* speedometer
'**tacito, a** ['tatʃito] *ag* silent; (*sottinteso*)
tacit, unspoken
ta'fano *sm* horsefly
taffe'ruglio [taffe'ruʎʎo] *sm* brawl, scuffle
taffettà *sm* taffeta
'**taglia** ['taʎʎa] *sf* (*statura*) height; (*misura*)
size; (*riscatto*) ransom; (*ricompensa*) reward;
~ **forte** (*di abito*) large size
taglia'carte [taʎʎa'karte] *sm inv* paperknife
tagli'ando [taʎ'ʎando] *sm* coupon
tagli'are [taʎ'ʎare] *vt* to cut; (*recidere*,

interrompere) to cut off; (*intersecare*) to cut
across, intersect; (*carne*) to carve; (*vini*) to
blend ♦ *vi* to cut; (*prendere una scorciatoia*)
to take a short-cut; ~ **corto** (*fig*) to cut
short
taglia'telle [taʎʎa'tɛlle] *sfpl* tagliatelle *pl*
taglia'unghie [taʎʎa'ungje] *sm inv* nail
clippers *pl*
tagli'ente [taʎ'ʎɛnte] *ag* sharp
'**taglio** ['taʎʎo] *sm* cutting *no pl*; cut; (*parte
tagliente*) cutting edge; (*di abito*) cut, style;
(*di stoffa: lunghezza*) length; (*di vini*)
blending; **di ~** on edge, edgeways;
banconote di piccolo/grosso ~ notes of
small/large denomination
tagli'ola [taʎ'ʎola] *sf* trap, snare
tail'leur [ta'jœr] *sm inv* suit (*for women*)
'**talco** *sm* talcum powder

PAROLA CHIAVE

'**tale** *det* **1** (*simile, così grande*) such; **un(a) ~
...** such (a) ...; **non accetto ~i discorsi** I
won't allow such talk; **è di una ~
arroganza** he is so arrogant; **fa una ~
confusione!** he makes such a mess!
2 (*persona o cosa indeterminata*) such-and-
such; **il giorno ~ all'ora ~** on such-and-
such a day at such-and-such a time; **la tal
persona** that person; **ha telefonato una ~
Giovanna** somebody called Giovanna
phoned
3 (*nelle similitudini*): ~ **...** ~ like ... like; ~
padre ~ figlio like father, like son; **hai il
vestito ~ quale il mio** your dress is just *o*
exactly like mine
♦ *pron* (*indefinito: persona*): **un(a) ~**
someone; **quel** (*o* **quella**) ~ that person,
that man (*o* woman); **il tal dei ~i** what's-
his-name

---

ta'lento *sm* talent
talis'mano *sm* talisman
tallon'cino [tallon'tʃino] *sm* counterfoil
tal'lone *sm* heel
tal'mente *av* so
ta'lora *av* = **talvolta**
'**talpa** *sf* (ZOOL) mole

tal'volta *av* sometimes, at times

tambu'rello *sm* tambourine

tam'buro *sm* drum

Ta'migi [ta'midʒi] *sm*: **il ~** the Thames

tampona'mento *sm* (AUT) collision; **~ a catena** pile-up

tampo'nare *vt* (otturare) to plug; (urtare: macchina) to crash *o* ram into

tam'pone *sm* (MED) wad, pad; (per timbri) ink-pad; (respingente) buffer; **~ assorbente** tampon

'tana *sf* lair, den

'tanfo *sm* stench; musty smell

tan'gente [tan'dʒɛnte] *ag* (MAT): **~ a** tangential to ♦ *sf* tangent; (quota) share

---
Tangentopoli

ⓘ **Tangentopoli** *describes the corruption scandal involving a large number of politicians, industrialists and businessmen. Investigations exposed a complex system of bribes, some paid from public funds, to gain benefits for private individuals and political parties. The scandal began in Milan which was subsequently called Tangentopoli or "Bribesville".*

---

tangenzi'ale [tandʒen'tsjale] *sf* (AUT) bypass

'tanica *sf* (contenitore) jerry can

tan'tino: **un ~** *av* a little, a bit

PAROLA CHIAVE

'tanto, a *det* **1** (molto: quantità) a lot of, much; (: numero) a lot of, many; (così ~: quantità) so much, such a lot of; (: numero) so many, such a lot of; **~e volte** so many times, so often; **~i auguri!** all the best!; **~e grazie** many thanks; **~ tempo** so long, such a long time; **ogni ~i chilometri** every so many kilometres

2: ~ ... quanto (quantità) as much ... as; (numero) as many ... as; **ho ~a pazienza quanta ne hai tu** I have as much patience as you have *o* as you; **ha ~i amici quanti nemici** he has as many friends as he has enemies

3 (rafforzativo) such; **ho aspettato per ~ tempo** I waited so long *o* for such a long time

♦ *pron* **1** (molto) much, a lot; (così ~) so much, such a lot; **~i, e** many, a lot; so many, such a lot; **credevo ce ne fosse ~** I thought there was (such) a lot, I thought there was plenty

2: ~ quanto (denaro) as much as; (cioccolatini) as many as; **ne ho ~ quanto basta** I have as much as I need; **due volte ~** twice as much

3 (indeterminato) so much; **~ per l'affitto, ~ per il gas** so much for the rent, so much for the gas; **costa un ~ al metro** it costs so much per metre; **di ~ in ~, ogni ~** every so often; **~ vale che ...** I (*o* we *etc*) may as well ...; **~ meglio!** so much the better!; **~ peggio per lui!** so much the worse for him!

♦ *av* **1** (molto) very; **vengo ~ volentieri** I'd be very glad to come; **non ci vuole ~ a capirlo** it doesn't take much to understand it

2 (così ~: con ag, av) so; (: con vb) so much, such a lot; **è ~ bella!** she's so beautiful!; **non urlare ~** don't shout so much; **sto ~ meglio adesso** I'm so much better now; **~ ... che** so ... (that); **~ ... da** so ... as

3: ~ ... quanto as ... as; **conosco ~ Carlo quanto suo padre** I know both Carlo and his father; **non è poi ~ complicato quanto sembri** it's not as difficult as it seems; **~ più insisti, ~ più non mollerà** the more you insist, the more stubborn he'll be; **quanto più ... ~ meno** the more ... the less

4 (solamente) just; **~ per cambiare/ scherzare** just for a change/a joke; **una volta ~** for once

5 (a lungo) (for) long

♦ *cong* after all

'tappa *sf* (luogo di sosta, fermata) stop, halt; (parte di un percorso) stage, leg; (SPORT) lap; **a ~e** in stages

tap'pare *vt* to plug, stop up; (*bottiglia*) to cork

tap'peto *sm* carpet; (*anche*: **tappettino**) rug; (*SPORT*): **andare al ~** to go down for the count; **mettere sul ~** (*fig*) to bring up for discussion

tappez'zare [tappet'tsare] *vt* (*con carta*) to paper; (*rivestire*): **~ qc (di)** to cover sth (with); **tappezze'ria** *sf* (*tessuto*) tapestry; (*carta da parati*) wallpaper; (*arte*) upholstery; **far da tappezzeria** (*fig*) to be a wallflower; **tappezzi'ere** *sm* upholsterer

'tappo *sm* stopper; (*in sughero*) cork

tarchi'ato, a [tar'kjato] *ag* stocky, thickset

tar'dare *vi* to be late ♦ *vt* to delay; **~ a fare** to delay doing

'tardi *av* late; **più ~** later (on); **al più ~** at the latest; **sul ~** (*verso sera*) late in the day; **far ~** to be late; (*restare alzato*) to stay up late

tar'divo, a *ag* (*primavera*) late; (*rimedio*) belated, tardy; (*fig*) retarded

'tardo, a *ag* (*lento, fig: ottuso*) slow; (*tempo: avanzato*) late

'targa, ghe *sf* plate; (*AUT*) number (*BRIT*) *o* license (*US*) plate; **tar'ghetta** *sf* (*su bagaglio*) name tag; (*su porta*) nameplate

ta'riffa *sf* (*gen*) rate, tariff; (*di trasporti*) fare; (*elenco*) price list; tariff

'tarlo *sm* woodworm

'tarma *sf* moth

ta'rocco, chi *sm* tarot card; **~chi** *smpl* (*gioco*) tarot *sg*

tartagli'are [tartaʎ'ʎare] *vi* to stutter, stammer

'tartaro, a *ag, sm* (*in tutti i sensi*) tartar

tarta'ruga, ghe *sf* tortoise; (*di mare*) turtle; (*materiale*) tortoiseshell

tar'tina *sf* canapé

tar'tufo *sm* (*BOT*) truffle

'tasca, sche *sf* pocket; **tas'cabile** *ag* (*libro*) pocket *cpd*; **tasca'pane** *sm* haversack; **tas'chino** *sm* breast pocket

'tassa *sf* (*imposta*) tax; (*doganale*) duty; (*per iscrizione: a scuola etc*) fee; **~ di circolazione/di soggiorno** road/tourist tax

tas'sametro *sm* taximeter

tas'sare *vt* to tax; to levy a duty on

tassa'tivo, a *ag* peremptory

tassazi'one [tassat'tsjone] *sf* taxation

tas'sello *sm* plug; wedge

tassì *sm inv* = **taxi**; **tas'sista, i, e** *sm/f* taxi driver

'tasso *sm* (*di natalità, d'interesse etc*) rate; (*BOT*) yew; (*ZOOL*) badger; **~ di cambio/ d'interesse** rate of exchange/interest

tas'tare *vt* to feel; **~ il terreno** (*fig*) to see how the land lies

tasti'era *sf* keyboard

'tasto *sm* key; (*tatto*) touch, feel

tas'toni *av*: **procedere (a) ~** to grope one's way forward

'tattica *sf* tactics *pl*

'tattico, a, ci, che *ag* tactical

'tatto *sm* (*senso*) touch; (*fig*) tact; **duro al ~** hard to the touch; **aver ~** to be tactful, have tact

tatu'aggio [tatu'addʒo] *sm* tattooing; (*disegno*) tattoo

tatu'are *vt* to tattoo

'tavola *sf* table; (*asse*) plank, board; (*lastra*) tablet; (*quadro*) panel (painting); (*illustrazione*) plate; **~ calda** snack bar; **~ a vela** windsurfer

tavo'lato *sm* boarding; (*pavimento*) wooden floor

tavo'letta *sf* tablet, bar; **a ~** (*AUT*) flat out

tavo'lino *sm* small table; (*scrivania*) desk

'tavolo *sm* table

tavo'lozza [tavo'lɔttsa] *sf* (*ARTE*) palette

'taxi *sm inv* taxi

'tazza ['tattsa] *sf* cup; **~ da caffè/tè** coffee/ tea cup; **una ~ di caffè/tè** a cup of coffee/tea

te *pron* (*soggetto: in forme comparative, oggetto*) you

tè *sm inv* tea; (*trattenimento*) tea party

tea'trale *ag* theatrical

te'atro *sm* theatre

'tecnica, che *sf* technique; (*tecnologia*) technology

'tecnico, a, ci, che *ag* technical ♦ *sm/f* technician

tecnolo'gia [teknolo'dʒia] *sf* technology

te'desco, a, schi, sche *ag, sm/f, sm* German

'tedio *sm* tedium, boredom

te'game *sm* (*CUC*) pan

'teglia ['teʎʎa] *sf* (*per dolci*) (baking) tin; (*per arrosti*) roasting) tin

'tegola *sf* tile

tei'era *sf* teapot

'tela *sf* (*tessuto*) cloth; (*per vele, quadri*) canvas; (*dipinto*) canvas, painting; **di ~** (*calzoni*) (heavy) cotton *cpd*; (*scarpe, borsa*) canvas *cpd*; **~ cerata** oilcloth

te'laio *sm* (*apparecchio*) loom; (*struttura*) frame

tele'camera *sf* television camera

teleco'mando *sm* remote control

telecopia'trice *sf* fax (machine)

tele'cronaca *sf* television report

tele'ferica, che *sf* cableway

telefo'nare *vi* to telephone, ring; to make a phone call ♦ *vt* to telephone; **~ a** to phone up, ring up, call up

telefo'nata *sf* (telephone) call; **~ a carico del destinatario** reverse-charge (*BRIT*) o collect (*US*) call

tele'fonico, a, ci, che *ag* (tele)phone *cpd*

telefon'ino *sm* mobile phone

telefo'nista, i, e *sm/f* telephonist; (*d'impresa*) switchboard operator

te'lefono *sm* telephone; **~ a gettoni** ≈ pay phone

telegior'nale [teledʒor'nale] *sm* television news (programme)

te'legrafo *sm* telegraph

tele'gramma, i *sm* telegram

telela'voro *sm* teleworking

tele'matica *sf* data transmission; telematics *sg*

teleobiet'tivo *sm* telephoto lens *sg*

telepa'tia *sf* telepathy

teles'copio *sm* telescope

teleselezi'one [teleselet'tsjone] *sf* direct dialling

telespetta'tore, 'trice *sm/f* (television) viewer

televisi'one *sf* television

televi'sore *sm* television set

'telex *sm inv* telex

'telo *sm* cloth; **~ da bagno** bath towel; **~ da spiaggia** beach towel

'tema, i *sm* theme; (*INS*) essay, composition

teme'rario, a *ag* rash, reckless

te'mere *vt* to fear, be afraid of; (*essere sensibile a: freddo, calore*) to be sensitive to ♦ *vi* to be afraid; (*essere preoccupato*): **~ per** to worry about, fear for; **~ di/che** to be afraid of/that

temperama'tite *sm inv* pencil sharpener

tempera'mento *sm* temperament

tempe'rato, a *ag* moderate, temperate

tempera'tura *sf* temperature

tempe'rino *sm* penknife

tem'pesta *sf* storm; **~ di sabbia/neve** sand/snowstorm

tempes'tare *vt*: **~ qn di domande** to bombard sb with questions; **~ qn di colpi** to rain blows on sb

tempes'tivo, a *ag* timely

tempes'toso, a *ag* stormy

'tempia *sf* (*ANAT*) temple

'tempio *sm* (*edificio*) temple

'tempo *sm* (*METEOR*) weather; (*cronologico*) time; (*epoca*) time, times *pl*; (*di film, gioco: parte*) part; (*MUS*) time; (: *battuta*) beat; (*LING*) tense; **un ~** once; **~ fa** some time ago; **al ~ stesso** o **a un ~** at the same time; **per ~** early; **ha fatto il suo ~** it has had its day; **~ libero** free time; **primo/secondo ~** (*TEATRO*) first/second part; (*SPORT*) first/second half; **in ~ utile** in due time o course; **a ~ pieno** full-time

tempo'rale *ag* temporal ♦ *sm* (*METEOR*) (thunder)storm

tempo'raneo, a *ag* temporary

temporeggi'are [tempored'dʒare] *vi* to play for time, temporize

tem'prare *vt* to temper

te'nace [te'natʃe] *ag* strong, tough; (*fig*) tenacious; **te'nacia** *sf* tenacity

te'naglie [te'naʎʎe] *sfpl* pincers *pl*

'tenda *sf* (*riparo*) awning; (*di finestra*) curtain; (*per campeggio etc*) tent

ten'denza [ten'dɛntsa] *sf* tendency; (*orientamento*) trend; **avere ~ a** *o* **per qc** to have a bent for sth

'tendere *vt* (*allungare al massimo*) to stretch, draw tight; (*porgere: mano*) to hold out; (*fig: trappola*) to lay, set ♦ *vi*: **~ a qc/a fare** to tend towards sth/to do; **~ l'orecchio** to prick up one's ears; **il tempo tende al caldo** the weather is getting hot; **un blu che tende al verde** a greenish blue

ten'dina *sf* curtain

'tendine *sm* tendon, sinew

ten'done *sm* (*da circo*) tent

'tenebre *sfpl* darkness *sg*; **tene'broso, a** *ag* dark, gloomy

te'nente *sm* lieutenant

te'nere *vt* to hold; (*conservare, mantenere*) to keep; (*ritenere, considerare*) to consider; (*spazio: occupare*) to take up, occupy; (*seguire: strada*) to keep to ♦ *vi* to hold; (*colori*) to be fast; (*dare importanza*): **~ a** to care about; **~ a fare** to want to do, be keen to do; **~rsi** *vr* (*stare in una determinata posizione*) to stand; (*stimarsi*) to consider o.s.; (*aggrapparsi*): **~rsi a** to hold on to; (*attenersi*): **~rsi a** to stick to; **~ una conferenza** to give a lecture; **~ conto di qc** to take sth into consideration; **~ presente qc** to bear sth in mind

'tenero, a *ag* tender; (*pietra, cera, colore*) soft; (*fig*) tender, loving

'tenia *sf* tapeworm

'tennis *sm* tennis

te'nore *sm* (*tono*) tone; (*MUS*) tenor; **~ di vita** (*livello*) standard of living

tensi'one *sf* tension

ten'tare *vt* (*indurre*) to tempt; (*provare*): **~ qc/di fare** to attempt *o* try sth/to do; **tenta'tivo** *sm* attempt; **tentazi'one** *sf* temptation

tenten'nare *vi* to shake, be unsteady; (*fig*) to hesitate, waver

ten'toni *av*: **andare a ~** (*anche fig*) to grope one's way

'tenue *ag* (*sottile*) fine; (*colore*) soft; (*fig*) slender, slight

te'nuta *sf* (*capacità*) capacity; (*divisa*) uniform; (*abito*) dress; (*AGR*) estate; **a ~ d'aria** airtight; **~ di strada** roadholding power

teolo'gia [teolo'dʒia] *sf* theology; **te'ologo, gi** *sm* theologian

teo'rema, i *sm* theorem

teo'ria *sf* theory; **te'orico, a, ci, che** *ag* theoretic(al)

te'pore *sm* warmth

'teppa *sf* mob, hooligans *pl*; **tep'pismo** *sm* hooliganism; **tep'pista, i** *sm* hooligan

tera'pia *sf* therapy

tergicris'tallo [terdʒikris'tallo] *sm* windscreen (*BRIT*) *o* windshield (*US*) wiper

tergiver'sare [terdʒiver'sare] *vi* to shilly-shally

'tergo *sm*: **a ~** behind; **vedi a ~** please turn over

ter'male *ag* thermal; **stazione** *sf* **~** spa

'terme *sfpl* thermal baths

'termico, a, ci, che *ag* thermic; (*unità*) thermal

termi'nale *ag*, *sm* terminal

termi'nare *vt* to end; (*lavoro*) to finish ♦ *vi* to end

'termine *sm* term; (*fine, estremità*) end; (*di territorio*) boundary, limit; **contratto a ~** (*COMM*) forward contract; **a breve/lungo ~** short-/long-term; **parlare senza mezzi ~i** to talk frankly, not to mince one's words

ter'mometro *sm* thermometer

termonucle'are *ag* thermonuclear

termosi'fone *sm* radiator

ter'mostato *sm* thermostat

'terra *sf* (*gen, ELETTR*) earth; (*sostanza*) soil, earth; (*opposto al mare*) land *no pl*; (*regione, paese*) land; (*argilla*) clay; **~e** *sfpl* (*possedimento*) lands, land *sg*; **a** *o* **per ~** (*stato*) on the ground (*o* floor); (*moto*) to the ground, down; **mettere a ~** (*ELETTR*) to earth

terra'cotta *sf* terracotta; **vasellame** *sm* **di ~** earthenware

terra'ferma *sf* dry land, terra firma; (*continente*) mainland

terrapi'eno *sm* embankment, bank

ter'razza [ter'rattsa] *sf* terrace

ter'razzo [ter'rattso] *sm* = **terrazza**

terre'moto *sm* earthquake

ter'reno, a *ag* (*vita, beni*) earthly ♦ *sm* (*suolo, fig*) ground; (*COMM*) land *no pl*, plot (of land); site; (*SPORT, MIL*) field

ter'restre *ag* (*superficie*) of the earth, earth's; (*di terra: battaglia, animale*) land *cpd*; (*REL*) earthly, worldly

ter'ribile *ag* terrible, dreadful

terrifi'cante *ag* terrifying

ter'rina *sf* tureen

territori'ale *ag* territorial

terri'torio *sm* territory

ter'rore *sm* terror; terro'rismo *sm* terrorism; terro'rista, i, e *sm/f* terrorist

'terso, a *ag* clear

'terzo, a ['tɛrtso] *ag* third ♦ *sm* (*frazione*) third; (*DIR*) third party; **la ~a pagina** (*STAMPA*) the Arts page

'tesa *sf* brim

'teschio ['teskjo] *sm* skull

'tesi *sf* thesis

'teso, a *pp di* tendere ♦ *ag* (*tirato*) taut, tight; (*fig*) tense

tesore'ria *sf* treasury

tesori'ere *sm* treasurer

te'soro *sm* treasure; **il Ministero del T~** the Treasury

'tessera *sf* (*documento*) card

'tessere *vt* to weave; 'tessile *ag, sm* textile; tessi'tore, 'trice *sm/f* weaver; tessi'tura *sf* weaving

tes'suto *sm* fabric, material; (*BIOL*) tissue

'testa *sf* head; (*di cose: estremità, parte anteriore*) head, front; **di ~** (*vettura etc*) front; **tenere ~ a qn** (*nemico etc*) to stand up to sb; **fare di ~ propria** to go one's own way; **in ~** (*SPORT*) in the lead; **~ o croce?** heads or tails?; **avere la ~ dura** to be stubborn; **~ di serie** (*TENNIS*) seed, seeded player

testa'mento *sm* (*atto*) will; **l'Antico/il Nuovo T~** (*REL*) the Old/New Testament

tes'tardo, a *ag* stubborn, pig-headed

tes'tata *sf* (*parte anteriore*) head; (*intestazione*) heading

'teste *sm/f* witness

tes'ticolo *sm* testicle

testi'mone *sm/f* (*DIR*) witness

testimoni'anza [testimo'njantsa] *sf* testimony

testimoni'are *vt* to testify; (*fig*) to bear witness to, testify to ♦ *vi* to give evidence, testify

tes'tina *sf* (*TECN*) head

'testo *sm* text; **fare ~** (*opera, autore*) to be authoritative; **questo libro non fa ~** this book is not essential reading; testu'ale *ag* textual; literal, word for word

tes'tuggine [tes'tuddʒine] *sf* tortoise; (*di mare*) turtle

'tetano *sm* (*MED*) tetanus

'tetro, a *ag* gloomy

'tetto *sm* roof; tet'toia *sf* roofing; canopy

'Tevere *sm*: **il ~** the Tiber

Tg *abbr* = **telegiornale**

'thermos ® ['tɛrmos] *sm inv* vacuum *o* Thermos ® flask

ti *pron* (*dav lo, la, li, le, ne diventa* te) *pron* (*oggetto*) you; (*complemento di termine*) (to) you; (*riflessivo*) yourself

'tibia *sf* tibia, shinbone

tic *sm inv* tic, (*nervous*) twitch; (*fig*) mannerism

ticchet'tio [tikket'tio] *sm* (*di macchina da scrivere*) clatter; (*di orologio*) ticking; (*della pioggia*) patter

'ticchio ['tikkjo] *sm* (*ghiribizzo*) whim; (*tic*) tic, (*nervous*) twitch

'ticket *sm inv* (*su farmaci*) prescription charge

ti'epido, a *ag* lukewarm, tepid

ti'fare *vi*: **~ per** to be a fan of; (*parteggiare*) to side with

'tifo *sm* (*MED*) typhus; (*fig*): **fare il ~ per** to be a fan of

tifoi'dea *sf* typhoid

ti'fone *sm* typhoon

ti'foso, a *sm/f* (*SPORT etc*) fan

'tiglio ['tiʎʎo] *sm* lime (tree), linden (tree)

'tigre *sf* tiger

tim'ballo *sm* (*strumento*) kettledrum; (*CUC*) timbale

'timbro *sm* stamp; (*MUS*) timbre, tone

'timido, a *ag* shy; timid

'timo *sm* thyme

ti'mone *sm* (*NAUT*) rudder; timoni'ere *sm* helmsman

ti'more *sm* (*paura*) fear; (*rispetto*) awe; timo'roso, a *ag* timid, timorous

'timpano *sm* (*ANAT*) eardrum; (*MUS*): ~i *smpl* kettledrums, timpani

ti'nello *sm* small dining room

'tingere ['tindʒere] *vt* to dye

'tino *sm* vat

ti'nozza [ti'nɔttsa] *sf* tub

'tinta *sf* (*materia colorante*) dye; (*colore*) colour, shade; tinta'rella (*fam*) *sf* (sun)tan

tintin'nare *vi* to tinkle

'tinto, a *pp di* tingere

tinto'ria *sf* (*lavasecco*) dry cleaner's (shop)

tin'tura *sf* (*operazione*) dyeing; (*colorante*) dye; ~ di iodio tincture of iodine

'tipico, a, ci, che *ag* typical

'tipo *sm* type; (*genere*) kind, type; (*fam*) chap, fellow

tipogra'fia *sf* typography; (*procedimento*) letterpress (printing); (*officina*) printing house; tipo'grafico, a, ci, che *ag* typographic(al); letterpress *cpd*; ti'pografo *sm* typographer

ti'ranno, a *ag* tyrannical ♦ *sm* tyrant

ti'rante *sm* (*per tenda*) guy

ti'rare *vt* (*gen*) to pull; (*estrarre*): ~ qc da to take *o* pull sth out of; to get sth out of; to extract sth from; (*chiudere: tenda etc*) to draw, pull; (*tracciare, disegnare*) to draw, trace; (*lanciare: sasso, palla*) to throw; (*stampare*) to print; (*pistola, freccia*) to fire ♦ *vi* (*pipa, camino*) to draw; (*vento*) to blow; (*abito*) to be tight; (*fare fuoco*) to fire; (*fare del tiro, CALCIO*) to shoot; ~ avanti *vi* to struggle on ♦ *vt* to keep going; ~ fuori (*estrarre*) to take out, pull out; ~ giù (*abbassare*) to bring down; ~ su to pull up; (*capelli*) to put up; (*fig: bambino*) to bring up; ~rsi indietro to move back

tira'tore *sm* gunman; un buon ~ a good shot; ~ scelto marksman

tira'tura *sf* (*azione*) printing; (*di libro*) (print) run; (*di giornale*) circulation

'tirchio, a ['tirkjo] *ag* mean, stingy

'tiro *sm* shooting *no pl*, firing *no pl*; (*colpo, sparo*) shot; (*di palla: lancio*) throwing *no pl*; throw; (*fig*) trick; cavallo da ~ draught (*BRIT*) *o* draft (*US*) horse; ~ a segno target shooting; (*luogo*) shooting range

tiro'cinio [tiro'tʃinjo] *sm* apprenticeship; (*professionale*) training

ti'roide *sf* thyroid (gland)

Tir'reno *sm*: il (mar) ~ the Tyrrhenian Sea

ti'sana *sf* herb tea

tito'lare *sm/f* incumbent; (*proprietario*) owner; (*CALCIO*) regular player

'titolo *sm* title; (*di giornale*) headline; (*diploma*) qualification; (*COMM*) security; (*: azione*) share; a che ~? for what reason?; a ~ di amicizia out of friendship; a ~ di premio as a prize; ~ di credito share

titu'bante *ag* hesitant, irresolute

'tizio, a ['tittsjo] *sm/f* fellow, chap

tiz'zone [tit'tsone] *sm* brand

toast [toust] *sm inv* toasted sandwich (*generally with ham and cheese*)

toc'cante *ag* touching

toc'care *vt* to touch; (*tastare*) to feel; (*fig: riguardare*) to concern; (*: commuovere*) to touch, move; (*: pungere*) to hurt, wound; (*: far cenno a: argomento*) to touch on, mention ♦ *vi*: ~ a (*accadere*) to happen to; (*spettare*) to be up to; ~ (il fondo) (*in acqua*) to touch the bottom; tocca a te difenderci it's up to you to defend us; a chi tocca? whose turn is it?; mi toccò pagare I had to pay

'tocco, chi *sm* touch; (*ARTE*) stroke, touch

'toga, ghe *sf* toga; (*di magistrato, professore*) gown

'togliere ['tɔʎʎere] *vt* (*rimuovere*) to take away (*o* off), remove; (*riprendere, non concedere più*) to take away, remove; (*MAT*) to take away, subtract; ~ qc a qn to take sth (away) from sb; ciò non toglie che nevertheless, be that as it may; ~rsi il cappello to take off one's hat

toi'lette [twa'lɛt] *sf inv* toilet; (*mobile*) dressing table

to'letta *sf* = toilette

tolle'ranza [tolle'rantsa] sf tolerance

tolle'rare vt to tolerate

'tolto, a pp di togliere

to'maia sf (di scarpa) upper

'tomba sf tomb

tom'bino sm manhole cover

'tombola sf (gioco) tombola; (ruzzolone) tumble

'tomo sm volume

'tonaca, che sf (REL) habit

'tondo, a ag round

'tonfo sm splash; (rumore sordo) thud; (caduta): fare un ~ to take a tumble

'tonico, a, ci, che ag, sm tonic

tonifi'care vt (muscoli, pelle) to tone up; (irrobustire) to invigorate, brace

tonnel'laggio [tonnel'laddʒo] sm (NAUT) tonnage

tonnel'lata sf ton

'tonno sm tuna (fish)

'tono sm (gen) tone; (MUS: di pezzo) key; (di colore) shade, tone

ton'silla sf tonsil; tonsil'lite sf tonsillitis

'tonto, a ag dull, stupid

to'pazio [to'pattsjo] sm topaz

'topo sm mouse

topogra'fia sf topography

'toppa sf (serratura) keyhole; (pezza) patch

to'race [to'ratʃe] sm chest

'torba sf peat

'torbido, a ag (liquido) cloudy; (: fiume) muddy; (fig) dark; troubled ♦ sm: pescare nel ~ (fig) to fish in troubled water

'torcere ['tɔrtʃere] vt to twist; ~rsi vr to twist, writhe

torchi'are [tor'kjare] vt to press; 'torchio sm press

'torcia, ce ['tɔrtʃa] sf torch; ~ elettrica torch (BRIT), flashlight (US)

torci'collo [tortʃi'kɔllo] sm stiff neck

'tordo sm thrush

To'rino sf Turin

tor'menta sf snowstorm

tormen'tare vt to torment; ~rsi vr to fret, worry o.s.; tor'mento sm torment

torna'conto sm advantage, benefit

tor'nado sm tornado

tor'nante sm hairpin bend

tor'nare vi to return, go (o come) back; (ridiventare: anche fig) to become (again); (riuscire giusto, esatto: conto) to work out; (risultare) to turn out (to be), prove (to be); ~ utile to prove o turn out (to be) useful; ~ a casa to go (o come) home

torna'sole sm inv litmus

tor'neo sm tournament

'tornio sm lathe

'toro sm bull; (dello zodiaco): T~ Taurus

tor'pedine sf torpedo; torpedini'era sf torpedo boat

'torre sf tower; (SCACCHI) rook, castle; ~ di controllo (AER) control tower

torrefazi'one [torrefat'tsjone] sf roasting

tor'rente sm torrent

tor'retta sf turret

torri'one sm keep

tor'rone sm nougat

torsi'one sf twisting; torsion

'torso sm torso, trunk; (ARTE) torso

'torsolo sm (di cavolo etc) stump; (di frutta) core

'torta sf cake

'torto, a pp di torcere ♦ ag (ritorto) twisted; (storto) twisted, crooked ♦ sm (ingiustizia) wrong; (colpa) fault; a ~ wrongly; aver ~ to be wrong

'tortora sf turtle dove

tortu'oso, a ag (strada) twisting; (fig) tortuous

tor'tura sf torture; tortu'rare vt to torture

'torvo, a ag menacing, grim

tosa'erba sm o f inv (lawn)mower

to'sare vt (pecora) to shear; (siepe) to clip

Tos'cana sf: la ~ Tuscany; tos'cano, a ag, sm/f Tuscan ♦ sm (sigaro) strong Italian cigar

'tosse sf cough

'tossico, a, ci, che ag toxic

tossicodipen'dente sm/f drug addict

tossi'comane sm/f drug addict

tos'sire vi to cough

tosta'pane sm inv toaster

tos'tare vt to toast; (caffè) to roast

'tosto, a ag: faccia ~a cheek

to'tale *ag, sm* total; totalità *sf*: **la totalità di** all of, the total amount (*o number*) of; the whole +*sg*; totaliz'zare *vt* to total; (*SPORT*: *punti*) to score

toto'calcio [toto'kaltʃo] *sm* gambling pool betting on football results, ≈ (football) pools *pl* (*BRIT*)

to'vaglia [to'vaʎʎa] *sf* tablecloth; tovagli'olo *sm* napkin

'tozzo, a ['tɔttso] *ag* squat ♦ *sm*: ~ **di pane** crust of bread

tra *prep* (*di due persone, cose*) between; (*di più persone, cose*) among(st); (*tempo: entro*) within, in; ~ **5 giorni** in 5 days' time; **sia detto ~ noi ...** between you and me ...; **litigano ~ (di) loro** they're fighting amongst themselves; ~ **breve** soon; ~ **sé e sé** (*parlare etc*) to oneself

trabal'lare *vi* to stagger, totter

traboc'care *vi* to overflow

traboc'chetto [trabok'ketto] *sm* (*fig*) trap

tracan'nare *vt* to gulp down

'traccia, ce ['trattʃa] *sf* (*segno, striscia*) trail, track; (*orma*) tracks *pl*; (*residuo, testimonianza*) trace, sign; (*abbozzo*) outline

tracci'are [trat'tʃare] *vt* to trace, mark (out); (*disegnare*) to draw; (*fig: abbozzare*) to outline; tracci'ato *sm* (*grafico*) layout, plan

tra'chea [tra'kea] *sf* windpipe, trachea

tra'colla *sf* shoulder strap; **borsa a ~** shoulder bag

tra'collo *sm* (*fig*) collapse, crash

tradi'mento *sm* betrayal; (*DIR, MIL*) treason

tra'dire *vt* to betray; (*coniuge*) to be unfaithful to; (*doveri: mancare*) to fail in; (*rivelare*) to give away, reveal; tradi'tore, 'trice *sm/f* traitor

tradizio'nale [tradittsjo'nale] *ag* traditional

tradizi'one [tradit'tsjone] *sf* tradition

tra'dotto, a *pp di* **tradurre**

tra'durre *vt* to translate; (*spiegare*) to render, convey; tradut'tore, 'trice *sm/f* translator; traduzi'one *sf* translation

trafe'lato, a *ag* out of breath

traffi'cante *sm/f* dealer; (*peg*) trafficker

traffi'care *vi* (*commerciare*): ~ **(in)** to trade (in), deal (in); (*affaccendarsi*) to busy o.s. ♦ *vt* (*peg*) to traffic in

'traffico, ci *sm* traffic; (*commercio*) trade, traffic

tra'figgere [tra'fiddʒere] *vt* to run through, stab; (*fig*) to pierce

tra'fitto, a *pp di* **trafiggere**

trafo'rare *vt* to bore, drill; tra'foro *sm* (*azione*) boring, drilling; (*galleria*) tunnel

tra'gedia [tra'dʒedja] *sf* tragedy

tra'ghetto [tra'getto] *sm* ferry(boat)

'tragico, a, ci, che ['tradʒiko] *ag* tragic

tra'gitto [tra'dʒitto] *sm* (*passaggio*) crossing; (*viaggio*) journey

tragu'ardo *sm* (*SPORT*) finishing line; (*fig*) goal, aim

traiet'toria *sf* trajectory

trai'nare *vt* to drag, haul; (*rimorchiare*) to tow; 'traino *sm* (*carro*) wagon; (*slitta*) sledge; (*carico*) load

tralasci'are [tralaʃ'ʃare] *vt* (*studi*) to neglect; (*dettagli*) to leave out, omit

'tralcio ['traltʃo] *sm* (*BOT*) shoot

tra'liccio [tra'littʃo] *sm* (*ELETTR*) pylon

tram *sm inv* tram

'trama *sf* (*filo*) weft, woof; (*fig: argomento, maneggio*) plot

traman'dare *vt* to pass on, hand down

tra'mare *vt* (*fig*) to scheme, plot

tram'busto *sm* turmoil

trames'tio *sm* bustle

tramez'zino [tramed'dzino] *sm* sandwich

tra'mezzo [tra'meddzo] *sm* (*EDIL*) partition

'tramite *prep* through

tramon'tare *vi* to set, go down; tra'monto *sm* setting; (*del sole*) sunset

tramor'tire *vi* to faint ♦ *vt* to stun

trampo'lino *sm* (*per tuffi*) springboard, diving board; (*per lo sci*) ski-jump

'trampolo *sm* stilt

tramu'tare *vt*: ~ **in** to change into, turn into

tra'nello *sm* trap

trangugi'are [trangu'dʒare] *vt* to gulp down

'tranne *prep* except (for), but (for); ~ **che**

unless

tranquil'lante *sm* (MED) tranquillizer

tranquillità *sf* calm, stillness; quietness; peace of mind

tranquilliz'zare [trankwillid'dzare] *vt* to reassure

tran'quillo, a *ag* calm, quiet; (*bambino, scolaro*) quiet; (*sereno*) with one's mind at rest; **sta'** ~ don't worry

transat'lantico, ci *sm* transatlantic liner

---

transatlantico

ⓘ The **transatlantico** *is a room in the* **Palazzo di Montecitorio.** *The* **deputati** *relax in it between parliamentary sessions and give media interviews and press conferences there.*

---

transazi'one [transat'tsjone] *sf* compromise; (DIR) settlement; (COMM) transaction, deal

tran'senna *sf* barrier

tran'sigere [tran'sidʒere] *vi* (*venire a patti*) to compromise, come to an agreement

tran'sistor *sm inv* transistor

transi'tabile *ag* passable

transi'tare *vi* to pass

transi'tivo, a *ag* transitive

'transito *sm* transit; **di** ~ (*merci*) in transit; (*stazione*) transit *cpd*; **"divieto di ~"** "no entry"

transi'torio, a *ag* transitory, transient; (*provvisorio*) provisional

'trapano *sm* (*utensile*) drill; (: MED) trepan

trapas'sare *vt* to pierce

tra'passo *sm* passage

trape'lare *vi* to leak, drip; (*fig*) to leak out

tra'pezio [tra'pettsjo] *sm* (MAT) trapezium; (*attrezzo ginnico*) trapeze

trapian'tare *vt* to transplant; **trapi'anto** *sm* transplanting; (MED) transplant

'trappola *sf* trap

tra'punta *sf* quilt

'trarre *vt* to draw, pull; (*portare*) to take; (*prendere, tirare fuori*) to take (out), draw; (*derivare*) to obtain; ~ **origine da qc** to have its origins *o* originate in sth

---

trasa'lire *vi* to start, jump

trasan'dato, a *ag* shabby

tras'bordo *sm* transfer

trasci'nare [traʃʃi'nare] *vt* to drag; **~rsi** *vr* to drag o.s. along; (*fig*) to drag on

tras'correre *vt* (*tempo*) to spend, pass ♦ *vi* to pass; **tras'corso, a** *pp di* **trascorrere**

tras'critto, a *pp di* **trascrivere**

tras'crivere *vt* to transcribe

trascu'rare *vt* to neglect; (*non considerare*) to disregard; **trascura'tezza** *sf* carelessness, negligence; **trascu'rato, a** *ag* (*casa*) neglected; (*persona*) careless, negligent

trasfe'ribile *ag* transferable; **"non ~"** (*su assegno*) "account payee only"

trasferi'mento *sm* transfer; (*trasloco*) removal, move

trasfe'rire *vt* to transfer; **~rsi** *vr* to move; **tras'ferta** *sf* transfer; (*indennità*) travelling expenses *pl*; (SPORT) away game

trasfigu'rare *vt* to transfigure

trasfor'mare *vt* to transform, change; **trasforma'tore** *sm* (ELEC) transformer

trasfusi'one *sf* (MED) transfusion

trasgre'dire *vt* to disobey, contravene

tras'lato, a *ag* metaphorical, figurative

traslo'care *vt* to move, transfer; **~rsi** *vr* to move; **tras'loco, chi** *sm* removal

tras'messo, a *pp di* **trasmettere**

tras'mettere *vt* (*passare*): ~ **qc a qn** to pass sth on to sb; (*mandare*) to send; (TECN, TEL, MED) to transmit; (TV, RADIO) to broadcast; **trasmetti'tore** *sm* transmitter; **trasmissi'one** *sf* (*gen, FISICA, TECN*) transmission; (*passaggio*) transmission, passing on; (TV, RADIO) broadcast; **trasmit'tente** *sf* transmitting *o* broadcasting station

traso'gnato, a [trason'nato] *ag* dreamy

traspa'rente *ag* transparent

traspa'rire *vi* to show (through)

traspi'rare *vi* to perspire; (*fig*) to come to light, leak out; **traspirazi'one** *sf* perspiration

traspor'tare *vt* to carry, move; (*merce*) to

transport, convey; **lasciarsi ~ (da qc)** (*fig*) to let o.s. be carried away (by sth); **tras'porto** *sm* transport

trastul'lare *vt* to amuse; **~rsi** *vr* to amuse o.s.

trasu'dare *vi* (*filtrare*) to ooze; (*sudare*) to sweat ♦ *vt* to ooze with

trasver'sale *ag* transverse, cross(-); running at right angles

trasvo'lare *vt* to fly over

'**tratta** *sf* (*ECON*) draft; (*di persone*): **la ~ delle bianche** the white slave trade

tratta'mento *sm* treatment; (*servizio*) service

trat'tare *vt* (*gen*) to treat; (*commerciare*) to deal in; (*svolgere: argomento*) to discuss, deal with; (*negoziare*) to negotiate ♦ *vi*: **~ di** to deal with; **~ con** (*persona*) to deal with; **si tratta di ...** it's about ...; **tratta'tive** *sfpl* negotiations; **trat'tato** *sm* (*testo*) treatise; (*accordo*) treaty; **trattazi'one** *sf* treatment

tratteggi'are [tratted'dʒare] *vt* (*disegnare: a tratti*) to sketch, outline; (*: col tratteggio*) to hatch

tratte'nere *vt* (*far rimanere: persona*) to detain; (*intrattenere: ospiti*) to entertain; (*tenere, frenare, reprimere*) to hold back, keep back; (*astenersi dal consegnare*) to hold, keep; (*detrarre: somma*) to deduct; **~rsi** *vr* (*astenersi*) to restrain o.s., stop o.s.; (*soffermarsi*) to stay, remain **tratteni'mento** *sm* entertainment; (*festa*) party

tratte'nuta *sf* deduction

trat'tino *sm* dash; (*in parole composte*) hyphen

'**tratto, a** *pp di* **trarre** ♦ *sm* (*di penna, matita*) stroke; (*parte*) part, piece; (*di strada*) stretch; (*di mare, cielo*) expanse; (*di tempo*) period (of time); **~i** *smpl* (*caratteristiche*) features; (*modo di fare*) ways, manners; **a un ~, d'un ~** suddenly

trat'tore *sm* tractor

tratto'ria *sf* restaurant

'**trauma, i** *sm* trauma; **trau'matico, a, ci, che** *ag* traumatic

tra'vaglio [tra'vaʎʎo] *sm* (*angoscia*) pain, suffering; (*MED*) pains *pl*

trava'sare *vt* to decant

'**trave** *sf* beam

tra'versa *sf* (*trave*) crosspiece; (*via*) sidestreet; (*FERR*) sleeper (*BRIT*), (railroad) tie (*US*); (*CALCIO*) crossbar

traver'sare *vt* to cross; **traver'sata** *sf* crossing; (*AER*) flight, trip

traver'sie *sfpl* mishaps, misfortunes

traver'sina *sf* (*FERR*) sleeper (*BRIT*), (railroad) tie (*US*)

tra'verso, a *ag* oblique; **di ~** *ag* askew ♦ *av* sideways; **andare di ~** (*cibo*) to go down the wrong way; **guardare di ~** to look askance at

travesti'mento *sm* disguise

traves'tire *vt* to disguise; **~rsi** *vr* to disguise o.s.

travi'are *vt* (*fig*) to lead astray

travi'sare *vt* (*fig*) to distort, misrepresent

tra'volgere [tra'vɔldʒere] *vt* to sweep away, carry away; (*fig*) to overwhelm; **tra'volto, a** *pp di* **travolgere**

tre *num* three

trebbi'are *vt* to thresh

'**treccia, ce** ['trettʃa] *sf* plait, braid

tre'cento [tre'tʃento] *num* three hundred ♦ *sm*: **il T~** the fourteenth century

'**tredici** ['treditʃi] *num* thirteen

'**tregua** *sf* truce; (*fig*) respite

tre'mare *vi*: **~ di** (*freddo etc*) to shiver *o* tremble with; (*paura, rabbia*) to shake *o* tremble with

tre'mendo, a *ag* terrible, awful

tre'mila *num* three thousand

'**tremito** *sm* trembling *no pl*; shaking *no pl*; shivering *no pl*

tremo'lare *vi* to tremble; (*luce*) to flicker; (*foglie*) to quiver

tre'more *sm* tremor

'**treno** *sm* train; **~ di gomme** set of tyres (*BRIT*) *o* tires (*US*); **~ merci** goods (*BRIT*) *o* freight train; **~ viaggiatori** passenger train

'**trenta** *num* thirty; **tren'tesimo, a** *num* thirtieth; **tren'tina** *sf*: **una trentina (di)** thirty or so, about thirty

'trepidante *ag* anxious

treppi'ede *sm* tripod; (*CUC*) trivet

'tresca, sche *sf* (*fig*) intrigue; (: *relazione amorosa*) affair

'trespolo *sm* trestle

tri'angolo *sm* triangle

tribù *sf inv* tribe

tri'buna *sf* (*podio*) platform; (*in aule etc*) gallery; (*di stadio*) stand

tribu'nale *sm* court

tribu'tare *vt* to bestow

tri'buto *sm* tax; (*fig*) tribute

tri'checo, chi [tri'kɛko] (*ZOOL*) walrus

tri'ciclo [tri'tʃiklo] *sm* tricycle

trico'lore *ag* three-coloured ♦ *sm* tricolour; (*bandiera italiana*) Italian flag

tri'dente *sm* trident

tri'foglio [tri'fɔʎʎo] *sm* clover

'triglia ['triʎʎa] *sf* red mullet

tril'lare *vi* (*MUS*) to trill

tri'mestre *sm* period of three months; (*INS*) term, quarter (*US*); (*COMM*) quarter

'trina *sf* lace

trin'cea [trin'tʃea] *sf* trench; **trince'rare** *vt* to entrench

trinci'are [trin'tʃare] *vt* to cut up

trion'fare *vi* to triumph, win; **~ su** to triumph over, overcome; **tri'onfo** *sm* triumph

tripli'care *vt* to triple

'triplice ['triplitʃe] *ag* triple; **in ~ copia** in triplicate

'triplo, a *ag* triple; treble ♦ *sm:* **il ~ (di)** three times as much (as); **la spesa è ~a** it costs three times as much

'trippa *sf* (*CUC*) tripe

'triste *ag* sad; (*luogo*) dreary, gloomy; **tris'tezza** *sf* sadness; gloominess

trita'carne *sm inv* mincer, grinder (*US*)

tri'tare *vt* to mince, grind (*US*)

'trito, a *ag* (*tritato*) minced, ground (*US*); **~ e ritrito** (*fig*) trite, hackneyed

'trittico, ci *sm* (*ARTE*) triptych

trivel'lare *vt* to drill

trivi'ale *ag* vulgar, low

tro'feo *sm* trophy

'tromba *sf* (*MUS*) trumpet; (*AUT*) horn; **~**

d'aria whirlwind; **~ delle scale** stairwell

trom'bone *sm* trombone

trom'bosi *sf* thrombosis

tron'care *vt* to cut off; (*spezzare*) to break off

'tronco, a, chi, che *ag* cut off; broken off; (*LING*) truncated; (*fig*) cut short ♦ *sm* (*BOT, ANAT*) trunk; (*fig: tratto*) section; **licenziare qn in ~** to fire sb on the spot

troneggi'are [troned'dʒare] *vi:* **~ (su)** to tower (over)

'tronfio, a *ag* conceited

'trono *sm* throne

tropi'cale *ag* tropical

'tropico, ci *sm* tropic; **~ci** *smpl* (*GEO*) tropics

PAROLA CHIAVE

'troppo, a *det* (*in eccesso: quantità*) too much; (: *numero*) too many; **c'era ~a gente** there were too many people; **fa ~ caldo** it's too hot

♦ *pron* (*in eccesso: quantità*) too much; (: *numero*) too many; **ne hai messo ~** you've put in too much; **meglio ~i che pochi** better too many than too few

♦ *av* (*eccessivamente: con ag, av*) too; (: *con vb*) too much; **~ amaro/tardi** too bitter/late; **lavora ~** he works too much; **di ~** too much; too many; **qualche tazza di ~** a few cups too many; **3000 lire di ~** 3000 lire too much; **essere di ~** to be in the way

---

'trota *sf* trout

trot'tare *vi* to trot; **trotterel'lare** *vi* to trot along; (*bambino*) to toddle; **'trotto** *sm* trot

'trottola *sf* spinning top

tro'vare *vt* to find; (*giudicare*): **trovo che** I find *o* think that; **~rsi** *vr* (*reciproco: incontrarsi*) to meet; (*essere, stare*) to be; (*arrivare, capitare*) to find o.s.; **andare a ~ qn** to go and see sb; **~ qn colpevole** to find sb guilty; **~rsi bene** (*in un luogo, con qn*) to get on well; **tro'vata** *sf* good idea

truc'care *vt* (*falsare*) to fake; (*attore etc*) to

make up; (*travestire*) to disguise; (*SPORT*) to fix; (*AUT*) to soup up; **~rsi** *vr* to make up (one's face); **trucca'tore**, **'trice** *sm/f* (*CINEMA, TEATRO*) make-up artist

'**trucco**, **chi** *sm* trick; (*cosmesi*) make-up

'**truce** ['trutʃe] *ag* fierce

truci'**dare** [trutʃi'dare] *vt* to slaughter

tru'**ciolo** ['trutʃolo] *sm* shaving

'**truffa** *sf* fraud, swindle; **truf'fare** *vt* to swindle, cheat

'**truppa** *sf* troop

tu *pron* you; **~ stesso(a)** you yourself; **dare del ~ a qn** to address sb as "tu"

'**tua** *vedi* **tuo**

'**tuba** *sf* (*MUS*) tuba; (*cappello*) top hat

tu'**bare** *vi* to coo

tuba'**tura** *sf* piping *no pl*, pipes *pl*

tu'**betto** *sm* tube

'**tubo** *sm* tube; pipe; **~ digerente** (*ANAT*) alimentary canal, digestive tract; **~ di scappamento** (*AUT*) exhaust pipe

'**tue** *vedi* **tuo**

tuf'**fare** *vt* to plunge, dip; **~rsi** *vr* to plunge, dive; '**tuffo** *sm* dive; (*breve bagno*) dip

tu'**gurio** *sm* hovel

tuli'**pano** *sm* tulip

tume'**farsi** *vr* (*MED*) to swell

'**tumido**, **a** *ag* swollen

tu'**more** *sm* (*MED*) tumour

tu'**multo** *sm* uproar, commotion; (*sommossa*) riot; (*fig*) turmoil; **tumultu'oso**, **a** *ag* rowdy, unruly; (*fig*) turbulent, stormy

'**tunica**, **che** *sf* tunic

Tuni'**sia** *sf*: **la ~** Tunisia

'**tuo** (*f* '**tua**, *pl* **tu'oi**, '**tue**) *det*: **il ~**, **la tua** *etc* your ♦ *pron*: **il ~**, **la tua** *etc* yours

tuo'**nare** *vi* to thunder; **tuona** it is thundering, there's some thunder

tu'**ono** *sm* thunder

tu'**orlo** *sm* yolk

tu'**racciolo** [tu'rattʃolo] *sm* cap, top; (*di sughero*) cork

tu'**rare** *vt* to stop, plug; (*con sughero*) to cork; **~rsi il naso** to hold one's nose

turba'**mento** *sm* disturbance; (*di animo*)

anxiety, agitation

tur'**bante** *sm* turban

tur'**bare** *vt* to disturb, trouble

'**turbine** *sm* whirlwind

turbo'**lento**, **a** *ag* turbulent; (*ragazzo*) boisterous, unruly

turbo'**lenza** [turbo'lentsa] *sf* turbulence

tur'**chese** [tur'kese] *sf* turquoise

Tur'**chia** [tur'kia] *sf*: **la ~** Turkey

tur'**chino**, **a** [tur'kino] *ag* deep blue

'**turco**, **a**, **chi**, **che** *ag* Turkish ♦ *sm/f* Turk/Turkish woman ♦ *sm* (*LING*) Turkish; **parlare ~** (*fig*) to talk double-dutch

tu'**rismo** *sm* tourism; tourist industry; tu'**rista**, **i**, **e** *sm/f* tourist; tu'**ristico**, **a**, **ci**, **che** *ag* tourist *cpd*

'**turno** *sm* turn; (*di lavoro*) shift; **di ~** (*soldato, medico, custode*) on duty; **a ~** (*rispondere*) in turn; (*lavorare*) in shifts; **fare a ~ a fare qc** to take turns to do sth; **è il suo ~** it's your (*o* his *etc*) turn

'**turpe** *ag* filthy, vile; **turpi'loquio** *sm* obscene language

'**tuta** *sf* overalls *pl*; (*SPORT*) tracksuit

tu'**tela** *sf* (*DIR: di minore*) guardianship; (*: protezione*) protection; (*difesa*) defence; **tute'lare** *vt* to protect, defend

tu'**tore**, '**trice** *sm/f* (*DIR*) guardian

tutta'**via** *cong* nevertheless, yet

PAROLA CHIAVE

'**tutto**, **a** *det* **1** (*intero*) all; **~ il latte** all the milk; **~a la notte** all night, the whole night; **~ il libro** the whole book; **~a una bottiglia** a whole bottle

2 (*pl, collettivo*) all; every; **~i i libri** all the books; **~e le notti** every night; **~i i venerdì** every Friday; **~i gli uomini** all the men; (*collettivo*) all men; **~ l'anno** all year long; **~i e due** both *o* each of us (*o* them *o* you); **~i e cinque** all five of us (*o* them *o* you)

3 (*completamente*): **era ~a sporca** she was all dirty; **tremava ~** he was trembling all over; **è ~a sua madre** she's just *o* exactly like her mother

4: **a tutt'oggi** so far, up till now; **a ~a velocità** at full *o* top speed

♦ *pron* **1** (*ogni cosa*) everything, all; (*qualsiasi cosa*) anything; **ha mangiato ~** he's eaten everything; **~ considerato** all things considered; **in ~: 10,000 lire in ~** 10.000 lire in all; **in ~ eravamo 50** there were 50 of us in all

2: ~i, e (*ognuno*) all, everybody; **vengono ~i** they are all coming, everybody's coming; **~i quanti** all and sundry

♦ *av* (*completamente*) entirely, quite; **è ~ il contrario** it's quite *o* exactly the opposite; **tutt'al più: saranno stati tutt'al più una cinquantina** there were about fifty of them at (the very) most; **tutt'al più possiamo prendere un treno** if the worst comes to the worst we can take a train; **tutt'altro** on the contrary; **è tutt'altro che felice** he's anything but happy; **tutt'a un tratto** suddenly

♦ *sm*: **il ~** the whole lot, all of it

tutto'fare *ag inv*: **domestica ~** general maid; **ragazzo ~** office boy ♦ *sm/f inv* handyman/woman

tut'tora *av* still

U, u

ubbidi'ente *ag* obedient; ubbidi'enza *sf* obedience

ubbi'dire *vi* to obey; **~ a** to obey; (*sog: veicolo, macchina*) to respond to

ubria'care *vt*: **~ qn** to get sb drunk; (*sog: alcool*) to make sb drunk; (*fig*) to make sb's head spin *o* reel; **~rsi** *vr* to get drunk; **~rsi di** (*fig*) to become intoxicated with

ubri'aco, a, chi, che *ag, sm/f* drunk

uccelli'era [utt∫el'ljɛra] *sf* aviary

uccel'lino [utt∫el'lino] *sm* baby bird, chick

uc'cello [ut't∫ɛllo] *sm* bird

uc'cidere [ut't∫idere] *vt* to kill; **~rsi** *vr* (*suicidarsi*) to kill o.s.; (*perdere la vita*) to be killed; uccisi'one *sf* killing; uc'ciso, a *pp di* **uccidere**; ucci'sore *sm* killer

udi'enza [u'djɛntsa] *sf* audience; (*DIR*) hearing

u'dire *vt* to hear; udi'tivo, a *ag* auditory; u'dito *sm* (sense of) hearing; udi'torio *sm* (*persone*) audience

UE *sigla f* (= *Unione Europea*) EU

UEM *sigla f* (= *Unione economica e monetaria*) EMU

'uffa *escl* tut!

uffici'ale [uffi't∫ale] *ag* official ♦ *sm* (*AMM*) official, officer; (*MIL*) officer; **~ di stato civile** registrar

uf'ficio [uf'fit∫o] *sm* (*gen*) office; (*dovere*) duty; (*mansione*) task, function, job; (*agenzia*) agency, bureau; (*REL*) service; **d'~** *ag* office *cpd*; official ♦ *av* officially; **~ di collocamento** employment office; **~ informazioni** information bureau; **~ oggetti smarriti** lost property office (*BRIT*), lost and found (*US*); **~ postale** post office

uffici'oso, a [uffi't∫oso] *ag* unofficial

'UFO *sm inv* UFO

'ufo: **a ~** *av* free, for nothing

uguagli'anza [ugwaλ'λantsa] *sf* equality

uguagli'are [ugwaλ'λare] *vt* to make equal; (*essere uguale*) to equal, be equal to; (*livellare*) to level; **~rsi a** *o* **con qn** (*paragonarsi*) to compare o.s. to sb

ugu'ale *ag* equal; (*identico*) identical, the same; (*uniforme*) level, even ♦ *av*: **costano ~** they cost the same; **sono bravi ~** they're equally good; ugual'mente *av* equally; (*lo stesso*) all the same

'ulcera ['ult∫era] *sf* ulcer

u'livo = **olivo**

ulteri'ore *ag* further

ulti'mare *vt* to finish, complete

'ultimo, a *ag* (*finale*) last; (*estremo*) farthest, utmost; (*recente: notizia, moda*) latest; (*fig*) ultimate ♦ *sm/f* last (one); **fino all'~** to the last, until the end; **da ~, in ~** in the end; **abitare all'~ piano** to live on the top floor; **per ~** (*entrare, arrivare*) last

ulu'lare *vi* to howl; ulu'lato *sm* howling *no pl*; howl

umanità *sf* humanity; umani'tario, a *ag* humanitarian

u'mano, a *ag* human; (*comprensivo*) humane

umet'tare vt to dampen, moisten

umidità sf dampness; humidity

'umido, a ag damp; (mano, occhi) moist; (clima) humid ♦ sm dampness, damp; **carne in ~** stew

'umile ag humble

umili'are vt to humiliate; **~rsi** vr to humble o.s.; **umiliazi'one** sf humiliation

umiltà sf humility, humbleness

u'more sm (disposizione d'animo) mood; (carattere) temper; **di buon/cattivo ~** in a good/bad mood

umo'rismo sm humour; **avere il senso dell'~** to have a sense of humour; **umo'ristico, a, ci, che** ag humorous, funny

un vedi **uno**

un' vedi **uno**

'una vedi **uno**

u'nanime ag unanimous; **unanimità** sf unanimity; **all'unanimità** unanimously

unci'netto [untʃi'netto] sm crochet hook

un'cino [un'tʃino] sm hook

'undici num eleven

'ungere ['undʒere] vt to grease, oil; (REL) to anoint; (fig) to flatter, butter up; **~rsi** vr (sporcarsi) to get covered in grease; **~rsi con la crema** to put on cream

unghe'rese [unge'rese] ag, sm/f, sm Hungarian

Unghe'ria [unge'ria] sf: **l'~** Hungary

'unghia ['ungja] sf (ANAT) nail; (di animale) claw; (di rapace) talon; (di cavallo) hoof; **unghi'ata** sf (graffio) scratch

ungu'ento sm ointment

'unico, a, ci, che ag (solo) only; (ineguagliabile) unique; (singolo: binario) single; **figlio(a) ~(a)** only son/daughter, only child

unifamili'are ag one-family cpd

unifi'care vt to unite, unify; (sistemi) to standardize; **unificazi'one** sf uniting; unification; standardization

uni'forme ag uniform; (superficie) even ♦ sf (divisa) uniform

unilate'rale ag one-sided; (DIR) unilateral

uni'one sf union; (fig: concordia) unity,
harmony

u'nire vt to unite; (congiungere) to join, connect; (: ingredienti, colori) to combine; (in matrimonio) to unite, join together; **~rsi** vr to unite; (in matrimonio) to be joined together; **~ qc a** to unite sth with; to join o connect sth with; to combine sth with; **~rsi a** (gruppo, società) to join

unità sf inv (unione, concordia) unity; (MAT, MIL, COMM, di misura) unit; **uni'tario, a** ag unitary; **prezzo unitario** price per unit

u'nito, a ag (paese) united; (amici, famiglia) close; **in tinta ~a** plain, self-coloured

univer'sale ag universal; general

università sf inv university; **universi'tario, a** ag university cpd ♦ sm/f (studente) university student; (insegnante) academic, university lecturer

uni'verso sm universe

PAROLA CHIAVE

'uno, a (dav sm **un** +C, V, **uno** +s impura, gn, pn, ps, x, z; dav sf **un'** +V, **una** +C) art indet **1** a; (dav vocale) an; **un bambino** a child; **~a strada** a street; **~ zingaro** a gypsy
2 (intensivo): **ho avuto ~a paura!** I got such a fright!
♦ pron **1** one; **prendine ~** take one (of them); **l'~ o l'altro** either (of them); **l'~ e l'altro** both (of them); **aiutarsi l'un l'altro** to help one another o each other; **sono entrati l'~ dopo l'altro** they came in one after the other
2 (un tale) someone, somebody
3 (con valore impersonale) one, you; **se ~ vuole** if one wants, if you want
♦ num one; **~a mela e due pere** one apple and two pears; **~ più ~ fa due** one plus one equals two, one and one are two
♦ sf: **è l'~a** it's one (o'clock)

'unto, a pp di **ungere** ♦ ag greasy, oily
♦ sm grease; **untu'oso, a** ag greasy, oily

u'omo (pl **u'omini**) sm man; **da ~** (abito, scarpe) men's, for men; **~ d'affari** businessman; **~ di paglia** stooge; **~ rana** frogman

u'ovo (pl(f) u'ova) sm egg; ~ affogato poached egg; ~ al tegame fried egg; ~ alla coque boiled egg; ~ bazzotto/sodo soft-/hard-boiled egg; ~ di Pasqua Easter egg; ~ in camicia poached egg; ~a strapazzate scrambled eggs

ura'gano sm hurricane

urba'nistica sf town planning

ur'bano, a ag urban, city cpd, town cpd; (TEL: chiamata) local; (fig) urbane

ur'gente [ur'dʒɛnte] ag urgent; ur'genza sf urgency; in caso d'urgenza (in case of) an emergency; d'urgenza ag emergency ♦ av urgently, as a matter of urgency

u'rina sf = orina

ur'lare vi (persona) to scream, yell; (animale, vento) to howl ♦ vt to scream, yell

'urlo (pl(m) 'urli, pl(f) 'urla) sm scream, yell; howl

'urna sf urn; (elettorale) ballot-box; andare alle ~e to go to the polls

urrà escl hurrah!

U.R.S.S. abbr f: l'~ the USSR

ur'tare vt to bump into, knock against; (fig: irritare) to annoy ♦ vi: ~ contro o in to bump into, knock against, crash into; (fig: imbattersi) to come up against; ~rsi vr (reciproco: scontrarsi) to collide; (: fig) to clash; (irritarsi) to get annoyed; 'urto sm (colpo) knock, bump; (scontro) crash, collision; (fig) clash

'U.S.A. ['uza] smpl: gli ~ the USA

u'sanza [u'zantsa] sf custom; (moda) fashion

u'sare vt to use, employ ♦ vi (servirsi): ~ di to use; (: diritto) to exercise; (essere di moda) to be fashionable; (essere solito): ~ fare to be in the habit of doing, be accustomed to doing ♦ vb impers: qui usa così it's the custom round here; u'sato, a ag used; (consumato) worn; (di seconda mano) used, second-hand ♦ sm second-hand goods pl

usci'ere [uʃˈʃɛre] sm usher

'uscio ['uʃʃo] sm door

u'scire [uʃˈʃire] vi (gen) to come out;

(partire, andare a passeggio, a uno spettacolo etc) to go out; (essere sorteggiato: numero) to come up; ~ da (gen) to leave; (posto) to go (o come) out of, leave; (solco, vasca etc) to come out of; (muro) to stick out of; (competenza etc) to be outside; (infanzia, adolescenza) to leave behind; (famiglia nobile etc) to come from; ~ da o di casa to go out; (fig) to leave home; ~ in automobile to go out in the car, go for a drive; ~ di strada (AUT) to go off o leave the road

u'scita [uʃˈʃita] sf (passaggio, varco) exit, way out; (per divertimento) outing; (ECON: somma) expenditure; (TEATRO) entrance; (fig: battuta) witty remark; ~ di sicurezza emergency exit

usi'gnolo [uziɲˈɲɔlo] sm nightingale

U.S.L. [uzl] sigla f (= unità sanitaria locale) local health centre

'uso sm (utilizzazione) use; (esercizio) practice; (abitudine) custom; a ~ di for (the use of); d'~ (corrente) in use; fuori ~ out of use

usti'one sf burn

usu'ale ag common, everyday

u'sura sf usury; (logoramento) wear (and tear)

uten'sile sm tool, implement; ~i da cucina kitchen utensils

u'tente sm/f user

'utero sm uterus

'utile ag useful ♦ sm (vantaggio) advantage, benefit; (ECON: profitto) profit; utilità sf usefulness no pl; use; (vantaggio) benefit; utili'taria sf (AUT) economy car

utiliz'zare [utilidˈdzare] vt to use, make use of, utilize

'uva sf grapes pl; ~ passa raisins pl; ~ spina gooseberry

V, v

v. *abbr* (= *vedi*) v

va *vb vedi* **andare**

va'cante *ag* vacant

va'canza [va'kantsa] *sf* (*l'essere vacante*) vacancy; (*riposo, ferie*) holiday(s *pl*) (*BRIT*), vacation (*US*); (*giorno di permesso*) day off, holiday; **~e** *sfpl* (*periodo di ferie*) holidays (*BRIT*), vacation *sg* (*US*); **essere/andare in ~** to be/go on holiday *o* vacation; **~e estive** summer holiday(s) *o* vacation

'vacca, che *sf* cow

vacci'nare [vattʃi'nare] *vt* to vaccinate

vac'cino [vat'tʃino] *sm* (*MED*) vaccine

vacil'lare [vatʃil'lare] *vi* to sway, wobble; (*luce*) to flicker; (*fig: memoria, coraggio*) to be failing, falter

'vacuo, a *ag* (*fig*) empty, vacuous

'vado *vb vedi* **andare**

vaga'bondo, a *sm/f* tramp, vagrant

va'gare *vi* to wander

va'gina [va'dʒina] *sf* vagina

va'gire [va'dʒire] *vi* to whimper

va'gito [va'dʒito] *sm* cry

'vaglia ['vaʎʎa] *sm inv* money order; **~ postale** postal order

vagli'are [vaʎ'ʎare] *vt* to sift; (*fig*) to weigh up; **'vaglio** *sm* sieve

'vago, a, ghi, ghe *ag* vague

va'gone *sm* (*FERR: per passeggeri*) coach; (: *per merci*) truck, wagon; **~ letto** sleeper, sleeping car; **~ ristorante** dining *o* restaurant car

'vai *vb vedi* **andare**

vai'olo *sm* smallpox

va'langa, ghe *sf* avalanche

va'lente *ag* able, talented

va'lere *vi* (*avere forza, potenza*) to have influence; (*essere valido*) to be valid; (*avere vigore, autorità*) to hold, apply; (*essere capace: poeta, studente*) to be good, be able ♦ *vt* (*prezzo, sforzo*) to be worth; (*corrispondere*) to correspond to; (*procurare*): **~ qc a qn** to earn sb sth; **~rsi**

di to make use of, take advantage of; **far ~** (*autorità etc*) to assert; **vale a dire** that is to say; **~ la pena** to be worth the effort *o* worth it

va'levole *ag* valid

vali'care *vt* to cross

'valico, chi *sm* (*passo*) pass

'valido, a *ag* valid; (*rimedio*) effective; (*aiuto*) real; (*persona*) worthwhile

valige'ria [validʒe'ria] *sf* leather goods *pl*; leather goods factory; leather goods shop

vali'getta [vali'dʒetta] *sf* briefcase

va'ligia, gie *o* **ge** [va'lidʒa] *sf* (suit)case; **fare le ~gie** to pack (up)

val'lata *sf* valley

'valle *sf* valley; **a ~** (*di fiume*) downstream; **scendere a ~** to go downhill

va'lore *sm* (*gen*) value; (*merito*) merit, worth; (*coraggio*) valour, courage; (*COMM: titolo*) security; **~i** *smpl* (*oggetti preziosi*) valuables

valoriz'zare [valorid'dzare] *vt* (*terreno*) to develop; (*fig*) to make the most of

'valso, a *pp di* **valere**

va'luta *sf* currency, money; (*BANCA*): **~ 15 gennaio** interest to run from January 15th

valu'tare *vt* (*casa, gioiello, fig*) to value; (*stabilire: peso, entrate, fig*) to estimate; **valutazi'one** *sf* valuation; estimate

'valvola *sf* (*TECN, ANAT*) valve; (*ELETTR*) fuse

'valzer ['valtser] *sm inv* waltz

vam'pata *sf* (*di fiamma*) blaze; (*di calore*) blast; (: *al viso*) flush

vam'piro *sm* vampire

vanda'lismo *sm* vandalism

'vandalo *sm* vandal

vaneggi'are [vaned'dʒare] *vi* to rave

'vanga, ghe *sf* spade; **van'gare** *vt* to dig

van'gelo [van'dʒelo] *sm* gospel

va'niglia [va'niʎʎa] *sf* vanilla

vanità *sf* vanity; (*di promessa*) emptiness; (*di sforzo*) futility; **vani'toso, a** *ag* vain, conceited

'vanno *vb vedi* **andare**

'vano, a *ag* vain ♦ *sm* (*spazio*) space; (*apertura*) opening; (*stanza*) room

van'taggio [van'taddʒo] *sm* advantage;

essere/portarsi in ~ (SPORT) to be in/take the lead; **vantaggi'oso, a** ag advantageous; favourable

van'tare vt to praise, speak highly of; **~rsi** vr: **~rsi (di/di aver fatto)** to boast o brag (about/about having done); **vante'ria** sf boasting; **'vanto** sm boasting; (merito) virtue; (gloria) pride

'vanvera sf: **a ~** haphazardly; **parlare a ~** to talk nonsense

va'pore sm vapour; (anche: **~ acqueo**) steam; (nave) steamer; **a ~** (turbina etc) steam cpd; **al ~** (CUC) steamed; **vapo'retto** sm steamer; **vaporiz'zare** vt to vaporize; **vapo'roso, a** ag (tessuto) filmy; (capelli) soft and full

va'rare vt (NAUT, fig) to launch; (DIR) to pass

var'care vt to cross

'varco, chi sm passage; **aprirsi un ~ tra la folla** to push one's way through the crowd

vari'abile ag variable; (tempo, umore) changeable, variable ♦ sf (MAT) variable

vari'are vt, vi to vary; **~ di opinione** to change one's mind; **variazi'one** sf variation; change

va'rice [va'ritʃe] sf varicose vein

vari'cella [vari'tʃella] sf chickenpox

vari'coso, a ag varicose

varie'gato, a ag variegated

varie'tà sf inv variety ♦ sm inv variety show

'vario, a ag varied; (parecchi: col sostantivo al pl) various; (mutevole: umore) changeable; **vario'pinto, a** ag multicoloured

'varo sm (NAUT, fig) launch; (di leggi) passing

va'saio sm potter

'vasca, sche sf basin; (anche: **~ da bagno**) bathtub, bath

va'scello [vaʃ'ʃello] sm vessel, ship

vase'lina sf vaseline

vasel'lame sm (stoviglie) crockery; (: di porcellana) china; **~ d'oro/d'argento** gold/silver plate

'vaso sm (recipiente) pot; (: barattolo) jar; (: decorativo) vase; (ANAT) vessel; **~ da fiori**

vase; (per piante) flowerpot

vas'soio sm tray

'vasto, a ag vast, immense

Vati'cano sm: **il ~** the Vatican

ve pron, av vedi **vi**

vecchi'aia [vek'kjaja] sf old age

'vecchio, a ['vekkjo] ag old ♦ sm/f old man/woman; **i ~i** the old

'vece ['vetʃe] sf: **in ~ di** in the place of, for; **fare le ~i di qn** to take sb's place

ve'dere vt, vi to see; **~rsi** vr to meet, see one another; **avere a che ~ con** to have something to do with; **far ~ qc a qn** to show sb sth; **farsi ~** to show o.s.; (farsi vivo) to show one's face; **vedi di non farlo** make sure o see you don't do it; **non (ci) si vede** (è buio etc) you can't see a thing; **non lo posso ~** (fig) I can't stand him

ve'detta sf (sentinella, posto) look-out; (NAUT) patrol boat

'vedovo, a sm/f widower/widow

ve'duta sf view

vee'mente ag vehement; violent

vege'tale [vedʒe'tale] ag, sm vegetable

vegetari'ano, a [vedʒeta'rjano] ag, sm/f vegetarian

'vegeto, a ['vedʒeto] ag (pianta) thriving; (persona) strong, vigorous

'veglia ['veʎʎa] sf wakefulness; (sorveglianza) watch; (trattenimento) evening gathering; **fare la ~ a un malato** to watch over a sick person

vegli'are [veʎ'ʎare] vi to be awake; to stay o sit up; (stare vigile) to watch; to keep watch ♦ vt (malato, morto) to watch over, sit up with

ve'icolo sm vehicle

'vela sf (NAUT: tela) sail; (sport) sailing

ve'lare vt to veil; **~rsi** vr (occhi, luna) to mist over; (voce) to become husky; **~rsi il viso** to cover one's face (with a veil); **ve'lato, a** ag veiled

veleggi'are [veled'dʒare] vi to sail; (AER) to glide

ve'leno sm poison; **vele'noso, a** ag poisonous

veli'ero sm sailing ship

ve'lina sf (anche: **carta ~**: per imballare) tissue paper

ve'livolo sm aircraft

velleità sf inv vain ambition, vain desire

vel'luto sm velvet; **~ a coste** cord

'velo sm veil; (tessuto) voile

ve'loce [ve'lotʃe] ag fast, quick ♦ av fast, quickly; velo'cista, i, e sm/f (SPORT) sprinter; velocità sf speed; **a forte velocità** at high speed; **velocità di crociera** cruising speed

'vena sf (gen) vein; (filone) vein, seam; (fig: ispirazione) inspiration; (: umore) mood; **essere in ~ di qc** to be in the mood for sth

ve'nale ag (prezzo, valore) market cpd; (fig) venal; mercenary

ven'demmia sf (raccolta) grape harvest; (quantità d'uva) grape crop, grapes pl; (vino ottenuto) vintage; vendemmi'are vt to harvest ♦ vi to harvest the grapes

'vendere vt to sell; **"vendesi"** "for sale"

ven'detta sf revenge

vendi'care vt to avenge; **~rsi** vr: **~rsi (di)** to avenge o.s. (for); (per rancore) to take one's revenge (for); **~rsi su qn** to revenge o.s. on sb; vendica'tivo, a ag vindictive

'vendita sf sale; **la ~** (attività) selling; (smercio) sales pl; **in ~** on sale; **~ all'asta** sale by auction; vendi'tore sm seller, vendor; (gestore di negozio) trader, dealer

vene'rabile ag venerable

venerando, a ag = **venerabile**

vene'rare vt to venerate

venerdì sm inv Friday; **di** o **il ~** on Fridays; **V~ Santo** Good Friday

ve'nereo, a ag venereal

'veneto, a ag, sm/f Venetian

Ve'nezia [ve'nettsja] sf Venice; venezi'ana sf Venetian blind; venezi'ano, a ag, sm/f Venetian

veni'ale ag venial

ve'nire vi to come; (riuscire: dolce, fotografia) to turn out; (come ausiliare: essere): **viene ammirato da tutti** he is admired by everyone; **~ da** to come from; **quanto viene?** how much does it cost?;

far ~ (mandare a chiamare) to send for; **~ giù** to come down; **~ meno** (svenire) to faint; **~ meno a qc** not to fulfil sth; **~ su** to come up; **~ a trovare qn** to come and see sb; **~ via** to come away

ven'taglio [ven'taʎʎo] sm fan

ven'tata sf gust (of wind)

ven'tenne ag: **una ragazza ~** a twenty-year-old girl, a girl of twenty

ven'tesimo, a num twentieth

'venti num twenty

venti'lare vt (stanza) to air, ventilate; (fig: idea, proposta) to air; ventila'tore sm ventilator, fan

ven'tina sf: **una ~ (di)** around twenty, twenty or so

venti'sette num twenty-seven

'vento sm wind

'ventola sf (AUT, TECN) fan

ven'tosa sf (ZOOL) sucker; (di gomma) suction pad

ven'toso, a ag windy

'ventre sm stomach

ven'tura sf: **soldato di ~** mercenary

ven'turo, a ag next, coming

ve'nuta sf coming, arrival

ve'nuto, a pp di **venire**

vera'mente av really

ver'bale ag verbal ♦ sm (di riunione) minutes pl

'verbo sm (LING) verb; (parola) word; (REL): **il V~** the Word

'verde ag, sm green; **essere al ~** to be broke; **~ bottiglia/oliva** bottle/olive green

verde'rame sm verdigris

ver'detto sm verdict

ver'dura sf vegetables pl

'verga, ghe sf rod

'vergine ['verdʒine] sf virgin; (dello zodiaco): **V~** Virgo ♦ ag virgin; (ragazza): **essere ~** to be a virgin

ver'gogna [ver'goɲɲa] sf shame; (timidezza) shyness, embarrassment; vergo'gnarsi vr: **vergognarsi (di)** to be o feel ashamed (of); to be shy (about), be embarrassed (about); vergo'gnoso, a ag ashamed; (timido) shy, embarrassed; (causa *di vergogna: azione*) shameful

ve'rifica, che *sf* checking *no pl*, check

verifi'care *vt* (*controllare*) to check; (*confermare*) to confirm, bear out

verità *sf inv* truth

veriti'ero, a *ag* (*che dice la verità*) truthful; (*conforme a verità*) true

'verme *sm* worm

vermi'celli [vermi'tʃelli] *smpl* vermicelli *sg*

ver'miglio [ver'miʎʎo] *sm* vermilion, scarlet

'vermut *sm inv* vermouth

ver'nice [ver'nitʃe] *sf* (*colorazione*) paint; (*trasparente*) varnish; (*pelle*) patent leather; "**~ fresca**" "wet paint"; **vernici'are** *vt* to paint; to varnish

'vero, a *ag* (*veridico: fatti, testimonianza*) true; (*autentico*) real ♦ *sm* (*verità*) truth; (*realtà*) (real) life; **un ~ e proprio delinquente** a real criminal, an out-and-out criminal

vero'simile *ag* likely, probable

ver'ruca, che *sf* wart

versa'mento *sm* (*pagamento*) payment; (*deposito di denaro*) deposit

ver'sante *sm* slopes *pl*, side

ver'sare *vt* (*fare uscire: vino, farina*) to pour (out); (*spargere: lacrime, sangue*) to shed; (*rovesciare*) to spill; (*ECON*) to pay; (*: depositare*) to deposit, pay in; **~rsi** *vr* (*rovesciarsi*) to spill; (*fiume, folla*): **~rsi (in)** to pour (into)

versa'tile *ag* versatile

ver'setto *sm* (*REL*) verse

versi'one *sf* version; (*traduzione*) translation

'verso *sm* (*di poesia*) verse, line; (*di animale, uccello*) cry; (*direzione*) direction; (*modo*) way; (*di foglio di carta*) verso; (*di moneta*) reverse; **~i** *smpl* (*poesia*) verse *sg*; **non c'è ~ di persuaderlo** there's no way of persuading him, he can't be persuaded ♦ *prep* (*in direzione di*) toward(s); (*nei pressi di*) near, around (about); (*in senso temporale*) about; around; (*nei confronti di*) for; **~ di me** towards me; **~ sera** towards evening

'vertebra *sf* vertebra

verti'cale *ag, sf* vertical

'vertice ['vertitʃe] *sm* summit, top; (*MAT*) vertex; **conferenza al ~** (*POL*) summit conference

ver'tigine [ver'tidʒine] *sf* dizziness *no pl*; dizzy spell; (*MED*) vertigo; **avere le ~i** to feel dizzy; **vertigi'noso, a** *ag* (*altezza*) dizzy; (*fig*) breathtakingly high (*o deep etc*)

ve'scica, che [veʃ'ʃika] *sf* (*ANAT*) bladder; (*MED*) blister

'vescovo *sm* bishop

'vespa *sf* wasp

'vespro *sm* (*REL*) vespers *pl*

ves'sillo *sm* standard; (*bandiera*) flag

ves'taglia [ves'taʎʎa] *sf* dressing gown

'veste *sf* garment; (*rivestimento*) covering; (*qualità, facoltà*) capacity; **in ~ ufficiale** (*fig*) in an official capacity; **in ~ di** in the guise of, as; **vesti'ario** *sm* wardrobe, clothes *pl*

ves'tire *vt* (*bambino, malato*) to dress; (*avere indosso*) to have on, wear; **~rsi** *vr* to dress, get dressed; **ves'tito, a** *ag* dressed ♦ *sm* garment; (*da donna*) dress; (*da uomo*) suit; **vestiti** *smpl* (*indumenti*) clothes; **vestito di bianco** dressed in white

Ve'suvio *sm*: **il ~** Vesuvius

vete'rano, a *ag, sm/f* veteran

veteri'naria *sf* veterinary medicine

veteri'nario, a *ag* veterinary ♦ *sm* veterinary surgeon (*BRIT*), veterinarian (*US*), vet

'veto *sm inv* veto

ve'traio *sm* glassmaker; glazier

ve'trata *sf* glass door (*o window*); (*di chiesa*) stained glass window

vetre'ria *sf* (*stabilimento*) glassworks *sg*; (*oggetti di vetro*) glassware

ve'trina *sf* (*di negozio*) (shop) window; (*armadio*) display cabinet; **vetri'nista, i, e** *sm/f* window dresser

vetri'olo *sm* vitriol

'vetro *sm* glass; (*per finestra, porta*) pane (of glass)

'vetta *sf* peak, summit, top

vet'tore *sm* (*MAT, FISICA*) vector; (*chi trasporta*) carrier

vetto'vaglie [vetto'vaʎʎe] _sfpl_ supplies

vet'tura _sf (carrozza)_ carriage; (FERR) carriage (BRIT), car (US); (auto) car (BRIT), automobile (US)

vezzeggia'tivo [vettseddʒa'tivo] _sm_ (LING) term of endearment

'vezzo ['vettso] _sm_ habit; **~i** _smpl_ (smancerie) affected ways; (leggiadria) charms; **vez'zoso, a** _ag (grazioso)_ charming, pretty; (lezioso) affected

vi _(dav lo, la, li, le, ne diventa_ **ve**) _pron_ (oggetto) you; (complemento di termine) (to) you; (riflessivo) yourselves; (reciproco) each other ♦ _av (lì)_ there; (qui) here; (per questo/quel luogo) through here/there; **~ è/sono** there is/are

'via _sf (strada)_ street; (sentiero, pista) path, track; (AMM: procedimento) channels _pl_ ♦ _prep (passando per)_ via, by way of ♦ _av_ away ♦ _escl_ go away!; (suvvia) come on!; (SPORT) go! ♦ _sm_ (SPORT) starting signal; **in ~ di guarigione** on the road to recovery; **per ~ di** (a causa di) because of, on account of; **in o per ~** on the way; **per ~ aerea** by air; (lettere) by airmail; **andare/essere ~** to go/be away; **~ ~ che** (a mano a mano) as; **dare il ~** (SPORT) to give the starting signal; **dare il ~ a** (fig) to start; **V~ lattea** (ASTR) Milky Way; **~ di mezzo** middle course; **in ~ provvisoria** provisionally

viabilità _sf (di strada)_ practicability; (rete stradale) roads _pl_, road network

via'dotto _sm_ viaduct

viaggi'are [viad'dʒare] _vi_ to travel; **viaggia'tore, 'trice** _ag_ travelling ♦ _sm_ traveller; (passeggero) passenger

vi'aggio ['vjaddʒo] _sm_ travel(ling); (tragitto) journey, trip; **buon ~!** have a good trip!; **~ di nozze** honeymoon

vi'ale _sm_ avenue

via'vai _sm_ coming and going, bustle

vi'brare _vi_ to vibrate

vi'cario _sm (apostolico etc)_ vicar

'vice ['vitʃe] _sm/f_ deputy ♦ _prefisso:_ **~'console** _sm_ vice-consul; **~diret'tore** _sm_ assistant manager

vi'cenda [vi'tʃɛnda] _sf_ event; **a ~** in turn; **vicen'devole** _ag_ mutual, reciprocal

vice'versa [vitʃe'vɛrsa] _av_ vice versa; **da Roma a Pisa e ~** from Rome to Pisa and back

vici'nanza [vitʃi'nantsa] _sf_ nearness, closeness; **~e** _sfpl (paraggi)_ neighbourhood, vicinity

vici'nato [vitʃi'nato] _sm_ neighbourhood; (vicini) neighbours _pl_

vi'cino, a [vi'tʃino] _ag (gen)_ near; (nello spazio) near, nearby; (accanto) next; (nel tempo) near, close at hand ♦ _sm/f_ neighbour ♦ _av_ near, close; **da ~** (guardare) close up; (esaminare, seguire) closely; (conoscere) well, intimately; **~ a** near (to), close to; (accanto a) beside; **~ di casa** neighbour

'vicolo _sm_ alley; **~ cieco** blind alley

'video _sm inv (TV: schermo)_ screen; **~'camera** _sf_ camcorder; **~cas'setta** _sf_ videocassette; **~registra'tore** _sm_ video (recorder)

vie'tare _vt_ to forbid; (AMM) to prohibit; **~ a qn di fare** to forbid sb to do; to prohibit sb from doing; **"vietato fumare/ l'ingresso"** "no smoking/admittance"

Viet'nam _sm:_ **il ~** Vietnam; **vietna'mita, i, e** _ag, sm/f, sm_ Vietnamese _inv_

vi'gente [vi'dʒɛnte] _ag_ in force

vigi'lare [vidʒi'lare] _vt_ to watch over, keep an eye on; **~ che** to make sure that, see to it that

'vigile ['vidʒile] _ag_ watchful ♦ _sm (anche: ~ urbano)_ policeman (in towns); **~ del fuoco** fireman

vi'gilia [vi'dʒilja] _sf (giorno antecedente)_ eve; **la ~ di Natale** Christmas Eve

vigli'acco, a, chi, che [viʎ'ʎakko] _ag_ cowardly ♦ _sm/f_ coward

'vigna ['viɲɲa] _sf =_ **vi'gneto**

vi'gneto [viɲ'ɲeto] _sm_ vineyard

vi'gnetta [viɲ'ɲetta] _sf_ cartoon

vi'gore _sm_ vigour; (DIR): **essere/entrare in ~** to be in/come into force; **vigo'roso, a** _ag_ vigorous

'vile _ag (spregevole)_ low, mean, base;

(*codardo*) cowardly

vili'pendio *sm* contempt, scorn; public insult

'villa *sf* villa

vil'laggio [vil'laddʒo] *sm* village

villa'nia *sf* rudeness, lack of manners; **fare** (*o* **dire**) **una ~ a qn** to be rude to sb

vil'lano, a *ag* rude, ill-mannered

villeggia'tura [villeddʒa'tura] *sf* holiday(s pl) (*BRIT*), vacation (*US*)

vil'lino *sm* small house (with a garden), cottage

vil'loso, a *ag* hairy

viltà *sf* cowardice *no pl*; cowardly act

'vimine *sm* wicker; **mobili di ~i** wicker furniture *sg*

'vincere ['vintʃere] *vt* (*in guerra, al gioco, a una gara*) to defeat, beat; (*premio, guerra, partita*) to win; (*fig*) to overcome, conquer ♦ *vi* to win; **~ qn in bellezza** to be better-looking than sb; 'vincita *sf* win; (*denaro vinto*) winnings *pl*; vinci'tore *sm* winner; (*MIL*) victor

vinco'lare *vt* to bind; (*COMM: denaro*) to tie up; 'vincolo *sm* (*fig*) bond, tie; (*DIR: servitù*) obligation

vi'nicolo, a *ag* wine *cpd*

'vino *sm* wine; **~ bianco/rosso** white/red wine; **~ da pasto** table wine

'vinto, a *pp di* vincere

vi'ola *sf* (*BOT*) violet; (*MUS*) viola ♦ *ag, sm inv* (*colore*) purple

vio'lare *vt* (*chiesa*) to desecrate, violate; (*giuramento, legge*) to violate

violen'tare *vt* to use violence on; (*donna*) to rape

vio'lento, a *ag* violent; vio'lenza *sf* violence; **violenza carnale** rape

vio'letta *sf* (*BOT*) violet

vio'letto, a *ag, sm* (*colore*) violet

violi'nista, i, e *sm/f* violinist

vio'lino *sm* violin

violon'cello [violon'tʃɛllo] *sm* cello

vi'ottolo *sm* path, track

'vipera *sf* viper, adder

vi'rare *vi* (*NAUT, AER*) to turn; (*FOT*) to tone; **~ di bordo** (*NAUT*) to tack

'virgola *sf* (*LING*) comma; (*MAT*) point; virgo'lette *sfpl* inverted commas, quotation marks

vi'rile *ag* (*proprio dell'uomo*) masculine; (*non puerile, da uomo*) manly, virile

virtù *sf inv* virtue; **in** *o* **per ~ di** by virtue of, by

virtu'ale *ag* virtual

virtu'oso, a *ag* virtuous ♦ *sm/f* (*MUS etc*) virtuoso

'virus *sm inv* (*anche COMPUT*) virus

'viscere ['viʃʃere] *sfpl* (*di animale*) entrails pl; (*fig*) bowels *pl*

'vischio ['viskjo] *sm* (*BOT*) mistletoe; (*pania*) birdlime; vischi'oso, a *ag* sticky

'viscido, a ['viʃʃido] *ag* slimy

vi'sibile *ag* visible

visi'bilio *sm*: **andare in ~** to go into raptures

visibilità *sf* visibility

visi'era *sf* (*di elmo*) visor; (*di berretto*) peak

visi'one *sf* vision; **prendere ~ di qc** to examine sth, look sth over; **prima/seconda ~** (*CINEMA*) first/second showing

'visita *sf* visit; (*MED*) visit, call; (: *esame*) examination; visi'tare *vt* to visit; (*MED*) to visit, call on; (: *esaminare*) to examine; visita'tore, 'trice *sm/f* visitor

vi'sivo, a *ag* visual

'viso *sm* face

vi'sone *sm* mink

'vispo, a *ag* quick, lively

vis'suto, a *pp di* vivere ♦ *ag* (*aria, modo di fare*) experienced

'vista *sf* (*facoltà*) (eye)sight; (*fatto di vedere*) sight; **la ~ di** the sight of; (*veduta*) view; **sparare a ~** to shoot on sight; **in ~** in sight; **perdere qn di ~** to lose sight of sb; (*fig*) to lose touch with sb; **a ~ d'occhio** as far as the eye can see; (*fig*) before one's

very eyes; **far ~ di fare** to pretend to do
'**visto, a** *pp di* **vedere** ♦ *sm* visa; **~ che**
seeing (that)
vis'**toso, a** *ag* gaudy, garish; (*ingente*)
considerable
visu'**ale** *ag* visual; visualizza'**tore** *sm*
(*INFORM*) visual display unit, VDU
'**vita** *sf* life; (*ANAT*) waist; **a ~** for life
vi'**tale** *ag* vital; vita'**lizio, a** *ag* life *cpd*
♦ *sm* life annuity
vita'**mina** *sf* vitamin
'**vite** *sf* (*BOT*) vine; (*TECN*) screw
vi'**tello** *sm* (*ZOOL*) calf; (*carne*) veal; (*pelle*)
calfskin
vi'**ticcio** [vi'tittʃo] *sm* (*BOT*) tendril
viticol'**tore** *sm* wine grower; viticol'**tura**
sf wine growing
'**vitreo, a** *ag* vitreous; (*occhio, sguardo*)
glassy
'**vittima** *sf* victim
'**vitto** *sm* food; (*in un albergo etc*) board; **~
e alloggio** board and lodging
vit'**toria** *sf* victory
'**viva** *escl*: **~ il re!** long live the king!
vi'**vace** [vi'vatʃe] *ag* (*vivo, animato*) lively;
(*: mente*) lively, sharp; (*colore*) bright;
vivacità *sf* vivacity; liveliness; brightness
vi'**vaio** *sm* (*di pesci*) hatchery; (*AGR*) nursery
vi'**vanda** *sf* food; (*piatto*) dish
vi'**vente** *ag* living, alive; **i ~i** the living
'**vivere** *vi* to live ♦ *vt* to live; (*passare:
brutto momento*) to live through, go
through; (*sentire: gioie, pene di qn*) to share
♦ *sm* life; (*anche: modo di ~*) way of life;
~i *smpl* (*cibo*) food *sg*, provisions; **~ di** to
live on
'**vivido, a** *ag* (*colore*) vivid, bright
'**vivo, a** *ag* (*vivente*) alive, living;
(*: animale*) live; (*fig*) lively; (*: colore*) bright,
brilliant; **i ~i** the living; **~ e vegeto** hale
and hearty; **farsi ~** to show one's face; to
be heard from; **ritrarre dal ~** to paint from
life; **pungere qn nel ~** (*fig*) to cut sb to the
quick
vizi'**are** [vit'tsjare] *vt* (*bambino*) to spoil;
(*corrompere moralmente*) to corrupt;
vizi'**ato, a** *ag* spoilt; (*aria, acqua*) polluted

'**vizio** [ˈvittsjo] *sm* (*morale*) vice; (*cattiva
abitudine*) bad habit; (*imperfezione*) flaw,
defect; (*errore*) fault, mistake; vizi'**oso, a**
ag depraved; defective; (*inesatto*) incorrect,
wrong
vocabo'**lario** *sm* (*dizionario*) dictionary;
(*lessico*) vocabulary
vo'**cabolo** *sm* word
vo'**cale** *ag* vocal ♦ *sf* vowel
vocazi'**one** [vokat'tsjone] *sf* vocation; (*fig*)
natural bent
'**voce** [ˈvotʃe] *sf* voice; (*diceria*) rumour; (*di
un elenco, in bilancio*) item; **~ in
capitolo** (*fig*) to have a say in the matter
voci'**are** [vo'tʃare] *vi* to shout, yell
'**voga** *sf* (*NAUT*) rowing; (*usanza*): **essere in
~** to be in fashion *o* in vogue
vo'**gare** *vi* to row
'**voglia** [ˈvɔʎʎa] *sf* desire, wish; (*macchia*)
birthmark; **aver ~ di qc/di fare** to feel like
sth/like doing; (*più forte*) to want sth/to do
'**voi** *pron* you; **voi'altri** *pron* you
vo'**lano** *sm* (*SPORT*) shuttlecock; (*TECN*)
flywheel
vo'**lante** *ag* flying ♦ *sm* (steering) wheel
volan'**tino** *sm* leaflet
vo'**lare** *vi* (*uccello, aereo, fig*) to fly;
(*cappello*) to blow away *o* off, fly away *o*
off; **~ via** to fly away *o* off
vo'**latile** *ag* (*CHIM*) volatile ♦ *sm* (*ZOOL*) bird
volente'**roso, a** *ag* willing
volenti'**eri** *av* willingly; "**~**" "with
pleasure", "I'd be glad to"

PAROLA CHIAVE

vo'**lere** *sm* will, wish(es); **contro il ~ di**
against the wishes of; **per ~ di qn** in
obedience to sb's will *o* wishes
♦ *vt* **1** (*esigere, desiderare*) to want; **voler
fare/che qn faccia** to want to do/sb to
do; **volete del caffè?** would you like *o* do
you want some coffee?; **vorrei questo/
fare** I would *o* I'd like this/to do; **come
vuoi** as you like; **senza ~** (*inavvertitamente*)
without meaning to, unintentionally
2 (*consentire*): **vogliate attendere, per
piacere** please wait; **vogliamo andare?**

shall we go?; **vuole essere così gentile da ...?** would you be so kind as to ...?; **non ha voluto ricevermi** he wouldn't see me **3: volerci** (*essere necessario: materiale, attenzione*) to need; (: *tempo*) to take; **quanta farina ci vuole per questa torta?** how much flour do you need for this cake?; **ci vuole un'ora per arrivare a Venezia** it takes an hour to get to Venice **4: voler bene a qn** (*amore*) to love sb; (*affetto*) to be fond of sb, like sb very much; **voler male a qn** to dislike sb; **volerne a qn** to bear sb a grudge; **voler dire** to mean

vol'gare *ag* vulgar; **volgariz'zare** *vt* to popularize

'volgere ['vɔldʒere] *vt* to turn ♦ *vi* to turn; (*tendere*): **~ a**: **il tempo volge al brutto** the weather is breaking; **un rosso che volge al viola** a red verging on purple; **~rsi** *vr* to turn; **~ al peggio** to take a turn for the worse; **~ al termine** to draw to an end

'volgo *sm* common people

voli'era *sf* aviary

voli'tivo, a *ag* strong-willed

'volo *sm* flight; **al ~: colpire qc al ~** to hit sth as it flies past; **capire al ~** to understand straight away

volontà *sf* will; **a ~** (*mangiare, bere*) as much as one likes; **buona/cattiva ~** goodwill/lack of goodwill

volon'tario, a *ag* voluntary ♦ *sm* (*MIL*) volunteer

'volpe *sf* fox

'volta *sf* (*momento, circostanza*) time; (*turno, giro*) turn; (*curva*) turn, bend; (*ARCHIT*) vault; (*direzione*): **partire alla ~ di** to set off for; **a mia** (*o* **tua** *etc*) **~** in turn; **una ~** once; **una ~ sola** only once; **due ~e** twice; **una cosa per ~** one thing at a time; **una ~ per tutte** once and for all; **a ~e** at times, sometimes; **una ~ che** (*temporale*) once; (*causale*) since; **3 ~e 4** 3 times 4

volta'faccia [vɔlta'fattʃa] *sm inv* (*fig*) volte-face

vol'taggio [vol'taddʒo] *sm* (*ELETTR*) voltage

vol'tare *vt* to turn; (*girare: moneta*) to turn over; (*rigirare*) to turn round ♦ *vi* to turn; **~rsi** *vr* to turn; to turn over; to turn round

volteggi'are [volted'dʒare] *vi* (*volare*) to circle; (*in equitazione*) to do trick riding; (*in ginnastica*) to vault; to perform acrobatics

'volto, a *pp di* **volgere** ♦ *sm* face

vo'lubile *ag* changeable, fickle

vo'lume *sm* volume; **volumi'noso, a** *ag* voluminous, bulky

voluttà *sf* sensual pleasure *o* delight; **voluttu'oso, a** *ag* voluptuous

vomi'tare *vt, vi* to vomit; **'vomito** *sm* vomiting *no pl*; vomit

'vongola *sf* clam

vo'race [vo'ratʃe] *ag* voracious, greedy

vo'ragine [vo'radʒine] *sf* abyss, chasm

'vortice ['vɔrtitʃe] *sm* whirlwind; whirlpool; (*fig*) whirl

'vostro, a *det*: **il(la) ~(a)** *etc* your ♦ *pron*: **il(la) ~(a)** *etc* yours

vo'tante *sm/f* voter

vo'tare *vi* to vote ♦ *vt* (*sottoporre a votazione*) to take a vote on; (*approvare*) to vote for; (*REL*): **~ qc a** to dedicate sth to; **votazi'one** *sf* vote, voting; **votazioni** *sfpl* (*POL*) votes; (*INS*) marks

'voto *sm* (*POL*) vote; (*INS*) mark; (*REL*) vow; (: *offerta*) votive offering; **aver ~i belli/ brutti** (*INS*) to get good/bad marks

vs. *abbr* (*COMM*) = **vostro**

vul'cano *sm* volcano

vulne'rabile *ag* vulnerable

vuo'tare *vt* to empty; **~rsi** *vr* to empty

vu'oto, a *ag* empty; (*fig: privo*): **~ di** (*senso etc*) devoid of ♦ *sm* empty space, gap; (*spazio in bianco*) blank; (*FISICA*) vacuum; (*fig: mancanza*) gap, void; **a mani ~e** empty-handed; **~ d'aria** air pocket; **~ a rendere** returnable bottle

PUZZLES AND WORDGAMES

Introduction

We are delighted that you have decided to invest in this Collins Italian Dictionary! Whether you intend to use it in school, at home, on holiday or at work, we are sure that you will find it very useful.

The purpose of this supplement is to help you become aware of the wealth of vocabulary and grammatical information your dictionary contains, to explain how this information is presented and also to point out some of the traps one can fall into when using an Italian-English English-Italian dictionary.

In the pages which follow you will find explanations and wordgames (not too difficult!) designed to give you practice in exploring the dictionary's contents and in retrieving information for a variety of purposes. Answers are provided at the end. If you spend a little time on these pages you should be able to use your dictionary more efficiently and effectively. Have fun!

Supplement by
Roy Simon
reproduced by kind permission of
Tayside Region Education Department

zuccheri'era [tsukke'rjera] *sf* sugar bowl

zuccheri'ficio [tsukkeri'fitʃo] *sm* sugar refinery

zucche'rino, a [tsukke'rino] *ag* sugary, sweet

'zucchero ['tsukkero] *sm* sugar

zuc'china [tsuk'kina] *sf* courgette (*BRIT*), zucchini (*US*)

zuc'chino [tsuk'kino] *sm* = **zucchina**

'zuffa ['tsuffa] *sf* brawl

'zuppa ['tsuppa] *sf* soup; (*fig*) mixture, muddle; ~ **inglese** (*CUC*) *dessert made with sponge cake, custard and chocolate,* ≈ trifle (*BRIT*); **zuppi'era** *sf* soup tureen

'zuppo, a ['tsuppo] *ag:* ~ **(di)** drenched (with), soaked (with)

W, X, Y

'**water** ['wɔːtə*] sm inv toilet
'**watt** [vat] sm inv watt
'**weekend** ['wiːkend] sm inv weekend
'**whisky** ['wiski] sm inv whisky
'**windsurf** ['windsəːf] sm inv (tavola)
  windsurfer; (sport) windsurfing
'**würstel** ['vyrstəl] sm inv frankfurter
xi'lofono [ksi'lɔfono] sm xylophone
yacht [jɔt] sm inv yacht
'**yoghurt** ['jɔgurt] sm inv yoghourt

Z, z

zabai'one [dzaba'jone] sm dessert made of
  egg yolks, sugar and marsala
zaf'fata [tsaf'fata] sf (tanfo) stench
zaffe'rano [dzaffe'rano] sm saffron
zaf'firo [dzaf'firo] sm sapphire
'**zaino** ['dzaino] sm rucksack
'**zampa** ['tsampa] sf (di animale: gamba) leg;
  (: piede) paw; **a quattro ~e** on all fours
zampil'lare [tsampil'lare] vi to gush, spurt;
  zam'pillo sm gush, spurt
zam'pogna [tsam'poɲɲa] sf instrument
  similar to bagpipes
'**zanna** ['tsanna] sf (di elefante) tusk; (di
  carnivori) fang
zan'zara [dzan'dzara] sf mosquito;
  zanzari'era sf mosquito net
'**zappa** ['tsappa] sf hoe; **zap'pare** vt to hoe
'**zapping** ['tsapin] sm (TV) channel-hopping
zar, za'rina [tsar, tsa'rina] sm/f tsar/tsarina
'**zattera** ['dzattera] sf raft
za'vorra [dza'vorra] sf ballast
'**zazzera** ['tsattsera] sf shock of hair
'**zebra** ['dzebra] sf zebra; **~e** sfpl (AUT) zebra
  crossing sg (BRIT), crosswalk sg (US)
'**zecca, che** ['tsekka] sf (ZOOL) tick; (officina
  di monete) mint
'**zelo** ['dzelo] sm zeal
ze'nit ['dzenit] sm zenith
'**zenzero** ['dzendzero] sm ginger

'**zeppa** ['tseppa] sf wedge
'**zeppo, a** ['tseppo] ag: **~ di** crammed o
  packed with
zer'bino [dzer'bino] sm doormat
'**zero** ['dzero] sm zero, nought; **vincere per
  tre a ~** (SPORT) to win three-nil
'**zeta** ['dzeta] sm o f zed, (the letter) z
'**zia** ['tsia] sf aunt
zibel'lino [dzibel'lino] sm sable
'**zigomo** ['dzigomo] sm cheekbone
zig'zag [dzig'dzag] sm inv zigzag; **andare a
  ~** to zigzag
zim'bello [dzim'bello] sm (oggetto di burle)
  laughing-stock
'**zinco** ['dzinko] sm zinc
'**zingaro, a** ['dzingaro] sm/f gipsy
'**zio** ['tsio] (pl **'zii**) sm uncle; **zii** smpl (zio e
  zia) uncle and aunt
zip'pare vt, vi (INFORM) to zip
zi'tella [dzi'tella] sf spinster; (peg) old maid
'**zitto, a** ['tsitto] ag quiet; **sta' ~!** be quiet!
ziz'zania [dzid'dzanja] sf (fig): **gettare** o
  seminare ~ to sow discord
'**zoccolo** ['tsɔkkolo] sm (calzatura) clog; (di
  cavallo etc) hoof; (basamento) base; plinth
zo'diaco [dzo'diako] sm zodiac
'**zolfo** ['tsolfo] sm sulphur
'**zolla** ['dzɔlla] sf clod (of earth)
zol'letta [dzol'letta] sf sugar lump
'**zona** ['dzɔna] sf zone, area; **~ di
  depressione** (METEOR) trough of low
  pressure; **~ disco** (AUT) ≈ meter zone; **~
  pedonale** pedestrian precinct; **~ verde** (di
  abitato) green area
'**zonzo** ['dzondzo]: **a ~** av: **andare a ~** to
  wander about, stroll about
zoo ['dzɔo] sm inv zoo
zoolo'gia [dzoolo'dʒia] sf zoology
zoppi'care [tsoppi'kare] vi to limp; to be
  shaky, rickety
'**zoppo, a** ['tsɔppo] ag lame; (fig: mobile)
  shaky, rickety
zoti'cone [dzoti'kone] sm lout
'**zucca, che** ['tsukka] sf (BOT) marrow;
  pumpkin
zucche'rare [tsukke'rare] vt to put sugar
  in; **zucche'rato, a** ag sweet, sweetened

PUZZLES AND WORDGAMES

Contents

HOW INFORMATION IS PRESENTED IN YOUR DICTIONARY

A great deal of information is packed into your Collins Italian Dictionary using colour, various typefaces, sizes of type, symbols, abbreviations and brackets. The purpose of this section is to acquaint you with the conventions used in presenting information.

Headwords

A headword is the word you look up in a dictionary. Headwords are listed in alphabetical order throughout the dictionary. They are printed in colour so that they stand out clearly from all the other words on the dictionary page.

Note that at the top of each page two headwords appear. These tell you which is the first and last word dealt with on the page in question. They are there to help you scan through the dictionary more quickly.

The Italian alphabet consists in practice of the same 26 letters as the English alphabet but j, k, w, x and y are found only in words of foreign origin. Where words are distinguised only by an accent, the unaccented form precedes the accented – e.g. te, tè.

A dictionary entry

An entry is made up of a headword and all the information about that headword. Entries will be short or long depending on how frequently a word is used in either English or Italian and how many meanings it has. Inevitably, the fuller the dictionary entry the more care is needed in sifting through it to find the information you require.

Meanings

The translations of a headword are given in ordinary type. Where there is more than one meaning or usage, a semi-colon separates one from the other.

cannocchi'ale [kannok'kjale] *sm* telescope
can'none *sm* (MIL) gun; (: STORIA) cannon;
(*tubo*) pipe, tube; (*piega*) box pleat; (*fig*)
ace
can'nuccia, ce [kan'nuttʃa] *sf* (drinking)
straw
ca'noa *sf* canoe

'prua *sf* (NAUT) = **prora**
pru'dente *ag* cautious, prudent;

puericul'tura *sf* paediatric nursing; infant
care

te *pron* (*soggetto: in forme comparative,
oggetto*) you
tè *sm inv* tea; (*trattenimento*) tea party

fragola *sf* strawberry

fu'ori *av* outside; (*all'aperto*) outdoors,
outside; (*fuori di casa*, SPORT) out;
(*esclamativo*) get out! ♦ *prep*: **~ (di)** out of,
outside ♦ *sm* outside; **lasciar ~ qc/qn** to
leave sth/sb out; **far ~ qn** (*fam*) to kill sb,
do sb in; **essere ~ di sé** to be beside o.s.;
~ luogo (*inopportuno*) out of place,
uncalled for; **~ mano** out of the way,
remote; **~ pericolo** out of danger; **~ uso**
old-fashioned; obsolete

'grande (*qualche volta* **gran** +C, **grand'** +V)
ag (*grosso, largo, vasto*) big, large; (*alto*)
tall; (*lungo*) long; (*in sensi astratti*) great
♦ *sm/f* (*persona adulta*) adult, grown-up;
(*chi ha ingegno e potenza*) great man/
woman; **fare le cose in ~** to do things in
style; **una gran bella donna** a very
beautiful woman; **non è una gran cosa** *o*
un gran che it's nothing special; **non ne
so gran che** I don't know very much
about it

289

In addition, you will often find other words appearing in *italics* in brackets before the translations. These either give some notion of the contexts in which the headword might appear (as with 'alto' opposite – 'una persona alta', 'un suono alto', etc.) or else they provide synonyms (as with 'reggere' opposite – 'tenere', 'sostenere', etc.).

Phonetic spellings

Where an Italian word contains a sound which is difficult for the English speaker, the phonetic spelling of the word – i.e. its pronunciation – is given in square brackets immediately after it. The phonetic transcription of Italian and English vowels and consonants is given on pages xiv to xv at the front of your dictionary.

Additional information about headwords

Information about the form or usage of certain headwords is given in brackets between the headword and the translation or translations. Have a look at the entries for 'A.C.I.', 'camerino', 'materia' and 'leccapiedi' opposite. This information is usually given in abbreviated form. A helpful list of abbreviations is given on pages xi to xiii at the front of your dictionary.

You should be particularly careful with colloquial words or phrases. Words labelled (*fam*) would not normally be used in formal speech, while those labelled (*fam!*) would be considered offensive. Careful consideration of such style labels will help you avoid many an embarrassing situation when using Italian!

Expressions in which the headword appears

An entry will often feature certain common expressions in which the headword appears. These expressions are in **bold** type, but in black as opposed to colour. A swung dash (~) is used instead of repeating a headword in an entry. 'Freno' and 'idea' opposite illustrate this point. Sometimes the swung dash is used with the appropriate ending shown after it; e.g. 'mano', where '~i' is used to indicate the plural form, 'mani'.

Related words

In the Italian Dictionary words related to certain headwords are sometimes given at the end of an entry, as with 'finestra' and 'accept' opposite. These are easily picked out as they are also in colour. These words are placed in alphabetical order after the headword to which they belong: cf. 'acceptable', 'acceptance' opposite.

'alto, a *ag* high; (*persona*) tall; (*tessuto*) wide, broad; (*sonno, acque*) deep; (*suono*) high(-pitched); (*GEO*) upper; (: *settentrionale*) northern ♦ *sm* top (part) ♦ *av* high; (*parlare*) aloud, loudly; **il palazzo è ~ 20 metri** the building is 20 metres high;

'reggere ['reddʒere] *vt* (*tenere*) to hold; (*sostenere*) to support, bear, hold up; (*portare*) to carry, bear; (*resistere*) to withstand; (*dirigere: impresa*) to manage, run; (*governare*) to rule, govern;

pron'tezza [pron'tettsa] *sf* readiness; quickness, promptness

reci'tare [retʃi'tare] *vt* (*poesia, lezione*) to recite; (*dramma*) to perform; (*ruolo*) to play *o* act (the part of); **recitazi'one** *sf* recitation; (*di attore*) acting

A.C.I. ['atʃi] *sigla m* = *Automobile Club d'Italia*

came'rino *sm* (*TEATRO*) dressing room

scocci'are [skot'tʃare] (*fam*) *vt* to bother, annoy; **~rsi** *vr* to be bothered *o* annoyed

fre'gare *vt* to rub; (*fam: truffare*) to take in, cheat; (: *rubare*) to swipe, pinch; **fregarsene** (*fam!*): **chi se ne frega?** who gives a damn (about it)?

'freno *sm* brake; (*morso*) bit; **~ a disco** disc brake; **~ a mano** handbrake; **tenere a ~ to** restrain

i'dea *sf* idea; (*opinione*) opinion, view; (*ideale*) ideal; **dare l'~ di** to seem, look like; **~ fissa** obsession; **neanche *o* neppure per ~!** certainly not!

fi'nestra *sf* window; **fines'trino** *sm* (*di treno, auto*) window

ma'teria *sf* (*FISICA*) matter; (*TECN, COMM*) material, matter *no pl*; (*disciplina*) subject; (*argomento*) subject matter, material;

leccapi'edi (*peg*) *sm/f inv* toady, bootlicker

'rompere *vt* to break; (*fidanzamento*) to break off ♦ *vi* to break; **~rsi** *vr* to break; **mi rompe le scatole** (*fam*) he (*o* she) is a pain in the neck; **~rsi un braccio** to break an arm;

'mano, i *sf* hand; (*strato: di vernice etc*) coat; **di prima ~** (*notizia*) first-hand; **di seconda ~** second-hand; **man ~** little by little, gradually; **man ~ che** as; **darsi *o* stringersi la ~** to shake hands; **mettere le ~i avanti** (*fig*) to safeguard o.s.; **restare a ~i vuote** to be left empty-handed; **venire alle ~i** to come to blows; **a ~** by hand; **~i in alto!** hands up!

accept [ək'sɛpt] *vt* accettare; **~able** *adj* accettabile; **~ance** *n* accettazione *f*

'Key' words

Your Collins Italian Dictionary gives special status to certain Italian and English words which can be looked on as 'key' words in each language. These are words which have many different usages. 'Molto', 'volere' and 'così' opposite are typical examples in Italian. You are likely to become familiar with them in your day-to-day language studies.

There will be occasions, however, when you want to check on a particular usage. Your dictionary can be very helpful here. Note how with 'volere', for example, different parts of speech and different usages are clearly indicated by a combination of lozenges – ♦ – and numbers. Additionally, further guides to usage are given in the language of the user who needs them. These are bracketed and in italics.

vo'lere *sm* will, wish(es); **contro il ~ di** against the wishes of; **per ~ di qn** in obedience to sb's will *o* wishes

♦ *vt* **1** (*esigere, desiderare*) to want; **voler fare/che qn faccia** to want to do/sb to do; **volete del caffè?** would you like *o* do you want some coffee?; **vorrei questo/ fare** I would *o* I'd like this/to do; **come vuoi** as you like; **senza ~** (*inavvertitamente*) without meaning to, unintentionally

2 (*consentire*): **vogliate attendere, per piacere** please wait; **vogliamo andare?** shall we go?; **vuole essere così gentile da ...?** would you be so kind as to ...?; **non ha voluto ricevermi** he wouldn't see me

3 **volerci** (*essere necessario: materiale, attenzione*) to need; (: *tempo*) to take; **quanta farina ci vuole per questa torta?** how much flour do you need for this cake?; **ci vuole un'ora per arrivare a Venezia** it takes an hour to get to Venice

4 **voler bene a qn** (*amore*) to love sb; (*affetto*) to be fond of sb, like sb very much; **voler male a qn** to dislike sb; **volerne a qn** to bear sb a grudge; **voler dire** to mean

---

'molto, a *det* (*quantità*) a lot of, much; (*numero*) a lot of, many; **~ pane/carbone** a lot of bread/coal; **~a gente** a lot of people, many people; **~i libri** a lot of books, many books; **non ho ~ tempo** I haven't got much time; **per ~ (tempo)** for a long time

♦ *av* **1** a lot, (very) much; **viaggia ~** he travels a lot; **non viaggia ~** he doesn't travel much *o* a lot

2 (*intensivo: con aggettivi, avverbi*) very; (: *con participio passato*) (very) much; **~ buono** very good; **~ migliore, ~ meglio** much *o* a lot better

♦ *pron* much, a lot; **~i, e** *pron pl* many, a lot; **~i pensano che ...** many (people) think ...

---

così *av* **1** (*in questo modo*) like this, (in) this way; (*in tal modo*) so; **le cose stanno ~** this is the way things stand; **non ho detto ~!** I didn't say that!; **come stai? – (e) ~** how are you? — so-so; **e ~ via** and so on; **per ~ dire** so to speak

2 (*tanto*) so; **~ lontano** so far away; **un ragazzo ~ intelligente** such an intelligent boy

♦ *ag inv* (*tale*): **non ho mai visto un film ~** I've never seen such a film

♦ *cong* **1** (*perciò*) so, therefore

2: **~ ... come** as ... as; **non è ~ bravo come te** he's not as good as you; **~ ... che** so ... that

HEADWORDS

Study the following sentences. In each sentence a wrong word spelt very similarly to the correct word has deliberately been put in and the sentence doesn't make sense. This word is shaded each time. Write out each sentence again, putting in the <u>correct</u> word which you will find in your dictionary near the wrong word.

Example: Vietato l'ingrosso agli estranei

['ingrosso' ('all'ingrosso' = 'wholesale') is the wrong word and should be replaced by 'ingresso' (= 'entry')]

1. Ha agito contro il volare della maggioranza.

2. Inserire la moneta e pigliare il pulsante.

3. Non dobbiamo molare proprio adesso.

4. Ho dovuto impanare la lezione a memoria.

5. Il prato era circondato da uno stecchito.

6. Vorrei sentire il tuo parare.

7. Vorrei un po' di panno sulle fragole.

8. Qual è l'oratorio d'apertura dell'ufficio?

9. Quel negoziante mi ha imbrigliato!

10. Sedevano fiasco a fiasco.

WORDGAME 2

DICTIONARY ENTRIES

Complete the crossword below by looking up the English words in the list and finding the correct Italian translations. There is a slight catch, however! All the English words can be translated several ways into Italian, but only one translation will fit correctly into each part of the crossword.

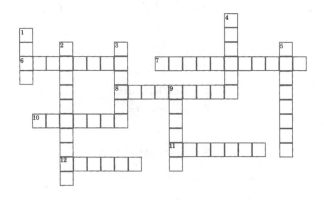

1. THREAD	7. COLD
2. PERMIT	8. WAIT
3. PRESENT	9. NOTICE
4. WANT	10. RETURN
5. JOURNEY	11. CUT
6. FREE	12. REST

WORDGAME 3

FINDING MEANINGS

In this list there are eight pairs of words that have some sort of connection with each other. For example, **'laurea'** (= 'degree') and **'studente'** (= 'student') are linked. Find the other pairs.

1. vestaglia
2. nido
3. pelletteria
4. pantofola
5. campanile
6. studente
7. libro
8. borsetta
9. passerella
10. pinna
11. laurea
12. scaffale
13. gazza
14. nave
15. campana
16. squalo

SYNONYMS

Complete the crossword by supplying SYNONYMS of the words below.
You will sometimes find the synonym you are looking for in italics and
bracketed at the entries for the words listed below. Sometimes you will
have to turn to the English-Italian section for help.

1. RIGUARDO
2. GALA
3. GALLERIA
4. CANCELLARE
5. GALERA

6. BUFFO
7. GIOCARE
8. RAPIDO
9. PAURA
10. MARRONE

WORDGAME 5

SPELLING

You will often use your dictionary to check spellings. The person who has compiled this list of ten Italian words has made <u>three</u> spelling mistakes. Find the three words which have been misspelt and write them out correctly.

1. uccello
2. docia
3. unghia
4. opportuno
5. temporale
6. ortica
7. ovest
8. arabiato
9. folio
10. ossigeno

WORDGAME 6

ANTONYMS

Complete the crossword by supplying ANTONYMS (i.e. opposites) in Italian of the words below. Use your dictionary to help you.

1. ricchezza
2. accettare
3. coraggioso
4. ridere
5. difendere
6. liscio
7. colpevole
8. chiaro
9. bello
10. aperto

WORDGAME 7

PHONETIC SPELLINGS

The phonetic transcriptions of ten Italian words are given below. If you study pages xiv to xv at the front of your dictionary you should be able to work out what the words are.

1. 'ridʒido

2. pit'tʃone

3. 'dʒɛlo

4. 'mattso

5. de'tʃennjo

6. 'kjave

7. 'fɔʎʎa

8. 'soɲɲo

9. 'aʃʃa

10. 'gjanda

WORDGAME 8

EXPRESSIONS IN WHICH THE HEADWORD APPEARS

If you look up the headword 'colpo' in the Italian-English section of your dictionary you will find that the word can have many meanings. Study the entry carefully and translate the following sentences into English.

1. La sua sconfitta è stata un duro colpo per tutti.

2. Ha preso un brutto colpo in testa.

3. Dammi un colpo di telefono domani mattina.

4. Sparò quattro colpi di pistola.

5. Il rumore cessò di colpo.

6. La sua fuga è stata un colpo di testa.

7. Un colpo di vento fece sbattere le persiane.

8. Gli è preso un colpo ed è morto.

9. Hai fatto colpo col tuo discorso, ieri.

10. Gli ho dato un colpo senza volere ed è caduto.

11. Con questo caldo è facile prendere un colpo di sole.

12. Hanno arrestato gli autori del fallito colpo di Stato.

WORDGAME 9

RELATED WORDS

Fill in the blanks in the pairs of sentences below. The missing words are
related to the words on the left. Choose the correct 'relative' each time.
You will find it in your dictionary near the headword provided.

HEADWORD	RELATED WORDS
impiegare	1. Fa l' _____ di banca. 2. Ha appena lasciato il suo _____ .
studiare	3. Ha vissuto a Firenze quand'era _____ . 4. Ha uno _____ in centro.
usare	5. Si raccomanda l' _____ delle cinture di sicurezza. 6. La tua macchina è nuova o _____ ?
unità	7. È una famiglia molto _____ . 8. Vi potete _____ a noi, se volete.
rifiuto	9. È un'offerta che non potrete _____ . 10. Dov'è il bidone dei _____ ?
festeggiare	11. Il negozio è chiuso nei giorni _____ . 12. Ha organizzato una _____ di compleanno.

WORDGAME 10

'KEY' WORDS

Study carefully the entry **'fare'** in your dictionary and find translations for the following:

1. the weather is fine

2. to do psychology

3. go ahead!

4. let me see

5. to get one's hair cut

6. this is the way it's done

7. to do the shopping

8. to be quick

9. to start up the engine

10. he made as if to leave

THE DICTIONARY AND GRAMMAR

While it is true that a dictionary can never be a substitute for a detailed grammar reference book, it nevertheless provides a great deal of grammatical information. If you know how to extract this information you will be able to use Italian more accurately both in speech and in writing.

The Collins Italian Dictionary presents grammatical information as follows.

Parts of speech

Parts of speech are given in italics immediately after the phonetic spellings of headwords. Abbreviated forms are used. Abbreviations can be checked on pages xi to xiii.

Changes in parts of speech within an entry – for example, from adjective to adverb to noun – are indicated by means of lozenges - ♦ - as with the Italian 'forte' and the English 'act' opposite.

Genders of Italian nouns

The gender of each noun in the Italian-English section of the dictionary is indicated in the following way:

> *sm* = sostantivo maschile
>
> *sf* = sostantivo femminile

You will occasionally see *'sm/f'* beside an entry. This indicates that a noun – 'insegnante', for example – can be either masculine or feminine.

Feminine and *irregular* plural forms of nouns are shown, as with 'bambino', 'autore' and 'bruco' opposite.

So many things depend on your knowing the correct gender of an Italian noun – whether you use 'il' or 'la' etc. to translate 'the'; the way you spell and pronounce certain adjectives; the changes you make to past participles, etc. If you are in any doubt as to the gender of a noun, it is always best to check it in your dictionary.

ono'rare *vt* to honour; (*far onore a*) to do credit to; **~rsi** *vr*: **~rsi di** to feel honoured at, be proud of

quassù *av* up here

perciò [per'tʃɔ] *cong* so, for this (*o* that) reason

'pranzo ['prandzo] *sm* dinner; (*a mezzogiorno*) lunch

'cena ['tʃena] *sf* dinner; (*leggera*) supper

bam'bino, a *sm/f* child

au'tore, 'trice *sm/f* author

'bruco, chi *sm* caterpillar; grub

'forte *ag* strong; (*suono*) loud; (*spesa*) considerable, great; (*passione, dolore*) great, deep ♦ *av* strongly; (*velocemente*) fast; (*a voce alta*) loud(ly); (*violentemente*) hard ♦ *sm* (*edificio*) fort; (*specialità*) forte, strong point; **essere ~ in qc** to be good at sth

act [ækt] *n* atto; (*in music-hall etc*) numero; (*LAW*) decreto ♦ *vi* agire; (*THEATRE*) recitare; (*pretend*) fingere ♦ *vt* (*part*) recitare; **to ~ as** agire da; **~ing** *adj* che fa le funzioni di ♦ *n* (*of actor*) recitazione *f*; (*activity*): **to do some ~ing** fare del teatro (*or* del cinema)

inse'gnante [inseɲ'ɲante] *ag* teaching ♦ *sm/f* teacher

305

Adjectives

Adjectives are given in both their masculine and feminine forms, where these are different. The usual rule is to drop the 'o' of the masculine form and add an 'a' to make an adjective feminine, as with 'nero' opposite.

Some adjectives have identical masculine and feminine forms, as with 'verde' opposite.

Many Italian adjectives, however, do not follow the regular pattern. Where an adjective has irregular plural forms, this information is clearly provided in your dictionary, usually with the irregular endings, being given. Consider the entries for 'bianco' and 'lungo' opposite.

Adverbs

Advebs are not always listed in your dictionary. The normal rule for forming adverbs in Italian is to add '-mente' to the feminine form of the adjective. Thus:

> vero > vera > veramente

The '-mente' ending is often the equivalent of the English '-ly':

> veramente – really
> certamente – certainly

Adjectives ending in '-e' and '-le' are slightly different:

> recente > recentemente
> reale > realmente

Where an adverb is very common in Italian, or where its translation(s) cannot be derived from translations for the adjective, it will be listed in alphabetical order, either as a headword or as a subentry. Compare 'solamente' and 'attualmente' opposite.

In many cases, however, Italian adverbs are not given, since the English translation can easily be derived from the relevant translation of the adjective headword: e.g. 'cortese' opposite.

Information about verbs

A major problem facing language learners is that the form of a verb will change according to the subject and/or the tense being used. A typical Italian verb can take on many different forms – too many to list in a dictionary entry.

'nero, a *ag* black; (*scuro*) dark ♦ *sm* black; il Mar N~ the Black Sea

'verde *ag, sm* green; essere al ~ to be broke; ~ bottiglia/oliva bottle/olive green

bi'anco, a, chi, che *ag* white; (*non scritto*) blank ♦ *sm* white; (*intonaco*) whitewash ♦ *sm/f* white, white man/woman; in ~ (*foglio, assegno*) blank; (*notte*) sleepless; in ~ e nero (*TV, FOT*) black and white; mangiare in ~ to follow a bland diet; pesce in ~ boiled fish; andare in ~ (*non riuscire*) to fail; ~ dell'uovo egg-white

'lungo, a, ghi, ghe *ag* long; (*lento: persona*) slow; (*diluito: caffè, brodo*) weak, watery, thin ♦ *sm* length ♦ *prep* along; ~ 3 metri 3 metres long; a ~ for a long time; a ~ andare in the long run; di gran ~a (*molto*) by far; andare in ~ *o* per le lunghe to drag on; saperla ~a to know what's what; in ~ e in largo far and wide, all over; ~ il corso dei secoli throughout the centuries

vera'mente *av* really

certa'mente [tʃerta'mente] *av* certainly

re'cente [re'tʃɛnte] *ag* recent; di ~ recently; recente'mente *av* recently

cor'tese *ag* courteous; corte'sia *sf* courtesy; per cortesia ... excuse me, please ...

sola'mente *av* only, just

'solo, a *ag* alone; (*in senso spirituale: isolato*) lonely; (*unico*): un ~ libro only one book, a single book; (*con ag numerale*): veniamo noi tre ~i just *o* only the three of us are coming ♦ *av* (*soltanto*) only, just; non ~ ... ma anche not only ... but also; fare qc da ~ to do sth (all) by oneself

attu'ale *ag* (*presente*) present; (*di attualità*) topical; (*che è in atto*) actual; attualità *sf inv* topicality; (*avvenimento*) current event; attual'mente *av* at the moment, at present

Yet, although verbs are listed in your dictionary in their infinitive forms only, this does not mean that the dictionary is of limited value when it comes to handling the verb system of the Italian language. On the contrary, it contains much valuable information.

First of all, your dictionary will help you with the meanings of unfamiliar verbs. If you came across the word 'riempie' in a text and looked it up in your dictionary you wouldn't find it. You must deduce that it is part of a verb and look for the infinitive form. Thus you will see that 'riempie' is a form of the verb 'riempire'. You now have the basic meaning of the word you are concerned with – something to do with the English verb 'fill' – and this should be enough to help you understand the text you are reading.

It is usually an easy task to make the connection between the form of a verb and the infinitive. For example, 'riempono', 'riempirò', 'riempissero' and 'reimpii' are all recognisable as parts of the infinitive 'riempire'. However, sometimes it is less obvious – for example, 'vengo', 'vieni' and 'verrò are all parts of 'venire'. The only real solution to this problem is to learn the various forms of the main Italian regular and irregular verbs.

And this is the second source of help offered by your dictionary. The verb tables on page 616 to 617 at the back of the Collins Italian Dictionary provide a summary of some of the main forms of the main tenses of regular and irregular verbs. Consider the verb 'venire' below where the following information is given:

2	venuto	–	Past Participle
3	vengo, vieni, viene, vengono	–	Present Tense forms
5	venni, venisti	–	Past Tense forms
6	verrò etc.	–	1st Person Singular of the Future Tense
8	venga	–	1st, 2nd, 3rd Person of Present Subjunctive

The regular '-are' verb 'parlare' is presented in greater detail, as are the regular '-ire' and '-ere' verbs. The main tenses and the different endings are given in full. This information can be transferred and applied to all verbs in the list. In addition, the main parts of the most common irregular verbs are listed in the body of the dictionary.

PARLARE

1 parlando
2 parlato
3 parlo, parli, parla, parliamo, parlate, parlano
4 parlavo, parlavi, parlava, parlavamo, parlavate, parlavano
5 parlai, parlasti, parlò, parlammo, parlaste, parlarono
6 parlerò, parlerai, parlerà, parleremo, parlerete, parleranno
7 parlerei, parleresti, parlerebbe, parleremmo, parlereste, parlerebbero
8 parli, parli, parli, parliamo, parliate, parlino
9 parlassi, parlassi, parlasse, parlassimo, parlaste, parlassero
10 parla!, parli!, parlate!, parlino!

In order to make maximum use of the information contained in these pages, a good working knowledge of the various rules affecting Italian verbs is required. You will acquire this in the course of your Italian studies and your Collins dictionary will serve as a useful reminder. If you happen to forget how to form the second person singular form of the Future Tense of 'venire' there will be no need to panic – your dictionary contains the information!

WORDGAME 11

PARTS OF SPEECH

In each sentence below a word has been shaded. Put a tick in the appropriate box to indicate the <u>part of speech</u> each time. Remember, different parts of speech are indicated by lozenges within entries.

SENTENCE	Noun	Adj	Adv	Verb
1. Studia diritto a Roma.				
2. Parla più piano! Il bambino dorme.				
3. Ho già versato la minestra nel piatto.				
4. Ho spento il televisore prima della fine del film.				
5. Ha finto di andarsene ed è rimasto ad ascoltare.				
6. Non gli ho permesso di venire.				
7. Vuoi una fetta di dolce?				
8. Abbassi il volume, per favore? Così è troppo forte.				
9. Dopo la notizia sembrava molto scossa.				
10. Hanno assunto un capo del personale per la nostra sezione.				

NOUNS

This list contains the feminine form of some Italian nouns. Use your dictionary to find the **masculine** form.

MASCULINE	FEMININE
	amica
	cantante
	direttrice
	straniera
	regista
	studentessa
	cugina
	lettrice
	professoressa
	collaboratrice

WORDGAME 13

MEANING CHANGES WITH GENDER

There are some pairs of Italian nouns which are distinguished only by
their ending and gender, e.g. 'il partito' and 'la partita'. Fill in the blanks
below with the appropriate member of each pair and the correct article –
'il, la, un' etc – where an article is required.

1. L'ho scritto su _____ da qualche parte   foglio *or*
   Guarda! Sulla pianta è spuntata _____   foglia?

2. Non è questo _____ di fare le cose!   moda *or*
   È un colore che non va più di _____   modo?

3. È arrivato di _____   corso *or*
   Credo che mi iscriverò ad _____   corsa?
   di spagnolo

4. In questa zona ci sono tanti _____   castagne *or*
   Ho comprato un sacchetto di _____   castagni?

5. Fammi vedere _____ della mano!   palma *or*
   Sedevano sulla spiaggia all'ombra di_____   palmo?

6. Ti va di fare _____ a tennis?   partito *or*
   _____ si sta preparando alle elezioni   partita?

7. Devo mettere _____ su questi pantaloni   pezzo *or*
   Vuoi _____ di torta?   pezza?

8. Per oggi basta lavorare! Vado a _____   caso *or*
   Ci siamo conosciuti per _____   casa?

WORDGAME 14

NOUN AND ADJECTIVE FORMS

Use your dictionary to find the following forms of these words.

MASCULINE	FEMININE
1. bianco	
2. fresco	
3. largo	
4. verde	
5. grave	

SINGULAR	PLURAL
6. poca	
7. giovane	
8. grande	
9. veloce	
10. poeta	
11. diadema	
12. triste	
13. tronco	
14. tromba	
15. dialogo	

WORDGAME 15

ADVERBS

Translate the following Italian adverbs into English. Put an asterisk next to those that don't appear in the Italian-English section of the Collins dictionary.

1. recentemente
2. redditiziamente
3. costantemente
4. gentilmente
5. mensilmente
6. naturalmente
7. aggressivamente
8. semplicemente
9. tenacemente
10. esattamente

WORDGAME 16

VERB TENSES

Use your dictionary to help you fill in the blanks in the table below.
(Remember the important pages at the back of your dictionary.)

INFINITIVE	PRESENT TENSE	PAST PARTICIPLE	FUTURE
venire			io
rimanere			
vedere			io
avere	io		
offrire			
muovere			io
finire	io		
uscire	io		
dovere			io
dormire			io
vivere			
potere	io		

WORDGAME 17

PAST PARTICIPLES

Use the verb tables at the back of your dictionary to work out the past participle of these verbs. Check that you have found the correct form by looking in the main text.

INFINITIVE	PAST PARTICIPLE
venire	
contrarre	
coprire	
vivere	
offrire	
sorridere	
prendere	
mettere	
sorprendere	
percorrere	
accogliere	
dipingere	
condurre	
scendere	

WORDGAME 18

IDENTIFYING INFINITIVES

In the sentences below you will see various Italian verbs shaded. Use your dictionary to help you find the **infinitive** form of each verb.

1. Quand'ero a Londra dividevo
   un appartamento con degli amici.

2. I miei amici mi raggiunsero in discoteca.

3. Sua madre lo accompagnava a scuola in macchina.

4. Domani mi alzerò alle nove.

5. Questo fine settimana andremo tutti in campagna.

6. Hanno già venduto la casa.

7. Entrò e si mise a sedere.

8. È nato in Germania.

9. Gli piacerebbe vivere negli Stati Uniti.

10. Faranno una partita a tennis.

11. Ha ricominciato a piovere.

12. Non so cosa gli sia successo.

13. Vorremmo visitare il castello.

14. I bambini avevano freddo.

15. Non so cosa sia meglio fare.

MORE ABOUT MEANING

In this section we will consider some of the problems associated with using a bilingual dictionary.

Overdependence on your dictionary

That the dictionary is an invaluable tool for the language learner is beyond dispute. Nevertheless, it is possible to become overdependent on your dictionary, turning to it in an almost automatic fashion every time you come up against a new Italian word or phrase. Tackling an unfamiliar text in this way will turn reading in Italian into an extremely tedious activity. If you stop to look up every new word you may actually be *hindering* your ability to read in Italian – you are so concerned with the individual words that you pay no attention to the text as a whole and to the context which gives them meaning. It is therefore important to develop appropriate reading skills – using clues such as titles, headlines, illustrations, etc., understanding relations within a sentence, etc. to predict or infer what a text is about.

A detailed study of the development of reading skills is not within the scope of this supplement; we are concerned with knowing how to use a dictionary, which is only one of several important skills involved in reading. Nevertheless, it may be instructive to look at one example. You see the following text in an Italian newspaper and are interested in working out what it is about.

Contextual clues here include the words in large type which you would probably recognise as an Italian name, something that looks like a date in the middle, and the name and address in the bottom right hand corner. The Italian words 'annunciare' and 'clinica' resemble closely the words 'announce' and

> Siamo lieti di annunciare
> la nascito di
>
> # Mario, Francesco
>
> il 29 marzo 1999
>
> Monica e Fraco ROSSI
> Clinca   corso Italia n° 18
> del Sole   34142 Padova

'clinic' in English, so you would not have to look them up in your dictionary. Other 'form' words such as 'siamo', 'la', 'il', and 'di' will be familiar to you from your general studies in Italian. Given that we are dealing with a newspaper, you will probably have worked out by now that this could be an announcement placed in the 'Personal Column'.

So you have used a series of cultural, contextual and word-formation clues to get you to the point where you have understood that Monica and Franco Rossi have placed this notice in the 'Personal Column' of the newspaper and that something happened to Francesco on 29 March 1999, something connected with a hospital. And you have reached this point *without* opening your dictionary once. Common sense and your knowledge of newspaper contents in this country might suggest that this must be an announcement of someone's birth or death. Thus 'lieti' ('happy') and 'nascita' ('birth') become the only words that you need to look up in order to confirm that this is indeed a birth announcement.

When learning Italian we are helped considerably by the fact that many Italian and English words look and sound alike and have exactly the same meaning. Such words are called 'COGNATES'. Many words which look similar in Italian and English come from a common Latin root. Other words are the same or nearly the same in both languages because Italian language has borrowed a word from English or vice versa. The dictionary will often not be necessary where cognates are concerned – provided you know the English word that the Italian word resembles!

Words with more than one meaning

The need to examine with care *all* the information contained in a dictionary entry must be stressed. This is particularly important with the many Italian words which have more than one meaning. For example, the Italian 'giornale' can mean 'diary' as well as 'newspaper'. How you translated the word would depend on the context in which you found it.

Similarly, if you were trying to translate a phrase such as 'era in corso ...', you would have to look through the whole entry for 'corso' to get the right translation. If you restricted your search to the first lines of the entry and saw that the meanings given are 'course' and 'main street', you might be tempted to assume that the phrase meant 'it was in the main street'. But if you examined the entry closely you would see that 'in corso' means 'in progress, under way'. So 'era in corso' means 'it was in progress', as in the phrase 'lavori in corso'.

The same need for care applies when you are using the English-Italian section of your dictionary to translate a word from English into Italian. Watch out in particular for the lozenges indicating changes in parts of speech.

The noun 'sink' is 'lavandino, aquaio', while the verb is 'affondare'. If you don't watch what you are doing, you could end up with ridiculous non-Italian e.g. 'Ha messo i piatti sporchi nell'affondare.'

Phrasal verbs

Another potential source of difficulty is English phrasal verbs. These consist of a common verb ('go', 'make', etc.) plus an adverb and/or a preposition to give English expressions such as 'to make out', 'to take after', etc. Entries for such verbs tend to be fairly full, so close examination of the contents is required. Note how these verbs appear in colour within the entry.

False friends

Many Italian and English words have similar forms *and* meanings. Many Italian words, however, *look* like English words but have a completely *different* meaning. For example, 'attualmente' means 'at the moment, at present'; 'eventuale' means 'possible'. This can easily lead to serious mistranslations.

make [meɪk] (*pt, pp* **made**) *vt* fare; (*manufacture*) fare, fabbricare; (*cause to be*): **to ~ sb sad** *etc* rendere qn triste *etc*; (*force*): **to ~ sb do sth** costringere qn a fare qc, far fare qc a qn; (*equal*): **2 and 2 ~ 4** 2 più 2 fa 4 ♦ *n* fabbricazione *f*; (*brand*) marca; **to ~ a fool of sb** far fare a qn la figura dello scemo; **to ~ a profit** realizzare un profitto; **to ~ a loss** subire una perdita; **to ~ it** (*arrive*) arrivare; (*achieve sth*) farcela; **what time do you ~ it?** che ora fai?; **to ~ do with** arrangiarsi con; **~ for** *vt fus* (*place*) avviarsi verso; **~ out** *vt* (*write out*) scrivere; (: *cheque*) emettere; (*understand*) capire; (*see*) distinguere; (: *numbers*) decifrare; **~ up** *vt* (*constitute*) formare; (*invent*) inventare; (*parcel*) fare ♦ *vi* conciliarsi; (*with cosmetics*) truccarsi; **~ up for** *vt fus* compensare; ricuperare; **~-believe** *n*: **a world of ~-believe** un mondo di favole;

Sometimes the meaning of the Italian word is *close* to the English. For example, 'la moneta' means 'small change' rather than 'money'; 'il soprannome' means 'nickname' not 'surname'. But some Italian words have two meanings, one the same as the English, the other completely different! 'L'editore' can mean 'publisher' as well as 'editor'; 'la marcia' can mean 'march/running/walking', but also 'the gear (of a car)'.

Such words are often referred to as 'false friends'. You will have to look at the context in which they appear to arrive at the correct meaning. If they seem to fit in with the sense of the passage as a whole, you will probably not need to look them up. If they don't make sense, however, you may well be dealing with 'false friends'.

WORDGAME 19

WORDS IN CONTEXT

Study the sentences below. Translations of the shaded words are given at the bottom. Match the number of the sentence and the letter of the translation correctly each time.

1. In questa zona è proibito cacciare.
2. L'ho visto cacciare i soldi in tasca.
3. È il ritratto di una dama del Settecento.
4. Facciamo una partita a dama?
5. Ha versato il vino nei bicchieri.
6. Hanno versato tutti i soldi sul loro conto.
7. Ti presento il mio fratello maggiore.
8. Aveva il grado di maggiore nell'esercito.
9. Ho finito i dadi per brodo.
10. In un angolo due uomini giocavano a dadi.
11. Sua madre è già partita per il mare.
12. Ti va di fare una partita a carte?
13. Il ladro è stato visto da un passante.
14. Devi infilare la cintura nel passante.
15. È corso verso di me.
16. Leggete ad alta voce il primo verso della poesia.

a. poured	e. loop	i. dice	m. passer-by
b. hunt	f. towards	j. major	n. draughts
c. left	g. paid	k. stock cubes	o. older
d. game	h. line	l. stick	p. lady

321

WORDGAME 20

WORDS WITH MORE THAN ONE MEANING

Look at the advertisements below. The words which are shaded can have more than one meaning. Use your dictionary to help you work out the correct translation in the context.

1

Desidero ricevere maggiori informazioni per un soggiorno al Lago di Garda

Nome e cognome: _____

Indirizzo: _____

2

Con il patrocinio della

REGIONE TOSCANA e CAMERA DI COMMERCIO DELLA TOSCANA

3

TRILLO
LA SVEGLIA ELETTRONICA
CHE NON TI TRADISCE
4 funzioni: ore, minuti, secondi, sveglia
Funzionamento a pile

4

ECONOMIA E
FINANZA
BORSA E FONDI

5

Albergo Ristorante
"La Cantina"
cucina casalinga
a 500 metri dalla piazza

6

SI PREGA DI RITIRARE LO SCONTRINO ALLA CASSA

7

Visite guidate al paese
di Alassio

8

CASSA
rurale ed artigiana
Via Basovizza 2
Trieste

9

Una casa in riva al mare
"CALA DEI TEMPLARI"
Soggiorno, una camera da letto,
bagno, balcone

10

PRATOLINI
la cucina su misura per te
Pratolini S.p.A. – 57480 Frascati – Roma
Tel (0733) 5581 (10 linee) –
Fax (0733) 5585

WORDGAME 21

FALSE FRIENDS

Look at the advertisements below. The words which are shaded resemble English words but have different meanings here. Find a correct translation for each word in the context.

1

Boutique "La Moda"
Liquidazione di tutti gli articoli

2

Pensione Miramonti

camere con bagno/doccia

parcheggio privato

bar, ristorante

3

ACCENDERE LE LUCI IN GALLERIA

4

LIBRERIA
Il Gabbiano
  Libri – Giornali – Articoli
  spiaggia – Guide turistiche
  – Cartoline

  SASSARI
  Via Mazzini 46

5

ITALMODA CRAVATTE
LE GRANDI FIRME
Divisione della BST,
Bergamo S.p.A

La direzione di questo albergo
declina ogni responsabilità per lo
smarrimento di oggetti lasciati
incustoditi

6

7

Questo **esercizio** resterà
chiuso nei giorni festivi
e il lunedì

8

"Le bollicine"
Locale notturno
    – pianobar
        – discoteca

9

**Lago di Garda
campeggi, sport acquatici,
gite in battello**

10

Attenzione: per l'uso leggere
attentamente l'istruzione
interna.
Da vendersi dietro
presentazione di **ricetta** medica.

HAVE FUN WITH YOUR DICTIONARY

Here are some word games for you to try. You will find your dictionary helpful as you attempt the activities.

WORDGAME 22

CODED WORDS

In the boxes below, the letters of eight Italian words have been replaced by numbers. A number represents the same letter each time.

Try to crack the code and find the eight words. If you need help, use your dictionary.

Here is a clue: all the words you are looking for have something to do with TRANSPORT.

1 | T¹ | R² | E³ | 4 | 5

2 | 6 | 7 | 8 | 9 | 5 | 4

3 | 4 | 7 | 10 | 3

4 | 7 | 11 | 1 | 5 | 12 | 11 | 16

5 | 1 | 2 | 7 | 13 | 14 | 3 | 1 | 1 | 5

6 | 8 | 5 | 1 | 5 | 6 | 9 | 6 | 15 | 3 | 1 | 1 | 7

7 | 12 | 7 | 2 | 6 | 7

8 | 7 | 11 | 1 | 5 | 8 | 5 | 12 | 9 | 15 | 3

HEADLESS WORDS

If you 'behead' certain Italian words, i.e. take away their first letter, you are left with another Italian word. For example, if you behead **'maglio'** (= 'mallet'), you get **'aglio'** (= 'garlic').

The following words have their heads chopped off, i.e. the first letter has been removed. Use your dictionary to help you form a new Italian word by adding one letter to the start of each word below. Write down the new Italian word and its meaning. There may be more than one new word you can form.

1. arto (= limb)
2. alto (= high)
3. esca (= bait)
4. unto (= greasy)
5. ora (= hour)
6. acca (= letter H)
7. orale (= oral)
8. otto (= eight)
9. orda (= horde)
10. alone (= halo)
11. oca (= goose)
12. anca (= hip)
13. ascia (= axe)
14. anno (= year)
15. rete (= net)

WORDGAME 24

CROSSWORD

Complete this crossword by looking up the words listed below in the English-Italian section of your dictionary. Remember to read through the entry carefully to find the word that will fit.

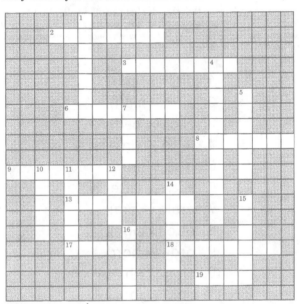

ACROSS

2. to dirty
3. to admire
6. relationship
8. deposit
9. strip
13. employ
17. ebony
18. to take off
19. night

DOWN

1. (a piece of) news
4. to reassure
5. story
7. porthole
10. rough
11. swarm
12. air
14. sad
15. adder
16. harbour

WORDGAME 25

SPLIT WORDS

There are twelve Italian words hidden in the grid below. Each word is made up of five letters but has been split into two parts. Find the Italian words. Each group of letters can only be used once. Use your dictionary to help you.

fer	ba	por	sce	za	che
an	mo	to	gam	se	duo
pri	ta	co	ro	fuo	na
fal	sen	men	so	for	mo

WORDGAME 26

KITCHEN WORDS

Here is a list of Italian words for things you will find in the kitchen. Unfortunately, the letters have all been jumbled up. Try to work out what each word is and put the word in the boxes on the right. You will see that there are six shaded boxes below. With the six letters in the shaded boxes make up <u>another</u> Italian word for an object you can find in the kitchen.

1. zazta   Vuoi una _____ di caffé?

2. grifo   Metti il burro nel _____!

3. vatloa   A _____! È pronto!

4. norfo   Cuocere in _____ per 20 minuti.

5. chiocciau   Assaggia la minestra col _____.

6. polacasta   Usa il _____ per gli spaghetti.

The word you are looking for is:

330

WORDGAME 27

GRID WORDS

Take the four letters given each time and put them in the four empty boxes in the centre of each grid. Arrange them in such a way that you form four six-letter words. Use your dictionary to check the words.

ANSWERS

WORDGAME 1

1	volere	6	parere
2	pigiare	7	panna
3	mollare	8	orario
4	imparare	9	imbrogliato
5	steccato	10	fianco

WORDGAME 2

1	filo	7	raffreddore
2	permettere	8	attendere
3	regalo	9	notare
4	volere	10	ritorno
5	tragitto	11	ridurre
6	liberare	12	riposo

WORDGAME 3

vestaglia + pantofola
nido + gazza
pelletteria + borsetta
campanile + campana
studente + laurea
libro + scaffale
passerella + nave
pinna + squalo

WORDGAME 4

1	attenzione	6	divertente
2	sfarzo	7	ingannare
3	traforo	8	veloce
4	annullare	9	timore
5	prigione	10	bruno

WORDGAME 5

1 doccia 2 arrabbiato 3 foglio

WORDGAME 6

1	povertà	6	ruvido
2	rifiutare	7	innocente
3	vigliacco	8	scuro
4	piangere	9	brutto
5	attaccare	10	chiuso

WORDGAME 7

1	rigido	6	chiave
2	piccione	7	foglia
3	gelo	8	sogno
4	mazzo	9	ascia
5	decennio	10	ghianda

WORDGAME 8

1 shock
2 blow
3 phone call
4 shot
5 suddenly
6 impulse *or* whim
7 gust of wind
8 stroke
9 strong impression
10 knock
11 sunstroke
12 coup d'état

WORDGAME 9

1	impiegato	7	unita
2	impiego	8	unire
3	studente	9	rifiutare
4	studio	10	rifiuti
5	uso	11	festivi
6	usata	12	festa

WORDGAME 10

1 fa bel tempo
2 fare psicologia
3 faccia pure
4 fammi vedere
5 farsi tagliare i capelli
6 si fa così
7 fare la spesa
8 fare presto
9 far partire il motore
10 fece per andarsene

WORDGAME 11

1	n	5	v	8	adj
2	adv	6	v	9	adj
3	n	7	n	10	n
4	n				

WORDGAME 12

1	amico	6	studente
2	cantante	7	cugino
3	direttore	8	lettore
4	straniero	9	professore
5	regista	10	collaboratore

WORDGAME 13

1	un foglio	5	il palmo
	una foglia		una palma
2	il modo	6	una partita
	moda		il partito
3	corsa	7	una pezza
	un corso		un pezzo
4	castagni	8	casa
	castagne		caso

WORDGAME 14

1	bianca	9	veloci
2	fresca	10	poeti
3	larga	11	diademi
4	verde	12	tristi
5	grave	13	tronchi
6	poche	14	trombe
7	giovani	15	dialoghi
8	grandi		

WORDGAME 16

1	io verrò	7	io finisco
2	rimasto	8	io esco
3	io vedrò	9	io dovrò
4	io ho	10	io dormirò
5	offerto	11	vissuto
6	mosso	12	io posso

WORDGAME 17

1	venuto	8	messo
2	contratto	9	sorpreso
3	coperto	10	percorso
4	vissuto	11	accolto
5	offerto	12	dipinto
6	sorriso	13	condotto
7	preso	14	sceso

WORDGAME 18

1	essere	9	piacere
2	raggiungere	10	fare
3	accompagnare	11	ricominciare
4	alzarsi	12	succedere
5	andare	13	volere
6	vendere	14	avere
7	mettersi	15	essere
8	nascere		

WORDGAME 19

1	b	5	a	9	k	13	m
2	l	6	g	10	i	14	e
3	p	7	o	11	c	15	f
4	n	8	j	12	d	16	h

WORDGAME 20

1	stay	7	village
2	chamber		(here; town)
3	alarm clock	8	bank
4	stock exchange;	9	living room
	funds	10	kitchen
5	cooking		
6	checkout		
	(here; till)		

WORDGAME 21

1	clearance sale	6	management
2	boarding house	7	business
3	tunnel	8	nightclub
4	newspapers	9	camp site
5	ties	10	prescription

WORDGAME 22

1	treno	5	traghetto
2	camion	6	motocicletta
3	nave	7	barca
4	autobus	8	automobile

WORDGAME 23

1 sarto (= tailor)
2 salto (= jump)
3 pesca (= peach)
4 punto (= dot)
5 mora (= blackberry)
6 vacca (= cow)
7 morale (= moral)
8 rotto (= broken)
9 corda (= cord)
10 salone (= sitting room)
11 foca (= seal)
12 panca (= bench)
13 fascia (= band)
14 danno (= damage)
15 prete (= priest)

WORDGAME 24

ACROSS		DOWN	
2	sporcare	1	notizia
3	ammirare	4	rassicurare
6	rapporto	5	favola
8	acconto	7	oblò
9	striscia	10	rozzo
13	impiegare	11	sciame
17	ebano	12	aria
18	togliere	14	triste
19	sera	15	vipera
		16	porto

WORDGAME 25

ferro	senza	duomo
gamba	anche	fuoco
porta	primo	falso
scena	mento	forse

WORDGAME 26

1	tazza	4	forno
2	frigo	5	cucchiaio
3	tavola	6	colapasta

Missing word – FRUSTA

WORDGAME 27

1	parere	1	podere	1	volere
2	triste	2	crosta	2	stagno
3	morire	3	pedone	3	volare
4	presto	4	cresta	4	fregio

ENGLISH – ITALIAN
INGLESE – ITALIANO

A, a

A [eɪ] *n* (MUS) la *m*; (letter) A, a *f or m inv*;
~-**road** *n* strada statale

a [ə] (before vowel or silent h: **an**) indef art
1 un (uno +s impure, gn, pn, ps, x, z), f
una (un' +vowel); ~ **book** un libro; ~ **mirror**
uno specchio; **an apple** una mela; **she's** ~
doctor è medico
2 (instead of the number ''one'') un(o), f
una; ~ **year ago** un anno fa; ~ **hundred/**
thousand etc **pounds** cento/mille etc
sterline
3 (in expressing ratios, prices etc) a, per; **3** ~
day/week 3 al giorno/alla settimana;
10 km an hour 10 km all'ora; **£5** ~ **person**
5 sterline a persona or per persona

A.A. *n abbr* (= Alcoholics Anonymous) AA;
(BRIT: = Automobile Association) ≈ A.C.I. *m*
A.A.A. (US) *n abbr* (= American Automobile
Association) ≈ A.C.I. *m*
aback [əˈbæk] *adv*: **to be taken** ~ essere
sbalordito(a)
abandon [əˈbændən] *vt* abbandonare ♦ *n*:
with ~ sfrenatamente, spensieratamente
abate [əˈbeɪt] *vi* calmarsi
abattoir [ˈæbətwɑː*] (BRIT) *n* mattatoio
abbey [ˈæbɪ] *n* abbazia, badia
abbot [ˈæbət] *n* abate *m*
abbreviation [əbriːvɪˈeɪʃən] *n* abbreviazione
f
abdicate [ˈæbdɪkeɪt] *vt* abdicare a ♦ *vi*
abdicare
abdomen [ˈæbdəmən] *n* addome *m*
abduct [æbˈdʌkt] *vt* rapire
abide [əˈbaɪd] *vt*: **I can't** ~ **it/him** non lo
posso soffrire or sopportare; ~ **by** *vt fus*
conformarsi a
ability [əˈbɪlɪtɪ] *n* abilità *f inv*

abject [ˈæbdʒɛkt] *adj* (poverty) abietto(a);
(apology) umiliante
ablaze [əˈbleɪz] *adj* in fiamme
able [ˈeɪbl] *adj* capace; **to be** ~ **to do sth**
essere capace di fare qc, poter fare qc; ~-
bodied *adj* robusto(a); **ably** *adv*
abilmente
abnormal [æbˈnɔːməl] *adj* anormale
aboard [əˈbɔːd] *adv* a bordo ♦ *prep* a bordo
di
abode [əˈbəʊd] *n*: **of no fixed** ~ senza fissa
dimora
abolish [əˈbɒlɪʃ] *vt* abolire
abominable [əˈbɒmɪnəbl] *adj* abominevole
aborigine [æbəˈrɪdʒɪnɪ] *n* aborigeno/a
abort [əˈbɔːt] *vt* abortire; ~**ion** [əˈbɔːʃən] *n*
aborto; **to have an** ~**ion** abortire; ~**ive** *adj*
abortivo/a
abound [əˈbaʊnd] *vi* abbondare; **to** ~ **in** or
with abbondare di

about [əˈbaʊt] *adv* **1** (approximately) circa,
quasi; ~ **a hundred/thousand** etc un
centinaio/migliaio etc, circa cento/mille etc;
it takes ~ **10 hours** ci vogliono circa 10
ore; **at** ~ **2 o'clock** verso le 2; **I've just** ~
finished ho quasi finito
2 (referring to place) qua e là, in giro; **to**
leave things lying ~ lasciare delle cose in
giro; **to run** ~ correre qua e là; **to walk** ~
camminare
3: **to be** ~ **to do sth** stare per fare qc
♦ *prep* **1** (relating to) su, di; **a book** ~
London un libro su Londra; **what is it** ~?
di che si tratta?; (book, film etc) di cosa
tratta?; **we talked** ~ **it** ne abbiamo parlato;
what or **how** ~ **doing this?** che ne dici di
fare questo?
2 (referring to place): **to walk** ~ **the town**

camminare per la città; **her clothes were scattered ~ the room** i suoi vestiti erano sparsi *or* in giro per tutta la stanza

about-face *n* dietro front *m inv*
about-turn *n* dietro front *m inv*
above [ə'bʌv] *adv, prep* sopra; **mentioned ~** suddetto; **~ all** soprattutto; **~board** *adj* aperto(a); onesto(a)
abrasive [ə'breɪzɪv] *adj* abrasivo(a); *(fig)* caustico(a)
abreast [ə'brɛst] *adv* di fianco; **to keep ~ of** tenersi aggiornato su
abroad [ə'brɔːd] *adv* all'estero
abrupt [ə'brʌpt] *adj (sudden)* improvviso(a); *(gruff, blunt)* brusco(a)
abscess ['æbsɪs] *n* ascesso
absence ['æbsəns] *n* assenza
absent ['æbsənt] *adj* assente; **~ee** [-'tiː] *n* assente *m/f*; **~-minded** *adj* distratto(a)
absolute ['æbsəluːt] *adj* assoluto(a); **~ly** [-'luːtlɪ] *adv* assolutamente
absolve [əb'zɒlv] *vt*: **to ~ sb (from)** *(sin)* assolvere qn (da); *(oath)* sciogliere qn (da)
absorb [əb'zɔːb] *vt* assorbire; **to be ~ed in a book** essere immerso in un libro; **~ent cotton** *(US)* n cotone *m* idrofilo
absorption [əb'sɔːpʃən] *n* assorbimento
abstain [əb'steɪn] *vi*: **to ~ (from)** astenersi (da)
abstract ['æbstrækt] *adj* astratto(a)
absurd [əb'sɜːd] *adj* assurdo(a)
abuse [*n* ə'bjuːs, *vb* ə'bjuːz] *n* abuso; *(insults)* ingiurie *fpl* ♦ *vt* abusare di; **abusive** *adj* ingiurioso(a)
abysmal [ə'bɪzməl] *adj* spaventoso(a)
abyss [ə'bɪs] *n* abisso
AC *abbr* (= *alternating current*) c.a.
academic [ækə'dɛmɪk] *adj* accademico(a); *(pej: issue)* puramente formale ♦ *n* universitario(a)
academy [ə'kædəmɪ] *n (learned body)* accademia; *(school)* scuola privata; **~ of music** conservatorio
accelerate [æk'sɛləreɪt] *vt, vi* accelerare; **acceleration** *n* accelerazione *f*; **accelerator** *n* acceleratore *m*

accent ['æksɛnt] *n* accento
accept [ək'sɛpt] *vt* accettare; **~able** *adj* accettabile; **~ance** *n* accettazione *f*
access ['æksɛs] *n* accesso; **~ible** [æk'sɛsəbl] *adj* accessibile
accessory [æk'sɛsərɪ] *n* accessorio; (LAW): **~ to** complice *m/f* di
accident ['æksɪdənt] *n* incidente *m*; *(chance)* caso; **by ~** per caso; **~al** [-'dɛntl] *adj* accidentale; **~ally** [-'dɛntəlɪ] *adv* per caso; **~ insurance** *n* assicurazione *f* contro gli infortuni; **~-prone** *adj*: **he's very ~-prone** è un vero passaguai
acclaim [ə'kleɪm] *n* acclamazione *f*
accommodate [ə'kɒmədeɪt] *vt* alloggiare; *(oblige, help)* favorire
accommodating [ə'kɒmədeɪtɪŋ] *adj* compiacente
accommodation [əkɒmə'deɪʃən] *n* alloggio; **~s** *(US)* npl alloggio
accompany [ə'kʌmpənɪ] *vt* accompagnare
accomplice [ə'kʌmplɪs] *n* complice *m/f*
accomplish [ə'kʌmplɪʃ] *vt* compiere; *(goal)* raggiungere; **~ed** *adj* esperto(a); **~ment** *n* compimento; realizzazione *f*
accord [ə'kɔːd] *n* accordo ♦ *vt* accordare; **of his own ~** di propria iniziativa; **~ance** *n*: **in ~ance with** in conformità con; **~ing**: **~ing to** *prep* secondo; **~ingly** *adv* in conformità
accordion [ə'kɔːdɪən] *n* fisarmonica
account [ə'kaunt] *n* (COMM) conto; *(report)* descrizione *f*; **~s** *npl* (COMM) conti *mpl*; **of no ~** di nessuna importanza; **on ~** in acconto; **on no ~** per nessun motivo; **on ~ of** a causa di; **to take into ~, take ~ of** tener conto di; **~ for** *vt fus* spiegare; giustificare; **~able** *adj*: **~able (to)** responsabile (verso)
accountancy [ə'kauntənsɪ] *n* ragioneria
accountant [ə'kauntənt] *n* ragioniere/a
account number *n* numero di conto
accrued interest [ə'kruːd-] *n* interesse *m* maturato
accumulate [ə'kjuːmjuleɪt] *vt* accumulare ♦ *vi* accumularsi
accuracy ['ækjurəsɪ] *n* precisione *f*

accurate ['ækjurɪt] *adj* preciso(a); **~ly** *adv* precisamente

accusation [ækju'zeɪʃən] *n* accusa

accuse [ə'kjuːz] *vt* accusare; **~d** *n* accusato/a

accustom [ə'kʌstəm] *vt* abituare; **~ed** *adj*: **~ed to** abituato(a) a

ace [eɪs] *n* asso

ache [eɪk] *n* male *m*, dolore *m* ♦ *vi* (*be sore*) far male, dolere; **my head ~s** mi fa male la testa

achieve [ə'tʃiːv] *vt* (*aim*) raggiungere; (*victory, success*) ottenere; **~ment** *n* compimento; successo

acid ['æsɪd] *adj* acido(a) ♦ *n* acido; **~ rain** *n* pioggia acida

acknowledge [ək'nɔlɪdʒ] *vt* (*letter: also*: **~ receipt of**) confermare la ricevuta di; (*fact*) riconoscere; **~ment** *n* conferma; riconoscimento

acne ['æknɪ] *n* acne *f*

acorn ['eɪkɔːn] *n* ghianda

acoustic [ə'kuːstɪk] *adj* acustico(a); **~s** *n, npl* acustica

acquaint [ə'kweɪnt] *vt*: **to ~ sb with sth** far sapere qc a qn; **to be ~ed with** (*person*) conoscere; **~ance** *n* conoscenza; (*person*) conoscente *m/f*

acquire [ə'kwaɪə*] *vt* acquistare

acquit [ə'kwɪt] *vt* assolvere; **to ~ o.s. well** comportarsi bene; **~tal** *n* assoluzione *f*

acre ['eɪkə*] *n* acro (= 4047 m²)

acrid ['ækrɪd] *adj* acre; pungente

acrobat ['ækrəbæt] *n* acrobata *m/f*

across [ə'krɔs] *prep* (*on the other side*) dall'altra parte di; (*crosswise*) attraverso ♦ *adv* dall'altra parte; in larghezza; **to run/swim ~** attraversare di corsa/a nuoto; **~ from** di fronte a

acrylic [ə'krɪlɪk] *adj* acrilico(a)

act [ækt] *n* atto; (*in music-hall etc*) numero; (*LAW*) decreto ♦ *vi* agire; (*THEATRE*) recitare; (*pretend*) fingere ♦ *vt* (*part*) recitare; **to ~ as** agire da; **~ing** *adj* che fa le funzioni di ♦ *n* (*of actor*) recitazione *f*; (*activity*): **to do some ~ing** fare del teatro (*or* del cinema)

action ['ækʃən] *n* azione *f*; (*MIL*) com-

battimento; (*LAW*) processo; **out of ~** fuori combattimento; fuori servizio; **to take ~** agire; **~ replay** *n* (*TV*) replay *m inv*

activate ['æktɪveɪt] *vt* (*mechanism*) attivare

active ['æktɪv] *adj* attivo(a); **~ly** *adv* (*participate*) attivamente; (*discourage, dislike*) vivamente

activity [æk'tɪvɪtɪ] *n* attività *f inv*; **~ holiday** *n* vacanza organizzata con attività ricreative per ragazzi

actor ['æktə*] *n* attore *m*

actress ['æktrɪs] *n* attrice *f*

actual ['æktjuəl] *adj* reale, vero(a); **~ly** *adv* veramente; (*even*) addirittura

acute [ə'kjuːt] *adj* acuto(a); (*mind, person*) perspicace

ad [æd] *n abbr* = **advertisement**

A.D. *adv abbr* (= *Anno Domini*) d.C.

adamant ['ædəmənt] *adj* irremovibile

adapt [ə'dæpt] *vt* adattare ♦ *vi*: **to ~ (to)** adattarsi (a); **~able** *adj* (*device*) adattabile; (*person*) che sa adattarsi; **~er** *or* **~or** *n* (*ELEC*) adattatore *m*

add [æd] *vt* aggiungere; (*figures: also*: **~ up**) addizionare ♦ *vi*: **to ~ to** (*increase*) aumentare; **it doesn't ~ up** (*fig*) non quadra, non ha senso

adder ['ædə*] *n* vipera

addict ['ædɪkt] *n* tossicomane *m/f*; (*fig*) fanatico/a; **~ed** [ə'dɪktɪd] *adj*: **to be ~ed to** (*drink etc*) essere dedito(a) a; (*fig: football etc*) essere tifoso(a) di; **~ion** [ə'dɪkʃən] *n* (*MED*) tossicodipendenza; **~ive** [ə'dɪktɪv] *adj* che dà assuefazione

addition [ə'dɪʃən] *n* addizione *f*; (*thing added*) aggiunta; **in ~** inoltre; **in ~ to** oltre; **~al** *adj* supplementare

additive ['ædɪtɪv] *n* additivo

address [ə'dres] *n* indirizzo; (*talk*) discorso ♦ *vt* indirizzare; (*speak to*) fare un discorso a; (*issue*) affrontare

adept ['ædept] *adj*: **~ at** esperto(a) in

adequate ['ædɪkwɪt] *adj* adeguato(a); sufficiente

adhere [əd'hɪə*] *vi*: **to ~ to** aderire a; (*fig: rule, decision*) seguire

adhesive [əd'hiːzɪv] *n* adesivo; **~ tape** *n*

(*BRIT: for parcels etc*) nastro adesivo; (*US: MED*) cerotto adesivo

adjective ['ædʒɛktɪv] *n* aggettivo

adjoining [ə'dʒɔɪnɪŋ] *adj* accanto *inv*, adiacente

adjourn [ə'dʒəːn] *vt* rimandare ♦ *vi* essere aggiornato(a)

adjust [ə'dʒʌst] *vt* aggiustare; (*change*) rettificare ♦ *vi*: **to ~ (to)** adattarsi (a); **~able** *adj* regolabile; **~ment** *n* (*PSYCH*) adattamento; (*of machine*) regolazione *f*; (*of prices, wages*) modifica

ad-lib [æd'lɪb] *vi* improvvisare ♦ *adv*: **ad lib** a piacere, a volontà

administer [əd'mɪnɪstə*] *vt* amministrare; (*justice, drug*) somministrare

administration [ədmɪnɪs'treɪʃən] *n* amministrazione *f*

administrative [əd'mɪnɪstrətɪv] *adj* amministrativo(a)

admiral ['ædmərəl] *n* ammiraglio; **A~ty** (*BRIT*) *n* Ministero della Marina

admiration [ædmə'reɪʃən] *n* ammirazione *f*

admire [əd'maɪə*] *vt* ammirare

admission [əd'mɪʃən] *n* ammissione *f*; (*to exhibition, night club etc*) ingresso; (*confession*) confessione *f*

admit [əd'mɪt] *vt* ammettere; far entrare; (*agree*) riconoscere; **to ~ to** riconoscere; **~tance** *n* ingresso; **~tedly** *adv* bisogna pur riconoscere (che)

ad nauseam [æd'nɔːsɪæm] *adv* fino alla nausea, a non finire

ado [ə'duː] *n*: **without (any) more ~** senza più indugi

adolescence [ædəu'lɛsns] *n* adolescenza

adolescent [ædəu'lɛsnt] *adj, n* adolescente *m/f*

adopt [ə'dɒpt] *vt* adottare; **~ed** *adj* adottivo(a); **~ion** [ə'dɒpʃən] *n* adozione *f*

adore [ə'dɔː*] *vt* adorare

Adriatic [eɪdrɪ'ætɪk] *n*: **the ~ (Sea)** il mare Adriatico, l'Adriatico

adrift [ə'drɪft] *adv* alla deriva

adult ['ædʌlt] *adj* adulto(a); (*work, education*) per adulti ♦ *n* adulto/a

adultery [ə'dʌltərɪ] *n* adulterio

advance [əd'vɑːns] *n* avanzamento; (*money*) anticipo ♦ *adj* (*booking etc*) in anticipo ♦ *vt* (*money*) anticipare ♦ *vi* avanzare; **in ~** in anticipo; **~d** *adj* avanzato(a); (*SCOL: studies*) superiore

advantage [əd'vɑːntɪdʒ] *n* (*also: TENNIS*) vantaggio; **to take ~ of** approfittarsi di

advent ['ædvənt] *n* avvento; (*REL*): **A~** Avvento

adventure [əd'vɛntʃə*] *n* avventura

adverb ['ædvəːb] *n* avverbio

adverse ['ædvəːs] *adj* avverso(a)

advert ['ædvəːt] (*BRIT*) *n abbr* = **advertisement**

advertise ['ædvətaɪz] *vi* (*vt*) fare pubblicità *or* réclame (a); fare un'inserzione (per vendere); **to ~ for** (*staff*) mettere un annuncio sul giornale per trovare

advertisement [əd'vəːtɪsmənt] *n* (*COMM*) réclame *f inv*, pubblicità *f inv*; (*in classified ads*) inserzione *f*

advertising ['ædvətaɪzɪŋ] *n* pubblicità

advice [əd'vaɪs] *n* consigli *mpl*; (*notification*) avviso; **piece of ~** consiglio; **to take legal ~** consultare un avvocato

advisable [əd'vaɪzəbl] *adj* consigliabile

advise [əd'vaɪz] *vt* consigliare; **to ~ sb of sth** informare qn di qc; **to ~ sb against sth/doing sth** sconsigliare qc a qn/a qn di fare qc; **~r** *or* **advisor** *n* consigliere/a; **advisory** [-ərɪ] *adj* consultivo(a)

advocate [*n* 'ædvəkɪt, *vb* 'ædvəkeɪt] *n* (*upholder*) sostenitore/trice; (*LAW*) avvocato (difensore) ♦ *vt* propugnare

Aegean [ɪ'dʒiːən] *n*: **the ~ (Sea)** il mar Egeo, l'Egeo

aerial ['ɛərɪəl] *n* antenna ♦ *adj* aereo(a)

aerobics [ɛə'rəubɪks] *n* aerobica

aeroplane ['ɛərəpleɪn] (*BRIT*) *n* aeroplano

aerosol ['ɛərəsɒl] (*BRIT*) *n* aerosol *m inv*

aesthetic [ɪs'θɛtɪk] *adj* estetico(a)

afar [ə'fɑː*] *adv*: **from ~** da lontano

affair [ə'fɛə*] *n* affare *m*; (*also: love ~*) relazione *f* amorosa; **~s** (*business*) affari

affect [ə'fɛkt] *vt* toccare; (*influence*) influire su, incidere su; (*feign*) fingere; **~ed** *adj* affettato(a)

affection [əˈfɛkʃən] n affezione f; ~**ate** adj affettuoso(a)

afflict [əˈflɪkt] vt affliggere

affluence [ˈæfluəns] n abbondanza; opulenza

affluent [ˈæfluənt] adj ricco(a); **the ~ society** la società del benessere

afford [əˈfɔːd] vt permettersi; (provide) fornire

afloat [əˈfləʊt] adv a galla

afoot [əˈfʊt] adv: **there is something ~** si sta preparando qualcosa

afraid [əˈfreɪd] adj impaurito(a); **to be ~ of** or **to/that** aver paura di/che; **I am ~ so/ not** ho paura di sì/no

Africa [ˈæfrɪkə] n Africa; ~**n** adj, n africano(a)

after [ˈɑːftə*] prep, adv dopo ♦ conj dopo che; **what/who are you ~?** che/chi cerca?; ~ **he left/having done** dopo che se ne fu andato/dopo aver fatto; **to name sb ~ sb** dare a qn il nome di qn; **it's twenty ~ eight** (US) sono le otto e venti; **to ask ~ sb** chiedere di qn; ~ **all** dopo tutto; ~ **you!** dopo di lei!; ~**effects** npl conseguenze fpl; (of illness) postumi mpl; ~**math** n conseguenze fpl; **in the ~math of** nel periodo dopo; ~**noon** n pomeriggio; ~**s** (inf: dessert) dessert m inv; ~**-shave (lotion)** n dopobarba m inv; ~**sun (lotion/cream)** n doposole m inv; ~**thought** n: **as an ~thought** come aggiunta; ~**wards** (US ~**ward**) adv dopo

again [əˈgɛn] adv di nuovo; **to begin/see ~** ricominciare/rivedere; **not ... ~** non ... più; ~ **and ~** ripetutamente

against [əˈgɛnst] prep contro

age [eɪdʒ] n età f inv ♦ vt, vi invecchiare; **it's been ~s since** sono secoli che; **he is 20 years of ~** ha 20 anni; **to come of ~** diventare maggiorenne; ~**d** [adj eɪdʒd, npl ˈeɪdʒɪd] adj: ~**d 10** di 10 anni ♦ npl **the ~d** gli anziani; ~ **group** n generazione f; ~ **limit** n limite m d'età

agency [ˈeɪdʒənsɪ] n agenzia

agenda [əˈdʒɛndə] n ordine m del giorno

agent [ˈeɪdʒənt] n agente m

aggravate [ˈægrəveɪt] vt aggravare; (person) irritare

aggregate [ˈægrɪgeɪt] n aggregato

aggressive [əˈgrɛsɪv] adj aggressivo(a)

agitate [ˈædʒɪteɪt] vt turbare; agitare ♦ vi: **to ~ for** agitarsi per

AGM n abbr = **annual general meeting**

ago [əˈgəʊ] adv: **2 days ~** 2 giorni fa; **not long ~** poco tempo fa; **how long ~?** quanto tempo fa?

agonizing [ˈægənaɪzɪŋ] adj straziante

agony [ˈægənɪ] n dolore m atroce; **to be in ~** avere dolori atroci

agree [əˈgriː] vt (price) pattuire ♦ vi: **to ~ (with)** essere d'accordo (con); (LING) concordare (con); **to ~ to sth/to do sth** accettare qc/di fare qc; **to ~ that** (admit) ammettere che; **to ~ on sth** accordarsi su qc; **garlic doesn't ~ with me** l'aglio non mi va; ~**able** adj gradevole; (willing) disposto(a); ~**d** adj (time, place) stabilito(a); ~**ment** n accordo; **in ~ment** d'accordo

agricultural [ægrɪˈkʌltʃərəl] adj agricolo(a)

agriculture [ˈægrɪkʌltʃə*] n agricoltura

aground [əˈgraʊnd] adv: **to run ~** arenarsi

ahead [əˈhɛd] adv avanti; davanti; ~ **of** davanti a; (fig: schedule etc) in anticipo su; ~ **of time** in anticipo; **go right** or **straight ~** tiri diritto

aid [eɪd] n aiuto ♦ vt aiutare; **in ~ of** a favore di

aide [eɪd] n (person) aiutante m

AIDS [eɪdz] n abbr (= acquired immune deficiency syndrome) AIDS f; ~**-related** adj (symptoms, illness) legato(a) all'AIDS; (research) sull'AIDS

aim [eɪm] vt: **to ~ sth at** (such as gun) mirare qc a, puntare qc a; (camera) rivolgere qc a; (missile) lanciare qc contro ♦ vi (also: **to take ~**) prendere la mira ♦ n mira; **to ~ at** mirare; **to ~ to do** aver l'intenzione di fare; ~**less** adj senza scopo

ain't [eɪnt] (inf) = **am not**; **aren't**; **isn't**

air [ɛə*] n aria ♦ vt (room) arieggiare; (clothes) far prendere aria a; (grievances, ideas) esprimere pubblicamente ♦ cpd (*currents*) d'aria; (*attack*) aereo(a); **to throw sth into the ~** lanciare qc in aria; **by ~** (*travel*) in aereo; **on the ~** (*RADIO, TV*) in onda; **~bed** (*BRIT*) n materassino; **~ conditioning** n condizionamento d'aria; **~craft** n inv apparecchio; **~craft carrier** n portaerei f inv; **~field** n campo d'aviazione; **A~ Force** n aviazione f militare; **~ freshener** n deodorante m per ambienti; **~gun** n fucile m ad aria compressa; **~ hostess** (*BRIT*) n hostess f inv; **~ letter** (*BRIT*) n aerogramma m; **~lift** n ponte m aereo; **~line** n linea aerea; **~liner** n aereo di linea; **~mail** n: **by ~mail** per via aerea; **~ mattress** n materassino gonfiabile; **~plane** (*US*) n aeroplano; **~port** n aeroporto; **~ raid** n incursione f aerea; **~sick** adj: **to be ~sick** soffrire di mal d'aria; **~tight** adj ermetico(a); **~ traffic controller** n controllore m del traffico aereo; **~y** adj arioso(a); (*manners*) noncurante

aisle [aɪl] n (*of church*) navata laterale; navata centrale; (*of plane*) corridoio; **~ seat** n (*on plane*) posto sul corridoio

ajar [ə'dʒɑː] adj socchiuso(a)

alarm [ə'lɑːm] n allarme m ♦ vt allarmare; **~ call** n (*in hotel etc*) sveglia; **~ clock** n sveglia

alas [ə'læs] excl ohimè!, ahimè!

albeit [ɔːl'biːɪt] conj sebbene +sub, benché +sub

album ['ælbəm] n album m inv

alcohol ['ælkəhɒl] n alcool m; **~ic** [-'hɒlɪk] adj alcolico(a) ♦ n alcolizzato/a

ale [eɪl] n birra

alert [ə'lɜːt] adj vigile ♦ n allarme m ♦ vt avvertire; mettere in guardia; **on the ~** all'erta

algebra ['ældʒɪbrə] n algebra

alias ['eɪlɪəs] adv alias ♦ n pseudonimo, falso nome m

alibi ['ælɪbaɪ] n alibi m inv

alien ['eɪlɪən] n straniero/a; (*extraterrestrial*) alieno/a ♦ adj: ~ **(to)** estraneo(a) (a); **~ate** vt alienare

alight [ə'laɪt] adj acceso(a) ♦ vi scendere;

(*bird*) posarsi

alike [ə'laɪk] adj simile ♦ adv sia ... sia; **to look ~** assomigliarsi

alimony ['ælɪmənɪ] n (*payment*) alimenti mpl

alive [ə'laɪv] adj vivo(a); (*lively*) vivace

KEYWORD

all [ɔːl] adj tutto(a); ~ **day** tutto il giorno; ~ **night** tutta la notte; ~ **men** tutti gli uomini; ~ **five came** sono venuti tutti e cinque; ~ **the books** tutti i libri; ~ **the food** tutto il cibo; ~ **the time** sempre; tutto il tempo; ~ **his life** tutta la vita

♦ pron 1 tutto(a); **I ate it ~, I ate ~ of it** l'ho mangiato tutto; ~ **of us went** tutti noi siamo andati; ~ **of the boys went** tutti i ragazzi sono andati

2 (*in phrases*): **above ~** soprattutto; **after ~** dopotutto; **at ~: not at ~** (*in answer to question*) niente affatto; (*in answer to thanks*) prego!, di niente!, s'immagini!; **I'm not at ~ tired** non sono affatto stanco(a); **anything at ~ will do** andrà bene qualsiasi cosa; ~ **in ~** tutto sommato

♦ adv: ~ **alone** tutto(a) solo(a); **it's not as hard as ~ that** non è poi così difficile; ~ **the more/the better** tanto più/meglio; ~ **but** quasi; **the score is two ~** il punteggio è di due a due

allay [ə'leɪ] vt (*fears*) dissipare

all clear n (*also fig*) segnale m di cessato allarme

allegation [ælɪ'geɪʃən] n asserzione f

allege [ə'ledʒ] vt asserire; **~dly** [ə'ledʒɪdlɪ] adv secondo quanto si asserisce

allegiance [ə'liːdʒəns] n fedeltà

allergic [ə'lɜːdʒɪk] adj: ~ **to** allergico(a) a

allergy ['ælədʒɪ] n allergia

alleviate [ə'liːvɪeɪt] vt sollevare

alley ['ælɪ] n vicolo

alliance [ə'laɪəns] n alleanza

allied ['ælaɪd] adj alleato(a)

all-in adj (*BRIT: also adv: charge*) tutto compreso

all-night adj aperto(a) (*or che dura*) tutta

la notte

allocate ['ælakeɪt] *vt* assegnare

allot [ə'lɒt] *vt* assegnare; **~ment** *n* assegnazione *f*; (*garden*) lotto di terra

all-out *adj* (*effort etc*) totale ♦ *adv*: **to go all out for** mettercela tutta per

allow [ə'lau] *vt* (*practice, behaviour*) permettere; (*allot*) accordare; (*sum, time estimated*) dare; (*concede*): **to ~ that** ammettere che; **to ~ sb to do** permettere a qn di fare; **he is ~ed to** lo può fare; **~ for** *vt fus* tener conto di; **~ance** *n* (*money received*) assegno; indennità *f inv*; (*TAX*) detrazione *f* di imposta; **to make ~ances for** tener conto di

alloy ['ælɔɪ] *n* lega

all right *adv* (*feel, work*) bene; (*as answer*) va bene

all-round *adj* completo(a)

all-time *adj* (*record*) assoluto(a)

alluring [ə'ljuərɪŋ] *adj* seducente

ally ['ælaɪ] *n* alleato

almighty [ɔːl'maɪtɪ] *adj* onnipotente; (*row etc*) colossale

almond ['ɑːmənd] *n* mandorla

almost ['ɔːlməust] *adv* quasi

alone [ə'ləun] *adj, adv* solo(a); **to leave sb ~** lasciare qn in pace; **to leave sth ~** lasciare stare qc; **let ~ ...** figuriamoci poi ..., tanto meno ....

along [ə'lɒŋ] *prep* lungo ♦ *adv*: **is he coming ~?** viene con noi?; **he was limping ~** veniva zoppicando; **~ with** insieme con; **all ~** (*all the time*) sempre, fin dall'inizio; **~side** *prep* accanto a; lungo ♦ *adv* accanto

aloof [ə'luːf] *adj* distaccato(a) ♦ *adv*: **to stand ~** tenersi a distanza *or* in disparte

aloud [ə'laud] *adv* ad alta voce

alphabet ['ælfəbet] *n* alfabeto

alpine ['ælpaɪn] *adj* alpino(a)

Alps [ælps] *npl*: **the ~** le Alpi

already [ɔːl'rɛdɪ] *adv* già

alright ['ɔːl'raɪt] (*BRIT*) *adv* = **all right**

Alsatian [æl'seɪʃən] (*BRIT*) *n* (*dog*) pastore *m* tedesco, (cane *m*) lupo

also ['ɔːlsəu] *adv* anche

altar ['ɔltə*] *n* altare *m*

alter ['ɔltə*] *vt, vi* alterare

alternate [*adj* ɔl'təːnɪt, *vb* 'ɔltəːneɪt] *adj* alterno(a); (*US: plan etc*) alternativo(a) ♦ *vi*: **to ~ (with)** alternarsi (a); **on ~ days** ogni due giorni; **alternating** ['ɔltəːneɪtɪŋ] *adj* (*current*) alternato(a)

alternative [ɔl'təːnətɪv] *adj* alternativo(a) ♦ *n* (*choice*) alternativa; **~ly** *adv*: **~ly one could ...** come alternativa si potrebbe ...; **~ medicine** *n* medicina alternativa

alternator ['ɔltəːneɪtə*] *n* (*AUT*) alternatore *m*

although [ɔːl'ðəu] *conj* benché +*sub*, sebbene +*sub*

altitude ['æltɪtjuːd] *n* altitudine *f*

alto ['æltəu] *n* contralto; (*male*) contraltino

altogether [ɔːltə'geðə*] *adv* del tutto, completamente; (*on the whole*) tutto considerato; (*in all*) in tutto

aluminium [æljuˈmɪnɪəm] *n* alluminio

aluminum [ə'luːmɪnəm] (*US*) *n* = **aluminium**

always ['ɔːlweɪz] *adv* sempre

Alzheimer's (disease) ['æltshaɪməz-] *n* (malattia di) Alzheimer

AM *n abbr* (= (*Welsh*) *Assembly Member*) deputato/a del Parlamento gallese

am [æm] *vb see* **be**

a.m. *adv abbr* (= *ante meridiem*) della mattina

amalgamate [ə'mælgəmeɪt] *vt* amalgamare ♦ *vi* amalgamarsi

amateur ['æmətə*] *n* dilettante *m/f* ♦ *adj* (*SPORT*) dilettante; **~ish** (*pej*) *adj* da dilettante

amaze [ə'meɪz] *vt* stupire; **to be ~d (at)** essere sbalordito (da); **~ment** *n* stupore *m*; **amazing** *adj* sorprendente, sbalorditivo(a)

ambassador [æm'bæsədə*] *n* ambasciatore/trice

amber ['æmbə*] *n* ambra; **at ~** (*BRIT: AUT*) giallo

ambiguous [æm'bɪgjuəs] *adj* ambiguo(a)

ambition [æm'bɪʃən] *n* ambizione *f*

ambitious [æm'bɪʃəs] *adj* ambizioso(a)

ambulance ['æmbjuləns] *n* ambulanza

ambush ['æmbuʃ] *n* imboscata ♦ *vt* fare un'imboscata a

amenable [ə'mi:nəbl] *adj*: ~ **to** (*advice etc*) ben disposto(a) a

amend [ə'mɛnd] *vt* (*law*) emendare; (*text*) correggere; **to make ~s** fare ammenda

amenities [ə'mi:nɪtɪz] *npl* attrezzature *fpl* ricreative e culturali

America [ə'mɛrɪkə] *n* America; **~n** *adj*, *n* americano(a)

amiable ['eɪmɪəbl] *adj* amabile, gentile

amicable ['æmɪkəbl] *adj* amichevole

amid(st) [ə'mɪd(st)] *prep* fra, tra, in mezzo a

amiss [ə'mɪs] *adj, adv*: **there's something ~** c'è qualcosa che non va bene; **don't take it ~** non prendertela (a male)

ammonia [ə'məunɪə] *n* ammoniaca

ammunition [æmju'nɪʃən] *n* munizioni *fpl*

amok [ə'mɔk] *adv*: **to run ~** diventare pazzo(a) furioso(a)

among(st) [ə'mʌŋ(st)] *prep* fra, tra, in mezzo a

amorous ['æmərəs] *adj* amoroso(a)

amount [ə'maunt] *n* somma; ammontare *m*; quantità *f inv* ♦ *vi*: **to ~ to** (*total*) ammontare a; (*be same as*) essere come

amp(ère) ['æmp(ɛə*)] *n* ampère *m inv*

ample ['æmpl] *adj* ampio(a); spazioso(a); (*enough*): **this is ~** questo è più che sufficiente

amplifier ['æmplɪfaɪə*] *n* amplificatore *m*

amuse [ə'mju:z] *vt* divertire; **~ment** *n* divertimento; **~ment arcade** *n* sala giochi; **~ment park** *n* luna park *m inv*

an [æn] *indef art see* **a**

anaemic [ə'ni:mɪk] *adj* anemico(a)

anaesthetic [ænɪs'θɛtɪk] *adj* anestetico(a) ♦ *n* anestetico

analog(ue) ['ænələg] *adj* (*watch, computer*) analogico(a)

analyse ['ænəlaɪz] (*BRIT*) *vt* analizzare

analysis [ə'næləsɪs] (*pl* **analyses**) *n* analisi *f inv*

analyst ['ænəlɪst] *n* (*POL etc*) analista *m/f*; (*US*) (psic)analista *m/f*

analyze ['ænəlaɪz] (*US*) *vt* = **analyse**

anarchy ['ænəkɪ] *n* anarchia

anatomy [ə'nætəmɪ] *n* anatomia

ancestor ['ænsɪstə*] *n* antenato/a

anchor ['æŋkə*] *n* ancora ♦ *vi* (*also*: **to drop ~**) gettare l'ancora ♦ *vt* ancorare; **to weigh ~** salpare *or* levare l'ancora

anchovy ['æntʃəvɪ] *n* acciuga

ancient ['eɪnʃənt] *adj* antico(a); (*person, car*) vecchissimo(a)

ancillary [æn'sɪlərɪ] *adj* ausiliario(a)

and [ænd] *conj* e (*often ed before vowel*); ~ **so on** e così via; **try ~ come** cerca di venire; **he talked ~ talked** non la finiva di parlare; **better ~ better** sempre meglio

anemic [ə'ni:mɪk] (*US*) *adj* = **anaemic**

anesthetic [ænɪs'θɛtɪk] (*US*) *adj, n* = **anaesthetic**

anew [ə'nju:] *adv* di nuovo

angel ['eɪndʒəl] *n* angelo

anger ['æŋgə*] *n* rabbia

angina [æn'dʒaɪnə] *n* angina pectoris

angle ['æŋgl] *n* angolo; **from their ~** dal loro punto di vista

Anglican ['æŋglɪkən] *adj, n* anglicano(a)

angling ['æŋglɪŋ] *n* pesca con la lenza

Anglo- ['æŋgləu] *prefix* anglo....

angrily ['æŋgrɪlɪ] *adv* con rabbia

angry ['æŋgrɪ] *adj* arrabbiato(a), furioso(a); (*wound*) infiammato(a); **to be ~ with sb/at sth** essere in collera con qn/per qc; **to get ~** arrabbiarsi; **to make sb ~** fare arrabbiare qn

anguish ['æŋgwɪʃ] *n* angoscia

animal ['ænɪməl] *adj* animale ♦ *n* animale *m*

animate ['ænɪmɪt] *adj* animato(a)

animated ['ænɪmeɪtɪd] *adj* animato(a)

aniseed ['ænɪsi:d] *n* semi *mpl* di anice

ankle ['æŋkl] *n* caviglia; **~ sock** *n* calzino

annex [*n* 'æneks, *vb* ə'neks] *n* (*also*: *BRIT*: **annexe**) (*edificio*) annesso ♦ *vt* annettere

anniversary [ænɪ'vɔ:sərɪ] *n* anniversario

announce [ə'nauns] *vt* annunciare; **~ment** *n* annuncio; (*letter, card*) partecipazione *f*; **~r** *n* (*RADIO, TV: between programmes*) annunciatore/ trice; (: *in a programme*) presentatore/trice

annoy [ə'nɔɪ] *vt* dare fastidio a; **don't get**

~ed! non irritarti!; **~ance** n fastidio; (*cause of ~ance*) noia; **~ing** adj noioso(a)
annual ['ænjuəl] adj annuale ♦ n (BOT) pianta annua; (*book*) annuario
annul [ə'nʌl] vt annullare
annum ['ænəm] n see **per**
anonymous [ə'nɔnɪməs] adj anonimo(a)
anorak ['ænəræk] n giacca a vento
anorexia [ænə'rɛksɪə] n (MED) anoressia
another [ə'nʌðə*] adj: ~ **book** (*one more*) un altro libro, ancora un libro; (*a different one*) un altro libro ♦ pron un altro(un'altra), ancora uno(a); see also **one**
answer ['ɑːnsə*] n risposta; soluzione f ♦ vi rispondere ♦ vt (*reply to*) rispondere a; (*problem*) risolvere; (*prayer*) esaudire; **in ~ to your letter** in risposta alla sua lettera; **to ~ the phone** rispondere (al telefono); **to ~ the bell** rispondere al campanello; **to ~ the door** aprire la porta; **~ back** vi ribattere; **~ for** vt fus essere responsabile di; **~ to** vt fus (*description*) corrispondere a; **~able** adj: **~able (to sb/for sth)** responsabile (verso qn/di qc); **~ing machine** n segreteria (telefonica) automatica
ant [ænt] n formica
antagonism [æn'tægənizəm] n antagonismo
antagonize [æn'tægənaiz] vt provocare l'ostilità di
Antarctic [ænt'ɑːktɪk] n: **the ~** l'Antartide f
antenatal ['æntɪ'neɪtl] adj prenatale; **~ clinic** n assistenza medica preparto
anthem ['ænθəm] n: **national ~** inno nazionale
antibiotic ['æntɪbaɪ'ɔtɪk] n antibiotico
antibody ['æntɪbɔdɪ] n anticorpo
anticipate [æn'tɪsɪpeɪt] vt prevedere; pregustare; (*wishes, request*) prevenire
anticipation [æntɪsɪ'peɪʃən] n anticipazione f; (*expectation*) aspettative fpl
anticlimax ['æntɪ'klaɪmæks] n: **it was an ~** fu una completa delusione
anticlockwise ['æntɪ'klɔkwaɪz] adj, adv in senso antiorario
antics ['æntɪks] npl buffonerie fpl
antidepressant ['æntɪdɪ'prɛsnt] n antidepressivo

antifreeze ['æntɪ'friːz] n anticongelante m
antihistamine [æntɪ'hɪstəmɪn] n antistaminico
antiquated ['æntɪkweɪtɪd] adj antiquato(a)
antique [æn'tiːk] n antichità f inv ♦ adj antico(a); **~ dealer** n antiquario/a; **~ shop** n negozio d'antichità
anti-Semitism ['æntɪ'sɛmɪtɪzəm] n antisemitismo
antiseptic [æntɪ'sɛptɪk] n antisettico
antisocial ['æntɪ'səʊʃəl] adj asociale
antlers ['æntləz] npl palchi mpl
anvil ['ænvɪl] n incudine f
anxiety [æŋ'zaɪətɪ] n ansia
anxious ['æŋkʃəs] adj ansioso(a), inquieto(a); (*worrying*) angosciante; (*keen*): **~ to do/that** impaziente di fare/che +sub

KEYWORD

any ['ɛnɪ] adj **1** (*in questions etc*): **have you ~ butter?** hai del burro?, hai un po' di burro?; **have you ~ children?** hai bambini?; **if there are ~ tickets left** se ci sono ancora (dei) biglietti, se c'è ancora qualche biglietto
2 (*with negative*): **I haven't ~ money/ books** non ho soldi/libri
3 (*no matter which*) qualsiasi, qualunque; **choose ~ book you like** scegli un libro qualsiasi
4 (*in phrases*): **in ~ case** in ogni caso; **~ day now** da un giorno all'altro; **at ~ moment** in qualsiasi momento, da un momento all'altro; **at ~ rate** ad ogni modo
♦ pron **1** (*in questions, with negative*): **have you got ~?** ne hai?; **can ~ of you sing?** qualcuno di voi sa cantare?; **I haven't ~ (of them)** non ne ho
2 (*no matter which one(s)*): **take ~ of those books (you like)** prendi uno qualsiasi di quei libri
♦ adv **1** (*in questions etc*): **do you want ~ more soup/sandwiches?** vuoi ancora un po' di minestra/degli altri panini?; **are you feeling ~ better?** ti senti meglio?
2 (*with negative*): **I can't hear him ~ more**

(for) *(permit, grant, job)* fare domanda (per); **to ~ o.s. to** dedicarsi a

appoint [ə'pɔɪnt] *vt* nominare; **~ed** *adj*: **at the ~ed time** all'ora stabilita; **~ment** *n* nomina; *(arrangement to meet)* appuntamento; **to make an ~ment (with)** prendere un appuntamento (con)

appraisal [ə'preɪzl] *n* valutazione *f*

appreciate [ə'priːʃieɪt] *vt (like)* apprezzare; *(be grateful for)* essere riconoscente di; *(be aware of)* rendersi conto di ♦ *vi (FINANCE)* aumentare; **I'd ~ your help** ti sono grato per l'aiuto

appreciation [əpriːʃi'eɪʃən] *n* apprezzamento; *(FINANCE)* aumento del valore

appreciative [ə'priːʃiətɪv] *adj (person)* sensibile; *(comment)* elogiativo(a)

apprehend [æprɪ'hɛnd] *vt (arrest)* arrestare

apprehension [æprɪ'hɛnʃən] *n (fear)* inquietudine *f*

apprehensive [æprɪ'hɛnsɪv] *adj* apprensivo(a)

apprentice [ə'prɛntɪs] *n* apprendista *m/f*; **~ship** *n* apprendistato

approach [ə'prəutʃ] *vi* avvicinarsi ♦ *vt (come near)* avvicinarsi a; *(ask, apply to)* rivolgersi a; *(subject, passer-by)* avvicinare ♦ *n* approccio; accesso; *(to problem)* modo di affrontare; **~able** *adj* accessibile

appropriate [*adj* ə'prəuprɪɪt, *vb* ə'prəuprɪeɪt] *adj* appropriato(a); adatto(a) ♦ *vt (take)* appropriarsi

approval [ə'pruːvəl] *n* approvazione *f*; **on ~** *(COMM)* in prova, in esame

approve [ə'pruːv] *vt, vi* approvare; **~ of** *vt fus* approvare

approximate [ə'prɔksɪmɪt] *adj* approssimativo(a); **~ly** *adv* circa

apricot ['eɪprɪkɔt] *n* albicocca

April ['eɪprəl] *n* aprile *m*; **~ fool!** pesce d'aprile!

April Fool's Day

---

i **April Fool's Day** è il primo aprile, il giorno degli scherzi e delle burle. Il nome deriva dal fatto che, se una persona cade nella trappola che gli è stata tesa, fa la

figura del **fool**, cioè dello sciocco.

---

apron ['eɪprən] *n* grembiule *m*

apt [æpt] *adj (suitable)* adatto(a); *(able)* capace; *(likely)*: **to be ~ to do** avere tendenza a fare

aquarium [ə'kwɛərɪəm] *n* acquario

Aquarius [ə'kwɛərɪəs] *n* Acquario

Arab ['ærəb] *adj*, *n* arabo(a)

Arabian [ə'reɪbɪən] *adj* arabo(a)

Arabic ['ærəbɪk] *adj* arabico(a), arabo(a) ♦ *n* arabo; **~ numerals** numeri *mpl* arabi

arbitrary ['aːbɪtrərɪ] *adj* arbitrario(a)

arbitration [aːbɪ'treɪʃən] *n (LAW)* arbitrato; *(INDUSTRY)* arbitraggio

arcade [aː'keɪd] *n* portico; *(passage with shops)* galleria

arch [aːtʃ] *n* arco; *(of foot)* arco plantare ♦ *vt* inarcare

archaeologist [aːkɪ'ɔlədʒɪst] *n* archeologo/a

archaeology [aːkɪ'ɔlədʒɪ] *n* archeologia

archbishop [aːtʃ'bɪʃəp] *n* arcivescovo

archeology [aːkɪ'ɔlədʒɪ] *etc (US)* = **archaeology** *etc*

archery ['aːtʃərɪ] *n* tiro all'arco

architect ['aːkɪtɛkt] *n* architetto; **~ure** ['aːkɪtɛktʃə*] *n* architettura

archives ['aːkaɪvz] *npl* archivi *mpl*

Arctic ['aːktɪk] *adj* artico(a) ♦ *n*: **the ~** l'Artico

ardent ['aːdənt] *adj* ardente

are [aː*] *vb see* **be**; **~n't** [aːnt] = **~ not**

area ['ɛərɪə] *n (GEOM)* area; *(zone)* zona; *(: smaller)* settore *m*

Argentina [aːdʒən'tiːnə] *n* Argentina; **Argentinian** [-'tɪnɪən] *adj*, *n* argentino(a)

arguably ['aːgjuəblɪ] *adv*: **it is ~ ...** si può sostenere che sia ....

argue ['aːgjuː] *vi (quarrel)* litigare; *(reason)* ragionare; **to ~ that** sostenere che

argument ['aːgjumənt] *n (reasons)* argomento; *(quarrel)* lite *f*; **~ative** [aːgju'mɛntətɪv] *adj* litigioso(a)

Aries ['ɛərɪz] *n* Ariete *m*

arise [ə'raɪz] *(pt* arose, *pp* arisen) *vi (opportunity, problem)* presentarsi

aristocrat [ˈærɪstəkræt] *n* aristocratico/a

arithmetic [əˈrɪθmətɪk] *n* aritmetica

ark [ɑːk] *n*: **Noah's A~** l'arca di Noè

arm [ɑːm] *n* braccio ♦ *vt* armare; **~s** *npl* (*weapons*) armi *fpl*; **in ~** a braccetto

armaments [ˈɑːməmənts] *npl* armamenti *mpl*

arm: ~chair *n* poltrona; **~ed** *adj* armato(a); **~ed robbery** *n* rapina a mano armata

armour [ˈɑːmə*] (*US* **armor**) *n* armatura; (*MIL: tanks*) mezzi *mpl* blindati; **~ed car** *n* autoblinda *f inv*

armpit [ˈɑːmpɪt] *n* ascella

armrest [ˈɑːmrɛst] *n* bracciolo

army [ˈɑːmɪ] *n* esercito

aroma [əˈrəʊmə] *n* aroma; **~therapy** *n* aromaterapia

arose [əˈrəʊz] *pt of* **arise**

around [əˈraʊnd] *adv* attorno, intorno ♦ *prep* intorno a; (*fig: about*): **~ £5/ 3 o'clock** circa 5 sterline/le 3; **is he ~?** è in giro?

arouse [əˈraʊz] *vt* (*sleeper*) svegliare; (*curiosity, passions*) suscitare

arrange [əˈreɪndʒ] *vt* sistemare; (*programme*) preparare; **to ~ to do sth** mettersi d'accordo per fare qc; **~ment** *n* sistemazione *f*; (*agreement*) accordo; **~ments** *npl* (*plans*) progetti *mpl*, piani *mpl*

array [əˈreɪ] *n*: **~ of** fila di

arrears [əˈrɪəz] *npl* arretrati *mpl*; **to be in ~ with one's rent** essere in arretrato con l'affitto

arrest [əˈrɛst] *vt* arrestare; (*sb's attention*) attirare ♦ *n* arresto; **under ~** in arresto

arrival [əˈraɪvl] *n* arrivo; (*person*) arrivato/a; **a new ~** un nuovo venuto; (*baby*) un neonato

arrive [əˈraɪv] *vi* arrivare

arrogant [ˈærəgənt] *adj* arrogante

arrow [ˈærəʊ] *n* freccia

arse [ɑːs] (*inf!*) *n* culo (!)

arson [ˈɑːsn] *n* incendio doloso

art [ɑːt] *n* arte *f*; (*craft*) mestiere *m*; **A~s** *npl* (*SCOL*) Lettere *fpl*

artery [ˈɑːtərɪ] *n* arteria

art gallery *n* galleria d'arte

arthritis [ɑːˈθraɪtɪs] *n* artrite *f*

artichoke [ˈɑːtɪtʃəʊk] *n* carciofo; **Jerusalem ~** topinambur *m inv*

article [ˈɑːtɪkl] *n* articolo; **~s** *npl* (*BRIT: LAW: training*) contratto di tirocinio; **~ of clothing** capo di vestiario

articulate [*adj* ɑːˈtɪkjulɪt, *vb* ɑːˈtɪkjuleɪt] *adj* (*person*) che si esprime forbitamente; (*speech*) articolato(a) ♦ *vi* articolare; **~d lorry** (*BRIT*) *n* autotreno

artificial [ɑːtɪˈfɪʃəl] *adj* artificiale; **~ respiration** *n* respirazione *f* artificiale

artist [ˈɑːtɪst] *n* artista *m/f*; **~ic** [ɑːˈtɪstɪk] *adj* artistico(a); **~ry** *n* arte *f*

art school *n* scuola d'arte

KEYWORD

as [æz] *conj* **1** (*referring to time*) mentre; **~ the years went by** col passare degli anni; **he came in ~ I was leaving** arrivò mentre stavo uscendo; **~ from tomorrow** da domani

2 (*in comparisons*): **~ big ~** grande come; **twice ~ big ~** due volte più grande di; **~ much/many ~** tanto quanto/tanti quanti; **~ soon ~ possible** prima possibile

3 (*since, because*) dal momento che, siccome

4 (*referring to manner, way*) come; **do ~ you wish** fa' come vuoi; **~ she said** come ha detto lei

5 (*concerning*): **~ for** *or* **to that** per quanto riguarda *or* quanto a quello

6: **~ if** *or* **though** come se; **he looked ~ if he was ill** sembrava stare male; *see also* **long**; **such**; **well**

♦ *prep*: **he works ~ a driver** fa l'autista; **~ chairman of the company, he ...** come presidente della compagnia, lui ...; **he gave me it ~ a present** me lo ha regalato

---

a.s.a.p. *abbr* = **as soon as possible**

ascend [əˈsɛnd] *vt* salire

ascertain [æsəˈteɪn] *vt* accertare

ash [æʃ] *n* (*dust*) cenere *f*; (*wood, tree*) frassino

non lo sento più; **don't wait ~ longer** non aspettare più

anybody ['ɛnɪbɔdɪ] *pron* (*in questions etc*) qualcuno, nessuno; (*with negative*) nessuno; (*no matter who*) chiunque; **can you see ~?** vedi qualcuno *or* nessuno?; **if ~ should phone ...** se telefona qualcuno ...; **I can't see ~** non vedo nessuno; **~ could do it** chiunque potrebbe farlo

anyhow ['ɛnɪhau] *adv* (*at any rate*) ad ogni modo, comunque; (*haphazard*): **do it ~ you like** fallo come ti pare; **I shall go ~** ci andrò lo stesso *or* comunque; **she leaves things just ~** lascia tutto come capita

anyone ['ɛnɪwʌn] *pron* = **anybody**

anything ['ɛnɪθɪŋ] *pron* (*in question etc*) qualcosa, niente; (*with negative*) niente; (*no matter what*): **you can say ~ you like** puoi dire quello che ti pare; **can you see ~?** vedi niente *or* qualcosa?; **if ~ happens to me ...** se mi dovesse succedere qualcosa ...; **I can't see ~** non vedo niente; **~ will do** va bene qualsiasi cosa *or* tutto

anyway ['ɛnɪweɪ] *adv* (*at any rate*) ad ogni modo, comunque; (*besides*) ad ogni modo

anywhere ['ɛnɪwɛə*] *adv* (*in questions etc*) da qualche parte; (*with negative*) da nessuna parte; (*no matter where*) da qualsiasi *or* qualunque parte, dovunque; **can you see him ~?** lo vedi da qualche parte?; **I can't see him ~** non lo vedo da nessuna parte; **~ in the world** dovunque nel mondo

apart [ə'pɑːt] *adv* (*to one side*) a parte; (*separately*) separatamente; **with one's legs ~** con le gambe divaricate; **10 miles ~** a 10 miglia di distanza (l'uno dall'altro); **to take ~** smontare; **~ from** a parte, eccetto

apartheid [ə'pɑːteɪt] *n* apartheid *f*

apartment [ə'pɑːtmənt] *n* (*US*) appartamento; (*room*) locale *m*; **~ building** (*US*) *n* stabile *m*, caseggiato

ape [eɪp] *n* scimmia ♦ *vt* scimmiottare

apéritif [ə'pɛrɪtɪv] *n* aperitivo

aperture ['æpətʃuə*] *n* apertura

APEX *n abbr* (= *advance purchase*

excursion) APEX *m inv*

apologetic [əpɔlə'dʒɛtɪk] *adj* (*tone, letter*) di scusa

apologize [ə'pɔlədʒaɪz] *vi*: **to ~ (for sth to sb)** scusarsi (di qc a qn), chiedere scusa (a qn per qc)

apology [ə'pɔlədʒɪ] *n* scuse *fpl*

apostle [ə'pɔsl] *n* apostolo

apostrophe [ə'pɔstrəfɪ] *n* (*sign*) apostrofo

appal [ə'pɔːl] *vt* scioccare; **~ling** *adj* spaventoso(a)

apparatus [æpə'reɪtəs] *n* apparato; (*in gymnasium*) attrezzatura

apparel [ə'pærl] (*US*) *n* abbigliamento, confezioni *fpl*

apparent [ə'pærənt] *adj* evidente; **~ly** *adv* evidentemente

appeal [ə'piːl] *vi* (*LAW*) appellarsi alla legge ♦ *n* (*LAW*) appello; (*request*) richiesta; (*charm*) attrattiva; **to ~ for** chiedere (con insistenza); **to ~ to** (*subj: person*) appellarsi a; (*subj: thing*) piacere a; **it doesn't ~ to me** mi dice poco; **~ing** *adj* (*nice*) attraente

appear [ə'pɪə*] *vi* apparire; (*LAW*) comparire; (*publication*) essere pubblicato(a); (*seem*) sembrare; **it would ~ that** sembra che; **~ance** *n* apparizione *f*; apparenza; (*look, aspect*) aspetto

appease [ə'piːz] *vt* calmare, appagare

appendicitis [əpɛndɪ'saɪtɪs] *n* appendicite *f*

appendix [ə'pɛndɪks] (*pl* **appendices**) *n* appendice *f*

appetite ['æpɪtaɪt] *n* appetito

appetizer ['æpɪtaɪzə*] *n* stuzzichino

applaud [ə'plɔːd] *vt, vi* applaudire

applause [ə'plɔːz] *n* applauso

apple ['æpl] *n* mela; **~ tree** *n* melo

appliance [ə'plaɪəns] *n* apparecchio

applicant ['æplɪkənt] *n* candidato/a

application [æplɪ'keɪʃən] *n* applicazione *f*; (*for a job, a grant etc*) domanda; **~ form** *n* modulo per la domanda

applied [ə'plaɪd] *adj* applicato(a)

apply [ə'plaɪ] *vt*: **to ~ (to)** (*paint, ointment*) dare (a); (*theory, technique*) applicare (a) ♦ *vi*: **to ~ to** (*ask*) rivolgersi a; (*be suitable for, relevant to*) riguardare, riferirsi a; **to ~**

ashamed [ə'feɪmd] *adj* vergognoso(a); **to be ~ of** vergognarsi di

ashore [ə'fɔ:*] *adv* a terra

ashtray ['æʃtreɪ] *n* portacenere *m*

Ash Wednesday *n* mercoledì *m inv* delle Ceneri

Asia ['eɪʃə] *n* Asia; **~n** *adj*, *n* asiatico(a)

aside [ə'saɪd] *adv* da parte ♦ *n* a parte *m*

ask [ɑ:sk] *vt* (*question*) domandare; (*invite*) invitare; **to ~ sb sth/sb to do sth** chiedere qc a qn/a qn di fare qc; **to ~ sb about sth** chiedere a qn di qc; **to ~ (sb) a question** fare una domanda (a qn); **to ~ sb out to dinner** invitare qn a mangiare fuori; **~ after** *vt fus* chiedere di; **~ for** *vt fus* chiedere; (*trouble etc*) cercare

asleep [ə'sli:p] *adj* addormentato(a); **to be ~** dormire; **to fall ~** addormentarsi

asparagus [əs'pærəgəs] *n* asparagi *mpl*

aspect ['æspekt] *n* aspetto

aspersions [əs'pə:ʃənz] *npl*: **to cast ~ on** diffamare

asphyxiation [æsfɪksɪ'eɪʃən] *n* asfissia

aspire [əs'paɪə*] *vi*: **to ~ to** aspirare a

aspirin ['æsprɪn] *n* aspirina

ass [æs] *n* asino; (*inf*) scemo/a; (*US: inf!*) culo (!)

assailant [ə'seɪlənt] *n* assalitore *m*

assassinate [ə'sæsɪneɪt] *vt* assassinare; **assassination** [əsæsɪ'neɪʃən] *n* assassinio

assault [ə'sɔ:lt] *n* (*MIL*) assalto; (*gen: attack*) aggressione *f* ♦ *vt* assaltare; aggredire; (*sexually*) violentare

assemble [ə'sembl] *vt* riunire; (*TECH*) montare ♦ *vi* riunirsi

assembly [ə'semblɪ] *n* (*meeting*) assemblea; (*construction*) montaggio; **~ line** *n* catena di montaggio

assent [ə'sent] *n* assenso, consenso

assert [ə'sə:t] *vt* asserire; (*insist on*) far valere

assess [ə'ses] *vt* valutare; **~ment** *n* valutazione *f*

asset ['æset] *n* vantaggio; **~s** *npl* (*FINANCE: of individual*) beni *mpl*; (: *of company*) attivo

assign [ə'saɪn] *vt*: **to ~ (to)** (*task*) assegnare

(a); (*resources*) riservare (a); (*cause, meaning*) attribuire (a); **to ~ a date to sth** fissare la data di qc; **~ment** *n* compito

assist [ə'sɪst] *vt* assistere, aiutare; **~ance** *n* assistenza, aiuto; **~ant** *n* assistente *m/f*; (*BRIT: also:* **shop ~ant**) commesso/a

associate [*adj, n* ə'səʊʃɪt, *vb* ə'səʊʃɪeɪt] *adj* associato(a); (*member*) aggiunto(a) ♦ *n* collega *m/f* ♦ *vt* associare ♦ *vi*: **to ~ with sb** frequentare qn

association [əsəʊsɪ'eɪʃən] *n* associazione *f*

assorted [ə'sɔ:tɪd] *adj* assortito(a)

assortment [ə'sɔ:tmənt] *n* assortimento

assume [ə'sju:m] *vt* supporre; (*responsibilities etc*) assumere; (*attitude, name*) prendere

assumption [ə'sʌmpʃən] *n* supposizione *f*, ipotesi *f inv*; (*of power*) assunzione *f*

assurance [ə'ʃuərəns] *n* assicurazione *f*; (*self-confidence*) fiducia in se stesso

assure [ə'ʃuə*] *vt* assicurare

asthma ['æsmə] *n* asma

astonish [ə'stɒnɪʃ] *vt* stupire; **~ment** *n* stupore *m*

astound [ə'staʊnd] *vt* sbalordire

astray [ə'streɪ] *adv*: **to go ~** smarrirsi; **to lead ~** portare sulla cattiva strada

astride [ə'straɪd] *prep* a cavalcioni di

astrology [əs'trɒlədʒɪ] *n* astrologia

astronaut ['æstrənɔ:t] *n* astronauta *m/f*

astronomy [əs'trɒnəmɪ] *n* astronomia

asylum [ə'saɪləm] *n* asilo; (*building*) manicomio

KEYWORD

---

at [æt] *prep* **1** (*referring to position, direction*) a; **~ the top** in cima; **~ the desk** al banco, alla scrivania; **~ home/school** a casa/ scuola; **~ the baker's** dal panettiere; **to look ~ sth** guardare qc; **to throw sth ~ sb** lanciare qc a qn

2 (*referring to time*) a; **~ 4 o'clock** alle 4; **~ night** di notte; **~ Christmas** a Natale; **~ times** a volte

3 (*referring to rates, speed etc*) a; **~ £1 a kilo** a 1 sterlina al chilo; **two ~ a time** due alla volta, due per volta; **~ 50 km/h** a

50 km/h
4 (*referring to manner*): ~ **a stroke** d'un solo colpo; ~ **peace** in pace
5 (*referring to activity*): **to be ~ work** essere al lavoro; **to play ~ cowboys** giocare ai cowboy; **to be good ~ sth/doing sth** essere bravo in qc/a fare qc
6 (*referring to cause*): **shocked/ surprised/annoyed ~ sth** colpito da/ sorpreso da/arrabbiato per qc; **I went ~ his suggestion** ci sono andato dietro suo consiglio

ate [eɪt] *pt of* **eat**
atheist ['eɪθɪɪst] *n* ateo/a
Athens ['æθɪnz] *n* Atene *f*
athlete ['æθliːt] *n* atleta *m/f*
athletic [æθ'letɪk] *adj* atletico(a); ~**s** *n* atletica
Atlantic [ət'læntɪk] *adj* atlantico(a) ♦ *n*: **the ~ (Ocean)** l'Atlantico, l'Oceano Atlantico
atlas ['ætləs] *n* atlante *m*
ATM *n abbr* (= *automated telling machine*) cassa automatica prelievi, sportello automatico
atmosphere ['ætməsfɪə*] *n* atmosfera
atom ['ætəm] *n* atomo; ~**ic** [ə'tɒmɪk] *adj* atomico(a); ~**(ic) bomb** *n* bomba atomica; ~**izer** ['ætəmaɪzə*] *n* atomizzatore *m*
atone [ə'təʊn] *vi*: **to ~ for** espiare
atrocious [ə'trəʊʃəs] *adj* pessimo(a), atroce
attach [ə'tætʃ] *vt* attaccare; (*document, letter*) allegare; (*importance etc*) attribuire; **to be ~ed to sb/sth** (*to like*) essere affezionato(a) a qn/qc
attaché case [ə'tæʃeɪ-] *n* valigetta per documenti
attachment [ə'tætʃmənt] *n* (*tool*) accessorio; (*love*): ~ **(to)** affetto (per)
attack [ə'tæk] *vt* attaccare; (*person*) aggredire; (*task etc*) iniziare; (*problem*) affrontare ♦ *n* attacco; **heart ~** infarto; ~**er** *n* aggressore *m*
attain [ə'teɪn] *vt* (*also*: **to ~ to**) arrivare a, raggiungere
attempt [ə'tempt] *n* tentativo ♦ *vt* tentare;

to make an ~ on sb's life attentare alla vita di qn
attend [ə'tend] *vt* frequentare; (*meeting, talk*) andare a; (*patient*) assistere; ~ **to** *vt fus* (*needs, affairs etc*) prendersi cura di; (*customer*) occuparsi di; ~**ance** *n* (*being present*) presenza; (*people present*) gente *f* presente; ~**ant** *n* custode *m/f*; persona di servizio ♦ *adj* concomitante
attention [ə'tenʃən] *n* attenzione *f* ♦ *excl* (*MIL*) attenti!; **for the ~ of** (*ADMIN*) per l'attenzione di
attentive [ə'tentɪv] *adj* attento(a); (*kind*) premuroso(a)
attic ['ætɪk] *n* soffitta
attitude ['ætɪtjuːd] *n* atteggiamento; posa
attorney [ə'tɜːnɪ] *n* (*lawyer*) avvocato; (*having proxy*) mandatario; **A~ General** *n* (*BRIT*) Procuratore *m* Generale; (*US*) Ministro della Giustizia
attract [ə'trækt] *vt* attirare; ~**ion** [ə'trækʃən] *n* (*gen pl: pleasant things*) attrattiva; (*PHYSICS, fig: towards sth*) attrazione *f*; ~**ive** *adj* attraente
attribute [*n* 'ætrɪbjuːt, *vb* ə'trɪbjuːt] *n* attributo ♦ *vt*: **to ~ sth to** attribuire qc a
attrition [ə'trɪʃən] *n*: **war of ~** guerra di logoramento
aubergine ['əʊbəʒiːn] *n* melanzana
auburn ['ɔːbən] *adj* tizianesco(a)
auction ['ɔːkʃən] *n* (*also*: **sale by ~**) asta ♦ *vt* (*also*: **to sell by ~**) vendere all'asta; (*also*: **to put up for ~**) mettere all'asta; ~**eer** [-'nɪə*] *n* banditore *m*
audible ['ɔːdɪbl] *adj* udibile
audience ['ɔːdɪəns] *n* (*people*) pubblico; spettatori *mpl*; ascoltatori *mpl*; (*interview*) udienza
audio-typist ['ɔːdɪəʊ'taɪpɪst] *n* dattilografo/a che trascrive da nastro
audio-visual [ɔːdɪəʊ'vɪzjuəl] *adj* audiovisivo(a); ~ **aid** *n* sussidio audiovisivo
audit ['ɔːdɪt] *vt* rivedere, verificare
audition [ɔː'dɪʃən] *n* audizione *f*
auditor ['ɔːdɪtə*] *n* revisore *m*
augment [ɔːg'ment] *vt, vi* aumentare
augur ['ɔːgə*] *vi*: **it ~s well** promette bene

August ['ɔːɡəst] *n* agosto

aunt [ɑːnt] *n* zia; **~ie** *or* **~y** *n* zietta

au pair ['əu'pεə*] *n* (*also*: **~ girl**) (ragazza *f*) alla pari *inv*

auspicious [ɔːs'pɪʃəs] *adj* propizio(a)

Australia [ɔs'treɪlɪə] *n* Australia; **~n** *adj, n* australiano(a)

Austria ['ɔstrɪə] *n* Austria; **~n** *adj, n* austriaco(a)

authentic [ɔː'θεntɪk] *adj* autentico(a)

author ['ɔːθə*] *n* autore/trice

authoritarian [ɔːθɔrɪ'tεərɪən] *adj* autoritario(a)

authoritative [ɔː'θɔrɪtətɪv] *adj* (*account etc*) autorevole; (*manner*) autoritario(a)

authority [ɔː'θɔrɪtɪ] *n* autorità *f inv*; (*permission*) autorizzazione *f*; **the authorities** *npl* (*government etc*) le autorità

authorize ['ɔːθəraɪz] *vt* autorizzare

auto ['ɔːtəu] (*US*) *n* auto *f inv*

autobiography [ɔːtəbaɪ'ɔɡrəfɪ] *n* autobiografia

autograph ['ɔːtəɡrɑːf] *n* autografo ♦ *vt* firmare

automatic [ɔːtə'mætɪk] *adj* automatico(a) ♦ *n* (*gun*) arma automatica; (*washing machine*) lavatrice *f* automatica; (*car*) automobile *f* con cambio automatico; **~ally** *adv* automaticamente

automation [ɔːtə'meɪʃən] *n* automazione *f*

automobile ['ɔːtəmɔbiːl] (*US*) *n* automobile *f*

autonomy [ɔː'tɔnəmɪ] *n* autonomia

autumn ['ɔːtəm] *n* autunno

auxiliary [ɔːɡ'zɪlɪərɪ] *adj* ausiliario(a) ♦ *n* ausiliare *m/f*

Av. *abbr* = **avenue**

avail [ə'veɪl] *vt*: **to ~ o.s. of** servirsi di; approfittarsi di ♦ *n*: **to no ~** inutilmente

available [ə'veɪləbl] *adj* disponibile

avalanche ['ævəlɑːnʃ] *n* valanga

avant-garde ['ævɑ̃n'ɡɑːd] *adj* d'avanguardia

Ave. *abbr* = **avenue**

avenge [ə'vεndʒ] *vt* vendicare

avenue ['ævənjuː] *n* viale *m*; (*fig*) strada, via

average ['ævərɪdʒ] *n* media ♦ *adj* medio(a)

♦ *vt* (*a certain figure*) fare di *or* in media; **on ~** in media; **~ out** *vi*: **to ~ out at** aggirarsi in media su, essere in media di

averse [ə'vəːs] *adj*: **to be ~ to sth/doing** essere contrario a qc/a fare

avert [ə'vəːt] *vt* evitare, prevenire; (*one's eyes*) distogliere

aviary ['eɪvɪərɪ] *n* voliera, uccelliera

avid ['ævɪd] *adj* (*supporter etc*) accanito(a)

avocado [ævə'kɑːdəu] *n* (*also*: *BRIT*: **~ pear**) avocado *m inv*

avoid [ə'vɔɪd] *vt* evitare

await [ə'weɪt] *vt* aspettare

awake [ə'weɪk] (*pt* awoke, *pp* awoken, awaked) *adj* sveglio(a) ♦ *vt* svegliare ♦ *vi* svegliarsi; **~ning** [ə'weɪknɪŋ] *n* risveglio

award [ə'wɔːd] *n* premio; (*LAW*) risarcimento ♦ *vt* assegnare; (*LAW*: *damages*) accordare

aware [ə'wεə*] *adj*: **~ of** (*conscious*) conscio(a) di; (*informed*) informato(a) di; **to become ~ of** accorgersi di; **~ness** *n* consapevolezza

away [ə'weɪ] *adj, adv* via; lontano(a); **two kilometres ~** a due chilometri di distanza; **two hours ~ by car** a due ore di distanza in macchina; **the holiday was two weeks ~** mancavano due settimane alle vacanze; **he's ~ for a week** è andato via per una settimana; **to take ~** togliere; **he was working/pedalling** *etc* ~ la particella *indica la continuità e l'energia dell'azione*: *lavorava/pedalava etc più che poteva*; **to fade/wither** *etc* ~ la particella *rinforza l'idea della diminuzione*; **~ game** *n* (*SPORT*) partita fuori casa

awe [ɔː] *n* timore *m*; **~-inspiring** imponente; **~some** *adj* imponente

awful ['ɔːfəl] *adj* terribile; **an ~ lot of** un mucchio di; **~ly** *adv* (*very*) terribilmente

awkward ['ɔːkwəd] *adj* (*clumsy*) goffo(a); (*inconvenient*) scomodo(a); (*embarrassing*) imbarazzante

awning ['ɔːnɪŋ] *n* (*of shop, hotel etc*) tenda

awoke [ə'wəuk] *pt of* **awake**

awoken [ə'wəukn] *pp of* **awake**

awry [ə'raɪ] *adv* di traverso

axe [æks] (*US* **ax**) *n* scure *f* ♦ *vt* (*project etc*) abolire; (jobs) sopprimere

axes ['æksiːz] npl of **axis**

axis ['æksɪs] (pl **axes**) n asse m

axle ['æksl] n (also: **~-tree**) asse m

ay(e) [aɪ] excl (yes) sì

B, b

B [biː] n (MUS) si m; (letter) B, b f or m inv; **~-road** n (BRIT: AUT) strada secondaria

B.A. n abbr = **Bachelor of Arts**

baby ['beɪbɪ] n bambino/a; **~ carriage** (US) n carrozzina; **~ food** n omogeneizzati mpl; **~-sit** vi fare il (or la) baby-sitter; **~-sitter** n baby-sitter m/f inv; **~-sitting** n: **to go ~-sitting** fare il (or la) baby-sitter; **~ wipe** n salvietta umidificata

bachelor ['bætʃələ*] n scapolo; **B~ of Arts/ Science** ≈ laureato/a in lettere/scienze

back [bæk] n (of person, horse) dorso, schiena; (as opposed to front) dietro; (of hand) dorso; (of train) coda; (of chair) schienale m; (of page) rovescio; (of book) retro; (FOOTBALL) difensore m ♦ vt (candidate: also: **~ up**) appoggiare; (horse: at races) puntare su; (car) guidare a marcia indietro ♦ vi indietreggiare; (car etc) fare marcia indietro ♦ cpd posteriore, di dietro; (AUT: seat, wheels) posteriore ♦ adv (not forward) indietro; (returned): **he's ~** è tornato; **he ran ~** tornò indietro di corsa; (restitution): **throw the ball ~** ritira la palla; **can I have it ~?** posso riaverlo?; (again): **he called ~** ha richiamato; **~ down** vi fare marcia indietro; **~ out** vi (of promise) tirarsi indietro; **~ up** vt (support) appoggiare, sostenere; (COMPUT) fare una copia di riserva di; **~bencher** (BRIT) n membro del Parlamento senza potere amministrativo; **~bone** n spina dorsale; **~date** vt (letter) retrodatare; **~dated pay rise** aumento retroattivo; **~fire** vi (AUT) dar ritorni di fiamma; (plans) fallire; **~ground** n sfondo; (of events) background m inv; (basic knowledge) base f; (experience) esperienza; **family ~ground** ambiente m familiare;

~hand n (TENNIS: also: **~hand stroke**) rovescio; **~handed** adj (fig) ambiguo(a); **~hander** (BRIT) n (bribe) bustarella; **~ing** n (fig) appoggio; **~lash** n contraccolpo, ripercussione f; **~log** n: **~log of work** lavoro arretrato; **~ number** n (of magazine etc) numero arretrato; **~pack** n zaino; **~packer** n chi viaggia con zaino e sacco a pelo; **~ pay** n arretrato di paga; **~ payments** npl arretrati mpl; **~side** (inf) n sedere m; **~stage** adv nel retroscena; **~stroke** n nuoto sul dorso; **~up** adj (train, plane) supplementare; (COMPUT) di riserva ♦ n (support) appoggio, sostegno; (also: **~up file**) file m inv di riserva; **~ward** adj (movement) indietro inv; (person) tardivo(a); (country) arretrato(a); **~wards** adv indietro; (fall, walk) all'indietro; **~yard** n cortile m dietro la casa

bacon ['beɪkən] n pancetta

bad [bæd] adj cattivo(a); (accident, injury) brutto(a); (meat, food) andato(a) a male; **his ~ leg** la sua gamba malata; **to go ~** andare a male

badge [bædʒ] n insegna; (of policeman) stemma m

badger ['bædʒə*] n tasso

badly ['bædlɪ] adv (work, dress etc) male; **~ wounded** gravemente ferito; **he needs it ~** ne ha un gran bisogno; **~ off** adj povero(a)

badminton ['bædmɪntən] n badminton m

bad-tempered ['bæd'tɛmpəd] adj irritabile; di malumore

baffle ['bæfl] vt (puzzle) confondere

bag [bæg] n sacco; (handbag etc) borsa; **~s of** (inf: lots of) un sacco di; **~gage** n bagagli mpl; **~gage allowance** n franchigia f bagaglio inv; **~gage reclaim** n ritiro m bagaglio inv; **~gy** adj largo(a), sformato(a); **~pipes** npl cornamusa

bail [beɪl] n cauzione f ♦ vt (prisoner: also: **grant~to**) concedere la libertà provvisoria su cauzione a; (boat: also: **~ out**) aggottare; **on ~** in libertà provvisoria su cauzione; **~ out** vt (prisoner) ottenere la libertà provvisoria su cauzione di; see also **bale**

bailiff ['beɪlɪf] n (LAW: BRIT) ufficiale m giudiziario; (: US) usciere m

bait [beɪt] n esca ♦ vt (hook) innescare; (trap) munire di esca; (fig) tormentare

bake [beɪk] vt cuocere al forno ♦ vi cuocersi al forno; ~**d beans** npl fagioli mpl in salsa di pomodoro; ~**d potato** npl patata cotta al forno con la buccia; ~**r** n fornaio/a, panettiere/a; ~**ry** n panetteria; **baking** n cottura (al forno); **baking powder** n lievito in polvere

balance ['bæləns] n equilibrio; (COMM: sum) bilancio; (remainder) resto; (scales) bilancia ♦ vt tenere in equilibrio; (budget) far quadrare; (account) pareggiare; (compensate) contrappesare; ~ **of trade/ payments** bilancia commerciale/dei pagamenti; ~**d** adj (personality, diet) equilibrato(a); ~ **sheet** n bilancio

balcony ['bælkənɪ] n balcone m; (in theatre) balconata

bald [bɔːld] adj calvo(a); (tyre) liscio(a)

bale [beɪl] n balla; ~ **out** vi (of a plane) gettarsi col paracadute

ball [bɔːl] n palla; (football) pallone m; (for golf) pallina; (of wool, string) gomitolo; (dance) ballo; **to play** ~ (fig) stare al gioco

ballast ['bæləst] n zavorra

ball bearings npl cuscinetti a sfere

ballerina [bælə'riːnə] n ballerina

ballet ['bæleɪ] n balletto; ~ **dancer** n ballerino/a classico/a

balloon [bə'luːn] n pallone m

ballot paper ['bælət-] n scheda

ball-point pen n penna a sfera

ballroom ['bɔːlrum] n sala da ballo

balm [bɑːm] n balsamo

ban [bæn] n interdizione f ♦ vt interdire

banana [bə'nɑːnə] n banana

band [bænd] n banda; (at a dance) orchestra; (MIL) fanfara; ~ **together** vi collegarsi

bandage ['bændɪdʒ] n benda, fascia

Bandaid ® ['bændeɪd] (US) n cerotto

bandy-legged [-'legɪd] adj dalle gambe storte

bang [bæŋ] n (of door) lo sbattere; (of gun, blow) colpo ♦ vt battere (violentemente); (door) sbattere ♦ vi scoppiare; sbattere

Bangladesh [bɑːŋglə'deʃ] n Bangladesh m

bangle ['bæŋgl] n braccialetto

bangs [bæŋz] (US) npl (fringe) frangia, frangetta

banish ['bænɪʃ] vt bandire

banister(s) ['bænɪstə(z)] n(pl) ringhiera

bank [bæŋk] n banca, banco; (of river, lake) riva, sponda; (of earth) banco ♦ vi (AVIAT) inclinarsi in virata; ~ **on** vt fus contare su; ~ **account** n conto in banca; ~ **card** n carta f assegni inv; ~**er** n banchiere m; ~**er's card** (BRIT) n = **bank card**; B~ **holiday** (BRIT) n giorno di festa; ~**ing** n attività bancaria; professione f di banchiere; ~**note** n banconota; ~ **rate** n tasso bancario

---

bank holiday

ⓘ Una **bank holiday**, in Gran Bretagna, è una giornata in cui banche e negozi sono chiusi. Generalmente le **bank holiday** cadono di lunedì e molti ne approfittano per fare una breve vacanza fuori città.

---

bankrupt ['bæŋkrʌpt] adj fallito(a); **to go** ~ fallire; ~**cy** n fallimento

bank statement n estratto conto

banner ['bænə*] n striscione m

baptism ['bæptɪzəm] n battesimo

bar [bɑː*] n (place) bar m inv; (counter) banco; (rod) barra; (of window etc) sbarra; (of chocolate) tavoletta; (fig) ostacolo; restrizione f; (MUS) battuta ♦ vt (road, window) sbarrare; (person) escludere; (activity) interdire; ~ **of soap** saponetta; **the B~** (LAW) l'Ordine m degli avvocati; **behind** ~**s** (prisoner) dietro le sbarre; ~ **none** senza eccezione

barbaric [bɑː'bærɪk] adj barbarico(a)

barbecue ['bɑːbɪkjuː] n barbecue m inv

barbed wire ['bɑːbd-] n filo spinato

barber ['bɑːbə*] n barbiere m

bar code n (on goods) codice m a barre

bare [bɛə*] adj nudo(a) ♦ vt scoprire,

denudare; (*teeth*) mostrare; **the ~ necessities** lo stretto necessario; **~back** *adv* senza sella; **~faced** *adj* sfacciato(a); **~foot** *adj, adv* scalzo(a); **~ly** *adv* appena

bargain ['bɑːgɪn] *n* (*transaction*) contratto; (*good buy*) affare *m* ♦ *vi* trattare; **into the ~** per giunta; **~ for** *vt fus*: **he got more than he ~ed for** gli è andata peggio di quel che si aspettasse

barge [bɑːdʒ] *n* chiatta; **~ in** *vi* (*walk in*) piombare dentro; (*interrupt talk*) intromettersi a sproposito

bark [bɑːk] *n* (*of tree*) corteccia; (*of dog*) abbaio ♦ *vi* abbaiare

barley ['bɑːlɪ] *n* orzo

barmaid ['bɑːmeɪd] *n* cameriera al banco

barman ['bɑːmən] *n* barista *m*

bar meal *n* spuntino servito al bar

barn [bɑːn] *n* granaio

barometer [bə'rɒmɪtə*] *n* barometro

baron ['bærən] *n* barone *m*; **~ess** *n* baronessa

barracks ['bærəks] *npl* caserma

barrage ['bærɑːʒ] *n* (*MIL, dam*) sbarramento; (*fig*) fiume *m*

barrel ['bærəl] *n* barile *m*; (*of gun*) canna

barren ['bærən] *adj* sterile; (*soil*) arido(a)

barricade [bærɪ'keɪd] *n* barricata

barrier ['bærɪə*] *n* barriera

barring ['bɑːrɪŋ] *prep* salvo

barrister ['bærɪstə*] (*BRIT*) *n* avvocato/essa (*con diritto di parlare davanti a tutte le corti*)

barrow ['bærəʊ] *n* (*cart*) carriola

bartender ['bɑːtendə*] (*US*) *n* barista *m*

barter ['bɑːtə*] *vt*: **to ~ sth for** barattare qc con

base [beɪs] *n* base *f* ♦ *vt*: **to ~ sth on** basare qc su ♦ *adj* vile

baseball ['beɪsbɔːl] *n* baseball *m*

basement ['beɪsmənt] *n* seminterrato; (*of shop*) interrato

bases[1] ['beɪsiːz] *npl of* **basis**

bases[2] ['beɪsɪz] *npl of* **base**

bash [bæʃ] (*inf*) *vt* picchiare

bashful ['bæʃful] *adj* timido(a)

basic ['beɪsɪk] *adj* rudimentale; essenziale; **~ally** [-lɪ] *adv* fondamentalmente;

sostanzialmente; **~s** *npl*: **the ~s** l'essenziale *m*

basil ['bæzl] *n* basilico

basin ['beɪsn] *n* (*vessel, also GEO*) bacino; (*also*: **wash~**) lavabo

basis ['beɪsɪs] (*pl* **bases**) *n* base *f*; **on a part-time ~** part-time; **on a trial ~** in prova

bask [bɑːsk] *vi*: **to ~ in the sun** crogiolarsi al sole

basket ['bɑːskɪt] *n* cesta; (*smaller*) cestino; (*with handle*) paniere *m*; **~ball** *n* pallacanestro *f*

bass [beɪs] *n* (*MUS*) basso

bassoon [bə'suːn] *n* fagotto

bastard ['bɑːstəd] *n* bastardo/a; (*inf!*) stronzo (*!*)

bat [bæt] *n* pipistrello; (*for baseball etc*) mazza; (*BRIT: for table tennis*) racchetta ♦ *vt*: **he didn't ~ an eyelid** non battè ciglio

batch [bætʃ] *n* (*of bread*) infornata; (*of papers*) cumulo

bated ['beɪtɪd] *adj*: **with ~ breath** col fiato sospeso

bath [bɑːθ] *n* bagno; (*bathtub*) vasca da bagno ♦ *vt* far fare il bagno a; **to have a ~** fare un bagno; *see also* **baths**

bathe [beɪð] *vi* fare il bagno ♦ *vt* (*wound*) lavare; **~r** *n* bagnante *m/f*

bathing ['beɪðɪŋ] *n* bagni *mpl*; **~ costume** (*US* **~ suit**) *n* costume *m* da bagno

bathrobe ['bɑːθrəʊb] *n* accappatoio

bathroom ['bɑːθrum] *n* stanza da bagno

baths [bɑːðz] *npl* bagni *mpl* pubblici

bath towel *n* asciugamano da bagno

baton ['bætən] *n* (*MUS*) bacchetta; (*ATHLETICS*) testimone *m*; (*club*) manganello

batter ['bætə*] *vt* battere ♦ *n* pastetta; **~ed** *adj* (*hat*) sformato(a); (*pan*) ammaccato(a)

battery ['bætərɪ] *n* batteria; (*of torch*) pila; **~ farming** *n* allevamento in batteria

battle ['bætl] *n* battaglia ♦ *vi* battagliare, lottare; **~field** *n* campo di battaglia; **~ship** *n* nave *f* da guerra

bawl [bɔːl] *vi* urlare

bay [beɪ] *n* (*of sea*) baia; **to hold sb at ~** tenere qn a bada; **~ leaf** *n* foglia d'alloro;

~ **window** *n* bovindo

bazaar [bə'zɑ:ˑ] *n* bazar *m inv*; vendita di beneficenza

B. & B. *abbr* = **bed and breakfast**

BBC *n abbr* (= *British Broadcasting Corporation*) rete nazionale di radiotelevisione in Gran Bretagna

B.C. *adv abbr* (= *before Christ*) a.C.

KEYWORD

---

be [biː] (*pt* **was, were,** *pp* **been**) *aux vb*
1 (*with present participle: forming continuous tenses*): **what are you doing?** che fa?, che sta facendo?; **they're coming tomorrow** vengono domani; **I've been waiting for her for hours** sono ore che l'aspetto
2 (*with pp: forming passives*) essere; **to ~ killed** essere *or* venire ucciso(a); **the box had been opened** la scatola era stata aperta; **the thief was nowhere to ~ seen** il ladro non si trovava da nessuna parte
3 (*in tag questions*): **it was fun, wasn't it?** è stato divertente, no?; **he's good-looking, isn't he?** è un bell'uomo, vero?; **she's back, is she?** così è tornata, eh?
4 (+*to* +*infinitive*): **the house is to ~ sold** abbiamo (*or* hanno *etc*) intenzione di vendere casa; **you're to ~ congratulated for all your work** dovremo farvi i complimenti per tutto il vostro lavoro; **he's not to open it** non deve aprirlo

♦ *vb* +*complement* 1 (*gen*) essere; **I'm English** sono inglese; **I'm tired** sono stanco(a); **I'm hot/cold** ho caldo/freddo; **he's a doctor** è un medico; **2 and 2 are 4** 2 più 2 fa 4; **~ careful!** sta attento(a)!; **~ good** sii buono(a)
2 (*of health*) stare; **how are you?** come sta?; **he's very ill** sta molto male
3 (*of age*): **how old are you?** quanti anni hai?; **I'm sixteen (years old)** ho sedici anni
4 (*cost*) costare; **how much was the meal?** quant'era *or* quanto costava il pranzo?; **that'll ~ £5, please** (fa) 5 sterline, per favore

♦ *vi* 1 (*exist, occur etc*) essere, esistere; **the**

best singer that ever was il migliore cantante mai esistito *or* di tutti tempi; **~ that as it may** comunque sia, sia come sia; **so ~ it** sia pure, e sia
2 (*referring to place*) essere, trovarsi; **I won't ~ here tomorrow** non ci sarò domani; **Edinburgh is in Scotland** Edimburgo si trova in Scozia
3 (*referring to movement*): **where have you been?** dov'è stato?; **I've been to China** sono stato in Cina

♦ *impers vb* 1 (*referring to time, distance*) essere; **it's 5 o'clock** sono le 5; **it's the 28th of April** è il 28 aprile; **it's 10 km to the village** di qui al paese sono 10 km
2 (*referring to the weather*) fare; **it's too hot/cold** fa troppo caldo/freddo; **it's windy** c'è vento
3 (*emphatic*): **it's me** sono io; **it was Maria who paid the bill** è stata Maria che ha pagato il conto

---

beach [biːtʃ] *n* spiaggia ♦ *vt* tirare in secco

beacon ['biːkən] *n* (*lighthouse*) faro; (*marker*) segnale *m*

bead [biːd] *n* perlina

beak [biːk] *n* becco

beaker ['biːkəˑ] *n* coppa

beam [biːm] *n* trave *f*; (*of light*) raggio ♦ *vi* brillare

bean [biːn] *n* fagiolo; (*of coffee*) chicco; **runner ~** fagiolino; **broad ~** fava; **~sprouts** *npl* germogli *mpl* di soia

bear [bɛəˑ] (*pt* **bore,** *pp* **borne**) *n* orso ♦ *vt* portare; (*endure*) sopportare; (*produce*) generare ♦ *vi*: **to ~ right/left** piegare a destra/sinistra; **~ out** *vt* (*suspicions*) confermare, convalidare; (*person*) dare il proprio appoggio a; **~ up** *vi* (*person*) fare buon viso a cattiva sorte

beard [biəd] *n* barba

bearer ['bɛərəˑ] *n* portatore *m*

bearing ['bɛərɪŋ] *n* portamento; (*connection*) rapporto; **~s** *npl* (*also*: **ball ~s**) cuscinetti *mpl* a sfere; **to take a ~** fare un rilevamento; **to find one's ~s** orientarsi

beast [biːst] *n* bestia; **~ly** *adj* meschino(a);

(*weather*) da cani

beat [bi:t] (*pt* **beat**, *pp* **beaten**) *n* colpo; (*of heart*) battito; (*MUS*) tempo; battuta; (*of policeman*) giro ♦ *vt* battere; (*eggs, cream*) sbattere ♦ *vi* battere; **off the ~en track** fuori mano; **~ it!** (*inf*) fila!, fuori dai piedi!; **~ off** *vt* respingere; **~ up** *vt* (*person*) picchiare; (*eggs*) sbattere; **beaten** *pp of* **beat**; **~ing** *n* bastonata

beautiful ['bju:tiful] *adj* bello(a); **~ly** *adv* splendidamente

beauty ['bju:ti] *n* bellezza; **~ salon** *n* istituto di bellezza; **~ spot** (*BRIT*) *n* (*TOURISM*) luogo pittoresco

beaver ['bi:və*] *n* castoro

became [bi'keim] *pt of* **become**

because [bi'kɔz] *conj* perché; **~ of** a causa di

beckon ['bekən] *vt* (*also:* **~ to**) chiamare con un cenno

become [bi'kʌm] (*irreg: like* **come**) *vt* diventare; **to ~ fat/thin** ingrassarsi/dimagrire

becoming [bi'kʌmiŋ] *adj* (*behaviour*) che si conviene; (*clothes*) grazioso(a)

bed [bed] *n* letto; (*of flowers*) aiuola; (*of coal, clay*) strato; **single/double ~** letto a una piazza/a due piazze *or* matrimoniale; **~ and breakfast** *n* (*place*) ≈ pensione *f* familiare; (*terms*) camera con colazione; **~clothes** ['bedkləuðz] *npl* biancheria e coperte *fpl* da letto; **~ding** *n* coperte e lenzuola *fpl*

---
bed and breakfast

ⓘ *I* **bed and breakfast**, *anche* B & B, *sono piccole pensioni a conduzione familiare, più economiche rispetto agli alberghi, dove al mattino viene servita la tradizionale colazione all'inglese.*

---

bed linen *n* biancheria da letto

bedraggled [bi'drægld] *adj* fradicio(a)

bed: **~ridden** *adj* costretto(a) a letto; **~room** *n* camera da letto; **~side** *n*: **at sb's ~side** al capezzale di qn; **~sit(ter)** (*BRIT*) *n* monolocale *m*; **~spread** *n*

copriletto; **~time** *n*: **it's ~time** è ora di andare a letto

bee [bi:] *n* ape *f*

beech [bi:tʃ] *n* faggio

beef [bi:f] *n* manzo; **roast ~** arrosto di manzo; **~burger** *n* hamburger *m inv*; **B~eater** *n* guardia della Torre di Londra

beehive ['bi:haiv] *n* alveare *m*

beeline ['bi:lain] *n*: **to make a ~ for** buttarsi a capo fitto verso

been [bi:n] *pp of* **be**

beer [biə*] *n* birra

beetle ['bi:tl] *n* scarafaggio; coleottero

beetroot ['bi:tru:t] (*BRIT*) *n* barbabietola

before [bi'fɔ:*] *prep* (*in time*) prima di; (*in space*) davanti a ♦ *conj* prima che +*sub*; prima di ♦ *adv* prima; **~ going** prima di andare; **~ she goes** prima che vada; **the week ~** la settimana prima; **I've seen it ~** l'ho già visto; **I've never seen it ~** è la prima volta che lo vedo; **~hand** *adv* in anticipo

beg [beg] *vi* chiedere l'elemosina ♦ *vt* (*also:* **~ for**) chiedere in elemosina; (*: favour*) chiedere; **to ~ sb to do** pregare qn di fare

began [bi'gæn] *pt of* **begin**

beggar ['begə*] *n* mendicante *m/f*

begin [bi'gin] (*pt* **began**, *pp* **begun**) *vt, vi* cominciare; **to ~ doing** *or* **to do sth** incominciare *or* iniziare a fare qc; **~ner** *n* principiante *m/f*; **~ning** *n* inizio, principio

begun [bi'gʌn] *pp of* **begin**

behalf [bi'hɑ:f] *n*: **on ~ of** per conto di; a nome di

behave [bi'heiv] *vi* comportarsi; (*well: also:* **~ o.s.**) comportarsi bene

behaviour [bi'heivjə*] (*US* **behavior**) *n* comportamento, condotta

behind [bi'haind] *prep* dietro; (*followed by pronoun*) dietro di; (*time*) in ritardo con ♦ *adv* dietro; (*leave, stay*) indietro ♦ *n* didietro; **to be ~ (schedule)** essere in ritardo rispetto al programma; **~ the scenes** (*fig*) dietro le quinte

behold [bi'həuld] (*irreg: like* **hold**) *vt* vedere, scorgere

beige [beiʒ] *adj* beige *inv*

Beijing ['beɪ'dʒɪŋ] *n* Pechino *f*

being ['biːɪŋ] *n* essere *m*

Beirut [beɪ'ruːt] *n* Beirut *f*

Belarus [bɛlə'rus] *n* Bielorussia

belated [bɪ'leɪtɪd] *adj* tardo(a)

belch [bɛltʃ] *vi* ruttare ♦ *vt* (*gen*: ~ **out**: *smoke etc*) eruttare

Belgian ['bɛldʒən] *adj, n* belga *m/f*

Belgium ['bɛldʒəm] *n* Belgio

belie [bɪ'laɪ] *vt* smentire

belief [bɪ'liːf] *n* (*opinion*) opinione *f*, convinzione *f*; (*trust, faith*) fede *f*

believe [bɪ'liːv] *vt, vi* credere; **to ~ in** (*God*) credere in; (*ghosts*) credere a; (*method*) avere fiducia in; **~r** *n* (*REL*) credente *m/f*; (*in idea, activity*): **to be a ~r in** credere in

belittle [bɪ'lɪtl] *vt* sminuire

bell [bɛl] *n* campana; (*small, on door, electric*) campanello

belligerent [bɪ'lɪdʒərənt] *adj* bellicoso(a)

bellow ['bɛləu] *vi* muggire

bellows ['bɛləuz] *npl* soffietto

belly ['bɛlɪ] *n* pancia

belong [bɪ'lɔŋ] *vi*: **to ~ to** appartenere a; (*club etc*) essere socio di; **this book ~s here** questo libro va qui; **~ings** *npl* cose *fpl*, roba

beloved [bɪ'lʌvɪd] *adj* adorato(a)

below [bɪ'ləu] *prep* sotto, al di sotto di ♦ *adv* sotto, di sotto; giù; **see ~** vedi sotto *or* oltre

belt [bɛlt] *n* cintura; (*TECH*) cinghia ♦ *vt* (*thrash*) picchiare ♦ *vi* (*inf*) filarsela; **~way** (*US*) *n* (*AUT*: *ring road*) circonvallazione *f*; (: *motorway*) autostrada

bemused [bɪ'mjuːzd] *adj* perplesso(a), stupito(a)

bench [bɛntʃ] *n* panca; (*in workshop, POL*) banco; **the B~** (*LAW*) la Corte

bend [bɛnd] (*pt, pp* **bent**) *vt* curvare; (*leg, arm*) piegare ♦ *vi* curvarsi; piegarsi ♦ *n* (*BRIT*: *in road*) curva; (*in pipe, river*) gomito; **~ down** *vi* chinarsi; **~ over** *vi* piegarsi

beneath [bɪ'niːθ] *prep* sotto, al di sotto di; (*unworthy of*) indegno(a) di ♦ *adv* sotto, di sotto

benefactor ['bɛnɪfæktə*] *n* benefattore *m*

beneficial [bɛnɪ'fɪʃəl] *adj* che fa bene; vantaggioso(a)

benefit ['bɛnɪfɪt] *n* beneficio, vantaggio; (*allowance of money*) indennità *f inv* ♦ *vt* far bene a ♦ *vi*: **he'll ~ from it** ne trarrà beneficio *or* profitto

benevolent [bɪ'nɛvələnt] *adj* benevolo(a)

benign [bɪ'naɪn] *adj* (*person, smile*) benevolo(a); (*MED*) benigno(a)

bent [bɛnt] *pt, pp of* **bend** ♦ *n* inclinazione *f* ♦ *adj* (*inf*: *dishonest*) losco(a); **to be ~ on** essere deciso(a) a

bequest [bɪ'kwɛst] *n* lascito

bereaved [bɪ'riːvd] *n*: **the ~** i familiari in lutto

beret ['bɛreɪ] *n* berretto

Berlin [bəː'lɪn] *n* Berlino *f*

berm [bəːm] (*US*) *n* (*AUT*) corsia d'emergenza

berry ['bɛrɪ] *n* bacca

berserk [bə'səːk] *adj*: **to go ~** montare su tutte le furie

berth [bəːθ] *n* (*bed*) cuccetta; (*for ship*) ormeggio ♦ *vi* (*in harbour*) entrare in porto; (*at anchor*) gettare l'ancora

beseech [bɪ'siːtʃ] (*pt, pp* **besought**) *vt* implorare

beset [bɪ'sɛt] (*pt, pp* **beset**) *vt* assalire

beside [bɪ'saɪd] *prep* accanto a; **to be ~ o.s. (with anger)** essere fuori di sé (dalla rabbia); **that's ~ the point** non c'entra

besides [bɪ'saɪdz] *adv* inoltre, per di più ♦ *prep* oltre a; a parte

besiege [bɪ'siːdʒ] *vt* (*town*) assediare; (*fig*) tempestare

best [bɛst] *adj* migliore ♦ *adv* meglio; **the ~ part of** (*quantity*) la maggior parte di; **at ~** tutt'al più; **to make the ~ of sth** cavare il meglio possibile da qc; **to do one's ~** fare del proprio meglio; **to the ~ of my knowledge** per quel che ne so; **to the ~ of my ability** al massimo delle mie capacità; **~-before date** *n* scadenza; **~ man** *n* testimone *m* dello sposo

bestow [bɪ'stəu] *vt* accordare; (*title*) conferire

bet [bɛt] (*pt, pp* **bet** *or* **betted**) *n* scommessa ♦ *vt, vi* scommettere; **to ~ sb sth**

scommettere qc con qn

betray [bɪ'treɪ] *vt* tradire; **~al** *n* tradimento

better ['bɛtə*] *adj* migliore ♦ *adv* meglio ♦ *vt* migliorare ♦ *n*: **to get the ~ of** avere la meglio su; **you had ~ do it** è meglio che lo faccia; **he thought ~ of it** cambiò idea; **to get ~** migliorare; **~ off** *adj* più ricco(a); *(fig)*: **you'd be ~ off this way** starebbe meglio così

betting ['bɛtɪŋ] *n* scommesse *fpl*; **~ shop** *(BRIT)* *n* ufficio dell'allibratore

between [bɪ'twiːn] *prep* tra ♦ *adv* in mezzo, nel mezzo

beverage ['bɛvərɪdʒ] *n* bevanda

beware [bɪ'wɛə*] *vt, vi*: **to ~ (of)** stare attento(a) (a); **"~ of the dog"** "attenti al cane"

bewildered [bɪ'wɪldəd] *adj* sconcertato(a), confuso(a)

beyond [bɪ'jɔnd] *prep* *(in space)* oltre; *(exceeding)* al di sopra di ♦ *adv* di là; **~ doubt** senza dubbio; **~ repair** irreparabile

bias ['baɪəs] *n* *(prejudice)* pregiudizio; *(preference)* preferenza; **~(s)ed** *adj* parziale

bib [bɪb] *n* bavaglino

Bible ['baɪbl] *n* Bibbia

bicarbonate of soda [baɪ'kɑːbənɪt-] *n* bicarbonato (di sodio)

bicker ['bɪkə*] *vi* bisticciare

bicycle ['baɪsɪkl] *n* bicicletta

bid [bɪd] *(pt* **bade** *or* **bid,** *pp* **bidden** *or* **bid)** *n* offerta; *(attempt)* tentativo ♦ *vi* fare un'offerta ♦ *vt* fare un'offerta di; **to ~ sb good day** dire buon giorno a qn; **bidden** *pp* of **bid;** **~der** *n*: **the highest ~der** il maggior offerente; **~ding** *n* offerte *fpl*

bide [baɪd] *vt*: **to ~ one's time** aspettare il momento giusto

bifocals [baɪ'fəuklz] *npl* occhiali *mpl* bifocali

big [bɪg] *adj* grande; grosso(a)

big dipper [-'dɪpə*] *n* montagne *fpl* russe, otto *m inv* volante

bigheaded ['bɪg'hɛdɪd] *adj* presuntuoso(a)

bigot ['bɪgət] *n* persona gretta; **~ed** *adj* gretto(a); **~ry** *n* grettezza

big top *n* tendone *m* del circo

bike [baɪk] *n* bici *f inv*

bikini [bɪ'kiːnɪ] *n* bikini *m inv*

bilingual [baɪ'lɪŋgwəl] *adj* bilingue

bill [bɪl] *n* conto; *(POL)* atto; *(US: banknote)* banconota; *(of bird)* becco; *(of show)* locandina; **"post no ~s"** "divieto di affissione"; **to fit** *or* **fill the ~** *(fig)* fare al caso; **~board** *n* tabellone *m*

billet ['bɪlɪt] *n* alloggio

billfold ['bɪlfəuld] *(US)* *n* portafoglio

billiards ['bɪljədz] *n* biliardo

billion ['bɪljən] *n* *(BRIT)* bilione *m*; *(US)* miliardo

bimbo ['bɪmbəu] *n* *(pej, col)* pollastrella, svampitella

bin [bɪn] *n* *(for coal, rubbish)* bidone *m*; *(for bread)* cassetta; *(dust~)* pattumiera; *(litter ~)* cestino

bind [baɪnd] *(pt, pp* **bound)** *vt* legare; *(oblige)* obbligare ♦ *n* *(inf)* scocciatura; **~ing** *adj* *(contract)* vincolante

binge [bɪndʒ] *(inf)* *n*: **to go on a ~** fare baldoria

bingo ['bɪŋgəu] *n* gioco simile alla tombola

binoculars [bɪ'nɔkjuləz] *npl* binocolo

bio... [baɪə'...] *prefix*: **~chemistry** *n* biochimica; **~degradable** *adj* biodegradabile; **~graphy** [baɪ'ɔgrəfɪ] *n* biografia; **~logical** *adj* biologico(a); **~logy** [baɪ'ɔlədʒɪ] *n* biologia

birch [bəːtʃ] *n* betulla

bird [bəːd] *n* uccello; *(BRIT: inf: girl)* bambola; **~'s eye view** *n* vista panoramica; **~ watcher** *n* ornitologo/a dilettante

Biro ® ['baɪrəu] *n* biro ® *f inv*

birth [bəːθ] *n* nascita; **to give ~ to** partorire; **~ certificate** *n* certificato di nascita; **~ control** *n* controllo delle nascite; contraccezione *f*; **~day** *n* compleanno ♦ *cpd* di compleanno; **~ rate** *n* indice *m* di natalità

biscuit ['bɪskɪt] *(BRIT)* *n* biscotto

bisect [baɪ'sɛkt] *vt* tagliare in due (parti)

bishop ['bɪʃəp] *n* vescovo

bit [bɪt] *pt* of **bite** ♦ *n* pezzo; *(COMPUT)* bit *m inv*; *(of horse)* morso; **a ~ of** un po' di; **a ~ mad** un po' matto; **~ by ~** a poco a poco

bitch [bɪtʃ] *n* *(dog)* cagna; *(inf!)* vacca

bite [baɪt] (pt bit, pp bitten) vt, vi mordere; (subj: insect) pungere ♦ n morso; (insect ~) puntura; (mouthful) boccone m; **let's have a ~ (to eat)** mangiamo un boccone; **to ~ one's nails** mangiarsi le unghie; **bitten** ['bɪtn] pp of **bite**

bitter ['bɪtə*] adj amaro(a); (wind, criticism) pungente ♦ n (BRIT: beer) birra amara; ~**ness** n amarezza; gusto amaro

black [blæk] adj nero(a) ♦ n nero; (person): B~ negro/a ♦ vt (BRIT: INDUSTRY) boicottare; **to give sb a ~ eye** fare un occhio nero a qn; **in the ~** (bank account) in attivo; ~ **and blue** adj tutto(a) pesto(a); ~**berry** n mora; ~**bird** n merlo; ~**board** n lavagna; ~ **coffee** n caffè m inv nero; ~**currant** n ribes m inv; ~**en** vt annerire; ~ **ice** n strato trasparente di ghiaccio; ~**leg** (BRIT) n crumiro; ~**list** n lista nera; ~**mail** n ricatto ♦ vt ricattare; ~ **market** n mercato nero; ~**out** n oscuramento; (TV, RADIO) interruzione f delle trasmissioni; (fainting) svenimento; B~ **Sea** n: **the B~ Sea** il Mar Nero; ~**sheep** n pecora nera; ~**smith** n fabbro ferraio; ~ **spot** n (AUT) luogo famigerato per gli incidenti; (for unemployment etc) zona critica

bladder ['blædə*] n vescica

blade [bleɪd] n lama; (of oar) pala; ~ **of grass** filo d'erba

blame [bleɪm] n colpa ♦ vt: **to ~ sb/sth for sth** dare la colpa di qc a qn/qc; **who's to ~?** chi è colpevole?

bland [blænd] adj mite; (taste) blando(a)

blank [blæŋk] adj bianco(a); (look) distratto(a) ♦ n spazio vuoto; (cartridge) cartuccia a salve; ~ **cheque** n assegno in bianco

blanket ['blæŋkɪt] n coperta

blare [bleə*] vi strombettare

blasphemy ['blæsfɪmɪ] n bestemmia

blast [blɑːst] n (of wind) raffica; (of bomb etc) esplosione f ♦ vt far saltare; ~**-off** n (SPACE) lancio

blatant ['bleɪtənt] adj flagrante

blaze [bleɪz] n (fire) incendio; (fig) vampata;

splendore m ♦ vi (fire) ardere, fiammeggiare; (guns) sparare senza sosta; (fig: eyes) ardere ♦ vt: **to ~ a trail** (fig) tracciare una via nuova; **in a ~ of publicity** circondato da grande pubblicità

blazer ['bleɪzə*] n blazer m inv

bleach [bliːtʃ] n (also: **household ~**) varechina ♦ vt (material) candeggiare; ~**ed** adj (hair) decolorato(a); ~**ers** (US) npl (SPORT) posti mpl di gradinata

bleak [bliːk] adj tetro(a)

bleat [bliːt] vi belare

bled [blɛd] pt, pp of **bleed**

bleed [bliːd] (pt, pp bled) vi sanguinare; **my nose is ~ing** mi viene fuori sangue dal naso

bleeper ['bliːpə*] n (device) cicalino

blemish ['blɛmɪʃ] n macchia

blend [blɛnd] n miscela ♦ vt mescolare ♦ vi (colours etc: also: ~ **in**) armonizzare

bless [blɛs] (pt, pp blessed or blest) vt benedire; ~ **you!** (after sneeze) salute!; ~**ing** n benedizione f; fortuna; **blest** [blɛst] pt, pp of **bless**

blew [bluː] pt of **blow**

blight [blaɪt] vt (hopes etc) deludere; (life) rovinare

blimey ['blaɪmɪ] (BRIT: inf) excl accidenti!

blind [blaɪnd] adj cieco(a) ♦ n (for window) avvolgibile m; (Venetian ~) veneziana ♦ vt accecare; **the ~** npl i ciechi; ~ **alley** n vicolo cieco; ~ **corner** (BRIT) n svolta cieca; ~**fold** n benda ♦ adj, adv bendato(a) ♦ vt bendare gli occhi a; ~**ly** adv ciecamente; ~**ness** n cecità; ~ **spot** n (AUT etc) punto cieco; (fig) punto debole

blink [blɪŋk] vi battere gli occhi; (light) lampeggiare; ~**ers** npl paraocchi mpl

bliss [blɪs] n estasi f

blister ['blɪstə*] n (on skin) vescica; (on paintwork) bolla ♦ vi (paint) coprirsi di bolle

blizzard ['blɪzəd] n bufera di neve

bloated ['bləʊtɪd] adj gonfio(a)

blob [blɒb] n (drop) goccia; (stain, spot) macchia

bloc [blɒk] n (POL) blocco

block [blɔk] *n* blocco; (*in pipes*) ingombro; (*toy*) cubo; (*of buildings*) isolato ♦ *vt* bloccare; **~ade** [-'keɪd] *n* blocco; **~age** *n* ostacolo; **~buster** *n* (*film, book*) grande successo; **~ letters** *npl* stampatello; **~ of flats** (*BRIT*) *n* caseggiato.

bloke [bləuk] (*BRIT: inf*) *n* tizio

blond(e) [blɔnd] *adj, n* biondo(a)

blood [blʌd] *n* sangue *m*; **~ donor** *n* donatore/trice di sangue; **~ group** *n* gruppo sanguigno; **~hound** *n* segugio; **~ poisoning** *n* setticemia; **~ pressure** *n* pressione *f* sanguigna; **~shed** *n* spargimento di sangue; **~shot** *adj*: **~shot eyes** occhi iniettati di sangue; **~stream** *n* flusso del sangue; **~ test** *n* analisi *f inv* del sangue; **~thirsty** *adj* assetato(a) di sangue; **~y** *adj* (*fight*) sanguinoso(a); (*nose*) sanguinante; (*BRIT: inf!*): **this ~y ...** questo maledetto ...; **~y awful / good** (*inf!*) veramente terribile/forte; **~y-minded** (*BRIT: inf*) *adj* indisponente

bloom [blu:m] *n* fiore *m* ♦ *vi* (*tree*) essere in fiore; (*flower*) aprirsi

blossom ['blɔsəm] *n* fiore *m*; (*with pl sense*) fiori *mpl* ♦ *vi* essere in fiore

blot [blɔt] *n* macchia ♦ *vt* macchiare; **~ out** *vt* (*memories*) cancellare; (*view*) nascondere

blotchy ['blɔtʃɪ] *adj* (*complexion*) coperto(a) di macchie

blotting paper ['blɔtɪŋ-] *n* carta assorbente

blouse [blauz] *n* (*feminine garment*) camicetta

blow [bləu] (*pt* **blew**, *pp* **blown**) *n* colpo ♦ *vi* soffiare ♦ *vt* (*fuse*) far saltare; (*subj: wind*) spingere; (*instrument*) suonare; **to ~ one's nose** soffiarsi il naso; **to ~ a whistle** fischiare; **~ away** *vt* portare via; **~ down** *vt* abbattere; **~ off** *vt* far volare via; **~ out** *vi* scoppiare; **~ over** *vi* calmarsi; **~ up** *vi* saltare in aria ♦ *vt* far saltare in aria; (*tyre*) gonfiare; (*PHOT*) ingrandire; **~-dry** *n* messa in piega a föhn; **~lamp** (*BRIT*) *n* lampada a benzina per saldare; **blown** *pp of* **blow**; **~-out** *n* (*of tyre*) scoppio; **~torch** *n* = **~lamp**

blue [blu:] *adj* azzurro(a); (*depressed*) giù *inv*; **~ film / joke** film/ barzelletta pornografico(a); **out of the ~** (*fig*) all'improvviso; **~bell** *n* giacinto dei boschi; **~bottle** *n* moscone *m*; **~print** *n* (*fig*): **~print (for)** formula (di)

bluff [blʌf] *vi* bluffare ♦ *n* bluff *m inv* ♦ *adj* (*person*) brusco(a); **to call sb's ~** mettere alla prova il bluff di qn

blunder ['blʌndə*] *n* abbaglio ♦ *vi* prendere un abbaglio

blunt [blʌnt] *adj* smussato(a); spuntato(a); (*person*) brusco(a)

blur [blə:*] *n* forma indistinta ♦ *vt* offuscare

blush [blʌʃ] *vi* arrossire ♦ *n* rossore *m*

blustering ['blʌstərɪŋ] *adj* infuriato(a)

blustery ['blʌstərɪ] *adj* (*weather*) burrascoso(a)

boar [bɔ:*] *n* cinghiale *m*

board [bɔ:d] *n* tavola; (*on wall*) tabellone *m*; (*committee*) consiglio, comitato; (*in firm*) consiglio d'amministrazione; (*NAUT, AVIAT*): **on ~** a bordo ♦ *vt* (*ship*) salire a bordo di; (*train*) salire su; **full ~** (*BRIT*) pensione completa; **half ~** (*BRIT*) mezza pensione; **~ and lodging** vitto e alloggio; **which goes by the ~** (*fig*) che viene abbandonato; **~ up** *vt* (*door*) chiudere con assi; **~er** *n* (*SCOL*) convittore/trice; **~ing card** *n* = **~ing pass**; **~ing house** *n* pensione *f*; **~ing pass** *n* (*AVIAT, NAUT*) carta d'imbarco; **~ing school** *n* collegio; **~ room** *n* sala del consiglio

boast [bəust] *vi*: **to ~ (about** *or* **of)** vantarsi (di)

boat [bəut] *n* nave *f*; (*small*) barca; **~swain** ['bəusn] *n* nostromo

bob [bɔb] *vi* (*boat, cork on water: also*: **~ up and down**) andare su e giù; **~ up** *vi* saltare fuori

bobby ['bɔbɪ] (*BRIT: inf*) *n* poliziotto

bobsleigh ['bɔbsleɪ] *n* bob *m inv*

bode [bəud] *vi*: **to ~ well / ill (for)** essere di buon/cattivo auspicio (per)

bodily ['bɔdɪlɪ] *adj* fisico(a), corporale ♦ *adv* corporalmente; interamente; in persona

body ['bɔdɪ] *n* corpo; (*of car*) carrozzeria; (*of*

plane) fusoliera; (*fig: group*) gruppo; (: *organization*) organizzazione *f*; (: *quantity*) quantità *f inv*; ~-**building** *n* culturismo; ~**guard** *n* guardia del corpo; ~**work** *n* carrozzeria

bog [bɔg] *n* palude *f* ♦ *vt*: **to get ~ged down** (*fig*) impantanarsi

bogus ['bəugəs] *adj* falso(a); finto(a)

boil [bɔɪl] *vt, vi* bollire ♦ *n* (*MED*) foruncolo; **to come to the** (*BRIT*) **or a** (*US*) ~ raggiungere l'ebollizione; ~ **down to** *vt fus* (*fig*) ridursi a; ~ **over** *vi* traboccare (bollendo); ~**ed egg** *n* uovo alla coque; ~**ed potatoes** *npl* patate *fpl* bollite *or* lesse; ~**er** *n* caldaia; ~**er suit** (*BRIT*) *n* tuta; ~**ing point** *n* punto di ebollizione

boisterous ['bɔɪstərəs] *adj* chiassoso(a)

bold [bəuld] *adj* audace; (*child*) impudente; (*colour*) deciso(a)

bollard ['bɔləd] (*BRIT*) *n* (*AUT*) colonnina luminosa

bolt [bəult] *n* chiavistello; (*with nut*) bullone *m* ♦ *adv*: ~ **upright** diritto(a) come un fuso ♦ *vt* serrare; (*also*: ~ **together**) imbullonare; (*food*) mangiare in fretta ♦ *vi* scappare via

bomb [bɔm] *n* bomba ♦ *vt* bombardare

bombastic [bɔm'bæstɪk] *adj* magniloquente

bomb: ~ **disposal unit** *n* corpo degli artificieri; ~**er** *n* (*AVIAT*) bombardiere *m*; ~**shell** *n* (*fig*) notizia bomba

bond [bɔnd] *n* legame *m*; (*binding promise, FINANCE*) obbligazione *f*; (*COMM*): **in** ~ in attesa di sdoganamento

bondage ['bɔndɪdʒ] *n* schiavitù *f*

bone [bəun] *n* osso; (*of fish*) spina, lisca ♦ *vt* disossare; togliere le spine a; ~ **idle** *adj* pigrissimo(a); ~ **marrow** *n* midollo osseo

bonfire ['bɔnfaɪə*] *n* falò *m inv*

bonnet ['bɔnɪt] *n* cuffia; (*BRIT: of car*) cofano

bonus ['bəunəs] *n* premio; (*fig*) sovrappiù *m inv*

bony ['bəunɪ] *adj* (*MED: tissue*) osseo(a); (*arm, face*) ossuto(a); (*meat*) pieno(a) di ossi; (*fish*) pieno(a) di spine

boo [bu:] *excl* ba! ♦ *vt* fischiare

booby trap ['bu:bɪ-] *n* trappola

book [buk] *n* libro; (*of stamps etc*)

blocchetto ♦ *vt* (*ticket, seat, room*) prenotare; (*driver*) multare; (*football player*) ammonire; ~**s** *npl* (*COMM*) conti *mpl*; ~**case** *n* scaffale *m*; ~**ing office** (*BRIT*) *n* (*RAIL*) biglietteria; (*THEATRE*) botteghino; ~-**keeping** *n* contabilità; ~**let** *n* libricino; ~**maker** *n* allibratore *m*; ~**seller** *n* libraio; ~**shop**, ~**store** *n* libreria

boom [bu:m] *n* (*noise*) rimbombo; (*in prices etc*) boom *m inv* ♦ *vi* rimbombare; andare a gonfie vele

boon [bu:n] *n* vantaggio

boost [bu:st] *n* spinta ♦ *vt* spingere; ~**er** *n* (*MED*) richiamo

boot [bu:t] *n* stivale *m*; (*for hiking*) scarpone *m* da montagna; (*for football etc*) scarpa; (*BRIT: of car*) portabagagli *m inv* ♦ *vt* (*COMPUT*) inizializzare; **to** ~ (*in addition*) per giunta, in più

booth [bu:ð] *n* cabina; (*at fair*) baraccone *m*

booty ['bu:tɪ] *n* bottino

booze [bu:z] (*inf*) *n* alcool *m*

border ['bɔ:də*] *n* orlo; margine *m*; (*of a country*) frontiera; (*for flowers*) aiuola (laterale) ♦ *vt* (*road*) costeggiare; (*another country: also*: ~ **on**) confinare con; **the B~s** la zona di confine tra l'Inghilterra e la Scozia; ~ **on** *vt fus* (*fig: insanity etc*) sfiorare; ~**line** *n* (*fig*): **on the ~line** incerto(a); ~**line case** *n* caso incerto

bore [bɔ:*] *pt of* **bear** ♦ *vt* (*hole etc*) scavare; (*person*) annoiare ♦ *n* (*person*) seccatore/trice; (*of gun*) calibro; **to be ~d** annoiarsi; ~**dom** *n* noia; **boring** *adj* noioso(a)

born [bɔ:n] *adj*: **to be** ~ nascere; **I was** ~ **in 1960** sono nato nel 1960

borne [bɔ:n] *pp of* **bear**

borough ['bʌrə] *n* comune *m*

borrow ['bɔrəu] *vt*: **to** ~ **sth (from sb)** prendere in prestito qc (da qn)

Bosnia(-Herzegovina) ['bɔznɪə-(hɜ:zə'gəuvi:nə)] *n* Bosnia-Erzegovina

Bosnian ['bɔznɪən] *n, adj* bosniaco(a) *m/f*

boss [bɔs] *n* capo ♦ *vt* comandare; ~**y** *adj* prepotente

bosun ['bəusn] *n* nostromo

botany ['bɔtənɪ] *n* botanica

botch [bɒtʃ] vt (*also*: **~ up**) fare un pasticcio di

both [bəuθ] *adj* entrambi(e), tutt'e due ♦ *pron*: **~ (of them)** entrambi(e); **~ of us went, we ~ went** ci siamo andati tutt'e due ♦ *adv*: **they sell ~ meat and poultry** vendono insieme la carne ed il pollame

bother ['bɒðə*] vt (*worry*) preoccupare; (*annoy*) infastidire ♦ vi (*also*: **~ o.s.**) preoccuparsi ♦ n: **it is a ~ to have to do** è una seccatura dover fare; **it was no ~** non c'era problema; **to ~ doing sth** darsi la pena di fare qc

bottle ['bɒtl] n bottiglia; (*baby's*) biberon m *inv* ♦ vt imbottigliare; **~ up** vt contenere; **~ bank** n contenitore m per la raccolta del vetro; **~neck** n imbottigliamento; **~-opener** n apribottiglie m *inv*

bottom ['bɒtəm] n fondo; (*buttocks*) sedere m ♦ *adj* più basso(a); ultimo(a); **at the ~ of** in fondo a

bough [bau] n ramo

bought [bɔːt] *pt, pp of* **buy**

boulder ['bəuldə*] n masso (tondeggiante)

bounce [bauns] vi (*ball*) rimbalzare; (*cheque*) essere restituito(a) ♦ vt far rimbalzare ♦ n (*rebound*) rimbalzo; **~r** (*inf*) n buttafuori m *inv*

bound [baund] *pt, pp of* **bind** ♦ n (*gen pl*) limite m; (*leap*) salto ♦ vi saltare ♦ vt (*limit*) delimitare ♦ *adj*: **~ by law** obbligato(a) per legge; **to be ~ to do sth** (*obliged*) essere costretto(a) a fare qc; **he's ~ to fail** (*likely*) fallirà di certo; **~ for** diretto(a) a; **out of ~s** il cui accesso è vietato

boundary ['baundrɪ] n confine m

boundless ['baundlɪs] *adj* senza limiti

bourgeois ['buəʒwɑː] *adj* borghese

bout [baut] n periodo; (*of malaria etc*) attacco; (*BOXING etc*) incontro

bow¹ [bəu] n nodo; (*weapon*) arco; (*MUS*) archetto

bow² [bau] n (*with body*) inchino; (*NAUT: also*: **~s**) prua ♦ vi inchinarsi; (*yield*): **to ~ to** *or* **before** sottomettersi a

bowels ['bauəlz] *npl* intestini *mpl*; (*fig*) viscere *fpl*

bowl [bəul] n (*for eating*) scodella; (*for washing*) bacino; (*ball*) boccia ♦ vi (*CRICKET*) servire (la palla)

bow-legged ['bəu'legɪd] *adj* dalle gambe storte

bowler ['bəulə*] n (*CRICKET, BASEBALL*) lanciatore m; (*BRIT: also*: **~ hat**) bombetta

bowling ['bəulɪŋ] n (*game*) gioco delle bocce; **~ alley** n pista da bowling; **~ green** n campo di bocce

bowls [bəulz] n gioco delle bocce

bow tie n cravatta a farfalla

box [bɒks] n scatola; (*also*: **cardboard ~**) cartone m; (*THEATRE*) palco ♦ vt inscatolare ♦ vi fare del pugilato; **~er** n (*person*) pugile m; **~ing** n (*SPORT*) pugilato; **B~ing Day** (*BRIT*) n ≈ Santo Stefano; **~ing gloves** *npl* guantoni *mpl* da pugile; **~ing ring** n ring m *inv*; **~ office** n biglietteria; **~ room** n ripostiglio

---

Boxing Day

---

i Il **Boxing Day** è il primo giorno infrasettimanale dopo Natale. Prende il nome dalla tradizionale usanza di donare pacchi regalo natalizi, un tempo chiamati "*Christmas boxes*", a fornitori e dipendenti.

---

boy [bɔɪ] n ragazzo

boycott ['bɔɪkɒt] n boicottaggio ♦ vt boicottare

boyfriend ['bɔɪfrend] n ragazzo

boyish ['bɔɪɪʃ] *adj* da ragazzo

B.R. *abbr* (*formerly*) = **British Rail**

bra [brɑː] n reggipetto, reggiseno

brace [breɪs] n (*on teeth*) apparecchio correttore; (*tool*) trapano ♦ vt rinforzare, sostenere; **~s** (*BRIT*) *npl* (*DRESS*) bretelle *fpl*; **to ~ o.s.** (*also fig*) tenersi forte

bracelet ['breɪslɪt] n braccialetto

bracing ['breɪsɪŋ] *adj* invigorante

bracken ['brækən] n felce f

bracket ['brækɪt] n (*TECH*) mensola; (*group*) gruppo; (*TYP*) parentesi f *inv* ♦ vt mettere fra parentesi

brag [bræg] vi vantarsi

braid [breɪd] n (*trimming*) passamano; (*of*

hair) treccia

brain [brein] *n* cervello; **~s** *npl* (*intelligence*) cervella *fpl*; **he's got ~s** è intelligente; **~wash** *vt* fare un lavaggio di cervello a; **~wave** *n* lampo di genio; **~y** *adj* intelligente

braise [breiz] *vt* brasare

brake [breik] *n* (*on vehicle*) freno ♦ *vi* frenare; **~ fluid** *n* liquido dei freni; **~ light** *n* (fanalino dello) stop *m inv*

bramble ['bræmbl] *n* rovo

bran [bræn] *n* crusca

branch [brɑːntʃ] *n* ramo; (*COMM*) succursale *f*; **~ out** *vi* (*fig*) intraprendere una nuova attività

brand [brænd] *n* (*also:* **~ name**) marca; (*fig*) tipo ♦ *vt* (*cattle*) marcare (a ferro rovente)

brand-new *adj* nuovo(a) di zecca

brandy ['brændi] *n* brandy *m inv*

brash [bræʃ] *adj* sfacciato(a)

brass [brɑːs] *n* ottone *m*; **the ~** (*MUS*) gli ottoni; **~ band** *n* fanfara

brat [bræt] (*pej*) *n* marmocchio, monello/a

bravado [brə'vɑːdəu] *n* spavalderia

brave [breiv] *adj* coraggioso(a) ♦ *vt* affrontare; **~ry** *n* coraggio

brawl [brɔːl] *n* rissa

brawny ['brɔːni] *adj* muscoloso(a)

bray [brei] *vi* ragliare

brazen ['breizn] *adj* sfacciato(a) ♦ *vt*: **to ~ it out** fare lo sfacciato

brazier ['breiziə*] *n* braciere *m*

Brazil [brə'zil] *n* Brasile *m*

breach [briːtʃ] *vt* aprire una breccia in ♦ *n* (*gap*) breccia, varco; (*breaking*): **~ of contract** rottura di contratto; **~ of the peace** violazione *f* dell'ordine pubblico

bread [brεd] *n* pane *m*; **~ and butter** *n* pane e burro; (*fig*) mezzi *mpl* di sussistenza; **~bin** *n* cassetta *f* portapane *inv*; **~crumbs** *npl* briciole *fpl*; (*CULIN*) pangrattato; **~line** *n*: **to be on the ~line** avere appena il denaro per vivere

breadth [brεtθ] *n* larghezza; (*fig: of knowledge etc*) ampiezza

breadwinner ['brεdwinə*] *n* chi guadagna il pane per tutta la famiglia

break [breik] (*pt* **broke**, *pp* **broken**) *vt* rompere; (*law*) violare; (*record*) battere ♦ *vi* rompersi; (*storm*) scoppiare; (*weather*) cambiare; (*dawn*) spuntare; (*news*) saltare fuori ♦ *n* (*gap*) breccia; (*fracture*) rottura; (*rest, also SCOL*) intervallo; (: *short*) pausa; (*chance*) possibilità *f inv*; **to ~ one's leg** *etc* rompersi la gamba *etc*; **to ~ the news to sb** comunicare per primo la notizia a qn; **to ~ even** coprire le spese; **to ~ free** or **loose** spezzare i legami; **to ~ open** (*door etc*) sfondare; **~ down** *vt* (*figures, data*) analizzare ♦ *vi* (*person*) avere un esaurimento (nervoso); (*AUT*) guastarsi; **~ in** *vt* (*horse etc*) domare ♦ *vi* (*burglar*) fare irruzione; (*interrupt*) interrompere; **~ into** *vt fus* (*house*) fare irruzione in; **~ off** *vi* (*speaker*) interrompersi; (*branch*) troncarsi; **~ out** *vi* evadere; (*war, fight*) scoppiare; **to ~ out in spots** coprirsi di macchie; **~ up** *vi* (*ship*) sfondarsi; (*meeting*) sciogliersi; (*crowd*) disperdersi; (*marriage*) andare a pezzi; (*SCOL*) chiudere ♦ *vt* fare a pezzi, spaccare; (*fight etc*) interrompere, far cessare; **~age** *n* rottura; (*object broken*) cosa rotta; **~down** *n* (*AUT*) guasto; (*in communications*) interruzione *f*; (*of marriage*) rottura; (*MED: also:* **nervous ~down**) esaurimento nervoso; (*of statistics*) resoconto; **~down van** (*BRIT*) *n* carro *m* attrezzi *inv*; **~er** *n* frangente *m*

breakfast ['brεkfəst] *n* colazione *f*

break: **~-in** *n* irruzione *f*; **~ing and entering** *n* (*LAW*) violazione *f* di domicilio con scasso; **~through** *n* (*fig*) passo avanti; **~water** *n* frangiflutti *m inv*

breast [brεst] *n* (*of woman*) seno; (*chest, CULIN*) petto; **~-feed** (*irreg: like* **feed**) *vt, vi* allattare (al seno); **~-stroke** *n* nuoto a rana

breath [brεθ] *n* respiro; **out of ~** senza fiato

Breathalyser ® ['brεθəlaizə*] (*BRIT*) *n* alcoltest *m inv*

breathe [briːð] *vt, vi* respirare; **~ in** *vt* respirare ♦ *vi* inspirare; **~ out** *vt, vi* espirare; **~r** *n* attimo di respiro; **breathing** *n* respiro, respirazione *f*

breathless ['brεθlɪs] *adj* senza fiato

breathtaking ['brεθteɪkɪŋ] *adj* mozzafiato *inv*

bred [brεd] *pt, pp of* **breed**

breed [briːd] (*pt, pp* **bred**) *vt* allevare ♦ *vi* riprodursi ♦ *n* razza; (*type, class*) varietà *f inv*; ~**ing** *n* riproduzione *f*; allevamento; (*upbringing*) educazione *f*

breeze [briːz] *n* brezza

breezy ['briːzɪ] *adj* allegro(a); ventilato(a)

brew [bruː] *vt* (*tea*) fare un infuso di; (*beer*) fare ♦ *vi* (*storm, fig: trouble etc*) prepararsi; ~**ery** *n* fabbrica di birra

bribe [braɪb] *n* bustarella ♦ *vt* comprare; ~**ry** *n* corruzione *f*

brick [brɪk] *n* mattone *m*; ~**layer** *n* muratore *m*

bridal ['braɪdl] *adj* nuziale

bride [braɪd] *n* sposa; ~**groom** *n* sposo; ~**smaid** *n* damigella d'onore

bridge [brɪdʒ] *n* ponte *m*; (*NAUT*) ponte di comando; (*of nose*) dorso; (*CARDS*) bridge *m inv* ♦ *vt* (*fig: gap*) colmare

bridle ['braɪdl] *n* briglia; ~ **path** *n* sentiero (per cavalli)

brief [briːf] *adj* breve ♦ *n* (*LAW*) comparsa; (*gen*) istruzioni *fpl* ♦ *vt* mettere al corrente; ~**s** *npl* (*underwear*) mutande *fpl*; ~**case** *n* cartella; ~**ing** *n* briefing *m inv*; ~**ly** *adv* (*glance*) di sfuggita; (*explain, say*) brevemente

bright [braɪt] *adj* luminoso(a); (*clever*) sveglio(a); (*lively*) vivace; ~**en** (*also:* ~**en up**) *vt* (*room*) rendere luminoso(a) ♦ *vi* schiarirsi; (*person*) rallegrarsi

brilliance ['brɪljəns] *n* splendore *m*

brilliant ['brɪljənt] *adj* brillante; (*light, smile*) radioso(a); (*inf*) splendido(a)

brim [brɪm] *n* orlo

brine [braɪn] *n* (*CULIN*) salamoia

bring [brɪŋ] (*pt, pp* **brought**) *vt* portare; ~ **about** *vt* causare; ~ **back** *vt* riportare; ~ **down** *vt* portare giù; abbattere; ~ **forward** *vt* (*proposal*) avanzare; (*meeting*) anticipare; ~ **off** *vt* (*task, plan*) portare a compimento; ~ **out** *vt* tirar fuori; (*meaning*) mettere in evidenza; (*book,*

album) far uscire; ~ **round** *vt* (*unconscious person*) far rinvenire; ~ **up** *vt* (*carry up*) portare su; (*child*) allevare; (*question*) introdurre; (*food: vomit*) rimettere, rigurgitare

brink [brɪŋk] *n* orlo

brisk [brɪsk] *adj* (*manner*) spiccio(a); (*trade*) vivace; (*pace*) svelto(a)

bristle ['brɪsl] *n* setola ♦ *vi* rizzarsi; **bristling with** irto(a) di

Britain ['brɪtən] *n* (*also:* **Great ~**) Gran Bretagna

British ['brɪtɪʃ] *adj* britannico(a); **the ~** *npl* i Britannici; **the ~ Isles** *npl* le Isole Britanniche; ~ **Rail** *n* compagnia *ferroviaria britannica*, ≈ Ferrovie *fpl* dello Stato

Briton ['brɪtən] *n* britannico/a

brittle ['brɪtl] *adj* fragile

broach [brəʊtʃ] *vt* (*subject*) affrontare

broad [brɔːd] *adj* largo(a); (*distinction*) generale; (*accent*) spiccato(a); **in ~ daylight** in pieno giorno; ~**cast** (*pt, pp* ~**cast**) *n* trasmissione *f* ♦ *vt* trasmettere per radio (*or* per televisione) ♦ *vi* fare una trasmissione; ~**en** *vt* allargare ♦ *vi* allargarsi; ~**ly** *adv* (*fig*) in generale; ~**-minded** *adj* di mente aperta

broccoli ['brɔkəlɪ] *n* broccoli *mpl*

brochure ['brəʊʃjʊə*] *n* dépliant *m inv*

broil [brɔɪl] *vt* cuocere a fuoco vivo

broke [brəʊk] *pt of* **break** ♦ *adj* (*inf*) squattrinato(a)

broken ['brəʊkn] *pp of* **break** ♦ *adj* rotto(a); **a ~ leg** una gamba rotta; **in ~ English** in un inglese stentato; ~**-hearted** *adj*: **to be ~-hearted** avere il cuore spezzato

broker ['brəʊkə*] *n* agente *m*

brolly ['brɔlɪ] (*BRIT: inf*) *n* ombrello

bronchitis [brɔŋ'kaɪtɪs] *n* bronchite *f*

bronze [brɔnz] *n* bronzo

brooch [brəʊtʃ] *n* spilla

brood [bruːd] *n* covata ♦ *vi* (*person*) rimuginare

brook [brʊk] *n* ruscello

broom [brʊm] *n* scopa; (*BOT*) ginestra

Bros. *abbr* (= *Brothers*) F.lli

broth [brɒθ] n brodo

brothel [ˈbrɒθl] n bordello

brother [ˈbrʌðə*] n fratello; **~-in-law** n
cognato

brought [brɔːt] pt, pp of **bring**

brow [brau] n fronte f; (rare, gen: eye~)
sopracciglio; (of hill) cima

brown [braun] adj bruno(a), marrone;
(tanned) abbronzato(a) ♦ n (colour) color m
bruno or marrone ♦ vt (CULIN) rosolare; ~
bread n pane m integrale, pane nero

Brownie [ˈbrauni] n giovane esploratrice f;
b~ (US: cake) dolce al cioccolato e nocciole

brown paper n carta da pacchi or da
imballaggio

brown sugar n zucchero greggio

browse [brauz] vi (among books) curiosare
fra i libri; **to ~ through a book** sfogliare un
libro; **~r** n (COMPUT) browser m inv

bruise [bruːz] n (on person) livido ♦ vt farsi
un livido a

brunette [bruːˈnɛt] n bruna

brunt [brʌnt] n: **the ~ of** (attack, criticism
etc) il peso maggiore di

brush [brʌʃ] n spazzola; (for painting,
shaving) pennello; (quarrel) schermaglia
♦ vt spazzolare; (also: **~ against**) sfiorare; **~
aside** vt scostare; **~ up** vt (knowledge)
rinfrescare; **~wood** n macchia

Brussels [ˈbrʌslz] n Bruxelles f; **~ sprout** n
cavolo di Bruxelles

brutal [ˈbruːtl] adj brutale

brute [bruːt] n bestia ♦ adj: **by ~ force** con
la forza, a viva forza

B.Sc. n abbr (UNIV) = **Bachelor of Science**

BSE n abbr (= bovine spongiform
encephalopathy) encefalite f bovina
spongiforme

BTW abbr a proposito

bubble [ˈbʌbl] n bolla ♦ vi ribollire; (sparkle,
fig) essere effervescente; **~ bath** n
bagnoschiuma m inv; **~ gum** n gomma
americana

buck [bʌk] n maschio (di camoscio, caprone,
coniglio etc); (US: inf) dollaro ♦ vi
sgroppare; **to pass the ~ (to sb)** scaricare
(su di qn) la propria responsabilità; **~ up** vi
(cheer up) rianimarsi

bucket [ˈbʌkɪt] n secchio

Buckingham Palace

ⓘ **Buckingham Palace** è la residenza
ufficiale a Londra del sovrano
britannico. Fu costruita nel 1703 per il duca
di Buckingham.

---

buckle [ˈbʌkl] n fibbia ♦ vt allacciare ♦ vi
(wheel etc) piegarsi

bud [bʌd] n gemma; (of flower) bocciolo
♦ vi germogliare; (flower) sbocciare

Buddhism [ˈbudɪzəm] n buddismo

budding [ˈbʌdɪŋ] adj (poet etc) in erba

buddy [ˈbʌdɪ] (US) n compagno

budge [bʌdʒ] vt scostare; (fig) smuovere
♦ vi spostarsi; smuoversi

budgerigar [ˈbʌdʒərɪgɑː*] n pappagallino

budget [ˈbʌdʒɪt] n bilancio preventivo ♦ vi:
to ~ for sth fare il bilancio per qc

budgie [ˈbʌdʒɪ] n = **budgerigar**

buff [bʌf] adj color camoscio ♦ n (inf:
enthusiast) appassionato/a

buffalo [ˈbʌfələu] (pl ~ or **~es**) n bufalo;
(US) bisonte m

buffer [ˈbʌfə*] n respingente m; (COMPUT)
memoria tampone, buffer m inv

buffet[1] [ˈbufeɪ] n (food, BRIT: bar) buffet m
inv; **~ car** (BRIT) n (RAIL) ≈ servizio ristoro

buffet[2] [ˈbʌfɪt] vt sferzare

bug [bʌg] n (esp US: insect) insetto; (COMPUT,
fig: germ) virus m inv; (spy device)
microfono spia ♦ vt mettere sotto
controllo; (inf: annoy) scocciare

buggy [ˈbʌgɪ] n (baby ~) passeggino

bugle [ˈbjuːgl] n tromba

build[bɪld] (pt, pp **built**) n (of person) corporatura ♦ vt costruire; **~ up** vt accumulare;
aumentare; **~er** n costruttore m; **~ing** n
costruzione f; edificio; (industry) edilizia; **~ing
society** (BRIT) n società f inv immobiliare

built [bɪlt] pt, pp of **build** ♦ adj: **~-in**
(cupboard) a muro; (device) incorporato(a);
~-up area n abitato

bulb [bʌlb] n (BOT) bulbo; (ELEC) lampadina

bulge [bʌldʒ] n rigonfiamento ♦ vi essere

protuberante or rigonfio(a); **to be bulging with** essere pieno(a) or zeppo(a) di

bulk [bʌlk] n massa, volume m; **in ~** a pacchi (or cassette etc); (COMM) all'ingrosso; **the ~ of** il grosso di; **~y** adj grosso(a); voluminoso(a)

bull [bul] n toro; (male elephant, whale) maschio; **~dog** n bulldog m inv

bulldozer ['buldəuzə*] n bulldozer m inv

bullet ['bulɪt] n pallottola

bulletin ['bulɪtɪn] n bollettino

bulletproof ['bulɪtpruːf] adj (car) blindato(a); (vest etc) antiproiettile inv

bullfight ['bulfaɪt] n corrida; **~er** n torero; **~ing** n tauromachia

bullion ['buljən] n oro or argento in lingotti

bullock ['bulək] n manzo

bullring ['bulrɪŋ] n arena (per corride)

bull's-eye ['bulzaɪ] n centro del bersaglio

bully ['bulɪ] n prepotente m ♦ vt angariare; (frighten) intimidire

bum [bʌm] n (inf) (backside) culo; (tramp) vagabondo/a

bumblebee ['bʌmblbiː] n bombo

bump [bʌmp] n (in car) piccolo tamponamento; (jolt) scossa; (on road etc) protuberanza; (on head) bernoccolo ♦ vt battere; **~ into** vt fus scontrarsi con; (person) imbattersi in; **~er** n paraurti m inv ♦ adj: **~er harvest** raccolto eccezionale; **~er cars** npl autoscontri mpl

bumpy ['bʌmpɪ] adj (road) dissestato(a)

bun [bʌn] n focaccia; (of hair) crocchia

bunch [bʌntʃ] n (of flowers, keys) mazzo; (of bananas) casco; (of people) gruppo; **~ of grapes** grappolo d'uva; **~es** npl (in hair) codine fpl

bundle ['bʌndl] n fascio ♦ vt (also: **~ up**) legare in un fascio; (put): **to ~ sth/sb into** spingere qc/qn in

bungalow ['bʌngələu] n bungalow m inv

bungle ['bʌngl] vt fare un pasticcio di

bunion ['bʌnjən] n callo (al piede)

bunk [bʌnk] n cuccetta; **~ beds** npl letti mpl a castello

bunker ['bʌnkə*] n (coal store) ripostiglio per il carbone; (MIL, GOLF) bunker m inv

bunny ['bʌnɪ] n (also: **~ rabbit**) coniglietto

bunting ['bʌntɪŋ] n pavesi mpl, bandierine fpl

buoy [bɔɪ] n boa; **~ant** adj galleggiante; (fig) vivace

burden ['bəːdn] n carico, fardello ♦ vt: **to ~ sb with** caricare qn di

bureau [bjuə'rəu] (pl **bureaux**) n (BRIT: writing desk) scrivania; (US: chest of drawers) cassettone m; (office) ufficio, agenzia

bureaucracy [bjuə'rɔkrəsɪ] n burocrazia

bureaux [bjuə'rəuz] npl of **bureau**

burglar ['bəːglə*] n scassinatore m; **~ alarm** n campanello antifurto; **~y** n furto con scasso

burial ['berɪəl] n sepoltura

burly ['bəːlɪ] adj robusto(a)

Burma ['bəːmə] n Birmania

burn [bəːn] (pt, pp **burned** or **burnt**) vt, vi bruciare ♦ n bruciatura, scottatura; **~ down** vt distruggere col fuoco; **~er** n (on cooker) fornello; (TECH) bruciatore m, becco (a gas); **~ing** adj in fiamme; (sand) che scotta; (ambition) bruciante; **burnt** pt, pp of **burn**

burrow ['bʌrəu] n tana ♦ vt scavare

bursary ['bəːsərɪ] (BRIT) n (SCOL) borsa di studio

burst [bəːst] (pt, pp **burst**) vt far scoppiare ♦ vi esplodere; (tyre) scoppiare ♦ n scoppio; (also: **~ pipe**) rottura nel tubo, perdita; **a ~ of speed** uno scatto di velocità; **to ~ into flames/tears** scoppiare in fiamme/lacrime; **to ~ out laughing** scoppiare a ridere; **to be ~ing with** scoppiare di; **~ into** vt fus (room etc) irrompere in

bury ['berɪ] vt seppellire

bus [bʌs] (pl **~es**) n autobus m inv

bush [buʃ] n cespuglio; (scrub land) macchia; **to beat about the ~** menare il cane per l'aia

bushy ['buʃɪ] adj cespuglioso(a)

busily ['bɪzɪlɪ] adv con impegno, alacremente

business ['bɪznɪs] n (matter) affare m; (trading) affari mpl; (firm) azienda; (job, duty) lavoro; **to be away on** ~ essere andato via per affari; **it's none of my** ~ questo non mi riguarda; **he means** ~ non scherza; ~**like** *adj* serio(a); efficiente; ~**man/woman** *(irreg)* n uomo/donna d'affari; ~ **trip** n viaggio d'affari

busker ['bʌskə*] *(BRIT)* n suonatore/trice ambulante

bus: ~ **shelter** n pensilina *(alla fermata dell'autobus)*; ~ **station** n stazione f delle corriere, autostazione f; ~-**stop** n fermata d'autobus

bust [bʌst] n busto m; *(ANAT)* seno ♦ *adj* (inf: broken) rotto(a); **to go** ~ fallire

bustle ['bʌsl] n movimento, attività ♦ *vi* darsi da fare; **bustling** *adj* movimentato(a)

busy ['bɪzɪ] *adj* occupato(a); *(shop, street)* molto frequentato(a) ♦ *vt*: **to** ~ **o.s.** darsi da fare; ~**body** n ficcanaso m/f *inv*; ~ **signal** *(US)* n *(TEL)* segnale m di occupato

but [bʌt] *conj* ma; **I'd love to come,** ~ **I'm busy** vorrei tanto venire, ma ho da fare ♦ *prep* (apart from, except) eccetto, tranne, meno; **he was nothing** ~ **trouble** non dava altro che guai; **no-one** ~ **him can do it** nessuno può farlo tranne lui; ~ **for you/your help** se non fosse per te/per il tuo aiuto; **anything** ~ **that** tutto ma non questo

♦ *adv* (just, only) solo, soltanto; **she's** ~ **a child** è solo una bambina; **had I** ~ **known** se solo avessi saputo; **I can** ~ **try** tentar non nuoce; **all** ~ **finished** quasi finito

butcher ['butʃə*] n macellaio ♦ *vt* macellare; ~'**s (shop)** n macelleria

butler ['bʌtlə*] n maggiordomo

butt [bʌt] n (cask) grossa botte f; (of gun) calcio; (of cigarette) mozzicone m; *(BRIT: fig: target)* oggetto ♦ *vt* cozzare; ~ **in** *vi* (interrupt) interrompere

butter ['bʌtə*] n burro ♦ *vt* imburrare; ~**cup** n ranuncolo

butterfly ['bʌtəflaɪ] n farfalla; *(SWIMMING:*

also: ~ **stroke**) (nuoto a) farfalla

buttocks ['bʌtəks] *npl* natiche *fpl*

button ['bʌtn] n bottone m; *(US: badge)* distintivo ♦ *vt* (also: ~ **up**) abbottonare ♦ *vi* abbottonarsi

buttress ['bʌtrɪs] n contrafforte f

buy [baɪ] *(pt, pp bought)* *vt* comprare ♦ n acquisto; **to** ~ **sb sth/sth from sb** comprare qc per qn/qc da qn; **to** ~ **sb a drink** offrire da bere a qn; ~**er** n compratore/trice

buzz [bʌz] n ronzio; (inf: phone call) colpo di telefono ♦ *vi* ronzare

buzzer ['bʌzə*] n cicalino

buzz word *(inf)* n termine m di gran moda

by [baɪ] *prep* 1 (referring to cause, agent) da; **killed** ~ **lightning** ucciso da un fulmine; **surrounded** ~ **a fence** circondato da uno steccato; **a painting** ~ **Picasso** un quadro di Picasso

2 (referring to method, manner, means): ~ **bus/car/train** in autobus/macchina/treno, con l'autobus/la macchina/il treno; **to pay** ~ **cheque** pagare con (un) assegno; ~ **moonlight** al chiaro di luna; ~ **saving hard, he ...** risparmiando molto, lui ...

3 (via, through) per; **we came** ~ **Dover** siamo venuti via Dover

4 (close to, past) accanto a; **the house** ~ **the river** la casa sul fiume; **a holiday** ~ **the sea** una vacanza al mare; **she sat** ~ **his bed** si sedette accanto al suo letto; **she rushed** ~ **me** mi è passata accanto correndo; **I go** ~ **the post office every day** passo davanti all'ufficio postale ogni giorno

5 (not later than) per; entro; ~ **4 o'clock** per *or* entro le 4; ~ **this time tomorrow** domani a quest'ora; ~ **the time I got here it was too late** quando sono arrivato era ormai troppo tardi

6 (during): ~ **day/night** di giorno/notte

7 (amount) a; ~ **the kilo/metre** a chili/metri; **paid** ~ **the hour** pagato all'ora; **one** ~ **one** uno per uno; **little** ~ **little** a poco a poco

8 (MATH, *measure*): **to divide/multiply ~ 3** dividere/moltiplicare per 3; **it's broader ~ a metre** è un metro più largo, è largo di un metro

9 (*according to*) per; **to play ~ the rules** attenersi alle regole; **it's all right ~ me** per me va bene

10: (all) **~ oneself** *etc* (tutto(a)) solo(a); **he did it (all) ~ himself** lo ha fatto (tutto) da solo

11: **~ the way** a proposito; **this wasn't my idea ~ the way** tra l'altro l'idea non è stata mia

♦ *adv* 1 *see* **go**; **pass** *etc*

2 **~ and ~** (*in past*) poco dopo; (*in future*) fra breve; **~ and large** nel complesso

bye(-bye) ['baɪ('baɪ)] *excl* ciao!, arrivederci!

by(e)-law *n* legge *f* locale

by-election (BRIT) *n* elezione *f* straordinaria

bygone ['baɪɡɒn] *adj* passato(a) ♦ *n*: **let ~s be ~s** mettiamoci una pietra sopra

bypass ['baɪpɑːs] *n* circonvallazione *f*; (MED) by-pass *m inv* ♦ *vt* fare una deviazione intorno a

by-product *n* sottoprodotto; (*fig*) conseguenza secondaria

bystander ['baɪstændə*] *n* spettatore/trice

byte [baɪt] *n* (COMPUT) byte *m inv*, bicarattere *m*

byword ['baɪwɜːd] *n*: **to be a ~ for** essere sinonimo di

C, c

C [siː] *n* (MUS) do

C. *abbr* (= centigrade) C.

C.A. *n abbr* = **chartered accountant**

cab [kæb] *n* taxi *m inv*; (*of truck*) cabina

cabaret ['kæbəreɪ] *n* cabaret *m inv*

cabbage ['kæbɪdʒ] *n* cavolo

cabin ['kæbɪn] *n* capanna; (*on ship*) cabina; **~ crew** *n* equipaggio; **~ cruiser** *n* cabinato

cabinet ['kæbɪnɪt] *n* (POL) consiglio dei ministri; (*furniture*) armadietto; (*also*:

display ~) vetrinetta

cable ['keɪbl] *n* cavo; fune *f*; (TEL) cablogramma *m* ♦ *vt* telegrafare; **~-car** *n* funivia; **~ television** *n* televisione *f* via cavo

cache [kæʃ] *n* deposito segreto

cackle ['kækl] *vi* schiamazzare

cactus ['kæktəs] (*pl* **cacti**) *n* cactus *m inv*

cadet [kə'dɛt] *n* (MIL) cadetto

cadge [kædʒ] (*inf*) *vt* scroccare

café ['kæfeɪ] *n* caffè *m inv*

cafeteria [kæfɪ'tɪərɪə] *n* self-service *m inv*

cage [keɪdʒ] *n* gabbia

cagey ['keɪdʒɪ] (*inf*) *adj* chiuso(a); guardingo(a)

cagoule [kə'ɡuːl] *n* K-way ® *m inv*

cajole [kə'dʒəul] *vt* allettare

cake [keɪk] *n* (*large*) torta; (*small*) pasticcino; **~ of soap** saponetta; **~d** *adj*: **~d with** incrostato(a) di

calculate ['kælkjuleɪt] *vt* calcolare; **calculation** [-'leɪʃən] *n* calcolo; **calculator** *n* calcolatrice *f*

calendar ['kæləndə*] *n* calendario; **~ year** *n* anno civile

calf [kɑːf] (*pl* **calves**) *n* (*of cow*) vitello; (*of other animals*) piccolo; (*also*: **~skin**) (pelle *f* di) vitello; (ANAT) polpaccio

calibre ['kælɪbə*] (US **caliber**) *n* calibro

call [kɔːl] *vt* (*gen, also* TEL) chiamare; (*meeting*) indire ♦ *vi* chiamare; (*visit: also*: **~ in, ~ round**) passare ♦ *n* (*shout*) grido, urlo; (TEL) telefonata; **to be ~ed** (*person, object*) chiamarsi; **to be on ~** essere a disposizione; **~ back** *vi* (*return*) ritornare; (TEL) ritelefonare, richiamare; **~ for** *vt fus* richiedere; (*fetch*) passare a prendere; **~ off** *vt* disdire; **~ on** *vt fus* (*visit*) passare da; (*appeal to*) chiedere a; **~ out** *vi* (*in pain*) urlare; (*to person*) chiamare; **~ up** *vt* (MIL) richiamare; (TEL) telefonare a; **~box** (BRIT) *n* cabina telefonica; **~ centre** *n* centro informazioni telefoniche; **~er** *n* persona che chiama; visitatore/trice; **~ girl** *n* ragazza *f* squillo *inv*; **~-in** (US) *n* (*phone-in*) trasmissione *f* a filo diretto con gli ascoltatori; **~ing** *n* vocazione *f*; **~ing card**

(*US*) *n* biglietto da visita

callous ['kæləs] *adj* indurito(a), insensibile

calm [kɑːm] *adj* calmo(a) ♦ *n* calma ♦ *vt* calmare; ~ **down** *vi* calmarsi ♦ *vt* calmare

Calor gas ® ['kælə*-] *n* butano

calorie ['kælərɪ] *n* caloria

calves [kɑːvz] *npl of* calf

Cambodia [kæm'bəudjə] *n* Cambogia

camcorder ['kæmkɔːdə*] *n* camcorder *f inv*

came [keɪm] *pt of* come

camel ['kæməl] *n* cammello

camera ['kæmərə] *n* macchina fotografica; (*CINEMA, TV*) cinepresa; **in ~** a porte chiuse; ~**man** (*irreg*) *n* cameraman *m inv*

camouflage ['kæməflɑːʒ] (*MIL, ZOOL*) mimetizzazione *f* ♦ *vt* mimetizzare

camp [kæmp] *n* campeggio; (*MIL*) campo ♦ *vi* accamparsi ♦ *adj* effeminato(a)

campaign [kæm'peɪn] *n* (*MIL, POL etc*) campagna ♦ *vi* (*also fig*) fare una campagna

camp bed (*BRIT*) *n* brandina

camper ['kæmpə*] *n* campeggiatore/trice; (*vehicle*) camper *m inv*

camping ['kæmpɪŋ] *n* campeggio; **to go ~** andare in campeggio

campsite ['kæmpsaɪt] *n* campeggio

campus ['kæmpəs] *n* campus *m inv*

can[1] [kæn] *n* (*of milk*) scatola; (*of oil*) bidone *m*; (*of water*) tanica; (*tin*) scatola ♦ *vt* mettere in scatola

KEYWORD

can[2] [kæn] (*negative* cannot, can't; *conditional and pt* could) *aux vb* 1 (*be able to*) potere; **I ~'t go any further** non posso andare oltre; **you ~ do it if you try** sei in grado di farlo — basta provarci; **I'll help you all I ~** ti aiuterò come potrò; **I ~'t see you** non ti vedo

2 (*know how to*) sapere, essere capace di; **I ~ swim** so nuotare; **~ you speak French?** parla francese?

3 (*may*) potere; **could I have a word with you?** posso parlarle un momento?

4 (*expressing disbelief, puzzlement etc*): **it ~'t be true!** non può essere vero!; **what**

CAN **he want?** cosa può mai volere?

5 (*expressing possibility, suggestion etc*): **he could be in the library** può darsi che sia in biblioteca; **she could have been delayed** può aver avuto un contrattempo

Canada ['kænədə] *n* Canada *m*

Canadian [kə'neɪdɪən] *adj, n* canadese *m/f*

canal [kə'næl] *n* canale *m*

canary [kə'nɛərɪ] *n* canarino

cancel ['kænsəl] *vt* annullare; (*train*) sopprimere; (*cross out*) cancellare; ~**lation** [-'leɪʃən] *n* annullamento; soppressione *f*; cancellazione *f*; (*TOURISM*) prenotazione *f* annullata

cancer ['kænsə*] *n* cancro; **C~** (*sign*) Cancro

candid ['kændɪd] *adj* onesto(a)

candidate ['kændɪdeɪt] *n* candidato/a

candle ['kændl] *n* candela; (*in church*) cero; ~**light** *n*: **by ~light** a lume di candela; ~**stick** *n* bugia; (*bigger, ornate*) candeliere *m*

candour ['kændə*] (*US* candor) *n* sincerità

candy ['kændɪ] *n* zucchero candito; (*US*) caramella, caramelle *fpl*; ~-**floss** (*BRIT*) *n* zucchero filato

cane [keɪn] *n* canna; (*for furniture*) bambù *m*; (*stick*) verga ♦ *vt* (*BRIT: SCOL*) punire a colpi di verga

canister ['kænɪstə*] *n* scatola metallica

cannabis ['kænəbɪs] *n* canapa indiana

canned ['kænd] *adj* (*food*) in scatola

cannon ['kænən] (*pl ~ or* ~**s**) *n* (*gun*) cannone *m*

cannot ['kænɔt] = can not

canny ['kænɪ] *adj* furbo(a)

canoe [kə'nuː] *n* canoa; ~**ing** *n* canottaggio

canon ['kænən] *n* (*clergyman*) canonico; (*standard*) canone *m*

can opener [-'əupnə*] *n* apriscatole *m inv*

canopy ['kænəpɪ] *n* baldacchino

cant [kænt] *n* gergo ♦ *vt* inclinare ♦ *vi* inclinarsi

can't [kænt] = can not

canteen [kæn'tiːn] *n* mensa; (*BRIT: of cutlery*) portaposate *m inv*

canter ['kæntə*] *vi* andare al piccolo

galoppo

canvas ['kænvəs] *n* tela

canvass ['kænvəs] *vi* (POL): **to ~ for** raccogliere voti per ♦ *vt* fare un sondaggio di

cap [kæp] *n* (hat) berretto; (of pen) coperchio; (of bottle, toy gun) tappo; (contraceptive) diaframma *m* ♦ *vt* (outdo) superare; (limit) fissare un tetto (a)

capability [keɪpə'bɪlɪtɪ] *n* capacità *f inv*, abilità *f inv*

capable ['keɪpəbl] *adj* capace

capacity [kə'pæsɪtɪ] *n* capacità *f inv*; (of lift etc) capienza

cape [keɪp] *n* (garment) cappa; (GEO) capo

caper ['keɪpə*] *n* (CULIN) cappero; (prank) scherzetto

capital ['kæpɪtl] *n* (also: ~ **city**) capitale *f*; (money) capitale *m*; (also: ~ **letter**) (lettera) maiuscola; ~ **gains tax** *n* imposta sulla plusvalenza; ~**ism** *n* capitalismo; ~**ist** *adj*, *n* capitalista (*m/f*); ~**ize**: **to ~ize on** *vt fus* trarre vantaggio da; ~ **punishment** *n* pena capitale

Capitol ['kæpɪtl] *n*: **the ~** il Campidoglio

```
Capitol
```

ⓘ Il **Capitol** è l'edificio dove si svolgono le riunioni del Congresso degli Stati Uniti. È situato sull'omonimo colle, Capitol Hill, a Washington D.C.

Capricorn ['kæprɪkɔːn] *n* Capricorno

capsize [kæp'saɪz] *vt* capovolgere ♦ *vi* capovolgersi

capsule ['kæpsjuːl] *n* capsula

captain ['kæptɪn] *n* capitano

caption ['kæpʃən] *n* leggenda

captivate ['kæptɪveɪt] *vt* avvincere

captive ['kæptɪv] *adj*, *n* prigioniero(a)

captivity [kæp'tɪvɪtɪ] *n* cattività

capture ['kæptʃə*] *vt* catturare; (COMPUT) registrare ♦ *n* cattura; (data ~) registrazione *f* or rilevazione *f* di dati

car [kɑː*] *n* (AUT) macchina, automobile *f*; (RAIL) vagone *m*

carafe [kə'ræf] *n* caraffa

caramel ['kærəməl] *n* caramello

caravan ['kærəvæn] *n* (BRIT) roulotte *f inv*; (of camels) carovana; ~**ning** *n* vacanze *fpl* in roulotte; ~ **site** (BRIT) *n* campeggio per roulotte

carbohydrates [kɑːbəu'haɪdreɪts] *npl* (foods) carboidrati *mpl*

carbon ['kɑːbən] *n* carbonio; ~ **paper** *n* carta carbone

car boot sale *n* mercatino dell'usato dove la merce viene esposta nei bagagliai delle macchine

carburettor [kɑːbju'retə*] (US **carburetor**) *n* carburatore *m*

card [kɑːd] *n* carta; (visiting ~ etc) biglietto; (Christmas ~ etc) cartolina; ~**board** *n* cartone *m*; ~ **game** *n* gioco di carte

cardiac ['kɑːdɪæk] *adj* cardiaco(a)

cardigan ['kɑːdɪgən] *n* cardigan *m inv*

cardinal ['kɑːdɪnl] *adj* cardinale ♦ *n* cardinale *m*

card index *n* schedario

cardphone ['kɑːdfəun] *n* telefono a scheda

care [kɛə*] *n* cura, attenzione *f*; (worry) preoccupazione *f* ♦ *vi*: **to ~ about** curarsi di; (thing, idea) interessarsi di; ~ **of** presso; **in sb's ~** alle cure di qn; **to take ~ (to do)** fare attenzione (a fare); **to take ~ of** curarsi di; (bill, problem) occuparsi di; **I don't ~** non me ne importa; **I couldn't ~ less** non m'interessa affatto; ~ **for** *vt fus* aver cura di; (like) volere bene a

career [kə'rɪə*] *n* carriera ♦ *vi* (also: ~ **along**) andare di (gran) carriera

carefree ['kɛəfriː] *adj* sgombro(a) di preoccupazioni

careful ['kɛəful] *adj* attento(a); (cautious) cauto(a); **(be) ~!** attenzione!; ~**ly** *adv* con cura; cautamente

careless ['kɛəlɪs] *adj* negligente; (heedless) spensierato(a)

carer ['kɛərə*] *n* assistente *m/f* (di persone malata o handicappata)

caress [kə'res] *n* carezza ♦ *vt* accarezzare

caretaker ['kɛəteɪkə*] *n* custode *m*

car-ferry *n* traghetto

cargo ['kɑːgəu] (*pl* ~**es**) *n* carico

car hire n autonoleggio

Caribbean [kærɪ'biːən] adj: **the ~ (Sea)** il Mar dei Caraibi

caring ['keərɪŋ] adj (person) premuroso(a); (society, organization) umanitario(a)

carnage ['kɑːnɪdʒ] n carneficina

carnation [kɑː'neɪʃən] n garofano

carnival ['kɑːnɪvəl] n (public celebration) carnevale m; (US: funfair) luna park m inv

carol ['kærəl] n: **(Christmas) ~** canto di Natale

carp [kɑːp] n (fish) carpa

car park (BRIT) n parcheggio

carpenter ['kɑːpɪntə*] n carpentiere m

carpentry ['kɑːpɪntrɪ] n carpenteria

carpet ['kɑːpɪt] n tappeto ♦ vt coprire con tappeto

car phone n telefonino per auto, cellulare m per auto

car rental (US) n autonoleggio

carriage ['kærɪdʒ] n (BRIT) vettura; (of goods) trasporto; **~way** (BRIT) n (part of road) carreggiata

carrier ['kærɪə*] n (of disease) portatore/ trice; (COMM) impresa di trasporti; **~ bag** (BRIT) n sacchetto

carrot ['kærət] n carota

carry ['kærɪ] vt (subj: person) portare; (: vehicle) trasportare; (involve: responsibilities etc) comportare; (MED) essere portatore/trice di ♦ vi (sound) farsi sentire; **to be** or **get carried away** (fig) entusiasmarsi; **~ on** vi: **to ~ on with sth/ doing** continuare qc/a fare ♦ vt mandare avanti; **~ out** vt (orders) eseguire; (investigation) svolgere; **~cot** (BRIT) n culla portabile; **~-on** (inf) n (fuss) casino, confusione f

cart [kɑːt] n carro ♦ vt (inf) trascinare

carton ['kɑːtən] n (box) scatola di cartone; (of yogurt) cartone m; (of cigarettes) stecca

cartoon [kɑː'tuːn] n (PRESS) disegno umoristico; (comic strip) fumetto; (CINEMA) disegno animato

cartridge ['kɑːtrɪdʒ] n (for gun, pen) cartuccia; (music tape) cassetta

carve [kɑːv] vt (meat) trinciare; (wood, stone) intagliare; **~ up** vt (fig: country) suddividere; **carving** n (in wood etc) scultura; **carving knife** n trinciante m

car wash n lavaggio auto

cascade [kæs'keɪd] n cascata

case [keɪs] n caso; (LAW) causa, processo; (box) scatola; (BRIT: also: **suit~**) valigia; **in ~ of** in caso di; **in ~ he** caso mai lui; **in any ~** in ogni caso; **just in ~** in caso di bisogno

cash [kæʃ] n denaro; (coins, notes) denaro liquido ♦ vt incassare; **to pay (in) ~** pagare in contanti; **~ on delivery** pagamento alla consegna; **~-book** n giornale m di cassa; **~ card** (BRIT) n tesserino di prelievo; **~ desk** (BRIT) n cassa; **~ dispenser** (BRIT) n sportello automatico

cashew [kæ'ʃuː] n (also: **~ nut**) anacardio

cashier [kæ'ʃɪə*] n cassiere/a

cashmere ['kæʃmɪə*] n cachemire m

cash register n registratore m di cassa

casing ['keɪsɪŋ] n rivestimento

casino [kə'siːnəu] n casinò m inv

cask [kɑːsk] n botte f

casket ['kɑːskɪt] n cofanetto; (US: coffin) bara

casserole ['kæsərəul] n casseruola; (food): **chicken ~** pollo in casseruola

cassette [kæ'set] n cassetta; **~ player** n riproduttore m a cassette; **~ recorder** n registratore m a cassette

cast [kɑːst] (pt, pp **cast**) vt (throw) gettare; (metal) gettare, fondere; (THEATRE): **to ~ sb as Hamlet** scegliere qn per la parte di Amleto ♦ n (THEATRE) cast m inv; (also: **plaster ~**) ingessatura; **to ~ one's vote** votare, dare il voto; **~ off** vi (NAUT) salpare; (KNITTING) calare; **~ on** vi (KNITTING) avviare le maglie

castaway ['kɑːstəwəɪ] n naufrago/a

caster sugar ['kɑːstə*-] (BRIT) n zucchero semolato

casting vote ['kɑːstɪŋ-] (BRIT) n voto decisivo

cast iron n ghisa

castle ['kɑːsl] n castello

castor oil ['kɑːstə*-] n olio di ricino

casual ['kæʒjul] adj (by chance) casuale,

fortuito(a); (*irregular: work etc*)
avventizio(a); (*unconcerned*) noncurante,
indifferente; ~ **wear** casual *m*; ~**ly** *adv* (*in
a relaxed way*) con noncuranza; (*dress*)
casual

casualty ['kæʒjʊltɪ] *n* ferito/a; (*dead*)
morto/a, vittima; (*MED: department*) pronto
soccorso

cat [kæt] *n* gatto

catalogue ['kætəlɔg] (*US* **catalog**) *n*
catalogo ♦ *vt* catalogare

catalyst ['kætəlɪst] *n* catalizzatore *m*

catalytic convertor [kætəlɪtɪk-] *n*
marmitta catalitica, catalizzatore *m*

catapult ['kætəpʌlt] *n* catapulta; fionda

cataract ['kætərækt] *n* (*also MED*) cateratta

catarrh [kə'tɑ:ʳ] *n* catarro

catastrophe [kə'tæstrəfɪ] *n* catastrofe *f*

catch [kætʃ] (*pt, pp* **caught**) *vt* prendere;
(*ball*) afferrare; (*surprise: person*)
sorprendere; (*attention*) attirare; (*comment,
whisper*) cogliere; (*person: also:* ~ **up**)
raggiungere ♦ *vi* (*fire*) prendere ♦ *n* (*fish
etc caught*) retata; (*of ball*) presa; (*trick*)
inganno; (*TECH*) gancio; (*game*) catch *m
inv*; **to ~ fire** prendere fuoco; **to ~ sight of**
scorgere; ~ **on** *vi* capire; (*become popular*)
affermarsi, far presa; ~ **up** *vi* mettersi in
pari ♦ *vt* (*also:* ~ **up with**) raggiungere

catching ['kætʃɪŋ] *adj* (*MED*) contagioso(a)

catchment area ['kætʃmənt-] (*BRIT*) *n*
(*SCOL*) circoscrizione *f* scolare

catch phrase *n* slogan *m inv*; frase *f* fatta

catchy ['kætʃɪ] *adj* orecchiabile

category ['kætɪgərɪ] *n* categoria

cater ['keɪtəʳ] *vi*: ~ **for** (*BRIT: needs*)
provvedere a; (: *readers, consumers*)
incontrare i gusti di; (*COMM: provide food*)
provvedere alla ristorazione di; ~**er** *n*
fornitore *m*; ~**ing** *n* approvvigionamento

caterpillar ['kætəpɪləʳ] *n* bruco

cathedral [kə'θi:drəl] *n* cattedrale *f*, duomo

catholic ['kæθəlɪk] *adj* universale; aperto(a);
eclettico(a); **C~** *adj*, *n* (*REL*) cattolico(a)

CAT scan *n* (= *computerized axial
tomography*) TAC *f inv*

Catseye ® [kæts'aɪ] (*BRIT*) *n* (*AUT*) cata-

rifrangente *m*

cattle ['kætl] *npl* bestiame *m*, bestie *fpl*

catty ['kætɪ] *adj* maligno(a), dispettoso(a)

caucus ['kɔ:kəs] *n* (*POL: group*) comitato di
dirigenti; (: *US*) (riunione *f* del) comitato
elettorale

caught [kɔ:t] *pt, pp of* **catch**

cauliflower ['kɔlɪflauəʳ] *n* cavolfiore *m*

cause [kɔ:z] *n* causa ♦ *vt* causare

caution ['kɔ:ʃən] *n* prudenza; (*warning*)
avvertimento ♦ *vt* avvertire; ammonire

cautious ['kɔ:ʃəs] *adj* cauto(a), prudente

cavalry ['kævəlrɪ] *n* cavalleria

cave [keɪv] *n* caverna, grotta; ~ **in** *vi* (*roof
etc*) crollare; ~**man** (*irreg*) *n* uomo delle
caverne

caviar(e) ['kævɪɑ:ʳ] *n* caviale *m*

CB *n abbr* (= *Citizens' Band (Radio)*): ~
radio (set) baracchino

CBI *n abbr* (= *Confederation of British
Industries*) ≈ Confindustria

cc *abbr* = **cubic centimetres; carbon copy**

CCTV *n abbr* (= *closed-circuit television*)
televisione *f* a circuito chiuso

CD *abbr* (*disc*) CD *m inv*

CDI *n abbr* (= *compact disk interactive*) CD-I
m inv, compact disc *m inv* interattivo

CD player *n* lettore *m* CD

CD-ROM [-rɔm] *n abbr* CD-ROM *m inv*

cease [si:s] *vt, vi* cessare; ~**fire** *n* cessate il
fuoco *m inv*; ~**less** *adj* incessante,
continuo(a)

cedar ['si:dəʳ] *n* cedro

ceiling ['si:lɪŋ] *n* soffitto; (*on wages etc*)
tetto

celebrate ['sɛlɪbreɪt] *vt, vi* celebrare; ~**d** *adj*
celebre; **celebration** [-'breɪʃən] *n*
celebrazione *f*

celery ['sɛlərɪ] *n* sedano

cell [sɛl] *n* cella; (*of revolutionaries, BIOL*)
cellula; (*ELEC*) elemento (di batteria)

cellar ['sɛləʳ] *n* sottosuolo; cantina

'cello ['tʃɛləu] *n* violoncello

cellphone [sɛl,fəun] *n* cellulare *m*

Celt [kɛlt, sɛlt] *n* celta *m/f*

cement [sə'mɛnt] *n* cemento; ~ **mixer** *n*
betoniera

cemetery ['sɛmɪtrɪ] *n* cimitero

censor ['sɛnsə*] *n* censore *m* ♦ *vt* censurare; **~ship** *n* censura

censure ['sɛnʃə*] *vt* riprovare, censurare

census ['sɛnsəs] *n* censimento

cent [sɛnt] *n* (*US: coin*) centesimo (= *1:100 di un dollaro*); (*unit of euro*) centesimo; *see also* **per**

centenary [sɛn'tiːnərɪ] *n* centenario

center ['sɛntə*] (*US*) *n, vt* = **centre**

centigrade ['sɛntɪgreɪd] *adj* centigrado(a)

centimetre ['sɛntɪmiːtə*] (*US* **centimeter**) *n* centimetro

centipede ['sɛntɪpiːd] *n* centopiedi *m inv*

central ['sɛntrəl] *adj* centrale; **C~ America** *n* America centrale; **~ heating** *n* riscaldamento centrale; **~ize** *vt* accentrare

centre ['sɛntə*] (*US* **center**) *n* centro ♦ *vt* centrare; **~-forward** *n* (*SPORT*) centroavanti *m inv*; **~-half** *n* (*SPORT*) centromediano

century ['sɛntjʊrɪ] *n* secolo; **20th ~** ventesimo secolo

ceramic [sɪ'ræmɪk] *adj* ceramico(a); **~s** *npl* ceramica

cereal ['siːrɪəl] *n* cereale *m*

ceremony ['sɛrɪmənɪ] *n* cerimonia; **to stand on ~** fare complimenti

certain ['sɜːtən] *adj* certo(a); **to make ~ of** assicurarsi di; **for ~** per certo, di sicuro; **~ly** *adv* certamente, certo; **~ty** *n* certezza

certificate [sə'tɪfɪkɪt] *n* certificato; diploma *m*

certified ['sɜːtɪfaɪd]: **~ mail** (*US*) *n* posta raccomandata con ricevuta di ritorno; **~ public accountant** (*US*) *n* ≈ commercialista *m/f*

certify ['sɜːtɪfaɪ] *vt* certificare; (*award diploma to*) conferire un diploma a; (*declare insane*) dichiarare pazzo(a)

cervical ['sɜːvɪkl] *adj*: **~ cancer** cancro della cervice; **~ smear** Pap-test *m inv*

cervix ['sɜːvɪks] *n* cervice *f*

cf. *abbr* (= *compare*) cfr

CFC *n* (= *chlorofluorocarbon*) CFC *m inv*

ch. *abbr* (= *chapter*) cap

chafe [tʃeɪf] *vt* fregare, irritare

chain [tʃeɪn] *n* catena ♦ *vt* (*also:* **~ up**) incatenare; **~ reaction** *n* reazione *f* a catena; **~-smoke** *vi* fumare una sigaretta dopo l'altra; **~ store** *n* negozio a catena

chair [tʃɛə*] *n* sedia; (*armchair*) poltrona; (*of university*) cattedra; (*of meeting*) presidenza ♦ *vt* (*meeting*) presiedere; **~lift** *n* seggiovia; **~man** (*irreg*) *n* presidente *m*

chalet ['ʃæleɪ] *n* chalet *m inv*

chalk [tʃɔːk] *n* gesso

challenge ['tʃælɪndʒ] *n* sfida ♦ *vt* sfidare; (*statement, right*) mettere in dubbio; **to ~ sb to do** sfidare qn a fare; **challenging** *adj* (*task*) impegnativo(a); (*look*) di sfida

chamber ['tʃeɪmbə*] *n* camera; **~ of commerce** *n* camera di commercio; **~maid** *n* cameriera; **~ music** *n* musica da camera

chamois ['ʃæmwɑː] *n* camoscio; (*also:* **~ leather**) panno in pelle di camoscio

champagne [ʃæm'peɪn] *n* champagne *m inv*

champion ['tʃæmpɪən] *n* campione/essa; **~ship** *n* campionato

chance [tʃɑːns] *n* caso; (*opportunity*) occasione *f*; (*likelihood*) possibilità *f inv* ♦ *vt*: **to~it** rischiare, provarci ♦ *adj* fortuito(a); **to take a ~** rischiare; **by ~** per caso

chancellor ['tʃɑːnsələ*] *n* cancelliere *m*; **C~ of the Exchequer** (*BRIT*) *n* Cancelliere dello Scacchiere

chandelier [ʃændə'lɪə*] *n* lampadario

change [tʃeɪndʒ] *vt* cambiare; (*transform*): **to ~ sb into** trasformare qn in ♦ *vi* cambiare; (*~ one's clothes*) cambiarsi; (*be transformed*): **to ~ into** trasformarsi in ♦ *n* cambiamento; (*of clothes*) cambio; (*money*) resto; **to ~ one's mind** cambiare idea; **for a ~** tanto per cambiare; **~able** *adj* (*weather*) variabile; **~ machine** *n* distributore automatico di monete; **~over** *n* cambiamento, passaggio

changing ['tʃeɪndʒɪŋ] *adj* che cambia; (*colours*) cangiante; **~ room** *n* (*BRIT: in shop*) camerino; (*: SPORT*) spogliatoio

channel ['tʃænl] *n* canale *m*; (*of river, sea*) alveo ♦ *vt* canalizzare; **the (English) C~**

n la Manica; **~-hopping** *n* (*TV*) zapping *m inv*; **the C~ Islands** *npl* le Isole Normanne; **the C~ Tunnel** *n* il tunnel sotto la Manica

chant [tʃɑ:nt] *n* canto; salmodia ♦ *vt* cantare; (*teeth*) battere ♦ *n* ciarle *fpl*; salmodiare

chaos ['keɪɒs] *n* caos *m*

chap [tʃæp] (*BRIT: inf*) *n* (*man*) tipo

chapel ['tʃæpəl] *n* cappella

chaperone ['ʃæpərəun] *n* accompagnatrice *f* ♦ *vt* accompagnare

chaplain ['tʃæplɪn] *n* cappellano

chapped [tʃæpt] *adj* (*skin, lips*) screpolato(a)

chapter ['tʃæptə*] *n* capitolo

char [tʃɑ:*] *vt* (*burn*) carbonizzare

character ['kærɪktə*] *n* carattere *m*; (*in novel, film*) personaggio; **~istic** [-'rɪstɪk] *adj* caratteristico(a) ♦ *n* caratteristica

charcoal ['tʃɑ:kəul] *n* carbone *m* di legna

charge [tʃɑ:dʒ] *n* accusa; (*cost*) prezzo; (*responsibility*) responsabilità ♦ *vt* (*gun, battery, MIL: enemy*) caricare; (*customer*) fare pagare a; (*sum*) fare pagare; (*LAW*): **to ~ sb (with)** accusare qn (di) ♦ *vi* (*gen with: up, along etc*) lanciarsi; **~s** *npl* (*bank ~s etc*) tariffe *fpl*; **to reverse the ~s** (*TEL*) fare una telefonata a carico del destinatario; **to take ~ of** incaricarsi di; **to be in ~ of** essere responsabile per; **how much do you ~?** quanto chiedete?; **to ~ an expense (up) to sb** addebitare una spesa a qn; **~ card** *n* carta *f* clienti *inv*

charitable ['tʃærɪtəbl] *adj* caritatevole

charity ['tʃærɪtɪ] *n* carità; (*organization*) opera pia

charm [tʃɑ:m] *n* fascino; (*on bracelet*) ciondolo ♦ *vt* affascinare, incantare; **~ing** *adj* affascinante

chart [tʃɑ:t] *n* tabella; grafico; (*map*) carta nautica ♦ *vt* fare una carta nautica di; **~s** *npl* (*MUS*) hit parade *f*

charter ['tʃɑ:tə*] *vt* (*plane*) noleggiare ♦ *n* (*document*) carta; **~ed accountant** (*BRIT*) *n* ragioniere/a professionista; **~ flight** *n* volo *m* charter *inv*

charwoman ['tʃɑ:wumən] *n* = **charlady**

chase [tʃeɪs] *vt* inseguire; (*also:* **~ away**) cacciare ♦ *n* caccia

chasm ['kæzəm] *n* abisso

chassis ['ʃæsɪ] *n* telaio

chat [tʃæt] *vi* (*also:* **have a ~**) chiacchierare ♦ *n* chiacchierata; **~ show** (*BRIT*) *n* talk show *m inv*

chatter ['tʃætə*] *vi* (*person*) ciarlare; (*bird*) cinguettare; (*teeth*) battere ♦ *n* ciarle *fpl*; cinguettio; **~box** (*inf*) *n* chiacchierone/a

chatty ['tʃætɪ] *adj* (*style*) familiare; (*person*) chiacchierino(a)

chauffeur ['ʃəufə*] *n* autista *m*

chauvinist ['ʃəuvɪnɪst] *n* (*male ~*) maschilista *m*; (*nationalist*) sciovinista *m/f*

cheap [tʃi:p] *adj* a buon mercato; (*joke*) grossolano(a); (*poor quality*) di cattiva qualità ♦ *adv* a buon mercato; **~ day return** *n* biglietto ridotto di andata e ritorno valido in giornata; **~er** *adj* meno caro(a); **~ly** *adv* a buon prezzo, a buon mercato

cheat [tʃi:t] *vi* imbrogliare; (*at school*) copiare ♦ *vt* ingannare ♦ *n* imbroglione *m*; **to ~ sb out of sth** defraudare qn di qc

check [tʃɛk] *vt* verificare; (*passport, ticket*) controllare; (*halt*) fermare; (*restrain*) contenere ♦ *n* verifica; controllo; (*curb*) freno; (*US: bill*) conto; (*pattern: gen pl*) quadretti *mpl*; (*US*) = **cheque** ♦ *adj* (*pattern, cloth*) a quadretti; **~ in** *vi* (*in hotel*) registrare; (*at airport*) presentarsi all'accettazione ♦ *vt* (*luggage*) depositare; **~ out** *vi* (*in hotel*) saldare il conto; **~ up** *vi*: **to ~ up (on sth)** investigare (qc); **to ~ up on sb** informarsi sul conto di qn; **~ered** (*US*) *adj* = **chequered**; **~ers** (*US*) *n* dama; **~-in (desk)** *n* check-in *m inv*, accettazione *f* (bagagli *inv*); **~ing account** (*US*) *n* conto corrente; **~mate** *n* scaccomatto; **~out** *n* (*in supermarket*) cassa; **~point** *n* posto di blocco; **~room** (*US*) *n* deposito *m* bagagli *inv*; **~up** *n* (*MED*) controllo medico

cheek [tʃi:k] *n* guancia; (*impudence*) faccia tosta; **~bone** *n* zigomo; **~y** *adj* sfacciato(a)

cheep [tʃiːp] vi pigolare
cheer [tʃɪə*] vt applaudire; (*gladden*) rallegrare ♦ vi applaudire ♦ n grido (di incoraggiamento); **~s** npl (*of approval, encouragement*) applausi mpl; evviva mpl; **~s!** salute!; **~ up** vi rallegrarsi, farsi animo ♦ vt rallegrare; **~ful** adj allegro(a)
cheerio ['tʃɪərɪ'əu] (BRIT) excl ciao!
cheese [tʃiːz] n formaggio; **~board** n piatto del (or per il) formaggio
cheetah ['tʃiːtə] n ghepardo
chef [ʃef] n capocuoco
chemical ['kemɪkəl] adj chimico(a) ♦ n prodotto chimico
chemist ['kemɪst] n (BRIT: *pharmacist*) farmacista m/f; (*scientist*) chimico/a; **~ry** n chimica; **~'s (shop)** (BRIT) n farmacia
cheque [tʃek] (BRIT) n assegno; **~book** n libretto degli assegni; **~ card** n carta f assegni inv
chequered ['tʃekəd] (US **checkered**) adj (*fig*) movimentato(a)
cherish ['tʃerɪʃ] vt aver caro
cherry ['tʃerɪ] n ciliegia; (*also:* **~tree**) ciliegio
chess [tʃes] n scacchi mpl; **~board** n scacchiera
chest [tʃest] n petto; (*box*) cassa; **~ of drawers** n cassettone m
chestnut ['tʃesnʌt] n castagna; (*also:* **~ tree**) castagno
chew [tʃuː] vt masticare; **~ing gum** n chewing gum m
chic [ʃiːk] adj elegante
chick [tʃɪk] n pulcino; (*inf*) pollastrella
chicken ['tʃɪkɪn] n pollo; (*inf: coward*) coniglio; **~ out** (*inf*) vi avere fifa; **~pox** n varicella
chicory ['tʃɪkərɪ] n cicoria
chief [tʃiːf] n capo ♦ adj principale; **~ executive** n direttore m generale; **~ly** adv per lo più, soprattutto
chilblain ['tʃɪlbleɪn] n gelone m
child [tʃaɪld] (pl **~ren**) n bambino/a; **~birth** n parto; **~hood** n infanzia; **~ish** adj puerile; **~like** adj fanciullesco(a); **~ minder** (BRIT) n bambinaia
children ['tʃɪldrən] npl of **child**

child seat n seggiolino per bambini (*in auto*)
Chile ['tʃɪlɪ] n Cile m
chill [tʃɪl] n freddo; (MED) infreddatura ♦ vt raffreddare
chilli ['tʃɪlɪ] n peperoncino
chilly ['tʃɪlɪ] adj freddo(a), fresco(a); **to feel ~** sentirsi infreddolito(a)
chime [tʃaɪm] n carillon m inv ♦ vi suonare, scampanare
chimney ['tʃɪmnɪ] n camino; **~ sweep** n spazzacamino
chimpanzee [tʃɪmpæn'ziː] n scimpanzé m inv
chin [tʃɪn] n mento
China ['tʃaɪnə] n Cina
china ['tʃaɪnə] n porcellana
Chinese [tʃaɪ'niːz] adj cinese ♦ n inv cinese m/f; (LING) cinese m
chink [tʃɪŋk] n (*opening*) fessura; (*noise*) tintinnio
chip [tʃɪp] n (*gen pl:* CULIN) patatina fritta; (: US: *also:* **potato ~**) patatina; (*of wood, glass, stone*) scheggia; (*also:* **micro~**) chip m inv ♦ vt (*cup, plate*) scheggiare

---
chip shop

i I **chip shops**, anche chiamati "fish and chip shops", sono friggitorie che vendono principalmente filetti di pesce impanati e patatine fritte.

---

chiropodist [kɪ'rɔpədɪst] (BRIT) n pedicure m/f inv
chirp [tʃəːp] vi cinguettare; fare cri cri
chisel ['tʃɪzl] n cesello
chit [tʃɪt] n biglietto
chitchat ['tʃɪttʃæt] n chiacchiere fpl
chivalry ['ʃɪvəlrɪ] n cavalleria, cortesia
chives [tʃaɪvz] npl erba cipollina
chock-a-block ['tʃɔk-] adj pieno(a) zeppo(a)
chock-full ['tʃɔk-] adj = **chock-a-block**
chocolate ['tʃɔklɪt] n (*substance*) cioccolato, cioccolata; (*drink*) cioccolata; (*a sweet*) cioccolatino
choice [tʃɔɪs] n scelta ♦ adj scelto(a)

choir ['kwaɪə*] *n* coro; **~boy** *n* corista *m* fanciullo

choke [tʃəuk] *vi* soffocare ♦ *vt* soffocare; (*block*): **to be ~d with** essere intasato(a) di ♦ *n* (*AUT*) valvola dell'aria

cholera ['kɔlərə] *n* colera *m*

cholesterol [kə'lestərɔl] *n* colesterolo

choose [tʃuːz] (*pt* **chose**, *pp* **chosen**) *vt* scegliere; **to ~ to do** decidere di fare; preferire fare

choosy ['tʃuːzɪ] *adj* schizzinoso(a)

chop [tʃɔp] *vt* (*wood*) spaccare; (*CULIN: also*: **~ up**) tritare ♦ *n* (*CULIN*) costoletta; **~s** *npl* (*jaws*) mascelle *fpl*

chopper ['tʃɔpə*] *n* (*helicopter*) elicottero

choppy ['tʃɔpɪ] *adj* (*sea*) mosso(a)

chopsticks ['tʃɔpstɪks] *npl* bastoncini *mpl* cinesi

choral ['kɔːrəl] *adj* corale

chord [kɔːd] *n* (*MUS*) accordo

chore [tʃɔː*] *n* faccenda; **household ~s** faccende *fpl* domestiche

chortle ['tʃɔːtl] *vi* ridacchiare

chorus ['kɔːrəs] *n* coro; (*repeated part of song, also fig*) ritornello

chose [tʃəuz] *pt of* **choose**

chosen ['tʃəuzn] *pp of* **choose**

chowder ['tʃaudə*] *n* (*esp US*) zuppa di pesce

Christ [kraɪst] *n* Cristo

christen ['krɪsn] *vt* battezzare

Christian ['krɪstɪən] *adj, n* cristiano(a); **~ity** [-'ænɪtɪ] *n* cristianesimo; **~ name** *n* nome *m* (di battesimo)

Christmas ['krɪsməs] *n* Natale *m*; **Merry ~!** Buon Natale!; **~ card** *n* cartolina di Natale; **~ Day** *n* il giorno di Natale; **~ Eve** *n* la vigilia di Natale; **~ tree** *n* albero di Natale

chrome [krəum] *n* cromo

chromium ['krəumɪəm] *n* cromo

chronic ['krɔnɪk] *adj* cronico(a)

chronological [krɔnə'lɔdʒɪkəl] *adj* cronologico(a)

chrysanthemum [krɪ'sænθəməm] *n* crisantemo

chubby ['tʃʌbɪ] *adj* paffuto(a)

chuck [tʃʌk] (*inf*) *vt* buttare, gettare; (*BRIT: also*: **~ up**) piantare; **~ out** *vt* buttar fuori

chuckle ['tʃʌkl] *vi* ridere sommessamente

chug [tʃʌg] *vi* fare ciuf ciuf

chum [tʃʌm] *n* compagno/a

chunk [tʃʌŋk] *n* pezzo

church [tʃəːtʃ] *n* chiesa; **~yard** *n* sagrato

churn [tʃəːn] *n* (*for butter*) zangola; (*for milk*) bidone *m*; **~ out** *vt* sfornare

chute [ʃuːt] *n* (*also*: **rubbish ~**) canale *m* di scarico; (*BRIT: children's slide*) scivolo

chutney ['tʃʌtnɪ] *n* salsa piccante (*di frutta, zucchero e spezie*)

CIA (*US*) *n abbr* (= *Central Intelligence Agency*) CIA *f*

CID (*BRIT*) *n abbr* (= *Criminal Investigation Department*) ≈ polizia giudiziaria

cider ['saɪdə*] *n* sidro

cigar [sɪ'gaː*] *n* sigaro

cigarette [sɪgə'ret] *n* sigaretta; **~ case** *n* portasigarette *m inv*; **~ end** *n* mozzicone *m*

Cinderella [sɪndə'relə] *n* Cenerentola

cinders ['sɪndəz] *npl* ceneri *fpl*

cine camera ['sɪnɪ-] (*BRIT*) *n* cinepresa

cine film ['sɪnɪ-] (*BRIT*) *n* pellicola

cinema ['sɪnəmə] *n* cinema *m inv*

cinnamon ['sɪnəmən] *n* cannella

cipher ['saɪfə*] *n* cifra

circle ['səːkl] *n* cerchio; (*of friends etc*) circolo; (*in cinema*) galleria ♦ *vi* girare in circolo ♦ *vt* (*surround*) circondare; (*move round*) girare intorno a

circuit ['səːkɪt] *n* circuito; **~ous** [səː'kjuɪtəs] *adj* indiretto(a)

circular ['səːkjulə*] *adj* circolare ♦ *n* circolare *f*

circulate ['səːkjuleɪt] *vi* circolare ♦ *vt* far circolare; **circulation** [-'leɪʃən] *n* circolazione *f*; (*of newspaper*) tiratura

circumstances ['səːkəmstənsɪz] *npl* circostanze *fpl*; (*financial condition*) condizioni *fpl* finanziarie

circus ['səːkəs] *n* circo

CIS *n abbr* (= *Commonwealth of Independent States*) CSI *f*

cistern ['sɪstən] *n* cisterna; (*in toilet*)

serbatoio d'acqua

citizen ['sɪtɪzn] n (of country) cittadino/a; (of town) abitante m/f; ~**ship** n cittadinanza

citrus fruit ['sɪtrəs-] n agrume m

city ['sɪtɪ] n città f inv; **the C~** la Città di Londra (centro commerciale)

civic ['sɪvɪk] adj civico(a); ~ **centre** (BRIT) n centro civico

civil ['sɪvɪl] adj civile; ~ **engineer** n ingegnere m civile; ~**ian** [sɪ'vɪlɪən] adj, n borghese m/f

civilization [sɪvɪlaɪ'zeɪʃən] n civiltà f inv

civilized ['sɪvɪlaɪzd] adj civilizzato(a); (fig) cortese

civil: ~ **law** n codice m civile; (study) diritto civile; ~ **servant** n impiegato/a statale; **C~ Service** n amministrazione f statale; ~ **war** n guerra civile

clad [klæd] adj: ~ **(in)** vestito(a) (di)

claim [kleɪm] vt (assert): **to ~ (that)/to be** sostenere (che)/di essere, (credit, rights etc) rivendicare; (damages) richiedere ♦ vi (for insurance) fare una domanda d'indennizzo ♦ n pretesa; rivendicazione f; richiesta; ~**ant** n (ADMIN, LAW) richiedente m/f

clairvoyant [kleə'vɔɪənt] n chiaroveggente m/f

clam [klæm] n vongola

clamber ['klæmbə*] vi arrampicarsi

clammy ['klæmɪ] adj (weather) caldo(a) umido(a); (hands) viscido(a)

clamour ['klæmə*] (US **clamor**) vi: **to ~ for** chiedere a gran voce

clamp [klæmp] n pinza, morsa ♦ vt stringere con una morsa; (AUT: wheel) applicare i ceppi bloccaruote a; ~ **down on** vt fus dare un giro di vite a

clan [klæn] n clan m inv

clang [klæŋ] vi emettere un suono metallico

clap [klæp] vi applaudire; ~**ping** n applausi mpl

claret ['klærət] n vino di Bordeaux

clarify ['klærɪfaɪ] vt chiarificare, chiarire

clarinet [klærɪ'net] n clarinetto

clarity ['klærɪtɪ] n clarità

clash [klæʃ] n frastuono; (fig) scontro ♦ vi scontrarsi; cozzare

clasp [klɑːsp] n (hold) stretta; (of necklace, bag) fermaglio, fibbia ♦ vt stringere

class [klɑːs] n classe f ♦ vt classificare

classic ['klæsɪk] adj classico(a) ♦ n classico; ~**al** adj classico(a)

classified ['klæsɪfaɪd] adj (information) segreto(a), riservato(a); ~ **advertise-ment** n annuncio economico

classmate ['klɑːsmeɪt] n compagno/a di classe

classroom ['klɑːsrum] n aula

clatter ['klætə*] n tintinnio; scalpitio ♦ vi tintinnare; scalpitare

clause [klɔːz] n clausola; (LING) proposizione f

claw [klɔː] n (of bird of prey) artiglio; (of lobster) pinza

clay [kleɪ] n argilla

clean [kliːn] adj pulito(a); (clear, smooth) liscio(a) ♦ vt pulire; ~ **out** vt ripulire; ~ **up** vt (also fig) ripulire; ~-**cut** adj (man) curato(a); ~**er** n (person) donna delle pulizie; ~**er's** n (also: **dry ~er's**) tintoria; ~**ing** n pulizia; ~**liness** ['klenlɪnɪs] n pulizia

cleanse [klenz] vt pulire; purificare; ~**r** n detergente m

clean-shaven [-'ʃeɪvn] adj sbarbato(a)

cleansing department ['klenzɪŋ-] (BRIT) n nettezza urbana

clear [klɪə*] adj chiaro(a); (glass etc) trasparente; (road, way) libero(a); (conscience) pulito(a) ♦ vt sgombrare; liberare; (table) sparecchiare; (cheque) fare la compensazione di; (LAW: suspect) discolpare; (obstacle) superare ♦ vi (weather) rasserenarsi; (fog) andarsene ♦ adv: ~ **of** distante da; ~ **up** vt mettere in ordine; (mystery) risolvere; ~**ance** n (removal) sgombro; (permission) autorizzazione f, permesso; ~-**cut** adj ben delineato(a), distinto(a); ~**ing** n radura; ~**ing bank** (BRIT) n banca (che fa uso della camera di compensazione); ~**ly** adv chiaramente; ~**way** (BRIT) n strada con divieto di sosta

cleaver ['kliːvə*] n mannaia

clef [klɛf] n (MUS) chiave f

cleft [klɛft] n (in rock) crepa, fenditura

clench [klɛntʃ] vt stringere

clergy ['klə:dʒi] n clero; ~man (irreg) n ecclesiastico

clerical ['klɛrɪkəl] adj d'impiegato; (REL) clericale

clerk [klɑːk, (US) kləːrk] n (BRIT) impiegato/a; (US) commesso/a

clever ['klɛvə*] adj (mentally) intelligente; (deft, skilful) abile; (device) ingegnoso(a)

click [klɪk] vi scattare ♦ vt (heels etc) battere; (tongue) far schioccare ♦ ~on vt (COMPUT) cliccare su

client ['klaɪənt] n cliente m/f

cliff [klɪf] n scogliera scoscesa, rupe f

climate ['klaɪmɪt] n clima m

climax ['klaɪmæks] n culmine m; (sexual) orgasmo

climb [klaɪm] vi salire; (clamber) arrampicarsi ♦ vt salire; (CLIMBING) scalare ♦ n salita; arrampicata; scalata; ~-down n marcia indietro; ~er n rocciatore/trice; alpinista m/f; ~ing n alpinismo

clinch [klɪntʃ] vt (deal) concludere

cling [klɪŋ] (pt, pp clung) vi: to ~ (to) aggrapparsi (a); (of clothes) aderire strettamente (a)

clinic ['klɪnɪk] n clinica; ~al adj clinico(a); (fig) distaccato(a); (: room) freddo(a)

clink [klɪŋk] vi tintinnare

clip [klɪp] n (for hair) forcina; (also: paper ~) graffetta; (TV, CINEMA) sequenza ♦ vt attaccare insieme; (hair, nails) tagliare; (hedge) tosare; ~pers npl (for gardening) cesoie fpl; (also: nail ~pers) forbicine fpl per le unghie; ~ping n (from newspaper) ritaglio

clique [kliːk] n cricca

cloak [kləuk] n mantello ♦ vt avvolgere; ~room n (for coats etc) guardaroba m inv; (BRIT: W.C.) gabinetti mpl

clock [klɔk] n orologio; ~ in or on vi timbrare il cartellino (all'entrata); ~ off or out vi timbrare il cartellino (all'uscita); ~wise adv in senso orario; ~work n movimento or meccanismo a orologeria

♦ adj a molla

clog [klɔg] n zoccolo ♦ vt intasare ♦ vi (also: ~ up) intasarsi, bloccarsi

cloister ['klɔɪstə*] n chiostro

clone [kləun] n clone m

close¹ [kləus] adj: ~ (to) vicino(a) (a); (watch, link, relative) stretto(a); (examination) attento(a); (contest) combattuto(a); (weather) afoso(a) ♦ adv vicino, dappresso; ~ to vicino a; ~ by, ~ at hand a portata di mano; a ~ friend un amico intimo; to have a ~ shave (fig) scamparla bella

close² [kləuz] vt chiudere ♦ vi (shop etc) chiudere; (lid, door etc) chiudersi; (end) finire ♦ n (end) fine f; ~ down vi cessare (definitivamente); ~d adj chiuso(a); ~d shop n azienda o fabbrica che impiega solo aderenti ai sindacati

close-knit [kləus'nɪt] adj (family, community) molto unito(a)

closely ['kləuslɪ] adv (examine, watch) da vicino; (related) strettamente

closet ['klɔzɪt] n (cupboard) armadio

close-up ['kləusʌp] n primo piano

closure ['kləuʒə*] n chiusura

clot [klɔt] n (also: blood ~) coagulo; (inf: idiot) scemo ♦ vi coagularsi

cloth [klɔθ] n (material) tessuto, stoffa; (rag) strofinaccio

clothe [kləuð] vt vestire; ~s npl abiti mpl, vestiti mpl; ~s brush n spazzola per abiti; ~s line n corda (per stendere il bucato); ~s peg (US ~s pin) n molletta

clothing ['kləuðɪŋ] n = clothes

cloud [klaud] n nuvola; ~burst n acquazzone m; ~y adj nuvoloso(a); (liquid) torbido(a)

clout [klaut] vt dare un colpo a

clove [kləuv] n chiodo di garofano; ~ of garlic spicchio d'aglio

clover ['kləuvə*] n trifoglio

clown [klaun] n pagliaccio ♦ vi (also: ~ about, ~ around) fare il pagliaccio

cloying ['klɔɪɪŋ] adj (taste, smell) nauseabondo(a)

club [klʌb] n (society) club m inv, circolo;

(weapon, GOLF) mazza ♦ vt bastonare ♦ vi:
to ~ together associarsi; ~s npl (CARDS) fiori
mpl; ~ class n (AVIAT) classe f club inv;
~house n sede f del circolo

cluck [klʌk] vi chiocciare

clue [kluː] n indizio; (in crosswords)
definizione f; I haven't a ~ non ho la
minima idea

clump [klʌmp] n (of flowers, trees) gruppo;
(of grass) ciuffo

clumsy ['klʌmzɪ] adj goffo(a)

clung [klʌŋ] pt, pp of cling

cluster ['klʌstə*] n gruppo ♦ vi
raggrupparsi

clutch [klʌtʃ] n (grip, grasp) presa, stretta;
(AUT) frizione f ♦ vt afferrare, stringere forte

clutter ['klʌtə*] vt ingombrare

CND n abbr = Campaign for Nuclear
Disarmament

Co. abbr = county; company

c/o abbr (= care of) presso

coach [kəutʃ] n (bus) pullman m inv;
(horse-drawn, of train) carrozza; (SPORT)
allenatore/trice; (tutor) chi dà ripetizioni
♦ vt allenare; dare ripetizioni a; ~ trip n
viaggio in pullman

coal [kəul] n carbone m; ~ face n fronte f;
~field n bacino carbonifero

coalition [kəuə'lɪʃən] n coalizione f

coalman ['kəulmən] (irreg) n negoziante m
di carbone

coalmine ['kəulmaɪn] n miniera di carbone

coarse [kɔːs] adj (salt, sand etc) grosso(a);
(cloth, person) rozzo(a)

coast [kəust] n costa ♦ vi (with cycle etc)
scendere a ruota libera; ~al adj costiero(a);
~guard n guardia costiera; ~line n linea
costiera

coat [kəut] n cappotto; (of animal) pelo; (of
paint) mano f ♦ vt coprire; ~ hanger n
attaccapanni m inv; ~ing n rivestimento;
~ of arms n stemma m

coax [kəuks] vt indurre (con moine)

cobbler ['kɔblə*] n calzolaio

cobbles ['kɔblz] npl ciottoli mpl

cobblestones ['kɔblstəunz] npl ciottoli
mpl

cobweb ['kɔbwɛb] n ragnatela

cocaine [kə'keɪn] n cocaina

cock [kɔk] n (rooster) gallo; (male bird)
maschio ♦ vt (gun) armare; ~erel n
galletto

cockle ['kɔkl] n cardio

cockney ['kɔknɪ] n cockney m/f inv
(abitante dei quartieri popolari dell'East End
di Londra)

cockpit ['kɔkpɪt] n abitacolo

cockroach ['kɔkrəutʃ] n blatta

cocktail ['kɔkteɪl] n cocktail m inv; ~
cabinet n mobile m bar inv; ~ party n
cocktail m inv

cocoa ['kəukəu] n cacao

coconut ['kəukənʌt] n noce f di cocco

cocoon [kə'kuːn] n bozzolo

cod [kɔd] n merluzzo

C.O.D. abbr = cash on delivery

code [kəud] n codice m

cod-liver oil n olio di fegato di merluzzo

coercion [kəu'əːʃən] n coercizione f

coffee ['kɔfɪ] n caffè m inv; ~ bar (BRIT) n
caffè m inv; ~ break n pausa per il caffè;
~pot n caffettiera; ~ table n tavolino

coffin ['kɔfɪn] n bara

cog [kɔg] n dente m

cogent ['kəudʒənt] adj convincente

coherent [kəu'hɪərənt] adj coerente

coil [kɔɪl] n rotolo; (ELEC) bobina;
(contraceptive) spirale f ♦ vt avvolgere

coin [kɔɪn] n moneta ♦ vt (word) coniare;
~age n sistema m monetario; ~-box
(BRIT) n telefono a gettoni

coincide [kəuɪn'saɪd] vi coincidere;
coincidence [kəu'ɪnsɪdəns] n
combinazione f

Coke ® [kəuk] n coca

coke [kəuk] n coke m

colander ['kɔləndə*] n colino

cold [kəuld] adj freddo(a) ♦ n freddo; (MED)
raffreddore m; it's ~ fa freddo; to be ~
(person) aver freddo; (object) essere
freddo(a); to catch ~ prendere freddo; to
catch a ~ prendere un raffreddore; in ~
blood a sangue freddo; ~-shoulder vt
trattare con freddezza; ~ sore n erpete m

coleslaw ['kəulslɔ:] n insalata di cavolo bianco

colic ['kɔlɪk] n colica

collapse [kə'læps] vi crollare ♦ n crollo; (MED) collasso

collapsible [kə'læpsəbl] adj pieghevole

collar ['kɔlə*] n (of coat, shirt) colletto; (of dog, cat) collare m; ~**bone** n clavicola

collateral [kə'lætərl] n garanzia

colleague ['kɔli:g] n collega m/f

collect [kə'lekt] vt (gen) raccogliere; (as a hobby) fare collezione di; (BRIT: call and pick up) prendere; (money owed, pension) riscuotere; (donations, subscriptions) fare una colletta di ♦ vi adunarsi, riunirsi; ammucchiarsi; **to call ~** (US: TEL) fare una chiamata a carico del destinatario; ~**ion** [kə'lekʃən] n raccolta; collezione f; (for money) colletta

collector [kə'lektə*] n collezionista m/f

college ['kɔlɪdʒ] n college m inv; (of technology etc) istituto superiore

collide [kə'laɪd] vi: **to ~ (with)** scontrarsi (con)

colliery ['kɔlɪərɪ] (BRIT) n miniera di carbone

collision [kə'lɪʒən] n collisione f, scontro

colloquial [kə'ləukwɪəl] adj familiare

colon ['kəulən] n (sign) due punti mpl; (MED) colon m inv

colonel ['kə:nl] n colonnello

colonial [kə'ləunɪəl] adj coloniale

colony ['kɔlənɪ] n colonia

colour ['kʌlə*] (US **color**) n colore m ♦ vt colorare; (tint, dye) tingere; (fig: affect) influenzare ♦ vi (blush) arrossire; ~**s** npl (of party, club) colori mpl; **in ~** a colori; **~ in** vt colorare; ~ **bar** n discriminazione f razziale (in locali etc); ~-**blind** adj daltonico; ~**ed** adj (photo) a colori; (person) di colore; ~ **film** n (for camera) pellicola a colori; ~**ful** adj pieno(a) di colore, a vivaci colori; (personality) colorato(a); ~**ing** n (substance) colorante m; (complexion) colorito; ~ **scheme** n combinazione f di colori; ~ **television** n televisione f a colori

colt [kəult] n puledro

column ['kɔləm] n colonna; ~**ist** ['kɔləmnɪst]

n articolista m/f

coma ['kəumə] n coma m inv

comb [kəum] n pettine m ♦ vt (hair) pettinare; (area) battere a tappeto

combat ['kɔmbæt] n combattimento ♦ vt combattere, lottare contro

combination [kɔmbɪ'neɪʃən] n combinazione f

combine [vb kəm'baɪn, n 'kɔmbaɪn] vt: **to ~ (with)** combinare (con); (one quality with another) unire (a) ♦ vi unirsi; (CHEM) combinarsi ♦ n (ECON) associazione f; ~ (**harvester**) n mietitrebbia

come [kʌm] (pt **came**, pp **come**) vi venire; arrivare; **to ~ to** (decision etc) raggiungere; **I've ~ to like him** ha cominciato a piacermi; **to ~ undone** slacciarsi; **to ~ loose** allentarsi; ~ **about** vi succedere; ~ **across** vt fus trovare per caso; ~ **away** vi venire via; staccarsi; ~ **back** vi ritornare; ~ **by** vt fus (acquire) ottenere; procurarsi; ~ **down** vi scendere; (prices) calare; (buildings) essere demolito(a); ~ **forward** vi farsi avanti; presentarsi; ~ **from** vt fus venire da; provenire da; ~ **in** vi entrare; ~ **in for** vt fus (criticism etc) ricevere; ~ **into** vt fus (money) ereditare; ~ **off** vi (button) staccarsi; (stain) andar via; (attempt) riuscire; ~ **on** vi (pupil, work, project) fare progressi; (lights) accendersi; (electricity) entrare in funzione; ~ **on!** avanti!, andiamo!, forza!; ~ **out** vi uscire; (stain) andare via; ~ **round** vi (after faint, operation) riprendere conoscenza, rinvenire; ~ **to** vi rinvenire; ~ **up** vi (sun) salire; (problem) sorgere; (event) essere in arrivo; (in conversation) saltar fuori; ~ **up against** vt fus (resistance, difficulties) urtare contro; ~ **up with** vt fus: **he came up with an idea** venne fuori con un'idea; ~ **upon** vt fus trovare per caso; ~**back** n (THEATRE etc) ritorno

comedian [kə'mi:dɪən] n comico

comedienne [kəmi:dɪ'ɛn] n attrice f comica

comedy ['kɔmɪdɪ] n commedia

comeuppance [kʌm'ʌpəns] n: **to get**

one's ~ ricevere ciò che si merita

comfort ['kʌmfət] n comodità f inv, benessere m; (relief) consolazione f, conforto ♦ vt consolare, confortare; ~s npl comodità fpl; ~**able** adj comodo(a); (financially) agiato(a); (live) bene; ~ **station** (US) n gabinetti mpl

comic ['kɒmɪk] adj (also: ~**al**) comico(a) ♦ n comico; (BRIT: magazine) giornaletto; ~ **strip** n fumetto

coming ['kʌmɪŋ] n arrivo ♦ adj (next) prossimo(a); (future) futuro(a); ~(**s**) **and going**(**s**) n(pl) andirivieni m inv

comma ['kɒmə] n virgola

command [kə'mɑːnd] n ordine m, comando; (MIL: authority) comando; (mastery) padronanza ♦ vt comandare; **to ~ sb to do** ordinare a qn di fare; ~**eer** [kɒmən'dɪə*] vt requisire; ~**er** n capo; (MIL) comandante m

commando [kə'mɑːndəu] n commando m inv; membro di un commando

commence [kə'mens] vt, vi cominciare

commend [kə'mend] vt lodare; raccomandare

commensurate [kə'menʃərɪt] adj: ~ **with** proporzionato(a) a

comment ['kɒment] n commento ♦ vi: **to ~ (on)** fare commenti (su); ~**ary** ['kɒməntəri] n commentario; (SPORT) radiocronaca; telecronaca; ~**ator** ['kɒmənteɪtə*] n commentatore/trice; radiocronista m/f; telecronista m/f

commerce ['kɒmə:s] n commercio

commercial [kə'mə:ʃəl] adj commerciale ♦ n (TV, RADIO: advertisement) pubblicità f inv; ~ **radio/television** n radio f inv/ televisione f privata

commiserate [kə'mɪzəreɪt] vi: **to ~ with** partecipare al dolore di

commission [kə'mɪʃən] n commissione f ♦ vt (work of art) commissionare; **out of ~** (NAUT) in disarmo; ~**aire** [kəmɪʃə'neə*] (BRIT) n (at shop, cinema etc) portiere m in livrea; ~**er** n (POLICE) questore m

commit [kə'mɪt] vt (act) commettere; (to

sb's care) affidare; **to ~ o.s. (to do)** impegnarsi (a fare); **to ~ suicide** suicidarsi; ~**ment** n impegno; promessa

committee [kə'mɪtɪ] n comitato

commodity [kə'mɒdɪtɪ] n prodotto, articolo

common ['kɒmən] adj comune; (pej) volgare; (usual) normale ♦ n terreno comune; **the C~s** (BRIT) npl la Camera dei Comuni; **in ~** in comune; ~**er** n cittadino/a (non nobile); ~ **law** n diritto consuetudinario; ~**ly** adv comunemente, usualmente; **C~ Market** n Mercato Comune; ~**place** adj banale, ordinario(a); ~**room** n sala di riunione; (SCOL) sala dei professori; ~ **sense** n buon senso; **the C~wealth** n il Commonwealth

commotion [kə'məuʃən] n confusione f, tumulto

communal ['kɒmjuːnl] adj (for common use) pubblico(a)

commune [n 'kɒmjuːn, vb kə'mjuːn] n (group) comune f ♦ vi: **to ~ with** mettersi in comunione con

communicate [kə'mjuːnɪkeɪt] vt comunicare, trasmettere ♦ vi: **to ~ (with)** comunicare (con)

communication [kəmjuːnɪ'keɪʃən] n comunicazione f; ~ **cord** (BRIT) n segnale m d'allarme

communion [kə'mjuːnɪən] n (also: **Holy C~**) comunione f

communiqué [kə'mjuːnɪkeɪ] n comunicato

communism ['kɒmjunɪzəm] n comunismo; **communist** adj, n comunista m/f

community [kə'mjuːnɪtɪ] n comunità f inv; ~ **centre** n circolo ricreativo; ~ **chest** (US) n fondo di beneficenza

commutation ticket [kɒmjuː'teɪʃən-] (US) n biglietto di abbonamento

commute [kə'mjuːt] vi fare il pendolare ♦ vt (LAW) commutare; ~**r** n pendolare m/f

compact [adj kəm'pækt, n 'kɒmpækt] adj compatto(a) ♦ n (also: **powder ~**) portacipria m inv; ~ **disc** n compact disc m inv; ~ **disc player** n lettore m CD inv

companion [kəm'pænɪən] n compagno/a; ~**ship** n compagnia

company ['kʌmpənɪ] *n* (*also* COMM, MIL, THEATRE) compagnia; **to keep sb ~** tenere compagnia a qn; **~ secretary** (BRIT) *n* segretario/a generale

comparable ['kɒmpərəbl] *adj* simile

comparative [kəm'pærətɪv] *adj* relativo(a); (*adjective etc*) comparativo(a); **~ly** *adv* relativamente

compare [kəm'pɛə*] *vt*: **to ~ sth/sb with/ to** confrontare qc/qn con/a ♦ *vi*: **to ~ (with)** reggere il confronto (con); **comparison** [-'pærɪsn] *n* confronto; **in comparison (with)** in confronto a (a)

compartment [kəm'pɑːtmənt] *n* compartimento; (RAIL) scompartimento

compass ['kʌmpəs] *n* bussola; **~es** *npl* (MATH) compasso

compassion [kəm'pæʃən] *n* compassione *f*

compatible [kəm'pætɪbl] *adj* compatibile

compel [kəm'pɛl] *vt* costringere, obbligare

compensate ['kɒmpənseɪt] *vt* risarcire ♦ *vi*: **to ~ for** compensare; **compensation** [-'seɪʃən] *n* compensazione *f*; (*money*) risarcimento

compère ['kɒmpɛə*] *n* presentatore/trice

compete [kəm'piːt] *vi* (*take part*) concorrere; (*vie*): **to ~ (with)** fare concorrenza (a)

competent ['kɒmpɪtənt] *adj* competente

competition [kɒmpɪ'tɪʃən] *n* gara; concorso; (ECON) concorrenza

competitive [kəm'petɪtɪv] *adj* (ECON) concorrenziale; (*sport*) agonistico(a); (*person*) che ha spirito di competizione; che ha spirito agonistico

competitor [kəm'petɪtə*] *n* concorrente *m/f*

complacency [kəm'pleɪsnsɪ] *n* compiacenza di sé

complain [kəm'pleɪn] *vi* lagnarsi, lamentarsi; **~t** *n* lamento; (*in shop etc*) reclamo; (MED) malattia

complement [*n* 'kɒmplɪmənt, *vb* 'kɒmplɪment] *n* complemento; (*especially of ship's crew etc*) effettivo ♦ *vt* (*enhance*) accompagnarsi bene a; **~ary** [kɒmplɪ'mentərɪ] *adj* complementare

complete [kəm'pliːt] *adj* completo(a) ♦ *vt*

completare; (*a form*) riempire; **~ly** *adv* completamente; **completion** [-'pliːʃən] *n* completamento

complex ['kɒmpleks] *adj* complesso(a) ♦ *n* (PSYCH, *buildings etc*) complesso

complexion [kəm'plekʃən] *n* (*of face*) carnagione *f*

compliance [kəm'plaɪəns] *n* acquiescenza; **in ~ with** (*orders, wishes etc*) in conformità con

complicate ['kɒmplɪkeɪt] *vt* complicare; **~d** *adj* complicato(a); **complication** [-'keɪʃən] *n* complicazione *f*

compliment [*n* 'kɒmplɪmənt, *vb* 'kɒmplɪment] *n* complimento ♦ *vt* fare un complimento a; **~s** *npl* (*greetings*) complimenti *mpl*; rispetti *mpl*; **to pay sb a ~** fare un complimento a qn; **~ary** [-'mentərɪ] *adj* complimentoso(a), elogiativo(a); (*free*) in omaggio; **~ary ticket** *n* biglietto omaggio

comply [kəm'plaɪ] *vi*: **to ~ with** assentire a; conformarsi a

component [kəm'pəunənt] *adj* componente ♦ *n* componente *m*

compose [kəm'pəuz] *vt* (*form*): **to be ~d of** essere composto di; (*music, poem etc*) comporre; **to ~ o.s.** ricomporsi; **~d** *adj* calmo(a); **~r** *n* (MUS) compositore/trice

composition [kɒmpə'zɪʃən] *n* composizione *f*

composure [kəm'pəuʒə*] *n* calma

compound ['kɒmpaund] *n* (CHEM, LING) composto; (*enclosure*) recinto ♦ *adj* composto(a); **~ fracture** *n* frattura esposta

comprehend [kɒmprɪ'hend] *vt* comprendere, capire; **comprehension** [-'henʃən] *n* comprensione *f*

comprehensive [kɒmprɪ'hensɪv] *adj* comprensivo(a); **~ policy** *n* (INSURANCE) polizza che copre tutti i rischi; **~ (school)** (BRIT) *n* scuola secondaria aperta a tutti

compress [*vb* kəm'pres, *n* 'kɒmpres] *vt* comprimere ♦ *n* (MED) compressa

comprise [kəm'praɪz] *vt* (*also*: **be ~d of**) comprendere

context [ˈkɒntɛkst] *n* contesto

continent [ˈkɒntɪnənt] *n* continente *m*; **the C~** (*BRIT*) l'Europa continentale; **~al** [-ˈnɛntl] *adj* continentale; **~al breakfast** *n* colazione *f* all'europea (*senza piatti caldi*); **~al quilt** (*BRIT*) *n* piumino

contingency [kənˈtɪndʒənsɪ] *n* eventualità *f inv*

continual [kənˈtɪnjuəl] *adj* continuo(a)

continuation [kəntɪnjuˈeɪʃən] *n* continuazione *f*; (*after interruption*) ripresa; (*of story*) seguito

continue [kənˈtɪnjuː] *vi* continuare ♦ *vt* continuare; (*start again*) riprendere

continuity [kɒntɪˈnjuːɪtɪ] *n* continuità *f*; (*TV, CINEMA*) (ordine *m* della) sceneggiatura

continuous [kənˈtɪnjuəs] *adj* continuo(a); ininterrotto(a)

contort [kənˈtɔːt] *vt* contorcere

contour [ˈkɒntuə*] *n* contorno, profilo; (*also: ~ line*) curva di livello

contraband [ˈkɒntrəbænd] *n* contrabbando

contraceptive [kɒntrəˈsɛptɪv] *adj* contraccettivo(a) ♦ *n* contraccettivo

contract [*n* ˈkɒntrækt, *vb* kənˈtrækt] *n* contratto ♦ *vi* (*become smaller*) contrarsi; (*COMM*): **to ~ to do sth** fare un contratto per fare qc ♦ *vt* (*illness*) contrarre; **~ion** [-ʃən] *n* contrazione *f*; **~or** *n* imprenditore *m*

contradict [kɒntrəˈdɪkt] *vt* contraddire

contraflow [ˈkɒntrəfləu] *n* (*AUT*) senso unico alternato

contraption [kənˈtræpʃən] (*pej*) *n* aggeggio

contrary[1] [ˈkɒntrərɪ] *adj* contrario(a); (*unfavourable*) avverso(a), contrario(a) ♦ *n* contrario; **on the ~** al contrario; **unless you hear to the ~** salvo contrordine

contrary[2] [kənˈtrɛərɪ] *adj* (*perverse*) bisbetico(a)

contrast [*n* ˈkɒntrɑːst, *vb* kənˈtrɑːst] *n* contrasto ♦ *vt* mettere in contrasto; **in ~ to** contrariamente a

contribute [kənˈtrɪbjuːt] *vi* contribuire ♦ *vt*: **to ~ £10/an article to** dare 10 sterline/un articolo a; **to ~ to** contribuire a; (*newspaper*) scrivere per; **contribution** [kɒntrɪˈbjuːʃən] *n* contributo; **contributor**

n (*to newspaper*) collaboratore/trice

contrivance [kənˈtraɪvəns] *n* congegno; espediente *m*

contrive [kənˈtraɪv] *vi*: **to ~ to do** fare in modo di fare

control [kənˈtrəul] *vt* controllare; (*firm, operation etc*) dirigere ♦ *n* controllo; **~s** *npl* (*of vehicle etc*) comandi *mpl*; (*governmental*) controlli *mpl*; **under ~** sotto controllo; **to be in ~ of** avere il controllo di; **to go out of ~** (*car*) non rispondere ai comandi; (*situation*) sfuggire di mano; **~led substance** *n* sostanza stupefacente; **~ panel** *n* quadro dei comandi; **~ room** *n* (*NAUT, MIL*) sala di comando; (*RADIO, TV*) sala di regia; **~ tower** *n* (*AVIAT*) torre *f* di controllo

controversial [kɒntrəˈvəːʃl] *adj* controverso(a), polemico(a)

controversy [ˈkɒntrəvəːsɪ] *n* controversia, polemica

convalesce [kɒnvəˈlɛs] *vi* rimettersi in salute

convene [kənˈviːn] *vt* convocare ♦ *vi* convenire, adunarsi

convenience [kənˈviːnɪəns] *n* comodità *f inv*; **at your ~** a suo comodo; **all modern ~s**, (*BRIT*) **all mod cons** tutte le comodità moderne

convenient [kənˈviːnɪənt] *adj* conveniente, comodo(a)

convent [ˈkɒnvənt] *n* convento

convention [kənˈvɛnʃən] *n* convenzione *f*; (*meeting*) convegno; **~al** *adj* convenzionale

conversant [kənˈvəːsnt] *adj*: **to be ~ with** essere al corrente di; essere pratico(a) di

conversation [kɒnvəˈseɪʃən] *n* conversazione *f*; **~al** *adj* non formale

converse[1] [ˈkɒnvəːs] *n* contrario, opposto; **~ly** [-ˈvəːslɪ] *adv* al contrario, per contro

convert [*vb* kənˈvəːt, *n* ˈkɒnvəːt] *vt* (*COMM, REL*) convertire; (*alter*) trasformare ♦ *n* convertito/a; **~ible** *n* macchina decappottabile

convex [ˈkɒnvɛks] *adj* convesso(a)

convey [kənˈveɪ] *vt* trasportare; (*thanks*)

compromise [ˈkɒmprəmaɪz] *n* compromesso ♦ *vt* compromettere ♦ *vi* venire a un compromesso

compulsion [kəmˈpʌlʃən] *n* costrizione *f*

compulsive [kəmˈpʌlsɪv] *adj* (*liar, gambler*) che non riesce a controllarsi; (*viewing, reading*) cui non si può fare a meno

compulsory [kəmˈpʌlsərɪ] *adj* obbligatorio(a)

computer [kəmˈpjuːtə*] *n* computer *m inv*, elaboratore *m* elettronico; **~ game** *n* gioco per computer; **~-generated** *adj* realizzato(a) al computer; **~ize** *vt* computerizzare; **~ programmer** *n* programmatore/trice; **~ programming** *n* programmazione *f* di computer; **~ science** *n* informatica; **computing** *n* informatica

comrade [ˈkɒmrɪd] *n* compagno/a; **~ship** *n* cameratismo

con [kɒn] (*inf*) *vt* truffare ♦ *n* truffa

conceal [kənˈsiːl] *vt* nascondere

concede [kənˈsiːd] *vt* ammettere

conceit [kənˈsiːt] *n* presunzione *f*, vanità; **~ed** *adj* presuntuoso(a), vanitoso(a)

conceive [kənˈsiːv] *vt* concepire ♦ *vi* concepire un bambino

concentrate [ˈkɒnsəntreɪt] *vi* concentrarsi ♦ *vt* concentrare

concentration [kɒnsənˈtreɪʃən] *n* concentrazione *f*; **~ camp** *n* campo di concentramento

concept [ˈkɒnsɛpt] *n* concetto

concern [kənˈsəːn] *n* affare *m*; (*COMM*) azienda, ditta; (*anxiety*) preoccupazione *f* ♦ *vt* riguardare; **to be ~ed (about)** preoccuparsi (di); **~ing** *prep* riguardo a, circa

concert [ˈkɒnsət] *n* concerto; **~ed** [kənˈsəːtɪd] *adj* concertato(a); **~ hall** *n* sala da concerti

concertina [kɒnsəˈtiːnə] *n* piccola fisarmonica

conclude [kənˈkluːd] *vt* concludere; **conclusion** [-ˈkluːʒən] *n* conclusione *f*; **conclusive** [-ˈkluːsɪv] *adj* conclusivo(a)

concoct [kənˈkɒkt] *vt* inventare; **~ion**

[-ˈkɒkʃən] *n* miscuglio

concourse [ˈkɒnkɔːs] *n* (*hall*) atrio

concrete [ˈkɒnkriːt] *n* calcestruzzo ♦ *adj* concreto(a); di calcestruzzo

concur [kənˈkəː*] *vi* concordare

concurrently [kənˈkʌrntlɪ] *adv* simultaneamente

concussion [kənˈkʌʃən] *n* commozione *f* cerebrale

condemn [kənˈdɛm] *vt* condannare; (*building*) dichiarare pericoloso(a)

condensation [kɒndɛnˈseɪʃən] *n* condensazione *f*

condense [kənˈdɛns] *vi* condensarsi ♦ *vt* condensare; **~d milk** *n* latte *m* condensato

condescending [kɒndɪˈsɛndɪŋ] *adj* (*person*) che ha un'aria di superiorità

condition [kənˈdɪʃən] *n* condizione *f*; (*MED*) malattia ♦ *vt* condizionare; **on ~ that** a condizione che +*sub*, a condizione di; **~er** *n* (*for hair*) balsamo; (*for fabrics*) ammorbidente *m*

condolences [kənˈdəulənsɪz] *npl* condoglianze *fpl*

condom [ˈkɒndəm] *n* preservativo

condominium [kɒndəˈmɪnɪəm] (*US*) *n* condominio

conducive [kənˈdjuːsɪv] *adj*: **~ to** favorevole a

conduct [*n* ˈkɒndʌkt, *vb* kənˈdʌkt] *n* condotta ♦ *vt* condurre; (*manage*) dirigere; amministrare; (*MUS*) dirigere; **to ~ o.s.** comportarsi; **~ed tour** *n* gita accompagnata; **~or** *n* (*of orchestra*) direttore *m* d'orchestra; (*on bus*) bigliettaio; (*US: on train*) controllore *m*; (*ELEC*) conduttore *m*; **~ress** *n* (*on bus*) bigliettaia

cone [kəun] *n* cono; (*BOT*) pigna; (*traffic ~*) birillo

confectioner [kənˈfɛkʃənə*] *n* pasticciere *m*; **~'s (shop)** *n* ≈ pasticceria; **~y** *n* dolciumi *mpl*

confer [kənˈfəː*] *vt*: **to ~ sth on** conferire qc a ♦ *vi* conferire

conference [ˈkɒnfərns] *n* congresso

confess [kənˈfɛs] *vt* confessare, ammettere

♦ vi confessare; **~ion** [-'feʃən] n confessione f

confetti [kən'feti] n coriandoli mpl

confide [kən'faɪd] vi: **to ~ in** confidarsi con

confidence ['kɒnfɪdns] n confidenza; (trust) fiducia; (self-assurance) sicurezza di sé; **in ~** (speak, write) in confidenza, confidenzialmente; **~ trick** n truffa;

confident adj sicuro(a); sicuro(a) di sé; **confidential** [kɒnfɪ'dɛnʃəl] adj riservato(a), confidenziale

confine [kən'faɪn] vt limitare; (shut up) rinchiudere; **~d** adj (space) ristretto(a); **~ment** n prigionia; **~s** ['kɒnfaɪnz] npl confini mpl

confirm [kən'fəːm] vt confermare; **~ation** [kɒnfə'meɪʃən] n (REL) cresima; **~ed** adj inveterato(a)

confiscate ['kɒnfɪskeɪt] vt confiscare

conflict [n 'kɒnflɪkt, vb kən'flɪkt] n conflitto ♦ vi essere in conflitto; **~ing** adj contrastante

conform [kən'fɔːm] vi: **to ~ (to)** conformarsi (a)

confound [kən'faund] vt confondere

confront [kən'frʌnt] vt (enemy, danger) affrontare; **~ation** [kɒnfrən'teɪʃən] n scontro

confuse [kən'fjuːz] vt (one thing with another) confondere; **~d** adj confuso(a); **confusing** adj che fa confondere; **confusion** [-'fjuːʒən] n confusione f

congeal [kən'dʒiːl] vi (blood) congelarsi

congenial [kən'dʒiːnɪəl] adj (person) simpatico(a); (thing) congeniale

congested [kən'dʒestɪd] adj congestionato(a)

congestion [kən'dʒestʃən] n congestione f

congratulate [kən'grætjuleɪt] vt: **to ~ sb (on)** congratularsi con qn (per o di); **congratulations** [-'leɪʃənz] npl auguri mpl; (on success) complimenti mpl, congratulazioni fpl

congregate ['kɒŋgrɪgeɪt] vi congregarsi, riunirsi

congress ['kɒŋgres] n congresso; **C~man** (US) n membro del Congresso

conjunction [kən'dʒʌŋkʃən] n congiunzione f

conjunctivitis [kəndʒʌŋktɪ'vaɪtɪs] n congiuntivite f

conjure ['kʌndʒə*] vi fare giochi di prestigio; **~ up** vt (ghost, spirit) evocare; (memories) rievocare; **~r** n prestidigitatore/trice, prestigiatore/trice

conk out [kɒŋk-] (inf) vi andare in panne

con man n truffatore m

connect [kə'nekt] vt connettere, collegare; (ELEC, TEL) collegare; (fig) associare ♦ vi (train): **to ~ with** essere in coincidenza con; **to be ~ed with** (associated) aver rapporti con; **~ion** [-ʃən] n relazione f, rapporto; (ELEC) connessione f; (train, plane) coincidenza; (TEL) collegamento

connive [kə'naɪv] vi: **to ~ at** essere connivente in

connoisseur [kɒnɪ'sə*] n conoscitore/trice

conquer ['kɒŋkə*] vt conquistare; (feelings) vincere

conquest ['kɒŋkwest] n conquista

cons [kɒnz] npl see **convenience; pro**

conscience ['kɒnʃəns] n coscienza

conscientious [kɒnʃɪ'enʃəs] adj coscienzioso(a)

conscious ['kɒnʃəs] adj consapevole; (MED) cosciente; **~ness** n consapevolezza; coscienza

conscript ['kɒnskrɪpt] n coscritto; **~ion** [-'skrɪpʃən] n arruolamento (obbligatorio)

consent [kən'sent] n consenso ♦ vi: **to ~ (to)** acconsentire (a)

consequence ['kɒnsɪkwəns] n conseguenza, risultato; importanza

consequently ['kɒnsɪkwəntlɪ] adv di conseguenza, dunque

conservation [kɒnsə'veɪʃən] n conservazione f

conservative [kən'səːvətɪv] adj conservatore(trice); (cautious) cauto(a); **C~** (BRIT) adj, n (POL) conservatore(trice)

conservatory [kən'səːvətrɪ] n (greenhouse) serra; (MUS) conservatorio

conserve [kən'səːv] vt conservare ♦ n conserva

consider [kən'sɪdə*] vt considerare; (take into account) tener conto di; **to ~ doing sth** considerare la possibilità di fare qc

considerable [kən'sɪdərəbl] adj considerevole, notevole; **considerably** adv notevolmente, decisamente

considerate [kən'sɪdərɪt] adj premuroso(a)

consideration [kənsɪdə'reɪʃən] n considerazione f

considering [kən'sɪdərɪŋ] prep in considerazione di

consign [kən'saɪn] vt: **to ~ to** (sth unwanted) relegare in; (person: to sb's care) consegnare a; (: to poverty) condannare a; **~ment** n (of goods) consegna; spedizione f

consist [kən'sɪst] vi: **to ~ of** constare di, essere composto(a) di

consistency [kən'sɪstənsɪ] n consistenza; (fig) coerenza

consistent [kən'sɪstənt] adj coerente

consolation [kɒnsə'leɪʃən] n consolazione f

console¹ [kən'səul] vt consolare

console² ['kɒnsəul] n quadro di comando

consonant ['kɒnsənənt] n consonante f

consortium [kən'sɔːtɪəm] n consorzio

conspicuous [kən'spɪkjuəs] adj cospicuo(a)

conspiracy [kən'spɪrəsɪ] n congiura, cospirazione f

constable ['kʌnstəbl] (BRIT) n ≈ poliziotto, agente m di polizia; **chief ~** ≈ questore m

constabulary [kən'stæbjulərɪ] n forze fpl dell'ordine

constant ['kɒnstənt] adj costante; continuo(a); **~ly** adv costantemente; continuamente

constipated ['kɒnstɪpeɪtɪd] adj stitico(a)

constipation [kɒnstɪ'peɪʃən] n stitichezza

constituency [kən'stɪtjuənsɪ] n collegio elettorale

constituent [kən'stɪtjuənt] n elettore/trice; (part) elemento componente

constitution [kɒnstɪ'tjuːʃən] n costituzione f; **~al** adj costituzionale

constraint [kən'streɪnt] n costrizione f

construct [kən'strʌkt] vt costruire; **~ion** [-ʃən] n costruzione f; **~ive** adj costruttivo(a)

consul ['kɒnsl] n console m; **~ate**

~ate ['kɒnsjulɪt] n consolato

consult [kən'sʌlt] vt consultare; **~ant** n (MED) consulente m medico; (other specialist) consulente; **~ation** [-'teɪʃən] n (MED) consulto; (discussion) consultazione f; **~ing room** (BRIT) n ambulatorio

consume [kən'sjuːm] vt consumare; **~r** n consumatore/trice; **~r goods** npl beni mpl di consumo; **~r society** n società dei consumi

consumption [kən'sʌmpʃən] n consumo

cont. abbr = **continued**

contact ['kɒntækt] n contatto; (person) conoscenza ♦ vt mettersi in contatto con; **~ lenses** npl lenti fpl a contatto

contagious [kən'teɪdʒəs] adj (also fig) contagioso(a)

contain [kən'teɪn] vt contenere; **to ~ o.s.** contenersi; **~er** n recipiente m; (for shipping etc) container m inv

contaminate [kən'tæmɪneɪt] vt contaminare

cont'd abbr = **continued**

contemplate ['kɒntəmpleɪt] vt contemplare; (consider) pensare a (o di)

contemporary [kən'tempərərɪ] adj, n contemporaneo(a)

contempt [kən'tempt] n disprezzo; **~ of court** (LAW) oltraggio alla Corte; **~ible** adj deprecabile

contend [kən'tend] vt: **to ~ that** sostenere che ♦ vi: **to ~ with** lottare contro; **~er** n contendente m/f; concorrente m/f

content¹ ['kɒntent] n contenuto; **~s** npl (of box, case etc) contenuto; **(table of) ~s** indice m

content² [kən'tent] adj contento(a), soddisfatto(a) ♦ vt contentare, soddisfare; **~ed** adj contento(a), soddisfatto(a)

contention [kən'tenʃən] n contesa; (assertion) tesi f inv

contentment [kən'tentmənt] n contentezza

contest [n 'kɒntest, vb kən'test] n lotta; (competition) gara, concorso ♦ vt contestare; impugnare; (compete for) essere in lizza per; **~ant** [kən'testənt] n concorrente m/f; (in fight) avversario/a

comunicare; (idea) dare; ~or belt n nastro trasportatore

convict [vb kən'vɪkt, n 'kɒnvɪkt] vt dichiarare colpevole ♦ n carcerato/a; ~ion [-ʃən] n condanna; (belief) convinzione f

convince [kən'vɪns] vt convincere, persuadere; convincing adj convincente

convoluted ['kɒnvə'luːtɪd] adj (argument etc) involuto(a)

convoy ['kɒnvɔɪ] n convoglio

convulse [kən'vʌls] vt: to be ~d with laughter contorcersi dalle risa

cook [kuk] vt cucinare, cuocere ♦ vi cuocere; (person) cucinare ♦ n cuoco/a; ~book n libro di cucina; ~er n fornello, cucina; ~ery n cucina; ~ery book (BRIT) n = book; ~ie (US) n biscotto; ~ing n cucina

cool [kuːl] adj fresco(a); (not afraid, calm) calmo(a); (unfriendly) freddo(a) ♦ vt raffreddare; (room) rinfrescare ♦ vi (water) raffreddarsi; (air) rinfrescarsi

coop [kuːp] n stia ♦ vt: to ~ up (fig) rinchiudere

cooperate [kəu'ɒpəreɪt] vi cooperare, collaborare; cooperation [-'reɪʃən] n cooperazione f, collaborazione f

cooperative [kəu'ɒpərətɪv] adj cooperativo(a) ♦ n cooperativa

coordinate [vb kəu'ɔːdɪneɪt, n kəu'ɔːdɪnət] vt coordinare ♦ n (MATH) coordinata; ~s npl (clothes) coordinati mpl

co-ownership [kəu'əunəʃɪp] n comproprietà

cop [kɒp] (inf) n sbirro

cope [kəup] vi: to ~ with (problems) far fronte a

copper ['kɒpə*] n rame m; (inf: policeman) sbirro; ~s npl (coins) spiccioli mpl

copse [kɒps] n bosco ceduo

copy ['kɒpɪ] n copia ♦ vt copiare; ~right n diritto d'autore

coral ['kɒrəl] n corallo

cord [kɔːd] n corda; (ELEC) filo

cordial ['kɔːdɪəl] adj cordiale ♦ n (BRIT) cordiale m

cordon ['kɔːdn] n cordone m; ~ off vt fare

cordone a

corduroy ['kɔːdərɔɪ] n fustagno

core [kɔː*] n (of fruit) torsolo; (of organization etc) cuore m ♦ vt estrarre il torsolo da

cork [kɔːk] n sughero; (of bottle) tappo; ~screw n cavatappi m inv

corn [kɔːn] n (BRIT: wheat) grano; (US: maize) granturco; (on foot) callo; ~ on the cob (CULIN) pannocchia cotta

corned beef ['kɔːnd-] n carne f di manzo in scatola

corner ['kɔːnə*] n angolo; (AUT) curva ♦ vt intrappolare; mettere con le spalle al muro; (COMM: market) accaparrare ♦ vi prendere una curva; ~stone n pietra angolare

cornet ['kɔːnɪt] n (MUS) cornetta; (BRIT: of ice-cream) cono

cornflakes ['kɔːnfleɪks] npl fiocchi mpl di granturco

cornflour ['kɔːnflauə*] (BRIT) n farina finissima di granturco

cornstarch ['kɔːnstɑːtʃ] (US) n = cornflour

Cornwall ['kɔːnwəl] n Cornovaglia

corny ['kɔːnɪ] (inf) adj trito(a)

coronary ['kɒrənərɪ] n: ~ (thrombosis) trombosi f coronaria

coronation [kɒrə'neɪʃən] n incoronazione f

coroner ['kɒrənə*] n magistrato incaricato di indagare la causa di morte in circostanze sospette

coronet ['kɒrənɪt] n diadema m

corporal ['kɔːpərl] n caporalmaggiore m ♦ adj: ~ punishment pena corporale

corporate ['kɔːpərɪt] adj costituito(a) (in corporazione); comune

corporation [kɔːpə'reɪʃən] n (of town) consiglio comunale; (COMM) ente m

corps [kɔː*, pl kɔːz] n inv corpo

corpse [kɔːps] n cadavere m

correct [kə'rɛkt] adj (accurate) corretto(a), esatto(a); (proper) corretto(a) ♦ vt correggere; ~ion [-ʃən] n correzione f

correspond [kɒrɪs'pɒnd] vi corrispondere; ~ence n corrispondenza; ~ence course n corso per corrispondenza; ~ent n corrispondente m/f

corridor ['kɔridɔ:ᵊ] *n* corridoio

corrode [kə'rəud] *vt* corrodere ♦ *vi* corrodersi

corrugated ['kɔrəgeitid] *adj* increspato(a); ondulato(a); ~ **iron** *n* lamiera di ferro ondulata

corrupt [kə'rʌpt] *adj* corrotto(a); (COMPUT) alterato(a) ♦ *vt* corrompere

corset ['kɔ:sit] *n* busto

Corsica ['kɔ:sikə] *n* Corsica

cosh [kɔʃ] (BRIT) *n* randello (corto)

cosmetic [kɔz'metik] *n* cosmetico ♦ *adj* (fig: measure etc) superficiale

cost [kɔst] (*pt, pp* **cost**) *n* costo ♦ *vt* costare; (find out the ~ of) stabilire il prezzo di; ~**s** *npl* (COMM, LAW) spese *fpl*; **how much does it ~?** quanto costa?; **at all ~s** a ogni costo

co-star ['kəu-] *n* attore/trice della stessa importanza del protagonista

cost-effective (BRIT) *adj* conveniente

costly ['kɔstli] *adj* costoso(a), caro(a)

cost-of-living *adj:* ~ **allowance** indennità *f inv* di contingenza

cost price (BRIT) *n* prezzo all'ingrosso

costume ['kɔstju:m] *n* costume *m*; (lady's suit) tailleur *m inv*; (BRIT: also: **swimming** ~) costume da bagno; ~ **jewellery** *n* bigiotteria

cosy ['kəuzi] (US **cozy**) *adj* intimo(a); **I'm very ~ here** sto proprio bene qui

cot [kɔt] *n* (BRIT: child's) lettino; (US: campbed) brandina

cottage ['kɔtidʒ] *n* cottage *m inv*; ~ **cheese** *n* fiocchi *mpl* di latte magro

cotton ['kɔtn] *n* cotone *m*; ~ **on to** (inf) *vt fus* afferrare; ~ **candy** (US) *n* zucchero filato; ~ **wool** (BRIT) *n* cotone idrofilo

couch [kautʃ] *n* sofà *m inv*

couchette [ku:'ʃet] *n* (on train, boat) cuccetta

cough [kɔf] *vi* tossire ♦ *n* tosse *f*; ~ **drop** *n* pasticca per la tosse

could [kud] *pt of* **can²**; ~**n't = could not**

council ['kaunsl] *n* consiglio; **city** *or* **town** ~ consiglio comunale; ~ **estate** (BRIT) *n* quartiere *m* di case popolari; ~ **house**

(BRIT) *n* casa popolare; ~**lor** *n* consigliere/a

counsel ['kaunsl] *n* avvocato; consultazione *f* ♦ *vt* consigliare; ~**lor** *n* (US: ~**or**) consigliere/a; (US) avvocato

count [kaunt] *vt, vi* contare ♦ *n* (of votes etc) conteggio; (of pollen etc) livello; (nobleman) conte *m*; ~ **on** *vt fus* contare su; ~**down** *n* conto alla rovescia

countenance ['kauntinəns] *n* volto, aspetto ♦ *vt* approvare

counter ['kauntəᵊ] *n* banco ♦ *vt* opporsi a ♦ *adv:* ~ **to** contro; in opposizione a; ~**act** *vt* agire in opposizione a; (poison etc) annullare gli effetti di; ~**-espionage** *n* controspionaggio

counterfeit ['kauntəfit] *n* contraffazione *f*, falso ♦ *vt* contraffare, falsificare ♦ *adj* falso(a)

counterfoil ['kauntəfɔil] *n* matrice *f*

counterpart ['kauntəpa:t] *n* (of document etc) copia; (of person) corrispondente *m/f*

counter-productive [-prə'dʌktiv] *adj* controproducente

countersign ['kauntəsain] *vt* controfirmare

countess ['kauntis] *n* contessa

countless ['kauntlis] *adj* innumerevole

country ['kʌntri] *n* paese *m*; (native land) patria; (as opposed to town) campagna; (region) regione *f;* ~ **dancing** (BRIT) *n* danza popolare; ~ **house** *n* villa in campagna; ~**man** (irreg) *n* (national) compatriota *m*; (rural) contadino; ~**side** *n* campagna

county ['kaunti] *n* contea

coup [ku:] (*pl* **coups**) *n* colpo; (also: ~ **d'état**) colpo di Stato

couple ['kʌpl] *n* coppia; **a ~ of** un paio di

coupon ['ku:pɔn] *n* buono; (detachable form) coupon *m inv*

courage ['kʌridʒ] *n* coraggio

courgette [kuə'ʒet] (BRIT) *n* zucchina

courier ['kuriəᵊ] *n* corriere *m*; (for tourists) guida

course [kɔ:s] *n* corso; (of ship) rotta; (for golf) campo; (part of meal) piatto; **of ~** senz'altro, naturalmente; ~ **of action** modo d'agire; **a ~ of treatment** (MED) una cura

court [kɔːt] *n* corte *f*; (*TENNIS*) campo ♦ *vt* (*woman*) fare la corte a; **to take to ~** citare in tribunale

courteous ['kəːtɪəs] *adj* cortese

courtesy ['kəːtəsɪ] *n* cortesia; **(by) ~ of** per gentile concessione di; **~ bus, ~ coach** *n* autobus *m inv* gratuito (*di hotel, aeroporto*)

court-house (*US*) *n* palazzo di giustizia

courtier ['kɔːtɪə*] *n* cortigiano/a

court-martial [-'mɑːʃəl] (*pl* **courts-martial**) *n* corte *f* marziale

courtroom ['kɔːtrum] *n* tribunale *m*

courtyard ['kɔːtjɑːd] *n* cortile *m*

cousin ['kʌzn] *n* cugino/a; **first ~** cugino di primo grado

cove [kəuv] *n* piccola baia

covenant ['kʌvənənt] *n* accordo

cover ['kʌvə*] *vt* coprire; (*book, table*) rivestire; (*include*) comprendere; (*PRESS*) fare un servizio su ♦ *n* (*of pan*) coperchio; (*over furniture*) fodera; (*of bed*) copriletto; (*of book*) copertina; (*shelter*) riparo; (*COMM, INSURANCE, of spy*) copertura; **to take ~** (*shelter*) ripararsi; **under ~** al riparo; **under ~ of darkness** protetto dall'oscurità; **under separate ~** (*COMM*) a parte, in plico separato; **~ up** *vi*: **to ~ up for sb** coprire qn; **~age** *n* (*PRESS, RADIO, TV*): **to give full ~age to sth** fare un ampio servizio su qc; **~ charge** *n* coperto; **~ing** *n* copertura; **~ing letter** (*US* **~ letter**) *n* lettera d'accompagnamento; **~ note** *n* (*INSURANCE*) polizza (di assicurazione) provvisoria

covert ['kʌvət] *adj* (*hidden*) nascosto(a); (*glance*) furtivo(a)

cover-up *n* occultamento (di informazioni)

cow [kau] *n* vacca ♦ *vt* (*person*) intimidire

coward ['kauəd] *n* vigliacco/a; **~ice** [-ɪs] *n* vigliaccheria; **~ly** *adj* vigliacco(a)

cowboy ['kaubɔɪ] *n* cow-boy *m inv*

cower ['kauə*] *vi* acquattarsi

coxswain ['kɔksn] (*abbr*: **cox**) *n* timoniere *m*

coy [kɔɪ] *adj* falsamente timido(a)

cozy ['kəuzɪ] (*US*) *adj* = **cosy**

CPA (*US*) *n abbr* = **certified public accountant**

crab [kræb] *n* granchio; **~ apple** *n* mela selvatica

crack [kræk] *n* fessura, crepa; incrinatura; (*noise*) schiocco; (: *of gun*) scoppio; (*drug*) crack *m inv* ♦ *vt* spaccare; incrinare; (*whip*) schioccare; (*nut*) schiacciare; (*problem*) risolvere; (*code*) decifrare ♦ *adj* (*troops*) fuori classe; **to ~ a joke** fare una battuta; **~ down on** *vt fus* porre freno a; **~ up** *vi* crollare; **~er** *n* cracker *m inv*; petardo

crackle ['krækl] *vi* crepitare

cradle ['kreɪdl] *n* culla

craft [krɑːft] *n* mestiere *m*; (*cunning*) astuzia; (*boat*) naviglio; **~sman** (*irreg*) *n* artigiano; **~smanship** *n* abilità; **~y** *adj* furbo(a), astuto(a)

crag [kræg] *n* roccia

cram [kræm] *vt* (*fill*): **to ~ sth with** riempire qc di; (*put*): **to ~ sth into** stipare qc in ♦ *vi* (*for exams*) prepararsi (in gran fretta)

cramp [kræmp] *n* crampo; **~ed** *adj* ristretto(a)

crampon ['kræmpən] *n* (*CLIMBING*) rampone *m*

cranberry ['krænbərɪ] *n* mirtillo

crane [kreɪn] *n* gru *f inv*

crank [kræŋk] *n* manovella; (*person*) persona stramba

cranny ['krænɪ] *n see* **nook**

crash [kræʃ] *n* fragore *m*; (*of car*) incidente *m*; (*of plane*) caduta; (*of business etc*) crollo ♦ *vt* fracassare ♦ *vi* (*plane*) fracassarsi; (*car*) avere un incidente; (*two cars*) scontrarsi; (*business etc*) fallire, andare in rovina; **~ course** *n* corso intensivo; **~ helmet** *n* casco; **~ landing** *n* atterraggio di fortuna

crate [kreɪt] *n* cassa

cravat(e) [krə'væt] *n* fazzoletto da collo

crave [kreɪv] *vt, vi*: **to ~ (for)** desiderare ardentemente

crawl [krɔːl] *vi* strisciare carponi; (*vehicle*) avanzare lentamente ♦ *n* (*SWIMMING*) crawl *m*

crayfish ['kreɪfɪʃ] *n inv* (*freshwater*) gambero (d'acqua dolce); (*saltwater*)

gambero
crayon ['kreɪən] n matita colorata
craze [kreɪz] n mania
crazy ['kreɪzɪ] adj matto(a); (inf: keen): ~ **about sb** pazzo(a) di qn; ~ **about sth** matto(a) per qc
creak [kriːk] vi cigolare, scricchiolare
cream [kriːm] n crema; (fresh) panna ♦ adj (colour) color crema inv; ~ **cake** n torta alla panna; ~ **cheese** n formaggio fresco; ~**y** adj cremoso(a)
crease [kriːs] n grinza; (deliberate) piega ♦ vt sgualcire ♦ vi sgualcirsi
create [kriː'eɪt] vt creare; **creation** [-ʃən] n creazione f; **creative** adj creativo(a)
creature ['kriːtʃə*] n creatura
crèche [kreʃ] n asilo infantile
credence ['kriːdns] n: **to lend** or **give ~ to** prestar fede a
credentials [krɪ'denʃlz] npl credenziali fpl
credit ['kredɪt] n credito; onore m ♦ vt (COMM) accreditare; (believe: also: **give ~ to**) credere, prestar fede a; ~**s** npl (CINEMA) titoli mpl; **to ~ sb with** (fig) attribuire a qn; **to be in ~** (person) essere creditore (trice); (bank account) essere coperto(a); ~ **card** n carta di credito; ~**or** n creditore/trice
creed [kriːd] n credo; dottrina
creek [kriːk] n insenatura; (US) piccolo fiume m
creep [kriːp] (pt, pp **crept**) vi avanzare furtivamente (or pian piano); ~**er** n pianta rampicante; ~**y** adj (frightening) che fa accapponare la pelle
crematorium [kremə'tɔːrɪəm] (pl **cremato-ria**) n forno crematorio
crêpe [kreɪp] n crespo; ~ **bandage** (BRIT) n fascia elastica
crept [krept] pt, pp of **creep**
crescent ['kresnt] n (shape) mezzaluna; (street) strada semicircolare
cress [kres] n crescione m
crest [krest] n cresta; (of coat of arms) cimiero; ~**fallen** adj mortificato(a)
Crete [kriːt] n Creta
crevasse [krɪ'væs] n crepaccio
crevice ['krevɪs] n fessura, crepa

crew [kruː] n equipaggio; ~**-cut** n: **to have a ~-cut** avere i capelli a spazzola; ~**-neck** n girocollo
crib [krɪb] n culla ♦ vt (inf) copiare
crick [krɪk] n crampo
cricket ['krɪkɪt] n (insect) grillo; (game) cricket m
crime [kraɪm] n crimine m; **criminal** ['krɪmɪnl] adj, n criminale m/f
crimson ['krɪmzn] adj color cremisi inv
cringe [krɪndʒ] vi acquattarsi; (in embarrassment) sentirsi sprofondare
crinkle ['krɪŋkl] vt arricciare, increspare
cripple ['krɪpl] n zoppo/a ♦ vt azzoppare
crises ['kraɪsiːz] npl of **crisis**
crisis ['kraɪsɪs] (pl **crises**) n crisi f inv
crisp [krɪsp] adj croccante; (fig) frizzante; vivace; deciso(a); ~**s** (BRIT) npl patatine fpl
criss-cross ['krɪs-] adj incrociato(a)
criteria [kraɪ'tɪərɪə] npl of **criterion**
criterion [kraɪ'tɪərɪən] (pl **criteria**) n criterio
critic ['krɪtɪk] n critico; ~**al** adj critico(a); ~**ally** adv (speak etc) criticamente; ~**ally ill** gravemente malato; ~**ism** ['krɪtɪsɪzm] n critica; ~**ize** ['krɪtɪsaɪz] vt criticare
croak [krəuk] vi gracchiare; (frog) gracidare
Croatia [krəu'eɪʃə] n Croazia
crochet ['krəuʃeɪ] n lavoro all'uncinetto
crockery ['krɒkərɪ] n vasellame m
crocodile ['krɒkədaɪl] n coccodrillo
crocus ['krəukəs] n croco
croft [krɒft] (BRIT) n piccolo podere m
crony ['krəunɪ] (inf: pej) n compare m
crook [kruk] n truffatore m; (of shepherd) bastone m; ~**ed** ['krukɪd] adj curvo(a), storto(a); (action) disonesto(a)
crop [krɒp] n (produce) coltivazione f; (amount produced) raccolto; (riding ~) frustino ♦ vt (hair) rapare; ~ **up** vi presentarsi
croquette [krə'ket] n crocchetta
cross [krɒs] n croce f; (BIOL) incrocio ♦ vt (street etc) attraversare; (arms, legs, BIOL) incrociare; (cheque) sbarrare ♦ adj di cattivo umore; ~ **out** vt cancellare; ~ **over** vi attraversare; ~**bar** n traversa; ~**country (race)** n cross-country m inv; ~**-examine**

vt (LAW) interrogare in contraddittorio; ~-
eyed adj strabico(a); ~**fire** n fuoco
incrociato; ~**ing** n incrocio; (sea passage)
traversata; (also: **pedestrian ~ing**) passaggio pedonale; ~**ing guard** (US) n dipendente comunale che aiuta i bambini ad
attraversare la strada; ~ **purposes** npl:
to be at ~ purposes non parlare della
stessa cosa; ~-**reference** n rinvio,
rimando; ~**roads** n incrocio; ~ **section** n
sezione f trasversale; (in population) settore
m rappresentativo; ~**walk** (US) n strisce fpl
pedonali, passaggio pedonale; ~**wind** n
vento di traverso; ~**word** n cruciverba m
inv

crotch [krɔtʃ] n (ANAT) inforcatura; (of
garment) pattina

crotchet ['krɔtʃit] n (MUS) semiminima

crouch [krautʃ] vi acquattarsi; rannicchiarsi

crow [krəu] n (bird) cornacchia; (of cock)
canto del gallo ♦ vi (cock) cantare

crowbar ['krəuba:*] n piede m di porco

crowd [kraud] n folla ♦ vt affollare, stipare
♦ vi: **to ~ round/in** affollarsi intorno a/in;
~**ed** adj affollato(a); ~**ed with** stipato(a) di

crown [kraun] n corona; (of head) calotta
cranica; (of hat) cocuzzolo; (of hill) cima
♦ vt incoronare; (fig: career) coronare; ~
jewels npl gioielli mpl della Corona; ~
prince n principe m ereditario

crow's feet npl zampe fpl di gallina

crucial ['kru:ʃl] adj cruciale, decisivo(a)

crucifix ['kru:sifiks] n crocifisso; ~**ion**
[-'fikʃən] n crocifissione f

crude [kru:d] adj (materials) greggio(a); non
raffinato(a); (fig: basic) crudo(a), primi-
tivo(a); (: vulgar) rozzo(a), grossolano(a);
~ **(oil)** n (petrolio) greggio

cruel ['kruəl] adj crudele; ~**ty** n crudeltà f
inv

cruise [kru:z] n crociera ♦ vi andare a
velocità di crociera; (taxi) circolare; ~**r** n
incrociatore m

crumb [krʌm] n briciola

crumble ['krʌmbl] vt sbriciolare ♦ vi
sbriciolarsi; (plaster etc) sgretolarsi; (land,
earth) franare; (building, fig) crollare;

crumbly adj friabile

crumpet ['krʌmpit] n specie di frittella

crumple ['krʌmpl] vt raggrinzare,
spiegazzare

crunch [krʌntʃ] vt sgranocchiare; (underfoot)
scricchiolare ♦ n (fig) punto or momento
cruciale; ~**y** adj croccante

crusade [kru:'seid] n crociata

crush [krʌʃ] n folla; (love): **to have a ~ on
sb** avere una cotta per qn; (drink): **lemon
~** spremuta di limone ♦ vt schiacciare;
(crumple) sgualcire

crust [krʌst] n crosta

crutch [krʌtʃ] n gruccia

crux [krʌks] n nodo

cry [krai] vi piangere; (shout: also: ~ **out**)
urlare ♦ n urlo, grido; ~ **off** vi ritirarsi

cryptic ['kriptik] adj ermetico(a)

crystal ['kristl] n cristallo; ~-**clear** adj
cristallino(a)

cub [kʌb] n cucciolo; (also: ~ **scout**) lupetto

Cuba ['kju:bə] n Cuba

cube [kju:b] n cubo ♦ vt (MATH) elevare al
cubo; **cubic** adj cubico(a); (metre, foot)
cubo(a); **cubic capacity** n cilindrata

cubicle ['kju:bikl] n scompartimento
separato; cabina

cuckoo ['kuku:] n cucù m inv; ~ **clock** n
orologio a cucù

cucumber ['kju:kʌmbə*] n cetriolo

cuddle ['kʌdl] vt abbracciare, coccolare ♦ vi
abbracciarsi

cue [kju:] n (snooker ~) stecca; (THEATRE etc)
segnale m

cuff [kʌf] n (BRIT: of shirt, coat etc) polsino;
(US: of trousers) risvolto; **off the ~**
improvvisando; ~**link** n gemello

cuisine [kwi'zi:n] n cucina

cul-de-sac ['kʌldəsæk] n vicolo cieco

cull [kʌl] vt (ideas etc) scegliere ♦ n (of
animals) abbattimento selettivo

culminate ['kʌlmineit] vi: **to ~ in**
culminare con; **culmination** [-'neiʃən] n
culmine m

culottes [kju:'lɔts] npl gonna f pantalone
inv

culpable ['kʌlpəbl] adj colpevole

culprit ['kʌlprɪt] n colpevole m/f
cult [kʌlt] n culto
cultivate ['kʌltɪveɪt] vt (also fig) coltivare; **cultivation** [-'veɪʃən] n coltivazione f
cultural ['kʌltʃərəl] adj culturale
culture ['kʌltʃə*] n (also fig) cultura; ~**d** adj colto(a)
cumbersome ['kʌmbəsəm] adj ingombrante
cunning ['kʌnɪŋ] n astuzia, furberia ♦ adj astuto(a), furbo(a)
cup [kʌp] n tazza; (prize, of bra) coppa
cupboard ['kʌbəd] n armadio
cup-tie (BRIT) n partita di coppa
curate ['kjuərɪt] n cappellano
curator [kjuə'reɪtə*] n direttore m (di museo etc)
curb [kə:b] vt tenere a freno ♦ n freno; (US) bordo del marciapiede
curdle ['kə:dl] vi cagliare
cure [kjuə*] vt guarire; (CULIN) trattare; affumicare; essiccare ♦ n rimedio
curfew ['kə:fju:] n coprifuoco
curiosity [kjuərɪ'ɒsɪtɪ] n curiosità
curious ['kjuərɪəs] adj curioso(a)
curl [kə:l] n riccio ♦ vt ondulare; (tightly) arricciare ♦ vi arricciarsi; ~ **up** vi rannicchiarsi; ~**er** n bigodino
curly ['kə:lɪ] adj ricciuto(a)
currant ['kʌrnt] n (dried) sultanina; (bush, fruit) ribes m inv
currency ['kʌrnsɪ] n moneta; **to gain** ~ (fig) acquistare larga diffusione
current ['kʌrnt] adj corrente ♦ n corrente f; ~ **account** (BRIT) n conto corrente; ~ **affairs** npl attualità fpl; ~**ly** adv attualmente
curricula [kə'rɪkjulə] npl of **curriculum**
curriculum [kə'rɪkjuləm] (pl ~**s** or **curricula**) n curriculum m inv; ~ **vitae** n curriculum vitae m inv
curry ['kʌrɪ] n curry m inv ♦ vt: **to** ~ **favour with** cercare di attirarsi i favori di; ~ **powder** n curry m
curse [kə:s] vt maledire ♦ vi bestemmiare ♦ n maledizione f; bestemmia
cursor ['kə:sə*] n (COMPUT) cursore m

cursory ['kə:sərɪ] adj superficiale
curt [kə:t] adj secco(a)
curtail [kə:'teɪl] vt (visit etc) accorciare; (expenses etc) ridurre
curtain ['kə:tn] n tenda; (THEATRE) sipario
curts(e)y ['kə:tsɪ] vi fare un inchino or una riverenza
curve [kə:v] n curva ♦ vi curvarsi
cushion ['kuʃən] n cuscino ♦ vt (shock) fare da cuscinetto a
custard ['kʌstəd] n (for pouring) crema
custodian [kʌs'təudɪən] n custode m/f
custody ['kʌstədɪ] n (of child) tutela; **to take into** ~ (suspect) mettere in detenzione preventiva
custom ['kʌstəm] n costume m, consuetudine f; (COMM) clientela; ~**ary** adj consueto(a)
customer ['kʌstəmə*] n cliente m/f
customized ['kʌstəmaɪzd] adj (car etc) fuoriserie inv
custom-made adj (clothes) fatto(a) su misura; (other goods) fatto(a) su ordinazione
customs ['kʌstəmz] npl dogana; ~ **duty** n tassa doganale; ~ **officer** n doganiere m
cut [kʌt] (pt, pp **cut**) vt tagliare; (shape, make) intagliare; (reduce) ridurre ♦ vi tagliare n taglio; (in salary etc) riduzione f; **to** ~ **a tooth** mettere un dente; ~ **down** vt (tree etc) abbattere ♦ vt fus (also: ~ **down on**) ridurre; ~ **off** vt tagliare; (fig) isolare; ~ **out** vt tagliare fuori; eliminare; ritagliare; ~ **up** vt tagliare a pezzi; ~**back** n riduzione f
cute [kju:t] adj (sweet) carino(a)
cuticle ['kju:tɪkl] n (on nail) pellicina, cuticola
cutlery ['kʌtlərɪ] n posate fpl
cutlet ['kʌtlɪt] n costoletta; (nut etc ~) cotoletta vegetariana
cut: ~**out** n interruttore m; (cardboard ~out) ritaglio; ~**price** (US ~**-rate**) adj a prezzo ridotto; ~**throat** n assassino ♦ adj (competition) spietato(a)
cutting ['kʌtɪŋ] adj tagliente ♦ n (from newspaper) ritaglio (di giornale); (from plant) talea

CV *n abbr* = **curriculum vitae**
cwt *abbr* = **hundredweight(s)**
cyanide ['saɪənaɪd] *n* cianuro
cybercafé ['saɪbəkæfeɪ] *n* cybercaffè *m inv*
cycle ['saɪkl] *n* ciclo; (*bicycle*) bicicletta ♦ *vi* andare in bicicletta; ~ **hire** *n* noleggio *m* biciclette *inv*; ~ **lane**, ~ **path** *n* pista ciclabile
cycling ['saɪklɪŋ] *n* ciclismo
cyclist ['saɪklɪst] *n* ciclista *m/f*
cygnet ['sɪgnɪt] *n* cigno giovane
cylinder ['sɪlɪndə*] *n* cilindro; ~**-head gasket** *n* guarnizione *f* della testata del cilindro
cymbals ['sɪmblz] *npl* cembali *mpl*
cynic ['sɪnɪk] *n* cinico/a; ~**al** *adj* cinico(a); ~**ism** ['sɪnɪsɪzəm] *n* cinismo
Cyprus ['saɪprəs] *n* Cipro
cyst [sɪst] *n* cisti *f inv*
cystitis [sɪs'taɪtɪs] *n* cistite *f*
czar [zɑ:*] *n* zar *m inv*
Czech [tʃɛk] *adj* ceco(a) ♦ *n* ceco/a; (*LING*) ceco
Czech Republic *n*: **the ~** la Repubblica Ceca

D, d

D [di:] *n* (*MUS*) re *m*
dab [dæb] *vt* (*eyes, wound*) tamponare; (*paint, cream*) applicare (con leggeri colpetti)
dabble ['dæbl] *vi*: **to ~ in** occuparsi (da dilettante) di
dad(dy) [dæd(ɪ)] (*inf*) *n* babbo, papà *m inv*
daffodil ['dæfədɪl] *n* trombone *m*, giunchiglia
daft [dɑ:ft] *adj* sciocco(a)
dagger ['dægə*] *n* pugnale *m*
daily ['deɪlɪ] *adj* quotidiano(a), giornaliero(a) ♦ *n* quotidiano ♦ *adv* tutti i giorni
dainty ['deɪntɪ] *adj* delicato(a), grazioso(a)
dairy ['dɛərɪ] *n* (*BRIT: shop*) latteria; (*on farm*) caseificio ♦ *adj* caseario(a); ~ **farm** *n* caseificio; ~ **products** *npl* latticini *mpl*; ~

store (*US*) *n* latteria
daisy ['deɪzɪ] *n* margherita
dale [deɪl] (*BRIT*) *n* valle *f*
dam [dæm] *n* diga ♦ *vt* sbarrare; costruire dighe su
damage ['dæmɪdʒ] *n* danno, danni *mpl*; (*fig*) danno ♦ *vt* danneggiare; ~**s** *npl* (*LAW*) danni
damn [dæm] *vt* condannare; (*curse*) maledire ♦ *n* (*inf*): **I don't give a ~** non me ne frega niente ♦ *adj* (*inf: also:* ~**ed**): **this ~ ...** questo maledetto ...; ~ **(it)!** accidenti!; ~**ing** *adj* (*evidence*) schiacciante
damp [dæmp] *adj* umido(a) ♦ *n* umidità, umido ♦ *vt* (*also:* ~**en:** *cloth, rag*) inumidire, bagnare; (: *enthusiasm etc*) spegnere
damson ['dæmzən] *n* susina damaschina
dance [dɑ:ns] *n* danza, ballo; (*ball*) ballo ♦ *vi* ballare; ~ **hall** *n* dancing *m inv*, sala da ballo; ~**r** *n* danzatore/trice; (*professional*) ballerino/a
dancing ['dɑ:nsɪŋ] *n* danza, ballo
dandelion ['dændɪlaɪən] *n* dente *m* di leone
dandruff ['dændrəf] *n* forfora
Dane [deɪn] *n* danese *m/f*
danger ['deɪndʒə*] *n* pericolo; **there is a ~ of fire** c'è pericolo di incendio; **in ~** in pericolo; **he was in ~ of falling** rischiava di cadere; ~**ous** *adj* pericoloso(a)
dangle ['dæŋgl] *vt* dondolare; (*fig*) far balenare ♦ *vi* pendolare
Danish ['deɪnɪʃ] *adj* danese ♦ *n* (*LING*) danese *m*
dare [dɛə*] *vt*: **to ~ sb to do** sfidare qn a fare ♦ *vi*: **to ~ (to) do sth** osare fare qc; **I ~ say** (*I suppose*) immagino (che); **daring** *adj* audace, ardito(a) ♦ *n* audacia
dark [dɑ:k] *adj* (*night, room*) buio(a), scuro(a); (*colour, complexion*) scuro(a); (*fig*) cupo(a), tetro(a), nero(a) ♦ *n*: **in the ~** al buio; **in the ~ about** (*fig*) all'oscuro di; **after ~** a notte fatta; ~**en** *vt* (*colour*) scurire ♦ *vi* (*sky, room*) oscurarsi; ~ **glasses** *npl* occhiali *mpl* scuri; ~**ness** *n* oscurità, buio; ~**room** *n* camera oscura
darling ['dɑ:lɪŋ] *adj* caro(a) ♦ *n* tesoro
darn [dɑ:n] *vt* rammendare

dart [dɑːt] *n* freccetta; (*SEWING*) pince *f inv* ♦ *vi*: **to ~ towards** precipitarsi verso; **to ~ away/along** sfrecciare via/lungo; **~board** *n* bersaglio (per freccette); **~s** *n* tiro al bersaglio (con freccette)

dash [dæʃ] *n* (*sign*) lineetta; (*small quantity*) punta ♦ *vt* (*missile*) gettare; (*hopes*) infrangere ♦ *vi*: **to ~ towards** precipitarsi verso; **~ away** *or* **off** *vi* scappare via

dashboard ['dæʃbɔːd] *n* (*AUT*) cruscotto

dashing ['dæʃɪŋ] *adj* ardito(a)

data ['deɪtə] *npl* dati *mpl*; **~base** *n* base *f* di dati, data base *m inv*; **~ processing** *n* elaborazione *f* (elettronica) dei dati

date [deɪt] *n* data; appuntamento; (*fruit*) dattero ♦ *vt* datare; (*person*) uscire con; **~ of birth** data di nascita; **to ~** (*until now*) fino a oggi; **~d** *adj* passato(a) di moda; **~ rape** *n* stupro perpetrato da persona conosciuta

daub [dɔːb] *vt* imbrattare

daughter ['dɔːtə*] *n* figlia; **~-in-law** *n* nuora

daunting ['dɔːntɪŋ] *adj* non invidiabile

dawdle ['dɔːdl] *vi* bighellonare

dawn [dɔːn] *n* alba ♦ *vi* (*day*) spuntare; (*fig*): **it ~ed on him that ...** gli è venuto in mente che ....

day [deɪ] *n* giorno; (*as duration*) giornata; (*period of time, age*) tempo, epoca; **the ~ before** il giorno avanti *or* prima; **the ~ after, the following ~** il giorno dopo *or* seguente; **the ~ after tomorrow** dopodomani; **the ~ before yesterday** l'altroieri; **by ~** di giorno; **~break** *n* spuntar *m* del giorno; **~dream** *vi* sognare a occhi aperti; **~light** *n* luce *f* del giorno; **~ return** (*BRIT*) *n* biglietto giornaliero di andata e ritorno; **~time** *n* giorno; **~-to-~** *adj* (*life, organization*) quotidiano(a)

daze [deɪz] *vt* (*subj: drug*) inebetire; (: *blow*) stordire ♦ *n*: **in a ~** inebetito(a); stordito(a)

dazzle ['dæzl] *vt* abbagliare

DC *abbr* (= *direct current*) c.c.

D-day *n* giorno dello sbarco alleato in Normandia

dead [dɛd] *adj* morto(a); (*numb*) intirizzito(a); (*telephone*) muto(a); (*battery*) scarico(a) ♦ *adv* assolutamente, perfettamente ♦ *npl*: **the ~** i morti; **he was shot ~** fu colpito a morte; **~ tired** stanco(a) morto(a); **to stop ~** fermarsi di colpo; **~en** *vt* (*blow, sound*) ammortire; **~ end** *n* vicolo cieco; **~ heat** *n* (*SPORT*): **to finish in a ~ heat** finire alla pari; **~line** *n* scadenza; **~ lock** *n* punto morto; **~ loss** *n*: **to be a ~ loss** (*inf: person, thing*) non valere niente; **~ly** *adj* mortale; (*weapon, poison*) micidiale; **~pan** *adj* a faccia impassibile

deaf [dɛf] *adj* sordo(a); **~en** *vt* assordare; **~ness** *n* sordità

deal [diːl] (*pt, pp* **dealt**) *n* accordo; (*business ~*) affare *m* ♦ *vt* (*blow, cards*) dare; **a great ~ (of)** molto(a); **~ in** *vt fus* occuparsi di; **~ with** *vt fus* (*COMM*) fare affari con, trattare con; (*handle*) occuparsi di; (*be about: book etc*) trattare di; **~er** *n* commerciante *m/f*; **~ings** *npl* (*COMM*) relazioni *fpl*; (*relations*) rapporti *mpl*; **dealt** [dɛlt] *pt, pp of* **deal**

dean [diːn] *n* (*REL*) decano; (*SCOL*) preside *m* di facoltà (*or* di collegio)

dear [dɪə*] *adj* caro(a) ♦ *n*: **my ~** caro mio/ cara mia ♦ *excl*: **~ me!** Dio mio!; **D~ Sir/ Madam** (*in letter*) Egregio Signore/Egregia Signora; **D~ Mr/Mrs X** Gentile Signor/ Signora X; **~ly** *adv* (*love*) moltissimo; (*pay*) a caro prezzo

death [dɛθ] *n* morte *f*; (*ADMIN*) decesso; **~ certificate** *n* atto di decesso; **~ly** *adj* di morte; **~ penalty** *n* pena di morte; **~ rate** *n* indice *m* di mortalità; **~ toll** *n* vittime *fpl*

debacle [dɪ'bækl] *n* fiasco

debase [dɪ'beɪs] *vt* (*currency*) adulterare; (*person*) degradare

debatable [dɪ'beɪtəbl] *adj* discutibile

debate [dɪ'beɪt] *n* dibattito ♦ *vt* dibattere; discutere

debit ['dɛbɪt] *n* debito ♦ *vt*: **to ~ a sum to sb** *or* **to sb's account** addebitare una somma a qn

debris ['dɛbriː] *n* detriti *mpl*

debt [dɛt] *n* debito; **to be in ~** essere

indebitato(a); **~or** n debitore/trice
début ['deɪbjuː] n debutto
decade ['dekeɪd] n decennio
decadence ['dekədəns] n decadenza
decaff ['diːkæf] (inf) n decaffeinato
decaffeinated [dɪ'kæfɪneɪtɪd] adj
  decaffeinato(a)
decanter [dɪ'kæntə*] n caraffa
decay [dɪ'keɪ] n decadimento; (also: **tooth**
  ~) carie f ♦ vi (rot) imputridire
deceased [dɪ'siːst] n defunto/a
deceit [dɪ'siːt] n inganno; **~ful** adj
  ingannevole, perfido(a)
deceive [dɪ'siːv] vt ingannare
December [dɪ'sembə*] n dicembre m
decent ['diːsənt] adj decente; (respectable)
  per bene; (kind) gentile
deception [dɪ'sepʃən] n inganno
deceptive [dɪ'septɪv] adj ingannevole
decide [dɪ'saɪd] vt (person) far prendere una
  decisione a; (question, argument) risolvere,
  decidere ♦ vi decidere, decidersi; **to ~ to**
  do/that decidere di fare/che; **to ~ on**
  decidere per; **~d** adj (resolute) deciso(a);
  (clear, definite) netto(a), chiaro(a); **~dly**
  [-dɪdlɪ] adv indubbiamente; decisamente
decimal ['desɪməl] adj decimale ♦ n
  decimale m; **~ point** n ≈ virgola
decipher [dɪ'saɪfə*] vt decifrare
decision [dɪ'sɪʒən] n decisione f
decisive [dɪ'saɪsɪv] adj decisivo(a); (person)
  deciso(a)
deck [dek] n (NAUT) ponte m; (of bus): **top ~**
  imperiale m; (record ~) piatto; (of cards)
  mazzo; **~chair** n sedia a sdraio
declaration [deklə'reɪʃən] n dichiarazione f
declare [dɪ'kleə*] vt dichiarare
decline [dɪ'klaɪn] n (decay) declino;
  (lessening) ribasso ♦ vt declinare; rifiutare
  ♦ vi declinare; diminuire
decode [diː'kəud] vt decifrare
decoder [diː'kəudə*] n (TV) decodificatore
  m
decompose [diːkəm'pəuz] vi decomporre
décor ['deɪkɔː*] n decorazione f
decorate ['dekəreɪt] vt (adorn, give a medal
  to) decorare; (paint and paper) tinteggiare

e tappezzare; **decoration** [-'reɪʃən] n
  (medal etc, adornment) decorazione f;
  decorator n decoratore m
decorum [dɪ'kɔːrəm] n decoro
decoy ['diːkɔɪ] n zimbello
decrease [n 'diːkriːs, vb diː'kriːs] n
  diminuzione f ♦ vt, vi diminuire
decree [dɪ'kriː] n decreto; **~ nisi** [-'naɪsaɪ] n
  sentenza provvisoria di divorzio
dedicate ['dedɪkeɪt] vt consacrare; (book
  etc) dedicare
dedication [dedɪ'keɪʃən] n (devotion)
  dedizione f; (in book etc) dedica
deduce [dɪ'djuːs] vt dedurre
deduct [dɪ'dʌkt] vt: **to ~ sth (from)** dedurre
  qc (da); **~ion** [dɪ'dʌkʃən] n deduzione f
deed [diːd] n azione f, atto; (LAW) atto
deep [diːp] adj profondo(a); **4 metres ~**
  profondo(a) 4 metri ♦ adv: **spectators**
  stood 20 ~ c'erano 20 file di spettatori;
  ~en vt (hole) approfondire ♦ vi
  approfondirsi; (darkness) farsi più buio; **~**
  end n: **the ~ end** (of swimming pool) la
  parte più profonda; **~-freeze** n
  congelatore m; **~-fry** vt friggere in olio
  abbondante; **~ly** adv profondamente; **~-**
  sea diving n immersione f in alto mare;
  ~-seated adj radicato(a)
deer [dɪə*] n inv: **the ~** i cervidi; (red) **~**
  cervo; (fallow) **~** daino; (roe) **~** capriolo;
  ~skin n pelle f di daino
deface [dɪ'feɪs] vt imbrattare
default [dɪ'fɔːlt] n (COMPUT: also: **~ value**)
  default m inv; **by ~** (SPORT) per abbandono
defeat [dɪ'fiːt] n sconfitta ♦ vt (team,
  opponents) sconfiggere; **~ist** adj, n
  disfattista m/f
defect [n 'diːfekt, vb dɪ'fekt] n difetto ♦ vi: **to**
  ~ to the enemy passare al nemico; **~ive**
  [dɪ'fektɪv] adj difettoso(a)
defence [dɪ'fens] (US **defense**) n difesa;
  ~less adj senza difesa
defend [dɪ'fend] vt difendere; **~ant** n
  imputato/a; **~er** n difensore/a
defense [dɪ'fens] (US) n = **defence**
defensive [dɪ'fensɪv] adj difensivo(a) ♦ n:
  on the ~ sulla difensiva

defer [dɪ'fəː*] vt (postpone) differire, rinviare

defiance [dɪ'faɪəns] n sfida; **in ~ of** a dispetto di

defiant [dɪ'faɪənt] adj (attitude) di sfida; (person) ribelle

deficiency [dɪ'fɪʃənsɪ] n deficienza; carenza

deficit ['dɛfɪsɪt] n deficit m inv

define [dɪ'faɪn] vt definire

definite ['dɛfɪnɪt] adj (fixed) definito(a), preciso(a); (clear, obvious) ben definito(a), esatto(a); (LING) determinativo(a); **he was ~ about it** ne era sicuro; **~ly** adv indubbiamente

definition [dɛfɪ'nɪʃən] n definizione f

deflate [diː'fleɪt] vt sgonfiare

deflect [dɪ'flɛkt] vt deflettere, deviare

deformed [dɪ'fɔːmd] adj deforme

defraud [dɪ'frɔːd] vt defraudare

defrost [diː'frɒst] vt (fridge) disgelare; **~er** (US) n (demister) sbrinatore m

deft [dɛft] adj svelto(a), destro(a)

defunct [dɪ'fʌŋkt] adj che non esiste più

defuse [diː'fjuːz] vt disinnescare; (fig) distendere

defy [dɪ'faɪ] vt sfidare; (efforts etc) resistere a; **it defies description** supera ogni descrizione

degenerate [vb dɪ'dʒɛnəreɪt, adj dɪ'dʒɛnərɪt] vi degenerare ♦ adj degenere

degree [dɪ'griː] n grado; (SCOL) laurea (universitaria); **a (first) ~ in maths** una laurea in matematica; **by ~s** (gradually) gradualmente, a poco a poco; **to some ~** fino a un certo punto, in certa misura

dehydrated [diːhaɪ'dreɪtɪd] adj disidratato(a); (milk, eggs) in polvere

de-ice [diː'aɪs] vt (windscreen) disgelare

deign [deɪn] vi: **to ~ to do** degnarsi di fare

deity ['diːɪtɪ] n divinità f inv

dejected [dɪ'dʒɛktɪd] adj abbattuto(a), avvilito(a)

delay [dɪ'leɪ] vt ritardare ♦ vi: **to ~ (in doing sth)** ritardare (a fare qc) ♦ n ritardo; **to be ~ed** subire un ritardo; (person) essere trattenuto(a)

delectable [dɪ'lɛktəbl] adj (person, food) delizioso(a)

delegate [n 'dɛlɪgɪt, vb 'dɛlɪgeɪt] n delegato/a ♦ vt delegare; **delegation** [-'geɪʃən] n (group) delegazione f; (by manager) delega

delete [dɪ'liːt] vt cancellare

deliberate [adj dɪ'lɪbərɪt, vb dɪ'lɪbəreɪt] adj (intentional) intenzionale; (slow) misurato(a) ♦ vi deliberare, riflettere; **~ly** adv (on purpose) deliberatamente

delicacy ['dɛlɪkəsɪ] n delicatezza

delicate ['dɛlɪkɪt] adj delicato(a)

delicatessen [dɛlɪkə'tɛsn] n ≈ salumeria

delicious [dɪ'lɪʃəs] adj delizioso(a), squisito(a)

delight [dɪ'laɪt] n delizia, gran piacere m ♦ vt dilettare; **to take (a) ~ in** dilettarsi in; **~ed** adj: **~ed (at or with)** contentissimo(a) (di), felice (di); **~ed to do** felice di fare; **~ful** adj delizioso(a); incantevole

delinquent [dɪ'lɪŋkwənt] adj, n delinquente m/f

delirious [dɪ'lɪrɪəs] adj: **to be ~** delirare

deliver [dɪ'lɪvə*] vt (mail) distribuire; (goods) consegnare; (speech) pronunciare; (MED) far partorire; **~y** n distribuzione f; consegna; (of speaker) dizione f; (MED) parto

delude [dɪ'luːd] vt illudere

deluge ['dɛljuːdʒ] n diluvio

delusion [dɪ'luːʒən] n illusione f

demand [dɪ'mɑːnd] vt richiedere; (rights) rivendicare ♦ n domanda; (claim) rivendicazione f; **in ~** ricercato(a), richiesto(a); **on ~** a richiesta; **~ing** adj (boss) esigente; (work) impegnativo(a)

demean [dɪ'miːn] vt: **to ~ o.s.** umiliarsi

demeanour [dɪ'miːnə*] (US **demeanor**) n comportamento; contegno

demented [dɪ'mɛntɪd] adj demente, impazzito(a)

demise [dɪ'maɪz] n decesso

demister [diː'mɪstə*] (BRIT) n (AUT) sbrinatore m

demo ['dɛməu] (inf) n abbr (= demonstration) manifestazione f

democracy [dɪ'mɔkrəsɪ] n democrazia

democrat ['dɛməkræt] n democratico/a; **~ic** [dɛmə'krætɪk] adj democratico(a)

demolish [dɪ'mɔlɪʃ] *vt* demolire
demonstrate ['dɛmənstreɪt] *vt* dimostrare,
provare ♦ *vi* dimostrare, manifestare;
demonstration [-'streɪʃən] *n*
dimostrazione *f*; (POL) dimostrazione,
manifestazione *f*; **demonstrator** *n* (POL)
dimostrante *m/f*; (COMM) dimostratore/trice
demote [dɪ'məut] *vt* far retrocedere
demure [dɪ'mjuə*] *adj* contegnoso(a)
den [dɛn] *n* tana, covo; (room) buco
denial [dɪ'naɪəl] *n* diniego; rifiuto
denim ['dɛnɪm] *n* tessuto di cotone ritorto;
~s *npl* (jeans) blue jeans *mpl*
Denmark ['dɛnmɑːk] *n* Danimarca
denomination [dɪnɔmɪ'neɪʃən] *n* (money)
valore *m*; (REL) confessione *f*
denounce [dɪ'nauns] *vt* denunciare
dense [dɛns] *adj* fitto(a); (smoke) denso(a);
(inf: person) ottuso(a), duro(a)
density ['dɛnsɪtɪ] *n* densità *f inv*
dent [dɛnt] *n* ammaccatura ♦ *vt* (also: **make
a ~ in**) ammaccare
dental ['dɛntl] *adj* dentale; **~ surgeon** *n*
medico/a dentista
dentist ['dɛntɪst] *n* dentista *m/f*
dentures ['dɛntʃəz] *npl* dentiera
deny [dɪ'naɪ] *vt* negare; (refuse) rifiutare
deodorant [diː'əudərənt] *n* deodorante *m*
depart [dɪ'pɑːt] *vi* partire; **to ~ from** (fig)
deviare da
department [dɪ'pɑːtmənt] *n* (COMM)
reparto; (SCOL) sezione *f*, dipartimento;
(POL) ministero; **~ store** *n* grande
magazzino
departure [dɪ'pɑːtʃə*] *n* partenza; (fig): **~
from** deviazione *f* da; **a new ~** una svolta
(decisiva); **~ lounge** *n* (at airport) sala
d'attesa
depend [dɪ'pɛnd] *vi*: **to ~ on** dipendere da;
(rely on) contare su; **it ~s** dipende; **~ing on
the result ...** a seconda del risultato ...;
~able *adj* fidato(a); (car etc) affidabile;
~ant *n* persona a carico; **~ent** *adj*: **to be
~ent on** dipendere da; (child, relative)
essere a carico di ♦ *n* = **~ant**
depict [dɪ'pɪkt] *vt* (in picture) dipingere; (in
words) descrivere

depleted [dɪ'pliːtɪd] *adj* diminuito(a)
deploy [dɪ'plɔɪ] *vt* dispiegare
depopulation ['diːpɔpju'leɪʃən] *n*
spopolamento
deport [dɪ'pɔːt] *vt* deportare; espellere
deportment [dɪ'pɔːtmənt] *n* portamento
deposit [dɪ'pɔzɪt] *n* (COMM, GEO) deposito;
(of ore, oil) giacimento; (CHEM) sedimento;
(part payment) acconto; (for hired goods
etc) cauzione *f* ♦ *vt* depositare; dare in
acconto; mettere *or* lasciare in deposito; **~
account** *n* conto vincolato
depot ['dɛpəu] *n* deposito; (US) stazione *f*
ferroviaria
depreciate [dɪ'priːʃɪeɪt] *vi* svalutarsi
depress [dɪ'prɛs] *vt* deprimere; (price,
wages) abbassare; (press down) premere;
~ed *adj* (person) depresso(a), abbattuto(a);
(price) in ribasso; (industry) in crisi; **~ing**
adj deprimente; **~ion** [dɪ'prɛʃən] *n*
depressione *f*
deprivation [dɛprɪ'veɪʃən] *n* privazione *f*
deprive [dɪ'praɪv] *vt*: **to ~ sb of** privare qn
di; **~d** *adj* disgraziato(a)
depth [dɛpθ] *n* profondità *f inv*; **in the ~s
of** nel profondo di; nel cuore di; **out of
one's ~** (in water) dove non si tocca; (fig) a
disagio
deputize ['dɛpjutaɪz] *vi*: **to ~ for** svolgere le
funzioni di
deputy ['dɛpjutɪ] *adj*: **~ head** (BRIT: SCOL)
vicepreside *m/f* ♦ *n* (assistant) vice *m/f inv*;
(US: also: **~ sheriff**) vice-sceriffo
derail [dɪ'reɪl] *vt*: **to be ~ed** deragliare
deranged [dɪ'reɪndʒd] *adj*: **to be
(mentally) ~** essere pazzo(a)
derby ['dɑːbɪ] (US) *n* (bowler hat) bombetta
derelict ['dɛrɪlɪkt] *adj* abbandonato(a)
derisory [dɪ'raɪsərɪ] *adj* (sum) irrisorio(a);
(laughter, person) beffardo(a)
derive [dɪ'raɪv] *vt*: **to ~ sth from** derivare qc
da; trarre qc da ♦ *vi*: **to ~ from** derivare da
derogatory [dɪ'rɔgətərɪ] *adj* denigratorio(a)
derv [dəːv] (BRIT) *n* gasolio
descend [dɪ'sɛnd] *vt*, *vi* discendere,
scendere; **to ~ from** discendere da; **to ~ to**
(lying, begging) abbassarsi a; **~ant** *n*

discendente m/f

descent [dɪ'sɛnt] n discesa; (origin) discendenza, famiglia

describe [dɪs'kraɪb] vt descrivere; **description** [-'krɪpʃən] n descrizione f; (sort) genere m, specie f

desecrate ['dɛsɪkreɪt] vt profanare

desert [n 'dɛzət, vb dɪ'zəːt] n deserto ♦ vt lasciare, abbandonare ♦ vi (MIL) disertare; ~**er** n disertore m; ~**ion** [dɪ'zəːʃən] n (MIL) diserzione f; (LAW) abbandono del tetto coniugale; ~ **island** n isola deserta; ~**s** [dɪ'zəːts] npl: **to get one's just ~s** avere ciò che si merita

deserve [dɪ'zəːv] vt meritare; **deserving** adj (person) meritevole, degno(a); (cause) meritorio(a)

design [dɪ'zaɪn] n (art, sketch) disegno; (layout, shape) linea; (pattern) fantasia; (intention) intenzione f ♦ vt disegnare; progettare

designer [dɪ'zaɪnə*] n (ART, TECH) disegnatore/trice; (of fashion) modellista m/f

desire [dɪ'zaɪə*] n desiderio, voglia ♦ vt desiderare, volere

desk [dɛsk] n (in office) scrivania; (for pupil) banco; (BRIT: in shop, restaurant) cassa; (in hotel) ricevimento; (at airport) accettazione f

desolate ['dɛsəlɪt] adj desolato(a)

despair [dɪs'pɛə*] n disperazione f ♦ vi: **to ~ of** disperare di

despatch [dɪs'pætʃ] n, vt = **dispatch**

desperate ['dɛspərɪt] adj disperato(a); (fugitive) capace di tutto; **to be ~ for sth/ to do** volere disperatamente qc/fare; ~**ly** adv disperatamente; (very) terribilmente, estremamente

desperation [dɛspə'reɪʃən] n disperazione f

despicable [dɪs'pɪkəbl] adj disprezzabile

despise [dɪs'paɪz] vt disprezzare, sdegnare

despite [dɪs'paɪt] prep malgrado, a dispetto di, nonostante

despondent [dɪs'pɔndənt] adj abbattuto(a), scoraggiato(a)

dessert [dɪ'zəːt] n dolce m; frutta; ~**spoon** n cucchiaio da dolci

destination [dɛstɪ'neɪʃən] n destinazione f

destined ['dɛstɪnd] adj: **to be ~ to do/for** essere destinato(a) a fare/per

destiny ['dɛstɪnɪ] n destino

destitute ['dɛstɪtjuːt] adj indigente, bisognoso(a)

destroy [dɪs'trɔɪ] vt distruggere; ~**er** n (NAUT) cacciatorpediniere m

destruction [dɪs'trʌkʃən] n distruzione f

detach [dɪ'tætʃ] vt staccare, distaccare; ~**ed** adj (attitude) distante; ~**ed house** n villa; ~**ment** n (MIL) distaccamento; (fig) distacco

detail ['diːteɪl] n particolare m, dettaglio ♦ vt dettagliare, particolareggiare; **in ~** nei particolari; ~**ed** adj particolareggiato(a)

detain [dɪ'teɪn] vt trattenere; (in captivity) detenere

detect [dɪ'tɛkt] vt scoprire, scorgere; (MED, POLICE, RADAR etc) individuare; ~**ion** [dɪ'tɛkʃən] n scoperta; individuazione f; ~**ive** n investigatore/trice; ~**ive story** n giallo

détente [deɪ'taːnt] n (POL) distensione f

detention [dɪ'tɛnʃən] n detenzione f; (SCOL) permanenza forzata per punizione

deter [dɪ'təː*] vt dissuadere

detergent [dɪ'təːdʒənt] n detersivo

deteriorate [dɪ'tɪərɪəreɪt] vi deteriorarsi

determine [dɪ'təːmɪn] vt determinare; ~**d** adj (person) risoluto(a), deciso(a); ~**d to do** deciso(a) a fare

detour ['diːtuə*] n deviazione f

detract [dɪ'trækt] vi: **to ~ from** detrarre da

detriment ['dɛtrɪmənt] n: **to the ~ of** detrimento di; ~**al** [dɛtrɪ'mɛntl] adj: ~**al to** dannoso(a) a, nocivo(a) a

devaluation [dɪvæljuː'eɪʃən] n svalutazione f

devastate ['dɛvəsteɪt] vt devastare; (fig): ~**d by** sconvolto(a) da; **devastating** adj devastatore(trice); sconvolgente

develop [dɪ'vɛləp] vt sviluppare; (habit) prendere (gradualmente) ♦ vi sviluppparsi; (facts, symptoms: appear) manifestarsi, rivelarsi; ~**er** n (also: **property ~er**) costruttore m edile; ~**ing country** n paese *m* in via di sviluppo; **~ment** *n* sviluppo

device [dɪ'vaɪs] *n* (*apparatus*) congegno

devil ['dɛvl] *n* diavolo; demonio

devious ['diːvɪəs] *adj* (*person*) subdolo(a)

devise [dɪ'vaɪz] *vt* escogitare, concepire

devoid [dɪ'vɔɪd] *adj*: **~ of** privo(a) di

devolution [diːvə'luːʃən] *n* (*POL*) decentramento

devote [dɪ'vəut] *vt*: **to ~ sth to** dedicare qc a; **~d** *adj* devoto(a); **to be ~d to sb** essere molto affezionato(a) a qn; **~e** [dɛvəu'tiː] *n* (*MUS, SPORT*) appassionato/a

devotion [dɪ'vəuʃən] *n* devozione *f*, attaccamento; (*REL*) atto di devozione, preghiera

devour [dɪ'vauə*] *vt* divorare

devout [dɪ'vaut] *adj* pio(a), devoto(a)

dew [djuː] *n* rugiada

dexterity [dɛks'tɛrɪtɪ] *n* destrezza

diabetes [daɪə'biːtiːz] *n* diabete *m*; **diabetic** [-'bɛtɪk] *adj*, *n* diabetico(a)

diabolical [daɪə'bɔlɪkl] (*inf*) *adj* orribile

diagnosis [daɪəg'nəusɪs] (*pl* **diagnoses**) *n* diagnosi *f inv*

diagonal [daɪ'ægənl] *adj* diagonale ♦ *n* diagonale *f*

diagram ['daɪəgræm] *n* diagramma *m*

dial ['daɪəl] *n* quadrante *m*; (*on radio*) lancetta; (*on telephone*) disco combinatore ♦ *vt* (*number*) fare

dialect ['daɪəlɛkt] *n* dialetto

dialling code ['daɪəlɪŋ-] (*US* **area code**) *n* prefisso

dialling tone ['daɪəlɪŋ-] (*US* **dial tone**) *n* segnale *m* di linea libera

dialogue ['daɪəlɔg] (*US* **dialog**) *n* dialogo

diameter [daɪ'æmɪtə*] *n* diametro

diamond ['daɪəmənd] *n* diamante *m*; (*shape*) rombo; **~s** *npl* (*CARDS*) quadri *mpl*

diaper ['daɪəpə*] (*US*) *n* pannolino

diaphragm ['daɪəfræm] *n* diaframma *m*

diarrhoea [daɪə'riːə] (*US* **diarrhea**) *n* diarrea

diary ['daɪərɪ] *n* (*daily account*) diario; (*book*) agenda

dice [daɪs] *n inv* dado ♦ *vt* (*CULIN*) tagliare a dadini

Dictaphone ® ['dɪktəfəun] *n* dittafono ®

dictate [dɪk'teɪt] *vt* dettare

dictation [dɪk'teɪʃən] *n* dettatura; (*SCOL*) dettato

dictator [dɪk'teɪtə*] *n* dittatore *m*; **~ship** *n* dittatura

dictionary ['dɪkʃənrɪ] *n* dizionario

did [dɪd] *pt of* **do**

didn't = **did not**

die [daɪ] *vi* morire; **to be dying for sth/to do sth** morire dalla voglia di qc/di fare qc; **~ away** *vi* spegnersi a poco a poco; **~ down** *vi* abbassarsi; **~ out** *vi* estinguersi

diesel ['diːzəl] *n* (*vehicle*) diesel *m inv*; **~ engine** *n* motore *m* diesel *inv*; **~ (oil)** *n* gasolio (per motori diesel), diesel *m inv*

diet ['daɪət] *n* alimentazione *f*; (*restricted food*) dieta ♦ *vi* (*also*: **be on a ~**) stare a dieta

differ ['dɪfə*] *vi*: **to ~ from sth** differire da qc; essere diverso(a) da qc; **to ~ from sb over sth** essere in disaccordo con qn su qc; **~ence** *n* differenza; (*disagreement*) screzio; **~ent** *adj* diverso(a); **~entiate** [-'rɛnʃɪeɪt] *vi*: **to ~entiate between** discriminare *or* fare differenza fra

difficult ['dɪfɪkəlt] *adj* difficile; **~y** *n* difficoltà *f inv*

diffident ['dɪfɪdənt] *adj* sfiduciato(a)

diffuse [*adj* dɪ'fjuːs, *vb* dɪ'fjuːz] *adj* diffuso(a) ♦ *vt* diffondere

dig [dɪg] (*pt, pp* **dug**) *vt* (*hole*) scavare; (*garden*) vangare ♦ *n* (*prod*) gomitata; (*archaeological*) scavo; **~ into** *vt fus* (*savings*) scavare in; **to ~ one's nails into** conficcare le unghie in; **~ up** *vt* (*tree etc*) sradicare; (*information*) scavare fuori

digest [*vb* daɪ'dʒɛst, *n* 'daɪdʒɛst] *vt* digerire ♦ *n* compendio; **~ion** [dɪ'dʒɛstʃən] *n* digestione *f*; **~ive** *adj* (*juices, system*) digerente

digit ['dɪdʒɪt] *n* cifra; (*finger*) dito; **~al** *adj* digitale; **~al camera** *n* macchina fotografica digitale; **~al TV** *n* televisione *f* digitale

dignified ['dɪgnɪfaɪd] *adj* dignitoso(a)

dignity ['dɪgnɪtɪ] *n* dignità

digress [daɪ'grɛs] *vi*: **to ~ from** divagare da

digs [dɪgz] (*BRIT: inf*) *npl* camera ammobiliata

dike [daɪk] *n* = **dyke**

dilapidated [dɪ'læpɪdeɪtɪd] *adj* cadente

dilemma [daɪ'lɛmə] *n* dilemma *m*

diligent ['dɪlɪdʒənt] *adj* diligente

dilute [daɪ'lu:t] *vt* diluire; (*with water*) annacquare

dim [dɪm] *adj* (*light*) debole; (*outline, figure*) vago(a); (*room*) in penombra; (*inf: person*) tonto(a) ♦ *vt* (*light*) abbassare

dime [daɪm] (*US*) *n = 10 cents*

dimension [daɪ'mɛnʃən] *n* dimensione *f*

diminish [dɪ'mɪnɪʃ] *vt, vi* diminuire

diminutive [dɪ'mɪnjutɪv] *adj* minuscolo(a) ♦ *n* (*LING*) diminutivo

dimmers ['dɪməz] (*US*) *npl* (*AUT*) anabbaglianti *mpl*; luci *fpl* di posizione

dimple ['dɪmpl] *n* fossetta

din [dɪn] *n* chiasso, fracasso

dine [daɪn] *vi* pranzare; **~r** *n* (*person*) cliente *m/f*; (*US: place*) tavola calda

dinghy ['dɪŋgɪ] *n* battello pneumatico; (*also:* **rubber ~**) gommone *m*

dingy ['dɪndʒɪ] *adj* grigio(a)

dining car ['daɪnɪŋ-] (*BRIT*) *n* vagone *m* ristorante

dining room ['daɪnɪŋ-] *n* sala da pranzo

dinner ['dɪnə*] *n* (*lunch*) pranzo; (*evening meal*) cena; (*public*) banchetto; **~ jacket** *n* smoking *m inv*; **~ party** *n* cena; **~ time** *n* ora di pranzo (*or* cena)

dip [dɪp] *n* discesa; (*in sea*) bagno; (*CULIN*) salsetta ♦ *vt* immergere; bagnare; (*BRIT: AUT: lights*) abbassare ♦ *vi* abbassarsi

diploma [dɪ'pləumə] *n* diploma *m*

diplomacy [dɪ'pləuməsɪ] *n* diplomazia

diplomat ['dɪpləmæt] *n* diplomatico; **~ic** [dɪplə'mætɪk] *adj* diplomatico(a)

diprod ['dɪprɔd] (*US*) *n* = **dipstick**

dipstick ['dɪpstɪk] *n* (*AUT*) indicatore *m* di livello dell'olio

dipswitch ['dɪpswɪtʃ] (*BRIT*) *n* (*AUT*) levetta dei fari

dire [daɪə*] *adj* terribile; estremo(a)

direct [daɪ'rɛkt] *adj* diretto(a) ♦ *vt* dirigere; (*order*): **to ~ sb to do sth** dare direttive a qn di fare qc ♦ *adv* direttamente; **can you ~ me to ...?** mi può indicare la strada per ...?

direction [dɪ'rɛkʃən] *n* direzione *f*; **~s** *npl* (*advice*) chiarimenti *mpl*; **sense of ~** senso dell'orientamento; **~s for use** istruzioni *fpl*

directly [dɪ'rɛktlɪ] *adv* (*in straight line*) direttamente; (*at once*) subito

director [dɪ'rɛktə*] *n* direttore/trice; amministratore/trice; (*THEATRE, CINEMA*) regista *m/f*

directory [dɪ'rɛktərɪ] *n* elenco; **~ enquiries**, **~ assistance** (*US*) *n* informazioni *fpl* elenco abbonati *inv*

dirt [də:t] *n* sporcizia; immondizia; (*earth*) terra; **~-cheap** *adj* a due soldi; **~y** *adj* sporco(a) ♦ *vt* sporcare; **~y trick** *n* brutto scherzo

disability [dɪsə'bɪlɪtɪ] *n* invalidità *f inv*; (*LAW*) incapacità *f inv*

disabled [dɪs'eɪbld] *adj* invalido(a); (*mentally*) ritardato(a) ♦ *npl*: **the ~** gli invalidi

disadvantage [dɪsəd'vɑːntɪdʒ] *n* svantaggio

disagree [dɪsə'gri:] *vi* (*differ*) discordare; (*be against, think otherwise*): **to ~ (with)** essere in disaccordo (con), dissentire (da); **~able** *adj* sgradevole; (*person*) antipatico(a); **~ment** *n* disaccordo; (*argument*) dissapore *m*

disallow [dɪsə'lau] *vt* (*appeal*) respingere

disappear [dɪsə'pɪə*] *vi* scomparire; **~ance** *n* scomparsa

disappoint [dɪsə'pɔɪnt] *vt* deludere; **~ed** *adj* deluso(a); **~ing** *adj* deludente; **~ment** *n* delusione *f*

disapproval [dɪsə'pru:vəl] *n* disapprovazione *f*

disapprove [dɪsə'pru:v] *vi*: **to ~ of** disapprovare

disarm [dɪs'ɑːm] *vt* disarmare; **~ament** *n* disarmo

disarray [dɪsə'reɪ] *n*: **in ~** (*army*) in rotta; (*organization*) in uno stato di confusione; (*clothes, hair*) in disordine

disaster [dɪ'zɑ:stə*] n disastro
disband [dɪs'bænd] vt sbandare; (MIL)
congedare ♦ vi sciogliersi
disbelief ['dɪsbə'li:f] n incredulità
disc [dɪsk] n disco; (COMPUT) = **disk**
discard [dɪs'kɑ:d] vt (old things) scartare;
(fig) abbandonare
discern [dɪ'sə:n] vt discernere, distinguere;
~**ing** adj perspicace
discharge [vb dɪs'tʃɑ:dʒ, n 'dɪstʃɑ:dʒ] vt
(duties) compiere; (ELEC, waste etc)
scaricare; (MED) emettere; (patient)
dimettere; (employee) licenziare; (soldier)
congedare; (defendant) liberare ♦ n (ELEC)
scarica; (MED) emissione f; (dismissal)
licenziamento; congedo; liberazione f
disciple [dɪ'saɪpl] n discepolo
discipline ['dɪsɪplɪn] n disciplina ♦ vt
disciplinare; (punish) punire
disc jockey n disc jockey m inv
disclaim [dɪs'kleɪm] vt negare, smentire
disclose [dɪs'kləʊz] vt rivelare, svelare;
disclosure [-'kləʊʒə*] n rivelazione f
disco ['dɪskəʊ] n abbr = **discotheque**
discoloured [dɪs'kʌləd] (US **discolored**) adj
scolorito(a); ingiallito(a)
discomfort [dɪs'kʌmfət] n disagio; (lack of
comfort) scomodità f inv
disconcert [dɪskən'sə:t] vt sconcertare
disconnect [dɪskə'nekt] vt sconnettere,
staccare; (ELEC, RADIO) staccare; (gas, water)
chiudere
discontent [dɪskən'tent] n scontentezza;
~**ed** adj scontento(a)
discontinue [dɪskən'tɪnju:] vt smettere,
cessare; **"~d"** (COMM) "fuori produzione"
discord ['dɪskɔ:d] n disaccordo; (MUS)
dissonanza
discotheque ['dɪskəʊtek] n discoteca
discount [n 'dɪskaunt, vb dɪs'kaunt] n sconto
♦ vt scontare; (idea) non badare a
discourage [dɪs'kʌrɪdʒ] vt scoraggiare
discourteous [dɪs'kə:tɪəs] adj scortese
discover [dɪs'kʌvə*] vt scoprire; ~**y** n
scoperta
discredit [dɪs'kredɪt] vt screditare; mettere
in dubbio

discreet [dɪ'skri:t] adj discreto(a)
discrepancy [dɪ'skrepənsɪ] n discrepanza
discriminate [dɪ'skrɪmɪneɪt] vi: **to ~
between** distinguere tra; **to ~ against**
discriminare contro; **discriminating** adj
fine, giudizioso(a); **discrimination**
[-'neɪʃən] n discriminazione f; (judgment)
discernimento
discuss [dɪ'skʌs] vt discutere; (debate)
dibattere; ~**ion** [dɪ'skʌʃən] n discussione f
disdain [dɪs'deɪn] n disdegno
disease [dɪ'zi:z] n malattia
disembark [dɪsɪm'bɑ:k] vt, vi sbarcare
disentangle [dɪsɪn'tæŋgl] vt liberare; (wool
etc) sbrogliare
disfigure [dɪs'fɪgə*] vt sfigurare
disgrace [dɪs'greɪs] n vergogna; (disfavour)
disgrazia ♦ vt disonorare, far cadere in
disgrazia; ~**ful** adj scandaloso(a),
vergognoso(a)
disgruntled [dɪs'grʌntld] adj scontento(a),
di cattivo umore
disguise [dɪs'gaɪz] n travestimento ♦ vt: **to
~ (as)** travestire (da); **in ~** travestito(a)
disgust [dɪs'gʌst] n disgusto, nausea ♦ vt
disgustare, far schifo a; ~**ing** adj
disgustoso(a); ripugnante
dish [dɪʃ] n piatto; **to do** or **wash the ~es**
fare i piatti; **~ out** distribuire; **~ up**
servire; ~**cloth** n strofinaccio
dishearten [dɪs'hɑ:tn] vt scoraggiare
dishevelled [dɪ'ʃevəld] (US **disheveled**) adj
arruffato(a); scapigliato(a)
dishonest [dɪs'ɒnɪst] adj disonesto(a)
dishonour [dɪs'ɒnə*] (US **dishonor**) n
disonore m; ~**able** adj disonorevole
dishtowel ['dɪʃtauəl] (US) n strofinaccio dei
piatti
dishwasher ['dɪʃwɒʃə*] n lavastoviglie f inv
disillusion [dɪsɪ'lu:ʒən] vt disilludere,
disingannare
disinfect [dɪsɪn'fekt] vt disinfettare; ~**ant** n
disinfettante m
disintegrate [dɪs'ɪntɪgreɪt] vi disintegrarsi
disinterested [dɪs'ɪntrəstɪd] adj
disinteressato(a)
disjointed [dɪs'dʒɔɪntɪd] adj sconnesso(a)

disk [dɪsk] n (COMPUT) disco; **single-/ double-sided ~** disco a facciata singola/ doppia; **~ drive** n lettore m; **~ette** (US) n = **disk**

dislike [dɪs'laɪk] n antipatia, avversione f; (gen pl) cosa che non piace ♦ vt: **he ~s it** non gli piace

dislocate ['dɪsləkeɪt] vt slogare

dislodge [dɪs'lɒdʒ] vt rimuovere

disloyal [dɪs'lɔɪəl] adj sleale

dismal ['dɪzml] adj triste, cupo(a)

dismantle [dɪs'mæntl] vt (machine) smontare

dismay [dɪs'meɪ] n costernazione f ♦ vt sgomentare

dismiss [dɪs'mɪs] vt congedare; (employee) licenziare; (idea) scacciare; (LAW) respingere; **~al** n congedo; licenziamento

dismount [dɪs'maunt] vi scendere

disobedience [dɪsə'biːdɪəns] n disubbidienza

disobedient [dɪsə'biːdɪənt] adj disubbidiente

disobey [dɪsə'beɪ] vt disubbidire a

disorder [dɪs'ɔːdə*] n disordine m; (rioting) tumulto; (MED) disturbo; **~ly** adj disordinato(a); tumultuoso(a)

disorientated [dɪs'ɔːrɪenteɪtd] adj disorientato(a)

disown [dɪs'əun] vt rinnegare

disparaging [dɪs'pærɪdʒɪŋ] adj spregiativo(a), sprezzante

dispassionate [dɪs'pæʃənət] adj calmo(a), freddo(a); imparziale

dispatch [dɪs'pætʃ] vt spedire, inviare ♦ n spedizione f, invio; (MIL, PRESS) dispaccio

dispel [dɪs'pel] vt dissipare, scacciare

dispense [dɪs'pens] vt distribuire, amministrare; **~ with** fus fare a meno di; **~r** n (container) distributore m; **dispensing chemist** (BRIT) n farmacista m/f

disperse [dɪs'pɜːs] vt disperdere; (knowledge) disseminare ♦ vi disperdersi

dispirited [dɪs'pɪrɪtɪd] adj scoraggiato(a), abbattuto(a)

displace [dɪs'pleɪs] vt spostare; **~d person**

n (POL) profugo/a

display [dɪs'pleɪ] n esposizione f; (of feeling etc) manifestazione f; (screen) schermo ♦ vt mostrare; (goods) esporre; (pej) ostentare

displease [dɪs'pliːz] vt dispiacere a, scontentare; **~d with** scontento di; **displeasure** [-'pleʒə*] n dispiacere m

disposable [dɪs'pəuzəbl] adj (pack etc) a perdere; (income) disponibile; **~ nappy** n pannolino di carta

disposal [dɪs'pəuzl] n eliminazione f; (of property) cessione f; **at one's ~** alla sua disposizione

dispose [dɪs'pəuz] vi: **~ of** sbarazzarsi di; **~d** adj: **~d to do** disposto(a) a fare; **disposition** [-'zɪʃən] n disposizione f; (temperament) carattere m

disproportionate [dɪsprə'pɔːʃənət] adj sproporzionato(a)

disprove [dɪs'pruːv] vt confutare

dispute [dɪs'pjuːt] n disputa; (also: **industrial ~**) controversia (sindacale) ♦ vt contestare; (matter) discutere; (victory) disputare

disqualify [dɪs'kwɒlɪfaɪ] vt (SPORT) squalificare; **to ~ sb from sth/from doing** rendere qn incapace a qc/a fare; squalificare qn da qc/da fare; **to ~ sb from driving** ritirare la patente a qn

disquiet [dɪs'kwaɪət] n inquietudine f

disregard [dɪsrɪ'gɑːd] vt non far caso a, non badare a

disrepair [dɪsrɪ'pɛə*] n: **to fall into ~** (building) andare in rovina; (machine) deteriorarsi

disreputable [dɪs'repjutəbl] adj poco raccomandabile; indecente

disrupt [dɪs'rʌpt] vt disturbare; creare scompiglio in

dissatisfaction [dɪssætɪsˈfækʃən] n scontentezza, insoddisfazione f

dissect [dɪ'sekt] vt sezionare

dissent [dɪ'sent] n dissenso

dissertation [dɪsə'teɪʃən] n tesi f inv, dissertazione f

disservice [dɪs'sɜːvɪs] n: **to do sb a ~** fare un cattivo servizio a qn

dissimilar [dɪ'sɪmɪlə*] adj: **~ (to)** dissimile

or diverso(a) (da)

dissipate ['dɪsɪpeɪt] *vt* dissipare

dissolve [dɪ'zɒlv] *vt* dissolvere, sciogliere; (*POL, marriage etc*) sciogliere ♦ *vi* dissolversi, sciogliersi

distance ['dɪstns] *n* distanza; **in the ~** in lontananza

distant ['dɪstnt] *adj* lontano(a), distante; (*manner*) riservato(a), freddo(a)

distaste [dɪs'teɪst] *n* ripugnanza; **~ful** *adj* ripugnante, sgradevole

distended [dɪs'tɛndɪd] *adj* (*stomach*) dilatato(a)

distil [dɪs'tɪl] (*US* **distill**) *vt* distillare; **~lery** *n* distilleria

distinct [dɪs'tɪŋkt] *adj* distinto(a); **as ~ from** a differenza di; **~ion** [dɪs'tɪŋkʃən] *n* distinzione *f*; (*in exam*) lode *f*; **~ive** *adj* distintivo(a)

distinguish [dɪs'tɪŋgwɪʃ] *vt* distinguere; discernere; **~ed** *adj* (*eminent*) eminente; **~ing** *adj* (*feature*) distinto(a), caratteristico(a)

distort [dɪs'tɔːt] *vt* distorcere; (*TECH*) deformare

distract [dɪs'trækt] *vt* distrarre; **~ed** *adj* distratto(a); **~ion** [dɪs'trækʃən] *n* distrazione *f*

distraught [dɪs'trɔːt] *adj* stravolto(a)

distress [dɪs'trɛs] *n* angoscia ♦ *vt* affliggere; **~ing** *adj* doloroso(a); **~ signal** *n* segnale *m* di soccorso

distribute [dɪs'trɪbjuːt] *vt* distribuire; **distribution** [-'bjuːʃən] *n* distribuzione *f*; **distributor** *n* distributore *m*

district ['dɪstrɪkt] *n* (*of country*) regione *f*; (*of town*) quartiere *m*; (*ADMIN*) distretto; **~ attorney** (*US*) *n* ≈ sostituto procuratore *m* della Repubblica; **~ nurse** (*BRIT*) *n* infermiera di quartiere

distrust [dɪs'trʌst] *n* diffidenza, sfiducia ♦ *vt* non aver fiducia in

disturb [dɪs'tɜːb] *vt* disturbare; **~ance** *n* disturbo; (*political etc*) disordini *mpl*; **~ed** *adj* (*worried, upset*) turbato(a); **emotionally ~ed** con turbe emotive; **~ing** *adj* sconvolgente

disuse [dɪs'juːs] *n*: **to fall into ~** cadere in disuso

disused [dɪs'juːzd] *adj* abbandonato(a)

ditch [dɪtʃ] *n* fossa ♦ *vt* (*inf*) piantare in asso

dither ['dɪðə*] (*pej*) *vi* vacillare

ditto ['dɪtəu] *adv* idem

dive [daɪv] *n* tuffo; (*of submarine*) immersione *f* ♦ *vi* tuffarsi; immergersi; **~r** *n* tuffatore/trice; palombaro

diverse [daɪ'vəːs] *adj* vario(a)

diversion [daɪ'vəːʃən] *n* (*BRIT: AUT*) deviazione *f*; (*distraction*) divertimento

divert [daɪ'vəːt] *vt* deviare

divide [dɪ'vaɪd] *vt* dividere; (*separate*) separare ♦ *vi* dividersi; **~d highway** (*US*) *n* strada a doppia carreggiata

dividend ['dɪvɪdɛnd] *n* dividendo; (*fig*): **to pay ~s** dare dei frutti

divine [dɪ'vaɪn] *adj* divino(a)

diving ['daɪvɪŋ] *n* tuffo; **~ board** *n* trampolino

divinity [dɪ'vɪnɪtɪ] *n* divinità *f inv*; teologia

division [dɪ'vɪʒən] *n* divisione *f*; separazione *f*; (*esp FOOTBALL*) serie *f*

divorce [dɪ'vɔːs] *n* divorzio ♦ *vt* divorziare da; (*dissociate*) separare; **~d** *adj* divorziato(a); **~e** [-'siː] *n* divorziato/a

D.I.Y. (*BRIT*) *n abbr* = **do-it-yourself**

dizzy ['dɪzɪ] *adj*: **to feel ~** avere il capogiro

DJ *n abbr* = **disc jockey**

KEYWORD

do [duː] (*pt* **did**, *pp* **done**) *n* (*inf: party etc*) festa; **it was rather a grand ~** è stato un ricevimento piuttosto importante
♦ *vb* **1** (*in negative constructions*) non tradotto; **I don't understand** non capisco
2 (*to form questions*) non tradotto; **didn't you know?** non lo sapevi?; **why didn't you come?** perché non sei venuto?
3 (*for emphasis, in polite expressions*): **she does seem rather late** sembra essere piuttosto in ritardo; **~ sit down** si accomodi la prego, prego si sieda; **~ take care!** mi raccomando, sta attento!
4 (*used to avoid repeating vb*): **she swims better than I ~** lei nuota meglio di me; **~**

you agree? – yes, I ~/no, I don't sei d'accordo? – sì/no; **she lives in Glasgow – so ~ I** lei vive a Glasgow — anch'io; **he asked me to help him and I did** mi ha chiesto di aiutarlo ed io l'ho fatto
5 (*in question tags*): **you like him, don't you?** ti piace, vero?; **I don't know him, ~ I?** non lo conosco, vero?
♦ *vt* (*gen, carry out, perform etc*) fare; **what are you ~ing tonight?** che fa stasera?; **to ~ the cooking** cucinare; **to ~ the washing-up** fare i piatti; **to ~ one's teeth** lavarsi i denti; **to ~ one's hair/nails** farsi i capelli/ le unghie; **the car was ~ing 100** la macchina faceva i 100 all'ora
♦ *vi* 1 (*act, behave*) fare; **~ as I ~** faccia come me, faccia come faccio io
2 (*get on, fare*) andare; **he's ~ing well/ badly at school** va bene/male a scuola; **how ~ you ~?** piacere!
3 (*suit*) andare bene; **this room will ~** questa stanza va bene
4 (*be sufficient*) bastare; **will £10 ~?** basteranno 10 sterline?; **that'll ~** basta così; **that'll ~!** (*in annoyance*) ora basta!; **to make ~ (with)** arrangiarsi (con)
do away with *vt fus* (*kill*) far fuori; (*abolish*) abolire
do up *vt* (*laces*) allacciare; (*dress, buttons*) abbottonare; (*renovate: room, house*) rimettere a nuovo, rifare
do with *vt fus* (*need*) aver bisogno di; (*be connected*): **what has it got to ~ with you?** e tu che c'entri?; **I won't have anything to ~ with it** non voglio avere niente a che farci; **it has to ~ with money** si tratta di soldi
do without *vi* fare senza ♦ *vt fus* fare a meno di

---

dock [dɔk] *n* (*NAUT*) bacino; (*LAW*) banco degli imputati ♦ *vi* entrare in bacino; (*SPACE*) agganciarsi; **~s** *npl* (*NAUT*) dock *m inv*; **~er** *n* scaricatore *m*; **~yard** *n* cantiere *m* (navale)
doctor ['dɔktə*] *n* medico/a; (*Ph.D. etc*) dottore/essa ♦ *vt* (*drink etc*) adulterare; **D~**

of Philosophy *n* dottorato di ricerca; (*person*) titolare *m/f* di un dottorato di ricerca
doctrine ['dɔktrɪn] *n* dottrina
document ['dɔkjumənt] *n* documento; **~ary** [-'mentəri] *adj* (*evidence*) documentato(a) ♦ *n* documentario
dodge [dɔdʒ] *n* trucco; schivata ♦ *vt* schivare, eludere
dodgems ['dɔdʒəmz] (*BRIT*) *npl* autoscontri *mpl*
doe [dəu] *n* (*deer*) femmina di daino; (*rabbit*) coniglia
does [dʌz] *vb see* **do**; **doesn't** = **does not**
dog [dɔg] *n* cane *m* ♦ *vt* (*follow closely*) pedinare; (*fig: memory etc*) perseguitare; **~ collar** *n* collare *m* di cane; (*fig*) collarino; **~-eared** *adj* (*book*) con orecchie
dogged ['dɔgɪd] *adj* ostinato(a), tenace
dogsbody ['dɔgzbɔdɪ] (*BRIT: inf*) *n* factotum *m inv*
doing ['du:ɪŋ] *n*: **this is your ~** è opera tua, sei stato tu
do-it-yourself *n* il far da sé
doldrums ['dɔldrəmz] *npl* (*fig*): **to be in the ~** avere un brutto periodo
dole [dəul] (*BRIT*) *n* sussidio di disoccu- pazione; **to be on the ~** vivere del sussidio; **~ out** *vt* distribuire
doll [dɔl] *n* bambola; **~ed up** (*inf*) *adj* in ghingheri
dollar ['dɔlə*] *n* dollaro
dolly ['dɔlɪ] *n* bambola
dolphin ['dɔlfɪn] *n* delfino
domain [də'meɪn] *n* dominio
dome [dəum] *n* cupola
domestic [də'mestɪk] *adj* (*duty, happiness, animal*) domestico(a); (*policy, affairs, flights*) nazionale; **~ated** *adj* addomesticato(a)
dominant ['dɔmɪnənt] *adj* dominante
dominate ['dɔmɪneɪt] *vt* dominare
domineering [dɔmɪ'nɪərɪŋ] *adj* dispotico(a), autoritario(a)
dominion [də'mɪnɪən] *n* dominio; sovranità; dominion *m inv*
domino ['dɔmɪnəu] (*pl* **~es**) *n* domino; **~es** *n* (*game*) gioco del domino

don [dɔn] (BRIT) n docente m/f universitario(a)

donate [dəˈneɪt] vt donare

done [dʌn] pp of **do**

donkey [ˈdɔŋkɪ] n asino

donor [ˈdəunə*] n donatore/trice; ~ **card** n tessera di donatore di organi

don't [dəunt] = **do not**

doodle [ˈduːdl] vi scarabocchiare

doom [duːm] n destino; rovina ♦ vt: **to be ~ed (to failure)** essere predestinato(a) (a fallire)

door [dɔː*] n porta; ~**bell** n campanello; ~ **handle** n maniglia; ~**man** (irreg) n (in hotel) portiere m in livrea; ~**mat** n stuoia della porta; ~**step** n gradino della porta; ~**way** n porta

dope [dəup] n (inf: drugs) roba ♦ vt drogare

dormant [ˈdɔːmənt] adj inattivo(a)

dormitory [ˈdɔːmɪtrɪ] n dormitorio; (US) casa dello studente

dormouse [ˈdɔːmaus] (pl **dormice**) n ghiro

dosage [ˈdəusɪdʒ] n posologia

dose [dəus] n dose f; (bout) attacco

doss house [ˈdɔs-] (BRIT) n asilo notturno

dot [dɔt] n punto; macchiolina ♦ vt: ~**ted with** punteggiato(a) di; **on the ~** in punto; ~**ted line** [ˈdɔtɪd-] n linea punteggiata

double [ˈdʌbl] adj doppio(a) ♦ adv (twice): **to cost ~ (sth)** costare il doppio (di qc) ♦ n sosia m inv ♦ vt raddoppiare; (fold) piegare doppio or in due ♦ vi raddoppiarsi; **at the ~** (BRIT), **on the ~** a passo di corsa; ~ **bass** n contrabbasso; ~ **bed** n letto matrimoniale; ~**-breasted** adj a doppio petto; ~**cross** vt fare il doppio gioco con; ~**decker** n autobus m inv a due piani; ~ **glazing** (BRIT) n doppi vetri mpl; ~ **room** n camera per due; ~**s** n (TENNIS) doppio; **doubly** adv doppiamente

doubt [daut] n dubbio ♦ vt dubitare di; **to ~ that** dubitare che +sub; ~**ful** adj dubbioso(a), incerto(a); (person) equivoco(a); ~**less** adv indubbiamente

dough [dəu] n pasta, impasto; ~**nut** n bombolone m

dove [dʌv] n colombo/a

Dover [ˈdəuvə*] n Dover f

dovetail [ˈdʌvteɪl] vi (fig) combaciare

dowdy [ˈdaudɪ] adj trasandato(a); malvestito(a)

down [daun] n piume fpl ♦ adv giù, di sotto ♦ prep giù per ♦ vt (inf: drink) scolarsi; ~ **with X!** abbasso X!; ~**-and-out** n barbone m; ~**-at-heel** adj scalcagnato(a); ~**cast** adj abbattuto(a); ~**fall** n caduta; rovina; ~**hearted** adj scoraggiato(a); ~**hill** adv: **to go ~hill** andare in discesa; (fig) lasciarsi andare; andare a rotoli; ~**load** vt (COMPUT) scaricare; ~ **payment** n acconto; ~**pour** n scroscio di pioggia; ~**right** adj franco(a); (refusal) assoluto(a); ~**size** vi (ECON: company) ridurre il personale; ~**stairs** adv di sotto; al piano inferiore; ~**stream** adv a valle; ~**-to-earth** adj pratico(a); ~**town** adv in città; ~ **under** adv (Australia etc) agli antipodi; ~**ward** [ˈdaunwəd] adj, adv in giù, in discesa; ~**wards** [ˈdaunwədz] adv = ~**ward**

Downing Street

i *Al numero 10 di* **Downing Street**, *nel quartiere di Westminster a Londra, si trova la residenza del primo ministro inglese, al numero 11 quella del* **Chancellor of the Exchequer**.

---

dowry [ˈdaurɪ] n dote f

doz. abbr = **dozen**

doze [dəuz] vi sonnecchiare; ~ **off** vi appisolarsi

dozen [ˈdʌzn] n dozzina; **a ~ books** una dozzina di libri; ~**s of** decine fpl di

Dr. abbr (= doctor) dott.; (in street names) = **drive**

drab [dræb] adj tetro(a), grigio(a)

draft [drɑːft] n abbozzo; (POL) bozza; (COMM) tratta; (US: call-up) leva ♦ vt abbozzare; see also **draught**

draftsman [ˈdrɑːftsmən] (US) n = **draughtsman**

drag [dræg] vt trascinare; (river) dragare ♦ vi trascinarsi ♦ n (inf) noioso/a; noia, fatica; (women's clothing): **in ~** travestito (da donna); **~ on** vi tirar avanti lentamente

dragon ['drægən] n drago

dragonfly ['drægənflaɪ] n libellula

drain [dreɪn] n (for sewage) fogna; (on resources) salasso ♦ vt (land, marshes) prosciugare; (vegetables) scolare ♦ vi (water) defluire (via); **~age** n prosciugamento; fognatura; **~ing board** (US **~board**) n piano del lavello; **~pipe** n tubo di scarico

drama ['drɑːmə] n (art) dramma m, teatro; (play) commedia; (event) dramma; **~tic** [drə'mætɪk] adj drammatico(a); **~tist** ['dræmətɪst] n drammaturgo/a; **~tize** ['dræmətaɪz] vt (events) drammatizzare

drank [dræŋk] pt of **drink**

drape [dreɪp] vt drappeggiare; **~r** (BRIT) n negoziante m/f di stoffe; **~s** (US) npl (curtains) tende fpl

drastic ['dræstɪk] adj drastico(a)

draught [drɑːft] (US **draft**) n corrente f d'aria; (NAUT) pescaggio; **on ~** (beer) alla spina; **~ beer** n birra alla spina; **~board** (BRIT) n scacchiera; **~s** (BRIT) n (gioco della) dama

draughtsman ['drɑːftsmən] (US **draftsman**) (irreg) n disegnatore m

draw [drɔː] (pt **drew**, pp **drawn**) vt tirare; (take out) estrarre; (attract) attirare; (picture) disegnare; (line, circle) tracciare; (money) ritirare ♦ vi (SPORT) pareggiare ♦ n pareggio; (in lottery) estrazione f; **to ~ near** avvicinarsi; **~ out** vi (lengthen) allungarsi ♦ vt (money) ritirare; **~ up** vi (stop) arrestarsi, fermarsi ♦ vt (chair) avvicinare; (document) compilare; **~back** n svantaggio, inconveniente m; **~bridge** n ponte m levatoio

drawer [drɔː*] n cassetto

drawing ['drɔːɪŋ] n disegno; **~ board** n tavola da disegno; **~ pin** (BRIT) n puntina da disegno; **~ room** n salotto

drawl [drɔːl] n pronuncia strascicata

drawn [drɔːn] pp of **draw**

dread [dred] n terrore m ♦ vt tremare all'idea di; **~ful** adj terribile

dream [driːm] (pt, pp **dreamed** or **dreamt**) n sogno ♦ vt, vi sognare; **~y** adj sognante

dreary ['drɪərɪ] adj tetro(a); monotono(a)

dredge [dredʒ] vt dragare

dregs [dregz] npl feccia

drench [drentʃ] vt inzuppare

dress [dres] n vestito; (no pl: clothing) abbigliamento ♦ vt vestire; (wound) fasciare ♦ vi vestirsi; **to get ~ed** vestirsi; **~ up** vi vestirsi a festa; (in fancy dress) vestirsi in costume; **~ circle** (BRIT) n prima galleria; **~er** n (BRIT: cupboard) credenza; (US) cassettone m; **~ing** n (MED) benda; (CULIN) condimento; **~ing gown** (BRIT) n vestaglia; **~ing room** n (THEATRE) camerino; (SPORT) spogliatoio; **~ing table** n toilette f inv; **~maker** n sarta; **~ rehearsal** n prova generale; **~y** (inf) adj elegante

drew [druː] pt of **draw**

dribble ['drɪbl] vi (baby) sbavare ♦ vt (ball) dribblare

dried [draɪd] adj (fruit, beans) secco(a); (eggs, milk) in polvere

drier ['draɪə*] n = **dryer**

drift [drɪft] n (of current etc) direzione f; forza; (of snow) cumulo; turbine m; (general meaning) senso ♦ vi (boat) essere trasportato(a) dalla corrente; (sand, snow) ammucchiarsi; **~wood** n resti mpl della mareggiata

drill [drɪl] n trapano; (MIL) esercitazione f ♦ vt trapanare; (troops) addestrare ♦ vi (for oil) fare trivellazioni

drink [drɪŋk] (pt **drank**, pp **drunk**) n bevanda, bibita; (alcoholic) bicchierino; (sip) sorso ♦ vt, vi bere; **to have a ~** bere qualcosa; **a ~ of water** un po' d'acqua; **~er** n bevitore/trice; **~ing water** n acqua potabile

drip [drɪp] n goccia; gocciolamento; (MED) fleboclisi f inv ♦ vi gocciolare; (tap) sgocciolare; **~-dry** adj (shirt) che non si stira; **~ping** n grasso d'arrosto

drive [draɪv] (pt **drove**, pp **driven**) n passeggiata or giro in macchina; (also: **~way**) viale m d'accesso; (energy) energia; (campaign) campagna; (also: **disk ~**) lettore *m* ♦ *vt* guidare; (*nail*) piantare; (*push*) cacciare, spingere; (*TECH: motor*) azionare; far funzionare ♦ *vi* (*AUT: at controls*) guidare; (: *travel*) andare in macchina; **left-/right-hand ~** guida a sinistra/destra; **to ~ sb mad** far impazzire qn

drivel ['drɪvl] (*inf*) *n* idiozie *fpl*

driven ['drɪvn] *pp of* **drive**

driver ['draɪvə*] *n* conducente *m/f*; (*of taxi*) tassista *m*; (*chauffeur, of bus*) autista *m/f*; **~'s license** (*US*) *n* patente *f* di guida

driveway ['draɪvweɪ] *n* viale *m* d'accesso

driving ['draɪvɪŋ] *n* guida; **~ instructor** *n* istruttore/trice di scuola guida; **~ lesson** *n* lezione *f* di guida; **~ licence** (*BRIT*) *n* patente *f* di guida; **~ mirror** *n* specchietto retrovisore; **~ school** *n* scuola *f* guida *inv*; **~ test** *n* esame *m* di guida

drizzle ['drɪzl] *n* pioggerella

drool [druːl] *vi* sbavare

droop [druːp] *vi* (*flower*) appassire; (*head, shoulders*) chinarsi

drop [drɒp] *n* (*of water*) goccia; (*lessening*) diminuzione *f*; (*fall*) caduta ♦ *vt* lasciare cadere; (*voice, eyes, price*) abbassare; (*set down from car*) far scendere; (*name from list*) lasciare fuori ♦ *vi* (*wind*) cascare; (*wind*) abbassarsi; **~s** *npl* (*MED*) gocce *fpl*; **~ off** *vi* (*sleep*) addormentarsi ♦ *vt* (*passenger*) far scendere; **~ out** *vi* (*withdraw*) ritirarsi; (*student etc*) smettere di studiare; **~-out** *n* (*from society/from university*) chi ha abbandonato (la società/gli studi); **~per** *n* contagocce *m inv*; **~pings** *npl* sterco

drought [draʊt] *n* siccità *f inv*

drove [drəʊv] *pt of* **drive**

drown [draʊn] *vt* affogare; (*fig: noise*) soffocare ♦ *vi* affogare

drowsy ['draʊzɪ] *adj* sonnolento(a), assonnato(a)

drug [drʌg] *n* farmaco; (*narcotic*) droga ♦ *vt* drogare; **to be on ~s** drogarsi; (*MED*) prendere medicinali; **hard/soft ~s** droghe pesanti/leggere; **~ addict** *n* tossicomane *m/f*; **~gist** (*US*) *n* persona che gestisce un *drugstore*; **~store** (*US*) *n* drugstore *m inv*

drum [drʌm] *n* tamburo; (*for oil, petrol*)

fusto ♦ *vi* tamburellare; **~s** *npl* (*set of ~s*) batteria; **~mer** *n* batterista *m/f*

drunk [drʌŋk] *pp of* **drink** ♦ *adj* ubriaco(a); ebbro(a) ♦ *n* (*also*: **~ard**) ubriacone/a; **~en** *adj* ubriaco(a); da ubriaco

dry [draɪ] *adj* secco(a); (*day, clothes*) asciutto(a) ♦ *vt* seccare; (*clothes, hair, hands*) asciugare ♦ *vi* asciugarsi; **~ up** *vi* seccarsi; **~-cleaner's** *n* lavasecco *m inv*; **~-cleaning** *n* pulitura a secco; **~er** *n* (*for hair*) föhn *m inv*, asciugacapelli *m inv*; (*for clothes*) asciugabiancheria; (*US: spin-dryer*) centrifuga; **~ goods store** (*US*) *n* negozio di stoffe; **~ rot** *n* fungo del legno

DSS *n abbr* (= *Department of Social Security*) ministero della Previdenza sociale

DTP *n abbr* (= *desk-top publishing*) desktop publishing *m inv*

dual ['djuəl] *adj* doppio(a); **~ carriageway** (*BRIT*) *n* strada a doppia carreggiata; **~-purpose** *adj* a doppio uso

dubbed [dʌbd] *adj* (*CINEMA*) doppiato(a)

dubious ['djuːbɪəs] *adj* dubbio(a)

Dublin ['dʌblɪn] *n* Dublino *f*

duchess ['dʌtʃɪs] *n* duchessa

duck [dʌk] *n* anatra ♦ *vi* abbassare la testa; **~ling** *n* anatroccolo

duct [dʌkt] *n* condotto; (*ANAT*) canale *m*

dud [dʌd] *n* (*object, tool*): **it's a ~** è inutile, non funziona ♦ *adj*: **~ cheque** (*BRIT*) assegno a vuoto

due [djuː] *adj* dovuto(a); (*expected*) atteso(a); (*fitting*) giusto(a) ♦ *n* dovuto ♦ *adv*: **~ north** diritto verso nord; **~s** *npl* (*for club, union*) quota; (*in harbour*) diritti *mpl* di porto; **in ~ course** a tempo debito; finalmente; **~ to** dovuto a; a causa di; **to be ~ to do** dover fare

duet [djuː'et] *n* duetto

duffel bag ['dʌfl-] *n* sacca da viaggio di tela

duffel coat ['dʌfl-] *n* montgomery *m inv*

dug [dʌg] *pt, pp of* **dig**

duke [djuːk] *n* duca *m*

dull [dʌl] *adj* (*light*) debole; (*boring*) noioso(a); (*slow-witted*) ottuso(a); (*sound, pain*) sordo(a); (*weather, day*) fosco(a), scuro(a) ♦ vt (*pain, grief*) attutire; (*mind, senses*) intorpidire

duly ['dju:lɪ] adv (*on time*) a tempo debito; (*as expected*) debitamente

dumb [dʌm] adj muto(a); (*pej*) stupido(a); **~founded** [dʌm'faundɪd] adj stupito(a), stordito(a)

dummy [dʌmɪ] n (*tailor's model*) manichino; (*TECH, COMM*) riproduzione f; (*BRIT: for baby*) tettarella ♦ adj falso(a), finto(a)

dump [dʌmp] n (*also:* **rubbish ~**) discarica di rifiuti; (*inf: place*) buco ♦ vt (*put down*) scaricare; (*get rid of*) buttar via

dumpling ['dʌmplɪŋ] n specie di gnocco

dumpy ['dʌmpɪ] adj tracagnotto(a)

dunce [dʌns] n (*SCOL*) somaro/a

dung [dʌŋ] n concime m

dungarees [dʌŋgə'ri:z] npl tuta

dungeon ['dʌndʒən] n prigione f sotterranea

dupe [dju:p] n zimbello ♦ vt gabbare, ingannare

duplex ['dju:pleks] (*US*) n (*house*) casa con muro divisorio in comune con un'altra; (*apartment*) appartamento su due piani

duplicate [n 'dju:plɪkət, vb 'dju:plɪkeɪt] n doppio ♦ vt duplicare; **in ~** in doppia copia

durable ['djuərəbl] adj durevole; (*clothes, metal*) resistente

duration [djuə'reɪʃən] n durata

during ['djuərɪŋ] prep durante, nel corso di

dusk [dʌsk] n crepuscolo

dust [dʌst] n polvere f ♦ vt (*furniture*) spolverare; (*cake etc*) to **~ with** cospargere con; **~bin** (*BRIT*) n pattumiera; **~er** n straccio per la polvere; **~man** (*BRIT: irreg*) n netturbino; **~y** adj polveroso(a)

Dutch [dʌtʃ] adj olandese ♦ n (*LING*) olandese m; **the ~** npl gli Olandesi; **to go ~** (*inf*) fare alla romana; **~man/woman** (*irreg*) n olandese m/f

duty ['dju:tɪ] n dovere m; (*tax*) dazio, tassa; **on ~** di servizio; **off ~** libero(a), fuori servizio; **~ chemist's** n farmacia di turno; **~-free** adj esente da dazio

duvet ['du:veɪ] (*BRIT*) n piumino, piumone m

DVD n abbr (= *digital versatile* (*or*) *video*

disk*) DVD m inv

dwarf [dwɔ:f] n nano/a ♦ vt far apparire piccolo

dwell [dwel] (*pt, pp* **dwelt**) vi dimorare; **~ on** vt fus indugiare su

dwindle ['dwɪndl] vi diminuire, decrescere

dye [daɪ] n tinta ♦ vt tingere

dying ['daɪɪŋ] adj morente, moribondo(a)

dyke [daɪk] (*BRIT*) n diga

dynamic [daɪ'næmɪk] adj dinamico(a)

dynamite ['daɪnəmaɪt] n dinamite f

dynamo ['daɪnəməu] n dinamo f inv

dyslexia [dɪs'leksɪə] n dislessia

E, e

E [i:] n (*MUS*) mi m

each [i:tʃ] adj ogni, ciascuno(a) ♦ pron ciascuno(a), ognuno(a); **~ one** ognuno(a); **~ other** si (*or* ci *etc*); **they hate ~ other** si odiano (l'un l'altro); **you are jealous of ~ other** siete gelosi l'uno dell'altro; **they have 2 books ~** hanno 2 libri ciascuno

eager ['i:gə*] adj impaziente; desideroso(a); ardente; **to be ~ for** essere desideroso di, aver gran voglia di

eagle ['i:gl] n aquila

ear [ɪə*] n orecchio; (*of corn*) pannocchia; **~ache** n mal m d'orecchi; **~drum** n timpano

earl [ə:l] (*BRIT*) n conte m

earlier ['ə:lɪə*] adj precedente ♦ adv prima

early ['ə:lɪ] adv presto, di buon'ora; (*ahead of time*) in anticipo ♦ adj (*near the start*) primo(a); (*sooner than expected*) prematuro(a); (*quick: reply*) veloce; **at an ~ hour** di buon'ora; **to have an ~ night** andare a letto presto; **in the ~** *or* **~ in the spring** all'inizio della primavera; **~ retirement** n ritiro anticipato

earmark ['ɪəmɑ:k] vt: **to ~ sth for** destinare qc a

earn [ə:n] vt guadagnare; (*rest, reward*) meritare

earnest ['ə:nɪst] adj serio(a); **in ~** sul serio

earnings ['ə:nɪŋz] npl guadagni mpl;

(salary) stipendio

earphones ['ɪəfəunz] *npl* cuffia

earring ['ɪərɪŋ] *n* orecchino

earshot ['ɪəʃɔt] *n*: **within ~** a portata d'orecchio

earth [ə:θ] *n* terra ♦ *vt (BRIT: ELEC)* mettere a terra; ~**enware** *n* terracotta; stoviglie *fpl* di terracotta; ~**quake** *n* terremoto; ~**y** *adj (fig)* grossolano(a)

ease [i:z] *n* agio, comodo ♦ *vt (soothe)* calmare; *(loosen)* allentare; **to ~ sth out/in** tirare fuori/infilare qc con delicatezza; facilitare l'uscita/l'entrata di qc; **at ~** a proprio agio; *(MIL)* a riposo; **~ off** *or* **up** *vi* diminuire; *(slow down)* rallentare

easel ['i:zl] *n* cavalletto

easily ['i:zɪlɪ] *adv* facilmente

east [i:st] *n* est *m* ♦ *adj* dell'est ♦ *adv* a oriente; **the E~** l'Oriente *m*; *(POL)* l'Est

Easter ['i:stə*] *n* Pasqua; ~ **egg** *n* uovo di Pasqua

easterly ['i:stəlɪ] *adj* dall'est, d'oriente

eastern ['i:stən] *adj* orientale, d'oriente; dell'est

East Germany *n* Germania dell'Est

eastward(s) ['i:stwəd(z)] *adv* verso est, verso levante

easy ['i:zɪ] *adj* facile; *(manner)* disinvolto(a) ♦ *adv*: **to take it** *or* **things ~** prendersela con calma; ~ **chair** *n* poltrona; ~**-going** *adj* accomodante

eat [i:t] *(pt* **ate**, *pp* **eaten**) *vt, vi* mangiare; ~ **away at** *vt fus* rodere; ~ **into** *vt fus* rodere

eaves [i:vz] *npl* gronda

eavesdrop ['i:vzdrɔp] *vi*: **to ~ (on a conversation)** origliare (una conversazione)

ebb [ɛb] *n* riflusso ♦ *vi* rifluire; *(fig: also:* ~ **away)** declinare

ebony ['ɛbənɪ] *n* ebano

EC *n abbr (= European Community)* CEE *f*

ECB *n abbr (= European Central Bank)* BCE *f*

eccentric [ɪk'sɛntrɪk] *adj, n* eccentrico(a)

echo ['ɛkəu] *(pl* ~**es**) *n* eco *m or f* ♦ *vt* ripetere; fare eco a ♦ *vi* echeggiare; dare

un eco

éclair [eɪ'kleə*] *n* ≈ bignè *m inv*

eclipse [ɪ'klɪps] *n* eclissi *f inv*

ecology [ɪ'kɔlədʒɪ] *n* ecologia

e-commerce *n* commercio elettronico

economic [i:kə'nɔmɪk] *adj* economico(a); ~**al** *adj* economico(a); *(person)* econo-mo(a); ~**s** *n* economia ♦ *npl* lato finanziario

economize [ɪ'kɔnəmaɪz] *vi* risparmiare, fare economia

economy [ɪ'kɔnəmɪ] *n* economia; ~ **class** *n (AVIAT)* classe *f* turistica; ~ **size** *n (COMM)* confezione *f* economica

ecstasy ['ɛkstəsɪ] *n* estasi *f inv*

ECU ['eɪkju:] *n abbr (= European Currency Unit)* ECU *m inv*

edge [ɛdʒ] *n* margine *m*; *(of table, plate, cup)* orlo; *(of knife etc)* taglio ♦ *vt* bordare; **on ~** *(fig)* = **edgy**; **to ~ away from** sgattaiolare da; ~**ways** *adv*: **he couldn't get a word in ~ways** non riuscì a dire una parola; **edgy** *adj* nervoso(a)

edible ['ɛdɪbl] *adj* commestibile; *(meal)* mangiabile

edict ['i:dɪkt] *n* editto

Edinburgh ['ɛdɪnbərə] *n* Edimburgo *f*

edit ['ɛdɪt] *vt* curare; ~**ion** [ɪ'dɪʃən] *n* edizione *f*; ~**or** *n (in newspaper)* redattore/ trice; redattore/trice capo; *(of sb's work)* curatore/trice; ~**orial** [-'tɔ:rɪəl] *adj* redazionale, editoriale ♦ *n* editoriale *m*

educate ['ɛdjukeɪt] *vt* istruire; educare

education [ɛdju'keɪʃən] *n* educazione *f*; *(schooling)* istruzione *f*; ~**al** *adj* pedagogico(a); scolastico(a); istruttivo(a)

EEC *n abbr* = **EC**

eel [i:l] *n* anguilla

eerie ['ɪərɪ] *adj* che fa accapponare la pelle

effect [ɪ'fɛkt] *n* effetto ♦ *vt* effettuare; **to take ~** *(law)* entrare in vigore; *(drug)* fare effetto; **in ~** effettivamente; ~**ive** *adj* efficace; *(actual)* effettivo(a); ~**ively** *adv* efficacemente; effettivamente; ~**iveness** *n* efficacia

effeminate [ɪ'fɛmɪnɪt] *adj* effeminato(a)

efficiency [ɪ'fɪʃənsɪ] *n* efficienza

efficient [ɪ'fɪʃənt] *adj* efficiente

effort [ˈɛfət] *n* sforzo

effusive [ɪˈfjuːsɪv] *adj* (*handshake, welcome*) caloroso(a)

e.g. *adv abbr* (= *exempli gratia*) per esempio, p.es.

egg [ɛg] *n* uovo; **hard-boiled/soft-boiled ~** uovo sodo/alla coque; **~ on** *vt* incitare; **~cup** *n* portauovo *m inv*; **~plant** *n* (*esp US*) melanzana; **~shell** *n* guscio d'uovo

ego [ˈiːgəʊ] *n* ego *m inv*

egotism [ˈɛgəʊtɪzəm] *n* egotismo

Egypt [ˈiːdʒɪpt] *n* Egitto; **~ian** [ɪˈdʒɪpʃən] *adj, n* egiziano(a)

eiderdown [ˈaɪdədaʊn] *n* piumino

eight [eɪt] *num* otto; **~een** *num* diciotto; **~h** [eɪtθ] *num* ottavo(a); **~y** *num* ottanta

Eire [ˈɛərə] *n* Repubblica d'Irlanda

either [ˈaɪðə*] *adj* l'uno(a) o l'altro(a); (*both, each*) ciascuno ♦ *pron:* **~ (of them)** (o) l'uno(a) o l'altro(a) ♦ *adv* neanche ♦ *conj:* **~ good or bad** o buono o cattivo; **on ~ side** su ciascun lato; **I don't like ~** non mi piace né l'uno né l'altro; **no, I don't ~** no, neanch'io

eject [ɪˈdʒɛkt] *vt* espellere; lanciare

elaborate [*adj* ɪˈlæbərɪt, *vb* ɪˈlæbəreɪt] *adj* elaborato(a), minuzioso(a) ♦ *vt* elaborare ♦ *vi* fornire i particolari

elastic [ɪˈlæstɪk] *adj* elastico(a) ♦ *n* elastico; **~ band** (*BRIT*) *n* elastico

elated [ɪˈleɪtɪd] *adj* pieno(a) di gioia

elbow [ˈɛlbəʊ] *n* gomito

elder [ˈɛldə*] *adj* maggiore, più vecchio(a) ♦ *n* (*tree*) sambuco; **one's ~s** i più anziani; **~ly** *adj* anziano(a) ♦ *npl:* **the ~ly** gli anziani

eldest [ˈɛldɪst] *adj, n:* **the ~ (child)** il(la) maggiore (dei bambini)

elect [ɪˈlɛkt] *vt* eleggere ♦ *adj:* **the president ~** il presidente designato; **to ~ to do** decidere di fare; **~ion** [ɪˈlɛkʃən] *n* elezione *f;* **~ioneering** [ɪlɛkʃəˈnɪərɪŋ] *n* propaganda elettorale; **~or** *n* elettore/trice; **~orate** *n* elettorato

electric [ɪˈlɛktrɪk] *adj* elettrico(a); **~al** *adj* elettrico(a); **~ blanket** *n* coperta elettrica;

~ fire *n* stufa elettrica

electrician [ɪlɛkˈtrɪʃən] *n* elettricista *m*

electricity [ɪlɛkˈtrɪsɪtɪ] *n* elettricità

electrify [ɪˈlɛktrɪfaɪ] *vt* (*RAIL*) elettrificare; (*audience*) elettrizzare

electrocute [ɪˈlɛktrəʊkjuːt] *vt* fulminare

electronic [ɪlɛkˈtrɒnɪk] *adj* elettronico(a); **~ mail** *n* posta elettronica; **~s** *n* elettronica

elegant [ˈɛlɪgənt] *adj* elegante

element [ˈɛlɪmənt] *n* elemento; (*of heater, kettle etc*) resistenza; **~ary** [-ˈmɛntərɪ] *adj* elementare

elephant [ˈɛlɪfənt] *n* elefante/essa

elevation [ɛlɪˈveɪʃən] *n* elevazione *f*

elevator [ˈɛlɪveɪtə*] *n* elevatore *m;* (*US: lift*) ascensore *m*

eleven [ɪˈlɛvn] *num* undici; **~ses** (*BRIT*) *n* caffè *m* a metà mattina; **~th** *adj* undicesimo(a)

elicit [ɪˈlɪsɪt] *vt:* **to ~ (from)** trarre (da), cavare fuori (da)

eligible [ˈɛlɪdʒəbl] *adj* eleggibile; (*for membership*) che ha i requisiti

elm [ɛlm] *n* olmo

elocution [ɛləˈkjuːʃən] *n* dizione *f*

elongated [ˈiːlɒŋgeɪtɪd] *adj* allungato(a)

elope [ɪˈləʊp] *vi* (*lovers*) scappare; **~ment** *n* fuga

eloquent [ˈɛləkwənt] *adj* eloquente

else [ɛls] *adv* altro; **something ~** qualcos'altro; **somewhere ~** altrove; **everywhere ~** in qualsiasi altro luogo; **nobody ~** nessun altro; **where ~?** in quale altro luogo?; **little ~** poco altro; **~where** *adv* altrove

elude [ɪˈluːd] *vt* eludere

elusive [ɪˈluːsɪv] *adj* elusivo(a)

emaciated [ɪˈmeɪsɪeɪtɪd] *adj* emaciato(a)

E-mail, e-mail *n abbr* (= *electronic mail*) posta elettronica ♦ *vt, vi* mandare un messaggio di posta elettronica a

emanate [ˈɛməneɪt] *vi:* **to ~ from** provenire da

emancipate [ɪˈmænsɪpeɪt] *vt* emancipare

embankment [ɪmˈbæŋkmənt] *n* (*of road, railway*) terrapieno

embark [ɪmˈbɑːk] *vi:* **to ~ (on)** imbarcarsi

(su) ♦ vt imbarcare; **to ~ on** (fig) imbarcarsi in; **~ation** [ɛmbɑː'keɪʃən] n imbarco

embarrass [ɪm'bærəs] vt imbarazzare; **~ed** adj imbarazzato(a); **~ing** adj imbarazzante; **~ment** n imbarazzo

embassy ['ɛmbəsɪ] n ambasciata

embedded [ɪm'bɛdɪd] adj incastrato(a)

embellish [ɪm'bɛlɪʃ] vt abbellire

embers ['ɛmbəz] npl braci fpl

embezzle [ɪm'bɛzl] vt appropriarsi indebitamente di

embitter [ɪm'bɪtə*] vt amareggiare; inasprire

embody [ɪm'bɔdɪ] vt (features) racchiudere, comprendere; (ideas) dar forma concreta a, esprimere

embossed [ɪm'bɔst] adj in rilievo; goffrato(a)

embrace [ɪm'breɪs] vt abbracciare ♦ vi abbracciarsi ♦ n abbraccio

embroider [ɪm'brɔɪdə*] vt ricamare; **~y** n ricamo

embryo ['ɛmbrɪəu] n embrione m

emerald ['ɛmərəld] n smeraldo

emerge [ɪ'mɜːdʒ] vi emergere

emergency [ɪ'mɜːdʒənsɪ] n emergenza; **in an ~** in caso di emergenza; **~ cord** n segnale m d'allarme; **~ exit** n uscita di sicurezza; **~ landing** n atterraggio forzato; **~ services** npl (fire, police, ambulance) servizi mpl di pronto intervento

emery board ['ɛmərɪ-] n limetta di carta smerigliata

emigrate ['ɛmɪgreɪt] vi emigrare

eminent ['ɛmɪnənt] adj eminente

emissions [ɪ'mɪʃənz] npl emissioni fpl

emit [ɪ'mɪt] vt emettere

emotion [ɪ'məuʃən] n emozione f; **~al** adj (person) emotivo(a); (scene) commovente; (tone, speech) carico(a) d'emozione

emperor ['ɛmpərə*] n imperatore m

emphasis ['ɛmfəsɪs] (pl -ases) n enfasi f inv; importanza

emphasize ['ɛmfəsaɪz] vt (word, point) sottolineare; (feature) mettere in evidenza

emphatic [ɛm'fætɪk] adj (strong) vigoroso(a); (unambiguous, clear) netto(a)

empire ['ɛmpaɪə*] n impero

employ [ɪm'plɔɪ] vt impiegare; **~ee** [-'iː] n impiegato/a; **~er** n principale m/f, datore m di lavoro; **~ment** n impiego; **~ment agency** n agenzia di collocamento

empower [ɪm'pauə*] vt: **to ~ sb to do** concedere autorità a qn di fare

empress ['ɛmprɪs] n imperatrice f

emptiness ['ɛmptɪnɪs] n vuoto

empty ['ɛmptɪ] adj vuoto(a); (threat, promise) vano(a) ♦ vt vuotare ♦ vi vuotarsi; (liquid) scaricarsi; **~-handed** adj a mani vuote

EMU n abbr (= economic and monetary union) unione f economica e monetaria

emulate ['ɛmjuleɪt] vt emulare

emulsion [ɪ'mʌlʃən] n emulsione f; **~ (paint)** n colore m a tempera

enable [ɪ'neɪbl] vt: **to ~ sb to do** permettere a qn di fare

enamel [ɪ'næməl] n smalto; (also: **~ paint**) vernice f a smalto

enchant [ɪn'tʃɑːnt] vt incantare; (subj: magic spell) catturare; **~ing** adj incantevole, affascinante

encircle [ɪn'sɜːkl] vt accerchiare

encl. abbr (= enclosed) all

enclave ['ɛnkleɪv] n enclave f

enclose [ɪn'kləuz] vt (land) circondare, recingere; (letter etc): **to ~ (with)** allegare (con); **please find ~d** trovi qui accluso

enclosure [ɪn'kləuʒə*] n recinto

encompass [ɪn'kʌmpəs] vt comprendere

encore [ɔŋ'kɔː*] excl bis ♦ n bis m inv

encounter [ɪn'kauntə*] n incontro ♦ vt incontrare

encourage [ɪn'kʌrɪdʒ] vt incoraggiare; **~ment** n incoraggiamento

encroach [ɪn'krəutʃ] vi: **to ~ (up)on** (rights) usurpare; (time) abusare di; (land) oltrepassare i limiti di

encyclop(a)edia [ensaɪkləu'piːdɪə] n enciclopedia

end [ɛnd] n fine f; (aim) fine m; (of table) bordo estremo; (of pointed object) punta ♦ vt finire; (also: **bring to an ~**, **put an ~ to**) mettere fine a ♦ vi finire; **in the ~** alla fine; **on ~** (*object*) ritto(a); **to stand on ~** (*hair*) rizzarsi; **for hours on ~** per ore ed ore; **~ up** *vi*: **to ~ up in** finire in

endanger [ɪn'deɪndʒə*] *vt* mettere in pericolo

endearing [ɪn'dɪərɪŋ] *adj* accattivante

endeavour [ɪn'devə*] (*US* **endeavor**) *n* sforzo, tentativo ♦ *vi*: **to ~ to do** cercare *or* sforzarsi di fare

ending ['endɪŋ] *n* fine *f*, conclusione *f*; (*LING*) desinenza

endive ['endaɪv] *n* (*curly*) indivia (riccia); (*smooth, flat*) indivia belga

endless ['endlɪs] *adj* senza fine

endorse [ɪn'dɔːs] *vt* (*cheque*) girare; (*approve*) approvare, appoggiare; **~ment** *n* approvazione *f*; (*on driving licence*) *contravvenzione registrata sulla patente*

endurance [ɪn'djuərəns] *n* resistenza; pazienza

endure [ɪn'djuə*] *vt* sopportare, resistere a ♦ *vi* durare

enemy ['enəmɪ] *adj, n* nemico(a)

energetic [enə'dʒetɪk] *adj* energico(a); attivo(a)

energy ['enədʒɪ] *n* energia

enforce [ɪn'fɔːs] *vt* (*LAW*) applicare, far osservare

engage [ɪn'geɪdʒ] *vt* (*hire*) assumere; (*lawyer*) incaricare; (*attention, interest*) assorbire; (*TECH*): **to ~ gear/the clutch** innestare la marcia/la frizione ♦ *vi* (*TECH*) ingranare; **to ~ in** impegnarsi in; **~d** *adj* (*BRIT: busy, in use*) occupato(a); (*betrothed*) fidanzato(a); **to get ~d** fidanzarsi; **~d tone** (*BRIT*) *n* (*TEL*) segnale *m* di occupato; **~ment** *n* impegno, obbligo; appuntamento; (*to marry*) fidanzamento; **~ment ring** *n* anello di fidanzamento

engaging [ɪn'geɪdʒɪŋ] *adj* attraente

engine ['endʒɪn] *n* (*AUT*) motore *m*; (*RAIL*) locomotiva; **~ driver** *n* (*of train*) macchinista *m*

engineer [endʒɪ'nɪə*] *n* ingegnere *m*; (*BRIT: for repairs*) tecnico; (*on ship, US: RAIL*) macchinista *m*; **~ing** *n* ingegneria

England ['ɪŋglənd] *n* Inghilterra

English ['ɪŋglɪʃ] *adj* inglese ♦ *n* (*LING*) inglese *m*; **the ~** *npl* gli Inglesi; **the ~ Channel** *n* la Manica; **~man/woman** (*irreg*) *n* inglese *m/f*

engraving [ɪn'greɪvɪŋ] *n* incisione *f*

engrossed [ɪn'grəust] *adj*: **~ in** assorbito(a) da, preso(a) da

engulf [ɪn'gʌlf] *vt* inghiottire

enhance [ɪn'hɑːns] *vt* accrescere

enjoy [ɪn'dʒɔɪ] *vt* godere; (*have: success, fortune*) avere; **to ~ o.s.** godersela, divertirsi; **~able** *adj* piacevole; **~ment** *n* piacere *m*, godimento

enlarge [ɪn'lɑːdʒ] *vt* ingrandire ♦ *vi*: **to ~ on** (*subject*) dilungarsi su

enlighten [ɪn'laɪtn] *vt* illuminare; dare schiarimenti a; **~ed** *adj* illuminato(a); **~ment** *n*: **the E~ment** (*HISTORY*) l'Illuminismo

enlist [ɪn'lɪst] *vt* arruolare; (*support*) procurare ♦ *vi* arruolarsi

enmity ['enmɪtɪ] *n* inimicizia

enormous [ɪ'nɔːməs] *adj* enorme

enough [ɪ'nʌf] *adj, n*: **~ time/books** assai tempo/libri; **have you got ~?** ne ha abbastanza *or* a sufficienza? ♦ *adv*: **big ~** abbastanza grande; **he has not worked ~** non ha lavorato abbastanza; **~!** basta!; **that's ~, thanks** basta così, grazie; **I've had ~ of him** ne ho abbastanza di lui; **... which, funnily** *or* **oddly ~** ... che, strano a dirsi

enquire [ɪn'kwaɪə*] *vt, vi* = **inquire**

enrage [ɪn'reɪdʒ] *vt* fare arrabbiare

enrich [ɪn'rɪtʃ] *vt* arricchire

enrol [ɪn'rəul] (*US* **enroll**) *vt* iscrivere ♦ *vi* iscriversi; **~ment** (*US* **enrollment**) *n* iscrizione *f*

en suite [ɔn'swiːt] *adj*: **room with ~ bathroom** camera con bagno

ensure [ɪn'ʃuə*] *vt* assicurare; garantire

entail [ɪn'teɪl] *vt* comportare

entangled [ɪn'tæŋgld] *adj*: **to become ~ (in)** impigliarsi (in)

enter ['entə*] *vt* entrare in; (*army*) arruolarsi in; (*competition*) partecipare a; (*sb for a competition*) iscrivere; (*write down*) registrare; (*COMPUT*) inserire ♦ *vi* entrare; ~ **for** *vt fus* iscriversi a; ~ **into** *vt fus* (*explanation*) cominciare a dare; (*debate*) partecipare a; (*agreement*) concludere

enterprise ['entəpraɪz] *n* (*undertaking, company*) impresa; (*spirit*) iniziativa; **free ~** liberalismo economico; **private ~** iniziativa privata

enterprising ['entəpraɪzɪŋ] *adj* intraprendente

entertain [entə'teɪn] *vt* divertire; (*invite*) ricevere; (*idea, plan*) nutrire; ~**er** *n* comico/a; ~**ing** *adj* divertente; ~**ment** *n* (*amusement*) divertimento; (*show*) spettacolo

enthralled [ɪn'θrɔːld] *adj* affascinato(a)

enthusiasm [ɪn'θuːzɪæzəm] *n* entusiasmo

enthusiast [ɪn'θuːzɪæst] *n* entusiasta *m/f*; ~**ic** [-'æstɪk] *adj* entusiasta, entusiastico(a); **to be ~ic about sth/sb** essere appassionato/a di qc/entusiasta di qn

entire [ɪn'taɪə*] *adj* intero(a); ~**ly** *adv* completamente, interamente; ~**ty** [ɪn'taɪərətɪ] *n*: **in its ~ty** nel suo complesso

entitle [ɪn'taɪtl] *vt* (*give right*): **to ~ sb to sth/to do** dare diritto a qn a qc/a fare; ~**d** *adj* (*book*) che si intitola; **to be ~d to do** avere il diritto di fare

entrails ['entreɪlz] *npl* interiora *fpl*

entrance [*n* 'entrns, *vb* ɪn'trɑːns] *n* entrata, ingresso; (*of person*) entrata ♦ *vt* incantare, rapire; **to gain ~ to** (*university etc*) essere ammesso a; ~ **examination** *n* esame *m* di ammissione; ~ **fee** *n* tassa d'iscrizione; (*to museum etc*) prezzo d'ingresso; ~ **ramp** (*US*) *n* (*AUT*) rampa di accesso

entrant ['entrnt] *n* partecipante *m/f*; concorrente *m/f*

entreat [en'triːt] *vt* supplicare

entrenched [en'trentʃt] *adj* radicato(a)

entrepreneur [ɒntrəprə'nɜː*] *n* imprenditore *m*

entrust [ɪn'trʌst] *vt*: **to ~ sth to** affidare qc a

entry ['entrɪ] *n* entrata; (*way in*) entrata, ingresso; (*item: on list*) iscrizione *f*; (*in dictionary*) voce *f*; **no ~** vietato l'ingresso; (*AUT*) divieto di accesso; ~ **form** *n* modulo

d'iscrizione; ~ **phone** *n* citofono

envelop [ɪn'veləp] *vt* avvolgere, avviluppare

envelope ['envələup] *n* busta

envious ['envɪəs] *adj* invidioso(a)

environment [ɪn'vaɪərnmənt] *n* ambiente *m*; ~**al** [-'mentl] *adj* ecologico(a); ambientale; ~**-friendly** *adj* che rispetta l'ambiente

envisage [ɪn'vɪzɪdʒ] *vt* immaginare; prevedere

envoy ['envɔɪ] *n* inviato/a

envy ['envɪ] *n* invidia ♦ *vt* invidiare; **to ~ sb sth** invidiare qn per qc

epic ['epɪk] *n* poema *m* epico ♦ *adj* epico(a)

epidemic [epɪ'demɪk] *n* epidemia

epilepsy ['epɪlepsɪ] *n* epilessia

episode ['epɪsəud] *n* episodio

epistle [ɪ'pɪsl] *n* epistola

epitome [ɪ'pɪtəmɪ] *n* epitome *f*; quintessenza; **epitomize** *vt* (*fig*) incarnare

equal ['iːkwl] *adj* uguale ♦ *n* pari *m/f inv* ♦ *vt* uguagliare; ~ **to** (*task*) all'altezza di; ~**ity** [iː'kwɔlɪtɪ] *n* uguaglianza; ~**ize** *vi* pareggiare; ~**ly** *adv* ugualmente

equanimity [ekwə'nɪmɪtɪ] *n* serenità

equate [ɪ'kweɪt] *vt*: **to ~ sth with** considerare qc uguale a; (*compare*) paragonare qc con; **equation** [ɪ'kweɪʃən] *n* (*MATH*) equazione *f*

equator [ɪ'kweɪtə*] *n* equatore *m*

equilibrium [iːkwɪ'lɪbrɪəm] *n* equilibrio

equip [ɪ'kwɪp] *vt* equipaggiare, attrezzare; **to ~ sb/sth with** fornire qn/qc di; **to be well ~ped** (*office etc*) essere ben attrezzato(a); **he is well ~ped for the job** ha i requisiti necessari per quel lavoro; ~**ment** *n* attrezzatura; (*electrical etc*) apparecchiatura

equitable ['ekwɪtəbl] *adj* equo(a), giusto(a)

equities ['ekwɪtɪz] (*BRIT*) *npl* (*COMM*) azioni *fpl* ordinarie

equivalent [ɪ'kwɪvəlnt] *adj* equivalente ♦ *n* equivalente *m*; **to be ~ to** equivalere a

era ['ɪərə] *n* era, età *f* inv

eradicate [ɪ'rædɪkeɪt] *vt* sradicare

erase [ɪ'reɪz] *vt* cancellare; ~**r** *n* gomma

erect [ɪ'rekt] *adj* eretto(a) ♦ *vt* costruire; (*assemble*) montare; ~**ion** [ɪ'rekʃən] *n* costruzione f; montaggio; (PHYSIOL) erezione f

ERM n (= Exchange Rate Mechanism) ERM m

ermine ['ɜːmɪn] n ermellino

erode [ɪ'rəʊd] vt erodere; (metal) corrodere

erotic [ɪ'rɒtɪk] adj erotico(a)

errand ['ɛrnd] n commissione f

erratic [ɪ'rætɪk] adj imprevedibile; (person, mood) incostante

error ['ɛrə*] n errore m

erupt [ɪ'rʌpt] vi (volcano) mettersi (or essere) in eruzione; (war, crisis) scoppiare; ~ion [ɪ'rʌpʃən] n eruzione f; scoppio

escalate ['ɛskəleɪt] vi intensificarsi

escalator ['ɛskəleɪtə*] n scala mobile

escapade [ɛskə'peɪd] n scappatella; avventura

escape [ɪ'skeɪp] n evasione f; fuga; (of gas etc) fuga, fuoriuscita ♦ vi fuggire; (from jail) evadere, scappare; (leak) uscire ♦ vt sfuggire a; **to ~ from** (place) fuggire da; (person) sfuggire a; **escapism** n evasione f (dalla realtà)

escort [n 'ɛskɔːt, vb ɪ'skɔːt] n scorta; (male companion) cavaliere m ♦ vt scortare; accompagnare

Eskimo ['ɛskɪməʊ] n eschimese m/f

especially [ɪ'spɛʃlɪ] adv specialmente, soprattutto; espressamente

espionage ['ɛspɪɒnɑːʒ] n spionaggio

esplanade [ɛsplə'neɪd] n lungomare m inv

Esq. abbr = **Esquire**

Esquire [ɪ'skwaɪə*] n: **J. Brown, ~** Signor J. Brown

essay ['ɛseɪ] n (SCOL) composizione f; (LITERATURE) saggio

essence ['ɛsns] n essenza

essential [ɪ'sɛnʃl] adj essenziale ♦ n elemento essenziale; **~ly** adv essenzialmente

establish [ɪ'stæblɪʃ] vt stabilire; (business) mettere su; (one's power etc) affermare; **~ed** adj (business etc) affermato(a); **~ment** n stabilimento; **the E~ment** la classe dirigente, l'establishment m

estate [ɪ'steɪt] n proprietà f inv; beni mpl, patrimonio; (BRIT: also: **housing ~**) complesso

edilizio; **~ agent** (BRIT) n agente m immobiliare; **~ car** (BRIT) n giardiniera

esteem [ɪ'stiːm] n stima ♦ vt (think highly of) stimare; (consider) considerare

esthetic [ɪs'θɛtɪk] (US) adj = **aesthetic**

estimate [n 'ɛstɪmət, vb 'ɛstɪmeɪt] n stima; (COMM) preventivo ♦ vt stimare, valutare; **estimation** [-'meɪʃən] n stima; opinione f

estranged [ɪ'streɪndʒd] adj separato(a)

etc abbr (= et cetera) etc, ecc

eternal [ɪ'tɜːnl] adj eterno(a)

eternity [ɪ'tɜːnɪtɪ] n eternità

ether ['iːθə*] n etere m

ethical ['ɛθɪkl] adj etico(a), morale

ethics ['ɛθɪks] n etica ♦ npl morale f

Ethiopia [iːθɪ'əʊpɪə] n Etiopia

ethnic ['ɛθnɪk] adj etnico(a); **~ minority** n minoranza etnica

ethos ['iːθɒs] n norma di vita

etiquette ['ɛtɪkɛt] n etichetta

EU n abbr (= European Union) UE

euro ['jʊərəʊ] n (currency) euro m inv

Euroland ['jʊərəʊlænd] n Eurolandia

Eurocheque ['jʊərəʊtʃɛk] n eurochèque m inv

Europe ['jʊərəp] n Europa; **European** [-'piːən] adj, n europeo(a); **European Community** n Comunità Europea

evacuate [ɪ'vækjʊeɪt] vt evacuare

evade [ɪ'veɪd] vt (tax) evadere; (duties etc) sottrarsi a; (person) schivare

evaluate [ɪ'væljʊeɪt] vt valutare

evaporate [ɪ'væpəreɪt] vi evaporare; **~d milk** n latte m concentrato

evasion [ɪ'veɪʒən] n evasione f

evasive [ɪ'veɪsɪv] adj evasivo(a)

eve [iːv] n: **on the ~ of** alla vigilia di

even ['iːvn] adj regolare; (number) pari inv ♦ adv anche, perfino; **~ if**, **~ though** anche se; **~ more** ancora di più; **~ so** ciò nonostante; **not ~** nemmeno; **to get ~ with sb** dare la pari a qn

evening ['iːvnɪŋ] n sera; (as duration, event) serata; **in the ~** la sera; **~ class** n corso serale; **~ dress** n (woman's) abito da sera; **in ~ dress** (man) in abito scuro; (woman) in abito lungo

event [ɪ'vɛnt] n avvenimento; (SPORT) gara; **in the ~ of** in caso di; **~ful** adj denso(a) di eventi

eventual [ɪ'vɛntʃuəl] adj finale; **~ity** [-'ælɪtɪ] n possibilità f inv, eventualità f inv; **~ly** adv alla fine

ever ['ɛvə*] adv mai; (at all times) sempre; **the best ~** il migliore che ci sia mai stato; **have you ~ seen it?** l'ha mai visto?; **~ since** adv da allora ♦ conj sin da quando; **~ so pretty** così bello(a); **~green** n sempreverde m; **~lasting** adj eterno(a)

every ['ɛvrɪ] adj ogni; **~ day** tutti i giorni, ogni giorno; **~ other/third day** ogni due/tre giorni; **~ other car** una macchina su due; **~ now and then** ogni tanto, di quando in quando; **~body** pron = **~one**; **~day** adj quotidiano(a); di ogni giorno; **~one** pron ognuno, tutti pl; **~thing** pron tutto, ogni cosa; **~where** adv (gen) dappertutto; (wherever) ovunque

evict [ɪ'vɪkt] vt sfrattare

evidence ['ɛvɪdns] n (proof) prova; (of witness) testimonianza; (sign): **to show ~ of** dare segni di; **to give ~** deporre

evident ['ɛvɪdnt] adj evidente; **~ly** adv evidentemente

evil ['i:vl] adj cattivo(a), maligno(a) ♦ n male m

evoke [ɪ'vəuk] vt evocare

evolution [i:və'lu:ʃən] n evoluzione f

evolve [ɪ'vɔlv] vt elaborare ♦ vi svilupparsi, evolversi

ewe [ju:] n pecora

ex- [ɛks] prefix ex

exacerbate [ɛks'æsəbeɪt] vt aggravare

exact [ɪg'zækt] adj esatto(a) ♦ vt: **to ~ sth (from)** estorcere qc (da); esigere qc (da); **~ing** adj esigente; (work) faticoso(a); **~ly** adv esattamente

exaggerate [ɪg'zædʒəreɪt] vt, vi esagerare; **exaggeration** [-'reɪʃən] n esagerazione f

exalted [ɪg'zɔ:ltɪd] adj esaltato(a); elevato(a)

exam [ɪg'zæm] n abbr (SCOL)
= **examination**

examination [ɪgzæmɪ'neɪʃən] n (SCOL) esame m; (MED) controllo

examine [ɪg'zæmɪn] vt esaminare; **~r** n esaminatore/trice

example [ɪg'zɑ:mpl] n esempio; **for ~** ad or per esempio

exasperate [ɪg'zɑ:spəreɪt] vt esasperare; **exasperating** adj esasperante; **exasperation** [-'reɪʃən] n esasperazione f

excavate ['ɛkskəveɪt] vt scavare

exceed [ɪk'si:d] vt superare; (one's powers, time limit) oltrepassare; **~ingly** adv eccessivamente

excellent ['ɛksələnt] adj eccellente

except [ɪk'sɛpt] prep (also: **~ for, ~ing**) salvo, all'infuori di, eccetto ♦ vt escludere; **~ if/when** salvo se/quando; **~ that** salvo che; **~ion** [ɪk'sɛpʃən] n eccezione f; **to take ~ion to** trovare a ridire su; **~ional** [ɪk'sɛpʃənl] adj eccezionale

excerpt ['ɛksə:pt] n estratto

excess [ɪk'sɛs] n eccesso; **~ baggage** n bagaglio in eccedenza; **~ fare** n supplemento; **~ive** adj eccessivo(a)

exchange [ɪks'tʃeɪndʒ] n scambio; (also: **telephone ~**) centralino ♦ vt: **to ~ (for)** scambiare (con); **~ rate** n tasso di cambio

Exchequer [ɪks'tʃɛkə*] n: **the ~** (BRIT) lo Scacchiere, ≈ il ministero delle Finanze

excise ['ɛksaɪz] n imposta, dazio

excite [ɪk'saɪt] vt eccitare; **to get ~d** eccitarsi; **~ment** n eccitazione f; agitazione f; **exciting** adj avventuroso(a); (film, book) appassionante

exclaim [ɪk'skleɪm] vi esclamare; **exclamation** [ɛksklə'meɪʃən] n esclamazione f; **exclamation mark** n punto esclamativo

exclude [ɪk'sklu:d] vt escludere

exclusive [ɪk'sklu:sɪv] adj esclusivo(a); **~ of VAT** I.V.A. esclusa

excommunicate [ɛkskə'mju:nɪkeɪt] vt scomunicare

excruciating [ɪk'skru:ʃɪeɪtɪŋ] adj straziante, atroce

excursion [ɪk'skə:ʃən] n escursione f, gita

excuse [n ɪk'skju:s, vb ɪk'skju:z] n scusa ♦ vt scusare; **to ~ sb from** (activity) dispensare qn da; **~ me!** mi scusi!; **now, if you will ~**

me ... ora, mi scusi ma ....

ex-directory (*BRIT*) *adj* (*TEL*): **to be ~** non essere sull'elenco

execute ['ɛksɪkjuːt] *vt* (*prisoner*) giustiziare; (*plan etc*) eseguire

execution [ɛksɪ'kjuːʃən] *n* esecuzione *f*; **~er** *n* boia *m inv*

executive [ɪg'zɛkjutɪv] *n* (*COMM*) dirigente *m*; (*POL*) esecutivo ♦ *adj* esecutivo(a)

exemplify [ɪg'zɛmplɪfaɪ] *vt* esemplificare

exempt [ɪg'zɛmpt] *adj* esentato(a) ♦ *vt*: **to ~ sb from** esentare qn da; **~ion** [ɪg'zɛmpʃən] *n* esenzione *f*

exercise ['ɛksəsaɪz] *n* (*keep fit*) moto; (*SCOL*, *MIL etc*) esercizio ♦ *vt* esercitare; (*patience*) usare; (*dog*) portar fuori ♦ *vi* (*also:* **take ~**) fare del moto; **~bike** *n* cyclette *f inv*; **~ book** *n* quaderno

exert [ɪg'zəːt] *vt* esercitare; **to ~ o.s.** sforzarsi; **~ion** [-ʃən] *n* sforzo

exhale [ɛks'heɪl] *vt*, *vi* espirare

exhaust [ɪg'zɔːst] *n* (*also:* **~ fumes**) scappamento; (*also:* **~ pipe**) tubo di scappamento ♦ *vt* esaurire; **~ed** *adj* esaurito(a); **~ion** [ɪg'zɔːstʃən] *n* esaurimento; **nervous ~ion** *n* sovraffaticamento mentale; **~ive** *adj* esauriente

exhibit [ɪg'zɪbɪt] *n* (*ART*) oggetto esposto; (*LAW*) documento *or* oggetto esibito ♦ *vt* esporre; (*courage, skill*) dimostrare; **~ion** [ɛksɪ'bɪʃən] *n* mostra, esposizione *f*

exhilarating [ɪg'zɪləreɪtɪŋ] *adj* esilarante; stimolante

exhort [ɪg'zɔːt] *vt* esortare

exile ['ɛksaɪl] *n* esilio; (*person*) esiliato/a ♦ *vt* esiliare

exist [ɪg'zɪst] *vi* esistere; **~ence** *n* esistenza; **~ing** *adj* esistente

exit ['ɛksɪt] *n* uscita ♦ *vi* (*THEATRE*, *COMPUT*) uscire; **~ poll** *n* exit poll *m inv*; **~ ramp** (*US*) *n* (*AUT*) rampa di uscita

exodus ['ɛksədəs] *n* esodo

exonerate [ɪg'zɔnəreɪt] *vt*: **to ~ from** discolpare da

exotic [ɪg'zɔtɪk] *adj* esotico(a)

expand [ɪk'spænd] *vt* espandere; estendere;

allargare ♦ *vi* (*business, gas*) espandersi; (*metal*) dilatarsi

expanse [ɪk'spæns] *n* distesa, estensione *f*

expansion [ɪk'spænʃən] *n* (*gen*) espansione *f*; (*of town, economy*) sviluppo; (*of metal*) dilatazione *f*

expect [ɪk'spɛkt] *vt* (*anticipate*) prevedere, aspettarsi, prevedere *or* aspettarsi che +*sub*; (*require*) richiedere, esigere; (*suppose*) supporre; (*await, also baby*) aspettare ♦ *vi*: **to be ~ing** essere in stato interessante; **to ~ sb to do** aspettarsi che qn faccia; **~ancy** *n* (*anticipation*) attesa; **life ~ancy** probabilità *fpl* di vita; **~ant mother** *n* gestante *f*; **~ation** [ɛkspɛk'teɪʃən] *n* aspettativa; speranza

expediency [ɪk'spiːdɪənsɪ] *n* convenienza

expedient [ɪk'spiːdɪənt] *adj* conveniente; vantaggioso(a) ♦ *n* espediente *m*

expedition [ɛkspə'dɪʃən] *n* spedizione *f*

expel [ɪk'spɛl] *vt* espellere

expend [ɪk'spɛnd] *vt* spendere; (*use up*) consumare; **~iture** [ɪk'spɛndɪtʃə*] *n* spesa

expense [ɪk'spɛns] *n* spesa; (*high cost*) costo; **~s** *npl* (*COMM*) spese *fpl*, indennità *fpl*; **at the ~ of** a spese di; **~ account** *n* conto *m* spese *inv*

expensive [ɪk'spɛnsɪv] *adj* caro(a), costoso(a)

experience [ɪk'spɪərɪəns] *n* esperienza ♦ *vt* (*pleasure*) provare; (*hardship*) soffrire; **~d** *adj* esperto(a)

experiment [*n* ɪk'spɛrɪmənt, *vb* ɪk'spɛrɪmɛnt] *n* esperimento, esperienza ♦ *vi*: **to ~ (with/on)** fare esperimenti (con/su)

expert ['ɛkspəːt] *adj*, *n* esperto(a); **~ise** [-'tiːz] *n* competenza

expire [ɪk'spaɪə*] *vi* (*period of time, licence*) scadere; **expiry** *n* scadenza

explain [ɪk'spleɪn] *vt* spiegare; **explanation** [ɛksplə'neɪʃən] *n* spiegazione *f*; **explanatory** [ɪk'splænətrɪ] *adj* esplicativo(a)

explicit [ɪk'splɪsɪt] *adj* esplicito(a)

explode [ɪk'spləud] *vi* esplodere

exploit [*n* 'ɛksplɔɪt, *vb* ɪk'splɔɪt] *n* impresa ♦ *vt* sfruttare; **~ation** [-'teɪʃən] *n* sfruttamento

exploratory [ɪkˈsplɔrətrɪ] *adj* esplorativo(a)

explore [ɪkˈsplɔːʳ] *vt* esplorare; (*possibilities*) esaminare; **~r** *n* esploratore/trice

explosion [ɪkˈspləʊʒən] *n* esplosione *f*

explosive [ɪkˈspləʊsɪv] *adj* esplosivo(a) ♦ *n* esplosivo

exponent [ɪkˈspəʊnənt] *n* esponente *m/f*

export [*vb* ɛkˈspɔːt, *n* ˈɛkspɔːt] *vt* esportare ♦ *n* esportazione *f*; articolo di esportazione ♦ *cpd* d'esportazione; **~er** *n* esportatore *m*

expose [ɪkˈspəʊz] *vt* esporre; (*unmask*) smascherare; **~d** *adj* (*position*) esposto(a)

exposure [ɪkˈspəʊʒəʳ] *n* esposizione *f*; (*PHOT*) posa; (*MED*) assideramento; **~ meter** *n* esposimetro

express [ɪkˈsprɛs] *adj* (*definite*) chiaro(a), espresso(a); (*BRIT: letter etc*) espresso *inv* ♦ *n* (*train*) espresso ♦ *vt* esprimere; **~ion** [ɪkˈsprɛʃən] *n* espressione *f*; **~ive** *adj* espressivo(a); **~ly** *adv* espressamente; **~way** (*US*) *n* (*urban motorway*) autostrada che attraversa la città

exquisite [ɛkˈskwɪzɪt] *adj* squisito(a)

extend [ɪkˈstɛnd] *vt* (*visit*) protrarre; (*road, deadline*) prolungare; (*building*) ampliare; (*offer*) offrire, porgere ♦ *vi* (*land, period*) estendersi

extension [ɪkˈstɛnʃən] *n* (*of road, term*) prolungamento; (*of contract, deadline*) proroga; (*building*) annesso; (*to wire, table*) prolunga; (*telephone*) interno; (: *in private house*) apparecchio supplementare

extensive [ɪkˈstɛnsɪv] *adj* esteso(a), ampio(a); (*damage*) su larga scala; (*coverage, discussion*) esauriente; (*use*) grande; **~ly** *adv*: **he's travelled ~ly** ha viaggiato molto

extent [ɪkˈstɛnt] *n* estensione *f*; **to some ~** fino a un certo punto; **to such an ~ that ...** a un tal punto che ...; **to what ~?** fino a che punto?; **to the ~ of ...** fino al punto di ...

extenuating [ɪksˈtɛnjueɪtɪŋ] *adj*: **~ circumstances** attenuanti *fpl*

exterior [ɛkˈstɪərɪəʳ] *adj* esteriore, esterno(a) ♦ *n* esteriore *m*, esterno; aspetto (esteriore)

exterminate [ɪkˈstəːmɪneɪt] *vt* sterminare

external [ɛkˈstəːnl] *adj* esterno(a), esteriore

extinct [ɪkˈstɪŋkt] *adj* estinto(a)

extinguish [ɪkˈstɪŋgwɪʃ] *vt* estinguere; **~er** *n* estintore *m*

extort [ɪkˈstɔːt] *vt*: **to ~ sth (from)** estorcere qc (da); **~ionate** [ɪkˈstɔːʃənɪt] *adj* esorbitante

extra [ˈɛkstrə] *adj* extra *inv*, supplementare ♦ *adv* (*in addition*) di più ♦ *n* extra *m inv*; (*surcharge*) supplemento; (*CINEMA, THEATRE*) comparsa

extra... [ˈɛkstrə] *prefix* extra...

extract [*vb* ɪkˈstrækt, *n* ˈɛkstrækt] *vt* estrarre; (*money, promise*) strappare ♦ *n* estratto; (*passage*) brano

extracurricular [ˈɛkstrəkəˈrɪkjuləʳ] *adj* extrascolastico(a)

extradite [ˈɛkstrədaɪt] *vt* estradare

extramarital [ɛkstrəˈmærɪtl] *adj* extraconiugale

extramural [ɛkstrəˈmjuərl] *adj* fuori dell'università

extraordinary [ɪkˈstrɔːdnrɪ] *adj* straordinario(a)

extravagance [ɪkˈstrævəgəns] *n* sperpero; stravaganza

extravagant [ɪkˈstrævəgənt] *adj* (*lavish*) prodigo(a); (*wasteful*) dispendioso(a)

extreme [ɪkˈstriːm] *adj* estremo(a) ♦ *n* estremo; **~ly** *adv* estremamente

extricate [ˈɛkstrɪkeɪt] *vt*: **to ~ sth (from)** districare qc (da)

extrovert [ˈɛkstrəvəːt] *n* estroverso/a

exude [ɪgˈzjuːd] *vt* trasudare; (*fig*) emanare

eye [aɪ] *n* occhio; (*of needle*) cruna ♦ *vt* osservare; **to keep an ~ on** tenere d'occhio; **~brow** *n* sopracciglio; **~drops** *npl* gocce *fpl* oculari, collirio; **~lash** *n* ciglio; **~lid** *n* palpebra; **~liner** *n* eye-liner *m inv*; **~-opener** *n* rivelazione *f*; **~shadow** *n* ombretto; **~sight** *n* vista; **~sore** *n* pugno nell'occhio; **~ witness** *n* testimone *m/f* oculare

F, f

F [ɛf] n (MUS) fa m

fable ['feɪbl] n favola

fabric ['fæbrɪk] n stoffa, tessuto

fabulous ['fæbjuləs] adj favoloso(a); (super) favoloso(a), fantastico(a)

façade [fə'sɑːd] n (also fig) facciata

face [feɪs] n faccia, viso, volto; (expression) faccia; (of clock) quadrante m; (of building) facciata ♦ vt essere di fronte a; (facts, situation) affrontare; ~ **down** a faccia in giù; **to make** or **pull a ~** fare una smorfia; **in the ~ of** (difficulties etc) di fronte a; **on the ~ of it** a prima vista; ~ **to ~** faccia a faccia; ~ **up to** vt fus affrontare, far fronte a; ~ **cloth** (BRIT) n guanto di spugna; ~ **cream** n crema per il viso; ~ **lift** n lifting m inv; (of façade etc) ripulita; ~ **powder** n cipria; ~-**saving** adj per salvare la faccia

facet ['fæsɪt] n sfaccettatura

facetious [fə'siːʃəs] adj faceto(a)

face value n (of coin) valore m facciale or nominale; **to take sth at ~** (fig) giudicare qc dalle apparenze

facial ['feɪʃəl] adj del viso

facile ['fæsaɪl] adj superficiale

facilities [fə'sɪlɪtɪz] npl attrezzature fpl; **credit ~** facilitazioni fpl di credito

facing ['feɪsɪŋ] prep di fronte a

facsimile [fæk'sɪmɪlɪ] n facsimile m inv; ~ **machine** n telecopiatrice f

fact [fækt] n fatto; **in ~** infatti

factor ['fæktə*] n fattore m

factory ['fæktərɪ] n fabbrica, stabilimento

factual ['fæktjuəl] adj che si attiene ai fatti

faculty ['fækəltɪ] n facoltà f inv; (US) corpo insegnante

fad [fæd] n mania; capriccio

fade [feɪd] vi sbiadire, sbiadirsi; (light, sound, hope) attenuarsi, affievolirsi; (flower) appassire

fag [fæg] (BRIT: inf) n (cigarette) cicca

fail [feɪl] vt (exam) non superare; (candidate) bocciare; (subj: courage, memory) mancare a ♦ vi fallire; (student) essere respinto(a); (eyesight, health, light) venire a mancare; **to ~ to do sth** (neglect) mancare di fare qc; (be unable) non riuscire a fare qc; **without ~** senza fallo; certamente; ~**ing** n difetto ♦ prep in mancanza di; ~**ure** ['feɪljə*] n fallimento; (person) fallito/a; (mechanical etc) guasto

faint [feɪnt] adj debole; (recollection) vago(a); (mark) indistinto(a) ♦ n (MED) svenimento ♦ vi svenire; **to feel ~** sentirsi svenire

fair [feə*] adj (person, decision) giusto(a), equo(a); (quite large, quite good) discreto(a); (hair etc) biondo(a); (skin, complexion) chiaro(a); (weather) bello(a), clemente ♦ adv (play) lealmente ♦ n fiera; (BRIT: funfair) luna park m inv; ~**ly** adv equamente; (quite) abbastanza; ~**ness** n equità, giustizia; ~ **play** n correttezza

fairy ['feərɪ] n fata; ~ **tale** n fiaba

faith [feɪθ] n fede f; (trust) fiducia; (sect) religione f, fede f; ~**ful** adj fedele; ~**fully** adv fedelmente; **yours ~fully** (BRIT: in letters) distinti saluti

fake [feɪk] n imitazione f; (picture) falso; (person) impostore/a ♦ adj falso(a) ♦ vt (accounts) falsificare; (illness) fingere; (painting) contraffare

fall [fɔːl] (pt **fell**, pp **fallen**) n caduta; (in temperature) abbassamento; (in price) ribasso; (US: autumn) autunno ♦ vi cadere; (temperature, price, night) scendere; ~**s** npl (waterfall) cascate fpl; **to ~ flat** (on one's face) cadere bocconi; (joke) fare cilecca; (plan) fallire; ~ **back** vi (retreat) indietreggiare; (MIL) ritirarsi; ~ **back on** vt fus (remedy etc) ripiegare su; ~ **behind** vi rimanere indietro; ~ **down** vi (person) cadere; (building) crollare; ~ **for** vt fus (person) prendere una cotta per; **to ~ for a trick** (or a story etc) cascarci; ~ **in** vi crollare; (MIL) mettersi in riga; ~ **off** vi cadere; (diminish) diminuire, abbassarsi; ~ **out** vi (hair, teeth) cadere; (friends etc) litigare; ~ **through** vi (plan, project) fallire

fallacy ['fæləsɪ] n errore m

fallen ['fɔːlən] *pp of* **fall**

fallout ['fɔːlaut] *n* fall-out *m*

fallow ['fæləu] *adj* incolto(a), a maggese

false [fɔːls] *adj* falso(a); **under ~ pretences** con l'inganno; **~ teeth** (*BRIT*) *npl* denti *mpl* finti

falter ['fɔːltəʳ] *vi* esitare, vacillare

fame [feɪm] *n* fama, celebrità

familiar [fəˈmɪlɪəʳ] *adj* familiare; (*close*) intimo(a); **to be ~ with** (*subject*) conoscere; **~ize** [fəˈmɪlɪəraɪz] *vt*: **to ~ize o.s. with** familiarizzare con

family ['fæmɪlɪ] *n* famiglia; **~ business** *n* ditta a conduzione familiare

famine ['fæmɪn] *n* carestia

famished ['fæmɪʃt] *adj* affamato(a)

famous ['feɪməs] *adj* famoso(a); **~ly** *adv* (*get on*) a meraviglia

fan [fæn] *n* (*folding*) ventaglio; (*ELEC*) ventilatore *m*; (*person*) ammiratore/trice; tifoso/a ♦ *vt* far vento a; (*fire, quarrel*) alimentare

fanatic [fəˈnætɪk] *n* fanatico/a

fan belt *n* cinghia del ventilatore

fanciful ['fænsɪful] *adj* fantasioso(a)

fancy ['fænsɪ] *n* immaginazione *f*, fantasia; (*whim*) capriccio ♦ *adj* (*hat*) stravagante; (*hotel, food*) speciale ♦ *vt* (*feel like, want*) aver voglia di; (*imagine, think*) immaginare; **to take a ~ to** incapricciarsi di; **he fancies her** (*inf*) gli piace; **~ dress** *n* costume *m* (per maschera); **~-dress ball** *n* ballo in maschera

fang [fæŋ] *n* zanna; (*of snake*) dente *m*

fantastic [fænˈtæstɪk] *adj* fantastico(a)

fantasy ['fæntəsɪ] *n* fantasia, immaginazione *f*; fantasticheria; chimera

far [fɑːʳ] *adj* lontano(a) ♦ *adv* lontano; (*much, greatly*) molto; **~ away, ~ off** lontano, distante; **~ better** assai migliore; **~ from** lontano da; **by ~** di gran lunga; **go as ~ as the farm** vada fino alla fattoria; **as ~ as I know** per quel che so; **how ~?** quanto lontano?; (*referring to activity etc*) fino a dove?; **~away** *adj* lontano(a)

farce [fɑːs] *n* farsa

fare [feəʳ] *n* (*on trains, buses*) tariffa; (*in taxi*) prezzo della corsa; (*food*) vitto, cibo; **half ~** metà tariffa; **full ~** tariffa intera

Far East *n*: **the ~** l'Estremo Oriente *m*

farewell [feəˈwel] *excl, n* addio

farm [fɑːm] *n* fattoria, podere *m* ♦ *vt* coltivare; **~er** *n* coltivatore/trice; agricoltore/trice; **~hand** *n* bracciante *m* agricolo; **~house** *n* fattoria; **~ing** *n* (*gen*) agricoltura; (*of crops*) coltivazione *f*; (*of animals*) allevamento; **~land** *n* terreno coltivabile; **~ worker** *n* = **~hand**; **~yard** *n* aia

far-reaching [-ˈriːtʃɪŋ] *adj* di vasta portata

fart [fɑːt] (*inf!*) *vi* scoreggiare (!)

farther ['fɑːðəʳ] *adv* più lontano ♦ *adj* più lontano(a)

farthest ['fɑːðɪst] *superl of* **far**

fascinate ['fæsɪneɪt] *vt* affascinare; **fascinating** *adj* affascinante; **fascination** [-'neɪʃən] *n* fascino

fascism ['fæʃɪzəm] *n* fascismo

fashion ['fæʃən] *n* moda; (*manner*) maniera, modo ♦ *vt* foggiare, formare; **in ~** alla moda; **out of ~** passato(a) di moda; **~able** *adj* alla moda, di moda; **~ show** *n* sfilata di moda

fast [fɑːst] *adj* rapido(a), svelto(a), veloce; (*clock*): **to be ~** andare avanti; (*dye, colour*) solido(a) ♦ *adv* rapidamente; (*stuck, held*) saldamente ♦ *n* digiuno ♦ *vi* digiunare; **~ asleep** profondamente addormentato

fasten ['fɑːsn] *vt* chiudere, fissare; (*coat*) abbottonare, allacciare ♦ *vi* chiudersi, fissarsi; abbottonarsi, allacciarsi; **~er** *n* fermaglio, chiusura; **~ing** *n* = **~er**

fast food *n* fast food *m*

fastidious [fæsˈtɪdɪəs] *adj* esigente, difficile

fat [fæt] *adj* grasso(a); (*book, profit etc*) grosso(a) ♦ *n* grasso

fatal ['feɪtl] *adj* fatale, mortale; disastroso(a); **~ity** [fəˈtælɪtɪ] *n* (*road death etc*) morto/a, vittima; **~ly** *adv* a morte

fate [feɪt] *n* destino; (*of person*) sorte *f*; **~ful** *adj* fatidico(a)

father ['fɑːðəʳ] *n* padre *m*; **~-in-law** *n* suocero; **~ly** *adj* paterno(a)

fathom ['fæðəm] *n* braccio (= *1828 mm*)

♦ *vt* (*mystery*) penetrare, sondare

fatigue [fə'ti:g] *n* stanchezza

fatten ['fætn] *vt, vi* ingrassare

fatty ['fæti] *adj* (*food*) grasso(a) ♦ *n* (*inf*) ciccione/a

fatuous ['fætjuəs] *adj* fatuo(a)

faucet ['fɔ:sɪt] (*US*) *n* rubinetto

fault [fɔ:lt] *n* colpa; (*TENNIS*) fallo; (*defect*) difetto; (*GEO*) faglia ♦ *vt* criticare; **it's my ~** è colpa mia; **to find ~ with** trovare da ridire su; **at ~** in fallo; **~y** *adj* difettoso(a)

fauna ['fɔ:nə] *n* fauna

favour ['feɪvə*] (*US* **favor**) *n* favore *m* ♦ *vt* (*proposition*) favorire, essere favorevole a; (*pupil etc*) favorire; (*team, horse*) dare per vincente; **to do sb a ~** fare un favore *or* una cortesia a qn; **to find ~ with** (*subj: person*) entrare nelle buone grazie di; (: *suggestion*) avere l'approvazione di; **in ~ of** in favore di; **~able** *adj* favorevole; **~ite** [-rɪt] *adj, n* favorito/a

fawn [fɔ:n] *n* daino ♦ *adj* (*also:* **~-coloured**) marrone chiaro *inv* ♦ *vi:* **to ~ (up)on** adulare servilmente

fax [fæks] *n* (*document*) facsimile *m inv*, telecopia; (*machine*) telecopiatrice *f* ♦ *vt* telecopiare, trasmettere in facsimile

FBI (*US*) *n abbr* (= *Federal Bureau of Investigation*) F.B.I. *f*

fear [fɪə*] *n* paura, timore *m* ♦ *vt* aver paura di, temere; **for ~ of** per paura di; **~ful** *adj* pauroso(a); (*sight, noise*) terribile, spaventoso(a)

feasible ['fi:zəbl] *adj* possibile, realizzabile

feast [fi:st] *n* festa, banchetto; (*REL: also:* **~ day**) festa ♦ *vi* banchettare

feat [fi:t] *n* impresa, fatto insigne

feather ['feðə*] *n* penna

feature ['fi:tʃə*] *n* caratteristica; (*PRESS, TV*) articolo ♦ *vt* (*subj: film*) avere come protagonista ♦ *vi* figurare; **~s** *npl* (*of face*) fisionomia; **~ film** *n* film *m inv* principale

February ['februərɪ] *n* febbraio

fed [fed] *pt, pp of* **feed**

federal ['fedərəl] *adj* federale

fed-up *adj:* **to be ~** essere stufo(a)

fee [fi:] *n* pagamento; (*of doctor, lawyer*) onorario; (*for examination*) tassa d'esame; **school ~s** tasse *fpl* scolastiche

feeble ['fi:bl] *adj* debole

feed [fi:d] (*pt, pp* **fed**) *n* (*of baby*) pappa; (*of animal*) mangime *m*; (*on printer*) meccanismo di alimentazione ♦ *vt* nutrire; (*baby*) allattare; (*horse etc*) dare da mangiare a; (*fire, machine*) alimentare; (*data, information*): **to ~ into** inserire in; **~ on** *vt fus* nutrirsi di; **~back** *n* feed-back *m*

feel [fi:l] (*pt, pp* **felt**) *n* consistenza; (*sense of touch*) tatto ♦ *vt* toccare; palpare; tastare; (*cold, pain, anger*) sentire; (*think, believe*): **to ~ (that)** pensare che; **to ~ hungry/cold** aver fame/freddo; **to ~ lonely/better** sentirsi solo/meglio; **I don't ~ well** non mi sento bene; **it ~s soft** è morbido al tatto; **to ~ like** (*want*) aver voglia di; **to ~ about** *or* **around for** cercare a tastoni; **~er** *n* (*of insect*) antenna; **~ing** *n* sensazione *f*; (*emotion*) sentimento

feet [fi:t] *npl of* **foot**

feign [feɪn] *vt* fingere, simulare

fell [fel] *pt of* **fall** ♦ *vt* (*tree*) abbattere

fellow ['feləu] *n* individuo, tipo; compagno; (*of learned society*) membro ♦ *cpd:* **~ citizen** *n* concittadino/a; **~ countryman** (*irreg*) *n* compatriota *m*; **~ men** *npl* simili *mpl*; **~ship** *n* associazione *f*; compagnia; *specie di borsa di studio universitaria*

felony ['felənɪ] *n* reato, crimine *m*

felt [felt] *pt, pp of* **feel** ♦ *n* feltro; **~-tip pen** *n* pennarello

female ['fi:meɪl] *n* (*ZOOL*) femmina; (*pej: woman*) donna, femmina ♦ *adj* (*BIOL, ELEC*) femmina *inv*; (*sex, character*) femminile; (*vote etc*) di donne

feminine ['femɪnɪn] *adj* femminile

feminist ['femɪnɪst] *n* femminista *m/f*

fence [fens] *n* recinto ♦ *vt* (*also:* **~ in**) recingere ♦ *vi* (*SPORT*) tirare di scherma; **fencing** *n* (*SPORT*) scherma

fend [fend] *vi:* **to ~ for o.s.** arrangiarsi; **~ off** *vt* (*attack, questions*) respingere, difendersi da

fender ['fendə*] *n* parafuoco; (*on boat*) parabordo; (*US*) parafango; paraurti *m inv*

ferment [*vb* fə'mɛnt, *n* 'fɜːmɛnt] *vi* fermentare ♦ *n* (*fig*) agitazione *f*, eccitazione *f*

fern [fɜːn] *n* felce *f*

ferocious [fə'rəʊʃəs] *adj* feroce

ferret ['fɛrɪt] *n* furetto; ~ **out** *vt* (*information*) scovare

ferry ['fɛrɪ] *n* (*small*) traghetto; (*large: also:* ~**boat**) nave *f* traghetto *inv* ♦ *vt* traghettare

fertile ['fɜːtaɪl] *adj* fertile; (*BIOL*) fecondo(a); **fertilizer** ['fɜːtɪlaɪzə*] *n* fertilizzante *m*

fester ['fɛstə*] *vi* suppurare

festival ['fɛstɪvəl] *n* (*REL*) festa; (*ART, MUS*) festival *m inv*

festive ['fɛstɪv] *adj* di festa; **the ~ season** (*BRIT: Christmas*) il periodo delle feste

festivities [fɛs'tɪvɪtɪz] *npl* festeggiamenti *mpl*

festoon [fɛs'tuːn] *vt*: **to ~ with** ornare di

fetch [fɛtʃ] *vt* andare a prendere; (*sell for*) essere venduto(a) per

fête [feɪt] *n* festa

fetus ['fiːtəs] (*US*) *n* = **foetus**

feud [fjuːd] *n* contesa, lotta

feudal ['fjuːdl] *adj* feudale

fever ['fiːvə*] *n* febbre *f*; ~**ish** *adj* febbrile

few [fjuː] *adj* pochi(e); **a ~** *adj* qualche *inv* ♦ *pron* alcuni(e); ~**er** *adj* meno *inv*; meno numerosi(e); ~**est** *adj* il minor numero di

fiancé [fɪ'ɑ̃ːŋseɪ] *n* fidanzato; ~**e** *n* fidanzata

fib [fɪb] *n* piccola bugia

fibre ['faɪbə*] (*US* **fiber**) *n* fibra; **F~glass** ® *n* fibra di vetro

fickle ['fɪkl] *adj* incostante, capriccioso(a)

fiction ['fɪkʃən] *n* narrativa, romanzi *mpl*; (*sth made up*) finzione *f*; ~**al** *adj* immaginario(a-)

fictitious [fɪk'tɪʃəs] *adj* fittizio(a)

fiddle ['fɪdl] *n* (*MUS*) violino; (*cheating*) imbroglio; truffa ♦ *vt* (*BRIT: accounts*) falsificare, falsare; ~ **with** *vt fus* gingillarsi con

fidelity [fɪ'dɛlɪtɪ] *n* fedeltà; (*accuracy*) esattezza

fidget ['fɪdʒɪt] *vi* agitarsi

field [fiːld] *n* campo; ~ **marshal** *n* feldmaresciallo; ~**work** *n* ricerche *fpl* esterne

fiend [fiːnd] *n* demonio

fierce [fɪəs] *adj* (*animal, person, fighting*) feroce; (*loyalty*) assoluto(a); (*wind*) furioso(a); (*heat*) intenso(a)

fiery ['faɪərɪ] *adj* ardente; infocato(a)

fifteen [fɪf'tiːn] *num* quindici

fifth [fɪfθ] *num* quinto(a)

fifty ['fɪftɪ] *num* cinquanta; ~-~ *adj*: **a ~-~ chance** una possibilità su due ♦ *adv* fifty-fifty, metà per ciascuno

fig [fɪg] *n* fico

fight [faɪt] (*pt, pp* **fought**) *n* zuffa, rissa; (*MIL*) battaglia, combattimento; (*against cancer etc*) lotta ♦ *vt* (*person*) azzuffarsi con; (*enemy: also: MIL*) combattere; (*cancer, alcoholism, emotion*) lottare contro, combattere; (*election*) partecipare a ♦ *vi* combattere; ~**er** *n* combattente *m*; (*plane*) aeroplano da caccia; ~**ing** *n* combattimento

figment ['fɪgmənt] *n*: **a ~ of the imagination** un parto della fantasia

figurative ['fɪgjʊrətɪv] *adj* figurato(a)

figure ['fɪgə*] *n* figura; (*number, cipher*) cifra ♦ *vt* (*think: esp US*) pensare ♦ *vi* (*appear*) figurare; ~ **out** *vt* riuscire a capire; calcolare; ~**head** *n* (*NAUT*) polena; (*pej*) prestanome *m/f inv*; ~ **of speech** *n* figura retorica

file [faɪl] *n* (*tool*) lima; (*dossier*) incartamento; (*folder*) cartellina; (*COMPUT*) archivio; (*row*) fila ♦ *vt* (*nails, wood*) limare; (*papers*) archiviare; (*LAW: claim*) presentare; passare agli atti; ~ **in/out** *vi* entrare/uscire in fila

filing cabinet ['faɪlɪŋ-] *n* casellario

fill [fɪl] *vt* riempire; (*job*) coprire ♦ *n*: **to eat one's ~** mangiare a sazietà; ~ **in** *vt* (*hole*) riempire; (*form*) compilare; ~ **up** *vt* riempire ♦ *vi* (*AUT*) fare il pieno

fillet ['fɪlɪt] *n* filetto; ~ **steak** *n* bistecca di filetto

filling ['fɪlɪŋ] *n* (*CULIN*) impasto, ripieno; (*for tooth*) otturazione *f*; ~ **station** *n* stazione *f* di rifornimento

film [fɪlm] n (CINEMA) film m inv; (PHOT) pellicola; (of powder, liquid) sottile strato ♦ vt, vi girare; **~ star** n divo/a dello schermo

filter ['fɪltə*] n filtro ♦ vt filtrare; **~ lane** (BRIT) n (AUT) corsia di svincolo; **~-tipped** adj con filtro

filth [fɪlθ] n sporcizia; **~y** adj lordo(a), sozzo(a); (language) osceno(a)

fin [fɪn] n (of fish) pinna

final ['faɪnl] adj finale, ultimo(a); definitivo(a) ♦ n (SPORT) finale f; **~s** npl (SCOL) esami mpl finali

finale [fɪ'nɑːlɪ] n finale m

finalize ['faɪnəlaɪz] vt mettere a punto

finally ['faɪnəlɪ] adv (lastly) alla fine; (eventually) finalmente

finance [faɪ'næns] n finanza; (capital) capitale m ♦ vt finanziare; **~s** npl (funds) finanze fpl

financial [faɪ'nænʃəl] adj finanziario(a)

financier [faɪ'nænsɪə*] n finanziatore m

find [faɪnd] (pt, pp **found**) vt trovare; (lost object) ritrovare ♦ n trovata, scoperta; **to ~ sb guilty** (LAW) giudicare qn colpevole; **~ out** vt (truth, secret) scoprire; (person) cogliere in fallo; **to ~ out about** informarsi su; (by chance) scoprire; **~ings** npl (LAW) sentenza, conclusioni fpl; (of report) conclusioni

fine [faɪn] adj bello(a); ottimo(a); (thin, subtle) fine ♦ adv (well) molto bene ♦ n (LAW) multa ♦ vt (LAW) multare; **to be ~** (person) stare bene; (weather) far bello; **~ arts** npl belle arti fpl

finery ['faɪnərɪ] n abiti mpl eleganti

finger ['fɪŋgə*] n dito ♦ vt toccare, tastare; **little/index ~** mignolo/(dito) indice m; **~nail** n unghia; **~print** n impronta digitale; **~tip** n punta del dito

finish ['fɪnɪʃ] n fine f; (polish etc) finitura ♦ vt, vi finire; **to ~ doing sth** finire di fare qc; **to ~ third** arrivare terzo(a); **~ off** vt compiere; (kill) uccidere; **~ up** vi, vt finire; **~ing line** n linea d'arrivo

finite ['faɪnaɪt] adj limitato(a); (verb) finito(a)

Finland ['fɪnlənd] n Finlandia

Finn [fɪn] n finlandese m/f; **~ish** adj finlandese ♦ n (LING) finlandese m

fir [fəː*] n abete m

fire [faɪə*] n fuoco; (destructive) incendio; (gas ~, electric ~) stufa ♦ vt (gun) far fuoco con; (arrow) sparare; (fig) infiammare; (inf: dismiss) licenziare ♦ vi sparare, far fuoco; **on ~** in fiamme; **~ alarm** n allarme m d'incendio; **~arm** n arma da fuoco; **~ brigade** (US **~ department**) n (corpo dei) pompieri mpl; **~ engine** n autopompa; **~ escape** n scala di sicurezza; **~ extinguisher** n estintore m; **~guard** n parafuoco; **~man** (irreg) n pompiere m; **~place** n focolare m; **~side** n angolo del focolare; **~ station** n caserma dei pompieri; **~wood** n legna; **~works** npl fuochi mpl d'artificio

firing squad ['faɪərɪŋ-] n plotone m d'esecuzione

firm [fəːm] adj fermo(a) ♦ n ditta, azienda; **~ly** adv fermamente

first [fəːst] adj primo(a) ♦ adv (before others) il primo, la prima; (before other things) per primo; (when listing reasons etc) per prima cosa ♦ n (person: in race) primo/a; (BRIT: SCOL) laurea con lode; (AUT) prima; **at ~** dapprima, all'inizio; **~ of all** prima di tutto; **~ aid** n pronto soccorso; **~-aid kit** n cassetta pronto soccorso; **~-class** adj di prima classe; **~ floor** n (BRIT) il primo piano (US); il pianterreno (US); **~-hand** adj di prima mano; **~ lady** (US) n moglie f del presidente; **~ly** adv in primo luogo; **~ name** n prenome m; **~-rate** adj di prima qualità, ottimo(a)

fish [fɪʃ] n inv pesce m ♦ vt (river, area) pescare in ♦ vi pescare; **to go ~ing** andare a pesca; **~erman** n pescatore m; **~ farm** n vivaio; **~ fingers** (BRIT) npl bastoncini mpl di pesce (surgelati); **~ing boat** n barca da pesca; **~ing line** n lenza; **~ing rod** n canna da pesca; **~monger** n pescivendolo; **~monger's (shop)** n pescheria; **~ sticks** (US) npl = **~ fingers**; **~y** (inf) adj (tale, story) sospetto(a)

fist [fɪst] n pugno

fit [fɪt] *adj* (MED, SPORT) in forma; (*proper*) adatto(a), appropriato(a); conveniente ♦ *vt* (*subj: clothes*) stare bene a; (*put in, attach*) mettere; installare; (*equip*) fornire, equipaggiare ♦ *vi* (*clothes*) stare bene; (*parts*) andare bene, adattarsi; (*in space, gap*) entrare ♦ *n* (MED) accesso, attacco; **~ to** in grado di; **~ for** adatto(a) a; degno(a) di; **a ~ of anger** un accesso d'ira; **this dress is a good ~** questo vestito sta bene; **by ~s and starts** a sbalzi; **~ in** *vi* accordarsi; adattarsi; **~ful** *adj* saltuario(a); **~ness** *n* (MED) forma fisica; **~ted carpet** *n* moquette *f*; **~ted kitchen** *n* cucina componibile; **~ter** *n* aggiustatore *m* or montatore *m* meccanico; **~ting** *adj* appropriato(a) ♦ *n* (*of dress*) prova; (*of piece of equipment*) montaggio, aggiustaggio; **~tings** *npl* (*in building*) impianti *mpl*; **~ting room** *n* camerino

five [faɪv] *num* cinque; **~r** (*inf*) *n* (BRIT) biglietto da cinque sterline; (US) biglietto da cinque dollari

fix [fɪks] *vt* fissare; (*mend*) riparare; (*meal, drink*) preparare ♦ *n*: **to be in a ~** essere nei guai; **~ up** *vt* (*meeting*) fissare; **to ~ sb up with sth** procurare qc a qn; **~ation** *n* fissazione *f*; **~ed** [fɪkst] *adj* (*prices etc*) fisso(a); **~ture** ['fɪkstʃə*] *n* impianto (fisso); (SPORT) incontro (del calendario sportivo)

fizzy ['fɪzɪ] *adj* frizzante; gassato(a)

flabbergasted ['flæbəgɑːstɪd] *adj* sbalordito(a)

flabby ['flæbɪ] *adj* flaccido(a)

flag [flæg] *n* bandiera; (*also:* **~stone**) pietra da lastricare ♦ *vi* stancarsi; affievolirsi; **~ down** *vt* fare segno (di fermarsi) a

flagpole ['flægpəul] *n* albero

flagship ['flægʃɪp] *n* nave *f* ammiraglia

flair [flɛə*] *n* (*for business etc*) fiuto; (*for languages etc*) facilità; (*style*) stile *m*

flak [flæk] *n* (MIL) fuoco d'artiglieria; (*inf: criticism*) critiche *fpl*

flake [fleɪk] *n* (*of rust, paint*) scaglia; (*of snow, soap powder*) fiocco ♦ *vi* (*also:* **~ off**) sfaldarsi

flamboyant [flæm'bɔɪənt] *adj* sgargiante

flame [fleɪm] *n* fiamma

flamingo [flə'mɪŋgəu] *n* fenicottero, fiammingo

flammable ['flæməbl] *adj* infiammabile

flan [flæn] *n* flan *m* inv

flank [flæŋk] *n* fianco ♦ *vt* fiancheggiare

flannel ['flænl] *n* (BRIT: *also:* **face ~**) guanto di spugna; (*fabric*) flanella

flap [flæp] *n* (*of pocket*) patta; (*of envelope*) lembo ♦ *vt* (*wings*) battere ♦ *vi* (*sail, flag*) sbattere; (*inf: also:* **be in a ~**) essere in agitazione

flare [flɛə*] *n* razzo; (*in skirt etc*) svasatura; **~ up** *vi* andare in fiamme; (*fig: person*) infiammarsi di rabbia; (: *revolt*) scoppiare

flash [flæʃ] *n* vampata; (PHOT) notizia *f* lampo inv; (PHOT) flash *m* inv ♦ *vt* accendere e spegnere; (*send: message*) trasmettere; (: *look, smile*) lanciare ♦ *vi* brillare; (*light on ambulance, eyes etc*) lampeggiare; **in a ~** in un lampo; **to ~ one's headlights** lampeggiare; **he ~ed by** or **past** ci passò davanti come un lampo; **~bulb** *n* cubo *m* flash inv; **~cube** *n* flash *m* inv; **~light** *n* lampadina tascabile

flashy ['flæʃɪ] (*pej*) *adj* vistoso(a)

flask [flɑːsk] *n* fiasco; (*also:* **vacuum ~**) thermos ® *m* inv

flat [flæt] *adj* piatto(a); (*tyre*) sgonfio(a), a terra; (*battery*) scarico(a); (*beer*) svampito(a); (*denial*) netto(a); (MUS) bemolle inv; (: *voice*) stonato(a); (*rate, fee*) unico(a) ♦ *n* (BRIT: *rooms*) appartamento; (AUT) pneumatico sgonfio; (MUS) bemolle *m*; **to work ~ out** lavorare a più non posso; **~ly** *adv* categoricamente; **~ten** *vt* (*also:* **~ten out**) appiattire; (*building, city*) spianare

flatter ['flætə*] *vt* lusingare; **~ing** *adj* lusinghiero(a); (*dress*) che dona; **~y** *n* adulazione *f*

flaunt [flɔːnt] *vt* fare mostra di

flavour ['fleɪvə*] (US **flavor**) *n* gusto ♦ *vt* insaporire, aggiungere sapore a; **strawberry-~ed** al gusto di fragola; **~ing** *n* essenza (artificiale)

flaw [flɔː] *n* difetto

flax [flæks] *n* lino

flea [fliː] n pulce f

fleck [flek] n (mark) macchiolina; (pattern) screziatura

fled [fled] pt, pp of **flee**

flee [fliː] (pt, pp **fled**) vt fuggire da ♦ vi fuggire, scappare

fleece [fliːs] n vello ♦ vt (inf) pelare

fleet [fliːt] n flotta; (of lorries etc) convoglio; parco

fleeting ['fliːtɪŋ] adj fugace, fuggitivo(a); (visit) volante

Flemish ['flemɪʃ] adj fiammingo(a)

flesh [fleʃ] n carne f; (of fruit) polpa; ~ **wound** n ferita superficiale

flew [fluː] pt of **fly**

flex [fleks] n filo (flessibile) ♦ vt flettere; (muscles) contrarre; ~**ible** adj flessibile

flick [flɪk] n colpetto; scarto ♦ vt dare un colpetto a; ~ **through** vt fus sfogliare

flicker ['flɪkə*] vi tremolare

flier ['flaɪə*] n aviatore m

flight [flaɪt] n volo; (escape) fuga; (also: ~ **of steps**) scalinata; ~ **attendant** (US) n steward m inv, hostess f inv; ~ **deck** n (AVIAT) cabina di controllo; (NAUT) ponte m di comando

flimsy ['flɪmzɪ] adj (shoes, clothes) leggero(a); (building) poco solido(a); (excuse) che non regge

flinch [flɪntʃ] vi ritirarsi; **to ~ from** tirarsi indietro di fronte a

fling [flɪŋ] (pt, pp **flung**) vt lanciare, gettare

flint [flɪnt] n selce f; (in lighter) pietrina

flip [flɪp] vt (switch) far scattare; (coin) lanciare in aria

flippant ['flɪpənt] adj senza rispetto, irriverente

flipper ['flɪpə*] n pinna

flirt [fləːt] vi flirtare ♦ n civetta

float [fləut] n galleggiante m; (in procession) carro; (money) somma ♦ vi galleggiare

flock [flɔk] n (of sheep, REL) gregge m; (of birds) stormo ♦ vi: **to ~ to** accorrere in massa a

flog [flɔg] vt flagellare

flood [flʌd] n alluvione m; (of letters etc) marea ♦ vt allagare; (subj: people) invadere

♦ vi (place) allagarsi; (people): **to ~ into** riversarsi in; ~**ing** n inondazione f; ~**light** n riflettore m ♦ vt illuminare a giorno

floor [flɔː*] n pavimento; (storey) piano; (of sea, valley) fondo ♦ vt (subj: blow) atterrare; (: question) ridurre al silenzio; **ground ~**, (US) **first ~** pianterreno; **first ~**, (US) **second ~** primo piano; ~**board** n tavellone m di legno; ~ **show** n spettacolo di varietà

flop [flɔp] n fiasco ♦ vi far fiasco; (fall) lasciarsi cadere

floppy ['flɔpɪ] adj floscio(a), molle; ~ **(disk)** n (COMPUT) floppy disk m inv

Florence ['flɔrəns] n Firenze f; **Florentine** ['flɔrəntaɪn] adj fiorentino(a)

florid ['flɔrɪd] adj (complexion) florido(a); (style) fiorito(a)

florist ['flɔrɪst] n fioraio/a

flounder ['flaundə*] vi annaspare ♦ n (ZOOL) passera di mare

flour ['flauə*] n farina

flourish ['flʌrɪʃ] vi fiorire ♦ n (bold gesture): **with a ~** con ostentazione; ~**ing** adj florido(a)

flout [flaut] vt (order) contravvenire a

flow [fləu] n flusso; circolazione f ♦ vi fluire; (traffic, blood in veins) circolare; (hair) scendere; ~ **chart** n schema m di flusso

flower ['flauə*] n fiore m ♦ vi fiorire; ~ **bed** n aiuola; ~**pot** n vaso da fiori; ~**y** adj (perfume) di fiori; (pattern) a fiori; (speech) fiorito(a)

flown [fləun] pp of **fly**

flu [fluː] n influenza

fluctuate ['flʌktjueɪt] vi fluttuare, oscillare

fluent ['fluːənt] adj (speech) facile, sciolto(a); corrente; **he speaks ~ Italian, he's ~ in Italian** parla l'italiano correntemente

fluff [flʌf] n lanugine f; ~**y** adj lanuginoso(a); (toy) di peluche

fluid ['fluːɪd] adj fluido(a) ♦ n fluido

fluke [fluːk] n (inf) colpo di fortuna

flung [flʌŋ] pt, pp of **fling**

fluoride ['fluəraɪd] n fluoruro; ~ **toothpaste** dentifricio al fluoro

flurry ['flʌrɪ] n (of snow) tempesta; **a ~ of**

activity uno scoppio di attività

flush [flʌʃ] n rossore m; (fig: of youth, beauty etc) rigoglio, pieno vigore ♦ vt ripulire con un getto d'acqua ♦ vi arrossire ♦ adj: ~ **with** a livello di, pari a; **to ~ the toilet** tirare l'acqua; **~ed** adj tutto(a) rosso(a)

flustered ['flʌstəd] adj sconvolto(a)

flute [fluːt] n flauto

flutter ['flʌtə*] n agitazione f; (of wings) battito ♦ vi (bird) battere le ali

flux [flʌks] n: **in a state of ~** in continuo mutamento

fly [flaɪ] (pt **flew**, pp **flown**) n (insect) mosca; (on trousers: also: **flies**) chiusura ♦ vt pilotare; (passengers, cargo) trasportare (in aereo); (distances) percorrere ♦ vi volare; (passengers) andare in aereo; (escape) fuggire; (flag) sventolare; ~ **away** or **off** vi volare via; **~ing** n (activity) aviazione f; (action) volo ♦ adj: **~ing visit** visita volante; **with ~ing colours** con risultati brillanti; **~ing saucer** n disco volante; **~ing start** n: **to get off to a ~ing start** partire come un razzo; **~over** (BRIT) n (bridge) cavalcavia m inv; **~sheet** n (for tent) sopratetto

foal [fəul] n puledro

foam [fəum] n schiuma; (also: ~ **rubber**) gommapiuma ® ♦ vi schiumare; (soapy water) fare la schiuma

fob [fɔb] vt: **to ~ sb off with** rifilare a qn

focus ['fəukəs] (pl **~es**) n fuoco; (of interest) centro ♦ vt (field glasses etc) mettere a fuoco ♦ vi: **to ~ on** (with camera) mettere a fuoco; (person) fissare lo sguardo su; **in ~** a fuoco; **out of ~** sfocato(a)

fodder ['fɔdə*] n foraggio

foe [fəu] n nemico

foetus ['fiːtəs] (US **fetus**) n feto

fog [fɔg] n nebbia; **~gy** adj: **it's ~gy** c'è nebbia; ~ **lamp** (US ~ **light**) n (AUT) faro m antinebbia inv

foil [fɔɪl] vt confondere, frustrare ♦ n lamina di metallo; (kitchen ~) foglio di alluminio; (FENCING) fioretto; **to act as a ~ to** (fig) far risaltare

fold [fəuld] n (bend, crease) piega; (AGR) ovile m; (fig) gregge m ♦ vt piegare; (arms)

incrociare; ~ **up** vi (map, bed, table) piegarsi; (business) crollare ♦ vt (map etc) piegare, ripiegare; **~er** n (for papers) cartella; cartellina; **~ing** adj (chair, bed) pieghevole

foliage ['fəulɪdʒ] n fogliame m

folk [fəuk] npl gente f ♦ adj popolare; **~s** npl (family) famiglia; **~lore** ['fəuklɔː*] n folclore m; ~ **song** n canto popolare

follow ['fɔləu] vt seguire ♦ vi seguire; (result) conseguire, risultare; **to ~ suit** fare lo stesso; ~ **up** vt (letter, offer) fare seguito a; (case) seguire; **~er** n seguace m/f, discepolo/a; **~ing** adj seguente ♦ n seguito, discepoli mpl; **~-on call** n chiamata successiva

folly ['fɔlɪ] n pazzia, follia

fond [fɔnd] adj (memory, look) tenero(a), affettuoso(a); **to be ~ of sb** volere bene a qn; **he's ~ of walking** gli piace fare camminate

fondle ['fɔndl] vt accarezzare

font [fɔnt] n (in church) fonte m battesimale; (TYP) caratteri mpl

food [fuːd] n cibo; ~ **mixer** n frullatore m; ~ **poisoning** n intossicazione f; ~ **processor** n tritatutto m inv elettrico; **~stuffs** npl generi fpl alimentari

fool [fuːl] n sciocco/a; (CULIN) frullato ♦ vt ingannare ♦ vi (gen: ~ **around**) fare lo sciocco; **~hardy** adj avventato(a); **~ish** adj scemo(a), stupido(a); imprudente; **~proof** adj (plan etc) sicurissimo(a)

foot [fut] (pl **feet**) n piede m; (measure) piede (= 304 mm; 12 inches); (of animal) zampa ♦ vt (bill) pagare; **on ~** a piedi; **~age** n (CINEMA: length) ≈ metraggio; (: material) sequenza; **~ball** n pallone m; (sport: BRIT) calcio; (: US) football m americano; **~ball player** n (BRIT: also: **~baller**) calciatore m; (US) giocatore m di football americano; **~brake** n freno a pedale; **~bridge** n passerella; **~hills** npl contrafforti fpl; **~hold** n punto d'appoggio; **~ing** n (fig) posizione f; **to lose one's ~ing** mettere un piede in fallo; **~note** n nota (a piè di pagina); **~path** n sentiero; (*in street*) marciapiede *m*; ~**print** *n* orma, impronta; ~**step** *n* passo; (~*print*) orma, impronta; ~**wear** *n* calzatura

---
KEYWORD
---

for [fɔ:*] *prep* **1** (*indicating destination, intention, purpose*) per; **the train ~ London** il treno è per Londra; **he went ~ the paper** è andato a prendere il giornale; **it's time ~ lunch** è ora di pranzo; **what's it ~?** a che serve?; **what ~?** (*why*) perché?

2 (*on behalf of, representing*) per; **to work ~ sb/sth** lavorare per qn/qc; **I'll ask him ~ you** glielo chiederò a nome tuo; **G ~ George** G come George

3 (*because of*) per, a causa di; **~ this reason** per questo motivo

4 (*with regard to*) per; **it's cold ~ July** è freddo per luglio; **~ everyone who voted yes, 50 voted no** per ogni voto a favore ce n'erano 50 contro

5 (*in exchange for*) per; **I sold it ~ £5** l'ho venduto per 5 sterline

6 (*in favour of*) per, a favore di; **are you ~ or against us?** è con noi o contro di noi?; **I'm all ~ it** sono completamente a favore

7 (*referring to distance, time*) per; **there are roadworks ~ 5 km** ci sono lavori in corso per 5 km; **he was away ~ 2 years** è stato via per 2 anni; **she will be away ~ a month** starà via un mese; **it hasn't rained ~ 3 weeks** non piove da 3 settimane; **can you do it ~ tomorrow?** può farlo per domani?

8 (*with infinitive clauses*): **it is not ~ me to decide** non sta a me decidere; **it would be best ~ you to leave** sarebbe meglio che lei se ne andasse; **there is still time ~ you to do it** ha ancora tempo per farlo; **~ this to be possible ...** perché ciò sia possibile ...

9 (*in spite of*) nonostante; **~ all his complaints, he's very fond of her** nonostante tutte le sue lamentele, le vuole molto bene

♦ *conj* (*since, as: rather formal*) dal momento che, poiché

forage ['fɔrɪdʒ] *vi*: **to ~ (for)** andare in cerca (di)

foray ['fɔreɪ] *n* incursione *f*

forbid [fə'bɪd] (*pt* **forbad(e)**, *pp* **forbidden**) *vt* vietare, interdire; **to ~ sb to do sth** proibire a qn di fare qc; ~**ding** *adj* minaccioso(a)

force [fɔ:s] *n* forza ♦ *vt* forzare; **the F~s** (*BRIT*) *npl* le forze armate; **to ~ o.s. to do** costringersi a fare; **in ~** (*in large numbers*) in gran numero; (*law*) in vigore; ~**d** *adj* forzato(a); ~**-feed** *vt* (*animal, prisoner*) sottoporre ad alimentazione forzata; ~**ful** *adj* forte, vigoroso(a)

forceps ['fɔ:seps] *npl* forcipe *m*

forcibly ['fɔ:səblɪ] *adv* con la forza; (*vigorously*) vigorosamente

ford [fɔ:d] *n* guado

fore [fɔ:*] *n*: **to come to the ~** mettersi in evidenza

forearm ['fɔ:rɑ:m] *n* avambraccio

foreboding [fɔ:'bəudɪŋ] *n* cattivo presagio

forecast ['fɔ:kɑ:st] (*irreg: like* **cast**) *n* previsione *f* ♦ *vt* prevedere

forecourt ['fɔ:kɔ:t] *n* (*of garage*) corte *f* esterna

forefinger ['fɔ:fɪŋgə*] *n* (dito) indice *m*

forefront ['fɔ:frʌnt] *n*: **in the ~ of** all'avanguardia in

forego [fɔ:'gəu] (*irreg: like* **go**) *vt* rinunciare a

foregone [fɔ:'gɔn] *pp* of **forego** ♦ *adj*: **it's a ~ conclusion** è una conclusione scontata

foreground ['fɔ:graund] *n* primo piano

forehead ['fɔrɪd] *n* fronte *f*

foreign ['fɔrɪn] *adj* straniero(a); (*trade*) estero(a); (*object, matter*) estraneo(a); ~**er** *n* straniero/a; ~ **exchange** *n* cambio con l'estero; (*currency*) valuta estera; **F~ Office** (*BRIT*) *n* Ministero degli Esteri; **F~ Secretary** (*BRIT*) *n* ministro degli Affari esteri

foreleg ['fɔ:leg] *n* zampa anteriore

foreman ['fɔ:mən] (*irreg*) *n* caposquadra *m*

foremost ['fɔ:məust] *adj* principale; più in vista ♦ *adv*: **first and ~** innanzitutto

forensic [fəˈrɛnsɪk] *adj*: **~ medicine** medicina legale

forerunner [ˈfɔːrʌnə*] *n* precursore *m*

foresaw [fɔːˈsɔː] *pt of* **foresee**

foresee [fɔːˈsiː] (*irreg: like* **see**) *vt* prevedere; **~able** *adj* prevedibile; **foreseen** *pp of* **foresee**

foreshadow [fɔːˈʃædəu] *vt* presagire, far prevedere

foresight [ˈfɔːsaɪt] *n* previdenza

forest [ˈfɒrɪst] *n* foresta

forestry [ˈfɒrɪstrɪ] *n* silvicoltura

foretaste [ˈfɔːteɪst] *n* pregustazione *f*

foretell [fɔːˈtɛl] (*irreg: like* **tell**) *vt* predire; **foretold** [fɔːˈtəuld] *pt, pp of* **foretell**

forever [fəˈrɛvə*] *adv* per sempre; (*endlessly*) sempre, di continuo

foreword [ˈfɔːwəːd] *n* prefazione *f*

forfeit [ˈfɔːfɪt] *vt* perdere; (*one's happiness, health*) giocarsi

forgave [fəˈgeɪv] *pt of* **forgive**

forge [fɔːdʒ] *n* fucina ♦ *vt* (*signature, money*) contraffare, falsificare; (*wrought iron*) fucinare, foggiare; **~ ahead** *vi* tirare avanti; **~ry** *n* falso; (*activity*) contraffazione *f*

forget [fəˈgɛt] (*pt* **forgot,** *pp* **forgotten**) *vt, vi* dimenticare; **~ful** *adj* di corta memoria; **~ful of** dimentico(a) di; **~-me-not** *n* nontiscordardimé *m inv*

forgive [fəˈgɪv] (*pt* **forgave,** *pp* **forgiven**) *vt* perdonare; **to ~ sb for sth** perdonare qc a qn; **~ness** *n* perdono

forgo [fɔːˈgəu] = **forego**

forgot [fəˈgɒt] *pt of* **forget**

forgotten [fəˈgɒtn] *pp of* **forget**

fork [fɔːk] *n* (*for eating*) forchetta; (*for gardening*) forca; (*of roads, rivers, railways*) biforcazione *f* ♦ *vi* (*road etc*) biforcarsi; **~ out** (*inf*) *vt* (*pay*) sborsare; **~-lift truck** *n* carrello elevatore

forlorn [fəˈlɔːn] *adj* (*person*) sconsolato(a); (*place*) abbandonato(a); (*attempt*) disperato(a); (*hope*) vano(a)

form [fɔːm] *n* forma; (*SCOL*) classe *f*; (*questionnaire*) scheda ♦ *vt* formare; **in top ~** in gran forma

formal [ˈfɔːməl] *adj* formale; (*gardens*) simmetrico(a), regolare; **~ly** *adv* formalmente

format [ˈfɔːmæt] *n* formato ♦ *vt* (*COMPUT*) formattare

formation [fɔːˈmeɪʃən] *n* formazione *f*

formative [ˈfɔːmətɪv] *adj*: **~ years** anni *mpl* formativi

former [ˈfɔːmə*] *adj* vecchio(a) (*before n*), ex *inv* (*before n*); **the ~ ... the latter** quello ... questo; **~ly** *adv* in passato

formula [ˈfɔːmjulə] *n* formula

forsake [fəˈseɪk] (*pt* **forsook,** *pp* **forsaken**) *vt* abbandonare

fort [fɔːt] *n* forte *m*

forth [fɔːθ] *adv* in avanti; **back and ~** avanti e indietro; **and so ~** e così via; **~coming** *adj* (*event*) prossimo(a); (*help*) disponibile; (*character*) aperto(a), comunicativo(a); **~right** *adj* franco(a), schietto(a); **~with** *adv* immediatamente, subito

fortify [ˈfɔːtɪfaɪ] *vt* (*city*) fortificare; (*person*) armare

fortitude [ˈfɔːtɪtjuːd] *n* forza d'animo

fortnight [ˈfɔːtnaɪt] (*BRIT*) *n* quindici giorni *mpl*, due settimane *fpl*; **~ly** *adj* bimensile ♦ *adv* ogni quindici giorni

fortress [ˈfɔːtrɪs] *n* fortezza, rocca

fortunate [ˈfɔːtʃənɪt] *adj* fortunato(a); **it is ~ that** è una fortuna che; **~ly** *adv* fortunatamente

fortune [ˈfɔːtʃən] *n* fortuna; **~-teller** *n* indovino/a

forty [ˈfɔːtɪ] *num* quaranta

forum [ˈfɔːrəm] *n* foro

forward [ˈfɔːwəd] *adj* (*ahead of schedule*) in anticipo; (*movement, position*) in avanti; (*not shy*) aperto(a); diretto(a) ♦ *n* (*SPORT*) avanti *m inv* ♦ *vt* (*letter*) inoltrare; (*parcel, goods*) spedire; (*career, plans*) promuovere, appoggiare; **to move ~** avanzare; **~(s)** *adv* avanti

fossil [ˈfɒsl] *adj* fossile ♦ *n* fossile *m*

foster [ˈfɒstə*] *vt* incoraggiare, nutrire; (*child*) avere in affidamento; **~ child** *n* bambino(a) preso(a) in affidamento

fought [fɔːt] *pt, pp of* **fight**

foul [faul] *adj* (*smell, food, temper etc*) cattivo(a); (*weather*) brutto(a); (*language*) osceno(a) ♦ *n* (*SPORT*) fallo ♦ *vt* sporcare; ~ **play** *n* (*LAW*): **the police suspect ~ play** la polizia sospetta un atto criminale

found [faund] *pt, pp of* **find** ♦ *vt* (*establish*) fondare; **~ation** [-'deɪʃən] *n* (*act*) fondazione *f*; (*base*) base *f*; (*also:* **~ation cream**) fondo tinta; **~ations** *npl* (*of building*) fondamenta *fpl*

founder ['faundə*] *n* fondatore/trice *f* ♦ *vi* affondare

foundry ['faundrɪ] *n* fonderia

fountain ['fauntɪn] *n* fontana; ~ **pen** *n* penna stilografica

four [fɔː*] *num* quattro; **on all ~s** a carponi; **~-poster** *n* (*also:* **~-poster bed**) letto a quattro colonne; **~teen** *num* quattordici; **~th** *num* quarto(a)

fowl [faul] *n* pollame *m*; volatile *m*

fox [fɔks] *n* volpe *f* ♦ *vt* confondere

foyer ['fɔɪeɪ] *n* atrio; (*THEATRE*) ridotto

fraction ['frækʃən] *n* frazione *f*

fracture ['fræktʃə*] *n* frattura

fragile ['frædʒaɪl] *adj* fragile

fragment ['frægmənt] *n* frammento

fragrant ['freɪgrənt] *adj* fragrante, profumato(a)

frail [freɪl] *adj* debole, delicato(a)

frame [freɪm] *n* (*of building*) armatura; (*of human, animal*) ossatura, corpo; (*of picture*) cornice *f*; (*of door, window*) telaio; (*of spectacles: also:* **~s**) montatura ♦ *vt* (*picture*) incorniciare; ~ **of mind** *n* stato d'animo; **~work** *n* struttura

France [frɑːns] *n* Francia

franchise ['fræntʃaɪz] *n* (*POL*) diritto di voto; (*COMM*) concessione *f*

frank [fræŋk] *adj* franco(a), aperto(a) ♦ *vt* (*letter*) affrancare; **~ly** *adv* francamente, sinceramente

frantic ['fræntɪk] *adj* frenetico(a)

fraternity [frə'tɜːnɪtɪ] *n* (*club*) associazione *f*; (*spirit*) fratellanza

fraud [frɔːd] *n* truffa; (*LAW*) frode *f*; (*person*) impostore/a

fraught [frɔːt] *adj*: ~ **with** pieno(a) di,

intriso(a) da

fray [freɪ] *vt* logorare ♦ *vi* logorarsi

freak [friːk] *n* fenomeno, mostro

freckle ['frekl] *n* lentiggine *f*

free [friː] *adj* libero(a); (*gratis*) gratuito(a) ♦ *vt* (*prisoner, jammed person*) liberare; (*jammed object*) districare; ~ (**of charge**), **for ~** gratuitamente; **~dom** ['friːdəm] *n* libertà; **F~fone** ® *n* numero verde; **~-for-all** *n* parapiglia *m* generale; ~ **gift** *n* regalo, omaggio; **~hold** *n* proprietà assoluta; ~ **kick** *n* calcio libero; **~lance** *adj* indipendente; **~ly** *adv* liberamente; (*liberally*) liberalmente; **F~mason** *n* massone *m*; **F~post** ® *n* affrancatura a carico del destinatario; **~-range** *adj* (*hen*) ruspante; (*eggs*) di gallina ruspante; **~style** *n* (*SPORT*) stile *m* libero; ~ **trade** *n* libero scambio; **~way** (*US*) *n* superstrada; ~ **will** *n* libero arbitrio; **of one's own ~ will** di spontanea volontà

freeze [friːz] (*pt* **froze,** *pp* **frozen**) *vi* gelare ♦ *vt* gelare; (*food*) congelare; (*prices, salaries*) bloccare ♦ *n* gelo; blocco; **~-dried** *adj* liofilizzato(a); **~r** *n* congelatore *m*

freezing ['friːzɪŋ] *adj* (*wind, weather*) gelido(a); ~ **point** *n* punto di congelamento; **3 degrees below ~ point** 3 gradi sotto zero

freight [freɪt] *n* (*goods*) merce *f*, merci *fpl*; (*money charged*) spese *fpl* di trasporto; ~ **train** (*US*) *n* treno *m* merci *inv*

French [frentʃ] *adj* francese ♦ *n* (*LING*) francese *m*; **the ~** *npl* i Francesi; ~ **bean** *n* fagiolino; ~ **fried potatoes** (*US* **~ fries**) *npl* patate *fpl* fritte; **~man** (*irreg*) *n* francese *m*; ~ **window** *n* portafinestra; **~woman** (*irreg*) *n* francese *f*

frenzy ['frenzɪ] *n* frenesia

frequency ['friːkwənsɪ] *n* frequenza

frequent [*adj* 'friːkwənt, *vb* frɪ'kwent] *adj* frequente ♦ *vt* frequentare; **~ly** *adv* frequentemente, spesso

fresco ['freskəu] *n* affresco

fresh [freʃ] *adj* fresco(a); (*new*) nuovo(a); (*cheeky*) sfacciato(a); **~en** *vi* (*wind, air*) rinfrescare; **~en up** vi rinfrescarsi; **~er** (BRIT: inf) n (SCOL) matricola; **~ly** adv di recente, di fresco; **~man** (irreg) (US) n = **~er**; **~ness** n freschezza; **~water** adj (fish) d'acqua dolce

fret [frɛt] vi agitarsi, affliggersi

friar ['fraɪə*] n frate m

friction ['frɪkʃən] n frizione f, attrito

Friday ['fraɪdɪ] n venerdì m

fridge [frɪdʒ] (BRIT) n frigo, frigorifero

fried [fraɪd] pt, pp of **fry** ♦ adj fritto(a)

friend [frɛnd] n amico/a; **~ly** adj amichevole; **~ly fire** n (MIL) fuoco amico; **~ship** n amicizia

frieze [fri:z] n fregio

fright [fraɪt] n paura, spavento; **to take ~** spaventarsi; **~en** vt spaventare, far paura a; **~ened** adj spaventato(a); **~ening** adj spaventoso(a), pauroso(a); **~ful** adj orribile

frill [frɪl] n balza

fringe [frɪndʒ] n (decoration, BRIT: of hair) frangia; (edge: of forest etc) margine m; **~ benefits** npl vantaggi mpl

frisk [frɪsk] vt perquisire

frisky ['frɪskɪ] adj vivace, vispo(a)

fritter ['frɪtə*] n frittella; **~ away** vt sprecare

frivolous ['frɪvələs] adj frivolo(a)

frizzy ['frɪzɪ] adj crespo(a)

fro [frəu] see **to**

frock [frɔk] n vestito

frog [frɔg] n rana; **~man** (irreg) n uomo m rana inv

frolic ['frɔlɪk] vi sgambettare

KEYWORD
---

from [frɔm] prep **1** (indicating starting place, origin etc) da; **where do you come ~?, where are you ~?** da dove viene?, di dov'è?; **~ London to Glasgow** da Londra a Glasgow; **a letter ~ my sister** una lettera da mia sorella; **tell him ~ me that ...** gli dica da parte mia che ...

2 (indicating time) da; **~ one o'clock to** or **until** or **till two** dall'una alle due; **~ January (on)** da gennaio, a partire da gennaio

3 (indicating distance) da; **the hotel is**

1 km ~ the beach l'albergo è a 1 km dalla spiaggia

4 (indicating price, number etc) da; **prices range ~ £10 to £50** i prezzi vanno dalle 10 alle 50 sterline

5 (indicating difference) da; **he can't tell red ~ green** non sa distinguere il rosso dal verde

6 (because of, on the basis of): **~ what he says** da quanto dice lui; **weak ~ hunger** debole per la fame

---

front [frʌnt] n (of house, dress) davanti m inv; (of train) testa; (of book) copertina; (promenade: also: **sea ~**) lungomare m; (MIL, POL, METEOR) fronte m; (fig: appearances) fronte f ♦ adj primo(a); anteriore, davanti inv; **in ~ of** davanti a; **~ door** n porta d'entrata; (of car) sportello anteriore; **~ier** ['frʌntɪə*] n frontiera; **~ page** n prima pagina; **~ room** (BRIT) n salotto; **~-wheel drive** n trasmissione f anteriore

frost [frɔst] n gelo; (also: **hoar~**) brina; **~bite** n congelamento; **~ed** adj (glass) smerigliato(a); **~y** adj (weather, look) gelido(a)

froth ['frɔθ] n spuma; schiuma

frown [fraun] vi acciglarsi

froze [frəuz] pt of **freeze**; **frozen** pp of **freeze**

fruit [fru:t] n inv (also fig) frutto; (collectively) frutta; **~erer** n fruttivendolo; **~erer's (shop)** n: **at the ~erer's (shop)** dal fruttivendolo; **~ful** adj fruttuoso(a); **~ion** [fru:'ɪʃən] n: **to come to ~ion** realizzarsi; **~ juice** n succo di frutta; **~ machine** (BRIT) n macchina f mangiasoldi inv; **~ salad** n macedonia

frustrate [frʌs'treɪt] vt frustrare

fry [fraɪ] (pt, pp fried) vt friggere; see also **small**; **~ing pan** n padella

ft. abbr = **foot**; **feet**

fudge [fʌdʒ] n (CULIN) specie di caramella a base di latte, burro e zucchero

fuel [fjuəl] n (for heating) combustibile m; (for propelling) carburante m; **~ tank** n deposito *m* nafta *inv*; (*on vehicle*) serbatoio (della benzina)

fugitive ['fjuːdʒɪtɪv] *n* fuggitivo/a, profugo/a

fulfil [ful'fɪl] *vt* (*function*) compiere; (*order*) eseguire; (*wish*, *desire*) soddisfare, appagare; **~ment** (*US* **fulfillment**) *n* (*of wishes*) soddisfazione *f*, appagamento; **sense of ~ment** soddisfazione

full [ful] *adj* pieno(a); (*details*, *skirt*) ampio(a) ♦ *adv*: **to know ~ well that** sapere benissimo che; **I'm ~ (up)** sono pieno; **a ~ two hours** due ore intere; **at ~ speed** a tutta velocità; **in ~** per intero; **~ board** (*BRIT*) *n* pensione *f* completa; **~ employment** *n* piena occupazione; **~-length** *adj* (*film*) a lungometraggio; (*coat*, *novel*) lungo(a); (*portrait*) in piedi; **~ moon** *n* luna piena; **~-scale** *adj* (*attack*, *war*) su larga scala; (*model*) in grandezza naturale; **~ stop** *n* punto; **~-time** *adj*, *adv* (*work*) a tempo pieno; **~y** *adv* interamente, pienamente, completamente; (*at least*) almeno; **~y-fledged** *adj* (*teacher*, *member etc*) a tutti gli effetti; **~y licensed** *adj* (*hotel*, *restaurant*) autorizzato(a) alla vendita di alcolici

fumble ['fʌmbl] *vi*: **to ~ with sth** armeggiare con qc

fume [fjuːm] *vi* essere furioso(a); **~s** *npl* esalazioni *fpl*, vapori *mpl*

fun [fʌn] *n* divertimento, spasso; **to have ~** divertirsi; **for ~** per scherzo; **to make ~ of** prendersi gioco di

function ['fʌŋkʃən] *n* funzione *f*; cerimonia, ricevimento ♦ *vi* funzionare; **~al** *adj* funzionale

fund [fʌnd] *n* fondo, cassa; (*source*) fondo; (*store*) riserva; **~s** *npl* (*money*) fondi *mpl*

fundamental [fʌndə'mɛntl] *adj* fondamentale

funeral ['fjuːnərəl] *n* funerale *m*; **~ parlour** *n* impresa di pompe funebri; **~ service** *n* ufficio funebre

fun fair (*BRIT*) *n* luna park *m inv*

fungus ['fʌŋgəs] (*pl* **fungi**) *n* fungo; (*mould*) muffa

funnel ['fʌnl] *n* imbuto; (*of ship*) ciminiera

funny ['fʌnɪ] *adj* divertente, buffo(a); (*strange*) strano(a), bizzarro(a)

fur [fəː*] *n* pelo; pelliccia; (*BRIT*: *in kettle etc*) deposito calcare; **~ coat** *n* pelliccia

furious ['fjuərɪəs] *adj* furioso(a); (*effort*) accanito(a)

furlong ['fəːlɔŋ] *n* = 201.17 m (*termine ippico*)

furnace ['fəːnɪs] *n* fornace *f*

furnish ['fəːnɪʃ] *vt* ammobiliare; (*supply*) fornire; **~ings** *npl* mobili *mpl*, mobilia

furniture ['fəːnɪtʃə*] *n* mobili *mpl*; **piece of ~** mobile *m*

furrow ['fʌrəu] *n* solco

furry ['fəːrɪ] *adj* (*animal*) peloso(a)

further ['fəːðə*] *adj* supplementare, altro(a); nuovo(a); più lontano(a) ♦ *adv* più lontano; (*more*) di più; (*moreover*) inoltre ♦ *vt* favorire, promuovere; **college of ~ education** *n* istituto statale con corsi specializzati (*di formazione professionale, aggiornamento professionale etc*); **~more** [fəːðə'mɔː*] *adv* inoltre, per di più

furthest ['fəːðɪst] *superl of* **far**

fury ['fjuərɪ] *n* furore *m*

fuse [fjuːz] *n* fusibile *m*; (*for bomb etc*) miccia, spoletta ♦ *vt* fondere ♦ *vi* fondersi; **to ~ the lights** (*BRIT*: *ELEC*) far saltare i fusibili; **~ box** *n* cassetta dei fusibili

fuselage ['fjuːzəlɑːʒ] *n* fusoliera

fuss [fʌs] *n* agitazione *f*; (*complaining*) storie *fpl*; **to make a ~** fare delle storie; **~y** *adj* (*person*) puntiglioso(a), esigente; che fa le storie; (*dress*) carico(a) di fronzoli; (*style*) elaborato(a)

future ['fjuːtʃə*] *adj* futuro(a) ♦ *n* futuro, avvenire *m*; (*LING*) futuro; **in ~** in futuro

fuze [fjuːz] (*US*) = **fuse**

fuzzy ['fʌzɪ] *adj* (*PHOT*) indistinto(a), sfocato(a); (*hair*) crespo(a)

G, g

G [dʒiː] n (MUS) sol m

G7 abbr (= Group of Seven) G7

gabble ['gæbl] vi borbottare; farfugliare

gable ['geɪbl] n frontone m

gadget ['gædʒɪt] n aggeggio

Gaelic ['geɪlɪk] adj gaelico(a) ♦ n (LING) gaelico

gag [gæg] n bavaglio; (joke) facezia, scherzo ♦ vt imbavagliare

gaiety ['geɪtɪ] n gaiezza

gaily ['geɪlɪ] adv allegramente

gain [geɪn] n guadagno, profitto ♦ vt guadagnare ♦ vi (clock, watch) andare avanti; (benefit): to ~ (from) trarre beneficio (da); to ~ 3lbs (in weight) aumentare di 3 libbre; to ~ on sb (in race etc) guadagnare su qn

gal. abbr = gallon

galaxy ['gæləksɪ] n galassia

gale [geɪl] n vento forte; burrasca

gallant ['gælənt] adj valoroso(a); (towards ladies) galante, cortese

gall bladder ['gɔːl-] n cistifellea

gallery ['gælərɪ] n galleria

gallon ['gælən] n gallone m (= 8 pints; BRIT = 4.543l; US = 3.785l)

gallop ['gæləp] n galoppo ♦ vi galoppare

gallows ['gæləuz] n forca

gallstone ['gɔːlstəun] n calcolo biliare

galore [gə'lɔː*] adv a iosa, a profusione

galvanize ['gælvənaɪz] vt galvanizzare

gambit ['gæmbɪt] n (fig): (opening) ~ prima mossa

gamble ['gæmbl] n azzardo, rischio calcolato ♦ vt, vi giocare; to ~ on (fig) giocare su; ~r n giocatore/trice d'azzardo; gambling n gioco d'azzardo

game [geɪm] n gioco; (event) partita; (TENNIS) game m inv; (CULIN, HUNTING) selvaggina ♦ adj (ready): to be ~ (for sth/ to do) essere pronto(a) (a qc/a fare); big ~ selvaggina grossa; ~keeper n guardacaccia m inv

gammon ['gæmən] n (bacon) quarto di maiale; (ham) prosciutto affumicato

gamut ['gæmət] n gamma

gang [gæŋ] n banda, squadra ♦ vi: to ~ up on sb far combutta contro qn

gangrene ['gæŋgriːn] n cancrena

gangster ['gæŋstə*] n gangster m inv

gangway ['gæŋweɪ] n passerella; (BRIT: of bus) corridoio

gaol [dʒeɪl] (BRIT) n, vt = jail

gap [gæp] n (space) buco; (in time) inter- vallo; (difference): ~ (between) divario (tra)

gape [geɪp] vi (person) restare a bocca aperta; (shirt, hole) essere spalancato(a); gaping adj spalancato(a)

gap year (SCOL) n anno di pausa durante il quale gli studenti viaggiano o lavorano

garage ['gæraːʒ] n garage m inv

garbage ['gaːbɪdʒ] n (US) immondizie fpl, rifiuti mpl; (inf) sciocchezze fpl; ~ can (US) n bidone m della spazzatura

garbled ['gaːbld] adj deformato(a); ingarbugliato(a)

garden ['gaːdn] n giardino; ~s npl (public park) giardini pubblici; ~er n giardiniere/a; ~ing n giardinaggio

gargle ['gaːgl] vi fare gargarismi

garish ['gɛərɪʃ] adj vistoso(a)

garland ['gaːlənd] n ghirlanda; corona

garlic ['gaːlɪk] n aglio

garment ['gaːmənt] n indumento

garnish ['gaːnɪʃ] vt (food) guarnire

garrison ['gærɪsn] n guarnigione f

garter ['gaːtə*] n giarrettiera

gas [gæs] n gas m inv; (US: gasoline) benzina ♦ vt asfissiare con il gas; ~ cooker (BRIT) n cucina a gas; ~ cylinder n bombola del gas; ~ fire (BRIT) n radiatore m a gas

gash [gæʃ] n sfregio ♦ vt sfregiare

gasket ['gæskɪt] n (AUT) guarnizione f

gas mask n maschera f antigas inv

gas meter n contatore m del gas

gasoline ['gæsəliːn] (US) n benzina

gasp [gaːsp] n respiro affannoso, ansito ♦ vi ansare, ansimare; (in surprise) restare senza fiato

gas station (US) n distributore m di benzina

gassy ['gæsɪ] *adj* gassoso(a)

gate [geɪt] *n* cancello; (*at airport*) uscita; **~crash** (*BRIT*) *vt* partecipare senza invito a; **~way** *n* porta

gather ['gæðə*] *vt* (*flowers, fruit*) cogliere; (*pick up*) raccogliere; (*assemble*) radunare; raccogliere; (*understand*) capire; (*SEWING*) increspare ♦ *vi* (*assemble*) radunarsi; **to ~ speed** acquistare velocità; **~ing** *n* adunanza

gauche [gəʊʃ] *adj* goffo(a), maldestro(a)

gaudy ['gɔːdɪ] *adj* vistoso(a)

gauge [geɪdʒ] *n* (*instrument*) indicatore *m* ♦ *vt* misurare; (*fig*) valutare

gaunt [gɔːnt] *adj* scarno(a); (*grim, desolate*) desolato(a)

gauntlet ['gɔːntlɪt] *n* guanto; (*fig*): **to run the ~ through an angry crowd** passare sotto il fuoco di una folla ostile; **to throw down the ~** gettare il guanto

gauze [gɔːz] *n* garza

gave [geɪv] *pt of* **give**

gay [geɪ] *adj* (*homosexual*) omosessuale; (*cheerful*) gaio(a), allegro(a); (*colour*) vivace, vivo(a)

gaze [geɪz] *n* sguardo fisso ♦ *vi*: **to ~ at** guardare fisso

GB *abbr* = **Great Britain**

GCE (*BRIT*) *n abbr* (= *General Certificate of Education*) ≈ maturità

GCSE (*BRIT*) *n abbr* = *General Certificate of Secondary Education*

gear [gɪə*] *n* attrezzi *mpl*, equipaggiamento; (*TECH*) ingranaggio; (*AUT*) marcia ♦ *vt* (*fig: adapt*): **to ~ sth to** adattare qc a; **in top** or (*US*) **high/low ~** in quarta (*or* quinta)/ seconda; **in ~** in marcia; **~ box** *n* scatola del cambio; **~ lever** (*US* **~ shift**) *n* leva del cambio

geese [giːs] *npl of* **goose**

gel [dʒel] *n* gel *m inv*

gem [dʒem] *n* gemma

Gemini ['dʒemɪnaɪ] *n* Gemelli *mpl*

gender ['dʒendə*] *n* genere *m*

general ['dʒenərl] *n* generale *m* ♦ *adj* generale; **in ~** in genere; **~ delivery** (*US*) *n* fermo posta *m*; **~ election** *n* elezioni

fpl generali; **~ly** *adv* generalmente; **~ practitioner** *n* medico generico

generate ['dʒenəreɪt] *vt* generare

generation [dʒenə'reɪʃən] *n* generazione *f*

generator ['dʒenəreɪtə*] *n* generatore *m*

generosity [dʒenə'rɔsɪtɪ] *n* generosità

generous ['dʒenərəs] *adj* generoso(a); (*copious*) abbondante

genetic engineering [dʒɪ'netɪk-] *n* ingegneria genetica

genetic fingerprinting [dʒɪ'netɪk-] *n* rilevamento delle impronte genetiche

Geneva [dʒɪ'niːvə] *n* Ginevra

genial ['dʒiːnɪəl] *adj* geniale, cordiale

genitals ['dʒenɪtlz] *npl* genitali *mpl*

genius ['dʒiːnɪəs] *n* genio

Genoa ['dʒenəuə] *n* Genova

gent [dʒent] *n abbr* = **gentleman**

genteel [dʒen'tiːl] *adj* raffinato(a), distinto(a)

gentle ['dʒentl] *adj* delicato(a); (*person*) dolce

gentleman ['dʒentlmən] *n* signore *m*; (*well-bred man*) gentiluomo

gently ['dʒentlɪ] *adv* delicatamente

gentry ['dʒentrɪ] *n* nobiltà minore

gents [dʒents] *n* W.C. *m* (per signori)

genuine ['dʒenjuɪn] *adj* autentico(a); sincero(a)

geography [dʒɪ'ɔgrəfɪ] *n* geografia

geology [dʒɪ'ɔlədʒɪ] *n* geologia

geometric(al) [dʒɪə'metrɪk(l)] *adj* geometrico(a)

geometry [dʒɪ'ɔmətrɪ] *n* geometria

geranium [dʒɪ'reɪnjəm] *n* geranio

geriatric [dʒerɪ'ætrɪk] *adj* geriatrico(a)

germ [dʒəːm] *n* (*MED*) microbo; (*BIOL, fig*) germe *m*

German ['dʒəːmən] *adj* tedesco(a) ♦ *n* tedesco/a; (*LING*) tedesco; **~ measles** (*BRIT*) *n* rosolia

Germany ['dʒəːmənɪ] *n* Germania

gesture ['dʒestjə*] *n* gesto

KEYWORD

get [get] (*pt, pp* **got**, (*US*) *pp* **gotten**) *vi* **1** (*become, be*) diventare, farsi; **to ~ old**

invecchiare; **to ~ tired** stancarsi; **to ~ drunk** ubriacarsi; **to ~ killed** venire or rimanere ucciso(a); **when do I ~ paid?** quando mi pagate?; **it's ~ting late** si sta facendo tardi
2 (go): **to ~ to/from** andare a/da; **to ~ home** arrivare or tornare a casa; **how did you ~ here?** come sei venuto?
3 (begin) mettersi a, cominciare a; **to ~ to know sb** incominciare a conoscere qn; **let's ~ going** or **started** muoviamoci
4 (modal aux vb): **you've got to do it** devi farlo
♦ vt 1: **to ~ sth done** (do) fare qc; (have done) far fare qc; **to ~ one's hair cut** farsi tagliare i capelli; **to ~ sb to do sth** far fare qc a qn
2 (obtain: money, permission, results) ottenere; (find: job, flat) trovare; (fetch: person, doctor) chiamare; (: object) prendere; **to ~ sth for sb** prendere or procurare qc a qn; **~ me Mr Jones, please** (TEL) mi passi il signor Jones, per favore; **can I ~ you a drink?** le posso offrire da bere?
3 (receive: present, letter, prize) ricevere; (acquire: reputation) farsi; **how much did you ~ for the painting?** quanto le hanno dato per il quadro?
4 (catch) prendere; (hit: target etc) colpire; **to ~ sb by the arm/throat** afferrare qn per un braccio/alla gola; **~ him!** prendetelo!
5 (take, move) portare; **to ~ sth to sb** far avere qc a qn; **do you think we'll ~ it through the door?** pensi che riusciremo a farlo passare per la porta?
6 (catch, take: plane, bus etc) prendere
7 (understand) afferrare; (hear) sentire; **I've got it!** ci sono arrivato!, ci sono!; **I'm sorry, I didn't ~ your name** scusi, non ho capito (or sentito) il suo nome
8 (have, possess): **to have got** avere; **how many have you got?** quanti ne ha?
get about vi muoversi; (news) diffondersi
get along vi (agree) andare d'accordo; (depart) andarsene; (manage) = **get by**
get at vt fus (attack) prendersela con; (reach) raggiungere, arrivare a

get away vi partire, andarsene; (escape) scappare
get away with vt fus cavarsela; farla franca
get back vi (return) ritornare, tornare ♦ vt riottenere, riavere
get by vi (pass) passare; (manage) farcela
get down vi, vt fus scendere ♦ vt far scendere; (depress) buttare giù
get down to vt fus (work) mettersi a (fare)
get in vi entrare; (train) arrivare; (arrive home) ritornare, tornare
get into vt fus entrare in; **to ~ into a rage** incavolarsi
get off vi (from train etc) scendere; (depart: person, car) andare via; (escape) cavarsela ♦ vt (remove: clothes, stain) levare ♦ vt fus (train, bus) scendere da
get on vi (at exam etc) andare; (agree): **to ~ on (with)** andare d'accordo (con) ♦ vt fus montare in; (horse) montare su
get out vi uscire; (of vehicle) scendere ♦ vt tirar fuori, far uscire
get out of vt fus uscire da; (duty etc) evitare
get over vt fus (illness) riaversi da
get round vt fus aggirare; (fig: person) rigirare
get through vi (TEL) avere la linea
get through to vt fus (TEL) parlare a
get together vi riunirsi ♦ vt raccogliere; (people) adunare
get up vi (rise) alzarsi ♦ vt fus salire su per
get up to vt fus (reach) raggiungere; (prank etc) fare

getaway ['getəweɪ] n fuga
geyser ['giːzə*] n (BRIT) scaldabagno; (GEO) geyser m inv
Ghana ['gɑːnə] n Ghana m
ghastly ['gɑːstlɪ] adj orribile, orrendo(a); (pale) spettrale
gherkin ['gəːkɪn] n cetriolino
ghetto blaster ['getəublɑːstə*] n maxistereo m inv portatile
ghost [gəust] n fantasma m, spettro

giant ['dʒaɪənt] *n* gigante *m* ♦ *adj* gigantesco(a), enorme

gibberish ['dʒɪbərɪʃ] *n* parole *fpl* senza senso

gibe [dʒaɪb] *n* = **jibe**

giblets ['dʒɪblɪts] *npl* frattaglie *fpl*

Gibraltar [dʒɪ'brɔːltə*] *n* Gibilterra

giddy ['gɪdɪ] *adj* (*dizzy*): **to be ~** aver le vertigini

gift [gɪft] *n* regalo; (*donation, ability*) dono; **~ed** *adj* dotato(a); **~ token** *n* buono *m* omaggio *inv*; **~ voucher** *n* = **~ token**

gigantic [dʒaɪ'gæntɪk] *adj* gigantesco(a)

giggle ['gɪgl] *vi* ridere scioccamente

gill [dʒɪl] *n* (*measure*) = 0.25 pints (*BRIT* = 0.148l, *US* = 0.118l)

gills [gɪlz] *npl* (*of fish*) branchie *fpl*

gilt [gɪlt] *n* doratura ♦ *adj* dorato(a); **~-edged** *adj* (*COMM*) della massima sicurezza

gimmick ['gɪmɪk] *n* trucco

gin [dʒɪn] *n* (*liquor*) gin *m inv*

ginger ['dʒɪndʒə*] *n* zenzero; **~ ale, ~ beer** *n* bibita gassosa allo zenzero; **~bread** *n* pan *m* di zenzero

gingerly ['dʒɪndʒəlɪ] *adv* cautamente

gipsy ['dʒɪpsɪ] *n* zingaro/a

giraffe [dʒɪ'rɑːf] *n* giraffa

girder ['gəːdə*] *n* trave *f*

girl [gəːl] *n* ragazza; (*young unmarried woman*) signorina; (*daughter*) figlia, figliola; **~friend** *n* (*of girl*) amica; (*of boy*) ragazza; **~ish** *adj* da ragazza

giro ['dʒaɪrəu] *n* (*bank ~*) versamento bancario; (*post office ~*) postagiro; (*BRIT: welfare cheque*) assegno del sussidio di assistenza sociale

gist [dʒɪst] *n* succo

give [gɪv] (*pt* **gave**, *pp* **given**) *vt* dare ♦ *vi* cedere; **to ~ sb sth, ~ sth to sb** dare qc a qn; **I'll ~ you £5 for it** te lo pago 5 sterline; **to ~ a cry/sigh** emettere un grido/sospiro; **to ~ a speech** fare un discorso; **~ away** *vt* dare via; (*disclose*) rivelare; (*bride*) condurre all'altare; **~ back** *vt* rendere; **~ in** *vi* cedere ♦ *vt* consegnare; **~ off** *vt* emettere; **~ out** *vt* distribuire;

annunciare; **~ up** *vi* rinunciare ♦ *vt* rinunciare a; **to ~ up smoking** smettere di fumare; **to ~ o.s. up** arrendersi; **~ way** *vi* cedere; (*BRIT: AUT*) dare la precedenza

glacier ['glæsɪə*] *n* ghiacciaio

glad [glæd] *adj* lieto(a), contento(a)

gladly ['glædlɪ] *adv* volentieri

glamorous ['glæmərəs] *adj* affascinante, seducente

glamour ['glæmə*] *n* fascino

glance [glɑːns] *n* occhiata, sguardo ♦ *vi*: **to ~ at** dare un'occhiata a; **to ~ off** (*bullet*) rimbalzare su; **glancing** *adj* (*blow*) che colpisce di striscio

gland [glænd] *n* ghiandola

glare [glɛə*] *n* (*of anger*) sguardo furioso; (*of light*) riverbero, luce *f* abbagliante; (*of publicity*) chiasso ♦ *vi* abbagliare; **to ~ at** guardare male; **glaring** *adj* (*mistake*) madornale

glass [glɑːs] *n* (*substance*) vetro; (*tumbler*) bicchiere *m*; **~es** *npl* (*spectacles*) occhiali *mpl*; **~ware** *n* vetrame *m*; **~y** *adj* (*eyes*) vitreo(a)

glaze [gleɪz] *vt* (*door*) fornire di vetri; (*pottery*) smaltare ♦ *n* smalto; **~d** *adj* (*eyes*) vitreo(a); (*pottery*) smaltato(a)

glazier ['gleɪzɪə*] *n* vetraio

gleam [gliːm] *vi* luccicare

glean [gliːn] *vt* (*information*) racimolare

glee [gliː] *n* allegrezza, gioia

glen [glɛn] *n* valletta

glib [glɪb] *adj* dalla parola facile; facile

glide [glaɪd] *vi* scivolare; (*AVIAT, birds*) planare; **~r** *n* (*AVIAT*) aliante *m*; **gliding** *n* (*AVIAT*) volo a vela

glimmer ['glɪmə*] *n* barlume *m*

glimpse [glɪmps] *n* impressione *f* fugace ♦ *vt* vedere al volo

glint [glɪnt] *vi* luccicare

glisten ['glɪsn] *vi* luccicare

glitter ['glɪtə*] *vi* scintillare

gloat [gləut] *vi*: **to ~ (over)** gongolare di piacere (per)

global ['gləubl] *adj* globale; **~ warming** *n* effetto *m* serra *inv*

globe [gləub] *n* globo, sfera

gloom [gluːm] n oscurità, buio; (sadness) tristezza, malinconia; ~y adj scuro(a); fosco(a), triste

glorious ['glɔːrɪəs] adj glorioso(a); magnifico(a)

glory ['glɔːrɪ] n gloria; splendore m

gloss [glɔs] n (shine) lucentezza; (paint) vernice f a olio; ~ **over** vt fus scivolare su

glossary ['glɔsərɪ] n glossario

glossy ['glɔsɪ] adj lucente

glove [glʌv] n guanto; ~ **compartment** n (AUT) vano portaoggetti

glow [gləu] vi ardere; (face) essere luminoso(a)

glower ['glauə*] vi: **to ~ (at sb)** guardare (qn) in cagnesco

glucose ['gluːkəus] n glucosio

glue [gluː] n colla ♦ vt incollare

glum [glʌm] adj abbattuto(a)

glut [glʌt] n eccesso

glutton ['glʌtn] n ghiottone/a; **a ~ for work** un(a) patito(a) del lavoro

GM adj abbr (= genetically modified) geneticamente modificato(a)

gnat [næt] n moscerino

gnaw [nɔː] vt rodere

go [gəu] (pt **went**, pp **gone**, pl **~es**) vi andare; (depart) partire, andarsene; (work) funzionare; (time) passare; (break etc) rompersi; (be sold): **to ~ for £10** essere venduto per 10 sterline; (fit, suit): **to ~ with** andare bene con; (become): **to ~ pale** diventare pallido(a); **to ~ mouldy** ammuffire ♦ n: **to have a ~ (at)** provare; **to be on the ~** essere in moto; **whose ~ is it?** a chi tocca?; **he's going to do** sta per fare; **to ~ for a walk** andare a fare una passeggiata; **to ~ dancing/shopping** andare a ballare/fare la spesa; **just then the bell went** proprio allora suonò il campanello; **how did it ~?** com'è andato?; **to ~ round the back/by the shop** passare da dietro/davanti al negozio; ~ **about** vi (also: ~ **round**: rumour) correre, circolare ♦ vt fus: **how do I ~ about this?** qual'è la prassi per questo?; ~ **ahead** vi andare avanti; ~ **along** vi andare, avanzare ♦ vt fus percorrere; **to ~ along with** (plan, idea) appoggiare; ~ **away** vi partire, andarsene; ~ **back** vi tornare, ritornare; ~ **back on** vt fus (promise) non mantenere; ~ **by** vi (time) scorrere ♦ vt fus attenersi a, seguire (alla lettera); prestar fede a; ~ **down** vi scendere; (ship) affondare; (sun) tramontare ♦ vt fus scendere; ~ **for** vt fus (fetch) andare a prendere; (like) andar matto(a) per; (attack) attaccare; saltare addosso a; ~ **in** vi entrare; ~ **in for** vt fus (competition) iscriversi a; (be interested in) interessarsi di; ~ **into** vt fus entrare in; (investigate) indagare, esaminare; (embark on) lanciarsi in; ~ **off** vi partire, andar via; (food) guastarsi; (explode) esplodere, scoppiare; (event) passare ♦ vt fus: **I've gone off chocolate** la cioccolata non mi piace più; **the gun went off** il fucile si scaricò; ~ **on** vi continuare; (happen) succedere; **to ~ on doing** continuare a fare; ~ **out** vi uscire; (couple): **they went out for 3 years** sono stati insieme per 3 anni; (fire, light) spegnersi; ~ **over** vt fus (check) esaminare; ~ **through** vt fus (town etc) attraversare; (files, papers) passare in rassegna; (examine: list etc) leggere da cima a fondo; ~ **up** vi salire; ~ **without** vt fus fare a meno di

goad [gəud] vt spronare

go-ahead adj intraprendente ♦ n via m

goal [gəul] n (SPORT) gol m, rete f; (: place) porta; (fig: aim) fine m, scopo; ~**keeper** n portiere m; ~**post** n palo (della porta)

goat [gəut] n capra

gobble ['gɔbl] vt (also: ~ **down**, ~ **up**) ingoiare

go-between n intermediario/a

god [gɔd] n dio; G~ n Dio; ~**child** n figlioccio/a; ~**daughter** n figlioccia; ~**dess** n dea; ~**father** n padrino; ~**forsaken** adj desolato(a), sperduto(a); ~**mother** n madrina; ~**send** n dono del cielo; ~**son** n figlioccio

goggles ['gɔglz] npl occhiali mpl (di protezione)

going ['gəuɪŋ] n (conditions) andare m, stato del terreno ♦ adj: **the ~ rate** la tariffa in vigore

gold [gəʊld] n oro ♦ adj d'oro; **~en** adj (made of ~) d'oro; (~ in colour) dorato(a); **~fish** n pesce m dorato or rosso; **~mine** n (also fig) miniera d'oro; **~-plated** adj placcato(a) oro inv; **~smith** n orefice m, orafo

golf [gɔlf] n golf m; ~ **ball** n (for game) pallina da golf; (on typewriter) pallina; ~ **club** n circolo di golf; (stick) bastone m or mazza da golf; ~ **course** n campo di golf; **~er** n giocatore/trice di golf

gondola ['gɔndələ] n gondola

gone [gɔn] pp of **go** ♦ adj partito(a)

gong [gɔŋ] n gong m inv

good [gʊd] adj buono(a); (kind) buono(a), gentile; (child) bravo(a) ♦ n bene m; **~s** npl (COMM etc) beni mpl, merci fpl; **~!** bene!, ottimo!; **to be ~ at** essere bravo(a) in; **to be ~ for** andare bene per; **it's ~ for you** fa bene; **would you be ~ enough to ...?** avrebbe la gentilezza di ...?; **a ~ deal (of)** molto(a), una buona quantità (di); **a ~ many** molti(e); **to make ~** (loss, damage) compensare; **it's no ~ complaining** brontolare non serve a niente; **for ~** per sempre, definitivamente; ~ **morning!** buon giorno!; ~ **afternoon/evening!** buona sera!; ~ **night!** buona notte!; **~bye** excl arrivederci!; **G~ Friday** n Venerdì Santo; **~-looking** adj bello(a); **~-natured** adj affabile; **~ness** n (of person) bontà; **for ~ness sake!** per amor di Dio!; **~ness gracious!** santo cielo!, mamma mia!; **~s train** (BRIT) n treno m merci inv; **~will** n amicizia, benevolenza

goose [guːs] (pl **geese**) n oca

gooseberry ['gʊzbəri] n uva spina; **to play ~** (BRIT) tenere la candela

gooseflesh ['guːsflɛʃ] n pelle f d'oca

goose pimples npl pelle f d'oca

gore [gɔː*] vt incornare ♦ n sangue m (coagulato)

gorge [gɔːdʒ] n gola ♦ vt: **to ~ o.s. (on)** ingozzarsi (di)

gorgeous ['gɔːdʒəs] adj magnifico(a)

gorilla [gə'rɪlə] n gorilla m inv

gorse [gɔːs] n ginestrone m

gory ['gɔːri] adj sanguinoso(a)

go-slow (BRIT) n rallentamento dei lavori (per agitazione sindacale)

gospel ['gɔspl] n vangelo

gossip ['gɔsɪp] n chiacchiere fpl; pettegolezzi mpl; (person) pettegolo/a ♦ vi chiacchierare

got [gɔt] pt, pp of **get**; **~ten** (US) pp of **get**

gout [gaʊt] n gotta

govern ['gʌvən] vt governare

governess ['gʌvənɪs] n governante f

government ['gʌvnmənt] n governo

governor ['gʌvənə*] n (of state, bank) governatore m; (of school, hospital) amministratore m; (BRIT: of prison) direttore/trice

gown [gaʊn] n vestito lungo; (of teacher, BRIT: of judge) toga

G.P. n abbr = **general practitioner**

grab [græb] vt afferrare, arraffare; (property, power) impadronirsi di ♦ vi: **to ~ at** cercare di afferrare

grace [greɪs] n grazia ♦ vt onorare; **5 days' ~** dilazione f di 5 giorni; **~ful** adj elegante, aggraziato(a); **gracious** ['greɪʃəs] adj grazioso(a); misericordioso(a)

grade [greɪd] n (COMM) qualità f inv; classe f; categoria; (in hierarchy) grado; (SCOL: mark) voto; (US: school class) classe ♦ vt classificare; ordinare; graduare; ~ **crossing** (US) n passaggio a livello; ~ **school** (US) n scuola elementare

gradient ['greɪdiənt] n pendenza, inclinazione f

gradual ['grædjuəl] adj graduale; **~ly** adv man mano, a poco a poco

graduate [n 'grædjut, vb 'grædjueɪt] n (of university) laureato/a; (US: of high school) diplomato/a ♦ vi laurearsi; diplomarsi; **graduation** [-'eɪʃən] n (ceremony) consegna delle lauree (or dei diplomi)

graffiti [grə'fiːti] npl graffiti mpl

graft [grɑːft] n (AGR, MED) innesto; (bribery) corruzione f; (BRIT: hard work): **it's hard ~** un lavoraccio ♦ vt innestare

grain [greɪn] n grano; (of sand) granello; (of

wood) venatura

gram [græm] *n* grammo

grammar ['græmə*] *n* grammatica; ~ **school** (*BRIT*) *n* ≈ liceo

grammatical [grə'mætɪkl] *adj* grammaticale

gramme [græm] *n* = **gram**

grand [grænd] *adj* grande, magnifico(a); grandioso(a); ~**children** *npl* nipoti *mpl*; ~**dad** (*inf*) *n* nonno; ~**daughter** *n* nipote *f*; ~**eur** ['grændjə*] *n* grandiosità; ~**father** *n* nonno; ~**ma** (*inf*) *n* nonna; ~**mother** *n* nonna; ~**pa** (*inf*) *n* = ~**dad**; ~**parents** *npl* nonni *mpl*; ~ **piano** *n* pianoforte *m* a coda; ~**son** *n* nipote *m*; ~**stand** *n* (*SPORT*) tribuna

granite ['grænɪt] *n* granito

granny ['grænɪ] (*inf*) *n* nonna

grant [grɑːnt] *vt* accordare; (*a request*) accogliere; (*admit*) ammettere, concedere ♦ *n* (*SCOL*) borsa; (*ADMIN*) sussidio, sovvenzione *f*; **to take sth for ~ed** dare qc per scontato; **to take sb for ~ed** dare per scontata la presenza di qn

granulated ['grænjuleɪtɪd] *adj*: ~ **sugar** zucchero cristallizzato

granule ['grænjuːl] *n* granello

grape [greɪp] *n* chicco d'uva, acino

grapefruit ['greɪpfruːt] *n* pompelmo

graph [grɑːf] *n* grafico; ~**ic** *adj* grafico(a); (*vivid*) vivido(a); ~**ics** *n* grafica ♦ *npl* illustrazioni *fpl*

grapple ['græpl] *vi*: **to ~ with** essere alle prese con

grasp [grɑːsp] *vt* afferrare ♦ *n* (*grip*) presa; (*fig*) potere *m*; comprensione *f*; ~**ing** *adj* avido(a)

grass [grɑːs] *n* erba; ~**hopper** *n* cavalletta; ~-**roots** *adj* di base

grate [greɪt] *n* graticola (del focolare) ♦ *vi* cigolare, stridere ♦ *vt* (*CULIN*) grattugiare

grateful ['greɪtful] *adj* grato(a), riconoscente

grater ['greɪtə*] *n* grattugia

grating ['greɪtɪŋ] *n* (*iron bars*) grata ♦ *adj* (*noise*) stridente, stridulo(a)

gratitude ['grætɪtjuːd] *n* gratitudine *f*

gratuity [grə'tjuːɪtɪ] *n* mancia

grave [greɪv] *n* tomba ♦ *adj* grave, serio(a)

gravel ['grævl] *n* ghiaia

gravestone ['greɪvstəun] *n* pietra tombale

graveyard ['greɪvjɑːd] *n* cimitero

gravity ['grævɪtɪ] *n* (*PHYSICS*) gravità; pesantezza; (*seriousness*) gravità, serietà

gravy ['greɪvɪ] *n* intingolo della carne; salsa

gray [greɪ] *adj* = **grey**

graze [greɪz] *vi* pascolare, pascere ♦ *vt* (*touch lightly*) sfiorare; (*scrape*) escoriare ♦ *n* (*MED*) escoriazione *f*

grease [griːs] *n* (*fat*) grasso; (*lubricant*) lubrificante *m* ♦ *vt* ingrassare; lubrificare; ~**proof paper** (*BRIT*) *n* carta oleata; **greasy** *adj* grasso(a), untuoso(a)

great [greɪt] *adj* grande; (*inf*) magnifico(a), meraviglioso(a); G~ **Britain** *n* Gran Bretagna; ~-**grandfather** *n* bisnonno; ~-**grandmother** *n* bisnonna; ~**ly** *adv* molto; ~**ness** *n* grandezza

Greece [griːs] *n* Grecia

greed [griːd] *n* (*also*: ~**iness**) avarizia; (*for food*) golosità, ghiottoneria; ~**y** *adj* avido(a); goloso(a), ghiotto(a)

Greek [griːk] *adj* greco(a) ♦ *n* greco/a; (*LING*) greco

green [griːn] *adj* verde; (*inexperienced*) inesperto(a), ingenuo(a) ♦ *n* verde *m*; (*stretch of grass*) prato; (*on golf course*) green *m inv*; ~**s** *npl* (*vegetables*) verdura; ~ **belt** *n* (*round town*) cintura di verde; ~ **card** *n* (*BRIT*: *AUT*) carta verde; (*US*: *ADMIN*) *permesso di soggiorno e di lavoro*; ~**ery** *n* verde *m*; ~**grocer** (*BRIT*) *n* fruttivendolo/a, erbivendolo/a; ~**house** *n* serra; ~**house effect** *n* effetto serra; ~**house gas** *n* gas responsabile dell'effetto serra; ~**ish** *adj* verdastro(a)

Greenland ['griːnlənd] *n* Groenlandia

greet [griːt] *vt* salutare; ~**ing** *n* saluto; ~**ing(s) card** *n* cartolina d'auguri

gregarious [grə'gɛərɪəs] *adj* (*person*) socievole

grenade [grə'neɪd] *n* (*also*: **hand** ~) granata

grew [gruː] *pt of* **grow**

grey [greɪ] *adj* grigio(a); ~**haired** *adj* dai

capelli grigi; **~hound** n levriere m
grid [grɪd] n grata; (ELEC) rete f
gridlock ['grɪdlɒk] n (traffic jam) paralisi f
inv del traffico; **~ed** adj paralizzato(a) dal
traffico; (talks etc) in fase di stallo
grief [griːf] n dolore m
grievance ['griːvəns] n lagnanza
grieve [griːv] vi addolorarsi; rattristarsi ♦ vt
addolorare; **to ~ for sb** (dead person)
piangere qn
grievous ['griːvəs] adj: **~ bodily harm** (LAW)
aggressione f
grill [grɪl] n (on cooker) griglia; (also: **mixed
~**) grigliata mista ♦ vt (BRIT) cuocere ai ferri;
(inf: question) interrogare senza sosta
grille [grɪl] n grata; (AUT) griglia
grim [grɪm] adj sinistro(a), brutto(a)
grimace [grɪ'meɪs] n smorfia ♦ vi fare
smorfie; fare boccacce
grime [graɪm] n sudiciume m
grin [grɪn] n sorriso smagliante ♦ vi fare un
gran sorriso
grind [graɪnd] (pt, pp **ground**) vt macinare;
(make sharp) arrotare ♦ n (work) sgobbata
gripping ['grɪpɪŋ] adj avvincente
grisly ['grɪzlɪ] adj macabro(a), orrido(a)
gristle ['grɪsl] n cartilagine f
grit [grɪt] n ghiaia; (courage) fegato ♦ vt
(road) coprire di sabbia; **to ~ one's teeth**
stringere i denti
groan [grəun] n gemito ♦ vi gemere
grocer ['grəusə•] n negoziante m di generi
alimentari; **~ies** npl provviste fpl; **~'s
(shop)** n negozio di (generi) alimentari
groggy ['grɒgɪ] adj barcollante
groin [grɔɪn] n inguine m
groom [gruːm] n palafreniere m; (also:
bride~) sposo ♦ vt (horse) strigliare; (fig):
to ~ sb for avviare qn a; **well-~ed** (person)
curato(a)
groove [gruːv] n scanalatura, solco
grope [grəup] vi: **to ~ for** cercare a tastoni
gross [grəus] adj grossolano(a); (COMM)

lordo(a); **~ly** adv (greatly) molto
grotesque [grəu'tɛsk] adj grottesco(a)
grotto ['grɒtəu] n grotta
grotty ['grɒtɪ] (inf) adj terribile
ground [graund] pt, pp of **grind** ♦ n suolo,
terra; (land) terreno; (SPORT) campo;
(reason: gen pl) ragione f; (US: also: **~ wire**)
terra ♦ vt (plane) tenere a terra; (US: ELEC)
mettere la presa a terra a; **~s** npl (of coffee
etc) fondi mpl; (gardens etc) terreno,
giardini mpl; **on/to the ~** per/a terra; **to
gain/lose ~** guadagnare/perdere terreno;
~ cloth (US) n = **~sheet**; **~ing** n (in
education) basi fpl; **~less** adj infondato(a);
~sheet (BRIT) n telone m impermeabile; **~
staff** n personale m di terra; **~work** n
preparazione f
group [gruːp] n gruppo ♦ vt (also: **~
together**) raggruppare ♦ vi (also: **~
together**) raggrupparsi
grouse [graus] n inv (bird) tetraone m ♦ vi
(complain) brontolare
grove [grəuv] n boschetto
grovel ['grɒvl] vi (fig): **to ~ (before)**
strisciare (di fronte a)
grow [grəu] (pt **grew**, pp **grown**) vi
crescere; (increase) aumentare; (develop)
svilupparsi; (become): **to ~ rich/weak**
arricchirsi/indebolirsi ♦ vt coltivare, far
crescere; **~ up** vi farsi grande, crescere;
~er n coltivatore/trice; **~ing** adj (fear,
amount) crescente
growl [graul] vi ringhiare
grown [grəun] pp of **grow**; **~-up** n adulto/
a, grande m/f
growth [grəuθ] n crescita, sviluppo; (what
has grown) crescita; (MED) escrescenza,
tumore m
grub [grʌb] n larva; (inf: food) roba (da
mangiare)
grubby ['grʌbɪ] adj sporco(a)
grudge [grʌdʒ] n rancore m ♦ vt: **to ~ sb
sth** dare qc a qn di malavoglia; invidiare qc
a qn; **to bear sb a ~ (for)** serbar rancore a
qn (per)
gruelling ['gruəlɪŋ] (US **grueling**) adj
estenuante

grip [grɪp] n impugnatura; presa; (holdall)
borsa da viaggio ♦ vt (object) afferrare;
(attention) catturare; **to come to ~s with**
affrontare; cercare di risolvere

gruesome ['gru:səm] adj orribile

gruff [grʌf] adj rozzo(a)

grumble ['grʌmbl] vi brontolare, lagnarsi

grumpy ['grʌmpɪ] adj scorbutico(a)

grunt [grʌnt] vi grugnire

G-string n tanga m inv

guarantee [gærən'ti:] n garanzia ♦ vt garantire

guard [ga:d] n guardia; (one man) guardia, sentinella; (BRIT: RAIL) capotreno; (on machine) schermo protettivo; (also: **fire~**) parafuoco ♦ vt fare la guardia a; (protect): **to ~ (against)** proteggere (da); **to be on one's ~** stare in guardia; **~ against** vt fus guardarsi da; **~ed** adj (fig) cauto(a), guardingo(a); **~ian** n custode m; (of minor) tutore/trice; **~'s van** (BRIT) n (RAIL) vagone m di servizio

guerrilla [gə'rɪlə] n guerrigliero

guess [gɛs] vi indovinare ♦ vt indovinare; (US) credere, pensare ♦ n: **to take** or **have a ~** provare a indovinare; **~work** n: **I got the answer by ~work** ho azzeccato la risposta

guest [gɛst] n ospite m/f; (in hotel) cliente m/f; **~-house** n pensione f; **~ room** n camera degli ospiti

guffaw [gʌ'fɔ:] vi scoppiare in una risata sonora

guidance ['gaɪdəns] n guida, direzione f

guide [gaɪd] n (person, book etc) guida; (BRIT: also: **girl ~**) giovane esploratrice f ♦ vt guidare; **~book** n guida; **~ dog** n cane m guida inv; **~lines** npl (fig) indicazioni fpl, linee fpl direttive

guild [gɪld] n arte f, corporazione f; associazione f

guillotine ['gɪləti:n] n ghigliottina; (for paper) taglierina

guilt [gɪlt] n colpevolezza; **~y** adj colpevole

guinea pig ['gɪnɪ-] n cavia

guise [gaɪz] n maschera

guitar [gɪ'ta:*] n chitarra

gulf [gʌlf] n golfo; (abyss) abisso

gull [gʌl] n gabbiano

gullible ['gʌlɪbl] adj credulo(a)

gully ['gʌlɪ] n burrone m; gola; canale m

gulp [gʌlp] vi deglutire; (from emotion) avere il nodo in gola ♦ vt (also: **~ down**) tracannare, inghiottire

gum [gʌm] n (ANAT) gengiva; (glue) colla; (also: **~drop**) caramella gommosa; (also: **chewing ~**) chewing-gum m ♦ vt: **to ~ (together)** incollare; **~boots** (BRIT) npl stivali mpl di gomma

gumption ['gʌmpʃən] n spirito d'iniziativa, buonsenso

gun [gʌn] n fucile m; (small) pistola, rivoltella; (rifle) carabina; (shotgun) fucile da caccia; (cannon) cannone m; **~boat** n cannoniera; **~fire** n spari mpl; **~man** n bandito armato; **~point** n: **at ~point** sotto minaccia di fucile; **~powder** n polvere f da sparo; **~shot** n sparo

gurgle ['gə:gl] vi gorgogliare

gush [gʌʃ] vi sgorgare; (fig) abbandonarsi ad effusioni

gusset ['gʌsɪt] n gherone m

gust [gʌst] n (of wind) raffica; (of smoke) buffata

gusto ['gʌstəu] n entusiasmo

gut [gʌt] n intestino, budello; **~s** npl (ANAT) interiora fpl; (courage) fegato

gutter ['gʌtə*] n (of roof) grondaia; (in street) cunetta

guy [gaɪ] n (inf: man) tipo, elemento; (also: **~rope**) cavo or corda di fissaggio; (figure) effigie di Guy Fawkes

---
Guy Fawkes' Night
---

i *Il 5 novembre si festeggia con falò e fuochi d'artificio la* **Guy Fawkes' Night**, *la notte in cui, nel 1605, fallì la Congiura delle Polveri contro Giacomo I;* **Guy Fawkes** *era il nome di uno dei cospiratori.*

---

guzzle ['gʌzl] vt tranguiare

gym [dʒɪm] n (also: **gymnasium**) palestra; (also: **gymnastics**) ginnastica

gymnast ['dʒɪmnæst] n ginnasta m/f; **~ics** [-'næstɪks] n, npl ginnastica

gym shoes npl scarpe fpl da ginnastica

gym slip (BRIT) n grembiule m da scuola

(per ragazze)

gynaecologist [gaɪnɪ'kɔlədʒɪst] *(US* **gynecologist)** *n* ginecologo/a

gypsy ['dʒɪpsɪ] *n* = **gipsy**

gyrate [dʒaɪ'reɪt] *vi* girare

H, h

haberdashery ['hæbə'dæʃərɪ] *(BRIT) n* merceria

habit ['hæbɪt] *n* abitudine *f*; *(costume)* abito; *(REL)* tonaca

habitual [hə'bɪtjuəl] *adj* abituale; *(drinker, liar)* inveterato(a)

hack [hæk] *vt* tagliare, fare a pezzi ♦ *n (pej: writer)* scribacchino/a

hacker ['hækə*] *n (COMPUT)* pirata *m* informatico

hackney cab ['hæknɪ-] *n* carrozza a nolo

hackneyed ['hæknɪd] *adj* comune, trito(a)

had [hæd] *pt, pp of* **have**

haddock ['hædək] *(pl ~ or ~s) n* eglefino

hadn't ['hædnt] = **had not**

haemorrhage ['hemərɪdʒ] *(US* **hemorrhage)** *n* emorragia

haemorrhoids ['hemərɔɪdz] *(US* **hemorrhoids)** *npl* emorroidi *fpl*

haggard ['hægəd] *adj* smunto(a)

haggle ['hægl] *vi* mercanteggiare

Hague [heɪg] *n*: **The ~** L'Aia

hail [heɪl] *n* grandine *f*; *(of criticism etc)* pioggia ♦ *vt (call)* chiamare; *(flag down: taxi)* fermare; *(greet)* salutare ♦ *vi* grandinare; **~stone** *n* chicco di grandine

hair [heə*] *n* capelli *mpl*; *(single hair: on head)* capello; *(: on body)* pelo; **to do one's ~** pettinarsi; **~brush** *n* spazzola per capelli; **~cut** *n* taglio di capelli; **~do** ['heədu:] *n* acconciatura, pettinatura; **~dresser** ['heə'dɛsə*] *n* parrucchiere/a; **~-dryer** *n* asciugacapelli *m inv*; **~ grip** *n* forcina; **~net** *n* retina per capelli; **~pin** *n* forcina; **~pin bend** *(US* **~pin curve)** *n* tornante *m*; **~raising** *adj* orripilante; **~ removing cream** *n* crema depilatoria; **~ spray** *n* lacca per capelli; **~style** *n* pettinatura,

acconciatura; **~y** *adj* irsuto(a); peloso(a); *(inf: frightening)* spaventoso(a)

hake [heɪk] *(pl ~ or ~s) n* nasello

half [hɑ:f] *(pl halves) n* mezzo, metà *f inv* ♦ *adj* mezzo(a) ♦ *adv* a mezzo, a metà; **~ an hour** mezz'ora; **~ a dozen** mezza dozzina; **~ a pound** mezza libbra; **two and a ~** due e mezzo; **a week and a ~** una settimana e mezza; **~ (of it)** la metà; **~ (of)** la metà di; **to cut sth in ~** tagliare qc in due; **~ asleep** mezzo(a) addormentato(a); **~-baked** *adj (scheme)* che non sta in piedi; **~ board** *(BRIT) n* mezza pensione; **~-caste** ['hɑ:fkɑ:st] *n* meticcio/a; **~ fare** *n* tariffa a metà prezzo; **~-hearted** *adj* tiepido(a); **~-hour** *n* mezz'ora; **~-mast**: **at ~-mast** *adv (flag)* a mezz'asta; **~penny** ['heɪpnɪ] *(BRIT) n* mezzo penny *m inv*; **~-price** *adj, adv* a metà prezzo; **~ term** *(BRIT) n (SCOL)* vacanza *a or* di metà trimestre; **~-time** *n (SPORT)* intervallo; **~way** *adv* a metà strada

halibut ['hælɪbət] *n inv* ippoglosso

hall [hɔ:l] *n* sala, salone *m*; *(entrance way)* entrata; **~ of residence** *(BRIT) n* casa dello studente

hallmark ['hɔ:lmɑ:k] *n* marchio di garanzia; *(fig)* caratteristica

hallo [hə'ləu] *excl* = **hello**

Hallowe'en [hæləu'i:n] *n* vigilia d'Ognissanti

Hallowe'en

i Negli Stati Uniti e in Scozia il 31 ottobre si festeggia **Hallowe'en**, *la notte delle streghe e dei fantasmi; i bambini, travestiti da fantasmi e con lanterne ricavate da zucche, bussano alle porte e raccolgono dolci e piccoli doni.*

---

hallucination [həlu:sɪ'neɪʃən] *n* allucinazione *f*

hallway ['hɔ:lweɪ] *n* corridoio; *(entrance)* ingresso

halo ['heɪləu] *n (of saint etc)* aureola

halt [hɔ:lt] *n* fermata ♦ *vt* fermare ♦ *vi* fermarsi

halve [hɑːv] vt (apple etc) dividere a metà; (expense) ridurre di metà

halves [hɑːvz] npl of **half**

ham [hæm] n prosciutto

Hamburg ['hæmbɜːg] n Amburgo f

hamburger ['hæmbɜːgə*] n hamburger m inv

hamlet ['hæmlɪt] n paesetto

hammer ['hæmə*] n martello ♦ vt martellare ♦ vi: **to ~ on** or **at the door** picchiare alla porta

hammock ['hæmək] n amaca

hamper ['hæmpə*] vt impedire ♦ n cesta

hamster ['hæmstə*] n criceto

hand [hænd] n mano f; (of clock) lancetta; (handwriting) scrittura; (at cards) mano; (: game) partita; (worker) operaio/a ♦ vt dare, passare; **to give sb a ~** dare una mano a qn; **at ~** a portata di mano; **in ~** a disposizione; (work) in corso; **on ~** (person) disponibile; (services) pronto(a) a intervenire; **to ~** (information etc) a portata di mano; **on the one ~ ..., on the other ~** da un lato ..., dall'altro; **~ in** vt consegnare; **~ out** vt distribuire; **~ over** vt passare; cedere; **~bag** n borsetta; **~book** n manuale m; **~brake** n freno a mano; **~cuffs** npl manette fpl; **~ful** n manciata, pugno

handicap ['hændɪkæp] n handicap m inv ♦ vt handicappare; **to be physically ~ped** essere handicappato(a); **to be mentally ~ped** essere un(a) handicappato(a) mentale

handicraft ['hændɪkrɑːft] n lavoro d'artigiano

handiwork ['hændɪwɜːk] n opera

handkerchief ['hæŋkətʃɪf] n fazzoletto

handle ['hændl] n (of door etc) maniglia; (of cup etc) ansa; (of knife etc) impugnatura; (of saucepan) manico; (for winding) manovella ♦ vt toccare, maneggiare; (deal with) occuparsi di; (treat: people) trattare; **"~ with care"** "fragile"; **to fly off the ~** (fig) perdere le staffe, uscire dai gangheri; **~bar(s)** n(pl) manubrio

hand: ~ luggage n bagagli mpl a mano;

~made adj fatto(a) a mano; **~out** n (money, food) elemosina; (leaflet) volantino; (at lecture) prospetto; **~rail** n corrimano; **~set** n (TEL) ricevitore m; **please replace the ~set** riagganciare il ricevitore; **~shake** n stretta di mano

handsome ['hænsəm] adj bello(a); (profit, fortune) considerevole

handwriting ['hændraɪtɪŋ] n scrittura

handy ['hændɪ] adj (person) bravo(a); (close at hand) a portata di mano; (convenient) comodo(a)

hang [hæŋ] (pt, pp **hung**) vt appendere; (criminal: pt, pp **hanged**) impiccare ♦ vi (painting) essere appeso(a); (hair) scendere; (drapery) cadere; **to get the ~ of sth** (inf) capire come qc funziona; **~ about** or **around** vi bighellonare, ciondolare; **~ on** vi (wait) aspettare; **~ up** vi (TEL) riattaccare ♦ vt appendere

hangar ['hæŋə*] n hangar m inv

hanger ['hæŋə*] n gruccia

hanger-on n parassita m

hang-gliding ['-glaɪdɪŋ] n volo col deltaplano

hangover ['hæŋəʊvə*] n (after drinking) postumi mpl di sbornia

hang-up n complesso

hanker ['hæŋkə*] vi: **to ~ after** bramare

hankie ['hæŋkɪ] n abbr = **handkerchief**

hanky ['hæŋkɪ] n abbr = **handkerchief**

haphazard [hæp'hæzəd] adj a casaccio, alla carlona

happen ['hæpən] vi accadere, succedere; (chance): **to ~ to do sth** fare qc per caso; **as it ~s** guarda caso; **~ing** n avvenimento

happily ['hæpɪlɪ] adv felicemente; fortunatamente

happiness ['hæpɪnɪs] n felicità, contentezza

happy ['hæpɪ] adj felice, contento(a); **~ with** (arrangements etc) soddisfatto(a) di; **to be ~ to do** (willing) fare volentieri; **~ birthday!** buon compleanno!; **~-go-lucky** adj spensierato(a); **~ hour** n orario in cui i bar hanno prezzi ridotti

harangue [hə'ræŋ] vt arringare

harass ['hærəs] vt molestare; **~ment** n

molestia

harbour ['hɑ:bə*] (*US* **harbor**) *n* porto ♦ *vt*
(*hope, fear*) nutrire; (*criminal*) dare rifugio a

hard [hɑ:d] *adj* duro(a) ♦ *adv* (*work*) sodo;
(*think, try*) bene; **to look ~ at** guardare
fissamente; esaminare attentamente; **no ~
feelings!** senza rancore!; **to be ~ of
hearing** essere duro(a) d'orecchio; **to be ~
done by** essere trattato(a) ingiustamente;
~**back** *n* libro rilegato; ~ **cash** *n* denaro
in contanti; ~ **disk** *n* (*COMPUT*) disco
rigido; ~**en** *vt, vi* indurire; ~**-headed** *adj*
pratico(a); ~ **labour** *n* lavori forzati *mpl*

hardly ['hɑ:dlɪ] *adv* (*scarcely*) appena; **it's ~
the case** non è proprio il caso; ~
anyone/anywhere quasi nessuno/da
nessuna parte; ~ **ever** quasi mai

hardship ['hɑ:dʃɪp] *n* avversità *f inv*;
privazioni *fpl*

hard shoulder (*BRIT*) *n* (*AUT*) corsia
d'emergenza

hard-up (*inf*) *adj* al verde

hardware ['hɑ:dwɛə*] *n* ferramenta *fpl*;
(*COMPUT*) hardware *m*; (*MIL*) armamenti
mpl; ~ **shop** *n* (negozio di) ferramenta *fpl*

hard-wearing [-'wɛərɪŋ] *adj* resistente;
(*shoes*) robusto(a)

hard-working [-'wə:kɪŋ] *adj* lavora-
tore(trice)

hardy ['hɑ:dɪ] *adj* robusto(a); (*plant*)
resistente al gelo

hare [hɛə*] *n* lepre *f*; ~**-brained** *adj* folle;
scervellato(a)

harm [hɑ:m] *n* male *m*; (*wrong*) danno ♦ *vt*
(*person*) fare male a; (*thing*) danneggiare;
out of ~'s way al sicuro; ~**ful** *adj*
dannoso(a); ~**less** *adj* innocuo(a);
inoffensivo(a)

harmonica [hɑ:'mɔnɪkə] *n* armonica

harmonious [hɑ:'məʊnɪəs] *adj*
armonioso(a)

harmony ['hɑ:mənɪ] *n* armonia

harness ['hɑ:nɪs] *n* (*for horse*) bardatura,
finimenti *mpl*; (*for child*) briglie *fpl*; (*safety
~*) imbracatura ♦ *vt* (*horse*) bardare;
(*resources*) sfruttare

harp [hɑ:p] *n* arpa ♦ *vi*: **to ~ on about**
insistere tediosamente su

harpoon [hɑ:'pu:n] *n* arpione *m*

harrowing ['hærəʊɪŋ] *adj* straziante

harsh [hɑ:ʃ] *adj* (*life, winter*) duro(a); (*judge,
criticism*) severo(a); (*sound*) rauco(a); (*light*)
violento(a)

harvest ['hɑ:vɪst] *n* raccolto; (*of grapes*)
vendemmia ♦ *vt* fare il raccolto di,
raccogliere; vendemmiare

has [hæz] *vb see* **have**

hash [hæʃ] *n* (*CULIN*) specie di spezzatino
fatto con carne già cotta; (*fig: mess*)
pasticcio

hasn't ['hæznt] = **has not**

hassle ['hæsl] (*inf*) *n* sacco di problemi

haste [heɪst] *n* fretta; precipitazione *f*; ~**n**
['heɪsn] *vt* affrettare ♦ *vi*: **to ~n (to)**
affrettarsi (a); ~**ily** *adv* in fretta;
precipitosamente; **hasty** *adj* affrettato(a);
precipitoso(a)

hat [hæt] *n* cappello

hatch [hætʃ] *n* (*NAUT: also:* ~**way**)
boccaporto; (*also:* **service ~**) portello di
servizio ♦ *vi* (*bird*) uscire dal guscio; (*egg*)
schiudersi

hatchback ['hætʃbæk] *n* (*AUT*) tre (*or*
cinque) porte *f inv*

hatchet ['hætʃɪt] *n* accetta

hate [heɪt] *vt* odiare, detestare ♦ *n* odio;
~**ful** *adj* odioso(a), detestabile

hatred ['heɪtrɪd] *n* odio

haughty ['hɔ:tɪ] *adj* altero(a), arrogante

haul [hɔ:l] *vt* trascinare, tirare ♦ *n* (*of fish*)
pescata; (*of stolen goods etc*) bottino; ~**age**
n trasporto; autotrasporto; ~**ier** (*US* ~**er**) *n*
trasportatore *m*

haunch [hɔ:ntʃ] *n* anca; (*of meat*) coscia

haunt [hɔ:nt] *vt* (*subj: fear*) pervadere;
(*: person*) frequentare ♦ *n* rifugio; **this
house is ~ed** questa casa è abitata da un
fantasma

KEYWORD

have [hæv] (*pt, pp* **had**) *aux vb* **1** (*gen*)
avere; essere; **to ~ arrived/gone** essere
arrivato(a)/andato(a); **to ~ eaten/slept**
avere mangiato/dormito; **he has been**

kind/promoted è stato gentile/promosso; **having finished** or **when he had finished, he left** dopo aver finito, se n'è andato **2** (in tag questions): **you've done it, ~n't you?** l'ha fatto, (non è vero)?; **he hasn't done it, has he?** non l'ha fatto, vero? **3** (in short answers and questions): **you've made a mistake – no I ~n't/so I ~** ha fatto un errore — ma no, niente affatto/sì, è vero; **we ~n't paid – yes we ~!** non abbiamo pagato — ma sì che abbiamo pagato!; **I've been there before, ~ you?** ci sono già stato, e lei?

♦ modal aux vb (be obliged): **to ~ (got) to do sth** dover fare qc; **I ~n't got** or **I don't ~ to wear glasses** non ho bisogno di portare gli occhiali

♦ vt **1** (possess, obtain) avere; **he has (got) blue eyes/dark hair** ha gli occhi azzurri/i capelli scuri; **do you ~** or **~ you got a car/ phone?** ha la macchina/il telefono?; **may I ~ your address?** potrebbe darmi il suo indirizzo?; **you can ~ it for £5** te lo lascio per 5 sterline

2 (+noun: take, hold etc): **to ~ breakfast/a swim/a bath** fare colazione/una nuotata/ un bagno; **to ~ lunch** pranzare; **to ~ dinner** cenare; **to ~ a drink** bere qualcosa; **to ~ a cigarette** fumare una sigaretta **3**: **to ~ sth done** far fare qc; **to ~ one's hair cut** farsi tagliare i capelli; **to ~ sb do sth** far fare qc a qn

4 (experience, suffer) avere; **to ~ a cold/flu** avere il raffreddore/l'influenza; **she had her bag stolen** le hanno rubato la borsa **5** (inf: dupe): **you've been had!** ci sei cascato!

have out vt: **to ~ it out with sb** (settle a problem etc) mettere le cose in chiaro con qn

---

haven ['heɪvn] n porto; (fig) rifugio **haven't** ['hævnt] = **have not** **havoc** ['hævək] n caos m **hawk** [hɔːk] n falco **hay** [heɪ] n fieno; **~ fever** n febbre f da fieno; **~stack** n pagliaio

haywire ['heɪwaɪə*] (inf) adj: **to go ~** impazzire **hazard** ['hæzəd] n azzardo, ventura; pericolo, rischio ♦ vt (guess etc) azzardare; **~ous** adj pericoloso(a); **~ (warning) lights** npl (AUT) luci fpl di emergenza **haze** [heɪz] n foschia **hazelnut** ['heɪzlnʌt] n nocciola **hazy** ['heɪzɪ] adj fosco(a); (idea) vago(a) **he** [hiː] pronoun lui, egli; **it is ~ who ...** è lui che ...

head [hed] n testa; (leader) capo; (of school) preside m/f ♦ vt (list) essere in testa a; (group) essere a capo di; **~s (or tails)** testa (o croce), pari (o dispari); **~ first** a capofitto, di testa; **~ over heels in love** pazzamente innamorato(a); **to ~ the ball** colpire una palla di testa; **~ for** vt fus dirigersi verso; **~ache** n mal m di testa; **~dress** (BRIT) n (of bride) acconciatura; **~ing** n titolo; intestazione f; **~lamp** (BRIT) n = **~light**; **~land** n promontorio; **~light** n fanale m; **~line** n titolo; **~long** adv (fall) a capofitto; (rush) precipitosamente; **~master/mistress** n preside m/f; **~ office** n sede f (centrale); **~-on** adj (collision) frontale; **~phones** npl cuffia; **~quarters** npl ufficio centrale; (MIL) quartiere m generale; **~-rest** n poggiacapo; **~room** n (in car) altezza dell'abitacolo; (under bridge) altezza limite; **~scarf** n foulard m inv; **~strong** adj testardo(a); **~ waiter** n capocameriere m; **~way** n: **to make ~way** fare progressi; **~wind** n controvento; **~y** adj (experience, period) inebriante **heal** [hiːl] vt, vi guarire **health** [helθ] n salute f; **~ centre** (BRIT) n poliambulatorio; **~ food(s)** n(pl) cibo macrobiotico; **~ food store** n negozio di alimenti dietetici e macrobiotici; **the H~ Service** (BRIT) n ≈ il Servizio Sanitario Statale; **~y** adj (person) sano(a), in buona salute; (climate) salubre; (appetite, economy etc) sano(a) **heap** [hiːp] n mucchio ♦ vt (stones, sand): **to ~ (up)** ammucchiare; (plate, sink): **to ~**

sth with riempire qc di; **~s of** (*inf*) un mucchio di

hear [hɪə*] (*pt, pp* **heard**) *vt* sentire; (*news*) ascoltare ♦ *vi* sentire; **to ~ about** avere notizie di; sentire parlare di; **to ~ from sb** ricevere notizie da qn; **~ing** *n* (*sense*) udito; (*of witnesses*) audizione *f*; (*of a case*) udienza; **~ing aid** *n* apparecchio acustico; **~say** *n* dicerie *fpl*, chiacchiere *fpl*

hearse [hɜːs] *n* carro funebre

heart [hɑːt] *n* cuore *m*; **~s** *npl* (*CARDS*) cuori *mpl*; **to lose ~** scoraggiarsi; **to take ~** farsi coraggio; **at ~** in fondo; **by ~** (*learn, know*) a memoria; **~ attack** *n* attacco di cuore; **~beat** *n* battito del cuore; **~breaking** *adj* straziante; **~broken** *adj*: **to be ~broken** avere il cuore spezzato; **~burn** *n* bruciore *m* di stomaco; **~ failure** *n* arresto cardiaco; **~felt** *adj* sincero(a)

hearth [hɑːθ] *n* focolare *m*

heartland ['hɑːtlænd] *n* regione *f* centrale

heartless ['hɑːtlɪs] *adj* senza cuore

hearty ['hɑːtɪ] *adj* caloroso(a); robusto(a), sano(a); vigoroso(a)

heat [hiːt] *n* calore *m*; (*fig*) ardore *m*; fuoco; (*SPORT: also:* **qualifying ~**) prova eliminatoria ♦ *vt* scaldare; **~ up** *vi* (*liquids*) scaldarsi; (*room*) riscaldarsi ♦ *vt* riscaldare; **~ed** *adj* riscaldato(a); (*argument*) acceso(a); **~er** *n* radiatore *m*; (*stove*) stufa

heath [hiːθ] (*BRIT*) *n* landa

heathen ['hiːðn] *n* pagano/a

heather ['hɛðə*] *n* erica

heating ['hiːtɪŋ] *n* riscaldamento

heatstroke ['hiːtstrəuk] *n* colpo di sole

heatwave ['hiːtweɪv] *n* ondata di caldo

heave [hiːv] *vt* (*pull*) tirare (con forza); (*push*) spingere (con forza); (*lift*) sollevare (con forza) ♦ *vi* sollevarsi; (*retch*) aver conati di vomito ♦ *n* (*push*) grande spinta; **to ~ a sigh** emettere un sospiro

heaven ['hɛvn] *n* paradiso, cielo; **~ly** *adj* divino(a), celeste

heavily ['hɛvɪlɪ] *adv* pesantemente; (*drink, smoke*) molto

heavy ['hɛvɪ] *adj* pesante; (*sea*) grosso(a); (*rain, blow*) forte; (*weather*) afoso(a);

(*drinker, smoker*) gran (*before noun*); **~ goods vehicle** *n* veicolo per trasporti pesanti; **~weight** *n* (*SPORT*) peso massimo

Hebrew ['hiːbruː] *adj* ebreo(a) ♦ *n* (*LING*) ebraico

Hebrides ['hɛbrɪdiːz] *npl*: **the ~** le Ebridi

heckle ['hɛkl] *vt* interpellare e dare noia a (*un oratore*)

hectic ['hɛktɪk] *adj* movimentato(a)

he'd [hiːd] = **he would; he had**

hedge [hɛdʒ] *n* siepe *f* ♦ *vi* essere elusivo(a); **to ~ one's bets** (*fig*) coprirsi dai rischi

hedgehog ['hɛdʒhɔg] *n* riccio

heed [hiːd] *vt* (*also:* **take ~ of**) badare a, far conto di; **~less** *adj*: **~less (of)** sordo(a) (a)

heel [hiːl] *n* (*ANAT*) calcagno; (*of shoe*) tacco ♦ *vt* (*shoe*) rifare i tacchi a

hefty ['hɛftɪ] *adj* (*person*) robusto(a); (*parcel*) pesante; (*profit*) grosso(a)

heifer ['hɛfə*] *n* giovenca

height [haɪt] *n* altezza; (*high ground*) altura; (*fig: of glory*) apice *m*; (: *of stupidity*) colmo; **~en** *vt* (*fig*) accrescere

heir [ɛə*] *n* erede *m*; **~ess** *n* erede *f*; **~loom** *n* mobile *m* (*or* gioiello *or* quadro) di famiglia

held [hɛld] *pt, pp of* **hold**

helicopter ['hɛlɪkɔptə*] *n* elicottero

heliport ['hɛlɪpɔːt] *n* eliporto

helium ['hiːlɪəm] *n* elio

hell [hɛl] *n* inferno; **~!** (*inf*) porca miseria!, accidenti!

he'll [hiːl] = **he will; he shall**

hellish ['hɛlɪʃ] (*inf*) *adj* infernale

hello [hə'ləu] *excl* buon giorno!; ciao! (*to sb one addresses as "tu"*); (*surprise*) ma guarda!

helm [hɛlm] *n* (*NAUT*) timone *m*

helmet ['hɛlmɪt] *n* casco

help [hɛlp] *n* aiuto; (*charwoman*) donna di servizio ♦ *vt* aiutare; **~!** aiuto!; **~ yourself (to bread)** si serva (del pane); **he can't ~ it** non ci può far niente; **~er** *n* aiutante *m/f*, assistente *m/f*; **~ful** *adj* di grande aiuto; (*useful*) utile; **~ing** *n* porzione *f*; **~less** *adj* impotente; debole

hem [hɛm] *n* orlo ♦ *vt* fare l'orlo a; ~ **in** *vt* cingere

hemisphere ['hɛmɪsfɪə*] *n* emisfero

hemorrhage ['hɛmərɪdʒ] (*US*) *n* = **haemorrhage**

hemorrhoids ['hɛmərɔɪdz] (*US*) *npl* = **haemorroids**

hen [hɛn] *n* gallina; (*female bird*) femmina

hence [hɛns] *adv* (*therefore*) dunque; **2 years** ~ di qui a 2 anni; ~**forth** *adv* d'ora in poi

henpecked ['hɛnpɛkt] *adj* dominato dalla moglie

hepatitis [hɛpə'taɪtɪs] *n* epatite *f*

her [həː*] *pron* (*direct*) la, l' +*vowel*; (*indirect*) le; (*stressed, after prep*) lei ♦ *adj* il(la) suo(a), i(le) suoi(sue); *see also* **me**; **my**

herald ['hɛrəld] *n* araldo ♦ *vt* annunciare

heraldry ['hɛrəldrɪ] *n* araldica

herb [həːb] *n* erba

herd [həːd] *n* mandria

here [hɪə*] *adv* qui, qua ♦ *excl* ehi!; ~! (*at roll call*) presente!; ~ **is/are** ecco; ~ **he/ she is** eccolo/eccola; ~**after** *adv* in futuro; dopo questo; ~**by** *adv* (*in letter*) con la presente

hereditary [hɪ'rɛdɪtrɪ] *adj* ereditario(a)

heresy ['hɛrəsɪ] *n* eresia

heretic ['hɛrətɪk] *n* eretico/a

heritage ['hɛrɪtɪdʒ] *n* eredità; (*fig*) retaggio

hermetically [həː'mɛtɪklɪ] *adv*: ~ **sealed** ermeticamente chiuso(a)

hermit ['həːmɪt] *n* eremita *m*

hernia ['həːnɪə] *n* ernia

hero ['hɪərəu] (*pl* ~**es**) *n* eroe *m*

heroin ['hɛrəuɪn] *n* eroina

heroine ['hɛrəuɪn] *n* eroina

heron ['hɛrən] *n* airone *m*

herring ['hɛrɪŋ] *n* aringa

hers [həːz] *pron* il(la) suo(a), i(le) suoi(sue); *see also* **mine**[1]

herself [həː'sɛlf] *pron* (*reflexive*) si; (*emphatic*) lei stessa; (*after prep*) se stessa, sé; *see also* **oneself**

he's [hiːz] = **he is**; **he has**

hesitant ['hɛzɪtənt] *adj* esitante, indeciso(a)

hesitate ['hɛzɪteɪt] *vi*: **to ~** (*about/to do*) esitare (su/a fare); **hesitation** [-'teɪʃən] *n* esitazione *f*

heterosexual ['hɛtərəu'sɛksjuəl] *adj, n* eterosessuale *m/f*

hexagonal [hɛk'sægənəl] *adj* esagonale

heyday ['heɪdeɪ] *n*: **the ~ of** i bei giorni di, l'età d'oro di

HGV *n abbr* = **heavy goods vehicle**

hi [haɪ] *excl* ciao!

hiatus [haɪ'eɪtəs] *n* vuoto; (*LING*) iato

hibernate ['haɪbəneɪt] *vi* ibernare

hiccough ['hɪkʌp] *vi* singhiozzare; ~**s** *npl*: **to have ~s** avere il singhiozzo

hiccup ['hɪkʌp] = **hiccough**

hid [hɪd] *pt of* **hide**; ~**den** ['hɪdn] *pp of* **hide**

hide [haɪd] (*pt* **hid**, *pp* **hidden**) *n* (*skin*) pelle *f* ♦ *vt*: **to ~ sth (from sb)** nascondere qc (a qn) ♦ *vi*: **to ~ (from sb)** nascondersi (da qn); ~**-and-seek** *n* rimpiattino

hideous ['hɪdɪəs] *adj* laido(a); orribile

hiding ['haɪdɪŋ] *n* (*beating*) bastonata; **to be in** ~ (*concealed*) tenersi nascosto(a)

hierarchy ['haɪərɑːkɪ] *n* gerarchia

hi-fi ['haɪfaɪ] *n* stereo ♦ *adj* ad alta fedeltà, hi-fi *inv*

high [haɪ] *adj* alto(a); (*speed, respect, number*) grande; (*wind*) forte; (*voice*) acuto(a) ♦ *adv* alto, in alto; **20m** ~ alto(a) 20m; ~**brow** *adj*, intellettuale *m/f*; ~**chair** *n* seggiolone *m*; ~**er education** *n* studi *mpl* superiori; ~**-handed** *adj* prepotente; ~**-heeled** *adj* con i tacchi alti; ~ **jump** *n* (*SPORT*) salto in alto; **the H~lands** *npl* le Highlands scozzesi; ~**light** *n* (*fig: of event*) momento culminante; (*in hair*) colpo di sole ♦ *vt* mettere in evidenza; ~**ly** *adv* molto; **to speak ~ly of** parlare molto bene di; ~**ly strung** *adj* teso(a) di nervi, eccitabile; ~**ness** *n*: **Her H~ness** Sua Altezza; ~**-pitched** *adj* acuto(a); ~**-rise block** *n* palazzone *m*; ~ **school** *n* scuola secondaria; (*US*) istituto superiore d'istruzione; ~ **season** (*BRIT*) *n* alta stagione; ~ **street** (*BRIT*) *n* strada principale

highway ['haɪweɪ] *n* strada maestra; **H~ Code** (*BRIT*) *n* codice *m* della strada

hijack ['haɪdʒæk] *vt* dirottare; **~er** *n* dirottatore/trice

hike [haɪk] *vi* fare un'escursione a piedi ♦ *n* escursione *f* a piedi; **~r** *n* escursionista *m/f*; **hiking** *n* escursioni *fpl* a piedi

hilarious [hɪ'lɛərɪəs] *adj* (*behaviour, event*) spassosissimo(a)

hill [hɪl] *n* collina, colle *m*; (*fairly high*) montagna; (*on road*) salita; **~side** *n* fianco della collina; **~ walking** *n* escursioni *fpl* in collina; **~y** *adj* collinoso(a); montagnoso(a)

hilt [hɪlt] *n* (*of sword*) elsa; **to the ~** (*fig: support*) fino in fondo

him [hɪm] *pron* (*direct*) lo, l' +*vowel*; (*indirect*) gli; (*stressed, after prep*) lui; *see also* **me**; **~self** *pron* (*reflexive*) si; (*emphatic*) lui stesso; (*after prep*) se stesso, sé; *see also* **oneself**

hinder ['hɪndə*] *vt* ostacolare; **hindrance** ['hɪndrəns] *n* ostacolo, impedimento

hindsight ['haɪndsaɪt] *n*: **with ~** con il senno di poi

Hindu ['hɪnduː] *n* indù *m/f inv*

hinge [hɪndʒ] *n* cardine *m* ♦ *vi* (*fig*): **to ~ on** dipendere da

hint [hɪnt] *n* (*suggestion*) allusione *f*; (*advice*) consiglio; (*sign*) accenno ♦ *vt*: **to ~ that** lasciar capire che ♦ *vi*: **to ~ at** alludere a

hip [hɪp] *n* anca, fianco

hippopotamus [hɪpə'pɒtəməs] (*pl* **~es** *or* **hippopotami**) *n* ippopotamo

hire ['haɪə*] *vt* (*BRIT: car, equipment*) noleggiare; (*worker*) assumere, dare lavoro a ♦ *n* nolo, noleggio; **for ~** da nolo; (*taxi*) libero(a); **~(d) car** (*BRIT*) *n* macchina a nolo; **~ purchase** (*BRIT*) *n* acquisto (*or* vendita) rateale

his [hɪz] *adj, pron* il(la) suo(sua), i(le) suoi(sue); *see also* **my**; **mine**[1]

hiss [hɪs] *vi* fischiare; (*cat, snake*) sibilare

historic(al) [hɪ'stɒrɪk(l)] *adj* storico(a)

history ['hɪstərɪ] *n* storia

hit [hɪt] (*pt, pp* **hit**) *vt* colpire, picchiare; (*knock against*) battere; (*reach: target*) raggiungere; (*collide with: car*) urtare contro; (*fig: affect*) colpire; (*find: problem etc*) incontrare ♦ *n* colpo; (*success, song*)

successo; **to ~ it off with sb** andare molto d'accordo con qn; **~-and-run driver** *n* pirata *m* della strada

hitch [hɪtʃ] *vt* (*fasten*) attaccare; (*also: ~ up*) tirare su ♦ *n* (*difficulty*) intoppo, difficoltà *f inv*; **to ~ a lift** fare l'autostop

hitch-hike *vi* fare l'autostop; **~r** *n* autostoppista *m/f*; **hitch-hiking** *n* autostop *m*

hi-tech ['haɪ'tɛk] *adj* di alta tecnologia ♦ *n* alta tecnologia

hitherto [hɪðə'tuː] *adv* in precedenza

HIV *abbr*: **HIV-negative/-positive** *adj* sieronegativo(a)/sieropositivo(a)

hive [haɪv] *n* alveare *m*

H.M.S. *abbr* = **His(Her) Majesty's Ship**

hoard [hɔːd] *n* (*of food*) provviste *fpl*; (*of money*) gruzzolo ♦ *vt* ammassare

hoarding ['hɔːdɪŋ] (*BRIT*) *n* (*for posters*) tabellone *m* per affissioni

hoarse [hɔːs] *adj* rauco(a)

hoax [həuks] *n* scherzo; falso allarme

hob [hɒb] *n* piastra (con fornelli)

hobble ['hɒbl] *vi* zoppicare

hobby ['hɒbɪ] *n* hobby *m inv*, passatempo

hobo ['həubəu] (*US*) *n* vagabondo

hockey ['hɒkɪ] *n* hockey *m*

hoe [həu] *n* zappa

hog [hɒg] *n* maiale *m* ♦ *vt* (*fig*) arraffare; **to go the whole ~** farlo fino in fondo

hoist [hɔɪst] *n* paranco ♦ *vt* issare

hold [həuld] (*pt, pp* **held**) *vt* tenere; (*contain*) contenere; (*keep back*) trattenere; (*believe*) mantenere; considerare; (*possess*) avere, possedere; detenere ♦ *vi* (*withstand pressure*) tenere; (*be valid*) essere valido(a) ♦ *n* presa; (*control*): **to have a ~ over** avere controllo su; (*NAUT*) stiva; **~ the line!** (*TEL*) resti in linea!; **to ~ one's own** (*fig*) difendersi bene; **to catch** *or* **get (a) ~ of** afferrare; **~ back** *vt* trattenere; (*secret*) tenere celato(a); **~ down** *vt* (*person*) tenere a terra; (*job*) tenere; **~ off** *vt* tener lontano; **~ on** *vi* tener fermo; (*wait*) aspettare; **~ on!** (*TEL*) resti in linea!; **~ on to** *vt fus* tenersi stretto(a) a; (*keep*) conservare; **~ out** *vt* offrire ♦ *vi* (*resist*) resistere; ~ **up** vt (raise) alzare; (support) sostenere; (delay) ritardare; (rob) assaltare; ~**all** (BRIT) n borsone m; ~**er** n (container) contenitore m; (of ticket, title) possessore/posseditrice; (of office etc) incaricato/a; (of record) detentore/trice; ~**ing** n (share) azioni fpl, titoli mpl; (farm) podere m, tenuta; ~**up** n (robbery) rapina a mano armata; (delay) ritardo; (BRIT: in traffic) blocco

hole [həul] n buco, buca

holiday ['hɔlədɪ] n vacanza; (day off) giorno di vacanza; (public) giorno festivo; **on ~** in vacanza; ~ **camp** (BRIT) (also: ~ **centre**) ≈ villaggio (di vacanze); ~**maker** (BRIT) n villeggiante m/f; ~ **resort** n luogo di villeggiatura

holiness ['həulɪnɪs] n santità

Holland ['hɔlənd] n Olanda

hollow ['hɔləu] adj cavo(a); (container, claim) vuoto(a); (laugh, sound) cupo(a) ♦ n cavità f inv; (in land) valletta, depressione f ♦ vt: **to ~ out** scavare

holly ['hɔlɪ] n agrifoglio

holocaust ['hɔləkɔːst] n olocausto

holster ['həulstə*] n fondina (di pistola)

holy ['həulɪ] adj santo(a); (bread) benedetto(a), consacrato(a); (ground) consacrato(a)

homage ['hɔmɪdʒ] n omaggio; **to pay ~ to** rendere omaggio a

home [həum] n casa; (country) patria; (institution) casa, ricovero ♦ cpd familiare; (cooking etc) casalingo(a); (ECON, POL) nazionale, interno(a); (SPORT) di casa ♦ adv a casa; in patria; (right in: nail etc) fino in fondo; **at ~** a casa; (in situation) a proprio agio; **to go** (or **come**) **~** tornare a casa (or in patria); **make yourself at ~** si metta a suo agio; ~ **address** n indirizzo di casa; ~**land** n patria; ~**less** adj senza tetto; spatriato(a); ~**ly** adj semplice, alla buona; accogliente; ~**-made** adj casalingo(a); **H~ Office** (BRIT) n ministero degli Interni; ~ **page** n (COMPUT) home page f inv; ~ **rule** n autogoverno; **H~ Secretary** (BRIT) n ministro degli Interni; ~**sick** adj: **to be ~sick** avere la nostalgia; ~ **town** n città f

inv natale; ~**ward** ['həumwəd] adj (journey) di ritorno; ~**work** n compiti mpl (per casa)

homicide ['hɔmɪsaɪd] (US) n omicidio

homoeopathic [həumɪə'pæθɪk] (US **homeopathic**) adj omeopatico(a)

homosexual [hɔməu'sɛksjuəl] adj, n omosessuale m/f

honest ['ɔnɪst] adj onesto(a); sincero(a); ~**ly** adv onestamente; sinceramente; ~**y** n onestà

honey ['hʌnɪ] n miele m; ~**comb** n favo; ~**moon** n luna di miele, viaggio di nozze; ~**suckle** n (BOT) caprifoglio

honk [hɔŋk] vi suonare il clacson

honorary ['ɔnərərɪ] adj onorario(a); (duty, title) onorifico(a)

honour ['ɔnə*] (US **honor**) vt onorare ♦ n onore m; ~**able** adj onorevole; ~**s degree** n (SCOL) laurea specializzata

hood [hud] n cappuccio; (on cooker) cappa; (BRIT: AUT) capote f; (US: AUT) cofano

hoodlum ['huːdləm] n teppista m/f

hoof [huːf] (pl **hooves**) n zoccolo

hook [huk] n gancio; (for fishing) amo ♦ vt uncinare; (dress) agganciare

hooligan ['huːlɪgən] n giovinastro, teppista m

hoop [huːp] n cerchio

hooray [huː'reɪ] excl = **hurray**

hoot [huːt] vi (AUT) suonare il clacson; (siren) ululare; (owl) gufare; ~**er** n (BRIT: AUT) clacson m inv; (NAUT) sirena

Hoover ® ['huːvə*] (BRIT) n aspirapolvere m inv ♦ vt: **h~** pulire con l'aspirapolvere

hooves [huːvz] npl of **hoof**

hop [hɔp] vi saltellare, saltare; (on one foot) saltare su una gamba

hope [həup] vt: **to ~ that/to do** sperare che/di fare ♦ vi sperare ♦ n speranza; **I ~ so/not** spero di sì/no; ~**ful** adj (person) pieno(a) di speranza; (situation) promettente; ~**fully** adv con speranza; ~**fully he will recover** speriamo che si riprenda; ~**less** adj senza speranza, disperato(a); (useless) inutile

hops [hɔps] npl luppoli mpl

horde [hɔːd] n orda

horizon [hə'raɪzn] n orizzonte m; **~tal** [hɔrɪ'zɔntl] adj orizzontale

hormone ['hɔːməʊn] n ormone m

horn [hɔːn] n (ZOOL, MUS) corno m; (AUT) clacson m inv

hornet ['hɔːnɪt] n calabrone m

horoscope ['hɔrəskəʊp] n oroscopo

horrendous [hə'rendəs] adj orrendo(a)

horrible ['hɔrɪbl] adj orribile, tremendo(a)

horrid ['hɔrɪd] adj orrido(a); (person) odioso(a)

horrify ['hɔrɪfaɪ] vt scandalizzare

horror ['hɔrə*] n orrore m; ~ **film** n film m inv dell'orrore

hors d'œuvre [ɔː'dəːvrə] n antipasto

horse [hɔːs] n cavallo m; **on ~back** adj, adv a cavallo; ~ **chestnut** n ippocastano; **~man** (irreg) n cavaliere m; **~power** n cavallo (vapore); **~-racing** n ippica; **~radish** n rafano; **~shoe** n ferro di cavallo; **~woman** (irreg) n amazzone f

horticulture ['hɔːtɪkʌltʃə*] n orticoltura

hose [həʊz] n (also: **~pipe**) tubo; (also: **garden ~**) tubo per annaffiare

hosiery ['həʊʒərɪ] n maglieria

hospice ['hɔspɪs] n ricovero, ospizio

hospitable [hɔs'pɪtəbl] adj ospitale

hospital ['hɔspɪtl] n ospedale m

hospitality [hɔspɪ'tælɪtɪ] n ospitalità

host [həʊst] n ospite m; (REL) ostia; (large number): **a ~ of** una schiera di

hostage ['hɔstɪdʒ] n ostaggio/a

hostel ['hɔstl] n ostello; (also: **youth ~**) ostello della gioventù

hostess ['həʊstɪs] n ospite f; (BRIT: air ~) hostess f inv

hostile ['hɔstaɪl] adj ostile

hostility [hɔ'stɪlɪtɪ] n ostilità f inv

hot [hɔt] adj caldo(a); (as opposed to only warm) molto caldo(a); (spicy) piccante; (fig) accanito(a); ardente; violento(a), focoso(a); **to be ~** (person) aver caldo(a); (object) essere caldo(a); (weather) far caldo; **~bed** n (fig) focolaio; ~ **dog** n hot dog m inv

hotel [həʊ'tɛl] n albergo; **~ier** n albergatore/trice

hot: ~house n serra; ~ **line** n (POL)

telefono rosso; **~ly** adv violentemente; **~plate** n piastra riscaldante; **~pot** (BRIT) n stufato coperto da uno strato di patate; **~-water bottle** n borsa dell'acqua calda

hound [haund] vt perseguitare ♦ n segugio

hour ['auə*] n ora; **~ly** adj all'ora

house [n haus, pl 'hauzɪz, vb hauz] n (also firm) casa; (POL) camera; (THEATRE) sala; pubblico; spettacolo ♦ vt (person) ospitare, alloggiare; **on the ~** (fig) offerto(a) dalla casa; ~ **arrest** n arresti mpl domiciliari; **~boat** n house boat f inv; **~bound** adj confinato(a) in casa; **~breaking** n furto con scasso; **~hold** n famiglia; casa; **~keeper** n governante f; **~keeping** n (work) governo della casa; (money) soldi mpl per le spese di casa; **~-warming party** n festa per inaugurare la casa nuova; **~wife** (irreg) n massaia, casalinga; **~work** n faccende fpl domestiche

housing ['hauzɪŋ] n alloggio; ~ **development** (BRIT ~ **estate**) n zona residenziale con case popolari e/o private

hovel ['hɔvl] n casupola

hover ['hɔvə*] vi (bird) librarsi; **~craft** n hovercraft m inv

how [hau] adv come; ~ **are you?** come sta?; ~ **do you do?** piacere!; ~ **far is it to the river?** quanto è lontano il fiume?; ~ **long have you been here?** da quando è qui?; ~ **lovely!/awful!** che bello!/orrore!; ~ **many?** quanti(e)?; ~ **much?** quanto(a)?; ~ **much milk?** quanto latte?; ~ **many people?** quante persone?; ~ **old are you?** quanti anni ha?; **~ever** adv in qualsiasi modo or maniera che; (+adjective) per quanto +sub; (in questions) come ♦ conj comunque, però

howl [haul] vi ululare; (baby, person) urlare

H.P. abbr = **hire purchase**; **horsepower**

h.p. n abbr = **H.P.**

HQ n abbr = **headquarters**

HTML abbr (= hypertext markup language) HTML m inv

hub [hʌb] n (of wheel) mozzo; (fig) fulcro

hubcap ['hʌbkæp] n coprimozzo

huddle ['hʌdl] vi: **to ~ together** rannicchiarsi l'uno contro l'altro

hue [hju:] *n* tinta

huff [hʌf] *n*: **in a ~** stizzito(a)

hug [hʌg] *vt* abbracciare; (*shore, kerb*) stringere

huge [hju:dʒ] *adj* enorme, immenso(a)

hulk [hʌlk] *n* (*ship*) nave *f* in disarmo; (*car*) carcassa; (*person*) mastodonte *m*

hull [hʌl] *n* (*of ship*) scafo

hullo [hə'ləu] *excl* = **hello**

hum [hʌm] *vt* (*tune*) canticchiare ♦ *vi* canticchiare; (*insect, plane, tool*) ronzare

human ['hju:mən] *adj* umano(a) ♦ *n* essere *m* umano

humane [hju:'meɪn] *adj* umanitario(a)

humanitarian [hju:mænɪ'tɛərɪən] *adj* umanitario(a)

humanity [hju:'mænɪtɪ] *n* umanità

humble ['hʌmbl] *adj* umile, modesto(a) ♦ *vt* umiliare

humdrum ['hʌmdrʌm] *adj* monotono(a), tedioso(a)

humid ['hju:mɪd] *adj* umido(a)

humiliate [hju:'mɪlɪeɪt] *vt* umiliare; **humiliation** [-'eɪʃən] *n* umiliazione *f*

humility [hju:'mɪlɪtɪ] *n* umiltà

humorous ['hju:mərəs] *adj* umoristico(a); (*person*) buffo(a)

humour ['hju:mə*] (*US* **humor**) *n* umore *m* ♦ *vt* accontentare

hump [hʌmp] *n* gobba

hunch [hʌntʃ] *n* (*premonition*) intuizione *f*; **~ed** *adj* ingobbito(a)

hundred ['hʌndrəd] *num* cento; **~s of** centinaia *fpl* di; **~weight** *n* (*BRIT*) = *50.8 kg; 112 lb*; (*US*) = *45.3 kg; 100 lb*

hung [hʌŋ] *pt, pp of* **hang**

Hungary ['hʌŋgərɪ] *n* Ungheria

hunger ['hʌŋgə*] *n* fame *f* ♦ *vi*: **to ~ for** desiderare ardentemente; **~ strike** *n* sciopero della fame

hungry ['hʌŋgrɪ] *adj* affamato(a); (*avid*): **~ for** avido(a) di; **to be ~** aver fame

hunk [hʌŋk] *n* (*of bread etc*) bel pezzo

hunt [hʌnt] *vt* (*seek*) cercare; (*SPORT*) cacciare ♦ *vi*: **to ~ (for)** andare a caccia (di) ♦ *n* caccia; **~er** *n* cacciatore *m*; **~ing** *n* caccia

hurdle ['hə:dl] *n* (*SPORT, fig*) ostacolo

hurl [hə:l] *vt* lanciare con violenza

hurrah [hu'rɑ:] *excl* = **hurray**

hurray [hu'reɪ] *excl* urrà!, evviva!

hurricane ['hʌrɪkən] *n* uragano

hurried ['hʌrɪd] *adj* affrettato(a); (*work*) fatto(a) in fretta; **~ly** *adv* in fretta

hurry ['hʌrɪ] *n* fretta ♦ *vi* (*also*: **~ up**) affrettarsi ♦ *vt* (*also*: **~ up**: *person*) affrettare; (: *work*) far in fretta; **to be in a ~** aver fretta

hurt [hə:t] (*pt, pp* **hurt**) *vt* (*cause pain to*) far male a; (*injure, fig*) ferire ♦ *vi* far male; **~ful** *adj* (*remark*) che ferisce

hurtle ['hə:tl] *vi*: **to ~ past/down** passare/scendere a razzo

husband ['hʌzbənd] *n* marito

hush [hʌʃ] *n* silenzio, calma ♦ *vt* zittire; **~!** zitto(a)!; **~ up** *vt* (*scandal*) mettere a tacere

husk [hʌsk] *n* (*of wheat*) cartoccio; (*of rice, maize*) buccia

husky ['hʌskɪ] *adj* roco(a) ♦ *n* cane *m* eschimese

hustle ['hʌsl] *vt* spingere, incalzare ♦ *n*: **~ and bustle** trambusto

hut [hʌt] *n* rifugio; (*shed*) ripostiglio

hutch [hʌtʃ] *n* gabbia

hyacinth ['haɪəsɪnθ] *n* giacinto

hybrid ['haɪbrɪd] *n* ibrido

hydrant ['haɪdrənt] *n* (*also*: **fire ~**) idrante *m*

hydraulic [haɪ'drɔ:lɪk] *adj* idraulico(a)

hydroelectric [haɪdrəu'lektrɪk] *adj* idroelettrico(a)

hydrofoil ['haɪdrəufɔɪl] *n* aliscafo

hydrogen ['haɪdrədʒən] *n* idrogeno

hyena [haɪ'i:nə] *n* iena

hygiene ['haɪdʒi:n] *n* igiene *f*

hymn [hɪm] *n* inno; cantica

hype [haɪp] *n* (*inf*) campagna pubblicitaria

hypermarket ['haɪpəmɑ:kɪt] (*BRIT*) *n* ipermercato

hypertext ['haɪpətekst] *n* (*COMPUT*) ipertesto

hyphen ['haɪfn] *n* trattino

hypnotize ['hɪpnətaɪz] *vt* ipnotizzare

hypocrisy [hɪ'pɔkrɪsɪ] *n* ipocrisia

hypocrite ['hɪpəkrɪt] *n* ipocrita *m/f*; **hypocritical** [-'krɪtɪkl] *adj* ipocrita

hypothesis [haɪ'pɔθɪsɪs] (*pl* **hypotheses**) *n* ipotesi *f inv*

hypothetical [haɪpəʊ'θɛtɪkl] *adj* ipotetico(a)

hysterical [hɪ'stɛrɪkl] *adj* isterico(a)

hysterics [hɪ'stɛrɪks] *npl* accesso di isteria; (*laughter*) attacco di riso

I, i

I [aɪ] *pron* io

ice [aɪs] *n* ghiaccio; (*on road*) gelo; (*~ cream*) gelato ♦ *vt* (*cake*) glassare ♦ *vi* (*also: ~ over*) ghiacciare; (*also: ~ up*) gelare; **~berg** *n* iceberg *m inv*; **~box** *n* (*US*) frigorifero; (*BRIT*) reparto ghiaccio; (*insulated box*) frigo portatile; **~ cream** *n* gelato; **~ hockey** *n* hockey *m* su ghiaccio

Iceland ['aɪslənd] *n* Islanda

ice: ~ lolly (*BRIT*) *n* ghiacciolo; **~ rink** *n* pista di pattinaggio; **~ skating** *n* pattinaggio sul ghiaccio

icicle ['aɪsɪkl] *n* ghiacciolo

icing ['aɪsɪŋ] *n* (*CULIN*) glassa; **~ sugar** (*BRIT*) *n* zucchero a velo

icon ['aɪkɔn] *n* icona

icy ['aɪsɪ] *adj* ghiacciato(a); (*weather, temperature*) gelido(a)

I'd [aɪd] = **I would**; **I had**

idea [aɪ'dɪə] *n* idea

ideal [aɪ'dɪəl] *adj* ideale ♦ *n* ideale *m*

identical [aɪ'dɛntɪkl] *adj* identico(a)

identification [aɪdɛntɪfɪ'keɪʃən] *n* identificazione *f*; (**means of**) **~** carta d'identità

identify [aɪ'dɛntɪfaɪ] *vt* identificare

Identikit picture ® [aɪ'dɛntɪkɪt-] *n* identikit *m inv*

identity [aɪ'dɛntɪtɪ] *n* identità *f inv*; **~ card** *n* carta d'identità

ideology [aɪdɪ'ɔlədʒɪ] *n* ideologia

idiom ['ɪdɪəm] *n* idioma *m*; (*phrase*) espressione *f* idiomatica

idiot ['ɪdɪət] *n* idiota *m/f*; **~ic** [-'ɔtɪk] *adj* idiota

idle ['aɪdl] *adj* inattivo(a); (*lazy*) pigro(a),

ozioso(a); (*unemployed*) disoccupato(a); (*question, pleasures*) ozioso(a) ♦ *vi* (*engine*) girare al minimo

idol ['aɪdl] *n* idolo; **~ize** *vt* idoleggiare

i.e. *adv abbr* (= *that is*) cioè

if [ɪf] *conj* se; **~ I were you ...** se fossi in te ..., io al tuo posto ...; **~ so** se è così; **~ not** se no; **~ only** se solo *or* soltanto

ignite [ɪg'naɪt] *vt* accendere ♦ *vi* accendersi

ignition [ɪg'nɪʃən] *n* (*AUT*) accensione *f*; **to switch on/off the ~** accendere/spegnere il motore; **~ key** *n* (*AUT*) chiave *f* dell'accensione

ignorant ['ɪgnərənt] *adj* ignorante; **to be ~ of** (*subject*) essere ignorante in; (*events*) essere ignaro(a) di

ignore [ɪg'nɔ:*] *vt* non tener conto di; (*person, fact*) ignorare

I'll [aɪl] = **I will**; **I shall**

ill [ɪl] *adj* (*sick*) malato(a); (*bad*) cattivo(a) ♦ *n* male *m* ♦ *adv*: **to speak** *etc* **~ of sb** parlare *etc* male di qn; **to take** *or* **be taken ~** ammalarsi; **~-advised** *adj* (*decision*) poco giudizioso(a); (*person*) mal consigliato(a); **~-at-ease** *adj* a disagio

illegal [ɪ'li:gl] *adj* illegale

illegible [ɪ'lɛdʒɪbl] *adj* illeggibile

illegitimate [ɪlɪ'dʒɪtɪmət] *adj* illegittimo(a)

ill-fated [ɪl'feɪtɪd] *adj* nefasto(a)

ill feeling *n* rancore *m*

illiterate [ɪ'lɪtərət] *adj* analfabeta, illetterato(a); (*letter*) scorretto(a)

ill-mannered [ɪl'mænəd] *adj* maleducato(a)

illness ['ɪlnɪs] *n* malattia

ill-treat *vt* maltrattare

illuminate [ɪ'lu:mɪneɪt] *vt* illuminare; **illumination** [-'neɪʃən] *n* illuminazione *f*; **illuminations** *npl* (*decorative*) luminarie *fpl*

illusion [ɪ'lu:ʒən] *n* illusione *f*

illustrate ['ɪləstreɪt] *vt* illustrare

illustration [ɪlə'streɪʃən] *n* illustrazione *f*

I'm [aɪm] = **I am**

image ['ɪmɪdʒ] *n* immagine *f*; (*public face*) immagine (pubblica); **~ry** *n* immagini *fpl*

imaginary [ɪ'mædʒɪnərɪ] *adj* immaginario(a)

imagination [ɪmædʒɪ'neɪʃən] *n* immaginazione *f*, fantasia

imaginative [ɪˈmædʒɪnətɪv] *adj* immaginoso(a)

imagine [ɪˈmædʒɪn] *vt* immaginare

imbalance [ɪmˈbæləns] *n* squilibrio

imbue [ɪmˈbjuː] *vt*: **to ~ sb/sth with** permeare qn/qc di

imitate [ˈɪmɪteɪt] *vt* imitare; **imitation** [-ˈteɪʃən] *n* imitazione *f*

immaculate [ɪˈmækjulət] *adj* immacolato(a); (*dress, appearance*) impeccabile

immaterial [ɪməˈtɪərɪəl] *adj* immateriale, indifferente

immature [ɪməˈtjuə*] *adj* immaturo(a)

immediate [ɪˈmiːdɪət] *adj* immediato(a); **~ly** *adv* (*at once*) subito, immediatamente; **~ly next to** proprio accanto a

immense [ɪˈmens] *adj* immenso(a); enorme

immerse [ɪˈmɜːs] *vt* immergere

immersion heater [ɪˈmɜːʃən-] (*BRIT*) *n* scaldaacqua *m inv* a immersione

immigrant [ˈɪmɪɡrənt] *n* immigrante *m/f*; immigrato/a

immigration [ɪmɪˈɡreɪʃən] *n* immigrazione *f*

imminent [ˈɪmɪnənt] *adj* imminente

immoral [ɪˈmɒrl] *adj* immorale

immortal [ɪˈmɔːtl] *adj*, *n* immortale *m/f*

immune [ɪˈmjuːn] *adj*: **~ (to)** immune (da); **immunity** *n* immunità

impact [ˈɪmpækt] *n* impatto

impair [ɪmˈpeə*] *vt* danneggiare

impart [ɪmˈpɑːt] *vt* (*make known*) comunicare; (*bestow*) impartire

impartial [ɪmˈpɑːʃl] *adj* imparziale

impassable [ɪmˈpɑːsəbl] *adj* insuperabile; (*road*) impraticabile

impassive [ɪmˈpæsɪv] *adj* impassibile

impatience [ɪmˈpeɪʃəns] *n* impazienza

impatient [ɪmˈpeɪʃənt] *adj* impaziente; **to get** *or* **grow ~** perdere la pazienza

impeccable [ɪmˈpekəbl] *adj* impeccabile

impede [ɪmˈpiːd] *vt* impedire

impediment [ɪmˈpedɪmənt] *n* impedimento; (*also*: **speech ~**) difetto di pronuncia

impending [ɪmˈpendɪŋ] *adj* imminente

imperative [ɪmˈperətɪv] *adj* imperativo(a); necessario(a), urgente; (*voice*) imperioso(a)

imperfect [ɪmˈpɜːfɪkt] *adj* imperfetto(a); (*goods etc*) difettoso(a) ♦ *n* (*LING*: *also*: **~ tense**) imperfetto

imperial [ɪmˈpɪərɪəl] *adj* imperiale; (*measure*) legale

impersonal [ɪmˈpɜːsənl] *adj* impersonale

impersonate [ɪmˈpɜːsəneɪt] *vt* impersonare; (*THEATRE*) fare la mimica di

impertinent [ɪmˈpɜːtɪnənt] *adj* insolente, impertinente

impervious [ɪmˈpɜːvɪəs] *adj* (*fig*): **~ to** insensibile a; impassibile di fronte a

impetuous [ɪmˈpetjuəs] *adj* impetuoso(a), precipitoso(a)

impetus [ˈɪmpətəs] *n* impeto

impinge on [ɪmˈpɪndʒ-] *vt fus* (*person*) colpire; (*rights*) ledere

implement [*n* ˈɪmplɪmənt, *vb* ˈɪmplɪment] *n* attrezzo; (*for cooking*) utensile *m* ♦ *vt* effettuare

implicit [ɪmˈplɪsɪt] *adj* implicito(a); (*complete*) completo(a)

imply [ɪmˈplaɪ] *vt* insinuare; suggerire

impolite [ɪmpəˈlaɪt] *adj* scortese

import [*vb* ɪmˈpɔːt, *n* ˈɪmpɔːt] *vt* importare ♦ *n* (*COMM*) importazione *f*

importance [ɪmˈpɔːtns] *n* importanza

important [ɪmˈpɔːtnt] *adj* importante; **it's not ~** non ha importanza

importer [ɪmˈpɔːtə*] *n* importatore/trice

impose [ɪmˈpəuz] *vt* imporre ♦ *vi*: **to ~ on sb** sfruttare la bontà di qn

imposing [ɪmˈpəuzɪŋ] *adj* imponente

imposition [ɪmpəˈzɪʃən] *n* (*of tax etc*) imposizione *f*; **to be an ~ on** (*person*) abusare della gentilezza di

impossibility [ɪmpɒsəˈbɪlɪtɪ] *n* impossibilità

impossible [ɪmˈpɒsɪbl] *adj* impossibile

impotent [ˈɪmpətnt] *adj* impotente

impound [ɪmˈpaund] *vt* confiscare

impoverished [ɪmˈpɒvərɪʃt] *adj* impoverito(a)

impracticable [ɪmˈpræktɪkəbl] *adj* inattuabile

impractical [ɪmˈpræktɪkl] *adj* non pratico(a)

impress [ɪmˈpres] *vt* impressionare; (*mark*)

imprimere, stampare; **to ~ sth on sb** far capire qc a qn

impression [ɪmˈprɛʃən] *n* impressione *f*; **to be under the ~ that** avere l'impressione che

impressive [ɪmˈprɛsɪv] *adj* notevole

imprint [ˈɪmprɪnt] *n* (*of hand etc*) impronta; (*PUBLISHING*) sigla editoriale

imprison [ɪmˈprɪzn] *vt* imprigionare; **~ment** *n* imprigionamento

improbable [ɪmˈprɔbəbl] *adj* improbabile; (*excuse*) inverosimile

impromptu [ɪmˈprɔmptjuː] *adj* improvvisato(a)

improper [ɪmˈprɔpə*] *adj* scorretto(a); (*unsuitable*) inadatto(a), improprio(a); sconveniente, indecente

improve [ɪmˈpruːv] *vt* migliorare ♦ *vi* migliorare; (*pupil etc*) fare progressi; **~ment** *n* miglioramento; progresso

improvise [ˈɪmprəvaɪz] *vt, vi* improvvisare

impudent [ˈɪmpjudnt] *adj* impudente, sfacciato(a)

impulse [ˈɪmpʌls] *n* impulso; **on ~** d'impulso, impulsivamente

impulsive [ɪmˈpʌlsɪv] *adj* impulsivo(a)

KEYWORD

in [ɪn] *prep* **1** (*indicating place, position*) in; **~ the house/garden** in casa/giardino; **~ the box** nella scatola; **~ the fridge** nel frigorifero; **I have it ~ my hand** ce l'ho in mano; **~ town/the country** in città/campagna; **~ school** a scuola; **~ here/there** qui/lì dentro

2 (*with place names: of town, region, country*): **~ London** a Londra; **~ England** in Inghilterra; **~ the United States** negli Stati Uniti; **~ Yorkshire** nello Yorkshire

3 (*indicating time: during, in the space of*) in; **~ spring/summer** in primavera/estate; **~ 1999** nel 1999; **~ May** in *or* a maggio; **I'll see you ~ July** ci vediamo a luglio; **~ the afternoon** nel pomeriggio; **at 4 o'clock ~ the afternoon** alle 4 del pomeriggio; **I did it ~ 3 hours/days** l'ho fatto in 3 ore/giorni; **I'll see you ~ 2**

weeks *or* **~ 2 weeks' time** ci vediamo tra 2 settimane

4 (*indicating manner etc*) a; **~ a loud/soft voice** a voce alta/bassa; **~ pencil** a matita; **~ English/French** in inglese/francese; **the boy ~ the blue shirt** il ragazzo con la camicia blu

5 (*indicating circumstances*): **~ the sun** al sole; **~ the shade** all'ombra; **~ the rain** sotto la pioggia; **a rise ~ prices** un aumento dei prezzi

6 (*indicating mood, state*): **~ tears** in lacrime; **~ anger** per la rabbia; **~ despair** disperato(a); **~ good condition** in buono stato, in buone condizioni; **to live ~ luxury** vivere nel lusso

7 (*with ratios, numbers*): **1 ~ 10** 1 su 10; **20 pence ~ the pound** 20 pence per sterlina; **they lined up ~ twos** si misero in fila a due a due

8 (*referring to people, works*) in; **the disease is common ~ children** la malattia è comune nei bambini; **~ (the works of) Dickens** in Dickens

9 (*indicating profession etc*) in; **to be ~ teaching** fare l'insegnante, insegnare; **to be ~ publishing** essere nell'editoria

10 (*after superlative*) di; **the best ~ the class** il migliore della classe

11 (*with present participle*): **~ saying this** dicendo questo, nel dire questo

♦ *adv*: **to be ~** (*person: at home, work*) esserci; (*train, ship, plane*) essere arrivato(a); (*in fashion*) essere di moda; **to ask sb ~** invitare qn ad entrare; **to run/limp etc ~** entrare di corsa/zoppicando *etc*

♦ *n*: **the ~s and outs of the problem** tutti i particolari del problema

---

in. *abbr* = **inch**

inability [ɪnəˈbɪlɪtɪ] *n*: **~ (to do)** incapacità (di fare)

inaccurate [ɪnˈækjurət] *adj* inesatto(a), impreciso(a)

inadequate [ɪnˈædɪkwət] *adj* insufficiente

inadvertently [ɪnədˈvɜːtntlɪ] *adv* senza volerlo

inadvisable [ɪnəd'vaɪzəbl] adj consigliabile
inane [ɪ'neɪn] adj vacuo(a), stupido(a)
inanimate [ɪn'ænɪmət] adj inanimato(a)
inappropriate [ɪnə'prəʊprɪət] adj non
adatto(a); (word, expression) improprio(a)
inarticulate [ɪnɑː'tɪkjulət] adj (person) che
si esprime male; (speech) inarticolato(a)
inasmuch as [ɪnəz'mʌtʃæz] adv in quanto
che; (insofar as) poiché
inaudible [ɪn'ɔːdɪbl] adj che non si riesce a
sentire
inauguration [ɪnɔːgju'reɪʃən] n
inaugurazione f; insediamento in carica
in-between adj fra i (or le) due
inborn [ɪn'bɔːn] adj innato(a)
inbred [ɪn'brɛd] adj innato(a); (family)
connaturato(a)
Inc. (US) abbr (= incorporated) S.A
incapable [ɪn'keɪpəbl] adj incapace
incapacitate [ɪnkə'pæsɪteɪt] vt: to ~ sb
from doing rendere qn incapace di fare
incense [n 'ɪnsɛns, vb ɪn'sɛns] n incenso ♦ vt
(anger) infuriare
incentive [ɪn'sɛntɪv] n incentivo
incessant [ɪn'sɛsnt] adj incessante; ~ly adv
di continuo, senza sosta
inch [ɪntʃ] n pollice m (= 25 mm; 12 in a
foot); within an ~ of a un pelo da; he
didn't give an ~ non ha ceduto di un
millimetro
incidence ['ɪnsɪdns] n (of crime, disease)
incidenza
incident ['ɪnsɪdnt] n incidente m; (in book)
episodio
incidental [ɪnsɪ'dɛntl] adj accessorio(a),
d'accompagnamento; (unplanned)
incidentale; ~ to marginale a; ~ly [-'dɛntəlɪ]
adv (by the way) a proposito
inclination [ɪnklɪ'neɪʃən] n inclinazione f
incline [n 'ɪnklaɪn, vb ɪn'klaɪn] n pendenza,
pendio ♦ vt inclinare ♦ vi (surface) essere
inclinato(a); to be ~d to do tendere a fare;
essere propenso(a) a fare
include [ɪn'kluːd] vt includere, comprendere; including prep compreso(a),
incluso(a)
inclusive [ɪn'kluːsɪv] adj incluso(a),

compreso(a); ~ of tax etc tasse etc
comprese
incoherent [ɪnkəʊ'hɪərənt] adj incoerente
income ['ɪnkʌm] n reddito; ~ tax n
imposta sul reddito
incoming ['ɪnkʌmɪŋ] adj (flight, mail) in
arrivo; (government) subentrante; (tide)
montante
incompetent [ɪn'kɔmpɪtnt] adj incompetente, incapace
incomplete [ɪnkəm'pliːt] adj incompleto(a)
incongruous [ɪn'kɔŋgruəs] adj poco
appropriato(a); (remark, act) incongruo(a)
inconsiderate [ɪnkən'sɪdərət] adj
sconsiderato(a)
inconsistency [ɪnkən'sɪstənsɪ] n incoerenza
inconsistent [ɪnkən'sɪstənt] adj incoerente;
~ with non coerente con
inconspicuous [ɪnkən'spɪkjuəs] adj
incospicuo(a); (colour) poco appariscente;
(dress) dimesso(a)
inconvenience [ɪnkən'viːnjəns] n
inconveniente m; (trouble) disturbo ♦ vt
disturbare
inconvenient [ɪnkən'viːnjənt] adj
scomodo(a)
incorporate [ɪn'kɔːpəreɪt] vt incorporare;
(contain) contenere; ~d adj: ~d company
(US) società f inv anonima
incorrect [ɪnkə'rɛkt] adj scorretto(a);
(statement) inesatto(a)
increase [n 'ɪnkriːs, vb ɪn'kriːs] n aumento
♦ vi, vt aumentare
increasing [ɪn'kriːsɪŋ] adj (number)
crescente; ~ly adv sempre più
incredible [ɪn'krɛdɪbl] adj incredibile
increment ['ɪnkrɪmənt] n aumento,
incremento
incriminate [ɪn'krɪmɪneɪt] vt compromettere
incubator ['ɪnkjubeɪtə*] n incubatrice f
incumbent [ɪn'kʌmbənt] adj: to be ~ on sb
spettare a qn
incur [ɪn'kɜː*] vt (expenses) incorrere; (anger,
risk) esporsi a; (debt) contrarre; (loss) subire
indebted [ɪn'dɛtɪd] adj: to be ~ to sb (for)
essere obbligato(a) verso qn (per)

indecent [ɪnˈdiːsnt] *adj* indecente; ~ **assault** (*BRIT*) *n* aggressione *f* a scopo di violenza sessuale; ~ **exposure** *n* atti *mpl* osceni in luogo pubblico

indecisive [ɪndɪˈsaɪsɪv] *adj* indeciso(a)

indeed [ɪnˈdiːd] *adv* infatti; veramente; **yes ~!** certamente!

indefinite [ɪnˈdefɪnɪt] *adj* indefinito(a); (*answer*) vago(a); (*period, number*) indeterminato(a); **~ly** *adv* (*wait*) indefinitamente

indemnity [ɪnˈdemnɪtɪ] *n* (*insurance*) assicurazione *f*; (*compensation*) indennità, indennizzo

independence [ɪndɪˈpendns] *n* indipendenza

Independence Day

i Negli Stati Uniti il 4 luglio si festeggia l'**Independence Day**, giorno in cui, nel 1776, 13 colonie britanniche proclamarono la propria indipendenza dalla Gran Bretagna ed entrarono ufficialmente a far parte degli Stati Uniti d'America.

independent [ɪndɪˈpendnt] *adj* indipendente

index [ˈɪndeks] (*pl* **~es**) *n* (*in book*) indice *m*; (*: in library etc*) catalogo; (*pl* **indices**: *ratio, sign*) indice *m*; ~ **card** *n* scheda; ~ **finger** *n* (dito) indice *m*; **~-linked** (*US* **~ed**) *adj* legato(a) al costo della vita

India [ˈɪndɪə] *n* India; **~n** *adj, n* indiano(a)

indicate [ˈɪndɪkeɪt] *vt* indicare; **indication** [-ˈkeɪʃən] *n* indicazione *f*, segno

indicative [ɪnˈdɪkətɪv] *adj*: ~ **of** indicativo(a) di

indicator [ˈɪndɪkeɪtə*] *n* indicatore *m*; (*AUT*) freccia

indices [ˈɪndɪsiːz] *npl of* **index**

indictment [ɪnˈdaɪtmənt] *n* accusa

indifference [ɪnˈdɪfrəns] *n* indifferenza

indifferent [ɪnˈdɪfrənt] *adj* indifferente; (*poor*) mediocre

indigenous [ɪnˈdɪdʒɪnəs] *adj* indigeno(a)

indigestion [ɪndɪˈdʒestʃən] *n* indigestione *f*

indignant [ɪnˈdɪgnənt] *adj*: ~ **(at sth / with sb**) indignato(a) (per qc/contro qn)

indignity [ɪnˈdɪgnɪtɪ] *n* umiliazione *f*

indigo [ˈɪndɪgəu] *n* indaco

indirect [ɪndɪˈrekt] *adj* indiretto(a)

indiscreet [ɪndɪˈskriːt] *adj* indiscreto(a); (*rash*) imprudente

indiscriminate [ɪndɪˈskrɪmɪnət] *adj* indiscriminato(a)

indisputable [ɪndɪˈspjuːtəbl] *adj* incontestabile, indiscutibile

individual [ɪndɪˈvɪdjuəl] *n* individuo ♦ *adj* individuale; (*characteristic*) particolare, originale

indoctrination [ɪndɒktrɪˈneɪʃən] *n* indottrinamento

Indonesia [ɪndəˈniːzɪə] *n* Indonesia

indoor [ˈɪndɔː*] *adj* da interno; (*plant*) d'appartamento; (*swimming pool*) coperto(a); (*sport, games*) fatto(a) al coperto; **~s** [ɪnˈdɔːz] *adv* all'interno

induce [ɪnˈdjuːs] *vt* persuadere; (*bring about, MED*) provocare

indulge [ɪnˈdʌldʒ] *vt* (*whim*) compiacere, soddisfare; (*child*) viziare ♦ *vi*: **to ~ in sth** concedersi qc; abbandonarsi a qc; **~nce** *n* lusso (che uno si permette); (*leniency*) indulgenza; **~nt** *adj* indulgente

industrial [ɪnˈdʌstrɪəl] *adj* industriale; (*injury*) sul lavoro; ~ **action** *n* azione *f* rivendicativa; ~ **estate** (*BRIT*) *n* zona industriale; ~ **park** (*US*) *n* = ~ **estate**

industrious [ɪnˈdʌstrɪəs] *adj* industrioso(a), assiduo(a)

industry [ˈɪndəstrɪ] *n* industria; (*diligence*) operosità

inedible [ɪnˈedɪbl] *adj* immangiabile; (*poisonous*) non commestibile

ineffective [ɪnɪˈfektɪv] *adj* inefficace; incompetente

ineffectual [ɪnɪˈfektʃuəl] *adj* inefficace; incompetente

inefficient [ɪnɪˈfɪʃənt] *adj* inefficiente

inept [ɪˈnept] *adj* inetto(a)

inequality [ɪnɪˈkwɒlɪtɪ] *n* ineguaglianza

inescapable [ɪnɪˈskeɪpəbl] *adj* inevitabile

inevitable [ɪnˈevɪtəbl] *adj* inevitabile; **inevitably** *adv* inevitabilmente

inexact [ɪnɪgˈzækt] *adj* inesatto(a)
inexcusable [ɪnɪksˈkjuːzəbl] *adj* ingiustificabile
inexpensive [ɪnɪksˈpɛnsɪv] *adj* poco costoso(a)
inexperienced [ɪnɪksˈpɪərɪənst] *adj* inesperto(a), senza esperienza
infallible [ɪnˈfælɪbl] *adj* infallibile
infamous [ˈɪnfəməs] *adj* infame
infancy [ˈɪnfənsɪ] *n* infanzia
infant [ˈɪnfənt] *n* bambino/a; **~ school** (*BRIT*) scuola elementare (*per bambini dall'età di 5 a 7 anni*)
infantry [ˈɪnfəntrɪ] *n* fanteria
infatuated [ɪnˈfætjueɪtɪd] *adj*: **~ with** infatuato(a) di
infatuation [ɪnfætjuˈeɪʃən] *n* infatuazione *f*
infect [ɪnˈfɛkt] *vt* infettare; **~ion** [ɪnˈfɛkʃən] *n* infezione *f*; **~ious** [ɪnˈfɛkʃəs] *adj* (*disease*) infettivo(a), contagioso(a); (*person, fig: enthusiasm*) contagioso(a)
infer [ɪnˈfəː*] *vt* inferire, dedurre
inferior [ɪnˈfɪərɪə*] *adj* inferiore; (*goods*) di qualità scadente ♦ *n* inferiore *m/f*; (*in rank*) subalterno/a; **~ity** [ɪnfɪərɪˈɔrətɪ] *n* inferiorità; **~ity complex** *n* complesso di inferiorità
infertile [ɪnˈfəːtaɪl] *adj* sterile
in-fighting [ˈɪnfaɪtɪŋ] *n* lotte *fpl* intestine
infiltrate [ˈɪnfɪltreɪt] *vt* infiltrarsi in
infinite [ˈɪnfɪnɪt] *adj* infinito(a)
infinitive [ɪnˈfɪnɪtɪv] *n* infinito
infinity [ɪnˈfɪnɪtɪ] *n* infinità; (*also MATH*) infinito
infirmary [ɪnˈfəːmərɪ] *n* ospedale *m*; (*in school, factory*) infermeria
inflamed [ɪnˈfleɪmd] *adj* infiammato(a)
inflammable [ɪnˈflæməbl] *adj* infiammabile
inflammation [ɪnfləˈmeɪʃən] *n* infiammazione *f*
inflatable [ɪnˈfleɪtəbl] *adj* gonfiabile
inflate [ɪnˈfleɪt] *vt* (*tyre, balloon*) gonfiare; (*fig*) esagerare; gonfiare; **inflation** [ɪnˈfleɪʃən] *n* (*ECON*) inflazione *f*; **inflationary** [ɪnˈfleɪʃnərɪ] *adj* inflazionistico(a)
inflict [ɪnˈflɪkt] *vt*: **to ~ on** infliggere a
influence [ˈɪnfluəns] *n* influenza ♦ *vt*

influenzare; **under the ~ of alcohol** sotto l'effetto dell'alcool
influential [ɪnfluˈɛnʃl] *adj* influente
influenza [ɪnfluˈɛnzə] *n* (*MED*) influenza
influx [ˈɪnflʌks] *n* afflusso
inform [ɪnˈfɔːm] *vt*: **to ~ sb (of)** informare qn (di) ♦ *vi*: **to ~ on sb** denunciare qn
informal [ɪnˈfɔːml] *adj* informale; (*announcement, invitation*) non ufficiale; **~ity** [-ˈmælɪtɪ] *n* informalità; carattere *m* non ufficiale
informant [ɪnˈfɔːmənt] *n* informatore/trice
information [ɪnfəˈmeɪʃən] *n* informazioni *fpl*; particolari *mpl*; **a piece of ~** un'informazione; **~ desk** *n* banco *m* informazioni; **~ office** *n* ufficio *m* informazioni
informative [ɪnˈfɔːmətɪv] *adj* istruttivo(a)
informer [ɪnˈfɔːmə*] *n* (*also: police ~*) informatore/trice
infringe [ɪnˈfrɪndʒ] *vt* infrangere ♦ *vi*: **to ~ on** calpestare; **~ment** *n* infrazione *f*
infuriating [ɪnˈfjuərɪeɪtɪŋ] *adj* molto irritante
ingenious [ɪnˈdʒiːnjəs] *adj* ingegnoso(a)
ingenuity [ɪndʒɪˈnjuːɪtɪ] *n* ingegnosità
ingenuous [ɪnˈdʒɛnjuəs] *adj* ingenuo(a)
ingot [ˈɪŋgət] *n* lingotto
ingrained [ɪnˈgreɪnd] *adj* radicato(a)
ingratiate [ɪnˈgreɪʃɪeɪt] *vt*: **to ~ o.s. with sb** ingraziarsi qn
ingredient [ɪnˈgriːdɪənt] *n* ingrediente *m*; elemento
inhabit [ɪnˈhæbɪt] *vt* abitare
inhabitant [ɪnˈhæbɪtnt] *n* abitante *m/f*
inhale [ɪnˈheɪl] *vt* inalare ♦ *vi* (*in smoking*) aspirare
inherent [ɪnˈhɪərənt] *adj*: **~ (in o. to)** inerente (a)
inherit [ɪnˈhɛrɪt] *vt* ereditare; **~ance** *n* eredità
inhibit [ɪnˈhɪbɪt] *vt* (*PSYCH*) inibire; **~ion** [-ˈbɪʃən] *n* inibizione *f*
inhospitable [ɪnhɔsˈpɪtəbl] *adj* inospitale
inhuman [ɪnˈhjuːmən] *adj* inumano(a).
initial [ɪˈnɪʃl] *adj* iniziale ♦ *n* iniziale *f* ♦ *vt* siglare; **~s** *npl* (*of name*) iniziali *fpl*; (*as signature*) sigla; **~ly** *adv* inizialmente,

all'inizio

initiate [ɪ'nɪʃɪeɪt] *vt* (*start*) avviare; intraprendere; iniziare; (*person*) iniziare; **to ~ sb into a secret** mettere qn a parte di un segreto; **to ~ proceedings against sb** (*LAW*) intentare causa contro qn

initiative [ɪ'nɪʃətɪv] *n* iniziativa

inject [ɪn'dʒɛkt] *vt* (*liquid*) iniettare; (*patient*): **to ~ sb with sth** fare a qn un'iniezione di qc; (*funds*) immettere; **~ion** [ɪn'dʒɛkʃən] *n* iniezione *f*, puntura

injure ['ɪndʒə*] *vt* ferire; (*damage: reputation etc*) nuocere a; **~d** *adj* ferito(a)

injury ['ɪndʒərɪ] *n* ferita; **~ time** *n* (*SPORT*) tempo di recupero

injustice [ɪn'dʒʌstɪs] *n* ingiustizia

ink [ɪŋk] *n* inchiostro

inkling ['ɪŋklɪŋ] *n* sentore *m*, vaga idea

inlaid ['ɪnleɪd] *adj* incrostato(a); (*table etc*) intarsiato(a)

inland [*adj* 'ɪnlənd, *adv* ɪn'lænd] *adj* interno(a) ♦ *adv* all'interno; **I~ Revenue** (*BRIT*) *n* Fisco

in-laws ['ɪnlɔːz] *npl* suoceri *mpl*; famiglia del marito (*or* della moglie)

inlet ['ɪnlɛt] *n* (*GEO*) insenatura, baia

inmate ['ɪnmeɪt] *n* (*in prison*) carcerato/a; (*in asylum*) ricoverato/a

inn [ɪn] *n* locanda

innate [ɪ'neɪt] *adj* innato(a)

inner ['ɪnə*] *adj* interno(a), interiore; **~ city** *n* centro di una zona urbana; **~ tube** *n* camera d'aria

innings ['ɪnɪŋz] *n* (*CRICKET*) turno di battuta

innocence ['ɪnəsns] *n* innocenza

innocent ['ɪnəsnt] *adj* innocente

innocuous [ɪ'nɔkjuəs] *adj* innocuo(a)

innuendo [ɪnju'ɛndəu] (*pl* **~es**) *n* insinuazione *f*

innumerable [ɪ'njuːmrəbl] *adj* innumerevole

in-patient *n* ricoverato/a

input ['ɪnput] *n* input *m*

inquest ['ɪnkwɛst] *n* inchiesta

inquire [ɪn'kwaɪə*] *vi* informarsi ♦ *vt* domandare, informarsi su; **~ about** *vt fus* informarsi di *or* su; **~ into** *vt fus* fare indagini su; **inquiry** *n* domanda; (*LAW*) indagine *f*, investigazione *f*; **"inquiries"** "informazioni"; **inquiry office** (*BRIT*) *n* ufficio *m* informazioni *inv*

inquisitive [ɪn'kwɪzɪtɪv] *adj* curioso(a)

ins. *abbr* = **inches**

insane [ɪn'seɪn] *adj* matto(a), pazzo(a); (*MED*) alienato(a)

insanity [ɪn'sænɪtɪ] *n* follia; (*MED*) alienazione *f* mentale

inscription [ɪn'skrɪpʃən] *n* iscrizione *f*, dedica

insect ['ɪnsɛkt] *n* insetto; **~icide** [ɪn'sɛktɪsaɪd] *n* insetticida *m*; **~ repellent** *n* insettifugo

insecure [ɪnsɪ'kjuə*] *adj* malsicuro(a); (*person*) insicuro(a)

insemination [ɪnsɛmɪ'neɪʃən] *n*: **artificial ~** fecondazione *f* artificiale

insensible [ɪn'sɛnsɪbl] *adj* (*unconscious*) privo(a) di sensi

insensitive [ɪn'sɛnsɪtɪv] *adj* insensibile

insert [ɪn'səːt] *vt* inserire, introdurre; **~ion** [ɪn'səːʃən] *n* inserzione *f*

in-service *adj* (*training, course*) durante l'orario di lavoro

inshore [ɪn'fɔː*] *adj* costiero(a) ♦ *adv* presso la riva; verso la riva

inside ['ɪn'saɪd] *n* interno, parte *f* interiore ♦ *adj* interno(a), interiore ♦ *adv* dentro, all'interno ♦ *prep* dentro, all'interno di; (*of time*): **~ 10 minutes** entro 10 minuti; **~s** *npl* (*inf: stomach*) ventre *m*; **~ forward** *n* (*SPORT*) mezzala, interno; **~ lane** *n* (*AUT*) corsia di marcia; **~ out** *adv* (*turn*) a rovescio; (*know*) in fondo; **~r dealing** *n* insider dealing *m inv*; **~r trading** *n* insider trading *m inv*

insight ['ɪnsaɪt] *n* acume *m*, perspicacia; (*glimpse, idea*) percezione *f*

insignia [ɪn'sɪgnɪə] *npl* insegne *fpl*

insignificant [ɪnsɪg'nɪfɪknt] *adj* insignificante

insincere [ɪnsɪn'sɪə*] *adj* insincero(a)

insinuate [ɪn'sɪnjueɪt] *vt* insinuare

insist [ɪn'sɪst] *vi* insistere; **to ~ on doing** insistere per fare; **to ~ that** insistere perché +*sub*; (*claim*) sostenere che; **~ent** *adj* insistente

insole ['ɪnsəʊl] *n* soletta

insolent ['ɪnsələnt] *adj* insolente

insomnia [ɪn'sɒmnɪə] *n* insonnia

inspect [ɪn'spekt] *vt* ispezionare; (*BRIT: ticket*) controllare; **~ion** [ɪn'spekʃən] *n* ispezione *f*; controllo; **~or** *n* ispettore/trice; (*BRIT: on buses, trains*) controllore *m*

inspire [ɪn'spaɪə*] *vt* ispirare

install [ɪn'stɔ:l] *vt* installare; **~ation** [ɪnstə'leɪʃən] *n* installazione *f*

instalment [ɪn'stɔ:lmənt] (*US* **installment**) *n* rata; (*of TV serial etc*) puntata; **in ~s** (*pay*) a rate; (*receive*) una parte per volta; (: *publication*) a fascicoli

instance ['ɪnstəns] *n* esempio, caso; **for ~** per *or* ad esempio; **in the first ~** in primo luogo

instant ['ɪnstənt] *n* istante *m*, attimo ♦ *adj* immediato(a); urgente; (*coffee, food*) in polvere; **~ly** *adv* immediatamente, subito

instead [ɪn'sted] *adv* invece; **~ of** invece di

instep ['ɪnstep] *n* collo del piede; (*of shoe*) collo della scarpa

instil [ɪn'stɪl] *vt*: **to ~ (into)** inculcare (in)

instinct ['ɪnstɪŋkt] *n* istinto

institute ['ɪnstɪtju:t] *n* istituto ♦ *vt* istituire, stabilire; (*inquiry*) avviare; (*proceedings*) iniziare

institution [ɪnstɪ'tju:ʃən] *n* istituzione *f*; (*educational ~, mental ~*) istituto

instruct [ɪn'strʌkt] *vt*: **to ~ sb in sth** insegnare qc a qn; **to ~ sb to do** dare ordini a qn di fare; **~ion** [ɪn'strʌkʃən] *n* istruzione *f*; **~ions (for use)** istruzioni per l'uso; **~or** *n* istruttore/trice; (*for skiing*) maestro/a

instrument ['ɪnstrəmənt] *n* strumento; **~al** [-'mentl] *adj* (*MUS*) strumentale; **to be ~al in** essere d'aiuto in; **~ panel** *n* quadro *m* portastrumenti *inv*

insufferable [ɪn'sʌfərəbl] *adj* insopportabile

insufficient [ɪnsə'fɪʃənt] *adj* insufficiente

insular ['ɪnsjulə*] *adj* insulare; (*person*) di mente ristretta

insulate ['ɪnsjuleɪt] *vt* isolare; **insulation** [-'leɪʃən] *n* isolamento

insulin ['ɪnsjulɪn] *n* insulina

insult [*n* 'ɪnsʌlt, *vb* ɪn'sʌlt] *n* insulto, affronto ♦ *vt* insultare; **~ing** *adj* offensivo(a), ingiurioso(a)

insuperable [ɪn'sju:prəbl] *adj* insormontabile, insuperabile

insurance [ɪn'ʃuərəns] *n* assicurazione *f*; **fire/life ~** assicurazione contro gli incendi/ sulla vita; **~ policy** *n* polizza d'assicu- razione

insure [ɪn'ʃuə*] *vt* assicurare

intact [ɪn'tækt] *adj* intatto(a)

intake ['ɪnteɪk] *n* (*TECH*) immissione *f*; (*of food*) consumo; (*BRIT: of pupils etc*) afflusso

integral ['ɪntɪgrəl] *adj* integrale; (*part*) integrante

integrate ['ɪntɪgreɪt] *vt* integrare ♦ *vi* integrarsi

integrity [ɪn'tegrɪtɪ] *n* integrità

intellect ['ɪntəlekt] *n* intelletto; **~ual** [-'lektjuəl] *adj, n* intellettuale *m/f*

intelligence [ɪn'telɪdʒəns] *n* intelligenza; (*MIL etc*) informazioni *fpl*; **~ service** *n* servizio segreto

intelligent [ɪn'telɪdʒənt] *adj* intelligente

intend [ɪn'tend] *vt* (*gift etc*): **to ~ sth for** destinare qc a; **to ~ to do** aver l'intenzione di fare; **~ed** *adj* (*effect*) voluto(a)

intense [ɪn'tens] *adj* intenso(a); (*person*) di forti sentimenti; **~ly** *adv* intensamente; profondamente

intensive [ɪn'tensɪv] *adj* intensivo(a); **~ care unit** *n* reparto terapia intensiva

intent [ɪn'tent] *n* intenzione *f* ♦ *adj*: **~ (on)** intento(a) (a), immerso(a) (in); **to all ~s and purposes** a tutti gli effetti; **to be ~ on doing sth** essere deciso a fare qc

intention [ɪn'tenʃən] *n* intenzione *f*; **~al** *adj* intenzionale, deliberato(a); **~ally** *adv* apposta

intently [ɪn'tentlɪ] *adv* attentamente

interact [ɪntər'ækt] *vi* interagire

interactive *adj* (*COMPUT*) interattivo(a)

interchange ['ɪntətʃeɪndʒ] *n* (*exchange*)

scambio; (_on motorway_) incrocio pluridirezionale; **~able** [-'tʃeɪndʒəbl] _adj_ intercambiabile

intercom ['ɪntəkɔm] _n_ interfono

intercourse ['ɪntəkɔːs] _n_ rapporti _mpl_

interest ['ɪntrɪst] _n_ interesse _m_; (COMM: _stake, share_) interessi _mpl_ ♦ _vt_ interessare; **~ed** _adj_ interessato(a); **to be ~ed in** interessarsi di; **~ing** _adj_ interessante; **~ rate** _n_ tasso di interesse

interface ['ɪntəfeɪs] _n_ (COMPUT) interfaccia

interfere [ɪntə'fɪə*] _vi_: **to ~ in** (_quarrel, other people's business_) immischiarsi in; **to ~ with** (_object_) toccare; (_plans, duty_) interferire con

interference [ɪntə'fɪərəns] _n_ interferenza

interim ['ɪntərɪm] _adj_ provvisorio(a) ♦ _n_: **in the ~** nel frattempo

interior [ɪn'tɪərɪə*] _n_ interno; (_of country_) entroterra ♦ _adj_ interno(a); (_minister_) degli Interni; **~ designer** _n_ arredatore/trice

interlock [ɪntə'lɔk] _vi_ ingranarsi

interlude ['ɪntəluːd] _n_ intervallo; (THEATRE) intermezzo

intermediate [ɪntə'miːdɪət] _adj_ intermedio(a)

intermission [ɪntə'mɪʃən] _n_ pausa; (THEATRE, CINEMA) intermissione _f_, intervallo

intern [_vb_ ɪn'təːn, _n_ 'ɪntəːn] _vt_ internare ♦ _n_ (US) medico interno

internal [ɪn'təːnl] _adj_ interno(a); **~ly** _adv_: **"not to be taken ~ly"** "per uso esterno"; **I~ Revenue Service** (US) _n_ Fisco

international [ɪntə'næʃənl] _adj_ internazionale ♦ _n_ (BRIT: SPORT) incontro internazionale

Internet ['ɪntənɛt] _n_: **the ~** Internet _f_; **~ café** _n_ cybercaffè _m inv_

interplay ['ɪntəpleɪ] _n_ azione e reazione _f_

interpret [ɪn'təːprɪt] _vt_ interpretare ♦ _vi_ fare da interprete; **~er** _n_ interprete _m/f_

interrogate [ɪn'tɛrəʊgeɪt] _vt_ interrogare; **interrogation** [-'geɪʃən] _n_ interrogazione _f_; (_of suspect etc_) interrogatorio

interrupt [ɪntə'rʌpt] _vt, vi_ interrompere; **~ion** [-'rʌpʃən] _n_ interruzione _f_

intersect [ɪntə'sɛkt] _vi_ (_roads_) incrociarsi; **~ion** [-'sɛkʃən] _n_ intersezione _f_; (_of roads_)

incrocio

intersperse [ɪntə'spəːs] _vt_: **to ~ with** costellare di

intertwine [ɪntə'twaɪn] _vi_ intrecciarsi

interval ['ɪntəvl] _n_ intervallo; **at ~s** a intervalli

intervene [ɪntə'viːn] _vi_ (_time_) intercorrere; (_event, person_) intervenire; **intervention** [-'vɛnʃən] _n_ intervento

interview ['ɪntəvjuː] _n_ (RADIO, TV etc) intervista; (_for job_) colloquio ♦ _vt_ intervistare; avere un colloquio con; **~er** _n_ intervistatore/trice

intestine [ɪn'tɛstɪn] _n_ intestino

intimacy ['ɪntɪməsɪ] _n_ intimità

intimate [_adj_ 'ɪntɪmət, _vb_ 'ɪntɪmeɪt] _adj_ intimo(a); (_knowledge_) profondo(a) ♦ _vt_ lasciar capire

into ['ɪntu:] _prep_ dentro, in; **come ~ the house** entra in casa; **he worked late ~ the night** lavorò fino a tarda notte; **~ Italian** in italiano

intolerable [ɪn'tɔlərəbl] _adj_ intollerabile

intolerance [ɪn'tɔlərns] _n_ intolleranza

intolerant [ɪn'tɔlərnt] _adj_: **~ of** intollerante di

intoxicated [ɪn'tɔksɪkeɪtɪd] _adj_ inebriato(a)

intractable [ɪn'træktəbl] _adj_ intrattabile

intranet ['ɪntrənɛt] _n_ intranet _f_

intransitive [ɪn'trænsɪtɪv] _adj_ intransitivo(a)

intravenous [ɪntrə'viːnəs] _adj_ endovenoso(a)

in-tray _n_ contenitore _m_ per la corrispondenza in arrivo

intricate ['ɪntrɪkət] _adj_ intricato(a), complicato(a)

intrigue [ɪn'triːg] _n_ intrigo ♦ _vt_ affascinare; **intriguing** _adj_ affascinante

intrinsic [ɪn'trɪnsɪk] _adj_ intrinseco(a)

introduce [ɪntrə'djuːs] _vt_ introdurre; **to ~ sb (to sb)** presentare qn (a qn); **to ~ sb to** (_pastime, technique_) iniziare qn a; **introduction** [-'dʌkʃən] _n_ introduzione _f_; (_of person_) presentazione _f_; (_to new experience_) iniziazione _f_; **introductory** _adj_ introduttivo(a)

intrude [ɪn'truːd] _vi_ (_person_): **to ~ (on)** intromettersi (in); **~r** _n_ intruso/a

intuition [ɪntjuː'ɪʃən] _n_ intuizione _f_

inundate ['ɪnʌndeɪt] *vt*: **to ~ with** inondare di

invade [ɪn'veɪd] *vt* invadere

invalid [*n* 'ɪnvəlɪd, *adj* ɪn'vælɪd] *n* malato/a; *(with disability)* invalido/a ♦ *adj (not valid)* invalido(a), non valido(a)

invaluable [ɪn'væljuəbl] *adj* prezioso(a); inestimabile

invariably [ɪn'vɛərɪəblɪ] *adv* invariabilmente; sempre

invasion [ɪn'veɪʒən] *n* invasione *f*

invent [ɪn'vɛnt] *vt* inventare; ~ion [ɪn'vɛnʃən] *n* invenzione *f*; ~ive *adj* inventivo(a); ~or *n* inventore *m*

inventory ['ɪnvəntrɪ] *n* inventario

invert [ɪn'vɜːt] *vt* invertire; *(cup, object)* rovesciare; ~ed commas *(BRIT) npl* virgolette *fpl*

invest [ɪn'vɛst] *vt* investire ♦ *vi*: **to ~ (in)** investire (in)

investigate [ɪn'vɛstɪgeɪt] *vt* investigare, indagare; *(crime)* fare indagini su; investigation [-'geɪʃən] *n* investigazione *f*; *(of crime)* indagine *f*

investment [ɪn'vɛstmənt] *n* investimento

investor [ɪn'vɛstə*] *n* investitore/trice; azionista *m/f*

invidious [ɪn'vɪdɪəs] *adj* odioso(a); *(task)* spiacevole

invigilator [ɪn'vɪdʒɪleɪtə*] *n* (in exam) sorvegliante *m/f*

invigorating [ɪn'vɪgəreɪtɪŋ] *adj* stimolante; vivificante

invisible [ɪn'vɪzɪbl] *adj* invisibile

invitation [ɪnvɪ'teɪʃən] *n* invito

invite [ɪn'vaɪt] *vt* invitare; *(opinions etc)* sollecitare; inviting *adj* invitante, attraente

invoice ['ɪnvɔɪs] *n* fattura ♦ *vt* fatturare

involuntary [ɪn'vɔləntrɪ] *adj* involontario(a)

involve [ɪn'vɔlv] *vt (entail)* richiedere, comportare; *(associate)*: **to ~ sb (in)** implicare qn (in); coinvolgere qn (in); ~d *adj* involuto(a), complesso(a); **to be ~d in** essere coinvolto(a) in; ~ment *n* implicazione *f*; coinvolgimento

inward ['ɪnwəd] *adj (movement)* verso l'interno; *(thought, feeling)* interiore,

intimo(a); ~(s) *adv* verso l'interno

I/O *abbr (COMPUT.* = *input/output)* I/O

iodine ['aɪəʊdiːn] *n* iodio

ioniser ['aɪənaɪzə*] *n* ionizzatore *m*

iota [aɪ'əʊtə] *n (fig)* briciolo

IOU *n abbr (*= I owe you) pagherò *m inv*

IQ *n abbr (*= intelligence quotient) quoziente *m* d'intelligenza

IRA *n abbr (*= Irish Republican Army) IRA *f*

Iran [ɪ'rɑːn] *n* Iran *m*; ~ian *adj, n* iraniano/a

Iraq [ɪ'rɑːk] *n* Iraq *m*; ~i *adj, n* iracheno(a)

irate [aɪ'reɪt] *adj* adirato(a)

Ireland ['aɪələnd] *n* Irlanda

iris ['aɪrɪs] (*pl* ~es) *n* iride *f*; (BOT) giaggiolo, iride

Irish ['aɪrɪʃ] *adj* irlandese ♦ *npl*: **the ~** gli Irlandesi; ~man *(irreg) n* irlandese *m*; ~ Sea *n* Mar *m* d'Irlanda; ~woman *(irreg) n* irlandese *f*

irksome ['əːksəm] *adj* seccante

iron ['aɪən] *n* ferro; *(for clothes)* ferro da stiro ♦ *adj* di *or* in ferro ♦ *vt (clothes)* stirare; ~ out *vt (crease)* appianare; *(fig)* spianare; far sparire

ironic(al) [aɪ'rɔnɪk(l)] *adj* ironico(a)

ironing ['aɪənɪŋ] *n (act)* stirare *m*; *(clothes)* roba da stirare; ~ board *n* asse *f* da stiro

ironmonger's (shop) ['aɪənmʌŋgəz-] *(BRIT) n* negozio di ferramenta

irony ['aɪrənɪ] *n* ironia

irrational [ɪ'ræʃənl] *adj* irrazionale

irregular [ɪ'regjulə*] *adj* irregolare

irrelevant [ɪ'reləvənt] *adj* non pertinente

irreplaceable [ɪrɪ'pleɪsəbl] *adj* insostituibile

irrepressible [ɪrɪ'presəbl] *adj* irrefrenabile

irresistible [ɪrɪ'zɪstɪbl] *adj* irresistibile

irrespective [ɪrɪ'spɛktɪv] *adj*: **~ of** *prep* senza riguardo a

irresponsible [ɪrɪ'spɔnsɪbl] *adj* irresponsabile

irrigate ['ɪrɪgeɪt] *vt* irrigare; irrigation [-'geɪʃən] *n* irrigazione *f*

irritable ['ɪrɪtəbl] *adj* irritabile

irritate ['ɪrɪteɪt] *vt* irritare; irritating *adj (person, sound etc)* irritante; irritation [-'teɪʃən] *n* irritazione *f*

IRS (US) n abbr = **Internal Revenue Service**

is [ɪz] vb see **be**

Islam ['ɪzlɑːm] n Islam m

island ['aɪlənd] n isola; ~**er** n isolano/a

isle [aɪl] n isola

isn't ['ɪznt] = **is not**

isolate ['aɪsəleɪt] vt isolare; ~**d** adj isolato(a); **isolation** [-'leɪʃən] n isolamento

ISP n abbr (= Internet Service Provider) provider m inv

Israel ['ɪzreɪl] n Israele m; ~**i** [ɪz'reɪlɪ] adj, n israeliano(a)

issue ['ɪʃjuː] n questione f, problema m; (of banknotes etc) emissione f; (of newspaper etc) numero ♦ vt (statement) rilasciare; (rations, equipment) distribuire; (book) pubblicare; (banknotes, cheques, stamps) emettere; **at ~** in gioco, in discussione; **to take ~ with sb (over sth)** prendere posizione contro qn (riguardo a qc); **to make an ~ of sth** fare un problema di qc

KEYWORD

it [ɪt] pron **1** (specific: subject) esso(a); (: direct object) lo(la), l'; (: indirect object) gli(le); **where's my book? – ~'s on the table** dov'è il mio libro? — è sulla tavola; **I can't find ~** non lo (or la) trovo; **give ~ to me** dammelo (or dammela); **about/from/ of ~** ne; **I spoke to him about ~** gliene ho parlato; **what did you learn from ~?** quale insegnamento ne hai tratto?; **I'm proud of ~** ne sono fiero; **did you go to ~?** ci sei andato?; **put the book in ~** mettici il libro

2 (impers): **~'s raining** piove; **~'s Friday tomorrow** domani è venerdì; **~'s 6 o'clock** sono le 6; **who is ~? – ~'s me** chi è? — sono io

Italian [ɪ'tæljən] adj italiano(a) ♦ n italiano/a; (LING) italiano; **the ~s** gli Italiani

italics [ɪ'tælɪks] npl corsivo

Italy ['ɪtəlɪ] n Italia

itch [ɪtʃ] n prurito ♦ vi (person) avere il prurito; (part of body) prudere; **to ~ to do sth** aver una gran voglia di fare qc; ~**y** adj

che prude; **to be ~y** = **to ~**

it'd ['ɪtd] = **it would**; **it had**

item ['aɪtəm] n articolo; (on agenda) punto; (also: **news ~**) notizia; ~**ize** vt specificare, dettagliare

itinerant [ɪ'tɪnərənt] adj ambulante

itinerary [aɪ'tɪnərərɪ] n itinerario

it'll ['ɪtl] = **it will**; **it shall**

its [ɪts] adj il(la) suo(a), i(le) suoi(sue)

it's [ɪts] = **it is**; **it has**

itself [ɪt'sɛlf] pron (emphatic) esso(a) stesso(a); (reflexive) si

ITV (BRIT) n abbr (= Independent Television) rete televisiva in concorrenza con la BBC

I.U.D. n abbr (= intra-uterine device) spirale f

I've [aɪv] = **I have**

ivory ['aɪvərɪ] n avorio

ivy ['aɪvɪ] n edera

J, j

jab [dʒæb] vt dare colpetti a ♦ n (MED: inf) puntura; **to ~ sth into** affondare or piantare qc dentro

jack [dʒæk] n (AUT) cricco; (CARDS) fante m; **~ up** vt sollevare col cricco

jackal ['dʒækl] n sciacallo

jackdaw ['dʒækdɔː] n taccola

jacket ['dʒækɪt] n giacca; (of book) copertura

jack-knife vi: **the lorry ~d** l'autotreno si è piegato su se stesso

jack plug n (ELEC) jack m inv

jackpot ['dʒækpɔt] n primo premio (in denaro)

jade [dʒeɪd] n (stone) giada

jaded ['dʒeɪdɪd] adj sfinito(a), spossato(a)

jagged ['dʒægɪd] adj seghettato(a); (cliffs etc) frastagliato(a)

jail [dʒeɪl] n prigione f ♦ vt mandare in prigione

jam [dʒæm] n marmellata; (also: **traffic ~**) ingorgo; (inf) pasticcio ♦ vt (passage etc) ingombrare, ostacolare; (mechanism, drawer etc) bloccare; (RADIO) disturbare con interferenze ♦ vi incepparsi; **to ~ sth into** forzare qc dentro; infilare qc a forza dentro

Jamaica [dʒə'meɪkə] n Giamaica

jangle ['dʒæŋgl] vi risuonare; (bracelet) tintinnare

janitor ['dʒænɪtə*] n (caretaker) portiere m; (: SCOL) bidello

January ['dʒænjuərɪ] n gennaio

Japan [dʒə'pæn] n Giappone m; ~ese [dʒæpə'niːz] adj giapponese ♦ n inv giapponese m/f; (LING) giapponese m

jar [dʒɑː*] n (glass) barattolo, vasetto ♦ vi (sound) stridere; (colours etc) stonare

jargon ['dʒɑːgən] n gergo

jasmin(e) ['dʒæzmɪn] n gelsomino

jaundice ['dʒɔːndɪs] n itterizia

jaunt [dʒɔːnt] n gita

javelin ['dʒævlɪn] n giavellotto

jaw [dʒɔː] n mascella

jay [dʒeɪ] n ghiandaia

jaywalker ['dʒeɪwɔːkə*] n pedone(a) indisciplinato(a)

jazz [dʒæz] n jazz m; ~ up vt rendere vivace

jealous ['dʒeləs] adj geloso(a); ~y n gelosia

jeans [dʒiːnz] npl (blue-)jeans mpl

jeer [dʒɪə*] vi: to ~ (at) fischiare; beffeggiare

jelly ['dʒelɪ] n gelatina; ~fish n medusa

jeopardy ['dʒepədɪ] n: in ~ in pericolo

jerk [dʒɜːk] n sobbalzo, scossa, sussulto; (inf: idiot) tonto/a ♦ vt dare una scossa a ♦ vi (vehicles) sobbalzare

jersey ['dʒɜːzɪ] n maglia; (fabric) jersey m

jest [dʒest] n scherzo

Jesus ['dʒiːzəs] n Gesù m

jet [dʒet] n (of gas, liquid) getto; (AVIAT) aviogetto; ~-black adj nero(a) come l'ebano, corvino(a); ~ engine n motore m a reazione; ~ lag n (problemi mpl dovuti allo) sbalzo dei fusi orari

jettison ['dʒetɪsn] vt gettare in mare

jetty ['dʒetɪ] n molo

Jew [dʒuː] n ebreo

jewel ['dʒuːəl] n gioiello; ~ler (US ~er) n orefice m, gioielliere/a; ~(l)er's (shop) n oreficeria, gioielleria; ~lery (US ~ery) n gioielli mpl

Jewess ['dʒuːɪs] n ebrea

Jewish ['dʒuːɪʃ] adj ebreo(a), ebraico(a)

jibe [dʒaɪb] n beffa

jiffy ['dʒɪfɪ] (inf) n: in a ~ in un batter d'occhio

jig [dʒɪg] n giga

jigsaw ['dʒɪgsɔː] n (also: ~ puzzle) puzzle m inv

jilt [dʒɪlt] vt piantare in asso

jingle ['dʒɪŋgl] n (for advert) sigla pubblicitaria ♦ vi tintinnare, scampanellare

jinx [dʒɪŋks] n iettatura; (person) iettatore/trice

jitters ['dʒɪtəz] (inf) npl: to get the ~ aver fifa

job [dʒɒb] n lavoro; (employment) impiego, posto; **it's not my ~** (duty) non è compito mio; **it's a good ~ that ...** meno male che ...; **just the ~!** proprio quello che ci vuole; ~ **centre** (BRIT) n ufficio di collocamento; ~less adj senza lavoro, disoccupato(a)

jockey ['dʒɒkɪ] n fantino, jockey m inv ♦ vi: to ~ for position manovrare per una posizione di vantaggio

jog [dʒɒg] vt urtare ♦ vi (SPORT) fare footing, fare jogging; to ~ sb's memory rinfrescare la memoria a qn; to ~ along trottare; (fig) andare avanti piano piano; ~ging n footing m, jogging m

join [dʒɔɪn] vt unire, congiungere; (become member of) iscriversi a; (meet) raggiungere; riunirsi a ♦ vi (roads, rivers) confluire ♦ n giuntura; ~ in vi partecipare ♦ vt fus unirsi a; ~ up vi incontrarsi; (MIL) arruolarsi

joiner ['dʒɔɪnə*] (BRIT) n falegname m

joint [dʒɔɪnt] n (TECH) giuntura, giunto; (ANAT) articolazione f, giuntura; (BRIT: CULIN) arrosto; (inf: place) locale m; (: of cannabis) spinello ♦ adj comune; ~ **account** n (at bank etc) conto in partecipazione, conto comune

joist [dʒɔɪst] n trave f

joke [dʒəuk] n scherzo; (funny story) barzelletta; (also: practical ~) beffa ♦ vi scherzare; to play a ~ on sb fare uno scherzo a qn; ~r n (CARDS) matta, jolly m inv

jolly ['dʒɒlɪ] adj allegro(a), gioioso(a) ♦ adv (BRIT: inf) veramente, proprio

jolt [dʒəult] n scossa, sobbalzo ♦ vt urtare

Jordan ['dʒɔːdən] n (country) Giordania; (river) Giordano

jostle ['dʒɔsl] vt spingere coi gomiti

jot [dʒɔt] n: **not one ~** nemmeno un po'; **~ down** vt annotare in fretta, buttare giù; **~ter** n blocco

journal ['dʒəːnl] n giornale m; rivista; diario; **~ism** n giornalismo; **~ist** n giornalista m/f

journey ['dʒəːni] n viaggio m; (distance covered) tragitto

joy [dʒɔɪ] n gioia; **~ful** adj gioioso(a), allegro(a); **~rider** n chi ruba un'auto per farvi un giro; **~stick** n (AVIAT) barra di comando; (COMPUT) joystick m inv

JP n abbr = **Justice of the Peace**

Jr abbr = **junior**

jubilant ['dʒuːbɪlnt] adj giubilante; trionfante

jubilee ['dʒuːbɪliː] n giubileo; **silver ~** venticinquesimo anniversario

judge [dʒʌdʒ] n giudice m/f ♦ vt giudicare; **judg(e)ment** n giudizio

judiciary [dʒuːˈdɪʃərɪ] n magistratura

judo ['dʒuːdəu] n judo

jug [dʒʌg] n brocca, bricco

juggernaut ['dʒʌgənɔːt] (BRIT) n (huge truck) bestione m

juggle ['dʒʌgl] vi fare giochi di destrezza; **~r** n giocoliere/a

juice [dʒuːs] n succo

juicy ['dʒuːsɪ] adj succoso(a)

jukebox ['dʒuːkbɔks] n juke-box m inv

July [dʒuːˈlaɪ] n luglio

jumble ['dʒʌmbl] n miscuglio ♦ vt (also: **~ up**) mischiare; **~ sale** (BRIT) n vendita di beneficenza

───────────────
jumble sale
───────────────

ⓘ Una **jumble sale** è un mercatino di oggetti di seconda mano organizzato in chiese, scuole o in circoli ricreativi, i cui proventi vengono devoluti in beneficenza.

───────────────

jumbo (jet) ['dʒʌmbəu-] n jumbo-jet m inv

jump [dʒʌmp] vi saltare, balzare; (start) sobbalzare; (increase) rincarare ♦ vt saltare ♦ n salto, balzo; sobbalzo

jumper ['dʒʌmpə*] n (BRIT: pullover) maglione m, pullover m inv; (US: dress) scamiciato; **~ cables** (US) npl = **jump leads**

jump leads (BRIT) npl cavi mpl per batteria

jumpy ['dʒʌmpɪ] adj nervoso(a), agitato(a)

Jun. abbr = **junior**

junction ['dʒʌŋkʃən] n (BRIT: of roads) incrocio; (of rails) nodo ferroviario

juncture ['dʒʌŋktʃə*] n: **at this ~** in questa congiuntura

June [dʒuːn] n giugno

jungle ['dʒʌŋgl] n giungla

junior ['dʒuːnɪə*] adj, n: **he's ~ to me (by 2 years), he's my ~ (by 2 years)** è più giovane di me (di 2 anni); **he's ~ to me** (seniority) è al di sotto di me, ho più anzianità di lui; **~ school** (BRIT) n scuola elementare (da 8 a 11 anni)

junk [dʒʌŋk] n cianfrusaglie fpl; (cheap goods) robaccia; **~ food** n porcherie fpl

junkie ['dʒʌŋkɪ] (inf) n drogato/a

junk mail n stampe fpl pubblicitarie

junk shop n chincaglieria

Junr abbr = **junior**

juror ['dʒuərə*] n giurato/a

jury ['dʒuərɪ] n giuria

just [dʒʌst] adj giusto(a) ♦ adv: **he's ~ done it/left** lo ha appena fatto/è appena partito; **~ right** proprio giusto; **~ 2 o'clock** le 2 precise; **she's ~ as clever as you** è in gamba proprio quanto te; **it's ~ as well that ...** meno male che ...; **~ as I arrived** proprio mentre arrivavo; **it was ~ before/ enough/here** era poco prima/appena assai/proprio qui; **it's ~ me** sono solo io; **~ missed/caught** appena perso/preso; **~ listen to this!** senta un po' questo!

justice ['dʒʌstɪs] n giustizia; **J~ of the Peace** n conciliatore

justify ['dʒʌstɪfaɪ] vt giustificare

jut [dʒʌt] vi (also: **~ out**) sporgersi

juvenile ['dʒuːvənaɪl] adj giovane, giovanile; (court) dei minorenni; (books) per ragazzi ♦ n giovane m/f, minorenne m/f

juxtapose ['dʒʌkstəpəuz] vt giustapporre

K, k

K *abbr* (= *one thousand*) mille; (= *kilobyte*) K

Kampuchea [kæmpə'tʃɪə] *n* Cambogia

kangaroo [kæŋgə'ruː] *n* canguro

karate [kə'rɑːtɪ] *n* karatè *m*

kebab [kə'bæb] *n* spiedino

keel [kiːl] *n* chiglia; **on an even ~** (*fig*) in uno stato normale

keen [kiːn] *adj* (*interest, desire*) vivo(a); (*eye, intelligence*) acuto(a); (*competition*) serrato(a); (*edge*) affilato(a); (*eager*) entusiasta; **to be ~ to do** *or* **doing sth** avere una gran voglia di fare qc; **to be ~ on sth** essere appassionato(a) di qc; **to be ~ on sb** avere un debole per qn

keep [kiːp] (*pt, pp* **kept**) *vt* tenere; (*hold back*) trattenere; (*feed: one's family etc*) mantenere, sostentare; (*a promise*) mantenere; (*chickens, bees, pigs etc*) allevare ♦ *vi* (*food*) mantenersi; (*remain: in a certain state or place*) restare ♦ *n* (*of castle*) maschio; (*food etc*): **enough for his ~** abbastanza per vitto e alloggio; (*inf*): **for ~s** per sempre; **to ~ doing sth** continuare a fare qc; fare qc di continuo; **to ~ sb from doing** impedire a qn di fare; **to ~ sb busy/a place tidy** tenere qn occupato(a)/ un luogo in ordine; **to ~ sth to o.s.** tenere qc per sé; **to ~ sth (back) from sb** celare qc a qn; **to ~ time** (*clock*) andar bene; **~ on** *vi*: **to ~ on doing** continuare a fare; **to ~ on (about sth)** continuare a insistere (su qc); **~ out** *vt* tener fuori; **"~ out"** "vietato l'accesso"; **~ up** *vt* continuare, mantenere ♦ *vi*: **to ~ up with** tener dietro a, andare di pari passo con; (*work etc*) farcela a seguire; **~er** *n* custode *m/f*, guardiano/a; **~-fit** *n* ginnastica; **~ing** *n* (*care*) custodia; **in ~ing with** in armonia con; in accordo con; **~sake** *n* ricordo

kennel ['kɛnl] *n* canile *m*; **to put a dog in ~s** mettere un cane al canile

kept [kɛpt] *pt, pp of* **keep**

kerb [kəːb] (*BRIT*) *n* orlo del marciapiede

kernel ['kəːnl] *n* nocciolo

kettle ['kɛtl] *n* bollitore *m*

kettle drum *n* timpano

key [kiː] *n* (*gen, MUS*) chiave *f*; (*of piano, typewriter*) tasto ♦ *adj* chiave *inv* ♦ *vt* (*also:* **~ in**) digitare; **~board** *n* tastiera; **~ed up** *adj* (*person*) agitato(a); **~hole** *n* buco della serratura; **~hole surgery** *n* chirurgia non invasiva; **~note** *n* (*MUS*) tonica; (*fig*) nota dominante; **~ring** *n* portachiavi *m inv*

khaki ['kɑːkɪ] *adj* cachi ♦ *n* cachi *m*

kick [kɪk] *vt* calciare, dare calci a; (*inf: habit etc*) liberarsi di ♦ *vi* (*horse*) tirar calci ♦ *n* calcio; (*thrill*): **he does it for ~s** lo fa giusto per il piacere di farlo; **~ off** *vi* (*SPORT*) dare il primo calcio

kid [kɪd] *n* (*inf: child*) ragazzino/a; (*animal, leather*) capretto ♦ *vi* (*inf*) scherzare

kidnap ['kɪdnæp] *vt* rapire, sequestrare; **~per** *n* rapitore/trice; **~ping** *n* sequestro (di persona)

kidney ['kɪdnɪ] *n* (*ANAT*) rene *m*; (*CULIN*) rognone *m*

kill [kɪl] *vt* uccidere, ammazzare ♦ *n* uccisione *f*; **~er** *n* uccisore *m*, killer *m inv*; assassino/a; **~ing** *n* assassinio; **to make a ~ing** (*inf*) fare un bel colpo; **~joy** *n* guastafeste *m/f inv*

kiln [kɪln] *n* forno

kilo ['kiːləʊ] *n* chilo; **~byte** *n* (*COMPUT*) kilobyte *m inv*; **~gram(me)** ['kɪləʊgræm] *n* chilogrammo; **~metre** ['kɪləmiːtə*] (*US* **~meter**) *n* chilometro; **~watt** ['kɪləʊwɔt] *n* chilowatt *m inv*

kilt [kɪlt] *n* gonnellino scozzese

kin [kɪn] *n see* **next; kith**

kind [kaɪnd] *adj* gentile, buono(a) ♦ *n* sorta, specie *f*; (*species*) genere *m*; **to be two of a ~** essere molto simili; **in ~** (*COMM*) in natura

kindergarten ['kɪndəgɑːtn] *n* giardino d'infanzia

kind-hearted [-'hɑːtɪd] *adj* di buon cuore

kindle ['kɪndl] *vt* accendere, infiammare

kindly ['kaɪndlɪ] *adj* pieno(a) di bontà, benevolo(a) ♦ *adv* con bontà, gentilmente; **will you ~ ...** vuole ... per favore

kindness ['kaɪndnɪs] *n* bontà, gentilezza

king [kɪŋ] n re m inv; **~dom** n regno, reame m; **~fisher** n martin m inv pescatore; **~-size** adj super inv; gigante

kiosk ['kiːɔsk] n edicola, chiosco; (BRIT: TEL) cabina (telefonica)

kipper ['kɪpə*] n aringa affumicata

kiss [kɪs] n bacio ♦ vt baciare; **to ~ (each other)** baciarsi; **~ of life** n respirazione f bocca a bocca

kit [kɪt] n equipaggiamento, corredo; (set of tools etc) attrezzi mpl; (for assembly) scatola di montaggio

kitchen ['kɪtʃɪn] n cucina; **~ sink** n acquaio

kite [kaɪt] n (toy) aquilone m

kitten ['kɪtn] n gattino/a, micino/a

kitty ['kɪtɪ] n (money) fondo comune

knack [næk] n: **to have the ~ of** avere l'abilità di

knapsack ['næpsæk] n zaino, sacco da montagna

knead [niːd] vt impastare

knee [niː] n ginocchio; **~cap** n rotula

kneel [niːl] (pt, pp **knelt**) vi (also: **~ down**) inginocchiarsi

knew [njuː] pt of **know**

knickers ['nɪkəz] (BRIT) npl mutandine fpl

knife [naɪf] (pl **knives**) n coltello ♦ vt accoltellare, dare una coltellata a

knight [naɪt] n cavaliere m; (CHESS) cavallo; **~hood** (BRIT) n (title): **to get a ~hood** essere fatto cavaliere

knit [nɪt] vt fare a maglia ♦ vi lavorare a maglia; (broken bones) saldarsi; **to ~ one's brows** aggrottare le sopracciglia; **~ting** n lavoro a maglia; **~ting machine** n macchina per maglieria; **~ting needle** n ferro (da calza); **~wear** n maglieria

knives [naɪvz] npl of **knife**

knob [nɔb] n bottone m; manopola

knock [nɔk] vt colpire; urtare; (fig: inf) criticare ♦ vi (at door etc): **to ~ at/on** bussare a ♦ n bussata; colpo, botta; **~ down** vt abbattere; **~ off** vi (inf: finish) smettere (di lavorare) ♦ vt (from price) far abbassare; (inf: steal) sgraffignare; **~ out** vt stendere; (BOXING) mettere K.O.; (defeat) battere; **~ over** vt (person) investire;

(object) far cadere; **~er** n (on door) battente m; **~out** n (BOXING) knock out m inv ♦ cpd a eliminazione

knot [nɔt] n nodo ♦ vt annodare

know [nəu] (pt **knew**, pp **known**) vt sapere; (person, author, place) conoscere; **to ~ how to do** sapere fare; **to ~ about** or **of sth/sb** conoscere qc/qn; **~-all** n sapientone/a; **~-how** n tecnica; pratica; **~ing** adj (look etc) d'intesa; **~ingly** adv (purposely) consapevolmente; (smile, look) con aria d'intesa

knowledge ['nɔlɪdʒ] n consapevolezza; (learning) conoscenza, sapere m; **~able** adj ben informato(a)

known [nəun] pp of **know**

knuckle ['nʌkl] n nocca

Koran [kɔ'rɑːn] n Corano

Korea [kə'rɪə] n Corea

kosher ['kəuʃə*] adj kasher inv

L, l

L (BRIT) abbr = **learner driver**

lab [læb] n abbr (= laboratory) laboratorio

label ['leɪbl] n etichetta, cartellino; (brand: of record) casa ♦ vt etichettare

labor etc ['leɪbə*] (US) = **labour** etc

laboratory [lə'bɔrətəri] n laboratorio

labour ['leɪbə*] (US **labor**) n (task) lavoro; (workmen) manodopera; (MED): **to be in ~** avere le doglie ♦ vi: **to ~ (at)** lavorare duro (a); **L~, the L~ party** (BRIT) il partito laburista, i laburisti; **hard ~** lavori mpl forzati; **~ed** adj (breathing) affannoso(a); **~er** n manovale m; **farm ~er** lavoratore m agricolo

lace [leɪs] n merletto, pizzo; (of shoe etc) laccio ♦ vt (shoe: also: **~ up**) allacciare

lack [læk] n mancanza ♦ vt mancare di; **through** or **for ~ of** per mancanza di; **to be ~ing** mancare; **to be ~ing in** mancare di

lackadaisical [lækə'deɪzɪkl] adj disinteressato(a), noncurante

lacquer ['lækə*] n lacca

lad [læd] n ragazzo, giovanotto

ladder ['lædə*] n scala; (BRIT: in tights) smagliatura

laden ['leɪdn] adj: ~ (with) carico(a) or caricato(a) (di)

ladle ['leɪdl] n mestolo

lady ['leɪdɪ] n signora; dama; **L~ Smith** lady Smith; **the ladies' (room)** i gabinetti per signore; ~**bird** (US ~**bug**) n coccinella; ~**like** adj da signora, distinto(a); ~**ship** n: **your ~ship** signora contessa (or baronessa etc)

lag [læg] n (of time) lasso, intervallo ♦ vi (also: ~ **behind**) trascinarsi ♦ vt (pipes) rivestire di materiale isolante

lager ['lɑːgə*] n lager m inv

lagoon [lə'guːn] n laguna

laid [leɪd] pt, pp of **lay**; ~ **back** (inf) adj rilassato(a), tranquillo(a); ~ **up** adj: ~ **up (with)** costretto(a) a letto (da)

lain [leɪn] pp of **lie**

lair [leə*] n covo, tana

lake [leɪk] n lago

lamb [læm] n agnello

lame [leɪm] adj zoppo(a); (excuse etc) zoppicante

lament [lə'mɛnt] n lamento ♦ vt lamentare, piangere

laminated ['læmɪneɪtɪd] adj laminato(a)

lamp [læmp] n lampada

lamppost ['læmppəʊst] (BRIT) n lampione m

lampshade ['læmpʃeɪd] n paralume m

lance [lɑːns] vt (MED) incidere

land [lænd] n (as opposed to sea) terra (ferma); (country) paese m; (soil) terreno; suolo; (estate) terreni mpl, terre fpl ♦ vi (from ship) sbarcare; (AVIAT) atterrare; (fig: fall) cadere ♦ vt (passengers) sbarcare; (goods) scaricare; **to ~ sb with sth** affibbiare qc a qn; ~ **up** vi andare a finire; ~**fill site** n discarica; ~**ing** n atterraggio; (of staircase) pianerottolo; ~**ing gear** n carrello di atterraggio; ~**lady** n padrona or proprietaria di casa; ~**locked** adj senza sbocco sul mare; ~**lord** n padrone m or proprietario di casa; (of pub etc) padrone m; ~**mark** n punto di riferimento; (fig) pietra miliare; ~**owner** n proprietario(a)

terriero(a); ~**scape** n paesaggio; ~**slide** n (GEO) frana; (fig: POL) valanga

lane [leɪn] n stradina; (AUT, in race) corsia; **"get in lane"** "immettersi in corsia"

language ['læŋgwɪdʒ] n lingua; (way one speaks) linguaggio; **bad ~** linguaggio volgare; ~ **laboratory** n laboratorio linguistico

languid ['læŋgwɪd] adj languido(a)

lank [læŋk] adj (hair) liscio(a) e opaco(a)

lanky ['læŋkɪ] adj allampanato(a)

lantern ['læntn] n lanterna

lap [læp] n (of track) giro; (of body): **in** or **on one's ~** in grembo ♦ vt (also: ~ **up**) papparsi, leccare ♦ vi (waves) sciabordare; ~ **up** vt (fig) bearsi di

lapel [lə'pɛl] n risvolto

Lapland ['læplænd] n Lapponia

lapse [læps] n lapsus m inv; (longer) caduta ♦ vi (law) cadere; (membership, contract) scadere; **to ~ into bad habits** pigliare cattive abitudini; ~ **of time** spazio di tempo

laptop (computer) ['læp,tɔp-] n laptop m inv

larch [lɑːtʃ] n larice m

lard [lɑːd] n lardo

larder ['lɑːdə*] n dispensa

large [lɑːdʒ] adj grande; (person, animal) grosso(a); **at ~** (free) in libertà; (generally) in generale; nell'insieme; ~**ly** adv in gran parte

largesse [lɑː'ʒɛs] n generosità

lark [lɑːk] n (bird) allodola; (joke) scherzo, gioco

laryngitis [lærɪn'dʒaɪtɪs] n laringite f

laser ['leɪzə*] n laser m; ~ **printer** n stampante f laser inv

lash [læʃ] n frustata; (also: eye~) ciglio ♦ vt frustare; (tie): **to ~ to/together** legare a/insieme; ~ **out** vi: **to ~ out (at** or **against sb)** attaccare violentemente (qn)

lass [læs] n ragazza

lasso [læ'suː] n laccio

last [lɑːst] adj ultimo(a); (week, month, year) scorso(a), passato(a) ♦ adv per ultimo ♦ vi durare; ~ **week** la settimana scorsa; ~ **night** ieri sera, la notte scorsa; **at ~** finalmente,

alla fine; **~ but one** penultimo(a); **~-ditch**
adj (*attempt*) estremo(a); **~ing** *adj*
durevole; **~ly** *adv* infine, per finire; **~-
minute** *adj* fatto(a) (*or* preso(a) *etc*)
all'ultimo momento

latch [lætʃ] *n* chiavistello

late [leɪt] *adj* (*not on time*) in ritardo; (*far on
in day etc*) tardi *inv*; tardo(a); (*former*) ex;
(*dead*) defunto(a) ♦ *adv* tardi; (*behind time,
schedule*) in ritardo; **of ~** di recente; **in the
~ afternoon** nel tardo pomeriggio; **in ~
May** verso la fine di maggio; **~comer** *n*
ritardatario/a; **~ly** *adv* recentemente

later ['leɪtə*] *adj* (*date etc*) posteriore;
(*version etc*) successivo(a) ♦ *adv* più tardi; **~
on** più avanti

lateral ['lætərl] *adj* laterale

latest ['leɪtɪst] *adj* ultimo(a), più recente; **at
the ~** al più tardi

lathe [leɪð] *n* tornio

lather ['lɑ:ðə*] *n* schiuma di sapone ♦ *vt*
insaponare

Latin ['lætɪn] *n* latino ♦ *adj* latino(a); **~
America** *n* America Latina; **~-American**
adj, n sudamericano(a)

latitude ['lætɪtjuːd] *n* latitudine *f*; (*fig*)
libertà d'azione

latter ['lætə*] *adj* secondo(a); più recente
♦ *n*: **the ~** quest'ultimo, il secondo; **~ly**
adv recentemente, negli ultimi tempi

lattice ['lætɪs] *n* traliccio; graticolato

laudable ['lɔ:dəbl] *adj* lodevole

laugh [lɑ:f] *n* risata ♦ *vi* ridere; **~ at** *fus*
(*misfortune etc*) ridere di; **~ off** *vt* prendere
alla leggera; **~able** *adj* ridicolo(a); **~ing
stock** *n*: **the ~ing stock of** lo zimbello di;
~ter *n* riso; risate *fpl*

launch [lɔ:ntʃ] *n* (*of rocket,* COMM) lancio;
(*of new ship*) varo; (*also:* **motor ~**) lancia
♦ *vt* (*rocket,* COMM) lanciare; (*ship, plan*)
varare; **~ into** *vt fus* lanciarsi in; **~(ing)
pad** *n* rampa di lancio

launder ['lɔ:ndə*] *vt* lavare e stirare

launderette [lɔ:n'dret] (*BRIT*) *n* lavanderia
(automatica)

Laundromat ® ['lɔ:ndrəmæt] (*US*) *n*
lavanderia automatica

laundry ['lɔ:ndrɪ] *n* lavanderia; (*clothes*)
biancheria; (: *dirty*) panni *mpl* da lavare

laurel ['lɒrl] *n* lauro

lava ['lɑ:və] *n* lava

lavatory ['lævətərɪ] *n* gabinetto

lavender ['lævəndə*] *n* lavanda

lavish ['lævɪʃ] *adj* copioso(a); abbondante;
(*giving freely*): **~ with** prodigo(a) di,
largo(a) in ♦ *vt*: **to ~ sth on sb** colmare qn
di qc

law [lɔ:] *n* legge *f*; **civil/criminal ~** diritto
civile/penale; **~-abiding** *adj* ubbidiente
alla legge; **~ and order** *n* l'ordine *m*
pubblico; **~ court** *n* tribunale *m*, corte *f* di
giustizia; **~ful** *adj* legale; lecito(a); **~less**
adj che non conosce nessuna legge

lawn [lɔ:n] *n* tappeto erboso; **~ mower** *n*
tosaerba *m or f inv*; **~ tennis** *n* tennis *m*
su prato

law school *n* facoltà *f inv* di legge

lawsuit ['lɔ:su:t] *n* processo, causa

lawyer ['lɔ:jə*] *n* (*for sales, wills etc*)
≈ notaio; (*partner, in court*) ≈ avvocato/
essa

lax [læks] *adj* rilassato(a); negligente

laxative ['læksətɪv] *n* lassativo

lay [leɪ] (*pt, pp* **laid**) *pt of* **lie** ♦ *adj* laico(a);
(*not expert*) profano(a) ♦ *vt* posare,
mettere; (*eggs*) fare; (*trap*) tendere; (*plans*)
fare, elaborare; **to ~ the table**
apparecchiare la tavola; **~ aside** *or* **by** *vt*
mettere da parte; **~ down** *vt* mettere giù;
(*rules etc*) formulare, fissare; **to ~ down the
law** dettar legge; **to ~ down one's life**
dare la propria vita; **~ off** *vt* (*workers*)
licenziare; **~ on** *vt* (*provide*) fornire; **~ out**
vt (*display*) presentare, disporre; **~about** *n*
sfaccendato/a, fannullone/a; **~-by** (*BRIT*) *n*
piazzola (di sosta)

layer ['leɪə*] *n* strato

layman ['leɪmən] *n* laico; profano

layout ['leɪaut] *n* lay-out *m inv*, disposizione
f; (*PRESS*) impaginazione *f*

laze [leɪz] *vi* oziare

lazy ['leɪzɪ] *adj* pigro(a)

lb. *abbr* = **pound** (*weight*)

lead¹ [liːd] (*pt, pp* **led**) *n* (*front position*)

posizione *f* di testa; (*distance, time ahead*) vantaggio; (*clue*) indizio; (*ELEC*) filo (elettrico); (*for dog*) guinzaglio; (*THEATRE*) parte *f* principale ♦ *vt* guidare, condurre; (*induce*) indurre; (*be leader of*) essere a capo di ♦ *vi* condurre; (*SPORT*) essere in testa; **in the ~** in testa; **to ~ the way** fare strada; **~ away** *vt* condurre via; **~ back** *vt*: **to ~ back to** ricondurre a; **~ on** *vt* (*tease*) tenere sulla corda; **~ to** *vt fus* condurre a; portare a; **~ up to** *vt fus* portare a

lead² [lɛd] *n* (*metal*) piombo; (*in pencil*) mina; **~ed petrol** *n* benzina con piombo

leaden ['lɛdn] *adj* (*sky, sea*) plumbeo(a)

leader ['liːdə*] *n* capo; leader *m inv*; (*in newspaper*) articolo di fondo; (*SPORT*) chi è in testa; **~ship** *n* direzione *f*; capacità di comando

leading ['liːdɪŋ] *adj* primo(a); principale; **~ light** *n* (*person*) personaggio di primo piano; **~ man/lady** *n* (*THEATRE*) primo attore/prima attrice

lead singer *n* cantante alla testa di un gruppo

leaf [liːf] (*pl* **leaves**) *n* foglia ♦ *vi*: **to ~ through sth** sfogliare qc; **to turn over a new ~** cambiar vita

leaflet ['liːflɪt] *n* dépliant *m inv*; (*POL, REL*) volantino

league [liːg] *n* lega; (*FOOTBALL*) campionato; **to be in ~ with** essere in lega con

leak [liːk] *n* (*out*) fuga; (*in*) infiltrazione *f*; (*security ~*) fuga d'informazioni ♦ *vi* (*roof, bucket*) perdere; (*liquid*) uscire; (*shoes*) lasciar passare l'acqua ♦ *vt* (*information*) divulgare; **~ out** *vi* uscire; (*information*) trapelare

lean [liːn] (*pt, pp* **leaned** *or* **leant**) *adj* magro(a) ♦ *vt*: **to ~ sth on sth** appoggiare qc su qc ♦ *vi* (*slope*) pendere; (*rest*): **to ~ against** appoggiarsi contro; essere appoggiato(a) a; **to ~ on** appoggiarsi a; **~ back/forward** *vi* sporgersi indietro/in avanti; **~ out** *vi* sporgersi; **~ over** *vi* inclinarsi; **~ing** *n*: **~ing (towards)** propensione *f* (per)

leap [liːp] (*pt, pp* **leaped** *or* **leapt**) *n* salto, balzo ♦ *vi* saltare, balzare; **~frog** *n* gioco della cavallina; **~ year** *n* anno bisestile

learn [ləːn] (*pt, pp* **learned** *or* **learnt**) *vt, vi* imparare; **to ~ about sth** (*hear, read*) apprendere qc; **to ~ to do sth** imparare a fare qc; **~ed** ['ləːnɪd] *adj* erudito(a), dotto(a); **~er** *n* principiante *m/f*; apprendista *m/f*; (*BRIT: also:* **~er driver**) guidatore/trice principiante; **~ing** *n* erudizione *f*, sapienza

lease [liːs] *n* contratto d'affitto ♦ *vt* affittare

leash [liːʃ] *n* guinzaglio

least [liːst] *adj*: **the ~** (+*noun*) il(la) più piccolo(a), il(la) minimo(a); (*smallest amount of*) il(la) meno ♦ *adv* (+*verb*) meno; **the ~** (+*adjective*): **the ~ beautiful girl** la ragazza meno bella; **the ~ possible effort** il minimo sforzo possibile; **I have the ~ money** ho meno denaro di tutti; **at ~** almeno; **not in the ~** affatto, per nulla

leather ['lɛðə*] *n* cuoio

leave [liːv] (*pt, pp* **left**) *vt* lasciare; (*go away from*) partire da ♦ *vi* partire, andarsene; (*bus, train*) partire ♦ *n* (*time off*) congedo; (*MIL, also: consent*) licenza; **to be left** rimanere; **there's some milk left over** c'è rimasto del latte; **on ~** in congedo; **~ behind** *vt* (*person, object*) lasciare; (*: forget*) dimenticare; **~ out** *vt* omettere, tralasciare; **~ of absence** *n* congedo

leaves [liːvz] *npl of* **leaf**

Lebanon ['lɛbənən] *n* Libano

lecherous ['lɛtʃərəs] *adj* lascivo(a), lubrico(a)

lecture ['lɛktʃə*] *n* conferenza; (*SCOL*) lezione *f* ♦ *vi* fare conferenze; fare lezioni ♦ *vt* (*scold*): **to ~ sb on** *or* **about sth** rimproverare qn *or* fare una ramanzina a qn per qc; **to give a ~ on** tenere una conferenza su

lecturer ['lɛktʃərə*] (*BRIT*) *n* (*at university*) professore/essa, docente *m/f*

led [lɛd] *pt, pp of* **lead**

ledge [lɛdʒ] *n* (*of window*) davanzale *m*; (*on wall etc*) sporgenza; (*of mountain*) cornice *f*, cengia

ledger ['lɛdʒə*] *n* libro maestro, registro

lee [li:] *n* lato sottovento

leech [li:tʃ] *n* sanguisuga

leek [li:k] *n* porro

leer [lɪə*] *vi*: **to ~ at sb** gettare uno sguardo voglioso (*or* maligno) su qn

leeway ['li:weɪ] *n* (*fig*): **to have some ~** avere una certa libertà di azione

left [lɛft] *pt, pp of* **leave** ♦ *adj* sinistro(a) ♦ *adv* a sinistra ♦ *n* sinistra; **on the ~, to the ~** a sinistra; **the L~** (*POL*) la sinistra; **~-hand drive** *n* guida a sinistra; **~-handed** *adj* mancino(a); **~-hand side** *n* lato *or* fianco sinistro; **~-luggage locker** *n* armadietto per deposito bagagli; **~ luggage (office)** (*BRIT*) *n* deposito *m* bagagli *inv*; **~overs** *npl* avanzi *mpl*, resti *mpl*; **~-wing** *adj* (*POL*) di sinistra

leg [lɛg] *n* gamba; (*of animal*) zampa; (*of furniture*) piede *m*; (*CULIN: of chicken*) coscia; (*of journey*) tappa; **1st/2nd ~** (*SPORT*) partita di andata/ritorno

legacy ['lɛgəsɪ] *n* eredità *f inv*

legal ['li:gl] *adj* legale; **~ holiday** (*US*) *n* giorno festivo, festa nazionale; **~ tender** *n* moneta legale

legend ['lɛdʒənd] *n* leggenda

legislation [lɛdʒɪs'leɪʃən] *n* legislazione *f*; **legislature** ['lɛdʒɪslətʃə*] *n* corpo legislativo

legitimate [lɪ'dʒɪtɪmət] *adj* legittimo(a)

leg-room *n* spazio per le gambe

leisure ['lɛʒə*] *n* agio, tempo libero; ricreazioni *fpl*; **at ~** con comodo; **~ centre** *n* centro di ricreazione; **~ly** *adj* tranquillo(a); fatto(a) con comodo *or* senza fretta

lemon ['lɛmən] *n* limone *m*; **~ade** [-'neɪd] *n* limonata; **~ tea** *n* tè *m inv* al limone

lend [lɛnd] (*pt, pp* **lent**) *vt*: **to ~ sth (to sb)** prestare qc (a qn); **~ing library** *n* biblioteca che consente prestiti di libri

length [lɛŋθ] *n* lunghezza; (*distance*) distanza; (*section: of road, pipe etc*) pezzo, tratto; (*of time*) periodo; **at ~** (*at last*) finalmente, alla fine; (*lengthily*) a lungo; **~en** *vt* allungare, prolungare ♦ *vi*

allungarsi; **~ways** *adv* per il lungo; **~y** *adj* molto lungo(a)

lenient ['li:nɪənt] *adj* indulgente, clemente

lens [lɛnz] *n* lente *f*; (*of camera*) obiettivo

Lent [lɛnt] *n* Quaresima

lent [lɛnt] *pt, pp of* **lend**

lentil ['lɛntl] *n* lenticchia

Leo ['li:əu] *n* Leone *m*

leotard ['li:ətɑ:d] *n* calzamaglia

leprosy ['lɛprəsɪ] *n* lebbra

lesbian ['lɛzbɪən] *n* lesbica

less [lɛs] *adj, pron, adv* meno ♦ *prep*: **~ tax/10% discount** meno tasse/il 10% di sconto; **~ than ever** meno che mai; **~ than half** meno della metà; **~ and ~** sempre meno; **the ~ he works ...** meno lavora ....

lessen ['lɛsn] *vi* diminuire, attenuarsi ♦ *vt* diminuire, ridurre

lesser ['lɛsə*] *adj* minore, più piccolo(a); **to a ~ extent** in grado *or* misura minore

lesson ['lɛsn] *n* lezione *f*; **to teach sb a ~** dare una lezione a qn

let [lɛt] (*pt, pp* **let**) *vt* lasciare; (*BRIT: lease*) dare in affitto; **to ~ sb do sth** lasciar fare qc a qn, lasciare che qn faccia qc; **to ~ sb know sth** far sapere qc a qn; **~'s go** andiamo; **~ him come** lo lasci venire; **"to ~"** "affittasi"; **~ down** *vt* (*lower*) abbassare; (*dress*) allungare; (*hair*) sciogliere; (*tyre*) sgonfiare; (*disappoint*) deludere; **~ go** *vt, vi* mollare; **~ in** *vt* lasciare entrare; (*visitor etc*) far entrare; **~ off** *vt* (*allow to go*) lasciare andare; (*firework etc*) far partire; **~ on** (*inf*) *vi* dire; **~ out** *vt* lasciare uscire; (*scream*) emettere; **~ up** *vi* diminuire

lethal ['li:θl] *adj* letale, mortale

lethargic [lɛ'θɑ:dʒɪk] *adj* letargico(a)

letter ['lɛtə*] *n* lettera; **~ bomb** *n* lettera esplosiva; **~box** (*BRIT*) *n* buca delle lettere; **~ing** *n* iscrizione *f*; caratteri *mpl*

lettuce ['lɛtɪs] *n* lattuga, insalata

let-up *n* pausa

leukaemia [lu:'ki:mɪə] (*US* **leukemia**) *n* leucemia

level ['lɛvl] *adj* piatto(a), piano(a); orizzontale ♦ *adv*: **to draw ~ with** mettersi alla pari di ♦ n livello ♦ vt livellare, spianare; **to be ~ with** essere alla pari di; **A ~s** (BRIT) npl ≈ esami mpl di maturità; **O ~s** (BRIT) npl esami fatti in Inghilterra all'età di 16 anni; **on the ~** piatto(a); (fig) onesto(a); **~ off** or **out** vi (prices etc) stabilizzarsi; **~ crossing** (BRIT) n passaggio a livello; **~-headed** adj equilibrato(a)

lever ['liːvə*] n leva; **~age** n: **~age (on** or **with)** forza (su); (fig) ascendente m (su)

levy ['lɛvɪ] n tassa, imposta ♦ vt imporre

lewd [luːd] adj osceno(a), lascivo(a)

liability [laɪə'bɪlətɪ] n responsabilità f inv; (handicap) peso; **liabilities** npl debiti mpl; (on balance sheet) passivo

liable ['laɪəbl] adj (subject): **~ to** soggetto(a) a; passibile di; (responsible): **~ (for)** responsabile (di); (likely): **~ to do** propenso(a) a fare

liaise [liː'eɪz] vi: **to ~ (with)** mantenere i contatti (con)

liaison [liː'eɪzɒn] n relazione f; (MIL) collegamento

liar ['laɪə*] n bugiardo/a

libel ['laɪbl] n libello, diffamazione f ♦ vt diffamare

liberal ['lɪbərl] adj liberale; (generous): **to be ~ with** distribuire liberalmente

liberation [lɪbə'reɪʃən] n liberazione f

liberty ['lɪbətɪ] n libertà f inv; **at ~** (criminal) in libertà; **at ~ to do** libero(a) di fare

Libra ['liːbrə] n Bilancia

librarian [laɪ'brɛərɪən] n bibliotecario/a

library ['laɪbrərɪ] n biblioteca

Libya ['lɪbɪə] n Libia; **~n** adj, n libico(a)

lice [laɪs] npl of **louse**

licence ['laɪsns] (US **license**) n autorizzazione f, permesso; (COMM) licenza; (RADIO, TV) canone m, abbonamento; (also: **driving ~**, (US) **driver's ~**) patente f di guida; (excessive freedom) licenza; **~ number** n numero di targa; **~ plate** n targa

license ['laɪsns] n (US) = **licence** ♦ vt dare una licenza a; **~d** adj (for alcohol) che ha la licenza di vendere bibite alcoliche

lick [lɪk] vt leccare; (inf: defeat) stracciare; **to**

~ one's lips (fig) leccarsi i baffi

licorice ['lɪkərɪs] (US) n = **liquorice**

lid [lɪd] n coperchio; (eye~) palpebra

lie [laɪ] (pt **lay**, pp **lain**) vi (rest) giacere; star disteso(a); (of object: be situated) trovarsi, essere; (tell lies: pt, pp **lied**) mentire, dire bugie ♦ n bugia, menzogna; **to ~ low** (fig) latitare; **~ about** or **around** vi (things) essere in giro; (person) bighellonare; **~-down** (BRIT) n: **to have a ~-down** sdraiarsi, riposarsi; **~-in** (BRIT) n: **to have a ~-in** rimanere a letto

lieu [luː]: **in ~ of** prep invece di, al posto di

lieutenant [lɛf'tɛnənt, (US) luː'tɛnənt] n tenente m

life [laɪf] (pl **lives**) n vita ♦ cpd di vita; della vita; a vita; **to come to ~** rianimarsi; **~ assurance** (BRIT) n = **~ insurance**; **~belt** (BRIT) n salvagente m; **~boat** n scialuppa di salvataggio; **~guard** n bagnino; **~ imprisonment** n carcere m a vita; **~ insurance** n assicurazione f sulla vita; **~ jacket** n giubbotto di salvataggio; **~less** adj senza vita; **~like** adj verosimile; rassomigliante; **~long** adj per tutta la vita; **~ preserver** (US) n salvagente m; giubbotto di salvataggio; **~ sentence** n ergastolo; **~-size(d)** adj a grandezza naturale; **~ span** n (durata della) vita; **~style** n stile m di vita; **~ support system** n respiratore m automatico; **~time** n: **in his ~time** durante la sua vita; **once in a ~time** una volta nella vita

lift [lɪft] vt sollevare; (ban, rule) levare ♦ vi (fog) alzarsi ♦ n (BRIT: elevator) ascensore m; **to give sb a ~** (BRIT) dare un passaggio a qn; **~-off** n decollo

light [laɪt] (pt, pp **lighted** or **lit**) n luce f, lume m; (daylight) luce f, giorno; (lamp) lampada; (AUT: rear ~) luce f di posizione; (: headlamp) fanale m; (for cigarette etc): **have you got a ~?** ha da accendere?; **~s** npl (AUT: traffic ~s) semaforo ♦ vt (candle, cigarette, fire) accendere; (room): **to be lit by** essere illuminato(a) da ♦ adj (room, colour) chiaro(a); (not heavy, also fig) leggero(a); **to come to ~** venire alla luce,

emergere; **~ up** vi illuminarsi ♦ vt
illuminare; **~ bulb** n lampadina; **~en** vt
(make less heavy) alleggerire; **~er** n (also:
cigarette ~er) accendino; **~-headed** adj
stordito(a); **~-hearted** adj gioioso(a),
gaio(a); **~house** n faro; **~ing** n
illuminazione f; **~ly** adv leggermente; **to
get off ~ly** cavarsela a buon mercato; **~
meter** n (PHOT) esposimetro; **~ness** n
chiarezza; (in weight) leggerezza

lightning ['laɪtnɪŋ] n lampo, fulmine m; **~
conductor** (US **~ rod**) n parafulmine m

light pen n penna ottica

lightweight ['laɪtweɪt] adj (suit) leggero(a)
♦ n (BOXING) peso leggero

light year n anno m luce inv

like [laɪk] vt (person) volere bene a; (activity,
object, food): **I ~ swimming/that book/
chocolate** mi piace nuotare/quel libro/il
cioccolato ♦ prep come ♦ adj simile,
uguale ♦ n: **the ~** uno(a) uguale; **his ~s
and dislikes** i suoi gusti; **I would ~, I'd ~**
mi piacerebbe, vorrei; **would you ~ a
coffee?** gradirebbe un caffè?; **to be/look ~
sb/sth** somigliare a qn/qc; **what does it
look/taste ~?** che aspetto/gusto ha?;
what does it sound ~? come fa?; **that's
just ~ him** è proprio da lui; **do it ~ this**
fallo così; **it is nothing ~ ...** non è affatto
come ...; **~able** adj simpatico(a)

likelihood ['laɪklɪhud] n probabilità

likely ['laɪklɪ] adj probabile, plausibile; **he's
~ to leave** probabilmente partirà, è
probabile che parta; **not ~!** neanche per
sogno!

likeness ['laɪknɪs] n somiglianza

likewise ['laɪkwaɪz] adv similmente, nello
stesso modo

liking ['laɪkɪŋ] n: **~ (for)** debole m (per); **to
be to sb's ~** piacere a qn

lilac ['laɪlək] n lilla m inv

lily ['lɪlɪ] n giglio; **~ of the valley** n
mughetto

limb [lɪm] n arto

limber up ['lɪmbə*-] vi riscaldarsi i muscoli

limbo ['lɪmbəu] n: **to be in ~** (fig) essere
lasciato(a) nel dimenticatoio

lime [laɪm] n (tree) tiglio; (fruit) limetta;
(GEO) calce f

limelight ['laɪmlaɪt] n: **in the ~** (fig) alla
ribalta, in vista

limerick ['lɪmərɪk] n poesiola umoristica di
5 versi

limestone ['laɪmstəun] n pietra calcarea;
(GEO) calcare m

limit ['lɪmɪt] n limite m ♦ vt limitare; **~ed**
adj limitato(a), ristretto(a); **to be ~ed to**
limitarsi a; **~ed (liability) company**
(BRIT) n ≈ società f inv a responsabilità
limitata

limp [lɪmp] n: **to have a ~** zoppicare ♦ vi
zoppicare ♦ adj floscio(a), flaccido(a)

limpet ['lɪmpɪt] n patella

line [laɪn] n linea; (rope) corda; (for fishing)
lenza; (wire) filo; (of poem) verso; (row,
series) fila, riga; coda; (on face) ruga ♦ vt
(clothes): **to ~ (with)** foderare (di); (box): **to
~ (with)** rivestire or foderare (di); (subj:
trees, crowd) fiancheggiare; **~ of business**
settore m or ramo d'attività; **in ~ with** in
linea con; **~ up** vi allinearsi, mettersi in fila
♦ vt mettere in fila; (event, celebration)
preparare

lined [laɪnd] adj (face) rugoso(a); (paper) a
righe, rigato(a)

linen ['lɪnɪn] n biancheria, panni mpl; (cloth)
tela di lino

liner ['laɪnə*] n nave f di linea; (for bin)
sacchetto

linesman ['laɪnzmən] n guardalinee m inv

line-up n allineamento, fila; (SPORT)
formazione f di gioco

linger ['lɪŋgə*] vi attardarsi; indugiare;
(smell, tradition) persistere

lingerie ['lænʒəriː] n biancheria intima
femminile

linguistics [lɪŋ'gwɪstɪks] n linguistica

lining ['laɪnɪŋ] n fodera

link [lɪŋk] n (of a chain) anello; (relationship)
legame m; (connection) collegamento ♦ vt
collegare, unire, congiungere; (associate):
to ~ with or **to** collegare a; **~s** npl (GOLF)
pista or terreno da golf; **~ up** vt collegare,
unire ♦ vi riunirsi; associarsi

lino ['laɪnəʊ] n = **linoleum**
linoleum [lɪ'nəʊlɪəm] n linoleum m inv
lion ['laɪən] n leone m; ~ess n leonessa
lip [lɪp] n labbro; (of cup etc) orlo
liposuction ['lɪpəʊsʌkʃən] n liposuzione f
lip: ~read vi leggere sulle labbra; ~ salve
n burro di cacao; ~ service n: to pay ~
service to sth essere favorevole a qc solo a
parole; ~stick n rossetto
liqueur [lɪ'kjʊə*] n liquore m
liquid ['lɪkwɪd] n liquido ♦ adj liquido(a)
liquidize ['lɪkwɪdaɪz] vt (CULIN) passare al
frullatore; ~r n frullatore m (a brocca)
liquor ['lɪkə*] n alcool m
liquorice ['lɪkərɪs] (BRIT) n liquirizia
liquor store (US) n negozio di liquori
lisp [lɪsp] n pronuncia blesa della ''s''
list [lɪst] n lista, elenco ♦ vt (write down)
mettere in lista; fare una lista di;
(enumerate) elencare; ~ed building (BRIT)
n edificio sotto la protezione delle Belle
Arti
listen ['lɪsn] vi ascoltare; to ~ to ascoltare;
~er n ascoltatore/trice
listless ['lɪstlɪs] adj apatico(a)
lit [lɪt] pt, pp of **light**
liter ['liːtə*] (US) n = **litre**
literacy ['lɪtərəsɪ] n il sapere leggere e
scrivere
literal ['lɪtərl] adj letterale; ~ly adv alla
lettera, letteralmente
literary ['lɪtərərɪ] adj letterario(a)
literate ['lɪtərət] adj che sa leggere e
scrivere
literature ['lɪtərɪtʃə*] n letteratura;
(brochures etc) materiale m
lithe [laɪð] adj agile, snello(a)
litigation [lɪtɪ'geɪʃən] n causa
litre ['liːtə*] (US liter) n litro
litter ['lɪtə*] n (rubbish) rifiuti mpl; (young
animals) figliata; ~ bin (BRIT) n cestino per
rifiuti; ~ed adj: ~ed with coperto(a) di
little ['lɪtl] adj (small) piccolo(a); (not much)
poco(a) ♦ adv poco; a ~ un po' (di); a ~
bit un pochino; ~ by ~ a poco a poco; ~
finger n mignolo
live[1] [lɪv] vi vivere; (reside) vivere, abitare;

~ down vt far dimenticare (alla gente); ~
on vt fus (food) vivere di; ~ together vi
vivere insieme, convivere; ~ up to vt fus
tener fede a, non venir meno a
live[2] [laɪv] adj (animal) vivo(a); (wire) sotto
tensione; (bullet, missile) inesploso(a);
(broadcast) diretto(a); (performance) dal
vivo
livelihood ['laɪvlɪhʊd] n mezzi mpl di
sostentamento
lively ['laɪvlɪ] adj vivace, vivo(a)
liven up ['laɪvn'ʌp] vt (discussion, evening)
animare ♦ vi ravvivarsi
liver ['lɪvə*] n fegato
lives [laɪvz] npl of **life**
livestock ['laɪvstɔk] n bestiame m
livid ['lɪvɪd] adj livido(a); (furious) livido(a) di
rabbia, furibondo(a)
living ['lɪvɪŋ] adj vivo(a), vivente ♦ n: to
earn or make a ~ guadagnarsi la vita; ~
conditions npl condizioni fpl di vita; ~
room n soggiorno; ~ standards npl
tenore m di vita; ~ wage n salario
sufficiente per vivere
lizard ['lɪzəd] n lucertola
load [ləʊd] n (weight) peso; (thing carried)
carico ♦ vt (also: ~ up): to ~ (with) (lorry,
ship) caricare (di); (gun, camera, COMPUT)
caricare (con); a ~ of, ~s of (fig) un sacco
di; ~ed adj (vehicle): ~ed (with) carico(a)
(di); (question) capzioso(a); (inf: rich)
carico(a) di soldi
loaf [ləʊf] (pl loaves) n pane m, pagnotta
loan [ləʊn] n prestito ♦ vt dare in prestito;
on ~ in prestito
loath [ləʊθ] adj: to be ~ to do essere
restio(a) a fare
loathe [ləʊð] vt detestare, aborrire
loaves [ləʊvz] npl of **loaf**
lobby ['lɔbɪ] n atrio, vestibolo; (POL: pressure
group) gruppo di pressione ♦ vt fare
pressione su
lobster ['lɔbstə*] n aragosta
local ['ləʊkl] adj locale ♦ n (BRIT: pub) ≈ bar
m inv all'angolo; the ~s npl (local
inhabitants) la gente della zona; ~
anaesthetic n anestesia locale; ~

authority *n* ente *m* locale; **~ call** *n* (TEL) telefonata urbana; **~ government** *n* amministrazione *f* locale

locality [ləu'kælɪtɪ] *n* località *f inv*; (*position*) posto, luogo

locally ['ləukəlɪ] *adv* da queste parti; nel vicinato

locate [ləu'keɪt] *vt* (*find*) trovare; (*situate*) collocare; situare

location [ləu'keɪʃən] *n* posizione *f*; **on ~** (CINEMA) all'esterno

loch [lɔx] *n* lago

lock [lɔk] *n* (*of door, box*) serratura; (*of canal*) chiusa; (*of hair*) ciocca, riccio ♦ *vt* (*with key*) chiudere a chiave ♦ *vi* (*door etc*) chiudersi; (*wheels*) bloccarsi, incepparsi; **~ in** *vt* chiudere dentro (a chiave); **~ out** *vt* chiudere fuori; **~ up** *vt* (*criminal, mental patient*) rinchiudere; (*house*) chiudere (a chiave) ♦ *vi* chiudere tutto (a chiave)

locker ['lɔkə*] *n* armadietto

locket ['lɔkɪt] *n* medaglione *m*

locksmith ['lɔksmɪθ] *n* magnano

lockup ['lɔkʌp] (US) *n* prigione *f*; guardina

locum ['ləukəm] *n* (MED) medico sostituto

lodge [lɔdʒ] *n* casetta, portineria; (*hunting ~*) casino di caccia ♦ *vi* (*person*): **to ~ (with)** essere a pensione (presso *or* da); (*bullet etc*) conficcarsi ♦ *vt* (*appeal etc*) presentare, fare; **to ~ a complaint** presentare un reclamo; **~r** *n* affittuario/a; (*with room and meals*) pensionante *m/f*

lodgings ['lɔdʒɪŋz] *npl* camera d'affitto; camera ammobiliata

loft [lɔft] *n* solaio, soffitta

lofty ['lɔftɪ] *adj* alto(a); (*haughty*) altezzoso(a)

log [lɔg] *n* (*of wood*) ceppo; (*book*) = **logbook** ♦ *vt* registrare; **~ in** *or* **on** (COMPUT) collegarsi; **~ off** *or* **out** *vi* (COMPUT) scollegarsi

logbook ['lɔgbuk] *n* (NAUT, AVIAT) diario di bordo; (AUT) libretto di circolazione

loggerheads ['lɔgəhedz] *npl*: **at ~ (with)** ai ferri corti (con)

logic ['lɔdʒɪk] *n* logica; **~al** *adj* logico(a)

loin [lɔɪn] *n* (CULIN) lombata

loiter ['lɔɪtə*] *vi* attardarsi

loll [lɔl] *vi* (*also*: **~ about**) essere stravaccato(a)

lollipop ['lɔlɪpɔp] *n* lecca lecca *m inv*; **~ man/lady** (BRIT: *irreg*) *n* see box

┌─────────────────────────┐
│ **lollipop man/lady** │
└─────────────────────────┘

i In Gran Bretagna il **lollipop man** e la **lollipop lady** sono persone incaricate di aiutare i bambini ad attraversare la strada in prossimità delle scuole; usano una paletta la cui forma ricorda quella di un lecca lecca, in inglese **lollipop**.

London ['lʌndən] *n* Londra; **~er** *n* londinese *m/f*

lone [ləun] *adj* solitario(a)

loneliness ['ləunlɪnɪs] *n* solitudine *f*, isolamento

lonely ['ləunlɪ] *adj* solo(a); solitario(a), isolato(a)

long [lɔŋ] *adj* lungo(a) ♦ *adv* a lungo, per molto tempo ♦ *vi*: **to ~ for sth/to do** desiderare qc/di fare; non veder l'ora di aver qc/di fare; **so** *or* **as ~ as** (*while*) finché; (*provided that*) sempre che +*sub*; **don't be ~!** fai presto!; **how ~ is this river/course?** quanto è lungo questo fiume/corso?; **6 metres ~** lungo 6 metri; **6 months ~** che dura 6 mesi, di 6 mesi; **all night ~** tutta la notte; **he no ~er comes** non viene più; **~ before** molto tempo prima; **before ~** (+*future*) presto, fra poco; (+*past*) poco tempo dopo; **at ~ last** finalmente; **~-distance** *adj* (*race*) di fondo; (*call*) interurbano(a); **~-haired** *adj* dai capelli lunghi; **~hand** *n* scrittura normale; **~ing** *n* desiderio, voglia, brama

longitude ['lɔŋgɪtjuːd] *n* longitudine *f*

long: **~ jump** *n* salto in lungo; **~-life** *adj* (*milk*) a lunga conservazione; (*batteries*) di lunga durata; **~-lost** *adj* perduto(a) da tempo; **~-range** *adj* a lunga portata; **~-sighted** *adj* presbite; **~-standing** *adj* di vecchia data; **~-suffering** *adj* estremamente paziente; infinitamente tollerante; **~-term** *adj* a lungo termine; **~**

wave n onde fpl lunghe; **~-winded** adj prolisso(a), interminabile

loo [lu:] (BRIT: inf) n W.C. m inv, cesso

look [luk] vi guardare; (seem) sembrare, parere; (building etc): **to ~ south/on to the sea** dare a sud/sul mare ♦ n sguardo; (appearance) aspetto, aria; **~s** npl (good ~s) bellezza; **~ after** vt fus occuparsi di, prendere cura di; (keep an eye on) guardare, badare a; **~ at** vt fus guardare; **~ back** vi: **to ~ back on** (event etc) ripensare a; **~ down on** vt fus (fig) guardare dall'alto, disprezzare; **~ for** vt fus cercare; **~ forward to** vt fus non veder l'ora di; (in letters): **we ~ forward to hearing from you** in attesa di una vostra gentile risposta; **~ into** vt fus esaminare; **~ on** vi fare da spettatore; **~ out** vi (beware): **to ~ out (for)** stare in guardia (per); **~ out for** vt fus cercare; **~ round** vi (turn) girarsi, voltarsi; (in shop) dare un'occhiata; **~ to** vt fus (rely on) contare su; **~ up** vi alzare gli occhi; (improve) migliorare ♦ vt (word) cercare; (friend) andare a trovare; **~ up to** vt fus avere rispetto per; **~-out** n posto d'osservazione; guardia; **to be on the ~-out (for)** stare in guardia (per)

loom [lu:m] n telaio ♦ vi (also: **~ up**) apparire minaccioso(a); (event) essere imminente

loony ['lu:nɪ] (inf) n pazzo/a

loop [lu:p] n cappio ♦ vt: **to ~ sth round sth** passare qc intorno a qc; **~hole** n via d'uscita; scappatoia

loose [lu:s] adj (knot) sciolto(a); (screw) allentato(a); (stone) cadente; (clothes) ampio(a), largo(a); (animal) in libertà, scappato(a); (life, morals) dissoluto(a) ♦ n: **to be on the ~** essere in libertà; **~ change** n spiccioli mpl, moneta; **~ chippings** npl (on road) ghiaino; **~ end** n: **to be at a ~ end** (BRIT) or **at ~ ends** (US) non saper che fare; **~ly** adv senza stringere; approssimativamente; **~n** vt sciogliere; (belt etc) allentare

loot [lu:t] n bottino ♦ vt saccheggiare

lop [lɒp] vt (also: **~ off**) tagliare via, recidere

lop-sided ['lɒp'saɪdɪd] adj non equilibrato(a), asimmetrico(a)

lord [lɔ:d] n signore m; **L~ Smith** lord Smith; **the L~** il Signore; **good L~!** buon Dio!; **the (House of) L~s** (BRIT) la Camera dei Lord; **~ship** n: **your L~ship** Sua Eccellenza

lore [lɔ:ʳ] n tradizioni fpl

lorry ['lɒrɪ] (BRIT) n camion m inv; **~ driver** (BRIT) n camionista m

lose [lu:z] (pt, pp **lost**) vt perdere ♦ vi perdere; **to ~ (time)** (clock) ritardare; **~r** n perdente m/f

loss [lɒs] n perdita; **to be at a ~** essere perplesso(a)

lost [lɒst] pt, pp of **lose** ♦ adj perduto(a); **~ property** (US **~ and found**) n oggetti mpl smarriti

lot [lɒt] n (at auctions) lotto; (destiny) destino, sorte f; **the ~** tutto(a) quanto(a); tutti(e) quanti(e); **a ~** molto; **a ~ of** una gran quantità di, un sacco di; **~s of** molto(a); **to draw ~s (for sth)** tirare a sorte (per qc)

lotion ['ləʊʃən] n lozione f

lottery ['lɒtərɪ] n lotteria

loud [laʊd] adj forte, alto(a); (gaudy) vistoso(a), sgargiante ♦ adv (speak etc) forte; **out ~** (read etc) ad alta voce; **~hailer** (BRIT) n portavoce m inv; **~ly** adv fortemente, ad alta voce; **~speaker** n altoparlante m

lounge [laʊndʒ] n salotto, soggiorno; (at airport, station) sala d'attesa; (BRIT: also: **~ bar**) bar m inv con servizio a tavolino ♦ vi oziare; **~ about** or **around** vi starsene colle mani in mano

louse [laʊs] (pl **lice**) n pidocchio

lousy ['laʊzɪ] (inf) adj orrendo(a), schifoso(a); **to feel ~** stare da cani

lout [laʊt] n zoticone m

lovable ['lʌvəbl] adj simpatico(a), carino(a); amabile

love [lʌv] n amore m ♦ vt amare; voler bene a; **to ~ to do: I ~ to do** mi piace fare; **to be/fall in ~ with** essere innamorato(a)/

innamorarsi di; **to make ~** fare l'amore;
"15 ~" (*TENNIS*) "15 a zero"; **~ affair** *n*
relazione *f*; **~ life** *n* vita sentimentale

lovely ['lʌvlɪ] *adj* bello(a); (*delicious: smell, meal*) buono(a)

lover ['lʌvə*] *n* amante *m/f*; (*person in love*) innamorato/a; (*amateur*): **a ~ of** un(un')amante di; un(un')appassionato(a) di

loving ['lʌvɪŋ] *adj* affettuoso(a)

low [ləu] *adj* basso(a) ♦ *adv* in basso ♦ *n* (*METEOR*) depressione *f*; **to be ~ on** (*supplies etc*) avere scarsità di; **to feel ~** sentirsi giù; **~-alcohol** *adj* a basso contenuto alcolico; **~-calorie** *adj* a basso contenuto calorico; **~-cut** *adj* (*dress*) scollato(a); **~er** *adj* (*bottom: of 2 things*) più basso; (*less important*) meno importante ♦ *vt* calare; (*prices, eyes, voice*) abbassare; **~-fat** *adj* magro(a); **~lands** *npl* (*GEO*) pianura *f*; **~ly** *adj* umile, modesto(a)

loyal ['lɔɪəl] *adj* fedele, leale; **~ty** *n* fedeltà, lealtà; **~ card** *n* carta che offre sconti a clienti abituali

lozenge ['lɔzɪndʒ] *n* (*MED*) pastiglia

L.P. *n abbr* = **long-playing record**

L-plates (*BRIT*) *npl* contrassegno P principiante

L-plates

i Le **L-plates** sono delle tabelle bianche con una L rossa che in Gran Bretagna i guidatori principianti, **learner drivers**, devono applicare alla propria autovettura finché non ottengono la patente.

Ltd *abbr* (= *limited*) ≈ S.r.l.

lubricate ['lu:brɪkeɪt] *vt* lubrificare

luck [lʌk] *n* fortuna, sorte *f*; **bad ~** sfortuna, mala sorte; **good ~!** buona fortuna!; **~ily** *adv* fortunatamente, per fortuna; **~y** *adj* fortunato(a); (*number etc*) che porta fortuna

ludicrous ['lu:dɪkrəs] *adj* ridicolo(a)

lug [lʌg] (*inf*) *vt* trascinare

luggage ['lʌgɪdʒ] *n* bagagli *mpl*; **~ rack** *n* portabagagli *m inv*

lukewarm ['lu:kwɔ:m] *adj* tiepido(a)

lull [lʌl] *n* intervallo di calma ♦ *vt*: **to ~ sb to sleep** cullare qn finché si addormenta

lullaby ['lʌləbaɪ] *n* ninnananna

lumbago [lʌm'beɪgəu] *n* (*MED*) lombaggine *f*

lumber ['lʌmbə*] *n* (*wood*) legname *m*; (*junk*) roba vecchia; **~ with** *vt*: **to be ~ed with sth** doversi sorbire qc; **~jack** *n* boscaiolo

luminous ['lu:mɪnəs] *adj* luminoso(a)

lump [lʌmp] *n* pezzo; (*in sauce*) grumo; (*swelling*) gonfiore *m*; (*also: sugar ~*) zolletta ♦ *vt* (*also: ~ together*) riunire, mettere insieme; **a ~ sum** una somma globale; **~y** *adj* (*sauce*) pieno(a) di grumi; (*bed*) bitorzoluto(a)

lunatic ['lu:nətɪk] *adj* pazzo(a), matto(a)

lunch [lʌntʃ] *n* pranzo, colazione *f*

luncheon ['lʌntʃən] *n* pranzo; **~ voucher** (*BRIT*) *n* buono *m* pasto *inv*

lunch time *n* ora di pranzo

lung [lʌŋ] *n* polmone *m*

lunge [lʌndʒ] *vi* (*also: ~ forward*) fare un balzo in avanti; **to ~ at** balzare su

lurch [lə:tʃ] *vi* vacillare, barcollare ♦ *n* scatto improvviso; **to leave sb in the ~** piantare in asso qn

lure [luə*] *n* richiamo; lusinga ♦ *vt* attirare (con l'inganno)

lurid ['luərɪd] *adj* sgargiante; (*details etc*) impressionante

lurk [lə:k] *vi* stare in agguato

luscious ['lʌʃəs] *adj* succulento(a); delizioso(a)

lush [lʌʃ] *adj* lussureggiante

lust [lʌst] *n* lussuria; cupidigia; desiderio; (*fig*): **~ for** sete *f* di

lusty ['lʌstɪ] *adj* vigoroso(a), robusto(a)

Luxembourg ['lʌksəmbə:g] *n* (*state*) Lussemburgo *m*; (*city*) Lussemburgo *f*

luxuriant [lʌg'zjuərɪənt] *adj* lussureggiante; (*hair*) folto(a)

luxurious [lʌg'zjuərɪəs] *adj* sontuoso(a), di lusso

luxury ['lʌkʃərɪ] *n* lusso ♦ *cpd* di lusso

lying ['laɪɪŋ] *n* bugie *fpl*, menzogne *fpl*

♦ *adj* bugiardo(a)
lynch [lɪntʃ] *vt* linciare
lyrical ['lɪrɪkl] *adj* lirico(a); (*fig*) entusiasta
lyrics ['lɪrɪks] *npl* (*of song*) parole *fpl*

M, m

m. *abbr* = **metre**; **mile**; **million**
M.A. *abbr* = **Master of Arts**
mac [mæk] (*BRIT*) *n* impermeabile *m*
macaroni [mækə'rəʊnɪ] *n* maccheroni *mpl*
machine [mə'ʃiːn] *n* macchina ♦ *vt* (*TECH*)
lavorare a macchina; (*dress etc*) cucire a
macchina; ~ **gun** *n* mitragliatrice *f*; ~**ry** *n*
macchinario, macchine *fpl*; (*fig*) macchina
mackerel ['mækrl] *n inv* sgombro
mackintosh ['mækɪntɒʃ] (*BRIT*) *n*
impermeabile *m*
mad [mæd] *adj* matto(a), pazzo(a); (*foolish*)
sciocco(a); (*angry*) furioso(a); **to be ~**
about (*keen*) andare pazzo(a) per
madam ['mædəm] *n* signora
madden ['mædn] *vt* fare infuriare
made [meɪd] *pt, pp of* **make**
Madeira [mə'dɪərə] *n* (*GEO*) Madera; (*wine*)
madera
made-to-measure (*BRIT*) *adj* fatto(a) su
misura
madly ['mædlɪ] *adv* follemente
madman ['mædmən] (*irreg*) *n* pazzo,
alienato
madness ['mædnɪs] *n* pazzia
magazine [mægə'ziːn] *n* (*PRESS*) rivista;
(*RADIO, TV*) rubrica
maggot ['mægət] *n* baco, verme *m*
magic ['mædʒɪk] *n* magia ♦ *adj* magico(a);
~**al** *adj* magico(a); ~**ian** [mə'dʒɪʃən] *n*
mago/a
magistrate ['mædʒɪstreɪt] *n* magistrato;
giudice *m/f*
magnet ['mægnɪt] *n* magnete *m*, calamita;
~**ic** [-'netɪk] *adj* magnetico(a)
magnificent [mæg'nɪfɪsnt] *adj* magnifico(a)
magnify ['mægnɪfaɪ] *vt* ingrandire; ~**ing**
glass *n* lente *f* d'ingrandimento
magnitude ['mægnɪtjuːd] *n* grandezza;

importanza
magpie ['mægpaɪ] *n* gazza
mahogany [mə'hɒgənɪ] *n* mogano
maid [meɪd] *n* domestica; (*in hotel*)
cameriera
maiden ['meɪdn] *n* fanciulla ♦ *adj* (*aunt etc*)
nubile; (*speech, voyage*) inaugurale; ~
name *n* nome *m* da nubile *or* da ragazza
mail [meɪl] *n* posta ♦ *vt* spedire (per posta);
~**box** (*US*) *n* cassetta delle lettere; ~**ing**
list *n* elenco d'indirizzi; ~**-order** *n* vendita
(*or* acquisto) per corrispondenza
maim [meɪm] *vt* mutilare
main [meɪn] *adj* principale ♦ *n* (*pipe*)
conduttura principale; **the ~s** *npl* (*ELEC*) la
linea principale; **in the ~** nel complesso,
nell'insieme; ~**frame** *n* (*COMPUT*)
mainframe *m inv*; ~**land** *n* continente *m*;
~**ly** *adv* principalmente, soprattutto; ~
road *n* strada principale; ~**stay** *n* (*fig*)
sostegno principale; ~**stream** *n* (*fig*)
corrente *f* principale
maintain [meɪn'teɪn] *vt* mantenere; (*affirm*)
sostenere; **maintenance** ['meɪntənəns] *n*
manutenzione *f*; (*alimony*) alimenti *mpl*
maize [meɪz] *n* granturco, mais *m*
majestic [mə'dʒestɪk] *adj* maestoso(a)
majesty ['mædʒɪstɪ] *n* maestà *f inv*
major ['meɪdʒə*] *n* (*MIL*) maggiore *m* ♦ *adj*
(*greater, MUS*) maggiore; (*in importance*)
principale, importante
Majorca [mə'jɔːkə] *n* Maiorca
majority [mə'dʒɒrɪtɪ] *n* maggioranza
make [meɪk] (*pt, pp* **made**) *vt* fare;
(*manufacture*) fare, fabbricare; (*cause to*
be): **to ~ sb sad** *etc* rendere qn triste *etc*;
(*force*): **to ~ sb do sth** costringere qn a fare
qc, far fare qc a qn; (*equal*): **2 and 2 ~ 4** 2
più 2 fa 4 ♦ *n* fabbricazione *f*; (*brand*)
marca; **to ~ a fool of sb** far fare a qn la
figura dello scemo; **to ~ a profit** realizzare
un profitto; **to ~ a loss** subire una perdita;
to ~ it (*arrive*) arrivare; (*achieve sth*) farcela;
what time do you ~ it? che ora fai?; **to ~**
do with arrangiarsi con; ~ **for** *vt fus*
(*place*) avviarsi verso; ~ **out** *vt* (*write out*)
scrivere; (: *cheque*) emettere; (*understand*)

capire; (*see*) distinguere; (: *numbers*)
decifrare; ~ **up** *vt* (*constitute*) formare;
(*invent*) inventare; (*parcel*) fare ♦ *vi*
conciliarsi; (*with cosmetics*) truccarsi; ~ **up**
for *vt fus* compensare; ricuperare; ~-
believe *n*: **a world of ~-believe** un
mondo di favole; **it's just ~-believe** è tutta
un'invenzione; ~**r** *n* (*of programme etc*)
creatore/trice; (*manufacturer*) fabbricante
m; ~**shift** *adj* improvvisato(a); ~-**up** *n*
trucco; ~-**up remover** *n* struccatore *m*

making ['meɪkɪŋ] *n* (*fig*): **in the ~** in
formazione; **to have the ~s of** (*actor*,
athlete etc) avere la stoffa di

maladjusted [mælə'dʒʌstɪd] *adj*
disadattato(a)

malaria [mə'lɛərɪə] *n* malaria

Malaysia [mə'leɪzɪə] *n* Malaysia

male [meɪl] *n* (*BIOL*) maschio ♦ *adj* maschile;
maschio(a)

malfunction [mæl'fʌŋkʃən] *n* funzione *f*
difettosa

malice ['mælɪs] *n* malevolenza; **malicious**
[mə'lɪʃəs] *adj* malevolo(a); (*LAW*) doloso(a)

malignant [mə'lɪgnənt] *adj* (*MED*)
maligno(a)

mall [mɔːl] *n* (*also*: **shopping ~**) centro
commerciale

mallet ['mælɪt] *n* maglio

malnutrition [mælnjuː'trɪʃən] *n*
denutrizione *f*

malpractice [mæl'præktɪs] *n* prevaricazione
f; negligenza

malt [mɔːlt] *n* malto

Malta ['mɔːltə] *n* Malta

mammal ['mæməl] *n* mammifero

mammoth ['mæməθ] *adj* enorme,
gigantesco(a)

man [mæn] (*pl* **men**) *n* uomo ♦ *vt* fornire
d'uomini; stare a; **an old ~** un vecchio; ~
and wife marito e moglie

manage ['mænɪdʒ] *vi* farcela ♦ *vt* (*be in
charge of*) occuparsi di; gestire; **to ~ to do
sth** riuscire a far qc; ~**able** *adj*
maneggevole; fattibile; ~**ment** *n*
amministrazione *f*, direzione *f*; ~**r** *n*
direttore *m*; (*of shop, restaurant*) gerente

m; (*of artist, SPORT*) manager *m inv*; ~**ress**
[-ə'rɛs] *n* direttrice *f*; gerente *f*; ~**rial**
[-ə'dʒɪərɪəl] *adj* dirigenziale; **managing
director** *n* amministratore *m* delegato

mandarin ['mændərɪn] *n* (*person, fruit*)
mandarino

mandatory ['mændətərɪ] *adj* obbli-
gatorio(a); ingiuntivo(a)

mane [meɪn] *n* criniera

maneuver *etc* [mə'nuːvə*] (*US*) =
manoeuvre *etc*

manfully ['mænfəlɪ] *adv* valorosamente

mangle ['mæŋgl] *vt* straziare; mutilare

mango ['mæŋgəu] (*pl* ~**es**) *n* mango

mangy ['meɪndʒɪ] *adj* rognoso(a)

manhandle ['mænhændl] *vt* malmenare

manhole ['mænhəul] *n* botola stradale

manhood ['mænhud] *n* età virile; virilità

man-hour *n* ora di lavoro

manhunt ['mænhʌnt] *n* caccia all'uomo

mania ['meɪnɪə] *n* mania; ~**c** ['meɪnɪæk] *n*
maniaco/a

manic ['mænɪk] *adj* (*behaviour, activity*)
maniacale

manicure ['mænɪkjuə*] *n* manicure *f inv*; ~
set *n* trousse *f inv* della manicure

manifest ['mænɪfɛst] *vt* manifestare ♦ *adj*
manifesto(a), palese

manifesto [mænɪ'fɛstəu] *n* manifesto

manipulate [mə'nɪpjuleɪt] *vt* manipolare

mankind [mæn'kaɪnd] *n* umanità, genere *m*
umano

manly ['mænlɪ] *adj* virile; coraggioso(a)

man-made *adj* sintetico(a); artificiale

manner ['mænə*] *n* maniera, modo;
(*behaviour*) modo di fare; (*type, sort*): **all ~
of things** ogni genere di cosa; ~**s** *npl*
(*conduct*) maniere *fpl*; **bad ~s**
maleducazione *f*; ~**ism** *n* vezzo, tic *m inv*

manoeuvre [mə'nuːvə*] (*US* **maneuver**) *vt*
manovrare ♦ *vi* far manovre ♦ *n* manovra

manor ['mænə*] *n* (*also*: ~ **house**) maniero

manpower ['mænpauə*] *n* manodopera

mansion ['mænʃən] *n* casa signorile

manslaughter ['mænslɔːtə*] *n* omicidio
preterintenzionale

mantelpiece ['mæntlpiːs] *n* mensola del

caminetto

manual ['mænjuəl] *adj* manuale ♦ *n* manuale *m*

manufacture [mænju'fæktʃə*] *vt* fabbricare ♦ *n* fabbricazione *f*, manifattura; **~r** *n* fabbricante *m*

manure [mə'njuə*] *n* concime *m*

manuscript ['mænjuskrɪpt] *n* manoscritto *m*

many ['mɛnɪ] *adj* molti(e) ♦ *pron* molti(e); **a great ~** moltissimi(e), un gran numero (di); **~ a time** molte volte

map [mæp] *n* carta (geografica); **~ out** *vt* tracciare un piano di

maple ['meɪpl] *n* acero

mar [mɑ:*] *vt* sciupare

marathon ['mærəθən] *n* maratona

marauder [mə'rɔ:də*] *n* saccheggiatore *m*

marble ['mɑ:bl] *n* marmo; (*toy*) pallina, bilia

March [mɑ:tʃ] *n* marzo

march [mɑ:tʃ] *vi* marciare; sfilare ♦ *n* marcia

mare [mɛə*] *n* giumenta

margarine [mɑ:dʒə'ri:n] *n* margarina

margin ['mɑ:dʒɪn] *n* margine *m*; **~al** (**seat**) *n* (POL) seggio elettorale ottenuto con una stretta maggioranza

marigold ['mærɪɡəʊld] *n* calendola

marina [mə'ri:nə] *n* marina

marine [mə'ri:n] *adj* (*animal, plant*) marino(a); (*forces, engineering*) marittimo(a) ♦ *n* (BRIT) fante *m* di marina; (US) marine *m inv*

marital ['mærɪtl] *adj* maritale, coniugale; **~ status** stato coniugale

mark [mɑ:k] *n* segno; (*stain*) macchia; (*of skid etc*) traccia; (BRIT: SCOL) voto; (SPORT) bersaglio; (*currency*) marco ♦ *vt* segnare; (*stain*) macchiare; (*indicate*) indicare; (BRIT: SCOL) dare un voto a; correggere; **to ~ time** segnare il passo; **~ed** *adj* spiccato(a), chiaro(a); **~er** *n* (*sign*) segno; (*bookmark*) segnalibro

market ['mɑ:kɪt] *n* mercato ♦ *vt* (COMM) mettere in vendita; **~ garden** (BRIT) *n* orto industriale; **~ing** *n* marketing *m*; **~ place** *n* piazza del mercato; (COMM) piazza, mercato; **~ research** *n* indagine *f or* ricerca di mercato

marksman ['mɑ:ksmən] *n* tiratore *m* scelto

marmalade ['mɑ:məleɪd] *n* marmellata d'arance

maroon [mə'ru:n] *vt* (*also fig*): **to be ~ed (in *or* at)** essere abbandonato(a) (in) ♦ *adj* bordeaux *inv*

marquee [mɑ:'ki:] *n* padiglione *m*

marquess ['mɑ:kwɪs] *n* = **marquis**

marquis ['mɑ:kwɪs] *n* marchese *m*

marriage ['mærɪdʒ] *n* matrimonio; **~ certificate** *n* certificato di matrimonio

married ['mærɪd] *adj* sposato(a); (*life, love*) coniugale, matrimoniale

marrow ['mærəʊ] *n* midollo; (*vegetable*) zucca

marry ['mærɪ] *vt* sposare, sposarsi con; (*subj: vicar, priest etc*) dare in matrimonio ♦ *vi* (*also:* **get married**) sposarsi

Mars [mɑ:z] *n* (*planet*) Marte *m*

marsh [mɑ:ʃ] *n* palude *f*

marshal ['mɑ:ʃl] *n* maresciallo; (US: *fire*) capo; (: *police*) capitano ♦ *vt* (*thoughts, support*) ordinare; (*soldiers*) adunare

martyr ['mɑ:tə*] *n* martire *m/f*; **~dom** *n* martirio

marvel ['mɑ:vl] *n* meraviglia ♦ *vi*: **to ~ (at)** meravigliarsi (di); **~lous** (US **~ous**) *adj* meraviglioso(a)

Marxist ['mɑ:ksɪst] *adj, n* marxista *m/f*

marzipan ['mɑ:zɪpæn] *n* marzapane *m*

mascara [mæs'kɑ:rə] *n* mascara *m*

masculine ['mæskjulɪn] *adj* maschile; (*woman*) mascolino(a)

mash [mæʃ] *vt* passare, schiacciare; **~ed potatoes** *npl* purè *m* di patate

mask [mɑ:sk] *n* maschera ♦ *vt* mascherare

mason ['meɪsn] *n* (*also:* **stone~**) scalpellino; (*also:* **free~**) massone *m*; **~ry** *n* muratura

masquerade [mæskə'reɪd] *vi*: **to ~ as** farsi passare per

mass [mæs] *n* moltitudine *f*, massa; (PHYSICS) massa; (REL) messa ♦ *cpd* di massa ♦ *vi* ammassarsi; **the ~es** *npl* (*ordinary people*) le masse; **~es of** (*inf*) una montagna di

massacre ['mæsəkə*] *n* massacro

massage ['mæsɑ:ʒ] *n* massaggio

masseur [mæˈsəːʳ] n massaggiatore m; **masseuse** [-ˈsəːz] n massaggiatrice f

massive [ˈmæsɪv] adj enorme, massiccio(a)

mass media npl mass media mpl

mass-production n produzione f in serie

mast [mɑːst] n albero

master [ˈmɑːstəʳ] n padrone m; (ART etc, teacher: in primary school) maestro; (: in secondary school) professore m; (title for boys): **M~ X** Signorino X ♦ vt domare; (learn) imparare a fondo; (understand) conoscere a fondo; **~ key** n chiave f maestra; **~ly** adj magistrale; **~mind** n mente f superiore ♦ vt essere il cervello di; **M~ of Arts/Science** n Master m inv in lettere/scienze; **~piece** n capolavoro; **~y** n dominio; padronanza

mat [mæt] n stuoia; (also: **door~**) stoino, zerbino; (also: **table ~**) sottopiatto ♦ adj = **matt**

match [mætʃ] n fiammifero; (game) partita, incontro; (fig) uguale m/f; matrimonio; partito ♦ vt intonare; (go well with) andare benissimo con; (equal) uguagliare; (correspond to) corrispondere a; (pair: also: **~ up**) accoppiare ♦ vi combaciare; **to be a good ~** andare bene; **~box** n scatola per fiammiferi; **~ing** adj ben assortito(a)

mate [meɪt] n compagno/a di lavoro; (inf: friend) amico/a; (animal) compagno/a; (in merchant navy) secondo ♦ vi accoppiarsi

material [məˈtɪərɪəl] n (substance) materiale m, materia; (cloth) stoffa ♦ adj materiale; **~s** npl (equipment) materiali mpl

maternal [məˈtəːnl] adj materno(a)

maternity [məˈtəːnɪtɪ] n maternità; **~ dress** n vestito m pre-maman inv; **~ hospital** n ≈ clinica ostetrica

math [mæθ] (US) n = **maths**

mathematical [mæθəˈmætɪkl] adj matematico(a)

mathematics [mæθəˈmætɪks] n matematica

maths [mæθs] (US **math**) n matematica

matinée [ˈmætɪneɪ] n matinée f inv

mating call [ˈmeɪtɪŋ-] n richiamo sessuale

matriculation [mətrɪkjuˈleɪʃən] n immatricolazione f

matrimonial [mætrɪˈməunɪəl] adj matrimoniale, coniugale

matrimony [ˈmætrɪmənɪ] n matrimonio

matron [ˈmeɪtrən] n (in hospital) capoinfermiera; (in school) infermiera

mat(t) [mæt] adj opaco(a)

matted [ˈmætɪd] adj ingarbugliato(a)

matter [ˈmætəʳ] n questione f; (PHYSICS) materia, sostanza; (content) contenuto; (MED: pus) pus m ♦ vi importare; **it doesn't ~** non importa; (I don't mind) non fa niente; **what's the ~?** che cosa c'è?; **no ~ what** qualsiasi cosa accada; **as a ~ of course** come cosa naturale; **as a ~ of fact** in verità; **~-of-fact** adj prosaico(a)

mattress [ˈmætrɪs] n materasso

mature [məˈtjuəʳ] adj maturo(a); (cheese) stagionato(a) ♦ vi maturare; stagionare

maul [mɔːl] vt lacerare

mauve [məuv] adj malva inv

maxim [ˈmæksɪm] n massima

maximum [ˈmæksɪməm] (pl **maxima**) adj massimo(a) ♦ n massimo

May [meɪ] n maggio

may [meɪ] (conditional: **might**) vi (indicating possibility): **he ~ come** può darsi che venga; (be allowed to): **~ I smoke?** posso fumare?; (wishes): **~ God bless you!** Dio la benedica!; **you ~ as well go** tanto vale che tu te ne vada

maybe [ˈmeɪbiː] adv forse, può darsi; **~ he'll ...** può darsi che lui ... +sub, forse lui ...

May Day n il primo maggio

mayhem [ˈmeɪhɛm] n cagnara

mayonnaise [meɪəˈneɪz] n maionese f

mayor [mɛəʳ] n sindaco; **~ess** n sindaco (donna); moglie f del sindaco

maze [meɪz] n labirinto, dedalo

M.D. abbr = **Doctor of Medicine**

me [miː] pron mi, m' +vowel or silent ''h''; (stressed, after prep) me; **he heard ~** mi ha or m'ha sentito; **give ~ a book** dammi (or mi dia) un libro; **it's ~** sono io; **with ~** con me; **without ~** senza di me

meadow [ˈmɛdəu] n prato

meagre [ˈmiːgəʳ] (US **meager**) adj magro(a)

meal [miːl] n pasto; (flour) farina; ~time n l'ora di mangiare

mean [miːn] (pt, pp meant) adj (with money) avaro(a), gretto(a); (unkind) meschino(a), maligno(a); (shabby) misero(a); (average) medio(a) ♦ vt (signify) significare, voler dire; (intend): to ~ to do aver l'intenzione di fare ♦ n mezzo; (MATH) media; ~s npl (way, money) mezzi mpl; by ~s of per mezzo di; by all ~s of per mezzo di; by all ~s ma certo, prego; to be meant for essere destinato(a) a; do you ~ it? dice sul serio?; what do you ~? che cosa vuol dire?

meander [mɪˈændə*] vi far meandri

meaning ['miːnɪŋ] n significato, senso; ~ful adj significativo(a); ~less adj senza senso

means [miːnz] npl mezzi mpl; by ~ of per mezzo di; (person) a mezzo di; by all ~ ma certo, prego

meant [mɛnt] pt, pp of mean

meantime ['miːntaɪm] adv (also: in the ~) nel frattempo

meanwhile ['miːnwaɪl] adv nel frattempo

measles ['miːzlz] n morbillo

measure ['mɛʒə*] vt, vi misurare ♦ n misura; (also: tape ~) metro; ~ments npl (size) misure fpl

meat [miːt] n carne f; cold ~ affettato; ~ball n polpetta di carne; ~ pie n pasticcio di carne in crosta

Mecca ['mɛkə] n (also fig) la Mecca

mechanic [mɪˈkænɪk] n meccanico; ~al adj meccanico(a); ~s n meccanica ♦ npl meccanismo

mechanism ['mɛkənɪzəm] n meccanismo

medal ['mɛdl] n medaglia; ~lion [mɪˈdæliən] n medaglione m; ~list (US ~ist) n (SPORT): to be a gold ~list essere medaglia d'oro

meddle ['mɛdl] vi: to ~ in immischiarsi in, mettere le mani in; to ~ with toccare

media ['miːdɪə] npl media mpl

mediaeval [mɛdɪˈiːvl] adj = medieval

median ['miːdɪən] (US) n (also: ~ strip) banchina f spartitraffico

mediate ['miːdɪeɪt] vi fare da mediatore/trice

Medicaid ® ['mɛdɪkeɪd] (US) n assistenza medica ai poveri

medical ['mɛdɪkl] adj medico(a) ♦ n visita medica

Medicare ® ['mɛdɪkeə*] (US) n assistenza medica agli anziani

medication [mɛdɪˈkeɪʃən] n medicinali mpl, farmaci mpl

medicine ['mɛdsɪn] n medicina

medieval [mɛdɪˈiːvl] adj medievale

mediocre [miːdɪˈəukə*] adj mediocre

meditate ['mɛdɪteɪt] vi: to ~ (on) meditare (su)

Mediterranean [mɛdɪtəˈreɪnɪən] adj mediterraneo(a); the ~ (Sea) il (mare) Mediterraneo

medium ['miːdɪəm] (pl media) adj medio(a) ♦ n (means) mezzo; (pl mediums: person) medium m inv; ~ wave n onde fpl medie

meek [miːk] adj dolce, umile

meet [miːt] (pt, pp met) vt incontrare; (for the first time) fare la conoscenza di; (go and fetch) andare a prendere; (fig) affrontare; soddisfare; raggiungere ♦ vi incontrarsi; (in session) riunirsi; (join: objects) unirsi; ~ with vt fus incontrare; ~ing n incontro; (session: of club etc) riunione f; (interview) intervista; she's at a ~ing (COMM) è in riunione

megabyte ['mɛgəbaɪt] n (COMPUT) megabyte m inv

megaphone ['mɛgəfəun] n megafono

melancholy ['mɛlənkəlɪ] n malinconia ♦ adj malinconico(a)

mellow ['mɛləu] adj (wine, sound) ricco(a); (light) dolce; (colour) caldo(a) ♦ vi (person) addolcirsi

melody ['mɛlədɪ] n melodia

melon ['mɛlən] n melone m

melt [mɛlt] vi (gen) sciogliersi, struggersi; (metals) fondersi ♦ vt sciogliere, struggere; fondere; ~ down vt fondere; ~down n (in nuclear reactor) fusione f (dovuta a surriscaldamento); ~ing pot n (fig) crogiolo

member ['mɛmbə*] n membro; M~ of the European Parliament (BRIT) n euro-deputato; M~ of Parliament (BRIT) n deputato/a; **M~ of the Scottish Parliament** (*BRIT*) *n* deputato/a del Parlamento scozzese; **~ship** *n* iscrizione *f*; (numero d')iscritti *mpl*, membri *mpl*; **~ship card** *n* tessera (di iscrizione)

memento [mə'mɛntəu] *n* ricordo, souvenir *m inv*

memo ['mɛməu] *n* appunto; (*COMM etc*) comunicazione *f* di servizio

memoirs ['mɛmwɑːz] *npl* memorie *fpl*, ricordi *mpl*

memorandum [mɛmə'rændəm] (*pl* **memoranda**) *n* appunto; (*COMM etc*) comunicazione *f* di servizio

memorial [mɪ'mɔːrɪəl] *n* monumento commemorativo ♦ *adj* commemorativo(a)

memorize ['mɛmərazz] *vt* memorizzare

memory ['mɛmərɪ] *n* (*also COMPUT*) memoria; (*recollection*) ricordo

men [mɛn] *npl of* **man**

menace ['mɛnəs] *n* minaccia ♦ *vt* minacciare

mend [mɛnd] *vt* aggiustare, riparare; (*darn*) rammendare ♦ *n*: **on the ~** in via di guarigione; **to ~ one's ways** correggersi

menial ['miːnɪəl] *adj* da servo, domestico(a); umile

meningitis [mɛnɪn'dʒaɪtɪs] *n* meningite *f*

menopause ['mɛnəupɔːz] *n* menopausa

menstruation [mɛnstru'eɪʃən] *n* mestruazione *f*

mental ['mɛntl] *adj* mentale

mentality [mɛn'tælɪtɪ] *n* mentalità *f inv*

menthol ['mɛnθɔl] *n* mentolo

mention ['mɛnʃən] *n* menzione *f* ♦ *vt* menzionare, far menzione di; **don't ~ it!** non c'è di che!, prego!

menu ['mɛnjuː] *n* (*set ~*, *COMPUT*) menù *m inv*; (*printed*) carta

MEP *n abbr* = **Member of the European Parliament**

merchandise ['mɜːtʃəndaɪz] *n* merci *fpl*

merchant ['mɜːtʃənt] *n* mercante *m*, commerciante *m*; **~ bank** (*BRIT*) *n* banca d'affari; **~ navy** (*US* = **marine**) *n* marina mercantile

merciful ['mɜːsɪful] *adj* pietoso(a), clemente

merciless ['mɜːsɪlɪs] *adj* spietato(a)

mercury ['mɜːkjurɪ] *n* mercurio

mercy ['mɜːsɪ] *n* pietà; (*REL*) misericordia; **at the ~ of** alla mercè di

mere [mɪə*] *adj* semplice; **by a ~ chance** per mero caso; **~ly** *adv* semplicemente, non ... che

merge [mɜːdʒ] *vt* unire ♦ *vi* fondersi, unirsi; (*COMM*) fondersi; **~r** *n* (*COMM*) fusione *f*

meringue [mə'ræŋ] *n* meringa

merit ['mɛrɪt] *n* merito, valore *m* ♦ *vt* meritare

mermaid ['mɜːmeɪd] *n* sirena

merry ['mɛrɪ] *adj* gaio(a), allegro(a); **M~ Christmas!** Buon Natale!; **~-go-round** *n* carosello

mesh [mɛʃ] *n* maglia; rete *f*

mesmerize ['mɛzməraɪz] *vt* ipnotizzare; affascinare

mess [mɛs] *n* confusione *f*, disordine *m*; (*fig*) pasticcio; (*dirt*) sporcizia; (*MIL*) mensa; **~ about** (*inf*) *vi* (*also*: **~ around**) trastullarsi; **~ about with** (*inf*) *vt fus* (*also*: **~ around with**) gingillarsi con; (*plans*) fare un pasticcio di; **~ up** *vt* sporcare; fare un pasticcio di; rovinare

message ['mɛsɪdʒ] *n* messaggio

messenger ['mɛsɪndʒə*] *n* messaggero/a

Messrs ['mɛsəz] *abbr* (*on letters*) Spett

messy ['mɛsɪ] *adj* sporco(a); disordinato(a)

met [mɛt] *pt*, *pp of* **meet**

metal ['mɛtl] *n* metallo; **~lic** [-'tælɪk] *adj* metallico(a)

metaphor ['mɛtəfə*] *n* metafora

meteorology [miːtɪə'rɔlədʒɪ] *n* meteorologia

meter ['miːtə*] *n* (*instrument*) contatore *m*; (*parking ~*) parchimetro; (*US: unit*) = **metre**

method ['mɛθəd] *n* metodo; **~ical** [mɪ'θɔdɪkl] *adj* metodico(a)

Methodist ['mɛθədɪst] *n* metodista *m/f*

meths [mɛθs] (*BRIT*) *n* = **methylated spirit**

methylated spirit ['mɛθɪleɪtɪd-] (*BRIT*) *n* alcool *m* denaturato

metre ['miːtə*] (*US* **meter**) *n* metro

metric ['mɛtrɪk] *adj* metrico(a)

metropolitan [mɛtrə'pɔlɪtən] *adj*

metropolitano(a); **the M~ Police** (*BRIT*) *n* la polizia di Londra

mettle ['mɛtl] *n*: **to be on one's ~** essere pronto(a) a dare il meglio di se stesso(a)

mew [mjuː] *vi* (*cat*) miagolare

mews [mjuːz] (*BRIT*) *n*: **~ flat** appartamento ricavato da un'antica scuderia

Mexico ['mɛksɪkəu] *n* Messico

miaow [miːˈau] *vi* miagolare

mice [maɪs] *npl of* **mouse**

micro... ['maɪkrəu] *prefix* micro...; **~chip** *n* microcircuito integrato; **~(computer)** *n* microcomputer *m inv*; **~phone** *n* microfono; **~scope** *n* microscopio; **~wave** *n* (*also*: **~wave oven**) forno a microonde

mid [mɪd] *adj*: **~ May** metà maggio; **~ afternoon** metà pomeriggio; **in ~ air** a mezz'aria; **~day** *n* mezzogiorno

middle ['mɪdl] *n* mezzo; centro; (*waist*) vita ♦ *adj* di mezzo; **in the ~ of the night** nel bel mezzo della notte; **~-aged** *adj* di mezza età; **the M~ Ages** *npl* il Medioevo; **~-class** *adj* ≈ borghese; **the ~ class(es)** *n(pl)* ≈ la borghesia; **M~ East** *n* Medio Oriente *m*; **~man** (*irreg*) *n* intermediario; agente *m* rivenditore; **~ name** *n* secondo nome *m*; **~-of-the-road** *adj* moderato(a); **~weight** *n* (*BOXING*) peso medio

middling ['mɪdlɪŋ] *adj* medio(a)

midge [mɪdʒ] *n* moscerino

midget ['mɪdʒɪt] *n* nano/a

Midlands ['mɪdləndz] *npl* contee del centro dell'Inghilterra

midnight ['mɪdnaɪt] *n* mezzanotte *f*

midriff ['mɪdrɪf] *n* diaframma *m*

midst [mɪdst] *n*: **in the ~ of** in mezzo a

midsummer [mɪdˈsʌmə*] *n* mezza *or* piena estate *f*

midway [mɪdˈweɪ] *adj, adv*: **~ (between)** a mezza strada (fra); **~ (through)** a metà (di)

midweek [mɪdˈwiːk] *adv* a metà settimana

midwife ['mɪdwaɪf] (*pl* **midwives**) *n* levatrice *f*

might [maɪt] *vb see* **may** ♦ *n* potere *m*, forza; **~y** *adj* forte, potente

migraine ['miːɡreɪn] *n* emicrania

migrant ['maɪɡrənt] *adj* (*bird*) migratore(trice); (*worker*) emigrato(a)

migrate [maɪˈɡreɪt] *vi* (*bird*) migrare; (*person*) emigrare

mike [maɪk] *n abbr* (= *microphone*) microfono

Milan [mɪˈlæn] *n* Milano *f*

mild [maɪld] *adj* mite; (*person, voice*) dolce; (*flavour*) delicato(a); (*illness*) leggero(a); (*interest*) blando(a) ♦ *n* (*beer*) birra leggera

mildew ['mɪldjuː] *n* muffa

mildly ['maɪldlɪ] *adv* mitemente; dolcemente; delicatamente; leggermente; blandamente; **to put it ~** a dire poco

mile [maɪl] *n* miglio; **~age** *n* distanza in miglia, ≈ chilometraggio

mileometer [maɪˈlɔmɪtə*] *n* ≈ conta-chilometri *m inv*

milestone ['maɪlstəun] *n* pietra miliare

milieu ['miːljəː] *n* ambiente *m*

militant ['mɪlɪtnt] *adj* militante

military ['mɪlɪtərɪ] *adj* militare

milk [mɪlk] *n* latte *m* ♦ *vt* (*cow*) mungere; (*fig*) sfruttare; **~ chocolate** *n* cioccolato al latte; **~man** (*irreg*) *n* lattaio; **~ shake** *n* frappé *m inv*; **~y** *adj* lattiginoso(a); (*colour*) latteo(a); **M~y Way** *n* Via Lattea

mill [mɪl] *n* mulino; (*small: for coffee, pepper etc*) macinino; (*factory*) fabbrica; (*spinning ~*) filatura ♦ *vt* macinare ♦ *vi* (*also*: **~ about**) brulicare

millennia [mɪˈlɛnɪə] *npl of* **millennium**

millennium [mɪˈlɛnɪəm] (*pl* **~s** *or* **millennia**) *n* millennio; **~ bug** *n* baco di fine millennio

miller ['mɪlə*] *n* mugnaio

milli... ['mɪlɪ] *prefix*: **~gram(me)** *n* milligrammo; **~metre** (*US* **~meter**) *n* millimetro

million ['mɪljən] *n* milione *m*; **~aire** *n* milionario, ≈ miliardario

milometer [maɪˈlɔmɪtə*] *n* = **mileometer**

mime [maɪm] *n* mimo ♦ *vt, vi* mimare

mimic ['mɪmɪk] *n* imitatore/trice ♦ *vt* fare la mimica di

min. *abbr* = **minute(s)**; **minimum**

mince [mɪns] *vt* tritare, macinare ♦ *n* (*BRIT*:

CULIN) carne *f* tritata *or* macinata; **~meat** *n* frutta secca tritata per uso in pasticceria; *(US)* carne *f* tritata *or* macinata; **~ pie** *n* specie di torta con frutta secca; **~r** *n* tritacarne *m inv*

mind [maɪnd] *n* mente *f* ♦ *vt (attend to, look after)* badare a, occuparsi di; *(be careful)* fare attenzione a, stare attento(a) a; *(object to):* **I don't ~ the noise** il rumore non mi dà alcun fastidio; **I don't ~** non m'importa; **it is on my ~** mi preoccupa; **to my ~** secondo me, a mio parere; **to be out of one's ~** essere uscito(a) di mente; **to keep** *or* **bear sth in ~** non dimenticare qc; **to make up one's ~** decidersi; **~ you, ...** sì, però va detto che ...; **never ~** non importa, non fa niente; *(don't worry)* non preoccuparti; **"~ the step"** "attenzione allo scalino"; **~er** *n (child ~er)* bambinaia; *(bodyguard)* guardia del corpo; **~less** *adj* idiota

mine[1] [maɪn] *pron* il(la) mio(a), *pl* i(le) miei(mie); **that book is ~** quel libro è mio; **yours is red, ~ is green** il tuo è rosso, il mio è verde; **a friend of ~** un mio amico

mine[2] [maɪn] *n* miniera; *(explosive)* mina ♦ *vt (coal)* estrarre; *(ship, beach)* minare; **~field** *n (also fig)* campo minato

miner [maɪnə*] *n* minatore *m*

mineral [mɪnərəl] *adj* minerale ♦ *n* minerale *m*; **~s** *npl (BRIT: soft drinks)* bevande *fpl* gasate; **~ water** *n* acqua minerale

mingle [mɪŋgl] *vi:* **to ~ with** mescolarsi a, mischiarsi con

miniature [mɪnətʃə*] *adj* in miniatura ♦ *n* miniatura

minibus [mɪnɪbʌs] *n* minibus *m inv*

Minidisc® [mɪnɪdɪsk] *n* minidisc *m inv*

minim [mɪnɪm] *n (MUS)* minima

minimum [mɪnɪməm] *(pl* **minima)** *n* minimo ♦ *adj* minimo(a)

mining [maɪnɪŋ] *n* industria mineraria

miniskirt [mɪnɪskəːt] *n* minigonna

minister [mɪnɪstə*] *n (BRIT: POL)* ministro; *(REL)* pastore *m;* **to ~ to sb's needs** provvedere ai bisogni di qn

ministry [mɪnɪstrɪ] *n (BRIT: POL)* ministero; *(REL):* **to go into the ~** diventare pastore

mink [mɪŋk] *n* visone *m*

minnow [mɪnəu] *n* pesciolino d'acqua dolce

minor [maɪnə*] *adj* minore, di poca importanza; *(MUS)* minore ♦ *n (LAW)* minorenne *m/f*

minority [maɪˈnɔrɪtɪ] *n* minoranza

mint [mɪnt] *n (plant)* menta; *(sweet)* pasticca di menta ♦ *vt (coins)* battere; **the (Royal) M~** *(BRIT)*, **the (US) M~** *(US)* la Zecca; **in ~ condition** come nuovo(a) di zecca

minus [maɪnəs] *n (also: ~ **sign)** segno meno ♦ *prep* meno

minute [*adj* maɪˈnjuːt, *n* ˈmɪnɪt] *adj* minuscolo(a); *(detail)* minuzioso(a) ♦ *n* minuto; **~s** *npl (of meeting)* verbale *m*

miracle [mɪrəkl] *n* miracolo

mirage [mɪrɑːʒ] *n* miraggio

mirror [mɪrə*] *n* specchio; *(in car)* specchietto

mirth [məːθ] *n* ilarità

misadventure [mɪsədˈventʃə*] *n* disavventura; **death by ~** morte *f* accidentale

misapprehension [mɪsæprɪˈhenʃən] *n* malinteso

misappropriate [mɪsəˈprəuprɪeɪt] *vt* appropriarsi indebitamente di

misbehave [mɪsbɪˈheɪv] *vi* comportarsi male

miscarriage [mɪskærɪdʒ] *n (MED)* aborto spontaneo; **~ of justice** errore *m* giudiziario

miscellaneous [mɪsɪˈleɪnɪəs] *adj (items)* vario(a); *(selection)* misto(a)

mischance [mɪsˈtʃɑːns] *n* sfortuna

mischief [mɪstʃɪf] *n (naughtiness)* birichineria; *(maliciousness)* malizia; **mischievous** *adj* birichino(a)

misconception [mɪskənˈsepʃən] *n* idea sbagliata

misconduct [mɪsˈkɔndʌkt] *n* cattiva condotta; **professional ~** reato professionale

misdemeanour [mɪsdɪˈmiːnə*] *(US* **misdemeanor)** *n* misfatto; infrazione *f*

miser [maɪzə*] *n* avaro

miserable ['mɪzərəbl] *adj* infelice; (*wretched*) miserabile; (*weather*) deprimente; (*offer, failure*) misero(a)

miserly ['maɪzəlɪ] *adj* avaro(a)

misery ['mɪzərɪ] *n* (*unhappiness*) tristezza; (*wretchedness*) miseria

misfire [mɪs'faɪə*] *vi* far cilecca; (*car engine*) perdere colpi

misfit ['mɪsfɪt] *n* (*person*) spostato/a

misfortune [mɪs'fɔ:tʃən] *n* sfortuna

misgiving [mɪs'gɪvɪŋ] *n* apprensione *f*; **to have ~s about** avere dei dubbi per quanto riguarda

misguided [mɪs'gaɪdɪd] *adj* sbagliato(a); poco giudizioso(a)

mishandle [mɪs'hændl] *vt* (*mismanage*) trattare male

mishap ['mɪshæp] *n* disgrazia

misinterpret [mɪsɪn'tə:prɪt] *vt* interpretare male

misjudge [mɪs'dʒʌdʒ] *vt* giudicare male

mislay [mɪs'leɪ] (*irreg*) *vt* smarrire

mislead [mɪs'li:d] (*irreg*) *vt* sviare; **~ing** *adj* ingannevole

mismanage [mɪs'mænɪdʒ] *vt* gestire male

misplace [mɪs'pleɪs] *vt* smarrire

misprint ['mɪsprɪnt] *n* errore *m* di stampa

Miss [mɪs] *n* Signorina

miss [mɪs] *vt* (*fail to get*) perdere; (*fail to hit*) mancare; (*fail to see*): **you can't ~ it** non puoi non vederlo; (*regret the absence of*): **I ~ him** sento la sua mancanza ♦ *vi* mancare ♦ *n* (*shot*) colpo mancato; **~ out** (*BRIT*) *vt* omettere

misshapen [mɪs'ʃeɪpən] *adj* deforme

missile ['mɪsaɪl] *n* (*MIL*) missile *m*; (*object thrown*) proiettile *m*

missing ['mɪsɪŋ] *adj* perso(a), smarrito(a); (*person*) scomparso(a); (: *after disaster, MIL*) disperso(a); (*removed*) mancante; **to be ~** mancare

mission ['mɪʃən] *n* missione *f*; **~ary** *n* missionario/a

mist [mɪst] *n* nebbia, foschia ♦ *vi* (*also: ~ over, ~ up*) annebbiarsi; (: *BRIT: windows*) appannarsi

mistake [mɪs'teɪk] (*irreg: like* **take**) *n* sbaglio, errore *m* ♦ *vt* sbagliarsi di; fraintendere; **to make a ~** fare uno sbaglio, sbagliare; **by ~** per sbaglio; **to ~ for** prendere per; **mistaken** *pp of* **mistake** ♦ *adj* (*idea etc*) sbagliato(a); **to be mistaken** sbagliarsi

mister ['mɪstə*] (*inf*) *n* signore *m*; *see* **Mr**

mistletoe ['mɪsltəʊ] *n* vischio

mistook [mɪs'tʊk] *pt of* **mistake**

mistress ['mɪstrɪs] *n* padrona; (*lover*) amante *f*; (*BRIT: SCOL*) insegnante *f*

mistrust [mɪs'trʌst] *vt* diffidare di

misty ['mɪstɪ] *adj* nebbioso(a), brumoso(a)

misunderstand [mɪsʌndə'stænd] (*irreg*) *vt*, *vi* capire male, fraintendere; **~ing** *n* malinteso, equivoco

misuse [*n* mɪs'ju:s, *vb* mɪs'ju:z] *n* cattivo uso; (*of power*) abuso ♦ *vt* far cattivo uso di; abusare di

mitigate ['mɪtɪgeɪt] *vt* mitigare

mitt(en) ['mɪt(n)] *n* mezzo guanto; manopola

mix [mɪks] *vt* mescolare ♦ *vi* (*people*): **to ~ with** avere a che fare con ♦ *n* mescolanza; preparato; **~ up** *vt* mescolare; (*confuse*) confondere; **~ed** *adj* misto(a); **~ed-up** *adj* (*confused*) confuso(a); **~er** *n* (*for food: electric*) frullatore *m*; (: *hand*) frullino; (*person*): **he is a good ~er** è molto socievole; **~ture** *n* mescolanza; (*blend: of tobacco etc*) miscela; (*MED*) sciroppo; **~-up** *n* confusione *f*

moan [məʊn] *n* gemito ♦ *vi* (*inf: complain*): **to ~ (about)** lamentarsi (di)

moat [məʊt] *n* fossato

mob [mɔb] *n* calca ♦ *vt* accalcarsi intorno a

mobile ['məʊbaɪl] *adj* mobile ♦ *n* (*decoration*) mobile *m*; **~ home** *n* grande roulotte *f inv* (utilizzata come domicilio); **~ phone** *n* telefono portatile, telefonino

mock [mɔk] *vt* deridere, burlarsi di ♦ *adj* falso(a); **~ery** *n* derisione *f*; **to make a ~ery of** burlarsi di; (*exam*) rendere una farsa; **~-up** *n* modello

mod [mɔd] *adj see* **convenience**

mode [məʊd] *n* modo

model ['mɔdl] *n* modello; (*person: for*

fashion) indossatore/trice; (: *for artist*)
modello/a ♦ *adj* (*small-scale: railway etc*) in
miniatura; (*child, factory*) modello *inv* ♦ *vt*
modellare ♦ *vi* fare l'indossatore (*or*
l'indossatrice); **to ~ clothes** presentare
degli abiti
modem ['məudɛm] *n* modem *m inv*
moderate [*adj* 'mɔdərət, *vb* 'mɔdəreɪt] *adj*
moderato(a) ♦ *vi* moderarsi, placarsi ♦ *vt*
moderare
modern ['mɔdən] *adj* moderno(a); **~ize** *vt*
modernizzare
modest ['mɔdɪst] *adj* modesto(a); **~y** *n*
modestia
modify ['mɔdɪfaɪ] *vt* modificare
mogul ['məugl] *n* (*fig*) magnate *m*, pezzo
grosso
mohair ['məuheə*] *n* mohair *m*
moist [mɔɪst] *adj* umido(a); **~en** ['mɔɪsn] *vt*
inumidire; **~ure** ['mɔɪstʃə*] *n* umidità; (*on
glass*) goccioline *fpl* di vapore; **~urizer**
['mɔɪstʃəraɪzə*] *n* idratante *f*
molar ['məulə*] *n* molare *m*
mold [məuld] (*US*) *n, vt* = **mould**
mole [məul] *n* (*animal, fig*) talpa; (*spot*) neo
molest [məu'lɛst] *vt* molestare
mollycoddle ['mɔlɪkɔdl] *vt* coccolare,
vezzeggiare
molt [məult] (*US*) *vi* = **moult**
molten ['məultən] *adj* fuso(a)
mom [mɔm] (*US*) *n* = **mum**
moment ['məumənt] *n* momento, istante
m; **at that ~** in quel momento; **at the ~** al
momento, in questo momento; **~ary** *adj*
momentaneo(a), passeggero(a); **~ous**
[-'mɛntəs] *adj* di grande importanza
momentum [məu'mɛntəm] *n* (*PHYSICS*)
momento; (*fig*) impeto; **to gather ~**
aumentare di velocità
mommy ['mɔmɪ] (*US*) *n* = **mummy**
Monaco ['mɔnəkəu] *n* Principato di Monaco
monarch ['mɔnək] *n* monarca *m*; **~y** *n*
monarchia
monastery ['mɔnəstərɪ] *n* monastero
Monday ['mʌndɪ] *n* lunedì *m inv*
monetary ['mʌnɪtərɪ] *adj* monetario(a)
money ['mʌnɪ] *n* denaro, soldi *mpl*; **~ belt**

n marsupio (*per soldi*); **~ order** *n* vaglia *m
inv*; **~-spinner** (*inf*) *n* miniera d'oro (*fig*)
mongol ['mɔŋgəl] *adj, n* (*MED*) mongoloide
m/f
mongrel ['mʌŋgrəl] *n* (*dog*) cane *m*
bastardo
monitor ['mɔnɪtə*] *n* (*TV, COMPUT*) monitor
m inv ♦ *vt* controllare
monk [mʌŋk] *n* monaco
monkey ['mʌŋkɪ] *n* scimmia; **~ nut** (*BRIT*) *n*
nocciolina americana; **~ wrench** *n* chiave
f a rullino
mono ['mɔnəu] *adj* (*recording*) (in) mono
inv
monopoly [mə'nɔpəlɪ] *n* monopolio
monotone ['mɔnətəun] *n* pronunzia (*or*
voce *f*) monotona
monotonous [mə'nɔtənəs] *adj*
monotono(a)
monsoon [mɔn'su:n] *n* monsone *m*
monster ['mɔnstə*] *n* mostro
monstrous ['mɔnstrəs] *adj* mostruoso(a);
(*huge*) gigantesco(a)
month [mʌnθ] *n* mese *m*; **~ly** *adj* mensile
♦ *adv* al mese; ogni mese
monument ['mɔnjumənt] *n* monumento
moo [mu:] *vi* muggire, mugghiare
mood [mu:d] *n* umore *m*; **to be in a
good/bad ~** essere di buon/cattivo umore;
~y *adj* (*variable*) capriccioso(a), lunatico(a);
(*sullen*) imbronciato(a)
moon [mu:n] *n* luna; **~light** *n* chiaro di
luna; **~lighting** *n* lavoro nero; **~lit** *adj*: **a
~lit night** una notte rischiarata dalla luna
Moor [muə*] *n* moro/a
moor [muə*] *n* brughiera ♦ *vt* (*ship*)
ormeggiare ♦ *vi* ormeggiarsi
moorland ['muələnd] *n* brughiera
moose [mu:s] *n inv* alce *m*
mop [mɔp] *n* lavapavimenti *m inv*; (*also: ~
of hair*) zazzera ♦ *vt* lavare con lo straccio;
(*face*) asciugare; **~ up** *vt* asciugare con
uno straccio
mope [məup] *vi* fare il broncio
moped ['məupɛd] *n* (*BRIT*) ciclomotore *m*
moral ['mɔrl] *adj* morale ♦ *n* morale *f*; **~s**
npl (*principles*) moralità

morality [mə'rælıtı] *n* moralità
morass [mə'ræs] *n* palude *f*, pantano
morbid ['mɔːbıd] *adj* morboso(a)

KEYWORD
---

more [mɔː*] *adj* 1 (*greater in number etc*)
più; **~ people/letters than we expected**
più persone/lettere di quante ne
aspettavamo; **I have ~ wine/money than
you** ho più vino/soldi di te; **I have ~ wine
than beer** ho più vino che birra
2 (*additional*) altro(a), ancora; **do you
want (some) ~ tea?** vuole dell'altro tè?,
vuole ancora del tè?; **I have no** *or* **I don't
have any ~ money** non ho più soldi
♦ *pron* 1 (*greater amount*) più; **~ than 10**
più di 10; **it cost ~ than we expected** ha
costato più di quanto ci aspettavamo
2 (*further or additional amount*) ancora; **is
there any ~?** ce n'è ancora?; **there's no ~**
non ce n'è più; **a little ~** ancora un po';
many/much ~ molti(e)/molto(a) di più
♦ *adv*: **~ dangerous/easily (than)** più
pericoloso/facilmente (di); **~ and ~** sempre
di più; **~ and ~ difficult** sempre più
difficile; **~ or less** più o meno; **~ than ever**
più che mai

---

moreover [mɔː'rəuvə*] *adv* inoltre, di più
morgue [mɔːg] *n* obitorio
morning ['mɔːnıŋ] *n* mattina, mattino;
(*duration*) mattinata ♦ *cpd* del mattino; **in
the ~** la mattina; **7 o'clock in the ~** le 7 di
or della mattina; **~ sickness** *n* nausee *fpl*
mattutine
Morocco [mə'rɔkəu] *n* Marocco
moron ['mɔːrɔn] (*inf*) *n* deficiente *m/f*
morose [mə'rəus] *adj* cupo(a), tetro(a)
Morse [mɔːs] *n* (*also*: **~ code**) alfabeto
Morse
morsel ['mɔːsl] *n* boccone *m*
mortal ['mɔːtl] *adj* mortale ♦ *n* mortale *m*
mortgage ['mɔːgıdʒ] *n* ipoteca; (*loan*)
prestito ipotecario ♦ *vt* ipotecare; **~
company** (*US*) *n* società *f inv* di credito
immobiliare
mortuary ['mɔːtjuərı] *n* camera mortuaria;

obitorio
mosaic [məu'zeıık] *n* mosaico
Moscow ['mɔskəu] *n* Mosca
Moslem ['mɔzləm] *adj*, *n* = **Muslim**
mosque [mɔsk] *n* moschea
mosquito [mɔs'kiːtəu] (*pl* **~es**) *n* zanzara
moss [mɔs] *n* muschio
most [məust] *adj* (*almost all*) la maggior
parte di; (*largest, greatest*): **who has (the)
~ money?** chi ha più soldi di tutti? ♦ *pron*
la maggior parte ♦ *adv* più; (*work, sleep
etc*) di più; (*very*) molto, estremamente;
the ~ (*also*: +*adjective*) il(la) più; **~ of** la
maggior parte di; **~ of them** quasi tutti; **I
saw (the) ~** ho visto più io; **at the (very) ~**
al massimo; **to make the ~ of** trarre il
massimo vantaggio da; **a ~ interesting
book** un libro estremamente interessante;
~ly *adv* per lo più
MOT (*BRIT*) *n abbr* (= *Ministry of Transport*):
the ~ (test) *revisione annuale obbligatoria
degli autoveicoli*
motel [məu'tel] *n* motel *m inv*
moth [mɔθ] *n* farfalla notturna; tarma
mother ['mʌðə*] *n* madre *f* ♦ *vt* (*care for*)
fare da madre a; **~hood** *n* maternità; **~-
in-law** *n* suocera; **~ly** *adj* materno(a); **~-
of-pearl** [mʌðərəv'pəːl] *n* madreperla; **~-
to-be** [mʌðətə'biː] *n* futura mamma; **~
tongue** *n* madrelingua
motion ['məuʃən] *n* movimento, moto;
(*gesture*) gesto; (*at meeting*) mozione *f*
♦ *vt, vi*: **to ~ (to) sb to do** fare cenno a qn
di fare; **~less** *adj* immobile; **~ picture** *n*
film *m inv*
motivated ['məutıveıtıd] *adj* motivato(a)
motive ['məutıv] *n* motivo
motley ['mɔtlı] *adj* eterogeneo(a), molto
vario(a)
motor ['məutə*] *n* motore *m*; (*BRIT*: *inf*:
vehicle) macchina ♦ *cpd* automobilistico(a);
~bike *n* moto *f inv*; **~boat** *n* motoscafo;
~car (*BRIT*) *n* automobile *f*; **~cycle** *n*
motocicletta; **~cyclist** *n* motociclista *m/f*;
~ing (*BRIT*) *n* turismo automobilistico; **~ist**
n automobilista *m/f*; **~ racing** (*BRIT*) *n*
corse *fpl* automobilistiche; **~way** (*BRIT*) *n*

autostrada

mottled ['mɔtld] *adj* chiazzato(a), marezzato(a)

motto ['mɔtəu] (*pl* **~es**) *n* motto

mould [məuld] (*US* **mold**) *n* forma, stampo; (*mildew*) muffa ♦ *vt* formare; (*fig*) foggiare; **~y** *adj* ammuffito(a); (*smell*) di muffa

moult [məult] (*US* **molt**) *vi* far la muta

mound [maund] *n* rialzo, collinetta; (*heap*) mucchio

mount [maunt] *n* (*GEO*) monte *m* ♦ *vt* montare; (*horse*) montare a ♦ *vi* (*increase*) aumentare; **~ up** *vi* (*build up*) accumularsi

mountain ['mauntɪn] *n* montagna ♦ *cpd* di montagna; **~ bike** *n* mountain bike *f inv*; **~eer** [-'nɪə*] *n* alpinista *m/f*; **~eering** [-'nɪərɪŋ] *n* alpinismo; **~ous** *adj* montagnoso(a); **~ rescue team** *n* squadra di soccorso alpino; **~side** *n* fianco della montagna

mourn [mɔ:n] *vt* piangere, lamentare ♦ *vi*: **to ~ (for sb)** piangere (la morte di qn); **~er** *n* parente *m/f* o amico/a del defunto; **~ing** *n* lutto; **in ~ing** in lutto

mouse [maus] (*pl* **mice**) *n* topo; (*COMPUT*) mouse *m inv*; **~ mat**, **~ pad** *n* (*COMPUT*) tappetino del mouse; **~trap** *n* trappola per i topi

mousse [mu:s] *n* mousse *f inv*

moustache [məs'tɑ:ʃ] (*US* **mustache**) *n* baffi *mpl*

mousy ['mausɪ] *adj* (*hair*) né chiaro né scuro(a)

mouth [mauθ, *pl* mauðz] *n* bocca; (*of river*) bocca, foce *f*; (*opening*) orifizio; **~ful** *n* boccata; **~ organ** *n* armonica; **~piece** *n* (*MUS*) imboccatura, bocchino; (*spokesman*) portavoce *m/f inv*; **~wash** *n* collutorio; **~-watering** *adj* che fa venire l'acquolina in bocca

movable ['mu:vəbl] *adj* mobile

move [mu:v] *n* (*movement*) movimento; (*in game*) mossa; (: *turn to play*) turno; (*change: of house*) trasloco; (: *of job*) cambiamento ♦ *vt* muovere, spostare; (*emotionally*) commuovere; (*POL: resolution etc*) proporre ♦ *vi* (*gen*) muoversi, spostarsi; (*also:* ~ **house**) cambiar casa, traslocare; **to get a ~ on**

affrettarsi, sbrigarsi; **to ~ sb to do sth** indurre *or* spingere qn a fare qc; **to ~ towards** andare verso; **~ about** *or* **around** *vi* spostarsi; **~ along** *vi* muoversi avanti; **~ away** *vi* allontanarsi, andarsene; **~ back** *vi* (*return*) ritornare; **~ forward** *vi* avanzare; **~ in** *vi* (*to a house*) entrare (in una nuova casa); (*police etc*) intervenire; **~ on** *vi* riprendere la strada; **~ out** *vi* (*of house*) sgombrare; **~ over** *vi* spostarsi; **~ up** *vi* avanzare

moveable ['mu:vəbl] *adj* = **movable**

movement ['mu:vmənt] *n* (*gen*) movimento; (*gesture*) gesto; (*of stars, water, physical*) moto

movie ['mu:vɪ] *n* film *m inv*; **the ~s** il cinema

moviecamera *n* cinepresa

moving ['mu:vɪŋ] *adj* mobile; (*causing emotion*) commovente

mow [məu] (*pt* **mowed**, *pp* **mowed** *or* **mown**) *vt* (*grass*) tagliare; (*corn*) mietere; **~ down** *vt* falciare; **~er** *n* (*also:* **lawnmower**) tagliaerba *m inv*

MP *n abbr* = **Member of Parliament**

MP3 *n abbr* M3

m.p.h. *n abbr* = *miles per hour* (60 m.p.h. = 96 km/h)

Mr ['mɪstə*] (*US* **Mr.**) *n*: **~ X** Signor X, Sig. X

Mrs ['mɪsɪz] (*US* **Mrs.**) *n*: **~ X** Signora X, Sig.ra X

Ms [mɪz] (*US* **Ms.**) *n* (= *Miss or Mrs*): **~ X** ≈ Signora X, Sig.ra X

M.Sc. *abbr* = **Master of Science**

MSP *n abbr* = **Member of the Scottish Parliament**

KEYWORD

---

much [mʌtʃ] *adj*, *pron* molto(a); **he's done so ~ work** ha lavorato così tanto; **I have as ~ money as you** ho tanti soldi quanti ne hai tu; **how ~ is it?** quant'è?; **it costs too ~** costa troppo; **as ~ as you want** quanto vuoi ♦ *adv* **1** (*greatly*) molto, tanto; **thank you very ~** molte grazie; **he's very ~ the gentleman** è il vero gentiluomo; **I read as ~ as I can** leggo quanto posso; **as ~ as you** tanto quanto te

2 (*by far*) molto; **it's ~ the biggest**

company in Europe è di gran lunga la più grossa società in Europa
3 (*almost*) grossomodo, praticamente; **they're ~ the same** sono praticamente uguali

---

muck [mʌk] *n* (*dirt*) sporcizia; **~ about** *or* **around** (*inf*) *vi* fare lo stupido; (*waste time*) gingillarsi; **~ up** (*inf*) *vt* (*ruin*) rovinare

mud [mʌd] *n* fango

muddle ['mʌdl] *n* confusione *f*, disordine *m*; pasticcio ♦ *vt* (*also*: **~ up**) confondere; **~ through** *vi* cavarsela alla meno peggio

muddy ['mʌdɪ] *adj* fangoso(a)

mudguard ['mʌdgɑːd] *n* parafango

muesli ['mjuːzlɪ] *n* muesli *m*

muffin ['mʌfɪn] *n specie di pasticcino soffice da tè*

muffle ['mʌfl] *vt* (*sound*) smorzare, attutire; (*against cold*) imbacuccare

muffler ['mʌflə*] (*US*) *n* (*AUT*) marmitta; (: *on motorbike*) silenziatore *m*

mug [mʌg] *n* (*cup*) tazzone *m*; (*for beer*) boccale *m*; (*inf*: *face*) muso; (: *fool*) scemo/a ♦ *vt* (*assault*) assalire; **~ging** *n* assalto

muggy ['mʌgɪ] *adj* afoso(a)

mule [mjuːl] *n* mulo

multi-level ['mʌltɪ-] (*US*) *adj* = **multistorey**

multiple ['mʌltɪpl] *adj* multiplo(a); molteplice ♦ *n* multiplo; **~ sclerosis** *n* sclerosi *f* a placche

multiplex cinema ['mʌltɪpleks-] *n* cinema *m inv* multisala *inv*

multiplication [mʌltɪplɪ'keɪʃən] *n* moltiplicazione *f*

multiply ['mʌltɪplaɪ] *vt* moltiplicare ♦ *vi* moltiplicarsi

multistorey ['mʌltɪ'stɔːrɪ] (*BRIT*) *adj* (*building, car park*) a più piani

mum [mʌm] (*BRIT*: *inf*) *n* mamma ♦ *adj*: **to keep ~** non aprire bocca

mumble ['mʌmbl] *vt*, *vi* borbottare

mummy ['mʌmɪ] *n* (*BRIT*: *mother*) mamma; (*embalmed*) mummia

mumps [mʌmps] *n* orecchioni *mpl*

munch [mʌntʃ] *vt*, *vi* sgranocchiare

mundane [mʌn'deɪn] *adj* terra a terra *inv*

municipal [mjuː'nɪsɪpl] *adj* municipale

mural ['mjuərl] *n* dipinto murale

murder ['mɜːdə*] *n* assassinio, omicidio ♦ *vt* assassinare; **~er** *n* omicida *m*, assassino; **~ous** *adj* omicida

murky ['mɜːkɪ] *adj* tenebroso(a)

murmur ['mɜːmə*] *n* mormorio ♦ *vt*, *vi* mormorare

muscle ['mʌsl] *n* muscolo; (*fig*) forza; **~ in** *vi* immischiarsi

muscular ['mʌskjulə*] *adj* muscolare; (*person, arm*) muscoloso(a)

muse [mjuːz] *vi* meditare, sognare ♦ *n* musa

museum [mjuː'zɪəm] *n* museo

mushroom ['mʌʃrum] *n* fungo ♦ *vi* crescere in fretta

music ['mjuːzɪk] *n* musica; **~al** *adj* musicale; (*person*) portato(a) per la musica ♦ *n* (*show*) commedia musicale; **~al instrument** *n* strumento musicale; **~ hall** *n* teatro di varietà; **~ian** [-'zɪʃən] *n* musicista *m/f*

Muslim ['mʌzlɪm] *adj*, *n* musulmano(a)

muslin ['mʌzlɪn] *n* mussola

mussel ['mʌsl] *n* cozza

must [mʌst] *aux vb* (*obligation*): **I ~ do it** devo farlo; (*probability*): **he ~ be there by now** dovrebbe essere arrivato ormai; **I ~ have made a mistake** devo essermi sbagliato ♦ *n*: **it's a ~** è d'obbligo

mustache ['mʌstæʃ] (*US*) *n* = **moustache**

mustard ['mʌstəd] *n* senape *f*, mostarda

muster ['mʌstə*] *vt* radunare

mustn't ['mʌsnt] = **must not**

musty ['mʌstɪ] *adj* che sa di muffa *or* di rinchiuso

mute [mjuːt] *adj*, *n* muto(a)

muted ['mjuːtɪd] *adj* smorzato(a)

mutiny ['mjuːtɪnɪ] *n* ammutinamento

mutter ['mʌtə*] *vt*, *vi* borbottare, brontolare

mutton ['mʌtn] *n* carne *f* di montone

mutual ['mjuːtʃuəl] *adj* mutuo(a), reciproco(a); **~ly** *adv* reciprocamente

muzzle ['mʌzl] *n* muso; (*protective device*) museruola; (*of gun*) bocca ♦ *vt* mettere la museruola a

my [maɪ] *adj* il(la) mio(a), *pl* i(le) miei(mie);
~ **house** la mia casa; ~ **books** i miei libri; ~
brother mio fratello; **I've washed ~ hair/
cut ~ finger** mi sono lavato i capelli/
tagliato il dito

myself [maɪ'sɛlf] *pron* (*reflexive*) mi;
(*emphatic*) io stesso(a); (*after prep*) me; *see
also* **oneself**

mysterious [mɪs'tɪərɪəs] *adj* misterioso(a)

mystery [ˈmɪstərɪ] *n* mistero

mystify [ˈmɪstɪfaɪ] *vt* mistificare; (*puzzle*)
confondere

mystique [mɪs'tiːk] *n* fascino

myth [mɪθ] *n* mito

mythology [mɪˈθɔlədʒɪ] *n* mitologia

N, n

n/a *abbr* = **not applicable**

nag [næg] *vt* tormentare ♦ *vi* brontolare in
continuazione; ~**ging** *adj* (*doubt, pain*)
persistente

nail [neɪl] *n* (*human*) unghia; (*metal*) chiodo
♦ *vt* inchiodare; **to ~ sb down to (doing)
sth** costringere qn a (fare) qc; ~**brush** *n*
spazzolino da *or* per unghie; ~**file** *n* lima
da *or* per unghie; ~ **polish** *n* smalto da *or*
per unghie; ~ **polish remover** *n* acetone
m, solvente *m*; ~ **scissors** *npl* forbici *fpl*
da *or* per unghie; ~ **varnish** (*BRIT*) *n* = ~
polish

naïve [naɪ'iːv] *adj* ingenuo(a)

naked [ˈneɪkɪd] *adj* nudo(a)

name [neɪm] *n* nome *m*; (*reputation*) nome,
reputazione *f* ♦ *vt* (*baby etc*) chiamare;
(*plant, illness*) nominare; (*person, object*)
identificare; (*price, date*) fissare; **what's
your ~?** come si chiama?; **by ~** di nome;
she knows them all by ~ li conosce tutti
per nome; ~**ly** *adv* cioè; ~**sake** *n*
omonimo

nanny [ˈnænɪ] *n* bambinaia

nap [næp] *n* (*sleep*) pisolino; (*of cloth*)
peluria; **to be caught ~ping** essere preso
alla sprovvista

nape [neɪp] *n*: ~ **of the neck** nuca

napkin [ˈnæpkɪn] *n* (*also*: **table ~**) tovagliolo

nappy [ˈnæpɪ] (*BRIT*) *n* pannolino; ~ **rash** *n*
arrossamento (causato dal pannolino)

narcissus [nɑːˈsɪsəs] (*pl* **narcissi**) *n* narciso

narcotic [nɑːˈkɔtɪk] *n* narcotico ♦ *adj*
narcotico(a)

narrative [ˈnærətɪv] *n* narrativa

narrow [ˈnærəu] *adj* stretto(a); (*fig*)
limitato(a), ristretto(a) ♦ *vi* restringersi; **to
have a ~ escape** farcela per un pelo; **to ~
sth down to** ridurre qc a; ~**ly** *adv* per un
pelo; (*time*) per poco; ~**-minded** *adj*
meschino(a)

nasty [ˈnɑːstɪ] *adj* (*person, remark*:
unpleasant) cattivo(a); (: *rude*) villano(a);
(*smell, wound, situation*) brutto(a)

nation [ˈneɪʃən] *n* nazione *f*

national [ˈnæʃənl] *adj* nazionale ♦ *n*
cittadino/a; ~ **dress** *n* costume *m*
nazionale; **N~ Health Service** (*BRIT*) *n*
servizio nazionale di assistenza sanitaria,
≈ S.S.N. *m*; **N~ Insurance** (*BRIT*) *n*
≈ Previdenza Sociale; ~**ism** *n*
nazionalismo; ~**ity** [-ˈnælɪtɪ] *n* nazionalità *f*
inv; ~**ize** *vt* nazionalizzare; ~**ly** *adv* a
livello nazionale; ~ **park** *n* parco nazionale

National Trust

Fondato nel 1895, il **National Trust** *è
un'organizzazione che si occupa della
tutela e della salvaguardia di luoghi di
interesse storico o ambientale*

---

nationwide [ˈneɪʃənwaɪd] *adj* diffuso(a) in
tutto il paese ♦ *adv* in tutto il paese

native [ˈneɪtɪv] *n* abitante *m/f* del paese
♦ *adj* indigeno(a); (*country*) natio(a);
(*ability*) innato(a); **a ~ of Russia** un nativo
della Russia; **a ~ speaker of French** una
persona di madrelingua francese; **N~
American** *n* discendente di tribù
dell'America settentrionale; ~ **language** *n*
madrelingua

Nativity [nə'tɪvɪtɪ] *n*: **the ~** la Natività

NATO [ˈneɪtəu] *n abbr* (= *North Atlantic
Treaty Organization*) N.A.T.O. *f*

natural [ˈnætʃrəl] *adj* naturale; (*ability*)

innato(a); (*manner*) semplice; ~ **gas** *n* gas *m* metano; **~ly** *adv* naturalmente; (*by nature: gifted*) di natura

nature ['neɪtʃə*] *n* natura; (*character*) natura, indole *f*; **by** ~ di natura

naught [nɔ:t] *n* = **nought**

naughty ['nɔ:tɪ] *adj* (*child*) birichino(a), cattivello(a); (*story, film*) spinto(a)

nausea ['nɔ:sɪə] *n* (*MED*) nausea; (*fig: disgust*) schifo

nautical ['nɔ:tɪkl] *adj* nautico(a)

naval ['neɪvl] *adj* navale; ~ **officer** *n* ufficiale *m* di marina

nave [neɪv] *n* navata centrale

navel ['neɪvl] *n* ombelico

navigate ['nævɪgeɪt] *vt* percorrere navigando ♦ *vi* navigare; (*AUT*) fare da navigatore; **navigation** [-'geɪʃən] *n* navigazione *f*; **navigator** *n* (*NAUT, AVIAT*) ufficiale *m* di rotta; (*explorer*) navigatore *m*; (*AUT*) copilota *m/f*

navvy ['nævɪ] (*BRIT*) *n* manovale *m*

navy ['neɪvɪ] *n* marina; **~(-blue)** *adj* blu scuro *inv*

Nazi ['nɑ:tsɪ] *n* nazista *m/f*

NB *abbr* (= *nota bene*) N.B.

near [nɪə*] *adj* vicino(a); (*relation*) prossimo(a) ♦ *adv* vicino ♦ *prep* (*also*: ~ **to**) vicino a, presso; (*: time*) verso ♦ *vt* avvicinarsi a; **~by** [nɪə'baɪ] *adj* vicino(a) ♦ *adv* vicino; **~ly** *adv* quasi; **I ~ly fell** per poco non sono caduto; ~ **miss** *n*: **that was a ~ miss** c'è mancato poco; **~side** *n* (*AUT: in Britain*) lato sinistro; (*: in US, Europe etc*) lato destro; **~-sighted** [nɪə'saɪtɪd] *adj* miope

neat [ni:t] *adj* (*person, room*) ordinato(a); (*work*) pulito(a); (*solution, plan*) ben indovinato(a), azzeccato(a); (*spirits*) liscio(a); **~ly** *adv* con ordine; (*skilfully*) abilmente

necessarily ['nɛsɪsrɪlɪ] *adv* necessariamente

necessary ['nɛsɪsrɪ] *adj* necessario(a)

necessity [nɪ'sɛsɪtɪ] *n* necessità *f inv*

neck [nɛk] *n* collo; (*of garment*) colletto ♦ *vi* (*inf*) pomiciare, sbaciucchiarsi; ~ **and** ~ testa a testa

necklace ['nɛklɪs] *n* collana

neckline ['nɛklaɪn] *n* scollatura

necktie ['nɛktaɪ] *n* cravatta

née [neɪ] *adj*: ~ **Scott** nata Scott

need [ni:d] *n* bisogno ♦ *vt* aver bisogno di; **to** ~ **to do** dover fare; aver bisogno di fare; **you don't** ~ **to go** non devi andare, non c'è bisogno che tu vada

needle ['ni:dl] *n* ago; (*on record player*) puntina ♦ *vt* punzecchiare

needless ['ni:dlɪs] *adj* inutile

needlework ['ni:dlwə:k] *n* cucito

needn't ['ni:dnt] = **need not**

needy ['ni:dɪ] *adj* bisognoso(a)

negative ['nɛgətɪv] *n* (*LING*) negazione *f*; (*PHOT*) negativo ♦ *adj* negativo(a); ~ **equity** *n* situazione in cui l'ammontare del mutuo su un immobile supera il suo valore sul mercato

neglect [nɪ'glɛkt] *vt* trascurare ♦ *n* (*of person, duty*) negligenza; (*of child, house etc*) scarsa cura; **state of** ~ stato di abbandono

negligence ['nɛglɪdʒəns] *n* negligenza

negligible ['nɛglɪdʒɪbl] *adj* insignificante, trascurabile

negotiable [nɪ'gəʊʃɪəbl] *adj* (*cheque*) trasferibile

negotiate [nɪ'gəʊʃɪeɪt] *vi*: **to** ~ **(with)** negoziare (con) ♦ *vt* (*COMM*) negoziare; (*obstacle*) superare; **negotiation** [-'eɪʃən] *n* negoziato, trattativa

Negro ['ni:grəʊ] (*pl* **~es**) *n* negro(a)

neigh [neɪ] *vi* nitrire

neighbour ['neɪbə*] (*US* **neighbor**) *n* vicino/a; **~hood** *n* vicinato; **~ing** *adj* vicino(a); **~ly** *adj*: **he is a ~ly person** è un buon vicino

neither ['naɪðə*] *adj, pron* né l'uno(a) né l'altro(a), nessuno(a) dei(delle) due ♦ *conj* neanche, nemmeno, neppure ♦ *adv*: ~ **good nor bad** né buono né cattivo; **I didn't move and** ~ **did Claude** io non mi mossi e nemmeno Claude; **...,** ~ **did I refuse** ..., ma non ho nemmeno rifiutato

neon light ['ni:ɔn-] *n* luce *f* al neon

nephew ['nɛvju:] *n* nipote *m*

nerve [nəːv] *n* nervo; (*fig*) coraggio; (*impudence*) faccia tosta; **a fit of ~s** una crisi di nervi; **~-racking** *adj* che spezza i nervi

nervous ['nəːvəs] *adj* nervoso(a); (*anxious*) agitato(a), in apprensione; **~ breakdown** *n* esaurimento nervoso

nest [nest] *n* nido ♦ *vi* fare il nido, nidificare; **~ egg** *n* (*fig*) gruzzolo

nestle ['nɛsl] *vi* accoccolarsi

net [net] *n* rete *f* ♦ *adj* netto(a) ♦ *vt* (*fish etc*) prendere con la rete; (*profit*) ricavare un utile netto di; **the N~** (*Internet*) Internet *f*; **~ball** *n* specie di pallacanestro

Netherlands ['nɛðələndz] *npl*: **the ~** i Paesi Bassi

nett [net] *adj* = **net**

netting ['netɪŋ] *n* (*for fence etc*) reticolato

nettle ['netl] *n* ortica

network ['netwəːk] *n* rete *f*

neurotic [njuə'rɔtɪk] *adj, n* nevrotico(a)

neuter ['njuːtə*] *adj* neutro(a) ♦ *vt* (*cat etc*) castrare

neutral ['njuːtrəl] *adj* neutro(a); (*person, nation*) neutrale ♦ *n* (*AUT*): **in ~** in folle; **~ize** *vt* neutralizzare

never ['nevə*] *adv* (non...) mai; **~ again** mai più; **I'll ~ go there again** non ci vado più; **~ in my life** mai in vita mia; *see also* **mind**; **~-ending** *adj* interminabile; **~theless** [nevəðə'lɛs] *adv* tuttavia, ciò nonostante, ciò nondimeno

new [njuː] *adj* nuovo(a); (*brand new*) nuovo(a) di zecca; **N~ Age** *n* New Age *f inv*; **~born** *adj* neonato(a); **~comer** ['njuːkʌmə*] *n* nuovo(a) venuto(a); **~-fangled** ['njuːfæŋgld] (*pej*) *adj* stramoderno(a); **~-found** *adj* nuovo(a); **~ly** *adv* di recente; **~ly-weds** *npl* sposini *mpl*, sposi *mpl* novelli

news [njuːz] *n* notizie *fpl*; (*RADIO*) giornale *m* radio; (*TV*) telegiornale *m*; **a piece of ~** una notizia; **~ agency** *n* agenzia di stampa; **~agent** (*BRIT*) *n* giornalaio; **~caster** *n* (*RADIO*, *TV*) annunciatore/trice; **~ flash** *n* notizia *f* lampo *inv*; **~letter** *n* bollettino; **~paper** *n* giornale *m*; **~print** *n*

carta da giornale; **~reader** *n* = **~caster**; **~reel** *n* cinegiornale *m*; **~ stand** *n* edicola

newt [njuːt] *n* tritone *m*

New Year *n* Anno Nuovo; **~'s Day** *n* il Capodanno; **~'s Eve** *n* la vigilia di Capodanno

New York [-'jɔːk] *n* New York *f*

New Zealand [-'ziːlənd] *n* Nuova Zelanda; **~er** *n* neozelandese *m/f*

next [nɛkst] *adj* prossimo(a) ♦ *adv* accanto; (*in time*) dopo; **the ~ day** il giorno dopo, l'indomani; **~ time** la prossima volta; **~ year** l'anno prossimo; **when do we meet ~?** quando ci rincontriamo?; **~ to** accanto a; **~ to nothing** quasi niente; **~ please!** (*avanti*) il prossimo!; **~ door** *adv*, *adj* accanto *inv*; **~-of-kin** *n* parente *m/f* prossimo(a)

NHS *n abbr* = **National Health Service**

nib [nib] *n* (*of pen*) pennino

nibble ['nibl] *vt* mordicchiare

Nicaragua [nikə'rægjuə] *n* Nicaragua *m*

nice [nais] *adj* (*holiday, trip*) piacevole; (*flat, picture*) bello(a); (*person*) simpatico(a), gentile; **~ly** *adv* bene

niceties ['naisɪtɪz] *npl* finezze *fpl*

nick [nik] *n* taglietto; tacca ♦ *vt* (*inf*) rubare; **in the ~ of time** appena in tempo

nickel ['nikl] *n* nichel *m*; (*US*) moneta da cinque centesimi di dollaro

nickname ['nikneim] *n* soprannome *m*

niece [niːs] *n* nipote *f*

Nigeria [nai'dʒiəriə] *n* Nigeria

niggling ['niglin] *adj* insignificante; (*annoying*) irritante

night [nait] *n* notte *f*; (*evening*) sera; **at ~** la sera; **by ~** di notte; **the ~ before last** l'altro ieri notte (*or* sera); **~cap** *n* bicchierino *prima di andare a letto*; **~ club** *n* locale *m* notturno; **~dress** *n* camicia da notte; **~fall** *n* crepuscolo; **~gown** *n* = **~dress**; **~ie** ['naiti] *n* = **~dress**

nightingale ['naitiŋgeil] *n* usignolo

nightlife ['naitlaif] *n* vita notturna

nightly ['naitli] *adj* di ogni notte *or* sera; (*by night*) notturno(a) ♦ *adv* ogni notte *or* sera

nightmare ['naɪtmɛə*] n incubo
night: ~ **porter** n portiere m di notte; ~
school n scuola serale; ~ **shift** n turno di
notte; **~-time** n notte f
nil [nɪl] n nulla m; (BRIT: SPORT) zero
Nile [naɪl] n: **the** ~ il Nilo
nimble ['nɪmbl] adj agile
nine [naɪn] num nove; **~teen** num
diciannove; **~ty** num novanta
ninth [naɪnθ] adj nono(a)
nip [nɪp] vt pizzicare; (bite) mordere
nipple ['nɪpl] n (ANAT) capezzolo
nitrogen ['naɪtrədʒən] n azoto

KEYWORD

no [nəu] (pl ~**es**) adv (opposite of "yes") no;
are you coming? – ~ (I'm not) viene? —
no (non vengo); **would you like some
more? – ~ thank you** ne vuole ancora un
po'? — no, grazie
♦ adj (not any) nessuno(a); **I have ~
money/time/books** non ho soldi/tempo/
libri; **~ student would have done it**
nessuno studente lo avrebbe fatto; **"~
parking"** "divieto di sosta"; **"~ smoking"**
"vietato fumare"
♦ n no m inv

nobility [nəu'bɪlɪtɪ] n nobiltà
noble ['nəubl] adj nobile
nobody ['nəubədɪ] pron nessuno
nod [nɔd] vi accennare col capo, fare un
cenno; (in agreement) annuire con un
cenno del capo; (sleep) sonnecchiare ♦ vt:
to ~ one's head fare di sì col capo ♦ n
cenno; ~ **off** vi assopirsi
noise [nɔɪz] n rumore m; (din, racket)
chiasso; **noisy** adj (street, car)
rumoroso(a); (person) chiassoso(a)
nominal ['nɔmɪnl] adj nominale; (rent)
simbolico(a)
nominate ['nɔmɪneɪt] vt (propose) proporre
come candidato; (elect) nominare
nominee [nɔmɪ'niː] n persona nominata;
candidato/a
non... [nɔn] prefix non...; **~-alcoholic** adj
analcolico(a)

nonchalant ['nɔnʃələnt] adj disinvolto(a),
noncurante
non-committal ['nɔnkə'mɪtl] adj evasivo(a)
nondescript ['nɔndɪskrɪpt] adj qualunque
inv
none [nʌn] pron (not one thing) niente; (not
one person) nessuno(a); ~ **of you**
nessuno(a) di voi; **I've ~ left** non ne ho
più; **he's ~ the worse for it** non ne ha
risentito
nonentity [nɔ'nentɪtɪ] n persona
insignificante
nonetheless [nʌnðə'les] adv nondimeno
non-existent [-ɪg'zɪstənt] adj inesistente
non-fiction n saggistica
nonplussed [nɔn'plʌst] adj sconcertato(a)
nonsense ['nɔnsəns] n sciocchezze fpl
non: **~-smoker** n non fumatore/trice; **~-
smoking** adj (person) che non fuma;
(area, section) per non fumatori; **~-stick**
adj antiaderente, antiadesivo(a); **~-stop**
adj continuo(a); (train, bus) direttissimo(a)
♦ adv senza sosta
noodles ['nuːdlz] npl taglierini mpl
nook [nuk] n: **~s and crannies** angoli mpl
noon [nuːn] n mezzogiorno
no one ['nəuwʌn] pron = **nobody**
noose [nuːs] n nodo scorsoio; (hangman's)
cappio
nor [nɔː*] conj = **neither** ♦ adv see **neither**
norm [nɔːm] n norma
normal ['nɔːml] adj normale; **~ly** adv
normalmente
north [nɔːθ] n nord m, settentrione m ♦ adj
nord inv, del nord, settentrionale ♦ adv
verso nord; **N~ America** n America del
Nord; **~-east** n nord-est m; **~erly**
['nɔːðəlɪ] adj (point, direction) verso nord;
~ern ['nɔːðən] adj del nord, settentrionale;
N~ern Ireland n Irlanda del Nord; **N~
Pole** n Polo Nord; **N~ Sea** n Mare m del
Nord; **~ward(s)** ['nɔːθwəd(z)] adv verso
nord; **~-west** n nord-ovest m
Norway ['nɔːweɪ] n Norvegia
Norwegian [nɔː'wiːdʒən] adj norvegese ♦ n
norvegese m/f; (LING) norvegese m
nose [nəuz] n naso; (of animal) muso ♦ vi:

to ~ about aggirarsi; **~bleed** *n* emorragia nasale; **~-dive** *n* picchiata; **~y** *(inf) adj* = **nosy**

nostalgia [nɔs'tældʒɪə] *n* nostalgia

nostril ['nɔstrɪl] *n* narice *f; (of horse)* frogia

nosy ['nəuzɪ] *(inf) adj* curioso(a)

not [nɔt] *adv* non; **he is ~** *or* **isn't here** non è qui, non c'è; **you must ~** *or* **you mustn't do that** non devi fare quello; **it's too late, isn't it** *or* **is it ~?** è troppo tardi, vero?; **~ that I don't like him** non che (lui) non mi piaccia; **~ yet/now** non ancora/ora; *see also* **all**; **only**

notably ['nəutəblɪ] *adv (markedly)* notevolmente; *(particularly)* in particolare

notary ['nəutərɪ] *n* notaio

notch [nɔtʃ] *n* tacca; *(in saw)* dente *m*

note [nəut] *n* nota; *(letter, banknote)* biglietto ♦ *vt (also:* **~ down)** prendere nota di; **to take ~s** prendere appunti; **~book** *n* taccuino; **~d** ['nəutɪd] *adj* celebre; **~pad** *n* bloc-notes *m inv;* **~paper** *n* carta da lettere

nothing ['nʌθɪŋ] *n* nulla *m,* niente *m; (zero)* zero; **he does ~** non fa niente; **~ new/ much** *etc* niente di nuovo/speciale *etc;* **for ~** per niente

notice ['nəutɪs] *n* avviso; *(of leaving)* preavviso ♦ *vt* notare, accorgersi di; **to take ~ of** fare attenzione a; **to bring sth to sb's ~** far notare qc a qn; **at short ~** con un breve preavviso; **until further ~** fino a nuovo avviso; **to hand in one's ~** licenziarsi; **~able** *adj* evidente; **~ board** *(BRIT) n* tabellone *m* per affissi

notify ['nəutɪfaɪ] *vt:* **to ~ sth to sb** far sapere qc a qn; **to ~ sb of sth** avvisare qn di qc

notion ['nəuʃən] *n* idea; *(concept)* nozione *f*

notorious [nəu'tɔ:rɪəs] *adj* famigerato(a)

nougat ['nu:ga:] *n* torrone *m*

nought [nɔ:t] *n* zero

noun [naun] *n* nome *m,* sostantivo

nourish ['nʌrɪʃ] *vt* nutrire

novel ['nɔvl] *n* romanzo ♦ *adj* nuovo(a); **~ist** *n* romanziere/a; **~ty** *n* novità *f inv*

November [nəu'vembə*] *n* novembre *m*

novice ['nɔvɪs] *n* principiante *m/f; (REL)* novizio/a

now [nau] *adv* ora, adesso ♦ *conj:* **~ (that)** adesso che, ora che; **by ~** ormai; **just ~** proprio ora; **right ~** subito, immediatamente; **~ and then, ~ and again** ogni tanto; **from ~ on** da ora in poi; **~adays** ['nauədeɪz] *adv* oggidì

nowhere ['nəuweə*] *adv* in nessun luogo, da nessuna parte

nozzle ['nɔzl] *n (of hose etc)* boccaglio; *(of fire extinguisher)* lancia

nuance ['nju:ɑ:ns] *n* sfumatura

nuclear ['nju:klɪə*] *adj* nucleare

nucleus ['nju:klɪəs] *(pl* **nuclei)** *n* nucleo

nude [nju:d] *adj* nudo(a) ♦ *n (ART)* nudo; **in the ~** tutto/a nudo(a)

nudge [nʌdʒ] *vt* dare una gomitata a

nudist ['nju:dɪst] *n* nudista *m/f*

nuisance ['nju:sns] *n:* **it's a ~** è una seccatura; **he's a ~** è uno scocciatore

null [nʌl] *adj:* **~ and void** nullo(a)

numb [nʌm] *adj:* **~ (with)** intorpidito(a) (da); *(with fear)* impietrito(a) (da); **~ with cold** intirizzito(a) (dal freddo)

number ['nʌmbə*] *n* numero ♦ *vt* numerare; *(include)* contare; **a ~ of** un certo numero di; **to be ~ed among** venire annoverato(a) tra; **they were 10 in ~** erano in tutto 10; **~ plate** *(BRIT) n (AUT)* targa

numeral ['nju:mərəl] *n* numero, cifra

numerate ['nju:mərɪt] *adj:* **to be ~** avere nozioni di aritmetica

numerical [nju:'merɪkl] *adj* numerico(a)

numerous ['nju:mərəs] *adj* numeroso(a)

nun [nʌn] *n* suora, monaca

nurse [nə:s] *n* infermiere/a; *(also:* **~maid)** bambinaia ♦ *vt (patient, cold)* curare; *(baby: BRIT)* cullare; *(: US)* allattare, dare il latte a

nursery ['nə:sərɪ] *n (room)* camera dei bambini; *(institution)* asilo; *(for plants)* vivaio; **~ rhyme** *n* filastrocca; **~ school** *n* scuola materna; **~ slope** *(BRIT) n (SKI)* pista per principianti

nursing ['nə:sɪŋ] *n (profession)* professione *f* di infermiere *(or* di infermiera); *(care)* cura; **~ home** *n* casa di cura

nurture ['nə:tʃə*] *vt* allevare; nutrire
nut [nʌt] *n* (*of metal*) dado; (*fruit*) noce *f*; **~crackers** *npl* schiaccianoci *m inv*
nutmeg ['nʌtmɛg] *n* noce *f* moscata
nutritious [nju:'trɪʃəs] *adj* nutriente
nuts [nʌts] (*inf*) *adj* matto(a)
nutshell ['nʌtʃɛl] *n*: **in a ~** in poche parole
nylon ['naɪlɔn] *n* nailon *m* ♦ *adj* di nailon

O, o

oak [əuk] *n* quercia ♦ *adj* di quercia
O.A.P. (*BRIT*) *n abbr* = **old age pensioner**
oar [ɔ:*] *n* remo
oasis [əu'eɪsɪs] (*pl* **oases**) *n* oasi *f inv*
oath [əuθ] *n* giuramento; (*swear word*) bestemmia
oatmeal ['əutmi:l] *n* farina d'avena
oats [əuts] *npl* avena
obedience [ə'bi:dɪəns] *n* ubbidienza
obedient [ə'bi:dɪənt] *adj* ubbidiente
obey [ə'beɪ] *vt* ubbidire a; (*instructions, regulations*) osservare
obituary [ə'bɪtjuərɪ] *n* necrologia
object [*n* 'ɔbdʒɪkt, *vb* əb'dʒɛkt] *n* oggetto; (*purpose*) scopo, intento; (*LING*) complemento oggetto ♦ *vi*: **to ~ to** (*attitude*) disapprovare; (*proposal*) protestare contro, sollevare delle obiezioni contro; **expense is no ~** non si bada a spese; **to ~ that** obiettare che; **I ~!** mi oppongo!; **~ion** [əb'dʒɛkʃən] *n* obiezione *f*; **~ionable** [əb'dʒɛkʃənəbl] *adj* antipatico(a); (*language*) scostumato(a); **~ive** *n* obiettivo
obligation [ɔblɪ'geɪʃən] *n* obbligo, dovere *m*; **without ~** senza impegno
oblige [ə'blaɪdʒ] *vt* (*force*): **to ~ sb to do** costringere qn a fare; (*do a favour*) fare una cortesia a; **to be ~d to sb for sth** essere grato a qn per qc; **obliging** *adj* servizievole, compiacente
oblique [ə'bli:k] *adj* obliquo(a); (*allusion*) indiretto(a)
obliterate [ə'blɪtəreɪt] *vt* cancellare
oblivion [ə'blɪvɪən] *n* oblio
oblivious [ə'blɪvɪəs] *adj*: **~ of** incurante di;

inconscio(a) di
oblong ['ɔblɔŋ] *adj* oblungo(a) ♦ *n* rettangolo
obnoxious [əb'nɔkʃəs] *adj* odioso(a); (*smell*) disgustoso(a), ripugnante
oboe ['əubəu] *n* oboe *m*
obscene [əb'si:n] *adj* osceno(a)
obscure [əb'skjuə*] *adj* oscuro(a) ♦ *vt* oscurare; (*hide: sun*) nascondere
observant [əb'zə:vnt] *adj* attento(a)
observation [ɔbzə'veɪʃən] *n* osservazione *f*; (*by police etc*) sorveglianza
observatory [əb'zə:vətrɪ] *n* osservatorio
observe [əb'zə:v] *vt* osservare; (*remark*) fare osservare; **~r** *n* osservatore/trice
obsess [əb'sɛs] *vt* ossessionare; **~ive** *adj* ossessivo(a)
obsolescence [ɔbsə'lɛsns] *n* obsolescenza
obsolete ['ɔbsəli:t] *adj* obsoleto(a)
obstacle ['ɔbstəkl] *n* ostacolo
obstinate ['ɔbstɪnɪt] *adj* ostinato(a)
obstruct [əb'strʌkt] *vt* (*block*) ostruire, ostacolare; (*halt*) fermare; (*hinder*) impedire
obtain [əb'teɪn] *vt* ottenere; **~able** *adj* ottenibile
obvious ['ɔbvɪəs] *adj* ovvio(a), evidente; **~ly** *adv* ovviamente; certo
occasion [ə'keɪʒən] *n* occasione *f*; (*event*) avvenimento; **~al** *adj* occasionale; **~ally** *adv* ogni tanto
occupation [ɔkju'peɪʃən] *n* occupazione *f*; (*job*) mestiere *m*, professione *f*; **~al hazard** *n* rischio del mestiere
occupier ['ɔkjupaɪə*] *n* occupante *m/f*
occupy ['ɔkjupaɪ] *vt* occupare; **to ~ o.s. in doing** occuparsi a fare
occur [ə'kə:*] *vi* accadere, capitare; **to ~ to sb** venire in mente a qn; **~rence** *n* caso, fatto; presenza
ocean ['əuʃən] *n* oceano
o'clock [ə'klɔk] *adv*: **it is 5 ~** sono le 5
OCR *n abbr* (= *optical character recognition*) lettura ottica; (= *optical character reader*) lettore *m* ottico
octave ['ɔktɪv] *n* ottavo
October [ɔk'təubə*] *n* ottobre *m*
octopus ['ɔktəpəs] *n* polpo, piovra

odd [ɔd] *adj* (*strange*) strano(a), bizzarro(a); (*number*) dispari *inv*; (*not of a set*) spaiato(a); **60-~** 60 e oltre; **at ~ times** di tanto in tanto; **the ~ one out** l'eccezione *f*; **~ity** *n* bizzarria; (*person*) originale *m*; **~-job man** *n* tuttofare *m inv*; **~ jobs** *npl* lavori *mpl* occasionali; **~ly** *adv* stranamente; **~ments** *npl* (*COMM*) rimanenze *fpl*; **~s** *npl* (*in betting*) quota; **~s and ends** *npl* avanzi *mpl*; **it makes no ~s** non importa; **at ~s** in contesa
odometer [ɔ'dɔmɪtə*] *n* odometro
odour ['əudə*] (*US* **odor**) *n* odore *m*; (*unpleasant*) cattivo odore

KEYWORD

of [ɔv, əv] *prep* 1 (*gen*) di; **a boy ~ 10** un ragazzo di 10 anni; **a friend ~ ours** un nostro amico; **that was kind ~ you** è stato molto gentile da parte sua
2 (*expressing quantity, amount, dates etc*) di; **a kilo ~ flour** un chilo di farina; **how much ~ this do you need?** quanto gliene serve?; **there were 3 ~ them** (*people*) erano in 3; (*objects*) ce n'erano 3; **3 ~ us went** 3 di noi sono andati; **the 5th ~ July** il 5 luglio
3 (*from, out of*) di, in; **made ~ wood** (*fatto*) di *or* in legno

KEYWORD

off [ɔf] *adv* 1 (*distance, time*): **it's a long way ~** è lontano; **the game is 3 days ~** la partita è tra 3 giorni
2 (*departure, removal*) via; **to go ~ to Paris** andarsene a Parigi; **I must be ~** devo andare via; **to take ~ one's coat** togliersi il cappotto; **the button came ~** il bottone è venuto via *or* si è staccato; **10% ~** con lo sconto del 10%
3 (*not at work*): **to have a day ~** avere un giorno libero; **to be ~ sick** essere assente per malattia
♦ *adj* (*engine*) spento(a); (*tap*) chiuso(a); (*cancelled*) sospeso(a); (*BRIT: food*) andato(a) a male; **on the ~ chance** nel caso; **to have**

an ~ day non essere in forma
♦ *prep* 1 (*motion, removal etc*) da; (*distant from*) a poca distanza da; **a street ~ the square** una strada che parte dalla piazza
2: **to be ~ meat** non mangiare più la carne

offal ['ɔfl] *n* (*CULIN*) frattaglie *fpl*
off-colour (*BRIT*) *adj* (*ill*) malato(a), indisposto(a)
offence [ə'fɛns] (*US* **offense**) *n* (*LAW*) contravvenzione *f*; (*: more serious*) reato; **to take ~ at** offendersi per
offend [ə'fɛnd] *vt* (*person*) offendere; **~er** *n* delinquente *m/f*; (*against regulations*) contravventore/trice
offense [ə'fɛns] (*US*) *n* = **offence**
offensive [ə'fɛnsɪv] *adj* offensivo(a); (*smell etc*) sgradevole, ripugnante ♦ *n* (*MIL*) offensiva
offer ['ɔfə*] *n* offerta, proposta ♦ *vt* offrire; **"on ~"** (*COMM*) "in offerta speciale"; **~ing** *n* offerta
offhand [ɔf'hænd] *adj* disinvolto(a), noncurante ♦ *adv* su due piedi
office ['ɔfɪs] *n* (*place*) ufficio; (*position*) carica; **doctor's ~** (*US*) studio; **to take ~** entrare in carica; **~ automation** *n* automazione *f* d'ufficio; burotica; **~ block** (*US* **~ building**) *n* complesso di uffici; **~ hours** *npl* orario d'ufficio; (*US: MED*) orario di visite
officer ['ɔfɪsə*] *n* (*MIL etc*) ufficiale *m*; (*also*: **police ~**) agente *m* di polizia; (*of organization*) funzionario
office worker *n* impiegato/a d'ufficio
official [ə'fɪʃl] *adj* (*authorized*) ufficiale ♦ *n* ufficiale *m*; (*civil servant*) impiegato/a statale; funzionario
officiate [ə'fɪʃɪeɪt] *vi* presenziare
officious [ə'fɪʃəs] *adj* invadente
offing ['ɔfɪŋ] *n*: **in the ~** (*fig*) in vista
off: ~-licence (*BRIT*) *n* (*shop*) spaccio di bevande alcoliche; **~-line** *adj, adv* (*COMPUT*) off-line *inv*, fuori linea; (*: switched off*) spento(a); **~-peak** *adj* (*ticket, heating etc*) a tariffa ridotta; (*time*) non di punta; **~-putting** (*BRIT*) *adj* sgradevole,

antipatico(a); **~-road vehicle** *n* fuoristrada *m inv*; **~-season** *adj, adv* fuori stagione

| off-licence |

> *In Gran Bretagna e in Irlanda, gli* **off-licence** *sono rivendite di vini, liquori e superalcolici, spesso aperti fino a tarda ora.*

offset ['ɔfset] (*irreg*) *vt* (*counteract*) controbilanciare, compensare

offshoot ['ɔfʃuːt] *n* (*fig*) diramazione *f*

offshore [ɔf'ʃɔː*] *adj* (*breeze*) di terra; (*island*) vicino alla costa; (*fishing*) costiero(a)

offside ['ɔf'saɪd] *adj* (*SPORT*) fuori gioco; (*AUT: in Britain*) destro(a); (*: in Italy etc*) sinistro(a)

offspring ['ɔfsprɪŋ] *n inv* prole *f*, discendenza

off: **~stage** *adv* dietro le quinte; **~-the-peg** (*US* **~-the-rack**) *adv* prêt-à-porter; **~-white** *adj* bianco sporco *inv*

often ['ɔfn] *adv* spesso; **how ~ do you go?** quanto spesso ci vai?

oh [əu] *excl* oh!

oil [ɔɪl] *n* olio; (*petroleum*) petrolio; (*for central heating*) nafta ♦ *vt* (*machine*) lubrificare; **~can** *n* oliatore *m* a mano; (*for storing*) latta da olio; **~field** *n* giacimento petrolifero; **~ filter** *n* (*AUT*) filtro dell'olio; **~ painting** *n* quadro a olio; **~ refinery** [-rɪ'faɪnərɪ] *n* raffineria di petrolio; **~ rig** *n* derrick *m inv*; (*at sea*) piattaforma per trivellazioni subacquee; **~ tanker** *n* (*ship*) petroliera; (*truck*) autocisterna per petrolio; **~ well** *n* pozzo petrolifero; **~y** *adj* unto(a), oleoso(a); (*food*) grasso(a)

ointment ['ɔɪntmənt] *n* unguento

O.K. ['əu'keɪ] *excl* d'accordo! ♦ *adj* non male *inv* ♦ *vt* approvare; **is it ~?, are you ~?** tutto bene?

okay ['əu'keɪ] *excl, adj, vt* = **O.K.**

old [əuld] *adj* vecchio(a); (*ancient*) antico(a), vecchio(a); (*person*) vecchio(a), anziano(a); **how ~ are you?** quanti anni ha?; **he's 10 years ~** ha 10 anni; **~er brother** fratello

maggiore; **~ age** *n* vecchiaia; **~ age pensioner** (*BRIT*) *n* pensionato/a; **~-fashioned** *adj* antiquato(a), fuori moda; (*person*) all'antica

olive ['ɔlɪv] *n* (*fruit*) oliva; (*tree*) olivo ♦ *adj* (*also:* **~-green**) verde oliva *inv*; **~ oil** *n* olio d'oliva

Olympic [əu'lɪmpɪk] *adj* olimpico(a); **the ~ Games, the ~s** i giochi olimpici, le Olimpiadi

omelet(te) ['ɔmlɪt] *n* omelette *f inv*

omen ['əumen] *n* presagio, augurio

ominous ['ɔmɪnəs] *adj* minaccioso(a); (*event*) di malaugurio

omit [əu'mɪt] *vt* omettere

| KEYWORD |

on [ɔn] *prep* 1 (*indicating position*) su; **~ the wall** sulla parete; **~ the left** a *or* sulla sinistra

2 (*indicating means, method, condition etc*): **~ foot** a piedi; **~ the train/plane** in treno/ aereo; **~ the telephone** al telefono; **~ the radio/television** alla radio/televisione; **to be ~ drugs** drogarsi; **~ holiday** in vacanza

3 (*of time*): **~ Friday** venerdì; **~ Fridays** il *or* di venerdì; **~ June 20th** il 20 giugno; **~ Friday, June 20th** venerdì, 20 giugno; **a week ~ Friday** venerdì a otto; **~ his arrival** al suo arrivo; **~ seeing this** vedendo ciò

4 (*about, concerning*): **information ~ train services** informazioni sui collegamenti ferroviari; **a book ~ Goldoni/physics** un libro su Goldoni/di *or* sulla fisica

♦ *adv* 1 (*referring to dress, covering*): **to have one's coat ~** avere indosso il cappotto; **to put one's coat ~** mettersi il cappotto; **what's she got ~?** cosa indossa?; **she put her boots/gloves/hat ~** si mise gli stivali/i guanti/il cappello; **screw the lid ~ tightly** avvita bene il coperchio

2 (*further, continuously*): **to walk ~, go ~** *etc* continuare, proseguire *etc*; **to read ~** continuare a leggere; **~ and off** ogni tanto

♦ *adj* 1 (*in operation: machine, TV, light*)

acceso(a); (: *tap*) aperto(a); (: *brake*) inserito(a); **is the meeting still ~?** (*in progress*) la riunione è ancora in corso?; (*not cancelled*) è confermato l'incontro?; **there's a good film ~ at the cinema** danno un buon film al cinema
2 (*inf*): **that's not ~!** (*not acceptable*) non si fa così!; (*not possible*) non se ne parla neanche!

once [wʌns] *adv* una volta ♦ *conj* non appena, quando; **~ he had left/it was done** dopo che se n'era andato/fu fatto; **at ~** subito; (*simultaneously*) a un tempo; **~ a week** una volta per settimana; **~ more** ancora una volta; **~ and for all** una volta per sempre; **~ upon a time** c'era una volta

oncoming ['ɒnkʌmɪŋ] *adj* (*traffic*) che viene in senso opposto

one [wʌn] *num* uno(a); **~ hundred and fifty** centocinquanta; **~ day** un giorno
♦ *adj* 1 (*sole*) unico(a); **the ~ book which** l'unico libro che; **the ~ man who** l'unico che 2 (*same*) stesso(a); **they came in the ~ car** sono venuti nella stessa macchina
♦ *pron* 1: **this ~** questo/a; **that ~** quello/a; **I've already got ~/a red ~** ne ho già uno/uno rosso; **~ by ~** uno per uno
2: **~ another** l'un l'altro; **to look at ~ another** guardarsi; **to help ~ another** aiutarsi l'un l'altro *or* a vicenda
3 (*impersonal*) si; **~ never knows** non si sa mai; **to cut ~'s finger** tagliarsi un dito; **~ needs to eat** bisogna mangiare

one: ~-day excursion (*US*) *n* biglietto giornaliero di andata e ritorno; **~-man** *adj* (*business*) diretto(a) *etc* da un solo uomo; **~-man band** *n* suonatore ambulante con vari strumenti; **~-off** (*BRIT: inf*) *n* fatto eccezionale

oneself [wʌnˈsɛlf] *pron* (*reflexive*) si; (*after prep*) se stesso(a), sé; **to do sth (by) ~** fare qc da sé; **to hurt ~** farsi male; **to keep sth for ~** tenere qc per sé; **to talk to ~** parlare

da solo

one: ~-sided *adj* (*argument*) unilaterale; **~-to-~** *adj* (*relationship*) univoco(a); **~-way** *adj* (*street, traffic*) a senso unico

ongoing ['ɒngəʊɪŋ] *adj* in corso; in attuazione

onion ['ʌnjən] *n* cipolla

on-line *adj, adv* (*COMPUT*) on-line *inv*

onlooker ['ɒnlʊkə*] *n* spettatore/trice

only ['əʊnlɪ] *adv* solo, soltanto ♦ *adj* solo(a), unico(a) ♦ *conj* solo che, ma; **an ~ child** un figlio unico; **not ~ ... but also** non solo ... ma anche

onset ['ɒnsɛt] *n* inizio

onshore ['ɒnʃɔː*] *adj* (*wind*) di mare

onslaught ['ɒnslɔːt] *n* attacco, assalto

onto ['ɒntu] *prep* = **on to**

onus ['əʊnəs] *n* onere *m*, peso

onward(s) ['ɒnwəd(z)] *adv* (*move*) in avanti; **from that time ~** da quella volta in poi

ooze [uːz] *vi* stillare

open ['əʊpn] *adj* aperto(a); (*road*) libero(a); (*meeting*) pubblico(a) ♦ *vt* aprire ♦ *vi* (*eyes, door, debate*) aprirsi; (*flower*) sbocciare; (*shop, bank, museum*) aprire; (*book etc: commence*) cominciare; **in the ~ (air)** all'aperto; **~ on to** *vt fus* (*subj: room, door*) dare su; **~ up** *vt* aprire; (*blocked road*) sgombrare ♦ *vi* (*shop, business*) aprire; **~ing** *adj* (*speech*) di apertura ♦ *n* apertura; (*opportunity*) occasione *f*, opportunità *f inv*; sbocco; **~ing hours** *npl* orario d'apertura; **~ learning centre** *n* sistema educativo nel quale lo studente ha maggiore controllo e gestione delle modalità di apprendimento; **~ly** *adv* apertamente; **~-minded** *adj* che ha la mente aperta; **~-necked** *adj* col collo slacciato; **~-plan** *adj* senza pareti divisorie

Open University

i La **Open University**, *fondata in Gran Bretagna nel 1969, organizza corsi universitari per corrispondenza, basati anche su lezioni trasmesse per radio e per televisione e su corsi estivi.*

opera ['ɔpərə] *n* opera

operate ['ɔpəreɪt] *vt* (*machine*) azionare, far funzionare; (*system*) usare ♦ *vi* funzionare; (*drug*) essere efficace; **to ~ on sb (for)** (*MED*) operare qn (di)

operatic [ɔpə'rætɪk] *adj* dell'opera, lirico(a)

operating ['ɔpəreɪtɪŋ] *adj*: **~ table** tavolo operatorio; **~ theatre** sala operatoria

operation [ɔpə'reɪʃən] *n* operazione *f*; **to be in ~** (*machine*) essere in azione *or* funzionamento; (*system*) essere in vigore; **to have an ~** (*MED*) subire un'operazione; **~al** *adj* in funzione; d'esercizio

operative ['ɔpərətɪv] *adj* (*measure*) operativo(a)

operator ['ɔpəreɪtə*] *n* (*of machine*) operatore/trice; (*TEL*) centralinista *m/f*

opinion [ə'pɪnɪən] *n* opinione *f*, parere *m*; **in my ~** secondo me, a mio avviso; **~ated** *adj* dogmatico(a); **~ poll** *n* sondaggio di opinioni

opium ['əupɪəm] *n* oppio

opponent [ə'pəunənt] *n* avversario/a

opportunist [ɔpə'tjuːnɪst] *n* opportunista *m/f*

opportunity [ɔpə'tjuːnɪtɪ] *n* opportunità *f inv*, occasione *f*; **to take the ~ of doing** cogliere l'occasione per fare

oppose [ə'pəuz] *vt* opporsi a; **~d to** contrario(a) a; **as ~d to** in contrasto con; **opposing** *adj* opposto(a); (*team*) avversario(a)

opposite ['ɔpəzɪt] *adj* opposto(a); (*house etc*) di fronte ♦ *adv* di fronte, dirimpetto ♦ *prep* di fronte a ♦ *n*: **the ~** il contrario, l'opposto; **the ~ sex** l'altro sesso

opposition [ɔpə'zɪʃən] *n* opposizione *f*

opt [ɔpt] *vi*: **to ~ for** optare per; **to ~ to do** scegliere di fare; **~ out** *vi*: **to ~ out of** ritirarsi da

optical ['ɔptɪkl] *adj* ottico(a)

optician [ɔp'tɪʃən] *n* ottico

optimist ['ɔptɪmɪst] *n* ottimista *m/f*; **~ic** [-'mɪstɪk] *adj* ottimistico(a)

optimum ['ɔptɪməm] *adj* ottimale

option ['ɔpʃən] *n* scelta; (*SCOL*) materia facoltativa; (*COMM*) opzione *f*; **~al** *adj*

facoltativo(a); (*COMM*) a scelta

or [ɔː*] *conj* o, oppure; (*with negative*): **he hasn't seen ~ heard anything** non ha visto né sentito niente; **~ else** se no, altrimenti; oppure

oral ['ɔːrəl] *adj* orale ♦ *n* esame *m* orale

orange ['ɔrɪndʒ] *n* (*fruit*) arancia ♦ *adj* arancione

orbit ['ɔːbɪt] *n* orbita ♦ *vt* orbitare intorno a

orbital (motorway) ['ɔːbɪtl-] *n* raccordo anulare

orchard ['ɔːtʃəd] *n* frutteto

orchestra ['ɔːkɪstrə] *n* orchestra; (*US: seating*) platea

orchid ['ɔːkɪd] *n* orchidea

ordain [ɔː'deɪn] *vt* (*REL*) ordinare; (*decide*) decretare

ordeal [ɔː'diːl] *n* prova, travaglio

order ['ɔːdə*] *n* ordine *m*; (*COMM*) ordinazione *f* ♦ *vt* ordinare; **in ~** in ordine; (*of document*) in regola; **in (working) ~** funzionante; **in ~ to do** per fare; **in ~ that** affinché +*sub*; **on ~** (*COMM*) in ordinazione; **out of ~** non in ordine; (*not working*) guasto; **to ~ sb to do** ordinare a qn di fare; **~ form** *n* modulo di ordinazione; **~ly** *n* (*MIL*) attendente *m*; (*MED*) inserviente *m* ♦ *adj* (*room*) in ordine; (*mind*) metodico(a); (*person*) ordinato(a), metodico(a)

ordinary ['ɔːdnrɪ] *adj* normale, comune; (*pej*) mediocre; **out of the ~** diverso dal solito, fuori dell'ordinario

Ordnance Survey ['ɔːdnəns-] (*BRIT*) *n* istituto cartografico britannico

ore [ɔː*] *n* minerale *m* grezzo

organ ['ɔːgən] *n* organo; **~ic** [ɔː'gænɪk] *adj* organico(a); (*of food*) biologico(a)

organization [ɔːgənaɪ'zeɪʃən] *n* organizzazione *f*

organize ['ɔːgənaɪz] *vt* organizzare; **to get ~d** organizzarsi; **~r** *n* organizzatore/trice

orgasm ['ɔːgæzm] *n* orgasmo

orgy ['ɔːdʒɪ] *n* orgia

Orient ['ɔːrɪənt] *n*: **the ~** l'Oriente *m*; **oriental** [-'entl] *adj*, *n* orientale *m/f*

origin ['ɔrɪdʒɪn] *n* origine *f*

original [ə'rɪdʒɪnl] *adj* originale; (*earliest*)

originario(a) ♦ n originale m; ~ly adv (at first) all'inizio

originate [əˈrɪdʒɪneɪt] vi: **to ~ from** essere originario(a) di; (suggestion) provenire da; **to ~ in** avere origine in

Orkneys [ˈɔːknɪz] npl: **the ~** (also: **the Orkney Islands**) le Orcadi

ornament [ˈɔːnəmənt] n ornamento; (trinket) ninnolo; ~al [-ˈmɛntl] adj ornamentale

ornate [ɔːˈneɪt] adj molto ornato(a)

orphan [ˈɔːfn] n orfano/a

orthodox [ˈɔːθədɒks] adj ortodosso(a)

orthopaedic [ɔːθəˈpiːdɪk] (US **orthopedic**) adj ortopedico(a)

ostensibly [ɔsˈtɛnsɪblɪ] adv all'apparenza

ostentatious [ɔstɛnˈteɪʃəs] adj pretenzioso(a); ostentato(a)

ostrich [ˈɔstrɪtʃ] n struzzo

other [ˈʌðə*] adj altro(a) ♦ pron: **the ~ (one)** l'altro(a); **~s** (~ people) altri mpl; **~ than** altro che; a parte; ~wise adv, conj altrimenti

otter [ˈɔtə*] n lontra

ouch [autʃ] excl ohi!, ahi!

ought [ɔːt] (pt ought) aux vb: **I ~ to do it** dovrei farlo; **this ~ to have been corrected** questo avrebbe dovuto essere corretto; **he ~ to win** dovrebbe vincere

ounce [auns] n oncia (= 28.35 g; 16 in a pound)

our [ˈauə*] adj il(la) nostro(a), pl i(le) nostri(e); see also **my**; ~s pron il(la) nostro(a), pl i(le) nostri(e); see also **mine**; ~**selves** pron pl (reflexive) ci; (after preposition) noi; (emphatic) noi stessi(e); see also **oneself**

oust [aust] vt cacciare, espellere

KEYWORD
---

out [aut] adv (gen) fuori; **~ here/there** qui/là fuori; **to speak ~ loud** parlare forte; **to have a night ~** uscire una sera; **the boat was 10 km ~** la barca era a 10 km dalla costa; **3 days ~ from Plymouth** a 3 giorni da Plymouth

♦ adj: **to be ~** (gen) essere fuori;

(unconscious) aver perso i sensi; (style, singer) essere fuori moda; **before the week was ~** prima che la settimana fosse finita; **to be ~ to do sth** avere intenzione di fare qc; **to be ~ in one's calculations** aver sbagliato i calcoli

♦ out of prep 1 (outside, beyond) fuori di; **to go ~ of the house** uscire di casa; **to look ~ of the window** guardare fuori dalla finestra

2 (because of) per

3 (origin) da; **to drink ~ of a cup** bere da una tazza

4 (from among): **~ of 10** su 10

5 (without) senza; **~ of petrol** senza benzina

---

out-and-out adj (liar, thief etc) vero(a) e proprio(a)

outback [ˈautbæk] n (in Australia) interno, entroterra

outboard [ˈautbɔːd] n: **~ (motor)** (motore m) fuoribordo

outbreak [ˈautbreɪk] n scoppio; epidemia

outburst [ˈautbɜːst] n scoppio

outcast [ˈautkɑːst] n esule m/f; (socially) paria m inv

outcome [ˈautkʌm] n esito, risultato

outcrop [ˈautkrɒp] n (of rock) affioramento

outcry [ˈautkraɪ] n protesta, clamore m

outdated [autˈdeɪtɪd] adj (custom, clothes) fuori moda; (idea) sorpassato(a)

outdo [autˈduː] (irreg) vt sorpassare

outdoor [autˈdɔː*] adj all'aperto; ~s adv fuori; all'aria aperta

outer [ˈautə*] adj esteriore; **~ space** n spazio cosmico

outfit [ˈautfɪt] n (clothes) completo; (: for sport) tenuta

outgoing [ˈautgəuɪŋ] adj (character) socievole; ~s (BRIT) npl (expenses) spese fpl, uscite fpl

outgrow [autˈgrəu] (irreg) vt: **he has ~n his clothes** tutti i vestiti gli sono diventati piccoli

outhouse [ˈauthaus] n costruzione f annessa

outing ['autɪŋ] n gita; escursione f
outlaw ['autlɔː] n fuorilegge m/f ♦ vt bandire
outlay ['autleɪ] n spese fpl; (investment) sborsa, spesa
outlet ['autlɛt] n (for liquid etc) sbocco, scarico; (US: ELEC) presa di corrente; (also: **retail ~**) punto di vendita
outline ['autlaɪn] n contorno, profilo; (summary) abbozzo, grandi linee fpl ♦ vt (fig) descrivere a grandi linee
outlive [aut'lɪv] vt sopravvivere a
outlook ['autluk] n prospettiva, vista
outlying ['autlaɪŋ] adj periferico(a)
outmoded [aut'məʊdɪd] adj passato(a) di moda; antiquato(a)
outnumber [aut'nʌmbə*] vt superare in numero
out-of-date adj (passport) scaduto(a); (clothes) fuori moda inv
out-of-the-way adj (place) fuori mano inv
outpatient ['autpeɪʃənt] n paziente m/f esterno(a)
outpost ['autpəʊst] n avamposto
output ['autput] n produzione f; (COMPUT) output m inv
outrage ['autreɪdʒ] n oltraggio; scandalo ♦ vt oltraggiare; **~ous** [-'reɪdʒəs] adj oltraggioso(a); scandaloso(a)
outreach worker ['autriːtʃ-] n assistente sociale che opera direttamente nei luoghi di aggregazione di emarginati, tossicodipendenti ecc
outright [adv aut'raɪt, adj 'autraɪt] adv completamente; schiettamente; apertamente; sul colpo ♦ adj completo(a); schietto(a) e netto(a)
outset ['autsɛt] n inizio
outside [aut'saɪd] n esterno, esteriore m ♦ adj esterno(a), esteriore ♦ adv fuori, all'esterno ♦ prep fuori di, all'esterno di; **at the ~** (fig) al massimo; **~ lane** n (AUT) corsia di sorpasso; **~ line** n (TEL) linea esterna; **~r** n (in race etc) outsider m inv; (stranger) estraneo(a)
outsize ['autsaɪz] adj (clothes) per taglie forti
outskirts ['autskəːts] npl sobborghi mpl

outspoken [aut'spəʊkən] adj molto franco(a)
outstanding [aut'stændɪŋ] adj eccezionale, di rilievo; (unfinished) non completo(a); non evaso(a); non regolato(a)
outstay [aut'steɪ] vt: **to ~ one's welcome** diventare un ospite sgradito
outstretched [aut'strɛtʃt] adj (hand) teso(a); (body) disteso(a)
outstrip [aut'strɪp] vt (competitors, demand) superare
out-tray n contenitore m per la corrispondenza in partenza
outward ['autwəd] adj (sign, appearances) esteriore; (journey) d'andata
outweigh [aut'weɪ] vt avere maggior peso di
outwit [aut'wɪt] vt superare in astuzia
oval ['əʊvl] adj ovale ♦ n ovale m

Oval Office

i L'**Oval Office** è una grande sala di forma ovale nella **White House**, la Casa Bianca, dove ha sede l'ufficio del Presidente degli Stati Uniti

---

ovary ['əʊvərɪ] n ovaia
oven ['ʌvn] n forno; **~proof** adj da forno
over ['əʊvə*] adv al di sopra ♦ adj (or adv) (finished) finito(a), terminato(a); (too) troppo; (remaining) che avanza ♦ prep su; sopra; (above) al di sopra di; (on the other side of) di là di; (more than) più di; (during) durante; **~ here** qui; **~ there** là; **all ~** (everywhere) dappertutto; (finished) tutto(a) finito(a); **~ and ~ (again)** più e più volte; **~ and above** oltre (a); **to ask sb ~** invitare qn (a passare)
overall [adj, n 'əʊvərɔːl, adv əʊvər'ɔːl] adj totale ♦ n (BRIT) grembiule m ♦ adv nell'insieme, complessivamente; **~s** npl (worker's ~s) tuta (da lavoro)
overawe [əʊvər'ɔː] vt intimidire
overbalance [əʊvə'bæləns] vi perdere l'equilibrio
overboard ['əʊvəbɔːd] adv (NAUT) fuori bordo, in mare

overbook [əuvə'buk] *vt*: **the hotel was ~ed** le prenotazioni all'albergo superavano i posti disponibili

overcast ['əuvəka:st] *adj* (*sky*) coperto(a)

overcharge [əuvə'tʃa:dʒ] *vt*: **to ~ sb for sth** far pagare troppo caro a qn per qc

overcoat ['əuvəkəut] *n* soprabito, cappotto

overcome [əuvə'kʌm] (*irreg*) *vt* superare; sopraffare

overcrowded [əuvə'kraudıd] *adj* sovraffollato(a)

overdo [əuvə'du:] (*irreg*) *vt* esagerare; (*overcook*) cuocere troppo

overdose ['əuvədəus] *n* dose *f* eccessiva

overdraft ['əuvədra:ft] *n* scoperto (di conto)

overdrawn [əuvə'drɔ:n] *adj* (*account*) scoperto(a)

overdue [əuvə'dju:] *adj* in ritardo

overestimate [əuvər'estımeıt] *vt* sopravvalutare

overflow [*vb* əuvə'fləu, *n* 'əuvəfləu] *vi* traboccare ♦ *n* (*also*: **~ pipe**) troppopieno

overgrown [əuvə'grəun] *adj* (*garden*) ricoperto(a) di vegetazione

overhaul [*vb* əuvə'hɔ:l, *n* 'əuvəhɔ:l] *vt* revisionare ♦ *n* revisione *f*

overhead [*adv* əuvə'hed, *adj, n* 'əuvəhed] *adv* di sopra ♦ *adj* aereo(a); (*lighting*) verticale ♦ *n* (*US*) = **~s**; **~s** *npl* spese *fpl* generali

overhear [əuvə'hıə*] (*irreg*) *vt* sentire (per caso)

overheat [əuvə'hi:t] *vi* (*engine*) surriscaldare

overjoyed [əuvə'dʒɔıd] *adj* pazzo(a) di gioia

overlap [əuvə'læp] *vi* sovrapporsi

overleaf [əuvə'li:f] *adv* a tergo

overload [əuvə'ləud] *vt* sovraccaricare

overlook [əuvə'luk] *vt* (*have view of*) dare su; (*miss*) trascurare; (*forgive*) passare sopra a

overnight [əuvə'naıt] *adv* (*happen*) durante la notte; (*fig*) tutto ad un tratto ♦ *adj* di notte; **he stayed there ~** ci ha passato la notte

overpass ['əuvəpɑ:s] *n* cavalcavia *m inv*

overpower [əuvə'pauə*] *vt* sopraffare; **~ing** *adj* irresistibile; (*heat, stench*) soffocante

overrate [əuvə'reıt] *vt* sopravvalutare

override [əuvə'raıd] (*irreg: like* **ride**) *vt* (*order, objection*) passar sopra a; (*decision*) annullare; **overriding** *adj* preponderante

overrule [əuvə'ru:l] *vt* (*decision*) annullare; (*claim*) respingere

overrun [əuvə'rʌn] (*irreg: like* **run**) *vt* (*country*) invadere; (*time limit*) superare

overseas [əuvə'si:z] *adv* oltremare; (*abroad*) all'estero ♦ *adj* (*trade*) estero(a); (*visitor*) straniero(a)

overshadow [əuvə'ʃædəu] *vt* far ombra su; (*fig*) eclissare

overshoot [əuvə'ʃu:t] (*irreg*) *vt* superare

oversight ['əuvəsaıt] *n* omissione *f*, svista

oversleep [əuvə'sli:p] (*irreg*) *vt* dormire troppo a lungo

overstep [əuvə'step] *vt*: **to ~ the mark** superare ogni limite

overt [əu'və:t] *adj* palese

overtake [əuvə'teık] (*irreg*) *vt* sorpassare

overthrow [əuvə'θrəu] (*irreg*) *vt* (*government*) rovesciare

overtime ['əuvətaım] *n* (*lavoro*) straordinario

overtone ['əuvətəun] *n* sfumatura

overture ['əuvətʃuə*] *n* (*MUS*) ouverture *f inv*; (*fig*) approccio

overturn [əuvə'tə:n] *vt* rovesciare ♦ *vi* rovesciarsi

overweight [əuvə'weıt] *adj* (*person*) troppo grasso(a)

overwhelm [əuvə'welm] *vt* sopraffare; sommergere; schiacciare; **~ing** *adj* (*victory, defeat*) schiacciante; (*heat, desire*) intenso(a)

overwrought [əuvə'rɔ:t] *adj* molto agitato(a)

owe [əu] *vt*: **to ~ sb sth, to ~ sth to sb** dovere qc a qn; **owing to** *prep* a causa di

owl [aul] *n* gufo

own [əun] *vt* possedere ♦ *adj* proprio(a); **a room of my ~** la mia propria camera; **to get one's ~ back** vendicarsi; **on one's ~** tutto(a) solo(a); **~ up** *vi* confessare; **~er** proprietario/a; **~ership** *n* possesso

ox [ɔks] (*pl* **oxen**) *n* bue *m*

oxen ['ɔksn] *npl of* **ox**

oxtail ['ɔksteɪl] *n*: ~ **soup** minestra di coda di bue

oxygen ['ɔksɪdʒən] *n* ossigeno; ~ **mask/tent** *n* maschera/tenda ad ossigeno

oyster ['ɔɪstə*] *n* ostrica

oz. *abbr* = **ounce(s)**

ozone ['əuzəun] *n* ozono; ~**-friendly** *adj* che non danneggia l'ozono; ~ **hole** *n* buco nell'ozono

P, p

p [pi:] *abbr* = **penny; pence**

P.A. *n abbr* = **personal assistant; public address system**

p.a. *abbr* = **per annum**

pa [pɑ:] (*inf*) *n* papà *m inv*, babbo

pace [peɪs] *n* passo; (*speed*) passo; velocità ♦ *vi*: **to ~ up and down** camminare su e giù; **to keep ~ with** camminare di pari passo a; (*events*) tenersi al corrente di; ~**maker** *n* (*MED*) segnapasso; (*SPORT: also*: ~ **setter**) battistrada *m inv*

pacific [pə'sɪfɪk] *n*: **the P~ (Ocean)** il Pacifico, l'Oceano Pacifico

pacify ['pæsɪfaɪ] *vt* calmare, placare

pack [pæk] *n* pacco; (*US: of cigarettes*) pacchetto; (*back~*) zaino; (*of hounds*) muta; (*of thieves etc*) banda; (*of cards*) mazzo ♦ *vt* (*in suitcase etc*) mettere; (*box*) riempire; (*cram*) stipare, pigiare; **to ~ (one's bags)** fare la valigia; **to ~ sb off** spedire via qn; ~ **it in!** (*inf*) dacci un taglio!

package ['pækɪdʒ] *n* pacco; balla; (*also*: ~ **deal**) pacchetto; forfait *m inv*; ~ **holiday** *n* vacanza organizzata; ~ **tour** *n* viaggio organizzato

packed lunch *n* pranzo al sacco

packet ['pækɪt] *n* pacchetto

packing ['pækɪŋ] *n* imballaggio; ~ **case** *n* cassa da imballaggio

pact [pækt] *n* patto, accordo; trattato

pad [pæd] *n* blocco; (*to prevent friction*) cuscinetto; (*inf: flat*) appartamentino ♦ *vt* imbottire; ~**ding** *n* imbottitura

paddle ['pædl] *n* (*oar*) pagaia; (*US: for table tennis*) racchetta da ping-pong ♦ *vi* squazzare ♦ *vt*: **to ~ a canoe** *etc* vogare con la pagaia; **paddling pool** (*BRIT*) *n* piscina per bambini

paddock ['pædək] *n* prato recintato; (*at racecourse*) paddock *m inv*

padlock ['pædlɔk] *n* lucchetto

paediatrics [pi:dɪ'ætrɪks] (*US* **pediatrics**) *n* pediatria

pagan ['peɪgən] *adj, n* pagano(a)

page [peɪdʒ] *n* pagina; (*also*: ~ **boy**) paggio ♦ *vt* (*in hotel etc*) chiamare

pageant ['pædʒənt] *n* spettacolo storico; grande cerimonia; ~**ry** *n* pompa

pager ['peɪdʒə*] *n* (*TEL*) cercapersone *m inv*

paging device ['peɪdʒɪŋ-] *n* (*TEL*) cercapersone *m inv*

paid [peɪd] *pt, pp of* **pay** ♦ *adj* (*work, official*) rimunerato(a); **to put ~ to** (*BRIT*) mettere fine a

pail [peɪl] *n* secchio

pain [peɪn] *n* dolore *m*; **to be in ~** soffrire, aver male; **to take ~s to do** mettercela tutta per fare; ~**ed** *adj* addolorato(a), afflitto(a); ~**ful** *adj* doloroso(a), che fa male; difficile, penoso(a); ~**fully** *adv* (*fig: very*) fin troppo; ~**killer** *n* antalgico, antidolorifico; ~**less** *adj* indolore

painstaking ['peɪnzteɪkɪŋ] *adj* (*person*) sollecito(a); (*work*) accurato(a)

paint [peɪnt] *n* vernice *f*, colore *m* ♦ *vt* dipingere; (*walls, door etc*) verniciare; **to ~ the door blue** verniciare la porta di azzurro; ~**brush** *n* pennello; ~**er** *n* (*artist*) pittore *m*; (*decorator*) imbianchino; ~**ing** *n* pittura; verniciatura; (*picture*) dipinto, quadro; ~**work** *n* tinta; (*of car*) vernice *f*

pair [pɛə*] *n* (*of shoes, gloves etc*) paio; (*of people*) coppia; duo *m inv*; **a ~ of scissors/trousers** un paio di forbici/pantaloni

pajamas [pɪ'dʒɑ:məz] (*US*) *npl* pigiama *m*

Pakistan [pɑ:kɪ'stɑ:n] *n* Pakistan *m*; ~**i** *adj, n* pakistano(a)

pal [pæl] (*inf*) *n* amico/a, compagno/a

palace ['pæləs] *n* palazzo

palatable ['pælɪtəbl] adj gustoso(a)

palate ['pælɪt] n palato

palatial [pə'leɪʃəl] adj sontuoso(a), sfarzoso(a)

pale [peɪl] adj pallido(a) ♦ n: **to be beyond the ~** aver oltrepassato ogni limite

Palestine ['pælɪstaɪn] n Palestina; **Palestinian** [-'tɪnɪən] adj, n palestinese m/f

palette ['pælɪt] n tavolozza

palings ['peɪlɪŋz] npl (fence) palizzata

pallet ['pælɪt] n (for goods) paletta

pallid ['pælɪd] adj pallido(a), smorto(a)

pallor ['pælə*] n pallore m

palm [pɑːm] n (ANAT) palma, palmo; (also: ~ **tree**) palma ♦ vt: **to ~ sth off on sb** (inf) rifilare qc a qn; **P~ Sunday** n Domenica delle Palme

paltry ['pɔːltrɪ] adj irrisorio(a); insignificante

pamper ['pæmpə*] vt viziare, coccolare

pamphlet ['pæmflət] n dépliant m inv

pan [pæn] n (also: **sauce~**) casseruola; (also: **frying ~**) padella

panache [pə'næʃ] n stile m

pancake ['pænkeɪk] n frittella

pancreas ['pæŋkrɪəs] n pancreas m inv

panda ['pændə] n panda m inv; ~ **car** (BRIT) n auto f della polizia

pandemonium [pændɪ'məʊnɪəm] n pandemonio

pander ['pændə*] vi: **to ~ to** lusingare; concedere tutto a

pane [peɪn] n vetro

panel ['pænl] n (of wood, cloth etc) pannello; (RADIO, TV) giuria; ~**ling** (US ~**ing**) n rivestimento a pannelli

pang [pæŋ] n: **a ~ of regret** un senso di rammarico; **hunger ~s** morsi mpl della fame

panic ['pænɪk] n panico ♦ vi perdere il sangue freddo; ~**ky** adj (person) pauroso(a); ~**-stricken** adj (person) preso(a) dal panico, in preda al panico; (look) terrorizzato(a)

pansy ['pænzɪ] n (BOT) viola del pensiero, pensée f inv; (inf: pej) femminuccia

pant [pænt] vi ansare

panther ['pænθə*] n pantera

panties ['pæntɪz] npl slip m, mutandine fpl

pantihose ['pæntɪhəʊz] (US) n collant m inv

pantomime ['pæntəmaɪm] (BRIT) n pantomima

---
pantomime
---

*In Gran Bretagna la **pantomime** è una sorta di libera interpretazione delle favole più conosciute, che vengono messe in scena a teatro durante il periodo natalizio. È uno spettacolo per tutta la famiglia che prevede la partecipazione del pubblico.*

---

pantry ['pæntrɪ] n dispensa

pants [pænts] npl mutande fpl, slip m; (US: trousers) pantaloni mpl

papal ['peɪpəl] adj papale, pontificio(a)

paper ['peɪpə*] n carta; (also: **wall~**) carta da parati, tappezzeria; (also: **news~**) giornale m; (study, article) saggio; (exam) prova scritta ♦ adj di carta ♦ vt tappezzare; ~**s** npl (also: **identity ~s**) carte fpl, documenti mpl; ~**back** n tascabile m; edizione f economica; ~ **bag** n sacchetto di carta; ~ **clip** n graffetta, clip f inv; ~ **hankie** n fazzolettino di carta; ~**weight** n fermacarte m inv; ~**work** n lavoro amministrativo

papier-mâché ['pæpɪeɪ'mæʃeɪ] n cartapesta

par [pɑː*] n parità, pari f; (GOLF) norma; **on a ~ with** alla pari con

parachute ['pærəʃuːt] n paracadute m inv

parade [pə'reɪd] n parata ♦ vt (fig) fare sfoggio di ♦ vi sfilare in parata

paradise ['pærədaɪs] n paradiso

paradox ['pærədɒks] n paradosso; ~**ically** [-'dɒksɪklɪ] adv paradossalmente

paraffin ['pærəfɪn] (BRIT) n: ~ **(oil)** paraffina

paragon ['pærəgən] n modello di perfezione or di virtù

paragraph ['pærəgrɑːf] n paragrafo

parallel ['pærəlɛl] adj parallelo(a); (fig) analogo(a) ♦ n (line) parallela; (fig, GEO) parallelo

paralyse ['pærəlaɪz] (US **paralyze**) vt paralizzare

paralysis [pə'rælɪsɪs] n paralisi f inv
paralyze ['pærəlaɪz] (US) vt = **paralyse**
paramount ['pærəmaunt] adj: **of ~ importance** di capitale importanza
paranoid ['pærənɔɪd] adj paranoico(a)
paraphernalia [pærəfə'neɪlɪə] n attrezzi mpl, roba
parasol ['pærəsɒl] n parasole m
paratrooper ['pærətruːpə*] n paracadutista m (soldato)
parcel ['pɑːsl] n pacco, pacchetto ♦ vt (also: **~ up**) impaccare
parched [pɑːtʃt] adj (person) assetato(a)
parchment ['pɑːtʃmənt] n pergamena
pardon ['pɑːdn] n perdono; grazia ♦ vt perdonare; (LAW) graziare; **~ me!** mi scusi!; **I beg your ~!** scusi!; **I beg your ~?** (BRIT), **~ me?** (US) prego?
parent ['pɛərənt] n genitore m; **~s** npl (mother and father) genitori mpl; **~al** [pə'rɛntl] adj dei genitori
parentheses [pə'rɛnθɪsiːz] npl of **parenthesis**
parenthesis [pə'rɛnθɪsɪs] (pl **parentheses**) n parentesi f inv
Paris ['pærɪs] n Parigi f
parish ['pærɪʃ] n parrocchia; (BRIT: civil) ≈ municipio
park [pɑːk] n parco ♦ vt, vi parcheggiare
parka ['pɑːkə] n eskimo
parking ['pɑːkɪŋ] n parcheggio; **"no ~"** "sosta vietata"; **~ lot** (US) n posteggio, parcheggio; **~ meter** n parchimetro; **~ ticket** n multa per sosta vietata
parliament ['pɑːləmənt] n parlamento
parliamentary [pɑːlə'mɛntərɪ] adj parlamentare
parlour ['pɑːlə*] (US **parlor**) n salotto
parochial [pə'rəukɪəl] (pej) adj provinciale
parole [pə'rəul] n: **on ~** in libertà per buona condotta
parrot ['pærət] n pappagallo
parry ['pærɪ] vt parare
parsley ['pɑːslɪ] n prezzemolo
parsnip ['pɑːsnɪp] n pastinaca
parson ['pɑːsn] n prete m; (Church of England) parroco

part [pɑːt] n parte f; (of machine) pezzo; (US: in hair) scriminatura ♦ adj in parte ♦ vt separare ♦ vi (people) separarsi; **to take ~ in** prendere parte a; **for my ~** per parte mia; **to take sth in good ~** prendere bene qc; **to take sb's ~** parteggiare per or prendere le parti di qn; **for the most ~** in generale; nella maggior parte dei casi; **~ with** vt fus separarsi da; rinunciare a; **~ exchange** (BRIT) n: **in ~ exchange** in pagamento parziale
partial ['pɑːʃl] adj parziale; **to be ~ to** avere un debole per
participate [pɑː'tɪsɪpeɪt] vi: **to ~ (in)** prendere parte (a), partecipare (a); **participation** [-'peɪʃən] n partecipazione f
participle ['pɑːtɪsɪpl] n participio
particle ['pɑːtɪkl] n particella
particular [pə'tɪkjulə*] adj particolare; speciale; (fussy) difficile; meticoloso(a); **in ~** in particolare, particolarmente; **~ly** adv particolarmente; in particolare; **~s** npl particolari mpl, dettagli mpl; (information) informazioni fpl
parting ['pɑːtɪŋ] n separazione f; (BRIT: in hair) scriminatura ♦ adj d'addio
partisan [pɑːtɪ'zæn] n partigiano/a ♦ adj partigiano(a); di parte
partition [pɑː'tɪʃən] n (POL) partizione f; (wall) tramezzo
partly ['pɑːtlɪ] adv parzialmente; in parte
partner ['pɑːtnə*] n (COMM) socio/a; (wife, husband etc, SPORT) compagno/a; (at dance) cavaliere/dama; **~ship** n associazione f; (COMM) società f inv
partridge ['pɑːtrɪdʒ] n pernice f
part-time adj, adv a orario ridotto
party ['pɑːtɪ] n (POL) partito; (group) gruppo; (LAW) parte f; (celebration) ricevimento; serata; festa ♦ cpd (POL) del partito, di partito; **~ dress** n vestito della festa
pass [pɑːs] vt (gen) passare; (place) passare davanti a; (exam) passare, superare; (candidate) promuovere; (overtake, surpass) sorpassare, superare; (approve) approvare ♦ vi passare ♦ n (permit) lasciapassare m inv; permesso; (in mountains) passo, gola;

(*SPORT*) passaggio; (*SCOL*): **to get a ~** prendere la sufficienza; **to ~ sth through a hole** *etc* far passare qc attraverso un buco *etc*; **to make a ~ at sb** (*inf*) fare delle proposte *or* delle avances a qn; **~ away** *vi* morire; **~ by** *vi* passare ♦ *vt* trascurare; **~ on** *vt* passare; **~ out** *vi* svenire; **~ up** *vt* (*opportunity*) lasciarsi sfuggire, perdere; **~able** *adj* (*road*) praticabile; (*work*) accettabile

passage ['pæsɪdʒ] *n* (*gen*) passaggio; (*also*: **~way**) corridoio; (*in book*) brano, passo; (*by boat*) traversata

passbook ['pɑːsbuk] *n* libretto di risparmio

passenger ['pæsɪndʒə*] *n* passeggero/a

passer-by [pɑːsə'baɪ] *n* passante *m/f*

passing ['pɑːsɪŋ] *adj* (*fig*) fuggevole; **to mention sth in ~** accennare a qc di sfuggita; **~ place** *n* (*AUT*) piazzola di sosta

passion ['pæʃən] *n* passione *f*; amore *m*; **~ate** *adj* appassionato(a)

passive ['pæsɪv] *adj* (*also LING*) passivo(a); **~ smoking** *n* fumo passivo

Passover ['pɑːsəuvə*] *n* Pasqua ebraica

passport ['pɑːspɔːt] *n* passaporto; **~ control** *n* controllo *m* passaporti *inv*; **~ office** *n* ufficio *m* passaporti *inv*

password ['pɑːswəːd] *n* parola d'ordine

past [pɑːst] *prep* (*further than*) oltre, di là di; dopo; (*later than*) dopo ♦ *adj* passato(a); (*president etc*) ex *inv* ♦ *n* passato; **he's ~ forty** ha più di quarant'anni; **ten ~ eight** le otto e dieci; **for the ~ few days** da qualche giorno; in questi ultimi giorni; **to run ~** passare di corsa

pasta ['pæstə] *n* pasta

paste [peɪst] *n* (*glue*) colla; (*CULIN*) pâté *inv*; pasta ♦ *vt* collare

pastel ['pæstl] *adj* pastello *inv*

pasteurized ['pæstəraɪzd] *adj* pastorizzato(a)

pastille ['pæstl] *n* pastiglia

pastime ['pɑːstaɪm] *n* passatempo

pastry ['peɪstrɪ] *n* pasta

pasture ['pɑːstʃə*] *n* pascolo

pasty¹ ['pæstɪ] *n* pasticcio di carne

pasty² ['peɪstɪ] *adj* (*face etc*) smorto(a)

pat [pæt] *vt* accarezzare, dare un colpetto (affettuoso) a

patch [pætʃ] *n* (*of material, on tyre*) toppa; (*eye ~*) benda; (*spot*) macchia ♦ *vt* (*clothes*) rattoppare; **(to go through) a bad ~** (*attraversare*) un brutto periodo; **~ up** *vt* rappezzare; (*quarrel*) appianare; **~y** *adj* irregolare

pâté ['pæteɪ] *n* pâté *m inv*

patent ['peɪtnt] *n* brevetto ♦ *vt* brevettare ♦ *adj* patente, manifesto(a); **~ leather** *n* cuoio verniciato

paternal [pə'təːnl] *adj* paterno(a)

path [pɑːθ] *n* sentiero, viottolo; viale *m*; (*fig*) via, strada; (*of planet, missile*) traiettoria

pathetic [pə'θetɪk] *adj* (*pitiful*) patetico(a); (*very bad*) penoso(a)

pathological [pæθə'lɔdʒɪkl] *adj* patologico(a)

pathway ['pɑːθweɪ] *n* sentiero

patience ['peɪʃns] *n* pazienza; (*BRIT: CARDS*) solitario

patient ['peɪʃnt] *n* paziente *m/f*; malato/a ♦ *adj* paziente

patio ['pætɪəu] *n* terrazza

patriot ['peɪtrɪət] *n* patriota *m/f*; **~ic** [pætrɪ'ɔtɪk] *adj* patriottico(a); **~ism** *n* patriottismo

patrol [pə'trəul] *n* pattuglia ♦ *vt* pattugliare; **~ car** *n* autoradio *f inv* (della polizia); **~man** (*US: irreg*) *n* poliziotto

patron ['peɪtrən] *n* (*in shop*) cliente *m/f*; (*of charity*) benefattore/trice; **~ of the arts** mecenate *m/f*; **~ize** ['pætrənaɪz] *vt* essere cliente abituale di; (*fig*) trattare dall'alto in basso

patter ['pætə*] *n* picchiettio; (*sales talk*) propaganda di vendita ♦ *vi* picchiettare; **a ~ of footsteps** un rumore di passi

pattern ['pætən] *n* modello; (*design*) disegno, motivo

pauper ['pɔːpə*] *n* indigente *m/f*

pause [pɔːz] *n* pausa ♦ *vi* fare una pausa, arrestarsi

pave [peɪv] *vt* pavimentare; **to ~ the way for** aprire la via a

pavement ['peɪvmənt] (*BRIT*) *n* marciapiede

m

pavilion [pəˈvɪlɪən] *n* (SPORT) *edificio annesso a campo sportivo*

paving [ˈpeɪvɪŋ] *n* pavimentazione *f*; ~ **stone** *n* lastra di pietra

paw [pɔː] *n* zampa

pawn [pɔːn] *n* (CHESS) pedone *m*; (*fig*) pedina ♦ *vt* dare in pegno; **~broker** *n* prestatore *m* su pegno; **~shop** *n* monte *m* di pietà

pay [peɪ] (*pt, pp* **paid**) *n* stipendio; paga ♦ *vt* pagare ♦ *vi* (*be profitable*) rendere; **to ~ attention (to)** fare attenzione (a); **to ~ sb a visit** far visita a qn; **to ~ one's respects to sb** porgere i propri rispetti a qn; ~ **back** *vt* rimborsare; ~ **for** *vt fus* pagare; ~ **in** *vt* versare; ~ **off** *vt* (*debt*) saldare; (*person*) pagare; (*employee*) pagare e licenziare ♦ *vi* (*scheme, decision*) dare dei frutti; ~ **up** *vt* saldare; **~able** *adj* pagabile; **~ee** *n* beneficiario/a; ~ **envelope** (US) *n* = ~ **packet**; **~ing** *adj*: **~ing guest** ospite *m/f* pagante, pensionante *m/f*; **~ment** *n* pagamento; versamento; saldo; ~ **packet** (BRIT) *n* busta *f* paga *inv*; ~ **phone** *n* cabina telefonica; **~roll** *n* ruolo (organico); ~ **slip** *n* foglio *m* paga *inv*; ~ **television** *n* televisione *f* a pagamento, pay-tv *f inv*

PC *n abbr* = **personal computer**; *adv abbr* = **politically correct**

p.c. *abbr* = **per cent**

pea [piː] *n* pisello

peace [piːs] *n* pace *f*; **~ful** *adj* pacifico(a), calmo(a)

peach [piːtʃ] *n* pesca

peacock [ˈpiːkɔk] *n* pavone *m*

peak [piːk] *n* (*of mountain*) cima, vetta; (*mountain itself*) picco; (*of cap*) visiera; (*fig*) apice *m*, culmine *m*; ~ **hours** *npl* ore *fpl* di punta; ~ **period** *n* = ~ **hours**

peal [piːl] *n* (*of bells*) scampanio, carillon *m inv*; **~s of laughter** scoppi *mpl* di risa

peanut [ˈpiːnʌt] *n* arachide *f*, nocciolina americana; ~ **butter** *n* burro di arachidi

pear [pɛə*] *n* pera

pearl [pɜːl] *n* perla

peasant [ˈpɛznt] *n* contadino/a

peat [piːt] *n* torba

pebble [ˈpɛbl] *n* ciottolo

peck [pɛk] *vt* (*also*: ~ **at**) beccare ♦ *n* colpo di becco; (*kiss*) bacetto; **~ing order** *n* ordine *m* gerarchico; **~ish** (BRIT: *inf*) *adj*: **I feel ~ish** ho un languorino

peculiar [pɪˈkjuːlɪə*] *adj* strano(a), bizzarro(a); peculiare; ~ **to** peculiare di

pedal [ˈpɛdl] *n* pedale *m* ♦ *vi* pedalare

pedantic [pɪˈdæntɪk] *adj* pedantesco(a)

peddler [ˈpɛdlə*] *n* (*also*: **drug ~**) spacciatore/trice

pedestal [ˈpɛdəstl] *n* piedestallo

pedestrian [pɪˈdɛstrɪən] *n* pedone/a ♦ *adj* pedonale; (*fig*) prosaico(a), pedestre; ~ **crossing** (BRIT) *n* passaggio pedonale; ~ **precinct** (BRIT), ~ **zone** (US) *n* zona pedonale

pediatrics [piːdɪˈætrɪks] (US) *n* = **paediatrics**

pedigree [ˈpɛdɪɡriː] *n* (*of animal*) pedigree *m inv*; (*fig*) background *m inv* ♦ *cpd* (*animal*) di razza

pee [piː] (*inf*) *vi* pisciare

peek [piːk] *vi* guardare furtivamente

peel [piːl] *n* buccia; (*of orange, lemon*) scorza ♦ *vt* sbucciare ♦ *vi* (*paint etc*) staccarsi

peep [piːp] *n* (BRIT: *look*) sguardo furtivo, sbirciata; (*sound*) pigolio ♦ *vi* (BRIT) guardare furtivamente; ~ **out** *vi* mostrarsi furtivamente; **~hole** *n* spioncino

peer [pɪə*] *vi*: **to ~ at** scrutare ♦ *n* (*noble*) pari *m inv*; (*equal*) pari *m/f inv*, uguale *m/f*; (*contemporary*) contemporaneo/a; **~age** *n* dignità di pari; pari *mpl*

peeved [piːvd] *adj* stizzito(a)

peevish [ˈpiːvɪʃ] *adj* stizzoso(a)

peg [pɛɡ] *n* caviglia; (*for coat etc*) attaccapanni *m inv*; (BRIT: *also*: **clothes ~**) molletta

Peking [piːˈkɪŋ] *n* Pechino *f*

pelican [ˈpɛlɪkən] *n* pellicano; ~ **crossing** (BRIT) *n* (AUT) attraversamento pedonale con semaforo a controllo manuale

pellet [ˈpɛlɪt] *n* pallottola, pallina

pelt [pɛlt] *vt*: **to ~ sb (with)** bombardare qn

(con) ♦ vi (rain) piovere a dirotto; (inf: run)
filare ♦ n pelle f

pelvis ['pɛlvɪs] n pelvi f inv, bacino

pen [pɛn] n penna; (for sheep) recinto

penal ['pi:nl] adj penale; ~**ize** vt punire;
(SPORT, fig) penalizzare

penalty ['pɛnltɪ] n penalità f inv; sanzione f
penale; (fine) ammenda; (SPORT)
penalizzazione f; ~ **(kick)** n (SPORT) calcio
di rigore

penance ['pɛnəns] n penitenza

pence [pɛns] (BRIT) npl of **penny**

pencil ['pɛnsl] n matita; ~ **case** n astuccio
per matite; ~ **sharpener** n
temperamatite m inv

pendant ['pɛndnt] n pendaglio

pending ['pɛndɪŋ] prep in attesa di ♦ adj in
sospeso

pendulum ['pɛndjuləm] n pendolo

penetrate ['pɛnɪtreɪt] vt penetrare

penfriend ['pɛnfrɛnd] (BRIT) n
corrispondente m/f

penguin ['pɛŋgwɪn] n pinguino

penicillin [pɛnɪ'sɪlɪn] n penicillina

peninsula [pə'nɪnsjulə] n penisola

penis ['pi:nɪs] n pene m

penitentiary [pɛnɪ'tɛnʃərɪ] (US) n carcere m

penknife ['pɛnnaɪf] n temperino

pen name n pseudonimo

penniless ['pɛnɪlɪs] adj senza un soldo

penny ['pɛnɪ] (pl **pennies** or **pence** (BRIT)) n
penny m; (US) centesimo

penpal ['pɛnpæl] n corrispondente m/f

pension ['pɛnʃən] n pensione f; ~**er** (BRIT)
n pensionato/a

pensive ['pɛnsɪv] adj pensoso(a)

penthouse ['pɛnthaus] n appartamento (di
lusso) nell'attico

pent-up ['pɛntʌp] adj (feelings) represso(a)

people ['pi:pl] npl gente f; persone fpl;
(citizens) popolo ♦ n (nation, race) popolo;
4/several ~ came 4/parecchie persone
sono venute; ~ **say that ...** si dice che ....

pep [pɛp] (inf): ~ **up** vt vivacizzare; (food)
rendere più gustoso(a)

pepper ['pɛpə*] n pepe m; (vegetable)
peperone m ♦ vt (fig): **to** ~ **with** spruzzare

di; ~**mint** n (sweet) pasticca di menta

peptalk ['pɛptɔ:k] (inf) n discorso di
incoraggiamento

per [pə:*] prep per; a; ~ **hour** all'ora; ~ **kilo**
etc il chilo etc; ~ **day** al giorno; ~ **annum**
adv all'anno; ~ **capita** adj, adv pro capite
inv

perceive [pə'si:v] vt percepire; (notice)
accorgersi di

per cent [pə'sɛnt] adv per cento

percentage [pə'sɛntɪdʒ] n percentuale f

perception [pə'sɛpʃən] n percezione f;
sensibilità; perspicacia

perceptive [pə'sɛptɪv] adj percettivo(a);
perspicace

perch [pə:tʃ] n (fish) pesce m persico; (for
bird) sostegno, ramo ♦ vi appollaiarsi

percolator ['pə:kəleɪtə*] n (also: **coffee** ~)
caffettiera a pressione; caffettiera elettrica

percussion [pə'kʌʃən] n percussione f;
(MUS) strumenti mpl a percussione

perennial [pə'rɛnɪəl] adj perenne

perfect [adj, n 'pə:fɪkt, vb pə'fɛkt] adj
perfetto(a) ♦ n (also: ~ **tense**) perfetto,
passato prossimo ♦ vt perfezionare;
mettere a punto ♦ ~**ly** adv perfettamente,
alla perfezione

perforate ['pə:fəreɪt] vt perforare;
perforation [-'reɪʃən] n perforazione f

perform [pə'fɔ:m] vt (carry out) eseguire,
fare; (symphony etc) suonare; (play, ballet)
dare; (opera) fare ♦ vi suonare; recitare;
~**ance** n esecuzione f; (at theatre etc)
rappresentazione f, spettacolo; (of an artist)
interpretazione f; (of player etc)
performance f; (of car, engine) prestazione
f; ~**er** n artista m/f

perfume ['pə:fju:m] n profumo

perhaps [pə'hæps] adv forse

peril ['pɛrɪl] n pericolo

perimeter [pə'rɪmɪtə*] n perimetro

period ['pɪərɪəd] n periodo; (HISTORY) epoca;
(SCOL) lezione f; (full stop) punto; (MED)
mestruazioni fpl ♦ adj (costume, furniture)
d'epoca; ~**ic(al)** [-'ɔdɪk(l)] adj periodico(a);
~**ical** [-'ɔdɪkl] n periodico

peripheral [pə'rɪfərəl] adj periferico(a) ♦ n

(COMPUT) unità f inv periferica
perish ['perɪʃ] vi perire, morire; (decay)
deteriorarsi; ~**able** adj deperibile
perjury ['pɜːdʒərɪ] n spergiuro
perk [pɜːk] (inf) n vantaggio; ~ **up** vi (cheer
up) rianimarsi
perm [pɜːm] n (for hair) permanente f
permanent ['pɜːmənənt] adj permanente
permeate ['pɜːmɪeɪt] vi penetrare ♦ vt
permeare
permissible [pə'mɪsɪbl] adj permissibile,
ammissibile
permission [pə'mɪʃən] n permesso
permissive [pə'mɪsɪv] adj permissivo(a)
permit [n 'pɜːmɪt, vb pə'mɪt] n permesso
♦ vt permettere; **to ~ sb to do** permettere
a qn di fare
perpendicular [pɜːpən'dɪkjulə*] adj
perpendicolare ♦ n perpendicolare f
perplex [pə'pleks] vt lasciare perplesso(a)
persecute ['pɜːsɪkjuːt] vt perseguitare
persevere [pɜːsɪ'vɪə*] vi perseverare
Persian ['pɜːʃən] adj persiano(a) ♦ n (LING)
persiano; **the (~) Gulf** n il Golfo Persico
persist [pə'sɪst] vi: **to ~ (in doing)** persistere
(nel fare); ostinarsi (a fare); ~**ent** adj
persistente; ostinato(a)
person ['pɜːsn] n persona; **in ~** di or in
persona, personalmente; ~**al** adj
personale; individuale; ~**al assistant** n
segretaria personale; ~**al column** n ≈
messaggi mpl personali; ~**al computer** n
personal computer m inv; ~**ality** [-'nælɪtɪ]
n personalità f inv; ~**ally** adv
personalmente; **to take sth ~ally** prendere
qc come una critica personale; ~**al
organizer** n (Filofax ®) Fulltime ®;
(electronic) agenda elettronica; ~**al stereo**
n Walkman ® m inv
personnel [pɜːsə'nel] n personale m
perspective [pə'spektɪv] n prospettiva
Perspex ® ['pɜːspeks] (BRIT) n tipo di resina
termoplastica
perspiration [pɜːspɪ'reɪʃən] n traspirazione
f, sudore m
persuade [pə'sweɪd] vt: **to ~ sb to do sth**
persuadere qn a fare qc

perturb [pə'tɜːb] vt turbare
pervert [n 'pɜːvɜːt, vb pə'vɜːt] n pervertito/a
♦ vt pervertire
pessimism ['pesɪmɪzəm] n pessimismo
pessimist ['pesɪmɪst] n pessimista m/f; ~**ic**
[-'mɪstɪk] adj pessimistico(a)
pest [pest] n animale m (or insetto)
pestifero; (fig) peste f
pester ['pestə*] vt tormentare, molestare
pet [pet] n animale m domestico ♦ cpd
favorito(a) ♦ vt accarezzare; **teacher's ~**
favorito/a del maestro
petal ['petl] n petalo
peter ['piːtə*]: **to ~ out** vi esaurirsi;
estinguersi
petite [pə'tiːt] adj piccolo(a) e aggraziato(a)
petition [pə'tɪʃən] n petizione f
petrified ['petrɪfaɪd] adj (fig) morto(a) di
paura
petrol ['petrəl] (BRIT) n benzina; **two/four-
star ~** ≈ benzina normale/super; ~ **can** n
tanica per benzina
petroleum [pə'trəuliəm] n petrolio
petrol: ~ **pump** (BRIT) n (in car, at garage)
pompa di benzina; ~ **station** (BRIT) n
stazione f di rifornimento; ~ **tank** (BRIT) n
serbatoio della benzina
petticoat ['petɪkəut] n sottana
petty ['petɪ] adj (mean) meschino(a);
(unimportant) insignificante; ~ **cash** n
piccola cassa; ~ **officer** n sottufficiale m di
marina
petulant ['petjulənt] adj irritabile
pew [pjuː] n panca (di chiesa)
pewter ['pjuːtə*] n peltro
phallic ['fælɪk] adj fallico(a)
phantom ['fæntəm] n fantasma m
pharmaceutical [fɑːmə'sjuːtɪkl] adj
farmaceutico(a)
pharmacy ['fɑːməsɪ] n farmacia
phase [feɪz] n fase f, periodo ♦ vt: **to ~ sth
in/out** introdurre/eliminare qc
progressivamente
Ph.D. n abbr = **Doctor of Philosophy**
pheasant ['feznt] n fagiano
phenomena [fə'nɒmɪnə] npl of
phenomenon

phenomenon [fə'nɔmɪnən] (*pl* **phenomena**) *n* fenomeno

Philippines ['fɪlɪpiːnz] *npl*: **the ~** le Filippine

philosophical [fɪlə'sɔfɪkl] *adj* filosofico(a)

philosophy [fɪ'lɔsəfɪ] *n* filosofia

phobia ['fəubjə] *n* fobia

phone [fəun] *n* telefono ♦ *vt* telefonare; **to be on the ~** avere il telefono; (*be calling*) essere al telefono; **~ back** *vt, vi* richiamare; **~ up** *vt* telefonare a ♦ *vi* telefonare; **~ book** *n* guida del telefono, elenco telefonico; **~ booth** *n* = **~ box**; **~ box** *n* cabina telefonica; **~ call** *n* telefonata; **~card** *n* scheda telefonica; **~-in** *n* (*BRIT: RADIO, TV*) trasmissione *f* a filo diretto con gli ascoltatori

phonetics [fə'nɛtɪks] *n* fonetica

phoney ['fəunɪ] *adj* falso(a), fasullo(a)

phosphorus ['fɔsfərəs] *n* fosforo

photo ['fəutəu] *n* foto *f inv*

photo... ['fəutəu] *prefix*: **~copier** *n* fotocopiatrice *f*; **~copy** *n* fotocopia ♦ *vt* fotocopiare; **~graph** *n* fotografia ♦ *vt* fotografare; **~grapher** [fə'tɔɡrəfə*] *n* fotografo; **~graphy** [fə'tɔɡrəfɪ] *n* fotografia

phrase [freɪz] *n* espressione *f*; (*LING*) locuzione *f*; (*MUS*) frase *f* ♦ *vt* esprimere; **~ book** *n* vocabolarietto

physical ['fɪzɪkl] *adj* fisico(a); **~ education** *n* educazione *f* fisica; **~ly** *adv* fisicamente

physician [fɪ'zɪʃən] *n* medico

physicist ['fɪzɪsɪst] *n* fisico

physics ['fɪzɪks] *n* fisica

physiology [fɪzɪ'ɔlədʒɪ] *n* fisiologia

physique [fɪ'ziːk] *n* fisico; costituzione *f*

pianist ['piːənɪst] *n* pianista *m/f*

piano [pɪ'ænəu] *n* pianoforte *m*

piccolo ['pɪkələu] *n* ottavino

pick [pɪk] *n* (*tool: also:* **~-axe**) piccone *m* ♦ *vt* scegliere; (*gather*) cogliere; (*remove*) togliere; (*lock*) far scattare; **take your ~** scelga; **the ~ of** il fior fiore di; **to ~ one's nose** mettersi le dita nel naso; **to ~ one's teeth** pulirsi i denti con lo stuzzicadenti; **to ~ a quarrel** attaccar briga; **~ at** *vt fus*: **to ~ at one's food** piluccare; **~ on** *vt fus*

(*person*) avercela con; **~ out** *vt* scegliere; (*distinguish*) distinguere; **~ up** *vi* (*improve*) migliorarsi ♦ *vt* raccogliere; (*POLICE, RADIO*) prendere; (*collect*) passare a prendere; (*AUT: give lift to*) far salire; (*person: for sexual encounter*) rimorchiare; (*learn*) imparare; **to ~ up speed** acquistare velocità; **to ~ o.s. up** rialzarsi

picket ['pɪkɪt] *n* (*in strike*) scioperante *m/f* che fa parte di un picchetto; picchetto ♦ *vt* picchettare

pickle ['pɪkl] *n* (*also:* **~s**: *as condiment*) sottaceti *mpl*; (*fig: mess*) pasticcio ♦ *vt* mettere sottaceto; mettere in salamoia

pickpocket ['pɪkpɔkɪt] *n* borsaiolo

pickup ['pɪkʌp] *n* (*small truck*) camioncino

picnic ['pɪknɪk] *n* picnic *m inv*

picture ['pɪktʃə*] *n* quadro; (*painting*) pittura; (*photograph*) foto(grafia) *f*; (*drawing*) disegno; (*film*) film *m inv* ♦ *vt* raffigurarsi; **~s** (*BRIT*) *npl* (*cinema*): **the ~s** il cinema; **~ book** *n* libro illustrato

picturesque [pɪktʃə'resk] *adj* pittoresco(a)

pie [paɪ] *n* torta; (*of meat*) pasticcio

piece [piːs] *n* pezzo; (*of land*) appezzamento; (*item*): **a ~ of furniture/ advice** un mobile/consiglio ♦ *vt*: **to ~ together** mettere insieme; **to take to ~s** smontare; **~meal** *adv* pezzo a pezzo, a spizzico; **~work** *n* (lavoro a) cottimo

pie chart *n* grafico a torta

pier [pɪə*] *n* molo; (*of bridge etc*) pila

pierce [pɪəs] *vt* forare; (*with arrow etc*) trafiggere

piercing ['pɪəsɪŋ] *adj* (*cry*) acuto(a); (*eyes*) penetrante; (*wind*) pungente

pig [pɪɡ] *n* maiale *m*, porco

pigeon ['pɪdʒən] *n* piccione *m*; **~hole** *n* casella

piggy bank ['pɪɡɪ-] *n* salvadanaio

pigheaded ['pɪɡ'hɛdɪd] *adj* caparbio(a), cocciuto(a)

piglet ['pɪɡlɪt] *n* porcellino

pigskin ['pɪɡskɪn] *n* cinghiale *m*

pigsty ['pɪɡstaɪ] *n* porcile *m*

pigtail ['pɪɡteɪl] *n* treccina

pike [paɪk] *n* (*fish*) luccio

pilchard ['pɪltʃəd] *n specie di sardina*

pile [paɪl] *n* (*pillar, of books*) pila; (*heap*) mucchio; (*of carpet*) pelo ♦ *vt* (*also:* ~ **up**) ammucchiare ♦ *vi* (*also:* ~ **up**) ammucchiarsi; **to ~ into** (*car*) stiparsi *or* ammucchiarsi in

piles [paɪlz] *npl* emorroidi *fpl*

pile-up ['paɪlʌp] *n* (*AUT*) tamponamento a catena

pilfering ['pɪlfərɪŋ] *n* rubacchiare *m*

pilgrim ['pɪlgrɪm] *n* pellegrino/a; **~age** *n* pellegrinaggio

pill [pɪl] *n* pillola; **the ~** la pillola

pillage ['pɪlɪdʒ] *vt* saccheggiare

pillar ['pɪlə*] *n* colonna; ~ **box** (*BRIT*) *n* cassetta postale

pillion ['pɪljən] *n*: **to ride ~** (*on motor cycle*) viaggiare dietro

pillow ['pɪləʊ] *n* guanciale *m*; **~case** *n* federa

pilot ['paɪlət] *n* pilota *m/f* ♦ *cpd* (*scheme etc*) pilota *inv* ♦ *vt* pilotare; ~ **light** *n* fiamma pilota

pimp [pɪmp] *n* mezzano

pimple ['pɪmpl] *n* foruncolo

pin [pɪn] *n* spillo; (*TECH*) perno ♦ *vt* attaccare con uno spillo; **~s and needles** formicolio; **to ~ sb down** (*fig*) obbligare qn a pronunziarsi; **to ~ sth on sb** (*fig*) addossare la colpa di qc a qn

pinafore ['pɪnəfɔ:*] *n* (*also:* ~ **dress**) grembiule *m* (senza maniche)

pinball ['pɪnbɔ:l] *n* flipper *m inv*

pincers ['pɪnsəz] *npl* pinzette *fpl*

pinch [pɪntʃ] *n* pizzicotto, pizzico ♦ *vt* pizzicare; (*inf: steal*) grattare; **at a ~** in caso di bisogno

pincushion ['pɪnkʊʃən] *n* puntaspilli *m inv*

pine [paɪn] *n* (*also:* ~ **tree**) pino ♦ *vi*: **to ~ for** struggersi dal desiderio di; ~ **away** *vi* languire

pineapple ['paɪnæpl] *n* ananas *m inv*

ping [pɪŋ] *n* (*noise*) tintinnio; **~-pong** ® *n* ping-pong ® *m*

pink [pɪŋk] *adj* rosa *inv* ♦ *n* (*colour*) rosa *m inv*; (*BOT*) garofano

PIN (number) [pɪn-] *n abbr* codice *m* segreto

pinpoint ['pɪnpɔɪnt] *vt* indicare con precisione

pint [paɪnt] *n* pinta (*BRIT = 0.57l*; *US = 0.47l*); (*BRIT: inf*) ≈ birra da mezzo

pioneer [paɪə'nɪə*] *n* pioniere/a

pious ['paɪəs] *adj* pio(a)

pip [pɪp] *n* (*seed*) seme *m*; (*BRIT: time signal on radio*) segnale *m* orario

pipe [paɪp] *n* tubo; (*for smoking*) pipa ♦ *vt* portare per mezzo di tubazione; **~s** *npl* (*also:* **bag~s**) cornamusa (scozzese); ~ **cleaner** *n* scovolino; ~ **dream** *n* vana speranza; **~line** *n* conduttura; (*for oil*) oleodotto; **~r** *n* piffero; suonatore/trice di cornamusa

piping ['paɪpɪŋ] *adv*: ~ **hot** caldo bollente

pique [pi:k] *n* picca

pirate ['paɪərət] *n* pirata *m* ♦ *vt* riprodurre abusivamente

Pisces ['paɪsi:z] *n* Pesci *mpl*

piss [pɪs] (*inf*) *vi* pisciare; **~ed** (*inf*) *adj* (*drunk*) ubriaco(a) fradicio(a)

pistol ['pɪstl] *n* pistola

piston ['pɪstən] *n* pistone *m*

pit [pɪt] *n* buca, fossa; (*also:* **coal ~**) miniera; (*quarry*) cava ♦ *vt*: **to ~ sb against sb** opporre qn a qn; **~s** *npl* (*AUT*) box *m*

pitch [pɪtʃ] *n* (*BRIT: SPORT*) campo; (*MUS*) tono; (*tar*) pece *f*; (*fig*) grado, punto ♦ *vt* (*throw*) lanciare ♦ *vi* (*fall*) cascare; **to ~ a tent** piantare una tenda; **~ed battle** *n* battaglia campale

pitfall ['pɪtfɔ:l] *n* trappola

pith [pɪθ] *n* (*of plant*) midollo; (*of orange*) parte *f* interna della scorza; (*fig*) essenza, succo; vigore *m*

pithy ['pɪθɪ] *adj* conciso(a); vigoroso(a)

pitiful ['pɪtɪful] *adj* (*touching*) pietoso(a)

pitiless ['pɪtɪlɪs] *adj* spietato(a)

pittance ['pɪtns] *n* miseria, magro salario

pity ['pɪtɪ] *n* pietà ♦ *vt* aver pietà di; **what a ~!** che peccato!

pivot ['pɪvət] *n* perno

pizza ['pi:tsə] *n* pizza

placard ['plækɑ:d] *n* affisso

placate [plə'keɪt] *vt* placare, calmare

place [pleɪs] *n* posto, luogo; (*proper position, rank, seat*) posto; (*house*) alloggio; (*home*): **at/to his ~** a casa sua ♦ *vt* (*object*) posare, mettere; (*identify*) riconoscere; individuare; **to take ~** aver luogo; succedere; **to change ~s with sb** scambiare il posto con qn; **out of ~** (*not suitable*) inopportuno(a); **in the first ~** in primo luogo; **to ~ an order** dare un'ordinazione; **to be ~d** (*in race, exam*) classificarsi

placid ['plæsɪd] *adj* placido(a), calmo(a)

plagiarism ['pleɪdʒərɪzəm] *n* plagio

plague [pleɪg] *n* peste *f* ♦ *vt* tormentare

plaice [pleɪs] *n inv* pianuzza

plaid [plæd] *n* plaid *m inv*

plain [pleɪn] *adj* (*clear*) chiaro(a), palese; (*simple*) semplice; (*frank*) franco(a), aperto(a); (*not handsome*) bruttino(a); (*without seasoning etc*) scondito(a); naturale; (*in one colour*) tinta unita *inv* ♦ *adv* francamente, chiaramente ♦ *n* pianura; **~ chocolate** *n* cioccolato fondente; **~ clothes** *npl*: **in ~ clothes** (*police*) in borghese; **~ly** *adv* chiaramente; (*frankly*) francamente

plaintiff ['pleɪntɪf] *n* attore/trice

plaintive ['pleɪntɪv] *adj* (*cry, voice*) dolente, lamentoso(a)

plait [plæt] *n* treccia

plan [plæn] *n* pianta; (*scheme*) progetto, piano ♦ *vt* (*think in advance*) progettare; (*prepare*) organizzare ♦ *vi* far piani *or* progetti; **to ~ to do** progettare di fare

plane [pleɪn] *n* (*AVIAT*) aereo; (*tree*) platano; (*tool*) pialla; (*ART, MATH etc*) piano ♦ *adj* piano(a), piatto(a) ♦ *vt* (*with tool*) piallare

planet ['plænɪt] *n* pianeta *m*

plank [plæŋk] *n* tavola, asse *f*

planner ['plænə*] *n* pianificatore/trice

planning ['plænɪŋ] *n* progettazione *f*; **family ~** pianificazione *f* delle nascite; **~ permission** *n* permesso di costruzione

plant [plɑːnt] *n* pianta; (*machinery*) impianto; (*factory*) fabbrica ♦ *vt* piantare; (*bomb*) mettere

plantation [plæn'teɪʃən] *n* piantagione *f*

plaque [plæk] *n* placca

plaster ['plɑːstə*] *n* intonaco; (*also*: **~ of Paris**) gesso; (*BRIT: also*: **sticking ~**) cerotto ♦ *vt* intonacare; ingessare; (*cover*): **to ~ with** coprire di; **~ed** (*inf*) *adj* ubriaco(a) fradicio(a)

plastic ['plæstɪk] *n* plastica ♦ *adj* (*made of ~*) di *or* in plastica; **~ bag** *n* sacchetto di plastica

Plasticine ® ['plæstɪsiːn] *n* plastilina ®

plastic surgery *n* chirurgia plastica

plate [pleɪt] *n* (*dish*) piatto; (*in book*) tavola; (*dental*) dentiera; **gold/silver ~** vasellame *m* d'oro/d'argento

plateau ['plætəu] (*pl* **~s** *or* **~x**) *n* altipiano

plateaux ['plætəuz] *npl of* **plateau**

plate glass *n* vetro piano

platform ['plætfɔːm] *n* (*stage, at meeting*) palco; (*RAIL*) marciapiede *m*; (*BRIT: of bus*) piattaforma

platinum ['plætɪnəm] *n* platino

platitude ['plætɪtjuːd] *n* luogo comune

platoon [plə'tuːn] *n* plotone *m*

platter ['plætə*] *n* piatto

plausible ['plɔːzɪbl] *adj* plausibile, credibile; (*person*) convincente

play [pleɪ] *n* gioco; (*THEATRE*) commedia ♦ *vt* (*game*) giocare a; (*team, opponent*) giocare contro; (*instrument, piece of music*) suonare; (*record, tape*) ascoltare; (*role, part*) interpretare ♦ *vi* giocare; suonare; recitare; **to ~ safe** giocare sul sicuro; **~ down** *vt* minimizzare; **~ up** *vi* (*cause trouble*) fare i capricci; **~boy** *n* playboy *m inv*; **~er** *n* giocatore/trice; (*THEATRE*) attore/trice; (*MUS*) musicista *m/f*; **~ful** *adj* giocoso(a); **~ground** *n* (*in school*) cortile *m* per la ricreazione; (*in park*) parco *m* giochi *inv*; **~group** *n* giardino d'infanzia; **~ing card** *n* carta da gioco; **~ing field** *n* campo sportivo; **~mate** *n* compagno/a di gioco; **~-off** *n* (*SPORT*) bella; **~pen** *n* box *m inv*; **~thing** *n* giocattolo; **~time** *n* (*SCOL*) ricreazione *f*; **~wright** *n* drammaturgo/a

plc *abbr* (= *public limited company*) società per azioni a responsabilità limitata quotata in borsa

plea [pli:] *n* (*request*) preghiera, domanda; (*LAW*) (argomento di) difesa; ~ **bargaining** *n* (*LAW*) patteggiamento (della pena)

plead [pli:d] *vt* patrocinare; (*give as excuse*) addurre a pretesto ♦ *vi* (*LAW*) perorare la causa; (*beg*): **to ~ with sb** implorare qn

pleasant ['plɛznt] *adj* piacevole, gradevole; ~**ries** *npl* (*polite remarks*): **to exchange ~ries** scambiarsi convenevoli

please [pli:z] *excl* per piacere!, per favore!; (*acceptance*): **yes, ~** sì, grazie ♦ *vt* piacere a ♦ *vi* piacere; (*think fit*): **do as you ~** faccia come le pare; ~ **yourself!** come ti (*or* le) pare!; ~**d** *adj*: ~**d (with)** contento(a) (di); ~**d to meet you!** piacere!; **pleasing** *adj* piacevole, che fa piacere

pleasure ['plɛʒə*] *n* piacere *m*; **"it's a ~"** "prego"

pleat [pli:t] *n* piega

pledge [plɛdʒ] *n* pegno; (*promise*) promessa ♦ *vt* impegnare; promettere

plentiful ['plɛntɪful] *adj* abbondante, copioso(a)

plenty ['plɛntɪ] *n*: ~ **of** tanto(a), molto(a); un'abbondanza di

pleurisy ['pluərɪsɪ] *n* pleurite *f*

pliable ['plaɪəbl] *adj* flessibile; (*fig: person*) malleabile

pliant [plaɪənt] *adj* = **pliable**

pliers ['plaɪəz] *npl* pinza

plight [plaɪt] *n* situazione *f* critica

plimsolls ['plɪmsəlz] (*BRIT*) *npl* scarpe *fpl* da tennis

plinth [plɪnθ] *n* plinto; piedistallo

plod [plɔd] *vi* camminare a stento; (*fig*) sgobbare

plonk [plɔŋk] (*inf*) *n* (*BRIT: wine*) vino da poco ♦ *vt*: **to ~ sth down** buttare giù qc bruscamente

plot [plɔt] *n* congiura, cospirazione *f*; (*of story, play*) trama; (*of land*) lotto ♦ *vt* (*mark out*) fare la pianta di; rilevare; (: *diagram etc*) tracciare; (*conspire*) congiurare, cospirare ♦ *vi* congiurare

plough [plau] (*US* **plow**) *n* aratro ♦ *vt* (*earth*) arare; **to ~ money into** (*company*

etc) investire danaro in; ~ **through** *vt fus* (*snow etc*) procedere a fatica in; ~**man's lunch** (*BRIT*) *n* pasto a base di pane, formaggio e birra

ploy [plɔɪ] *n* stratagemma *m*

pluck [plʌk] *vt* (*fruit*) cogliere; (*musical instrument*) pizzicare; (*bird*) spennare; (*hairs*) togliere ♦ *n* coraggio, fegato; **to ~ up courage** farsi coraggio

plug [plʌg] *n* tappo; (*ELEC*) spina; (*AUT: also*: **spark(ing) ~**) candela ♦ *vt* (*hole*) tappare; (*inf: advertise*) spingere; ~ **in** *vt* (*ELEC*) attaccare a una presa

plum [plʌm] *n* (*fruit*) susina

plumb [plʌm] *vt*: **to ~ the depths** (*fig*) toccare il fondo

plumber ['plʌmə*] *n* idraulico

plumbing ['plʌmɪŋ] *n* (*trade*) lavoro di idraulico; (*piping*) tubature *fpl*

plummet ['plʌmɪt] *vi*: **to ~ (down)** cadere a piombo

plump [plʌmp] *adj* grassoccio(a) ♦ *vi*: **to ~ for** (*inf: choose*) decidersi per; ~ **up** *vt* (*cushion etc*) sprimacciare

plunder ['plʌndə*] *n* saccheggio ♦ *vt* saccheggiare

plunge [plʌndʒ] *n* tuffo; (*fig*) caduta ♦ *vt* immergere ♦ *vi* (*fall*) cadere, precipitare; (*dive*) tuffarsi; **to take the ~** saltare il fosso; **plunging** *adj* (*neckline*) profondo(a)

pluperfect [plu:'pə:fɪkt] *n* piucchepperfetto

plural ['pluərl] *adj* plurale ♦ *n* plurale *m*

plus [plʌs] *n* (*also*: ~ **sign**) segno più ♦ *prep* più; **ten/twenty ~** piùr di dieci/venti

plush [plʌʃ] *adj* lussuoso(a)

ply [plaɪ] *vt* (*a trade*) esercitare ♦ *vi* (*ship*) fare il servizio ♦ *n* (*of wool, rope*) capo; **to ~ sb with drink** dare di bere continuamente a qn; ~**wood** *n* legno compensato

P.M. *n abbr* = **prime minister**

p.m. *adv abbr* (= *post meridiem*) del pomeriggio

pneumatic drill [nju:'mætɪk-] *n* martello pneumatico

pneumonia [nju:'məunɪə] *n* polmonite *f*

poach [pəutʃ] *vt* (*cook: egg*) affogare; (: *fish*) cuocere in bianco; (*steal*) cacciare (*or* pescare) di frodo ♦ *vi* fare il bracconiere; **~er** *n* bracconiere *m*

P.O. Box *n abbr* = **Post Office Box**

pocket ['pɔkɪt] *n* tasca ♦ *vt* intascare; **to be out of ~** (*BRIT*) rimetterci; **~book** (*US*) *n* (*wallet*) portafoglio; **~ knife** *n* temperino; **~ money** *n* paghetta, settimana

pod [pɔd] *n* guscio

podgy ['pɔdʒɪ] *adj* grassoccio(a)

podiatrist [pɔ'di:ətrɪst] (*US*) *n* callista *m/f*, pedicure *m/f*

poem ['pəuɪm] *n* poesia

poet ['pəuɪt] *n* poeta/essa; **~ic** [-'ɛtɪk] *adj* poetico(a); **~ry** *n* poesia

poignant ['pɔɪnjənt] *adj* struggente

point [pɔɪnt] *n* (*gen*) punto; (*tip: of needle etc*) punta; (*in time*) punto, momento; (*SCOL*) voto; (*main idea, important part*) nocciolo; (*ELEC*) presa (di corrente); (*also*: **decimal ~**): **2 ~ 3 (2.3)** 2 virgola 3 (2,3) ♦ *vt* (*show*) indicare; (*gun etc*): **to ~ sth at** puntare qc contro ♦ *vi*: **to ~ at** mostrare a dito; **~s** *npl* (*AUT*) puntine *fpl*; (*RAIL*) scambio; **to be on the ~ of doing sth** essere sul punto di *or* stare per fare qc; **to make a ~** fare un'osservazione; **to get/ miss the ~** capire/non capire; **to come to the ~** venire al fatto; **there's no ~ (in doing)** è inutile (fare); **~ out** *vt* far notare; **~ to** *vt fus* indicare; (*fig*) dimostrare; **~-blank** *adv* (*also*: **at ~-blank range**) a bruciapelo; (*fig*) categoricamente; **~ed** *adj* (*shape*) aguzzo(a), appuntito(a); (*remark*) specifico(a); **~edly** *adv* in maniera inequivocabile; **~er** *n* (*needle*) lancetta; (*fig*) indicazione *f*, consiglio; **~less** *adj* inutile, vano(a); **~ of view** *n* punto di vista

poise [pɔɪz] *n* (*composure*) portamento; **~d** *adj*: **to be ~d to do** tenersi pronto(a) a fare

poison ['pɔɪzn] *n* veleno ♦ *vt* avvelenare; **~ing** *n* avvelenamento; **~ous** *adj* velenoso(a)

poke [pəuk] *vt* (*fire*) attizzare; (*jab with finger, stick etc*) punzecchiare; (*put*): **to ~ sth in(to)** spingere qc dentro; **~ about** *vi* frugare

poker ['pəukə*] *n* attizzatoio; (*CARDS*) poker *m*

poky ['pəukɪ] *adj* piccolo(a) e stretto(a)

Poland ['pəulənd] *n* Polonia

polar ['pəulə*] *adj* polare; **~ bear** *n* orso bianco

Pole [pəul] *n* polacco/a

pole [pəul] *n* (*of wood*) palo; (*ELEC, GEO*) polo; **~ bean** (*US*) *n* (*runner bean*) fagiolino; **~ vault** *n* salto con l'asta

police [pə'li:s] *n* polizia ♦ *vt* mantenere l'ordine in; **~ car** *n* macchina della polizia; **~man** (*irreg*) *n* poliziotto, agente *m* di polizia; **~ station** *n* posto di polizia; **~woman** (*irreg*) *n* donna *f* poliziotto *inv*

policy ['pɔlɪsɪ] *n* politica; (*also*: **insurance ~**) polizza (d'assicurazione)

polio ['pəulɪəu] *n* polio *f*

Polish ['pəulɪʃ] *adj* polacco(a) ♦ *n* (*LING*) polacco

polish ['pɔlɪʃ] *n* (*for shoes*) lucido; (*for floor*) cera; (*for nails*) smalto; (*shine*) lucentezza, lustro; (*fig: refinement*) raffinatezza ♦ *vt* lucidare; (*fig: improve*) raffinare; **~ off** *vt* (*food*) mangiarsi; **~ed** *adj* (*fig*) raffinato(a)

polite [pə'laɪt] *adj* cortese; **~ness** *n* cortesia

political [pə'lɪtɪkl] *adj* politico(a); **~ly** *adv* politicamente; **~ly correct** politicamente corretto(a)

politician [pɔlɪ'tɪʃən] *n* politico

politics ['pɔlɪtɪks] *n* politica ♦ *npl* (*views, policies*) idee *fpl* politiche

poll [pəul] *n* scrutinio; (*votes cast*) voti *mpl*; (*also*: **opinion ~**) sondaggio (d'opinioni) ♦ *vt* ottenere

pollen ['pɔlən] *n* polline *m*

polling day ['pəulɪŋ-] (*BRIT*) *n* giorno delle elezioni

polling station ['pəulɪŋ-] (*BRIT*) *n* sezione *f* elettorale

pollute [pə'lu:t] *vt* inquinare

pollution [pə'lu:ʃən] *n* inquinamento

polo ['pəuləu] *n* polo; **~-necked** *adj* a collo alto risvoltato; **~ shirt** *n* polo *f inv*

polyester [pɔlɪ'ɛstə*] *n* poliestere *m*

polystyrene [pɔlɪ'staɪri:n] *n* polistirolo

polytechnic [pɔlɪ'tɛknɪk] *n* (*college*) istituto

superiore ad indirizzo tecnologico
polythene ['pɒliθiːn] *n* politene *m*; ~ **bag** *n* sacco di plastica
pomegranate ['pɒmɪgrænɪt] *n* melagrana
pomp [pɒmp] *n* pompa, fasto
pompom ['pɒmpɒm] *n* pompon *m inv*
pompon ['pɒmpɒn] *n* = **pompom**
pompous ['pɒmpəs] *adj* pomposo(a)
pond [pɒnd] *n* pozza; stagno
ponder ['pɒndə*] *vt* ponderare, riflettere su; ~**ous** *adj* ponderoso(a), pesante
pong [pɒŋ] (*BRIT: inf*) *n* puzzo
pony ['pəʊnɪ] *n* pony *m inv*; ~**tail** *n* coda di cavallo; ~ **trekking** (*BRIT*) *n* escursione *f* a cavallo
poodle ['puːdl] *n* barboncino, barbone *m*
pool [puːl] *n* (*puddle*) pozza; (*pond*) stagno; (*also*: **swimming ~**) piscina; (*fig: of light*) cerchio; (*billiards*) *specie di biliardo a buca* ♦ *vt* mettere in comune; ~**s** *npl* (*football ~s*) ≈ totocalcio; **typing ~** servizio comune di dattilografia
poor [pʊə*] *adj* povero(a); (*mediocre*) mediocre, cattivo(a) ♦ *npl*: **the ~** i poveri; ~ **in** povero(a) di; ~**ly** *adv* poveramente; male ♦ *adj* indisposto(a), malato(a)
pop [pɒp] *n* (*noise*) schiocco; (*MUS*) musica pop; (*drink*) bibita gasata; (*US: inf: father*) babbo ♦ *vt* (*put*) mettere (in fretta) ♦ *vi* scoppiare; (*cork*) schioccare; ~ **in** *vi* passare; ~ **out** *vi* fare un salto fuori; ~ **up** *vi* apparire, sorgere; ~**corn** *n* pop-corn *m*
pope [pəʊp] *n* papa *m*
poplar ['pɒplə*] *n* pioppo
popper ['pɒpə*] *n* bottone *m* a pressione
poppy ['pɒpɪ] *n* papavero
Popsicle ® ['pɒpsɪkl] (*US*) *n* (*ice lolly*) ghiacciolo
populace ['pɒpjʊlɪs] *n* popolino
popular ['pɒpjʊlə*] *adj* popolare; (*fashionable*) in voga; ~**ity** [-'lærɪtɪ] *n* popolarità
population [pɒpjʊ'leɪʃən] *n* popolazione *f*
porcelain ['pɔːslɪn] *n* porcellana
porch [pɔːtʃ] *n* veranda
porcupine ['pɔːkjʊpaɪn] *n* porcospino
pore [pɔː*] *n* poro ♦ *vi*: **to ~ over** essere immerso(a) in

pork [pɔːk] *n* carne *f* di maiale
pornographic [pɔːnə'græfɪk] *adj* pornografico(a)
pornography [pɔː'nɒgrəfɪ] *n* pornografia
porpoise ['pɔːpəs] *n* focena
porridge ['pɒrɪdʒ] *n* porridge *m*
port [pɔːt] *n* (*gen, wine*) porto; (*NAUT: left side*) babordo; ~ **of call** (porto di) scalo
portable ['pɔːtəbl] *adj* portatile
porter ['pɔːtə*] *n* (*for luggage*) facchino, portabagagli *m inv*; (*doorkeeper*) portiere *m*, portinaio
portfolio [pɔːt'fəʊlɪəʊ] *n* (*case*) cartella; (*POL, FINANCE*) portafoglio; (*of artist*) raccolta dei propri lavori
porthole ['pɔːthəʊl] *n* oblò *m inv*
portion ['pɔːʃən] *n* porzione *f*
portrait ['pɔːtreɪt] *n* ritratto
portray [pɔː'treɪ] *vt* fare il ritratto di; (*character on stage*) rappresentare; (*in writing*) ritrarre
Portugal ['pɔːtjʊgl] *n* Portogallo
Portuguese [pɔːtjʊ'giːz] *adj* portoghese ♦ *n inv* portoghese *m/f*; (*LING*) portoghese *m*
pose [pəʊz] *n* posa ♦ *vi* posare; (*pretend*): **to ~ as** atteggiarsi a, posare a ♦ *vt* porre
posh [pɒʃ] (*inf*) *adj* elegante; (*family*) per bene
position [pə'zɪʃən] *n* posizione *f*; (*job*) posto ♦ *vt* sistemare
positive ['pɒzɪtɪv] *adj* positivo(a); (*certain*) sicuro(a), certo(a); (*definite*) preciso(a); definitivo(a)
posse ['pɒsɪ] (*US*) *n* drappello
possess [pə'zɛs] *vt* possedere; ~**ion** [pə'zɛʃən] *n* possesso; ~**ions** *npl* (*belongings*) beni *mpl*; ~**ive** *adj* possessivo(a)
possibility [pɒsɪ'bɪlɪtɪ] *n* possibilità *f inv*
possible ['pɒsɪbl] *adj* possibile; **as big as ~** il più grande possibile
possibly ['pɒsɪblɪ] *adv* (*perhaps*) forse; **if you ~ can** se le è possibile; **I cannot ~ come** proprio non posso venire
post [pəʊst] *n* (*BRIT*) posta; (: *collection*) levata; (*job, situation*) posto; (*MIL*)

postazione f; (*pole*) palo ♦ vt (*BRIT: send by post*) impostare; (: *appoint*): **to ~ to** assegnare a; **~age** n affrancatura; **~age stamp** n francobollo; **~al order** n vaglia m inv postale; **~box** (*BRIT*) n cassetta postale; **~card** n cartolina; **~ code** (*BRIT*) n codice m (di avviamento) postale

poster ['pəustə*] n manifesto, affisso

poste restante [pəust'rɛstɑ̃:nt] (*BRIT*) n fermo posta m

postgraduate ['pəust'grædjuət] n laureato/a che continua gli studi

posthumous ['pɔstjuməs] adj postumo(a)

postman ['pəustmən] (*irreg*) n postino

postmark ['pəustmɑ:k] n bollo *or* timbro postale

post-mortem [-'mɔ:təm] n autopsia

post office n (*building*) ufficio postale; (*organization*): **the Post Office** ≈ le Poste e Telecomunicazioni; **Post Office Box** n casella postale

postpone [pəs'pəun] vt rinviare

postscript ['pəustskrɪpt] n poscritto

posture ['pɔstʃə*] n portamento; (*pose*) posa, atteggiamento

postwar ['pəust'wɔ:*] adj del dopoguerra

posy ['pəuzɪ] n mazzetto di fiori

pot [pɔt] n (*for cooking*) pentola; casseruola; (*tea*~) teiera; (*coffee*~) caffettiera; (*for plants, jam*) vaso; (*inf: marijuana*) erba ♦ vt (*plant*) piantare in vaso; **a ~ of tea for two** tè per due; **to go to ~** (*inf: work, performance*) andare in malora

potato [pə'teɪtəu] (*pl* **~es**) n patata; **~ peeler** n sbucciapatate m inv

potent ['pəutnt] adj potente, forte

potential [pə'tɛnʃl] adj potenziale ♦ n possibilità fpl

pothole ['pɔthəul] n (*in road*) buca; (*BRIT: underground*) caverna; **potholing** (*BRIT*) n: **to go potholing** fare speleologia

potluck [pɔt'lʌk] n: **to take ~** tentare la sorte

potted ['pɔtɪd] adj (*food*) in conserva; (*plant*) in vaso; (*account etc*) condensato(a)

potter ['pɔtə*] n vasaio ♦ vi: **to ~ around, ~ about** (*BRIT*) lavoracchiare; **~y** n ceramiche

fpl; (*factory*) fabbrica di ceramiche

potty ['pɔtɪ] adj (*inf: mad*) tocco(a) ♦ n (*child's*) vasino

pouch [pautʃ] n borsa; (*ZOOL*) marsupio

poultry ['pəultrɪ] n pollame m

pounce [pauns] vi: **to ~ (on)** piombare (su)

pound [paund] n (*weight*) libbra; (*money*) (*lira*) sterlina ♦ vt (*beat*) battere; (*crush*) pestare, polverizzare ♦ vi (*beat*) battere, martellare; **~ sterling** n sterlina (*inglese*)

pour [pɔ:*] vt versare ♦ vi riversarsi; (*rain*) piovere a dirotto; **~ away** vt vuotare; **~ in** vi affluire in gran quantità; **~ off** vt vuotare; **~ out** vi (*people*) uscire a fiumi ♦ vt vuotare; versare; (*fig*) sfogare; **~ing** adj: **~ing rain** pioggia torrenziale

pout [paut] vi sporgere le labbra; fare il broncio

poverty ['pɔvətɪ] n povertà, miseria; **~-stricken** adj molto povero(a), misero(a)

powder ['paudə*] n polvere f ♦ vt: **to ~ one's face** incipriarsi il viso; **~ compact** n portacipria m inv; **~ed milk** n latte m in polvere; **~ room** n toilette f inv (*per signore*)

power ['pauə*] n (*strength*) potenza, forza; (*ability, POL: of party, leader*) potere m; (*ELEC*) corrente f; **to be in ~** (*POL etc*) essere al potere; **~ cut** (*BRIT*) n interruzione f *or* mancanza di corrente; **~ed** adj: **~ed by** azionato(a) da; **~ failure** n interruzione f della corrente elettrica; **~ful** adj potente, forte; **~less** adj impotente; **~less to do** impossibilitato(a) a fare; **~ point** (*BRIT*) n presa di corrente; **~ station** n centrale f elettrica

p.p. abbr (= *per procurationem*): **~ J. Smith** per J. Smith; (= *pages*) p.p.

PR abbr = **public relations**

practicable ['præktɪkəbl] adj (*scheme*) praticabile

practical ['præktɪkl] adj pratico(a); **~ity** [-'kælɪtɪ] (*no pl*) n (*of situation etc*) lato pratico; **~ joke** n beffa; **~ly** adv praticamente

practice ['præktɪs] n pratica; (*of profession*) esercizio; (*at football etc*) allenamento;

(*business*) gabinetto; clientela ♦ *vt*, *vi* (*US*) = **practise**; **in ~** (*in reality*) in pratica; **out of ~** fuori esercizio

practise ['præktɪs] (*US* **practice**) *vt* (*work at: piano, one's backhand etc*) esercitarsi a; (*train for: skiing, running etc*) allenarsi a; (*a sport, religion*) praticare; (*method*) usare; (*profession*) esercitare ♦ *vi* esercitarsi; (*train*) allenarsi; (*lawyer, doctor*) esercitare; **practising** *adj* (*Christian etc*) praticante; (*lawyer*) che esercita la professione

practitioner [præk'tɪʃənə*] *n* professionista *m/f*

pragmatic [præg'mætɪk] *adj* pragmatico(a)

prairie ['prɛərɪ] *n* prateria

praise [preɪz] *n* elogio, lode *f* ♦ *vt* elogiare, lodare; **~worthy** *adj* lodevole

pram [præm] (*BRIT*) *n* carrozzina

prank [præŋk] *n* burla

prawn [prɔːn] *n* gamberetto

pray [preɪ] *vi* pregare

prayer [prɛə*] *n* preghiera

preach [priːtʃ] *vt*, *vi* predicare

precarious [prɪ'kɛərɪəs] *adj* precario(a)

precaution [prɪ'kɔːʃən] *n* precauzione *f*

precede [prɪ'siːd] *vt* precedere

precedent ['presɪdənt] *n* precedente *m*

precept ['priːsept] *n* precetto

precinct ['priːsɪŋkt] *n* (*US*) circoscrizione *f*; **~s** *npl* (*of building*) zona recintata; **pedestrian ~** (*BRIT*) zona pedonale; **shopping ~** (*BRIT*) centro commerciale (chiuso al traffico)

precious ['preʃəs] *adj* prezioso(a)

precipitate [prɪ'sɪpɪteɪt] *vt* precipitare

precise [prɪ'saɪs] *adj* preciso(a); **~ly** *adv* precisamente

precocious [prɪ'kəʊʃəs] *adj* precoce

precondition [priːkən'dɪʃən] *n* condizione *f* necessaria

predecessor ['priːdɪsesə*] *n* predecessore/a

predicament [prɪ'dɪkəmənt] *n* situazione *f* difficile

predict [prɪ'dɪkt] *vt* predire; **~able** *adj* prevedibile

predominantly [prɪ'dɒmɪnəntlɪ] *adv* in maggior parte; soprattutto

predominate [prɪ'dɒmɪneɪt] *vi* predominare

pre-empt [priː'empt] *vt* pregiudicare

preen [priːn] *vt*: **to ~ itself** (*bird*) lisciarsi le penne; **to ~ o.s.** agghindarsi

prefab ['priːfæb] *n* casa prefabbricata

preface ['prefəs] *n* prefazione *f*

prefect ['priːfekt] *n* (*BRIT: in school*) studente/essa con funzioni disciplinari; (*French etc, Admin*) prefetto

prefer [prɪ'fɜː*] *vt* preferire; **to ~ doing** *or* **to do** preferire fare; **~ably** ['prefrəblɪ] *adv* preferibilmente; **~ence** ['prefrəns] *n* preferenza; **~ential** [prefə'renʃəl] *adj* preferenziale

prefix ['priːfɪks] *n* prefisso

pregnancy ['pregnənsɪ] *n* gravidanza

pregnant ['pregnənt] *adj* incinta *af*

prehistoric ['priːhɪs'tɒrɪk] *adj* preistorico(a)

prejudice ['predʒudɪs] *n* pregiudizio; (*harm*) torto, danno; **~d** *adj*: **~d (against)** prevenuto(a) (contro); **~d (in favour of)** ben disposto(a) (verso)

preliminary [prɪ'lɪmɪnərɪ] *adj* preliminare

premarital ['priː'mærɪtl] *adj* prematrimoniale

premature ['premətʃʊə*] *adj* prematuro(a)

premenstrual syndrome [priː'menstruəl-] *n* (*MED*) sindrome *f* premestruale

premier ['premɪə*] *adj* primo(a) ♦ *n* (*POL*) primo ministro

première ['premɪɛə*] *n* prima

premise ['premɪs] *n* premessa; **~s** *npl* (*of business, institution*) locale *m*; **on the ~s** sul posto

premium ['priːmɪəm] *n* premio; **to be at a ~** essere ricercatissimo; **~ bond** (*BRIT*) *n* obbligazione *f* a premio

premonition [premə'nɪʃən] *n* premonizione *f*

preoccupied [priː'ɒkjupaɪd] *adj* preoccupato(a)

prep [prep] *n* (*SCOL: study*) studio

prepaid [priː'peɪd] *adj* pagato(a) in anticipo

preparation [prepə'reɪʃən] *n* preparazione *f*; **~s** *npl* (*for trip, war*) preparativi *mpl*

preparatory [prɪ'pærətərɪ] *adj*
preparatorio(a); **~ school** *n* scuola
elementare privata

prepare [prɪ'peə*] *vt* preparare ♦ *vi*: **to ~
for** prepararsi a; **~d to** pronto(a) a

preposition [prepə'zɪʃən] *n* preposizione *f*

preposterous [prɪ'pɔstərəs] *adj* assurdo(a)

prep school *n* = **preparatory school**

prerequisite [priː'rekwɪzɪt] *n* requisito
indispensabile

prescribe [prɪ'skraɪb] *vt* (MED) prescrivere

prescription [prɪ'skrɪpʃən] *n* prescrizione *f*;
(MED) ricetta

presence ['prezns] *n* presenza; **~ of mind**
presenza di spirito

present [*adj, n* 'preznt, *vb* prɪ'zent] *adj*
presente; (*wife, residence, job*) attuale ♦ *n*
(*actuality*): **the ~** il presente; (*gift*) regalo
♦ *vt* presentare; (*give*): **to ~ sb with sth**
offrire qc a qn; **to give sb a ~** fare un
regalo a qn; **at ~** al momento; **~ation**
[-'teɪʃən] *n* presentazione *f*; (*ceremony*)
consegna ufficiale; **~-day** *adj* attuale,
d'oggigiorno; **~er** *n* (RADIO, TV)
presentatore/trice; **~ly** *adv* (*soon*) fra poco,
presto; (*at present*) al momento

preservative [prɪ'zəːvətɪv] *n* conservante *m*

preserve [prɪ'zəːv] *vt* (*keep safe*) preservare,
proteggere; (*maintain*) conservare; (*food*)
mettere in conserva ♦ *n* (*often pl: jam*)
marmellata; (: *fruit*) frutta sciroppata

preside [prɪ'zaɪd] *vi*: **to ~ (over)** presiedere
(a)

president ['prezɪdənt] *n* presidente *m*; **~ial**
[-'denʃl] *adj* presidenziale

press [pres] *n* (*newspapers etc*): **the P~** la
stampa; (*tool, machine*) pressa; (*for wine*)
torchio ♦ *vt* (*push*) premere, pigiare;
(*squeeze*) spremere; (: *hand*) stringere;
(*clothes: iron*) stirare; (*pursue*) incalzare;
(*insist*): **to ~ sth on sb** far accettare qc da
qn ♦ *vi* premere; accalcare; **we are ~ed
for time** ci manca il tempo; **to ~ for sth**
insistere per avere qc; **~ on** *vi* continuare;
~ conference *n* conferenza *f* stampa *inv*;
~ing *adj* urgente; **~ stud** (BRIT) *n* bottone
m a pressione; **~-up** (BRIT) *n* flessione *f*

sulle braccia

pressure ['preʃə*] *n* pressione *f*; **to put ~
on sb (to do)** mettere qn sotto pressione
(affinché faccia); **~ cooker** *n* pentola a
pressione; **~ gauge** *n* manometro; **~
group** *n* gruppo di pressione

prestige [pres'tiːʒ] *n* prestigio

presumably [prɪ'zjuːməblɪ] *adv*
presumibilmente

presume [prɪ'zjuːm] *vt* supporre

presumption [prɪ'zʌmpʃən] *n* presunzione
f

presumptuous [prɪ'zʌmpʃəs] *adj*
presuntuoso(a)

pretence [prɪ'tens] (US **pretense**) *n* (*claim*)
pretesa; **to make a ~ of doing** far finta di
fare; **under false ~s** con l'inganno

pretend [prɪ'tend] *vt* (*feign*) fingere ♦ *vi* far
finta; **to ~ to do** far finta di fare

pretense [prɪ'tens] (US) *n* = **pretence**

pretentious [prɪ'tenʃəs] *adj* pretenzioso(a)

pretext ['priːtekst] *n* pretesto

pretty ['prɪtɪ] *adj* grazioso(a), carino(a)
♦ *adv* abbastanza, assai

prevail [prɪ'veɪl] *vi* (*win, be usual*) prevalere;
(*persuade*): **to ~ (up)on sb to do**
persuadere qn a fare; **~ing** *adj* dominante

prevalent ['prevələnt] *adj* (*belief*)
predominante; (*customs*) diffuso(a);
(*fashion*) corrente; (*disease*) comune

prevent [prɪ'vent] *vt*: **to ~ sb from doing**
impedire a qn di fare; **to ~ sth from
happening** impedire che qc succeda;
~ative *adj* = **~ive**; **~ion** [-'venʃən] *n*
prevenzione *f*; **~ive** *adj* preventivo(a)

preview ['priːvjuː] *n* (*of film*) anteprima

previous ['priːvɪəs] *adj* precedente;
anteriore; **~ly** *adv* prima

prewar ['priː'wɔː*] *adj* anteguerra *inv*

prey [preɪ] *n* preda ♦ *vi*: **to ~ on** far preda
di; **it was ~ing on his mind** lo stava
ossessionando

price [praɪs] *n* prezzo ♦ *vt* (*goods*) fissare il
prezzo di; valutare; **~less** *adj*
inapprezzabile; **~ list** *n* listino (dei) prezzi

prick [prɪk] *n* puntura ♦ *vt* pungere; **to ~ up
one's ears** drizzare gli orecchi

prickle ['prɪkl] n (of plant) spina; (sensation) pizzicore m

prickly ['prɪklɪ] adj spinoso(a); **~ heat** n sudamina

pride [praɪd] n orgoglio; superbia ♦ vt: **to ~ o.s. on** essere orgoglioso(a) di; vantarsi di

priest [priːst] n prete m, sacerdote m; **~hood** n sacerdozio

prim [prɪm] adj pudico(a); contegnoso(a)

primarily ['praɪmərɪlɪ] adv principalmente, essenzialmente

primary ['praɪmərɪ] adj primario(a); (first in importance) primo(a) ♦ n (US: election) primarie fpl; **~ school** (BRIT) n scuola elementare

prime [praɪm] adj primario(a), fondamentale; (excellent) di prima qualità ♦ vt (wood) preparare; (fig) mettere al corrente ♦ n: **in the ~ of life** nel fiore della vita; **P~ Minister** n primo ministro

primeval [praɪˈmiːvl] adj primitivo(a)

primitive ['prɪmɪtɪv] adj primitivo(a)

primrose ['prɪmrəʊz] n primavera

primus (stove) ® ['praɪməs(-)] (BRIT) n fornello a petrolio

prince [prɪns] n principe m

princess [prɪnˈses] n principessa

principal ['prɪnsɪpl] adj principale ♦ n (headmaster) preside m

principle ['prɪnsɪpl] n principio; **in ~** in linea di principio; **on ~** per principio

print [prɪnt] n (mark) impronta; (letters) caratteri mpl; (fabric) tessuto stampato; (ART, PHOT) stampa ♦ vt imprimere; (publish) stampare, pubblicare; (write in capitals) scrivere in stampatello; **out of ~** esaurito(a); **~ed matter** n stampe fpl; **~er** n tipografo; (machine) stampante f; **~ing** n stampa; **~-out** n (COMPUT) tabulato

prior ['praɪə*] adj precedente; (claim etc) più importante; **~ to doing** prima di fare

priority [praɪˈɒrɪtɪ] n priorità f inv; precedenza

prise [praɪz] vt: **to ~ open** forzare

prison ['prɪzn] n prigione f ♦ cpd (system) carcerario(a); (conditions, food) nelle or delle prigioni; **~er** n prigioniero/a

pristine ['prɪstiːn] adj immacolato(a)

privacy ['prɪvəsɪ] n solitudine f, intimità

private ['praɪvɪt] adj privato(a); personale ♦ n soldato semplice; **"~"** (on envelope) "riservata"; (on door) "privato"; **in ~** in privato; **~ enterprise** n iniziativa privata; **~ eye** n investigatore m privato; **~ly** adv in privato; (within oneself) dentro di sé; **~ property** n proprietà privata; **privatize** vt privatizzare

privet ['prɪvɪt] n ligustro

privilege ['prɪvɪlɪdʒ] n privilegio

privy ['prɪvɪ] adj: **to be ~ to** essere al corrente di

prize [praɪz] n premio ♦ adj (example, idiot) perfetto(a); (bull, novel) premiato(a) ♦ vt apprezzare, pregiare; **~-giving** n premiazione f; **~winner** n premiato/a

pro [prəʊ] n (SPORT) professionista m/f ♦ prep pro; **the ~s and cons** il pro e il contro

probability [prɒbəˈbɪlɪtɪ] n probabilità f inv; **in all ~** con tutta probabilità

probable ['prɒbəbl] adj probabile; **probably** adv probabilmente

probation [prəˈbeɪʃən] n: **on ~** (employee) in prova; (LAW) in libertà vigilata

probe [prəʊb] n (MED, SPACE) sonda; (enquiry) indagine f, investigazione f ♦ vt sondare, esplorare; indagare

problem ['prɒbləm] n problema m

procedure [prəˈsiːdʒə*] n (ADMIN, LAW) procedura; (method) metodo, procedimento

proceed [prəˈsiːd] vi (go forward) avanzare, andare avanti; (go about it) procedere; (continue): **to ~ (with)** continuare; **to ~ to** andare a; passare a; **to ~ to do** mettersi a fare; **~ings** npl misure fpl; (LAW) procedimento; (meeting) riunione f; (records) rendiconti mpl; atti mpl; **~s** ['prəʊsiːdz] npl profitto, incasso

process ['prəʊses] n processo; (method) metodo, sistema m ♦ vt trattare; (information) elaborare; **~ing** n trattamento; elaborazione f

procession [prəˈseʃən] n processione f,

corteo; **funeral** ~ corteo funebre

pro-choice [prəʊ'tʃɔɪs] *adj* per la libertà di scelta di gravidanza

proclaim [prə'kleɪm] *vt* proclamare, dichiarare

procrastinate [prəʊ'kræstɪneɪt] *vi* procrastinare

prod [prɒd] *vt* dare un colpetto a; pungolare ♦ *n* colpetto

prodigal ['prɒdɪgl] *adj* prodigo(a)

prodigy ['prɒdɪdʒɪ] *n* prodigio

produce [*n* 'prɒdjuːs, *vb* prə'djuːs] *n* (AGR) prodotto, prodotti *mpl* ♦ *vt* produrre; (*to show*) esibire, mostrare; (*cause*) cagionare, causare; ~**r** *n* (THEATRE) regista *m/f*; (AGR, CINEMA) produttore *m*

product ['prɒdʌkt] *n* prodotto

production [prə'dʌkʃən] *n* produzione *f*; ~ **line** *n* catena di lavorazione

productivity [prɒdʌk'tɪvɪtɪ] *n* produttività

profane [prə'feɪn] *adj* profano(a); (*language*) empio(a)

profess [prə'fes] *vt* (*claim*) dichiarare; (*opinion etc*) professare

profession [prə'feʃən] *n* professione *f*; ~**al** *n* professionista *m/f* ♦ *adj* professionale; (*work*) da professionista

professor [prə'fesə*] *n* professore *m* (*titolare di una cattedra*); (US) professore/essa

proficiency [prə'fɪʃənsɪ] *n* competenza, abilità

profile ['prəʊfaɪl] *n* profilo

profit ['prɒfɪt] *n* profitto; beneficio ♦ *vi*: **to ~ (by** *or* **from**) approfittare (di); ~**ability** [-'bɪlɪtɪ] *n* redditività; ~**able** *adj* redditizio(a)

profound [prə'faʊnd] *adj* profondo(a)

profusely [prə'fjuːslɪ] *adv* con grande effusione

programme ['prəʊgræm] (US **program**) *n* programma *m* ♦ *vt* programmare; ~**r** (US **programer**) *n* programmatore/trice

progress [*n* 'prəʊgres, *vb* prə'gres] *n* progresso ♦ *vi* avanzare, procedere; **in** ~ in corso; **to make** ~ far progressi; ~**ive** [-'gresɪv] *adj* progressivo(a); (*person*) progressista

prohibit [prə'hɪbɪt] *vt* proibire, vietare; ~**ion** [prəʊɪ'bɪʃən] *n* proibizione *f*, divieto; (US): **P~ion** proibizionismo; ~**ive** *adj* (*price etc*) proibitivo(a)

project [*n* 'prɒdʒekt, *vb* prə'dʒekt] *n* (*plan*) piano; (*venture*) progetto; (SCOL) studio ♦ *vt* proiettare ♦ *vi* (*stick out*) sporgere

projectile [prə'dʒektaɪl] *n* proiettile *m*

projector [prə'dʒektə*] *n* proiettore *m*

pro-life [prəʊ'laɪf] *adj* per il diritto alla vita

prolific [prə'lɪfɪk] *adj* (*artist etc*) fecondo(a)

prolong [prə'lɒŋ] *vt* prolungare

Prom

i In Gran Bretagna i **Prom (promenade concert)** *sono concerti di musica classica, i più noti dei quali sono quelli eseguiti nella Royal Albert Hall a Londra. Un tempo il pubblico seguiva i concerti in piedi, passeggiando. Negli Stati Uniti, invece, con* **prom** *si intende il ballo studentesco di un'università o di un college.*

---

prom [prɒm] *n abbr* = **promenade**; (US: *ball*) ballo studentesco

promenade [prɒmə'nɑːd] *n* (*by sea*) lungomare *m*; ~ **concert** *n* concerto (*con posti in piedi*)

prominent ['prɒmɪnənt] *adj* (*standing out*) prominente; (*important*) importante

promiscuous [prə'mɪskjuəs] *adj* (*sexually*) di facili costumi

promise ['prɒmɪs] *n* promessa ♦ *vt, vi* promettere; **to ~ sb sth, ~ sth to sb** promettere qc a qn; **to ~ (sb) that/to do sth** promettere (a qn) che/di fare qc; **promising** *adj* promettente

promote [prə'məʊt] *vt* promuovere; (*venture, event*) organizzare; ~**r** *n* promotore/trice; (*of sporting event*) organizzatore/trice; **promotion** [-'məʊʃən] *n* promozione *f*

prompt [prɒmpt] *adj* rapido(a), svelto(a); puntuale; (*reply*) sollecito(a) ♦ *adv* (*punctually*) in punto ♦ *n* (COMPUT) prompt *m* ♦ *vt* incitare; provocare; (THEATRE) suggerire a; **to ~ sb to do** incitare qn a

fare; ~ly *adv* prontamente; puntualmente
prone [prəun] *adj* (*lying*) prono(a); ~ **to**
propenso(a) a, incline a
prong [prɔŋ] *n* rebbio, punta
pronoun [ˈprəunaun] *n* pronome *m*
pronounce [prəˈnauns] *vt* pronunciare
pronunciation [prənʌnsɪˈeɪʃən] *n*
pronuncia
proof [pruːf] *n* prova; (*of book*) bozza;
(*PHOT*) provino ♦ *adj*: ~ **against** a prova di
prop [prɔp] *n* sostegno, appoggio ♦ *vt* (*also*:
~ **up**) sostenere, appoggiare; (*lean*): **to** ~
sth against appoggiare qc contro *or* a
propaganda [prɔpəˈɡændə] *n* propaganda
propel [prəˈpel] *vt* spingere (in avanti),
muovere; ~**ler** *n* elica
propensity [prəˈpensɪtɪ] *n* tendenza
proper [ˈprɔpə*] *adj* (*suited, right*) adatto(a),
appropriato(a); (*seemly*) decente;
(*authentic*) vero(a); (*inf: real*) noun +vero(a)
e proprio(a); ~**ly** [ˈprɔpəlɪ] *adv* (*eat, study*)
bene; (*behave*) come si deve; ~ **noun** *n*
nome *m* proprio
property [ˈprɔpətɪ] *n* (*things owned*) beni
mpl; (*land, building*) proprietà *f inv*; (*CHEM*
etc: quality) proprietà; ~ **owner** *n*
proprietario/a
prophecy [ˈprɔfɪsɪ] *n* profezia
prophesy [ˈprɔfɪsaɪ] *vt* predire
prophet [ˈprɔfɪt] *n* profeta *m*
proportion [prəˈpɔːʃən] *n* proporzione *f*;
(*share*) parte *f*; ~**al** *adj* proporzionale;
~**ate** *adj* proporzionato(a)
proposal [prəˈpəuzl] *n* proposta; (*plan*)
progetto; (*of marriage*) proposta di
matrimonio
propose [prəˈpəuz] *vt* proporre, suggerire
♦ *vi* fare una proposta di matrimonio; **to** ~ **to**
do proporsi di fare, aver l'intenzione di fare
proposition [prɔpəˈzɪʃən] *n* proposizione *f*;
(*offer*) proposta
proprietor [prəˈpraɪətə*] *n* proprietario/a
propriety [prəˈpraɪətɪ] *n* (*seemliness*) decoro,
rispetto delle convenienze sociali
pro rata [ˈprəuˈrɑːtə] *adv* in proporzione
prose [prəuz] *n* prosa
prosecute [ˈprɔsɪkjuːt] *vt* processare;

prosecution [-ˈkjuːʃən] *n* processo;
(*accusing side*) accusa; **prosecutor** *n*
(*also: public prosecutor*) ≈ procuratore *m*
della Repubblica
prospect [*n* ˈprɔspekt, *vb* prəˈspekt] *n*
prospettiva; (*hope*) speranza ♦ *vi*: **to** ~ **for**
cercare; ~**s** *npl* (*for work etc*) prospettive
fpl; ~**ive** [-ˈspektɪv] *adj* possibile; futuro(a)
prospectus [prəˈspektəs] *n* prospetto,
programma *m*
prosperity [prɔˈsperɪtɪ] *n* prosperità
prostitute [ˈprɔstɪtjuːt] *n* prostituta; **male**
~ uomo che si prostituisce
protect [prəˈtekt] *vt* proteggere,
salvaguardare; ~**ed species** *n* specie *f*
protetta; ~**ion** *n* protezione *f*; ~**ive** *adj*
protettivo(a)
protégé [ˈprəutəʒeɪ] *n* protetto
protein [ˈprəutiːn] *n* proteina
protest [*n* ˈprəutest, *vb* prəˈtest] *n* protesta
♦ *vt, vi* protestare
Protestant [ˈprɔtɪstənt] *adj, n* protestante
m/f
protester [prəˈtestə*] *n* dimostrante *m/f*
prototype [ˈprəutətaɪp] *n* prototipo
protracted [prəˈtræktɪd] *adj* tirato(a) per le
lunghe
protrude [prəˈtruːd] *vi* sporgere
proud [praud] *adj* fiero(a), orgoglioso(a);
(*pej*) superbo(a)
prove [pruːv] *vt* provare, dimostrare ♦ *vi*: **to**
~ (**to be**) **correct** *etc* risultare vero(a) *etc*;
to ~ **o.s.** mostrare le proprie capacità
proverb [ˈprɔvəːb] *n* proverbio
provide [prəˈvaɪd] *vt* fornire, provvedere; **to**
~ **sb with sth** fornire *or* provvedere qn di
qc; ~ **for** *vt fus* provvedere a; (*future*
event) prevedere; ~**d (that)** *conj* purché
+*sub*, a condizione che +*sub*
providing [prəˈvaɪdɪŋ] *conj* purché +*sub*, a
condizione che +*sub*
province [ˈprɔvɪns] *n* provincia; **provincial**
[prəˈvɪnʃəl] *adj* provinciale
provision [prəˈvɪʒən] *n* (*supply*) riserva;
(*supplying*) provvista; rifornimento;
(*stipulation*) condizione *f*; ~**s** *npl* (*food*)
provviste *fpl*; ~**al** *adj* provvisorio(a)

proviso [prə'vaızəʊ] n condizione f
provocative [prə'vɔkətıv] adj (aggressive) provocatorio(a); (thought-provoking) stimolante; (seductive) provocante
provoke [prə'vəʊk] vt provocare; incitare
prowess ['praʊıs] n prodezza
prowl [praʊl] vi (also: ~ about, ~ around) aggirarsi ♦ n: to be on the ~ aggirarsi; ~er n tipo sospetto (che s'aggira con l'intenzione di rubare, aggredire etc)
proximity [prɔk'sımıtı] n prossimità
proxy ['prɔksı] n: by ~ per procura
prude [pru:d] n puritano/a
prudent ['pru:dnt] adj prudente
prudish ['pru:dıʃ] adj puritano(a)
prune [pru:n] n prugna secca ♦ vt potare
pry [praı] vi: to ~ into ficcare il naso in
PS abbr (= postscript) P.S.
psalm [sɑ:m] n salmo
pseudonym ['sju:dənım] n pseudonimo
psyche ['saıkı] n psiche f
psychiatric [saıkı'ætrık] adj psichiatrico(a)
psychiatrist [saı'kaıətrıst] n psichiatra m/f
psychic ['saıkık] adj (also: ~al) psichico(a); (person) dotato(a) di qualità telepatiche
psychoanalyst [saıkəʊ'ænəlıst] n psicanalista m/f
psychological [saıkə'lɔdʒıkl] adj psicologico(a)
psychologist [saı'kɔlədʒıst] n psicologo/a
psychology [saı'kɔlədʒı] n psicologia
psychopath ['saıkəʊpæθ] n psicopatico/a
P.T.O. abbr (= please turn over) v.r.
pub [pʌb] n abbr (= public house) pub m inv

---
pub

ⓘ In Gran Bretagna e in Irlanda i pub sono locali dove vengono servite bevande alcoliche ed analcoliche e dove spesso è possibile anche mangiare, giocare a biliardo o a freccette e guardare la televisione.

---

pubic ['pju:bık] adj pubico(a), del pube
public ['pʌblık] adj pubblico(a) ♦ n pubblico; **in ~** in pubblico; **~ address system** n impianto di amplificazione

publican ['pʌblıkən] n proprietario di un pub
publication [pʌblı'keıʃən] n pubblicazione f
public: ~ company n società f inv per azioni (costituita tramite pubblica sottoscrizione); **~ convenience** (BRIT) n gabinetti mpl; **~ holiday** n giorno festivo, festa nazionale; **~ house** (BRIT) n pub m inv
publicity [pʌb'lısıtı] n pubblicità
publicize ['pʌblısaız] vt rendere pubblico(a)
publicly ['pʌblıklı] adv pubblicamente
public: ~ opinion n opinione f pubblica; **~ relations** n pubbliche relazioni fpl; **~ school** n (BRIT) scuola privata; (US) scuola statale; **~-spirited** adj che ha senso civico; **~ transport** n mezzi mpl pubblici
publish ['pʌblıʃ] vt pubblicare; **~er** n editore m; **~ing** n (industry) editoria; (of a book) pubblicazione f
pub lunch n pranzo semplice ed economico servito nei pub
puce [pju:s] adj marroncino rosato inv
pucker ['pʌkə*] vt corrugare
pudding ['pʊdıŋ] n budino; (BRIT: dessert) dolce m; **black ~**, (US) **blood ~** sanguinaccio
puddle ['pʌdl] n pozza, pozzanghera
puff [pʌf] n sbuffo ♦ vt: to ~ one's pipe tirare sboccate di fumo ♦ vi (pant) ansare; **~ out** vt (cheeks etc) gonfiare; **~ pastry** n pasta sfoglia; **~y** adj gonfio(a)
pull [pʊl] n (tug): **to give sth a ~** tirare su qc ♦ vt tirare; (muscle) strappare; (trigger) premere ♦ vi tirare; **to ~ to pieces** fare a pezzi; **to ~ one's punches** (BOXING) risparmiare l'avversario; **to ~ one's weight** dare il proprio contributo; **to ~ o.s. together** ricomporsi, riprendersi; **to ~ sb's leg** prendere in giro qn; **~ apart** vt (break) fare a pezzi; **~ down** vt (house) demolire; (tree) abbattere; **~ in** vi (AUT: at the kerb) accostarsi; (RAIL) entrare in stazione; **~ off** vt (clothes) togliere; (deal etc) portare a compimento; **~ out** vi partire; (AUT: come out of line) spostarsi sulla mezzeria ♦ vt staccare; far uscire; (withdraw) ritirare; **~**

over *vi* (*AUT*) accostare; **~ through** *vi* farcela; **~ up** *vi* (*stop*) fermarsi ♦ *vt* (*raise*) sollevare; (*uproot*) sradicare

pulley ['pulɪ] *n* puleggia, carrucola

pullover ['puləuvə*] *n* pullover *m inv*

pulp [pʌlp] *n* (*of fruit*) polpa

pulpit ['pulpɪt] *n* pulpito

pulsate [pʌl'seɪt] *vi* battere, palpitare

pulse [pʌls] *n* polso; (*BOT*) legume *m*

pummel ['pʌml] *vt* dare pugni a

pump [pʌmp] *n* pompa; (*shoe*) scarpetta ♦ *vt* pompare; **~ up** *vt* gonfiare

pumpkin ['pʌmpkɪn] *n* zucca

pun [pʌn] *n* gioco di parole

punch [pʌntʃ] *n* (*blow*) pugno; (*tool*) punzone *m*; (*drink*) ponce *m* ♦ *vt* (*hit*): **to ~ sb/sth** dare un pugno a qn/qc; **~ line** *n* (*of joke*) battuta finale; **~-up** (*BRIT*: *inf*) *n* rissa

punctual ['pʌŋktjuəl] *adj* puntuale

punctuation [pʌŋktju'eɪʃən] *n* interpunzione *f*, punteggiatura

puncture ['pʌŋktʃə*] *n* foratura ♦ *vt* forare

pundit ['pʌndɪt] *n* sapientone *m*

pungent ['pʌndʒənt] *adj* pungente

punish ['pʌnɪʃ] *vt* punire; **~ment** *n* punizione *f*

punk [pʌŋk] *n* (*also*: **~ rocker**) punk *m/f inv*; (*also*: **~ rock**) musica punk, punk rock *m*; (*US*: *inf*: *hoodlum*) teppista *m*

punt [pʌnt] *n* (*boat*) barchino

punter ['pʌntə*] (*BRIT*) *n* (*gambler*) scommettitore/trice; (*: inf*) cliente *m/f*

puny ['pjuːnɪ] *adj* gracile

pup [pʌp] *n* cucciolo/a

pupil ['pjuːpl] *n* allievo/a; (*ANAT*) pupilla

puppet ['pʌpɪt] *n* burattino

puppy ['pʌpɪ] *n* cucciolo/a, cagnolino/a

purchase ['pəːtʃɪs] *n* acquisto, compera ♦ *vt* comprare; **~r** *n* compratore/trice

pure [pjuə*] *adj* puro(a)

purée ['pjuəreɪ] *n* (*of potatoes*) purè *m*; (*of tomatoes*) passato; (*of apples*) crema

purely ['pjuəlɪ] *adv* puramente

purge [pəːdʒ] *n* (*MED*) purga; (*POL*) epurazione *f* ♦ *vt* purgare

puritan ['pjuərɪtən] *adj*, *n* puritano(a)

purity ['pjuərɪtɪ] *n* purezza

purple ['pəːpl] *adj* di porpora; viola *inv*

purpose ['pəːpəs] *n* intenzione *f*, scopo; **on ~** apposta; **~ful** *adj* deciso(a), risoluto(a)

purr [pəː*] *vi* fare le fusa

purse [pəːs] *n* (*BRIT*) borsellino; (*US*) borsetta ♦ *vt* contrarre

purser ['pəːsə*] *n* (*NAUT*) commissario di bordo

pursue [pə'sjuː] *vt* inseguire; (*fig*: *activity etc*) continuare con; (*: aim etc*) perseguire

pursuit [pə'sjuːt] *n* inseguimento; (*fig*) ricerca; (*pastime*) passatempo

push [puʃ] *n* spinta; (*effort*) grande sforzo; (*drive*) energia ♦ *vt* spingere; (*button*) premere; (*thrust*): **to ~ sth (into)** ficcare qc (in); (*fig*) fare pubblicità a ♦ *vi* spingere; premere; **to ~ for** (*fig*) insistere per; **~ aside** *vt* scostare; **~ off** (*inf*) *vi* filare; **~ on** *vi* (*continue*) continuare; **~ through** *vi* farsi largo spingendo ♦ *vt* (*measure*) far approvare; **~ up** *vt* (*total*, *prices*) far salire; **~chair** (*BRIT*) *n* passeggino; **~er** *n* (*drug ~er*) spacciatore/trice; **~over** (*inf*) *n*: **it's a ~over** è un lavoro da bambini; **~-up** (*US*) *n* (*press-up*) flessione *f* sulle braccia; **~y** (*pej*) *adj* opportunista

puss [pus] (*inf*) *n* = **pussy(-cat)**

pussy(-cat) ['pusɪ(-)] (*inf*) *n* micio

put [put] (*pt*, *pp* **put**) *vt* mettere, porre; (*say*) dire, esprimere; (*a question*) fare; (*estimate*) stimare; **~ about** *or* **around** *vt* (*rumour*) diffondere; **~ across** *vt* (*ideas etc*) comunicare; far capire; **~ away** *vt* (*return*) mettere a posto; **~ back** *vt* (*replace*) rimettere a posto; (*postpone*) rinviare; (*delay*) ritardare; **~ by** *vt* (*money*) mettere da parte; **~ down** *vt* (*parcel etc*) posare, mettere giù; (*pay*) versare; (*in writing*) mettere per iscritto; (*revolt*, *animal*) sopprimere; (*attribute*) attribuire; **~ forward** *vt* (*ideas*) avanzare, proporre; **~ in** *vt* (*application*, *complaint*) presentare; (*time*, *effort*) mettere; **~ off** *vt* (*postpone*) rimandare, rinviare; (*discourage*) dissuadere; **~ on** *vt* (*clothes*, *lipstick etc*) mettere; (*light etc*) accendere; (*play etc*) mettere in scena;

(*food, meal*) mettere su; (*brake*) mettere; **to ~ on weight** ingrassare; **to ~ on airs** darsi delle arie; **~ out** *vt* mettere fuori; (*one's hand*) porgere; (*light etc*) spegnere; (*person: inconvenience*) scomodare; **~ through** *vt* (*TEL: call*) passare; (: *person*) mettere in comunicazione; (*plan*) far approvare; **~ up** *vt* (*raise*) sollevare, alzare; (: *umbrella*) aprire; (: *tent*) montare; (*pin up*) affiggere; (*hang*) appendere; (*build*) costruire, erigere; (*increase*) aumentare; (*accommodate*) alloggiare; **~ up with** *vt fus* sopportare

putt [pʌt] *n* colpo leggero; **~ing green** *n* green *m inv*; campo da putting

putty ['pʌti] *n* stucco

puzzle ['pʌzl] *n* enigma *m*, mistero; (*jigsaw*) puzzle *m*; (*also*: **crossword ~**) parole *fpl* incrociate, cruciverba *m inv* ♦ *vt* confondere, rendere perplesso(a) ♦ *vi* scervellarsi

pyjamas [pɪ'dʒɑːməz] (*BRIT*) *npl* pigiama *m*

pylon ['paɪlən] *n* pilone *m*

pyramid ['pɪrəmɪd] *n* piramide *f*

Pyrenees [pɪrɪ'niːz] *npl*: **the ~** i Pirenei

Q, q

quack [kwæk] *n* (*of duck*) qua qua *m inv*; (*pej: doctor*) dottoruccio/a

quad [kwɒd] *n abbr* = **quadrangle; quadruplet**

quadrangle ['kwɒdræŋgl] *n* (*courtyard*) cortile *m*

quadruple [kwɒ'druːpl] *vt* quadruplicare ♦ *vi* quadruplicarsi

quadruplets [kwɒ'druːplɪts] *npl* quattro gemelli *mpl*

quail [kweɪl] *n* (*ZOOL*) quaglia ♦ *vi* (*person*): **to ~ at** *or* **before** perdersi d'animo davanti a

quaint [kweɪnt] *adj* bizzarro(a); (*old-fashioned*) antiquato(a); grazioso(a), pittoresco(a)

quake [kweɪk] *vi* tremare ♦ *n abbr* = **earthquake**

Quaker ['kweɪkə*] *n* quacchero/a

qualification [kwɒlɪfɪ'keɪʃən] *n* (*degree etc*) qualifica, titolo; (*ability*) competenza, qualificazione *f*; (*limitation*) riserva, restrizione *f*

qualified ['kwɒlɪfaɪd] *adj* qualificato(a); (*able*): **~ to** competente in, qualificato(a) a; (*limited*) condizionato(a)

qualify ['kwɒlɪfaɪ] *vt* abilitare; (*limit: statement*) modificare, precisare ♦ *vi*: **to ~ (as)** qualificarsi (come); **to ~ (for)** acquistare i requisiti necessari (per); (*SPORT*) qualificarsi (per *or* a)

quality ['kwɒlɪti] *n* qualità *f inv*

> **quality press**

i *Il termine* **quality press** *si riferisce ai quotidiani e ai settimanali che offrono un'informazione più seria ed approfondita rispetto ai* **tabloid**, *i giornali popolari; vedi anche* **tabloid press**.

qualm [kwɑːm] *n* dubbio; scrupolo

quandary ['kwɒndrɪ] *n*: **in a ~** in un dilemma

quantity ['kwɒntɪti] *n* quantità *f inv*

quantity surveyor [-sə'veɪə*] *n* geometra *m* (*specializzato nel calcolare la quantità e il costo del materiale da costruzione*)

quarantine ['kwɒrntiːn] *n* quarantena *f*

quarrel ['kwɒrl] *n* lite *f*, disputa ♦ *vi* litigare

quarry ['kwɒri] *n* (*for stone*) cava; (*animal*) preda

quart [kwɔːt] *n* ≈ litro

quarter ['kwɔːtə*] *n* quarto; (*US: coin*) quarto di dollaro; (*of year*) trimestre *m*; (*district*) quartiere *m* ♦ *vt* dividere in quattro; (*MIL*) alloggiare; **~s** *npl* (*living ~s*) alloggio; (*MIL*) alloggi *mpl*, quadrato; **a ~ of an hour** un quarto d'ora; **~ final** *n* quarto di finale; **~ly** *adj* trimestrale ♦ *adv* trimestralmente

quartet(te) [kwɔː'tɛt] *n* quartetto

quartz [kwɔːts] *n* quarzo

quash [kwɒʃ] *vt* (*verdict*) annullare

quaver ['kweɪvə*] *n* (*BRIT: MUS*) croma ♦ *vi* tremolare

quay [kiː] *n* (*also*: **~side**) banchina

queasy ['kwiːzɪ] *adj* (*stomach*) delicato(a); **to feel ~** aver la nausea

queen [kwiːn] *n* (*gen*) regina; (*CARDS etc*) regina, donna; **~ mother** *n* regina madre

queer [kwɪə*] *adj* strano(a), curioso(a) ♦ *n* (*inf*) finocchio

quell [kwɛl] *vt* domare

quench [kwɛntʃ] *vt*: **to ~ one's thirst** dissetarsi

query ['kwɪərɪ] *n* domanda, questione *f* ♦ *vt* mettere in questione

quest [kwɛst] *n* cerca, ricerca

question ['kwɛstʃən] *n* domanda, questione *f* ♦ *vt* (*person*) interrogare; (*plan, idea*) mettere in questione *or* in dubbio; **it's a ~ of doing** si tratta di fare; **beyond ~** fuori di dubbio; **out of the ~** fuori discussione, impossibile; **~able** *adj* discutibile; **~ mark** *n* punto interrogativo

questionnaire [kwɛstʃə'nɛə*] *n* questionario

queue [kjuː] (*BRIT*) *n* coda, fila ♦ *vi* fare la coda

quibble ['kwɪbl] *vi* cavillare

quiche [kiːʃ] *n* torta salata a base di uova, formaggio, prosciutto o altro

quick [kwɪk] *adj* rapido(a), veloce; (*reply*) pronto(a); (*mind*) pronto(a), acuto(a) ♦ *n*: **cut to the ~** (*fig*) toccato(a) sul vivo; **be ~!** fa presto!; **~en** *vt* accelerare, affrettare ♦ *vi* accelerare, affrettarsi; **~ly** *adv* rapidamente, velocemente; **~sand** *n* sabbie *fpl* mobili; **~-witted** *adj* pronto(a) d'ingegno

quid [kwɪd] (*BRIT: inf*) *n inv* sterlina

quiet ['kwaɪət] *adj* tranquillo(a), quieto(a); (*ceremony*) semplice ♦ *n* tranquillità, calma ♦ *vt, vi* (*US*) = **~en; keep ~!** sta zitto!; **~en** (*also*: **~en down**) *vi* calmarsi, chetarsi ♦ *vt* calmare, chetare; **~ly** *adv* tranquillamente, calmamente; sommessamente

quilt [kwɪlt] *n* trapunta; (*continental ~*) piumino

quin [kwɪn] *n abbr* = **quintuplet**

quintuplets [kwɪn'tjuːplɪts] *npl* cinque gemelli *mpl*

quip [kwɪp] *n* frizzo

quirk [kwəːk] *n* ghiribizzo

quit [kwɪt] (*pt, pp* **quit** *or* **quitted**) *vt* mollare; (*premises*) lasciare, partire da ♦ *vi* (*give up*) mollare; (*resign*) dimettersi

quite [kwaɪt] *adv* (*rather*) assai; (*entirely*) completamente, del tutto; **I ~ understand** capisco perfettamente; **that's not ~ big enough** non è proprio sufficiente; **~ a few of them** non pochi di loro; **~ (so)!** esatto!

quits [kwɪts] *adj*: **~ (with)** pari (con); **let's call it ~** adesso siamo pari

quiver ['kwɪvə*] *vi* tremare, fremere

quiz [kwɪz] *n* (*game*) quiz *m inv*; indovinello ♦ *vt* interrogare; **~zical** *adj* enigmatico(a)

quota ['kwəʊtə] *n* quota

quotation [kwəʊ'teɪʃən] *n* citazione *f*; (*of shares etc*) quotazione *f*; (*estimate*) preventivo; **~ marks** *npl* virgolette *fpl*

quote [kwəʊt] *n* citazione *f* ♦ *vt* (*sentence*) citare; (*price*) dare, fissare; (*shares*) quotare ♦ *vi*: **to ~ from** citare; **~s** *npl* = **quotation marks**

R, r

rabbi ['ræbaɪ] *n* rabbino

rabbit ['ræbɪt] *n* coniglio; **~ hutch** *n* conigliera

rabble ['ræbl] (*pej*) *n* canaglia, plebaglia

rabies ['reɪbiːz] *n* rabbia

RAC (*BRIT*) *n abbr* = **Royal Automobile Club**

rac(c)oon [rə'kuːn] *n* procione *m*

race [reɪs] *n* razza; (*competition, rush*) corsa ♦ *vt* (*horse*) far correre ♦ *vi* correre; (*engine*) imballarsi; **~ car** (*US*) *n* = **racing car**; **~ car driver** (*US*) *n* = **racing driver**; **~course** *n* campo di corse, ippodromo; **~horse** *n* cavallo da corsa; **~track** *n* pista

racial ['reɪʃl] *adj* razziale

racing ['reɪsɪŋ] *n* corsa; **~ car** (*BRIT*) *n* macchina da corsa; **~ driver** (*BRIT*) *n* corridore *m* automobilista

racism ['reɪsɪzəm] *n* razzismo; **racist** *adj, n* razzista *m/f*

rack [ræk] *n* rastrelliera; (*also*: **luggage ~**) rete *f*, portabagagli *m inv*; (*also*: **roof ~**)

portabagagli; (*dish* ~) scolapiatti *m inv*
♦ *vt*: **~ed by** torturato(a) da; **to ~ one's brains** scervellarsi

racket ['rækɪt] *n* (*for tennis*) racchetta; (*noise*) fracasso; baccano; (*swindle*) imbroglio, truffa; (*organized crime*) racket *m inv*

racoon [rə'kuːn] *n* = **raccoon**

racquet ['rækɪt] *n* racchetta

racy ['reɪsɪ] *adj* brioso(a); piccante

radar ['reɪdɑː*] *n* radar *m*

radial ['reɪdɪəl] *adj* (*also*: **~-ply**) radiale

radiant ['reɪdɪənt] *adj* raggiante; (*PHYSICS*) radiante

radiate ['reɪdɪeɪt] *vt* (*heat*) irraggiare, irradiare ♦ *vi* (*lines*) irradiarsi

radiation [reɪdɪ'eɪʃən] *n* irradiamento; (*radioactive*) radiazione *f*

radiator ['reɪdɪeɪtə*] *n* radiatore *m*

radical ['rædɪkl] *adj* radicale

radii ['reɪdɪaɪ] *npl of* **radius**

radio ['reɪdɪəu] *n* radio *f inv*; **on the ~** alla radio

radioactive [reɪdɪəu'æktɪv] *adj* radioattivo(a)

radio station *n* stazione *f* radio *inv*

radish ['rædɪʃ] *n* ravanello

radius ['reɪdɪəs] (*pl* **radii**) *n* raggio

RAF *n abbr* = **Royal Air Force**

raffle ['ræfl] *n* lotteria

raft [rɑːft] *n* zattera; (*also*: **life ~**) zattera di salvataggio

rafter ['rɑːftə*] *n* trave *f*

rag [ræg] *n* straccio, cencio; (*pej: newspaper*) giornalaccio, bandiera; (*for charity*) *iniziativa studentesca a scopo benefico*; **~s** *npl* (*torn clothes*) stracci *mpl*, brandelli *mpl*; **~ doll** *n* bambola di pezza

rage [reɪdʒ] *n* (*fury*) collera, furia ♦ *vi* (*person*) andare su tutte le furie; (*storm*) infuriare; **it's all the ~** fa furore

ragged ['rægɪd] *adj* (*edge*) irregolare; (*clothes*) logoro(a); (*appearance*) pezzente

raid [reɪd] *n* (*MIL*) incursione *f*; (*criminal*) rapina; (*by police*) irruzione *f* ♦ *vt* fare un'incursione in; rapinare; fare irruzione in

rail [reɪl] *n* (*on stair*) ringhiera; (*on bridge,*

balcony) parapetto; (*of ship*) battagliola; **~s** *npl* (*for train*) binario, rotaie *fpl*; **by ~** per ferrovia; **~ing(s)** *n(pl)* ringhiere *fpl*; **~road** (*US*) *n* = **~way**; **~way** (*BRIT*) *n* ferrovia; **~way line** (*BRIT*) *n* linea ferroviaria; **~wayman** (*BRIT: irreg*) *n* ferroviere *m*; **~way station** (*BRIT*) *n* stazione *f* ferroviaria

rain [reɪn] *n* pioggia ♦ *vi* piovere; **in the ~** sotto la pioggia; **it's ~ing** piove; **~bow** *n* arcobaleno; **~coat** *n* impermeabile *m*; **~drop** *n* goccia di pioggia; **~fall** *n* pioggia; (*measurement*) piovosità; **~forest** *n* foresta pluviale; **~y** *adj* piovoso(a)

raise [reɪz] *n* aumento ♦ *vt* (*lift*) alzare; sollevare; (*increase*) aumentare; (*a protest, doubt, question*) sollevare; (*cattle, family*) allevare; (*crop*) coltivare; (*army, funds*) raccogliere; (*loan*) ottenere; **to ~ one's voice** alzare la voce

raisin ['reɪzn] *n* uva secca

rake [reɪk] *n* (*tool*) rastrello ♦ *vt* (*garden*) rastrellare

rally ['rælɪ] *n* (*POL etc*) riunione *f*; (*AUT*) rally *m inv*; (*TENNIS*) scambio ♦ *vt* riunire, radunare ♦ *vi* (*sick person, Stock Exchange*) riprendersi; **~ round** *vt fus* raggrupparsi intorno a; venire in aiuto di

RAM [ræm] *n abbr* (= *random access memory*) memoria ad accesso casuale

ram [ræm] *n* montone *m*, ariete *m* ♦ *vt* conficcare; (*crash into*) cozzare, sbattere contro; percuotere; speronare

ramble ['ræmbl] *n* escursione *f* ♦ *vi* (*pej: also*: **~ on**) divagare; **~r** *n* escursionista *m/f*; (*BOT*) rosa rampicante; **rambling** *adj* (*speech*) sconnesso(a); (*house*) tutto(a) a nicchie e corridoi; (*BOT*) rampicante

ramp [ræmp] *n* rampa; **on/off ~** (*US: AUT*) raccordo di entrata/uscita

rampage [ræm'peɪdʒ] *n*: **to go on the ~** scatenarsi in modo violento

rampant ['ræmpənt] *adj* (*disease etc*) che infierisce

rampart ['ræmpɑːt] *n* bastione *m*

ram raiding *n* il rapinare un negozio o una banca sfondandone la vetrina con un'auto-ariete

ramshackle ['ræmʃækl] *adj* (*house*) cadente; (*car etc*) sgangherato(a)

ran [ræn] *pt of* **run**

ranch [rɑːntʃ] *n* ranch *m inv*; **~er** *n* proprietario di un ranch; cowboy *m inv*

rancid ['rænsɪd] *adj* rancido(a)

rancour ['ræŋkə*] (*US* **rancor**) *n* rancore *m*

random ['rændəm] *adj* fatto(a) *or* detto(a) per caso; (*COMPUT, MATH*) casuale ♦ *n*: **at ~** a casaccio; **~ access** *n* (*COMPUT*) accesso casuale

randy ['rændɪ] (*BRIT: inf*) *adj* arrapato(a); lascivo(a)

rang [ræŋ] *pt of* **ring**

range [reɪndʒ] *n* (*of mountains*) catena; (*of missile, voice*) portata; (*of proposals, products*) gamma; (*MIL: also*: **shooting ~**) campo di tiro; (*also*: **kitchen ~**) fornello, cucina economica ♦ *vt* disporre ♦ *vi*: **to ~ over** coprire; **to ~ from ... to** andare da ... a

ranger ['reɪndʒə*] *n* guardia forestale

rank [ræŋk] *n* fila; (*status, MIL*) grado; (*BRIT: also*: **taxi ~**) posteggio di taxi ♦ *vi*: **to ~ among** essere tra ♦ *adj* puzzolente; vero(a) e proprio(a); **the ~ and file** (*fig*) la gran massa

ransack ['rænsæk] *vt* rovistare; (*plunder*) saccheggiare

ransom ['rænsəm] *n* riscatto; **to hold sb to ~** (*fig*) esercitare pressione su qn

rant [rænt] *vi* vociare

rap [ræp] *vt* bussare a; picchiare su ♦ *n* (*music*) rap *m inv*

rape [reɪp] *n* violenza carnale, stupro; (*BOT*) ravizzone *m* ♦ *vt* violentare; **~(seed) oil** *n* olio di ravizzone

rapid ['ræpɪd] *adj* rapido(a); **~s** *npl* (*GEO*) rapida; **~ly** *adv* rapidamente

rapist ['reɪpɪst] *n* violentatore *m*

rapport [ræ'pɔː*] *n* rapporto

rare [rɛə*] *adj* raro(a); (*CULIN: steak*) al sangue

rarely ['rɛəlɪ] *adv* raramente

raring ['rɛərɪŋ] *adj*: **to be ~ to go** (*inf*) non veder l'ora di cominciare

rascal ['rɑːskl] *n* mascalzone *m*

rash [ræʃ] *adj* imprudente, sconsiderato(a) ♦ *n* (*MED*) eruzione *f*; (*of events etc*) scoppio

rasher ['ræʃə*] *n* fetta sottile (di lardo *or* prosciutto)

raspberry ['rɑːzbərɪ] *n* lampone *m*

rasping ['rɑːspɪŋ] *adj* stridulo(a)

rat [ræt] *n* ratto

rate [reɪt] *n* (*proportion*) tasso, percentuale *f*; (*speed*) velocità *f inv*; (*price*) tariffa ♦ *vt* giudicare; stimare; **~s** *npl* (*BRIT: property tax*) imposte *fpl* comunali; (*fees*) tariffe *fpl*; **to ~ sb/sth as** valutare qn/qc come; **~able value** (*BRIT*) *n* valore *m* imponibile *or* locativo (di una proprietà); **~payer** (*BRIT*) *n* contribuente *m/f* (che paga le imposte comunali)

rather ['rɑːðə*] *adv* piuttosto; **it's ~ expensive** è piuttosto caro; (*too*) è un po' caro; **there's ~ a lot** ce n'è parecchio; **I would** *or* **I'd ~ go** preferirei andare

rating ['reɪtɪŋ] *n* (*assessment*) valutazione *f*; (*score*) punteggio di merito

ratio ['reɪʃɪəu] *n* proporzione *f*, rapporto

ration ['ræʃən] *n* (*gen pl*) razioni *fpl* ♦ *vt* razionare

rational ['ræʃənl] *adj* razionale, ragionevole; (*solution, reasoning*) logico(a); **~e** [-'nɑːl] *n* fondamento logico; giustificazione *f*; **~ize** *vt* razionalizzare

rat race *n* carrierismo, corsa al successo

rattle ['rætl] *n* tintinnio; (*louder*) strepito; (*for baby*) sonaglino ♦ *vi* risuonare, tintinnare; fare un rumore di ferraglia ♦ *vt* scuotere (con strepito); **~snake** *n* serpente *m* a sonagli

raucous ['rɔːkəs] *adj* rumoroso(a), fragoroso(a)

ravage ['rævɪdʒ] *vt* devastare; **~s** *npl* danni *mpl*

rave [reɪv] *vi* (*in anger*) infuriarsi; (*with enthusiasm*) andare in estasi; (*MED*) delirare ♦ (*BRIT: inf*) *n* (*party*) rave *m inv*

raven ['reɪvən] *n* corvo

ravenous ['rævənəs] *adj* affamato(a)

ravine [rə'viːn] *n* burrone *m*

raving ['reɪvɪŋ] *adj*: **~ lunatic** pazzo(a)

furioso(a)

ravishing ['rævɪʃɪŋ] *adj* incantevole

raw [rɔː] *adj* (*uncooked*) crudo(a); (*not processed*) greggio(a); (*sore*) vivo(a); (*inexperienced*) inesperto(a); (*weather, day*) gelido(a); ~ **deal** (*inf*) n bidonata; ~ **material** n materia prima

ray [reɪ] *n* raggio; **a ~ of hope** un barlume di speranza

rayon ['reɪɔn] *n* raion *m*

raze [reɪz] *vt* radere, distruggere

razor ['reɪzə*] *n* rasoio; ~ **blade** *n* lama di rasoio

Rd *abbr* = **road**

re [riː] *prep* con riferimento a

reach [riːtʃ] *n* portata; (*of river etc*) tratto ♦ *vt* raggiungere; arrivare a ♦ *vi* stendersi; **out of/within ~** fuori/a portata di mano; **within ~ of the shops/station** vicino ai negozi/alla stazione; ~ **out** *vt* (*hand*) allungare ♦ *vi*: **to ~ out for** stendere la mano per prendere

react [riː'ækt] *vi* reagire; ~**ion** [-'ækʃən] *n* reazione *f*

reactor [riː'æktə*] *n* reattore *m*

read [riːd, *pt, pp* rɛd] (*pt, pp* **read**) *vi* leggere ♦ *vt* leggere; (*understand*) intendere, interpretare; (*study*) studiare; ~ **out** *vt* leggere ad alta voce; ~**able** *adj* (*writing*) leggibile; (*book etc*) che si legge volentieri; ~**er** *n* lettore/trice; (*BRIT: at university*) professore con funzioni preminenti di ricerca; ~**ership** *n* (*of paper etc*) numero di lettori

readily ['rɛdɪlɪ] *adv* volentieri; (*easily*) facilmente; (*quickly*) prontamente

readiness ['rɛdɪnɪs] *n* prontezza; **in ~** (*prepared*) pronto(a)

reading ['riːdɪŋ] *n* lettura; (*understanding*) interpretazione *f*; (*on instrument*) indicazione *f*

readjust [riːə'dʒʌst] *vt* riaggiustare ♦ *vi* (*person*): **to ~ (to)** riadattarsi (a)

ready ['rɛdɪ] *adj* pronto(a); (*willing*) pronto(a), disposto(a); (*available*) disponibile ♦ *n*: **at the ~** (*MIL*) pronto a sparare; **to get ~** *vi* prepararsi ♦ *vt*

preparare; ~**-made** *adj* prefabbricato(a); (*clothes*) confezionato(a); ~ **reckoner** *n* prontuario di calcolo; ~**-to-wear** *adj* prêt-à-porter *inv*

reaffirm [riːə'fəːm] *vt* riaffermare

real [rɪəl] *adj* reale; vero(a); **in ~ terms** in realtà; ~ **estate** *n* beni *mpl* immobili; ~**ism** *n* (*also ART*) realismo; ~**ist** *n* realista *m/f*; ~**istic** [-'lɪstɪk] *adj* realistico(a)

reality [riː'ælɪtɪ] *n* realtà *f inv*

realization [rɪəlaɪ'zeɪʃən] *n* presa di coscienza; realizzazione *f*

realize ['rɪəlaɪz] *vt* (*understand*) rendersi conto di

really ['rɪəlɪ] *adv* veramente, davvero; ~! (*indicating annoyance*) oh, insomma!

realm [rɛlm] *n* reame *m*, regno

Realtor ® ['rɪəltɔː*] (*US*) *n* agente *m* immobiliare

reap [riːp] *vt* mietere; (*fig*) raccogliere

reappear [riːə'pɪə*] *vi* ricomparire, riapparire

rear [rɪə*] *adj* di dietro; (*AUT: wheel etc*) posteriore ♦ *n* didietro, parte *f* posteriore ♦ *vt* (*cattle, family*) allevare ♦ *vi* (*also*: ~ **up**: *animal*) impennarsi

rearmament [riː'ɑːməmənt] *n* riarmo

rearrange [riːə'reɪndʒ] *vt* riordinare

rear-view: ~ **mirror** *n* (*AUT*) specchio retrovisore

reason ['riːzn] *n* ragione *f*; (*cause, motive*) ragione, motivo ♦ *vi*: **to ~ with sb** far ragionare qn; **it stands to ~ that** è ovvio che; ~**able** *adj* ragionevole; (*not bad*) accettabile; ~**ably** *adv* ragionevolmente; ~**ed** *adj*: **a well-~ed argument** una forte argomentazione; ~**ing** *n* ragionamento

reassurance [riːə'ʃuərəns] *n* rassicurazione *f*

reassure [riːə'ʃuə*] *vt* rassicurare; **to ~ sb of** rassicurare qn di *or* su

rebate ['riːbeɪt] *n* (*on tax etc*) sgravio

rebel [*n* 'rɛbl, *vb* rɪ'bɛl] *n* ribelle *m/f* ♦ *vi* ribellarsi; ~**lion** *n* ribellione *f*; ~**lious** *adj* ribelle

rebound [*vb* rɪ'baund, *n* 'riːbaund] *vi* (*ball*) rimbalzare ♦ *n*: **on the ~** di rimbalzo

rebuff [rɪˈbʌf] *n* secco rifiuto

rebuke [rɪˈbjuːk] *vt* rimproverare

rebut [rɪˈbʌt] *vt* rifiutare

recall [rɪˈkɔːl] *vt* richiamare; (*remember*) ricordare, richiamare alla mente ♦ *n* richiamo

recap [ˈriːkæp], **recapitulate** [riːkəˈpɪtjuleɪt] *vt* ricapitolare ♦ *vi* riassumere

rec'd *abbr* = **received**

recede [rɪˈsiːd] *vi* allontanarsi; ritirarsi; calare; **receding** *adj* (*forehead, chin*) sfuggente; **he's got a receding hairline** sta stempiando

receipt [rɪˈsiːt] *n* (*document*) ricevuta; (*act of receiving*) ricevimento; **~s** *npl* (*COMM*) introiti *mpl*

receive [rɪˈsiːv] *vt* ricevere; (*guest*) ricevere, accogliere

receiver [rɪˈsiːvə*] *n* (*TEL*) ricevitore *m*; (*RADIO, TV*) apparecchio ricevente; (*of stolen goods*) ricettatore/trice; (*COMM*) curatore *m* fallimentare

recent [ˈriːsnt] *adj* recente; **~ly** *adv* recentemente

receptacle [rɪˈseptɪkl] *n* recipiente *m*

reception [rɪˈsepʃən] *n* ricevimento; (*welcome*) accoglienza; (*TV etc*) ricezione *f*; **~ desk** *n* (*in hotel*) reception *f inv*; (*in hospital, at doctor's*) accettazione *f*; (*in offices etc*) portineria; **~ist** *n* receptionist *m/f inv*

receptive [rɪˈseptɪv] *adj* ricettivo(a)

recess [rɪˈses] *n* (*in room, secret place*) alcova; (*POL etc: holiday*) vacanze *fpl*; **~ion** [-ˈseʃən] *n* recessione *f*

recharge [riːˈtʃɑːdʒ] *vt* (*battery*) ricaricare

recipe [ˈresɪpɪ] *n* ricetta

recipient [rɪˈsɪpɪənt] *n* beneficiario/a; (*of letter*) destinatario/a

recital [rɪˈsaɪtl] *n* recital *m inv*

recite [rɪˈsaɪt] *vt* (*poem*) recitare

reckless [ˈrekləs] *adj* (*driver etc*) spericolato(a); (*spending*) folle

reckon [ˈrekən] *vt* (*count*) calcolare; (*think*): **I ~ that ...** penso che ...; **~ on** *vt fus* contare su; **~ing** *n* conto, stima

reclaim [rɪˈkleɪm] *vt* (*demand back*) richiedere, reclamare; (*land*) bonificare; (*materials*) recuperare; **reclamation** [rekləˈmeɪʃən] *n* bonifica

recline [rɪˈklaɪn] *vi* stare sdraiato(a); **reclining** *adj* (*seat*) ribaltabile

recognition [rekəgˈnɪʃən] *n* riconoscimento; **transformed beyond ~** irriconoscibile

recognize [ˈrekəgnaɪz] *vt*: **to ~ (by/as)** riconoscere (a *or* da/come)

recoil [rɪˈkɔɪl] *vi* (*person*): **to ~ from doing sth** rifuggire dal fare qc ♦ *n* (*of gun*) rinculo

recollect [rekəˈlekt] *vt* ricordare; **~ion** [-ˈlekʃən] *n* ricordo

recommend [rekəˈmend] *vt* raccomandare; (*advise*) consigliare

reconcile [ˈrekənsaɪl] *vt* (*two people*) riconciliare; (*two facts*) conciliare, quadrare; **to ~ o.s. to** rassegnarsi a

recondition [riːkənˈdɪʃən] *vt* rimettere a nuovo

reconnoitre [rekəˈnɔɪtə*] (*US* **reconnoiter**) *vt* (*MIL*) fare una ricognizione di

reconstruct [riːkənˈstrʌkt] *vt* ricostruire

record [*n* ˈrekɔːd, *vb* rɪˈkɔːd] *n* ricordo, documento; (*of meeting etc*) nota, verbale *m*; (*register*) registro; (*file*) pratica, dossier *m inv*; (*COMPUT*) record *m inv*; (*also:* **criminal ~**) fedina penale sporca; (*MUS: disc*) disco; (*SPORT*) record *m inv*, primato ♦ *vt* (*set down*) prendere nota di, registrare; (*MUS: song etc*) registrare; **in ~ time** a tempo di record; **off the ~** *adj* ufficioso(a) ♦ *adv* ufficiosamente; **~ card** *n* (*in file*) scheda; **~ed delivery** (*BRIT*) *n* (*POST*): **~ed delivery letter** *etc* lettera *etc* raccomandata; **~er** *n* (*MUS*) flauto diritto; **~ holder** *n* (*SPORT*) primatista *m/f*; **~ing** *n* (*MUS*) registrazione *f*; **~ player** *n* giradischi *m inv*

recount [rɪˈkaunt] *vt* raccontare, narrare

re-count [ˈriːkaunt] *n* (*POL: of votes*) nuovo computo

recoup [rɪˈkuːp] *vt* ricuperare

recourse [rɪˈkɔːs] *n*: **to have ~ to** ricorrere a, far ricorso a

recover [rɪˈkʌvə*] *vt* ricuperare ♦ *vi*: **to ~**

(from) riprendersi (da)

recovery [rɪ'kʌvərɪ] *n* ricupero; ristabilimento; ripresa

recreation [rɛkrɪ'eɪʃən] *n* ricreazione *f*; svago; **~al** *adj* ricreativo(a); **~al drug** *n* sostanza stupefacente usata a scopo ricreativo

recrimination [rɪkrɪmɪ'neɪʃən] *n* recriminazione *f*

recruit [rɪ'kruːt] *n* recluta; *(in company)* nuovo(a) assunto(a) ♦ *vt* reclutare

rectangle ['rɛktæŋgl] *n* rettangolo; **rectangular** [-'tæŋgjulə*] *adj* rettangolare

rectify ['rɛktɪfaɪ] *vt* (error) rettificare; (omission) riparare

rector ['rɛktə*] *n* (REL) parroco (anglicano); **~y** *n* presbiterio

recuperate [rɪ'kjuːpəreɪt] *vi* ristabilirsi

recur [rɪ'kə:*] *vi* riaccadere; *(symptoms)* ripresentarsi; **~rent** *adj* ricorrente, periodico(a)

recycle [ri:'saɪkl] *vt* riciclare

red [rɛd] *n* rosso; *(POL: pej)* rosso/a ♦ *adj* rosso(a); **in the ~** (account) scoperto; (business) in deficit; **~ carpet treatment** *n* cerimonia col gran pavese; **R~ Cross** *n* Croce *f* Rossa; **~currant** *n* ribes *m inv*; **~den** *vt* arrossare ♦ *vi* arrossire

redeem [rɪ'diːm] *vt* (debt) riscattare; (sth in pawn) ritirare; (fig, also REL) redimere; **~ing** *adj*: **~ing feature** unico aspetto positivo

redeploy [riːdɪ'plɔɪ] *vt* (resources) riorganizzare

red-haired [-'hɛəd] *adj* dai capelli rossi

red-handed [-'hændɪd] *adj*: **to be caught ~** essere preso(a) in flagrante *or* con le mani nel sacco

redhead ['rɛdhɛd] *n* rosso/a

red herring *n* (fig) falsa pista

red-hot *adj* arroventato(a)

redirect [riːdaɪ'rɛkt] *vt* (mail) far seguire

red light *n*: **to go through a ~** (AUT) passare col rosso; **red-light district** *n* quartiere *m* a luci rosse

redo [riː'duː] (irreg) *vt* rifare

redouble [riː'dʌbl] *vt*: **to ~ one's efforts** raddoppiare gli sforzi

redress [rɪ'drɛs] *vt* riparare

Red Sea *n*: **the ~** il Mar Rosso

redskin ['rɛdskɪn] *n* pellerossa *m/f*

red tape *n* (fig) burocrazia

reduce [rɪ'djuːs] *vt* ridurre; (lower) ridurre, abbassare; **"~ speed now"** (AUT) "rallentare"; **at a ~d price** scontato(a); **reduction** [rɪ'dʌkʃən] *n* riduzione *f*; (of price) ribasso; (discount) sconto

redundancy [rɪ'dʌndənsɪ] *n* licenziamento

redundant [rɪ'dʌndnt] *adj* (worker) licenziato(a); (detail, object) superfluo(a); **to be made ~** essere licenziato (per eccesso di personale)

reed [riːd] *n* (BOT) canna; (MUS: of clarinet etc) ancia

reef [riːf] *n* (at sea) scogliera

reek [riːk] *vi*: **to ~ (of)** puzzare (di)

reel [riːl] *n* bobina, rocchetto; (FISHING) mulinello; (CINEMA) rotolo; (dance) danza veloce scozzese ♦ *vi* (sway) barcollare; **~ in** *vt* tirare su

ref [rɛf] (inf) *n abbr* (= referee) arbitro

refectory [rɪ'fɛktərɪ] *n* refettorio

refer [rɪ'fə:*] *vt*: **to ~ sth to** (dispute, decision) deferire qc a; **to ~ sb to** (inquirer, MED: patient) indirizzare qn a; (reader: to text) rimandare qn a ♦ *vi*: **to ~** (allude to) accennare a; (consult) rivolgersi a

referee [rɛfə'riː] *n* arbitro; (BRIT: for job application) referenza ♦ *vt* arbitrare

reference ['rɛfrəns] *n* riferimento; (mention) menzione *f*, allusione *f*; (for job application) referenza; **with ~ to** (COMM: in letter) in or con riferimento a; **~ book** *n* libro di consultazione; **~ number** *n* numero di riferimento

referenda [rɛfə'rɛndə] *npl of* **referendum**

referendum [rɛfə'rɛndəm] (pl **referenda**) *n* referendum *m inv*

refill [vb riː'fɪl, *n* 'riːfɪl] *vt* riempire di nuovo; (pen, lighter etc) ricaricare ♦ *n* (for pen etc) ricambio

refine [rɪ'faɪn] *vt* raffinare; **~d** *adj* (person, taste) raffinato(a)

reflect [rɪ'flɛkt] *vt* (light, image) riflettere; (fig) rispecchiare ♦ *vi* (think) riflettere, considerare; **it ~s badly/well on him** si ripercuote su di lui in senso negativo/positivo; **~ion** [-'flɛkʃən] n riflessione f; (*image*) riflesso; (*criticism*): **~ion on** giudizio su; attacco a; **on ~ion** pensandoci sopra

reflex ['riːflɛks] adj n riflesso ♦ vt riflesso; **~ive** [rɪ'flɛksɪv] adj (LING) riflessivo(a)

reform [rɪ'fɔːm] n (*of sinner etc*) correzione f; (*of law etc*) riforma ♦ vt correggere; riformare; **~atory** (US) n riformatorio

refrain [rɪ'freɪn] vi: **to ~ from doing** trattenersi dal fare ♦ n ritornello

refresh [rɪ'frɛʃ] vt rinfrescare; (*subj: food, sleep*) ristorare; **~er course** (BRIT) n corso di aggiornamento; **~ing** adj (*drink*) rinfrescante; (*sleep*) riposante, ristoratore(trice); **~ments** npl rinfreschi mpl

refrigerator [rɪ'frɪdʒəreɪtə*] n frigorifero

refuel [riː'fjuəl] vi far rifornimento (di carburante)

refuge ['rɛfjuːdʒ] n rifugio; **to take ~ in** rifugiarsi in

refugee [rɛfju'dʒiː] n rifugiato/a, profugo/a

refund [n 'riːfʌnd, vb rɪ'fʌnd] n rimborso ♦ vt rimborsare

refurbish [riː'fɜːbɪʃ] vt rimettere a nuovo

refusal [rɪ'fjuːzəl] n rifiuto; **to have first ~ on** avere il diritto d'opzione su

refuse [n 'rɛfjuːs, vb rɪ'fjuːz] n rifiuti mpl ♦ vt, vi rifiutare; **to ~ to do** rifiutare di fare; **~ collection** n raccolta di rifiuti

refute [rɪ'fjuːt] vt confutare

regain [rɪ'geɪn] vt riguadagnare; riacquistare, ricuperare

regal ['riːgl] adj regale; **~ia** [rɪ'geɪlɪə] n insegne fpl regie

regard [rɪ'gɑːd] n riguardo, stima ♦ vt considerare, stimare; **to give one's ~s to** porgere i suoi saluti a; **"with kindest ~s"** "cordiali saluti"; **~ing, as ~s, with ~ to** riguardo a; **~less** adv lo stesso; **~less of** a dispetto di, nonostante

regenerate [rɪ'dʒɛnəreɪt] vt rigenerare

régime [reɪ'ʒiːm] n regime m

regiment ['rɛdʒɪmənt] n reggimento; **~al** [-'mɛntl] adj reggimentale

region ['riːdʒən] n regione f; **in the ~ of** (*fig*) all'incirca di; **~al** adj regionale

register ['rɛdʒɪstə*] n registro; (*also:* **electoral ~**) lista elettorale ♦ vt registrare; (*vehicle*) immatricolare; (*letter*) assicurare; (*subj: instrument*) segnare ♦ vi iscriversi; (*at hotel*) firmare il registro; (*make impression*) entrare in testa; **~ed** (BRIT) adj (*letter*) assicurato(a); **~ed trademark** n marchio depositato

registrar ['rɛdʒɪstrɑː*] n ufficiale m di stato civile; segretario

registration [rɛdʒɪs'treɪʃən] n (*act*) registrazione f; iscrizione f; (AUT: *also:* **~ number**) numero di targa

registry ['rɛdʒɪstrɪ] n ufficio del registro; **~ office** (BRIT) n anagrafe f; **to get married in a ~ office** ≈ sposarsi in municipio

regret [rɪ'grɛt] n rimpianto, rincrescimento ♦ vt rimpiangere; **~fully** adv con rincrescimento; **~table** adj deplorevole

regular ['rɛgjulə*] adj regolare; (*usual*) abituale, normale; (*soldier*) dell'esercito regolare ♦ n (*client etc*) cliente m/f abituale; **~ly** adv regolarmente

regulate ['rɛgjuleɪt] vt regolare; **regulation** [-'leɪʃən] n regolazione f; (*rule*) regola, regolamento

rehabilitation ['riːhəbɪlɪ'teɪʃən] n (*of offender*) riabilitazione f; (*of disabled*) riadattamento

rehearsal [rɪ'hɜːsəl] n prova

rehearse [rɪ'hɜːs] vt provare

reign [reɪn] n regno ♦ vi regnare

reimburse [riːɪm'bɜːs] vt rimborsare

rein [reɪn] n (*for horse*) briglia

reindeer ['reɪndɪə*] n inv renna

reinforce [riːɪn'fɔːs] vt rinforzare; **~d concrete** n cemento armato; **~ment** n rinforzo; **~ments** npl (MIL) rinforzi mpl

reinstate [riːɪn'steɪt] vt reintegrare

reiterate [riː'ɪtəreɪt] vt reiterare, ripetere

reject [n 'riːdʒɛkt, vb rɪ'dʒɛkt] n (COMM) scarto ♦ vt rifiutare, respingere; (COMM: *goods*) scartare; **~ion** [rɪ'dʒɛkʃən] n rifiuto

rejoice [rɪ'dʒɔɪs] vi: **to ~ (at or over)** provare diletto in

rejuvenate [rɪ'dʒuːvəneɪt] *vt* ringiovanire

relapse [rɪ'læps] *n* (MED) ricaduta

relate [rɪ'leɪt] *vt* (*tell*) raccontare; (*connect*) collegare ♦ *vi*: **to ~ to** (*connect*) riferirsi a; (*get on with*) stabilire un rapporto con; **relating to** che riguarda, rispetto a; **~d** *adj*: **~d (to)** imparentato(a) (con); collegato(a) *or* connesso(a) (a)

relation [rɪ'leɪʃən] *n* (*person*) parente *m/f*; (*link*) rapporto, relazione *f*; **~ship** *n* rapporto; (*personal ties*) rapporti *mpl*, relazioni *fpl*; (*also*: **family ~ship**) legami *mpl* di parentela

relative ['rɛlətɪv] *n* parente *m/f* ♦ *adj* relativo(a); (*respective*) rispettivo(a); **~ly** *adv* relativamente; (*fairly, rather*) abbastanza

relax [rɪ'læks] *vi* rilasciarsi; (*person: unwind*) rilassarsi ♦ *vt* rilasciare; (*mind, person*) rilassare; **~ation** [riːlæk'seɪʃən] *n* rilasciamento; rilassamento; (*entertainment*) ricreazione *f*, svago; **~ed** *adj* rilassato(a); **~ing** *adj* rilassante

relay ['riːleɪ] *n* (SPORT) corsa a staffetta ♦ *vt* (*message*) trasmettere

release [rɪ'liːs] *n* (*from prison*) rilascio; (*from obligation*) liberazione *f*; (*of gas etc*) emissione *f*; (*of film etc*) distribuzione *f*; (*record*) disco; (*device*) disinnesto ♦ *vt* (*prisoner*) rilasciare; (*from obligation, wreckage etc*) liberare; (*book, film*) fare uscire; (*news*) rendere pubblico(a); (*gas etc*) emettere; (TECH: *catch, spring etc*) disinnestare

relegate ['rɛləgeɪt] *vt* relegare; (BRIT: SPORT): **to be ~d** essere retrocesso(a)

relent [rɪ'lɛnt] *vi* cedere; **~less** *adj* implacabile

relevant ['rɛləvənt] *adj* pertinente; (*chapter*) in questione; **~ to** pertinente a

reliability [rɪlaɪə'bɪlɪtɪ] *n* (*of person*) serietà; (*of machine*) affidabilità

reliable [rɪ'laɪəbl] *adj* (*person, firm*) fidato(a), che dà affidamento; (*method*) sicuro(a); (*machine*) affidabile; **reliably** *adv*: **to be reliably informed** sapere da fonti sicure

reliance [rɪ'laɪəns] *n*: **~ (on)** fiducia (in); bisogno (di)

relic ['rɛlɪk] *n* (REL) reliquia; (*of the past*) resto

relief [rɪ'liːf] *n* (*from pain, anxiety*) sollievo; (*help, supplies*) soccorsi *mpl*; (ART, GEO) rilievo

relieve [rɪ'liːv] *vt* (*pain, patient*) sollevare; (*bring help*) soccorrere; (*take over from: gen*) sostituire; (: *guard*) rilevare; **to ~ sb of sth** (*load*) alleggerire qn di qc; **to ~ o.s.** fare i propri bisogni

religion [rɪ'lɪdʒən] *n* religione *f*; **religious** *adj* religioso(a)

relinquish [rɪ'lɪŋkwɪʃ] *vt* abbandonare; (*plan, habit*) rinunziare a

relish ['rɛlɪʃ] *n* (CULIN) condimento; (*enjoyment*) gran piacere *m* ♦ *vt* (*food etc*) godere; **to ~ doing** adorare fare

relocate ['riːləʊkeɪt] *vt* trasferire ♦ *vi* trasferirsi

reluctance [rɪ'lʌktəns] *n* riluttanza

reluctant [rɪ'lʌktənt] *adj* riluttante, mal disposto(a); **~ly** *adv* di mala voglia, a malincuore

rely [rɪ'laɪ]: **to ~ on** *vt fus* contare su; (*be dependent*) dipendere da

remain [rɪ'meɪn] *vi* restare, rimanere; **~der** *n* resto; (COMM) rimanenza; **~ing** *adj* che rimane; **~s** *npl* resti *mpl*

remand [rɪ'mɑːnd] *n*: **on ~** in detenzione preventiva ♦ *vt*: **to ~ in custody** rinviare in carcere; trattenere a disposizione della legge; **~ home** (BRIT) *n* riformatorio, casa di correzione

remark [rɪ'mɑːk] *n* osservazione *f* ♦ *vt* osservare, dire; **~able** *adj* notevole; eccezionale

remedial [rɪ'miːdɪəl] *adj* (*tuition, classes*) di riparazione; (*exercise*) correttivo(a)

remedy ['rɛmədɪ] *n*: **~ (for)** rimedio (per) ♦ *vt* rimediare a

remember [rɪ'mɛmbə*] *vt* ricordare, ricordarsi di; **~ me to him** salutalo da parte mia; **remembrance** *n* memoria; ricordo; **Remembrance Day** *n* 11 novembre, giorno della commemorazione dei caduti in *guerra*

┌─────────────────────┐
│ **Remembrance Day** │
└─────────────────────┘

i *In Gran Bretagna, il* **Remembrance Day** *è un giorno di commemorazione dei caduti in guerra. Si celebra ogni anno la domenica più vicina all'11 novembre, anniversario della firma dell'armistizio con la Germania nel 1918.*

remind [rɪ'maɪnd] *vt*: **to ~ sb of sth** ricordare qc a qn; **to ~ sb to do** ricordare a qn di fare; **~er** *n* richiamo; (*note etc*) promemoria *m inv*

reminisce [rɛmɪ'nɪs] *vi*: **to ~ (about)** abbandonarsi ai ricordi (di)

reminiscent [rɛmɪ'nɪsnt] *adj*: **~ of** che fa pensare a, che richiama

remiss [rɪ'mɪs] *adj* negligente

remission [rɪ'mɪʃən] *n* remissione *f*

remit [rɪ'mɪt] *vt* (*send: money*) rimettere; **~tance** *n* rimessa

remnant ['rɛmnənt] *n* resto, avanzo; **~s** *npl* (*COMM*) scampoli *mpl*; fine *f* serie

remorse [rɪ'mɔːs] *n* rimorso; **~ful** *adj* pieno(a) di rimorsi; **~less** *adj* (*fig*) spietato(a)

remote [rɪ'məut] *adj* remoto(a), lontano(a); (*person*) distaccato(a); **~ control** *n* telecomando; **~ly** *adv* remotamente; (*slightly*) vagamente

remould ['riːməuld] (*BRIT*) *n* (*tyre*) gomma rivestita

removable [rɪ'muːvəbl] *adj* (*detachable*) staccabile

removal [rɪ'muːvəl] *n* (*taking away*) rimozione *f*; soppressione *f*; (*BRIT: from house*) trasloco; (*from office: dismissal*) destituzione *f*; (*MED*) ablazione *f*; **~ van** (*BRIT*) *n* furgone *m* per traslochi

remove [rɪ'muːv] *vt* togliere, rimuovere; (*employee*) destituire; (*stain*) far sparire; (*doubt, abuse*) sopprimere, eliminare; **~rs** (*BRIT*) *npl* (*company*) ditta *or* impresa di traslochi

Renaissance [rɪ'neɪsɑ̃ːns] *n*: **the ~** il Rinascimento

render ['rɛndə*] *vt* rendere; **~ing** *n* (*MUS etc*) interpretazione *f*

rendez-vous ['rɔndɪvuː] *n* appuntamento; (*place*) luogo d'incontro; (*meeting*) incontro

renegade ['rɛnɪgeɪd] *n* rinnegato/a

renew [rɪ'njuː] *vt* rinnovare; (*negotiations*) riprendere; **~able** *adj* rinnovabile; **~al** *n* rinnovo; ripresa

renounce [rɪ'nauns] *vt* rinunziare a

renovate ['rɛnəveɪt] *vt* rinnovare; (*art work*) restaurare; **renovation** [-'veɪʃən] *n* rinnovamento; restauro

renown [rɪ'naun] *n* rinomanza; **~ed** *adj* rinomato(a)

rent [rɛnt] *n* affitto ♦ *vt* (*take for ~*) prendere in affitto; (*also:* **~ out**) dare in affitto; **~al** *n* (*for television, car*) fitto

renunciation [rɪnʌnsɪ'eɪʃən] *n* rinunzia

rep [rɛp] *n abbr* (*COMM*: = *representative*) rappresentante *m/f*; (*THEATRE*: = *repertory*) teatro di repertorio

repair [rɪ'pɛə*] *n* riparazione *f* ♦ *vt* riparare; **in good/bad ~** in buone/cattive condizioni; **~ kit** *n* corredo per riparazioni

repatriate [riː'pætrɪeɪt] *vt* rimpatriare

repay [riː'peɪ] (*irreg*) *vt* (*money, creditor*) rimborsare, ripagare; (*sb's efforts*) ricompensare; (*favour*) ricambiare; **~ment** *n* pagamento; rimborso

repeal [rɪ'piːl] *n* (*of law*) abrogazione *f* ♦ *vt* abrogare

repeat [rɪ'piːt] *n* (*RADIO, TV*) replica ♦ *vt* ripetere; (*pattern*) riprodurre; (*promise, attack, also COMM: order*) rinnovare ♦ *vi* ripetere; **~edly** *adv* ripetutamente, spesso

repel [rɪ'pɛl] *vt* respingere; (*disgust*) ripugnare a; **~lent** *adj* repellente ♦ *n*: **insect ~lent** prodotto *m* anti-insetti *inv*

repent [rɪ'pɛnt] *vi*: **to ~ (of)** pentirsi (di); **~ance** *n* pentimento

repertoire ['rɛpətwɑː*] *n* repertorio

repertory ['rɛpətərɪ] *n* (*also:* **~ theatre**) teatro di repertorio

repetition [rɛpɪ'tɪʃən] *n* ripetizione *f*

repetitive [rɪ'pɛtɪtɪv] *adj* (*movement*) che si ripete; (*work*) monotono(a); (*speech*) pieno(a) di ripetizioni

replace [rɪ'pleɪs] vt (put back) rimettere a posto; (take the place of) sostituire; ~**ment** n rimessa; sostituzione f; (person) sostituto/a

replay ['riːpleɪ] n (of match) partita ripetuta; (of tape, film) replay m inv

replenish [rɪ'plenɪʃ] vt (glass) riempire; (stock etc) rifornire

replete [rɪ'pliːt] adj (well-fed) sazio(a)

replica ['replɪkə] n replica, copia

reply [rɪ'plaɪ] n risposta ♦ vi rispondere; ~ **coupon** n buono di risposta

report [rɪ'pɔːt] n rapporto; (PRESS etc) cronaca; (BRIT: also: **school ~**) pagella; (of gun) sparo ♦ vt riportare; (PRESS etc) fare una cronaca su; (bring to notice: occurrence) segnalare; (: person) denunciare ♦ vi (make a report) fare un rapporto (or una cronaca); (present o.s.): **to ~ (to sb)** presentarsi (a qn); ~ **card** n (US, SCOTTISH) pagella; ~**edly** adv stando a quanto si dice; **he ~edly told them to ...** avrebbe detto loro di ...; ~**er** n reporter m inv

repose [rɪ'pəuz] n: **in ~** (face, mouth) in riposo

reprehensible [reprɪ'hensɪbl] adj riprovevole

represent [reprɪ'zent] vt rappresentare; ~**ation** [-'teɪʃən] n rappresentazione f; (petition) rappresentanza; ~**ations** npl (protest) protesta; ~**ative** n rappresentante m/f; (US: POL) deputato/a ♦ adj rappresentativo(a)

repress [rɪ'pres] vt reprimere; ~**ion** [-'preʃən] n repressione f

reprieve [rɪ'priːv] n (LAW) sospensione f dell'esecuzione della condanna; (fig) dilazione f

reprimand ['reprɪmɑːnd] n rimprovero ♦ vt rimproverare

reprint ['riːprɪnt] n ristampa

reprisal [rɪ'praɪzl] n rappresaglia

reproach [rɪ'prəutʃ] n rimprovero ♦ vt: **to ~ sb for sth** rimproverare qn di qc; ~**ful** adj di rimprovero

reproduce [riːprə'djuːs] vt riprodurre ♦ vi riprodursi; **reproduction** [-'dʌkʃən] n riproduzione f

reproof [rɪ'pruːf] n riprovazione f

reprove [rɪ'pruːv] vt: **to ~ (for)** biasimare (per)

reptile ['reptaɪl] n rettile m

republic [rɪ'pʌblɪk] n repubblica; ~**an** adj, n repubblicano(a)

repudiate [rɪ'pjuːdɪeɪt] vt (accusation) respingere

repulse [rɪ'pʌls] vt respingere

repulsive [rɪ'pʌlsɪv] adj ripugnante, ripulsivo(a)

reputable ['repjutəbl] adj di buona reputazione; (occupation) rispettabile

reputation [repju'teɪʃən] n reputazione f

reputed [rɪ'pjuːtɪd] adj reputato(a); ~**ly** adv secondo quanto si dice

request [rɪ'kwest] n domanda; (formal) richiesta ♦ vt: **to ~ (of or from sb)** chiedere (a qn); ~ **stop** (BRIT) n (for bus) fermata facoltativa or a richiesta

require [rɪ'kwaɪə*] vt (need: subj: person) aver bisogno di; (: thing, situation) richiedere; (want) volere; esigere; (order): **to ~ sb to do sth** ordinare a qn di fare qc; ~**ment** n esigenza; bisogno; requisito

requisition [rekwɪ'zɪʃən] n: ~ **(for)** richiesta (di) ♦ vt (MIL) requisire

rescue ['reskjuː] n salvataggio; (help) soccorso ♦ vt salvare; ~ **party** n squadra di salvataggio; ~**r** n salvatore/trice

research [rɪ'səːtʃ] n ricerca, ricerche fpl ♦ vt fare ricerche su; ~**er** n ricercatore/trice

resemblance [rɪ'zembləns] n somiglianza

resemble [rɪ'zembl] vt assomigliare a

resent [rɪ'zent] vt risentirsi di; ~**ful** adj pieno(a) di risentimento; ~**ment** n risentimento

reservation [rezə'veɪʃən] n (booking) prenotazione f; (doubt) dubbio; (protected area) riserva; (BRIT: on road: also: **central ~**) spartitraffico m inv

reserve [rɪ'zəːv] n riserva ♦ vt (seats etc) prenotare; ~**s** npl (MIL) riserve fpl; **in ~** in serbo; ~**d** adj (shy) riservato(a)

reservoir ['rezəvwɑː*] n serbatoio

reshuffle [riːˈʃʌfl] *n*: **Cabinet ~** (*POL*) rimpasto governativo

reside [rɪˈzaɪd] *vi* risiedere

residence [ˈrezɪdəns] *n* residenza; **~ permit** (*BRIT*) *n* permesso di soggiorno

resident [ˈrezɪdənt] *n* residente *m/f*; (*in hotel*) cliente *m/f* fisso(a) ♦ *adj* residente; (*doctor*) fisso(a); (*course, college*) a tempo pieno con pernottamento; **~ial** [-ˈdenʃəl] *adj* di residenza; (*area*) residenziale

residue [ˈrezɪdjuː] *n* resto; (*CHEM, PHYSICS*) residuo

resign [rɪˈzaɪn] *vt* (*one's post*) dimettersi da ♦ *vi* dimettersi; **to ~ o.s. to** rassegnarsi a; **~ation** [rezɪgˈneɪʃən] *n* dimissioni *fpl*; rassegnazione *f*; **~ed** *adj* rassegnato(a)

resilience [rɪˈzɪlɪəns] *n* (*of material*) elasticità, resilienza; (*of person*) capacità di recupero

resilient [rɪˈzɪlɪənt] *adj* elastico(a); (*person*) che si riprende facilmente

resin [ˈrezɪn] *n* resina

resist [rɪˈzɪst] *vt* resistere a; **~ance** *n* resistenza

resolution [rezəˈluːʃən] *n* risoluzione *f*

resolve [rɪˈzɔlv] *n* risoluzione *f* ♦ *vi* (*decide*): **to ~ to do** decidere di fare ♦ *vt* (*problem*) risolvere

resort [rɪˈzɔːt] *n* (*town*) stazione *f*; (*recourse*) ricorso ♦ *vi*: **to ~ to** aver ricorso a; **in the last ~** come ultima risorsa

resounding [rɪˈzaundɪŋ] *adj* risonante; (*fig*) clamoroso(a)

resource [rɪˈsɔːs] *n* risorsa; **~s** *npl* (*coal, iron etc*) risorse *fpl*; **~ful** *adj* pieno(a) di risorse, intraprendente

respect [rɪsˈpekt] *n* rispetto ♦ *vt* rispettare; **~s** *npl* (*greetings*) ossequi *mpl*; **with ~ to** rispetto a, riguardo a; **in this ~** per questo riguardo; **~able** *adj* rispettabile; **~ful** *adj* rispettoso(a)

respective [rɪsˈpektɪv] *adj* rispettivo(a)

respite [ˈrespaɪt] *n* respiro, tregua

respond [rɪsˈpɔnd] *vi* rispondere

response [rɪsˈpɔns] *n* risposta

responsibility [rɪspɔnsɪˈbɪlɪtɪ] *n* responsabilità *f inv*

responsible [rɪsˈpɔnsɪbl] *adj* (*trustworthy*) fidato(a); (*job*) di (grande) responsabilità; **~ (for)** responsabile (di)

responsive [rɪsˈpɔnsɪv] *adj* che reagisce

rest [rest] *n* (*repose*) riposo, sosta, pausa; (*stop*) sosta, pausa; (*MUS*) pausa; (*object: to support sth*) appoggio, sostegno; (*remainder*) resto, avanzi *mpl* ♦ *vi* riposarsi; (*remain*) rimanere, restare; (*be supported*): **to ~ on** appoggiarsi su ♦ *vt* (far) riposare; (*lean*): **to ~ sth on/against** appoggiare qc su/contro; **the ~ of them** gli altri; **it ~s with him to decide** sta a lui decidere

restaurant [ˈrestərɔŋ] *n* ristorante *m*; **~ car** (*BRIT*) *n* vagone *m* ristorante

restful [ˈrestful] *adj* riposante

rest home *n* casa di riposo

restitution [restɪˈtjuːʃən] *n*: **to make ~ to sb for sth** compensare qn di qc

restive [ˈrestɪv] *adj* agitato(a), impaziente

restless [ˈrestlɪs] *adj* agitato(a), irrequieto(a)

restoration [restəˈreɪʃən] *n* restauro; restituzione *f*

restore [rɪˈstɔː*] *vt* (*building, to power*) restaurare; (*sth stolen*) restituire; (*peace, health*) ristorare

restrain [rɪsˈtreɪn] *vt* (*feeling, growth*) contenere, frenare; (*person*): **to ~ (from doing)** trattenere (dal fare); **~ed** *adj* (*style*) contenuto(a), sobrio(a); (*person*) riservato(a); **~t** *n* (*restriction*) limitazione *f*; (*moderation*) ritegno; (*of style*) contenutezza

restrict [rɪsˈtrɪkt] *vt* restringere, limitare; **~ion** [-kʃən] *n*: **~ion (on)** restrizione *f* (di), limitazione *f*

rest room (*US*) *n* toletta

restructure [riːˈstrʌktʃə*] *vt* ristrutturare

result [rɪˈzʌlt] *n* risultato ♦ *vi*: **to ~ in** avere per risultato; **as a ~ of** in *or* di conseguenza a, in seguito a

resume [rɪˈzjuːm] *vt, vi* (*work, journey*) riprendere

résumé [ˈreɪzjumeɪ] *n* riassunto; (*US*) curriculum *m inv* vitae

resumption [rɪˈzʌmpʃən] *n* ripresa

resurgence [rɪ'səːdʒəns] *n* rinascita

resurrection [rɛzə'rɛkʃən] *n* risurrezione *f*

resuscitate [rɪ'sʌsɪteɪt] *vt* (*MED*) risuscitare; **resuscitation** [-'teɪʃən] *n* rianimazione *f*

retail ['riːteɪl] *adj, adv* al minuto ♦ *vt* vendere al minuto; **~er** *n* commerciante *m/f* al minuto, dettagliante *m/f*; **~ price** *n* prezzo al minuto

retain [rɪ'teɪn] *vt* (*keep*) tenere, serbare; **~er** *n* (*fee*) onorario

retaliate [rɪ'tælɪeɪt] *vi*: **to ~ (against)** vendicarsi (di); **retaliation** [-'eɪʃən] *n* rappresaglie *fpl*

retarded [rɪ'tɑːdɪd] *adj* ritardato(a)

retch [rɛtʃ] *vi* aver conati di vomito

retire [rɪ'taɪə*] *vi* (*give up work*) andare in pensione; (*withdraw*) ritirarsi, andarsene; (*go to bed*) andare a letto, ritirarsi; **~d** *adj* (*person*) pensionato(a); **~ment** *n* pensione *f*; (*act*) pensionamento; **retiring** *adj* (*leaving*) uscente; (*shy*) riservato(a)

retort [rɪ'tɔːt] *vi* rimbeccare

retrace [riː'treɪs] *vt*: **to ~ one's steps** tornare sui passi

retract [rɪ'trækt] *vt* (*statement*) ritrattare; (*claws, undercarriage, aerial*) ritrarre, ritirare

retrain [riː'treɪn] *vt* (*worker*) riaddestrare

retread ['riːtrɛd] *n* (*tyre*) gomma rigenerata

retreat [rɪ'triːt] *n* ritirata; (*place*) rifugio ♦ *vi* battere in ritirata

retribution [rɛtrɪ'bjuːʃən] *n* castigo

retrieval [rɪ'triːvəl] *n* (*see vb*) ricupero; riparazione *f*

retrieve [rɪ'triːv] *vt* (*sth lost*) ricuperare, ritrovare; (*situation, honour*) salvare; (*error, loss*) rimediare a; **~r** *n* cane *m* da riporto

retrospect ['rɛtrəspɛkt] *n*: **in ~** guardando indietro; **~ive** [-'spɛktɪv] *adj* retrospettivo(a); (*law*) retroattivo(a)

return [rɪ'təːn] *n* (*going or coming back*) ritorno; (*of sth stolen etc*) restituzione *f*; (*FINANCE: from land, shares*) profitto, reddito ♦ *cpd* (*journey, match*) di ritorno; (*BRIT: ticket*) di andata e ritorno ♦ *vi* tornare, ritornare ♦ *vt* rendere, restituire; (*bring back*) riportare; (*send back*) mandare indietro; (*put back*) rimettere; (*POL:*

candidate) eleggere; **~s** *npl* (*COMM*) incassi *mpl*; profitti *mpl*; **in ~ (for)** in cambio (di); **by ~ of post** a stretto giro di posta; **many happy ~s (of the day)!** cento di questi giorni!

reunion [riː'juːnɪən] *n* riunione *f*

reunite [riːju'naɪt] *vt* riunire

rev [rɛv] *n abbr* (*AUT*: = *revolution*) giro ♦ *vt* (*also: ~ up*) imballare

revamp ['riː'væmp] *vt* (*firm*) riorganizzare

reveal [rɪ'viːl] *vt* (*make known*) rivelare, svelare; (*display*) rivelare, mostrare; **~ing** *adj* rivelatore(trice); (*dress*) scollato(a)

revel ['rɛvl] *vi*: **to ~ in sth/in doing** dilettarsi di qc/a fare

revelation [rɛvə'leɪʃən] *n* rivelazione *f*

revenge [rɪ'vɛndʒ] *n* vendetta ♦ *vt* vendicare; **to take ~ on** vendicarsi di

revenue ['rɛvənjuː] *n* reddito

reverberate [rɪ'vəːbəreɪt] *vi* (*sound*) rimbombare; (*light*) riverberarsi; (*fig*) ripercuotersi

revere [rɪ'vɪə*] *vt* venerare

reverence ['rɛvərəns] *n* venerazione *f*, riverenza

Reverend ['rɛvərənd] *adj* (*in titles*) reverendo(a)

reverie ['rɛvərɪ] *n* fantasticheria

reversal [rɪ'vəːsl] *n* capovolgimento

reverse [rɪ'vəːs] *n* contrario, opposto; (*back, defeat*) rovescio; (*AUT*: *also*: **~ gear**) marcia indietro ♦ *adj* (*order, direction*) contrario(a), opposto(a) ♦ *vt* (*turn*) invertire, rivoltare; (*change*) capovolgere, rovesciare; (*LAW: judgment*) cassare; (*car*) fare marcia indietro con ♦ *vi* (*BRIT: AUT, person etc*) fare marcia indietro; **~-charge call** (*BRIT*) *n* (*TEL*) telefonata con addebito al ricevente; **reversing lights** (*BRIT*) *npl* (*AUT*) luci *fpl* per la retromarcia

revert [rɪ'vəːt] *vi*: **to ~ to** tornare a

review [rɪ'vjuː] *n* rivista; (*of book, film*) recensione *f*; (*of situation*) esame *m* ♦ *vt* passare in rivista; fare la recensione di; fare il punto di; **~er** *n* recensore/a

revise [rɪ'vaɪz] *vt* (*manuscript*) rivedere, correggere; (*opinion*) emendare,

modificare; (*study: subject, notes*) ripassare; **revision** [rɪ'vɪʒən] *n* revisione *f*; ripasso
revitalize [ri:'vaɪtəlaɪz] *vt* ravvivare
revival [rɪ'vaɪvl] *n* ripresa; ristabilimento; (*of faith*) risveglio
revive [rɪ'vaɪv] *vt* (*person*) rianimare; (*custom*) far rivivere; (*hope, courage, economy*) ravvivare; (*play, fashion*) riesumare ♦ *vi* (*person*) rianimarsi; (*hope*) ravvivarsi; (*activity*) riprendersi
revolt [rɪ'vəʊlt] *n* rivolta, ribellione *f* ♦ *vi* rivoltarsi, ribellarsi ♦ *vt* (far) rivoltare; **~ing** *adj* ripugnante
revolution [revə'lu:ʃən] *n* rivoluzione *f*; (*of wheel etc*) rivoluzione, giro; **~ary** *adj*, *n* rivoluzionario(a)
revolve [rɪ'vɒlv] *vi* girare
revolver [rɪ'vɒlvə*] *n* rivoltella
revolving [rɪ'vɒlvɪŋ] *adj* girevole
revue [rɪ'vju:] *n* (THEATRE) rivista
revulsion [rɪ'vʌlʃən] *n* ripugnanza
reward [rɪ'wɔ:d] *n* ricompensa, premio ♦ *vt*: **to ~ (for)** ricompensare (per); **~ing** *adj* (*fig*) gratificante
rewind [ri:'waɪnd] (*irreg*) *vt* (*watch*) ricaricare; (*ribbon etc*) riavvolgere
rewire [ri:'waɪə*] *vt* (*house*) rifare l'impianto elettrico di
reword [ri:'wə:d] *vt* formulare *or* esprimere con altre parole
rheumatism ['ru:mətɪzəm] *n* reumatismo
Rhine [raɪn] *n*: **the ~** il Reno
rhinoceros [raɪ'nɒsərəs] *n* rinoceronte *m*
rhododendron [rəʊdə'dendrən] *n* rododendro
Rhone [rəʊn] *n*: **the ~** il Rodano
rhubarb ['ru:bɑ:b] *n* rabarbaro
rhyme [raɪm] *n* rima; (*verse*) poesia
rhythm ['rɪðm] *n* ritmo
rib [rɪb] *n* (ANAT) costola ♦ *vt* (*tease*) punzecchiare
ribbon ['rɪbən] *n* nastro; **in ~s** (*torn*) a brandelli
rice [raɪs] *n* riso; **~ pudding** *n* budino di riso
rich [rɪtʃ] *adj* ricco(a); (*clothes*) sontuoso(a); (*abundant*): **~ in** ricco(a) di; **the ~** *npl*

(*wealthy people*) i ricchi; **~es** *npl* ricchezze *fpl*; **~ly** *adv* riccamente; (*dressed*) sontuosamente; (*deserved*) pienamente
rickets ['rɪkɪts] *n* rachitismo
ricochet ['rɪkəʃeɪ] *vi* rimbalzare
rid [rɪd] (*pt, pp rid*) *vt*: **to ~ sb of** sbarazzare *or* liberare qn di; **to get ~ of** sbarazzarsi di
ridden ['rɪdn] *pp of* **ride**
riddle ['rɪdl] *n* (*puzzle*) indovinello ♦ *vt*: **to be ~d with** (*holes*) essere crivellato(a) di; (*doubts*) essere pieno(a) di
ride [raɪd] (*pt rode, pp ridden*) *n* (*on horse*) cavalcata; (*outing*) passeggiata; (*distance covered*) cavalcata; corsa ♦ *vi* (*as sport*) cavalcare; (*go somewhere: on horse, bicycle*) andare (a cavallo *or* in bicicletta *etc*); (*journey: on bicycle, motorcycle, bus*) andare, viaggiare ♦ *vt* (*a horse*) montare, cavalcare; **to take sb for a ~** (*fig*) prendere in giro qn; fregare qn; **to ~ a horse/bicycle/ camel** montare a cavallo/in bicicletta/in groppa a un cammello; **~r** *n* cavalcatore/ trice; (*in race*) fantino; (*on bicycle*) ciclista *m/f*; (*on motorcycle*) motociclista *m/f*
ridge [rɪdʒ] *n* (*of hill*) cresta; (*of roof*) colmo; (*on object*) riga (in rilievo)
ridicule ['rɪdɪkju:l] *n* ridicolo; scherno ♦ *vt* mettere in ridicolo
ridiculous [rɪ'dɪkjʊləs] *adj* ridicolo(a)
riding ['raɪdɪŋ] *n* equitazione *f*; **~ school** *n* scuola d'equitazione
rife [raɪf] *adj* diffuso(a); **to be ~ with** abbondare di
riffraff ['rɪfræf] *n* canaglia
rifle ['raɪfl] *n* carabina ♦ *vt* vuotare; **~ through** *vt fus* frugare tra; **~ range** *n* campo di tiro; (*at fair*) tiro a segno
rift [rɪft] *n* fessura, crepatura; (*fig: disagreement*) incrinatura, disaccordo
rig [rɪg] *n* (*also*: **oil ~**: *on land*) derrick *m inv*; (: *at sea*) piattaforma di trivellazione ♦ *vt* (*election etc*) truccare; **~ out** (BRIT) *vt*: **to ~ out as/in** vestire da/in; **~ up** *vt* allestire; **~ging** *n* (NAUT) attrezzatura
right [raɪt] *adj* giusto(a); (*suitable*) appropriato(a); (*not left*) destro(a) ♦ *n* giusto; (*title, claim*) diritto; (*not left*) destra

♦ *adv* (*answer*) correttamente; (*not on the left*) a destra ♦ *vt* raddrizzare; (*fig*) riparare ♦ *excl* bene!; **to be ~** (*person*) aver ragione; (*answer*) essere giusto(a) *or* corretto(a); **by ~s** di diritto; **on the ~** a destra; **to be in the ~** aver ragione, essere nel giusto; **~ now** proprio adesso; subito; **~ away** subito; **~ angle** *n* angolo retto; **~eous** ['raɪtʃəs] *adj* retto(a), virtuoso(a); (*anger*) giusto(a), giustificato(a); **~ful** *adj* (*heir*) legittimo(a); **~-handed** *adj* (*person*) che adopera la mano destra; **~-hand man** *n* braccio destro; **~-hand side** *n* il lato destro; **~ly** *adv* bene, correttamente; (*with reason*) a ragione; **~ of way** *n* diritto di passaggio; (*AUT*) precedenza; **~-wing** *adj* (*POL*) di destra

rigid ['rɪdʒɪd] *adj* rigido(a); (*principle*) rigoroso(a)

rigmarole ['rɪgmərəʊl] *n* tiritera; commedia

rile [raɪl] *vt* irritare, seccare

rim [rɪm] *n* orlo; (*of spectacles*) montatura; (*of wheel*) cerchione *m*

rind [raɪnd] *n* (*of bacon*) cotenna; (*of lemon etc*) scorza

ring [rɪŋ] (*pt* **rang**, *pp* **rung**) *n* anello; (*of people, objects*) cerchio; (*of spies*) giro; (*of smoke etc*) spirale *m*; (*arena*) pista, arena; (*for boxing*) ring *m inv*; (*sound of bell*) scampanio ♦ *vi* (*person, bell, telephone*) suonare; (*also:* **~ out**: *voice, words*) risuonare; (*TEL*) telefonare; (*ears*) fischiare ♦ *vt* (*BRIT*: *TEL*) telefonare a; (*bell, doorbell*) suonare; **to give sb a ~** (*BRIT*: *TEL*) dare un colpo di telefono a qn; **~ back** *vt, vi* (*TEL*) richiamare; **~ off** (*BRIT*) *vi* (*TEL*) mettere giù, riattaccare; **~ up** (*BRIT*) *vt* (*TEL*) telefonare a; **~ing** *n* (*of bell*) scampanio; (*of telephone*) squillo; (*in ears*) ronzio; **~ing tone** (*BRIT*) *n* (*TEL*) segnale *m* di libero; **~leader** *n* (*of gang*) capobanda *m*

ringlets ['rɪŋlɪts] *npl* boccoli *mpl*

ring road (*BRIT*) *n* raccordo anulare

rink [rɪŋk] *n* (*also:* **ice ~**) pista di pattinaggio

rinse [rɪns] *n* risciacquatura; (*hair tint*) cachet *m inv* ♦ *vt* sciacquare

riot ['raɪət] *n* sommossa, tumulto; (*of colours*) orgia ♦ *vi* tumultuare; **to run ~** creare disordine; **~ous** *adj* tumultuoso(a); (*living*) sfrenato(a); (*party*) scatenato(a)

rip [rɪp] *n* strappo ♦ *vt* strappare ♦ *vi* strapparsi; **~cord** *n* cavo di sfilamento

ripe [raɪp] *adj* (*fruit, grain*) maturo(a); (*cheese*) stagionato(a); **~n** *vt* maturare ♦ *vi* maturarsi

ripple ['rɪpl] *n* increspamento, ondulazione *f*; mormorio ♦ *vi* incresparsi

rise [raɪz] (*pt* **rose**, *pp* **risen**) *n* (*slope*) salita, pendio; (*hill*) altura; (*increase: in wages*: *BRIT*) aumento; (: *in prices, temperature*) rialzo, aumento; (*fig: to power etc*) ascesa ♦ *vi* alzarsi, levarsi; (*prices*) aumentare; (*waters, river*) crescere; (*sun, wind, person: from chair, bed*) levarsi; (*also:* **~ up**: *building*) ergersi; (: *rebel*) insorgere; ribellarsi; (*in rank*) salire; **to give ~ to** provocare, dare origine a; **to ~ to the occasion** essere all'altezza; **risen** ['rɪzn] *pp of* **rise**; **rising** *adj* (*increasing: number*) sempre crescente; (: *prices*) in aumento; (*tide*) montante; (*sun, moon*) nascente, che sorge

risk [rɪsk] *n* rischio; pericolo ♦ *vt* rischiare; **to take** *or* **run the ~ of doing** correre il rischio di fare; **at ~** in pericolo; **at one's own ~** a proprio rischio e pericolo; **~y** *adj* rischioso(a)

risqué ['riːskeɪ] *adj* (*joke*) spinto(a)

rissole ['rɪsəʊl] *n* crocchetta

rite [raɪt] *n* rito; **last ~s** l'estrema unzione

ritual ['rɪtjʊəl] *adj* rituale ♦ *n* rituale *m*

rival ['raɪvl] *n* rivale *m/f*; (*in business*) concorrente *m/f* ♦ *adj* rivale; che fa concorrenza ♦ *vt* essere in concorrenza con; **to ~ sb/sth in** competere con qn/qc in; **~ry** *n* rivalità; concorrenza

river ['rɪvə*] *n* fiume *m* ♦ *cpd* (*port, traffic*) fluviale; **up/down ~** a monte/valle; **~bank** *n* argine *m*; **~bed** *n* letto di fiume

rivet ['rɪvɪt] *n* ribattino, rivetto ♦ *vt* (*fig*) concentrare, fissare

Riviera [rɪvɪˈɛərə] *n*: **the (French) ~** la Costa Azzurra; **the Italian ~** la Riviera

road [rəʊd] *n* strada; (*small*) cammino; (*in town*) via ♦ *cpd* stradale; **major/minor ~**

strada con/senza diritto di precedenza; ~ **accident** n incidente m stradale; ~**block** n blocco stradale; ~**hog** n guidatore m egoista e spericolato; ~ **map** n carta stradale; ~ **rage** n comportamento aggressivo al volante; ~ **safety** n sicurezza sulle strade; ~**side** n margine m della strada; ~**sign** n cartello stradale; ~**user** n chi usa la strada; ~**way** n carreggiata; ~**works** npl lavori mpl stradali; ~**worthy** adj in buono stato di marcia

roam [rəum] vi errare, vagabondare

roar [rɔ:*] n ruggito; (of crowd) tumulto; (of thunder, storm) muggito; (of laughter) scoppio ♦ vi ruggire; tumultuare; muggire; **to ~ with laughter** scoppiare dalle risa; **to do a ~ing trade** fare affari d'oro

roast [rəust] n arrosto ♦ vt arrostire; (coffee) tostare, torrefare; ~ **beef** n arrosto di manzo

rob [rɔb] vt (person) rubare; (bank) svaligiare; **to ~ sb of sth** derubare qn di qc; (fig: deprive) privare qn di qc; ~**ber** n ladro; (armed) rapinatore m; ~**bery** n furto, rapina

robe [rəub] n (for ceremony etc) abito; (also: **bath** ~) accappatoio; (US: also: **lap** ~) coperta

robin ['rɔbɪn] n pettirosso

robot ['rəubɔt] n robot m inv

robust [rəu'bʌst] adj robusto(a); (economy) solido(a)

rock [rɔk] n (substance) roccia; (boulder) masso; roccia; (in sea) scoglio; (US: pebble) ciottolo; (BRIT: sweet) zucchero candito ♦ vt (swing gently: cradle) dondolare; (: child) cullare; (shake) scrollare, far tremare ♦ vi dondolarsi; scrollarsi, tremare; **on the ~s** (drink) col ghiaccio; (marriage etc) in crisi; ~ **and roll** n rock and roll m; ~**-bottom** adj bassissimo(a); ~**ery** n giardino roccioso

rocket ['rɔkɪt] n razzo

rock fall n parete f della roccia

rocking ['rɔkɪŋ]: ~ **chair** n sedia a dondolo; ~ **horse** n cavallo a dondolo

rocky ['rɔkɪ] adj (hill) roccioso(a); (path) sassoso(a); (marriage etc) instabile

rod [rɔd] n (metallic, TECH) asta; (wooden) bacchetta; (also: **fishing** ~) canna da pesca

rode [rəud] pt of **ride**

rodent ['rəudnt] n roditore m

rodeo ['rəudɪəu] n rodeo

roe [rəu] n (species: also: ~ **deer**) capriolo; (of fish, also: **hard** ~) uova fpl di pesce; **soft** ~ latte m di pesce

rogue [rəug] n mascalzone m

role [rəul] n ruolo

roll [rəul] n rotolo; (of banknotes) mazzo; (also: **bread** ~) panino; (register) lista; (sound: of drums etc) rullo ♦ vt rotolare; (also: ~ **up**: string) aggomitolare; (also: ~ **up**: sleeves) rimboccare; (cigarettes) arrotolare; (eyes) roteare; (also: ~ **out**: pastry) stendere; (lawn, road etc) spianare ♦ vi rotolare; (wheel) girare; (drum) rullare; (vehicle: also: ~ **along**) avanzare; (ship) rollare; ~ **about** or **around** vi rotolare qua e là; (person) rotolarsi; ~ **by** vi (time) passare; ~ **over** vi rivoltarsi; ~ **up** (inf) vi (arrive) arrivare ♦ vt (carpet) arrotolare; ~ **call** n appello; ~**er** n rullo; (wheel) rotella; (for hair) bigodino; ~**er blades** npl pattini mpl in linea; ~**er coaster** n montagne fpl russe; ~**er skates** npl pattini mpl a rotelle

rolling ['rəulɪŋ] adj (landscape) ondulato(a); ~ **pin** n matterello; ~ **stock** n (RAIL) materiale m rotabile

ROM [rɔm] n abbr (= read only memory) memoria di sola lettura

Roman ['rəumən] adj, n romano(a); ~ **Catholic** adj, n cattolico(a)

romance [rə'mæns] n storia (or avventura or film m inv) romantico(a); (charm) poesia; (love affair) idillio

Romania [rəu'meɪnɪə] n = **Rumania**

Roman numeral n numero romano

romantic [rə'mæntɪk] adj romantico(a); sentimentale

Rome [rəum] n Roma

romp [rɔmp] n gioco rumoroso ♦ vi (also: ~ **about**) far chiasso, giocare in un modo rumoroso

rompers ['rɔmpəz] npl pagliaccetto

roof [ru:f] n tetto; (of tunnel, cave) volta ♦ vt

coprire (con un tetto); **~ of the mouth** palato; **~ing** *n* materiale *m* per copertura; **~ rack** *n* (*AUT*) portabagagli *m inv*

rook [ruk] *n* (*bird*) corvo nero; (*CHESS*) torre *f*

room [ruːm] *n* (*in house*) stanza; (*bed~*, *in hotel*) camera; (*in school etc*) sala; (*space*) posto, spazio; **~s** *npl* (*lodging*) alloggio; **"~s to let"** (*BRIT*), **"~s for rent"** (*US*) "si affittano camere"; **there is ~ for improvement** si potrebbe migliorare; **~ing house** (*US*) *n* casa in cui si affittano camere o appartamentini ammobiliati; **~mate** *n* compagno/a di stanza; **~ service** *n* servizio da camera; **~y** *adj* spazioso(a); (*garment*) ampio(a)

roost [ruːst] *vi* appollaiarsi

rooster ['ruːstə*] *n* gallo

root [ruːt] *n* radice *f* ♦ *vi* (*plant, belief*) attecchire; **~ about** *vi* (*fig*) frugare; **~ for** *vt fus* fare il tifo per; **~ out** *vt* estirpare

rope [rəup] *n* corda, fune *f*; (*NAUT*) cavo ♦ *vt* (*box*) legare; (*climbers*) legare in cordata; (*area: also:* **~ off**) isolare cingendo con cordoni; **to know the ~s** (*fig*) conoscere i trucchi del mestiere; **~ in** *vt* (*fig*) coinvolgere; **~ ladder** *n* scala a corda

rosary ['rəuzərɪ] *n* rosario; roseto

rose [rəuz] *pt of* **rise** ♦ *n* rosa; (*also:* **~ bush**) rosaio; (*on watering can*) rosetta

rosé ['rəuzeɪ] *n* vino rosato

rosebud ['rəuzbʌd] *n* bocciolo di rosa

rosebush ['rəuzbuʃ] *n* rosaio

rosemary ['rəuzmərɪ] *n* rosmarino

rosette [rəu'zɛt] *n* coccarda

roster ['rɔstə*] *n*: **duty ~** ruolino di servizio

rostrum ['rɔstrəm] *n* tribuna

rosy ['rəuzɪ] *adj* roseo(a)

rot [rɔt] *n* (*decay*) putrefazione *f*; (*inf*: *nonsense*) stupidaggini *fpl* ♦ *vt*, *vi* imputridire, marcire

rota ['rəutə] *n* tabella dei turni

rotary ['rəutərɪ] *adj* rotante

rotate [rəu'teɪt] *vt* (*revolve*) far girare; (*change round*: *jobs*) fare a turno ♦ *vi* (*revolve*) girare; **rotating** *adj* (*movement*) rotante

rotten ['rɔtn] *adj* (*decayed*) putrido(a),

marcio(a); (*dishonest*) corrotto(a); (*inf*: *bad*) brutto(a); (: *action*) vigliacco(a); **to feel ~** (*ill*) sentirsi da cani

rouble ['ruːbl] (*US* **ruble**) *n* rublo

rouge [ruːʒ] *n* belletto

rough [rʌf] *adj* (*skin, surface*) ruvido(a); (*terrain, road*) accidentato(a); (*voice*) rauco(a); (*person, manner: coarse*) rozzo(a), aspro(a); (: *violent*) brutale; (*district*) malfamato(a); (*weather*) cattivo(a); (*sea*) mosso(a); (*plan*) abbozzato(a); (*guess*) approssimativo(a) ♦ *n* (*GOLF*) macchia; **to ~ it** far vita dura; **to sleep ~** (*BRIT*) dormire all'addiaccio; **~age** *n* alimenti *mpl* ricchi in cellulosa; **~-and-ready** *adj* rudimentale; **~cast** *n* intonaco grezzo; **~ copy** *n* brutta copia; **~ly** *adv* (*handle*) rudemente, brutalmente; (*make*) grossolanamente; (*speak*) bruscamente; (*approximately*) approssimativamente; **~ness** *n* ruvidità; (*of manner*) rozzezza

roulette [ruː'lɛt] *n* roulette *f*

Roumania [ruː'meɪnɪə] *n* = **Rumania**

round [raund] *adj* rotondo(a); (*figures*) tondo(a) ♦ *n* (*BRIT*: *of toast*) fetta; (*duty*: *of policeman, milkman etc*) giro; (: *of doctor*) visite *fpl*; (*game*: *of cards, golf, in competition*) partita; (*of ammunition*) cartuccia; (*BOXING*) round *m inv*; (*of talks*) serie *f inv* ♦ *vt* (*corner*) girare; (*bend*) prendere ♦ *prep* intorno a ♦ *adv*: **all ~** tutt'attorno; **to go the long way ~** fare il giro più lungo; **all the year ~** tutto l'anno; **it's just ~ the corner** (*also fig*) è dietro l'angolo; **~ the clock** ininterrottamente; **to go ~ to sb's house** andare da qn; **go ~ the back** passi dietro; **enough to go ~** abbastanza per tutti; **~ of applause** applausi *mpl*; **~ of drinks** giro di bibite; **~ of sandwiches** sandwich *m inv*; **~ off** *vt* (*speech etc*) finire; **~ up** *vt* radunare; (*criminals*) fare una retata di; (*prices*) arrotondare; **~about** *n* (*BRIT*: *AUT*) rotatoria; (: *at fair*) giostra ♦ *adj* (*route, means*) indiretto(a); **~ers** *npl* (*game*) gioco simile al baseball; **~ly** *adv* (*fig*) chiaro e tondo; **~ trip** *n* (viaggio di) andata e ritorno; ~**up** n raduno; (of criminals) retata

rouse [rauz] vt (wake up) svegliare; (stir up) destare; provocare; risvegliare; **rousing** adj (speech, applause) entusiastico(a)

route [ru:t] n itinerario; (of bus) percorso

routine [ru:'ti:n] adj (work) corrente, abituale; (procedure) solito(a) ♦ n (pej) routine f, tran tran m; (THEATRE) numero

rove [rəuv] vt vagabondare per

row[1] [rəu] n (line) riga, fila; (KNITTING) ferro; (behind one another: of cars, people) fila; (in boat) remata ♦ vi (in boat) remare; (as sport) vogare ♦ vt (boat) manovrare a remi; **in a ~** (fig) di fila

row[2] [rau] n (racket) baccano, chiasso; (dispute) lite f; (scolding) sgridata ♦ vi (argue) litigare

rowboat ['rəubaut] (US) n barca a remi

rowdy ['raudɪ] adj chiassoso(a); turbolento(a) ♦ n teppista m/f

rowing ['rəuɪŋ] n canottaggio; ~ **boat** (BRIT) n barca a remi

royal ['rɔɪəl] adj reale; **R~ Air Force** n aeronautica militare britannica

royalty ['rɔɪəltɪ] n (royal persons) (membri mpl della) famiglia reale; (payment: to author) diritti mpl d'autore

r.p.m. abbr (= revolutions per minute) giri/min

R.S.V.P. abbr (= répondez s'il vous plaît) R.S.V.P.

Rt Hon. (BRIT) abbr (= Right Honourable) ≈ Onorevole

rub [rʌb] n: **to give sth a ~** strofinare qc; (sore place) massaggiare qc ♦ vt strofinare; massaggiare; (hands: also: ~ **together**) sfregarsi; **to ~ sb up** (BRIT) or ~ **sb the wrong way** (US) lisciare qn contro pelo; ~ **off** vi andare via; ~ **off on** vt fus lasciare una traccia su; ~ **out** vt cancellare

rubber ['rʌbə*] n gomma; ~ **band** n elastico; ~ **plant** n ficus m inv

rubbish ['rʌbɪʃ] n (from household) immondizie fpl, rifiuti mpl; (fig: pej) cose fpl senza valore; robaccia; sciocchezze fpl; ~ **bin** (BRIT) n pattumiera; ~ **dump** n (in town) immondezzaio

rubble ['rʌbl] n macerie fpl; (smaller) pietrisco

ruble ['ru:bl] (US) n = **rouble**

ruby ['ru:bɪ] n rubino

rucksack ['rʌksæk] n zaino

rudder ['rʌdə*] n timone m

ruddy ['rʌdɪ] adj (face) rubicondo(a); (inf: damned) maledetto(a)

rude [ru:d] adj (impolite: person) scortese, rozzo(a); (: word, manners) grossolano(a), rozzo(a); (shocking) indecente; ~**ness** n scortesia; grossolanità

ruffle ['rʌfl] vt (hair) scompigliare; (clothes, water) increspare; (fig: person) turbare

rug [rʌg] n tappeto; (BRIT: for knees) coperta

rugby ['rʌgbɪ] n (also: ~ **football**) rugby m

rugged ['rʌgɪd] adj (landscape) aspro(a); (features, determination) duro(a); (character) brusco(a)

ruin ['ru:ɪn] n rovina ♦ vt rovinare; ~**s** npl (of building, castle etc) rovine fpl, ruderi mpl; ~**ous** adj rovinoso(a); (expenditure) inverosimile

rule [ru:l] n regola; (regulation) regolamento, regola; (government) governo; (~r) riga ♦ vt (country) governare; (person) dominare ♦ vi regnare; decidere; (LAW) dichiarare; **as a ~** normalmente; ~ **out** vt escludere; ~**d** adj (paper) vergato(a); ~**r** n (sovereign) sovrano/a; (for measuring) regolo, riga; **ruling** adj (party) al potere; (class) dirigente ♦ n (LAW) decisione f

rum [rʌm] n rum m

Rumania [ru:'meɪnɪə] n Romania

rumble ['rʌmbl] n rimbombo; brontolio ♦ vi rimbombare; (stomach, pipe) brontolare

rummage ['rʌmɪdʒ] vi frugare

rumour ['ru:mə*] (US **rumor**) n voce f ♦ vt: **it is ~ed that** corre voce che

rump [rʌmp] n groppa; ~ **steak** n bistecca di girello

rumpus ['rʌmpəs] (inf) n baccano; (quarrel) rissa

run [rʌn] (pt **ran**, pp **run**) n corsa; (outing) gita (in macchina); (distance travelled) percorso, tragitto; (SKI) pista; (CRICKET,

BASEBALL) meta; (*series*) serie *f*; (*THEATRE*) periodo di rappresentazione; (*in tights, stockings*) smagliatura ♦ *vt* (*distance*) correre; (*operate: business*) gestire, dirigere; (*: competition, course*) organizzare; (*: hotel*) gestire; (*: house*) governare; (*COMPUT*) eseguire; (*water, bath*) far scorrere; (*force through: rope, pipe*): **to ~ sth through** far passare qc attraverso; (*pass: hand, finger*): **to ~ sth over** passare qc su; (*PRESS: feature*) presentare ♦ *vi* correre; (*flee*) scappare; (*pass: road etc*) passare; (*work: machine, factory*) funzionare, andare; (*bus, train: operate*) far servizio; (*: travel*) circolare; (*continue: play, contract*) durare; (*slide: drawer, flow: river, bath*) scorrere; (*colours, washing*) stemperarsi; (*in election*) presentarsi candidato; (*nose*) colare; **there was a ~ on ...** c'era una corsa a ...; **in the long ~** a lungo andare; **on the ~** in fuga; **to ~ a race** partecipare ad una gara; **I'll ~ you to the station** la porto alla stazione; **to ~ a risk** correre un rischio; **~ about** *or* **around** *vi* (*children*) correre qua e là; **~ across** *vt fus* (*find*) trovare per caso; **~ away** *vi* fuggire; **~ down** *vt* (*production*) ridurre gradualmente; (*factory*) rallentare l'attività di; (*AUT*) investire; (*criticize*) criticare; **to be ~ down** (*person: tired*) essere esausto(a); **~ in** (*BRIT*) *vt* (*car*) rodare, fare il rodaggio di; **~ into** *vt fus* (*meet: person*) incontrare per caso; (*: trouble*) incontrare, trovare; (*collide with*) andare a sbattere contro; **~ off** *vi* fuggire ♦ *vt* (*water*) far scolare; (*copies*) fare; **~ out** *vi* (*person*) uscire di corsa; (*liquid*) colare; (*lease*) scadere; (*money*) esaurirsi; **~ out of** *vt fus* rimanere a corto di; **~ over** *vt* (*AUT*) investire, mettere sotto ♦ *vt fus* (*revise*) rivedere; **~ through** *vt fus* (*instructions*) dare una scorsa a; (*rehearse: play*) riprovare, ripetere; **~ up** *vt* (*debt*) lasciar accumulare; **to ~ up against** (*difficulties*) incontrare; **~away** *adj* (*person*) fuggiasco(a); (*horse*) in libertà; (*truck*) fuori controllo

rung [rʌŋ] *pp of* **ring** ♦ *n* (*of ladder*) piolo

runner [ˈrʌnə*] *n* (*in race*) corridore *m*; (*: horse*) partente *m/f*; (*on sledge*) pattino; (*for drawer etc*) guida; **~ bean** (*BRIT*) *n* fagiolo rampicante; **~-up** *n* secondo(a) arrivato(a)

running [ˈrʌnɪŋ] *n* corsa; direzione *f*; organizzazione *f*; funzionamento ♦ *adj* (*water*) corrente; (*commentary*) simultaneo(a); **to be in/out of the ~ for sth** essere/non essere più in lizza per qc; **6 days ~** 6 giorni di seguito; **~ costs** *npl* costi *mpl* d'esercizio; (*of car*) spese *fpl* di mantenimento

runny [ˈrʌnɪ] *adj* che cola

run-of-the-mill *adj* solito(a), banale

runt [rʌnt] *n* (*also pej*) omuncolo; (*ZOOL*) animale *m* più piccolo del normale

run-through *n* prova

run-up *n*: **~ to** (*election etc*) periodo che precede

runway [ˈrʌnweɪ] *n* (*AVIAT*) pista (di decollo)

rupture [ˈrʌptʃə*] *n* (*MED*) ernia

rural [ˈrʊərəl] *adj* rurale

ruse [ruːz] *n* trucco

rush [rʌʃ] *n* corsa precipitosa; (*hurry*) furia, fretta; (*sudden demand*): **~ for** corsa a; (*current*) flusso; (*of emotion*) impeto; (*BOT*) giunco ♦ *vt* mandare *or* spedire velocemente; (*attack: town etc*) prendere d'assalto ♦ *vi* precipitarsi; **~ hour** *n* ora di punta

rusk [rʌsk] *n* biscotto

Russia [ˈrʌʃə] *n* Russia; **~n** *adj* russo(a) ♦ *n* russo/a; (*LING*) russo

rust [rʌst] *n* ruggine *f* ♦ *vi* arrugginirsi

rustic [ˈrʌstɪk] *adj* rustico(a)

rustle [ˈrʌsl] *vi* frusciare ♦ *vt* (*paper*) far frusciare

rustproof [ˈrʌstpruːf] *adj* inossidabile

rusty [ˈrʌstɪ] *adj* arrugginito(a)

rut [rʌt] *n* solco; (*ZOOL*) fregola; **to get into a ~** (*fig*) adagiarsi troppo

ruthless [ˈruːθlɪs] *adj* spietato(a)

rye [raɪ] *n* segale *f*; **~ bread** *n* pane *m* di segale

S, s

Sabbath ['sæbəθ] n (Jewish) sabato; (Christian) domenica

sabotage ['sæbətɑːʒ] n sabotaggio ♦ vt sabotare

saccharin(e) ['sækərɪn] n saccarina

sachet ['sæʃeɪ] n bustina

sack [sæk] n (bag) sacco ♦ vt (dismiss) licenziare, mandare a spasso; (plunder) saccheggiare; **to get the ~** essere mandato a spasso; **~ing** n tela di sacco; (dismissal) licenziamento

sacrament ['sækrəmənt] n sacramento

sacred ['seɪkrɪd] adj sacro(a)

sacrifice ['sækrɪfaɪs] n sacrificio ♦ vt sacrificare

sad [sæd] adj triste

saddle ['sædl] n sella ♦ vt (horse) sellare; **to be ~d with sth** (inf) avere qc sulle spalle; **~bag** n (on bicycle) borsa

sadistic [sə'dɪstɪk] adj sadico(a)

sadness ['sædnɪs] n tristezza

s.a.e. n abbr = **stamped addressed envelope**

safe [seɪf] adj sicuro(a); (out of danger) salvo(a), al sicuro; (cautious) prudente ♦ n cassaforte f; **~ from** al sicuro da; **~ and sound** sano(a) e salvo(a); **(just) to be on the ~ side** per non correre rischi; **~-conduct** n salvacondotto; **~-deposit** n (vault) caveau m inv; (box) cassetta di sicurezza; **~guard** n salvaguardia ♦ vt salvaguardare; **~keeping** n custodia; **~ly** adv sicuramente; sano(a) e salvo(a); prudentemente; **~ sex** n sesso sicuro

safety ['seɪftɪ] n sicurezza; **~ belt** n cintura di sicurezza; **~ pin** n spilla di sicurezza; **~ valve** n valvola di sicurezza

saffron ['sæfrən] n zafferano

sag [sæg] vi incurvarsi; afflosciarsi

sage [seɪdʒ] n (herb) salvia; (man) saggio

Sagittarius [sædʒɪ'tɛərɪəs] n Sagittario

Sahara [sə'hɑːrə] n: **the ~ (Desert)** il (deserto del) Sahara

said [sɛd] pt, pp of **say**

sail [seɪl] n (on boat) vela; (trip): **to go for a ~** fare un giro in barca a vela ♦ vt (boat) condurre, governare ♦ vi (travel: ship) navigare; (: passenger) viaggiare per mare; (set off) salpare; (sport) fare della vela; **they ~ed into Genoa** entrarono nel porto di Genova; **~ through** vt fus (fig) superare senza difficoltà; **~boat** (US) n barca a vela; **~ing** n (sport) vela; **to go ~ing** fare della vela; **~ing boat** n barca a vela; **~ing ship** n veliero; **~or** n marinaio

saint [seɪnt] n santo(a); **S~ John** adj santo(a)

sake [seɪk] n: **for the ~ of** per, per amore di

salad ['sæləd] n insalata; **~ bowl** n insalatiera; **~ cream** (BRIT) n (tipo di) maionese f; **~ dressing** n condimento per insalata

salami [sə'lɑːmɪ] n salame m

salary ['sælərɪ] n stipendio

sale [seɪl] n vendita; (at reduced prices) svendita, liquidazione f; (auction) vendita all'asta; **"for ~"** "in vendita"; **on ~** in vendita; **on ~ or return** vendere o rimandare; **~room** n sala delle aste; **~s assistant** (US **~s clerk**) n commesso/a; **~sman/swoman** (irreg) n commesso/a; (representative) rappresentante m/f

salmon ['sæmən] n inv salmone m

saloon [sə'luːn] n (US) saloon m inv; bar m inv; (BRIT: AUT) berlina; (ship's lounge) salone m

salt [sɔːlt] n sale m ♦ vt salare; **~ cellar** n saliera; **~water** adj di mare; **~y** adj salato(a)

salute [sə'luːt] n saluto ♦ vt salutare

salvage ['sælvɪdʒ] n (saving) salvataggio; (things saved) beni mpl salvati or recuperati ♦ vt salvare, mettere in salvo

salvation [sæl'veɪʃən] n salvezza; **S~ Army** n Esercito della Salvezza

same [seɪm] adj stesso(a), medesimo(a) ♦ pron: **the ~** lo(la) stesso(a), gli(le) stessi(e); **the ~ book as** lo stesso libro di (o che); **at the ~ time** allo stesso tempo; **all** or **just the ~** tuttavia; **to do the ~ as sb** fare come qn; **the ~ to you!** altrettanto a te!

sample ['sɑːmpl] n campione m ♦ vt (food) assaggiare; (wine) degustare

sanction ['sæŋkʃən] n sanzione f ♦ vt sancire, sanzionare

sanctity ['sæŋktɪtɪ] n santità

sanctuary ['sæŋktjuarɪ] n (holy place) santuario; (refuge) rifugio; (for wildlife) riserva

sand [sænd] n sabbia ♦ vt (also: ~ **down**) cartavetrare

sandal ['sændl] n sandalo

sandbox ['sændbɔks] (US) n = **sandpit**

sandcastle ['sændkɑːsl] n castello di sabbia

sandpaper ['sændpeɪpə*] n carta vetrata

sandpit ['sændpɪt] n (for children) buca di sabbia

sandstone ['sændstəun] n arenaria

sandwich ['sændwɪtʃ] n tramezzino, panino, sandwich m inv ♦ vt: **~ed between** incastrato(a) fra; **cheese/ham ~** sandwich al formaggio/prosciutto; **~ course** (BRIT) n corso di formazione professionale

sandy ['sændɪ] adj sabbioso(a); (colour) color sabbia inv, biondo(a) rossiccio(a)

sane [seɪn] adj (person) sano(a) di mente; (outlook) sensato(a)

sang [sæŋ] pt of **sing**

sanitary ['sænɪtərɪ] adj (system, arrangements) sanitario(a); (clean) igienico(a); **~ towel** (US **~ napkin**) n assorbente m (igienico)

sanitation [sænɪ'teɪʃən] n (in house) impianti mpl sanitari; (in town) fognature fpl; **~ department** (US) n nettezza urbana

sanity ['sænɪtɪ] n sanità mentale; (common sense) buon senso

sank [sæŋk] pt of **sink**

Santa Claus [sæntə'klɔːz] n Babbo Natale

sap [sæp] n (of plants) linfa ♦ vt (strength) fiaccare

sapling ['sæplɪŋ] n alberello

sapphire ['sæfaɪə*] n zaffiro

sarcasm ['sɑːkæzm] n sarcasmo

sardine [sɑː'diːn] n sardina

Sardinia [sɑː'dɪnɪə] n Sardegna

sash [sæʃ] n fascia

sat [sæt] pt, pp of **sit**

Satan ['seɪtən] n Satana m

satchel ['sætʃl] n cartella

satellite ['sætəlaɪt] adj satellite ♦ n satellite m; **~ dish** n antenna parabolica; **~ television** n televisione f via satellite

satin ['sætɪn] n raso ♦ adj di raso

satire ['sætaɪə*] n satira

satisfaction [sætɪs'fækʃən] n soddisfazione f

satisfactory [sætɪs'fæktərɪ] adj soddisfacente

satisfy ['sætɪsfaɪ] vt soddisfare; (convince) convincere; **~ing** adj soddisfacente

Saturday ['sætədɪ] n sabato

sauce [sɔːs] n salsa; (containing meat, fish) sugo; **~pan** n casseruola

saucer ['sɔːsə*] n sottocoppa m, piattino

Saudi ['saudɪ]: **~ Arabia** n Arabia Saudita; **~ (Arabian)** adj, n arabo(a) saudita

sauna ['sɔːnə] n sauna

saunter ['sɔːntə*] vi andare a zonzo, bighellonare

sausage ['sɔsɪdʒ] n salsiccia; **~ roll** n rotolo di pasta sfoglia ripieno di salsiccia

sauté ['səuteɪ] adj: **~ potatoes** patate fpl saltate in padella

savage ['sævɪdʒ] adj (cruel, fierce) selvaggio(a), feroce; (primitive) primitivo(a) ♦ n selvaggio/a ♦ vt attaccare selvaggiamente

save [seɪv] vt (person, belongings, COMPUT) salvare; (money) risparmiare, mettere da parte; (time) risparmiare; (food) conservare; (avoid: trouble) evitare; (SPORT) parare ♦ vi (also: **~ up**) economizzare ♦ n (SPORT) parata ♦ prep salvo, a eccezione di

saving ['seɪvɪŋ] n risparmio ♦ adj: **the ~ grace of** l'unica cosa buona di; **~s** npl (money) risparmi mpl; **~s account** n libretto di risparmio; **~s bank** n cassa di risparmio

saviour ['seɪvjə*] (US **savior**) n salvatore m

savour ['seɪvə*] (US **savor**) vt gustare; **~y** adj (dish: not sweet) salato(a)

saw [sɔː] (pt **sawed**, pp **sawed** or **sawn**) pt of **see** ♦ n (tool) sega ♦ vt segare; **~dust** n segatura; **~mill** n segheria; **sawn** pp of

saw; **~n-off shotgun** n fucile m a canne mozze

saxophone ['sæksəfəun] n sassofono

say [seɪ] (pt, pp **said**) n: **to have one's ~** fare sentire il proprio parere; **to have a** or **some ~** avere voce in capitolo ♦ vt dire; **could you ~ that again?** potrebbe ripeterlo?; **that goes without ~ing** va da sé; **~ing** n proverbio, detto

scab [skæb] n crosta; (pej) crumiro/a

scaffold ['skæfəuld] n (gallows) patibolo; **~ing** n impalcatura

scald [skɔːld] n scottatura ♦ vt scottare

scale [skeɪl] n scala; (of fish) squama ♦ vt (mountain) scalare; **~s** npl (for weighing) bilancia; **on a large ~** su vasta scala; **~ of charges** tariffa; **~ down** vt ridurre (proporzionalmente)

scallop ['skɔləp] n (ZOOL) pettine m; (SEWING) smerlo

scalp [skælp] n cuoio capelluto ♦ vt scotennare

scalpel ['skælpl] n bisturi m inv

scampi ['skæmpɪ] npl scampi mpl

scan [skæn] vt scrutare; (glance at quickly) scorrere, dare un'occhiata a; (TV) analizzare; (RADAR) esplorare ♦ n (MED) ecografia

scandal ['skændl] n scandalo; (gossip) pettegolezzi mpl

Scandinavia [skændɪ'neɪvɪə] n Scandinavia; **~n** adj, n scandinavo/a

scant [skænt] adj scarso(a); **~y** adj insufficiente; (swimsuit) ridotto(a)

scapegoat ['skeɪpgəut] n capro espiatorio

scar [skɑː] n cicatrice f ♦ vt sfregiare

scarce [skɛəs] adj scarso(a); (copy, edition) raro(a); **to make o.s. ~** (inf) squagliarsela; **~ly** adv appena; **scarcity** n scarsità, mancanza

scare [skɛə] n spavento; panico ♦ vt spaventare, atterrire; **there was a bomb ~ at the bank** hanno evacuato la banca per paura di un attentato dinamitardo; **to ~ sb stiff** spaventare a morte qn; **~ off** or **away** vt mettere in fuga; **~crow** n spaventapasseri m inv; **~d** adj: **to be ~d** aver paura

scarf [skɑːf] (pl **scarves** or **~s**) n (long) sciarpa; (square) fazzoletto da testa, foulard m inv

scarlet ['skɑːlɪt] adj scarlatto(a); **~ fever** n scarlattina

scarves [skɑːvz] npl of **scarf**

scary ['skɛərɪ] adj che spaventa

scathing ['skeɪðɪŋ] adj aspro(a)

scatter ['skætə] vt spargere; (crowd) disperdere ♦ vi disperdersi; **~brained** adj sbadato(a)

scavenger ['skævəndʒə] n (person) accattone/a

scenario [sɪ'nɑːrɪəu] n (THEATRE, CINEMA) copione m; (fig) situazione f

scene [siːn] n (THEATRE, fig etc) scena; (of crime, accident) scena, luogo; (sight, view) vista, veduta; **~ry** n (THEATRE) scenario; (landscape) panorama m; **scenic** adj scenico(a); panoramico(a)

scent [sɛnt] n profumo; (sense of smell) olfatto, odorato; (fig: track) pista

sceptical ['skɛptɪkəl] (US **skeptical**) adj scettico(a)

sceptre ['sɛptə] (US **scepter**) n scettro

schedule ['ʃɛdjuːl, (US) 'skɛdjuːl] n programma m, piano; (of trains) orario; (of prices etc) lista, tabella ♦ vt fissare; **on ~** in orario; **to be ahead of/behind ~** essere in anticipo/ritardo sul previsto; **~d flight** n volo di linea

scheme [skiːm] n piano, progetto; (method) sistema m; (dishonest plan, plot) intrigo, trama; (arrangement) disposizione f, sistemazione f; (pension ~ etc) programma m ♦ vi fare progetti; (intrigue) complottare; **scheming** adj intrigante ♦ n intrighi mpl, macchinazioni fpl

schism ['skɪzəm] n scisma m

scholar ['skɔlə] n erudito/a; (pupil) scolaro/a; **~ship** n erudizione f; (grant) borsa di studio

school [skuːl] n (primary, secondary) scuola; (university: US) università f inv ♦ cpd scolare, scolastico(a) ♦ vt (animal) addestrare; **~ age** n età scolare; **~bag** n cartella; **~book** n libro scolastico; **~boy** n scolaro; **~children** npl scolari mpl; **~girl** n scolara; **~ing** n istruzione f; **~master** n (primary) maestro; (secondary) insegnante m; **~mistress** n maestra; insegnante f; **~teacher** n insegnante m/f, docente m/f; (primary) maestro/a

sciatica [saɪ'ætɪkə] n sciatica

science ['saɪəns] n scienza; **~ fiction** n fantascienza, notizia (in) esclusiva; **scientific** [-'tɪfɪk] adj scientifico(a); **scientist** n scienziato/a

scissors ['sɪzəz] npl forbici fpl

scoff [skɔf] vt (BRIT: inf: eat) tranguiare, ingozzare ♦ vi: **to ~ (at)** (mock) farsi beffe (di)

scold [skəuld] vt rimproverare

scone [skɔn] n focaccina da tè

scoop [sku:p] n mestolo; (for ice cream) cucchiaio dosatore; (PRESS) colpo giornalistico, notizia (in) esclusiva; **~ out** vt scavare; **~ up** vt tirare su, sollevare

scooter ['sku:tə*] n (motor cycle) motoretta, scooter m inv; (toy) monopattino

scope [skəup] n (capacity: of plan, undertaking) portata; (: of person) capacità fpl; (opportunity) possibilità fpl

scorch [skɔ:tʃ] vt (clothes) strinare, bruciacchiare; (earth, grass) seccare, bruciare

score [skɔ:*] n punti mpl, punteggio; (MUS) partitura, spartito; (twenty) venti ♦ vt (goal, point) segnare, fare; (success) ottenere ♦ vi segnare; (FOOTBALL) fare un goal; (keep score) segnare i punti; **~s of** (very many) un sacco di; **on that ~** a questo riguardo; **to ~ 6 out of 10** prendere 6 su 10; **~ out** vt cancellare con un segno; **~board** n tabellone m segnapunti

scorn [skɔ:n] n disprezzo ♦ vt disprezzare

scornful ['skɔ:nful] adj sprezzante

Scorpio ['skɔ:pɪəu] n Scorpione m

scorpion ['skɔ:pɪən] n scorpione m

Scot [skɔt] n scozzese m/f

Scotch [skɔtʃ] n whisky m scozzese, scotch m

scot-free adv: **to get off ~** farla franca

Scotland ['skɔtlənd] n Scozia

Scots [skɔts] adj scozzese; **~man/woman** (irreg) n scozzese m/f

Scottish ['skɔtɪʃ] adj scozzese

scoundrel ['skaundrl] n farabutto/a; (child) furfantello/a

scour ['skauə*] vt (search) battere, perlustrare

scout [skaut] n (MIL) esploratore m; (also: boy ~) giovane esploratore, scout m inv; **~ around** vi cercare in giro; **girl ~** (US) n giovane esploratrice f

scowl [skaul] vi accigliarsi, aggrottare le sopracciglia; **to ~ at** guardare torvo

scrabble ['skræbl] vi (claw): **to ~ (at)** graffiare, grattare; (also: **~ around**: search) cercare a tentoni ♦ n: **S~** ® Scarabeo ®

scraggy ['skrægɪ] adj scarno(a), molto magro(a)

scram [skræm] (inf) vi filare via

scramble ['skræmbl] n arrampicata ♦ vi inerpicarsi; **to ~ out** etc uscire etc in fretta; **to ~ for** azzuffarsi per; **~d eggs** npl uova fpl strapazzate

scrap [skræp] n pezzo, pezzetto; (fight) zuffa; (also: ~ iron) rottami mpl di ferro, ferraglia ♦ vt demolire; (fig) scartare ♦ vi: **to ~ (with sb)** fare a botte (con qn); **~s** npl (waste) scarti mpl; **~book** n album m inv di ritagli; **~ dealer** n commerciante m di ferraglia

scrape [skreɪp] vt, vi raschiare, grattare ♦ n: **to get into a ~** cacciarsi in un guaio; **~ through** vi farcela per un pelo; **~ together** vt (money) raggranellare; **~r** n raschietto

scrap: ~ heap n: **on the ~ heap** (fig) nel dimenticatoio; **~ merchant** (BRIT) n commerciante m di ferraglia; **~ paper** n cartaccia

scratch [skrætʃ] n graffio ♦ cpd: **~ team** squadra raccogliticcia ♦ vt graffiare, rigare ♦ vi grattare; (paint, car) graffiare; **to start from ~** cominciare or partire da zero; **to be up to ~** essere all'altezza

scrawl [skrɔ:l] n scarabocchio ♦ vi scarabocchiare

scrawny ['skrɔ:nɪ] adj scarno(a)

scream [skri:m] n grido, urlo ♦ vi urlare, gridare

scree [skri:] n ghiaione m

screech [skri:tʃ] vi stridere

screen [skri:n] n schermo; (fig) muro, cortina, velo ♦ vt schermare, fare schermo a; (from the wind etc) riparare; (film) proiettare; (book) adattare per lo schermo; (candidates etc) selezionare; ~ing n (MED) dépistage m inv; ~play n sceneggiatura; ~ saver n (COMPUT) screen saver m inv

screw [skru:] n vite f ♦ vt avvitare; ~ up vt (paper etc) spiegazzare; (inf: ruin) rovinare; to ~ up one's eyes strizzare gli occhi; ~driver n cacciavite m

scribble ['skrɪbl] n scarabocchio ♦ vt scribacchiare in fretta ♦ vi scarabocchiare

script [skrɪpt] n (CINEMA etc) copione m; (in exam) elaborato or compito d'esame

scripture(s) ['skrɪptʃə(z)] n(pl) sacre Scritture fpl

scroll [skrəul] n rotolo di carta

scrounge [skraundʒ] (inf) vt: to ~ sth (off or from sb) scroccare qc (a qn) ♦ n: on the ~ a sbafo

scrub [skrʌb] n (land) boscaglia ♦ vt pulire strofinando; (reject) annullare

scruff [skrʌf] n: by the ~ of the neck per la collottola

scruffy ['skrʌfɪ] adj sciatto(a)

scrum(mage) ['skrʌm(ɪdʒ)] n mischia

scruple ['skru:pl] n scrupolo

scrutiny ['skru:tɪnɪ] n esame m accurato

scuff [skʌf] vt (shoes) consumare strascicando

scuffle ['skʌfl] n baruffa, tafferuglio

sculptor ['skʌlptə*] n scultore m

sculpture ['skʌlptʃə*] n scultura

scum [skʌm] n schiuma; (pej: people) feccia

scupper ['skʌpə*] (BRIT: inf) vt far naufragare

scurry ['skʌrɪ] vi sgambare, affrettarsi; ~ off vi andarsene a tutta velocità

scuttle ['skʌtl] n (also: coal ~) secchio del carbone ♦ vt (ship) autoaffondare ♦ vi (scamper): to ~ away, ~ off darsela a gambe, scappare

scythe [saɪð] n falce f

SDP (BRIT) n abbr = **Social Democratic Party**

sea [si:] n mare m ♦ cpd marino(a), del mare; (bird, fish) di mare; (route, transport) marittimo(a); by ~ per mare; on the ~ (boat) in mare; (town) di mare; to be all at ~ (fig) non sapere che pesci pigliare; out to ~ al largo; (out) at ~ in mare; ~board n costa; ~food n frutti mpl di mare; ~ front n lungomare m; ~gull n gabbiano

seal [si:l] n (animal) foca; (stamp) sigillo; (impression) impronta del sigillo ♦ vt sigillare; ~ off vt (close) sigillare; (forbid entry to) bloccare l'accesso a

sea level n livello del mare

seam [si:m] n cucitura; (of coal) filone m

seaman ['si:mən] (irreg) n marinaio

seance ['seɪɒns] n seduta spiritica

seaplane ['si:pleɪn] n idrovolante m

seaport ['si:pɔ:t] n porto di mare

search [sə:tʃ] n ricerca; (LAW: at sb's home) perquisizione f ♦ vt frugare ♦ vi: to ~ for ricercare; in ~ of alla ricerca di; ~ through vt fus frugare; ~ engine n (COMPUT) motore m di ricerca; ~ing adj minuzioso(a); penetrante; ~light n proiettore m; ~ party n squadra di soccorso; ~ warrant n mandato di perquisizione

seashore ['si:ʃɔ:*] n spiaggia

seasick ['si:sɪk] adj che soffre il mal di mare

seaside ['si:saɪd] n spiaggia; ~ resort n stazione f balneare

season ['si:zn] n stagione f ♦ vt condire, insaporire; ~al adj stagionale; ~ed adj (fig) con esperienza; ~ing n condimento; ~ ticket n abbonamento

seat [si:t] n sedile m; (in bus, train: place) posto; (PARLIAMENT) seggio; (buttocks) didietro; (of trousers) fondo ♦ vt far sedere; (have room for) avere or essere fornito(a) di posti a sedere per; to be ~ed essere seduto(a); ~ belt n cintura di sicurezza

sea water n acqua di mare

seaweed ['si:wi:d] n alghe fpl

seaworthy ['si:wə:ðɪ] adj atto(a) alla navigazione

sec. *abbr* = **second(s)**

secluded [sɪ'kluːdɪd] *adj* isolato(a), appartato(a)

seclusion [sɪ'kluːʒən] *n* isolamento

second[1] [sɪ'kɔnd] (BRIT) *vt* (*worker*) distaccare

second[2] ['sɛkənd] *num* secondo(a) ♦ *adv* (*in race etc*) al secondo posto ♦ *n* (*unit of time*) secondo; (AUT: *also:* **~ gear**) seconda; (COMM: *imperfect*) scarto; (BRIT: SCOL: *degree*) laurea con punteggio discreto ♦ *vt* (*motion*) appoggiare; **~ary** *adj* secondario(a); **~ary school** *n* scuola secondaria; **~-class** *adj* di seconda classe ♦ *adv* in seconda classe; **~er** *n* sostenitore/trice; **~hand** *adj* di seconda mano, usato(a); **~ hand** *n* (*on clock*) lancetta dei secondi; **~ly** *adv* in secondo luogo; **~-rate** *adj* scadente; **~ thoughts** *npl* ripensamenti *mpl*; **on ~ thoughts** (BRIT) *or* **thought** (US) ripensandoci bene

secrecy ['siːkrəsɪ] *n* segretezza

secret ['siːkrɪt] *adj* segreto(a) ♦ *n* segreto; **in ~** in segreto

secretarial [sɛkrɪ'tɛərɪəl] *adj* di segretario(a)

secretariat [sɛkrɪ'tɛərɪət] *n* segretariato

secretary ['sɛkrətrɪ] *n* segretario/a; **S~ of State (for)** (BRIT: POL) ministro (di)

secretive ['siːkrətɪv] *adj* riservato(a)

sect [sɛkt] *n* setta; **~arian** [-'tɛərɪən] *adj* settario(a)

section ['sɛkʃən] *n* sezione *f*

sector ['sɛktə*] *n* settore *m*

secure [sɪ'kjuə*] *adj* sicuro(a); (*firmly fixed*) assicurato(a), ben fermato(a); (*in safe place*) al sicuro ♦ *vt* (*fix*) fissare, assicurare; (*get*) ottenere, assicurarsi

security [sɪ'kjuərɪtɪ] *n* sicurezza; (*for loan*) garanzia

sedate [sɪ'deɪt] *adj* posato(a); calmo(a) ♦ *vt* calmare

sedation [sɪ'deɪʃən] *n* (MED) effetto dei sedativi

sedative ['sɛdɪtɪv] *n* sedativo, calmante *m*

seduce [sɪ'djuːs] *vt* sedurre; **seduction** [-'dʌkʃən] *n* seduzione *f*; **seductive** [-'dʌktɪv] *adj* seducente

see [siː] (*pt* **saw**, *pp* **seen**) *vt* vedere; (*accompany*): **to ~ sb to the door** accompagnare qn alla porta ♦ *vi* vedere; (*understand*) capire ♦ *n* sede *f* vescovile; **to ~ that** (*ensure*) badare che +*sub*, fare in modo che +*sub*; **~ you soon!** a presto!; **~ about** *vt fus* occuparsi di; **~ off** *vt* salutare alla partenza; **~ through** *vt* portare a termine ♦ *vt fus* non lasciarsi ingannare da; **~ to** *vt fus* occuparsi di

seed [siːd] *n* seme *m*; (*fig*) germe *m*; (TENNIS *etc*) testa di serie; **to go to ~** fare seme; (*fig*) scadere; **~ling** *n* piantina di semenzaio; **~y** *adj* (*shabby: person*) sciatto(a); (: *place*) cadente

seeing ['siːɪŋ] *conj:* **~ (that)** visto che

seek [siːk] (*pt*, *pp* **sought**) *vt* cercare

seem [siːm] *vi* sembrare, parere; **there ~s to be ...** sembra che ci sia ...; **~ingly** *adv* apparentemente

seen [siːn] *pp of* **see**

seep [siːp] *vi* filtrare, trapelare

seesaw ['siːsɔː] *n* altalena a bilico

seethe [siːð] *vi* ribollire; **to ~ with anger** fremere di rabbia

see-through *adj* trasparente

segregate ['sɛgrɪgeɪt] *vt* segregare, isolare

seize [siːz] *vt* (*grasp*) afferrare; (*take possession of*) impadronirsi di; (LAW) sequestrare; **~ (up)on** *vt fus* ricorrere a; **~ up** *vi* (TECH) grippare

seizure ['siːʒə*] *n* (MED) attacco; (LAW) confisca, sequestro

seldom ['sɛldəm] *adv* raramente

select [sɪ'lɛkt] *adj* scelto(a) ♦ *vt* scegliere, selezionare; **~ion** [-'lɛkʃən] *n* selezione *f*, scelta

self [sɛlf] *n*: **the ~** l'io *m* ♦ *prefix* auto...; **~-assured** *adj* sicuro(a) di sé; **~-catering** (BRIT) *adj* in cui ci si cucina da sé; **~-centred** (US **~-centered**) *adj* egocentrico(a); **~-confidence** *n* sicurezza di sé; **~-conscious** *adj* timido(a); **~-contained** (BRIT) *adj* (*flat*) indipendente; **~-control** *n* autocontrollo; **~-defence** (US **~-defense**) *n* autodifesa; (LAW) legittima difesa; **~-discipline** *n* autodisciplina; ~-**employed** *adj* che lavora in proprio; ~-**evident** *adj* evidente; ~-**governing** *adj* autonomo(a); ~-**indulgent** *adj* indulgente verso se stesso(a); ~-**interest** *n* interesse *m* personale; ~-**ish** *adj* egoista; ~**ishness** *n* egoismo; ~**less** *adj* dimentico(a) di sé, altruista; ~-**pity** *n* autocommiserazione *f*; ~-**portrait** *n* autoritratto; ~-**possessed** *adj* controllato(a); ~-**preservation** *n* istinto di conservazione; ~-**respect** *n* rispetto di sé, amor proprio; ~-**righteous** *adj* soddisfatto(a) di sé; ~-**sacrifice** *n* abnegazione *f*; ~-**satisfied** *adj* compiaciuto(a) di sé; ~-**service** *n* autoservizio, self-service *m*; ~-**sufficient** *adj* autosufficiente; ~-**taught** *adj* autodidatta

sell [sɛl] (*pt, pp* **sold**) *vt* vendere ♦ *vi* vendersi; **to ~ at** *or* **for 1000 lire** essere in vendita a 1000 lire; ~ **off** *vt* svendere, liquidare; ~ **out** *vi*: **to ~ out (of sth)** esaurire (qc); **the tickets are all sold out** i biglietti sono esauriti; ~-**by date** *n* data di scadenza; ~**er** *n* venditore/trice; ~**ing price** *n* prezzo di vendita

Sellotape ® ['sɛləuteɪp] (*BRIT*) *n* nastro adesivo, scotch ® *m*

selves [sɛlvz] *npl of* **self**

semaphore ['sɛməfɔ:*] *n* segnalazioni *fpl* con bandierine; (*RAIL*) semaforo (ferroviario)

semblance ['sɛmbləns] *n* parvenza, apparenza

semen ['si:mən] *n* sperma *m*

semester [sɪ'mɛstə*] (*US*) *n* semestre *m*

semi... ['sɛmɪ] *prefix* semi...; ~**circle** *n* semicerchio; ~**colon** *n* punto e virgola; ~**detached (house)** (*BRIT*) *n* casa gemella; ~**final** *n* semifinale *f*

seminar ['sɛmɪnɑ:*] *n* seminario

seminary ['sɛmɪnərɪ] *n* (*REL*) seminario

semiskilled ['sɛmɪ'skɪld] *adj* (*worker*) parzialmente qualificato(a); (*work*) che richiede una qualificazione parziale

semi-skimmed ['sɛmɪ'skɪmd] *adj* (*milk*) parzialmente scremato(a)

senate ['sɛnɪt] *n* senato; **senator** *n*

senatore/trice

send [sɛnd] (*pt, pp* **sent**) *vt* mandare; ~ **away** *vt* (*letter, goods*) spedire; (*person*) mandare via; ~ **away for** *vt fus* richiedere per posta, farsi spedire; ~ **back** *vt* rimandare; ~ **for** *vt fus* mandare a chiamare, far venire; ~ **off** *vt* (*goods*) spedire; (*BRIT: SPORT: player*) espellere; ~ **out** *vt* (*invitation*) diramare; ~ **up** *vt* (*person, price*) far salire; (*BRIT: parody*) mettere in ridicolo; ~**er** *n* mittente *m/f*; ~-**off** *n*: **to give sb a good ~-off** festeggiare la partenza di qn

senior ['si:nɪə*] *adj* (*older*) più vecchio(a); (*of higher rank*) di grado più elevato; ~ **citizen** *n* persona anziana; ~**ity** [-'ɔrɪtɪ] *n* anzianità

sensation [sɛn'seɪʃən] *n* sensazione *f*; ~**al** *adj* sensazionale; (*marvellous*) eccezionale

sense [sɛns] *n* senso; (*feeling*) sensazione *f*, senso; (*meaning*) senso, significato; (*wisdom*) buonsenso ♦ *vt* sentire, percepire; **it makes ~** ha senso; ~**less** *adj* sciocco(a); (*unconscious*) privo(a) di sensi

sensible ['sɛnsɪbl] *adj* sensato(a), ragionevole

sensitive ['sɛnsɪtɪv] *adj* sensibile; (*skin, question*) delicato(a)

sensual ['sɛnsjuəl] *adj* sensuale

sensuous ['sɛnsjuəs] *adj* sensuale

sent [sɛnt] *pt, pp of* **send**

sentence ['sɛntns] *n* (*LING*) frase *f*; (*LAW: judgment*) sentenza; (: *punishment*) condanna ♦ *vt*: **to ~ sb to death/to 5 years** condannare qn a morte/a 5 anni

sentiment ['sɛntɪmənt] *n* sentimento; (*opinion*) opinione *f*; ~**al** [-'mɛntl] *adj* sentimentale

sentry ['sɛntrɪ] *n* sentinella

separate [*adj* 'sɛprɪt, *vb* 'sɛpəreɪt] *adj* separato(a) ♦ *vt* separare ♦ *vi* separarsi; ~**ly** *adv* separatamente; ~**s** *npl* (*clothes*) coordinati *mpl*; **separation** [-'reɪʃən] *n* separazione *f*

September [sɛp'tɛmbə*] *n* settembre *m*

septic ['sɛptɪk] *adj* settico(a); (*wound*) infettato(a); ~ **tank** *n* fossa settica

sequel ['si:kwl] n conseguenza; (of story) seguito; (of film) sequenza

sequence ['si:kwəns] n (series) serie f; (order) ordine m

sequin ['si:kwɪn] n lustrino, paillette f inv

serene [sə'ri:n] adj sereno(a), calmo(a)

sergeant ['sɑ:dʒənt] n sergente m; (POLICE) brigadiere m

serial ['sɪərɪəl] n (PRESS) romanzo a puntate; (RADIO, TV) trasmissione f a puntate, serial m inv; ~ize vt pubblicare (or trasmettere) a puntate; ~ killer n serial-killer m/f inv; ~ number n numero di serie

series ['sɪəri:z] n inv serie f inv; (PUBLISHING) collana

serious ['sɪərɪəs] adj serio(a), grave; ~ly adv seriamente

sermon ['sə:mən] n sermone m

serrated [sɪ'reɪtɪd] adj seghettato(a)

serum ['sɪərəm] n siero

servant ['sə:vənt] n domestico/a

serve [sə:v] vt (employer etc) servire, essere a servizio di; (purpose) servire a; (customer, food, meal) servire; (apprenticeship) fare; (prison term) scontare ♦ vi (also TENNIS) servire; (be useful): to ~ as/for/to do servire da/per/per fare ♦ n (TENNIS) servizio; it ~s him right ben gli sta, se l'è meritata; ~ out, ~ up vt (food) servire

service ['sə:vɪs] n servizio; (AUT: maintenance) assistenza, revisione f ♦ vt (car, washing machine) revisionare; the S~s le forze armate; to be of ~ to sb essere d'aiuto a qn; ~ included/not included servizio compreso/escluso; ~able adj pratico(a), utile; ~ area n (on motorway) area di servizio; ~ charge (BRIT) n servizio; ~man (irreg) n militare m; ~ station n stazione f di servizio

serviette [sə:vɪ'et] (BRIT) n tovagliolo

session ['seʃən] n (sitting) seduta, sessione f; (SCOL) anno scolastico (or accademico)

set [set] (pt, pp set) n serie f inv; (of cutlery etc) servizio; (RADIO, TV) apparecchio; (TENNIS) set m inv; (group of people) mondo, ambiente m; (CINEMA) scenario; (THEATRE: stage) scene fpl; (: scenery)

scenario; (MATH) insieme m; (HAIRDRESSING) messa in piega ♦ adj (fixed) stabilito(a), determinato(a); (ready) pronto(a) ♦ vt (place) posare, mettere; (arrange) sistemare; (fix) fissare; (adjust) regolare; (decide: rules etc) stabilire, fissare ♦ vi (sun) tramontare; (jam, jelly) rapprendersi; (concrete) fare presa; to be ~ on doing essere deciso a fare; to ~ to music mettere in musica; to ~ on fire dare fuoco a; to ~ free liberare; to ~ sth going mettere in moto qc; to ~ sail prendere il mare; ~ about vt fus (task) intraprendere, mettersi a; ~ aside vt mettere da parte; ~ back vt (in time): to ~ back (by) mettere indietro (di); (inf: cost): it ~ me back £5 mi è costato la bellezza di 5 sterline; ~ off vi partire ♦ vt (bomb) far scoppiare; (cause to start) mettere in moto; (show up well) dare risalto a; ~ out vi partire ♦ vt (arrange) disporre; (state) esporre, presentare; to ~ out to do proporsi di fare; ~ up vt (organization) fondare, costituire; ~back n (hitch) contrattempo, inconveniente m; ~ menu n menù m inv fisso

settee [se'ti:] n divano, sofà m inv

setting ['setɪŋ] n (background) ambiente m; (of controls) posizione f; (of sun) tramonto; (of jewel) montatura

settle ['setl] vt (argument, matter) appianare; (accounts) regolare; (MED: calm) calmare ♦ vi (bird, dust etc) posarsi; (sediment) depositarsi; (also: ~ down) sistemarsi, stabilirsi; calmarsi; to ~ for sth accontentarsi di qc; to ~ on sth decidersi per qc; ~ in vi sistemarsi; ~ up vi: to ~ up with sb regolare i conti con qn; ~ment n (payment) pagamento, saldo; (agreement) accordo; (colony) colonia; (village etc) villaggio, comunità f inv; ~r n colonizzatore/trice

setup ['setʌp] n (arrangement) sistemazione f; (situation) situazione f

seven ['sevn] num sette; ~teen num diciassette; ~th num settimo(a); ~ty num settanta

sever ['sevə*] vt recidere, tagliare; (relations)

troncare

several ['sɛvərl] *adj, pron* alcuni(e), diversi(e); **~ of us** alcuni di noi

severance ['sɛvərəns] *n (of relations)* rottura; **~ pay** *n* indennità di licenziamento

severe [sɪ'vɪə*] *adj* severo(a); *(serious)* serio(a), grave; *(hard)* duro(a); *(plain)* semplice, sobrio(a); **severity** [sɪ'vɛrɪtɪ] *n* severità; gravità; *(of weather)* rigore *m*

sew [səu] *(pt* **sewed**, *pp* **sewn**) *vt, vi* cucire; **~ up** *vt* ricucire

sewage ['su:ɪdʒ] *n* acque *fpl* di scolo

sewer ['su:ə*] *n* fogna

sewing ['səuɪŋ] *n* cucitura; cucito; **~ machine** *n* macchina da cucire

sewn [səun] *pp of* **sew**

sex [sɛks] *n* sesso; **to have ~ with** avere rapporti sessuali con; **~ist** *adj, n* sessista *m/f*

sexual ['sɛksjuəl] *adj* sessuale

sexy ['sɛksɪ] *adj* provocante, sexy *inv*

shabby ['ʃæbɪ] *adj* malandato(a); *(behaviour)* vergognoso(a)

shack [ʃæk] *n* baracca, capanna

shackles ['ʃæklz] *npl* ferri *mpl*, catene *fpl*

shade [ʃeɪd] *n* ombra; *(for lamp)* paralume *m*; *(of colour)* tonalità *f inv*; *(small quantity)*: **a ~ (more/too large)** un po' (di più/troppo grande) ♦ *vt* ombreggiare, fare ombra a; **in the ~** all'ombra

shadow ['ʃædəu] *n* ombra ♦ *vt (follow)* pedinare; **~ cabinet** *(BRIT)* *n* *(POL)* governo *m* ombra *inv*; **~y** *adj* ombreggiato(a), ombroso(a); *(dim)* vago(a), indistinto(a)

shady ['ʃeɪdɪ] *adj* ombroso(a); *(fig: dishonest)* losco(a), equivoco(a)

shaft [ʃɑːft] *n (of arrow, spear)* asta; *(AUT, TECH)* albero; *(of mine)* pozzo; *(of lift)* tromba; *(of light)* raggio

shaggy ['ʃægɪ] *adj* ispido(a)

shake [ʃeɪk] *(pt* **shook**, *pp* **shaken**) *vt* scuotere; *(bottle, cocktail)* agitare ♦ *vi* tremare; **to ~ one's head** *(in refusal, dismay)* scuotere la testa; **to ~ hands with sb** stringere *or* dare la mano a qn; **~ off** *vt* scrollare (via); *(fig)* sbarazzarsi di; **~ up** *vt*

scuotere; **~n** *pp of* **shake**; **shaky** *adj (hand, voice)* tremante; *(building)* traballante

shall [ʃæl] *aux vb*: **I ~ go** andrò; **~ I open the door?** apro io la porta?; **I'll get some, ~ I?** ne prendo un po', va bene?

shallow ['ʃæləu] *adj* poco profondo(a); *(fig)* superficiale

sham [ʃæm] *n* finzione *f*, messinscena; *(jewellery, furniture)* imitazione *f*

shambles ['ʃæmblz] *n* confusione *f*, baraonda, scompiglio

shame [ʃeɪm] *n* vergogna ♦ *vt* far vergognare; **it is a ~ (that/to do)** è un peccato (che +*sub*/fare); **what a ~!** che peccato!; **~ful** *adj* vergognoso(a); **~less** *adj* sfrontato(a); *(immodest)* spudorato(a)

shampoo [ʃæm'pu:] *n* shampoo *m inv* ♦ *vt* fare lo shampoo a; **~ and set** *n* shampoo e messa in piega

shamrock ['ʃæmrɔk] *n* trifoglio *(simbolo nazionale dell'Irlanda)*

shandy ['ʃændɪ] *n* birra con gassosa

shan't [ʃɑːnt] = **shall not**

shanty town ['ʃæntɪ-] *n* bidonville *f inv*

shape [ʃeɪp] *n* forma ♦ *vt* formare; *(statement)* formulare; *(sb's ideas)* condizionare; **to take ~** prendere forma; **~ up** *vi (events)* andare, mettersi; *(person)* cavarsela; **-shaped** *suffix*: **heart-shaped** a forma di cuore; **~less** *adj* senza forma, informe; **~ly** *adj* ben proporzionato(a)

share [ʃɛə*] *n (thing received, contribution)* parte *f*; *(COMM)* azione *f* ♦ *vt* dividere; *(have in common)* condividere, avere in comune; **~ out** *vi* dividere; **~holder** *n* azionista *m/f*

shark [ʃɑːk] *n* squalo, pescecane *m*

sharp [ʃɑːp] *adj (razor, knife)* affilato(a); *(point)* acuto(a), acuminato(a); *(nose, chin)* aguzzo(a); *(outline, contrast)* netto(a); *(cold, pain)* pungente; *(voice)* stridulo(a); *(person: quick-witted)* sveglio(a); *(: unscrupulous)* disonesto(a); *(MUS)*: **C ~** do diesis ♦ *n (MUS)* diesis *m inv* ♦ *adv*: **at 2 o'clock ~** alle due in punto; **~en** *vt* affilare; *(pencil)* fare la punta a; *(fig)* acuire; **~ener** *n (also:* **pencil**

~ener) temperamatite *m inv*; **~-eyed** *adj* dalla vista acuta; **~ly** *adv* (*turn, stop*) bruscamente; (*stand out, contrast*) nettamente; (*criticize, retort*) duramente, aspramente

shatter ['ʃætə*] *vt* mandare in frantumi, frantumare; (*fig: upset*) distruggere; (: *ruin*) rovinare ♦ *vi* frantumarsi, andare in pezzi

shave [ʃeɪv] *vt* radere, rasare ♦ *vi* radersi, farsi la barba ♦ *n*: **to have a ~** farsi la barba; **~r** *n* (*also*: **electric ~r**) rasoio elettrico

shaving ['ʃeɪvɪŋ] *n* (*action*) rasatura; **~s** *npl* (*of wood etc*) trucioli *mpl*; **~ brush** *n* pennello da barba; **~ cream** *n* crema da barba; **~ foam** *n* = **~ cream**

shawl [ʃɔːl] *n* scialle *m*

she [ʃiː] *pron* ella, lei; **~-cat** gatta; **~-elephant** elefantessa

sheaf [ʃiːf] (*pl* **sheaves**) *n* covone *m*; (*of papers*) fascio

shear [ʃɪə*] (*pt* **~ed**, *pp* **~ed** *or* **shorn**) *vt* (*sheep*) tosare; **~s** *npl* (*for hedge*) cesoie *fpl*

sheath [ʃiːθ] *n* fodero, guaina; (*contraceptive*) preservativo

sheaves [ʃiːvz] *npl of* **sheaf**

shed [ʃed] (*pt, pp* **shed**) *n* capannone *m* ♦ *vt* (*leaves, fur etc*) perdere; (*tears, blood*) versare; (*workers*) liberarsi di

she'd [ʃiːd] = **she had**; **she would**

sheen [ʃiːn] *n* lucentezza

sheep [ʃiːp] *n inv* pecora; **~dog** *n* cane *m* da pastore; **~skin** *n* pelle *f* di pecora

sheer [ʃɪə*] *adj* (*utter*) vero(a) (e proprio(a)); (*steep*) a picco, perpendicolare; (*almost transparent*) sottile ♦ *adv* a picco

sheet [ʃiːt] *n* (*on bed*) lenzuolo; (*of paper*) foglio; (*of glass, ice*) lastra; (*of metal*) foglio, lamina; **~ lightning** *n* lampo diffuso

sheik(h) [ʃeɪk] *n* sceicco

shelf [ʃelf] (*pl* **shelves**) *n* scaffale *m*, mensola

shell [ʃel] *n* (*on beach*) conchiglia; (*of egg, nut etc*) guscio; (*explosive*) granata; (*of building*) scheletro ♦ *vt* (*peas*) sgranare; (*MIL*) bombardare; **~ suit** *n* (*lightweight*) tuta di acetato; (*heavier*) tuta di trilobato

she'll [ʃiːl] = **she will**; **she shall**

shellfish ['ʃelfɪʃ] *n inv* (*crab etc*) crostaceo; (*scallop etc*) mollusco; (*pl: as food*) crostacei; molluschi

shelter ['ʃeltə*] *n* riparo, rifugio ♦ *vt* riparare, proteggere; (*give lodging to*) dare rifugio *or* asilo a ♦ *vi* ripararsi, mettersi al riparo; **~ed** *adj* riparato(a); **~ed housing** (*BRIT*) *n* alloggi dotati di strutture per anziani o handicappati

shelve [ʃelv] *vt* (*fig*) accantonare, rimandare; **~s** *npl of* **shelf**

shepherd ['ʃepəd] *n* pastore *m* ♦ *vt* (*guide*) guidare; **~'s pie** (*BRIT*) *n* timballo di carne macinata e purè di patate

sheriff ['ʃerɪf] (*US*) *n* sceriffo

sherry ['ʃerɪ] *n* sherry *m inv*

she's [ʃiːz] = **she is**; **she has**

Shetland ['ʃetlənd] *n* (*also*: **the ~s, the ~ Isles**) le isole Shetland, le Shetland

shield [ʃiːld] *n* scudo; (*trophy*) scudetto; (*protection*) schermo ♦ *vt*: **to ~ (from)** riparare (da), proteggere (da *or* contro)

shift [ʃɪft] *n* (*change*) cambiamento; (*of workers*) turno ♦ *vt* spostare, muovere; (*remove*) rimuovere ♦ *vi* spostarsi, muoversi; **~ work** *n* lavoro a squadre; **~y** *adj* ambiguo(a); (*eyes*) sfuggente

shilling ['ʃɪlɪŋ] (*BRIT*) *n* scellino (= *12 old pence; 20 in a pound*)

shimmer ['ʃɪmə*] *vi* brillare, luccicare

shin [ʃɪn] *n* tibia

shine [ʃaɪn] (*pt, pp* **shone**) *n* splendore *m*, lucentezza ♦ *vi* (ri)splendere, brillare ♦ *vt* far brillare, far risplendere; (*torch*): **to ~ sth on** puntare qc verso

shingle ['ʃɪŋgl] *n* (*on beach*) ciottoli *mpl*; **~s** *n* (*MED*) herpes zoster *m*

shiny ['ʃaɪnɪ] *adj* lucente, lucido(a)

ship [ʃɪp] *n* nave *f* ♦ *vt* trasportare (via mare); (*send*) spedire (via mare); **~building** *n* costruzione *f* navale; **~ment** *n* carico; **~ping** *n* (*ships*) naviglio; (*traffic*) navigazione *f*; **~shape** *adj* in perfetto ordine; **~wreck** *n* relitto; (*event*) naufragio ♦ *vt*: **to be ~wrecked** naufragare, fare naufragio; **~yard** *n* cantiere *m* navale

shire [ˈʃaɪə*] (BRIT) n contea

shirt [ʃəːt] n camicia; **in ~ sleeves** in maniche di camicia

shit [ʃɪt] (infl) excl merda (!)

shiver [ˈʃɪvə*] n brivido ♦ vi rabbrividire, tremare

shoal [ʃəul] n (of fish) banco; (fig) massa

shock [ʃɔk] n (impact) urto, scossa; (ELEC) scossa; (emotional) colpo, shock m inv; (MED) shock ♦ vt colpire, scioccare; scandalizzare; ~ **absorber** n ammortizzatore m; ~**ing** adj scioccante, traumatizzante; scandaloso(a)

shoddy [ˈʃɔdɪ] adj scadente

shoe [ʃuː] (pt, pp **shod**) n scarpa; (also: **horse~**) ferro di cavallo ♦ vt (horse) ferrare; ~**brush** n spazzola per scarpe; ~**lace** n stringa; ~ **polish** n lucido per scarpe; ~**shop** n calzoleria; ~**string** n (fig): **on a ~string** con quattro soldi

shone [ʃɔn] pt, pp of **shine**

shook [ʃuk] pt of **shake**

shoot [ʃuːt] (pt, pp **shot**) n (on branch, seedling) germoglio ♦ vt (game) cacciare, andare a caccia di; (person) sparare a; (execute) fucilare; (film) girare ♦ vi (with gun): **to ~ (at)** sparare (a), fare fuoco (su); (with bow): **to ~ (at)** tirare (su); (FOOTBALL) sparare, tirare (forte); ~ **down** vt (plane) abbattere; ~ **in/out** vi entrare/uscire come una freccia; ~ **up** vi (fig) salire alle stelle; ~**ing** n (shots) sparatoria; (HUNTING) caccia; ~**ing star** n stella cadente

shop [ʃɔp] n negozio; (workshop) officina ♦ vi (also: **go ~ping**) fare spese; ~ **assistant** (BRIT) n commesso/a; ~ **floor** n officina; (BRIT: fig) operai mpl, maestranze fpl; ~**keeper** n negoziante m/f, bottegaio/a; ~**lifting** n taccheggio; ~**per** n compratore/trice; ~**ping** n (goods) spesa, acquisti mpl; ~**ping bag** n borsa per la spesa; ~**ping centre** (US ~**ping center**) n centro commerciale; ~-**soiled** adj sciupato(a) a forza di stare in vetrina; ~ **steward** (BRIT) n (INDUSTRY) rappresentante m sindacale; ~ **window** n vetrina

shore [ʃɔː*] n (of sea) riva, spiaggia; (of lake) riva ♦ vt: **to ~ (up)** puntellare; **on ~** a riva

shorn [ʃɔːn] pp of **shear**

short [ʃɔːt] adj (not long) corto(a); (soon finished) breve; (person) basso(a); (curt) brusco(a), secco(a); (insufficient) insufficiente ♦ n (also: ~ **film**) cortometraggio; **(a pair of) ~s** (i) calzoncini; **to be ~ of sth** essere a corto di or mancare di qc; **in ~** in breve; ~ **of doing** a meno che non si faccia; **everything ~ of** tutto fuorché; **it is ~ for** è l'abbreviazione or il diminutivo di; **to cut ~** (speech, visit) accorciare, abbreviare; **to fall ~ of** venir meno a; non soddisfare; **to run ~ of** rimanere senza; **to stop ~** fermarsi di colpo; **to stop ~ of** non arrivare fino a; ~**age** n scarsezza, carenza; ~**bread** n biscotto di pasta frolla; ~-**change** vt: **to ~-change sb** imbrogliare qn sul resto; ~-**circuit** n cortocircuito; ~-**coming** n difetto; ~**(crust) pastry** (BRIT) n pasta frolla; ~**cut** n scorciatoia; ~**en** vt accorciare, ridurre; ~**fall** n deficit m; ~**hand** (BRIT) n stenografia; ~**hand typist** (BRIT) n stenodattilografo/a; ~ **list** (BRIT) n (for job) rosa dei candidati; ~-**lived** adj di breve durata; ~**ly** adv fra poco; ~-**sighted** (BRIT) adj miope; ~-**staffed** adj a corto di personale; ~-**stay** adj (car park) a tempo limitato; ~ **story** n racconto, novella; ~-**tempered** adj irascibile; ~-**term** adj (effect) di or a breve durata; (borrowing) a breve scadenza; ~ **wave** (RADIO) onde fpl corte

shot [ʃɔt] pt, pp of **shoot** ♦ n sparo, colpo; (try) prova; (FOOTBALL) tiro; (injection) iniezione f; (PHOT) foto f inv; **like a ~** come un razzo; (very readily) immediatamente; ~**gun** n fucile m da caccia

should [ʃud] aux vb: **I ~ go now** dovrei andare ora; **he ~ be there now** dovrebbe essere arrivato ora; **I ~ go if I were you** se fossi in te andrei; **I ~ like to** mi piacerebbe

shoulder [ˈʃəuldə*] n spalla; (BRIT: of road): **hard ~** banchina ♦ vt (fig) addossarsi, prendere sulle proprie spalle; ~ **bag** n

borsa a tracolla; ~ **blade** *n* scapola
shouldn't ['ʃudnt] = **should not**
shout [ʃaut] *n* urlo, grido ♦ *vt* gridare ♦ *vi*
(*also:* ~ **out**) urlare, gridare; ~ **down** *vt*
zittire gridando; ~**ing** *n* urli *mpl*
shove [ʃʌv] *vt* spingere; (*inf: put*): **to ~ sth
in** ficcare qc in; ~ **off** (*inf*) *vi* sloggiare,
smammare
shovel ['ʃʌvl] *n* pala ♦ *vt* spalare
show [ʃəu] (*pt* ~**ed**, *pp* **shown**) *n* (*of
emotion*) dimostrazione *f*, manifestazione *f*;
(*semblance*) apparenza; (*exhibition*) mostra,
esposizione *f*; (*THEATRE, CINEMA*) spettacolo
♦ *vt* far vedere, mostrare; (*courage etc*)
dimostrare, dar prova di; (*exhibit*) esporre
♦ *vi* vedersi, essere visibile; **for ~** per fare
scena; **on ~** (*exhibits etc*) esposto(a); ~ **in**
vt (*person*) far entrare; ~ **off** *vi* (*pej*)
esibirsi, mettersi in mostra ♦ *vt* (*display*)
mettere in risalto; (*pej*) mettere in mostra;
~ **out** *vt* (*person*) accompagnare alla porta;
~ **up** *vi* (*stand out*) essere ben visibile; (*inf:
turn up*) farsi vedere ♦ *vt* mettere in risalto;
~ **business** *n* industria dello spettacolo;
~**down** *n* prova di forza
shower ['ʃauə*] *n* (*rain*) acquazzone *m*; (*of
stones etc*) pioggia; (*also:* ~**bath**) doccia
♦ *vi* fare la doccia ♦ *vt:* **to ~ sb with** (*gifts,
abuse etc*) coprire qn di; (*missiles*) lanciare
contro qn una pioggia di; **to have a ~** fare
la doccia; ~**proof** *adj* impermeabile
showing ['ʃəuɪŋ] *n* (*of film*) proiezione *f*
show jumping *n* concorso ippico (di salto
ad ostacoli)
shown [ʃəun] *pp of* **show**
show-off (*inf*) *n* (*person*) esibizionista *m/f*
showpiece ['ʃəupiːs] *n* pezzo forte
showroom ['ʃəurum] *n* sala d'esposizione
shrank [ʃræŋk] *pt of* **shrink**
shrapnel ['ʃræpnl] *n* shrapnel *m*
shred [ʃred] *n* (*gen pl*) brandello ♦ *vt* fare a
brandelli; (*CULIN*) sminuzzare, tagliuzzare;
~**der** *n* (*vegetable* ~**der**) grattugia;
(*document* ~**der**) distruttore *m* di
documenti
shrewd [ʃruːd] *adj* astuto(a), scaltro(a)
shriek [ʃriːk] *n* strillo ♦ *vi* strillare

shrill [ʃrɪl] *adj* acuto(a), stridulo(a), stridente
shrimp [ʃrɪmp] *n* gamberetto
shrine [ʃraɪn] *n* reliquario; (*place*) santuario
shrink [ʃrɪŋk] (*pt* **shrank**, *pp* **shrunk**) *vi*
restringersi; (*fig*) ridursi; (*also:* ~ **away**)
ritrarsi ♦ *vt* (*wool*) far restringere ♦ *n* (*inf:
pej*) psicanalista *m/f*; **to ~ from doing sth**
rifuggire dal fare qc; ~**wrap** *vt*
confezionare con pellicola di plastica
shrivel ['ʃrɪvl] (*also:* ~ **up**) *vt* raggrinzare,
avvizzire ♦ *vi* raggrinzirsi, avvizzire
shroud [ʃraud] *n* lenzuolo funebre ♦ *vt:* ~**ed
in mystery** avvolto(a) nel mistero
Shrove Tuesday ['ʃrəuv-] *n* martedì *m*
grasso
shrub [ʃrʌb] *n* arbusto; ~**bery** *n* arbusti *mpl*
shrug [ʃrʌg] *n* scrollata di spalle ♦ *vt, vi:* **to
~ (one's shoulders)** alzare le spalle, fare
spallucce; ~ **off** *vt* passare sopra a
shrunk [ʃrʌŋk] *pp of* **shrink**
shudder ['ʃʌdə*] *n* brivido ♦ *vi* rabbrividire
shuffle ['ʃʌfl] *vt* (*cards*) mescolare; **to ~
(one's feet)** strascicare i piedi
shun [ʃʌn] *vt* sfuggire, evitare
shunt [ʃʌnt] *vt* (*RAIL: direct*) smistare;
(: *divert*) deviare; (*object*) spostare
shut [ʃʌt] (*pt, pp* **shut**) *vt* chiudere ♦ *vi*
chiudersi, chiudere; ~ **down** *vt, vi*
chiudere definitivamente; ~ **off** *vt* fermare,
bloccare; ~ **up** *vi* (*inf: keep quiet*) stare
zitto(a), fare silenzio ♦ *vt* (*close*) chiudere;
(*silence*) far tacere; ~**ter** *n* imposta; (*PHOT*)
otturatore *m*
shuttle ['ʃʌtl] *n* spola, navetta; (*space* ~)
navetta (spaziale); (*also:* ~ **service**) servizio
m navetta *inv*
shuttlecock ['ʃʌtlkɔk] *n* volano
shuttle diplomacy *n la gestione dei
rapporti diplomatici caratterizzata da
frequenti viaggi e incontri dei
rappresentanti del governo*
shy [ʃaɪ] *adj* timido(a)
Sicily ['sɪsɪlɪ] *n* Sicilia
sick [sɪk] *adj* (*ill*) malato(a); (*vomiting*): **to be
~** vomitare; (*humour*) macabro(a); **to feel ~**
avere la nausea; **to be ~ of** (*fig*) averne
abbastanza di; ~ **bay** *n* infermeria; ~**en** *vt*

nauseare ♦ vi: **to be ~ening for sth** (*cold etc*) covare qc
sickle ['sɪkl] n falcetto
sick: ~ **leave** n congedo per malattia; **~ly** adj malaticcio(a); (*causing nausea*) nauseante; **~ness** n malattia; (*vomiting*) vomito; ~ **pay** n sussidio per malattia
side [saɪd] n lato; (*of lake*) riva; (*team*) squadra ♦ cpd (*door, entrance*) laterale ♦ vi: **to ~ with sb** parteggiare per qn, prendere le parti di qn; **by the ~ of** a fianco di; (*road*) sul ciglio di; ~ **by ~** fianco a fianco; **from ~ to ~** da una parte all'altra; **to take ~s (with)** schierarsi (con); **~board** n credenza; **~burns** (*BRIT* **~boards**) npl (*whiskers*) basette fpl; ~ **effect** n (*MED*) effetto collaterale; **~light** n (*AUT*) luce f di posizione; **~line** n (*SPORT*) linea laterale; (*fig*) attività secondaria; **~long** adj obliquo(a); ~ **order** n contorno (*pietanza*); ~ **show** n attrazione f; **~step** vt (*question*) eludere; (*problem*) scavalcare; ~ **street** n traversa; **~track** vt (*fig*) distrarre; **~walk** (*US*) n marciapiede m; **~ways** adv (*move*) di lato, di fianco
siding ['saɪdɪŋ] n (*RAIL*) binario di raccordo
siege [siːdʒ] n assedio
sieve [sɪv] n setaccio ♦ vt setacciare
sift [sɪft] vt passare al crivello; (*fig*) vagliare
sigh [saɪ] n sospiro ♦ vi sospirare
sight [saɪt] n (*faculty*) vista; (*spectacle*) spettacolo; (*on gun*) mira ♦ vt avvistare; **in ~** in vista; **on ~** a vista; **out of ~** non visibile; **~seeing** n giro turistico; **to go ~seeing** visitare una località
sign [saɪn] n segno; (*with hand etc*) segno, gesto; (*notice*) insegna, cartello ♦ vt firmare; (*player*) ingaggiare; ~ **on** vi (*MIL*) arruolarsi; (*as unemployed*) iscriversi sulla lista (dell'ufficio di collocamento) ♦ vt (*MIL*) arruolare; (*employee*) assumere; ~ **over** vt: **to ~ sth over to sb** cedere qc con scrittura legale a qn; ~ **up** vi (*MIL*) arruolarsi; (*for course*) iscriversi ♦ vt (*player*) ingaggiare; (*recruits*) reclutare
signal ['sɪɡnl] n segnale m ♦ vi (*AUT*) segnalare, mettere la freccia ♦ vt (*person*) fare segno a; (*message*) comunicare per mezzo di segnali; **~man** (*irreg*) n (*RAIL*) deviatore m
signature ['sɪɡnətʃə*] n firma; ~ **tune** n sigla musicale
signet ring ['sɪɡnət-] n anello con sigillo
significance [sɪɡ'nɪfɪkəns] n significato; importanza
significant [sɪɡ'nɪfɪkənt] adj significativo(a)
sign language n linguaggio dei muti
signpost ['saɪnpəust] n cartello indicatore
silence ['saɪlns] n silenzio ♦ vt far tacere, ridurre al silenzio; **~r** n (*on gun, BRIT: AUT*) silenziatore m
silent ['saɪlnt] adj silenzioso(a); (*film*) muto(a); **to remain ~** tacere, stare zitto; ~ **partner** n (*COMM*) socio inattivo
silhouette [sɪluːˈet] n silhouette f inv
silicon chip ['sɪlɪkən-] n piastrina di silicio
silk [sɪlk] n seta ♦ adj di seta; **~y** adj di seta
silly ['sɪlɪ] adj stupido(a), sciocco(a)
silt [sɪlt] n limo
silver ['sɪlvə*] n argento; (*money*) monete da 5, 10 or 50 pence; (*also*: **~ware**) argenteria ♦ adj d'argento; ~ **paper** n (*BRIT*) n carta argentata, (carta stagnola); **~-plated** adj argentato(a); **~smith** n argentiere m; **~y** adj (*colour*) argenteo(a); (*sound*) argentino(a)
similar ['sɪmɪlə*] adj: ~ **(to)** simile (a); **~ly** adv allo stesso modo; così pure
simmer ['sɪmə*] vi cuocere a fuoco lento
simple ['sɪmpl] adj semplice; **simplicity** [-'plɪsɪtɪ] n semplicità; **simply** adv semplicemente
simultaneous [sɪməl'teɪnɪəs] adj simultaneo(a)
sin [sɪn] n peccato ♦ vi peccare
since [sɪns] adv da allora ♦ prep da ♦ conj (*time*) da quando; (*because*) poiché, dato che; ~ **then, ever ~** da allora
sincere [sɪn'sɪə*] adj sincero(a); **~ly** adv: **yours ~ly** (*in letters*) distinti saluti; **sincerity** [-'sɛrɪtɪ] n sincerità
sinew ['sɪnjuː] n tendine m
sing [sɪŋ] (*pt* **sang**, *pp* **sung**) vt, vi cantare
singe [sɪndʒ] vt bruciacchiare

singer ['sɪŋə*] n cantante m/f

singing ['sɪŋɪŋ] n canto

single ['sɪŋgl] adj solo(a), unico(a); (*unmarried: man*) celibe; (*: woman*) nubile; (*not double*) semplice ♦ n (BRIT: *also*: ~ **ticket**) biglietto di (sola) andata; (*record*) 45 giri m; **~s** n (TENNIS) singolo; ~ **out** vt scegliere; (*distinguish*) distinguere; ~ **bed** n letto singolo; ~-**breasted** adj a un petto; ~ **file** n: **in ~ file** in fila indiana; ~-**handed** adv senza aiuto, da solo(a); ~-**minded** adj tenace, risoluto(a); ~ **parent** n (*mother*) ragazza f madre inv; (*father*) ragazzo m padre inv; ~ **room** n camera singola; ~-**track road** n strada a una carreggiata

singly ['sɪŋglɪ] adv separatamente

singular ['sɪŋgjulə*] adj (*exceptional, LING*) singolare ♦ n (LING) singolare m

sinister ['sɪnɪstə*] adj sinistro(a)

sink [sɪŋk] (*pt* **sank**, *pp* **sunk**) n lavandino, acquaio ♦ vt (*ship*) (fare) affondare, colare a picco; (*foundations*) scavare; (*piles etc*): **to ~ sth into** conficcare qc in ♦ vi affondare, andare a fondo; (*ground etc*) cedere, avvallarsi; **my heart sank** mi sentii venir meno; ~ **in** vi penetrare

sinner ['sɪnə*] n peccatore/trice

sinus ['saɪnəs] n (ANAT) seno

sip [sɪp] n sorso ♦ vt sorseggiare

siphon ['saɪfən] n sifone m; ~ **off** vt travasare (con un sifone)

sir [sə*] n signore m; **S~ John Smith** Sir John Smith; **yes ~** sì, signore

sirloin ['sə:lɔɪn] n controfiletto

sissy ['sɪsɪ] n (*inf*) femminuccia

sister ['sɪstə*] n sorella; (*nun*) suora; (BRIT: *nurse*) infermiera f caposala inv; ~-**in-law** n cognata

sit [sɪt] (*pt, pp* **sat**) vi sedere, sedersi; (*assembly*) essere in seduta; (*for painter*) posare ♦ vt (*exam*) sostenere, dare; ~ **down** vi sedersi; ~ **in on** vt fus assistere a; ~ **up** vi tirarsi su a sedere; (*not go to bed*) stare alzato(a) fino a tardi

sitcom ['sɪtkɔm] n abbr (= **situation comedy**) commedia di situazione

site [saɪt] n posto; (*also*: **building** ~) cantiere m ♦ vt situare

sit-in n (*demonstration*) sit-in m inv

sitting ['sɪtɪŋ] n (*of assembly etc*) seduta; (*in canteen*) turno; ~ **room** n soggiorno

situated ['sɪtjueɪtɪd] adj situato(a)

situation [sɪtju'eɪʃən] n situazione f; (*job*) lavoro; (*location*) posizione f; **"~s vacant"** (BRIT) "offerte fpl di impiego"

six [sɪks] num sei; ~**teen** num sedici; ~**th** num sesto(a); ~**ty** num sessanta

size [saɪz] n dimensioni fpl; (*of clothing*) taglia, misura; (*of shoes*) numero; (*glue*) colla; ~ **up** vt giudicare, farsi un'idea di; ~**able** adj considerevole

sizzle ['sɪzl] vi sfrigolare

skate [skeɪt] n pattino; (*fish: pl inv*) razza ♦ vi pattinare; ~**board** n skateboard m inv; ~**r** n pattinatore/trice; **skating** n pattinaggio; **skating rink** n pista di pattinaggio

skeleton ['skelɪtn] n scheletro; ~ **staff** n personale m ridotto

skeptical ['skeptɪkl] (*US*) adj = **sceptical**

sketch [sketʃ] n (*drawing*) schizzo, abbozzo; (THEATRE) scenetta comica, sketch m inv ♦ vt abbozzare, schizzare; ~ **book** n album m inv per schizzi; ~**y** adj incompleto(a), lacunoso(a)

skewer ['skju:ə*] n spiedo

ski [ski:] n sci m inv ♦ vi sciare; ~ **boot** n scarpone m da sci; ~ **pass** n ski pass m inv

skid [skɪd] n slittamento ♦ vi slittare

skier ['ski:ə*] n sciatore/trice

skiing ['ski:ɪŋ] n sci m

ski jump n (*ramp*) trampolino; (*event*) salto con gli sci

skilful ['skɪlful] (*US* **skillful**) adj abile

ski lift n ['ski:lɪft] n sciovia

skill [skɪl] n abilità f inv, capacità f inv; ~**ed** adj esperto(a); (*worker*) qualificato(a), specializzato(a); ~**ful** (*US*) adj = **skilful**

skim [skɪm] vt (*milk*) scremare; (*glide over*) sfiorare ♦ vi: **to ~ through** (*fig*) scorrere, dare una scorsa a; ~**med milk** n latte m scremato

skimp [skɪmp] *vt* (*work: also:* ~ **on**) fare alla carlona; (*cloth etc*) lesinare; **~y** *adj* misero(a); striminzito(a); frugale

skin [skɪn] *n* pelle *f* ♦ *vt* (*fruit etc*) sbucciare; (*animal*) scuoiare, spellare; ~ **cancer** *n* cancro alla pelle; **~-deep** *adj* superficiale; ~ **diving** *n* nuoto subacqueo; **~ny** *adj* molto magro(a), pelle e ossa *inv*; **~tight** *adj* (*dress etc*) aderente

skip [skɪp] *n* saltello, balzo; (*BRIT: container*) benna ♦ *vi* saltare; (*with rope*) saltare la corda ♦ *vt* saltare

ski pole *n* racchetta (da sci)

skipper ['skɪpə*] *n* (*NAUT, SPORT*) capitano

skipping rope ['skɪpɪŋ-] (*BRIT*) *n* corda per saltare

skirmish ['skə:mɪʃ] *n* scaramuccia

skirt [skə:t] *n* gonna, sottana ♦ *vt* fiancheggiare, costeggiare; **~ing board** (*BRIT*) *n* zoccolo

ski slope *n* pista da sci

ski suit *n* tuta da sci

skit [skɪt] *n* parodia; scenetta satirica

ski tow *n* sciovia, ski-lift *m inv*

skittle ['skɪtl] *n* birillo; **~s** *n* (*game*) (gioco dei) birilli *mpl*

skive [skaɪv] (*BRIT: inf*) *vi* fare il lavativo

skull [skʌl] *n* cranio, teschio

skunk [skʌŋk] *n* moffetta

sky [skaɪ] *n* cielo; **~light** *n* lucernario; **~scraper** *n* grattacielo

slab [slæb] *n* lastra; (*of cake, cheese*) fetta

slack [slæk] *adj* (*loose*) allentato(a); (*slow*) lento(a); (*careless*) negligente; **~en** (*also:* **~en off**) *vi* rallentare, diminuire ♦ *vt* allentare; (*speed*) diminuire; **~s** *npl* (*trousers*) pantaloni *mpl*

slag heap [slæg-] *n* ammasso di scorie

slag off [slæg-] (*BRIT: inf*) *vt* sparlare di

slam [slæm] *vt* (*door*) sbattere; (*throw*) scaraventare; (*criticize*) stroncare ♦ *vi* sbattere

slander ['slɑ:ndə*] *n* calunnia; diffamazione *f*

slang [slæŋ] *n* gergo, slang *m*

slant [slɑ:nt] *n* pendenza, inclinazione *f*; (*fig*) angolazione *f*, punto di vista; **~ed** *adj*

in pendenza, inclinato(a); (*eyes*) obliquo(a); **~ing** *adj* = **~ed**

slap [slæp] *n* manata, pacca; (*on face*) schiaffo ♦ *vt* dare una manata a; schiaffeggiare ♦ *adv* (*directly*) in pieno; ~ **a coat of paint on it** dagli una mano di vernice; **~dash** *adj* negligente; (*work*) raffazzonato(a); **~stick** *n* (*comedy*) farsa grossolana; **~-up** (*BRIT*) *adj*: **a ~-up meal** un pranzo (*or* una cena) coi fiocchi

slash [slæʃ] *vt* tagliare; (*face*) sfregiare; (*fig: prices*) ridurre drasticamente, tagliare

slat [slæt] *n* (*of wood*) stecca; (*of plastic*) lamina

slate [sleɪt] *n* ardesia; (*piece*) lastra di ardesia ♦ *vt* (*fig: criticize*) stroncare, distruggere

slaughter ['slɔ:tə*] *n* strage *f*, massacro ♦ *vt* (*animal*) macellare; (*people*) trucidare, massacrare

slave [sleɪv] *n* schiavo/a ♦ *vi* (*also:* ~ **away**) lavorare come uno schiavo; **~ry** *n* schiavitù *f*; **slavish** *adj* servile; (*copy*) pedissequo(a)

slay [sleɪ] (*pt* **slew**, *pp* **slain**) *vt* (*formal*) uccidere

sleazy ['sli:zɪ] *adj* trasandato(a)

sledge [sledʒ] *n* slitta; **~hammer** *n* mazza, martello da fabbro

sleek [sli:k] *adj* (*hair, fur*) lucido(a), lucente; (*car, boat*) slanciato(a), affusolato(a)

sleep [sli:p] (*pt, pp* **slept**) *n* sonno ♦ *vi* dormire; **to go to** ~ addormentarsi; ~ **around** *vi* andare a letto con tutti; ~ **in** *vi* (*oversleep*) dormire fino a tardi; **~er** (*BRIT*) *n* (*RAIL: on track*) traversina; (*: train*) treno di vagoni letto; **~ing bag** *n* sacco a pelo; **~ing car** *n* vagone *m* letto *inv*, carrozza *f* letto *inv*; **~ing partner** (*BRIT*) *n* (*COMM*) socio inattivo; **~ing pill** *n* sonnifero; **~less** *adj*: **a ~less night** una notte in bianco; **~walker** *n* sonnambulo/a; **~y** *adj* assonnato(a), sonnolento(a); (*fig*) addormentato(a)

sleet [sli:t] *n* nevischio

sleeve [sli:v] *n* manica; (*of record*) copertina

sleigh [sleɪ] *n* slitta

sleight [slaɪt] *n*: ~ **of hand** gioco di destrezza

slender ['slɛndə*] adj snello(a), sottile; (not enough) scarso(a), esiguo(a)

slept [slɛpt] pt, pp of **sleep**

slew [slu:] pt of **slay** ♦ vi (BRIT) girare

slice [slaɪs] n fetta ♦ vt affettare, tagliare a fette

slick [slɪk] adj (skilful) brillante; (clever) furbo(a) ♦ n (also: **oil ~**) chiazza di petrolio

slide [slaɪd] (pt, pp **slid**) n scivolone m; (in playground) scivolo; (PHOT) diapositiva; (BRIT: also: **hair ~**) fermaglio (per capelli) ♦ vt far scivolare ♦ vi scivolare; **~ rule** n regolo calcolatore; **sliding** adj (door) scorrevole; **sliding scale** n scala mobile

slight [slaɪt] adj (slim) snello(a), sottile; (frail) delicato(a), fragile; (trivial) insignificante; (small) piccolo(a) ♦ n offesa, affronto; **not in the ~est** affatto, neppure per sogno; **~ly** adv lievemente, un po'

slim [slɪm] adj magro(a), snello(a) ♦ vi dimagrire; fare (or seguire) una dieta dimagrante

slime [slaɪm] n limo, melma; viscidume m

slimming ['slɪmɪŋ] adj (diet) dimagrante; (food) ipocalorico(a)

sling [slɪŋ] (pt, pp **slung**) n (MED) fascia al collo; (for baby) marsupio ♦ vt lanciare, tirare

slip [slɪp] n scivolata, scivolone m; (mistake) errore m, sbaglio; (underskirt) sottoveste f; (of paper) striscia di carta; tagliando, scontrino ♦ vt (slide) far scivolare ♦ vi (slide) scivolare; (move smoothly): **to ~ into/out of** scivolare in/fuori da; (decline) declinare; **to ~ sth on/off** infilarsi/togliersi qc; **to give sb the ~** sfuggire qn; **a ~ of the tongue** un lapsus linguae; **~ away** vi svignarsela; **~ in** vt infilare ♦ vi (error) scivolare; **~ out** vi scivolare fuori; **~ up** vi sbagliarsi; **~ped disc** n spostamento delle vertebre

slipper ['slɪpə*] n pantofola

slippery ['slɪpərɪ] adj scivoloso(a)

slip road (BRIT) n (to motorway) rampa di accesso

slip-up n granchio (fig)

slipway ['slɪpweɪ] n scalo di costruzione

slit [slɪt] (pt, pp **slit**) n fessura, fenditura; (cut) taglio ♦ vt fendere; tagliare

slither ['slɪðə*] vi scivolare, sdrucciolare

sliver ['slɪvə*] n (of glass, wood) scheggia; (of cheese etc) fettina

slob [slɔb] (inf) n sciattone/a

slog [slɔg] (BRIT) n faticata ♦ vi lavorare con accanimento, sgobbare

slogan ['sləugən] n motto, slogan m inv

slope [sləup] n pendio; (side of mountain) versante m; (ski ~) pista; (of roof) pendenza; (of floor) inclinazione f ♦ vi: **to ~ down** declinare; **to ~ up** essere in salita; **sloping** adj inclinato(a)

sloppy ['slɔpɪ] adj (work) tirato(a) via; (appearance) sciatto(a)

slot [slɔt] n fessura ♦ vt: **to ~ sth into** infilare qc in

sloth [sləuθ] n (laziness) pigrizia, accidia

slot machine n (BRIT: vending machine) distributore m automatico; (for gambling) slot-machine f inv

slouch [slautʃ] vi (when walking) camminare dinoccolato(a); **she was ~ing in a chair** era sprofondata in una poltrona

Slovenia [sləu'vi:nɪə] n Slovenia

slovenly ['slʌvənlɪ] adj sciatto(a), trasandato(a)

slow [sləu] adj lento(a); (watch): **to be ~** essere indietro ♦ adv lentamente ♦ vt, vi (also: **~ down, ~ up**) rallentare; "**~**" (road sign) "rallentare"; **~ly** adv lentamente; **~ motion** n: **in ~ motion** al rallentatore

sludge [slʌdʒ] n fanghiglia

slug [slʌg] n lumaca; (bullet) pallottola; **~gish** adj lento(a); (trading) stagnante

sluice [slu:s] n chiusa

slum [slʌm] n catapecchia

slumber ['slʌmbə*] n sonno

slump [slʌmp] n crollo, caduta; (economic) depressione f, crisi f inv ♦ vi crollare

slung [slʌŋ] pt, pp of **sling**

slur [slə:*] n (fig): **~ (on)** calunnia (su) ♦ vt pronunciare in modo indistinto

slush [slʌʃ] n neve f mista a fango; **~ fund** n fondi mpl neri

slut [slʌt] n donna trasandata, sciattona

sly [slaɪ] *adj* (*smile, remark*) sornione(a); (*person*) furbo(a)

smack [smæk] *n* (*slap*) pacca; (*on face*) schiaffo ♦ *vt* schiaffeggiare; (*child*) picchiare ♦ *vi*: **to ~ of** puzzare di

small [smɔːl] *adj* piccolo(a); **~ ads** (BRIT) *npl* piccola pubblicità; **~ change** *n* moneta, spiccioli *mpl*; **~-holder** *n* piccolo proprietario; **~ hours** *npl*: **in the ~ hours** alle ore piccole; **~pox** *n* vaiolo; **~ talk** *n* chiacchiere *fpl*

smart [smɑːt] *adj* elegante; (*fashionable*) alla moda; (*clever*) intelligente; (*quick*) sveglio(a) ♦ *vi* bruciare; **~ card** *n* carta intelligente; **~en up** *vi* farsi bello(a) ♦ *vt* (*people*) fare bello(a); (*things*) abbellire

smash [smæʃ] *n* (*also*: **~-up**) scontro, collisione *f*; (*~ hit*) successone *m* ♦ *vt* frantumare, fracassare; (*SPORT: record*) battere ♦ *vi* frantumarsi, andare in pezzi; **~ing** (*inf*) *adj* favoloso(a), formidabile

smattering ['smætərɪŋ] *n*: **a ~ of** un'infarinatura di

smear [smɪə*] *n* macchia; (MED) striscio ♦ *vt* spalmare; (*make dirty*) sporcare; **~ campaign** *n* campagna diffamatoria

smell [smel] (*pt, pp* **smelt** *or* **smelled**) *n* odore *m*; (*sense*) olfatto, odorato ♦ *vt* sentire (l')odore di ♦ *vi* (*food etc*): **to ~ (of)** avere odore (di); (*pej*) puzzare, avere un cattivo odore; **~y** *adj* puzzolente

smile [smaɪl] *n* sorriso ♦ *vi* sorridere

smirk [smɜːk] *n* sorriso furbo; sorriso compiaciuto

smog [smɒg] *n* smog *m*

smoke [sməʊk] *n* fumo ♦ *vt, vi* fumare; **~d** *adj* (*bacon, glass*) affumicato(a); **~r** *n* (*person*) fumatore/trice; (RAIL) carrozza per fumatori; **~ screen** *n* (MIL) cortina fumogena *or* di fumo; (*fig*) copertura; **smoking** *n* fumo; **"no smoking"** (*sign*) "vietato fumare"; **smoking compartment** (BRIT), **smoking car** (US) *n* scompartimento (per) fumatori; **smoky** *adj* fumoso(a); (*taste*) affumicato(a)

smolder ['sməʊldə*] (US) *vi* = **smoulder**

smooth [smuːð] *adj* liscio(a); (*sauce*) omogeneo(a); (*flavour, whisky*) amabile; (*movement*) regolare; (*person*) mellifluo(a) ♦ *vt* (*also*: **~ out**) lisciare, spianare; (: *difficulties*) appianare

smother ['smʌðə*] *vt* soffocare

smoulder ['sməʊldə*] (US **smolder**) *vi* covare sotto la cenere

smudge [smʌdʒ] *n* macchia; sbavatura ♦ *vt* imbrattare, sporcare

smug [smʌg] *adj* soddisfatto(a), compiaciuto(a)

smuggle ['smʌgl] *vt* contrabbandare; **~r** *n* contrabbandiere/a; **smuggling** *n* contrabbando

smutty ['smʌtɪ] *adj* (*fig*) osceno(a), indecente

snack [snæk] *n* spuntino; **~ bar** *n* tavola calda, snack bar *m inv*

snag [snæg] *n* intoppo, ostacolo imprevisto

snail [sneɪl] *n* chiocciola

snake [sneɪk] *n* serpente *m*

snap [snæp] *n* (*sound*) schianto, colpo secco; (*photograph*) istantanea ♦ *adj* improvviso(a) ♦ *vt* (*far*) schioccare; (*break*) spezzare di netto ♦ *vi* spezzarsi con un rumore secco; (*fig: person*) parlare con tono secco; **to ~ shut** chiudersi di scatto; **~ at** *vt fus* (*subj: dog*) cercare di mordere; **~ off** *vt* (*break*) schiantare; **~ up** *vt* afferrare; **~py** (*inf*) *adj* (*answer, slogan*) d'effetto; **make it ~py!** (*hurry up*) sbrigati!, svelto!; **~shot** *n* istantanea

snare [snɛə*] *n* trappola

snarl [snɑːl] *vi* ringhiare

snatch [snætʃ] *n* (*small amount*) frammento ♦ *vt* strappare (con violenza); (*fig*) rubare

sneak [sniːk] (*pt* (US) **snuck**) *vi*: **to ~ in/out** entrare/uscire di nascosto ♦ *n* spione/a; **to ~ up on sb** avvicinarsi quatto quatto a qn; **~ers** *npl* scarpe *fpl* da ginnastica

sneer [snɪə*] *vi* sogghignare; **to ~ at** farsi beffe di

sneeze [sniːz] *n* starnuto ♦ *vi* starnutire

sniff [snɪf] *n* fiutata, annusata ♦ *vi* tirare su col naso ♦ *vt* fiutare, annusare

snigger ['snɪgə*] *vi* ridacchiare, ridere sotto i baffi

snip [snɪp] *n* pezzetto; (*bargain*) (buon) affare *m*, occasione *f* ♦ *vt* tagliare

sniper ['snaɪpə*] *n* (*marksman*) franco tiratore *m*, cecchino

snippet ['snɪpɪt] *n* frammento

snob [snɔb] *n* snob *m/f inv*; **~bery** *n* snobismo; **~bish** *adj* snob *inv*

snooker ['snu:kə*] *n* tipo di gioco del biliardo

snoop ['snu:p] *vi*: **to ~ about** curiosare

snooze [snu:z] *n* sonnellino, pisolino ♦ *vi* fare un sonnellino

snore [snɔ:*] *vi* russare

snorkel ['snɔ:kl] *n* (*of swimmer*) respiratore *m* a tubo

snort [snɔ:t] *n* sbuffo ♦ *vi* sbuffare

snout [snaut] *n* muso

snow [snəu] *n* neve *f* ♦ *vi* nevicare; **~ball** *n* palla di neve ♦ *vi* (*fig*) crescere a vista d'occhio; **~bound** *adj* bloccato(a) dalla neve; **~drift** *n* cumulo di neve (ammucchiato dal vento); **~drop** *n* bucaneve *m inv*; **~fall** *n* nevicata; **~flake** *n* fiocco di neve; **~man** (*irreg*) *n* pupazzo di neve; **~plough** (*US* **~plow**) *n* spazzaneve *m inv*; **~shoe** *n* racchetta da neve; **~storm** *n* tormenta

snub [snʌb] *vt* snobbare ♦ *n* offesa, affronto; **~-nosed** *adj* dal naso camuso

snuff [snʌf] *n* tabacco da fiuto

snug [snʌg] *adj* comodo(a); (*room, house*) accogliente, comodo(a)

snuggle ['snʌgl] *vi*: **to ~ up to sb** stringersi a qn

KEYWORD

so [səu] *adv* 1 (*thus, likewise*) così; **if ~** se è così, quand'è così; **I didn't do it — you did ~!** non l'ho fatto io — sì che l'hai fatto!; **~ do I, ~ am I** *etc* anch'io; **it's 5 o'clock — ~ it is!** sono le 5 — davvero!; **I hope ~** lo spero; **I think ~** penso di sì; **~ far** finora, fin qui; (*in past*) fino ad allora

2 (*in comparisons etc: to such a degree*) così; **~ big (that)** così grande (che); **she's not ~ clever as her brother** lei non è (così) intelligente come suo fratello

3: **~ much** *adj* tanto(a) ♦ *adv* tanto; **I've got ~ much work/money** ho tanto lavoro/tanti soldi; **I love you ~ much** ti amo tanto; **~ many** tanti(e)

4 (*phrases*): **10 or ~** circa 10; **~ long!** (*inf: goodbye*) ciao!, ci vediamo!

♦ *conj* 1 (*expressing purpose*): **~ as to do** in modo *or* così da fare; **we hurried ~ as not to be late** ci affrettammo per non fare tardi; **~ (that)** affinché +*sub*, perché +*sub*

2 (*expressing result*): **he didn't arrive ~ I left** non è venuto così me ne sono andata; **~ you see, I could have gone** vedi, sarei potuto andare

---

soak [səuk] *vt* inzuppare; (*clothes*) mettere a mollo ♦ *vi* (*clothes etc*) essere a mollo; **~ in** *vi* penetrare; **~ up** *vt* assorbire

soap [səup] *n* sapone *m*; **~flakes** *npl* sapone *m* in scaglie; **~ opera** *n* soap opera *f inv*; **~ powder** *n* detersivo; **~y** *adj* insaponato(a)

soar [sɔ:*] *vi* volare in alto; (*price etc*) salire alle stelle; (*building*) ergersi

sob [sɔb] *n* singhiozzo ♦ *vi* singhiozzare

sober ['səubə*] *adj* sobrio(a); (*not drunk*) non ubriaco(a); (*moderate*) moderato(a); **~ up** *vt* far passare la sbornia a ♦ *vi* farsi passare la sbornia

so-called ['səu'kɔ:ld] *adj* cosiddetto(a)

soccer ['sɔkə*] *n* calcio

sociable ['səuʃəbl] *adj* socievole

social ['səuʃl] *adj* sociale ♦ *n* festa, serata; **~ club** *n* club *m inv* sociale; **~ism** *n* socialismo; **~ist** *adj, n* socialista *m/f*; **~ize** *vi*: **to ~ize (with)** socializzare (con); **~ security** (*BRIT*) *n* previdenza sociale; **~ work** *n* servizio sociale; **~ worker** *n* assistente *m/f* sociale

society [sə'saɪətɪ] *n* società *f inv*; (*club*) società, associazione *f*; (*also:* **high ~**) alta società

sociology [səusɪ'ɔlədʒɪ] *n* sociologia

sock [sɔk] *n* calzino

socket ['sɔkɪt] *n* cavità *f inv*; (*of eye*) orbita; (*BRIT: ELEC: also:* **wall ~**) presa di corrente

sod [sɔd] *n* (*of earth*) zolla erbosa; (*BRIT: inf!*)

bastardo/a (!)

soda ['səʊdə] n (CHEM) soda; (also: ~ **water**) acqua di seltz; (US: also: ~ **pop**) gassosa

sodium ['səʊdɪəm] n sodio

sofa ['səʊfə] n sofà m inv

soft [sɒft] adj (not rough) morbido(a); (not hard) soffice; (not loud) sommesso(a); (not bright) tenue; (kind) gentile; ~ **drink** n analcolico; ~**en** ['sɒfn] vt ammorbidire; addolcire; attenuare ♦ vi ammorbidirsi; addolcirsi; attenuarsi; ~**ly** adv dolcemente; morbidamente; ~**ness** n dolcezza; morbidezza

software ['sɒftwɛə*] n (COMPUT) software m

soggy ['sɒgɪ] adj inzuppato(a)

soil [sɔɪl] n terreno ♦ vt sporcare

solar ['səʊlə*] adj solare; ~ **panel** n pannello solare; ~ **power** n energie solare

sold [səʊld] pt, pp of **sell**; ~ **out** adj (COMM) esaurito(a)

solder ['səʊldə*] vt saldare ♦ n saldatura

soldier ['səʊldʒə*] n soldato, militare m

sole [səʊl] n (of foot) pianta (del piede); (of shoe) suola; (fish: pl inv) sogliola ♦ adj solo(a), unico(a)

solemn ['sɒləm] adj solenne

sole trader n (COMM) commerciante m in proprio

solicit [sə'lɪsɪt] vt (request) richiedere, sollecitare ♦ vi (prostitute) adescare i passanti

solicitor [sə'lɪsɪtə*] (BRIT) n (for wills etc) ≈ notaio; (in court) ≈ avvocato

solid ['sɒlɪd] adj solido(a); (not hollow) pieno(a); (meal) sostanzioso(a) ♦ n solido

solidarity [sɒlɪ'dærɪtɪ] n solidarietà

solitaire [sɒlɪ'tɛə*] n (games, gem) solitario

solitary ['sɒlɪtərɪ] adj solitario(a); ~ **confinement** n (LAW) isolamento

solo ['səʊləʊ] n assolo; ~**ist** n solista m/f

soluble ['sɒljʊbl] adj solubile

solution [sə'luːʃən] n soluzione f

solve [sɒlv] vt risolvere

solvent ['sɒlvənt] adj (COMM) solvibile ♦ n (CHEM) solvente m

sombre ['sɒmbə*] (US **somber**) adj scuro(a); (mood, person) triste

some [sʌm] adj 1 (a certain amount or number of): ~ **tea/water/cream** del tè/dell'acqua/della panna; ~ **children/apples** dei bambini/delle mele

2 (certain: in contrasts) certo(a); ~ **people say that ...** alcuni dicono che ..., certa gente dice che ...

3 (unspecified) un(a) certo(a), qualche; ~ **woman was asking for you** una tale chiedeva di lei; ~ **day** un giorno; ~ **day next week** un giorno della prossima settimana

♦ pron 1 (a certain number) alcuni(e), certi(e); I've got ~ (books etc) ne ho alcuni; ~ (of them) have been sold alcuni sono stati venduti

2 (a certain amount) un po'; I've got ~ (money, milk) ne ho un po'; I've read ~ of the book ho letto parte del libro

♦ adv: ~ **10 people** circa 10 persone

somebody ['sʌmbədɪ] pron = **someone**

somehow ['sʌmhaʊ] adv in un modo o nell'altro, in qualche modo; (for some reason) per qualche ragione

someone ['sʌmwʌn] pron qualcuno

someplace ['sʌmpleɪs] (US) adv = **somewhere**

somersault ['sʌməsɔːlt] n capriola; salto mortale ♦ vi fare una capriola (or un salto mortale); (car) cappottare

something ['sʌmθɪŋ] pron qualcosa, qualche cosa; ~ **nice** qualcosa di bello; ~ **to do** qualcosa da fare

sometime ['sʌmtaɪm] adv (in future) una volta o l'altra; (in past): ~ **last month** durante il mese scorso

sometimes ['sʌmtaɪmz] adv qualche volta

somewhat ['sʌmwɒt] adv piuttosto

somewhere ['sʌmwɛə*] adv in or da qualche parte

son [sʌn] n figlio

song [sɒŋ] n canzone f

sonic ['sɒnɪk] adj (boom) sonico(a)

son-in-law n genero

sonnet ['sɒnɪt] *n* sonetto

sonny ['sʌnɪ] (*inf*) *n* ragazzo mio

soon [suːn] *adv* presto, fra poco; (*early, a short time after*) presto; **~ afterwards** poco dopo; *see also* **as;** **~er** *adv* (*time*) prima; (*preference*): **I would ~er do** preferirei fare; **~er or later** prima o poi

soot [sʊt] *n* fuliggine *f*

soothe [suːð] *vt* calmare

sophisticated [sə'fɪstɪkeɪtɪd] *adj* sofisticato(a); raffinato(a); complesso(a)

sophomore ['sɒfəmɔː*] (*US*) *n* studente/ essa del secondo anno

sopping ['sɒpɪŋ] *adj* (*also:* **~ wet**) bagnato(a) fradicio(a)

soppy ['sɒpɪ] (*pej*) *adj* sentimentale

soprano [sə'prɑːnəʊ] *n* (*voice*) soprano *m*; (*singer*) soprano *m/f*

sorcerer ['sɔːsərə*] *n* stregone *m*, mago

sore [sɔː*] *adj* (*painful*) dolorante ♦ *n* piaga; **~ly** *adv* (*tempted*) fortemente

sorrow ['sɒrəʊ] *n* dolore *m*; **~ful** *adj* doloroso(a)

sorry ['sɒrɪ] *adj* spiacente; (*condition, excuse*) misero(a); **~!** scusa! (*or* scusi! *or* scusate!); **to feel ~ for sb** rincrescersi per qn

sort [sɔːt] *n* specie *f*, genere *m* ♦ *vt* (*also:* **~ out:** *papers*) classificare; ordinare; (: *letters etc*) smistare; (: *problems*) risolvere; **~ing office** *n* ufficio *m* smistamento *inv*

SOS *n abbr* (= *save our souls*) S.O.S. *m inv*

so-so *adv* così così

sought [sɔːt] *pt, pp of* **seek**

soul [səʊl] *n* anima; **~ful** *adj* pieno(a) di sentimento

sound [saʊnd] *adj* (*healthy*) sano(a); (*safe, not damaged*) solido(a), in buono stato; (*reliable, not superficial*) solido(a); (*sensible*) giudizioso(a), di buon senso ♦ *adv:* **~ asleep** profondamente addormentato ♦ *n* suono; (*noise*) rumore *m*; (*GEO*) stretto ♦ *vt* (*alarm*) suonare ♦ *vi* suonare; (*fig: seem*) sembrare; **to ~ like** rassomigliare a; **~ out** *vt* sondare; **~ barrier** *n* muro del suono; **~bite** *n* dichiarazione breve ed incisiva (*trasmessa per radio o per TV*); **~ effects** *npl* effetti sonori; **~ly** *adv* (*sleep*)

profondamente; (*beat*) duramente; **~proof** *adj* insonorizzato(a), isolato(a) acusticamente; **~track** *n* (*of film*) colonna sonora

soup [suːp] *n* minestra; brodo; zuppa; **~ plate** *n* piatto fondo; **~spoon** *n* cucchiaio da minestra

sour ['saʊə*] *adj* aspro(a); (*fruit*) acerbo(a); (*milk*) acido(a); (*fig*) arcigno(a); acido(a); **it's ~ grapes** è soltanto invidia

source [sɔːs] *n* fonte *f*, sorgente *f*; (*fig*) fonte

south [saʊθ] *n* sud *m*, meridione *m*, mezzogiorno ♦ *adj* del sud, sud *inv*, meridionale ♦ *adv* verso sud; **S~ Africa** *n* Sudafrica *m*; **S~ African** *adj, n* sudafricano(a); **S~ America** *n* Sudamerica *m*, America del sud; **S~ American** *adj, n* sudamericano(a); **~-east** *n* sud-est *m*; **~erly** ['sʌðəlɪ] *adj* del sud; **~ern** ['sʌðən] *adj* del sud, meridionale; esposto(a) a sud; **S~ Pole** *n* Polo Sud; **~ward(s)** *adv* verso sud; **~-west** *n* sud-ovest *m*

souvenir [suːvə'nɪə*] *n* ricordo, souvenir *m inv*

sovereign ['sɒvrɪn] *adj, n* sovrano(a)

soviet ['səʊvɪət] *adj* sovietico(a); **the S~ Union** l'Unione *f* Sovietica

sow[1] [səʊ] (*pt* **~ed,** *pp* **sown**) *vt* seminare

sow[2] [saʊ] *n* scrofa

sown [səʊn] *pp of* **sow**

soy [sɔɪ] (*US*) *n* = **soya**

soya ['sɔɪə] (*US* **soy**) *n:* **~ bean** *n* seme *m* di soia; **~ sauce** *n* salsa di soia

spa [spɑː] *n* (*resort*) stazione *f* termale; (*US: also:* **health ~**) centro di cure estetiche

space [speɪs] *n* spazio; (*room*) posto; spazio; (*length of time*) intervallo ♦ *cpd* spaziale ♦ *vt* (*also:* **~ out**) distanziare; **~craft** *n inv* veicolo spaziale; **~man/woman** (*irreg*) *n* astronauta *m/f*, cosmonauta *m/f*; **~ship** *n* = **~craft**; **spacing** *n* spaziatura

spacious ['speɪʃəs] *adj* spazioso(a), ampio(a)

spade [speɪd] *n* (*tool*) vanga; pala; (*child's*) paletta; **~s** *npl* (*CARDS*) picche *fpl*

Spain [speɪn] n Spagna
span [spæn] n (of bird, plane) apertura alare; (of arch) campata; (in time) periodo; durata ♦ vt attraversare; (fig) abbracciare
Spaniard ['spænjəd] n spagnolo/a
spaniel ['spænjəl] n spaniel m inv
Spanish ['spænɪʃ] adj spagnolo(a) ♦ n (LING) spagnolo; **the ~** npl gli Spagnoli
spank [spæŋk] vt sculacciare
spanner ['spænə*] (BRIT) n chiave f inglese
spare [speə*] adj di riserva, di scorta; (surplus) in più, d'avanzo ♦ n (part) pezzo di ricambio ♦ vt (do without) fare a meno di; (afford to give) concedere; (refrain from hurting, using) risparmiare; **to ~** (surplus) d'avanzo; **~ part** n pezzo di ricambio; **~ time** n tempo libero; **~ wheel** n (AUT) ruota di scorta
sparingly ['speərɪŋlɪ] adv moderatamente
spark [spɑːk] n scintilla; **~(ing) plug** n candela
sparkle ['spɑːkl] n scintillio, sfavillio ♦ vi scintillare, sfavillare; **sparkling** adj scintillante, sfavillante; (conversation, wine, water) frizzante
sparrow ['spærəu] n passero
sparse [spɑːs] adj sparso(a), rado(a)
spartan ['spɑːtən] adj (fig) spartano(a)
spasm ['spæzəm] n (MED) spasmo; (fig) accesso, attacco; **~odic** [spæz'mɔdɪk] adj spasmodico(a); (fig) intermittente
spastic ['spæstɪk] n spastico/a
spat [spæt] pt, pp of **spit**
spate [speɪt] n (fig): **~ of** diluvio or fiume m di
spawn [spɔːn] vi deporre le uova ♦ n uova fpl
speak [spiːk] (pt **spoke**, pp **spoken**) vt (language) parlare; (truth) dire ♦ vi parlare; **to ~ to sb/of or about sth** parlare a qn/di qc; **~ up!** parla più forte!; **~er** n (in public) oratore/trice; (also: **loud~er**) altoparlante m; (POL): **the S~er** il presidente della Camera dei Comuni (BRIT) or dei Rappresentanti (US)
spear [spɪə*] n lancia ♦ vt infilzare; **~head** vt (attack etc) condurre

spec [spek] (inf) n: **on ~** sperando bene
special ['speʃl] adj speciale; **~ist** n specialista m/f; **~ity** [speʃɪˈælɪtɪ] n specialità f inv; **~ize** vi: **to ~ize (in)** specializzarsi (in); **~ly** adv specialmente, particolarmente; **~ needs** adj: **~ needs children** bambini mpl con difficoltà di apprendimento; **~ty** n = **speciality**
species ['spiːʃiːz] n inv specie f inv
specific [spə'sɪfɪk] adj specifico(a); preciso(a); **~ally** adv esplicitamente; (especially) appositamente
specimen ['spesɪmən] n esemplare m, modello; (MED) campione m
speck [spek] n puntino, macchiolina; (particle) granello
speckled ['spekld] adj macchiettato(a)
specs [speks] (inf) npl occhiali mpl
spectacle ['spektəkl] n spettacolo; **~s** npl (glasses) occhiali mpl; **spectacular** [-ˈtækjulə*] adj spettacolare
spectator [spek'teɪtə*] n spettatore m
spectra ['spektrə] npl of **spectrum**
spectre ['spektə*] (US **specter**) n spettro
spectrum ['spektrəm] (pl **spectra**) n spettro
speculation [spekjuˈleɪʃən] n speculazione f; congettura fpl
speech [spiːtʃ] n (faculty) parola; (talk, THEATRE) discorso; (manner of speaking) parlata; **~less** adj ammutolito(a), muto(a)
speed [spiːd] n velocità f inv; (promptness) prontezza; **at full** or **top ~** a tutta velocità; **~ up** vi, vt accelerare; **~boat** n motoscafo; **~ily** adv velocemente; prontamente; **~ing** n (AUT) eccesso di velocità; **~ limit** n limite m di velocità; **~ometer** [spɪ'dɔmɪtə*] n tachimetro; **~way** n (sport) corsa motociclistica (su pista); **~y** adj veloce, rapido(a); pronto(a)
spell [spel] (pt, pp **spelt** (BRIT) or **~ed**) n (also: **magic ~**) incantesimo; (period of time) (breve) periodo ♦ vt (in writing) scrivere (lettera per lettera); (aloud) dire lettera per lettera; (fig) significare; **to cast a ~ on sb** fare un incantesimo a qn; **he can't ~** fa errori di ortografia; **~bound** adj

incantato(a); affascinato(a); ~ing n ortografia; spelt (BRIT) pt, pp of spell

spend [spɛnd] (pt, pp spent) vt (money) spendere; (time, life) passare; ~thrift n spendaccione/a; spent pt, pp of spend

sperm [spə:m] n sperma m

sphere [sfɪə*] n sfera

spice [spaɪs] n spezia ♦ vt aromatizzare

spicy ['spaɪsɪ] adj piccante

spider ['spaɪdə*] n ragno

spike [spaɪk] n punta

spill [spɪl] (pt, pp spilt or ~ed) vt versare, rovesciare ♦ vi versarsi, rovesciarsi; ~ over vi (liquid) versarsi; (crowd) riversarsi; spilt pt, pp of spill

spin [spɪn] (pt, pp spun) n (revolution of wheel) rotazione f; (AVIAT) avvitamento; (trip in car) giretto ♦ vt (wool etc) filare; (wheel) far girare ♦ vi girare

spinach ['spɪnɪtʃ] n spinacio; (as food) spinaci mpl

spinal ['spaɪnl] adj spinale; ~ cord n midollo spinale

spin doctor (inf) n esperto di comunicazioni responsabile dell'immagine di un partito politico

spin-dryer (BRIT) n centrifuga

spine [spaɪn] n spina dorsale; (thorn) spina

spinning ['spɪnɪŋ] n filatura; ~ top n trottola

spin-off n (product) prodotto secondario

spinster ['spɪnstə*] n nubile f; zitella

spiral ['spaɪərl] n spirale f ♦ vi (fig) salire a spirale; ~ staircase n scala a chiocciola

spire ['spaɪə*] n guglia

spirit ['spɪrɪt] n spirito; (ghost) spirito, fantasma m; (mood) stato d'animo, umore m; (courage) coraggio; ~s npl (drink) alcolici mpl; in good ~s di buon umore; ~ed adj vivace, vigoroso(a); (horse) focoso(a); ~ level n livella a bolla (d'aria)

spiritual ['spɪrɪtjuəl] adj spirituale

spit [spɪt] (pt, pp spat) n (for roasting) spiedo; (saliva) sputo; saliva ♦ vi sputare; (fire, fat) scoppiettare

spite [spaɪt] n dispetto ♦ vt contrariare, far dispetto a; in ~ of nonostante, malgrado;

~ful adj dispettoso(a)

spittle ['spɪtl] n saliva; sputo

splash [splæʃ] n spruzzo; (sound) splash m inv; (of colour) schizzo ♦ vt spruzzare ♦ vi (also: ~ about) sguazzare

spleen [spli:n] n (ANAT) milza

splendid ['splɛndɪd] adj splendido(a), magnifico(a)

splint [splɪnt] n (MED) stecca

splinter ['splɪntə*] n scheggia ♦ vi scheggiarsi

split [splɪt] (pt, pp split) n spaccatura; (fig: division, quarrel) scissione f ♦ vt spaccare; (party) dividere; (work, profits) spartire, ripartire ♦ vi (divide) dividersi; ~ up vi (couple) separarsi, rompere; (meeting) sciogliersi

spoil [spɔɪl] (pt, pp spoilt or ~ed) vt (damage) rovinare, guastare; (mar) sciupare; (child) viziare; ~s npl bottino; ~sport n guastafeste m/f inv; spoilt pt, pp of spoil

spoke [spəuk] pt of speak ♦ n raggio

spoken ['spəukn] pp of speak

spokesman ['spəuksmən] (irreg) n portavoce m inv

spokeswoman ['spəukswumən] (irreg) n portavoce f inv

sponge [spʌndʒ] n spugna; (also: ~ cake) pan m di spagna ♦ vt spugnare, pulire con una spugna ♦ vi: to ~ off or on scroccare a; ~ bag (BRIT) n nécessaire m inv

sponsor ['spɒnsə*] n (RADIO, TV, SPORT etc) sponsor m inv; (POL: of bill) promotore/trice ♦ vt sponsorizzare; (bill) presentare; ~ship n sponsorizzazione f

spontaneous [spɒn'teɪnɪəs] adj spontaneo(a)

spooky ['spu:kɪ] (inf) adj che fa accapponare la pelle

spool [spu:l] n bobina

spoon [spu:n] n cucchiaio; ~-feed vt nutrire con il cucchiaio; (fig) imboccare; ~ful n cucchiaiata

sport [spɔ:t] n sport m inv; (person) persona di spirito ♦ vt sfoggiare; ~ing adj sportivo(a); to give sb a ~ing chance dare a qn una possibilità (di vincere); ~ **jacket** (*US*) n = ~**s jacket**; ~**s car** n automobile f sportiva; ~**s jacket** (*BRIT*) *n* giacca sportiva; ~**sman** (*irreg*) *n* sportivo; ~**smanship** *n* spirito sportivo; ~**swear** *n* abiti *mpl* sportivi; ~**swoman** (*irreg*) *n* sportiva; ~**y** *adj* sportivo(a)

spot [spɔt] *n* punto; (*mark*) macchia; (*dot: on pattern*) pallino; (*pimple*) foruncolo; (*place*) posto; (*RADIO, TV*) spot *m inv*; (*small amount*): **a ~ of** un po' di ♦ *vt* (*notice*) individuare, distinguere; **on the ~** sul posto; (*immediately*) su due piedi; (*in difficulty*) nei guai; ~ **check** *n* controllo senza preavviso; ~**less** *adj* immacolato(a); ~**light** *n* proiettore *m*; (*AUT*) faro ausiliario; ~**ted** *adj* macchiato(a); a puntini, a pallini; ~**ty** *adj* (*face*) foruncoloso(a)

spouse [spauz] *n* sposo/a

spout [spaut] *n* (*of jug*) beccuccio; (*of pipe*) scarico ♦ *vi* zampillare

sprain [sprein] *n* storta, distorsione *f* ♦ *vt*: **to ~ one's ankle** storcersi una caviglia

sprang [spræŋ] *pt of* **spring**

sprawl [sprɔːl] *vi* sdraiarsi (in modo scomposto); (*place*) estendersi (disordinatamente)

spray [sprei] *n* spruzzo; (*container*) nebulizzatore *m*, spray *m inv*; (*of flowers*) mazzetto ♦ *vt* spruzzare; (*crops*) irrorare

spread [spred] (*pt, pp* **spread**) *n* diffusione *f*; (*distribution*) distribuzione *f*; (*CULIN*) pasta (da spalmare); (*inf: food*) banchetto ♦ *vt* (*cloth*) stendere, distendere; (*butter etc*) spalmare; (*disease, knowledge*) propagare, diffondere ♦ *vi* stendersi, distendersi; spalmarsi; propagarsi, diffondersi; ~ **out** *vi* (*move apart*) separarsi; ~**eagled** ['spredi:gld] *adj* a gambe e braccia aperte; ~**sheet** *n* foglio elettronico ad espansione

spree [spriː] *n*: **to go on a ~** fare baldoria

sprightly ['spraitli] *adj* vivace

spring [spriŋ] (*pt* **sprang**, *pp* **sprung**) *n* (*leap*) salto, balzo; (*coiled metal*) molla; (*season*) primavera; (*of water*) sorgente *f* ♦ *vi* saltare, balzare; ~ **up** *vi* (*problem*) presentarsi; ~**board** *n* trampolino; ~-

clean(ing) *n* grandi pulizie *fpl* di primavera; ~**time** *n* primavera

sprinkle ['spriŋkl] *vt* spruzzare; spargere; **to ~ water** *etc* **on**, ~ **with water** *etc* spruzzare dell'acqua *etc* su; ~**r** *n* (*for lawn*) irrigatore *m*; (*to put out fire*) sprinkler *m inv*

sprint [sprint] *n* scatto ♦ *vi* scattare; ~**er** *n* (*SPORT*) velocista *m/f*

sprout [spraut] *vi* germogliare; ~**s** *npl* (*also:* **Brussels ~s**) cavolini *mpl* di Bruxelles

spruce [spruːs] *n inv* abete *m* rosso ♦ *adj* lindo(a); azzimato(a)

sprung [sprʌŋ] *pp of* **spring**

spun [spʌn] *pt, pp of* **spin**

spur [spəː*] *n* sperone *m*; (*fig*) sprone *m*, incentivo ♦ *vt* (*also:* ~ **on**) spronare; **on the ~ of the moment** lì per lì

spurious ['spjuəriəs] *adj* falso(a)

spurn [spəːn] *vt* rifiutare con disprezzo, sdegnare

spurt [spəːt] *n* (*of water*) getto; (*of energy*) scatto ♦ *vi* sgorgare

spy [spai] *n* spia ♦ *vi*: **to ~ on** spiare ♦ *vt* (*see*) scorgere; ~**ing** *n* spionaggio

sq. *abbr* = **square**

squabble ['skwɔbl] *vi* bisticciarsi

squad [skwɔd] *n* (*MIL*) plotone *m*; (*POLICE*) squadra

squadron ['skwɔdrn] *n* (*MIL*) squadrone *m*; (*AVIAT, NAUT*) squadriglia

squalid ['skwɔlid] *adj* squallido(a)

squall [skwɔːl] *n* raffica; burrasca

squalor ['skwɔlə*] *n* squallore *m*

squander ['skwɔndə*] *vt* dissipare

square [skwɛə*] *n* quadrato; (*in town*) piazza ♦ *adj* quadrato(a); (*inf: ideas, person*) di vecchio stampo ♦ *vt* (*arrange*) regolare; (*MATH*) elevare al quadrato; (*reconcile*) conciliare; **all ~** pari; **a ~ meal** un pasto abbondante; **2 metres ~** di 2 metri per 2; **1 ~ metre** 1 metro quadrato; ~**ly** *adv* diritto; fermamente

squash [skwɔʃ] *n* (*SPORT*) squash *m*; (*BRIT: drink*): **lemon/orange ~** sciroppo di limone/arancia; (*US*) zucca; (*SPORT*) squash *m* ♦ *vt* schiacciare

squat [skwɔt] *adj* tarchiato(a), tozzo(a) ♦ *vi*

(*also*: **~ down**) accovacciarsi; **~ter** *n* occupante *m/f* abusivo(a)

squeak [skwi:k] *vi* squittire

squeal [skwi:l] *vi* strillare

squeamish ['skwi:mɪʃ] *adj* schizzinoso(a); disgustato(a)

squeeze [skwi:z] *n* pressione *f*; (*also* ECON) stretta ♦ *vt* premere; (*hand, arm*) stringere; **~ out** *vt* spremere

squelch [skwɛltʃ] *vi* fare ciac; sguazzare

squid [skwɪd] *n* calamaro

squiggle ['skwɪgl] *n* ghirigoro

squint [skwɪnt] *vi* essere strabico(a) ♦ *n*: **he has a ~** è strabico

squirm [skwə:m] *vi* contorcersi

squirrel ['skwɪrəl] *n* scoiattolo

squirt [skwə:t] *vi* schizzare; zampillare ♦ *vt* spruzzare

Sr *abbr* = **senior**

St *abbr* = **saint; street**

stab [stæb] *n* (*with knife etc*) pugnalata; (*of pain*) fitta; (*inf: try*): **to have a ~ at (doing) sth** provare a (fare) qc ♦ *vt* pugnalare

stable ['steɪbl] *n* (*for horses*) scuderia; (*for cattle*) stalla ♦ *adj* stabile

stack [stæk] *n* catasta, pila ♦ *vt* accatastare, ammucchiare

stadium ['steɪdɪəm] *n* stadio

staff [stɑ:f] *n* (*work force: gen*) personale *m*; (*: BRIT: SCOL*) personale insegnante ♦ *vt* fornire di personale

stag [stæg] *n* cervo

stage [steɪdʒ] *n* palcoscenico; (*profession*): **the ~** il teatro, la scena; (*point*) punto; (*platform*) palco ♦ *vt* (*play*) allestire, mettere in scena; (*demonstration*) organizzare; **in ~s** per gradi; a tappe; **~coach** *n* diligenza; **~ manager** *n* direttore *m* di scena

stagger ['stægə*] *vi* barcollare ♦ *vt* (*person*) sbalordire; (*hours, holidays*) scaglionare; **~ing** *adj* (*amazing*) sbalorditivo(a)

stagnate [stæg'neɪt] *vi* stagnare

stag party *n* festa di addio al celibato

staid [steɪd] *adj* posato(a), serio(a)

stain [steɪn] *n* macchia; (*colouring*) colorante *m* ♦ *vt* macchiare; (*wood*) tingere; **~ed**

glass window *n* vetrata; **~less** *adj* (*steel*) inossidabile; **~ remover** *n* smacchiatore *m*

stair [steə*] *n* (*step*) gradino; **~s** *npl* (*flight of ~s*) scale *fpl*, scala; **~case** *n* scale *fpl*, scala; **~way** *n* = **~case**

stake [steɪk] *n* palo, piolo; (*COMM*) interesse *m*; (*BETTING*) puntata, scommessa ♦ *vt* (*bet*) scommettere; (*risk*) rischiare; **to be at ~** essere in gioco

stale [steɪl] *adj* (*bread*) raffermo(a); (*food*) stantio(a); (*air*) viziato(a); (*beer*) svaporato(a); (*smell*) di chiuso

stalemate ['steɪlmeɪt] *n* stallo; (*fig*) punto morto

stalk [stɔ:k] *n* gambo, stelo ♦ *vt* inseguire; **~ off** *vi* andarsene impettito(a)

stall [stɔ:l] *n* bancarella; (*in stable*) box *m inv* di stalla ♦ *vt* (*AUT*) far spegnere; (*fig*) bloccare ♦ *vi* (*AUT*) spegnersi, fermarsi; (*fig*) temporeggiare; **~s** *npl* (*BRIT: in cinema, theatre*) platea

stallion ['stælɪən] *n* stallone *m*

stalwart ['stɔ:lwət] *adj* fidato(a); risoluto(a)

stamina ['stæmɪnə] *n* vigore *m*, resistenza

stammer ['stæmə*] *n* balbuzie *f* ♦ *vi* balbettare

stamp [stæmp] *n* (*postage ~*) francobollo; (*implement*) timbro; (*mark, also fig*) marchio, impronta; (*on document*) bollo; timbro ♦ *vi* (*also*: **~ one's foot**) battere il piede ♦ *vt* battere; (*letter*) affrancare; (*mark with a ~*) timbrare; **~ album** *n* album *m inv* per francobolli; **~ collecting** *n* filatelia

stampede [stæm'pi:d] *n* fuggi fuggi *m inv*

stance [stæns] *n* posizione *f*

stand [stænd] (*pt, pp* **stood**) *n* (*position*) posizione *f*; (*for taxis*) posteggio; (*structure*) supporto, sostegno; (*at exhibition*) stand *m inv*; (*in shop*) banco; (*at market*) bancarella; (*booth*) chiosco; (*SPORT*) tribuna ♦ *vi* stare in piedi; (*rise*) alzarsi in piedi; (*be placed*) trovarsi ♦ *vt* (*place*) mettere, porre; (*tolerate, withstand*) resistere, sopportare; (*treat*) offrire; **to make a ~** prendere posizione; **to ~ for parliament** (*BRIT*) presentarsi come candidato (per il parlamento); ~ **by** vi (be ready) tenersi pronto(a) ♦ vt fus (opinion) sostenere; ~ **down** vi (withdraw) ritirarsi; ~ **for** vt fus (signify) rappresentare, significare; (tolerate) sopportare, tollerare; ~ **in for** vt fus sostituire; ~ **out** vi (be prominent) spiccare; ~ **up** vi (rise) alzarsi in piedi; ~ **up for** vt fus difendere; ~ **up to** vt fus tener testa a, resistere a

standard ['stændəd] n modello, standard m inv; (level) livello; (flag) stendardo ♦ adj (size etc) normale, standard inv; ~**s** npl (morals) principi mpl, valori mpl; ~ **lamp** (BRIT) n lampada a stelo; ~ **of living** n livello di vita

stand-by n riserva, sostituto; **to be on** ~ (gen) tenersi pronto(a); (doctor) essere di guardia; ~ **ticket** n (AVIAT) biglietto senza garanzia

stand-in n sostituto/a

standing ['stændɪŋ] adj diritto(a), in piedi; (permanent) permanente ♦ n rango, condizione f, posizione f; **of many years'** ~ che esiste da molti anni; ~ **joke** n barzelletta; ~ **order** (BRIT) n (at bank) ordine m di pagamento (permanente); ~ **room** n posto all'impiedi

standpoint ['stændpɔɪnt] n punto di vista

standstill ['stændstɪl] n: **at a** ~ fermo(a); (fig) a un punto morto; **to come to a** ~ fermarsi; giungere a un punto morto

stank [stæŋk] pt of **stink**

staple ['steɪpl] n (for papers) graffetta ♦ adj (food etc) di base ♦ vt cucire; ~**r** n cucitrice f

star [stɑː*] n stella; (celebrity) divo/a ♦ vi: **to** ~ **(in)** essere il (or la) protagonista (di) ♦ vt (CINEMA) essere interpretato(a) da

starboard ['stɑːbəd] n dritta

starch [stɑːtʃ] n amido

stardom ['stɑːdəm] n celebrità

stare [stɛə*] n sguardo fisso ♦ vi: **to** ~ **at** fissare

starfish ['stɑːfɪʃ] n stella di mare

stark [stɑːk] adj (bleak) desolato(a) ♦ adv: ~ **naked** completamente nudo(a)

starling ['stɑːlɪŋ] n storno

starry ['stɑːrɪ] adj stellato(a); ~-**eyed** adj (innocent) ingenuo(a)

start [stɑːt] n inizio; (of race) partenza; (sudden movement) sobbalzo; (advantage) vantaggio ♦ vt cominciare, iniziare; (car) mettere in moto ♦ vi cominciare; (on journey) partire, mettersi in viaggio; (jump) sobbalzare; **to** ~ **doing** or **to do sth** (in)cominciare a fare qc; ~ **off** vi cominciare; (leave) partire; ~ **up** vi cominciare; (car) avviarsi ♦ vt iniziare; (car) avviare; ~**er** n (AUT) motorino d'avviamento; (SPORT: official) starter m inv; (BRIT: CULIN) primo piatto; ~**ing point** n punto di partenza

startle ['stɑːtl] vt far trasalire; **startling** adj sorprendente

starvation [stɑːˈveɪʃən] n fame f, inedia

starve [stɑːv] vi morire di fame; soffrire la fame ♦ vt far morire di fame, affamare

state [steɪt] n stato ♦ vt dichiarare, affermare; annunciare; **the S~s** (USA) gli Stati Uniti; **to be in a** ~ essere agitato(a); ~**ly** adj maestoso(a), imponente; ~**ly home** n residenza nobiliare (d'interesse storico e artistico); ~**ment** n dichiarazione f; ~**sman** (irreg) n statista m

static ['stætɪk] n (RADIO) scariche fpl ♦ adj statico(a)

station ['steɪʃən] n stazione f ♦ vt collocare, disporre

stationary ['steɪʃənərɪ] adj fermo(a), immobile

stationer ['steɪʃənə*] n cartolaio/a; ~'**s (shop)** n cartoleria; ~**y** n articoli mpl di cancelleria

station master n (RAIL) capostazione m

station wagon (US) n giardinetta

statistic [stəˈtɪstɪk] n statistica; ~**s** n (science) statistica

statue ['stætjuː] n statua

status ['steɪtəs] n posizione f, condizione f sociale; prestigio; stato; ~ **symbol** n simbolo di prestigio

statute ['stætjuːt] n legge f; **statutory** adj stabilito(a) dalla legge, statutario(a)

staunch [stɔːntʃ] *adj* fidato(a), leale

stay [steɪ] *n* (*period of time*) soggiorno, permanenza ♦ *vi* rimanere; (*reside*) alloggiare, stare; (*spend some time*) trattenersi, soggiornare; **to ~ put** non muoversi; **to ~ the night** fermarsi per la notte; **~ behind** *vi* restare indietro; **~ in** *vi* (*at home*) stare in casa; **~ on** *vi* restare, rimanere; **~ out** *vi* (*of house*) rimanere fuori (di casa); **~ up** *vi* (*at night*) rimanere alzato(a); **~ing power** *n* capacità di resistenza

stead [stɛd] *n*: **in sb's ~** al posto di qn; **to stand sb in good ~** essere utile a qn

steadfast [ˈstɛdfɑːst] *adj* fermo(a), risoluto(a)

steadily [ˈstɛdɪlɪ] *adv* (*firmly*) saldamente; (*constantly*) continuamente; (*fixedly*) fisso; (*walk*) con passo sicuro

steady [ˈstɛdɪ] *adj* (*not wobbling*) fermo(a); (*regular*) costante; (*person, character*) serio(a); (: *calm*) calmo(a), tranquillo(a) ♦ *vt* stabilizzare; calmare

steak [steɪk] *n* (*meat*) bistecca; (*fish*) trancia

steal [stiːl] (*pt* **stole**, *pp* **stolen**) *vt* rubare ♦ *vi* rubare; (*move*) muoversi furtivamente

stealth [stɛlθ] *n*: **by ~** furtivamente; **~y** *adj* furtivo(a)

steam [stiːm] *n* vapore *m* ♦ *vt* (*CULIN*) cuocere a vapore ♦ *vi* fumare; **~ engine** *n* macchina a vapore; (*RAIL*) locomotiva a vapore; **~er** *n* piroscafo, vapore *m*; **~roller** *n* rullo compressore; **~ship** *n* = **~er**; **~y** *adj* (*room*) pieno(a) di vapore; (*window*) appannato(a)

steel [stiːl] *n* acciaio ♦ *adj* di acciaio; **~works** *n* acciaieria

steep [stiːp] *adj* ripido(a), scosceso(a); (*price*) eccessivo(a) ♦ *vt* inzuppare; (*washing*) mettere a mollo

steeple [ˈstiːpl] *n* campanile *m*

steer [stɪə*] *vt* guidare ♦ *vi* (*NAUT: person*) governare; (*car*) guidarsi; **~ing** *n* (*AUT*) sterzo; **~ing wheel** *n* volante *m*

stem [stɛm] *n* (*of flower, plant*) stelo; (*of tree*) fusto; (*of glass*) gambo; (*of fruit, leaf*) picciolo ♦ *vt* contenere, arginare; **~ from**

vt fus provenire da, derivare da

stench [stɛntʃ] *n* puzzo, fetore *m*

stencil [ˈstɛnsl] *n* (*of metal, cardboard*) stampino, mascherina; (*in typing*) matrice *f* ♦ *vt* disegnare con stampino

stenographer [stɛˈnɔɡrəfə*] (*US*) *n* stenografo/a

step [stɛp] *n* passo; (*stair*) gradino, scalino; (*action*) mossa, azione *f* ♦ *vi*: **to ~ forward/back** fare un passo avanti/indietro; **~s** *npl* (*BRIT*) = **stepladder**; **to be in/out of ~ (with)** stare/non stare al passo (con); **~ down** *vi* (*fig*) ritirarsi; **~ on** *vt fus* calpestare; **~ up** *vt* aumentare; intensificare; **~brother** *n* fratellastro; **~daughter** *n* figliastra; **~father** *n* patrigno; **~ladder** *n* scala a libretto; **~mother** *n* matrigna; **~ping stone** *n* pietra di un guado; **~sister** *n* sorellastra; **~son** *n* figliastro

stereo [ˈstɛrɪəʊ] *n* (*system*) sistema *m* stereofonico; (*record player*) stereo *m inv* ♦ *adj* (*also*: **~phonic**) stereofonico(a)

sterile [ˈstɛraɪl] *adj* sterile; **sterilize** [ˈstɛrɪlaɪz] *vt* sterilizzare

sterling [ˈstɜːlɪŋ] *adj* (*gold, silver*) di buona lega ♦ *n* (*ECON*) (lira) sterlina; **a pound ~** una lira sterlina

stern [stɜːn] *adj* severo(a) ♦ *n* (*NAUT*) poppa

stew [stjuː] *n* stufato ♦ *vt* cuocere in umido

steward [ˈstjuːəd] *n* (*AVIAT, NAUT, RAIL*) steward *m inv*; (*in club etc*) dispensiere *m*; **~ess** *n* assistente *f* di volo, hostess *f inv*

stick [stɪk] (*pt, pp* **stuck**) *n* bastone *m*; (*of rhubarb, celery*) gambo; (*of dynamite*) candelotto ♦ *vt* (*glue*) attaccare; (*thrust*): **to ~ sth into** conficcare *or* piantare *or* infiggere qc in; (*inf: put*) ficcare; (*inf: tolerate*) sopportare ♦ *vi* attaccarsi; (*remain*) restare, rimanere; **~ out** *vi* sporgere, spuntare; **~ up** *vi* sporgere, spuntare; **~ up for** *vt fus* difendere; **~er** *n* cartellino adesivo; **~ing plaster** *n* cerotto adesivo

stick-up [stɪk] (*inf*) *n* rapina a mano armata

sticky [ˈstɪkɪ] *adj* attaccaticcio(a), vischioso(a); (*label*) adesivo(a); (*fig: situation*) difficile

stiff [stɪf] *adj* rigido(a), duro(a); (*muscle*) legato(a), indolenzito(a); (*difficult*) difficile, arduo(a); (*cold*) freddo(a), formale; (*strong*) forte; (*high: price*) molto alto(a) ♦ *adv*: **bored ~** annoiato(a) a morte; **~en** *vt* irrigidire; rinforzare ♦ *vi* irrigidirsi; indurirsi; **~ neck** *n* torcicollo

stifle ['staɪfl] *vt* soffocare

stigma ['stɪgmə] *n* (*fig*) stigma *m*

stile [staɪl] *n* cavalcasiepe *m*; cavalcasteccato

stiletto [stɪ'lɛtəu] (*BRIT*) *n* (*also*: **~ heel**) tacco a spillo

still [stɪl] *adj* fermo(a); silenzioso(a) ♦ *adv* (*up to this time, even*) ancora; (*nonetheless*) tuttavia, ciò nonostante; **~born** *adj* nato(a) morto(a); **~ life** *n* natura morta

stilt [stɪlt] *n* trampolo; (*pile*) palo

stilted ['stɪltɪd] *adj* freddo(a), formale; artificiale

stimulate ['stɪmjuleɪt] *vt* stimolare

stimuli ['stɪmjulaɪ] *npl of* **stimulus**

stimulus ['stɪmjuləs] (*pl* **stimuli**) *n* stimolo

sting [stɪŋ] (*pt, pp* **stung**) *n* puntura; (*organ*) pungiglione *m* ♦ *vt* pungere

stingy ['stɪndʒɪ] *adj* spilorcio(a), tirchio(a)

stink [stɪŋk] (*pt* **stank**, *pp* **stunk**) *n* fetore *m*, puzzo ♦ *vi* puzzare; **~ing** (*inf*) *adj* (*fig*): **a ~ing ...** uno schifo di ..., un(a) maledetto(a) ...

stint [stɪnt] *n* lavoro, compito ♦ *vi*: **to ~ on** lesinare su

stir [stəːʳ] *n* agitazione *f*, clamore *m* ♦ *vt* mescolare; (*fig*) risvegliare ♦ *vi* muoversi; **~ up** *vt* provocare, suscitare

stirrup ['stɪrəp] *n* staffa

stitch [stɪtʃ] *n* (*SEWING*) punto; (*KNITTING*) maglia; (*MED*) punto (di sutura); (*pain*) fitta ♦ *vt* cucire, attaccare; suturare

stoat [stəut] *n* ermellino

stock [stɔk] *n* riserva, provvista; (*COMM*) giacenza, stock *m inv*; (*AGR*) bestiame *m*; (*CULIN*) brodo; (*descent*) stirpe *f*; (*FINANCE*) titoli *mpl*, azioni *fpl* ♦ *adj* (*fig: reply etc*) consueto(a); classico(a) ♦ *vt* (*have in stock*) avere, vendere; **~s and shares** valori *mpl* di borsa; **in ~** in magazzino; **out of ~** esaurito(a); **~ up** *vi*: **to ~ up (with)** fare provvista (di)

stockbroker ['stɔkbrəukəʳ] *n* agente *m* di cambio

stock cube (*BRIT*) *n* dado

stock exchange *n* Borsa (valori)

stocking ['stɔkɪŋ] *n* calza

stock: ~ market *n* Borsa, mercato finanziario; **~pile** *n* riserva ♦ *vt* accumulare riserve di; **~taking** (*BRIT*) *n* (*COMM*) inventario

stocky ['stɔkɪ] *adj* tarchiato(a), tozzo(a)

stodgy ['stɔdʒɪ] *adj* pesante, indigesto(a)

stoke [stəuk] *vt* alimentare

stole [stəul] *pt of* **steal** ♦ *n* stola

stolen ['stəuln] *pp of* **steal**

stomach ['stʌmək] *n* stomaco; (*belly*) pancia ♦ *vt* sopportare, digerire; **~ ache** *n* mal *m* di stomaco

stone [stəun] *n* pietra; (*pebble*) sasso, ciottolo; (*in fruit*) nocciolo; (*MED*) calcolo; (*BRIT: weight*) = 6.348 kg.; 14 libbre ♦ *adj* di pietra ♦ *vt* lapidare; (*fruit*) togliere il nocciolo a; **~-cold** *adj* gelido(a); **~-deaf** *adj* sordo(a) come una campana; **~work** *n* muratura; **stony** *adj* sassoso(a); (*fig*) di pietra

stood [stud] *pt, pp of* **stand**

stool [stuːl] *n* sgabello

stoop [stuːp] *vi* (*also*: **have a ~**) avere una curvatura; (*also*: **~ down**) chinarsi, curvarsi

stop [stɔp] *n* arresto; (*stopping place*) fermata; (*in punctuation*) punto ♦ *vt* arrestare, fermare; (*break off*) interrompere; (*also*: **put a ~ to**) porre fine a ♦ *vi* fermarsi; (*rain, noise etc*) cessare, finire; **to ~ doing sth** cessare *or* finire di fare qc; **to ~ dead** fermarsi di colpo; **~ off** *vi* sostare brevemente; **~ up** *vt* (*hole*) chiudere, turare; **~gap** *n* tappabuchi *m inv*; **~lights** *npl* (*AUT*) stop *mpl*; **~over** *n* breve sosta; (*AVIAT*) scalo

stoppage ['stɔpɪdʒ] *n* arresto, fermata; (*of pay*) trattenuta; (*strike*) interruzione *f* del lavoro

stopper ['stɔpəʳ] *n* tappo

stop press *n* ultimissime *fpl*

stopwatch ['stɔpwɔtʃ] *n* cronometro

storage ['stɔ:rɪdʒ] *n* immagazzinamento; ~ **heater** *n* radiatore *m* elettrico che accumula calore

store [stɔ:*] *n* provvista, riserva; (*depot*) deposito; (*BRIT: department* ~) grande magazzino; (*US: shop*) negozio ♦ *vt* immagazzinare; ~**s** *npl* (*provisions*) rifornimenti *mpl*, scorte *fpl*; **in** ~ di riserva; in serbo; ~ **up** *vt* conservare; mettere in serbo; ~**room** *n* dispensa

storey ['stɔ:rɪ] (*US* **story**) *n* piano

stork [stɔ:k] *n* cicogna

storm [stɔ:m] *n* tempesta, temporale *m*, burrasca; uragano ♦ *vi* (*fig*) infuriarsi ♦ *vt* prendere d'assalto; ~**y** *adj* tempestoso(a), burrascoso(a)

story ['stɔ:rɪ] *n* storia; favola; racconto; (*US*) = **storey**; ~**book** *n* libro di racconti

stout [staut] *adj* solido(a), robusto(a); (*friend, supporter*) tenace; (*fat*) corpulento(a), grasso(a) ♦ *n* birra scura

stove [stəuv] *n* (*for cooking*) fornello; (*: small*) fornelletto; (*for heating*) stufa

stow [stəu] *vt* (*also:* ~ **away**) mettere via; ~**away** *n* passeggero(a) clandestino(a)

straddle ['strædl] *vt* stare a cavalcioni di; (*fig*) essere a cavallo di

straggle ['strægl] *vi* crescere (*or* estendersi) disordinatamente; trascinarsi; rimanere indietro; **straggly** *adj* (*hair*) in disordine

straight [streɪt] *adj* dritto(a); (*frank*) onesto(a), franco(a); (*simple*) semplice ♦ *adv* diritto; (*drink*) liscio; **to put** *or* **get** ~ mettere in ordine, mettere ordine in; ~ **away, ~ off** (*at once*) immediatamente; ~**en** *vt* (*also:* ~**en out**) raddrizzare; ~-**faced** *adj* impassibile, imperturbabile; ~**forward** *adj* semplice; onesto(a), franco(a)

strain [streɪn] *n* (*TECH*) sollecitazione *f*; (*physical*) sforzo; (*mental*) tensione *f*; (*MED*) strappo; distorsione *f*; (*streak, trace*) tendenza; elemento ♦ *vt* tendere; (*muscle*) sforzare; (*ankle*) storcere; (*resources*) pesare su; (*food*) colare; passare; ~**s** *npl* (*MUS*) note *fpl*; ~**ed** *adj* (*muscle*) stirato(a); (*laugh etc*) forzato(a); (*relations*) teso(a); ~**er** *n*

passino, colino

strait [streɪt] *n* (*GEO*) stretto; ~**s** *npl*: **to be in dire** ~**s** (*fig*) essere nei guai; ~**jacket** *n* camicia di forza; ~-**laced** *adj* bacchettone(a)

strand [strænd] *n* (*of thread*) filo; ~**ed** *adj* nei guai; senza mezzi di trasporto

strange [streɪndʒ] *adj* (*not known*) sconosciuto(a); (*odd*) strano(a), bizzarro(a); ~**ly** *adv* stranamente; ~**r** *n* sconosciuto/a; estraneo/a

strangle ['stræŋgl] *vt* strangolare; ~**hold** *n* (*fig*) stretta (mortale)

strap [stræp] *n* cinghia; (*of slip, dress*) spallina, bretella

strategic [strə'ti:dʒɪk] *adj* strategico(a)

strategy ['strætɪdʒɪ] *n* strategia

straw [strɔ:] *n* paglia; (*drinking* ~) cannuccia; **that's the last** ~! è la goccia che fa traboccare il vaso!

strawberry ['strɔ:bərɪ] *n* fragola

stray [streɪ] *adj* (*animal*) randagio(a); (*bullet*) vagante; (*scattered*) sparso(a) ♦ *vi* perdersi

streak [stri:k] *n* striscia; (*of hair*) mèche *f inv* ♦ *vt* striare, screziare ♦ *vi*: **to** ~ **past** passare come un fulmine

stream [stri:m] *n* ruscello; corrente *f*; (*of people, smoke etc*) fiume *m* ♦ *vt* (*SCOL*) dividere in livelli di rendimento ♦ *vi* scorrere; **to** ~ **in/out** entrare/uscire a fiotti

streamer ['stri:mə*] *n* (*of paper*) stella filante

streamlined ['stri:mlaɪnd] *adj* aerodinamico(a), affusolato(a)

street [stri:t] *n* strada, via; ~**car** (*US*) *n* tram *m inv*; ~ **lamp** *n* lampione *m*; ~ **plan** *n* pianta (di una città); ~**wise** (*inf*) *adj* esperto(a) dei bassifondi

strength [streŋθ] *n* forza; ~**en** *vt* rinforzare; fortificare; consolidare

strenuous ['strenjuəs] *adj* vigoroso(a), energico(a); (*tiring*) duro(a), pesante

stress [stres] *n* (*force, pressure*) pressione *f*; (*mental strain*) tensione *f*; (*accent*) accento ♦ *vt* insistere su, sottolineare; accentare

stretch [stretʃ] *n* (*of sand etc*) distesa ♦ *vi* stirarsi; (*extend*): **to** ~ **to** *or* **as far as**

estendersi fino a ♦ vt tendere, allungare; (spread) distendere; (fig) spingere (al massimo); ~ out vi allungarsi, estendersi ♦ vt (arm etc) allungare, tendere; (to spread) distendere

stretcher ['stretʃə*] n barella, lettiga

strewn [struːn] adj: ~ with cosparso(a) di

stricken ['strɪkən] adj (person) provato(a); (city, industry etc) colpito(a); ~ with (disease etc) colpito(a) da

strict [strɪkt] adj (severe) rigido(a), severo(a); (precise) preciso(a), stretto(a); ~ly adv severamente; rigorosamente; strettamente

stridden ['strɪdn] pp of stride

stride [straɪd] (pt strode, pp stridden) n passo lungo ♦ vi camminare a grandi passi

strife [straɪf] n conflitto; litigi mpl

strike [straɪk] (pt, pp struck) n sciopero; (of oil etc) scoperta; (attack) attacco ♦ vt colpire; (oil etc) scoprire, trovare (bargain) fare; (fig): the thought or it ~s me that ... mi viene in mente che ... ♦ vi scioperare; (attack) attaccare; (clock) suonare; on ~ (workers) in sciopero; to ~ a match accendere un fiammifero; ~ down vt (fig) atterrare; ~ up vt (MUS, conversation) attaccare; to ~ up a friendship with fare amicizia con; ~r n scioperante m/f; (SPORT) attaccante m; striking adj che colpisce

string [strɪŋ] (pt, pp strung) n spago; (row) fila; sequenza; catena; (MUS) corda ♦ vt: to ~ out disporre di fianco; to ~ together (words, ideas) mettere insieme; the ~s npl (MUS) gli archi; to pull ~s for sb (fig) raccomandare qn; ~ bean n fagiolino; ~(ed) instrument n (MUS) strumento a corda

stringent ['strɪndʒənt] adj rigoroso(a)

strip [strɪp] n striscia ♦ vt spogliare; (paint) togliere; (also: ~ down: machine) smontare ♦ vi spogliarsi; ~ cartoon n fumetto

stripe [straɪp] n striscia, riga; (MIL, POLICE) gallone m; ~d adj a strisce or righe

strip lighting n illuminazione f al neon

stripper ['strɪpə*] n spogliarellista m/f

strip-search ['strɪpsəːtʃ] vt: to ~ sb perquisire qn facendolo(a) spogliare ♦ n

perquisizione (facendo spogliare il perquisto)

striptease ['strɪptiːz] n spogliarello

strive [straɪv] (pt strove, pp striven) vi: to ~ to do sforzarsi di fare; striven ['strɪvn] pp of strive

strode [strəud] pt of stride

stroke [strəuk] n colpo; (SWIMMING) bracciata; (: style) stile m; (MED) colpo apoplettico ♦ vt accarezzare; at a ~ in un attimo

stroll [strəul] n giretto, passeggiatina ♦ vi andare a spasso; ~er n (US) passeggino

strong [strɔŋ] adj (gen) forte; (sturdy: table, fabric etc) robusto(a); they are 50 ~ sono in 50; ~box n cassaforte f; ~hold n (also fig) roccaforte f; ~ly adv fortemente, con forza; energicamente; vivamente; ~room n camera di sicurezza

strove [strəuv] pt of strive

struck [strʌk] pt, pp of strike

structural ['strʌktʃərəl] adj strutturale

structure ['strʌktʃə*] n struttura; (building) costruzione f, fabbricato

struggle ['strʌgl] n lotta ♦ vi lottare

strum [strʌm] vt (guitar) strimpellare

strung [strʌŋ] pt, pp of string

strut [strʌt] n sostegno, supporto ♦ vi pavoneggiarsi

stub [stʌb] n mozzicone m; (of ticket etc) matrice f, talloncino ♦ vt: to ~ one's toe urtare or sbattere il dito del piede; ~ out vt schiacciare

stubble ['stʌbl] n stoppia; (on chin) barba ispida

stubborn ['stʌbən] adj testardo(a), ostinato(a)

stuck [stʌk] pt, pp of stick ♦ adj (jammed) bloccato(a); ~-up adj presuntuoso(a)

stud [stʌd] n bottoncino; borchia; (also: ~ earring) orecchino a pressione; (also: ~ farm) scuderia, allevamento di cavalli; (also: ~ horse) stallone m ♦ vt (fig): ~ded with tempestato(a) di

student ['stjuːdənt] n studente/essa ♦ cpd studentesco(a); universitario(a); degli studenti; ~ driver n (US) conducente m/f principiante

studio ['stju:dɪəu] *n* studio; ~ **flat** (*US* ~ **apartment**) *n* monolocale *m*

studious ['stju:dɪəs] *adj* studioso(a); (*studied*) studiato(a), voluto(a); ~**ly** *adv* (*carefully*) deliberatamente, di proposito

study ['stʌdɪ] *n* studio ♦ *vt* studiare; esaminare ♦ *vi* studiare

stuff [stʌf] *n* roba; (*substance*) sostanza, materiale *m* ♦ *vt* imbottire; (*CULIN*) farcire; (*dead animal*) impagliare; (*inf: push*) ficcare; ~**ing** *n* imbottitura; (*CULIN*) ripieno; ~**y** *adj* (*room*) mal ventilato(a), senz'aria; (*ideas*) antiquato(a)

stumble ['stʌmbl] *vi* inciampare; **to ~ across** (*fig*) imbattersi in; **stumbling block** *n* ostacolo, scoglio

stump [stʌmp] *n* ceppo; (*of limb*) moncone *m* ♦ *vt*: **to be ~ed** essere sconcertato(a)

stun [stʌn] *vt* stordire; (*amaze*) sbalordire

stung [stʌŋ] *pt, pp of* **sting**

stunk [stʌŋk] *pp of* **stink**

stunning ['stʌnɪŋ] *adj* sbalorditivo(a); (*girl etc*) fantastico(a)

stunt [stʌnt] *n* bravata; trucco pubblicitario; ~**man** (*irreg*) *n* cascatore *m*

stupefy ['stju:pɪfaɪ] *vt* stordire; intontire; (*fig*) stupire

stupendous [stju:'pɛndəs] *adj* stupendo(a), meraviglioso(a)

stupid ['stju:pɪd] *adj* stupido(a); ~**ity** [-'pɪdɪtɪ] *n* stupidità *f inv*, stupidaggine *f*

stupor ['stju:pə*] *n* torpore *m*

sturdy ['stə:dɪ] *adj* robusto(a), vigoroso(a); solido(a)

stutter ['stʌtə*] *n* balbuzie *f* ♦ *vi* balbettare

sty [staɪ] *n* (*of pigs*) porcile *m*

stye [staɪ] *n* (*MED*) orzaiolo

style [staɪl] *n* stile *m*; (*distinction*) eleganza, classe *f*; **stylish** *adj* elegante

stylus ['staɪləs] *n* (*of record player*) puntina

suave [swɑ:v] *adj* untuoso(a)

sub... [sʌb] *prefix* sub..., sotto...; ~**conscious** *adj* subcosciente ♦ *n* subcosciente *m*; ~**contract** *vt* subappaltare

subdue [səb'dju:] *vt* sottomettere, soggiogare; ~**d** *adj* pacato(a); (*light*)

attenuato(a)

subject [*n* 'sʌbdʒɪkt, *vb* səb'dʒɛkt] *n* soggetto; (*citizen etc*) cittadino/a; (*SCOL*) materia ♦ *vt*: **to ~ to** sottomettere a; esporre a; **to be ~ to** (*law*) essere sottomesso(a) a; (*disease*) essere soggetto(a) a; ~**ive** [-'dʒɛktɪv] *adj* soggettivo(a); ~ **matter** *n* argomento; contenuto

sublet [sʌb'lɛt] *vt* subaffittare

submachine gun ['sʌbmə'ʃi:n-] *n* mitra *m inv*

submarine [sʌbmə'ri:n] *n* sommergibile *m*

submerge [səb'mə:dʒ] *vt* sommergere; immergere ♦ *vi* immergersi

submission [səb'mɪʃən] *n* sottomissione *f*; (*claim*) richiesta

submissive [səb'mɪsɪv] *adj* remissivo(a)

submit [səb'mɪt] *vt* sottomettere ♦ *vi* sottomettersi

subnormal [sʌb'nɔ:məl] *adj* subnormale

subordinate [sə'bɔ:dɪnət] *adj, n* subordinato(a)

subpoena [səb'pi:nə] *n* (*LAW*) citazione *f*, mandato di comparizione

subscribe [səb'skraɪb] *vi* contribuire; **to ~ to** (*opinion*) approvare, condividere; (*fund*) sottoscrivere a; (*newspaper*) abbonarsi a; essere abbonato a; ~**r** *n* (*to periodical, telephone*) abbonato/a

subscription [səb'skrɪpʃən] *n* sottoscrizione *f*; abbonamento

subsequent ['sʌbsɪkwənt] *adj* successivo(a), seguente; conseguente; ~**ly** *adv* in seguito, successivamente

subside [səb'saɪd] *vi* cedere, abbassarsi; (*flood*) decrescere; (*wind*) calmarsi; ~**nce** [-'saɪdns] *n* cedimento, abbassamento

subsidiary [səb'sɪdɪərɪ] *adj* sussidiario(a); accessorio(a) ♦ *n* filiale *f*

subsidize ['sʌbsɪdaɪz] *vt* sovvenzionare

subsidy ['sʌbsɪdɪ] *n* sovvenzione *f*

subsistence [səb'sɪstəns] *n* esistenza; mezzi *mpl* di sostentamento; ~ **allowance** *n* indennità *f inv* di trasferta

substance ['sʌbstəns] *n* sostanza

substantial [səb'stænʃl] *adj* solido(a);

(*amount, progress etc*) notevole; (*meal*)
sostanzioso(a)
substantiate [səb'stænʃɪeɪt] *vt* comprovare
substitute ['sʌbstɪtjuːt] *n* (*person*)
sostituto/a; (*thing*) succedaneo, surrogato
♦ *vt*: **to ~ sth/sb for** sostituire qc/qn a
subterfuge ['sʌbtəfjuːdʒ] *n* sotterfugio
subterranean [sʌbtə'reɪnɪən] *adj*
sotterraneo(a)
subtitle ['sʌbtaɪtl] *n* (*CINEMA*) sottotitolo; ~d
adj sottotitolato(a)
subtle ['sʌtl] *adj* sottile; ~ty *n* sottigliezza
subtotal [sʌb'təutl] *n* somma parziale
subtract [səb'trækt] *vt* sottrarre; ~ion
[-'trækʃən] *n* sottrazione *f*
suburb ['sʌbəːb] *n* sobborgo; **the ~s** la
periferia; ~**an** [sə'bəːbən] *adj* suburbano(a);
~**ia** *n* periferia, sobborghi *mpl*
subversive [səb'vəːsɪv] *adj* sovversivo(a)
subway ['sʌbweɪ] *n* (*US: underground*)
metropolitana; (*BRIT: underpass*)
sottopassaggio
succeed [sək'siːd] *vi* riuscire; avere successo
♦ *vt* succedere a; **to ~ in doing** riuscire a
fare; ~**ing** (*following*) successivo(a)
success [sək'ses] *n* successo; ~**ful** *adj*
(*venture*) coronato(a) da successo,
riuscito(a); **to be ~ful (in doing)** riuscire (a
fare); ~**fully** *adv* con successo
succession [sək'seʃən] *n* successione *f*
successive [sək'sesɪv] *adj* successivo(a);
consecutivo(a)
succumb [sə'kʌm] *vi* soccombere
such [sʌtʃ] *adj* tale; (*of that kind*): **~ a book**
un tale libro, un libro del genere; **~ books**
tali libri, libri del genere; (*so much*): **~
courage** tanto coraggio ♦ *adv* talmente,
così; **~ a long trip** un viaggio così lungo; **~
a lot of** talmente or così tanto(a); **~ as**
(*like*) come; **as ~** come or in quanto tale;
~**-and-~** *adj* tale (*after noun*)
suck [sʌk] *vt* succhiare; (*breast, bottle*)
poppare; ~**er** *n* (*ZOOL, TECH*) ventosa; (*inf*)
gonzo/a, babbeo/a
suction ['sʌkʃən] *n* succhiamento; (*TECH*)
aspirazione *f*
sudden ['sʌdn] *adj* improvviso(a); **all of a ~**

improvvisamente, all'improvviso; ~**ly** *adv*
bruscamente, improvvisamente, di colpo
suds [sʌdz] *npl* schiuma (di sapone)
sue [suː] *vt* citare in giudizio
suede [sweɪd] *n* pelle *f* scamosciata
suet ['suːɪt] *n* grasso di rognone
suffer ['sʌfə*] *vt* soffrire, patire; (*bear*)
sopportare, tollerare ♦ *vi* soffrire; **to ~ from**
soffrire di; ~**er** *n* malato/a; ~**ing** *n*
sofferenza
suffice [sə'faɪs] *vi* essere sufficiente, bastare
sufficient [sə'fɪʃənt] *adj* sufficiente; **~
money** abbastanza soldi; ~**ly** *adv*
sufficientemente, abbastanza
suffocate ['sʌfəkeɪt] *vi* (*have difficulty
breathing*) soffocare; (*die through lack of air*)
asfissiare
sugar ['ʃugə*] *n* zucchero ♦ *vt* zuccherare; **~
beet** *n* barbabietola da zucchero; **~ cane**
n canna da zucchero
suggest [sə'dʒest] *vt* proporre, suggerire;
indicare; ~**ion** [-'dʒestʃən] *n* suggerimento,
proposta; indicazione *f*; ~**ive** (*pej*) *adj*
indecente
suicide ['suɪsaɪd] *n* (*person*) suicida *m/f*;
(*act*) suicidio; *see also* **commit**
suit [suːt] *n* (*man's*) vestito; (*woman's*)
completo, tailleur *m inv*; (*LAW*) causa;
(*CARDS*) seme *m*, colore *m* ♦ *vt* andar bene
a *or* per; essere adatto(a) a *or* per; (*adapt*):
to ~ sth to adattare qc a; **well ~ed** ben
assortito(a); ~**able** *adj* adatto(a);
appropriato(a); ~**ably** *adv* (*dress*) in modo
adatto; (*impressed*) favorevolmente
suitcase ['suːtkeɪs] *n* valigia
suite [swiːt] *n* (*of rooms*) appartamento;
(*MUS*) suite *f inv*; (*furniture*): **bedroom/
dining room ~** arredo *or* mobilia per la
camera da letto/sala da pranzo
suitor ['suːtə*] *n* corteggiatore *m*,
spasimante *m*
sulfur ['sʌlfə*] (*US*) *n* = **sulphur**
sulk [sʌlk] *vi* fare il broncio; ~**y** *adj*
imbronciato(a)
sullen ['sʌlən] *adj* scontroso(a); cupo(a)
sulphur ['sʌlfə*] (*US* **sulfur**) *n* zolfo
sultana [sʌl'tɑːnə] *n* (*fruit*) uva (secca)

sultanina

sultry ['sʌltrɪ] *adj* afoso(a)

sum [sʌm] *n* somma; (*SCOL etc*) addizione *f*; ~ **up** *vt, vi* riassumere

summarize ['sʌməraɪz] *vt* riassumere, riepilogare

summary ['sʌmərɪ] *n* riassunto

summer ['sʌmə*] *n* estate *f* ♦ *cpd* d'estate, estivo(a); ~ **holidays** *npl* vacanze *fpl* estive; ~**house** *n* (*in garden*) padiglione *m*; ~**time** *n* (*season*) estate *f*; ~ **time** *n* (*by clock*) ora legale (estiva)

summit ['sʌmɪt] *n* cima, sommità; (*POL*) vertice *m*

summon ['sʌmən] *vt* chiamare, convocare; ~ **up** *vt* raccogliere, fare appello a; ~**s** *n* ordine *m* di comparizione ♦ *vt* citare

sump [sʌmp] (*BRIT*) *n* (*AUT*) coppa dell'olio

sumptuous ['sʌmptjuəs] *adj* sontuoso(a)

sun [sʌn] *n* sole *m*; ~**bathe** *vi* prendere un bagno di sole; ~**block** *n* protezione *f* solare totale; ~**burn** *n* (*painful*) scottatura; ~**burnt** *adj* abbronzato(a); (*painfully*) scottato(a)

Sunday ['sʌndɪ] *n* domenica; ~ **school** *n* ≈ scuola di catechismo

sundial ['sʌndaɪəl] *n* meridiana

sundown ['sʌndaun] *n* tramonto

sundry ['sʌndrɪ] *adj* vari(e), diversi(e); **all and** ~ tutti quanti; **sundries** *npl* articoli diversi, cose diverse

sunflower ['sʌnflauə*] *n* girasole *m*

sung [sʌŋ] *pp of* **sing**

sunglasses ['sʌnglɑːsɪz] *npl* occhiali *mpl* da sole

sunk [sʌŋk] *pp of* **sink**

sun: ~**light** *n* (luce *f* del) sole *m*; ~**lit** *adj* soleggiato(a); ~**ny** *adj* assolato(a), soleggiato(a); (*fig*) allegro(a), felice; ~**rise** *n* levata del sole, alba; ~ **roof** *n* (*AUT*) tetto apribile; ~**screen** *n* (*protective ingredient*) filtro solare; (*cream*) crema solare protettiva; ~**set** *n* tramonto; ~**shade** *n* parasole *m*; ~**shine** *n* (luce *f* del) sole *m*; ~**stroke** *n* insolazione *f*, colpo di sole; ~**tan** *n* abbronzatura; ~**tan lotion** *n* lozione *f* solare; ~**tan oil** *n* olio solare

super ['suːpə*] (*inf*) *adj* fantastico(a)

superannuation [suːpərænjuˈeɪʃən] *n* contributi *mpl* pensionistici; pensione *f*

superb [suːˈpəːb] *adj* magnifico(a)

supercilious [suːpəˈsɪlɪəs] *adj* sprezzante, sdegnoso(a)

superficial [suːpəˈfɪʃəl] *adj* superficiale

superhuman [suːpəˈhjuːmən] *adj* sovrumano(a)

superimpose ['suːpərɪmˈpəuz] *vt* sovrapporre

superintendent [suːpərɪnˈtendənt] *n* direttore/trice; (*POLICE*) ≈ commissario (capo)

superior [suˈpɪərɪə*] *adj, n* superiore *m/f*; ~**ity** [-ˈɔrɪtɪ] *n* superiorità

superlative [suˈpəːlətɪv] *adj* superlativo(a), supremo(a) ♦ *n* (*LING*) superlativo

superman ['suːpəmæn] (*irreg*) *n* superuomo

supermarket ['suːpəmɑːkɪt] *n* supermercato

supernatural [suːpəˈnætʃərəl] *adj* soprannaturale ♦ *n* soprannaturale *m*

superpower ['suːpəpauə*] *n* (*POL*) superpotenza

supersede [suːpəˈsiːd] *vt* sostituire, soppiantare

superstitious [suːpəˈstɪʃəs] *adj* superstizioso(a)

supertanker ['suːpətæŋkə*] *n* superpetroliera

supervise ['suːpəvaɪz] *vt* (*person etc*) sorvegliare; (*organization*) soprintendere a; **supervision** [-ˈvɪʒən] *n* sorveglianza; supervisione *f*; **supervisor** *n* sorvegliante *m/f*; soprintendente *m/f*; (*in shop*) capocommesso/a

supine ['suːpaɪn] *adj* supino(a)

supper ['sʌpə*] *n* cena

supplant [səˈplɑːnt] *vt* (*person, thing*) soppiantare

supple ['sʌpl] *adj* flessibile; agile

supplement [*n* 'sʌplɪmənt, *vb* sʌplɪˈment] *n* supplemento ♦ *vt* completare, integrare; ~**ary** [-ˈmentərɪ] *adj* supplementare

supplier [səˈplaɪə*] *n* fornitore *m*

supply [səˈplaɪ] *vt* (*provide*) fornire; (*equip*):

to ~ (with) approvvigionare (di); attrezzare (con) ♦ *n* riserva, provvista; *(supplying)* approvvigionamento; *(TECH)* alimentazione *f*; **supplies** *npl (food)* viveri *mpl*; *(MIL)* sussistenza; ~ **teacher** *(BRIT)* *n* supplente *m/f*

support [sə'pɔːt] *n (moral, financial etc)* sostegno, appoggio; *(TECH)* supporto ♦ *vt* sostenere; *(financially)* mantenere; *(uphold)* sostenere, difendere; ~**er** *n (POL etc)* sostenitore/trice, fautore/trice; *(SPORT)* tifoso/a

suppose [sə'pəuz] *vt* supporre; immaginare; **to be ~d to do** essere tenuto(a) a fare; ~**dly** [sə'pəuzɪdlɪ] *adv* presumibilmente; **supposing** *conj* se, ammesso che +*sub*

suppository [sə'pɔzɪtərɪ] *n* suppositorio

suppress [sə'prɛs] *vt* reprimere; sopprimere; occultare

supreme [su'priːm] *adj* supremo(a)

surcharge ['sɜːtʃɑːdʒ] *n* supplemento

sure [ʃuə*] *adj* sicuro(a); *(definite, convinced)* sicuro(a), certo(a); ~**!** *(of course)* senz'altro!, certo!; ~ **enough** infatti; **to make ~ of sth/that** assicurarsi di qc/che; ~**-footed** *adj* dal passo sicuro; ~**ly** *adv* sicuramente; certamente

surf [sɜːf] *n (waves)* cavalloni *mpl*; *(foam)* spuma

surface ['sɜːfɪs] *n* superficie *f* ♦ *vt (road)* asfaltare ♦ *vi* risalire alla superficie; *(fig: news, feeling)* venire a galla; ~ **mail** *n* posta ordinaria

surfboard ['sɜːfbɔːd] *n* tavola per surfing

surfeit ['sɜːfɪt] *n*: **a ~ of** un eccesso di; un'indigestione di

surfing ['sɜːfɪŋ] *n* surfing *m*

surge [sɜːdʒ] *n (strong movement)* ondata; *(of feeling)* impeto ♦ *vi* gonfiarsi; *(people)* riversarsi

surgeon ['sɜːdʒən] *n* chirurgo

surgery ['sɜːdʒərɪ] *n* chirurgia; *(BRIT: room)* studio *or* gabinetto medico, ambulatorio; *(: also:* ~ **hours)** orario delle visite *or* di consultazione; **to undergo** ~ subire un intervento chirurgico

surgical ['sɜːdʒɪkl] *adj* chirurgico(a); ~

spirit *(BRIT)* *n* alcool *m* denaturato

surname ['sɜːneɪm] *n* cognome *m*

surpass [sɜː'pɑːs] *vt* superare

surplus ['sɜːpləs] *n* eccedenza; *(ECON)* surplus *m inv* ♦ *adj* eccedente, d'avanzo

surprise [sə'praɪz] *n* sorpresa; *(astonishment)* stupore *m* ♦ *vt* sorprendere; stupire; **surprising** *adj* sorprendente, stupefacente; **surprisingly** *adv (easy, helpful)* sorprendentemente

surrender [sə'rɛndə*] *n* resa, capitolazione *f* ♦ *vi* arrendersi

surreptitious [sʌrəp'tɪʃəs] *adj* furtivo(a)

surrogate ['sʌrəgɪt] *n* surrogato; ~ **mother** *n* madre *f* provetta

surround [sə'raund] *vt* circondare; *(MIL etc)* accerchiare; ~**ing** *adj* circostante; ~**ings** *npl* dintorni *mpl*; *(fig)* ambiente *m*

surveillance [sɜː'veɪləns] *n* sorveglianza, controllo

survey [*n* 'sɜːveɪ, *vb* sɜː'veɪ] *n* quadro generale; *(study)* esame *m*; *(in housebuying etc)* perizia; *(of land)* rilevamento, rilievo topografico ♦ *vt* osservare; esaminare; valutare; rilevare; ~**or** *n* perito; geometra *m*; *(of land)* agrimensore

survival [sə'vaɪvl] *n* sopravvivenza; *(relic)* reliquia, vestigio

survive [sə'vaɪv] *vi* sopravvivere ♦ *vt* sopravvivere a; **survivor** *n* superstite *m/f*, sopravvissuto/a

susceptible [sə'sɛptəbl] *adj*: ~ **(to)** sensibile (a); *(disease)* predisposto(a) (a)

suspect [*adj, n* 'sʌspɛkt, *vb* səs'pɛkt] *adj* sospetto(a) ♦ *n* persona sospetta ♦ *vt* sospettare; *(think likely)* supporre; *(doubt)* dubitare

suspend [səs'pɛnd] *vt* sospendere; ~**ed sentence** *n* condanna con la condizionale; ~**er belt** *n* reggicalze *m inv*; ~**ers** *npl (BRIT)* giarrettiere *fpl*; *(US)* bretelle *fpl*

suspense [səs'pɛns] *n* apprensione *f*; *(in film etc)* suspense *m*; **to keep sb in** ~ tenere qn in sospeso

suspension [səs'pɛnʃən] *n (gen AUT)* sospensione *f*; *(of driving licence)* ritiro temporaneo; **~ bridge** *n* ponte *m* sospeso

suspicion [səs'pɪʃən] *n* sospetto

suspicious [səs'pɪʃəs] *adj* (*suspecting*) sospettoso(a); (*causing suspicion*) sospetto(a)

sustain [səs'teɪn] *vt* sostenere; sopportare; (*LAW: charge*) confermare; (*suffer*) subire; **~able** *adj* sostenibile; **~ed** *adj* (*effort*) prolungato(a)

sustenance ['sʌstɪnəns] *n* nutrimento; mezzi *mpl* di sostentamento

swab [swɔb] *n* (*MED*) tampone *m*

swagger ['swægə*] *vi* pavoneggiarsi

swallow ['swɔləu] *n* (*bird*) rondine *f* ♦ *vt* inghiottire; (*fig: story*) bere; **~ up** *vt* inghiottire

swam [swæm] *pt of* **swim**

swamp [swɔmp] *n* palude *f* ♦ *vt* sommergere

swan [swɔn] *n* cigno

swap [swɔp] *vt*: **to ~ (for)** scambiare (con)

swarm [swɔːm] *n* sciame *m* ♦ *vi* (*bees*) sciamare; (*people*) brulicare; (*place*): **to be ~ing with** brulicare di

swastika ['swɔstɪkə] *n* croce *f* uncinata, svastica

swat [swɔt] *vt* schiacciare

sway [sweɪ] *vi* (*tree*) ondeggiare; (*person*) barcollare ♦ *vt* (*influence*) influenzare, dominare

swear [swɛə*] (*pt* **swore**, *pp* **sworn**) *vi* (*curse*) bestemmiare, imprecare ♦ *vt* (*promise*) giurare; **~word** *n* parolaccia

sweat [swɛt] *n* sudore *m*, traspirazione *f* ♦ *vi* sudare

sweater ['swɛtə*] *n* maglione *m*

sweatshirt ['swɛtʃəːt] *n* felpa

sweaty ['swɛtɪ] *adj* sudato(a); bagnato(a) di sudore

Swede [swiːd] *n* svedese *m/f*

swede [swiːd] (*BRIT*) *n* rapa svedese

Sweden ['swiːdn] *n* Svezia

Swedish ['swiːdɪʃ] *adj* svedese ♦ *n* (*LING*) svedese *m*

sweep [swiːp] (*pt*, *pp* **swept**) *n* spazzata; (*also*: **chimney ~**) spazzacamino ♦ *vt* spazzare, scopare; (*current*) spazzare ♦ *vi*

(*hand*) muoversi con gesto ampio; (*wind*) infuriare; **~ away** *vt* spazzare via; trascinare via; **~ past** *vi* sfrecciare accanto; passare accanto maestosamente; **~ up** *vt*, *vi* spazzare; **~ing** *adj* (*gesture*) ampio(a); circolare; **a ~ing statement** un'affermazione generica

sweet [swiːt] *n* (*BRIT: pudding*) dolce *m*; (*candy*) caramella ♦ *adj* dolce; (*fresh*) fresco(a); (*fig*) piacevole; delicato(a), grazioso(a); gentile; **~corn** *n* granturco dolce; **~en** *vt* addolcire; zuccherare; **~heart** *n* innamorato/a; **~ness** *n* sapore *m* dolce; dolcezza; **~ pea** *n* pisello odoroso

swell [swɛl] (*pt* **~ed**, *pp* **swollen**, **~ed**) *n* (*of sea*) mare *m* lungo ♦ *adj* (*US: inf: excellent*) favoloso(a) ♦ *vt* gonfiare, ingrossare; aumentare ♦ *vi* gonfiarsi, ingrossarsi; (*sound*) crescere; (*also*: **~ up**) gonfiarsi; **~ing** *n* (*MED*) tumefazione *f*, gonfiore *m*

sweltering ['swɛltərɪŋ] *adj* soffocante

swept [swɛpt] *pt*, *pp of* **sweep**

swerve [swəːv] *vi* deviare; (*driver*) sterzare; (*boxer*) scartare

swift [swɪft] *n* (*bird*) rondone *m* ♦ *adj* rapido(a), veloce

swig [swɪg] (*inf*) *n* (*drink*) sorsata

swill [swɪl] *vt* (*also*: **~ out**, **~ down**) risciacquare

swim [swɪm] (*pt* **swam**, *pp* **swum**) *n*: **to go for a ~** andare a fare una nuotata ♦ *vi* nuotare; (*SPORT*) fare del nuoto; (*head, room*) girare ♦ *vt* (*river, channel*) attraversare *or* percorrere a nuoto; (*length*) nuotare; **~mer** *n* nuotatore/trice; **~ming** *n* nuoto; **~ming cap** *n* cuffia; **~ming costume** (*BRIT*) *n* costume *m* da bagno; **~ming pool** *n* piscina; **~ming trunks** *npl* costume *m* da bagno (da uomo); **~suit** *n* costume *m* da bagno

swindle ['swɪndl] *n* truffa ♦ *vt* truffare

swine [swaɪn] (*inf!*) *n inv* porco (!)

swing [swɪŋ] (*pt*, *pp* **swung**) *n* altalena; (*movement*) oscillazione *f*; (*MUS*) ritmo; swing *m* ♦ *vt* dondolare, far oscillare; (*also*: **~ round**) far girare ♦ *vi* oscillare, dondolare; (*also*: ~ **round**: *object*) roteare; (: *person*) girarsi, voltarsi; **to be in full ~** (*activity*) essere in piena attività; (*party etc*) essere nel pieno; ~ **door** (*US* **~ing door**) *n* porta battente

swingeing ['swɪndʒɪn] *adj* (*BRIT: defeat*) violento(a); (: *cuts*) enorme

swipe [swaɪp] *vt* (*hit*) colpire con forza; dare uno schiaffo a; (*inf: steal*) sgraffignare; **~card** *n* tessera magnetica

swirl [swəːl] *vi* turbinare, far mulinello

Swiss [swɪs] *adj, n inv* svizzero(a)

switch [swɪtʃ] *n* (*for light, radio etc*) interruttore *m*; (*change*) cambiamento ♦ *vt* (*change*) cambiare; scambiare; ~ **off** *vt* spegnere; ~ **on** *vt* accendere; (*engine, machine*) mettere in moto, avviare; **~board** *n* (*TEL*) centralino

Switzerland ['swɪtsələnd] *n* Svizzera

swivel ['swɪvl] *vi* (*also*: ~ **round**) girare

swollen ['swəulən] *pp of* **swell**

swoon [swuːn] *vi* svenire

swoop [swuːp] *n* incursione *f* ♦ *vi* (*also*: ~ *down*) scendere in picchiata, piombare

swop [swɔp] *n, vt* = **swap**

sword [sɔːd] *n* spada; **~fish** *n* pesce *m* spada *inv*

swore [swɔː*] *pt of* **swear**

sworn [swɔːn] *pp of* **swear** ♦ *adj* giurato(a)

swot [swɔt] *vi* sgobbare

swum [swʌm] *pp of* **swim**

swung [swʌŋ] *pt, pp of* **swing**

syllable ['sɪləbl] *n* sillaba

syllabus ['sɪləbəs] *n* programma *m*

symbol ['sɪmbl] *n* simbolo

symmetry ['sɪmɪtrɪ] *n* simmetria

sympathetic [sɪmpə'θɛtɪk] *adj* (*showing pity*) compassionevole; (*kind*) comprensivo(a); ~ **towards** ben disposto(a) verso

sympathize ['sɪmpəθaɪz] *vi*: **to ~ with** (*person*) compatire; partecipare al dolore di; (*cause*) simpatizzare per; **~r** *n* (*POL*) simpatizzante *m/f*

sympathy ['sɪmpəθɪ] *n* compassione *f*; **sympathies** *npl* (*support, tendencies*) simpatie *fpl*; **in ~ with** (*strike*) per

solidarietà con; **with our deepest ~** con le nostre più sincere condoglianze

symphony ['sɪmfənɪ] *n* sinfonia

symptom ['sɪmptəm] *n* sintomo; indizio

synagogue ['sɪnəgɔg] *n* sinagoga

syndicate ['sɪndɪkɪt] *n* sindacato

synopses [sɪ'nɔpsiːz] *npl of* **synopsis**

synopsis [sɪ'nɔpsɪs] (*pl* **synopses**) *n* sommario, sinossi *f inv*

syntheses ['sɪnθəsiːz] *npl of* **synthesis**

synthesis ['sɪnθəsɪs] (*pl* **syntheses**) *n* sintesi *f inv*

synthetic [sɪn'θɛtɪk] *adj* sintetico(a)

syphon ['saɪfən] *n, vb* = **siphon**

Syria ['sɪrɪə] *n* Siria

syringe [sɪ'rɪndʒ] *n* siringa

syrup ['sɪrəp] *n* sciroppo; (*also*: **golden ~**) melassa raffinata

system ['sɪstəm] *n* sistema *m*; (*order*) metodo; (*ANAT*) organismo; **~atic** [-'mætɪk] *adj* sistematico(a); metodico(a); ~ **disk** *n* (*COMPUT*) disco del sistema; **~s analyst** *n* analista *m* di sistemi

T, t

ta [taː] (*BRIT: inf*) *excl* grazie!

tab [tæb] *n* (*loop on coat etc*) laccetto; (*label*) etichetta; **to keep ~s on** (*fig*) tenere d'occhio

tabby ['tæbɪ] *n* (*also*: ~ **cat**) (gatto) soriano, gatto tigrato

table ['teɪbl] *n* tavolo, tavola; (*MATH, CHEM etc*) tavola ♦ *vt* (*BRIT: motion etc*) presentare; **to lay** *or* **set the ~** apparecchiare *or* preparare la tavola; **~cloth** *n* tovaglia; ~ **d'hôte** [taːbl'dəut] *adj* (*meal*) a prezzo fisso; ~ **lamp** *n* lampada da tavolo; **~mat** *n* sottopiatto; ~ **of contents** *n* indice *m*; **~spoon** *n* cucchiaio da tavola; (*also*: **~spoonful**: *as measurement*) cucchiaiata

tablet ['tæblɪt] *n* (*MED*) compressa; (*of stone*) targa

table: ~ **tennis** *n* tennis *m* da tavolo, ping-pong ® *m*; ~ **wine** *n* vino da tavola

---
tabloid press
---

i *Il termine* **tabloid press** *si riferisce ai giornali popolari, che hanno un formato ridotto e pubblicano le notizie in modo sensazionalistico; vedi anche* **quality press**.

---

tacit ['tæsɪt] *adj* tacito(a)

tack [tæk] *n* (*nail*) bulletta; (*fig*) approccio ♦ *vt* imbullettare; imbastire ♦ *vi* bordeggiare

tackle ['tækl] *n* attrezzatura, equipaggiamento; (*for lifting*) paranco; (*FOOTBALL*) contrasto; (*RUGBY*) placcaggio ♦ *vt* (*difficulty*) affrontare; (*FOOTBALL*) contrastare; (*RUGBY*) placcare

tacky ['tækɪ] *adj* appiccicaticcio(a); (*pej*) scadente

tact [tækt] *n* tatto; ~**ful** *adj* delicato(a), discreto(a)

tactical ['tæktɪkl] *adj* tattico(a)

tactics ['tæktɪks] *n, npl* tattica

tactless ['tæktlɪs] *adj* che manca di tatto

tadpole ['tædpəʊl] *n* girino

tag [tæg] *n* etichetta; ~ **along** *vi* seguire

tail [teɪl] *n* coda; (*of shirt*) falda ♦ *vt* (*follow*) seguire, pedinare; ~ **away** *vi* = ~ **off**; ~ **off** *vi* (*in size, quality etc*) diminuire gradatamente; ~**back** (*BRIT*) *n* (*AUT*) ingorgo; ~ **end** *n* (*of train, procession etc*) coda; (*of meeting etc*) fine *f*; ~**gate** *n* (*AUT*) portellone *m* posteriore

tailor ['teɪlə*] *n* sarto; ~**ing** *n* (*cut*) stile *m*; (*craft*) sartoria; ~-**made** *adj* (*also fig*) fatto(a) su misura

tailwind ['teɪlwɪnd] *n* vento di coda

tainted ['teɪntɪd] *adj* (*food*) guasto(a); (*water, air*) infetto(a); (*fig*) corrotto(a)

take [teɪk] (*pt* **took**, *pp* **taken**) *vt* prendere; (*gain: prize*) ottenere, vincere; (*require: effort, courage*) occorrere, volerci; (*tolerate*) accettare, sopportare; (*hold: passengers etc*) contenere; (*accompany*) accompagnare; (*bring, carry*) portare; (*exam*) sostenere, presentarsi a; **to ~ a photo/a shower** fare una fotografia/una doccia; **I ~ it that** suppongo che; ~ **after** *vt fus* assomigliare

a; ~ **apart** *vt* smontare; ~ **away** *vt* portare via; togliere; ~ **back** *vt* (*return*) restituire; riportare; (*one's words*) ritirare; ~ **down** *vt* (*building*) demolire; (*letter etc*) scrivere; ~ **in** *vt* (*deceive*) imbrogliare, abbindolare; (*understand*) capire; (*include*) comprendere, includere; (*lodger*) prendere, ospitare; ~ **off** *vi* (*AVIAT*) decollare; (*go away*) andarsene ♦ *vt* (*remove*) togliere; ~ **on** *vt* (*work*) accettare, intraprendere; (*employee*) assumere; (*opponent*) sfidare, affrontare; ~ **out** *vt* portare fuori; (*remove*) togliere; (*licence*) prendere, ottenere; **to ~ sth out of sth** (*drawer, pocket etc*) tirare qc fuori da qc; estrarre qc da qc; ~ **over** *vt* (*business*) rilevare ♦ *vi*: **to ~ over from sb** prendere le consegne *or* il controllo da qn; ~ **to** *vt fus* (*person*) prendere in simpatia; (*activity*) prendere gusto a; ~ **up** *vt* (*dress*) accorciare; (*occupy: time, space*) occupare; (*engage in: hobby etc*) mettersi a; **to ~ sb up on sth** accettare qc da qn; ~**away** (*BRIT*) *n* (*shop etc*) ≈ rosticceria; (*food*) pasto per asporto; ~**off** *n* (*AVIAT*) decollo; ~**out** (*US*) *n* = ~**away**; ~**over** *n* (*COMM*) assorbimento

takings ['teɪkɪnz] *npl* (*COMM*) incasso

talc [tælk] *n* (*also:* ~**um powder**) talco

tale [teɪl] *n* racconto, storia; **to tell ~s** (*fig: to teacher, parent etc*) fare la spia

talent ['tælnt] *n* talento; ~**ed** *adj* di talento

talk [tɔːk] *n* discorso; (*gossip*) chiacchiere *fpl*; (*conversation*) conversazione *f*; (*interview*) discussione *f* ♦ *vi* parlare; ~**s** *npl* (*POL etc*) colloqui *mpl*; **to ~ about** parlare di; **to ~ sb out of/into doing** dissuadere qn da/ convincere qn a fare; **to ~ shop** parlare di lavoro *or* di affari; ~ **over** *vt* discutere; ~**ative** *adj* loquace, ciarliero(a); ~ **show** *n* conversazione *f* televisiva, talk show *m inv*

tall [tɔːl] *adj* alto(a); **to be 6 feet ~** ≈ essere alto 1 metro e 80; ~ **story** *n* panzana, frottola

tally ['tælɪ] *n* conto, conteggio ♦ *vi*: **to ~ (with)** corrispondere (a)

talon ['tælən] *n* artiglio

tambourine [tæmbə'ri:n] *n* tamburello
tame [teɪm] *adj* addomesticato(a); (*fig: story, style*) insipido(a), scialbo(a)
tamper ['tæmpə*] *vi*: **to ~ with** manomettere
tampon ['tæmpɔn] *n* tampone *m*
tan [tæn] *n* (*also:* **sun~**) abbronzatura ♦ *vi* abbronzarsi ♦ *adj* (*colour*) marrone rossiccio *inv*
tang [tæŋ] *n* odore *m* penetrante; sapore *m* piccante
tangent ['tændʒənt] *n*: **to go off at a ~** (*fig*) partire per la tangente
tangerine [tændʒə'ri:n] *n* mandarino
tangle ['tæŋgl] *n* groviglio; **to get into a ~** aggrovigliarsi; (*fig*) combinare un pasticcio
tank [tæŋk] *n* serbatoio; (*for fish*) acquario; (*MIL*) carro armato
tanker ['tæŋkə*] *n* (*ship*) nave *f* cisterna *inv*; (*truck*) autobotte *f*, autocisterna
tanned [tænd] *adj* abbronzato(a)
tantalizing ['tæntəlaɪzɪŋ] *adj* allettante
tantamount ['tæntəmaunt] *adj*: **~ to** equivalente a
tantrum ['tæntrəm] *n* accesso di collera
tap [tæp] *n* (*on sink etc*) rubinetto; (*gentle blow*) colpetto ♦ *vt* dare un colpetto a; (*resources*) sfruttare, utilizzare; (*telephone*) mettere sotto controllo; **on ~** (*fig: resources*) a disposizione; **~ dancing** *n* tip tap *m*
tape [teɪp] *n* nastro; (*also:* **magnetic ~**) nastro (magnetico); (*sticky ~*) nastro adesivo ♦ *vt* (*record*) registrare (su nastro); (*stick*) attaccare con nastro adesivo; **~ deck** *n* piastra; **~ measure** *n* metro a nastro
taper ['teɪpə*] *n* candelina ♦ *vi* assottigliarsi
tape recorder *n* registratore *m* (a nastro)
tapestry ['tæpɪstrɪ] *n* arazzo; tappezzeria
tar [tɑ:*] *n* catrame *m*
target ['tɑ:gɪt] *n* bersaglio; (*fig: objective*) obiettivo
tariff ['tærɪf] *n* tariffa
tarmac ['tɑ:mæk] *n* (*BRIT: on road*) macadam *m* al catrame; (*AVIAT*) pista di decollo
tarnish ['tɑ:nɪʃ] *vt* offuscare, annerire; (*fig*) macchiare
tarpaulin [tɑ:'pɔ:lɪn] *n* tela incatramata
tarragon ['tærəgən] *n* dragoncello
tart [tɑ:t] *n* (*CULIN*) crostata; (*BRIT: inf: pej: woman*) sgualdrina ♦ *adj* (*flavour*) aspro(a), agro(a); **~ up** (*inf*) *vt* agghindare
tartan ['tɑ:tn] *n* tartan *m inv*
tartar ['tɑ:tə*] *n* (*on teeth*) tartaro; **~(e) sauce** *n* salsa tartara
task [tɑ:sk] *n* compito; **to take to ~** rimproverare; **~ force** *n* (*MIL, POLICE*) unità operativa
taste [teɪst] *n* gusto; (*flavour*) sapore *m*, gusto; (*sample*) assaggio; (*fig: glimpse, idea*) idea ♦ *vt* gustare; (*sample*) assaggiare ♦ *vi*: **to ~ of** *or* **like** (*fish etc*) sapere *or* avere sapore di; **you can ~ the garlic (in it)** (ci) si sente il sapore dell'aglio; **in good/bad ~** di buon/cattivo gusto; **~ful** *adj* di buon gusto; **~less** *adj* (*food*) insipido(a); (*remark*) di cattivo gusto; **tasty** *adj* saporito(a), gustoso(a)
tatters ['tætəz] *npl*: **in ~** a brandelli
tattoo [tə'tu:] *n* tatuaggio; (*spectacle*) parata militare ♦ *vt* tatuare
tatty ['tætɪ] *adj* malridotto(a)
taught [tɔ:t] *pt, pp of* **teach**
taunt [tɔ:nt] *n* scherno ♦ *vt* schernire
Taurus ['tɔ:rəs] *n* Toro
taut [tɔ:t] *adj* teso(a)
tax [tæks] *n* (*on goods*) imposta; (*on services*) tassa; (*on income*) imposte *fpl*, tasse *fpl* ♦ *vt* tassare; (*fig: strain: patience etc*) mettere alla prova; **~able** *adj* (*income*) imponibile; **~ation** [-'seɪʃən] *n* tassazione *f*; tasse *fpl*, imposte *fpl*; **~ avoidance** *n* elusione *f* fiscale; **~ disc** (*BRIT*) *n* (*AUT*) ≈ bollo; **~ evasion** *n* evasione *f* fiscale; **~-free** *adj* esente da imposte
taxi ['tæksɪ] *n* taxi *m inv* ♦ *vi* (*AVIAT*) rullare; **~ driver** *n* tassista *m/f*; **~ rank** (*BRIT*) *n* = **~ stand**; **~ stand** *n* posteggio dei taxi
tax: **~ payer** *n* contribuente *m/f*; **~ relief** *n* agevolazioni *fpl* fiscali; **~ return** *n* dichiarazione *f* dei redditi
TB *n abbr* = **tuberculosis**
tea [ti:] *n* tè *m inv*; (*BRIT: snack: for children*)

merenda; **high ~** (*BRIT*) cena leggera (*presa nel tardo pomeriggio*); **~ bag** n bustina di tè; **~ break** (*BRIT*) n intervallo per il tè

teach [tiːtʃ] (*pt, pp* **taught**) *vt*: **to ~ sb sth, ~ sth to sb** insegnare qc a qn ♦ *vi* insegnare; **~er** n insegnante *m/f*; (*in secondary school*) professore/essa; (*in primary school*) maestro/a; **~ing** n insegnamento

tea cosy n copriteiera *m inv*

teacup ['tiːkʌp] n tazza da tè

teak [tiːk] n teak *m*

tea leaves *npl* foglie *fpl* di tè

team [tiːm] n squadra; (*of animals*) tiro; **~work** n lavoro di squadra

teapot ['tiːpɔt] n teiera

tear[1] [tɛə*] (*pt* **tore**, *pp* **torn**) n strappo ♦ *vt* strappare ♦ *vi* strapparsi; **~ along** *vi* (*rush*) correre all'impazzata; **~ up** *vt* (*sheet of paper etc*) strappare

tear[2] [tɪə*] n lacrima; **in ~s** in lacrime; **~ful** *adj* piangente, lacrimoso(a); **~ gas** n gas *m* lacrimogeno

tearoom ['tiːruːm] n sala da tè

tease [tiːz] *vt* canzonare; (*unkindly*) tormentare

tea set n servizio da tè

teaspoon ['tiːspuːn] n cucchiaino da tè; (*also*: **~ful**: *as measurement*) cucchiaino

teat [tiːt] n capezzolo

teatime ['tiːtaɪm] n ora del tè

tea towel (*BRIT*) n strofinaccio (per i piatti)

technical ['tɛknɪkl] *adj* tecnico(a); **~ college** (*BRIT*) n ≈ istituto tecnico; **~ity** [-'kælɪtɪ] n tecnicità; (*detail*) dettaglio tecnico; (*legal*) cavillo

technician [tɛk'nɪʃən] n tecnico/a

technique [tɛk'niːk] n tecnica

technological [tɛknə'lɔdʒɪkl] *adj* tecnologico(a)

technology [tɛk'nɔlədʒɪ] n tecnologia

teddy (bear) ['tɛdɪ-] n orsacchiotto

tedious ['tiːdɪəs] *adj* noioso(a), tedioso(a)

tee [tiː] n (*GOLF*) tee *m inv*

teem [tiːm] *vi*: **to ~ with** brulicare di; **it is ~ing (with rain)** piove a dirotto

teenage ['tiːneɪdʒ] *adj* (*fashions etc*) per giovani, per adolescenti; **~r** n adolescente

m/f

teens [tiːnz] *npl*: **to be in one's ~** essere adolescente

tee-shirt ['tiːʃəːt] n = **T-shirt**

teeter ['tiːtə*] *vi* barcollare, vacillare

teeth [tiːθ] *npl* of **tooth**

teethe [tiːð] *vi* mettere i denti

teething ring ['tiːðɪŋ-] n dentaruolo

teething troubles ['tiːðɪŋ-] *npl* (*fig*) difficoltà *fpl* iniziali

teetotal ['tiː'təutl] *adj* astemio(a)

tele: **~conferencing** n teleconferenza; **~gram** n telegramma *m*; **~graph** n telegrafo; **~pathy** [tə'lɛpəθɪ] n telepatia

telephone ['tɛlɪfəun] n telefono ♦ *vt* (*person*) telefonare a; (*message*) comunicare per telefono; **~ booth** (*BRIT* **~ box**) n cabina telefonica; **~ call** n telefonata; **~ directory** n elenco telefonico; **~ number** n numero di telefono; **telephonist** [tə'lɛfənɪst] (*BRIT*) n telefonista *m/f*

telescope ['tɛlɪskəup] n telescopio

telesales ['tɛlɪseɪlz] n vendita per telefono

television ['tɛlɪvɪʒən] n televisione *f*; **on ~** alla televisione; **~ set** n televisore *m*

teleworking ['tɛlɪwəːkɪŋ] n telelavoro

telex ['tɛlɛks] n telex *m inv* ♦ *vt* trasmettere per telex

tell [tɛl] (*pt, pp* **told**) *vt* dire; (*relate: story*) raccontare; (*distinguish*): **to ~ sth from** distinguere qc da ♦ *vi* (*talk*): **to ~ (of)** parlare (di); (*have effect*) farsi sentire, avere effetto; **to ~ sb to do** dire a qn di fare; **~ off** *vt* rimproverare, sgridare; **~er** n (*in bank*) cassiere/a; **~ing** *adj* (*remark, detail*) rivelatore(trice); **~tale** *adj* (*sign*) rivelatore(trice)

telly ['tɛlɪ] (*BRIT*: *inf*) n abbr (= *television*) tivù *f inv*

temerity [tə'mɛrɪtɪ] n temerarietà

temp [tɛmp] n abbr (= *temporary*) segretaria temporanea

temper ['tɛmpə*] n (*nature*) carattere *m*; (*mood*) umore *m*; (*fit of anger*) collera ♦ *vt* (*moderate*) moderare; **to be in a ~** essere in collera; **to lose one's ~** andare in collera

temperament ['tɛmprəmənt] n (*nature*)

temperamento; **~al** [-'mɛntl] *adj* capriccioso(a)

temperate ['tɛmprət] *adj* moderato(a); (*climate*) temperato(a)

temperature ['tɛmprətʃə*] *n* temperatura; **to have** *or* **run a ~** avere la febbre

tempest ['tɛmpɪst] *n* tempesta

template ['tɛmplɪt] *n* sagoma

temple ['tɛmpl] *n* (*building*) tempio; (ANAT) tempia

temporary ['tɛmpərərɪ] *adj* temporaneo(a); (*job, worker*) avventizio(a), temporaneo(a)

tempt [tɛmpt] *vt* tentare; **to ~ sb into doing** indurre qn a fare; **~ation** [-'teɪʃən] *n* tentazione *f*; **~ing** *adj* allettante

ten [tɛn] *num* dieci

tenacity [tə'næsɪtɪ] *n* tenacia

tenancy ['tɛnənsɪ] *n* affitto; condizione *f* di inquilino

tenant ['tɛnənt] *n* inquilino/a

tend [tɛnd] *vt* badare a, occuparsi di ♦ *vi*: **to ~ to do** tendere a fare

tendency ['tɛndənsɪ] *n* tendenza

tender ['tɛndə*] *adj* tenero(a); (*sore*) dolorante ♦ *n* (COMM: *offer*) offerta; (*money*): **legal ~** moneta in corso legale ♦ *vt* offrire

tendon ['tɛndən] *n* tendine *m*

tenement ['tɛnəmənt] *n* casamento

tennis ['tɛnɪs] *n* tennis *m*; **~ ball** *n* palla da tennis; **~ court** *n* campo da tennis; **~ player** *n* tennista *m/f*; **~ racket** *n* racchetta da tennis; **~ shoes** *npl* scarpe *fpl* da tennis

tenor ['tɛnə*] *n* (MUS) tenore *m*

tenpin bowling ['tɛnpɪn-] *n* bowling *m*

tense [tɛns] *adj* teso(a) ♦ *n* (LING) tempo

tension ['tɛnʃən] *n* tensione *f*

tent [tɛnt] *n* tenda

tentative ['tɛntətɪv] *adj* esitante, incerto(a); (*conclusion*) provvisorio(a)

tenterhooks ['tɛntəhuks] *npl*: **on ~** sulle spine

tenth [tɛnθ] *num* decimo(a)

tent: **~ peg** *n* picchetto da tenda; **~ pole** *n* palo da tenda, montante *m*

tenuous ['tɛnjuəs] *adj* tenue

tenure ['tɛnjuə*] *n* (*of property*) possesso; (*of job*) permanenza; titolarità

tepid ['tɛpɪd] *adj* tiepido(a)

term [tɜːm] *n* termine *m*; (SCOL) trimestre *m*; (LAW) sessione *f* ♦ *vt* chiamare, definire; **~s** *npl* (*conditions*) condizioni *fpl*; (COMM) prezzi *mpl*, tariffe *fpl*; **in the short/long ~** a breve/lunga scadenza; **to be on good ~s with sb** essere in buoni rapporti con qn; **to come to ~s with** (*problem*) affrontare

terminal ['tɜːmɪnl] *adj* finale, terminale; (*disease*) terminale ♦ *n* (ELEC) morsetto; (COMPUT) terminale *m*; (AVIAT, for oil, ore etc) terminal *m inv*; (BRIT: *also*: **coach ~**) capolinea *m*

terminate ['tɜːmɪneɪt] *vt* mettere fine a

termini ['tɜːmɪnaɪ] *npl of* **terminus**

terminus ['tɜːmɪnəs] (*pl* **termini**) *n* (*for buses*) capolinea *m*; (*for trains*) stazione *f* terminale

terrace ['tɛrəs] *n* terrazza; (BRIT: *row of houses*) fila di case a schiera; **the ~s** *npl* (BRIT: SPORT) le gradinate; **~d** *adj* (*garden*) a terrazze

terracotta ['tɛrə'kɔtə] *n* terracotta

terrain [tɛ'reɪn] *n* terreno

terrible ['tɛrɪbl] *adj* terribile; **terribly** *adv* terribilmente; (*very badly*) malissimo

terrier ['tɛrɪə*] *n* terrier *m inv*

terrific [tə'rɪfɪk] *adj* incredibile, fantastico(a); (*wonderful*) formidabile, eccezionale

terrify ['tɛrɪfaɪ] *vt* terrorizzare

territory ['tɛrɪtərɪ] *n* territorio

terror ['tɛrə*] *n* terrore *m*; **~ism** *n* terrorismo; **~ist** *n* terrorista *m/f*

Terylene ® ['tɛrɪliːn] *n* terital ® *m*, terilene ® *m*

test [tɛst] *n* (*trial, check, of courage etc*) prova; (MED) esame *m*; (CHEM) analisi *f inv*; (*exam: of intelligence etc*) test *m inv*; (: *in school*) compito in classe; (*also*: **driving ~**) esame *m* di guida ♦ *vt* provare; esaminare; analizzare; sottoporre ad esame; **to ~ sb in history** esaminare qn in storia

testament ['tɛstəmənt] *n* testamento; **the Old/New T~** il Vecchio/Nuovo testamento

testicle ['tɛstɪkl] *n* testicolo

testify ['testɪfaɪ] vi (LAW) testimoniare, deporre; **to ~ to sth** (LAW) testimoniare qc; (gen) comprovare or dimostrare qc

testimony ['testɪmənɪ] n (LAW) testimonianza, deposizione f

test match n (CRICKET, RUGBY) partita internazionale

test tube n provetta

tetanus ['tetənəs] n tetano

tether ['teðə*] vt legare ♦ n: **at the end of one's ~** al limite (della pazienza)

text [tekst] n testo; **~book** n libro di testo

textiles ['tekstaɪlz] npl tessuti mpl; (industry) industria tessile

texting ['tekstɪŋ] n il mandare messaggi con il telefono

texture ['tekstfə*] n tessitura; (of skin, paper etc) struttura

Thames [temz] n: **the ~** il Tamigi

than [ðæn, ðən] conj (in comparisons) che; (with numerals, pronouns, proper names) di; **more ~ 10/once** più di 10/una volta; **I have more/less ~ you** ne ho più/meno di te; **I have more pens ~ pencils** ho più penne che matite; **she is older ~ you think** è più vecchia di quanto tu (non) pensi

thank [θæŋk] vt ringraziare; **~ you (very much)** grazie (tante); **~s** npl ringraziamenti mpl, grazie fpl ♦ excl grazie!; **~s to** grazie a; **~ful** adj: **~ful (for)** riconoscente (per); **~less** adj ingrato(a); **T~sgiving (Day)** n see box

┌─ *KEYWORD* ────────────────────────┐

that [ðæt] (pl **those**) adj (demonstrative) quel(quell', quello) m; quella(quell') f; **~ man/woman/book** quell'uomo/quella donna/quel libro; (not "this") quell'uomo/

quella donna/quel libro là; **~ one** quello(a) là

♦ pron **1** (demonstrative) ciò; (not "this one") quello(a); **who's ~?** chi è?; **what's ~?** cos'è quello?; **is ~ you?** sei tu?; **I prefer this to ~** preferisco questo a quello; **~'s what he said** questo è ciò che ha detto; **what happened after ~?** che è successo dopo?; **~ is (to say)** cioè

2 (relative: direct) che; (: indirect) cui; **the book (~) I read** il libro che ho letto; **the box (~) I put it in** la scatola in cui l'ho messo; **the people (~) I spoke to** le persone con cui or con le quali ho parlato

3 (relative: of time) in cui; **the day (~) he came** il giorno in cui è venuto

♦ conj che; **he thought ~ I was ill** pensava che io fossi malato

♦ adv (demonstrative) così; **I can't work ~ much** non posso lavorare (così) tanto; **~ high** così alto; **the wall's about ~ high and ~ thick** il muro è alto circa così e spesso circa così

└────────────────────────────────────┘

thatched [θætʃt] adj (roof) di paglia; **~ cottage** n cottage m inv col tetto di paglia

thaw [θɔ:] n disgelo ♦ vi (ice) sciogliersi; (food) scongelarsi ♦ vt (food: also: **~ out**) (fare) scongelare

┌─ *KEYWORD* ────────────────────────┐

the [ði:, ðə] def art **1** (gen) il(lo, l') m; la(l') f; i(gli) mpl; le fpl; **~ boy/girl/ink** il ragazzo/la ragazza/l'inchiostro; **~ books/pencils** i libri/le matite; **~ history of ~ world** la storia del mondo; **give it to ~ postman** dallo al postino; **I haven't ~ time/money** non ho tempo/soldi; **~ rich and ~ poor** i ricchi e i poveri

2 (in titles): **Elizabeth ~ First** Elisabetta prima; **Peter ~ Great** Pietro il grande

3 (in comparisons): **~ more he works, ~ more he earns** più lavora più guadagna

└────────────────────────────────────┘

theatre ['θɪətə*] (US **theater**) n teatro; (also: **lecture ~**) aula magna; (also: **operating ~**)

sala operatoria; **~-goer** n frequentatore/trice di teatri
theatrical [θɪ'ætrɪkl] adj teatrale
theft [θɛft] n furto
their [ðɛə*] adj il(la) loro, pl i(le) loro; **~s** pron il(la) loro, pl i(le) loro; see also **my**; **mine**
them [ðɛm, ðəm] pron (direct) li(le); (indirect) gli, loro (after vb); (stressed, after prep: people) loro; (: people, things) essi(e); see also **me**
theme [θi:m] n tema m; **~ park** n parco di divertimenti (intorno a un tema centrale); **~ song** n tema musicale
themselves [ðəm'sɛlvz] pl pron (reflexive) si; (emphatic) loro stessi(e); (after prep) se stessi(e)
then [ðɛn] adv (at that time) allora; (next) poi, dopo; (and also) e poi ♦ conj (therefore) perciò, dunque, quindi ♦ adj: **the ~ president** il presidente di allora; **by ~** allora; **from ~ on** da allora in poi
theology [θɪ'ɔlədʒɪ] n teologia
theorem ['θɪərəm] n teorema m
theoretical [θɪə'rɛtɪkl] adj teorico(a)
theory ['θɪərɪ] n teoria
therapy ['θɛrəpɪ] n terapia

KEYWORD
---

there [ðɛə*] adv 1: **~ is, ~ are** c'è, ci sono; **~ are 3 of them** (people) sono in 3; (things) ce ne sono 3; **~ is no-one here** non c'è nessuno qui; **~ has been an accident** c'è stato un incidente
2 (referring to place) là, lì; **up/in/down ~** lassù/là dentro/laggiù; **he went ~ on Friday** ci è andato venerdì; **I want that book ~** voglio quel libro là or lì; **~ he is!** eccolo!
3: **~, ~** (esp to child) su, su

thereabouts [ðɛərə'bauts] adv (place) nei pressi, da quelle parti; (amount) giù di lì, all'incirca
thereafter [ðɛər'ɑːftə*] adv da allora in poi
thereby [ðɛə'baɪ] adv con ciò
therefore ['ðɛəfɔː*] adv perciò, quindi

there's [ðɛəz] = **there is**; **there has**
thermal ['θə:ml] adj termico(a)
thermometer [θə'mɔmɪtə*] n termometro
Thermos ® ['θə:məs] n (also: **~ flask**) thermos ® m inv
thesaurus [θɪ'sɔːrəs] n dizionario dei sinonimi
these [ði:z] pl pron, adj questi(e)
theses ['θi:si:z] npl of **thesis**
thesis ['θi:sɪs] (pl **theses**) n tesi f inv
they [ðeɪ] pl pron essi(esse); (people only) loro; **~ say that ...** (it is said that) si dice che ...; **~'d** = **they had; they would; ~'ll** = **they shall; they will; ~'re** = **they are; ~'ve** = **they have**
thick [θɪk] adj spesso(a); (crowd) compatto(a); (stupid) ottuso(a), lento(a) ♦ n: **in the ~ of** nel folto di; **it's 20 cm ~** ha uno spessore di 20 cm; **~en** vi ispessire ♦ vt (sauce etc) ispessire, rendere più denso(a); **~ly** adv (spread) a strati spessi; (cut) a fette grosse; (populated) densamente; **~ness** n spessore m; **~set** adj tarchiato(a), tozzo(a)
thief [θi:f] (pl **thieves**) n ladro/a
thieves [θi:vz] npl of **thief**
thigh [θaɪ] n coscia
thimble ['θɪmbl] n ditale m
thin [θɪn] adj sottile; (person) magro(a); (soup) poco denso(a) ♦ vt: **to ~ (down)** (sauce, paint) diluire
thing [θɪŋ] n cosa; (object) oggetto; (mania): **to have a ~ about** essere fissato(a) con; **~s** npl (belongings) cose fpl; **poor ~** poverino(a); **the best ~ would be to** la cosa migliore sarebbe di; **how are ~s?** come va?
think [θɪŋk] (pt, pp **thought**) vi pensare, riflettere ♦ vt pensare, credere; (imagine) immaginare; **to ~ of** pensare a; **what did you ~ of them?** cosa ne ha pensato?; **to ~ about sth/sb** pensare a qc/qn; **I'll ~ about it** ci penserò; **to ~ of doing** pensare di fare; **I ~ so/not** penso di sì/no; **to ~ well of** avere una buona opinione di; **~ out** vt (plan) elaborare; (solution) trovare; **~ over** vt riflettere su; **~ through** vt riflettere a

fondo su; **~ up** vt ideare; **~ tank** n commissione f di esperti

third [θəːd] num terzo(a) ♦ n terzo/a; (*fraction*) terzo, terza parte f; (AUT) terza; (BRIT: SCOL: *degree*) laurea col minimo dei voti; **~ly** adv in terzo luogo; **~ party insurance** (BRIT) n assicurazione f contro terzi; **~-rate** adj di qualità scadente; **the T~ World** n il Terzo Mondo

thirst [θəːst] n sete f; **~y** adj (*person*) assetato(a), che ha sete

thirteen [θəːˈtiːn] num tredici

thirty [ˈθəːtɪ] num trenta

KEYWORD

this [ðɪs] (pl **these**) adj (*demonstrative*) questo(a); **~ man/woman/book** quest'uomo/questa donna/questo libro; (*not "that"*) quest'uomo/questa donna/ questo libro qui; **~ one** questo(a) qui ♦ pron (*demonstrative*) questo(a); (*not "that one"*) questo(a) qui; **who/what is ~?** chi è/che cos'è questo?; **I prefer ~ to that** preferisco questo a quello; **~ is where I live** io abito qui; **~ is what he said** questo è ciò che ha detto; **~ is Mr Brown** (*in introductions, photo*) questo è il signor Brown; (*on telephone*) sono il signor Brown ♦ adv (*demonstrative*): **~ high/long** etc alto/lungo etc così; **I didn't know things were ~ bad** non sapevo andasse così male

thistle [ˈθɪsl] n cardo

thong [θɔŋ] n cinghia

thorn [θɔːn] n spina; **~y** adj spinoso(a)

thorough [ˈθʌrə] adj (*search*) minuzioso(a); (*knowledge, research*) approfondito(a), profondo(a); (*person*) coscienzioso(a); (*cleaning*) a fondo; **~bred** n (*horse*) purosangue m/f inv; **~fare** n strada transitabile; **"no ~fare"** "divieto di transito"; **~ly** adv (*search*) minuziosamente; (*wash, study*) a fondo; (*very*) assolutamente

those [ðəuz] pl pron quelli(e) ♦ pl adj quei(quegli) mpl; quelle fpl

though [ðəu] conj benché, sebbene ♦ adv

comunque

thought [θɔːt] pt, pp of **think** ♦ n pensiero; (*opinion*) opinione f; **~ful** adj pensieroso(a), pensoso(a); (*considerate*) premuroso(a); **~less** adj sconsiderato(a); (*behaviour*) scortese

thousand [ˈθauzənd] num mille; **one ~** mille; **~s of** migliaia di; **~th** num millesimo(a)

thrash [θræʃ] vt picchiare; bastonare; (*defeat*) battere; **~ about** vi dibattersi; **~ out** vt dibattere

thread [θrɛd] n filo; (*of screw*) filetto ♦ vt (*needle*) infilare; **~bare** adj consumato(a), logoro(a)

threat [θrɛt] n minaccia; **~en** vi (*storm*) minacciare ♦ vt: **to ~en sb with/to do** minacciare qn con/di fare

three [θriː] num tre; **~-dimensional** adj tridimensionale; (*film*) stereoscopico(a); **~-piece suit** n completo (con gilè); **~-piece suite** n salotto comprendente un divano e due poltrone; **~-ply** adj (*wool*) a tre fili

threshold [ˈθrɛʃhəuld] n soglia

threw [θruː] pt of **throw**

thrifty [ˈθrɪftɪ] adj economico(a)

thrill [θrɪl] n brivido ♦ vt (*audience*) elettrizzare; **to be ~ed** (*with gift etc*) essere elettrizzato(a); **~er** n thriller m inv; **~ing** adj (*book*) pieno(a) di suspense; (*news, discovery*) elettrizzante

thrive [θraɪv] (pt **thrived**, pp **thrived**) vi crescere or svilupparsi bene; (*business*) prosperare; **he ~s on it** gli fa bene, ne gode; **thriving** adj fiorente

throat [θrəut] n gola; **to have a sore ~** avere (un or il) mal di gola

throb [θrɔb] vi palpitare; pulsare; vibrare

throes [θrəuz] npl: **in the ~ of** alle prese con; in preda a

thrombosis [θrɔmˈbəusɪs] n trombosi f

throne [θrəun] n trono

throng [θrɔŋ] n moltitudine f ♦ vt affollare

throttle [ˈθrɔtl] n (AUT) valvola a farfalla ♦ vt strangolare

through [θruː] prep attraverso; (*time*) per,

durante; (*by means of*) per mezzo di; (*owing to*) a causa di ♦ *adj* (*ticket, train, passage*) diretto(a) ♦ *adv* attraverso; **to put sb ~ to sb** (*TEL*) passare qn a qn; **to be ~** (*TEL*) ottenere la comunicazione; (*have finished*) essere finito(a); **"no ~ road"** (*BRIT*) "strada senza sbocco"; **~out** *prep* (*place*) dappertutto in; (*time*) per *or* durante tutto(a) ♦ *adv* dappertutto; sempre

throw [θrəu] (*pt* **threw**, *pp* **thrown**) *n* (*SPORT*) lancio, tiro ♦ *vt* tirare, gettare; (*SPORT*) lanciare, tirare; (*rider*) disarcionare; (*fig*) confondere; **to ~ a party** dare una festa; **~ away** *vt* gettare *or* buttare via; **~ off** *vt* sbarazzarsi di; **~ out** *vt* buttare fuori; (*reject*) respingere; **~ up** *vi* vomitare; **~away** *adj* da buttare; **~-in** *n* (*SPORT*) rimessa in gioco; **thrown** *pp* of **throw**

thru [θru:] (*US*) *prep, adj, adv* = **through**

thrush [θrʌʃ] *n* tordo

thrust [θrʌst] (*pt, pp* **thrust**) *vt* spingere con forza; (*push in*) conficcare

thud [θʌd] *n* tonfo

thug [θʌg] *n* delinquente *m*

thumb [θʌm] *n* (*ANAT*) pollice *m*; **to ~ a lift** fare l'autostop; **~ through** *vt fus* (*book*) sfogliare; **~tack** (*US*) *n* puntina da disegno

thump [θʌmp] *n* colpo forte; (*sound*) tonfo ♦ *vt* (*person*) picchiare; (*object*) battere su ♦ *vi* picchiare; battere

thunder ['θʌndə*] *n* tuono ♦ *vi* tuonare; (*train etc*): **to ~ past** passare con un rombo; **~bolt** *n* fulmine *m*; **~clap** *n* rombo di tuono; **~storm** *n* temporale *m*; **~y** *adj* temporalesco(a)

Thursday ['θə:zdɪ] *n* giovedì *m inv*

thus [ðʌs] *adv* così

thwart [θwɔ:t] *vt* contrastare

thyme [taɪm] *n* timo

thyroid ['θaɪrɔɪd] *n* (*also:* **~ gland**) tiroide *f*

tiara [tɪ'ɑːrə] (*woman's*) *n* diadema *m*

Tiber ['taɪbə*] *n*: **the ~** il Tevere

tick [tɪk] *n* (*sound: of clock*) tic tac *m inv*; (*mark*) segno; spunta; (*ZOOL*) zecca; (*BRIT: inf*): **in a ~** in un attimo ♦ *vi* fare tic tac ♦ *vt* spuntare; **~ off** *vt* spuntare; (*person*) sgridare; **~ over** *vi* (*engine*) andare al

minimo; (*fig*) andare avanti come al solito

ticket ['tɪkɪt] *n* biglietto; (*in shop: on goods*) etichetta; (*parking ~*) multa; (*for library*) scheda; **~ collector** *n* bigliettaio; **~ office** *n* biglietteria

tickle ['tɪkl] *vt* fare il solletico a; (*fig*) solleticare ♦ *vi*: **it ~s** mi (*or* gli *etc*) fa il solletico; **ticklish** [-lɪʃ] *adj* che soffre il solletico; (*problem*) delicato(a)

tidal ['taɪdl] *adj* di marea; (*estuary*) soggetto(a) alla marea; **~ wave** *n* onda anomala

tidbit ['tɪdbɪt] (*US*) *n* (*food*) leccornia; (*news*) notizia ghiotta

tiddlywinks ['tɪdlɪwɪŋks] *n* gioco della pulce

tide [taɪd] *n* marea; (*fig: of events*) corso; **high/low ~** alta/bassa marea; **~ over** *vt* dare una mano a

tidy ['taɪdɪ] *adj* (*room*) ordinato(a), lindo(a); (*dress, work*) curato(a), in ordine; (*person*) ordinato(a) ♦ *vt* (*also:* **~ up**) riordinare, mettere in ordine

tie [taɪ] *n* (*string etc*) legaccio; (*BRIT: also:* **neck~**) cravatta; (*fig: link*) legame *m*; (*SPORT: draw*) pareggio ♦ *vt* (*parcel*) legare; (*ribbon*) annodare ♦ *vi* (*SPORT*) pareggiare; **to ~ sth in a bow** annodare qc; **to ~ a knot in sth** fare un nodo a qc; **~ down** *vt* legare; (*to price etc*) costringere ad accettare; **~ up** *vt* (*parcel, dog*) legare; (*boat*) ormeggiare; (*arrangements*) concludere; **to be ~d up** (*busy*) essere occupato(a) *or* preso(a)

tier [tɪə*] *n* fila; (*of cake*) piano, strato

tiger ['taɪgə*] *n* tigre *f*

tight [taɪt] *adj* (*rope*) teso(a), tirato(a); (*money*) poco(a); (*clothes, budget, bend etc*) stretto(a); (*control*) severo(a), fermo(a); (*inf: drunk*) sbronzo(a) ♦ *adv* (*squeeze*) fortemente; (*shut*) ermeticamente; **~s** (*BRIT*) *npl* collant *m inv*; **~en** *vt* (*rope*) tendere; (*screw*) stringere; (*control*) rinforzare ♦ *vi* tendersi; stringersi; **~-fisted** *adj* avaro(a); **~ly** *adv* (*grasp*) bene, saldamente; **~rope** *n* corda (da acrobata)

tile [taɪl] *n* (*on roof*) tegola; (*on wall or floor*) piastrella, mattonella; ~d adj di tegole; a piastrelle, a mattonelle

till [tɪl] n registratore m di cassa ♦ vt (land) coltivare ♦ prep, conj = until

tiller ['tɪlə*] n (NAUT) barra del timone

tilt [tɪlt] vt inclinare, far pendere ♦ vi inclinarsi, pendere

timber ['tɪmbə*] n (material) legname m

time [taɪm] n tempo; (epoch: often pl) epoca, tempo; (by clock) ora; (moment) momento; (occasion) volta; (MUS) tempo ♦ vt (race) cronometrare; (programme) calcolare la durata di; (fix moment for) programmare; (remark etc) dire (or fare) al momento giusto; **a long ~** molto tempo; **for the ~ being** per il momento; **4 at a ~** 4 per or alla volta; **from ~ to ~** ogni tanto; **at ~s** a volte; **in ~** (soon enough) in tempo; (after some ~) col tempo; (MUS) a tempo; **in a week's ~** fra una settimana; **in no ~** in un attimo; **any ~** in qualsiasi momento; **on ~** puntualmente; **5 ~s 5** 5 volte 5, 5 per 5; **what ~ is it?** che ora è?, che ore sono?; **to have a good ~** divertirsi; ~ **bomb** n bomba a orologeria; ~**less** adj eterno(a); ~**ly** adj opportuno(a); ~ **off** n tempo libero; ~**r** n (~ switch) temporizzatore m; (in kitchen) contaminuti m inv; ~ **scale** n periodo; ~**-share** adj: ~**-share apartment/villa** appartamento/villa in multiproprietà; ~ **switch** (BRIT) n temporizzatore m; ~**table** n orario; ~ **zone** n fuso orario

timid ['tɪmɪd] adj timido(a); (easily scared) pauroso(a)

timing ['taɪmɪŋ] n (SPORT) cronometraggio; (fig) scelta del momento opportuno

timpani ['tɪmpənɪ] npl timpani mpl

tin [tɪn] n stagno; (also: ~ **plate**) latta; (container) scatola; (BRIT: can) barattolo (di latta), lattina; ~**foil** n stagnola

tinge [tɪndʒ] n sfumatura ♦ vt: ~**d with** tinto(a) di

tingle ['tɪŋgl] vi pizzicare

tinker ['tɪŋkə*]: ~ **with** vt fus armeggiare intorno a; cercare di riparare

tinned [tɪnd] (BRIT) adj (food) in scatola

tin opener ['-əʊpnə*] (BRIT) n apriscatole m inv

tinsel ['tɪnsl] n decorazioni fpl natalizie (argentate)

tint [tɪnt] n tinta; ~**ed** adj (hair) tinto(a); (spectacles, glass) colorato(a)

tiny ['taɪnɪ] adj minuscolo(a)

tip [tɪp] n (end) punta; (gratuity) mancia; (BRIT: for rubbish) immondezzaio; (advice) suggerimento ♦ vt (waiter) dare la mancia a; (tilt) inclinare; (overturn: also: ~ **over**) capovolgere; (empty: also: ~ **out**) scaricare; ~**-off** n (hint) soffiata; ~**ped** (BRIT) adj (cigarette) col filtro

Tipp-Ex ® ['tɪpeks] n correttore m

tipsy ['tɪpsɪ] adj brillo(a)

tiptoe ['tɪptəʊ] n: **on** ~ in punta di piedi

tiptop ['tɪp'tɒp] adj: **in** ~ **condition** in ottime condizioni

tire ['taɪə*] n (US) = tyre ♦ vt stancare ♦ vi stancarsi; ~**d** adj stanco(a); **to be** ~**d of** essere stanco or stufo di; ~**less** adj instancabile; ~**some** adj noioso(a); tiring adj faticoso(a)

tissue ['tɪʃuː] n tessuto; (paper handkerchief) fazzoletto di carta; ~ **paper** n carta velina

tit [tɪt] n (bird) cinciallegra; **to give** ~ **for tat** rendere pan per focaccia

titbit ['tɪtbɪt] (BRIT) n (food) leccornia; (news) notizia ghiotta

title ['taɪtl] n titolo; ~ **deed** n (LAW) titolo di proprietà; ~ **role** n ruolo or parte f principale

TM abbr = trademark

KEYWORD

---

to [tuː, tə] prep 1 (direction) a; **to go** ~ **France/London/school** andare in Francia/a Londra/a scuola; **to go** ~ **Paul's/the doctor's** andare da Paul/dal dottore; **the road** ~ **Edinburgh** la strada per Edimburgo; ~ **the left/right** a sinistra/destra

2 (as far as) (fino) a; **from here** ~ **London** da qui a Londra; **to count** ~ **10** contare fino a 10; **from 40** ~ **50 people** da 40 a 50 persone

3 (*with expressions of time*): **a quarter ~ 5** le 5 meno un quarto; **it's twenty ~ 3** sono le 3 meno venti

4 (*for, of*): **the key ~ the front door** la chiave della porta d'ingresso; **a letter ~ his wife** una lettera per la moglie

5 (*expressing indirect object*) a; **to give sth ~ sb** dare qc a qn; **to talk ~ sb** parlare a qn; **to be a danger ~ sb/sth** rappresentare un pericolo per qn/qc

6 (*in relation to*) a; **3 goals ~ 2** 3 goal a 2; **30 miles ~ the gallon** ≈ 11 chilometri con un litro

7 (*purpose, result*): **to come ~ sb's aid** venire in aiuto a qn; **to sentence sb ~ death** condannare a morte qn; **~ my surprise** con mia sorpresa

♦ *with vb* 1 (*simple infinitive*): **~ go/eat** *etc* andare/mangiare *etc*

2 (*following another vb*): **to want/try/start ~ do** volere/cercare di/cominciare a fare

3 (*with vb omitted*): **I don't want ~** non voglio (farlo); **you ought ~** devi (farlo)

4 (*purpose, result*) per; **I did it ~ help you** l'ho fatto per aiutarti

5 (*equivalent to relative clause*): **I have things ~ do** ho da fare; **the main thing is ~ try** la cosa più importante è provare

6 (*after adjective etc*): **ready ~ go** pronto a partire; **too old/young ~ ...** troppo vecchio/giovane per ...

♦ *adv*: **to push the door ~** accostare la porta

toad [təud] *n* rospo; **~stool** *n* fungo (velenoso)

toast [təust] *n* (CULIN) pane *m* tostato; (*drink, speech*) brindisi *m inv* ♦ *vt* (CULIN) tostare; (*drink to*) brindare a; **a piece** *or* **slice of ~** una fetta di pane tostato; **~er** *n* tostapane *m inv*

tobacco [tə'bækəu] *n* tabacco; **~nist** *n* tabaccaio/a; **~nist's (shop)** *n* tabaccheria

toboggan [tə'bɔgən] *n* toboga *m inv*

today [tə'deı] *adv* oggi ♦ *n* (*also fig*) oggi *m*

toddler ['tɔdlə*] *n* bambino/a che impara a camminare

toe [təu] *n* dito del piede; (*of shoe*) punta; **to ~ the line** (*fig*) stare in riga, conformarsi; **~nail** *n* unghia del piede

toffee ['tɔfı] *n* caramella; **~ apple** *n* mela caramellata

toga ['təugə] *n* toga

together [tə'geðə*] *adv* insieme; (*at same time*) allo stesso tempo; **~ with** insieme a

toil [tɔıl] *n* travaglio, fatica ♦ *vi* affannarsi; sgobbare

toilet ['tɔılət] *n* (BRIT: *lavatory*) gabinetto ♦ *cpd* (*bag, soap etc*) da toletta; **~ paper** *n* carta igienica; **~ries** *npl* articoli *mpl* da toletta; **~ roll** *n* rotolo di carta igienica; **~ water** *n* acqua di colonia

token ['təukən] *n* (*sign*) segno; (*substitute coin*) gettone *m*; **book/record/gift ~** (BRIT) buono-libro/disco/regalo

told [təuld] *pt, pp of* **tell**

tolerable ['tɔlərəbl] *adj* (*bearable*) tollerabile; (*fairly good*) passabile

tolerant ['tɔlərnt] *adj*: **~ (of)** tollerante (nei confronti di)

tolerate ['tɔləreıt] *vt* sopportare; (MED, TECH) tollerare

toll [təul] *n* (*tax, charge*) pedaggio ♦ *vi* (*bell*) suonare; **the accident ~ on the roads** il numero delle vittime della strada

tomato [tə'mɑːtəu] (*pl* **~es**) *n* pomodoro

tomb [tuːm] *n* tomba

tomboy ['tɔmbɔı] *n* maschiaccio

tombstone ['tuːmstəun] *n* pietra tombale

tomcat ['tɔmkæt] *n* gatto

tomorrow [tə'mɔrəu] *adv* domani ♦ *n* (*also fig*) domani *m inv*; **the day after ~** dopodomani; **~ morning** domani mattina

ton [tʌn] *n* tonnellata (BRIT = 1016 kg; US = 907 kg; *metric* = 1000 kg); **~s of** (*inf*) un mucchio *or* sacco di

tone [təun] *n* tono ♦ *vi* (*also:* **~ in**) intonarsi; **~ down** *vt* (*colour, criticism, sound*) attenuare; **~ up** *vt* (*muscles*) tonificare; **~-deaf** *adj* che non ha orecchio (musicale)

tongs [tɔnz] *npl* tenaglie *fpl*; (*for coal*) molle *fpl*; (*for hair*) arricciacapelli *m inv*

tongue [tʌn] *n* lingua; **~ in cheek** (*say, speak*) ironicamente; **~-tied** *adj* (*fig*) muto(a); ~-**twister** n scioglilingua m inv

tonic ['tɒnɪk] n (MED) tonico(a); (also: ~ **water**) acqua tonica

tonight [təˈnaɪt] adv stanotte; (this evening) stasera ♦ n questa notte; questa sera

tonnage ['tʌnɪdʒ] n (NAUT) tonnellaggio, stazza

tonsil ['tɒnsl] n tonsilla; ~**litis** [-ˈlaɪtɪs] n tonsillite f

too [tuː] adv (excessively) troppo; (also) anche; ~ **much** adv troppo ♦ adj troppo(a); ~ **many** troppi(e)

took [tuk] pt of **take**

tool [tuːl] n utensile m, attrezzo; ~ **box** n cassetta f portautensili

toot [tuːt] n (of horn) colpo di clacson; (of whistle) fischio ♦ vi suonare; (with car horn) suonare il clacson

tooth [tuːθ] (pl **teeth**) n (ANAT, TECH) dente m; ~**ache** n mal di denti; ~**brush** n spazzolino da denti; ~**paste** n dentifricio; ~**pick** n stuzzicadenti m inv

top [tɒp] n (of mountain, page, ladder) cima; (of box, cupboard, table) sopra m inv, parte f superiore; (lid: of box, jar) coperchio; (: of bottle) tappo; (blouse etc) sopra m inv; (toy) trottola ♦ adj più alto(a); (in rank) primo(a); (best) migliore ♦ vt (exceed) superare; (be first in) essere in testa a; **on ~ of** sopra, in cima a; (in addition to) oltre a; **from ~ to bottom** da cima a fondo; ~ **up** (US ~ **off**) vt riempire; (salary) integrare; ~ **floor** n ultimo piano; ~ **hat** n cilindro; ~-**heavy** adj (object) con la parte superiore troppo pesante

topic ['tɒpɪk] n argomento; ~**al** adj d'attualità

top: ~**less** adj (bather etc) col seno scoperto; ~-**level** adj (talks) ad alto livello; ~**most** adj il(la) più alto(a)

topple ['tɒpl] vt rovesciare, far cadere ♦ vi cadere; traballare

top-secret adj segretissimo(a)

topsy-turvy ['tɒpsɪˈtəːvɪ] adj, adv sottosopra inv

torch [tɔːtʃ] n torcia; (BRIT: electric) lampadina tascabile

tore [tɔː] pt of **tear**¹

torment [n 'tɔːment, vb tɔːˈment] n tormento ♦ vt tormentare

torn [tɔːn] pp of **tear**¹

torpedo [tɔːˈpiːdəu] (pl ~**es**) n siluro

torrent ['tɒrnt] n torrente m

torrid ['tɒrɪd] adj torrido(a); (love affair) infuocato(a)

tortoise ['tɔːtəs] n tartaruga; ~**shell** ['tɔːtəʃɛl] adj di tartaruga

torture ['tɔːtʃə*] n tortura ♦ vt torturare

Tory ['tɔːrɪ] (BRIT: POL) adj dei tories, conservatore(trice) ♦ n tory m/f inv, conservatore/trice

toss [tɒs] vt gettare, lanciare; (one's head) scuotere; **to ~ a coin** fare a testa o croce; **to ~ up for sth** fare a testa o croce per qc; **to ~ and turn** (in bed) girarsi e rigirarsi

tot [tɒt] n (BRIT: drink) bicchierino; (child) bimbo/a

total ['təutl] adj totale ♦ n totale m ♦ vt (add up) sommare; (amount to) ammontare a

totally ['təutəlɪ] adv completamente

touch [tʌtʃ] n tocco; (sense) tatto; (contact) contatto ♦ vt toccare; **a ~ of** (fig) un tocco di; un pizzico di; **to get in ~ with** mettersi in contatto con; **to lose ~** (friends) perdersi di vista; ~ **on** vt fus (topic) sfiorare, accennare a; ~ **up** vt (paint) ritoccare; ~-**and-go** adj incerto(a); ~**down** n atterraggio; (on sea) ammaraggio; (US: FOOTBALL) meta; ~**ed** adj commosso(a); ~**ing** adj commovente; ~**line** n (SPORT) linea laterale; ~**y** adj (person) suscettibile

tough [tʌf] adj duro(a); (resistant) resistente; ~**en** vt rinforzare

toupee ['tuːpeɪ] n parrucchino

tour ['tuə*] n viaggio; (also: **package** ~) viaggio organizzato or tutto compreso; (of town, museum) visita; (by artist) tournée f inv ♦ vt visitare; ~ **guide** n guida turistica; ~**ing** n turismo

tourism ['tuərɪzəm] n turismo

tourist ['tuərɪst] n turista m/f ♦ adv (travel) in classe turistica ♦ cpd turistico(a); ~ **office** n pro loco f inv

tournament ['tuənəmənt] n torneo

tousled ['tauzld] adj (hair) arruffato(a)

tout [taut] vi: **to ~ for** procacciare, raccogliere; cercare clienti per ♦ n (also: **ticket ~**) bagarino

tow [tau] vt rimorchiare; **"on ~"** (BRIT), **"in ~"** (US) "veicolo rimorchiato"

toward(s) [tə'wɔːd(z)] prep verso; (of attitude) nei confronti di; (of purpose) per

towel ['tauəl] n asciugamano; (also: **tea ~**) strofinaccio; ~ling n (fabric) spugna; ~ rail (US ~ rack) n portasciugamano

tower ['tauə*] n torre f; ~ block (BRIT) n palazzone m; ~ing adj altissimo(a), imponente

town [taun] n città f inv; **to go to ~** andare in città; (fig) mettercela tutta; ~ centre n centro (città); ~ council n consiglio comunale; ~ hall n ≈ municipio; ~ plan n pianta della città; ~ planning n urbanistica

towrope ['tauraup] n (cavo da) rimorchio

tow truck (US) n carro m attrezzi inv

toxic ['tɔksɪk] adj tossico(a)

toy [tɔɪ] n giocattolo; ~ with vt fus giocare con; (idea) accarezzare, trastullarsi con; ~ shop n negozio di giocattoli

trace [treɪs] n traccia ♦ vt (draw) tracciare; (follow) seguire; (locate) rintracciare; **tracing paper** n carta da ricalco

track [træk] n (of person, animal) traccia; (on tape, SPORT, path: gen) pista; (: of bullet etc) traiettoria; (: of suspect, animal) pista, tracce fpl; (RAIL) binario, rotaie fpl ♦ vt seguire le tracce di; **to keep ~ of** seguire; ~ down vt (prey) scovare; snidare; (sth lost) rintracciare; ~suit n tuta sportiva

tract [trækt] n (GEO) tratto, estensione f

tractor ['træktə*] n trattore m

trade [treɪd] n commercio; (skill, job) mestiere m ♦ vi commerciare ♦ vt: **to ~ sth (for sth)** barattare qc (con qc); **to ~ with/ in** commerciare con/in; ~ in vt (old car etc) dare come pagamento parziale; ~ fair n fiera commerciale; ~mark n marchio di fabbrica; ~ name n marca, nome m depositato; ~r n commerciante m/f;

~sman (irreg) n fornitore m; (shopkeeper) negoziante m; ~ union n sindacato; ~ unionist n sindacalista m/f

tradition [trə'dɪʃən] n tradizione f; ~al adj tradizionale

traffic ['træfɪk] n traffico ♦ vi: **to ~ in** (pej: liquor, drugs) trafficare in; ~ circle (US) n isola rotatoria; ~ jam n ingorgo (del traffico); ~ lights npl semaforo; ~ warden n addetto/a al controllo del traffico e del parcheggio

tragedy ['trædʒədɪ] n tragedia

tragic ['trædʒɪk] adj tragico(a)

trail [treɪl] n (tracks) tracce fpl, pista; (path) sentiero; (of smoke etc) scia ♦ vt trascinare, strascicare; (follow) seguire ♦ vi essere al traino; (dress etc) strusciare; (plant) arrampicarsi; strisciare; (in game) essere in svantaggio; ~ behind vi essere al traino; ~er n (AUT) rimorchio; (US) roulotte f inv; (CINEMA) prossimamente m inv; ~ truck (US) n (articulated lorry) autoarticolato

train [treɪn] n treno; (of dress) coda, strascico ♦ vt (apprentice, doctor etc) formare; (sportsman) allenare; (dog) addestrare; (memory) esercitare; (point: gun etc): **to ~ sth on** puntare qc contro ♦ vi formarsi; allenarsi; **one's ~ of thought** il filo dei propri pensieri; ~ed adj qualificato(a); allenato(a); addestrato(a); ~ee [treɪ'niː] n (in trade) apprendista m/f; ~er n (SPORT) allenatore/trice; (: shoe) scarpa da ginnastica; (of dogs etc) addestratore/trice; ~ing n formazione f; allenamento; addestramento; **in ~ing** (SPORT) in allenamento; ~ing college n istituto professionale; (for teachers) ≈ istituto magistrale; ~ing shoes npl scarpe fpl da ginnastica

trait [treɪt] n tratto

traitor ['treɪtə*] n traditore m

tram [træm] (BRIT) n (also: ~car) tram m inv

tramp [træmp] n (person) vagabondo/a; (inf: pej: woman) sgualdrina

trample ['træmpl] vt: **to ~ (underfoot)** calpestare

trampoline ['træmpəliːn] n trampolino

tranquil ['træŋkwɪl] *adj* tranquillo(a); **~lizer** *n* (*MED*) tranquillante *m*

transact [træn'zækt] *vt* (*business*) trattare; **~ion** [-'zækʃən] *n* transazione *f*

transatlantic ['trænzət'læntɪk] *adj* transatlantico(a)

transfer [*n* 'trænsfə*, *vb* træns'fə:*] *n* (*gen, also SPORT*) trasferimento; (*POL: of power*) passaggio; (*picture, design*) decalcomania; (: *stick-on*) autoadesivo ♦ *vt* trasferire; passare; **to ~ the charges** (*BRIT: TEL*) fare una chiamata a carico del destinatario; **~ desk** *n* (*AVIAT*) banco *m* transiti *inv*

transform [træns'fɔ:m] *vt* trasformare

transfusion [træns'fju:ʒən] *n* trasfusione *f*

transient ['trænzɪənt] *adj* transitorio(a), fugace

transistor [træn'zɪstə*] *n* (*ELEC*) transistor *m inv*; (*also:* **~ radio**) radio *f inv* a transistor

transit ['trænzɪt] *n*: **in ~** in transito

transitive ['trænzɪtɪv] *adj* (*LING*) transitivo(a)

translate [trænz'leɪt] *vt* tradurre; **translation** [-'leɪʃən] *n* traduzione *f*; **translator** *n* traduttore/trice

transmission [trænz'mɪʃən] *n* trasmissione *f*

transmit [trænz'mɪt] *vt* trasmettere; **~ter** *n* trasmettitore *m*

transparency [træns'pɛərənsɪ] *n* trasparenza; (*BRIT: PHOT*) diapositiva

transparent [træns'pærnt] *adj* trasparente

transpire [træn'spaɪə*] *vi* (*happen*) succedere; (*turn out*): **it ~d that** si venne a sapere che

transplant [*vb* træns'plɑ:nt, *n* 'trænsplɑ:nt] *vt* trapiantare ♦ *n* (*MED*) trapianto

transport [*n* 'trænspɔ:t, *vb* træns'pɔ:t] *n* trasporto ♦ *vt* trasportare; **~ation** [-'teɪʃən] *n* (*mezzo di*) trasporto; **~ café** (*BRIT*) *n* trattoria per camionisti

trap [træp] *n* (*snare, trick*) trappola; (*carriage*) calesse *m* ♦ *vt* prendere in trappola, intrappolare; **~ door** *n* botola

trapeze [trə'pi:z] *n* trapezio

trappings ['træpɪŋz] *npl* ornamenti *mpl*; indoratura, sfarzo

trash [træʃ] (*pej*) *n* (*goods*) ciarpame *m*; (*nonsense*) sciocchezze *fpl*; **~ can** (*US*) *n* secchio della spazzatura

trauma ['trɔ:mə] *n* trauma *m*; **~tic** [-'mætɪk] *adj* traumatico(a)

travel ['trævl] *n* viaggio; viaggi *mpl* ♦ *vi* viaggiare ♦ *vt* (*distance*) percorrere; **~ agency** *n* agenzia (di) viaggi; **~ agent** *n* agente *m* di viaggio; **~ler** (*US* **~er**) *n* viaggiatore/trice; **~ler's cheque** (*US* **~er's check**) *n* assegno turistico; **~ling** (*US* **~ing**) *n* viaggi *mpl*; **~ sickness** *n* mal *m* d'auto (*or di mare or d'aria*)

travesty ['trævəstɪ] *n* parodia

trawler ['trɔ:lə*] *n* peschereccio (a strascico)

tray [treɪ] *n* (*for carrying*) vassoio; (*on desk*) vaschetta

treacherous ['tretʃərəs] *adj* infido(a)

treachery ['tretʃərɪ] *n* tradimento

treacle ['tri:kl] *n* melassa

tread [tred] (*pt* **trod**, *pp* **trodden**) *n* passo; (*sound*) rumore *m* di passi; (*of stairs*) pedata; (*of tyre*) battistrada *m inv* ♦ *vi* camminare; **~ on** *vt fus* calpestare

treason ['tri:zn] *n* tradimento

treasure ['treʒə*] *n* tesoro ♦ *vt* (*value*) tenere in gran conto, apprezzare molto; (*store*) custodire gelosamente

treasurer ['treʒərə*] *n* tesoriere/a

treasury ['treʒərɪ] *n*: **the T~** (*BRIT*), **the T~ Department** (*US*) il ministero del Tesoro

treat [tri:t] *n* regalo ♦ *vt* trattare; (*MED*) curare; **to ~ sb to sth** offrire qc a qn

treatment ['tri:tmənt] *n* trattamento

treaty ['tri:tɪ] *n* patto, trattato

treble ['trebl] *adj* triplo(a), triplice ♦ *vt* triplicare ♦ *vi* triplicarsi; **~ clef** *n* chiave *f* di violino

tree [tri:] *n* albero; **~ trunk** *n* tronco d'albero

trek [trek] *n* escursione *f* a piedi; escursione *f* in macchina; (*tiring walk*) camminata sfiancante ♦ *vi* (*as holiday*) fare dell'escursionismo

trellis ['trelɪs] *n* graticcio

tremble ['trembl] *vi* tremare

tremendous [trɪ'mendəs] *adj* (*enormous*) enorme; (*excellent*) meraviglioso(a), formidabile

tremor ['tremə*] *n* tremore *m*, tremito; (*also*: **earth ~**) scossa sismica

trench [trentʃ] *n* trincea

trend [trend] *n* (*tendency*) tendenza; (*of events*) corso; (*fashion*) moda; **~y** *adj* (*idea*) di moda; (*clothes*) all'ultima moda

trespass ['trespəs] *vi*: **to ~ on** entrare abusivamente in; **"no ~ing"** "proprietà privata", "vietato l'accesso"

trestle ['tresl] *n* cavalletto

trial ['traɪəl] *n* (*LAW*) processo; (*test: of machine etc*) collaudo; **~s** *npl* (*unpleasant experiences*) dure prove *fpl*; **on ~** (*LAW*) sotto processo; **by ~ and error** a tentoni; **~ period** periodo di prova

triangle ['traɪæŋgl] *n* (*MATH, MUS*) triangolo

tribe [traɪb] *n* tribù *f inv*; **~sman** (*irreg*) *n* membro di tribù

tribunal [traɪˈbjuːnl] *n* tribunale *m*

tributary ['trɪbjutəri] *n* (*river*) tributario, affluente *m*

tribute ['trɪbjuːt] *n* tributo, omaggio; **to pay ~ to** rendere omaggio a

trick [trɪk] *n* trucco; (*joke*) tiro; (*CARDS*) presa ♦ *vt* imbrogliare, ingannare; **to play a ~ on sb** giocare un tiro a qn; **that should do the ~** vedrai che funziona; **~ery** *n* inganno

trickle ['trɪkl] *n* (*of water etc*) rivolo; gocciolio ♦ *vi* gocciolare

tricky ['trɪkɪ] *adj* difficile, delicato(a)

tricycle ['traɪsɪkl] *n* triciclo

trifle ['traɪfl] *n* sciocchezza; (*BRIT: CULIN*) ≈ zuppa inglese ♦ *adv*: **a ~ long** un po' lungo; **trifling** *adj* insignificante

trigger ['trɪgə*] *n* (*of gun*) grilletto; **~ off** *vt* dare l'avvio a

trim [trɪm] *adj* (*house, garden*) ben tenuto(a); (*figure*) snello(a) ♦ *n* (*haircut etc*) spuntata, regolata; (*embellishment*) finiture *fpl*; (*on car*) guarnizioni *fpl* ♦ *vt* spuntare; (*decorate*): **to ~ (with)** decorare (con); (*NAUT: a sail*) orientare; **~mings** *npl* decorazioni *fpl*; (*extras: gen CULIN*) guarnizione *f*

trinket ['trɪŋkɪt] *n* gingillo; (*piece of jewellery*) ciondolo

trip [trɪp] *n* viaggio; (*excursion*) gita, escursione *f*; (*stumble*) passo falso ♦ *vi* inciampare; (*go lightly*) camminare con passo leggero; **on a ~** in viaggio; **~ up** *vi* inciampare ♦ *vt* fare lo sgambetto a

tripe [traɪp] *n* (*CULIN*) trippa; (*pej: rubbish*) sciocchezze *fpl*, fesserie *fpl*

triple ['trɪpl] *adj* triplo(a)

triplets ['trɪplɪts] *npl* bambini(e) trigemini(e)

triplicate ['trɪplɪkət] *n*: **in ~** in triplice copia

tripod ['traɪpɔd] *n* treppiede *m*

trite [traɪt] *adj* banale, trito(a)

triumph ['traɪʌmf] *n* trionfo ♦ *vi*: **to ~ (over)** trionfare (su)

trivia ['trɪvɪə] *npl* banalità *fpl*

trivial ['trɪvɪəl] *adj* insignificante; (*commonplace*) banale

trod [trɔd] *pt of* **tread**; **~den** *pp of* **tread**

trolley ['trɔlɪ] *n* carrello; **~ bus** *n* filobus *m inv*

trombone [trɔmˈbəun] *n* trombone *m*

troop [truːp] *n* gruppo; (*MIL*) squadrone *m*; **~s** *npl* (*MIL*) truppe *fpl*; **~ in/out** *vi* entrare/uscire a frotte; **~ing the colour** *n* (*ceremony*) sfilata della bandiera

trophy ['trəufɪ] *n* trofeo

tropic ['trɔpɪk] *n* tropico; **~al** *adj* tropicale

trot [trɔt] *n* trotto ♦ *vi* trottare; **on the ~** (*BRIT: fig*) di fila, uno(a) dopo l'altro(a)

trouble ['trʌbl] *n* difficoltà *f inv*, problema *m*; difficoltà *fpl*, problemi *f*; (*worry*) preoccupazione *f*; (*bother, effort*) sforzo; (*POL*) conflitti *mpl*; disordine *m*; (*MED*): **stomach** *etc* **~** disturbi *mpl* gastrici *etc* ♦ *vt* disturbare; (*worry*) preoccupare ♦ *vi*: **to ~ to do** disturbarsi a fare; **~s** *npl* (*POL etc*) disordini *mpl*; **to be in ~** avere dei problemi; **it's no ~!** di niente!; **what's the ~?** cosa c'è che non va?; **~d** *adj* (*person*) preoccupato(a), inquieto(a); (*epoch, life*) agitato(a), difficile; **~maker** *n* elemento disturbatore, agitatore/trice; (*child*) disloco/a; **~shooter** *n* (*in conflict*) conciliatore *m*; **~some** *adj* fastidioso(a), seccante

trough [trɔf] *n* (*also*: **drinking ~**) abbeveratoio; (*also*: **feeding ~**) trogolo, mangiatoia; (*channel*) canale *m*

trousers ['trauzəz] *npl* pantaloni *mpl*, calzoni *mpl*; **short ~** calzoncini *mpl*

trousseau ['truːsəu] (*pl* **~x** *or* **~s**) *n* corredo da sposa

trousseaux ['truːsəuz] *npl of* **trousseau**

trout [traut] *n inv* trota

trowel ['trauəl] *n* cazzuola

truant ['truːənt] (*BRIT*) *n*: **to play ~** marinare la scuola

truce [truːs] *n* tregua

truck [trʌk] *n* autocarro, camion *m inv*; (*RAIL*) carro merci aperto; (*for luggage*) carrello *m* portabagagli *inv*; **~ driver** *n* camionista *m/f*; **~ farm** (*US*) *n* orto industriale

true [truː] *adj* vero(a); (*accurate*) accurato(a), esatto(a); (*genuine*) reale; (*faithful*) fedele; **to come ~** avverarsi

truffle ['trʌfl] *n* tartufo

truly ['truːlɪ] *adv* veramente; (*truthfully*) sinceramente; (*faithfully*): **yours ~** (*in letter*) distinti saluti

trump [trʌmp] *n* (*also*: **~ card**) atout *m inv*

trumpet ['trʌmpɪt] *n* tromba

truncheon ['trʌntʃən] *n* sfollagente *m inv*

trundle ['trʌndl] *vt* far rotolare rumorosamente ♦ *vi*: **to ~ along** rotolare rumorosamente

trunk [trʌŋk] *n* (*of tree, person*) tronco; (*of elephant*) proboscide *f*; (*case*) baule *m*; (*US: AUT*) bagagliaio; **~s** *npl* (*also*: **swimming ~s**) calzoncini *mpl* da bagno

truss [trʌs] *vt*: **~ (up)** (*CULIN*) legare

trust [trʌst] *n* fiducia; (*LAW*) amministrazione *f* fiduciaria; (*COMM*) trust *m inv* ♦ *vt* (*rely on*) contare su; (*hope*) sperare; (*entrust*): **to ~ sth to sb** affidare qc a qn; **~ed** *adj* fidato(a); **~ee** [trʌs'tiː] *n* (*LAW*) amministratore(trice) fiduciario(a); (*of school etc*) amministratore/trice; **~ful** *adj* fiducioso(a); **~ing** *adj* = **~ful**; **~worthy** *adj* fidato(a), degno(a) di fiducia

truth [truːθ, *pl* truːðz] *n* verità *f inv*; **~ful** *adj* (*person*) sincero(a); (*description*) veritiero(a), esatto(a)

try [traɪ] *n* prova, tentativo; (*RUGBY*) meta

♦ *vt* (*LAW*) giudicare; (*test: also*: **~ out**) provare; (*strain*) mettere alla prova ♦ *vi* provare; **to have a ~** fare un tentativo; **to ~ to do** (*seek*) cercare di fare; **~ on** *vt* (*clothes*) provare; **~ing** *adj* (*day, experience*) logorante, pesante; (*child*) difficile, insopportabile

tsar [zɑː*] *n* zar *m inv*

T-shirt ['tiː-] *n* maglietta

T-square ['tiː-] *n* riga a T

tub [tʌb] *n* tinozza; mastello; (*bath*) bagno

tuba ['tjuːbə] *n* tuba

tubby ['tʌbɪ] *adj* grassoccio(a)

tube [tjuːb] *n* tubo; (*BRIT: underground*) metropolitana, metrò *m inv*; (*for tyre*) camera d'aria; **~ station** (*BRIT*) *n* stazione *f* della metropolitana

tubular ['tjuːbjulə*] *adj* tubolare

TUC (*BRIT*) *n abbr* (= *Trades Union Congress*) confederazione *f* dei sindacati britannici

tuck [tʌk] *vt* (*put*) mettere; **~ away** *vt* riporre; (*building*): **to be ~ed away** essere in un luogo isolato; **~ in** *vt* mettere dentro; (*food*) rimboccare ♦ *vi* (*eat*) mangiare di buon appetito; abbuffarsi; **~ up** *vt* (*child*) rimboccare le coperte a; **~ shop** *n* negozio di pasticceria (*in una scuola*)

Tuesday ['tjuːzdɪ] *n* martedì *m inv*

tuft [tʌft] *n* ciuffo

tug [tʌg] *n* (*ship*) rimorchiatore *m* ♦ *vt* tirare con forza; **~-of-war** *n* tiro alla fune

tuition [tjuː'ɪʃən] *n* (*BRIT*) lezioni *fpl*; (*: private ~*) lezioni *fpl* private; (*US: school fees*) tasse *fpl* scolastiche

tulip ['tjuːlɪp] *n* tulipano

tumble ['tʌmbl] *n* (*fall*) capitombolo ♦ *vi* capitombolare, ruzzolare; **to ~ to sth** (*inf*) realizzare qc; **~down** *adj* cadente, diroccato(a); **~ dryer** (*BRIT*) *n* asciugatrice *f*

tumbler ['tʌmblə*] *n* bicchiere *m* (*senza stelo*)

tummy ['tʌmɪ] (*inf*) *n* pancia; **~ upset** *n* mal *m* di pancia

tumour ['tjuːmə*] (*US* **tumor**) *n* tumore *m*

tuna ['tjuːnə] *n inv* (*also*: **~ fish**) tonno

tune [tjuːn] *n* (*melody*) melodia, aria ♦ *vt* (*MUS*) accordare; (*RADIO, TV, AUT*) regolare, mettere a punto; **to be in/out of ~** (*instrument*) essere accordata(a)/ scordata(a); (*singer*) essere intonato(a)/ stonato(a); **~ in** *vi*: **to ~ in (to)** (*RADIO, TV*) sintonizzarsi (su); **~ up** *vi* (*musician*) accordare lo strumento; **~ful** *adj* melodioso(a); **~r** *n*: **piano ~r** accordatore *m*

tunic ['tjuːnɪk] *n* tunica

Tunisia [tjuːˈnɪzɪə] *n* Tunisia

tunnel ['tʌnl] *n* galleria ♦ *vi* scavare una galleria

turban ['təːbən] *n* turbante *m*

turbulence ['təːbjuləns] *n* (*AVIAT*) turbolenza

tureen [təˈriːn] *n* zuppiera

turf [təːf] *n* terreno erboso; (*clod*) zolla ♦ *vt* coprire di zolle erbose; **~ out** (*inf*) *vt* buttar fuori

Turin [tjuəˈrɪn] *n* Torino *f*

Turk [təːk] *n* turco/a

Turkey ['təːkɪ] *n* Turchia

turkey ['təːkɪ] *n* tacchino

Turkish ['təːkɪʃ] *adj* turco(a) ♦ *n* (*LING*) turco

turmoil ['təːmɔɪl] *n* confusione *f*, tumulto

turn [təːn] *n* giro; (*change*) cambiamento; (*in road*) curva; (*tendency: of mind, events*) tendenza; (*performance*) numero; (*chance*) turno; (*MED*) crisi *f inv*, attacco ♦ *vt* girare, voltare; (*change*): **to ~ sth into** trasformare qc in ♦ *vi* girare; (*person: look back*) girarsi, voltarsi; (*reverse direction*) girare; (*change*) cambiare; (*milk*) andare a male; (*become*) diventare; **a good ~** un buon servizio; **it gave me quite a ~** mi ha fatto prendere un bello spavento; **"no left ~"** (*AUT*) "divieto di svolta a sinistra"; **it's your ~** tocca a lei; **in ~** a sua volta; a turno; **to take ~s (at sth)** fare (qc) a turno; **~ away** *vi* girarsi dall'altra parte) ♦ *vt* mandare via; **~ back** *vi* ritornare, tornare indietro ♦ *vt* far tornare indietro; (*clock*) spostare indietro; **~ down** *vt* (*refuse*) rifiutare; (*reduce*) abbassare; (*fold*) ripiegare; **~ in** *vi* (*inf: go to bed*) andare a letto ♦ *vt* (*fold*) voltare in dentro; **~ off** *vi* (*from road*) girare, voltare ♦ *vt* (*light, radio, engine etc*) spegnere; **~ on** *vt* (*light, radio etc*) accendere; **~ out** *vt* (*light, gas*) chiudere; spegnere ♦ *vi* (*voters*) presentarsi; **to ~ out to be ...** rivelarsi ..., risultare ...; **~ over** *vi* (*person*) girarsi ♦ *vt* girare; **~ round** *vi* girare; (*person*) girarsi; **~ up** *vi* (*person*) arrivare, presentarsi; (*lost object*) saltar fuori ♦ *vt* (*collar, sound*) alzare; **~ing** *n* (*in road*) curva; **~ing point** *n* (*fig*) svolta decisiva

turnip ['təːnɪp] *n* rapa

turnout ['təːnaut] *n* presenza, affluenza

turnover ['təːnəuvə*] *n* (*COMM*) turnover *m inv*; (*CULIN*): **apple** *etc* **~** sfogliatella alle mele *ecc*

turnpike ['təːnpaɪk] (*US*) *n* autostrada a pedaggio

turnstile ['təːnstaɪl] *n* tornella

turntable ['təːnteɪbl] *n* (*on record player*) piatto

turn-up (*BRIT*) *n* (*on trousers*) risvolto

turpentine ['təːpəntaɪn] *n* (*also*: **turps**) acqua ragia

turquoise ['təːkwɔɪz] *n* turchese *m* ♦ *adj* turchese

turret ['tʌrɪt] *n* torretta

turtle ['təːtl] *n* testuggine *f*; **~neck (sweater)** *n* maglione *m* con il collo alto

Tuscany ['tʌskənɪ] *n* Toscana

tusk [tʌsk] *n* zanna

tutor ['tjuːtə*] *n* (*in college*) docente *m/f* (*responsabile di un gruppo di studenti*); (*private teacher*) precettore *m*; **~ial** [-ˈtɔːrɪəl] *n* (*SCOL*) lezione *f* con discussione (*a un gruppo limitato*)

tuxedo [tʌkˈsiːdəu] (*US*) *n* smoking *m inv*

TV [tiːˈviː] *n abbr* (= *television*) tivù *f inv*

twang [twæŋ] *n* (*of instrument*) suono vibrante; (*of voice*) accento nasale

tweed [twiːd] *n* tweed *m inv*

tweezers ['twiːzəz] *npl* pinzette *fpl*

twelfth [twelfθ] *num* dodicesimo(a)

twelve [twelv] *num* dodici; **at ~ (o'clock)** alle dodici, a mezzogiorno; (*midnight*) a mezzanotte

twentieth ['twentɪɪθ] *num* ventesimo(a)

twenty ['twentɪ] *num* venti

twice [twaɪs] *adv* due volte; ~ **as much** due volte tanto; ~ **a week** due volte alla settimana

twiddle ['twɪdl] *vt, vi*: **to ~ (with) sth** giocherellare con qc; **to ~ one's thumbs** (*fig*) girarsi i pollici

twig [twɪg] *n* ramoscello ♦ *vt, vi* (*inf*) capire

twilight ['twaɪlaɪt] *n* crepuscolo

twin [twɪn] *adj, n* gemello(a) ♦ *vt*: **to ~ one town with another** fare il gemellaggio di una città con un'altra; ~**-bedded room** *n* stanza con letti gemelli; ~ **beds** *npl* letti *mpl* gemelli

twine [twaɪn] *n* spago, cordicella ♦ *vi* attorcigliarsi

twinge [twɪndʒ] *n* (*of pain*) fitta; **a ~ of conscience/regret** un rimorso/rimpianto

twinkle ['twɪŋkl] *vi* scintillare; (*eyes*) brillare

twirl [twə:l] *vt* far roteare ♦ *vi* roteare

twist [twɪst] *n* torsione *f*; (*in wire, flex*) piega; (*in road*) curva; (*in story*) colpo di scena ♦ *vt* attorcigliare; (*ankle*) slogare; (*weave*) intrecciare; (*roll around*) arrotolare; (*fig*) distorcere ♦ *vi* (*road*) serpeggiare

twit [twɪt] (*inf*) *n* cretino(a)

twitch [twɪtʃ] *n* tiratina; (*nervous*) tic *m inv* ♦ *vi* contrarsi

two [tu:] *num* due; **to put ~ and ~ together** (*fig*) fare uno più uno; ~**-door** *adj* (*AUT*) a due porte; ~**-faced** (*pej*) *adj* (*person*) falso(a); ~**fold** *adv*: **to increase ~fold** aumentare del doppio; ~**-piece** (*suit*) *n* due pezzi *m inv*; ~**-piece** (*swimsuit*) *n* (costume *m* da bagno a) due pezzi *m inv*; ~**some** *n* (*people*) coppia; ~**-way** *adj* (*traffic*) a due sensi

tycoon [taɪ'ku:n] *n*: **(business) ~** magnate *m*

type [taɪp] *n* (*category*) genere *m*; (*model*) modello; (*example*) tipo; (*TYP*) tipo, carattere *m* ♦ *vt* (*letter etc*) battere (a macchina), dattilografare; ~**-cast** *adj* (*actor*) a ruolo fisso; ~**face** *n* carattere *m* tipografico; ~**script** *n* dattiloscritto;

~**writer** *n* macchina da scrivere; ~**written** *adj* dattiloscritto(a), battuto(a) a macchina

typhoid ['taɪfɔɪd] *n* tifoidea

typhoon [taɪ'fu:n] *n* tifone *m*

typical ['tɪpɪkl] *adj* tipico(a)

typify ['tɪpɪfaɪ] *vt* caratterizzare; (*person*) impersonare

typing ['taɪpɪŋ] *n* dattilografia

typist ['taɪpɪst] *n* dattilografo/a

tyrant ['taɪərnt] *n* tiranno

tyre ['taɪə*] (*US* **tire**) *n* pneumatico, gomma; ~ **pressure** *n* pressione *f* (delle gomme)

tzar [zɑ:*] *n* = **tsar**

U, u

U-bend ['ju:'-] *n* (*in pipe*) sifone *m*

ubiquitous [ju:'bɪkwɪtəs] *adj* onnipresente

udder ['ʌdə*] *n* mammella

UFO ['ju:fəu] *n abbr* (= *unidentified flying object*) UFO *m inv*

ugh [ə:h] *excl* puah!

ugly ['ʌglɪ] *adj* brutto(a)

UHT *abbr* (= *ultra heat treated*) UHT *inv*, a lunga conservazione

UK *n abbr* = **United Kingdom**

ulcer ['ʌlsə*] *n* ulcera; (*also*: **mouth ~**) afta

Ulster ['ʌlstə*] *n* Ulster *m*

ulterior [ʌl'tɪərɪə*] *adj* ulteriore; ~ **motive** *n* secondo fine *m*

ultimate ['ʌltɪmət] *adj* ultimo(a), finale; (*authority*) massimo(a), supremo(a); ~**ly** *adv* alla fine; in definitiva, in fin dei conti

ultrasound [ʌltrə'saund] *n* (*MED*) ultrasuono

umbilical cord [ʌmbɪ'laɪkl-] *n* cordone *m* ombelicale

umbrella [ʌm'brelə] *n* ombrello

umpire ['ʌmpaɪə*] *n* arbitro

umpteen [ʌmp'ti:n] *adj* non so quanti(e); **for the ~th time** per l'ennesima volta

UN *n abbr* (= *United Nations*) ONU *f*

unable [ʌn'eɪbl] *adj*: **to be ~ to** non potere, essere nell'impossibilità di; essere incapace di

unaccompanied [ʌnə'kʌmpənɪd] *adj* (*child, lady*) non accompagnato(a)

unaccustomed [ʌnə'kʌstəmd] *adj*: **to be ~ to sth** non essere abituato a qc
unanimous [ju:'nænıməs] *adj* unanime; **~ly** *adv* all'unanimità
unarmed [ʌn'ɑ:md] *adj* (*without a weapon*) disarmato(a); (*combat*) senz'armi
unattached [ʌnə'tætʃt] *adj* senza legami, libero(a)
unattended [ʌnə'tendıd] *adj* (*car, child, luggage*) incustodito(a)
unattractive [ʌnə'træktıv] *adj* poco attraente
unauthorized [ʌn'ɔ:θəraızd] *adj* non autorizzato(a)
unavoidable [ʌnə'vɔıdəbl] *adj* inevitabile
unaware [ʌnə'weə*] *adj*: **to be ~ of** non sapere, ignorare; **~s** *adv* di sorpresa, alla sprovvista
unbalanced [ʌn'bælənst] *adj* squilibrato(a)
unbearable [ʌn'beərəbl] *adj* insopportabile
unbeknown(st) [ʌnbı'nəun(st)] *adv*: **~ to** all'insaputa di
unbelievable [ʌnbı'li:vəbl] *adj* incredibile
unbend [ʌn'bend] (*irreg: like* **bend**) *vi* distendersi ♦ *vt* (*wire*) raddrizzare
unbias(s)ed [ʌn'baıəst] *adj* (*person, report*) obiettivo(a), imparziale
unborn [ʌn'bɔ:n] *adj* non ancora nato(a)
unbreakable [ʌn'breıkəbl] *adj* infrangibile
unbroken [ʌn'brəukən] *adj* intero(a); (*series*) continuo(a); (*record*) imbattuto(a)
unbutton [ʌn'bʌtn] *vt* sbottonare
uncalled-for [ʌn'kɔ:ld-] *adj* (*remark*) fuori luogo *inv*; (*action*) ingiustificato(a)
uncanny [ʌn'kænı] *adj* misterioso(a), strano(a)
unceasing [ʌn'si:sıŋ] *adj* incessante
unceremonious ['ʌnserı'məunıəs] *adj* (*abrupt, rude*) senza tante cerimonie
uncertain [ʌn'sə:tn] *adj* incerto(a); dubbio(a); **~ty** *n* incertezza
unchanged [ʌn'tʃeındʒd] *adj* invariato(a)
uncivilized [ʌn'sıvılaızd] *adj* (*gen*) selvaggio(a); (*fig*) incivile, barbaro(a)
uncle [ʌŋkl] *n* zio
uncomfortable [ʌn'kʌmfətəbl] *adj* scomodo(a); (*uneasy*) a disagio, agitato(a);

(*unpleasant*) fastidioso(a)
uncommon [ʌn'kɔmən] *adj* raro(a), insolito(a), non comune
uncompromising [ʌn'kɔmprəmaızıŋ] *adj* intransigente, inflessibile
unconcerned [ʌnkən'sə:nd] *adj*: **to be ~ (about)** non preoccuparsi (di *or* per)
unconditional [ʌnkən'dıʃənl] *adj* incondizionato(a), senza condizioni
unconscious [ʌn'kɔnʃəs] *adj* privo(a) di sensi, svenuto(a); (*unaware*) inconsapevole, inconscio(a) ♦ *n*: **the ~** l'inconscio; **~ly** *adv* inconsciamente
uncontrollable [ʌnkən'trəuləbl] *adj* incontrollabile; indisciplinato(a)
unconventional [ʌnkən'venʃənl] *adj* poco convenzionale
uncouth [ʌn'ku:θ] *adj* maleducato(a), grossolano(a)
uncover [ʌn'kʌvə*] *vt* scoprire
undecided [ʌndı'saıdıd] *adj* indeciso(a)
under ['ʌndə*] *prep* sotto; (*less than*) meno di; al disotto di; (*according to*) secondo, in conformità a ♦ *adv* (al) disotto; **~ there** là sotto; **~ repair** in riparazione
under... ['ʌndə*] *prefix* sotto..., sub...; **~-age** *adj* minorenne; **~carriage** (*BRIT*) *n* carrello (d'atterraggio); **~charge** *vt* far pagare di meno a; **~clothes** *npl* biancheria (intima); **~coat** *n* (*paint*) mano *f* di fondo; **~cover** *adj* segreto(a), clandestino(a); **~current** *n* corrente *f* sottomarina; **~cut** *vt irreg* vendere a prezzo minore di; **~developed** *adj* sottosviluppato(a); **~dog** *n* oppresso/a; **~done** *adj* (*CULIN*) al sangue; (*pej*) poco cotto(a); **~estimate** *vt* sottovalutare; **~fed** *adj* denutrito(a); **~foot** *adv* sotto i piedi; **~go** *vt irreg* subire; (*treatment*) sottoporsi a; **~graduate** *n* studente(essa) universitario(a); **~ground** *n* (*BRIT: railway*) metropolitana; (*POL*) movimento clandestino ♦ *adj* sotterraneo(a); (*fig*) clandestino(a) ♦ *adv* sottoterra; **to go ~ground** (*fig*) darsi alla macchia; **~growth** *n* sottobosco; **~hand(ed)** *adj* (*fig*) furtivo(a), subdolo(a); **~lie** *vt irreg* essere

alla base di; **~line** *vt* sottolineare; **~mine** *vt* minare; **~neath** [ʌndə'niːθ] *adv* sotto, disotto ♦ *prep* sotto, al di sotto di; **~paid** *adj* sottopagato(a); **~pants** *npl* mutande *fpl*, slip *m inv*; **~pass** (*BRIT*) *n* sottopassaggio; **~privileged** *adj* non abbiente; meno favorito(a); **~rate** *vt* sottovalutare; **~shirt** (*US*) *n* maglietta; **~shorts** (*US*) *npl* mutande *fpl*, slip *m inv*; **~side** *n* disotto; **~skirt** (*BRIT*) *n* sottoveste *f*

understand [ʌndə'stænd] (*irreg: like* **stand**) *vt, vi* capire, comprendere; **I ~ that ...** sento che ...; credo di capire che ...; **~able** *adj* comprensibile; **~ing** *adj* comprensivo(a) ♦ *n* comprensione *f*; (*agreement*) accordo

understatement [ʌndə'steɪtmənt] *n*: **that's an ~!** a dire poco!

understood [ʌndə'stud] *pt, pp of* **understand** ♦ *adj* inteso(a); (*implied*) sottinteso(a)

understudy ['ʌndəstʌdɪ] *n* sostituto/a, attore/trice supplente

undertake [ʌndə'teɪk] (*irreg: like* **take**) *vt* intraprendere; **to ~ to do sth** impegnarsi a fare qc

undertaker ['ʌndəteɪkə*] *n* impresario di pompe funebri

undertaking [ʌndə'teɪkɪŋ] *n* impresa; (*promise*) promessa

undertone ['ʌndətəun] *n*: **in an ~** a mezza voce, a voce bassa

underwater [ʌndə'wɔːtə*] *adv* sott'acqua ♦ *adj* subacqueo(a)

underwear ['ʌndəweə*] *n* biancheria (intima)

underworld ['ʌndəwəːld] *n* (*of crime*) malavita

underwriter ['ʌndəraɪtə*] *n* (*INSURANCE*) sottoscrittore/trice

undesirable [ʌndɪ'zaɪərəbl] *adj* sgradevole

undies ['ʌndɪz] (*inf*) *npl* biancheria intima da donna

undo [ʌn'duː] *vt irreg* disfare; **~ing** *n* rovina, perdita

undoubted [ʌn'dautɪd] *adj* sicuro(a),

certo(a); **~ly** *adv* senza alcun dubbio

undress [ʌn'dres] *vi* spogliarsi

undue [ʌn'djuː] *adj* eccessivo(a)

undulating ['ʌndjuleɪtɪŋ] *adj* ondeggiante; ondulato(a)

unduly [ʌn'djuːlɪ] *adv* eccessivamente

unearth [ʌn'əːθ] *vt* dissotterrare; (*fig*) scoprire

unearthly [ʌn'əːθlɪ] *adj* (*hour*) impossibile

uneasy [ʌn'iːzɪ] *adj* a disagio; (*worried*) preoccupato(a); (*peace*) precario(a)

uneconomic(al) ['ʌniːkə'nɔmɪk(l)] *adj* antieconomico(a)

unemployed [ʌnɪm'plɔɪd] *adj* disoccupato(a) ♦ *npl*: **the ~** i disoccupati

unemployment [ʌnɪm'plɔɪmənt] *n* disoccupazione *f*

unending [ʌn'ɛndɪŋ] *adj* senza fine

unerring [ʌn'əːrɪŋ] *adj* infallibile

uneven [ʌn'iːvn] *adj* ineguale; irregolare

unexpected [ʌnɪk'spɛktɪd] *adj* inatteso(a), imprevisto(a); **~ly** *adv* inaspettatamente

unfailing [ʌn'feɪlɪŋ] *adj* (*supply, energy*) inesauribile; (*remedy*) infallibile

unfair [ʌn'feə*] *adj*: **~ (to)** ingiusto(a) (nei confronti di)

unfaithful [ʌn'feɪθful] *adj* infedele

unfamiliar [ʌnfə'mɪlɪə*] *adj* sconosciuto(a), strano(a); **to be ~ with** non avere familiarità con

unfashionable [ʌn'fæʃnəbl] *adj* (*clothes*) fuori moda; (*district*) non alla moda

unfasten [ʌn'fɑːsn] *vt* slacciare; sciogliere

unfavourable [ʌn'feɪvərəbl] (*US* **unfavorable**) *adj* sfavorevole

unfeeling [ʌn'fiːlɪŋ] *adj* insensibile, duro(a)

unfinished [ʌn'fɪnɪʃt] *adj* incompleto(a)

unfit [ʌn'fɪt] *adj* (*ill*) malato(a), in cattiva salute; (*incompetent*): **~ (for)** incompetente (in); (: *work, MIL*) inabile (a)

unfold [ʌn'fəuld] *vt* spiegare ♦ *vi* (*story, plot*) svelarsi

unforeseen ['ʌnfɔː'siːn] *adj* imprevisto(a)

unforgettable [ʌnfə'gɛtəbl] *adj* indimenticabile

unfortunate [ʌn'fɔːtʃnət] *adj* sfortunato(a); (*event, remark*) infelice; **~ly** *adv* sfortunatamente, purtroppo

unfounded [ʌnˈfaundɪd] *adj* infondato(a)

unfriendly [ʌnˈfrɛndlɪ] *adj* poco amichevole, freddo(a)

ungainly [ʌnˈgeɪnlɪ] *adj* goffo(a), impacciato(a)

ungodly [ʌnˈgɒdlɪ] *adj*: **at an ~ hour** a un'ora impossibile

ungrateful [ʌnˈgreɪtful] *adj* ingrato(a)

unhappiness [ʌnˈhæpɪnɪs] *n* infelicità

unhappy [ʌnˈhæpɪ] *adj* infelice; **~ about/ with** (*arrangements etc*) insoddisfatto(a) di

unharmed [ʌnˈhɑːmd] *adj* incolume, sano(a) e salvo(a)

unhealthy [ʌnˈhɛlθɪ] *adj* (*gen*) malsano(a); (*person*) malaticcio(a)

unheard-of [ʌnˈhɑːdɒv] *adj* inaudito(a), senza precedenti

unhurt [ʌnˈhɑːt] *adj* illeso(a)

uniform [ˈjuːnɪfɔːm] *n* uniforme *f*, divisa ♦ *adj* uniforme

uninhabited [ʌnɪnˈhæbɪtɪd] *adj* disabitato(a)

unintentional [ʌnɪnˈtɛnʃənəl] *adj* involontario(a)

union [ˈjuːnjən] *n* unione *f*; (*also*: **trade ~**) sindacato ♦ *cpd* sindacale, dei sindacati; **U~ Jack** *n* bandiera nazionale britannica

unique [juːˈniːk] *adj* unico(a)

unit [ˈjuːnɪt] *n* unità *f inv*; (*section: of furniture etc*) elemento; (*team, squad*) reparto, squadra

unite [juːˈnaɪt] *vt* unire ♦ *vi* unirsi; **~d** unito(a); unificato(a); (*efforts*) congiunto(a); **U~d Kingdom** *n* Regno Unito; **U~d Nations (Organization)** *n* (Organizzazione *f* delle) Nazioni Unite; **U~d States (of America)** *n* Stati *mpl* Uniti (d'America)

unit trust (*BRIT*) *n* fondo d'investimento

unity [ˈjuːnɪtɪ] *n* unità

universal [juːnɪˈvɛːsl] *adj* universale

universe [ˈjuːnɪvɛːs] *n* universo

university [juːnɪˈvɛːsɪtɪ] *n* università *f inv*

unjust [ʌnˈdʒʌst] *adj* ingiusto(a)

unkempt [ʌnˈkɛmpt] *adj* trasandato(a); spettinato(a)

unkind [ʌnˈkaɪnd] *adj* scortese; crudele

unknown [ʌnˈnəun] *adj* sconosciuto(a)

unlawful [ʌnˈlɔːful] *adj* illecito(a), illegale

unleaded [ʌnˈlɛdɪd] *adj* (*petrol, fuel*) verde, senza piombo

unleash [ʌnˈliːʃ] *vt* (*fig*) scatenare

unless [ʌnˈlɛs] *conj* a meno che (non) +*sub*

unlike [ʌnˈlaɪk] *adj* diverso(a) ♦ *prep* a differenza di, contrariamente a

unlikely [ʌnˈlaɪklɪ] *adj* improbabile

unlisted [ʌnˈlɪstɪd] (*US*) *adj* (*TEL*): **to be ~** non essere sull'elenco

unload [ʌnˈləud] *vt* scaricare

unlock [ʌnˈlɒk] *vt* aprire

unlucky [ʌnˈlʌkɪ] *adj* sfortunato(a); (*object, number*) che porta sfortuna

unmarried [ʌnˈmærɪd] *adj* non sposato(a); (*man only*) scapolo, celibe; (*woman only*) nubile

unmistak(e)able [ʌnmɪsˈteɪkəbl] *adj* inconfondibile

unmitigated [ʌnˈmɪtɪgeɪtɪd] *adj* non mitigato(a), assoluto(a), vero(a) e proprio(a)

unnatural [ʌnˈnætʃrəl] *adj* innaturale; contro natura

unnecessary [ʌnˈnɛsəsərɪ] *adj* inutile, superfluo(a)

unnoticed [ʌnˈnəutɪst] *adj*: **(to go) ~** (passare) inosservato(a)

UNO [ˈjuːnəu] *n abbr* (= *United Nations Organization*) ONU *f*

unobtainable [ʌnəbˈteɪnəbl] *adj* (*TEL*) non ottenibile

unobtrusive [ʌnəbˈtruːsɪv] *adj* discreto(a)

unofficial [ʌnəˈfɪʃl] *adj* non ufficiale; (*strike*) non dichiarato(a) dal sindacato

unpack [ʌnˈpæk] *vi* disfare la valigia (*or* le valigie) ♦ *vt* disfare

unpalatable [ʌnˈpælətəbl] *adj* sgradevole

unparalleled [ʌnˈpærəlɛld] *adj* incomparabile, impareggiabile

unpleasant [ʌnˈplɛznt] *adj* spiacevole

unplug [ʌnˈplʌg] *vt* staccare

unpopular [ʌnˈpɒpjulə*] *adj* impopolare

unprecedented [ʌnˈprɛsɪdəntɪd] *adj* senza precedenti

unpredictable [ʌnprɪ'dɪktəbl] *adj* imprevedibile

unprofessional [ʌnprə'fɛʃənl] *adj* poco professionale

unqualified [ʌnɪ'kwɔlɪfaɪd] *adj* (*teacher*) non abilitato(a); (*success*) assoluto(a), senza riserve

unquestionably [ʌn'kwɛstʃənəblɪ] *adv* indiscutibilmente

unravel [ʌn'rævl] *vt* dipanare, districare

unreal [ʌn'rɪəl] *adj* irreale

unrealistic [ʌnrɪə'lɪstɪk] *adj* non realistico(a)

unreasonable [ʌn'riːznəbl] *adj* irragionevole

unrelated [ʌnrɪ'leɪtɪd] *adj*: ~ **(to)** senza rapporto (con); non imparentato(a) (con)

unreliable [ʌnrɪ'laɪəbl] *adj* (*person, machine*) che non dà affidamento; (*news, source of information*) inattendibile

unremitting [ʌnrɪ'mɪtɪŋ] *adj* incessante

unreservedly [ʌnrɪ'zɜːvɪdlɪ] *adv* senza riserve

unrest [ʌn'rɛst] *n* agitazione *f*

unroll [ʌn'rəul] *vt* srotolare

unruly [ʌn'ruːlɪ] *adj* indisciplinato(a)

unsafe [ʌn'seɪf] *adj* pericoloso(a), rischioso(a)

unsaid [ʌn'sɛd] *adj*: **to leave sth ~** passare qc sotto silenzio

unsatisfactory ['ʌnsætɪs'fæktərɪ] *adj* che lascia a desiderare, insufficiente

unsavoury [ʌn'seɪvərɪ] (*US* **unsavory**) *adj* (*fig: person, place*) losco(a)

unscathed [ʌn'skeɪðd] *adj* incolume

unscrew [ʌn'skruː] *vt* svitare

unscrupulous [ʌn'skruːpjuləs] *adj* senza scrupoli

unsettled [ʌn'sɛtld] *adj* (*person*) turbato(a); indeciso(a); (*weather*) instabile

unshaven [ʌn'ʃeɪvn] *adj* non rasato(a)

unsightly [ʌn'saɪtlɪ] *adj* brutto(a), sgradevole a vedersi

unskilled [ʌn'skɪld] *adj* non specializzato(a)

unspeakable [ʌn'spiːkəbl] *adj* (*indescribable*) indicibile; (*awful*) abominevole

unstable [ʌn'steɪbl] *adj* (*gen*) instabile;

(*mentally*) squilibrato(a)

unsteady [ʌn'stɛdɪ] *adj* instabile, malsicuro(a)

unstuck [ʌn'stʌk] *adj*: **to come ~** scollarsi; (*fig*) fare fiasco

unsuccessful [ʌnsək'sɛsful] *adj* (*writer, proposal*) che non ha successo; (*marriage, attempt*) mal riuscito(a), fallito(a); **to be ~** (*in attempting sth*) non avere successo

unsuitable [ʌn'suːtəbl] *adj* inadatto(a); inopportuno(a); sconveniente

unsure [ʌn'ʃuə*] *adj* incerto(a); **to be ~ of o.s.** essere insicuro(a)

unsuspecting [ʌnsə'spɛktɪŋ] *adj* che non sospetta nulla

unsympathetic [ʌnsɪmpə'θɛtɪk] *adj* (*person*) antipatico(a); (*attitude*) poco incoraggiante

untapped [ʌn'tæpt] *adj* (*resources*) non sfruttato(a)

unthinkable [ʌn'θɪŋkəbl] *adj* impensabile, inconcepibile

untidy [ʌn'taɪdɪ] *adj* (*room*) in disordine; (*appearance*) trascurato(a); (*person*) disordinato(a)

untie [ʌn'taɪ] *vt* (*knot, parcel*) disfare; (*prisoner, dog*) slegare

until [ʌn'tɪl] *prep* fino a; (*after negative*) prima di ♦ *conj* finché, fino a quando; (*in past, after negative*) prima che +*sub*, prima di +*infinitive*; ~ **he comes** finché *or* fino a quando non arriva; ~ **now** finora; ~ **then** fino ad allora

untimely [ʌn'taɪmlɪ] *adj* intempestivo(a), inopportuno(a); (*death*) prematuro(a)

untold [ʌn'təuld] *adj* (*story*) mai rivelato(a); (*wealth*) incalcolabile; (*joy, suffering*) indescrivibile

untoward [ʌntə'wɔːd] *adj* sfortunato(a), sconveniente

unused [ʌn'juːzd] *adj* nuovo(a)

unusual [ʌn'juːʒuəl] *adj* insolito(a), eccezionale, raro(a)

unveil [ʌn'veɪl] *vt* scoprire; svelare

unwanted [ʌn'wɔntɪd] *adj* (*clothing*) smesso(a); (*child*) non desiderato(a)

unwavering [ʌn'weɪvərɪŋ] *adj* fermo(a),

incrollabile

unwelcome [ʌn'wɛlkəm] *adj* non gradito(a)

unwell [ʌn'wɛl] *adj* indisposto(a); **to feel ~** non sentirsi bene

unwieldy [ʌn'wiːldɪ] *adj* poco maneggevole

unwilling [ʌn'wɪlɪŋ] *adj*: **to be ~ to do** non voler fare; **~ly** *adv* malvolentieri

unwind [ʌn'waɪnd] (*irreg: like* **wind**[1]) *vt* svolgere, srotolare ♦ *vi* (*relax*) rilassarsi

unwise [ʌn'waɪz] *adj* poco saggio(a)

unwitting [ʌn'wɪtɪŋ] *adj* involontario(a)

unworkable [ʌn'wəːkəbl] *adj* (*plan*) inattuabile

unworthy [ʌn'wəːðɪ] *adj* indegno(a)

unwrap [ʌn'ræp] *vt* disfare; aprire

unwritten [ʌn'rɪtn] *adj* (*agreement*) tacito(a); (*law*) non scritto(a)

KEYWORD

up [ʌp] *prep*: **he went ~ the stairs/the hill** è salito su per le scale/sulla collina; **the cat was ~ a tree** il gatto era su un albero; **they live further ~ the street** vivono un po' più su nella stessa strada

♦ *adv* **1** (*upwards, higher*) su, in alto; **~ in the sky/the mountains** su nel cielo/in montagna; **~ there** lassù; **~ above** su in alto

2: **to be ~** (*out of bed*) essere alzato(a); (*prices, level*) essere salito(a)

3: **~ to** (*as far as*) fino a; **~ to now** finora

4: **to be ~ to** (*depending on*): **it's ~ to you** sta a lei, dipende da lei; (*equal to*): **he's not ~ to it** (*job, task etc*) non ne è all'altezza; (*inf: be doing*): **what is he ~ to?** cosa sta combinando?

♦ *n*: **~s and downs** alti e bassi *mpl*

---

upbringing ['ʌpbrɪŋɪŋ] *n* educazione *f*

update [ʌp'deɪt] *vt* aggiornare

upgrade [ʌp'greɪd] *vt* (*house, job*) migliorare; (*employee*) avanzare di grado

upheaval [ʌp'hiːvl] *n* sconvolgimento; tumulto

uphill [ʌp'hɪl] *adj* in salita; (*fig: task*) difficile ♦ *adv*: **to go ~** andare in salita, salire

uphold [ʌp'həʊld] (*irreg: like* **hold**) *vt* approvare; sostenere

upholstery [ʌp'həʊlstərɪ] *n* tappezzeria

upkeep ['ʌpkiːp] *n* manutenzione *f*

upon [ə'pɔn] *prep* su

upper ['ʌpə*] *adj* superiore ♦ *n* (*of shoe*) tomaia; **~-class** *adj* dell'alta borghesia; **~ hand** *n*: **to have the ~ hand** avere il coltello dalla parte del manico; **~most** *adj* il(la) più alto(a); predominante

upright ['ʌpraɪt] *adj* diritto(a); verticale; (*fig*) diritto(a), onesto(a)

uprising ['ʌpraɪzɪŋ] *n* insurrezione *f*, rivolta

uproar ['ʌprɔː*] *n* tumulto, clamore *m*

uproot [ʌp'ruːt] *vt* sradicare

upset [*n* 'ʌpsɛt, *vb, adj* ʌp'sɛt] (*irreg: like* **set**) *n* (*to plan etc*) contrattempo; (*stomach ~*) disturbo ♦ *vt* (*glass etc*) rovesciare; (*plan, stomach*) scombussolare; (*person: offend*) contrariare; (: *grieve*) addolorare; sconvolgere ♦ *adj* contrariato(a); addolorato(a); (*stomach*) scombussolato(a)

upshot ['ʌpʃɔt] *n* risultato

upside down ['ʌpsaɪd-] *adv* sottosopra

upstairs [ʌp'stɛəz] *adv, adj* di sopra, al piano superiore ♦ *n* piano di sopra

upstart ['ʌpstɑːt] *n* parvenu *m inv*

upstream [ʌp'striːm] *adv* a monte

uptake ['ʌpteɪk] *n*: **he is quick/slow on the ~** è pronto/lento di comprendonio

uptight [ʌp'taɪt] (*inf*) *adj* teso(a)

up-to-date *adj* moderno(a); aggiornato(a)

upturn ['ʌptəːn] *n* (*in luck*) svolta favorevole; (*COMM: in market*) rialzo

upward ['ʌpwəd] *adj* ascendente; verso l'alto; **~(s)** *adv* in su, verso l'alto

urban ['əːbən] *adj* urbano(a); **~ clearway** *n* strada di scorrimento (*in cui è vietata la sosta*)

urbane [əː'beɪn] *adj* civile, urbano(a), educato(a)

urchin ['əːtʃɪn] *n* monello

urge [əːdʒ] *n* impulso; stimolo; forte desiderio ♦ *vt*: **to ~ sb to do** esortare qn a fare, spingere qn a fare; raccomandare a qn di fare

urgency ['əːdʒənsɪ] *n* urgenza; (*of tone*)

insistenza

urgent ['ɔːdʒənt] *adj* urgente; (*voice*) insistente

urinate ['juərɪneɪt] *vi* orinare

urine ['juərɪn] *n* orina

urn [əːn] *n* urna; (*also:* **tea ~**) bollitore *m* per il tè

us [ʌs] *pron* ci; (*stressed, after prep*) noi; *see also* **me**

US(A) *n abbr* (= *United States (of America)*) USA *mpl*

usage ['juːzɪdʒ] *n* uso

use [*n* juːs, *vb* juːz] *n* uso; impiego, utilizzazione *f* ♦ *vt* usare, utilizzare, servirsi di; **in ~** in uso; **out of ~** fuori uso; **to be of ~** essere utile, servire; **it's no ~** non serve, è inutile; **she ~d to do it** lo faceva (una volta), era solita farlo; **to be ~d to** avere l'abitudine di; **~ up** *vt* consumare; esaurire; **~d** *adj* (*object, car*) usato(a); **~ful** *adj* utile; **~fulness** *n* utilità; **~less** *adj* inutile; (*person*) inetto(a); **~r** *n* utente *m/f*; **~r-friendly** *adj* (*computer*) di facile uso

usher ['ʌʃə*] *n* usciere *m*; **~ette** [-'rɛt] *n* (*in cinema*) maschera

USSR *n* (*HIST*): **the ~** l'URSS *f*

usual ['juːʒuəl] *adj* solito(a); **as ~** come al solito, come d'abitudine; **~ly** *adv* di solito

utensil [juː'tɛnsl] *n* utensile *m*; **kitchen ~s** utensili da cucina

uterus ['juːtərəs] *n* utero

utility [juː'tɪlɪtɪ] *n* utilità; (*also:* **public ~**) servizio pubblico; **~ room** *n* locale adibito alla stiratura dei panni etc

utmost ['ʌtməust] *adj* estremo(a) ♦ *n*: **to do one's ~** fare il possibile *or* di tutto

utter ['ʌtə*] *adj* assoluto(a), totale ♦ *vt* pronunciare, proferire; emettere; **~ance** *n* espressione *f*; parole *fpl*; **~ly** *adv* completamente, del tutto

U-turn ['juː'təːn] *n* inversione *f* a U

V, v

v. *abbr* = **verse**; **versus**; **volt**; (= *vide*) vedi, vedere

vacancy ['veɪkənsɪ] *n* (*BRIT: job*) posto libero; (*room*) stanza libera; **"no vacancies"** "completo"

vacant ['veɪkənt] *adj* (*job, seat etc*) libero(a); (*expression*) assente

vacate [və'keɪt] *vt* lasciare libero(a)

vacation [və'keɪʃən] *n* (*esp US*) vacanze *fpl*

vaccinate ['væksɪneɪt] *vt* vaccinare

vaccination [væksɪ'neɪʃən] *n* vaccinazione *f*

vacuum ['vækjum] *n* vuoto; **~ cleaner** *n* aspirapolvere *m inv*; **~ flask** (*BRIT*) *n* thermos ® *m inv*; **~-packed** *adj* confezionato(a) sottovuoto

vagina [və'dʒaɪnə] *n* vagina

vagrant ['veɪgrnt] *n* vagabondo/a

vague [veɪg] *adj* vago(a); (*blurred: photo, memory*) sfocato(a); **~ly** *adv* vagamente

vain [veɪn] *adj* (*useless*) inutile, vano(a); (*conceited*) vanitoso(a); **in ~** inutilmente, invano

valentine ['væləntaɪn] *n* (*also:* **~ card**) cartolina *or* biglietto di San Valentino; (*person*) innamorato/a

valet ['væleɪ] *n* cameriere *m* personale

valiant ['vælɪənt] *adj* valoroso(a), coraggioso(a)

valid ['vælɪd] *adj* valido(a), valevole; (*excuse*) valido(a)

valley ['vælɪ] *n* valle *f*

valour ['vælə*] (*US* **valor**) *n* valore *m*

valuable ['væljuəbl] *adj* (*jewel*) di (grande) valore; (*time, help*) prezioso(a); **~s** *npl* oggetti *mpl* di valore

valuation [vælju'eɪʃən] *n* valutazione *f*, stima

value ['væljuː] *n* valore *m* ♦ *vt* (*fix price*) valutare, dare un prezzo a; (*cherish*) apprezzare, tenere a; **~ added tax** (*BRIT*) *n* imposta sul valore aggiunto; **~d** *adj* (*appreciated*) stimato(a), apprezzato(a)

valve [vælv] *n* valvola

van [væn] *n* (AUT) furgone *m*; (BRIT: RAIL) vagone *m*

vandal ['vændl] *n* vandalo/a; **~ism** *n* vandalismo

vanilla [və'nɪlə] *n* vaniglia ♦ *cpd* (ice cream) alla vaniglia

vanish ['vænɪʃ] *vi* svanire, scomparire

vanity ['vænɪtɪ] *n* vanità

vantage ['vɑːntɪdʒ] *n*: **~ point** posizione *f* or punto di osservazione; (fig) posizione vantaggiosa

vapour ['veɪpə*] (US **vapor**) *n* vapore *m*

variable ['vɛərɪəbl] *adj* variabile; (mood) mutevole

variance ['vɛərɪəns] *n*: **to be at ~ (with)** essere in disaccordo (con); (facts) essere in contraddizione (con)

varicose ['værɪkəus] *adj*: **~ veins** vene *fpl* varicose

varied ['vɛərɪd] *adj* vario(a), diverso(a)

variety [və'raɪətɪ] *n* varietà *f inv*; (quantity) quantità, numero; **~ show** *n* varietà *m inv*

various ['vɛərɪəs] *adj* vario(a), diverso(a); (several) parecchi(e), molti(e)

varnish ['vɑːnɪʃ] *n* vernice *f*; (nail ~) smalto ♦ *vt* verniciare; mettere lo smalto su

vary ['vɛərɪ] *vt*, *vi* variare, mutare

vase [vɑːz] *n* vaso

Vaseline ® ['væsɪliːn] *n* vaselina

vast [vɑːst] *adj* vasto(a); (amount, success) enorme

VAT [væt] *n abbr* (= value added tax) I.V.A. *f*

vat [væt] *n* tino

Vatican ['vætɪkən] *n*: **the ~** il Vaticano

vault [vɔːlt] *n* (of roof) volta; (tomb) tomba; (in bank) camera blindata ♦ *vt* (also: **~ over**) saltare (d'un balzo)

vaunted ['vɔːntɪd] *adj*: **much-~** tanto celebrato(a)

VCR *n abbr* = **video cassette recorder**

VD *n abbr* = **venereal disease**

VDU *n abbr* = **visual display unit**

veal [viːl] *n* vitello

veer [vɪə*] *vi* girare; virare

vegan ['viːgən] *n* vegetaliano(a)

vegeburger ['vedʒɪbɜːgɜ*] *n* hamburger *m* inv vegetariano

vegetable ['vedʒtəbl] *n* verdura, ortaggio ♦ *adj* vegetale

vegetarian [vedʒɪ'tɛərɪən] *adj*, *n* vegetariano(a)

vehement ['viːɪmənt] *adj* veemente, violento(a)

vehicle ['viːɪkl] *n* veicolo

veil [veɪl] *n* velo; **~ed** *adj* (fig: threat) velato(a)

vein [veɪn] *n* vena; (on leaf) nervatura

velvet ['vɛlvɪt] *n* velluto ♦ *adj* di velluto

vending machine ['vɛndɪŋ-] *n* distributore *m* automatico

vendor ['vɛndə*] *n* venditore/trice

veneer [və'nɪə*] *n* impiallacciatura; (fig) vernice *f*

venereal [vɪ'nɪərɪəl] *adj*: **~ disease** malattia venerea

Venetian [vɪ'niːʃən] *adj* veneziano(a); **~ blind** *n* (tenda alla) veneziana

vengeance ['vɛndʒəns] *n* vendetta; **with a ~** (fig) davvero; furiosamente

Venice ['vɛnɪs] *n* Venezia

venison ['vɛnɪsn] *n* carne *f* di cervo

venom ['vɛnəm] *n* veleno

vent [vɛnt] *n* foro, apertura; (in dress, jacket) spacco ♦ *vt* (fig: one's feelings) sfogare, dare sfogo a

ventilate ['vɛntɪleɪt] *vt* (room) dare aria a, arieggiare; **ventilator** *n* ventilatore *m*

ventriloquist [vɛn'trɪləkwɪst] *n* ventriloquo/a

venture ['vɛntʃə*] *n* impresa (rischiosa) ♦ *vt* rischiare, azzardare ♦ *vi* avventurarsi; **business ~** iniziativa commerciale

venue ['vɛnjuː] *n* luogo (designato) per l'incontro

verb [vɜːb] *n* verbo; **~al** *adj* verbale; (translation) orale

verbatim [vɜː'beɪtɪm] *adj*, *adv* parola per parola

verdict ['vɜːdɪkt] *n* verdetto

verge [vɜːdʒ] (BRIT) *n* bordo, orlo; **"soft ~s"** (BRIT: AUT) banchine *fpl* cedevoli; **on the ~ of doing** sul punto di fare; **~ on** *vt fus* rasentare

veritable ['vɛrɪtəbl] *adj* vero(a)
vermin ['vəːmɪn] *npl* animali *mpl* nocivi; (*insects*) insetti *mpl* parassiti
vermouth ['vəːməθ] *n* vermut *m inv*
versatile ['vəːsətaɪl] *adj* (*person*) versatile; (*machine, tool etc*) (che si presta) a molti usi
verse [vəːs] *n* versi *mpl*; (*stanza*) stanza, strofa; (*in bible*) versetto
version ['vəːʃən] *n* versione *f*
versus ['vəːsəs] *prep* contro
vertical ['vəːtɪkl] *adj* verticale ♦ *n* verticale *m*; ~**ly** *adv* verticalmente
vertigo ['vəːtɪgəu] *n* vertigine *f*
verve [vəːv] *n* brio; entusiasmo
very ['vɛrɪ] *adv* molto ♦ *adj*: **the ~ book which** proprio il libro che; **the ~ last** proprio l'ultimo; **at the ~ least** almeno; ~ **much** moltissimo
vessel ['vɛsl] *n* (*ANAT*) vaso; (*NAUT*) nave *f*; (*container*) recipiente *m*
vest [vɛst] *n* (*BRIT*) maglia; (: *sleeveless*) canottiera; (*US: waistcoat*) gilè *m inv*
vested interests ['vɛstɪd-] *npl* (*COMM*) diritti *mpl* acquisiti
vet [vɛt] *n abbr* (*BRIT*: = *veterinary surgeon*) veterinario ♦ *vt* esaminare minuziosamente
veteran ['vɛtərn] *n* (*also*: **war ~**) veterano
veterinary ['vɛtrɪnərɪ] *adj* veterinario(a); ~ **surgeon** (*US* **veterinarian**) *n* veterinario
veto ['viːtəu] *n* (*pl* ~**es**) *n* veto ♦ *vt* opporre il veto a
vex [vɛks] *vt* irritare, contrariare; ~**ed** *adj* (*question*) controverso(a), dibattuto(a)
via ['vaɪə] *prep* (*by way of*) via; (*by means of*) tramite
viable ['vaɪəbl] *adj* attuabile; vitale
viaduct ['vaɪədʌkt] *n* viadotto
vibrant ['vaɪbrənt] *adj* (*lively, bright*) vivace; (*voice*) vibrante
vibrate [vaɪ'breɪt] *vi*: **to ~ (with)** vibrare (di); (*resound*) risonare (di)
vicar ['vɪkə*] *n* pastore *m*; ~**age** *n* presbiterio
vicarious [vɪ'kɛərɪəs] *adj* indiretto(a)
vice [vaɪs] *n* (*evil*) vizio; (*TECH*) morsa
vice- [vaɪs] *prefix* vice...

vice squad *n* (squadra del) buon costume *f*
vice versa ['vaɪsɪ'vəːsə] *adv* viceversa
vicinity [vɪ'sɪnɪtɪ] *n* vicinanze *fpl*
vicious ['vɪʃəs] *adj* (*remark, dog*) cattivo(a); (*blow*) violento(a); ~ **circle** *n* circolo vizioso
victim ['vɪktɪm] *n* vittima
victor ['vɪktə*] *n* vincitore *m*
Victorian [vɪk'tɔːrɪən] *adj* vittoriano(a)
victory ['vɪktərɪ] *n* vittoria
video ['vɪdɪəu] *cpd* video... ♦ *n* (~ *film*) video *m inv*; (*also*: ~ **cassette**) videocassetta; (*also*: ~ **cassette recorder**) videoregistratore *m*; ~ **tape** *n* videotape *m inv*; ~ **wall** *n* schermo *m* multivideo *inv*
vie [vaɪ] *vi*: **to ~ with** competere con, rivaleggiare con
Vienna [vɪ'ɛnə] *n* Vienna
Vietnam [vjɛt'næm] *n* Vietnam *m*; ~**ese** *adj*, *n inv* vietnamita *m/f*
view [vjuː] *n* vista, veduta; (*opinion*) opinione *f* ♦ *vt* (*look at*: *also fig*) considerare; (*house*) visitare; **on ~** (*in museum etc*) esposto(a); **in full ~ of** sotto gli occhi di; **in ~ of the weather/the fact that** considerato il tempo/che; **in my ~** a mio parere; ~**er** *n* spettatore/trice; ~**finder** *n* mirino; ~**point** *n* punto di vista; (*place*) posizione *f*
vigil ['vɪdʒɪl] *n* veglia
vigorous ['vɪgərəs] *adj* vigoroso(a)
vile [vaɪl] *adj* (*action*) vile; (*smell*) disgustoso(a), nauseante; (*temper*) pessimo(a)
villa ['vɪlə] *n* villa
village ['vɪlɪdʒ] *n* villaggio; ~**r** *n* abitante *m/f* di villaggio
villain ['vɪlən] *n* (*scoundrel*) canaglia; (*BRIT*: *criminal*) criminale *m*; (*in novel etc*) cattivo
vindicate ['vɪndɪkeɪt] *vt* comprovare; giustificare
vindictive [vɪn'dɪktɪv] *adj* vendicativo(a)
vine [vaɪn] *n* vite *f*; (*climbing plant*) rampicante *m*
vinegar ['vɪnɪgə*] *n* aceto
vineyard ['vɪnjɑːd] *n* vigna, vigneto

vintage ['vɪntɪdʒ] n (year) annata, produzione f ♦ cpd d'annata; ~ **car** n auto f inv d'epoca; ~ **wine** n vino d'annata

vinyl ['vaɪnl] n vinile m

violate ['vaɪəleɪt] vt violare

violence ['vaɪələns] n violenza

violent ['vaɪələnt] adj violento(a)

violet ['vaɪələt] adj (colour) viola inv, violetto(a) ♦ n (plant) violetta; (colour) violetto

violin [vaɪə'lɪn] n violino; ~**ist** n violinista m/f

VIP n abbr (= very important person) V.I.P. m/f inv

virgin ['vɜ:dʒɪn] n vergine f ♦ adj vergine inv

Virgo ['vɜ:gəu] n (sign) Vergine f

virile ['vɪraɪl] adj virile

virtually ['vɜ:tjuəlɪ] adv (almost) praticamente

virtual reality ['vɜ:tʃuəl -] n (COMPUT) realtà virtuale

virtue ['vɜ:tju:] n virtù f inv; (advantage) pregio, vantaggio; **by ~ of** grazie a

virtuous ['vɜ:tjuəs] adj virtuoso(a)

virus ['vaɪərəs] n (also COMPUT) virus m inv

visa ['vi:zə] n visto

vis-à-vis [vi:zə'vi:] prep rispetto a, nei riguardi di

visibility [vɪzɪ'bɪlɪtɪ] n visibilità

visible ['vɪzəbl] adj visibile

vision ['vɪʒən] n (sight) vista; (foresight, in dream) visione f

visit ['vɪzɪt] n visita; (stay) soggiorno ♦ vt (person: US also: ~ **with**) andare a trovare; (place) visitare; ~**ing hours** npl (in hospital etc) orario delle visite; ~**or** n visitatore/trice; (guest) ospite m/f; ~**or centre** n centro informazioni per visitatori di museo, zoo, parco ecc

visor ['vaɪzə*] n visiera

visual ['vɪzjuəl] adj visivo(a); visuale; ottico(a); ~ **aid** n sussidio visivo; ~ **display unit** n visualizzatore m

visualize ['vɪzjuəlaɪz] vt immaginare, figurarsi; (foresee) prevedere

visually-impaired ['vɪzjuəlɪ-] adj videoleso(a)

vital ['vaɪtl] adj vitale; ~**ly** adv estremamente; ~ **statistics** npl (fig) misure fpl

vitamin ['vɪtəmɪn] n vitamina

vivacious [vɪ'veɪʃəs] adj vivace

vivid ['vɪvɪd] adj vivido(a); ~**ly** adv (describe) vividamente; (remember) con precisione

V-neck ['vi:nɛk] n maglione m con lo scollo a V

vocabulary [vəu'kæbjulərɪ] n vocabolario

vocal ['vəukl] adj (MUS) vocale; (communication) verbale; ~ **cords** npl corde fpl vocali

vocation [vəu'keɪʃən] n vocazione f; ~**al** adj professionale

vociferous [və'sɪfərəs] adj rumoroso(a)

vodka ['vɔdkə] n vodka f inv

vogue [vəug] n moda; (popularity) popolarità, voga

voice [vɔɪs] n voce f ♦ vt (opinion) esprimere; ~ **mail** n servizio di segreteria telefonica

void [vɔɪd] n vuoto ♦ adj (invalid) nullo(a); (empty): ~ **of** privo(a) di

volatile ['vɔlətaɪl] adj volatile; (fig) volubile

volcano [vɔl'keɪnəu] (pl ~**es**) n vulcano

volition [və'lɪʃən] n: **of one's own ~** di sua volontà

volley ['vɔlɪ] n (of gunfire) salva; (of stones, questions etc) raffica; (TENNIS etc) volata; ~**ball** n pallavolo f

volt [vəult] n volt m inv; ~**age** n tensione f, voltaggio

voluble ['vɔljubl] adj loquace, ciarliero(a)

volume ['vɔlju:m] n volume m

voluntarily ['vɔləntrɪlɪ] adv volontariamente; gratuitamente

voluntary ['vɔləntərɪ] adj volontario(a); (unpaid) gratuito(a), non retribuito(a)

volunteer [vɔlən'tɪə*] n volontario/a ♦ vt offrire volontariamente ♦ vi (MIL) arruolarsi volontario; **to ~ to do** offrire (volontariamente) di fare

voluptuous [və'lʌptjuəs] adj voluttuoso(a)

vomit ['vɔmɪt] n vomito ♦ vt, vi vomitare

vote [vəut] n voto, suffragio; (cast) voto; (franchise) diritto di voto ♦ vt: **to be ~d**

chairman *etc* venir eletto presidente *etc*; (*propose*): **to ~ that** approvare la proposta che ♦ *vi* votare; **~ of thanks** discorso di ringraziamento; **~r** *n* elettore/trice; **voting** *n* scrutinio

vouch [vautʃ]: **to ~ for** *vt fus* farsi garante di

voucher ['vautʃə*] *n* (*for meal, petrol etc*) buono

vow [vau] *n* voto, promessa solenne ♦ *vt*: **to ~ to do/that** giurare di fare/che

vowel ['vauəl] *n* vocale *f*

voyage ['vɔɪɪdʒ] *n* viaggio per mare, traversata

V-sign ['viː-] (*BRIT*) *n* gesto volgare con le dita

vulgar ['vʌlɡə*] *adj* volgare

vulnerable ['vʌlnərəbl] *adj* vulnerabile

vulture ['vʌltʃə*] *n* avvoltoio

W, w

wad [wɔd] *n* (*of cotton wool, paper*) tampone *m*; (*of banknotes etc*) fascio

waddle ['wɔdl] *vi* camminare come una papera

wade [weid] *vi*: **to ~ through** camminare a stento in; (*fig: book*) leggere con fatica

wafer ['weifə*] *n* (*CULIN*) cialda

waffle ['wɔfl] *n* (*CULIN*) cialda; (*inf*) ciance *fpl* ♦ *vi* cianciare

waft [wɔft] *vt* portare ♦ *vi* diffondersi

wag [wæɡ] *vt* agitare, muovere ♦ *vi* agitarsi

wage [weidʒ] *n* (*also*: **~s**) salario, paga ♦ *vt*: **to ~ war** fare la guerra; **~ earner** *n* salariato/a; **~ packet** *n* busta *f* paga *inv*

wager ['weidʒə*] *n* scommessa

wag(g)on ['wæɡən] *n* (*horse-drawn*) carro; (*BRIT: RAIL*) vagone *m* (*merci*)

wail [weil] *n* gemito; (*of siren*) urlo ♦ *vi* gemere; urlare

waist [weist] *n* vita, cintola; **~coat** (*BRIT*) *n* panciotto, gilè *m inv*; **~line** *n* (giro di) vita

wait [weit] *n* attesa ♦ *vi* aspettare, attendere; **to lie in ~ for** stare in agguato a; **to ~ for** aspettare; **I can't ~ to** (*fig*) non vedo l'ora di; **~ behind** *vi* rimanere (ad aspettare); **~ on** *vt fus* servire; **~er** *n* cameriere *m*; **~ing** *n*: **"no ~ing"** (*BRIT: AUT*) "divieto di sosta"; **~ing list** *n* lista di attesa; **~ing room** *n* sala d'aspetto *or* d'attesa; **~ress** *n* cameriera

waive [weiv] *vt* rinunciare a, abbandonare

wake [weik] (*pt* **woke**, **~d**, *pp* **woken**, **~d**) *vt* (*also*: **~ up**) svegliare ♦ *vi* (*also*: **~ up**) svegliarsi ♦ *n* (*for dead person*) veglia funebre; (*NAUT*) scia; **waken** *vt*, *vi* = **wake**

Wales [weilz] *n* Galles *m*

walk [wɔːk] *n* passeggiata; (*short*) giretto; (*gait*) passo, andatura; (*path*) sentiero; (*in park etc*) sentiero, vialetto ♦ *vi* camminare; (*for pleasure, exercise*) passeggiare ♦ *vt* (*distance*) fare *o* percorrere a piedi; (*dog*) accompagnare, portare a passeggiare; **10 minutes' ~ from** 10 minuti di cammino *or* a piedi da; **from all ~s of life** di tutte le condizioni sociali; **~ out** *vi* (*audience*) andarsene; (*workers*) scendere in sciopero; **~ out on** (*inf*) *vt fus* piantare in asso; **~er** *n* (*person*) camminatore/trice; **~ie-talkie** ['wɔːkɪ'tɔːkɪ] *n* walkie-talkie *m inv*; **~ing** *n* camminare *m*; **~ing shoes** *npl* pedule *fpl*; **~ing stick** *n* bastone *m* da passeggio; **W~man** ® ['wɔːkmən] *n* Walkman ® *m inv*; **~out** *n* (*of workers*) sciopero senza preavviso *or* a sorpresa; **~over** (*inf*) *n* vittoria facile, gioco da ragazzi; **~way** *n* passaggio pedonale

wall [wɔːl] *n* muro; (*internal, of tunnel, cave*) parete *f*; **~ed** *adj* (*city*) fortificato(a); (*garden*) cintato(a)

wallet ['wɔlɪt] *n* portafoglio

wallflower ['wɔːlflauə*] *n* violacciocca; **to be a ~** (*fig*) fare da tappezzeria

wallow ['wɔləu] *vi* sguazzare

wallpaper ['wɔːlpeipə*] *n* carta da parati ♦ *vt* (*room*) mettere la carta da parati in

wally ['wɔlɪ] (*inf*) *n* imbecille *m/f*

walnut ['wɔːlnʌt] *n* noce *f*; (*tree, wood*) noce *m*

walrus ['wɔːlrəs] (*pl* **~** *or* **~es**) *n* tricheco

waltz [wɔːlts] *n* valzer *m inv* ♦ *vi* ballare il valzer

wand [wɔnd] *n* (*also*: **magic ~**) bacchetta

(magica)

wander ['wɔndə*] vi (person) girare senza meta, girovagare; (thoughts) vagare ♦ vt girovagare per

wane [weɪn] vi calare

wangle ['wæŋgl] (BRIT: inf) vt procurare con l'astuzia

want [wɔnt] vt volere; (need) aver bisogno di ♦ n: **for ~** per mancanza di; **~s** npl (needs) bisogni mpl; **to ~ to do** volere fare; **to ~ sb to do** volere che qn faccia; **~ed** adj (criminal) ricercato(a); **''~ed''** (in adverts) "cercasi"; **~ing** adj: **to be found ~ing** non risultare all'altezza

WAP n abbr (= wireless application protocol) WAP

war [wɔː*] n guerra; **to make ~ (on)** far guerra (a)

ward [wɔːd] n (in hospital: room) corsia; (: section) reparto; (POL) circoscrizione f; (LAW: child: also: ~ **of court**) pupillo/a; ~ **off** vt parare, schivare

warden ['wɔːdn] n (of park, game reserve, youth hostel) guardiano/a; (BRIT: of institution) direttore/trice; (BRIT: also: **traffic** ~) addetto/a al controllo del traffico e del parcheggio

warder ['wɔːdə*] (BRIT) n guardia carceraria

wardrobe ['wɔːdrəub] n (cupboard) guardaroba m inv, armadio; (clothes) guardaroba; (CINEMA, THEATRE) costumi mpl

warehouse ['wɛəhaus] n magazzino

wares [wɛəz] npl merci fpl

warfare ['wɔːfɛə*] n guerra

warhead ['wɔːhɛd] n (MIL) testata

warily ['wɛərɪlɪ] adv cautamente, con prudenza

warlike ['wɔːlaɪk] adj bellicoso(a)

warm [wɔːm] adj caldo(a); (thanks, welcome, applause) caloroso(a); (person) cordiale; **it's ~** fa caldo; **I'm ~** ho caldo; ~ **up** vi scaldarsi, riscaldarsi ♦ vt scaldare, riscaldare; (engine) far scaldare; **~-hearted** adj affettuoso(a); **~ly** adv (applaud, welcome) calorosamente; (dress) con abiti pesanti; **~th** n calore m

warn [wɔːn] vt: **to ~ sb that/(not) to do/of**

avvertire or avvisare qn che/di (non) fare/ di; **~ing** n avvertimento; (notice) avviso; (signal) segnalazione f; **~ing light** n spia luminosa; **~ing triangle** n (AUT) triangolo

warp [wɔːp] vi deformarsi ♦ vt (fig) corrompere

warrant ['wɔrnt] n (voucher) buono; (LAW: to arrest) mandato di cattura; (: to search) mandato di perquisizione

warranty ['wɔrəntɪ] n garanzia

warren ['wɔrən] n (of rabbits) tana; (fig: of streets etc) dedalo

warrior ['wɔrɪə*] n guerriero/a

Warsaw ['wɔːsɔː] n Varsavia

warship ['wɔːʃɪp] n nave f da guerra

wart [wɔːt] n verruca

wartime ['wɔːtaɪm] n: **in ~** in tempo di guerra

wary ['wɛərɪ] adj prudente

was [wɔz] pt of **be**

wash [wɔʃ] vt lavare ♦ vi lavarsi; (sea): **to ~ over/against sth** infrangersi su/contro qc ♦ n lavaggio; (of ship) scia; **to give sth a ~** lavare qc, dare una lavata a qc; **to have a ~** lavarsi; ~ **away** vt (stain) togliere lavando; (subj: river) trascinare via; ~ **off** vi andare via con il lavaggio; ~ **up** vi (BRIT) lavare i piatti; (US) darsi una lavata; **~able** adj lavabile; **~basin** (US **~bowl**) n lavabo; **~cloth** (US) n pezzuola (per lavarsi); **~er** n (TECH) rondella; **~ing** n (linen etc) bucato; **~ing machine** n lavatrice f; **~ing powder** (BRIT) n detersivo (in polvere)

wash: **~ing up** n rigovernatura, lavatura dei piatti; **~ing-up liquid** n detersivo liquido (per stoviglie); **~-out** (inf) n disastro; **~room** n gabinetto

wasn't ['wɔznt] = **was not**

wasp [wɔsp] n vespa

wastage ['weɪstɪdʒ] n spreco; (in manufacturing) scarti mpl; **natural ~** diminuzione f di manodopera (per pensionamento, decesso etc)

waste [weɪst] n spreco; (of time) perdita; (rubbish) rifiuti mpl; (also: **household ~**) immondizie fpl ♦ adj (material) di scarto; (food) avanzato(a); (land) incolto(a) ♦ vt sprecare; **~s** npl (area of land) distesa desolata; ~ **away** *vi* deperire; ~ **disposal unit** (*BRIT*) *n* eliminatore *m* di rifiuti; ~**ful** *adj* sprecone(a); (*process*) dispendioso(a); ~ **ground** (*BRIT*) *n* terreno incolto or abbandonato; ~**paper basket** *n* cestino per la carta straccia; ~**pipe** *n* tubo di scarico

watch [wɔtʃ] *n* (*also*: **wrist** ~) orologio (da polso); (*act of watching, vigilance*) sorveglianza; (*guard*: *MIL*, *NAUT*) guardia; (*NAUT*: *spell of duty*) quarto ♦ *vt* (*look at*) osservare; (: *match, programme*) guardare; (*spy on, guard*) sorvegliare, tenere d'occhio; (*be careful of*) fare attenzione a ♦ *vi* osservare, guardare; (*keep guard*) fare or montare la guardia; ~ **out** *vi* fare attenzione; ~**dog** *n* (*also fig*) cane *m* da guardia; ~**ful** *adj* attento(a), vigile; ~**man** (*irreg*) *n* see **night**; ~ **strap** *n* cinturino da orologio

water [wɔːtə*] *n* acqua ♦ *vt* (*plant*) annaffiare ♦ *vi* (*eyes*) lacrimare; (*mouth*): to **make sb's mouth** ~ far venire l'acquolina in bocca a qn; **in British** ~s nelle acque territoriali britanniche; ~ **down** *vt* (*milk*) diluire; (*fig*: *story*) edulcorare; ~ **cannon** *n* idrante *m*; ~ **closet** (*BRIT*) *n* water *m inv*; ~**colour** *n* acquerello; ~**cress** *n* crescione *m*; ~**fall** *n* cascata; ~**heater** *n* scaldabagno; ~**ing can** *n* annaffiatoio; ~ **lily** *n* ninfea; ~**line** *n* (*NAUT*) linea di galleggiamento; ~**logged** *adj* saturo(a) d'acqua; imbevuto(a) d'acqua; (*football pitch etc*) allagato(a); ~ **main** *n* conduttura dell'acqua; ~**melon** *n* anguria, cocomero; ~**proof** *adj* impermeabile; ~**shed** *n* (*GEO, fig*) spartiacque *m*; ~-**skiing** *n* sci *m* acquatico; ~**tight** *adj* stagno(a); ~**way** *n* corso d'acqua navigabile; ~**works** *npl* impianto idrico; ~**y** *adj* (*colour*) slavato(a); (*coffee*) acquoso(a); (*eyes*) umido(a)

watt [wɔt] *n* watt *m inv*

wave [weɪv] *n* (*of hand*) gesto, segno; (*in hair*) ondulazione *f*; (*fig*: *surge*) ondata ♦ *vi* fare un cenno con la mano; (*branches, grass*) ondeggiare; (*flag*) sventolare ♦ *vt* (*hand*) fare un gesto con; (*handkerchief*) sventolare; (*stick*) brandire; ~**length** *n* lunghezza d'onda

waver [weɪvə*] *vi* esitare; (*voice*) tremolare
wavy [weɪvɪ] *adj* ondulato(a); ondeggiante
wax [wæks] *n* cera ♦ *vt* dare la cera a; (*car*) lucidare ♦ *vi* (*moon*) crescere; ~**works** *npl* cere *fpl* ♦ *n* museo delle cere

way [weɪ] *n* via, strada; (*path, access*) passaggio; (*distance*) distanza; (*direction*) parte *f*, direzione *f*; (*manner*) modo, stile *m*; (*habit*) abitudine *f*; **which ~? – this ~** da che parte or in quale direzione? – da questa parte or per di qua; **on the ~** (*en route*) per strada; **to be on one's ~** essere in cammino or sulla strada; **to be in the ~** bloccare il passaggio; (*fig*) essere tra i piedi or d'impiccio; **to go out of one's ~ to do** (*fig*) mettercela tutta or fare di tutto per fare; **under ~** (*project*) in corso; **to lose one's ~** perdere la strada; **in a ~** in un certo senso; **in some ~s** sotto certi aspetti; **no ~!** (*inf*) neanche per idea!; **by the ~ ...** a proposito ...; **"~ in"** (*BRIT*) "entrata", "ingresso"; **"~ out"** (*BRIT*) "uscita"; **the ~ back** la strada del ritorno; **"give ~"** (*BRIT*: *AUT*) "dare la precedenza"

waylay [weɪˈleɪ] (*irreg*: *like* **lay**) *vt* tendere un agguato a; attendere al passaggio
wayward [weɪwəd] *adj* capriccioso(a); testardo(a)
W.C. [dʌblju'si:] (*BRIT*) *n* W.C. *m inv*, gabinetto
we [wiː] *pl pron* noi
weak [wiːk] *adj* debole; (*health*) precario(a); (*beam etc*) fragile; (*tea*) leggero(a); ~**en** *vi* indebolirsi ♦ *vt* indebolire; ~**ling** [wiːklɪŋ] *n* smidollato/a; debole *m/f*; ~**ness** *n* debolezza; (*fault*) punto debole, difetto; **to have a ~ness for** avere un debole per
wealth [wɛlθ] *n* (*money, resources*) ricchezza, ricchezze *fpl*; (*of details*) abbondanza, profusione *f*; ~**y** *adj* ricco(a)
wean [wiːn] *vt* svezzare
weapon [wɛpən] *n* arma
wear [wɛə*] (*pt* **wore**, *pp* **worn**) *n* (*use*) uso; (*damage through use*) logorio, usura; (*clothing*): **sports/baby** ~ abbigliamento sportivo/per neonati ♦ *vt* (*clothes*) portare; (*put on*) mettersi; (*damage*) consumare ♦ *vi*

(*last*) durare; (*rub etc through*) consumarsi; **evening ~** abiti *mpl or* tenuta da sera; ~ **away** *vt* consumare; erodere ♦ *vi* consumarsi; essere eroso(a); ~ **down** *vt* consumare; (*strength*) esaurire; ~ **off** *vi* sparire lentamente; ~ **out** *vt* consumare; (*person*) esaurire; ~ **and tear** *n* usura, consumo

weary ['wɪərɪ] *adj* stanco(a) ♦ *vi*: **to ~ of** stancarsi di

weasel ['wiːzl] *n* (*ZOOL*) donnola

weather ['weðə*] *n* tempo ♦ *vt* (*storm, crisis*) superare; **under the ~** (*fig: ill*) poco bene; **~-beaten** *adj* (*face, skin*) segnato(a) dalle intemperie; (*building*) logorato(a) dalle intemperie; **~cock** *n* banderuola; ~ **forecast** *n* previsioni *fpl* del tempo, bollettino meteorologico; **~man** (*irreg inf*) *n* meteorologo; ~ **vane** *n* = **~cock**

weave [wiːv] (*pt* **wove**, *pp* **woven**) *vt* (*cloth*) tessere; (*basket*) intrecciare; **~r** *n* tessitore/trice; **weaving** *n* tessitura

web [web] *n* (*of spider*) ragnatela; (*on foot*) palma; (*fabric, also fig*) tessuto; **the (World Wide) Web** la Rete

webcam ['wɛbkæm] *n abbr* (= webcamera) webcamera

webcast ['wɛbkɑːst] *n* spettacolo cui si può assistere in Internet

website ['wɛbsaɪt] *n* (*COMPUT*) sitio (Internet)

wed [wɛd] (*pt*, *pp* **wedded**) *vt* sposare ♦ *vi* sposarsi

we'd [wiːd] = **we had**; **we would**

wedding ['wɛdɪŋ] *n* matrimonio; **silver ~ (anniversary)** *n* nozze *fpl* d'argento; ~ **day** *n* giorno delle nozze *or* del matrimonio; ~ **dress** *n* abito nuziale; ~ **ring** *n* fede *f*

wedge [wɛdʒ] *n* (*of wood etc*) zeppa; (*of cake*) fetta ♦ *vt* (*fix*) fissare con zeppe; (*pack tightly*) incastrare

Wednesday ['wɛdnzdɪ] *n* mercoledì *m inv*

wee [wiː] (*SCOTTISH*) *adj* piccolo(a)

weed [wiːd] *n* erbaccia ♦ *vt* diserbare; **~killer** *n* diserbante *m*; **~y** *adj* (*person*) allampanato(a)

week [wiːk] *n* settimana; **a ~ today / on Friday** oggi / venerdì a otto; **~day** *n* giorno feriale; (*COMM*) giornata lavorativa; **~end** *n*

fine settimana *m or f inv*, weekend *m inv*; **~ly** *adv* ogni settimana, settimanalmente ♦ *adj* settimanale ♦ *n* settimanale *m*

weep [wiːp] (*pt*, *pp* **wept**) *vi* piangere; **~ing willow** *n* salice *m* piangente

weigh [weɪ] *vt*, *vi* pesare; **to ~ anchor** salpare l'ancora; ~ **down** *vt* (*branch*) piegare; (*fig: with worry*) opprimere, caricare; ~ **up** *vt* valutare

weight [weɪt] *n* peso; **to lose / put on ~** dimagrire / ingrassare; **~ing** *n* (*allowance*) indennità; ~ **lifter** *n* pesista *m*; **~y** *adj* pesante; (*fig*) importante, grave

weir [wɪə*] *n* diga

weird [wɪəd] *adj* strano(a), bizzarro(a); (*eerie*) soprannaturale

welcome ['wɛlkəm] *adj* benvenuto(a) ♦ *n* accoglienza, benvenuto ♦ *vt* dare il benvenuto a; (*be glad of*) rallegrarsi di; **thank you – you're ~!** grazie – prego!

welfare ['wɛlfɛə*] *n* benessere *m*; ~ **state** *n* stato assistenziale

well [wɛl] *n* pozzo ♦ *adv* bene ♦ *adj*: **to be ~** (*person*) stare bene ♦ *excl* allora!; ma!; ebbene!; **as ~** anche; **as ~ as** così come; oltre a; ~ **done!** bravo(a)!; **get ~ soon!** guarisci presto!; **to do ~** andare bene; ~ **up** *vi* sgorgare

we'll [wiːl] = **we will**; **we shall**

well: **~-behaved** *adj* ubbidiente; **~-being** *n* benessere *m*; **~-built** *adj* (*person*) ben fatto(a); **~-deserved** *adj* meritato(a); **~-dressed** *adj* ben vestito(a), vestito(a) bene; **~-heeled** (*inf*) *adj* agiato(a), facoltoso(a)

wellingtons ['wɛlɪŋtənz] *npl* (*also*: **wellington boots**) stivali *mpl* di gomma

well: **~-known** *adj* noto(a), famoso(a); **~-mannered** *adj* ben educato(a); **~-meaning** *adj* ben intenzionato(a); **~-off** *adj* benestante, danaroso(a); **~-read** *adj* colto(a); **~-to-do** *adj* abbiente, benestante; **~-wisher** *n* ammiratore/trice

Welsh [wɛlʃ] *adj* gallese ♦ *n* (*LING*) gallese *m*; **the ~** *npl* i Gallesi; ~ **Assembly** *n* Parlamento gallese; **~man / woman** (*irreg*) *n* gallese *m/f*; ~ **rarebit** *n* crostino al formaggio

went [wɛnt] *pt of* **go**

wept [wɛpt] *pt, pp of* **weep**

were [wəː*] *pt of* **be**

we're [wɪə*] = **we are**

weren't [wəːnt] = **were not**

west [wɛst] *n* ovest *m*, occidente *m*, ponente *m* ♦ *adj* (a) ovest *inv*, occidentale ♦ *adv* verso ovest; **the W~** l'Occidente *m*; **the W~ Country** (*BRIT*) *n* il sud-ovest dell'Inghilterra; **~erly** *adj* (*point*) a ovest; (*wind*) occidentale, da ovest; **~ern** *adj* occidentale, dell'ovest ♦ *n* (*CINEMA*) western *m inv*; **W~ Germany** *n* Germania Occidentale; **W~ Indian** *adj* delle Indie Occidentali ♦ *n* abitante *m/f* delle Indie Occidentali; **W~ Indies** *npl* Indie *fpl* Occidentali; **~ward(s)** *adv* verso ovest

wet [wɛt] *adj* umido(a), bagnato(a); (*soaked*) fradicio(a); (*rainy*) piovoso(a) ♦ *n* (*BRIT*: *POL*) politico moderato; **to get ~** bagnarsi; **"~ paint"** "vernice fresca"; **~ suit** *n* tuta da sub

we've [wiːv] = **we have**

whack [wæk] *vt* picchiare, battere

whale [weɪl] *n* (*ZOOL*) balena

wharf [wɔːf] (*pl* **wharves**) *n* banchina

wharves [wɔːvz] *npl of* **wharf**

─── KEYWORD ───

what [wɔt] *adj* 1 (*in direct/indirect questions*) che; quale; **~ size is it?** che taglia è?; **~ colour is it?** di che colore è?; **~ books do you want?** quali *or* che libri vuole?
2 (*in exclamations*) che; **~ a mess!** che disordine!

♦ *pron* 1 (*interrogative*) che cosa, cosa, che; **~ are you doing?** che *or* (che) cosa fai?; **~ are you talking about?** di che cosa parli?; **~ is it called?** come si chiama?; **~ about me?** e io?; **~ about doing ...?** e se facessimo ...?
2 (*relative*) ciò che, quello che; **I saw ~ you did/was on the table** ho visto quello che hai fatto/quello che era sul tavolo
3 (*indirect use*) (che) cosa; **he asked me ~ she had said** mi ha chiesto che cosa avesse detto; **tell me ~ you're thinking about** dimmi a cosa stai pensando

♦ *excl* (*disbelieving*) cosa!, come!

─── ───

whatever [wɔt'ɛvə*] *adj*: **~ book** qualunque *or* qualsiasi libro +*sub* ♦ *pron*: **do ~ is necessary/you want** faccia qualunque *or* qualsiasi cosa sia necessaria/lei voglia; **~ happens** qualunque cosa accada; **no reason ~** *or* **whatsoever** nessuna ragione affatto *or* al mondo; **nothing ~** proprio niente

whatsoever [wɔtsəu'ɛvə*] *adj* = **whatever**

wheat [wiːt] *n* grano, frumento

wheedle ['wiːdl] *vt*: **to ~ sb into doing sth** convincere qn a fare qc (con lusinghe); **to ~ sth out of sb** ottenere qc da qn (con lusinghe)

wheel [wiːl] *n* ruota; (*AUT*: *also*: **steering ~**) volante *m*; (*NAUT*) (ruota del) timone *m* ♦ *vt* spingere ♦ *vi* (*birds*) roteare; (*also*: **~ round**) girare; **~barrow** *n* carriola; **~chair** *n* sedia a rotelle; **~ clamp** *n* (*AUT*) morsa che blocca la ruota di una vettura in sosta vietata

wheeze [wiːz] *vi* ansimare

─── KEYWORD ───

when [wɛn] *adv* quando; **~ did it happen?** quando è successo?

♦ *conj* 1 (*at, during, after the time that*) quando; **she was reading ~ I came in** quando sono entrato lei leggeva; **that was ~ I needed you** era allora che avevo bisogno di te
2 (*on, at which*): **on the day ~ I met him** il giorno in cui l'ho incontrato; **one day ~ it was raining** un giorno che pioveva
3 (*whereas*) quando, mentre; **you said I was wrong ~ in fact I was right** mi hai detto che avevo torto, quando in realtà avevo ragione

─── ───

whenever [wɛn'ɛvə*] *adv* quando mai ♦ *conj* quando; (*every time that*) ogni volta che

where [wɛə*] *adv*, *conj* dove; **this is ~** è qui che; **~abouts** *adv* dove ♦ *n*: **sb's**

~abouts luogo dove qn si trova; **~as** *conj*
mentre; **~by** *pron* per cui; **wherever**
[-'ɛvə*] *conj* dovunque +*sub*; (*interrogative*)
dove mai; **~withal** *n* mezzi *mpl*
whet [wɛt] *vt* (*appetite etc*) stimolare
whether ['wɛðə*] *conj* se; **I don't know ~ to
accept or not** non so se accettare o no;
it's doubtful ~ è poco probabile che; **~
you go or not** che lei vada o no

╔═══════════╗
║ *KEYWORD* ║
╚═══════════╝

which [wɪtʃ] *adj* **1** (*interrogative: direct,
indirect*) quale; **~ picture do you want?**
quale quadro vuole?; **~ one?** quale?; **~ one
of you did it?** chi di voi lo ha fatto?
2: in ~ case nel qual caso
♦ *pron* **1** (*interrogative*) quale; **~ (of these)
are yours?** quali di questi sono suoi?; **~ of
you are coming?** chi di voi viene?
2 (*relative*) che; (: *indirect*) cui, il (la) quale;
the apple ~ you ate/~ is on the table la
mela che hai mangiato/che è sul tavolo;
the chair on ~ you are sitting la sedia
sulla quale *or* su cui sei seduto; **he said he
knew, ~ is true** ha detto che lo sapeva, il
che è vero; **after ~** dopo di che

whichever [wɪtʃ'ɛvə*] *adj*: **take ~ book you
prefer** prenda qualsiasi libro che preferisce;
~ book you take qualsiasi libro prenda
whiff [wɪf] *n* soffio; sbuffo; odore *m*
while [waɪl] *n* momento ♦ *conj* mentre; (*as
long as*) finché; (*although*) sebbene +*sub*;
per quanto +*sub*; **for a ~** per un po'; **~
away** *vt* (*time*) far passare
whim [wɪm] *n* capriccio
whimper ['wɪmpə*] *n* piagnucolio ♦ *vi*
piagnucolare
whimsical ['wɪmzɪkl] *adj* (*person*)
capriccioso(a); (*look*) strano(a)
whine [waɪn] *n* gemito ♦ *vi* gemere;
uggiolare; piagnucolare
whip [wɪp] *n* frusta; (*for riding*) frustino; (*POL:
person*) capogruppo (*che sovrintende alla
disciplina dei colleghi di partito*) ♦ *vt*
frustare; (*cream, eggs*) sbattere; **~ped
cream** *n* panna montata; **~-round** (*BRIT*)

n colletta
whirl [wə:l] *vt* (*far*) girare rapidamente; (*far*)
turbinare ♦ *vi* (*dancers*) volteggiare; (*leaves,
water*) sollevarsi in vortice; **~pool** *n*
mulinello; **~wind** *n* turbine *m*
whirr [wə:*] *vi* ronzare; rombare; frullare
whisk [wɪsk] *n* (*CULIN*) frusta; frullino ♦ *vt*
sbattere, frullare; **to ~ sb away** *or* **off**
portar via qn a tutta velocità
whiskers ['wɪskəz] *npl* (*of animal*) baffi *mpl*;
(*of man*) favoriti *mpl*
whisky ['wɪskɪ] (*US, IRELAND* **whiskey**) *n*
whisky *m inv*
whisper ['wɪspə*] *n* sussurro ♦ *vt, vi*
sussurrare
whist [wɪst] *n* whist *m*
whistle ['wɪsl] *n* (*sound*) fischio; (*object*)
fischietto ♦ *vi* fischiare
white [waɪt] *adj* bianco(a); (*with fear*)
pallido(a) ♦ *n* bianco; (*person*) bianco/a; **~
coffee** (*BRIT*) *n* caffellatte *m inv*; **~-collar
worker** *n* impiegato; **~ elephant** *n* (*fig*)
oggetto (*or* progetto) costoso ma inutile;
W~ House *n* Casa Bianca; **~ lie** *n* bugia
pietosa; **~ness** *n* bianchezza; **~ paper** *n*
(*POL*) libro bianco; **~wash** *n* (*paint*) bianco
di calce ♦ *vt* imbiancare; (*fig*) coprire
whiting ['waɪtɪŋ] *n inv* (*fish*) merlango
Whitsun ['wɪtsn] *n* Pentecoste *f*
whittle ['wɪtl] *vt*: **to ~ away, ~ down**
ridurre, tagliare
whizz [wɪz] *vi*: **to ~ past** *or* **by** passare
sfrecciando; **~ kid** (*inf*) *n* prodigio

╔═══════════╗
║ *KEYWORD* ║
╚═══════════╝

who [hu:] *pron* **1** (*interrogative*) chi; **~ is it?,
~'s there?** chi è?
2 (*relative*) che; **the man ~ spoke to me**
l'uomo che ha parlato con me; **those ~
can swim** quelli che sanno nuotare

whodunit [hu:'dʌnɪt] (*inf*) *n* giallo
whoever [hu:'ɛvə*] *pron*: **~ finds it**
chiunque lo trovi; **ask ~ you like** lo chieda
a chiunque vuole; **~ she marries** chiunque
sposerà, non importa chi sposerà; **~ told
you that?** chi mai gliel'ha detto?

whole [həʊl] *adj* (*complete*) tutto(a), completo(a); (*not broken*) intero(a), intatto(a) ♦ *n* (*all*): **the ~ of** tutto(a) il(la); (*entire unit*) tutto; (*not broken*) tutto; **the ~ of the town** tutta la città; la città intera; **on the ~, as a ~** nel complesso, nell'insieme; ~ **food(s)** *n(pl)* cibo integrale; **~hearted** *adj* sincero(a); **~meal** *adj* (*bread, flour*) integrale; **~sale** *n* commercio or vendita all'ingrosso ♦ *adj* all'ingrosso; (*destruction*) totale; **~saler** *n* grossista *m/f*; **~some** *adj* sano(a); salutare; **~wheat** *adj* = **~meal**; **wholly** *adv* completamente, del tutto

whom [huːm] *pron* **1** (*interrogative*) chi; ~ **did you see?** chi hai visto?; **to ~ did you give it?** a chi lo hai dato?
2 (*relative*) che, *prep* +il (la) quale (*check syntax of Italian verb used*); **the man ~ I saw/to ~ I spoke** l'uomo che ho visto/al quale ho parlato

whooping cough ['huːpɪŋ-] *n* pertosse *f*
whore [hɔː*] (*inf: pej*) *n* puttana

whose [huːz] *adj* **1** (*possessive: interrogative*) di chi; ~ **book is this?, ~ is this book?** di chi è questo libro?; ~ **daughter are you?** di chi sei figlia?
2 (*possessive: relative*): **the man ~ son you rescued** l'uomo il cui figlio hai salvato; **the girl ~ sister you were speaking to** la ragazza alla cui sorella stavi parlando ♦ *pron* di chi; ~ **is this?** di chi è questo?; **I know ~ it is** so di chi è

why [waɪ] *adv, conj* perché ♦ *excl* (*surprise*) ma guarda un po'!; (*remonstrating*) ma (via)!; (*explaining*) ebbene!; ~ **not?** perché no?; ~ **not do it now?** perché non farlo adesso?; **that's not ~ I'm here** non è questo il motivo per cui sono qui; **the reason ~** il motivo per cui; **~ever** *adv* perché mai
wicked ['wɪkɪd] *adj* cattivo(a), malvagio(a);

maligno(a); perfido(a)
wickerwork ['wɪkəwɜːk] *adj* di vimini ♦ *n* articoli *mpl* di vimini
wicket ['wɪkɪt] *n* (*CRICKET*) porta; area tra le due porte
wide [waɪd] *adj* largo(a); (*area, knowledge*) vasto(a); (*choice*) ampio(a) ♦ *adv*: **to open ~** spalancare; **to shoot ~** tirare a vuoto or fuori bersaglio; **~-angle lens** *n* grandangolare *m*; **~-awake** *adj* completamente sveglio(a); **~ly** *adv* (*differing*) molto, completamente; (*travelled, spaced*) molto; (*believed*) generalmente; **~n** *vt* allargare, ampliare; ~ **open** *adj* spalancato(a); **~spread** *adj* (*belief etc*) molto or assai diffuso(a)
widow ['wɪdəʊ] *n* vedova; **~ed** *adj*: **to be ~ed** restare vedovo(a); **~er** *n* vedovo
width [wɪdθ] *n* larghezza
wield [wiːld] *vt* (*sword*) maneggiare; (*power*) esercitare
wife [waɪf] (*pl* **wives**) *n* moglie *f*
wig [wɪg] *n* parrucca
wiggle ['wɪgl] *vt* dimenare, agitare
wild [waɪld] *adj* selvatico(a); selvaggio(a); (*sea, weather*) tempestoso(a); (*idea, life*) folle; stravagante; (*applause*) frenetico(a); **~erness** ['wɪldənɪs] *n* deserto; **~life** *n* natura; **~ly** *adv* selvaggiamente; (*applaud*) freneticamente; (*hit, guess*) a casaccio; (*happy*) follemente; **~s** *npl* regione *f* selvaggia
wilful ['wɪlful] (*US* **willful**) *adj* (*person*) testardo(a), ostinato(a); (*action*) intenzionale; (*crime*) premeditato(a)

will [wɪl] (*pt, pp* **~ed**) *aux vb* **1** (*forming future tense*): **I ~ finish it tomorrow** lo finirò domani; **I ~ have finished it by tomorrow** lo finirò entro domani; ~ **you do it?** – **yes I ~/no I won't** lo farai? – sì (lo farò)/no (non lo farò)
2 (*in conjectures, predictions*): **he ~** or **he'll be there by now** dovrebbe essere arrivato ora; **that ~ be the postman** sarà il postino
3 (*in commands, requests, offers*): ~ **you be**

quiet! vuoi stare zitto?; **~ you come?** vieni anche tu?; **~ you help me?** mi aiuti?, mi puoi aiutare?; **~ you have a cup of tea?** vorrebbe una tazza di tè?; **I won't put up with it!** non lo accetterò!
♦ *vt*: **to ~ sb to do** volere che qn faccia; **he ~ed himself to go on** continuò grazie a un grande sforzo di volontà
♦ *n* volontà; testamento

willful ['wɪlful] (*US*) *adj* = **wilful**
willing ['wɪlɪŋ] *adj* volenteroso(a); **~ to do** disposto(a) a fare; **~ly** *adv* volentieri; **~ness** *n* buona volontà
willow ['wɪləu] *n* salice *m*
will power *n* forza di volontà
willy-nilly [wɪlɪ'nɪlɪ] *adv* volente o nolente
wilt [wɪlt] *vi* appassire
win [wɪn] (*pt, pp* **won**) *n* (*in sports etc*) vittoria ♦ *vt* (*battle, prize, money*) vincere; (*popularity*) conquistare ♦ *vi* vincere; **~ over** *vt* convincere; **~ round** (*BRIT*) *vt* convincere
wince [wɪns] *vi* trasalire
winch [wɪntʃ] *n* verricello, argano
wind[1] [waɪnd] (*pt, pp* **wound**) *vt* attorcigliare; (*wrap*) avvolgere; (*clock, toy*) caricare ♦ *vi* (*road, river*) serpeggiare; **~ up** *vt* (*clock*) caricare; (*debate*) concludere
wind[2] [wɪnd] *n* vento; (*MED*) flatulenza; (*breath*) respiro, fiato ♦ *vt* (*take breath away*) far restare senza fiato; **~ power** energia eolica; **~fall** *n* (*money*) guadagno insperato
winding ['waɪndɪŋ] *adj* (*road*) serpeggiante; (*staircase*) a chiocciola
wind instrument *n* (*MUS*) strumento a fiato
windmill ['wɪndmɪl] *n* mulino a vento
window ['wɪndəu] *n* finestra; (*in car, train*) finestrino; (*in shop etc*) vetrina; (*also: ~* **pane**) vetro; **~ box** *n* cassetta da fiori; **~ cleaner** *n* (*person*) pulitore *m* di finestre; **~ envelope** *n* busta a finestra; **~ ledge** *n* davanzale *m*; **~ pane** *n* vetro; **~-shopping** *n*: **to go ~-shopping** andare a vedere le vetrine; **~sill** *n* davanzale *m*

windpipe ['wɪndpaɪp] *n* trachea
windscreen ['wɪndskriːn] *n* parabrezza *m inv*; **~ washer** *n* lavacristallo; **~ wiper** *n* tergicristallo
windshield ['wɪndʃiːld] (*US*) *n* = **windscreen**
windswept ['wɪndswɛpt] *adj* spazzato(a) dal vento
windy ['wɪndɪ] *adj* ventoso(a); **it's ~** c'è vento
wine [waɪn] *n* vino; **~ bar** *n* enoteca (*per degustazione*); **~ cellar** *n* cantina; **~ glass** *n* bicchiere *m* da vino; **~ list** *n* lista dei vini; **~ merchant** *n* commerciante *m* di vini; **~ tasting** *n* degustazione *f* dei vini; **~ waiter** *n* sommelier *m inv*
wing [wɪŋ] *n* ala; (*AUT*) fiancata; **~s** *npl* (*THEATRE*) quinte *fpl*; **~er** *n* (*SPORT*) ala
wink [wɪŋk] *n* ammiccamento ♦ *vi* ammiccare, fare l'occhiolino; (*light*) balugìnare
winner ['wɪnə*] *n* vincitore/trice
winning ['wɪnɪŋ] *adj* (*team, goal*) vincente; (*smile*) affascinante; **~s** *npl* vincite *fpl*
winter ['wɪntə*] *n* inverno; **~ sports** *npl* sport *mpl* invernali
wintry ['wɪntrɪ] *adj* invernale
wipe [waɪp] *n* pulita, passata ♦ *vt* pulire (strofinando); (*erase: tape*) cancellare; **~ off** *vt* cancellare; (*stains*) togliere strofinando; **~ out** *vt* (*debt*) pagare, liquidare; (*memory*) cancellare; (*destroy*) annientare; **~ up** *vt* asciugare
wire ['waɪə*] *n* filo; (*ELEC*) filo elettrico; (*TEL*) telegramma *m* ♦ *vt* (*house*) fare l'impianto elettrico di; (*also: ~* **up**) collegare, allacciare; (*person*) telegrafare a
wireless ['waɪəlɪs] (*BRIT*) *n* (*set*) (apparecchio *m*) radio *f inv*
wiring ['waɪərɪŋ] *n* impianto elettrico
wiry ['waɪərɪ] *adj* magro(a) e nerboruto(a); (*hair*) ispido(a)
wisdom ['wɪzdəm] *n* saggezza; (*of action*) prudenza; **~ tooth** *n* dente *m* del giudizio
wise [waɪz] *adj* saggio(a); prudente; giudizioso(a)
...wise [waɪz] *suffix*: **time~** per quanto

riguarda il tempo, in termini di tempo

wish [wɪʃ] *n* (*desire*) desiderio; (*specific desire*) richiesta ♦ *vt* desiderare, volere; **best ~es** (*on birthday etc*) i migliori auguri; **with best ~es** (*in letter*) cordiali saluti, con i migliori saluti; **to ~ sb goodbye** dire arrivederci a qn; **he ~ed me well** mi augurò di riuscire; **to ~ to do/sb to do** desiderare *or* volere fare/che qn faccia; **to ~ for** desiderare; **~ful** *adj*: **it's ~ful thinking** è prendere i desideri per realtà

wishy-washy [wɪʃi'wɔʃi] (*inf*) *adj* (*colour*) slavato(a); (*ideas, argument*) insulso(a)

wisp [wɪsp] *n* ciuffo, ciocca; (*of smoke*) filo

wistful ['wɪstful] *adj* malinconico(a)

wit [wɪt] *n* (*also*: **~s**) intelligenza; presenza di spirito; (*wittiness*) spirito, arguzia; (*person*) bello spirito

witch [wɪtʃ] *n* strega

---KEYWORD---

with [wɪð, wɪθ] *prep* **1** (*in the company of*) con; **I was ~ him** ero con lui; **we stayed ~ friends** siamo stati da amici; **I'll be ~ you in a minute** vengo subito

2 (*descriptive*) con; **a room ~ a view** una stanza con vista sul mare (*or* sulle montagne *etc*); **the man ~ the grey hat/blue eyes** l'uomo con il cappello grigio/gli occhi blu

3 (*indicating manner, means, cause*): **~ tears in her eyes** con le lacrime agli occhi; **red ~ anger** rosso dalla rabbia; **to shake ~ fear** tremare di paura

4: **I'm ~ you** (*I understand*) la seguo; **to be ~ it** (*inf: up-to-date*) essere alla moda; (*: alert*) essere sveglio(a)

---

withdraw [wɪθ'drɔ:] (*irreg: like* **draw**) *vt* ritirare; (*money from bank*) ritirare; prelevare ♦ *vi* ritirarsi; **~al** *n* ritiro; prelievo; (*of army*) ritirata; **~al symptoms** (*MED*) crisi *f* di astinenza; **~n** *adj* (*person*) distaccato(a)

wither ['wɪðə*] *vi* appassire

withhold [wɪθ'həʊld] (*irreg: like* **hold**) *vt* (*money*) trattenere; (*permission*): **to ~ (from)** rifiutare (a); (*information*): **to ~**

(from) nascondere (a)

within [wɪð'ɪn] *prep* all'interno; (*in time, distances*) entro ♦ *adv* all'interno, dentro; **~ reach (of)** alla portata (di); **~ sight (of)** in vista (di); **~ a mile of** entro un miglio da; **~ the week** prima della fine della settimana

without [wɪð'aut] *prep* senza; **to go ~ sth** fare a meno di qc

withstand [wɪθ'stænd] (*irreg: like* **stand**) *vt* resistere a

witness ['wɪtnɪs] *n* (*person, also LAW*) testimone *m/f* ♦ *vt* (*event*) essere testimone di; (*document*) attestare l'autenticità di; **~ box** (*US* **~ stand**) *n* banco dei testimoni

witticism ['wɪtɪsɪzm] *n* spiritosaggine *f*

witty ['wɪti] *adj* spiritoso(a)

wives [waɪvz] *npl of* **wife**

wizard ['wɪzəd] *n* mago

wk *abbr* = **week**

wobble ['wɔbl] *vi* tremare; (*chair*) traballare

woe [wəʊ] *n* dolore *m*; disgrazia

woke [wəʊk] *pt of* **wake**; **woken** *pp of* **wake**

wolf [wʊlf] (*pl* **wolves**) *n* lupo

wolves [wʊlvz] *npl of* **wolf**

woman ['wʊmən] (*pl* **women**) *n* donna; **~ doctor** *n* dottoressa; **women's lib** (*inf*) *n* movimento femminista

womb [wu:m] *n* (*ANAT*) utero

women ['wɪmɪn] *npl of* **woman**

won [wʌn] *pt, pp of* **win**

wonder ['wʌndə*] *n* meraviglia ♦ *vi*: **to ~ whether/why** domandarsi se/perché; **to ~ at** essere sorpreso(a) di; meravigliarsi di; **to ~ about** domandarsi di; pensare a; **it's no ~ that** c'è poco *or* non c'è da meravigliarsi che +*sub*; **~ful** *adj* meraviglioso(a)

won't [wəʊnt] = **will not**

wood [wʊd] *n* legno; (*timber*) legname *m*; (*forest*) bosco; **~ carving** *n* scultura in legno, intaglio; **~ed** *adj* boschivo(a); boscoso(a); **~en** *adj* di legno; (*fig*) rigido(a); inespressivo(a); **~pecker** *n* picchio; **~wind** *npl* (*MUS*): **the ~wind** i legni; **~work** *n* (*craft, subject*) falegnameria; **~worm** *n* tarlo del legno

wool [wʊl] *n* lana; **to pull the ~ over sb's**

eyes (fig) imbrogliare qn; ~**len** (US ~**en**) adj di lana; (industry) laniero(a); ~**lens** npl indumenti mpl di lana; ~**ly** (US ~**y**) adj di lana; (fig: ideas) confuso(a)

word [wə:d] n parola; (news) notizie fpl ♦ vt esprimere, formulare; **in other ~s** in altre parole; **to break/keep one's ~** non mantenere/mantenere la propria parola; **to have ~s with sb** avere un diverbio con qn; ~**ing** n formulazione f; ~ **processing** n elaborazione f di testi, word processing m; ~ **processor** n word processor m inv

wore [wɔ:ʳ] pt of **wear**

work [wə:k] n lavoro; (ART, LITERATURE) opera ♦ vi lavorare; (mechanism, plan etc) funzionare; (medicine) essere efficace ♦ vt (clay, wood etc) lavorare; (mine etc) sfruttare; (machine) far funzionare; (cause: effect, miracle) fare; **to be out of ~** essere disoccupato(a); ~**s** n (BRIT: factory) fabbrica ♦ npl (of clock, machine) meccanismo; **to ~ loose** allentarsi; ~ **on** vt fus lavorare a; (person) lavorarsi; (principle) basarsi su; ~ **out** vi (plans etc) riuscire, andare bene ♦ vt (problem) risolvere; (plan) elaborare; **it ~s out at £100** fa 100 sterline; ~ **up** vt: **to get ~ed up** andare su tutte le furie; eccitarsi; ~**able** adj (solution) realizzabile; ~**aholic** n maniaco del lavoro; ~**er** n lavoratore/trice, operaio/a; ~**force** n forza lavoro; ~**ing class** n classe f operaia; ~**ing-class** adj operaio(a); ~**ing order** n: **in ~ing order** funzionante; ~**man** (irreg) n operaio; ~**manship** n abilità; ~**sheet** n foglio col programma di lavoro; ~**shop** n officina; (practical session) gruppo di lavoro; ~ **station** n stazione f di lavoro; ~**-to-rule** (BRIT) n sciopero bianco

world [wə:ld] n mondo ♦ cpd (champion) del mondo; (power, war) mondiale; **to think the ~ of sb** (fig) pensare un gran bene di qn; ~**ly** adj di questo mondo; (knowledgeable) di mondo; ~**-wide** adj universale; **W~-Wide Web** n World Wide Web m

worm [wə:m] n (also: **earth~**) verme m

worn [wɔ:n] pp of **wear** ♦ adj usato(a); ~**out** adj (object) consumato(a), logoro(a); (person) sfinito(a)

worried ['wʌrɪd] adj preoccupato(a)

worry ['wʌrɪ] n preoccupazione f ♦ vt preoccupare ♦ vi preoccuparsi

worse [wə:s] adj peggiore ♦ adv, n peggio; **a change for the ~** un peggioramento; ~**n** vt, vi peggiorare; ~ **off** adj in condizioni (economiche) peggiori

worship ['wə:ʃɪp] n culto ♦ vt (God) adorare, venerare; (person) adorare; **Your W~** (BRIT: to mayor) signor sindaco; (: to judge) signor giudice

worst [wə:st] adj il(la) peggiore ♦ adv, n peggio; **at ~** al peggio, per male che vada

worth [wə:θ] n valore m ♦ adj: **to be ~** valere; **it's ~ it** ne vale la pena; **it is ~ one's while (to do)** vale la pena (fare); ~**less** adj di nessun valore; ~**while** adj (activity) utile; (cause) lodevole

worthy ['wə:ðɪ] adj (person) degno(a); (motive) lodevole; ~ **of** degno di

---

KEYWORD

---

would [wʊd] aux vb 1 (conditional tense): **if you asked him he ~ do it** se glielo chiedesse lo farebbe; **if you had asked him he ~ have done it** se glielo avesse chiesto lo avrebbe fatto

2 (in offers, invitations, requests): ~ **you like a biscuit?** vorrebbe or vuole un biscotto?; ~ **you ask him to come in?** lo faccia entrare, per cortesia; ~ **you open the window please?** apra la finestra, per favore

3 (in indirect speech): **I said I ~ do it** ho detto che l'avrei fatto

4 (emphatic): **it WOULD have to snow today!** doveva proprio nevicare oggi!

5 (insistence): **she ~n't do it** non ha voluto farlo

6 (conjecture): **it ~ have been midnight** sarà stato mezzanotte; **it ~ seem so** sembrerebbe proprio di sì

7 (indicating habit): **he ~ go there on Mondays** andava lì ogni lunedì

would-be (pej) adj sedicente
wouldn't ['wudnt] = **would not**
wound[1] [waund] pt, pp of **wind**[1]
wound[2] [wu:nd] n ferita ♦ vt ferire
wove [wəuv] pt of **weave**; **woven** pp of **weave**
wrangle ['ræŋgl] n litigio
wrap [ræp] vt avvolgere; (pack: also: ~ **up**) incartare; ~**per** n (on chocolate) carta; (BRIT: of book) copertina; ~**ping paper** n carta da pacchi; (for gift) carta da regali
wreak [ri:k] vt (havoc) portare, causare; **to ~ vengeance on** vendicarsi su
wreath [ri:θ, pl ri:ðz] n corona
wreck [rɛk] n (sea disaster) naufragio; (ship) relitto; (pej: person) rottame m ♦ vt demolire; (ship) far naufragare; (fig) rovinare; ~**age** n rottami mpl; (of building) macerie fpl; (of ship) relitti mpl
wren [rɛn] n (ZOOL) scricciolo
wrench [rɛntʃ] n (TECH) chiave f; (tug) torsione f brusca; (fig) strazio ♦ vt strappare; storcere; **to ~ sth from** strappare qc a or da
wrestle ['rɛsl] vi: **to ~ (with sb)** lottare (con qn); ~**r** n lottatore/trice; **wrestling** n lotta
wretched ['rɛtʃɪd] adj disgraziato(a); (inf: weather, holiday) orrendo(a), orribile; (: child, dog) pestifero(a)
wriggle ['rɪgl] vi (also: ~ **about**) dimenarsi; (: snake, worm) serpeggiare
wring [rɪŋ] (pt, pp **wrung**) vt torcere; (wet clothes) strizzare; (fig): **to ~ sth out of** strappare qc a
wrinkle ['rɪŋkl] n (on skin) ruga; (on paper etc) grinza ♦ vt (nose) torcere; (forehead) corrugare ♦ vi (skin, paint) raggrinzirsi
wrist [rɪst] n polso; ~**watch** n orologio da polso
writ [rɪt] n ordine m; mandato
write [raɪt] (pt **wrote**, pp **written**) vt, vi scrivere; ~ **down** vt annotare; (put in writing) mettere per iscritto; ~ **off** vt (debt, plan) cancellare; ~ **out** vt mettere per iscritto; (cheque, receipt) scrivere; ~ **up** vt redigere; ~**-off** n perdita completa; ~**r** n autore/trice, scrittore/trice
writhe [raɪð] vi contorcersi

writing ['raɪtɪŋ] n scrittura; (of author) scritto, opera; **in ~** per iscritto; ~ **paper** n carta da lettere
written ['rɪtn] pp of **write**
wrong [rɒŋ] adj sbagliato(a); (not suitable) inadatto(a); (wicked) cattivo(a); (unfair) ingiusto(a) ♦ adv in modo sbagliato, erroneamente ♦ n (injustice) torto ♦ vt fare torto a; **you are ~ to do it** ha torto a farlo; **you are ~ about that, you've got it ~** si sbaglia; **to be in the ~** avere torto; **what's ~?** cosa c'è che non va?; **to go ~** (person) sbagliarsi; (plan) fallire, non riuscire; (machine) guastarsi; ~**ful** adj illegittimo(a); ingiusto(a); ~**ly** adv (incorrectly, by mistake) in modo sbagliato; ~ **number** n (TEL): **you've got the ~ number** ha sbagliato numero
wrote [rəut] pt of **write**
wrought iron [rɔ:t-] n ferro battuto
wrung [rʌŋ] pt, pp of **wring**
WWW n abbr (= World Wide Web): **the ~** la Rete

X, x

Xmas ['ɛksməs] n abbr = **Christmas**
X-ray ['ɛksreɪ] n raggio X; (photograph) radiografia ♦ vt radiografare
xylophone ['zaɪləfəun] n xilofono

Y, y

yacht [jɒt] n panfilo, yacht m inv; ~**ing** n yachting m, sport m della vela
Yank [jæŋk] (pej) n yankee m/f inv
Yankee ['jæŋkɪ] (pej) n = **Yank**
yap [jæp] vi (dog) guaire
yard [jɑ:d] n (of house etc) cortile m; (measure) iarda (= 914 mm; 3 feet); ~**stick** n (fig) misura, criterio
yarn [jɑ:n] n filato; (tale) lunga storia
yawn [jɔ:n] n sbadiglio ♦ vi sbadigliare; ~**ing** adj (gap) spalancato(a)
yd. abbr = **yard(s)**

yeah [jeə] (*inf*) *adv* sì

year [jɪə*] *n* anno; (*referring to harvest, wine etc*) annata; **he is 8 ~s old** ha 8 anni; **an eight-~-old child** un(a) bambino(a) di otto anni; **~ly** *adj* annuale ♦ *adv* annualmente

yearn [jə:n] *vi*: **to ~ for sth/to do** desiderare ardentemente qc/di fare

yeast [ji:st] *n* lievito

yell [jɛl] *n* urlo ♦ *vi* urlare

yellow ['jɛləʊ] *adj* giallo(a)

yelp [jɛlp] *vi* guaire, uggiolare

yeoman ['jəʊmən] *n*: **~ of the guard** guardiano della Torre di Londra

yes [jɛs] *adv* sì ♦ *n* sì *m inv*; **to say/answer ~** dire/rispondere di sì

yesterday ['jɛstədɪ] *adv* ieri ♦ *n* ieri *m inv*; **~ morning/evening** ieri mattina/sera; **all day ~** ieri per tutta la giornata

yet [jɛt] *adv* ancora; già ♦ *conj* ma, tuttavia; **it is not finished ~** non è ancora finito; **the best ~** finora il migliore; **as ~** finora

yew [ju:] *n* tasso (*albero*)

yield [ji:ld] *n* produzione *f*, resa; reddito ♦ *vt* produrre, rendere; (*surrender*) cedere ♦ *vi* cedere; (*US: AUT*) dare la precedenza

YMCA *n abbr* (= *Young Men's Christian Association*) Y.M.C.A. *m*

yoga ['jəʊgə] *n* yoga *m*

yog(h)ourt ['jəʊgət] *n* = **yog(h)urt**

yog(h)urt ['jəʊgət] *n* iogurt *m inv*

yoke [jəʊk] *n* (*also fig*) giogo

yolk [jəʊk] *n* tuorlo, rosso d'uovo

KEYWORD

you [ju:] *pron* **1** (*subject*) tu; (: *polite form*) lei; (: *pl*) voi; (: *very formal*) loro; **~ Italians enjoy your food** a voi Italiani piace mangiare bene; **~ and I will go** tu ed io *or* lei ed io andiamo

2 (*object: direct*) ti; la; vi; loro (*after vb*); (: *indirect*) ti; le; vi; loro (*after vb*); **I know ~** ti *or* la *or* vi conosco; **I gave it to ~** te l'ho dato; gliel'ho dato; ve l'ho dato; l'ho dato loro

3 (*stressed, after prep, in comparisons*) te; lei; voi; loro; **I told YOU to do it** ho detto a *TE* (*or* a *LEI etc*) di farlo; **she's younger**

---

than ~ è più giovane di te (*or* lei *etc*)

4 (*impers: one*) si; **fresh air does ~ good** l'aria fresca fa bene; **~ never know** non si sa mai

---

you'd [ju:d] = **you had**; **you would**

you'll [ju:l] = **you will**; **you shall**

young [jʌŋ] *adj* giovane ♦ *npl* (*of animal*) piccoli *mpl*; (*people*): **the ~** i giovani, la gioventù; **~er** *adj* più giovane; (*brother*) minore, più giovane; **~ster** *n* giovanotto, ragazzo; (*child*) bambino/a

your [jɔ:*] *adj* il(la) tuo(a), *pl* i(le) tuoi(tue); (*polite form*) il(la) suo(a), *pl* i(le) suoi(sue); il(la) vostro(a), *pl* i(le) vostri(e); il(la) loro, *pl* i(le) loro; *see also* **my**

you're [juə*] = **you are**

yours [jɔ:z] *pron* il(la) tuo(a), *pl* i(le) tuoi(tue); (*polite form*) il(la) suo(a), *pl* i(le) suoi(sue); (*pl*) il(la) vostro(a), *pl* i(le) vostri(e); (: *very formal*) il(la) loro, *pl* i(le) loro; *see also* **mine**; **faithfully**; **sincerely**

yourself [jɔ:'sɛlf] *pron* (*reflexive*) ti; si; (*after prep*) te; sé; (*emphatic*) tu stesso(a); lei stesso(a); **yourselves** *pl pron* (*reflexive*) vi; si; (*after prep*) voi; loro; (*emphatic*) voi stessi(e); loro stessi(e); *see also* **oneself**

youth [ju:θ, *pl* ju:ðz] *n* gioventù *f*; (*young man*) giovane *m*, ragazzo; **~ club** *n* centro giovanile; **~ful** *adj* giovane; da giovane; giovanile; **~ hostel** *n* ostello della gioventù

you've [ju:v] = **you have**

Yugoslav ['ju:gəʊ'sla:v] *adj, n* jugoslavo(a)

Yugoslavia ['ju:gəʊ'sla:vɪə] *n* Jugoslavia

yuppie ['jʌpɪ] (*inf*) *n, adj* yuppie *m/f inv*

YWCA *n abbr* (= *Young Women's Christian Association*) Y.W.C.A. *m*

Z, z

zany ['zeɪnɪ] *adj* un po' pazzo(a)

zap [zæp] *vt* (*COMPUT*) cancellare

zeal [zi:l] *n* zelo; entusiasmo

zebra ['zi:brə] *n* zebra; **~ crossing** (*BRIT*) *n* (passaggio pedonale a) strisce *fpl*, zebre *fpl*

zero [ˈzɪərəʊ] *n* zero

zest [zɛst] *n* gusto; (*CULIN*) buccia

zigzag [ˈzɪgzæg] *n* zigzag *m inv* ♦ *vi* zigzagare

Zimbabwe [zɪmˈbɑːbwɪ] *n* Zimbabwe *m*

zinc [zɪŋk] *n* zinco

zip [zɪp] *n* (*also*: **~ fastener,** (*US*) **~per**) chiusura *f or* cerniera *f* lampo *inv* ♦ *vt* (*also*: **~ up**) chiudere con una cerniera lampo; **~ code** (*US*) *n* codice *m* di avviamento postale

zodiac [ˈzəʊdɪæk] *n* zodiaco

zombie [ˈzɔmbɪ] *n* (*fig*): **like a ~** come un morto che cammina

zone [zəʊn] *n* (*also MIL*) zona

zoo [zuː] *n* zoo *m inv*

zoology [zuːˈɔlədʒɪ] *n* zoologia

zoom [zuːm] *vi*: **to ~ past** sfrecciare; **~ lens** *n* zoom *m inv*, obiettivo a focale variabile

zucchini [zuːˈkiːnɪ] (*US*) *npl* (*courgettes*) zucchine *fpl*

ITALIAN VERBS

1 Gerundio *2* Participio passato *3* Presente *4* Imperfetto *5* Passato remoto *6* Futuro *7* Condizionale *8* Congiuntivo presente *9* Congiuntivo passato *10* Imperativo

andare *3* vado, vai, va, andiamo, andate, vanno *6* andrò *etc 8* vada *10* va'!, vada!, andate!, vadano!

apparire *2* apparso *3* appaio, appari *o* apparisci, appare *o* apparisce, appaiono *o* appariscono *5* apparvi *o* apparsi, apparisti, apparve *o* apparì *o* apparse, apparvero *o* apparirono *o* apparsero *8* appaia *o* apparisca

aprire *2* aperto *3* apro *5* aprii *o* apersi, apristi *8* apra

AVERE *3* ho, hai, ha, abbiamo, avete, hanno *5* ebbi, avesti, ebbe, avemmo, aveste, ebbero *6* avrò *etc 8* abbia *etc 10* abbi!, abbia!, abbiate!, abbiano!

bere *1* bevendo *2* bevuto *3* bevo *etc 4* bevevo *etc 8* beva *etc 9* bevessi *etc*

cadere *5* caddi, cadesti *6* cadrò *etc*

cogliere *2* colto *3* colgo, colgono *5* colsi, cogliesti *8* colga

correre *2* corso *5* corsi, corresti

cuocere *2* cotto *3* cuocio, cociamo, cuociono *5* cossi, cocesti

dare *3* do, dai, dà, diamo, date, danno *5* diedi *o* detti, desti *6* darò *etc 8* dia *etc 9* dessi *etc 10* da'!, dia!, date!, diano!

dire *1* dicendo *2* detto *3* dico, dici, dice, diciamo, dite, dicono *4* dicevo *etc 5* dissi, dicesti *6* dirò *etc 8* dica, diciamo, diciate, dicano *9* dicessi *etc 10* di'!, dica!, dite!, dicano!

dolere *3* dolgo, duoli, duole, dolgono *5* dolsi, dolesti *6* dorrò *etc 8* dolga

dovere *3* devo *o* debbo, devi, deve, dobbiamo, dovete, devono *o* debbono *6* dovrò *etc 8* debba, dobbiamo, dobbiate, devano *o* debbano

ESSERE *2* stato *3* sono, sei, è, siamo, siete, sono *4* ero, eri, era, eravamo, eravate, erano *5* fui, fosti, fu, fummo, foste, furono *6* sarò *etc 8* sia *etc 9* fossi, fossi, fosse, fossimo, foste, fossero *10* sii!, sia!, siate!, siano!

fare *1* facendo *2* fatto *3* faccio, fai, fa, facciamo, fate, fanno *4* facevo *etc 5* feci, facesti *6* farò *etc 8* faccia *etc 9* facessi *etc 10* fa'!, faccia!, fate!, facciano!

FINIRE *1* finendo *2* finito *3* finisco, finisci, finisce, finiamo, finite, finiscono *4* finivo, finivi, finiva, finivamo, finivate, finivano *5* finii, finisti, finì, finimmo, finiste, finirono *6* finirò, finirai, finirà, finiremo, finirete, finiranno *7* finirei, finiresti, finirebbe, finiremmo, finireste, finirebbero *8* finisca, finisca, finisca, finiamo, finiate, finiscano *9* finissi, finissi, finisse, finissimo, finiste, finissero *10* finisci!, finisca!, finite!, finiscano!

giungere *2* giunto *5* giunsi, giungesti

leggere *2* letto *5* lessi, leggesti

mettere *2* messo *5* misi, mettesti

morire *2* morto *3* muoio, muori, muore, moriamo, morite, muoiono *6* morirò *o* morrò *etc 8* muoia

muovere *2* mosso *5* mossi, movesti

nascere *2* nato *5* nacqui, nascesti

nuocere *2* nuociuto *3* nuoccio, nuoci, nuoce, nociamo *o* nuociamo, nuocete, nuocciono *4* nuocevo *etc 5* nocqui, nuocesti *6* nuocerò *etc 7* nuoccia

offrire *2* offerto *3* offro *5* offersi *o* offrii, offristi *8* offra

parere *2* parso *3* paio, paiamo, paiono *5* parvi *o* parsi, paresti *6* parrò *etc 8* paia, paiamo, paiate, paiano

PARLARE *1* parlando *2* parlato *3* parlo, parli, parla, parliamo, parlate, parlano *4* parlavo, parlavi, parlava, parlavamo, parlavate, parlavano *5* parlai, parlasti, parlò, parlammo, parlaste, parlarono *6* parlerò, parlerai, parlerà, parleremo, parlerete, parleranno *7* parlerei, parleresti, parlerebbe, parleremmo, parlereste, parlerebbero *8* parli, parli, parli, parliamo, parliate, parlino *9* parlassi, parlassi, parlasse, parlassimo, parlaste, parlassero *10* parla!, parli!, parlate!, parlino!

piacere *2* piaciuto *3* piaccio, piacciamo, piacciono *5* piacqui, piacesti *8* piaccia *etc*

porre *1* ponendo *2* posto *3* pongo, poni, pone, poniamo, ponete, pongono *4* ponevo *etc 5* posi, ponesti *6* porrò *etc 8* ponga, poniamo, poniate, pongano *9* ponessi *etc*

potere *3* posso, puoi, può, possiamo, potete, possono *6* potrò *etc 8* possa, possiamo, possiate, possano

prendere *2* preso *5* presi, prendesti

ridurre *1* riducendo *2* ridotto *3* riduco *etc 4* riducevo *etc 5* ridussi, riducesti *6* ridurrò *etc 8* riduca *etc 9* riducessi *etc*

riempire *1* riempiendo *3* riempio, riempi, riempie, riempiono

rimanere *2* rimasto *3* rimango, rimangono *5* rimasi, rimanesti *6* rimarrò *etc 8* rimanga

rispondere *2* risposto *5* risposi, rispondesti

salire *3* salgo, sali, salgono *8* salga

sapere *3* so, sai, sa, sappiamo, sapete, sanno *5* seppi, sapesti *6* saprò *etc 8* sappia *etc 10* sappi!, sappia!, sappiate!, sappiano!

scrivere *2* scritto *5* scrissi, scrivesti

sedere *3* siedo, siedi, siede, siedono *8* sieda

spegnere *2* spento *3* spengo, spengono *5* spensi, spegnesti *8* spenga

stare *2* stato *3* sto, stai, sta, stiamo, state, stanno *5* stetti, stesti *6* starò *etc*

8 stia *etc 9* stessi *etc 10* sta'!, stia!, state!, stiano!

tacere *2* taciuto *3* taccio, tacciono *5* tacqui, tacesti *8* taccia

tenere *3* tengo, tieni, tiene, tengono *5* tenni, tenesti *6* terrò *etc 8* tenga

trarre *1* traendo *2* tratto *3* traggo, trai, trae, traiamo, traete, traggono *4* traevo *etc 5* trassi, traesti *6* trarrò *etc 8* tragga *9* traessi *etc*

udire *3* odo, odi, ode, odono *8* oda

uscire *3* esco, esci, esce, escono *8* esca

valere *2* valso *3* valgo, valgono *5* valsi, valesti *6* varrò *etc 8* valga

vedere *2* visto *o* veduto *5* vidi, vedesti *6* vedrò *etc*

VENDERE *1* vendendo *2* venduto *3* vendo, vendi, vende, vendiamo, vendete, vendono *4* vendevo, vendevi, vendeva, vendevamo, vendevate, vendevano *5* vendei *o* vendetti, vendesti, vendé *o* vendette, vendemmo, vendeste, venderono *o* vendettero *6* venderò, venderai, venderà, venderemo, venderete, venderanno *7* venderei, venderesti, venderebbe, venderemmo, vendereste, venderebbero *8* venda, venda, venda, vendiamo, vendiate, vendano *9* vendessi, vendessi, vendesse, vendessimo, vendeste, vendessero *10* vendi!, venda!, vendete!, vendano!

venire *2* venuto *3* vengo, vieni, viene, vengono *5* venni, venisti *6* verrò *etc 8* venga

vivere *2* vissuto *5* vissi, vivesti

volere *3* voglio, vuoi, vuole, vogliamo, volete, vogliono *5* volli, volesti *6* vorrò *etc 8* voglia *etc 10* vogli!, voglia!, vogliate!, vogliano!

VERBI INGLESI

present	pt	pp	present	pt	pp
arise	arose	arisen	feed	fed	fed
awake	awoke	awoken	feel	felt	felt
be (am, is,	was,	been	fight	fought	fought
are; being)	were		find	found	found
bear	bore	born(e)	flee	fled	fled
beat	beat	beaten	fling	flung	flung
become	became	become	fly (flies)	flew	flown
begin	began	begun	forbid	forbade	forbidden
behold	beheld	beheld	forecast	forecast	forecast
bend	bent	bent	forego	forewent	foregone
beseech	besought	besought	foresee	foresaw	foreseen
beset	beset	beset	foretell	foretold	foretold
bet	bet, betted	bet, betted	forget	forgot	forgotten
bid	bid, bade	bid, bidden	forgive	forgave	forgiven
bind	bound	bound	forsake	forsook	forsaken
bite	bit	bitten	freeze	froze	frozen
bleed	bled	bled	get	got	got, (US)
blow	blew	blown			gotten
break	broke	broken	give	gave	given
breed	bred	bred	go (goes)	went	gone
bring	brought	brought	grind	ground	ground
build	built	built	grow	grew	grown
burn	burnt,	burnt, burned	hang	hung,	hung,
	burned			hanged	hanged
burst	burst	burst	have (has;	had	had
buy	bought	bought	having)		
can	could	(been able)	hear	heard	heard
cast	cast	cast	hide	hid	hidden
catch	caught	caught	hit	hit	hit
choose	chose	chosen	hold	held	held
cling	clung	clung	hurt	hurt	hurt
come	came	come	keep	kept	kept
cost	cost	cost	kneel	knelt,	knelt,
creep	crept	crept		kneeled	kneeled
cut	cut	cut	know	knew	known
deal	dealt	dealt	lay	laid	laid
dig	dug	dug	lead	led	led
do (3rd	did	done	lean	leant,	leant, leaned
person:he/				leaned	
she/it does)			leap	leapt,	leapt, leaped
draw	drew	drawn		leaped	
dream	dreamed,	dreamed,	learn	learnt,	learnt,
	dreamt	dreamt		learned	learned
drink	drank	drunk	leave	left	left
drive	drove	driven	lend	lent	lent
dwell	dwelt	dwelt	let	let	let
eat	ate	eaten	lie (lying)	lay	lain
fall	fell	fallen	light	lit, lighted	lit, lighted

present	pt	pp	present	pt	pp
lose	lost	lost	spell	spelt, spelled	spelt, spelled
make	made	made			
may	might	—	spend	spent	spent
mean	meant	meant	spill	spilt, spilled	spilt, spilled
meet	met	met			
mistake	mistook	mistaken	spin	spun	spun
mow	mowed	mown, mowed	spit	spat	spat
must	(had to)	(had to)	split	split	split
pay	paid	paid	spoil	spoiled, spoilt	spoiled, spoilt
put	put	put			
quit	quit, quitted	quit, quitted	spread	spread	spread
			spring	sprang	sprung
read	read	read	stand	stood	stood
rid	rid	rid	steal	stole	stolen
ride	rode	ridden	stick	stuck	stuck
ring	rang	rung	sting	stung	stung
rise	rose	risen	stink	stank	stunk
run	ran	run	stride	strode	stridden
saw	sawed	sawn	strike	struck	struck, stricken
say	said	said			
see	saw	seen	strive	strove	striven
seek	sought	sought	swear	swore	sworn
sell	sold	sold	sweep	swept	swept
send	sent	sent	swell	swelled	swollen, swelled
set	set	set			
shake	shook	shaken	swim	swam	swum
shall	should	—	swing	swung	swung
shear	sheared	shorn, sheared	take	took	taken
shed	shed	shed	teach	taught	taught
shine	shone	shone	tear	tore	torn
shoot	shot	shot	tell	told	told
show	showed	shown	think	thought	thought
shrink	shrank	shrunk	throw	threw	thrown
shut	shut	shut	thrust	thrust	thrust
sing	sang	sung	tread	trod	trodden
sink	sank	sunk	wake	woke	woken
sit	sat	sat	waylay	waylaid	waylaid
slay	slew	slain	wear	wore	worn
sleep	slept	slept	weave	wove, weaved	woven, weaved
slide	slid	slid			
sling	slung	slung	wed	wedded, wed	wedded, wed
slit	slit	slit			
smell	smelt, smelled	smelt, smelled	weep	wept	wept
			win	won	won
sow	sowed	sown, sowed	wind	wound	wound
speak	spoke	spoken	wring	wrung	wrung
speed	sped, speeded	sped, speeded	write	wrote	written

I NUMERI

NUMBERS

uno(a)	1	one
due	2	two
tre	3	three
quattro	4	four
cinque	5	five
sei	6	six
sette	7	seven
otto	8	eight
nove	9	nine
dieci	10	ten
undici	11	eleven
dodici	12	twelve
tredici	13	thirteen
quattordici	14	fourteen
quindici	15	fifteen
sedici	16	sixteen
diciassette	17	seventeen
diciotto	18	eighteen
diciannove	19	nineteen
venti	20	twenty
ventuno	21	twenty-one
ventidue	22	twenty-two
ventitré	23	twenty-three
ventotto	28	twenty-eight
trenta	30	thirty
quaranta	40	forty
cinquanta	50	fifty
sessanta	60	sixty
settanta	70	seventy
ottanta	80	eighty
novanta	90	ninety
cento	100	a hundred, one hundred
cento uno	101	a hundred and one
duecento	200	two hundred
mille	1 000	a thousand, one thousand
milleduecentodue	1 202	one thousand two hundred and two
cinquemila	5 000	five thousand
un milione	1 000 000	a million, one million

primo(a), 1º		first, 1st
secondo(a), 2º		second, 2nd
terzo(a), 3º		third, 3rd
quarto(a)		fourth, 4th
quinto(a)		fifth, 5th
sesto(a)		sixth, 6th

I NUMERI

settimo(a)
ottavo(a)
nono(a)
decimo(a)
undicesimo(a)
dodicesimo(a)
tredicesimo(a)
quattordicesimo(a)
quindicesimo(a)
sedicesimo(a)
diciassettesimo(a)
diciottesimo(a)
diciannovesimo(a)
ventesimo(a)
ventunesimo(a)
ventiduesimo(a)
ventitreesimo(a)
ventottesimo(a)
trentesimo(a)
centesimo(a)
centunesimo(a)
millesimo(a)
milionesimo(a)

Frazioni etc

mezzo
terzo
due terzi
quarto
quinto
zero virgola cinque, 0,5
tre virgola quattro, 3,4
dieci per cento
cento per cento

Esempi

abita al numero dieci
si trova nel capitolo sette, a
  pagina sette
abita al terzo piano
arrivò quarto
scala uno a venticinquemila

NUMBERS

seventh
eighth
ninth
tenth
eleventh
twelfth
thirteenth
fourteenth
fifteenth
sixteenth
seventeenth
eighteenth
nineteenth
twentieth
twenty-first
twenty-second
twenty-third
twenty-eighth
thirtieth
hundredth
hundred-and-first
thousandth
millionth

Fractions etc

half
third
two thirds
quarter
fifth
(nought) point five, 0.5
three point four, 3.4
ten per cent
a hundred per cent

Examples

he lives at number 10
it's in chapter 7, on page 7

he lives on the 3rd floor
he came in 4th
scale 1:25,000

L'ORA

THE TIME

che ora è?, che ore sono?

what time is it?

è ..., sono ...

it is ...

mezzanotte	midnight, twelve p.m.
l'una (della mattina)	one o'clock (in the morning), one (a.m.)
l'una e cinque	five past one
l'una e dieci	ten past one
l'una e un quarto, l'una e quindici	a quarter past one, one fifteen
l'una e venticinque	twenty-five past one, one twenty-five
l'una e mezzo *or* mezza, l'una e trenta	half-past one, one thirty
le due meno venticinque, l'una e trentacinque	twenty-five to two, one thirty-five
le due meno venti, l'una e quaranta	twenty to two, one forty
le due meno un quarto, l'una e quarantacinque	a quarter to two, one forty-five
le due meno dieci, l'una e cinquanta	ten to two, one fifty
mezzogiorno	twelve o'clock, midday, noon
l'una, le tredici	one o'clock (in the afternoon), one (p.m.)
le sette (di sera), le diciannove	seven o'clock (in the evening), seven (p.m.)

a che ora?

at what time?

a mezzanotte	at midnight
all'una, alle tredici	at one o'clock
fra venti minuti	in twenty minutes
venti minuti fa	twenty minutes ago